D0575012

SAMPLE OUR EXCITING NEW LINE-UP OF CASE STUDIES

STEP INTO THE REAL WORLD OF BUSINESS TODAY—WITH VIDEOS

TENTH EDITION

BUSINESS TODAY

Michael H. Mescon

Founder and Chairman, The Mescon Group
Atlanta, Georgia

Regents Professor of Management, Ramsey Chair of Private Enterprise
Andrew Young School of Policy Studies, Georgia State University

Courtland L. Bovée

Professor of Business Administration
C. Allen Paul Distinguished Chair
Grossmont College

John V. Thill

Chief Executive Officer
Communication Specialists of America

Prentice
Hall

Upper Saddle River, New Jersey 07458

Library of Congress Cataloging-in-Publication Data

Mescon, Michael, H.
  Business today / Michael H. Mescon, Courtland L. Bovée, John V. Thill. --10th ed.
    p. cm.
  Includes Index.
  ISBN 0-13-091263-8
  1. Business. 2. Management--United States. I. Bovée, Courtland L. II. Thill, John V.
  III. Title.

  HF5351 .M376 2001
  658--dc21

                    2001021619

Editor-in-Chief: Jeff Shelstad
Assistant Editor: Jennifer Surich
Editorial Assistant: Virginia Sheridan
Media Project Manager: Cindy Harford
Senior Marketing Manager: Debbie Clare
Marketing Assistant: Brian Rappelfeld
Managing Editor (Production): Judy Leale
Production Editor: Emma Moore
Production Assistant: Dianne Falcone
Permissions Coordinator: Suzanne Grappi
Associate Director, Manufacturing: Vincent Scelta
Production Manager: Arnold Vila
Design Manager: Pat Smythe
Art Director: Cheryl Asherman
Interior Design: Donna Wickes
Cover Design: Amanda Wilson
Cover Illustration/Photo: Ivan Lee Sanford/SIS
Illustrator (Interior): Electragraphics
Associate Director, Multimedia Production: Karen Goldsmith
Manager, Print Production: Christy Mahon
Composition: Carlisle Communications
Full-Service Project Management: Lynn Steines/Carlisle Communications
Printer/Binder: Quebecor/World Color

Credits and acknowledgments borrowed from other sources and reproduced, with permission, in this textbook appear on pages R-25–R-33. Photo credits appear on page R-33–R-34.

Copyright © 2002, 1999, 1997 by Bovée & Thill LLC. All rights reserved. Printed in the United States of America. This publication is protected by Copyright and permission should be obtained from the publisher prior to any prohibited reproduction, storage in a retrieval system, or transmission in any form or by any means, electronic, mechanical, photocopying, recording, or likewise. For information regarding permission(s), write to: Rights and Permissions Department, Prentice Hall.

10 9 8 7 6 5 4 3 2 1
ISBN 0-13-091263-8

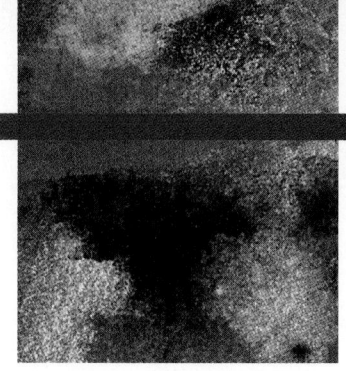

CONTENTS IN BRIEF

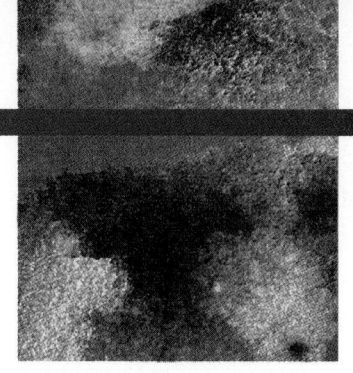

CONTENTS

INSIDE BUSINESS TODAY

Webtime Stories: Yahoo!—The Search Engine That Could

Best of the Web

Find the Right Stuff

Best of the Web

Step Inside the Economic Statistics Briefing Room

Best of the Web

Discover What's in the CPI

Competing in the Global Marketplace

Enterprise Rent-A-Car Tries Harder, and It Pays Off

Keeping Pace with Technology and Electronic Commerce

Milking the Net

INSIDE BUSINESS TODAY

Beyond the Pursuit of Profits: Patagonia Gears Up to Save the Environment

Best of the Web

Build a Better Business

Best of the Web

Go for the Green

Best of the Web

Surf Safely

Keeping Pace with Technology and Electronic Commerce

Recruiting the Thief to Protect the Jewels

Thinking about Ethics

Firestone and Ford: Failure to Yield . . . or Asleep at the Wheel?

INSIDE BUSINESS TODAY

Trek Bikes: Trekking Around the Globe

Best of the Web

Navigating Global Business Differences

Best of the Web

Going Global

Best of the Web

Banking on the World Bank

Competing in the Global Marketplace

When Will China Get Real?

Competing in the Global Marketplace

How to Avoid Business Blunders Abroad

INSIDE BUSINESS TODAY

Ideas by the Dozen: Hatching Internet Companies at Idealab!

Best of the Web

Get Smart

Best of the Web

Start a Small Business

Best of the Web

Learn the ABCs of IPOs

Managing in the 21st Century

Create a Winning Business Plan

Competing in the Global Marketplace

Are You Crazy?

INSIDE BUSINESS TODAY

Restructuring Kinko's Partnerships to Duplicate Success

Best of the Web

Planning Your Online Business

Best of the Web

Choosing a Form of Ownership

■ PART 3 MANAGING A BUSINESS, INFORMATION SYSTEMS,
        AND PRODUCTION 150

Chapter 6   Functions and Skills of Management 150

Chapter 7   Organization, Teamwork, and Communication 176

Best of the Web

Attending a Communications
Master Class Online

**Competing in the
Global Marketplace**

Mervyn's Calls SWAT Team to
the Rescue

Thinking about Ethics

Office Ethics: Teams Make It
Hard to Tattle

INSIDE BUSINESS TODAY

Meet Mr. Internet: John
Chambers—Cisco's Live Wire

Best of the Web

Stay Informed with CIO

Best of the Web

Ride the Technology Wave

Best of the Web

Learn the Rules of the Road

**Keeping Pace with Technology
and Electronic Commerce**

Using Information to Make
a ScrubaDub Difference

**Keeping Pace with Technology
and Electronic Commerce**

Wait, Don't Punch That
Computer Monitor!

INSIDE BUSINESS TODAY

Sweet Success: Producing Perfect
Krispy Kreme Doughnuts

Best of the Web

Learn What It Takes to Manage
a CD Operation

Best of the Web

Step Inside ISO Online

■ PART 4 MANAGING EMPLOYEES 260

Chapter 10   *Motivation, Today's Workforce, and Employee-Management Relations 260*

INSIDE BUSINESS TODAY

Blending a Successful Workforce: Jamba Juice Whips Up Creative Recruiting Strategies

Best of the Web

Staying on Top of the HR World

Best of the Web

Digging Deeper at the Bureau of Labor Statistics

Best of the Web

Understanding Employee Ownership

Managing in the 21st Century

Are Temp Workers Becoming a Full-Time Headache?

Managing in the 21st Century

It's Okay to Fall Asleep on the Job

INSIDE BUSINESS TODAY

Driven by Data: Banking on Information at Capital One

Best of the Web

Fasten Your Seatbelt

Best of the Web

Sign Up For Electronic Commerce 101

Best of the Web

Demographics for Your
Marketing Toolbox

Managing in the 21st Century

Move Over Boomers and
Gen Xers: Here Comes
Generation Y

Thinking about Ethics

Questionable Marketing Tactics
on Campus

Chapter 13 Product and Pricing Strategies 344

INSIDE BUSINESS TODAY

A Living Brand: Martha
Stewart, America's Lifestyle
Queen

Best of the Web

Be a Sharp Shopper

Best of the Web

Protect Your Trademark

Best of the Web

Uncovering Hidden Costs

**Competing in the
Global Marketplace**

After You: Sometimes It Pays to
Be Second

**Competing in the
Global Marketplace**

Winning at the Name Game

Chapter 14 Distribution Strategies 368

INSIDE BUSINESS TODAY

Building a Distribution
Strategy: Home Depot, the
Ultimate Category Killer

Best of the Web

Explore the World of
Wholesaling

Best of the Web
Explore the World of Retailing

Best of the Web
Get a Move On

Keeping Pace with Technology and Electronic Commerce
Smart Car Dealers Say, "Follow That Mouse"

Managing in the 21st Century
Gateway's Big Gamble

INSIDE BUSINESS TODAY
Flooring It: Mini-Billboards at Your Feet from Floorgraphics

Best of the Web
Learn the Consumer Marketing Laws

Best of the Web
Take an Idea Journey

Best of the Web
Sample Success on the Sales Marketing Network

Competing in the Global Marketplace
Three Steps to an Effective Sales Presentation

Keeping Pace with Technology and Electronic Commerce
Should Marketers Trash the Banner?

■ PART 6 MANAGING ACCOUNTING AND FINANCIAL RESOURCES 426

INSIDE BUSINESS TODAY

Drilling for Dollars at Dental Limited

Best of the Web

Size Them Up

Best of the Web

Link Your Way to the World of Accounting

Best of the Web

Sharpen Your Pencil

Thinking about Ethics

Auditors and Clients: Too Close for Comfort?

Managing in the 21st Century

How to Read an Annual Report

INSIDE BUSINESS TODAY

Virtual Financial Management: Intuit's One-Stop Money Shop

Best of the Web

Plan Ahead

Best of the Web

Take a Field Trip to the Fed

Best of the Web

Tour the U.S. Treasury

Thinking about Ethics

Surprise! You've Been Swiped

Keeping Pace with Technology and Electronic Commerce

How Will You Be Paying for That?

INSIDE BUSINESS TODAY

Tricks of E*Trade

Best of the Web

Best of the Web

Best of the Web

Thinking about Ethics

**Keeping Pace with Technology
and Electronic Commerce**

■ PART 7 FOCUSING ON SPECIAL TOPICS IN BUSINESS 510

Component Chapter B   Business Law, Taxes, and the U.S. Legal System 510

Component Chapter C   Risk Management and Insurance 524

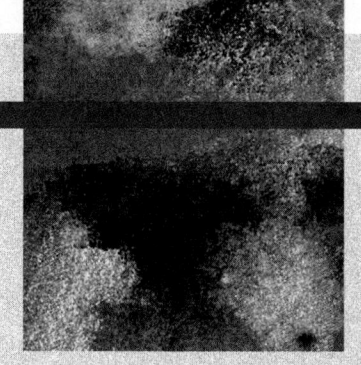

PREFACE

Business Today
TENTH EDITION

MICHAEL H. MESCON • COURTLAND L. BOVÉE • JOHN V. THILL

A text of the highest quality backed by superior authorship, this new edition of **Business Today enables your students to not only read about business, but actually experience it– first hand**–through a variety of highly involving activities in every chapter. Students will appreciate its currency, real-life examples, in-depth coverage, lively conversational writing style, colorful graphics, entrepreneurial focus, and broad selection of featured companies. Literally millions of students have learned about business from **Business Today**, and this edition continues its respected tradition of excellence. Take this opportunity to explore the features of **Business Today, Tenth Edition**. With an active-learning approach that launches students into the real world of business, this text offers today's most compelling look at the business world. We think this is the text that instructors and students alike have been looking for!

All-New Features in This Edition!

Inside Business TODAY

TREK BIKES: TREKKING AROUND THE GLOBE

www.trekbikes.com

Lance Armstrong, winner of the 1999 and 2000 Tour de France, boldly displays his affiliation.

It's a world away from the bright lights of Paris. But the little town of Waterloo, Wisconsin, captured the world's attention during the 1999 Tour de France. When Lance Armstrong zoomed across the finish line on Paris's Champs-Elysées, the American cycler raced to victory on an American bike—a bike made by Trek Bicycle Corporation of Waterloo.

At first glance, Waterloo seems an unlikely place for the headquarters of an international business. Dairy farms dominate the rural landscape. And when Green Bay Packers' fans support their favorite team, they also promote the state's most famous commodity by wearing foam cheese wedges on their heads. Even so, Waterloo is where Trek opened for business in 1976 with five workers assembling bicycle frames by hand in an old wooden barn.

During the company's first few years, Trek sold its bicycles exclusively in the United States. But all that changed in 1985 when Joyce Keehn, now Trek's worldwide sales director, received several inquiries about exporting Treks to Canada. A novice in international trade, Keehn consulted the state's export agency and sought advice from local exporters at state-sponsored trade seminars. After considering Trek's close proximity to Canada, Keehn decided that selling directly to Canadian bicycle shops was the company's best option for international expansion.

As more exporting opportunities opened up, Keehn experimented with other foreign distribution methods. For instance, to minimize cultural and language barriers, she relied on the expertise and knowledge of local distributors instead of approaching retailers directly. In other countries, she advised Trek to create wholly owned subsidiaries for handling sales, inventory, warranties, customer service, and direct distribution to retail outlets. Such subsidiary offices allowed Trek to maintain higher profits and more control over its products.

Still, Keehn hit some bumps in the road as she ventured into the global marketplace. For example, customs delays created frequent insurance and financial problems; some shipments even disappeared during customs clearances in Mexico. On one occasion, Trek halted distribution of its catalog after discovering that a featured cartoon character was offensive to Germans. And customizing bikes for the European markets increased Trek's production costs.

Cyberspace presented even more challenges for Keehn. Trek's international dealers must charge higher prices than those charged by U.S. sellers to cover such costs as shipping and tariffs. Moreover, international prices must allow for fluctuating foreign exchange rates. To avoid this confusion and to protect its international sellers, Trek does not sell bicycles or reveal prices on its Web site. Instead, it refers customers to authorized dealers in their area.

Today, whether you're in cyberspace, Cincinnati, or Cyprus, you won't have to travel far to find a Trek. Keehn has established a network of 65 distributors on six continents and seven wholly owned subsidiaries in Europe and Japan. From its humble beginnings in Waterloo, Trek is now the world's largest maker of racing bikes, mountain bikes, and other types of specialty bikes. The company sells more than a half million bikes in more than 70 countries every year. In 10 years, annual revenues have grown from $18 million to over $400 million, of which 40 percent now come from international business.[1]

INSIDE BUSINESS TODAY

Each chapter begins with a vignette, **"Inside Business Today,"** that attracts student interest by vividly portraying the business challenges faced by real businesspeople at companies such as Krispy Creme, Yahoo!, Jamba Juice, and Kinko's. Each vignette ends with thought-provoking questions that draw students into the chapter.

@ FOCUSING ON E-BUSINESS TODAY

Roadblocks on the European and Asian Superhighways

Late to the Internet and electronic commerce, Europe and Asia have trailed the United States in its use and enthusiasm for the Web. But now they are trying to catch up. Young firms in Europe and Asia are bursting through the gates at lightning pace, taking ideas originally conceived and launched in the United States and adapting them for the local market. But many roadblocks exist for these foreign companies.

E-COMMERCE IN EUROPE

The Internet in Europe is still in its infancy. Though rapidly growing, only 10 percent of Europeans currently use the Web. The pattern of e-commerce development varies country by country. Scandinavians are early adopters, driven partly by the excellence of local telecommunications manufacturers such as Ericsson of Sweden and Nokia of Finland. France, on the other hand, has been slow to take to the Web, partly because of cultural resistance and partly because of high telecommunications prices and tariffs, as well as inefficient phone systems.

> **LEARNING OBJECTIVE** @8
>
> Summarize the challenges European and Asian countries are facing as they attempt to narrow the U.S. lead in global e-commerce

Improvements to the European Highway

In spite of these obstacles, recent advancements in Europe's digital, cable, and satellite services are vastly improving the continent's telecommunications infrastructure. Europe is building on its strength in mobile telephones and will likely lead the world in mobile e-commerce (as Chapter 8 points out). Moreover, Europe's transition to the new economy is being fueled by a shift in career preferences from big traditional corporations to smaller start-ups due to a growing acceptance of entrepreneurship, as the exhibit on Bootstrap Capitalism suggests. Experts predict that e-commerce sales in Europe will skyrocket from a mere $5.6 billion in 1998 to $430 billion by 2003. Still, roadblocks exist.

Surfing a Web of Red Tape

European leaders say they support the rise of the Internet economy. Nonetheless, their governments burden e-commerce with a maze of rules, regulations, and tax laws from another era. For instance, to protect neighborhood stores, German regulations prohibit most price discounting on consumer goods. The same laws keep airlines from dumping unsold seats at the last minute with fire-sale fares. Online auctions run into legal tangles because laws require the physical display of goods to be sold at the auction. And legislative mazes turn the simple act of registering a Web address into a long and complex process. Moreover, they discourage e-commerce entrepreneurs.

E-COMMERCE IN ASIA

Asia is home to half the world's population but is even further behind Europe. Like Europe, Asia is not a homogeneous market. It varies widely by language, culture, literacy, and wealth. For instance, Singapore's and Hong Kong's wired societies have little in common with Sumatran villages of Indonesia or the rusting industrial ports of mainland China. In order to develop and thrive, e-commerce must jump several hurdles in Asia.

Hurdles on the Asian Highway

Lack of access to investment capital and expensive, uneven telecommunications service contribute to the Internet's lag in Asia. Getting a decent phone connection, let alone a net linkup, is a challenge in some parts of Asia. Worse, most commercial transactions in Asia still require cash and written receipts. A lack of comprehensive credit services also means that each e-marketplace buyer and seller must be painstakingly screened, which can take weeks. "It's difficult enough in the real world, but on the Internet, it can be even harder," says one Asian e-business owner.

BOOTSTRAP CAPITALISM

Polls show that Europe remains far less fertile ground for entrepreneurship than the United States, though entrepreneurs themselves are gaining respect.

Percent of respondents. . .

	. . .involved in creating a new company in the previous year	. . .expecting good opportunities to start a business in the next six months	. . .who say successful entrepreneurs have high status and are respected in their country
U.S.	8.4%	57%	91%
Britain	3.3	16	38
Germany	2.2	15	73
France	1.8	15	83
Japan	1.6	1	8

FOCUSING ON E-BUSINESS TODAY

From the smallest dot-coms to lumbering global giants, e-business is affecting the way all companies do business today. **"Focusing on E-Business Today"** is a dedicated section that appears at the end of each chapter and expands student learning by explaining in depth the important challenges companies are facing in the world of e-business.

VIDEO CASES AND EXERCISES

Each chapter concludes with an engaging **"Video Case and Exercises."** Professionally produced videos take students behind the scenes at some of the world's most fascinating companies, such as Lands' End, Ritz-Carlton, Terra Chips, Amy's Ice Creams, and IHOP. Each set of exercises contains nine labeled parts: analysis, application, decision, communication, integration, ethics, debate, teamwork, and online research.

VIDEO CASE AND EXERCISES

▪ Yahoo! and Lands' End
Think Global, Act Local

SYNOPSIS

Although Internet media pioneer Yahoo! is headquartered in California, and apparel retailer Lands' End is based in Wisconsin, both see international business activity as a way to fuel growth. Lands' End, founded in 1963, started its global expansion in 1987 by sending catalogs to customers in Canada. Soon the company was selling by mail in 175 countries. As global sales increased, the company opened offices in the United Kingdom and Japan and learned, through trial and error, how to navigate cultural differences. For its part, Yahoo! moved into global markets just two years after it was founded in 1994, starting with a Web site with language and content customized for Japan. Yahoo! has continued opening several new international Web sites every year, carefully tailoring the offerings on each site to fit local customs and culture.

EXERCISES

Analysis

1. What forms of international business activity have Lands' End and Yahoo! used to enter global markets?

2. Why do Lands' End managers say that "the United States and the United Kingdom are two countries divided by a common language?"

3. How do the sales made by U.S. companies offering products on international Yahoo! sites affect the U.S. balance of trade?

4. If a country in which Lands' End operates decides to devalue its currency, what is the likely effect on Lands' End?

5. Managers at Yahoo! say that services such as their Web sites are "apolitical," yet they are careful to abide by each country's customs. Why?

Application

Companies choosing among the five types of international business activities must consider the degree of risk, ownership, and financial commitment they find acceptable. What risks might Lands' End encounter in opening facilities in South Africa to handle local customers' orders? How might the company research these risks in more detail?

Decision

Assume that an Egyptian entrepreneur has asked to license the Yahoo! name for a local Web site. What are the advantages and disadvantages of licensing the Yahoo! brand? What decision would you recommend to the top management of Yahoo!—and why?

Communication

Write a one-page memo to Jasmine Kem, international marketing manager for Yahoo!, explaining the decision you recommend concerning whether Yahoo! should license its name to the entrepreneur in Egypt.

Integration

Turn back to the discussion of labor-intensive and capital-intensive businesses in Chapter 1. How would you categorize Yahoo! and Lands' End? Why?

Ethics

Does Yahoo! have an ethical obligation to prevent its users in Japan, China, and other countries from falling victim to Internet scams such as fraudulent sales offers?

Debate

Many successful e-businesses have been founded in the United States, especially in and around Silicon Valley. Does the United States have a comparative advantage in e-business? Use this question as the subject of a debate, offering evidence to support your stand for or against.

Teamwork

In a team of three students, consider how Lands' End would be affected if Japan decided to pursue a protectionist strategy. What kinds of trade restrictions would hurt Lands' End? Could any restrictions help Lands' End?

Online Research

Using Internet sources, identify all the countries and languages in which Yahoo! sites are available. Also research the company's plans for opening new international sites in the coming year. Summarize your findings in a paragraph or two.

The Match

FedEx is the leader in overnight air delivery. Arch-rival United Parcel Service (UPS), also known as "Big Brown," practically owns the business of moving packages by truck and delivering them to any address in the United States. Both companies compete in the same transportation industry sector—air delivery, freight, and parcel services. Several years ago UPS began going after FedEx's profitable core business—next day air express, with surprising success. Acknowledging that it is losing ground to UPS, FedEx is counterattacking.

1999 Revenue
$17.5 billion $27.2 billion

	FedEx	UPS
	$7.4	$5.2
		$2.7
	$2.3	
	$3.0	$14.4
	$3.8	
		$3.6
	$1.0	

- ■ Other
- ■ U.S. ground
- ■ U.S. overnight
- ■ International operations
- ■ U.S. two-day air

FedEx Hits the Ground

In 1997 FedEx acquired RPS, a trucking company, to wage a ground turf war against UPS. But FedEx feared that combining the two companies could tarnish the FedEx image, so it kept RPS at arm's length. Meanwhile, poor integration of the FedEx air and RPS ground units made things tough for corporate customers who wanted to ship by both truck and overnight air. They had to deal with two salespeople, call two numbers, and so on. By contrast, UPS offers both services seamlessly. So UPS captured the lion's share of e-commerce delivery traffic.

Realizing that customers wanted both ground and air services, FedEx combined the two operations in early 2000. Then it renamed RPS to FedEx Ground, changed RPS's focus to business-to-business deliveries, and developed FedEx Home to beef up deliveries to residential neighborhoods—going right after the heart of UPS. FedEx is increasing its aggressive counterattack against UPS by engaging in talks to acquire American Freightways, a large U.S. ground shipper.

30

UPS Flexes Its Muscle

Even though FedEx is making inroads with its acquisition of RPS, UPS still has the advantage. With three times the number of trucks of FedEx, UPS delivers to virtually every U.S. address. Moreover, UPS's massive volume of ground-based shipments keeps its residential package delivery costs low. So UPS can pass the savings on to customers and still make money. Furthermore, UPS has poured a stunning $11 billion into technology to improve its package-tracking systems and on-time delivery performance. Like FedEx, UPS customers can track the exact location of their packages.

Fighting a Battle in the Sky and on the Ground!

	FedEx www.fedex.com	UPS www.ups.com
Sales (annual)	$17.5 billion	$27.2 billion
Daily Packages	4.5 million	13 million
Delivered Market Share	25% of package delivery market	55% of package delivery market
Employees	149,000	344,000
Equipment	43,500 trucks; 637 planes	150,000 trucks; 610 planes

The Fight Goes Airborne

For years UPS's air-express business lagged far behind FedEx's, and UPS could not match FedEx's reputation for reliability. But UPS has improved its air delivery service and is gradually cutting into FedEx's business. Furthermore, when possible, UPS shifts packages from expensive airplane delivery to less-expensive truck delivery, then passes the savings on to the customer.

Duking it Out in China

Both UPS and FedEx are major players in the global marketplace, but their approach in China differs significantly. FedEx has poured money into an all-out China blitz in advance of market demand. The company flies its own jets to and from China and is keeping its American identity. FedEx's operations, trucks, and employees in China look identical to those in the United States and the company is promoting its service with U.S.-style, and at times abrasive, advertising.

UPS, by contrast, took a go-slow approach, putting its packages on others' planes (even though this adds one day to delivery time). In fact, UPS hopes that Chinese customers won't even notice that it is a U.S. company. UPS's advertising is understated and old-fashioned, and the company is focusing on developing personal relationships with Chinese businesses while keeping a low profile.

When the Asian economy was suffering, it appeared that UPS made a smarter move. But now UPS would like to be in FedEx's shoes. China, with 1.4 billion people, is the fastest-growing freight market. To catch up, UPS is trying to acquire its own air

"FACE-OFF" CASES

In end-of-part **"Face-Off"** cases, students compare and contrast the performance results of two companies in the same industry who compete against each other by adopting different approaches and methods for executing their strategies, such as UPS vs.FedEx, Airbus vs. Boeing, and Barnesandnoble.com vs. Amazon. As the two companies battle it out, students will gain an understanding of the challenges of competing in today's global marketplace.

BUSINESS PLANPRO EXERCISES

The end-of-part **"Business PlanPro Exercises"** enable students to use the knowledge they've gained from reading chapters within that part. Each exercise has two tasks: **"Think Like a Pro"** tasks require students to navigate the software, find and review information in sample business plans, and evaluate and critique some of the thinking that went behind these plans. **"Create Your Own Business Plan"** tasks provide students with an opportunity to apply their skills to creating their own winning business plan.

Business PlanPro

■ CONDUCTING BUSINESS IN THE GLOBAL ECONOMY

Think Like a Pro

OBJECTIVE: By completing these exercises you will become acquainted with the sections of a business plan that address forms of competition, company and product/service descriptions, and the economic outlook for the related industry. You will use the sample business plan for Adventure Travel International (ATI) in this exercise.

Open the BPP software and explore the sample business plan Travel Agency.spd. Click on the "Plan Outline" icon to access the plan's Task Manager. Find the headings "What You're Selling" and "The Business You're In" and double click on each of the sections under these headings to read the text portion of the business plan that discusses these topics.

1. What products and services does ATI provide? Will ATI compete on price, speed, quality, service, or innovation to gain a competitive advantage?
2. What is the economic outlook for the travel industry? What are the principal categories of this industry? What percentage of the industry involves international travel?

3. How has the Internet affected this industry?
4. Find the heading "What You're Selling." Double click on "Product and Service Description." The text view of BPP software provides helpful instructions for each section of a business plan. Click on the "Instructions" tab located at the top of your screen. What information should you include about a company's product and service in a business plan? Now return to the Task Manager and double click on "Competitive Comparison." Click on the "Instructions" tab. What are some of the things you should discuss about your competition in a business plan?

Create Your Own Business Plan

Think about your own business. Describe in detail the product or service your company will provide. Indicate whether you will compete on price, speed, quality, service, or innovation. In what industry will you compete? What is the economic outlook for that industry? What kinds of competition do you expect to face?

Greater Emphasis on E-Business

When preparing the Tenth Edition, the authors dedicated themselves to the most extensive revision ever. The most significant change is the expanded coverage of the technological revolution in business. **Business Today's** nine-way integrated approach to e-business reinforces its importance to students.

1 **A substantial, dedicated section at the end of each chapter.** Focusing on E-Business Today is a feature that appears at the end of each chapter just before the end-of-chapter Summary of Learning Objectives.

2 **Full-chapter coverage.** Internet technology and its impact on the way companies do business is explored in detail in Component Chapter A, which follows Chapter 1.

3 **"Keeping Pace with Technology and Electronic Commerce" boxes.** Special feature boxes highlight the differences between conducting business in the e-world and in a traditional business environment.

4 **Featured e-businesses.** Chapter vignettes, case studies, boxes, and in-text and online examples feature popular e-businesses such as AOL Time Warner, Cisco, Dell, E*Trade, eSchwab, Priceline, 1-800 Flowers, iPrint, eBay, Amazon, and more.

5 **Online Supplement.** Written to accompany this text, this supplement focuses entirely on e-business hot topics and the latest trends in e-commerce.

6 **"Video Case with Exercises."** Many of the video cases give students a first-hand look at critical e-commerce issues that companies are facing.

7 **Internet exercises**. Students become acquainted with the wealth of information on the Web by completing the text's **"Best of the Web," "Explore on Your Own,"** and supplemental online Internet exercises.

8 **Learning objectives.** One e-business learning objective appears in the "Learning Objectives" list at the beginning of each chapter.

9 **Photo and exhibit program.** Photographs and exhibits throughout the book that relate to e-business give students an intimate glimpse into the real-life application of the topic being portrayed.

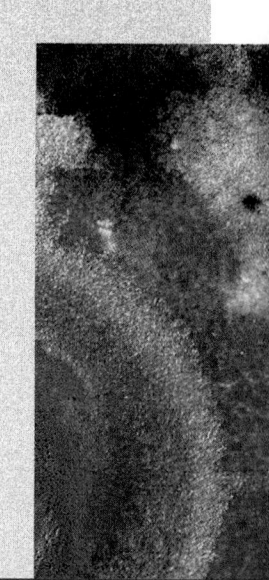

Spotlight on Five Major Business Challenges

This edition places special emphasis on five major challenges facing businesses in today's highly competitive, fast-paced, and changing environment. The material is woven into chapter text, where explanation and analysis offer students vivid insights into how businesspeople cope with these challenges on a daily basis. A list of the examples associated with each of the following well-integrated themes can be found in a special "Guide to Thematic Examples" following this Preface:

1 PRODUCING QUALITY PRODUCTS AND SERVICES THAT SATISFY CUSTOMERS' CHANGING NEEDS

2 STARTING AND MANAGING A SMALL BUSINESS IN TODAY'S COMPETITIVE ENVIRONMENT

3 THINKING GLOBALLY AND COMMITTING TO A CULTURALLY DIVERSE WORK FORCE

4 BEHAVING IN AN ETHICALLY AND SOCIALLY RESPONSIBLE MANNER

5 KEEPING PACE WITH TECHNOLOGY AND ELECTRONIC COMMERCE

Trademark Features— All Updated for This Edition

SPECIAL FEATURE BOXES

Special feature boxes make the world of business come alive with fresh, never-before-seen examples that are carefully placed in each chapter to further enhance student learning. Each box includes two critical-thinking questions that are ideal for developing individual or team problem-solving skills. The four themes include the following:

KEEPING PACE WITH TECHNOLOGY AND ELECTRONIC COMMERCE

MILKING THE NET

In 1999 Ted Farnsworth was trolling the Internet, looking for farming equipment for his brother-in-law's New York dairy farm. Frustrated that he could not find what he needed online, Farnsworth decided to fill his own needs and start a farming Web site. Now CEO and founder of Farmbid.com, Farnsworth traverses the country signing up farmers at one trade show after another. The company has about 90,000 registered customers who use the site to buy and sell seed, chemicals, machinery, and other agricultural supplies.

Farmbid is one of more than a dozen business-to-business farming Web sites that try to cash in on the isolation of many rural farmers by giving them a one-stop shop for their farming needs. Some auction cattle, pigs, sheep, and horses, while others sell everything from seed to animal vaccinations to farm insurance. But competition is increasing. Major agricultural firms Cenex Harvest States Cooperatives, Cargill, and DuPont are challenging the newcomers with their own joint venture Rooster.com, an electronic mall where farmers can buy and sell seed, fertilizer, crops, farm chemicals, and other goods.

The Web sites are welcome news for farmers. Most farmers live in remote places and conduct their affairs in the nearest town. A consolidation wave in agribusiness is shrinking their local choices for everything from seed suppliers to grain handlers. The Internet might be the farmers' solution to the local monopolies they face. It gives farmers the means to connect with distant businesses. For example, on a recent afternoon Mark Gunn, a Janesville, Wisconsin farmer, fired up his computer and headed for a swine auction at Farms.com in search of 230 pigs to stock his 2,000-acre farm. Instead of running off to another farm or a crowded auction house—sometimes two or three states away—to look for pigs, Gunn sat in his office and found what he was looking for in a few minutes.

The Web sites make money through advertising, from transaction fees, or by taking a percentage of each sale made over the site. But few are profitable, and most don't expect to be for at least a year. Moreover, while there appears to be a strong market for Internet farming, industry analysts agree that there is room for only two or three players. Farmbid expects a tough battle now that the big guys such as DuPont and Cargill have awakened. Meanwhile, as more and more farmers discover what the Internet can do for this ancient industry, one thing is for certain: it may never be the same down on the farm.

■ QUESTIONS FOR CRITICAL THINKING

1. Review the Farmbid.com Web site at www.farmbid.com/. How does this site provide value to the farm community?

2. How is Internet technology changing the agricultural industry?

Keeping Pace with Technology and Electronic Commerce

COMPETING IN THE GLOBAL MARKETPLACE

WHEN WILL CHINA GET REAL?

Welcome to the People's Republic of China, where everything from soap to software is pirated. China produces more fakes than any other nation—everything from autos to aircraft parts, beer to razor blades, soap to shampoo, TVs to toilets. China produces nearly half of the world's 14 billion batteries. But most of them are fake versions of Panasonic, Gillette, and other big brands. Moreover, it is estimated that a quarter of the world's watch production (perhaps a third of which is counterfeit) is concentrated in Guangdong—China's richest and fastest-growing region.

Fake-making has infiltrated nearly every sector of China's economy. Most counterfeiters work at small to mid-sized factories, but many stay at home, doing things like filling Head & Shoulders bottles from large vats in their living rooms. Overall, the amount of China's manufacturing base that is dependent on fakes and other illegal knockoffs is es-

Dove soap is making its way from China into Europe. Bose (a maker of highend audio systems), is finding Chinese fakes in overseas markets. Indeed, the pirates have moved to a whole new level of sophistication. Ten years ago, China's knockoffs were below Western standards. Today, many fake Duracells look so genuine that Gillette has to send them to a forensics lab to analyze them. Fake watches even contain full-sized Swiss movements and real gems.

So what are pirated brand owners to do? For the most part, companies are trying to boost government enforcement, a tough task. For example, U.S. sunglasses maker Oakley has gotten Chinese authorities to close counterfeiters' factories, but new ones pop up in their place. Many multinationals are shutting or shrinking some product lines in China because these products are overrun by counterfeits. But China's market is so vast and promising, few companies are willing to pull out entirely.

Competing

in the Global

Marketplace

MANAGING IN THE 21ST CENTURY

CREATE A WINNING BUSINESS PLAN

Although the business plan has a simple, straightforward purpose, it still requires a great deal of thought. For example, before you open your doors, you have to make important decisions about personnel, marketing, facilities, suppliers, and distribution. A written business plan forces you to think about those issues and develop programs that will help you succeed. If you are starting out on a small scale and using your own money, your business plan may be relatively informal. But at a minimum, you should describe the basic concept of the business and outline its specific goals, objectives, and resource requirements. A formal plan, suitable for use with banks or investors, should cover these points:

ment personnel in your company. Include résumés in the appendix.

- *Marketing strategy.* Provide projections of sales and market share, and outline a strategy for identifying and contacting customers, setting prices, providing customer services, advertising, and so forth. Whenever possible, include evidence of customer acceptance, such as advance product orders.
- *Design and development plans.* If your product requires design or development, describe the nature and extent of what needs to be done, including costs and possible problems.

Managing

in the 21st

Century

THINKING ABOUT ETHICS

FIRESTONE AND FORD: FAILURE TO YIELD . . . OR ASLEEP AT THE WHEEL?

For nearly a decade, lawsuits claimed that treads on tires manufactured by Bridgestone/Firestone were peeling off without warning, causing Ford Explorers to flip over. Mounting consumer complaints and damaging media reports led to a federal investigation in 2000, putting pressure on Firestone to recall 6.5 million defective tires. But the public soon learned that trouble had started long before the massive tire recall.

As early as 1998, Ford Motor Company received reports of Firestone tire tread separations on Ford Explorers in countries with hot climates, such as Saudi Arabia and Venezuela. Ford took the complaints to Firestone because it didn't have enough information to investigate the problem itself. (Tires are the only significant part of the car that is guaranteed by the tire supplier, not the automaker.) Firestone reassured Ford that the tire problems resulted

Meanwhile, simmering tensions between the longtime partners burst into open hostilities as Ford and Firestone engaged in bitter finger-pointing over who was responsible for the tire problems and why they didn't come to light sooner. Convinced that tread separations were related to inadequate tire pressures, Firestone claimed Ford had ignored the tire maker's warnings to boost the recommended tire pressure for Explorers. But Ford pinned the blame on Firestone, claiming the company stalled in analyzing and sharing its warranty-claims data. Firestone executives, in turn, argued that Explorers had been involved in 16,000 rollover accidents within the past decade—but fewer than 10 percent had involved tread separation of Firestone tires.

In spite of over 100 deaths from accidents involving Explorers with Firestone radials, Firestone and Ford admitted they didn't realize the extent of the lethal tire prob-

Thinking

About Ethics

BEST OF THE WEB

Students become acquainted with the Web and its wealth of information that relates to the content of *Business Today*. In each chapter, three **"Best of the Web"** features describe Web sites that reinforce and extend chapter material.

Best of the Web Best of the Web Best of

GOING GLOBAL

Have you ever thought about getting into the world of exporting? Where would you go for information and help? Many small and large companies have gotten valuable export assistance from online material such as the *Basic Guide to Exporting*. This joint publication by the U.S. Department of Commerce and Unz & Company has a wealth of information about export procedures; foreign markets, industries, companies, and products; export financing; unfair trade practices; trade statistics; and more.
www.unzco.com/basicguide/index.html

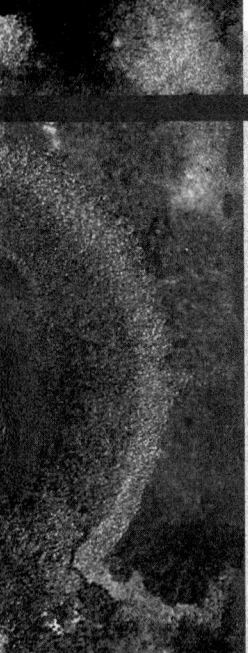

A CASE FOR CRITICAL THINKING

At the end of each chapter, **"A Case for Critical Thinking"** reinforces points made in the chapter. This classic device assists students in evaluating situations, using good judgment, learning to make decisions, and developing critical thinking skills. These cases are 100% new!

A CASE FOR CRITICAL THINKING

■ Doing Everybody's Wash— Whirlpool's Global Lesson

Everybody is talking about going global these days, but most people don't understand what that really means. David Whitwam, chairman and CEO of Whirlpool, does. When he first began eyeing the global marketplace, this Michigan-based appliance maker was concentrating only on the U.S. market, producing and marketing washers, refrigerators, and other household appliances under the Whirlpool, KitchenAid, Roper, and Kenmore brand names.

THE RIGHT WAY TO GO GLOBAL

Determined to convert Whirlpool from essentially a U.S. company to a major global player, Whitwam purchased N. V. Philips's floundering European appliance business in 1989. The CEO's first challenge was to integrate and coordinate the many European operations with the U.S. operation. Some companies accomplish this task by imposing the parent's systems on the acquired companies, but Whitwam started down a more ambitious path. He created cross-cultural teams with members from the European and North American operations, and together they designed a program to ensure quality and productivity throughout Whirlpool's worldwide operation. In the eyes of other corporate leaders, Whirlpool was doing everything right. The company was even featured in a 1994 *Harvard Business Review* article titled "The Right Way to Go Global."

SPINNING OUT OF CONTROL

Whitwam soon discovered, however, that developing global strategies was far easier than executing them. Whirlpool had not counted on the difficulty in marketing appliances—a largely homogeneous process in the United States—to the fragmented cultures of Europe, Asia, and Latin America. For instance, clothes washers sold in northern European countries such as Denmark must spin-dry clothes much better than in southern Italy, where consumers often line-dry clothes in warmer weather. And consumers in India and southern China prefer small refrigerators because they must fit in tight kitchens.

Despite these challenges, Whitwam was convinced that he could remake Whirlpool into a truly global company. But Whirlpool's timing couldn't have been worse. Just as the company

was planting its feet in international markets, economic turmoil hit Asia and Europe. Wildly fluctuating foreign exchange rates wreaked havoc in Asia, where Whirlpool had participated in several joint ventures. Fortunately, less than 5 percent of Whirlpool's sales came from Asia, so the company was not seriously hurt. Still, ongoing global economic woes contributed to Whirlpool's multimillion-dollar losses overseas.

REARRANGING THE GLOBAL LOAD

The global economic crisis forced Whitwam to fine-tune his expansion plans. Whirlpool dropped one joint venture in China (costing the company $350 million) and rearranged others as intense competition and weak economic conditions drove appliance prices down and sapped profits. "The thing we misjudged was how rapidly Chinese manufacturers could improve their quality," notes Whitwam.

In Brazil, where Whirlpool had long been profitable, a currency crisis slowed appliance sales to a trickle. Still, Whitwam remained committed to the market. Anticipating future growth opportunities in this emerging market, Whirlpool invested hundreds of millions of dollars to modernize operations, cut costs, and solidify its position as the country's market leader in refrigerators, room air conditioners, and washers.

To expedite its entry into foreign markets, Whirlpool kept things simple. The company used licensing arrangements and formed strategic alliances with others. It also developed standardized products, which it could modify to meet specific market needs. For instance, front-loading washing machines were scaled down for European homes as were refrigerators for India. Despite their widely different exteriors and sizes, the appliances had plenty of common "innards."

ULTIMATE REWARD

In less than a decade, Whitwam transformed Whirlpool from essentially a U.S. company into the world's leading manufacturer of major home appliances. With 11 major brands sold in 170 countries, international sales now account for about 45 percent of the company's $10 billion annual revenue. Moreover, the outlook for growth in the global appliance industry looks promising. Still, Whitwam understands that doing business in the global marketplace is fraught with risk; conditions can change at the drop of a baht, ruble, or dollar.

End-of-Chapter Skill-Building Activities and Exercises

As stated in the SCANS (Secretary's Commission on Achieving Necessary Skills) report from the Department of Labor, it is essential that students meet national standards of academic and occupational skills. Like no other introduction to business text, **Business Today** emphasizes the skills and competencies necessary for students to make the transition from academia to the workplace.

Business Today includes an extraordinary number of pedagogical devices that simplify teaching, facilitate learning, stimulate critical thinking, maintain interest and enjoyment, and illustrate the practical application of chapter concepts.

▇▇▇▇▇ T E S T   Y O U R   K N O W L E D G E

QUESTIONS FOR REVIEW

1. How can a company use a licensing agreement to enter world markets?
2. What is the balance of trade, and how is it related to the balance of payments?
3. What is intrafirm trade?
4. What is dumping, and how does the United States respond to this practice?
5. What is a floating exchange rate?

QUESTIONS FOR ANALYSIS

6. Why would a company choose to work through intermediaries when selling products in a foreign country?
7. How do companies benefit from forming international joint ventures and strategic alliances?
8. What types of situations might cause the U.S. government to implement protectionist measures?
9. How do tariffs and quotas protect a country's own industries?
10. @ Why is it important to understand other cultures when designing an e-commerce Web site?
11. ▣ Should the U.S. government more closely regulate the practice of giving trips and other incentives to foreign managers to win their business? Is this bribery?

QUESTIONS FOR APPLICATION

12. Suppose you own a small company that manufactures baseball equipment. You are aware that Russia is a large market, and you are considering exporting your products there. What steps should you take? Who might be able to give you assistance?
13. Because your Brazilian restaurant caters to Western businesspeople and tourists, much of the food you buy is imported from the United States. Lately, the value of the real (Brazil's currency) has been falling relative to the dollar. This change makes your food imports much more costly, and it negatively affects your profitability. You have three options: Which one will you choose? (a) Raise menu prices across the board. (b) Accept only U.S. dollars from customers. (c) Try to purchase more of your food items locally. Please explain your selection.
14. ▨ Review the theory of supply and demand discussed in Chapter 1. Using this theory, explain how a country's currency is valued and why governments sometimes adjust the values of their currency.
15. ▨ You just received notice that a large shipment of manufacturing supplies you have been waiting for has been held up in customs for two weeks. A local business associate tells you that you are expected to give customs agents some "incentive money" to see that everything clears easily. How will you handle this situation? Evaluate the ethical merits of your decision by answering the questions outlined in Exhibit 2.1 on page 00.

"Questions for Review" reinforce learning and help students review chapter material.

"Questions for Application" give students the opportunity to apply principles presented in the chapter material; two of these questions are integrated to help students apply principles learned in earlier chapters.

"Questions for Analysis" help students analyze chapter material; one question focuses on e-business and the other focuses on ethics. Each is marked with a special icon.

PRACTICE YOUR KNOWLEDGE

NEW! Sharpening Your Communication Skills
These exercises call on students to practice a wide range of communication activities, including one-on-one and group discussions, personal interviews, panel sessions, oral and written papers, and letter- and memo-writing assignments.

NEW! Handling Difficult Situations on the Job
Students learn to handle difficult situations on the job through short, experimental exercises. They must use the knowledge they've gained from the text, along with their good judgment, to solve a challenging workplace dilemma. Taken from actual events, these exercises are designed to develop student problem-solving and critical thinking skills.

▇▇▇▇▇ P R A C T I C E   Y O U R   K N O W L E D G E

SHARPENING YOUR COMMUNICATION SKILLS

Languages never translate on a word-for-word basis. When doing business in the global marketplace, choose words that convey only their most specific denotative meaning. Avoid using slang or idioms (words that can have meanings far different from their individual components when translated literally). For example, if a U.S. executive tells an Egyptian executive that a certain product "doesn't cut the mustard," chances are that communication will fail.

Team up with two other students and list 10 examples of slang (in your own language) that would probably be misinterpreted or misunderstood during a business conversation with someone from another culture. Next to each example, suggest other words you might use to convey the same message. Make sure the alternatives mean exactly the same as the original slang or idiom. Compare your list with those of your classmates.

HANDLING DIFFICULT SITUATIONS ON THE JOB: SHOULD COMPANIES STRESS ENGLISH ONLY ON THE JOB?

When Frances Arreola read the memo announcing that employees should speak only English on the job, she was outraged. Arreola, a lens inspector for Signet Amoralite, a lens-manufacturing firm in southern California, is fluent in both English and Spanish but feels that the English-only rules constitute discrimination.

More than half of Signet's 900 employees are Asian, Filipino, or Hispanic. The company defends its English-only rule on the ground that "speaking in another language that associates cannot fully understand can lead to misunderstandings, is impolite, and can even be unsafe." While the policy carries no punishment, it is considered by some critics to violate federal discrimination laws.[59]

1. If you were a manager at Signet Amoralite, how would you defend the company's English-only policy?
2. If a company knowingly hires an employee who is not fluent in English, should the company have a right to require English only on the job?
3. If you took a job in another country where you weren't fluent in the native language, would you feel compelled to learn the language even if your employer did not require you to?

BUILDING YOUR TEAM SKILLS

In today's interdependent global economy, fluctuations in a country's currency can have a profound effect on the flow of products across borders. The U.S. steel industry, for example, has been feeling intense competition from an influx of Korean, Brazilian, and Russian steel imports. After the currencies of those countries plummeted in value, the price of steel products exported to the United States dropped as well, making U.S. steel much more expensive by comparison.

Fueled by low prices, steel flooded into the United States, hurting sales of U.S. steel. Over the course of several months, the volume of steel imports nearly doubled. Stung, U.S. steelmakers slashed production and laid off more than 10,000 U.S. workers. U.S. trade officials charge that the cheap imported steel is being

NEW! Building Your Team Skills
Students have the opportunity to form team-building skills through innovative exercises that teach brainstorming, collaborative decision making, developing a consensus, debating, role-playing, and resolving conflict.

EXPAND YOUR KNOWLEDGE

"Keeping Current Using The Wall Street Journal."

To emphasize the link between today's business news and Business Today, a "Keeping Current Using The Wall Street Journal" exercise is provided at the end of each chapter. Students are asked to choose an article they are interested in and are provided with a structure for analyzing the article in the context of the material covered in the chapter.

New! Discovering Career Opportunities

Students can explore career resources on campus, observe businesspeople on their jobs, interview businesspeople, and perform self-evaluations to assess their own career skills and interests.

EXPAND YOUR KNOWLEDGE

KEEPING CURRENT USING *THE WALL STREET JOURNAL*

Find a *Wall Street Journal* article describing an experience of a U.S. company or division that conducts business in a foreign country. As an alternative, look for an article describing how a company or division based in another country has started doing business in the United States. If you are using the *Wall Street Journal* Interactive edition on the Web, search past editions (click on Past Editions and Articles) using key terms such as "joint venture," "licensing," or "strategic alliance."

1. Describe in your own words the company's experience. Was it positive, negative, or mixed? Why?

2. What legal or political barriers did the company have to overcome? What cultural or business differences did the company encounter? What problems did these difference create for the company? What did the company do to overcome the obstacles?

3. Companies involved in international trade have to watch the foreign exchange rates of the countries in which they do business. Find yesterday's foreign exchange rates for the euro, Japanese yen, Brazilian real, and Russian ruble relative to the U.S. dollar. If you were a U.S. exporter, how might a stronger dollar affect demand for your products? How might a weaker dollar affect demand? (Note: one Internet source for foreign exchange rates is www.x-rates.com/.)

DISCOVERING CAREER OPPORTUNITIES

If global business interests you, consider working for a U.S. government agency that supports or regulates international trade. For example, here are the duties performed by an international trade specialist at the International Trade Administration of the U.S. Department of Commerce: "The incumbent will assist senior specialists in coordination and support of government trade programs and events; perform research and analysis of trade data and information on specific topics or issues within a larger project or assignment; and disseminate trade information and materials on government products/services to U.S. businesses and associations. Incumbent will attend meetings and engage in other activities for developmental purposes. As a condition of employment, applicants must be available for reassignment and relocation within the United States."[61]

1. On the basis of this description, what education and skills (personal and professional) would you need to succeed as an international trade specialist? Why? How does this job description fit your qualifications and interests?

3. What sources would you contact to locate trade-related jobs with government agencies such as the International Trade Administration?

EXPLORING THE BEST OF THE WEB

URLs for all Internet exercises are provided at the Web site for this book, www.prenhall.com/mescon. Log on to the text Web site, select Chapter 3, click on the name of the featured Web site, and follow the detailed navigational directions to complete these exercises.

Navigating Global Business Differences, page 000

The resources available at USA Trade.gov will start your journey into the world of global business on the right foot. Log on to this site, and access the Country Commercial Guide for a specific country you would like to learn more about.

1. What are the economic trends and future outlook for that country?

2. What role does the government play in the country's economy?

3. How do the business customs of that country differ from those of the United States? What is the country's official language?

Going Global, page 000

Many factors must be considered before exporting a product. The information in the *Basic Guide to Exporting*, available online, can help you make sense of it all. Explore the publication to increase your knowledge about export procedures, foreign markets, and more.

1. Describe the general factors you should examine before reaching a decision to enter the global marketplace.

2. What kinds of information can you find at U.S. Export Assistance Centers?

3. What questions should a company consider before preparing a product for export? Why do governments impose foreign product regulations on imported goods?

Banking on the World Bank, page 000

Log on to the World Bank Web site and learn about the important role this organization plays in today's global economy.

1. What is the goal of the World Bank? What does the World Bank do?

Exploring the Best of the Web

These exercises are directly tied to the "Best of the Web" features within the chapters and give students experience with the rich resources of the Web. Students who complete these exercises will learn how to use the Internet proficiently and productively.

MASTERING GLOBAL AND GEOGRAPHICAL SKILLS

MASTERING GLOBAL AND GEOGRAPHICAL SKILLS: ADIOS, ARGENTINA—HELLO, BRAZIL

"Love thy neighbor" is not an easy commandment to live by for Argentina. The 35 percent slide of the Brazilian real against the Argentine peso at the end of the twentieth century made Argentine products comparatively more expensive both at home and abroad. Worse, the cost of doing business became far cheaper in Brazil than in Argentina, spurring some two-dozen companies to jump the border. One manufacturer after another moved north to Brazil. At least 15 auto-parts companies have left, taking with them 7,000 jobs or one-fifth of the industry's workforce. And the stampede isn't limited to the auto industry.

You are the owner of a U.S.-based home security equipment manufacturing company with a local operation in Argentina, and your Argentine workers have been bolting for Brazil like everyone else. So now you're thinking of packing it up and moving your Argentine operation to São Paulo Brazil. Not only is the cost of doing business more affordable there, but with all the people migrating north, you'll have no trouble finding customers and employees.[62]

You heard (unofficially) that the market for home security equipment is good in Brazil. But you know very little about the Brazilian laws, culture, and infrastructure. You speak fluent Spanish, but not a word of Portuguese. And you think it would be a good idea to research the Brazilian marketplace before making such an important decision. Fortunately, many good Internet resources can provide you with information on foreign countries and markets around the world. These sites include:

- CIA World Factbook
- U.S. State Department Background Notes
- Big Emerging Markets Resource Page

Log on to this text's Web site, Chapter 3—Mastering Global and Geographic Skills, for current links to these resources and directions. Use these resources and others you may find on the Internet or at the library to answer the following questions:

1. Briefly describe Brazil's infrastructure. How do most products reach Brazil? Is internal transportation primarily by air or truck? Which state in Brazil has the best highways? Which transportation-related industries have been privatized or are scheduled to be privatized? In which area of Brazil does the majority of the population live? How does the size of Brazil compare to that of the United States? Which countries border Brazil?

2. How does the size of Brazil's economy compare to other nations in the world? What industries are strongest in Brazil?

3. Briefly outline the typical steps required for importing products into Brazil?

4. Discuss the overall economic outlook for sales of security and safety equipment in Brazil?

Now that so many businesses are affected by global affairs, students need a stronger understanding of geography. Each of these end-of-part exercises (of which one always focuses on cultural diversity) describes a real-world business situation and asks students to complete an activity.

Learning Tools That Help Develop Skills and Enhance Comprehension

Business Today uses a variety of helpful learning tools to reinforce and apply chapter material as well as stimulate higher-level thinking skills. These learning tools include:

Learning Objectives. Each numbered objective at the opening of the chapter signals important concepts students are expected to master. The numbered objectives reappear in the text margins close to the related material. The end-of-chapter "Summary of Learning Objectives" reinforces basic concepts by capsulizing chapter highlights for students.

Four-Way Approach to Vocabulary Development. The text's four-way method of vocabulary reinforcement helps students learn basic business vocabulary with ease. First, each term is printed in boldface within the text. Second, a definition appears in the margin adjacent to the term. Third, an alphabetical list of key terms appears at the end of each chapter, with convenient cross-references to the pages where the terms are defined. Fourth, all marginal definitions are assembled in an alphabetical Glossary at the end of the book.

Team Building Skills. In addition to the "Building Your Team Skills" exercises, many of the exercises included in **Business Today** are designed to be worked on in teams. This is especially true for application and critical thinking questions, in addition to all cases and Web-based exercises.

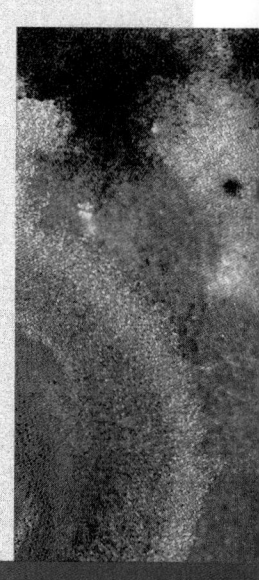

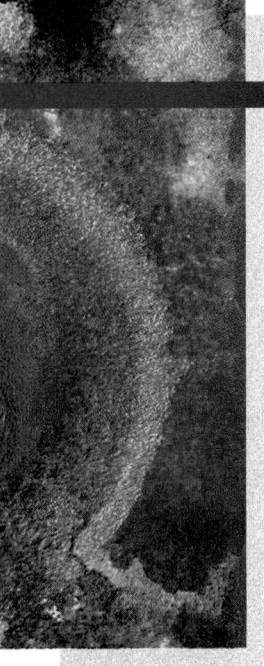

Lively, Conversational Writing Style

Read a few pages of this textbook and then read a few pages of another introduction to business textbook. We think you will immediately notice how the lucid writing style in **Business Today** makes the material pleasing to read and easy to comprehend. The Authors carefully monitored the text's content and reading level to make sure they are neither too simple nor too difficult.

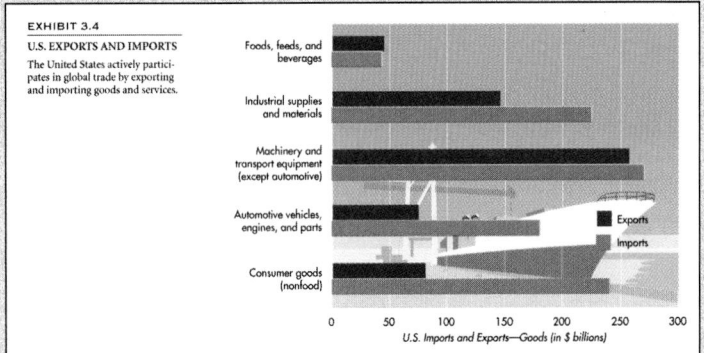

EXHIBIT 3.4

U.S. EXPORTS AND IMPORTS
The United States actively participates in global trade by exporting and importing goods and services.

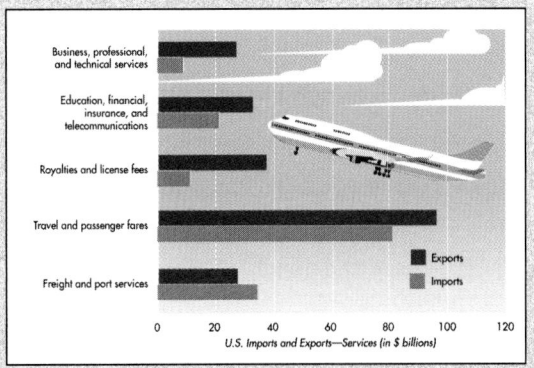

State-of-the-Art Design with New Exhibits. An inspiring new text design is engrossing and attractive, yet businesslike and professional. And, a striking new selection of exhibits (which the authors refer to as "Visuals 2000+) have been created especially for this new edition. Exhibits appear frequently throughout the text to highlight and reinforce key chapter concepts and to provide students with more useful ways for remembering the information presented. The art program—numerous exhibits and photographs—amounts to a course in itself.

An Unparalleled Supplements Package Offers a Fully Integrated Teaching System

The instructional resource package accompanying this text is specially designed to simplify the tasks of teaching and learning. Several new and exciting items have been added.

ALL NEW! Instructor's Resource Manual

This all-new, comprehensive manual written by Judy Bulin, Monroe Community College, and Bud Kolter, Winthrop University, contains a set of completely integrated support materials. It is designed to assist instructors in quickly finding and assembling the resources available for each chapter of the text and includes the following new material:

- brief chapter outline and chapter summaries
- changes to the new edition
- detailed lecture outlines and notes customized for both PowerPoint users and acetate users
- sample syllabi
- pop quizzes for every chapter
- answers to all end-of-chapter questions, problems, and assignments
- a detailed Video Guide with answers to video exercise questions
- suggested classroom exercises, classroom projects, and supplemental cases
- useful Web sites

ALL NEW! Test Item File

This new two-volume Test Item File contains approximately 4,000 questions, all of which have been carefully checked for accuracy and quality. This comprehensive set written by Jay Whitlock, Cantonville Community College, consists of multiple-choice, true/false, and essay questions. Each test question is ranked by level of difficulty (easy, moderate, or difficult) and contains section and learning objective references to allow the instructor a quick and easy way to balance the level of exams or quizzes. In addition, a special section contains test questions for all boxed features and vignettes in each chapter. The Test Item File reinforces students' understanding of key terms and concepts and requires them to apply their critical-thinking and analytical skills. In addition, it features two precreated sample tests for every part plus a mid-term and final exam for immediate use or distribution—an arrangement that provides both maximum flexibility and ease of use.

ALL NEW! Prentice Hall's Computerized Test Manager 4.2—ESATEST 2000 (Windows Version)

User-friendly software allows you to generate error-free tests quickly and easily by previewing questions individually on the screen and then selecting randomly by query or by number. The Computerized Test Manager allows you to generate random tests from an extensive bank of questions. You can also edit the questions/answers and even add some of your own. You can create an exam, administer it traditionally or online, and analyze your success with a simple click of the mouse. The newest version of the Computerized Test Manager, ESATEST 2000, has been improved to provide users with a vast array of new options. Enhancements now allow you to:

- Import test questions from word processors
- Import/export tests
- Correlate charts
- Select by query
- Select by review (redesigned)
- Select by criteria
- Archive database capability
- Analyze test bank items
- Export grades to Excel
- Weight grades
- Record grades in a new spreadsheet format and create a grade database
- Control online testing

ALL NEW! Telephone Test Preparation

For those instructors who prefer not to use the Computerized Test Item File, Prentice Hall provides a special 800 call-in service for ease of use. All you need to do is call the 800 Testing Help Desk to have a customized test created. The test can then be delivered by e-mail, U.S. mail, or overnight carrier.

ALL NEW! Color Acetate Transparency Program

A set of color transparency acetates, created by Steve Peters, Walla Walla Community College, available to instructors on request, highlights text concepts and supply additional facts and information to help bring concepts alive in the classroom and enhance the classroom experience. All are keyed to the Instructor's Resource Manual.

ALL NEW! Videos

A set of 18 specially selected videos (one for each chapter) is available to adopters.

ALL NEW! PowerPoint Presentation

Enhance your classroom presentations with this well-developed PowerPoint presentation set created by Steve Peters, Walla Walla Community College. More than 500 text-specific PowerPoint slides highlight fundamental concepts by integrating key graphs, figures, and illustrations from the text. PowerPoint slides come complete with lecture notes, which are available in the Instructor's Resource Manual or on the Instructor's Resource CD. Free to adopters, PowerPoint slides are available on CD or can be downloaded from the Instructor's Resource Web site at **www.prenhall.com/mescon**.

Business PlanPro Software and Exercises

Business PlanPro 4.0 software provides students with a step-by-step approach to creating a comprehensive business plan. Preformatted report templates, charts, and tables handle the mechanics so students can focus on the thinking. Business PlanPro software can be packaged with the textbook for a nominal fee of $10.

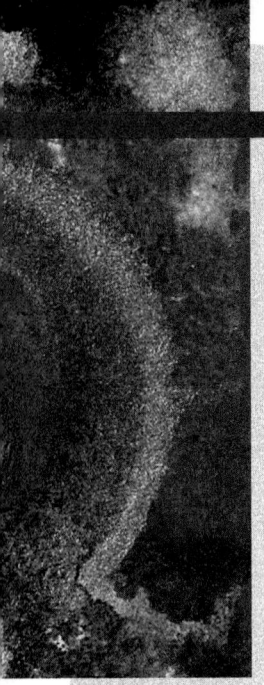

ALL NEW! Mastering Business Essentials CD

This innovative, interactive CD gives students an introduction to the wide range of concerns facing businesses today. The CD contains 12 episodes that use a series of videos with enhanced interactive exercises that help students apply the lessons of the classroom to all the key areas of business at an e-business called CanGo. The Mastering Business Essentials CD can be value-packed with this text for a special price. Please contact your Prentice Hall representative for details. The following topics are covered:

- The Goal of the Firm and Social Responsibility
- The Economic Way of Thinking
- Ethical Issues
- Concepts of Strategic Management
- Working in Groups and Teams
- Managerial Accounting and Cost Behavior

- Raising Capital
- Work Motivation
- Leadership
- Marketing Concepts/Strategy
- Understanding Consumer Behavior
- Strategy and Operations

ALL NEW! E-Business Online Supplement

Each chapter in the online supplement, located at **www.prenhall.com/mescon,** is keyed to the text parts and includes learning objectives, real-world examples, discussion questions, a group activity, Internet exercises, and a "mystery" exercise. In-depth coverage of the latest trends and concepts in e-commerce include:

- Internet Privacy and Security
- Internet Davids vs. Goliaths
- Managing the Virtual Organization
- Virtual Training and Development
- Hot Online Pricing Strategies
- Internet IPOs
- Emerging Legal Issues In
  E-Commerce

Plus a special feature: Preparing
for a Career in E-Commerce

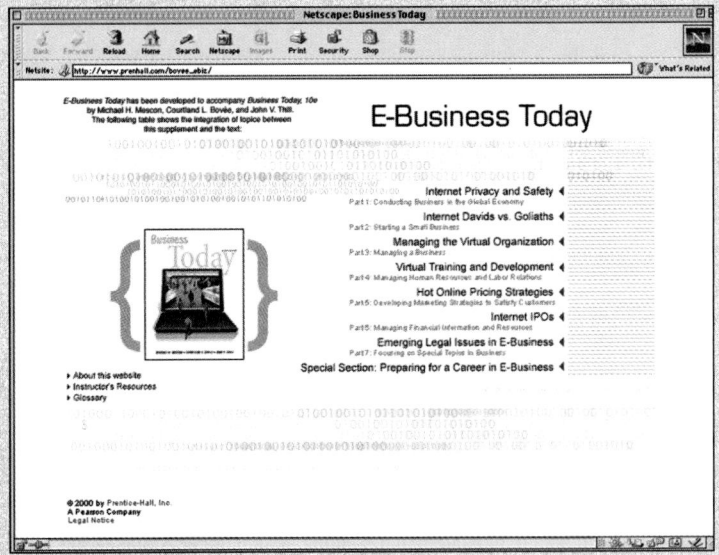

ALL NEW! E-Business and E-Commerce Supplement

In the new world of business, you'll run into e-commerce no matter what direction you turn. Take your students behind the scenes to explore the dynamic world of e-business with this new value-pack supplement. This unique print supplement provides an overview of the basic concepts of e-business and e-commerce, an introduction to popular search sites, a look at wide range of business-related sites and addresses, and an up-to-the-minute look at online job searches and career sites. The Web component of this supplement provides updated coverage of the latest trends, challenges, and hot concepts in e-commerce, plus additional interactive exercises. Go to **www.prenhall.com/ebiz**. This great supplement can be value-packed with the text for free.

FINANCIAL TIMES
World business newspaper.

ALL NEW! Financial Times Offer

We are pleased to announce our new partnership with the Financial Times to offer a 15-week print subscription for $10 with this text. The Prentice Hall textbook + subscription package will contain a 16-page, full-color **Financial Times Student Guide** shrink-wrapped with the textbook. Bound inside the Student Guide will be a postcard that entitles the student to claim a prepaid 15-week subscription. When the student mails in the reply card, the subscription should begin in 5 to 7 business days.

Study Guide

The **Study Guide for Business Today** by Doug Copeland, Johnson Community College, is designed to increase your students' comprehension of the concepts presented in this text. The guide provides chapter-by-chapter explanations and exercises designed to reinforce comprehension of key terms and concepts, and to promote concept-application skills.

Beginning Your Career Search, Second Edition

This concise book by James S. O'Rourke IV offers some straightforward, practical information on how to write a résumé, where and how to find company information, how to conduct oneself during an interview, and how the interview process works. Included in the book are copies of sample introductory, cover, follow-up, and thank-you letters. This great supplement can be value-packed with the text for free.

Introduction to Business Insights Newsletter for Faculty

Delivered exclusively by e-mail every month, this newsletter provides interesting materials that can be used in class and offers a wealth of practical ideas about teaching methods. To receive a complimentary subscription, send an e-mail to bovee-thill@uia.net. In the subject line, put "IBI Subscription Request." In the message area, please list your name and institutional affiliation.

Authors' E-Mail Hotline for Faculty

Integrity, excellence, and responsiveness are the authors' hallmarks. This means providing you with textbooks that are academically sound, creative, timely, and sensitive to instructor and student needs. As an adopter of Business Today, you are invited to use the authors' E-Mail Hotline. The authors want to be sure you're completely satisfied, so if you ever have a question or concern related to the text or its supplements, or want to give them your feedback, please e-mail them at bovee-thill@uia.net. The authors will get back to you as quickly as possible.

Introducing the myPHLIP Companion Web Site for Business Today, Tenth Edition

The myPHLIP (Prentice Hall's Learning on the Internet Partnership) Companion Web site is your personal guide to the free online resources for your book and is located at **www.prenhall.com/mescon**. It's the most advanced, text-specific site available on the Web!

myPhlip features one-click access to all of the resources created by an award-winning team of educators. Here is a preview of its exciting features:

- **myPHLIP pages** –Your personal access page unites all your myPHLIP texts.

- **Notes** – Add personal notes to our resources for personal reminders and references.

- **Messages** – Instructors can send messages to individual students or all students linked to a course.

- **Student Resources** – Add premium myPHLIP resources for your students to view and download (such as PowerPoint slides, videos, and spreadsheets).

- **Business Headlines** – Check out links to articles in today's business news.

- **Search** – Search all myPHLIP resources for relevant articles and exercises.

- **Instructor's Manual** – For instructors, the myPHLIP Instructor's Manual provides tips and suggestions from the myPHLIP faculty for integrating myPHLIP resources into your course.

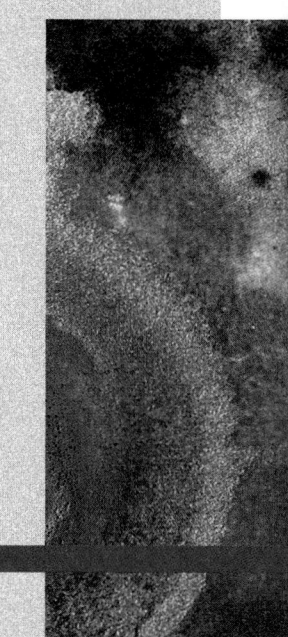

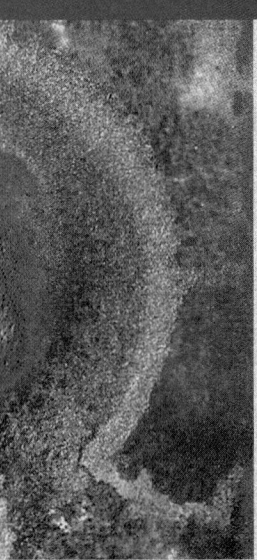

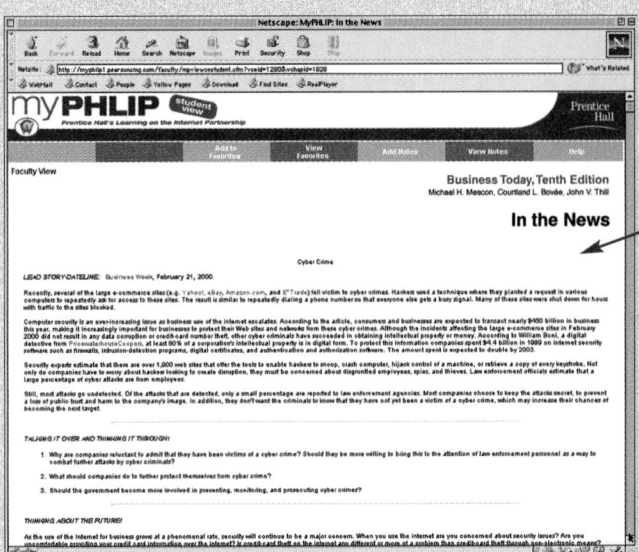

■ In the News – These articles and exercises, linked to relevant chapters, are added throughout the year. Each article is summarized by teams of expert professors. Group activities, critical thinking questions, discussion questions, and reference citations follow each article, all supported by instructor materials.

■ Study Guide – An interactive, online study guide offers a wide variety of self-assessment questions for every chapter. Results from the automatically graded questions for every chapter provide immediate feedback for students that can be e-mailed to the instructor for extra credit or can serve as practice.

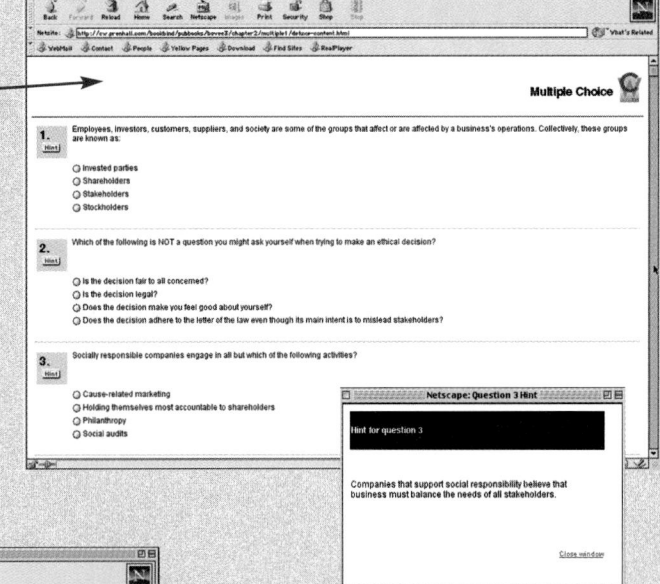

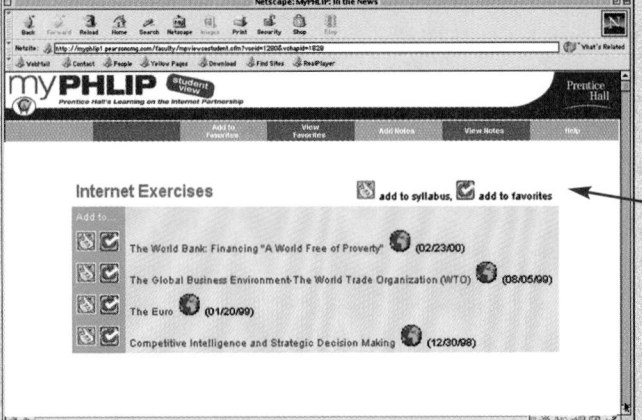

■ Research Area – Let myPHLIP save you time finding the most valuable and relevant material available on the Web. The Research Area provides a resource library that includes links to tutorials, virtual libraries, Internet resources, and more. Each link is annotated to expedite your research.

■ Internet Resources – New Internet Exercises, created by the myPHLIP team of professors, are continually added to the site. These exercises are designed to promote students' critical thinking skills as they utilize the Internet to explore current business issues.

FOR THE STUDENT

■ **Talk to the Tutor** has virtual office hours that allow students to post questions from any supported discipline and receive responses from the dedicated PHLIP/Companion Web site faculty team.

■ **Writing Resource Center** is an on-line writing center that provides links to online directories, thesauruses, writing tutors, style and grammar guides, and additional tools.

■ **Career Resource Center** helps students access career information, view sample résumés, even apply for jobs online.

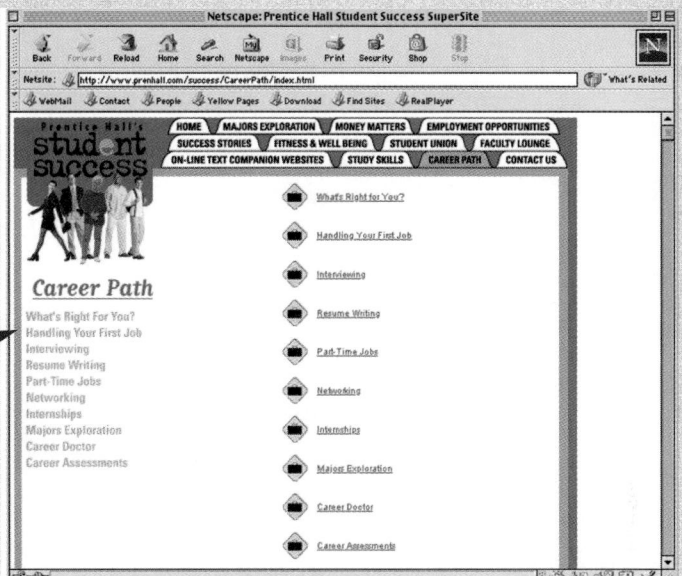

FOR THE INSTRUCTOR

■ **Syllabus Manager**
An improved online syllabus manager is an easy-to-use program that allows faculty to create online custom syllabi hosted by Prentice Hall servers. Syllabus Manager provides instructors with a step-by-step process for creating and revising syllabi, with direct links into Companion Web Sites and other online content. Changes you make to your syllabus are immediately available to your students at their next login. Your students need only know the Web address for the Companion Web Site and the password you've assigned to your syllabus, and they may log on to your syllabus during any study session.

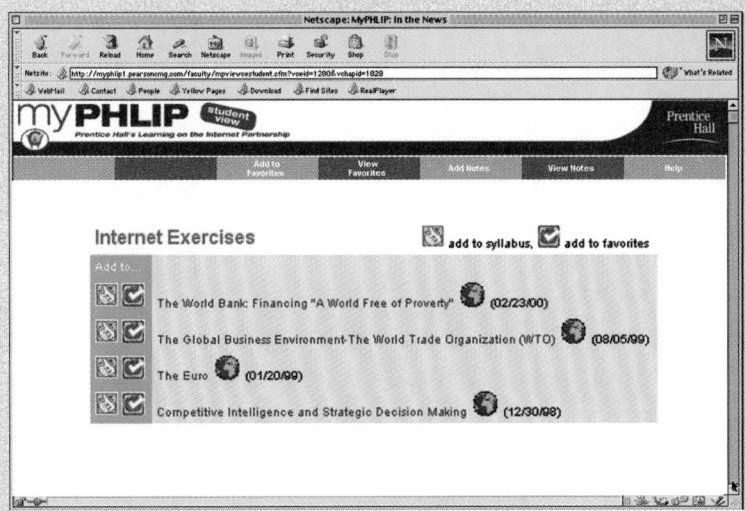

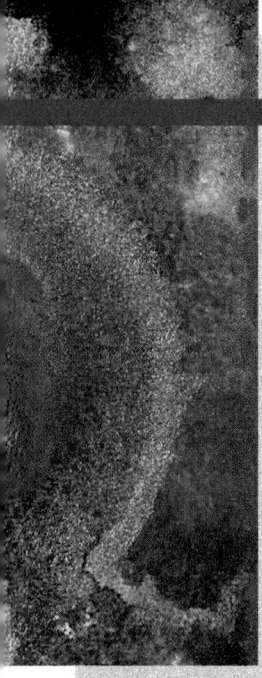

■ **Faculty Resources** include resources contributed by professors throughout the world, including teaching tips, techniques, academic papers, and sample syllabuses.

■ **What's New** gives you one-click access to all newly posted myPHLIP resources.

■ **Talk to the Team** is a moderated faculty chat room.

■ **Online Faculty Support** is a password protected area that provides faculty with the most current and advanced support material available, including downloadable supplements, additional cases, articles, links, and suggested answers to current events activities.

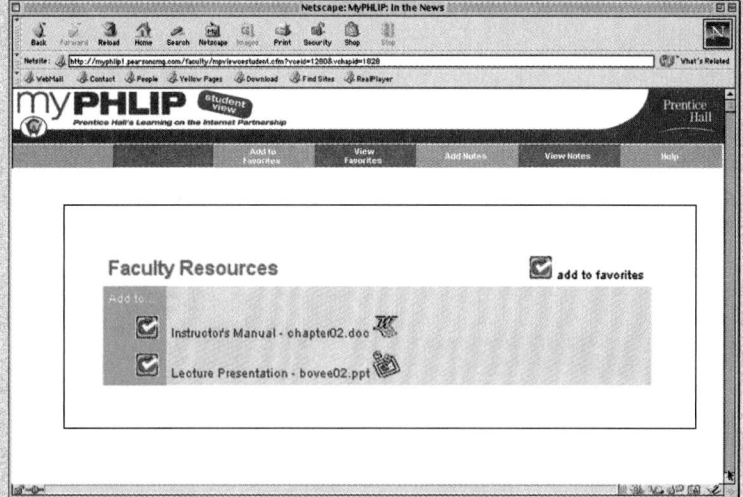

Offering Business Today, Tenth Edition, As an Online Course

Are you interested in offering a complete and fully functional online course? Would you like to take advantage of existing technology to better communicate with your students, post supplementary course materials, or conduct online testing and grading?

As the leading college textbook publisher, Prentice Hall has formed close alliances with each of the leading online platform provider—Blackboard, WebCT, and our own Pearson CourseCompass.

WEBCT

www.prenhall.com/webct

Gold Level Customer Support, available exclusively to adopters of Prentice Hall courses, is awarded free-of-charge upon adoption and provides you with priority assistance, training discounts, and dedicated technical support from WebCT.

BLACKBOARD

www.prenhall.com/blackboard

Prentice Hall's abundant online content, combined with Blackboard's popular tools and interface, result in robust Web-based courses that are easy to implement, manage, and us—taking your courses to new heights in student interaction and learning.

COURSECOMPASS

www.prenhall.com/coursecompass

CourseCompass™ is a dynamic, interactive online course management tool powered by Blackboard. This exciting product allows you to teach with market-leading Pearson Education content in an easy-to-use customizable format.

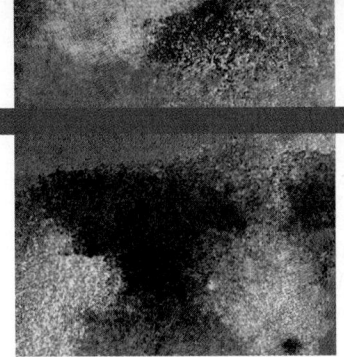

ACKNOWLEDGMENTS

A key reason for the continued success of *Business Today* is an extensive market research effort. The advice of hundreds of instructors around the country aided us in our attempt to create a textbook suited to the unique needs of the introductory business market. Our sincere thanks are extended to the individuals who responded to our surveys as well as to the individuals who provided us with their insights through detailed market reviews.

▪ SURVEY REVIEWERS

Lee Adami, Northern Wyoming College; **Robert Alliston,** Davenport College of Business; **Lorraine Anderson,** Marshall University; **Doug Ashby,** Lewis and Clark Community College; **Fay Avery,** Northern Virginia Community College; **Sandra Bailey,** Indiana Vocational Technical College; **James Baskfleld,** Northern Hennepin Community College; **Gregory Baxter,** Southeastern Oklahoma State University; **Charles Beavin,** Miami-Dade Community College; **Larry Beck,** Cohin County Community College; **Joseph Berger,** Monroe Community College; **James Boeger,** Rock Valley College; **Riccardo Boehm,** Hostos Community College; **Mary Jo Boehms,** Jackson State Community College; **Glennis Boyd,** Cisco Junior College; **Jeffrey Bruehl,** Bryan College; **Carl Buckel,** College of the Canyons; **Howard Budner,** Borough of Manhattan Community College; **John Bunnell,** Broome Community College; **Van Bushnell,** Southern Utah University; **William Carman,** Bucks County Community College; **Paul Caruso,** Richard Bland College; **Eloise Chester,** Suffolk County Community College; **Carmin Cimino,** Mitchell College; **Ellen Clemens,** Bloomsburg University of Pennsylvania; **James Cleveland,** Sage Junior College of Albany; **Debra Clingerman,** California University of Pennsylvania; **Herbert Coolidge,** Southern College of Seventh-Day Adventists; **Gary Cutler,** Dyersburg State Community College; **Giles Dail,** Edgecombe Community College; **Joe Damato,** Cuyamaca College; **James Day,** Shawnee State University; **Patrick Ellsberg,** Lower Columbia College; **Alfred Fabian,** Indiana Vocational College; **Jennifer Friestad,** Anoka-Ramsey Community College; **Joan Gailey,** Kent State University, East; **Joyce Goetz,** Austin Community College; **Barbara Goza,** Southern Florida Community College; **Phyllis Graff,** Kauai Community College;

Hugh Graham, Loras College; **Vance Gray,** Bishop State Community College; **Gary Greene,** Manatee Community College; **Marciano Guerrero,** LaGuardia Community College; **Delia Haak,** John Brown University; **Maurice Hamington,** Mount St. Mary's College; **E.C. Hamm,** Tidewater Community College; **Carnella Hardin,** Glendale Community College; **Marie Hardink,** Anne Arundel Community College; **Diana Hayden,** Northeastern University; **Elizabeth Haynes,** Haywood Community College; **Sheila Devoe Heidman,** Cochise College; **Diana Henke,** University of Wisconsin at Sheboygan; **Norman Humble,** Kirkwood Community College; **Liz Jackson,** Keystone Junior College; **Michael Johnson,** Chippewa Valley Technical College; **Carol Jones,** Cuyahoga Community College; **Lonora Keas,** Del Mar College; **Sylvia Keyes,** Northeastern University; **Sharon Kolstad,** Fort Peck Community College; **Ken LaFave,** Mt. San Jacinto Community College; **Richard Larsen,** University of Maine at Machias; **Philip Lee,** Campbellsville College; **Richard Lenoir,** George Washington University; **Martha Leva,** Pennsylvania State University; **Kathy Lorencz,** Oakland Community College; **James Loricchio,** Ulster County Community College; **Tricia McConville,** Northeastern University; **Cheryl Macon,** Butler County Community College; **Ann Maddox,** Angelo State University; **Marie Madison,** Harry S. Truman College; **Barry Marshall,** Northeastern University; **George Michaehides,** Franklin Pierce College; **Norman Muller,** Greenfield Community College; **Lucia Murphy,** Ursinus College; **Alita Myers,** Copiah-Lincoln Community College; **Eric Nielsen,** College of Charleston; **Patricia Parker,** Maryville University of St. Louis; **Clyde Patterson,** Shawnee State University; **Corey Pfaffe,** Marantha Baptist Bible College; **Noel Powell,** West Georgia College; **Allen Rager,** Southwestern Community College; **Roy Roddy,** Yakima Valley Community College; **Ehsan Salek,** Virginia Wesleyan College; **Bernard Saperstein,** Passaic County Community College; **Kurk Schindler,** Wilbur Wright College; **Mark Schultz,** Rocky Mountain College; **Arnold Scolnick,** Borough of Manhattan Community College; **David Shepard,** Virginia Western Community College; **Stephanie Smith,** Lander University; **Susan Smith,** Finger Lakes Community College; **George Stook,** Anne Arundel Community College; **David Stringer,** DeAnza College; **Ben Tanksley,** Sul Ross State University; **John Taylor,** University of Alaska, Fairbanks; **Chris Tomas,** Northeast Iowa Community College; **Palmina**

Uzzolino, Montclair State University; **Martha Valentine,** Regis University; **Juanita Vertrees,** Sinclair Community College; **IngoVon Ruckteschel,** Long Island University; **Chuck Wall,** Bakersfield College; **Jay Weiner,** Adams State College; **Lewis Welshofer,** Miami University of Ohio; **Charles White,** Edison Community College; **Richard Williams,** Laramie County Community College; **Clay Willis,** Oklahoma Baptist University; **Ira Wilsker,** Lamar University; **Ron Young,** Kalamazoo Valley Community College; **Sandra Young,** Jones County Junior College; **Harold Zarr,** Des Moines Area Community College; **Nancy Zeliff,** Northwest Missouri State University; and **Gene Zeller,** Jordan College.

■ MARKET REVIEWERS

Harvey Bronstein, Oakland Community College; **Debra Clingerman,** California University of Pennsylvania; **Bill Dempkey,** Bakersfield College; **John Heinsius,** Modesto Junior College; **Alan Hollander,** Suffolk Community College; **Bob Matthews,** Oakton Community College; **Jerry Myers,** Stark Technical College; **Dianne Osborne,** Broward Community College; **Mary Rousseau,** Delta College; **Martin St. John,** Westmoreland Community College; **Patricia Setlik,** William Rainey Harper College; **Richard Shapiro,** Cuyahoga Community College; **Shafi Ullah,** Broward Community College; **Randy Barker,** Virginia Commonwealth University; **James D. Bell,** Southwest State University; **Joe Brum,** Fayetteville Technical Community College; **Steven Cassidy,** Howard University; **Jan Feldbauer,** Austin Community College; **Lorraine Hartley,** Franklin University; **Donald Johnson,** College for Financial Planning; **Jeffery Klivans,** University of Maine-Augusta; **Paul Londrigan,** Mott Community College; **Ted Valvoda,** Lakeland Community College; and **William Warfeld,** Indiana State University.

■ MARKET REVIEWERS FOR TENTH EDITION

Lewis Schlossinger, Community College of Aurora; **Ronald Cereola,** James Madison University; **Dr. Mohammed Ahmed,** Webster University; **Dr. Dennis Foster,** Northern Arizona University; **Dr. Marshall Wick,** Gallaudet University; **Dr. Anthony Cafarelli,** Ursuline University; **Sandra Johnson,** Shasta College; **Robert Fouquette,** New Hampshire College; **Judy Domalewski,** Community College of Aurora, SD; **Gerald Crawford,** University of North Alabama; **Gary Walk,** Lima Technical College; **Pamela Shindler,** Wittenburg University; **John Mozingo,** University of Wisconsin, Oshkosh; **C. Russell Edwards,** Valencia Community College; and **David Sollars,** Auburn University, Montgomery.

■ PERSONAL ACKNOWLEDGMENTS

A very special acknowledgment goes to Barbara Schatzman, whose superb communication skills, distinguished background, and wealth of business experience assured this project of clarity and completeness.

Recognition and thanks to Marian Burk Wood for her highly valuable contributions; to Susan Sawyer for her noteworthy talents; to Terry Anderson for her outstanding editorial skills; to Jackie Estrada for her excellent attention to details; to Stef Gould for her artistry; and to Joe Glidden for his research efforts and database supervision.

The authors wish to acknowledge the contributions of Dr. David Rachman, including his work on the outline for the First Edition of *Business Today.* Dr. Rachman was a named author for editions One through Eight of *Business Today.*

The supplements package for *Business Today* has benefited from the able contributions of numerous individuals. We would like to express our thanks to them for creating the finest set of instructional supplements in the field.

We also wish to extend our warmest appreciation to the devoted professionals at Prentice Hall. They include Jerome Grant, president; Jeff Shelstad, editor in chief; Elisa Adams, editor; Debbie Clare, senior marketing manager; Jennifer Surich, supplements manager; and Virginia Sheridan, editorial assistant; all of Prentice Hall Business Publishing; and the outstanding Prentice Hall sales representatives. Finally, we thank Judy Leale, managing editor of production, and Emma Moore, production editor, for their dedication, and we are grateful to Lynn Steines, Project Manager at Carlisle Communications; Suzanne Grappi, permissions editor; Melinda Alexander, photo researcher; and Cheryl Asherman, art director, for their superb work.

Michael H. Mescon
Courtland L. Bovée
John V. Thill

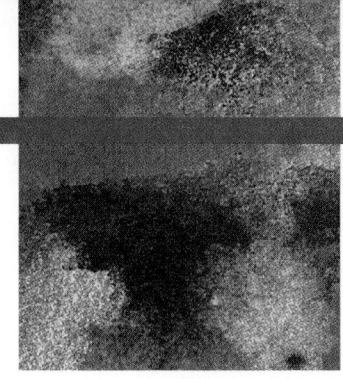

GUIDE TO THEMATIC EXAMPLES

PRODUCING QUALITY PRODUCTS AND SERVICES THAT SATISFY CUSTOMERS' CHANGING NEEDS

KEEPING PACE WITH TECHNOLOGY AND ELECTRONIC COMMERCE

STARTING AND MANAGING A SMALL BUSINESS IN TODAY'S COMPETITIVE ENVIRONMENT

BEHAVING IN AN ETHICALLY AND SOCIALLY RESPONSIBLE MANNER

THINKING GLOBALLY AND COMMITTING TO A CULTURALLY DIVERSE WORKFORCE

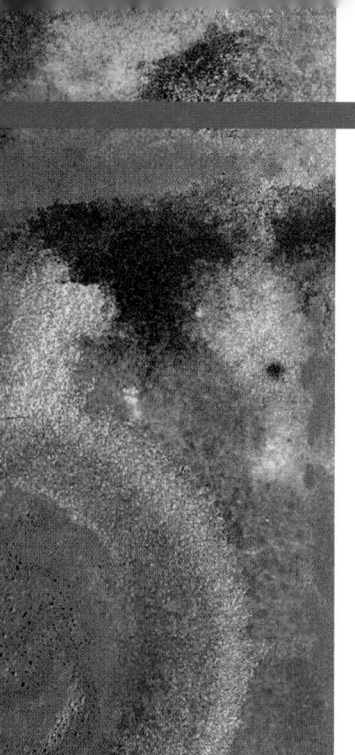

FUNDAMENTALS OF BUSINESS AND ECONOMICS

1

LEARNING OBJECTIVES

After studying this chapter, you will be able to

1. Identify four key social and economic roles that businesses serve

2. List six factors that are contributing to the increase in the number of service businesses

3. Differentiate between a free-market system and a planned system

4. Explain how supply and demand interact to affect price

5. List the three major economic roles of the U.S. government

6. Define the gross domestic product and explain what it is used for

7. Identify five challenges that businesses are facing in the global economy

@ 8. Highlight six ways in which the new economy differs from the old economy, and discuss whether the old economy rules are obsolete

Inside Business

Jerry Yang and David Filo transformed their hobby into a new kind of media company when they developed Yahoo!

WEBTIME STORIES: YAHOO!—THE SEARCH ENGINE THAT COULD

w w w . y a h o o . c o m

Successful entrepreneurs are by definition creative people. They invent new technologies, and they figure out how to open new windows of opportunity in a marketplace. Sometimes they even unleash whole new industries, like Jerry Yang and David Filo did.

Just as Net mania was beginning to flower in 1994, Yang and Filo, two Stanford Ph.D. candidates, noticed that the rich and diverse World Wide Web was becoming increasingly impossible for users to navigate. So for fun they built a straightforward system that sorted and classified their favorite Web sites into categories. Then they posted their lists onto the university's Web site and named their site Yahoo!, an acronym for "Yet Another Hierarchical Officious Oracle."

Working around the clock, the two strained to make sense of the tidal wave of information people were posting online. But they never thought of making a business out of their hobby until university officials asked them to find a company that was willing to host their Web site. That's when Yang and Filo knew they were onto something big. Like most entrepreneurs, they needed money. And they needed people who could help them with the aspects of a business they didn't understand. Yang and Filo found both.

With a million dollars and a new CEO, Timothy Koogle, Yahoo! set up shop in Silicon Valley, and recruited a staff to help categorize the Web sites. In 1996 company stock was sold to the investing public. Yahoo! was on the road to billions. Still, Yang and Filo stuck with the fundamentals of business. That is, they listened to customers and gave them abundant reasons to visit the Yahoo! site and to stay for awhile. They also kept the Yahoo! site fast, current, and easy to use. Moreover, Yahoo! set itself apart from competitors by using humans to filter, categorize, and add Web sites to its directory. Excite, Infoseek, and Lycos use computer software programs to catalog Web sites and automate the search process.

Today Yahoo! is much more than a mere directory. Responding to customer requests, Yahoo! has metamorphosed into an interactive information service. Millions of people use Yahoo! every day for e-mail, instant messaging, Web photo albums, personal homepages, shopping, bill paying, games, auctions, news, and much more. In fact, Yahoo! generates more than $1 billion in annual sales and over $60 million in profits by selling absolutely nothing. Instead, Yahoo! charges for advertising on its Web site, providing advertisers with instant feedback on every ad—such as how many people saw the ad, how many clicked futher, and the target group to which they belong. Yahoo! also takes a small percentage of sales earned by featured e-merchants who sign on to hawk their goods and services in one of the largest marketplaces on the Internet. But with 90 percent of its revenue coming from advertising—most of which comes from other Internet companies—Yahoo's stock was clobbered in the early twenty-first century Internet shakeout .

Still, Yang and Filo are confident that Yahoo! will remain profitable and achieve long-term success. After all, with over 166 million registered users, and Web sites in more than 12 languages and 24 countries, Yahoo! is indeed a promising young company. Moreover, Yang and Filo know that to compete in today's economy you must be innovative and fast, and you must anticipate whatever opportunities and challenges the restless Internet may present.[1]

■ WHY STUDY BUSINESS?

Business is everywhere. Whether you're logged on to the Yahoo! Web site, flying in an airplane, watching a movie, buying a CD over the Internet, enjoying your favorite coffee drink, or withdrawing money from an ATM machine, you're involved in someone else's business. In fact, you engage in business just about every day of your life. But like many college students, for most of your life you've been observing and enjoying the efforts of others. Now that you're taking an introduction to business course, however, your perspective is about to change.

In this course you'll learn what it takes to run a successful business such as Yahoo! As you progress though this course, you'll begin to look at things from the eyes of an employee or a manager instead of a consumer. You'll develop a fundamental business vocabulary that will help you keep up with the latest news and make more informed decisions. By participating in classroom discussions and completing the chapter exercises you'll gain some valuable critical-thinking, problem-solving, team-building, and communication skills that you can use on the job and throughout your life.

Should you decide to pursue a career in business, this course will introduce you to a variety of jobs that exist in fields such as accounting, economics, human resources, management, finance, marketing, and so on. You'll see how people who work in these business functions contribute to the success of a company as a whole. You'll gain insight into the types of skills and knowledge these jobs require. And most important, you'll discover that a career in business today is fascinating, challenging, and oftentimes quite rewarding.

LEARNING OBJECTIVE 1

Identify four key social and economic roles that businesses serve

■ WHAT IS A BUSINESS?

business
Activity and enterprise that provides goods and services that a society needs

Like David Filo and Jerry Yang, many people start a new **business**—a profit-seeking activity that provides goods and services that satisfy consumers' needs. Businesses play a number of key roles in society and the economy: They provide society with necessities such as housing, clothing, food, transportation, communication, and health care; they provide people with jobs and a means to prosper; they pay taxes that are used to build highways, fund education, and provide grants for scientific research; and they reinvest their profits in the economy, thereby creating a higher standard of living and quality of life for society as a whole.

profit
Money left over after expenses and taxes have been deducted from revenue generated by selling goods and services

The driving force behind most businesses is the prospect of earning a **profit**—what remains after all expenses have been deducted from business revenue. Still, not every business exists to earn a profit. Some organizations exist to provide society with a social or educational service instead. Such **not-for-profit organizations** include museums, schools, public universities, symphonies, libraries, and government agencies. Even though these organizations do not have a profit motive, they must still run efficiently and effectively to achieve their goals. Thus, the business principles discussed throughout this textbook—competition, marketing, finance, management, quality, and so on—apply to both profit-seeking and not-for-profit organizations.

not-for-profit organizations
Firms whose primary objective is something other than returning a profit to their owners

Best of the Web Best of the Web Best of

FIND THE RIGHT STUFF

...A tip for finding Web sites: If you get an error message when you try to get to a site, go to www.ixquick.com or www.brightgate.com. Insert the name of the site or the URL in the space provided, and press "search." If the site you're seeking is still operating, the results of this search will usually provide a hot link to it.

Finding company information on the Internet can be an overwhelming task if you don't know where to begin. One of the best starting points is Hoover's Online. This Web site provides an incredible gateway to over 10,000 companies and the latest information on each (such as brief profiles, financial data, history, and current events). So log on, type in the full name of a company, and check it out. Read the capsule, follow the links, catch up on latest company news, and learn about the company's history. Don't leave without finding out what the company's competition is up to. www.hoovers.com/

Note: To reach the Web sites listed in this book, you don't have to type the URLs into your browser. Just go to the Web site for this book at www.prenhall.com/mescon. There, you'll find live links that take you straight to the site of your choice.

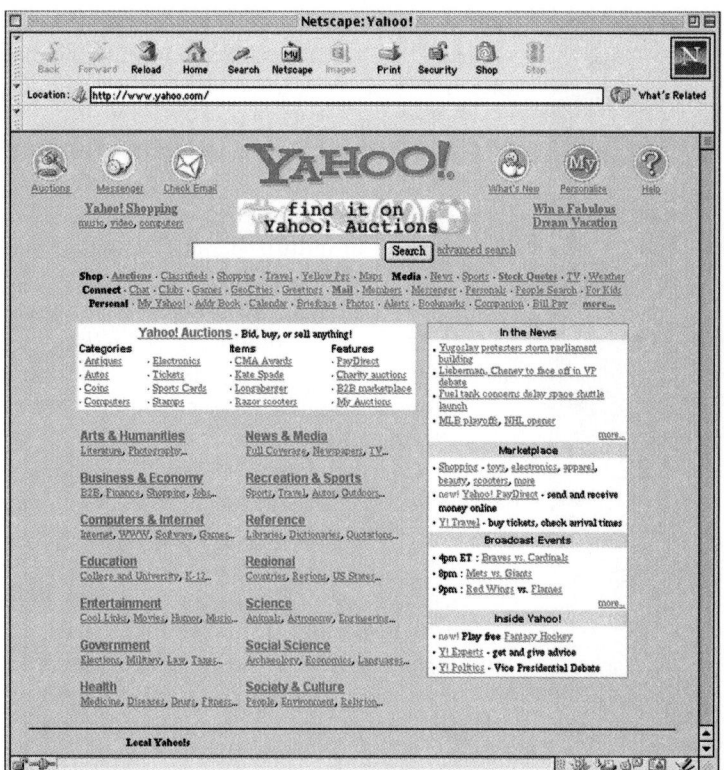

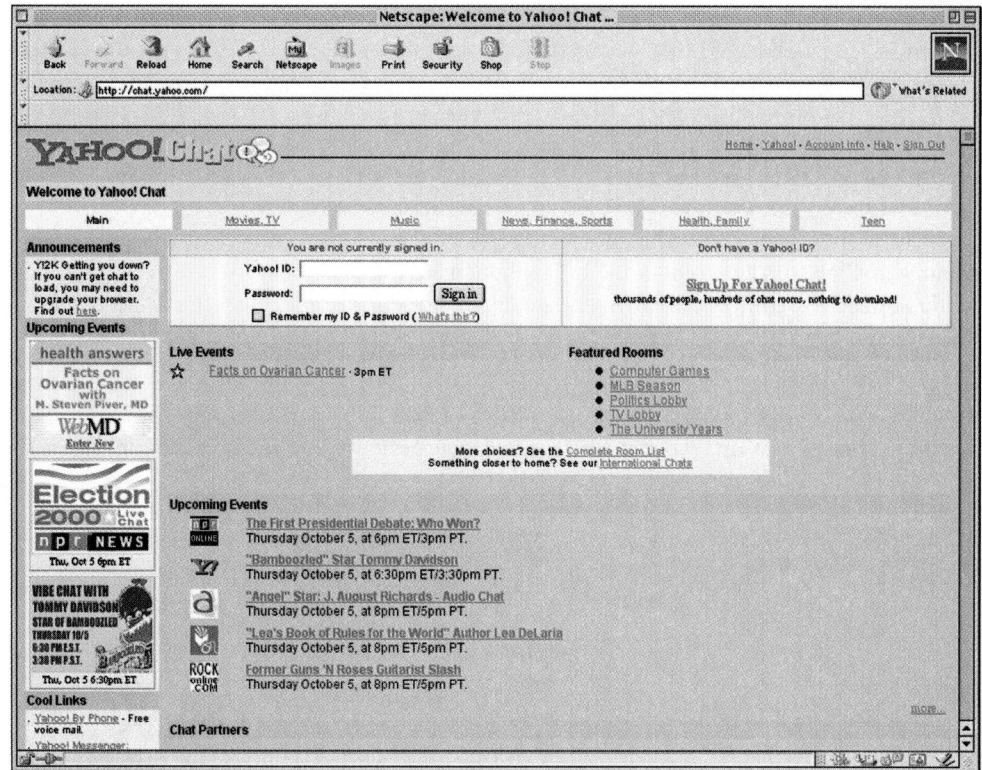

Like many service businesses, Yahoo! must respond to customers' changing needs. A glance at these Web site images shows how Yahoo! has progressed from a directory to an interactive information service—in less than one decade.

Goods-Producing Businesses versus Service Businesses

Most businesses can be classified into two broad categories (or industry sectors): goods-producing businesses and service businesses. **Goods-producing businesses** produce tangible goods by engaging in activities such as manufacturing, construction, mining, and agriculture. **Service businesses** produce intangible products (ones that cannot be held in your hand) and include

goods-producing businesses
Businesses that produce tangible products

service businesses
Businesses that provide intangible products or perform useful labor on behalf of another

Manufacturers of resistance-training machines have characteristics of both goods-producing and service-producing businesses. In addition to producing high-quality equipment, they must provide product training, technical support, warranties, and on-site repair and maintenance; some manufacturers even offer seminars on resistance training and how to maintain a healthy lifestyle.

labor-intensive businesses
Businesses in which labor costs are more significant than capital costs

capital-intensive businesses
Businesses that require large investments in capital assets

those whose principal product is finance, insurance, transportation, utilities, wholesale and retail trade, banking, entertainment, health care, repairs, and information.

Of course, many companies produce both services and goods. Consider IBM, for example. IBM manufactures computers and other business machines, but at least one-third of IBM's sales come from computer-related services such as systems design, consulting, and product support.[2] Similarly, a manufacturer of industrial and farm equipment such as Caterpillar must provide its customers with services such as product training and technical support. Even though it becomes more and more difficult to classify a company as either a goods-producing business or a service business, such classification is useful for reporting and analysis purposes.

Most service businesses are **labor-intensive businesses;** that is, they rely predominantly on human resources to prosper. A consulting firm is an example of a labor-intensive business because its existence is heavily dependent on the knowledge and skills of its consultants. Even though the firm requires money to operate, a group of consultants can go into business simply by purchasing some computers and some telephones. Businesses that require large amounts of money or equipment to get started and to operate are **capital-intensive businesses.** Airlines, electric utilities, telecommunications companies, and automobile manufacturers are examples of capital-intensive businesses. Although each of these businesses requires a large pool of labor to operate, it would be difficult to start them without substantial investments in buildings, machinery, and equipment.

Growth of the Service Sector

Services have always played an important role in the U.S. economy. For more than 60 years, they accounted for half of all U.S. employment. In the mid-1980s services became the engine of growth for the U.S. economy (see Exhibit 1.1).[3] In fact, most of the increase in U.S. employment from 1985 to the present has been generated by the service sector. Today about half of the 1,000 largest U.S. companies are service-based.[4]

Economists project that the number of service-related jobs will continue to increase—from about 94 million (or 72 percent of the 130 million or so people in today's workforce) to about 112 million by 2006. In contrast, employment growth in the goods-producing sector is projected to remain flat through 2006 (see Exhibit 1.2).[5] The projected growth in the service sector is attributable to several factors:

■ *Consumers have more disposable income.* The 76 million baby boomers in the United States (people born between 1946 and 1964) are in their peak earning years. These consumers find

EXHIBIT 1.1

SECTORS OF THE U.S. ECONOMY

The service sector accounts for 72 percent of U.S. economic output, and the goods-producing sector accounts for the remaining 28 percent.

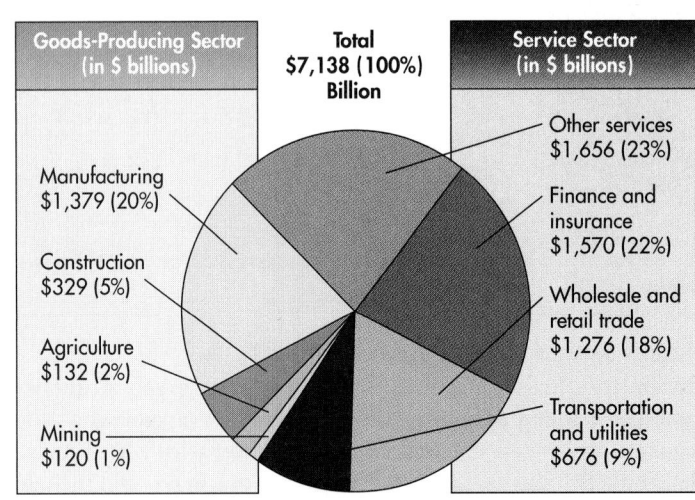

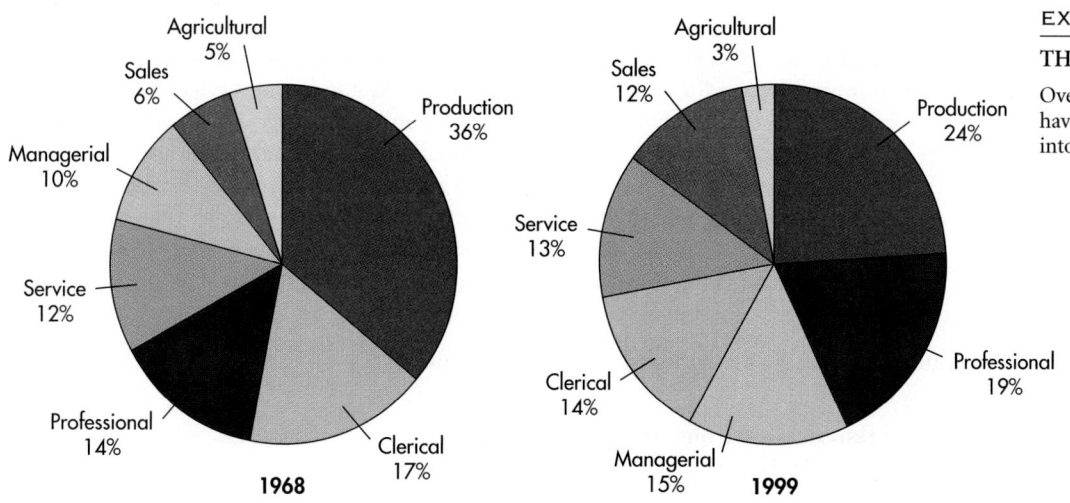

EXHIBIT 1.2

THE SHIFTING ECONOMY

Over the past 30 years, workers have moved out of production and into professional jobs.

themselves with more disposable income and look for services to help them invest, travel, relax, and stay fit.

- *Services target changing demographic patterns and lifestyle trends.* The United States has more elderly people, more single people living alone, more two-career households, and more single parents than ever before. These trends create opportunities for service companies that can help people with all the tasks they no longer have time for, including home maintenance, food service, and child care.[6]

- *Services are needed to support complex goods and new technology.* Computers, home entertainment centers, recreational vehicles, security systems, and automated production equipment are examples of products that require specialized installation, repair, user training, or extensive support services. As new technology is incorporated into more and more products, companies will need to provide more of these types of product-support services to remain competitive.

- *Companies are seeking professional advice to remain competitive.* Many firms turn to consultants to find ways to cut costs, refine business processes, and become more competitive. In addition, the continued growth of global marketing and e-commerce requires more professional support services.

- *Barriers to entry are low for services conducting e-commerce.* Capital-intensive businesses generally have high barriers to entry, which means that conditions exist that make entry into these businesses extremely difficult. Such conditions include significant capital requirements, high learning curves, tightly controlled markets, strict licensing procedures, the need for highly skilled employees or the use of specialized facilities. By contrast, the barriers to entry for most companies transacting electronic commerce are low. Just about any company can build a Web site and enter the electronic marketplace.

- *Internet economy is growing at an unprecedented rate.* Companies or parts of companies that generate revenue from **electronic commerce (e-commerce)**—buying and selling over the Internet—account for more than 2.5 million jobs. Although these jobs employ just a fraction of the 130 million-member U.S. workforce, they are jobs that did not previously exist, and many are service-related.[7]

LEARNING OBJECTIVE 2

List six factors that are contributing to the increase in the number of service businesses

barriers to entry
Factors that make it difficult to launch a business in a particular industry

electronic commerce (e-commerce)
The general term for the buying and selling of goods and services on the Internet

WHAT IS AN ECONOMIC SYSTEM?

Whether you're running a service or a goods-producing business, a capital-intensive or a labor-intensive business, world economic situations affect all businesses that compete in the global economy. Thus, running a successful business today requires a firm understanding of basic economic principles, of the different economic systems in the world, and of how businesses compete in the global economy.

economics
The study of how society uses scarce resources to produce and distribute goods and services

Economics is the study of how a society uses its scarce resources to produce and distribute goods and services. All societies must deal with the same basic questions: How should limited economic resources be used to satisfy society's needs? What goods and services should be produced? Who should produce them? How should these goods and services be divided among the population? In some countries these decisions are made by individuals (or households) when they decide how to spend or invest their income and by businesses when they decide what kinds of goods and services to produce; in other countries these decisions are made by governments.

Economists call the resources that societies use to produce goods and services *factors of production*. To maximize a company's profit, businesses use five **factors of production** in the most efficient way possible:

factors of production
Basic inputs that a society uses to produce goods and services, including natural resources, labor, capital, entrepreneurship, and knowledge

- ■ **Natural resources**—things that are useful in their natural state, such as land, forests, minerals, and water

natural resources
Land, forests, minerals, water, and other tangible assets usable in their natural state

- ■ **Human resources**—anyone (from company presidents to grocery clerks) who works to produce goods and services
- ■ **Capital**—resources (such as money, computers, machines, tools, and buildings) that a business needs to produce goods and services

human resources
All the people who work for an organization

- ■ **Entrepreneurs**—people such as Jerry Yang and David Filo who are innovative and willing to take risks to create and operate new businesses (see Exhibit 1.3)

capital
The physical, human-made elements used to produce goods and services, such as factories and computers; can also refer to the funds that finance the operations of a business

- ■ **Knowledge**—the collective intelligence of an organization

Traditionally, a business was considered to have an advantage if it was located in a country with a plentiful supply of natural resources, human resources, capital, and entrepreneurs. But in a global economy, companies can obtain capital from one part of the world, purchase supplies from another, and locate production facilities in still another. Furthermore, companies can relocate their operations to wherever they find a steady supply of affordable workers. Thus, economists no longer point to the proximity of these four factors of production as a requirement for success. Instead, they consider knowledge to be the key economic resource.[8] Today, minds rather than mines are the source of economic prosperity.

entrepreneurs
People who accept the risk of failure in the private enterprise system

knowledge
Expertise gained through experience or association

How important is knowledge in the global economy? Consider this: Economists agree that the seven key industries of the next few decades will be microelectronics, biotechnology, composite materials, telecommunications, civilian aviation, robotics, and computers.[9] All of these are brainpower industries. Tomorrow's workers will be freelancers, contractors, and analysts-for-hire, and their work will be brain-intensive instead of labor-intensive. Thus, countries with the greatest supply of knowledge workers and ones with economic systems that give workers the freedom to pursue their own economic interests will have the greatest advantage in the global marketplace.

LEARNING
OBJECTIVE   3
Differentiate between a free-market system and a planned system

Types of Economic Systems

The role that individuals and government play in allocating a society's resources depend on the society's **economic system,** the basic set of rules for allocating a society's resources to satisfy its citizens' needs. Two main economic systems exist in the world today: *free-market systems* and *planned systems.*

economic system
Means by which a society distributes its resources to satisfy its people's needs

free-market system
Economic system in which decisions about what to produce and in what quantities are decided by the market's buyers and sellers

Free-Market System In a **free-market system,** individuals are free to decide what products to produce, how to produce them, whom to sell them to, and at what price to sell them. Thus, they have the chance to succeed—or to fail—by their own efforts. **Capitalism** is the term most often used to describe the free-market system, which owes its philosophical origins to eighteenth-century philosophers such as Adam Smith. According to Smith, in the ideal capitalist economy (pure capitalism) the *market* (an arrangement between buyer and seller to trade goods and services) serves as a self-correcting mechanism—an "invisible hand" to ensure the production of the goods that society wants in the quantities that society wants, without regulation of any kind.[10]

capitalism
Economic system based on economic freedom and competition

Because the market is its own regulator, Smith was opposed to government intervention. He believed that if anyone's prices or wages strayed from acceptable levels that were set for everyone, the force of competition would drive them back. In modern practice, however, the government sometimes intervenes in free-market systems to influence prices and wages or to change the

THE COMPANY	ITS START
Clorox	In May 1913, five men pooled $100 each and started Clorox. The group had no experience in bleach-making chemistry but suspected that the brine found in salt ponds in San Francisco Bay could be converted into bleach.
The Limited	In 1963, 26-year-old Leslie Wexner left his family's retail store after having an argument with his father. He opened one small store in a strip mall in Columbus, Ohio. Today the company operates more than 5,000 stores in the United States.
Gateway 2000	Using $10,000 he borrowed from his grandmother, Ted Waitt started the company in his father's South Dakota barn in 1985. Because a typical computer-industry campaign would have been too costly, Waitt invented its now-famous faux-cowhide boxes. Today Gateway's revenues exceed $5 billion.
Coca-Cola	Pharmacist John Pemberton invented a soft drink in his backyard in 1886. Asa Chandler bought the company for $2,300 in 1891. Today it is worth over $170 billion.
E & J Gallo Winery	The brothers invested $6,000 but had no wine-making experience when they rented their first warehouse in California. They learned wine making by studying pamphlets at the local library.
Marriott	Willard Marriott and his fiancee-partner started a 9-seat A & W soda fountain with $3,000 in 1927. They demonstrated a knack for hospitality and clever marketing from the beginning.
Nike	In the early 1960s, Philip Knight and his college track coach sold imported Japanese sneakers from the trunk of a station wagon. Start-up costs totaled $1,000.
United Parcel Service	In 1907 two Seattle teenagers pooled their cash, came up with $100, and began a message and parcel delivery service for local merchants.
William Wrigley Jr.	In 1891 young Wrigley Jr. started selling baking soda in Chicago. To entice new customers, he threw in two packages of chewing gum with every sale. Guess what the customers were more excited about?
Amazon.com	In 1994 Jeff Bezos came across a report projecting annual Web growth at 2,300 percent. So Bezos left his Wall Street job, headed to Seattle in an aging Chevy Blazer, and drafted his business plan enroute. His e-business Amazon.com initially focused on selling books over the Internet, but Bezos later expanded his product offerings to include toys, consumer electronics, software, home improvement products, and more. Today Amazon.com is exploding in size. Although the company is still profitless, it generates over $1.6 billion in annual revenue.

EXHIBIT 1.3

RAGS TO RICHES

Few start-up companies are resource rich. Often they become successful because ingenuity is substituted for capital.

way resources are allocated. This practice of limited intervention is called *mixed capitalism,* which is the economic system of the United States. Other countries with variations of this economic system include Canada, Germany, and Japan. Under mixed capitalism, the pursuit of private gain is regarded as a worthwhile goal that ultimately benefits society as a whole. This is not the case in a planned system.

Planned System In a **planned system,** governments control all or part of the allocation of resources and limit the freedom of choice in order to accomplish government goals. Because social equality is a major goal of planned systems, private enterprise and the pursuit of private gain are generally regarded as wasteful and exploitative.

The planned system that allows individuals the least degree of economic freedom is **communism,** which still exists in such countries as North Korea and Cuba. (Keep in mind that even though communism and socialism are discussed here as economic systems, they can be political and social systems as well.) The degree to which communism is actually practiced varies. In its purest form, almost all resources are under government control. Private ownership is restricted largely to personal and household items. Resource allocation is handled through rigid centralized

planned system
Economic system in which the government controls most of the factors of production and regulates their allocation

communism
Economic system in which all productive resources are owned and operated by the government, to the elimination of private property

More than half of Russia's economy operates on a barter system. These shoppers at a Moscow market are trading goods for food.

planning by a handful of government officials who decide what goods to produce, how to produce them, and to whom they should be distributed.[11] Although pure communism still has its supporters, the future of communism is dismal. As economists Lester Thurow and Robert Heilbroner put it, "It's a great deal easier to design and assemble the skeleton of a mighty economy than to run it."[12]

Look at Russia. After decades of economic failure and the associated public unrest, the republics that were formerly part of the Soviet Union began restructuring their communist economies. Overnight, the entire Soviet system—its ideology, institutions, and embracing party apparatus—was dismantled. Despite the fervent efforts of Westerners and Russian reformers to shift to a more market-driven system, internal financial and economic turmoil forced the country to throw on the brakes (as Chapter 3 discusses in detail). As a result, Russia moved only partly down the path to a free-market system. Now the country is operating on a system of barters and IOUs fueled by shortages of money and supplies—a system that some economists say grows stranger by the day.[13]

socialism
Economic system characterized by public ownership and operation of key industries combined with private ownership and operation of less-vital industries

Socialism, by contrast, lies somewhere between capitalism and communism in the degree of economic freedom that it permits. Like communism, socialism involves a relatively high degree of government planning and some government ownership of land and capital resources (such as buildings and equipment). However, government involvement is limited to industries considered vital to the common welfare, such as transportation, utilities, medicine, steel, and communications. In these industries, the government owns or controls all the facilities and determines what will be produced and how the output will be distributed. Private ownership is permitted in industries that are not considered vital, and both businesses and individuals are allowed to benefit from their own efforts. However, taxes are high in socialist states because the government absorbs the costs of medical care, education, subsidized housing, and other social services.

The Trend Toward Privatization

Although varying degrees of socialism and communism are practiced around the world today, several socialist and communist economies are moving toward free-market economic systems. Anxious to unload unprofitable businesses for badly needed cash and to experiment with free-market capitalism, countries such as Great Britain, Mexico, Argentina, Israel, France, Sweden, and China are **privatizing** some of their government-owned enterprises by selling them to privately held firms. Great Britain, for example, has sold the national phone company, the national steel company, the national sugar company, Heathrow Airport, water suppliers, and the company that makes Rover automobiles. Hopes are high that converting certain industries to private ownership will enable them to compete more effectively in the global marketplace.[14]

privatizing
The conversion of public ownership to private ownership

Nevertheless, many planned economic systems are discovering that moving toward a free-market system and converting state-owned enterprises into world-class corporations is a formidable task without existing blueprints. Some countries are rushing forward without building effective banking or legal systems to protect their emerging private industries. Others, such as China, are being met with strong resistance from hard-line communists. Still, China expects to privatize more than 60 percent of its state-owned enterprises by 2005. If successful in its privatization attempts, China will indeed serve as a role model.[15]

HOW DOES A FREE-MARKET ECONOMIC ■ SYSTEM WORK?

Earlier in this chapter we noted that in a free-market system the marketplace determines what goods and services get produced. In this section we will discuss the underlying elements or principles that must be present for the free market to work in an orderly fashion. These concepts include the theory of supply and demand, competition, and government intervention.

The Theory of Supply and Demand in a Free-Market System

The theory of supply and demand is the immediate driving force of the free-market system. It is the basic tool that economists use to describe how the market works in determining prices and the quantity of goods produced. **Demand** refers to the amount of a good or service that consumers will buy at a given time at various prices. **Supply** refers to the quantities of a good or service that producers will provide on a particular date at various prices. Simply put, *demand* refers to the behavior of buyers, whereas *supply* refers to the behavior of sellers. Exhibit 1.4 shows how the two work together to impose a kind of order on the free-market system.

On the surface, the theory of supply and demand seems little more than common sense. Consumers would buy more when the price is low and buy less when the price is high. Producers would offer more when the price is high and offer less when the price is low. In other words, the quantity supplied and the quantity demanded would continuously interact, and the balance between them at any given moment would be reflected by the current price on the open market.

However, a quick look at any real-life market situation shows you that pricing isn't that simple. To a large degree, pricing depends on the type of product being sold. When the price of gasoline goes up, consumers may cut down a little, but most wouldn't stop driving, even if the price were to double. Moreover, a rise in housing prices could set off rumors that prices will rise even more. As a result consumers might rush to buy available homes, forcing the prices to rise higher still.

Nevertheless, in broad terms, the interaction of supply and demand regulates a free-market system by determining what is produced and in what amounts. For example, a movie studio might produce more comedies if ticket sales for similar films are brisk. On the other hand, it might decide to produce fewer comedies and more action-adventure movies if attendance at comedies lags. The result of such decisions—in theory, at least—is that consumers will get what they want and producers will earn a profit by keeping up with public demand.

Buyer's Perspective The forces of supply and demand determine the market price for products and services. Say that you're shopping for blue jeans, and the pair you want is priced at $35. This is more than you can afford, so you don't make the purchase. When the store puts them on sale the following week for $18, however, you run right in and buy a pair.

But what if the store had to buy the jeans from the manufacturer for $20? It would have made a profit selling them to you for $35, but it would lose money selling them for $18. What if the store asks to buy more from the manufacturer at $10 or $15 but the manufacturer refuses? Is

demand
Buyers' willingness and ability to purchase products

supply
Specific quantity of a product that the seller is able and willing to provide

LEARNING
OBJECTIVE 4

Explain how supply and demand interact to affect price

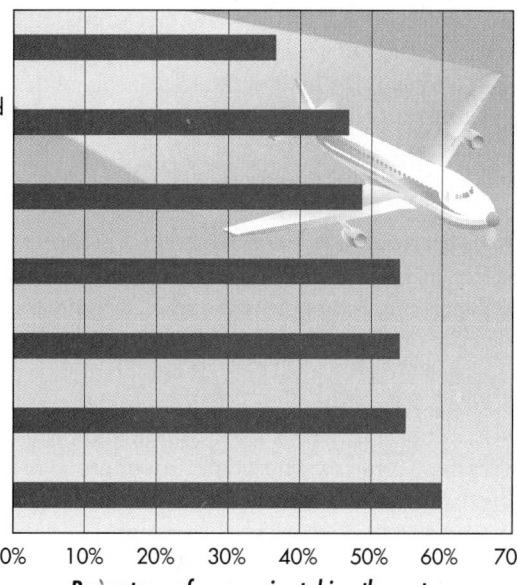

Increase use of corporate or chartered aircraft

Reduce number of conventions and conferences employees attend

Use alternative airports, even if less convenient

Reduce number of employees traveling

Reduce number of domestic trips

Increase use of Saturday-night stayovers

Increase use of videoconferencing and teleconferencing

0% 10% 20% 30% 40% 50% 60% 70%
Percentage of companies taking these steps

EXHIBIT 1.4

EFFECTS OF HIGHER AIR FARE ON DEMAND FOR BUSINESS TRAVEL

When airlines raise their prices, demand for business travel softens as companies take steps to reduce their travel costs.

EXHIBIT 1.5

THE RELATIONSHIP
BETWEEN SUPPLY AND
DEMAND

In a free-market system, prices
aren't set by the government; nor
do producers alone have the final
say. Instead, prices reflect the
interaction of supply (**S**) and
demand (**D**). The equilibrium
price (**E**) is established when the
amount of a product that
producers are willing to sell at a
given price equals the amount that
consumers are willing to buy at
that price.

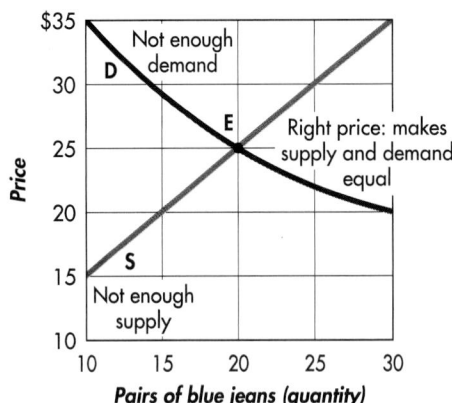

demand curve
Graph of relationship between various
prices and the quantity demanded at
each price

supply curve
Graph of relationship between various
prices and the quantity supplied at
each price

equilibrium price
Point at which quantity supplied equals
quantity demanded

competition
Rivalry among businesses for the same
customer

pure competition
Situation in which so many buyers and
sellers exist that no single buyer or
seller can individually influence market
prices

monopoly
Market in which there are no direct
competitors so that one company
dominates

oligopoly
Market dominated by a few producers

there a price that will make both the supplier and the customer happy? The answer is yes—the
price at which the quantity of jeans demanded equals the quantity supplied.

This relationship is shown in Exhibit 1.5. A range of possible prices is listed vertically at the
left of the graph, with the lowest at the bottom and the highest at the top. Quantity of blue jeans
is represented along the horizontal axis. The points plotted on the curve labeled **D** indicate that
on a given day the store would sell 10 pairs of jeans if they were priced at $35, 15 pairs if they were
priced at $27, and so on. The curve that describes this relationship between price and quantity
demanded is a **demand curve.** (Demand curves are not necessarily curved; they may be straight
lines.)

Seller's Perspective Now think about the situation from the seller's point of view. In general, the
more profit the store can make on a particular item, the more of that item it will want to sell. This
relationship can also be depicted graphically. Again, look at Exhibit 1.5. The line labeled **S** shows
that the store would be willing to offer 30 pairs of jeans at $35, 25 pairs at $30, and so on. The
store's willingness to carry the item increases as the price it can charge and its profit potential per
item increase. In other words, as the price goes up, the quantity supplied goes up. The line tracing
the relationship between price and quantity supplied is called a **supply curve.**

As much as the store would like to sell 30 pairs of jeans at $35, you and your fellow con-
sumers are likely to want only 10 pairs at that price. If the store offered 30 pairs, therefore, it
would probably be stuck with some that it would have to mark down. How does the store avoid
this problem? It looks for the point at which the demand curve and the supply curve intersect, the
point at which the intentions of buyers and sellers coincide. The point marked **E** in Exhibit 1.5
shows that when jeans are priced at $25, consumers are willing to buy 20 pairs of them and the
store is willing to sell 20 pairs. In other words, at the price of $25, the quantity supplied and the
quantity demanded are in balance. The price at this point is known as the **equilibrium price.**

Note that this intersection represents both a specific price—$25 in our example—and a
specific quantity of goods—here, 20 pairs of jeans. It is also tied to a specific point in time. Note
also that it is the mutual interaction between quantity demanded and quantity supplied that determines the equilibrium price.

Competition in a Free-Market System

In a free-market system, customers are free to buy whatever and wherever they please. Therefore,
companies must compete with rivals for potential customers. **Competition** is the situation in
which two or more suppliers of a product are rivals in the pursuit of the same customers.

In theory, the ideal type of competition is **pure competition,** which is characterized by
marketplace conditions in which multiple buyers and sellers exist; a product or service with
nearly identical features such as wheat; and the ability to easily enter and exit the marketplace.
Under these conditions no single firm or group of firms in an industry becomes large enough to
influence prices and thereby distort the workings of the free-market system. By contrast, a **monopoly** is a scenario in which there is only one producer of a product in a given market, and thus
the producer is able to determine the price. A situation in which an industry (such as commercial
aircraft manufacturing) is dominated by only a few producers is called an **oligopoly.**

Between pure competition and a monopoly lie a number of firms with varying degrees of competitive power. Most of the competition in advanced free-market economic systems is **monopolistic competition,** in which a large number of sellers (none of which dominates the market) offers products that can be distinguished from competing products in at least some small way. Toothpaste, cosmetics, soft drinks, Internet search engines, and restaurants are examples of products with distinguishable features.

When markets become filled with competitors and products start to look alike, companies use price, speed, quality, service, or innovation to gain a **competitive advantage**—something that sets one company apart from its rivals and makes its products more appealing to consumers. For example, Southwest Airlines competes on price by offering the lowest fares of any of its competitors. And American Airlines sends e-mail listing rock-bottom fares for undersubscribed flights to more than a million Net SAAver subscribers.[16] Competing on price may seem like an obvious and easy choice to make, but the consequences can be devastating to individual companies and to entire industries. During a three-year period in the early 1990s, price wars caused the U.S. airline industry to lose more money than it had made since the Wright brothers' first flight. Unfortunately, the harsh truth of many price wars is that sooner or later everybody sells at a loss. For this reason, companies try to find other ways to compete.

Jiffy Lube, for instance, competes on speed. Mechanics change a car's oil and filter in 15 minutes or less while customers wait. Starbucks competes on quality by delivering a premium product that has changed the definition of "a good cup of coffee." And Enterprise Rent-A-Car blows past its competitors by competing on service. The company establishes convenient rental offices just about everywhere. If your car needs repair service, Enterprise will provide you with a

monopolistic competition
Situation in which many sellers differentiate their products from those of competitors in at least some small way

competitive advantage
Ability to perform in one or more ways that competitors cannot match

COMPETING IN THE GLOBAL MARKETPLACE

ENTERPRISE RENT-A-CAR TRIES HARDER, AND IT PAYS OFF

How does a small, private company in a highly competitive industry enter the marketplace and zoom past all its competitors? For Enterprise Rent-A-Car, the answer was "be different." Winner of the 1997 Ernst and Young Entrepreneur of the Year Award, and named one of the "100 Best Companies to Work For" by *Fortune* magazine, Enterprise now owns more cars (over 500,000) and operates in more locations than Hertz. Here's how Enterprise did it.

Enterprise is innovative. While Hertz, Avis, and lots of little companies were cutting one another's throats to win more business from corporate and vacation travelers at airports, Enterprise invaded the market with a completely different strategy and an astoundingly simple approach. Instead of amassing 10,000 cars at a few dozen airports, Enterprise recognized that many people can't live a day without their car. So the company set out to deliver wheels to people whose family cars were being repaired or whose cars were too small or unreliable for special occasions.

Enterprise is convenient. The company sets up inexpensive rental offices just about everywhere. As soon as an Enterprise site grows to about 150 cars, another is opened a few miles away. Enterprise now claims to be within 15 minutes of 90 percent of the U.S. population. And at major accounts such as auto repair shops, the company sets

up an office on the premises, staffs it during peak hours, and keeps a supply of cars parked outside so customers can fill out the paperwork and conveniently pick up and return rental cars.

Enterprise is aggressive. The company knows that when your car is being towed, you're in no mood to figure out which local rent-a-car company to use. Instead you'll probably rely on the recommendation of the garage service manager. So once Enterprise opens a new site, employees fan out to develop chummy relationships with the service managers of every good-sized auto dealership and body shop in the area—bringing them pizza and doughnuts on most Wednesdays.

Enterprise is affordable. It charges less than competitors but is able to generate high profits because it sets up operations away from expensive airport locations. And higher profits mean that Enterprise won't be needing a jump start to keep its business running in the future.

■ QUESTIONS FOR CRITICAL THINKING

1. Use Enterprise as an example to explain why the free-market system works.

2. How does Enterprise provide value to their customers?

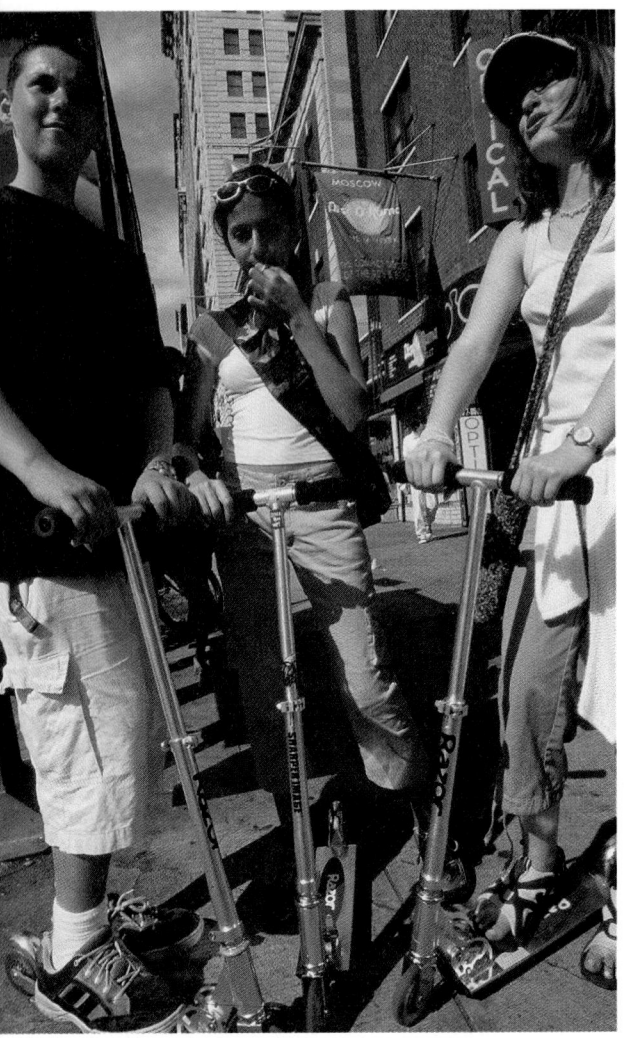

It doesn't take long before innovative products such as scooters catch on. But just rolling out a "me-too" product in today's competitive marketplace will not guarantee success. Today's products must be exciting and create perceived consumer value to catch the savvy buyer's eye.

LEARNING
OBJECTIVE   5

List the three major economic roles of the U.S. government

deregulation
Removal or relaxation of rules and restrictions affecting businesses

rental car right at the dealer's service center. And the company bets that you won't be in the mood to quibble about prices.[17]

Product innovation is another way that companies compete in the free-market economy. For nearly a century, 3M's management has promoted innovation by giving employees the freedom to take risks and try new ideas. Beginning with the invention of sandpaper in 1904, 3M has produced such staples as masking tape, cellophane tape, magnetic tape, videotape, and Post-it Notes. Sometimes product innovation can revolutionize an entire industry, just as Razor aluminum scooters, Rollerblades, AbFlex, Atomic hour-glass skis, and Burton & Sims snowboards did by creating new market opportunities for the sporting goods industry.[18]

Government's Role in a Free-Market System

Although the free-market system generally works well, it's far from perfect. If left unchecked, the economic forces that make capitalism succeed may also create severe problems for some groups or individuals. To correct these types of problems, the government intervenes in free-market systems by enforcing laws and regulations to protect consumers and foster competition, by contributing to economic stability, and by spending for the public good.

Enforcing Laws and Regulations to Protect Consumers and Foster Competition The U.S. federal government and state and local governments create thousands of new laws and regulations every year, many of which limit what businesses and consumers can and cannot do. These laws are intended to protect the consumer and foster competition. As a consumer, for example, you can't buy some medications without a doctor's prescription; you can't buy alcoholic beverages without a certificate proving that you're old enough; and you can't buy certain products lacking safety features, such as cars without seatbelts and medication without childproof tops.

Just as governments can create laws, they can also remove or relax existing laws and regulations through a process known as **deregulation.** Industries such as airlines, banking, and telecommunications have been deregulated in order to promote industry competition in hopes of providing consumers with lower prices and improved products or services.

Because competition generally benefits the U.S. economy, the federal government tries to preserve competition and ensure that no single enterprise becomes too powerful. If a company has a monopoly, it can harm consumers by raising prices, cutting output, or stifling innovation. Furthermore, because monopolies have total control over certain products and prices and the total market share for those products, it's extremely difficult for competitors to enter markets where monopolies exist. For these reasons, true monopolies are prohibited by federal antitrust laws. (Some monopolies, such as utilities, are legal but closely regulated.)

The United States versus Microsoft The government's heavy hand with monopolies has been a subject of continuing concern since the turn of the century. One of the highest-profile antitrust cases of the 1990s involved the software giant Microsoft. Microsoft makes the operating-system software used by 90 percent of personal computers as well as a wide array of application software that runs on those operating systems. In the late 1990s, the U.S. Justice Department accused Microsoft of using its vast clout to give itself an unfair advantage in the application-software business by bundling its popular Internet Explorer Web browser with its Windows operating system. Competitors such as Netscape alleged that Microsoft was willing to use every tool at its disposal to damage competition by forcing or persuading companies to install its Internet Explorer as a condition of licensing the Windows operating system.

Subsequently, in 1998 the U.S. government and 19 states filed lawsuits claiming that Microsoft's practices were in violation of antitrust law. After a much-publicized two-year trial, on June 7, 2000, U.S. District Judge Thomas Jackson ruled that Microsoft had repeatedly and willfully violated antitrust laws and should be broken up to restore competition to the computer software industry. Microsoft, of course, appealed Jackson's ruling and Jackson agreed not to impose any court-ordered restrictions on Microsoft's conduct while the case was under appeal. The final outcome of the Microsoft case will eventually be resolved by the Supreme Court. But until that time, Microsoft is free to forge ahead with major business initiatives and conduct business as usual.[19]

Government Opposition to Mergers While monopolies are illegal, oligopolies are not. Still, the U.S. government has the power to prevent a combination of firms if it would reduce competition in the marketplace. The $120 billion merger between WorldCom and Sprint was called off because U.S. regulators were concerned that merging the second- and third-biggest long-distance services would stop the decline of long-distance rates.[20] Similarly, bookstore chain Barnes & Noble scrapped its planned $600 million acquisition of Ingram Book Group, the largest book wholesaler in the United States, in the face of regulatory opposition. Regulators alleged that the merger would stifle competition by giving Barnes & Noble an advantage over smaller booksellers.[21]

Contributing to Economic Stability Another important role the government assumes in a free-market system is to contribute to the economy's stability. A nation's economy never stays exactly the same size. Instead, it grows and contracts in response to the combined effects of such factors as technological breakthroughs, changes in investment patterns, shifts in consumer attitudes, world events, and basic economic forces. During periods of downward swing, or **recession,** consumers buy less and factories produce less, so companies must lay off workers, who in turn buy less—and so on. During periods of *recovery* companies buy more, factories produce more, employment is high, and workers spend their earnings.

Bill Gates, chairman of Microsoft, called Judge Jackson's ruling "unreasonable" and "clearly the most massive attempt at government regulation of the technology industry ever."

These recurrent up-and-down swings are known as the **business cycle.** Although such swings are natural and to some degree predictable, they cause hardship. In an attempt to avoid such hardship and to foster economic stability, the government can levy new taxes or adjust the current tax rates, raise or lower interest rates, and regulate the total amount of money circulating in our economy. These government actions have two facets: fiscal policy and monetary policy. **Fiscal policy** involves changes in the government's revenues and expenditures to stimulate or dampen the economy. **Monetary policy** involves adjustments to the nation's money supply by increasing or decreasing interest rates to help control inflation. In the United States, monetary policy is controlled primarily by the Federal Reserve Board, a group of appointed government officials who oversee the country's central banking system. (Monetary policy is discussed more fully in Chapter 17.)

Spending for the Public Good Although everybody hates to pay taxes, most of us are willing to admit they're a necessary evil. If the government didn't take your tax money and repair our nation's roads, would you be inclined to fix them yourself? Similarly, it might not be practical to rely on individual demand to provide police and fire protection or to launch satellites. Instead, the government steps in and collects a variety of taxes so it can supply such *public goods* (see Exhibit 1.6).

For many years the U.S. government spent more money than it took in, creating annual budget deficits on the order of several hundred billion dollars. The accumulated amount of annual budget deficits (the U.S. national debt) now amounts to almost $6 trillion. As a result, interest payments alone on the national debt cost U.S. taxpayers about $340 billion a year—or $10,000 per second. In 1997 Congress approved a plan to pare down future deficits to balance the budget by 2002.[22] Strong economic growth accompanied by budget modifications put the United States ahead of schedule. For the first time since 1835, the United States is on a path to becoming debt free by 2013.[23]

Although reducing government spending might seem like a practical step, keep in mind that such reduction can have rippling economic consequences. That's because government

recession
Period during which national income, employment, and production all fall

business cycle
Fluctuations in the rate of growth that an economy experiences over a period of several years

fiscal policy
Use of government revenue collection and spending to influence the business cycle

monetary policy
Government policy and actions taken by the Federal Reserve Board to regulate the nation's money supply

EXHIBIT 1.6

THE FEDERAL DOLLAR

Here's a breakdown of the federal dollar—how it's collected and how it's spent.

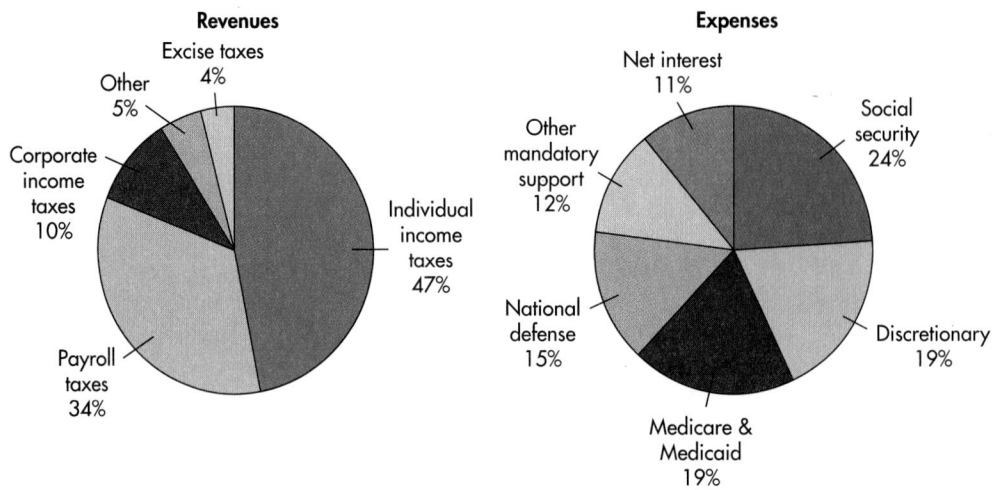

EXHIBIT 1.6

THE FEDERAL DOLLAR

Here's a breakdown of the federal dollar—how it's collected and how it's spent.

spending boosts the economy and has a *multiplier effect* as it makes its way through the economy. For example, if the government decides to fund new highway projects, thousands of construction workers will be gainfully employed and earn wages. If some of these workers decide to spend their extra income to buy new cars, car dealers will have more income. The car dealers, in turn, might spend their income on new clothes, and the salesclerks (who earn commissions) might buy compact disks, and so on. This *circular flow* of money through the economic system links all elements of the U.S. economy by exchanging goods and services for money, which is then used to buy more goods and services, and so on.

How Does a Free-Market System Monitor Its Economic Performance?

Each day we are deluged with complex statistical data that depict the current status and past performance of the economy. Sorting, understanding, and interpreting these data are difficult tasks even for professional economists. **Economic indicators** are statistics such as interest rates, unemployment rates, and housing data that are used to monitor and measure economic performance. Statistics that point to what may happen to the economy in the future are called *leading indicators;* statistics that signal a swing in the economy after the movement has begun are called *lagging indicators* (see Exhibit 1.7).

economic indicators
Statistics that measure variables in the economy

Unemployment statistics, for example, are leading economic indicators because they are a signal of future changes in consumer spending. When unemployment rises, people have less money to spend, and the economy suffers. Housing starts are another leading indicator because they show where construction and manufacturing is headed. Housing is very sensitive to interest rate changes. If mortgage rates are high, fewer people can afford to build new homes. When housing starts drop, builders stop hiring, and may even lay off workers. Meanwhile, orders fall for plumbing fixtures, carpets, and appliances, so manufacturers decrease production and workers' hours. These cutbacks ripple through the economy and lead to slower income and job growth,

Best of the Web Best of the Web Best of

STEP INSIDE THE ECONOMIC STATISTICS BRIEFING ROOM

Want to know where the economy is heading? Visit the White House Economic Statistics Briefing Room to get the latest economic indicators compiled by a number of U.S. agencies. Click on Federal Statistics by category to enter the room, and check out the stats and graphs for new housing starts; manufacturers' shipments, inventories, and orders; unemployment; average hourly earnings; and more. Then point your mouse to "SSBR" and drop by the Social Statistics Briefing Room for some data on crime, demography, education, and health.
www.whitehouse.gov/fsbr/esbr.html

EXHIBIT 1.7

MAJOR ECONOMIC
INDICATORS

Businesses and government leaders rely on these major economic
indicators to make decisions.

LEADING INDICATORS	LAGGING INDICATORS
Changes in the money supply in circulation	Changes in the prime rate
Number of building permits issued by private housing units	Number of commercial and industrial loans to be repaid
New orders for consumer goods	Change in the Consumer Price Index for services
Number of contracts and orders for equipment	Size of manufacturing and trade inventories
Weekly initial claims for unemployment insurance	Average length of unemployment
Average weekly hours for production workers in manufacturing	Labor cost per unit of output in manufacturing

and weaker consumer spending.[24] Besides housing starts and unemployment data, economists closely monitor a nation's output and price changes.

LEARNING OBJECTIVE 6

Define the gross domestic product and explain what it is used for

Measuring a Nation's Output The broadest measure of an economy's health is the **gross domestic product (GDP).** The GDP measures a country's output—its production, distribution, and use of goods and services—by computing the sum of all goods and services produced for *final* use in a market during a specified period (usually a year). The goods may be produced by either domestic or foreign companies as long as these companies are located within a nation's boundaries. Sales from a Honda assembly plant in California, for instance, would be included in the GDP.

gross domestic product (GDP)
Dollar value of all the final goods and services produced by businesses located within a nation's borders; excludes receipts from overseas operations of domestic companies

A less popular measure of a country's output is the **gross national product (GNP).** This measure excludes the value of production from foreign-owned businesses within a nation's boundaries (such as Honda U.S.), but it includes receipts from the overseas operations of domestic companies—such as McDonald's in Switzerland. Put another way, GNP considers *who* is responsible for the production; GDP considers *where* the production occurs. Although far from perfect, the GDP enables a nation to evaluate its economic policies and to compare its current performance with prior periods or with the performance of other nations.[25]

gross national product (GNP)
Dollar value of all the final goods and services produced by domestic businesses; includes receipts from overseas operations and excludes receipts from foreign-owned businesses within a nation's borders

Measuring Price Changes Price changes, especially price increases, are another important economic indicator. In a period of rising prices, the purchasing power of a dollar erodes, which means that you can purchase fewer things with today's dollar than you could in a prior period. Over time, price increases tend to lead to wage increases, which in turn add pressures for higher prices, setting a vicious cycle in motion.

Inflation and Deflation **Inflation** is a steady rise in the prices of goods and services throughout the economy. When the inflation rate begins to decline, economists use the term *disinflation.* **Deflation,** on the other hand, is the sustained fall in the general price level for goods and services. It is the opposite of inflation; that is, purchasing power increases because a dollar held today will buy more tomorrow. In a deflationary period, investors postpone major purchases in anticipation of lower prices in the future. Keep in mind that although prices in the overall economy tend to increase year after year, not all industries and product categories necessarily follow this trend. In the electronics industry, for instance, prices tend to drop as technology advances and production becomes more efficient.

inflation
Economic condition in which prices rise steadily throughout the economy

deflation
Economic condition in which prices fall steadily throughout the economy

Consumer Price Index The **consumer price index (CPI)** measures the rate of inflation by comparing the change in prices of a representative basket of goods and services such as clothing, food, housing, and utilities over time. A numerical weight is assigned to each item in the representative basket to adjust for each item's relative importance in the marketplace. As are most economic indicators, the CPI is far from perfect. For one thing, the representative basket of goods may not accurately represent the prices and consumption patterns of the area in which you live. For another, the mix in this basket may not include new innovations, which often play a major role in consumer spending patterns. Nonetheless, many businesses use the CPI to adjust rent increases and to keep employees' wages in line with the pace of inflation.

consumer price index (CPI)
Monthly statistic that measures changes in the prices of about 400 goods and services that consumers buy

Best of the Web Best of the Web Best of

DISCOVER WHAT'S IN THE CPI

The CPI is an important tool that allows analysts to track the change in prices over time. But the CPI doesn't always match a given individual's inflation experience. Find out why by visiting the official CPI Web site maintained by the U.S. Bureau of Labor Statistics. Be sure to check out how the CPI measures homeowners' costs, and don't leave without getting some data. Click on the Most Requested Series, find your region, and trace the CPI for your area by entering some information in the boxes.

stats.bls.gov/cpihome.htm

LEARNING OBJECTIVE 7

Identify five challenges that businesses are facing in the global economy

globalization
Tendency of the world's economies to act as a single interdependent system

---

■ CHALLENGES OF A GLOBAL ECONOMY

Even though economic indicators suggest that the United States is in a period of great economic strength, businesses today are facing a raft of new challenges. Today, financial and product markets are far more interconnected than ever before. **Globalization**—the increasing tendency of the world to act as one market instead of a series of national ones—opens new markets for a company's goods and services while simultaneously producing tougher competition. Thus, doing business in the twenty-first century means working in a world of increasing uncertainty where change is the norm, not the exception. In the coming chapters we will explore each of the challenges that businesses are facing in the global economy and we will provide real-world examples of how companies are tackling and meeting these challenges:

■ *Producing quality products and services that satisfy customers' changing needs.* Today's customer is well-informed and has many product choices. For many businesses, such as Yahoo!, competing in the global economy means competing on the basis of *speed* (getting products to market sooner), *quality* (doing a better job of meeting customer expectations), and *customer satisfaction* (making sure buyers are happy with every aspect of the purchase, from the shopping experience until they're through using the product).

■ *Starting and managing a small business in today's competitive environment.* Starting a new business or successfully managing a small company in today's global economy requires creativity and a willingness to exploit new opportunities. Small companies often lack the resources to buffer themselves from competition. Furthermore, once a new product or process is brought to the market, competitors need only a short time to be up and running with something similar. Thus, the biggest challenge for small businesses today is to make a product or provide a service that is hard to imitate.

■ *Thinking globally and committing to a culturally diverse workforce.* Globalization opens new markets for a company's goods, increases competition, and changes the composition of the workforce into one that is more diverse in race, gender, age, physical and mental abilities, lifestyle, culture, education, ideas, and background. By 2010 minorities will account for 50 percent of the U.S. population, and immigrants will account for half of all new U.S. workers.[26] Thus, to be competitive in the global economy, companies must commit to a culturally diverse workforce, think globally, and adopt global standards of excellence.

■ *Behaving in an ethically and socially responsible manner.* As businesses become more complex through global expansion and technological change, they must deal with an increasing number of ethical and social issues. These include the marketing of unhealthful products, the use of questionable accounting practices to compute financial results, and the pollution of the environment (as Chapter 2 discusses). In the future, businesses can expect continued pressure from environmental groups, consumers, employees, and government regulators to act ethically and responsibly.

■ *Keeping pace with technology and electronic commerce.* Everywhere we look, technology is reshaping the world (see Exhibit 1.8). The Internet and innovations in computerization, miniaturization, and telecommunication have made it possible for people anywhere in the world to exchange information and goods. Such technologies are collapsing boundaries and changing

YEAR	EVENT
1960	Xerox sells the first convenient office copier using xerography—Greek for "dry writing."
1965	Gordon Moore predicts exponential growth in chip power.
1969	Internet started by U.S. Department of Defense.
1971	Intel produces first microprocessor.
1975	First commercial personal computers are sold.
1977	Ken Olsen, founder of Digital Equipment, declares that "there is no reason anyone would want a computer in their home."
1981	First portable computer introduced.
1983	Motorola brings out first portable cellular phone system.
1990	World Wide Web developed; debuts to public two years later.
1991	IBM reports its first-ever annual loss of $2.8 billion.
1992	America Online goes public; Microsoft's Bill Gates becomes the richest man in America.
1994	Jerry Yang and David Filo create Yahoo!
1995	Netscape goes public.
1997	More than 50 percent of Schwab's brokerage business is being done online.
1998	Number of telecommuters in United States reaches 16 million.
1999	Vodafone acquires AirTouch for $70 billion, creating the world's biggest wireless-communications firm.
2000	U.S. Justice Department rules that Microsoft is a monopoly and orders it split into two separate and competing companies.

EXHIBIT 1.8

FORTY YEARS OF TECHNOLOGICAL CHANGE

Technological advancement over the last 40 years has been dramatic.

the way customers, suppliers, and companies interact. Not only are fledgling Internet companies becoming global competitors overnight, but they're changing the way people shop for books, cars, vacations, advice—just about everything. Meanwhile, the Internet is forcing traditional enterprises to explore new ways of doing business—including launching products and services that compete with their existing ones.[27] In short, the Internet has touched every business and industry and is changing all facets of business life.[28] (Consult Component Chapter A for a discussion of Internet fundamentals.)

Customer satisfaction, competition, cultural diversity, ethics, and technology are indeed the key challenges of the twenty-first century. But a closer look at U.S. business history will show that meeting new challenges has been a recurring theme for decades.

■ HISTORY OF U.S. ECONOMIC GROWTH

The first economic base in the United States was the small family farm. People grew enough food for their families and used any surplus to trade for necessary goods provided by independent craftspeople and merchants. Business operated on a small scale, and much of the population was self-employed. With fertile, flat terrain and adequate rainfall, farmers soon prospered, and their prosperity spread to the townspeople who served them.

In the early nineteenth century, people began making greater use of rivers, harbors, and rich mineral deposits. Excellent natural resources helped businesspeople accumulate the capital they needed to increase production—fueling the transition of the United States from a farm-based economy to an industrial economy.

KEEPING PACE WITH TECHNOLOGY AND ELECTRONIC COMMERCE

MILKING THE NET

In 1999 Ted Farnsworth was trolling the Internet, looking for farming equipment for his brother-in-law's New York dairy farm. Frustrated that he could not find what he needed online, Farnsworth decided to fill his own needs and start a farming Web site. Now CEO and founder of Farmbid.com, Farnsworth traverses the country signing up farmers at one trade show after another. The company has about 90,000 registered customers who use the site to buy and sell seed, chemicals, machinery, and other agricultural supplies.

Farmbid is one of more than a dozen business-to-business farming Web sites that try to cash in on the isolation of many rural farmers by giving them a one-stop shop for their farming needs. Some auction cattle, pigs, sheep, and horses, while others sell everything from seed to animal vaccinations to farm insurance. But competition is increasing. Major agricultural firms Cenex Harvest States Cooperatives, Cargill, and DuPont are challenging the newcomers with their own joint venture Rooster.com, an electronic mall where farmers can buy and sell seed, fertilizer, crops, farm chemicals, and other goods.

The Web sites are welcome news for farmers. Most farmers live in remote places and conduct their affairs in the nearest town. A consolidation wave in agribusiness is shrinking their local choices for everything from seed suppliers to grain handlers. The Internet might be the farmers' solution to the local monopolies they face. It gives farmers the means to connect with distant businesses. For example, on a recent afternoon Mark Gunn, a Janesville, Wisconsin farmer, fired up his computer and headed for a swine auction at Farms.com in search of 230 pigs to stock his 2,000-acre farm. Instead of running off to another farm or a crowded auction house—sometimes two or three states away—to look for pigs, Gunn sat in his office and found what he was looking for in a few minutes.

The Web sites make money through advertising, from transaction fees, or by taking a percentage of each sale made over the site. But few are profitable, and most don't expect to be for at least a year. Moreover, while there appears to be a strong market for Internet farming, industry analysts agree that there is room for only two or three players. Farmbid expects a tough battle now that the big guys such as DuPont and Cargill have awakened. Meanwhile, as more and more farmers discover what the Internet can do for this ancient industry, one thing is for certain: it may never be the same down on the farm.

■ QUESTIONS FOR CRITICAL THINKING

1. Review the Farmbid.com Web site at www.farmbid.com/. How does this site provide value to the farm community?

2. How is Internet technology changing the agricultural industry?

Age of Industrialization: 1900–1944

During the nineteenth century, new technology gave birth to the factory and the industrial revolution. Millions of new workers came to the United States from abroad to work in factories where each person performed one simple task over and over. Separating the manufacturing process into distinct tasks and producing large quantities of similar products allowed businesses to achieve cost and operating efficiencies known as **economies of scale.**

economies of scale
Savings from manufacturing, marketing, or buying in large quantities

As businesses increased in size, they also became more powerful. In the early 1920s more and more industrial assets were concentrated into fewer and fewer hands, putting smaller competitors, workers, and consumers at a disadvantage. By popular mandate, the government passed laws and regulations to prevent the abuse of power by big business. At the same time, workers began to organize into labor unions to balance the power of their employers. Meanwhile, U.S. businesses enjoyed such an enormously diverse market within the country's borders that they didn't need to trade overseas. But prosperity soon ended. In 1929 the U.S. stock market crashed, ushering in a period of economic collapse known as the Great Depression. Millions of people lost their jobs. By 1941, one in 10 workers remained unemployed, the birthrate was stagnant, and the hand of the U.S. government strengthened as people lost confidence in the power of business to pull the country out of hard times. That same year the United States entered World War II.

The Postwar Golden Era: 1945–1969

The postwar reconstruction, which started in 1945, revived the economy and renewed the trend toward large-scale enterprises. The G.I. Bill of Rights opened advanced education to the working classes. The middle class grew and prospered. By 1950 the birthrate had jumped, and the baby boom was on. Accustomed to playing a major role in the war effort, the government continued to exert a large measure of control over business and the economy. President Eisenhower's highway system fueled expansion and the growth of the suburbs. Sales of new homes and U.S.-manufactured automobiles skyrocketed.

Stimulated by a boom in world demand and an expansive political climate, the United States prospered throughout the 1960s. Expanding world trade provided limitless markets for U.S. goods. But once Europe and Japan had recovered from the war, they began challenging U.S. industries—Italy with shoes, Switzerland with watches, and Japan with cameras. By the end of the 1960s, Japanese transistor radios dominated the world market. Still, the more advanced technological industries and their products—televisions, copying machines, and aircraft—remained U.S. preserves.

The Turbulent Years: 1970–1979

In the early 1970s, inflation depressed demand and U.S. economic growth began to slump. In 1973 the price of a barrel of oil skyrocketed from $3 to $11, forcing companies to invest in ways to save energy instead of investing in new manufacturing equipment. Meanwhile, with virtually no investment money floating around, and no money for new business start-ups, the U.S. economy wasn't particularly competitive. Companies had no incentive to lower their costs and consumers had fewer product choices, which helped sustain higher prices.

The U.S. economy had barely recovered from the 1973 oil shock when it got hit again in 1979 (oil jumped from $13 to $23 per barrel), resulting in galloping inflation and sky-high interest rates. Exports from Asia began to pour into the United States—some bearing U.S. labels—and the United States entered an era of diminishing growth.[29] Meanwhile, a takeover binge was changing the structure of corporate America. Giant organizations called *conglomerates* emerged as companies acquired strings of unrelated businesses to grow and diversify their enterprises. At the same time, deregulation in several large markets, including transportation and financial services, made it possible for newcomers such as People Express (airline) to enter the marketplace. Even though some of these companies failed, their presence forced significant restructuring in the industries they entered.

Rise of Global Competition: 1980–1989

During the 1980s, global competition slowly crept up on the United States. Since the 1950s, Japanese firms had been refining their manufacturing processes to become more efficient, and by 1980 they had a 30-year head start on the United States. (Ironically, the United States had supplied its foreign competitors with the resources and know-how to stake a claim in the world marketplace.) Sony moved into the fast lane and introduced new product innovations such as the Walkman and the VCR, while pricing them affordably. By the mid-1980s, it became almost impossible to buy a consumer electronic device that was made in the United States.

To regain a competitive edge, many U.S. companies restructured their operations. Some corporations merged with others to produce economies of scale; others splintered into smaller fragments to focus on a single industry or a narrower customer base. The tough times of the 1970s planted the seeds for entrepreneurship of the early 1980s. Little companies such as Staples, Dell, and Home Depot started popping up with founders who said, "We went to work for the safe, big company and it wasn't safe at all."[30] Meanwhile, new technological developments such as the microprocessor and genetic engineering tools were embraced, not by leading companies of the day but by new entrants (such as Microsoft, Cisco, and Oracle) who swiftly attacked the status quo, as Exhibit 1.9 shows.[31]

Highway to the New Economy: 1990 and Beyond

In the early 1990s, U.S. businesses got hit again. The U.S. economy went into full-blown recession, and many companies that had loaded up on debt in the 1980s to expand their operations or to acquire other companies went bankrupt. During this period of upheaval, unemployment

The Top 25 U.S. Companies by Market Value*

■ High-tech/telecom   ■ Natural resources   ■ Finance   ■ Manufacturing
■ Pharmaceuticals   ■ Consumer products   ■ Retail   ■ Chemicals

	1969			1979			1989			1999	
Rank	Company	Market value (billions)	Rank	Company	Market value (billions)	Rank	Company	Market value (billions)	Rank	Company	Market value (billions)
1	IBM	$41.5	1	IBM	$37.6	1	Exxon	$62.5	1	Microsoft	$601.0
2	AT&T	26.7	2	AT&T	36.6	2	GE	58.4	2	GE	507.2
3	General Motors	19.8	3	Exxon	24.2	3	IBM	54.1	3	Cisco	355.1
4	Eastman Kodak	13.3	4	General Motors	14.5	4	AT&T	48.9	4	Wal-Mart	307.9
5	Exxon	13.3	5	Schlumberger	11.9	5	Philip Morris	38.7	5	ExxonMobil	278.7
6	Sears, Roebuck	10.5	6	Amoco	11.8	6	Merck	30.6	6	Intel	275.0
7	Texaco	8.3	7	Mobil	11.7	7	Bristol-Myers Squibb	29.4	7	Lucent	228.7
8	Xerox	8.2	8	GE	11.5	8	Dupont	28.1	8	AT&T	226.7
9	Ge	7.0	9	Sohio	10.8	9	Amoco	27.9	9	IBM	196.6
10	Gulf Oil	6.4	10	Chevron	9.6	10	BellSouth	27.9	10	Citigroup	187.5
11	3M	6.0	11	Atlantic Richfield	9.3	11	Coca-Cola	26.0	11	America Online	169.5
12	Dupont	4.9	12	Texaco	7.8	12	General Motors	25.6	12	AIG	167.4
13	Avon Products	4.9	13	Eastman Kodak	7.8	13	Mobil	25.6	13	Oracle	159.5
14	Coca-Cola	4.7	14	Phillips Petroleum	7.4	14	Wal-Mart	25.4	14	Home Depot	158.2
15	Mobil Oil	4.7	15	Gulf Oil	6.8	15	Procter & Gamble	24.3	15	Merck	157.1
16	Procter & Gamble	4.5	16	Procter & Gamble	6.1	16	Chevron	24.1	16	MCI WorldCom	149.3
17	Chevron	4.3	17	Getty Oil	6.1	17	GTE	23.1	17	Procter & Gamble	144.2
18	Polaroid	4.1	18	3M	5.9	18	Bell Atlantic	21.9	18	Coca-Cola	143.9
19	Merck	4.1	19	Dupont	5.8	19	Pacific Telesis	21.0	19	Dell Computer	130.1
20	Atlantic Richfield	3.8	20	Dow Chemical	5.8	20	Ford Motor	20.6	20	Bristol-Myers Squibb	127.3
21	American Home Prod.	3.6	21	Sears, Roebuck	5.7	21	Johnson & Johnson	19.8	21	Pfizer	125.6
22	ITT	3.5	22	Merck	5.4	22	Dow Chemical	19.2	22	Johnson & Johnson	125.3
23	Amoco	3.4	23	Xerox	5.2	23	SBC Communications	19.2	23	Sun Microsystems	121.0
24	Johnson & Johnson	3.3	24	Conoco	5.1	24	Eli Lilly	19.1	24	Hewlett-Packard	115.9
25	GTE	3.2	25	Halliburton	5.0	25	Ameritech	18.4	25	Yahoo!	113.9

*Market value is equal to year-end share price multiplied by shares outstanding.

EXHIBIT 1.9

INCREASING IMPORTANCE OF TECHNOLOGY TO THE U.S. ECONOMY

Need proof that the new economy is more than just a buzzword? Take a good look at the top 25 companies (ranked by market value) at the end of each of the past four decades.

soared as hundreds of thousands of jobs were eliminated. General Motors alone laid off 130,000 workers—enough to fill two football stadiums. Had the United States continued in the direction it was headed at the beginning of the 1990s, it might well have experienced the disaster that many economists feared. But it didn't.

Manufacturing improvements helped move the United States from a position of near-terminal decline to renewed world dominance.[32] Managers at IBM and AT&T breathed new life into these two U.S. manufacturing classics. Meanwhile, Motorola struck back with its pagers and cell phones, Hewlett-Packard took over the high-volume market in low-cost computer printers, and once-sleepy Kodak challenged the Japanese with digital and disposable cameras.[33] As more and more U.S. companies reengineered their operations to improve productivity and to focus on product quality, U.S. industries experienced remarkable turnarounds. But it was investments in new technology and the promise of e-commerce that ultimately pushed the U.S. economy into a remarkable period of prosperity. Characterized by faster growth, lower inflation, technology-driven expansion, and thrift, this new era is referred as the *new economy*.

FOCUSING ON E-BUSINESS TODAY

What's New About the New Economy?

People talk about a new economy—one where the Internet is supposed to change everything. But in reality, no single technology can fulfill such an extravagant promise. In fact, when e-businesses that were supposed to topple industry giants began to vanish at the beginning of the twenty-first century, the once limitless promise of the Internet faded. Now some even question whether a "new economy" exists, and if so, how does it differ from the old economy.

HOW DOES THE NEW ECONOMY DIFFER FROM THE OLD ECONOMY?

Whether labeled a revolution or an evolution, the new economy differs from the old economy in a number of key ways.

- *The new economy is less concerned with physical goods.* Almost 93 million workers (80 percent of the workforce) do not spend their days making things. Instead they work in jobs that require them to move things, process or generate information, or provide services to people. In the old economy, information flow was physical: cash, checks, invoices, reports, and face-to-face meetings. But in the new economy, information in all its forms becomes digital—reduced to bits stored in computers and racing at the speed of light across networks.

 LEARNING OBJECTIVE @ 8

Highlight six ways in which the new economy differs from the old economy, and discuss whether the old economy rules are obsolete

- *The new economy has no geographical boundaries.* In the old economy, geography played a key role in determining who competed with whom. In the new economy,

distance and time differences have vanished. In a world where everyone and everything is connected, the shortest distance between a customer and a firm is one mouse click.

- *The new economy operates at a faster pace.* Besides compressing distance, the Internet compresses time. In the new economy, the ability to innovate and get to market faster is a key competitive advantage. Companies today move quickly and aggressively to develop new products and services, find capital, and win Web customers. In the new economy, a week is equivalent to three months in the old economy. Consider this: In less than 18 months after its launch, Hotmail had signed up 12 million subscribers. A few days later its founders sold the company to Microsoft for $400 million in Microsoft stock. Today, with 50 million registered users, Hotmail is the largest Web-based e-mail service in the world.

- *Companies in the new economy can easily enter and exit the marketplace.* In the old economy, setting up a nursery to sell plants might involve leasing a shed, buying various types of trees and plants, hiring a sales clerk, passing out fliers, and more. But on the Internet, setting up a nursery can be as simple as registering a domain name, hiring an artist to design some Web pages, and making arrangements with a plant wholesaler. In short, barriers to entry for companies selling over the Internet are virtually nonexistent. Industries that were once sheltered from significant competition, such as transportation, utilities, communications, health care, and legal services, are now facing growing competition from firms conducting e-commerce.

- *The pursuit of monopoly power is the driving thrust of the new economy.* More than two centuries ago, Adam Smith claimed that monopolies tended to stifle competition. But in the new economy, the quest for monopoly can actually prompt competition—thanks to low barriers to entry. Thus, the emergence of a temporary monopolistic leader with a stronghold in a particular e-commerce category tends to ignite a fury of "me too" entrants who can swiftly catch up, offer near-identical products and services, and push the prices down sharply.

- *Competitors are joining forces.* In the old economy, competitors were just that. But in the new economy rivals join forces to create business-to-business Internet operations. The Marriott–Hyatt joint Internet venture, for instance, will provide one-stop shopping for hotel supplies. The General Motors, Ford Motor, and Daimler Chrysler joint venture will do the same for auto parts and auto supplies.

| New Economy versus Old Economy ||
Digital Age (New Economy)	Industrial Age (Old Economy)
Brick-and-click business	Brick-and-mortar business
Knowledge is shared	Knowledge is scattered
Virtual communication	Face-to-face meetings
Business alliances are fundamental	Business alliances when necessary
Constant innovation	Innovate when necessary
Direct access to manufacturer	Limited access to manufacturer
Manage for change	Manage for efficiency
Teams run business	Teams run projects
Launch and learn	Learn and launch
Working 24/7	Working 9 to 5

ARE OLD ECONOMY RULES OBSOLETE?

Of course, not everything in the new economy is new. Many companies have learned the hard way that indeed the fundamental rules of the old economy still apply. For instance, if you want to do business on the Internet, it helps to have a trusted brand name; it helps to have customers; and it helps to have some business to do. Furthermore, it helps to earn a profit. In the beginning of the new economy, Internet companies did a remarkably good job of convincing people otherwise. They played a game of "don't look there, look here," by conjuring up a host of new ways to gauge a company's performance. They even convinced investors that market share, growth, number of people who see a Web page, and length of each site visit had a greater value than profitability. But these new measures soon turned out to be largely irrelevant.

Today, Internet companies (dot-coms) are compared to the traditional companies they once promised to trounce. Gone is the assumption that being Net-based gives a company a competitive edge over its real-world rivals. The new economy may be less concerned with the physical, and it may be more global, faster, and more competitive, but E*Trade is still a broker, Priceline.com is still a travel agent, Yahoo! is still a media company, and Amazon.com is still a retailer. In fact, as the Internet weaves itself into the fabric of the economy and touches every business and industry, the new economy will not replace the old economy; instead it will make the old economy better.[34]

FOCUSING ON E-BUSINESS TODAY

In each end-of-chapter Focusing on E-Business Today special feature we take a closer look at some of the issues and challenges businesses are facing in the new economy as they explore the exciting world of electronic commerce. Moreover, we explain how the important concepts discussed in that chapter are being affected by the Internet. But first you'll need some Internet and e-commerce fundamentals. You'll find them in Component Chapter A. Think of this chapter as your entry ticket to the exciting world of e-business today.

SUMMARY OF LEARNING OBJECTIVES

1. **Identify four key social and economic roles that businesses serve.**
Businesses provide society with necessities; they provide people with jobs and a means to prosper; they pay taxes that are used by the government to provide services for its citizens; and they reinvest their profits in the economy, thereby increasing a nation's wealth.

2. **List six factors that are contributing to the increase in the number of service businesses.**
The number of service businesses is increasing because (1) consumers have more disposable income to spend on taking care of themselves; (2) many services target consumers' needs brought about by changing demographic patterns and lifestyle trends; (3) consumers need assistance with using and integrating new technology into their business operations and lifestyle; (4) companies are turning to consultants and other professionals for advice to remain competitive; (5) barriers to entry for companies transacting e-commerce are low; and (6) the Internet economy is growing at an unprecedented rate.

3. **Differentiate between a free-market system and a planned system.**
In a free-market system, individuals have a high degree of freedom to decide what is produced, by whom, and for whom. Moreover, the pursuit of private gain is regarded as a worthwhile goal. In a planned system, governments limit the individual's freedom of choice in order to accomplish government goals, control the allocation of resources, and restrict private ownership to personal and household items. The pursuit of private gain is nonexistent under a planned system.

4. **Explain how supply and demand interact to affect price.**
In the simplest sense, supply and demand affect price in the following manner: When the price goes up, the quantity demanded goes down but the supplier's incentive to produce more goes up. When the price goes down, the quantity demanded increases, whereas the quantity supplied may (or may not) decline. When the interests of buyers and sellers are in balance, an equilibrium price is established. However, pricing involves more than the simple notions of supply and demand, as the examples of gasoline and housing illustrate.

5. **List three major economic roles of the U.S. government.**
The U.S. government enforces rules and regulations to protect consumers and foster competition; it contributes to economic stability by adjusting tax and interest rates by regulating the money supply; and it provides its citizens with public services.

6. **Define the gross domestic product and explain what it is used for.**
The gross domestic product (GDP) is the sum of all goods and services produced by both domestic and foreign companies as long as they are located within a nation's boundaries. The GDP is used to measure the productivity of a nation and to evaluate the effectiveness of a government's policies and economic systems.

7. **Identify five challenges that businesses are facing in the global economy.**
The five challenges identified in the chapter are (1) producing quality products and services that satisfy customers' changing needs; (2) starting and managing a small business in today's competitive environment; (3) committing to a culturally diverse work-

force; (4) behaving in an ethically and socially responsible manner; and (5) keeping pace with technology and e-commerce.

8. **Highlight six ways in which the new economy differs from the old economy, and discuss whether the rules of the old economy still apply.**

    @ The new economy is less reliant on physical goods, and it has no geographical boundaries. Companies in the new economy must operate at a faster pace, and they can easily enter and exit the marketplace. Moreover, in the new economy monopolies can actually prompt competition, and it's not uncommon for competitors to join forces. In spite of these differences, the rules of the old economy still apply. It is still important to have a trusted brand name, customers, to have a viable business model, and to generate a profit.

KEY TERMS

barriers to entry (7)

business (4)

business cycle (15)

capital (8)

capital-intensive business (6)

capitalism (8)

communism (9)

competition (12)

competitive advantage (13)

consumer price index (CPI) (17)

deflation (17)

demand (11)

demand curve (12)

deregulation (14)

economic indicators (16)

economic system (8)

economics (8)

economies of scale (20)

electronic commerce (e-commerce) (7)

entrepreneurs (8)

equilibrium price (12)

factors of production (8)

fiscal policy (15)

free-market system (8)

globalization (18)

goods-producing businesses (5)

gross domestic product (GDP) (17)

gross national product (GNP) (17)

human resources (8)

inflation (17)

knowledge (8)

labor-intensive businesses (6)

monetary policy (15)

monopolistic competition (13)

monopoly (12)

natural resources (8)

not-for-profit organizations (4)

oligopoly (12)

planned system (9)

privatizing (10)

profit (4)

pure competition (12)

recession (15)

service businesses (5)

socialism (10)

supply (11)

supply curve (12)

TEST YOUR KNOWLEDGE

QUESTIONS FOR REVIEW

1. Why do businesspeople study economics?

2. Why are the barriers to entry low for most e-commerce companies?

3. Why are knowledge workers the key economic resource?

4. Why are planned economies privatizing some of their industries?

5. What is the definition for the demand curve, the supply curve, and the equilibrium price?

QUESTIONS FOR ANALYSIS

6. Why is it often easier to start a service business than a goods-producing business?

7. Why is knowledge a factor of production?

8. Why do governments intervene in a free-market system?

9. How do countries know if their economic system is working?

10. Why does the new economy operate at a faster pace?

11. Because knowledge workers are in such high demand, you decide to enroll in an evening MBA program. Your company has agreed to reimburse you for 80 percent of your tuition. You haven't told them, however, that once you earn your degree, you plan to apply for a management position at a different company. Is it ethical for you to accept your company's tuition reimbursement, given your intentions?

QUESTIONS FOR APPLICATION

12. Company sales are skyrocketing, and projections show that your computer consulting business will outgrow its current location by next year. What factors should you consider when selecting a new site for your business?

13. How would a decrease in Social Security benefits to the elderly affect the economy?

14. One of the five economic challenges in this century is "starting and managing a small business in today's global economy." Review "Enterprise Rent-A-Car Tries Harder, and It Pays Off" (see page 13) and explain how Enterprise Rent-A-Car is meeting this challenge.

15. @ Think about the many ways that the Internet and e-commerce have changed your life as a consumer. Record your thoughts on a sheet of paper. On that same sheet of paper, make a second list of how you envision the Internet and e-commerce will change your life in the near future. Compare your thoughts to those of your classmates.

PRACTICE YOUR KNOWLEDGE

SHARPENING YOUR COMMUNICATION SKILLS

Select a local service business you are familiar with. How does that business try to gain a competitive advantage in the marketplace? Write a brief summary, as directed by your instructor, describing whether the company competes on speed, quality, price, innovation, service, or a combination of those attributes. Be prepared to present your analysis to your classmates.

HANDLING DIFFICULT SITUATIONS ON THE JOB: COPING WITH WAKEBOARD MANIA

Bill Porter, owner of the Performance Ski & Surf store, hasn't seen sporting equipment sell this rapidly in Orlando, Florida, since in-line skating became popular. But now his store, where you are the assistant manager, has been unable to keep wakeboards in stock. It doesn't seem to matter which brand—Wake Tech, Neptune, or Full Tilt—is available, only that locals and tourists alike are snapping them up and heading out to the water. These boards are outselling traditional trick water skis by 20 to 1.

This unusually strong demand has been fueled, in part, by media coverage of professional wakeboarders such as Dean Lavelle, who recently exhibited his wakeboard skills at nearby Lake Butler. You and Porter saw a photo of Lavelle in action, holding the same kind of rope as any water skier—except he was 15 feet in the air. His short, stubby, fiberglass wakeboard (which was strapped to his feet) was higher than his head, and from the grimace on his face, it looked as if he was mid-flip.

Porter does not want to keep disappointing shoppers who come in asking for wakeboards, so he has asked you to order another 12 Wake Techs, 8 Neptunes, and 10 Full Tilts. "Don't worry about colors or models; we'll be lucky to get this order filled at all from what I hear," he says. With such strong demand, however, you wonder whether the store should adjust the price of these wakeboards to reflect the skimpy and uncertain supply.[35]

1. According to the theory of supply and demand, how do you think consumers would react if your store set higher prices on the new order of wakeboards? What are the advantages and disadvantages of increasing the price to customers? In the end, what would you advise Porter to do?

2. If you do mark a higher price on the next shipment of wakeboards, what will you tell shoppers who comment on the increase?

3. What would you do if a competitor started selling wakeboards over the Internet at a much lower price?

BUILDING YOUR TEAM SKILLS

Economic indicators help businesses and governments determine where the economy is headed. You may have noticed news headlines such as the following, each of which offers clues to the direction of the U.S. economy:

1. Housing Starts Lowest in Months
2. Fed Lowers Discount Rate and Interest Rates Tumble
3. Retail Sales Up 4 Percent Over Last Month
4. Business Debt Down from Last Year
5. Businesses Are Buying More Electronic Equipment
6. Industry Jobs Go Unfilled as Area Unemployment Rate Sinks to 3 Percent
7. Telephone Reports 30-Day Backlog in Installing Business Systems

Discuss each of those headlines with the other students on your team. Is each item good news or bad news for the economy? Why? What does each news item mean for large and small businesses? Report your team's findings to the class as a whole. Did all the teams come to the same conclusions about each headline? Why or why not? With your team, discuss how these different perspectives might influence the way you interpret economic news in the future.

EXPAND YOUR KNOWLEDGE

KEEPING CURRENT USING *THE WALL STREET JOURNAL*

Gaining a competitive advantage in today's marketplace is critical to a company's success. Look in recent issues of *The Wall Street Journal* (print or online editions) and find a company whose practices have set that company apart from its competitors. If you are using the online edition at www.wsj.com, go to the "Select a Page" drop-down menu in the upper left-hand corner of the screen, and select "Search." Enter key terms such as *customer service, innovation, competitive advantage,* or *discount.*

1. What products or services does the company manufacture or sell?

2. How does the company set its goods or services apart from its competitors? Does the company compete on price, quality, service, or innovation?

3. Does the company have a Web site, and if so, how does the company use it? What kinds of information does the company include on its Web site?

DISCOVERING CAREER OPPORTUNITIES

Thinking about a career in economics.? Find out what economists do by reviewing the *Occupational Outlook Handbook* in your library or online at stats.bls.gov/ocohome.htm. This is an authoritative resource for information about all kinds of occupations. Under Search By Occupation, enter "economists."

1. Briefly describe what economists do and their typical working conditions.

2. What is the job outlook for economists? What is the average salary for starting economists?

3. What training and qualifications are required for a career as an economist? Are the qualifications different for jobs in the private sector as opposed to those in the government?

EXPLORING THE BEST OF THE WEB

URLs for all Internet exercises are provided at the Web site for this book, www.prenhall.com/mescon. When you log on to the text Web site, select Chapter 1, then select "Student Resources," click on the name of the featured Web site, and follow the detailed navigational directions to complete these exercises.

Find the Right Stuff, page 4

Hoover's Online provides a wealth of company and industry information. Browse Hoover's Online to get the latest information about IBM, Wrigley, Marriott International, and thousands of other companies.

1. Which industry and sector are IBM, Wrigley, and Marriott assigned to? Are the companies mainly service or goods-producing businesses? List each company's three main competitors.

2. Review IBM's, Wrigley's and Marriott's histories and read their current news articles and press releases. How is Hoover's Online an effective tool for gathering information about companies and industries?

3. Review the data for any five companies listed on Fortune's Most Admired Companies. On which criteria are these companies judged? Of the categories listed, which ones are discussed in this chapter?

Step Inside the Economic Statistics Briefing Room, page 16

Get the latest economic indicators by visiting the Economic Statistics Briefing Room. Check the stats and make your own projections as to which direction the economy is heading.

1. Are monthly housing starts increasing or decreasing? Why are housing starts a leading economic indicator?

2. Is unemployment for the month increasing or decreasing? What is the current unemployment rate for this year? In what year was unemployment the highest?

3. Is annual median household income increasing or decreasing? Is the trend the same for all population segments tracked?

Discover What's in the CPI, page 18

Find out what's in the consumer price index (CPI) and how it is calculated by visiting the CPI Web site. Track the CPI for several areas and compare your results.

1. How is the CPI used?

2. What goods and services does the CPI cover, and how are they categorized?

3. Use the CPI calculator at the Dismal Scientist Web site to see the power of inflation by answering the following: If you had $100 in 1913, how much would it be worth today? (Use the latest year available.)

Explore on Your Own

Review these chapter-related Web sites on your own to learn more about economics and business.

1. The Electronic Commerce Page, www.mtmercy.edu/advance/advelec.htm, has multiple links to e-commerce resources and data. The site is maintained by the Virtual Library.

2. Corporate Information, www.corporateinformation.com/, is a good starting point to find corporate information from around the world.

3. New Economy Index, www.neweconomyindex.org/, is a series of indicators gathered from existing public and private data to illustrate changes in the U.S. economy.

A CASE FOR CRITICAL THINKING

■ How Tyco Hooked the Industry

Although essential to the retail clothing industry, garment hangers aren't items most people notice. Most hangers are purchased at wholesale by garment manufacturers who hang their finished products on them, ready for display at retail outlets. Some big retailers negotiate hanger prices and tell garment makers whom to buy from; others give garment makers a list of acceptable hanger suppliers. Although dozens of smaller hanger manufacturers exist around the world, retailers and garment companies say it's time-consuming and costly to buy from scattered suppliers of uneven quality. Thus, large hanger manufacturers with global networks have a competitive edge.

HANGING UP THE COMPETITION

For years, the two biggest hanger manufacturers were A&E, a division of Phoenix plastics company, and Batts, a family-owned Michigan company. With about 35 percent of the U.S. garment-hanger market each, they had a sharp rivalry. But this rivalry helped keep hanger prices in line.

In 1996 Tyco International, a $22 billion manufacturer of fire and safety systems, electrical connectors, disposable medical products, and valves for water systems, bought its way into the plastic hanger business when it purchased Phoenix, A&E's parent company.

Executives at stores like Kmart weren't troubled by the acquisition at first. But then Tyco snapped up another hanger company. Then in 1999 Tyco bought Batts, and within weeks announced a hanger price increase. Angry retailers forced Tyco to rescind the price increase—but not for long. Fearful that Tyco could corner the market, Kmart started funneling much of its $40 million hanger account to one of the remaining independent suppliers, a small New York outfit called WAF Group. In September 1999 Tyco gobbled up WAF.

IF YOU CAN'T BEAT THEM, BUY THEM

Tyco denies buying WAF to remove a pesky competitor. Tyco was more interested in WAF's other business—distributing jacket linings, zippers, and other trim—says Andrew Zuckerman, head of Tyco's hanger division. After all, acquisitions were Tyco's lifeblood. In the late 1990s the company spent some $30 billion to acquire more than 120 companies. So when Tyco bought A&E's parent and then bought other hanger manufacturers, it was business as usual. Nevertheless, shortly after absorbing WAF, Tyco told hanger customers it was raising prices because raw-material costs had "risen dramatically." This time the price increase stuck.

HUNG OUT TO DRY

John Davis, a hanger buyer at J.C. Penney, was stunned that the federal government allowed Tyco to buy Batts and others because as he saw it, this "created a monopoly." Davis complained to the Federal Trade Commission but got no response. Meanwhile, Tyco's service slipped after the Batts acquisition. At one point hanger deliveries were so late that some stores had to buy hangers in smaller batches from local distributors at 50 percent higher prices. Tyco blamed the service glitches on a computer software problem.

"Consolidation in this industry is going just a little too far," notes a Kmart vice president. In less than four years Tyco has amassed a hanger business with annual revenue of more than $400 million and about 70 to 80 percent of the U.S. market for plastic garment hangers. Only a handful of rivals remain in the United States—none with the global manufacturing reach that big retailers and garment makers prefer. Tyco "has basically monopolized the market . . . they have us over a barrel," notes one hanger buyer for Lee Wrangler garments, who claims she would switch to another supplier in a minute if that were possible.

SKIRTING THE ISSUE

As Zuckerman sees it, customers still have plenty of choices. For instance, retailers could finance the expansion of rival hanger companies, or they could "choose to manufacture hangers themselves." Discount stores could even follow in the footsteps of high-end retailer Federated Department Stores. Federated establishes an industry standard for hangers, then certifies smaller suppliers who are able to meet that standard. This keeps competition alive. But some think Tyco would like to change this too.

Tyco has tried to convince some large retail clothing chains that it should be their sole approved hanger supplier. No deal, says

Nordstrom. If Tyco buys all the remaining smaller manufacturers it would be in a position to create a shortage in the marketplace. While rejection is hard to swallow—even for Tyco—at least it proves one thing: "There is competition in the market," says Zuckerman.

CRITICAL THINKING QUESTIONS

1. Are the barriers to entry in the garment-hanger manufacturing business high or low?

2. Locate other plastic hanger suppliers by using a meta search engine such as Ixquick at www.ixquick.com. Enter the key words "plastic garment hangers," and review your search results. Do you think Tyco has a monopoly in the garment-hanger industry?

3. Should the federal government have paid more attention to concerns voiced by garment-hanger users?

4. Go to this text's Web site at www.prenhall.com/mescon, select Chapter 1, and click on the hot link to Tyco's Web site. Follow the online instructions to answer these questions: Are hanger manufacturers listed among the company's acquisitions? Does Tyco actively promote its involvement in the plastic hanger industry? Now read about A&E. How important do you think hangers are to Tyco's overall business? Now that you know more about the company, would you change your answers to questions 2 or 3?

VIDEO CASE AND EXERCISES

■ Lands' End Catalogs Its Global Business

SYNOPSIS

The largest specialty catalog company in the United States is helping to fuel the movement toward a global economy—as well as providing support for the local economy. Founded in 1963, Lands' End (www.landsend.com), employs 7,000 in its Dodgeville, Wisconsin, headquarters. In 1987 the company began to expand by mailing catalogs to customers across the border in Canada. Soon Lands' End was selling by mail in 175 countries, with telephone centers in Wisconsin, the United Kingdom, and Japan to handle the rising volume of customer orders. Today, the company has 7.5 million customers and rings up nearly $1 billion in annual sales around the world. Management continues to build the business by asking customers what they want—then following through with new and improved products and friendly, helpful sales assistance.

EXERCISES
Analysis

1. Can Lands' End be categorized as a goods-producing business or a service business?

2. Does Lands' End operate in a situation of monopoly, oligopoly, or monopolistic competition?

3. What is Lands' End doing to gain a competitive advantage in the marketplace?

4. Is Lands' End likely to experience inflation or deflation over the years?

5. How do you think economies of scale affect Lands' End's pricing and profits?

Application
Which of the factors of production are most important to the global success of Lands' End today?

Decision
Assume that a recession has just started, and Lands' End wants to avoid seeing sales drop. Should the company lower the quality of its products in order to lower prices so it can draw from a broader group of customers across the economic spectrum?

Communication
Imagine that Lands' End has decided to expand into South America. Draft a memo to staff members announcing the reasons for this expansion (making up any details you need to complete this exercise).

Integration
Look ahead to the discussion of responsibility toward consumers in Chapter 2. Write a one-paragraph response to the statement that the consumer should also be guaranteed reasonable prices (you can agree or disagree with the statement).

Ethics

Knowing that much of the economy of the Dodgeville area depends on Lands' End, is it ethical for the company to lay off employees if a recession hurts its sales?

Debate

Eyeing the growing number of consumers who buy online, should Lands' End stop mailing catalogs and concentrate all its efforts on selling through its Web site? As your instructor directs, prepare to defend one side of this question in a classroom debate or outline at least two arguments supporting one side of this question.

Teamwork

With two other students, identify the barriers to entry for companies seeking to compete with Lands' End. Do the barriers to entry seem high or low?

Online Research

Where is Lands' End selling its products today, and how is the business doing? Use Internet sources to find out. See Component Chapter A, Exhibit A.1, for search engines to use in doing your research.

MYPHLIP COMPANION WEB SITE

Learning Interactively

Visit the myPHLIP Web site at www.prenhall.com/mescon. For Chapter 1, take advantage of the interactive "Study Guide" to test your changer knowledge. Get instant feedback on whether you need additional studying. Read the "Current Events" articles to get the latest on chapter topics, and complete the exercises as specified by your instructor. Expand your learning with a visit to the "Research Area." There you will find a wealth of information you can use to complete your course assignments.

MASTERING BUSINESS ESSENTIALS

Go to "The Economic Way of Thinking" episode on the Mastering Business Essentials interactive, video-enhanced CD-ROM to help the managers at CanGo (an e-business start-up) plan for the company's future by solving an economic dilemma: how to expand the business without the needed resources.

EXPLANATION OF ICONS

 Signifies a question related to ethics.

 Signifies a question related to e-business, or to a learning objective relating to e-business.

 Signifies integration, which means the question gives you the opportunity to apply principles learned in earlier chapters to the chapter you're currently studying.

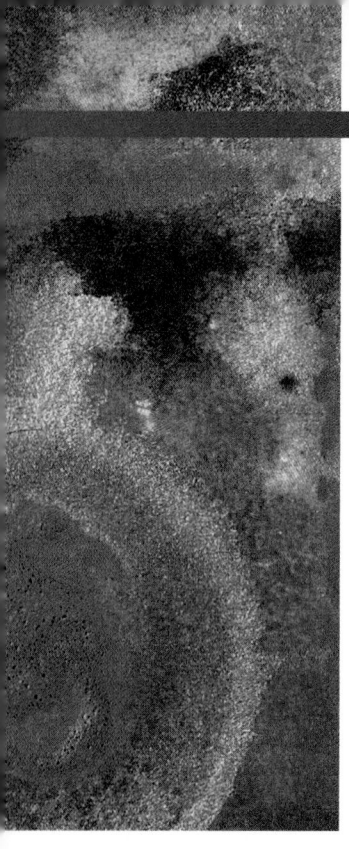

COMPONENT CHAPTER A

FUNDAMENTALS OF THE INTERNET AND E-COMMERCE

■ WHAT IS THE INTERNET?

As Chapter 1 demonstrates, it's pretty difficult to study business today without understanding the Internet and electronic commerce. This component chapter will give you the Internet and e-commerce basics you will need to complete the readings and assignments in this introduction-to-business course. We begin this chapter by explaining some Internet fundamentals.

The **Internet** is the world's largest computer network. Started in 1969 by the U.S. Department of Defense, the Internet is a voluntary, cooperative undertaking; no one individual, organization, or government owns it. The Internet is accessible to individuals, companies, colleges, government agencies, and other institutions in countries all over the world. It links thousands of smaller computer networks and millions of individual computer users in homes, businesses, government offices, and schools worldwide. You can learn more about the Internet by taking the tour at www.learnthenet.com, netforbeginners.about.com/internet/netforbeginners, or www.provide.net/~bfield/polaris/tour0000.htm.

To connect to the Internet, all you need is a computer with a modem, a standard telephone line, and an **Internet service provider (ISP)**—a company that provides access to the Internet. For a flat monthly fee or a per-use fee, you can dial into one of the ISP's host computers, which will link you to any number of the computers that make up the Internet network. Organizations can also lease their own direct Internet access lines, which provide Internet access to every user wired to the organization's network. See Chapter 8 for a detailed discussion of network transmission media used to connect to the Internet.

The most widely used part of the Internet is the **World Wide Web (WWW** or **Web)**. Developed in 1990, the Web uses a graphical user interface (GUI) system rather than text commands, enabling users to search for, display, and save **multimedia** resources such as graphics, text, audio, and video files. This information is typically stored in a **Web site,** which consists of one or more Web pages located on one of the Internet's many networked computers. To read Web pages, you need a Web **browser**—software such as Netscape Navigator or Microsoft's Internet Explorer.

The **homepage** of a Web site is the primary screen that users first access when visiting a site. Furthermore, each page in a Web site is identified by a unique address known as a **uniform resource locator (URL).** Take http://www.yahoo.com, for example. The address begins with *http,* which is the abbreviation for **hypertext transfer protocol,** the communications protocol that allows you to navigate the Web. The address continues with *www,* indicating that the site is located on the World Wide Web. The next part of the address is the site's registered **domain name** (in this case *yahoo.com*). No other Web site may use this name. The abbreviation following the *period* is the top-level domain (TLD). To keep up with increasing demand, new TLDs (such as pro, biz, coop, info, museum, aero, and name) are in the works. Expect to see even more TLDs now that the original seven have been exhausted: business (com), an educational institution (edu), a government (gov), an international source (int), the military (mil), network resources (net), or a not-for-profit organization (org).

Fortunately, you don't have to remember URLs, because just about every bit of information on the Web has a **hyperlink** or *hot link,* which means you can click on words in **hypertext markup language (HTML)**—colored, underlined, or highlighted words—with your mouse and automatically jump to another Web page or a different Internet site. Once you get to

Each Procter & Gamble product has its own Web site. The Crisco site offers consumers product information, tips, recipes, and a newsletter, in addition to reinforcing the product's quality and versatility.

your new destination you can **bookmark** the site by using a browser feature that places the site's URL in a file on your computer for future use. Then, whenever you click on a bookmark while online, you automatically go to that site's address. Another handy browser feature is the ability to navigate your trail backward or forward at any time by using the *back* and *forward* buttons on your browser software.

Of course, you can't really get a picture of what the Internet is until you have a better idea of how you can use it, how it facilitates communication, and how it is changing the way companies do business.

How Do You Find Information on the Internet?

The Internet is rich in business information. It contains current news, business issues, industry trends, and company information such as financial performance, products, goals, and employment. In fact, the Web is so vast and changes so constantly that it's easy to get sidetracked. If you've ever been lost in cyberspace, take heart—it happens to everybody. Chances are good that you'll find information on the Internet about almost any research topic. However, finding that information can be frustrating if you don't know how to conduct an effective search.

One important thing to keep in mind when looking for business information on the Internet is that anyone (including you) can post anything on a Web site. No one filters it. No one checks it for accuracy. And no one can be sure of who is pro-

ducing the information or why they are placing it on the Internet. For that reason, it's best to refrain from seriously surfing the Web for business information until you've had a chance to learn a bit about your topic from journals, books, and other sources that are carefully edited for the accuracy of their content. That way you'll be able to detect skewed or erroneous information, and you can be more selective about the Web sites and documents you choose to use as a resource.

If you are looking for specific company **data** (recorded facts and statistics), your best source may be the company's own Web site (assuming it maintains one). Web sites generally include detailed information about the company's products, services, history, mission, strategy, financial performance, and employment needs. Furthermore, many sites provide links to related company information, such as public records and financial statements, news releases, and more.

Keep in mind that a lot of the information that you may want simply isn't on the Web. If you're researching small organizations, for instance, you may find nothing or just an address and phone number. Furthermore, even if the information you're seeking does exist on the Web, you may not be able to locate it. The Internet holds more than 800 million Web pages, with hundreds of pages being added every day. But even the best **search engines**—Internet tools that identify and screen resources—manage to index only about a third of the pages on the Web.[1] Then again, when a search engine turns up what you're looking for, it will probably also turn up a mountain of stuff you won't need. Suppose you're looking for information about available jobs for writers. The search engine may turn up information on being an accountant at an insurance company. Why? Because the insurance company described itself on the Web as one of the largest *writers* of insurance policies. You can produce more targeted search results by learning how to conduct an effective database search.

Conducting an Effective Database Search A **database** is a collection of data that are usually stored in a computerized format. Whether you are using a library database or an Internet search engine such as the ones listed in Exhibit A.1, follow these search strategies and tips to conduct an effective database search:[2]

■ *Select an appropriate database or databases.* In most cases you'll want a good business database. However, it could be that the journals covering your topic are located in the database that includes journals on psychology, computers, or medicine.

■ *Use multiple search engines.* Not all search engines are the same. Don't limit yourself to a *single search engine*—especially if you are looking for less popular topics. To improve your results, read the help file and learn how the search engine works.

■ *Choose search terms by translating concepts into keywords and phrases.* For instance, if you want to explore "how the Internet is affecting the economy," select keywords such as *Internet, economy, e-business,* and *e-commerce* and phrases such as *Internet economy, new economy, electronic economy,*

MAJOR SEARCH ENGINES

Alta Vista
www.altavista.com
Indexes data from millions of Web pages and articles from thousands of Usenet newsgroups.

Ask Jeeves
www.ask.com
Finds answers to natural-language questions such as "Who won Super Bowl XXV?"

Excite
www.excite.com
All-purpose site loaded with options.

Fedstats
www.fedstats.gov/search.html
Simultaneously queries 14 federal agencies for specified statistics and numerical data.

Google
www.google.com
A simple directory that is especially useful for finding homepages of companies and organizations.

GoTo
www.goto.com
Companies can pay to be placed higher in this engine's search results.

HotBot
www.hotbot.com
Wired magazine packs all kinds of searching possibilities into this site.

LookSmart
www.looksmart.com
Closest rival to Yahoo! in terms of being a human-compiled directory. Choose "Your Town" for local directories.

Lycos
www.lycos.com
One of the oldest of the major search engines, provides short abstracts for each match.

Northern Light
www.northernlight.com
Categorizes returns by subject. Has "special collection" of over 2 million documents not readily accessible to search engine spiders.

WebCrawler
www.webcrawler.com
Allows you to either search the entire site or browse any of the preselected categories.

Yahoo!
www.yahoo.com
The oldest major Web site directory, listing over 500,000 sites.

MULTIPLE SEARCH ENGINE SITES—METACRAWLERS

C4 Total Search
www.c4search.com
Search up to 20 search engines at the same time. Customized search options are available.

Cyber411
www.cyber411.com
Search up to 16 popular search engines at the same time. The query is reformulated to fit the syntax of each search engine.

Dogpile
www.dogpile.com
Despite the silly name, just enter one query and this hound sniffs through dozens of FTP, Usenet, and Web sites.

IXQuick
www.ixquick.com
Search up to 14 search engines at the same time. Results are ranked by relevancy.

Mamma
www.mamma.com
Claiming to be the "Mother of All Search Engines," this multilegged spiker queries the major search engines for fast results.

ProFusion
www.profusion.com
The University of Kansas spider retrieves only the "best" results from selected search engines.

Zworks
www.zworks.com
Results are ranked based on the cumulative score of all the engines used in the search. Duplicate results are eliminated.

EXHIBIT A.1

BEST OF INTERNET SEARCHING

Searchers can get the most dependable results from well-known, commercially backed search engines. These major search engines (and directories) are likely to be well maintained and upgraded when necessary, to keep pace with the growing Web. Most have simple or advanced search features, plus extras such as interactive maps and weather, travel information, phone and e-mail directories, and company profiles.

and *digital economy.* Remember, use quotes around phrases to look for the entire phrase instead of separate words.

■ *Enter variations of your terms.* Use acronyms (*CEO, CPA*), synonyms (*man, male*), related terms (*e-commerce, e-business*), different spellings (*dialog, dialogue*), singular and plural forms (*man, men*), nouns and adjectives (*manager, management, managerial*), and simple and compound forms (*online, on line, on-line*).

■ *Avoid using a long phrase when a short phrase or single term will do.* The computer searches for the words exactly as you have keyed them in. If the words occur, but not in the same order, you may miss relevant hits.

■ *Avoid using words that are implied in the database.* Words such as *business* or *economics* in a business database will work, but they will slow down the processing time and generally yield no better results.

■ *Evaluate the precision and quality of your search results, and refine or redo your search if necessary.* If you end up with more than 60 to 100 references to sort through, you probably need to refine your search strategy. Experts recommend that if your first page of results doesn't have something of value, you've probably entered the wrong words or too few words. In addition, pay attention to whether you are searching in

the title, subject, or document fields of the database. Each will return different results.

Of course, having too much information can be just as bad as having no information. To enhance your search results, use Boolean operators, proximity operators, and wildcards.

Enhancing Your Search Results **Boolean operators** include the words AND, OR, and NOT. As Exhibit A.2 shows, the AND operator narrows a search because it indicates that all the keywords (joined by the word AND) must be found in the same document or Web page. By contrast, the OR operator broadens the search because it indicates that either keyword must be present. Finally, the NOT operator (sometimes expressed as AND NOT) narrows a search because it indicates that a certain keyword must not appear in the document or Web page.

Boolean operators can help you create complex, precise search strategies. For example you could create a search strategy such as "(marketing OR advertising) AND (organizations OR associations) AND NOT consultants." In plain English this means that qualifying documents or Web sites must have either the word *marketing* or *advertising* and must have either the word *organizations* or *associations,* but they can't have the word *consultants.* For example, say that you are trying to search for the *gross national product of Jordan,* and you keep getting sports

SEARCH OPERATOR	EFFECT	STRATEGY	RESULTS
AND	Narrows the results. Searches for records containing both of the words it separates. Words separated by AND may be anywhere in the document—and far away from each other.	Rock AND roll	Music
OR	Broadens the results. This is a scattergun search that will turn up lots of matches and is not particularly precise. Searches for records containing either of the words it separates.	Rock OR roll	Igneous rocks; gemstones; crescent rolls; music
NOT, AND NOT	Limits the results. Searches for records containing the first word(s) but not the second one. Depending on the database, AND is not always included in combination with NOT.	Snow skiing NOT water skiing; Snow skiing AND NOT water skiing	Snow skiing; cross-country skiing
WITHIN OR NEAR	Proximity operators. Searches for words that all appear in a specified word range.	Snow WITHIN/ 2 skiing	Terms in which *skiing* is within 2 words of *snow*
ADJ	Adjacency operator. Searches for records in which second word immediately follows first word (two words are next to each other).	Ski ADJ patrol	Ski patrol
?	Wildcard operator for single character; matches any one character.	Ski?	Skit; skid; skin;skip
*	Wildcard operator for string of characters.	Ski*	Ski; skiing; skies; skill; skirt; skit; skinny, skimpy
""	Exact match. Searches for string of words placed within quotation marks.	"2002 budget deficit"	2002 budget deficit

EXHIBIT A.2

IMPROVING YOUR SEARCH RESULTS

Using these Boolean operators, proximity operators, and wildcards will vastly improve the effectiveness of your electronic searches.

sites about Michael Jordan. By using the operator NOT to exclude the word *Michael,* you'll trim a few hundred thousand irrelevant results right away.

Many search engines automatically include Boolean operators in their search strategies even though you can't see them on the screen. For instance, some search engines insert the OR operator between keywords. Others may insert the word AND. For this reason, either insert these operators yourself (in most cases they will override the automatic operators inserted by the engine) or review the instructions to learn the inner workings of the specific search engine you are using.

Proximity operators let you specify how close one of your keywords should be to another. The most common proximity operator is NEAR, which tells the database engine to find documents in which one key word is a certain number of words away from another. For example the search phrase "marketing NEAR2 organizations" means *marketing* must be within 2 words of *organi?ations.*

Wildcard characters help you find plurals and alternate spellings of your keywords. For example, by using a question mark in the word *organi?ations,* you'll find documents with both *organisations* (British spelling) and *organizations.* Similarly, by using an asterisk at the end of the stem *chair*,* you'll find *chairman, chairperson, chairs,* and *chairlift.*

How Does the Internet Facilitate Communication?

Businesses are using the Internet to communicate with employees, customers, and suppliers anywhere in the world. Keep in mind that the Internet is platform independent. This means that all computers can link to the Internet and communicate with each other even if they use different internal operating systems such as Microsoft Windows or Mac. The Internet makes these types of communications possible:

■ E-*mail.* Electronic mail, generally called **e-mail,** enables users to create, transmit, and read written messages entirely on computer. An e-mail document may be a simple text message, or it might include long and complex files or programs. In addition to facilitating communication, e-mail also offers speed, low cost, portability, convenience, and ease of record keeping.

■ *Telnet.* As Chapter 8 will discuss in detail, a **network** is a collection of hardware, software, and communication media that enables computers to communicate and share information. **Telnet** is a class of Internet application program that allows you to communicate with other computers on a remote network even if your computer is not a permanent part of that network. For instance, you would use Telnet to access your county library's electronic card catalog from your home computer.

■ *Internet telephony.* It is now possible for Internet users to converse vocally over the Internet. Although the telephone has handled this job for decades, converting traditional voice calls to digital signals and sending them over the Internet is much less expensive than calling over standard analog phone lines. It can also be more efficient, allowing an organization

to accommodate more users on a single line at once. Experts say that Internet telephony could soon capture 4 percent of U.S. telephone company revenues.[3]

■ *File transfers.* **File transfer protocol (FTP)** is an Internet service that enables you to **download** files or transfer data from a server to your computer, and **upload** files, or transfer data from your computer to a server or host system.[4] Millions of useful files, including art, music, educational materials, games, maps, photos, software, and books, are available on the Internet. FTP also allows you to attach formatted documents to your e-mail messages. When you download a file, the FTP software breaks it down and reassembles it on your computer in a usable form.[5] Sometimes users compress or *zip* large files into smaller packets to make them easier and faster to transfer. If you receive a zipped file, you must use special software (usually provided with your Web browser) to unzip it before you can read it. The Internet also makes *peer-to-peer file sharing* possible. By using the Internet and software, users can exchange files directly (from user to user) without going through a central server.

■ *Discussion mailing lists.* **Discussion mailing lists,** also known as *listservs,* are discussion groups to which you subscribe by sending a message to the list's e-mail address. From then on, copies of all messages posted by any other subscriber are sent to you via e-mail. It's like subscribing to an electronic newsletter to which everyone can contribute.

■ *Newsgroups.* **Usenet newsgroups** consist of posted messages on a particular subject and responses to them. They differ from discussion mailing lists in two key ways. First, messages are posted at the newsgroup site, which you must access by using a news reader program. Second, messages posted to a newsgroup can be viewed by anyone. In other words, think of a newsgroup as a *place* you visit to read posted messages, whereas a discussion mailing list *delivers* posted messages to you.

■ *Chat.* **Chat** is an online conversation in which any number of computer users can type in messages to each other and receive responses in real time.

Intranets Not all Web sites are available to anyone cruising the Net. Some are reserved for private use. An **intranet** is a private internal corporate network. Intranets use the same technologies as the Internet and the World Wide Web, but the information provided and the access allowed are restricted to members of the organization (regardless of their actual location). Sensitive corporate data (recorded facts and statistics) that reside on intranets are protected from unauthorized access via the Internet by security software called a **firewall,** a special type of gateway that controls access to the company's local network. When anyone tries to get into the internal web, the firewall requests a password and other forms of identification. Whereas people on an intranet can get out to the Internet, unauthorized people on the Internet can't get in.

More than half of companies with 500 employees or more have corporate intranets. One of the biggest advantages of an intranet is that it enables employees to communicate and collaborate. At Arthur Andersen, for instance, employees use the company's intranet, *AA Online,* to access the company's wealth of expert knowledge and to search the company's online databases. Ford Motor Company uses its intranet to enable engineers and designers worldwide to collaborate in real time on the design of new car models. Every car and truck model has its own internal Web site to track design, production, quality control, and delivery processes.[6]

Besides sharing information, other uses for these networks include sending e-mail, filing electronic forms and reports, gaining access to the company information from remote locations, and publishing electronic phone directories, company newsletters, and other company material:[7]

■ *Policy manuals.* The most current version is always available to all employees without having to reprint hundreds of copies when policies change.

■ *Employee benefits information.* Employees can find out what their benefits are, reallocate the funds in their employee benefit plans, fill out electronic W-4 forms, view an electronic pay stub, and sign up for employee training programs.

■ *Job openings.* New positions are posted, and current employees can submit job applications over the intranet.

■ *Presentation materials used by marketing and sales departments.* Sales representatives can download sales and marketing materials at customer sites all over the world. In addition, changes made by marketing representatives at company headquarters are immediately available to field salespeople.

■ *Company records and information.* Company directories, customer information, employee skills inventories, project status reports, company calendars and events, and many other records are stored on an intranet and are accessible from anywhere in the world; all you need is an Internet connection and the right password.

Putting this material on an intranet allows employees to find information quickly and easily. Companies are finding that performing an electronic search on a well-designed intranet is far more efficient than digging through multiple filing cabinets stuffed with papers.

Extranets Once a company has an intranet in place, the cost of adding external capabilities is minimal, but the benefits can be substantial. An **extranet** is simply an external intranet that allows people to communicate and exchange data within a secured network.[8] Unlike intranets, which limit network access to a single organization, extranets allow qualified people from the outside—such as suppliers and customers—to use the network. Extranets can increase communication with clients, suppliers, and colleagues, and they can save companies time and money.

Consider Boeing. Every year the Seattle aerospace giant would ship a mountain of technical manuals, parts lists, and other maintenance documents to its 600 airline customers—enough papers to make a stack 130,000 feet tall. Printing and mailing costs alone ran into millions of dollars each year. But now Boeing places this material on a private Web site. Using an extranet, customers can access this information, obtain updates and news sources, and discuss maintenance issues in chat areas.[9]

An intranet set up by his law firm enables attorney David Beckman to view documents and other legal resources whether he's in the office or in the courtroom.

Like Boeing, some executive search firms and employment agencies are allowing clients to tap into their private Web sites to search for job prospects. Doctors and hospitals are also using extranets to share best practices among their individual organizations. In the past they faxed this information to each other, but there was no guarantee that the right person would see a fax or even know it existed before the information became obsolete.

How Is the Internet Changing the Way Companies Do Business?

The Internet is revolutionizing all facets of business life. In the space of just a few years, the Internet has penetrated virtually every aspect of the economy. It's changing the way customers, suppliers, and companies interact, creating huge opportunities as well as unforeseen competitive threats. It's changing the way companies work internally—collapsing boundaries and redefining relationships among different functions, departments, and divisions. It's the fastest-growing marketplace in the world economy, spawning new businesses, transforming existing ones, and creating enormous wealth, opportunities, and risk.[10]

Companies are using the Internet to

■ Find information

■ Work collaboratively

■ Find new business partners

■ Conduct electronic commerce

■ Attract new customers

■ Order supplies

■ Operate more efficiently

■ Communicate with their manufacturers, suppliers, customers, employees, and investors

■ Determine customer preferences

■ Recruit employees

Egghead.com of Menlo Park, California, operates a network of Web sites that sell everything from computer products to sporting goods, it also features an auction service. The sites ring up more than $500 million in annual sales.

Although the Internet has many business functions, corporate executives see improved communication and enhanced customer service as its two biggest benefits, as Exhibit A.3 suggests.

Of course, companies aren't the only ones benefiting from the Internet. In subsequent chapters we'll discuss how customers are also benefiting from Internet technology. Specifically, the Internet provides customers with information that is difficult and expensive to obtain in other ways. Additionally, it provides customers with affordable pricing options, enhanced product selections, convenience, and in some cases entertainment.

What Is Electronic Commerce?

In Chapter 1 we defined electronic commerce (e-commerce) as the buying and selling of goods and services over an electronic network. Specifically, e-commerce is classified into three broad categories:

■ **Business-to-consumer e-commerce.** Referred to as B2C, e-tailing, or electronic retailing, this form of e-commerce involves interactions and transactions between a company and consumers, with a strong focus on selling goods and services and marketing to the consumer (see Exhibit A.4). Typical business-to-consumer transactions include such functions as sales, marketing (promotions, advertising, coupons, catalogs), order processing and tracking, credit authorization, customer service, and electronic payments.

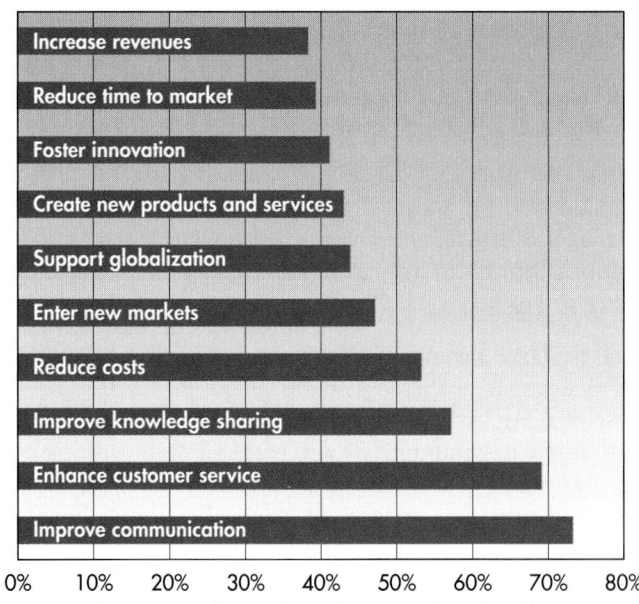

Percentage of executives who expect these benefits from the Internet

EXHIBIT A.3

GREATEST INTERNET BENEFITS

Over 525 executives who responded to a survey by Booz-Allen & Hamilton and the Economist Intelligent Unit listed these business benefits as the key contributions of the Internet.

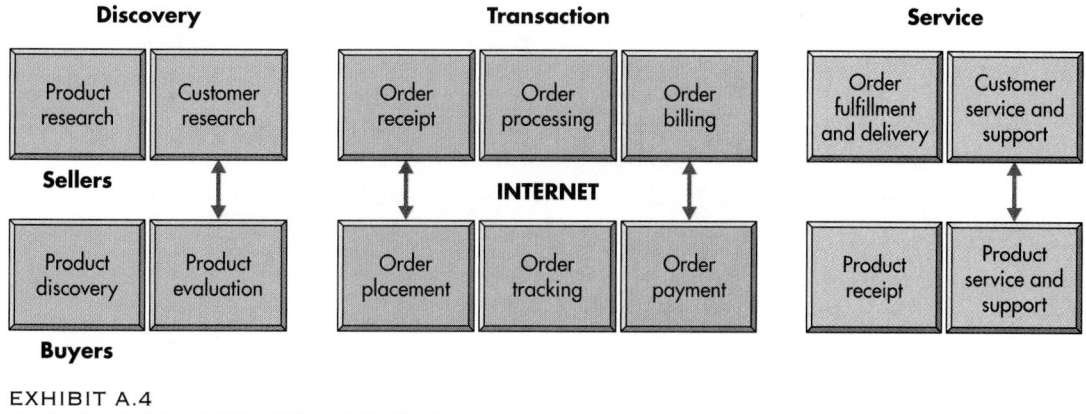

EXHIBIT A.4

WHAT IS E-COMMERCE?

In general, e-commerce enables both the buying and selling of goods and services over the Internet.

■ **Business-to-business e-commerce.** Known as B2B, this form of e-commerce uses the Internet to conduct transactions between businesses. Business-to-business e-commerce typically involves a company and its suppliers, distributors, manufacturers, and retailers, but not consumers. Generally, the types of goods sold in business-to-business transactions include office materials, manufacturing supplies, equipment, and other goods a company needs for operations. Companies from Honeywell to Chevron, W.W. Grainger, Sears, and the Big Three automakers (Ford, GM, and DaimlerChrysler) have all started electronic marketplaces to purchase supplies and transact business, as discussed in Chapter 9's Focusing on E-Business Today.[11] Industry experts predict that the business-to-business segment of e-commerce will grow five times faster than transactions between businesses and consumers. By 2006, it could represent more than 9 percent of all business conducted in the United States.[12]

■ **Consumer-to-consumer e-commerce.** In this category of e-commerce consumers sell products directly to each other using the Internet as the intermediary. Auction sites such as eBay are consumer-to-consumer electronic channels. Sellers list their products with the auction site and buyers bid on listed sellers' products. Once a bid is accepted, the seller ships the product directly to the buyer.

Mobile commerce (m-commerce) is the transaction of e-commerce using wireless portable devices, such as cell phones, palm pilots, pagers, and wireless Internet access. As Chapter 8 will discuss, m-commerce is becoming increasingly popular in Europe and will become more popular in the United States once the required technology is in place.

What Is the Difference Between E-Commerce and E-Business?

As discussed earlier, e-commerce involves buying and selling over electronic networks. By contrast, an **electronic business (e-business)** uses Internet technology to do much more than set up a Web site to sell or deliver goods. An e-business takes full advantage of Internet technology to transform the way it does business, with one goal in mind: to maximize customer value. E-commerce is indeed an important part of becoming an e-business, but it is only one step in the evolutionary process.

How a Typical E-Business Evolves Typically, a company moves through three distinct stages to become an e-business:[13]

■ *Stage 1: The e-aware company.* The company feels a sense of urgency about the Internet. It launches a Web site, provides information to prospective customers and other interested parties, and then wonders what to do next. It has not yet developed specific e-commerce strategies; nor has it addressed the internal changes that must be made to transact e-commerce successfully.

■ *Stage 2: The e-launch company.* The company begins to sell goods over the Internet and begins making some noticeable changes: it shifts to a paperless order-to-delivery process; it rapidly acknowledges the profound opportunity e-commerce offers; and it develops some new strategies and makes operational changes to take advantage of these opportunities.

■ *Stage 3: The e-business.* The company's e-commerce vision is now apparent to all employees and business partners. An entrepreneurial culture takes root and knowledge is shared freely throughout the organization and at all levels, facilitated by intranets and extranets. Business units seamlessly access needed resources from both inside and outside the organization. The company adopts a flexible, efficient organizational structure and begins to integrate technology into every part of the company's operation. It reorganizes the company's operation, creating a fundamentally new enterprise and making "e" such a core part of its business operation that the difference between "e" and everything else is nonexistent.

In short, visionary companies understand that they must radically change their current systems and operations to meet the challenges of doing business in the e-commerce era.

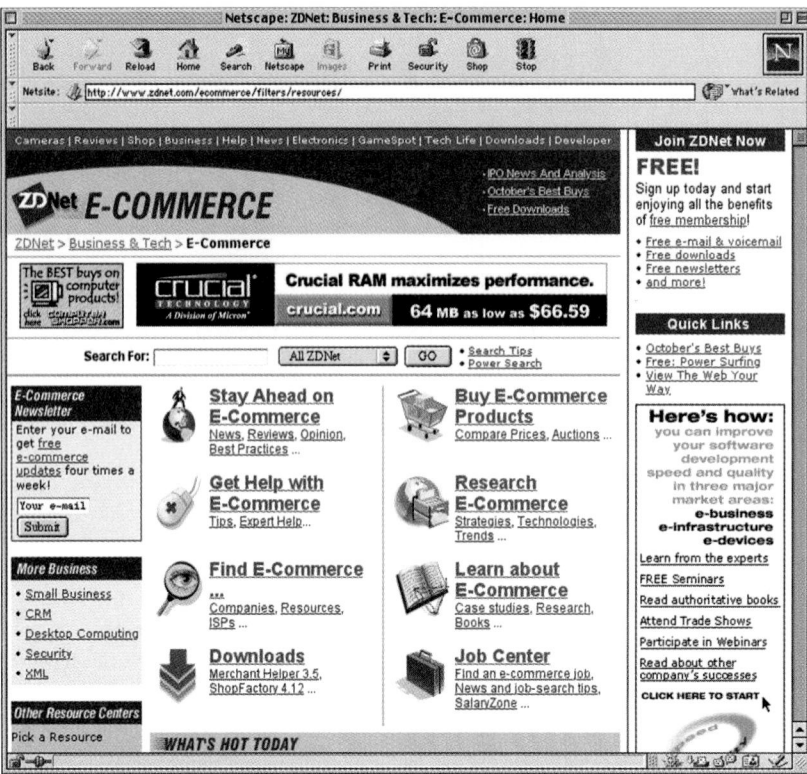

ZDNet E-Commerce is one of the many Web sites you can visit to get the latest information on e-commerce strategies, trends, products, practices, and more.

To become an e-business, they must develop systems and structures that facilitate the company's ability to innovate constantly, react rapidly, and handle dynamic change. The company begins the transformation process by asking some difficult questions. Then it uses the answers to those questions to reinvent the enterprise one piece at a time, as Exhibit A.5 suggests.[14]

The Role of Technology in the Evolution Process   In an e-business, technology is no longer an afterthought; rather, it is the driver for change. A company evolves into an e-business by integrating technology and the Internet into every phase of the business process—production, marketing, sales, customer support, advertising, public relations, and more—with one goal in mind: to meet customers' changing needs and priorities.[15]

Running a successful e-business means seamlessly coordinating all of these processes so that they are transparent to the customer. Studies show that companies that have woven technology and the Internet into every part of their operations are more successful in transacting e-commerce.[16] Look at Amazon.com, for example. The company started with two employees in a rundown Seattle warehouse, grew revenues in just three short years to more than $600 million, and outmaneuvered the two industry giants, Barnes & Noble and Borders Books & Music.[17] Here's how they did it.

To create a satisfying shopping experience, Amazon's Web site includes author interviews, sales information, customized book recommendations, instant order confirmation, editorial analysis, sample chapters, and more. If a customer inquires about an out-of-print book, the special orders department contacts suppliers to check availability and, if a copy is located, notifies the customer by e-mail for price approval. Amazon's order-fulfillment process is built around state-of-the-art high-tech distribution centers that operate seamlessly with the company's Web site. As a result, Amazon can provide a level of customer service that is unprecedented in the book retailing industry.[18]

Still, successfully weaving technology into every part of an operation is a huge undertaking. *Fortune* magazine reports that less than 10 percent of e-business strategies are effectively executed. Moreover, for a business to become a successful e-business, it must not only meet the needs and priorities of its customers but also anticipate and prepare for the unexpected.[19] Consider the debacle online auctioneer eBay faced in June 1999 when its computers went down for 22 hours. This outage was the cyber equivalent of hanging a huge "closed" sign on eBay's front door. Ebay was unprepared for such a major technological failure, even though its entire business operation depends on functioning computer systems. The event cost eBay an estimated $3 to $5 million in potential revenue, drove down its stock price by 9 percent, and created a round of unimaginable headaches—not to mention a huge public embarrassment.[20]

What Is Driving the Growth of E-Commerce?
The Internet (the backbone of electronic commerce), faster computers, and faster connections via high-speed modems and cable lines are binding consumers and companies in a low-cost

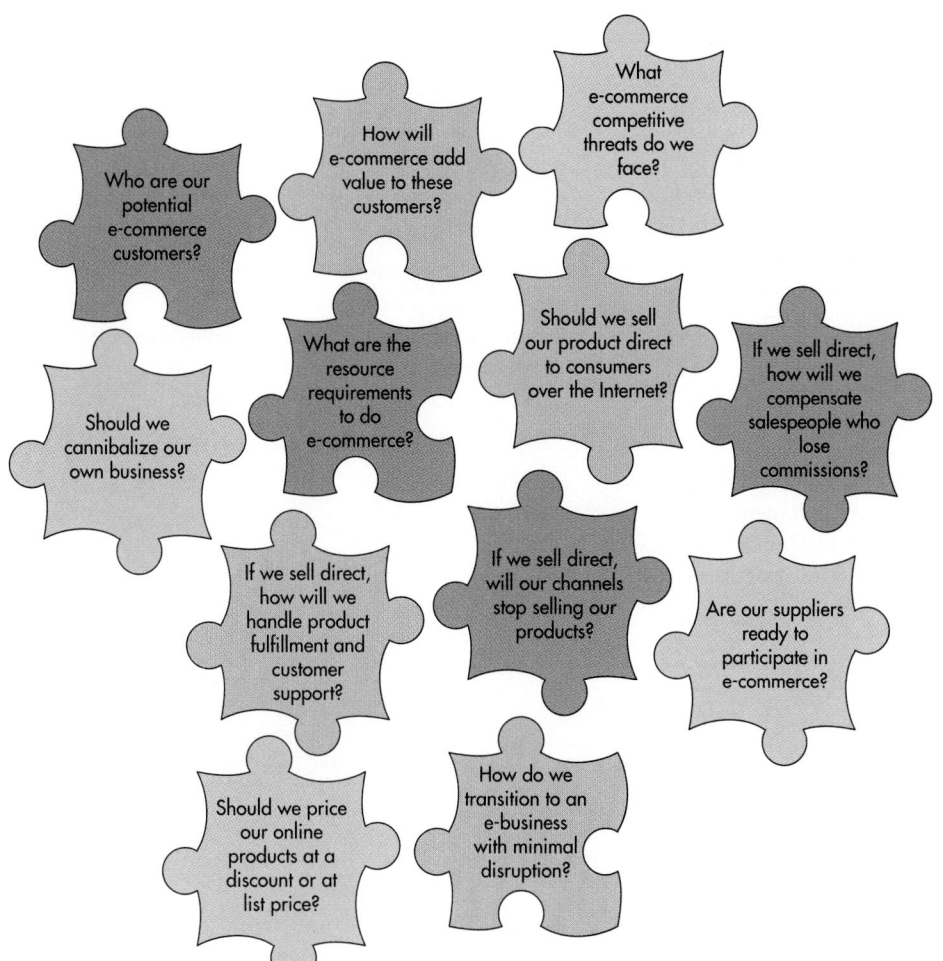

EXHIBIT A.5

BECOMING AN E-BUSINESS

Puzzled by what it takes to become an e-business? So are many of today's leading companies. Experts advise companies to start the transformation process by asking the right questions and by making sure they have all the right pieces. Then it's a matter of trial and error until everything fits in the right place.

way just as the inventions of the steam engine, electricity, and the telephone did (see Chapter 8). Affordable technology facilitates the growth of electronic commerce by making it accessible to more and more people. Additionally, the costs to build a Web site and transact business electronically can be relatively small when compared to setting up a physical warehouse and stocking it with inventory. As a result, the barriers to entry in the electronic marketplace are low.

As more and more businesses set up shop on the Web, competition increases. In some cases, it even forces reluctant traditional businesses to migrate their business to the Web. Barnesandnobel.com is a perfect example of a traditional chain that was forced to sell books online because of the rapid consumer acceptance and enthusiasm for online book retailer Amazon. Nevertheless, most companies today aren't being forced into electronic commerce. Instead, they're marching into cyberspace willingly and at unprecedented speeds because e-commerce offers substantial benefits to both companies and consumers.

Company Benefits   Companies are using e-commerce to improve their image, improve customer service, simplify processes, compress time, increase productivity, eliminate paper transactions, expedite access to information, reduce transportation costs, find new benefits, increase flexibility, and locate new customers.[21] By shifting attention to the new Internet markets,

companies can (1) create new online markets for existing products, (2) create new products specifically designed for online markets, and (3) expand existing or new products into international markets.[22]

At the same time electronic commerce can reduce the costs of publishing, processing, distributing, storing, and retrieving information. Although designing and creating online catalogs can be as costly as creating a print catalog, the costs to distribute 100 electronic catalogs or 100,000 are about the same. Similarly, the electronic processing of customer orders can be done at the fraction of the cost of doing business with traditional paper-based and labor-intensive processes. Dell Computer reports that prior to its Web site launch, customers called an average of once or twice per purchase to check on the status of their orders. Now with online order tracing, customers check their order status electronically instead of calling a customer service rep. This reduces Dell's costs significantly.[23]

Customer Benefits   Customers stand to gain as much if not more from e-commerce than companies do. Electronic commerce[24]

- Enables customers to shop or conduct other transactions 24 hours a day, every day, from almost any location

- Provides customers with more choices; they can select from many vendors and from more products and price levels

■ Allows for quick delivery of digitized products and information

■ Allows customers to interact with other customers and exchange ideas as well as compare experiences

■ Facilitates competition—which can keep prices in line

With a click of the mouse, for example, travelers can plan and price trips, purchase tickets, receive travel confirmations, review current reservations, and review the status of their mileage rewards accounts. In short, today's customers can make buying decisions as if they had an army of intelligent helpers running to all the stores around the world to find the best products and prices. And as Chapter 12 discusses, this ability is putting customers in a position of unprecedented control.

Learn More About E-Commerce On Your Own

This chapter was designed to teach you the fundamentals of the Internet and electronic commerce that you will need for this course. To learn more about these subjects, consider the following electronic sources:

1. Beginner's Guide to Starting a Business on the Internet, at www.homebusinessresearch.com, provides basic information on how to start an online business.

2. Setting Up an Online Business, at www.netquest1.com/ecommerce1.htm, provides a seven-part online course explaining the basics of e-commerce, with models of e-commerce sites.

3. Cornell University's Guide to E-Commerce, at www.ilr.cornell.edu/library/reference/guides/ecommerce/, is a beginner's introduction to e-commerce with links to sources of technical information, online journals and newspapers, and industry associations and guides.

4. E-Commerce Guidebook, at www.online-commerce.com, is a step-by-step guide to the process of becoming e-commerce enabled.

KEY TERMS

bookmark (31)

boolean operators (33)

browser (30)

business-to-business electronic
    commerce (37)

business-to-consumer electronic
    commerce (36)

chat (34)

consumer-to-consumer electronic
    commerce (37)

data (31)

database (31)

discussion mailing lists (34)

domain name (30)

download (34)

electronic business (e-business) (35)

e-mail (34)

extranet (35)

file transfer protocol (FTP) (34)

firewall (34)

graphical user interface (GUI) (30)

homepage (30)

hyperlink (30)

hypertext markup language (HTML) (30)

hypertext transfer protocol (HTTP) (30)

Internet (30)

Internet service provider (ISP) (30)

intranet (34)

mobile commerce (m-commerce) (37)

multimedia (30)

network (34)

search engines (31)

Telnet (34)

uniform resource locator (URL) (30)

upload (34)

Usenet newsgroups (34)

Web site (30)

World Wide Web (WWW) (30)

TEST YOUR KNOWLEDGE

QUESTIONS FOR REVIEW

1. Besides the World Wide Web, what else resides on the Internet?

2. How can you maximize your database search results?

3. How do newsgroups differ from discussion mailing lists?

4. What function does a firewall serve?

5. What is driving the growth of e-commerce?

QUESTIONS FOR ANALYSIS

6. What concerns might you have when citing information from a Web site?

7. What are some of the key benefits of company intranets?

8. What kinds of information might a company want to place on its intranet and why?

9. What is the difference between e-commerce and e-business?

10. When constructing a Web site, is it ethical to use the same design features and functions you find on another company's Web site?

11. Select a well-known e-commerce Web site and use Exhibit A.4 as a guide to help answer these questions:

a. What kinds of product and company information does the Web site provide?

b. What information does the Web site ask customers to provide about themselves?

c. What are some of the features the site includes to facilitate the product ordering process? For instance, can you check the status of your order? Does the site advise you if the product is out of stock?

d. How does the Web site provide customers with assistance if they have a question or concern?

CHAPTER GLOSSARY

Boolean operators
The term *boolean* refers to a system of logical thought developed by the English mathematician George Boole; it uses the operators AND, OR, and NOT

bookmark
A browser feature that places selected URLs in a file for quick access, allowing you to automatically return to the Web site by clicking on the site's name

browser
Software, such as Netscape Navigator or Microsoft's Internet Explorer, that enables a computer to search for, display, and download the multimedia information that appears on the World Wide Web

business-to-business e-commerce
Electronic commerce that involves transactions between companies and their suppliers, manufacturers, or other companies

business-to-consumer e-commerce
Electronic commerce that involves transactions between businesses and the end user or consumer

chat
A form of interactive communication that enables computer users in separate locations to have real-time conversations. Usually takes place at Web sites called chat rooms

consumer-to-consumer e-commerce
Electronic commerce that involves transactions between consumers

data
Recorded facts and statistics; data need to be converted to information before they can help people solve business problems

database
A collection of related data that can be cross-referenced in order to extract information

discussion mailing lists
E-mail lists that allow people to discuss a common interest by posting messages that are received by everyone in the group

domain name
The portion of an Internet address that identifies the host and indicates the type of organization it is

download
Transmitting a file from one computer system to another; on the Internet, bringing data from the Internet into your computer

electronic business (e-business)
A company that has transformed its key business processes to incorporate Internet technology into every phase of the operation

e-mail
Communication system that enables computers to transmit and receive written messages over electronic networks

extranet
Similar to an intranet, but extending the network to select people outside the organization

file transfer protocol (FTP)
A software protocol that lets you copy or move files from a remote computer—called an FTP site—to your computer over the Internet; it is the Internet facility for downloading and uploading files

firewall
Computer hardware and software that protects part or all of a private computer network attached to the Internet by preventing public Internet users from accessing it

graphical user interface (GUI)
A user-friendly program that enables computer operators to enter commands by clicking on icons and menus with a mouse

homepage
The primary Web site for an organization or individual; the first hypertext document displayed on a Web site

hyperlink
A highlighted word or image on a Web page or document that automatically allows people to move to another Web page or document when clicked on with a mouse

hypertext markup language (HTML)
The software language used to create, present, and link pages on the World Wide Web

hypertext transfer protocol (HTTP)
A communications protocol that allows people to navigate among documents or pages linked by hypertext and to download pages from the World Wide Web

Internet
A worldwide collection of interconnected networks that enables users to share information electronically and provides digital access to a wide variety of services

Internet service provider (ISP)
A company that provides access to the Internet, usually for a monthly fee, via telephone lines or cable; ISPs can be local companies or specialists such as America Online

intranet
A private network, set up within a corporation or organization, that operates over the Internet and may be used to link geographically remote sites

mobile commerce (m-commerce)
Transaction of electronic commerce using wireless devices and wireless Internet access instead of PC-based technology

multimedia
Typically used to mean the combination of more than one presentation medium—such as text, sound, graphics, and video

network
Collection of computers, communications software, and transmission media (such as telephone lines) that allows computers to communicate

search engines
Internet tools for finding Web sites on the topics of your choice

Telnet
A way to access someone else's computer (the host computer) and to use it as if it were right on your desk

uniform resource locator (URL)
Web address that gives the exact location of an Internet resource

upload
To send a file from your computer to a server or host system

Usenet newsgroups
One or more discussion groups on the Internet where people with similar interests can post articles and reply to messages

Web site
A related collection of files on the World Wide Web

World Wide Web (Web)
A hypertext-based system for finding and accessing Internet resources such as text, graphics, sound, and other multimedia resources

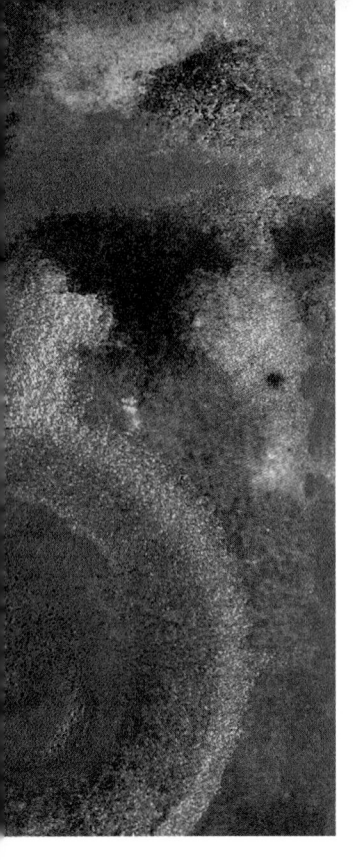

ETHICS AND SOCIAL RESPONSIBILITY OF BUSINESS

2

LEARNING OBJECTIVES

After studying this chapter, you will be able to

1. Explain the difference between an ethical dilemma and an ethical lapse

2. List four questions you might ask yourself when trying to make an ethical decision

3. Identify three steps that businesses are taking to encourage ethical behavior

4. Discuss three activities in which socially responsible companies might engage

5. Name three kinds of pollution and outline activities to control them

6. Highlight at least five actions that some businesses are taking to address environmental problems

7. Discuss the four rights of consumers

@ 8. Discuss four governing principles proposed by *Business Week* to address privacy concerns of individuals conducting e-commerce

BEYOND THE PURSUIT OF PROFITS: PATAGONIA GEARS UP TO SAVE THE ENVIRONMENT

www.patagonia.com

Environment-friendly products such as those sold by Patagonia give consumers a chance to make a difference while meeting their needs.

Some business executives believe they have to concentrate on the bottom line before they can turn their attention to worthy causes. But as founder and owner of Patagonia, leading designer and distributor of outdoor gear, Yvon Chouinard sees things differently. A passionate environmentalist, Chouinard believes everyone—from consumers to corporations—should do their part to save the earth's resources. In fact, Chouinard refuses to sacrifice the environment for the sake of his company's profitability. Instead, Chouinard strives for the best of both worlds—profits and environmental responsibility—by making both a key part of his business strategy.

Patagonia works hard to develop production techniques that reduce the environmental impact of the company's operations. Employees also reap the benefits of the company's environmental values. For instance, employees receive full pay for two-month internships at environmental not-for-profit organizations. Moreover, through a self-imposed "earth tax" on annual profits, Patagonia gives environmental groups about $1 million each year—more money than the company allocates for advertising.

Nevertheless, blending profitability with social responsibility isn't always easy. In the 1990s, the company's adherence to rigid environmental standards in the production of its high-priced goods created enormous operating expenses. Faced with sagging sales and a severe cash crunch, Patagonia was forced to scale back its operations and lay off one-fifth of its workforce.

Consultants advised Chouinard to sell the company and create a charitable foundation for environmental causes instead of donating a million or so from company profits each year. But Chouinard had established Patagonia to do more than donate money to environmental groups. He wanted to "use the company as a tool for social change" and was convinced that Patagonia could serve as an example for others.

So Chouinard launched an extensive effort to improve Patagonia's bottom line while also focusing on saving the earth's resources. First, he took his case to the public, educating consumers on environmental issues. Lengthy catalog essays by Chouinard explained the company's philosophies about saving the earth's resources and its rationale for developing environmentally sensitive production techniques. Then he refined Patagonia's public image of a "green" business, creating an internal assessment group to evaluate the company's environmental performance. He also constructed a new distribution center with recycled materials and an energy-saving heating system.

Next Chouinard focused on his suppliers. He challenged them to improve their performance and helped them develop techniques for meeting Patagonia's environmental standards. Working with outside contractors, Patagonia developed Synchilla fleece (a fabric made from recycled plastic soda bottles), which now accounts for the recycling of some 8 million plastic bottles each year. Patagonia also worked with farmers to produce organic cotton—grown without artificial pesticides or fertilizers. To offset higher production costs for the cotton, the company split the increased costs with consumers, hoping that they would find value in an environmentally sensitive product. They did. Once the catalogs reached consumers, Patagonia immediately sold out of the new line of all-organic cotton sweaters.

Today, Patagonia is a leader and pioneer of "green" profits. With annual sales exceeding $160 million, Chouinard has proven that Patagonia could achieve success while supporting its environmental values.[1]

■ ETHICS IN THE WORKPLACE

Yvon Chouinard works hard to make sure that Patagonia does the right thing. But as Chouinard knows, a business can't take action or make decisions; only the individuals within a business can do that. From the CEO to the newest entry-level clerk, individuals make decisions every day that affect their company and its **stakeholders**—groups that are affected by (or that affect) a business's operations, including colleagues, employees, supervisors, investors, customers, suppliers, governments, and society at large. These decisions ultimately determine whether the company is recognized as a responsible corporate citizen.

What Is Ethical Behavior?

Guided by written policies, unwritten standards, and examples set by top managers, every individual in an organization makes choices that have moral implications. We define **ethics** as the principles and standards of moral behavior that are accepted by society as right versus wrong. To make the "right" choice individuals must think through the consequences of their actions. *Business ethics* is the application of moral standards to business situations.

Ethical Dilemmas versus Ethical Lapses Ethical decisions can be divided into two general types: ethical dilemmas and ethical lapses. An **ethical dilemma** is a situation in which one must choose between two conflicting but arguably valid sides. For example, Johnson & Johnson (J&J) faced an ethical dilemma when it had to decide how to keep its Tylenol customers well informed without scaring them away altogether. Tylenol is certainly safe enough for all the millions of people who take it each year without ill effects. However, more than 100 deaths per year are caused by acetaminophen, the active ingredient in Tylenol.[2]

Even though J&J strengthened label warnings about not giving Tylenol to children and not taking it in combination with alcohol, the labels did not mention the possibility of death from liver failure when the recommended dose is exceeded. The company believed that such warnings would confuse people and that mentioning the risk of death would promote the use of Tylenol in suicides.[3] Should J&J include organ-specific warnings? Or is it enough to caution users about sticking to the proper dose? J&J decided to clarify the dangers by mentioning that mixing alcohol with painkillers can lead to liver damage and stomach bleeding.[4]

All ethical dilemmas have a common theme: the conflict between the rights of two or more important groups of people. Consumers have the right to be informed about any risks from using over-the-counter medications, and J&J has the right to profit by selling a beneficial medication that is used safely by millions. Similarly, recording artists have the right to earn royalties from the songs they publish, and consumers have the right to copy music for their own enjoyment.

The second type of decision is an **ethical lapse,** in which an individual makes a decision that is clearly wrong, such as divulging trade secrets to a competitor. Be careful not to confuse ethical dilemmas with ethical lapses. A company faces an ethical dilemma when it must decide whether to continue operating a production facility that is suspected, but not proven, to be unsafe. A company makes an ethical lapse when it continues to operate the facility even after the site has been proven unsafe. Other examples of ethical lapses would include inflating prices for certain customers or selling technological secrets to unfriendly foreign governments.

Cyberethics The Internet's ability to reach millions of people, combined with its protective cloak of anonymity, makes it a breeding ground for all sorts of ethical lapses. Cyberspace abounds with stories about top company executives who steal one another's intellectual property, auction rip-offs, Internet stock fraud, and e-commerce sites that fail to deliver what they promise. Not long ago Internet scams were rare, but now they are so rampant that regulators are finding themselves blitzed with complaints. The Federal Trade Commission alone identified 18,660 instances of potential Internet fraud in 1999. One-fourth of all its consumer complaints are now about the Internet, up from just 3 percent in 1997.[5] "Never underestimate people's ability to do bad," warns one ethics professional. "Technology is just going to make it easier."[6]

It's not just gullible consumers who are being duped. Businesses of all sizes are becoming targets. The hot Internet business scams include hijacking Web pages and diverting traffic to sites that can charge higher ad fees based on their new audience, fraudulent Internet access offers, and bogus Web page design outfits that prey on small companies. Part of the problem is that ethics

---

stakeholders
Individuals or groups to whom business has a responsibility

ethics
The rules or standards governing the conduct of a person or group

ethical dilemma
Situation in which both sides of an issue can be supported with valid arguments

LEARNING
OBJECTIVE 1
Explain the difference between an ethical dilemma and an ethical lapse.

ethical lapse
Situation in which an individual makes a decision that is morally wrong, illegal, or unethical

KEEPING PACE WITH TECHNOLOGY AND ELECTRONIC COMMERCE

RECRUITING THE THIEF TO PROTECT THE JEWELS

Shawn Fanning wasn't trying to change the world—or break the law—when he wrote a software program that allowed computer users to swap music files with each other. Fascinated by technology, the 18-year-old just wanted to create a program that would allow users to get great music over the Internet—for free. But Fanning's simple idea, known as Napster, turned out to be much more than just another software program.

Napster showcased the potential for "peer-to-peer file sharing," which is the direct transfer of files from one computer to another without passing through a central server. Napster users would access a directory stored on the company's central server, and use Napster's free software to easily swap music files stored on the personal computers of other users. Napster merely serves as a clearinghouse that facilitates the exchange.

Outraged by the potential loss of royalties from music sales, recording companies and artists slapped multiple lawsuits on Napster, insisting the site violated copyright laws by illegally distributing copyrighted music. The industry also claimed that both Napster and Napsterites committed piracy by stealing intellectual property and robbing artists of payment for copyrighted work. But Napster argued that it wasn't doing anything illegal or unethical. After all, it wasn't storing any songs on its central server or distributing music directly from its Web site. Napster was just the go-between for users who were sim-

ply sharing music files for personal use—not stealing or distributing songs for commercial profit. Furthermore, the availability of free music had not harmed CD sales and profits. In fact, CD sales actually *increased* with Napster's soaring popularity.

Although both sides offered valid arguments, in 2001 a U.S. Federal District judge shut Napster down. Still, Fanning's invention has far-reaching possibilities—well beyond snagging free copies of the latest Metallica song. For instance, Thomas Middelhoff, CEO of Bertelsmann (the world's third-largest media company), sees Napster's technology as a possible way to transform his publishing house into a powerhouse for the Internet Age. Middleoff invested $50 million in Napster to fund the development of technology that will require users to pay a small fee to download media files, and give peer-to-peer file sharing the media industry's *Good Housekeeping* seal of approval. Developing such technology, of course, is no easy feat. But, if Fanning is successful, Napster could bring rock and roll to much more than the music industry.

■ QUESTIONS FOR CRITICAL THINKING

1. What ethical dilemmas surfaced as Napster gained popularity?

2. Why did Middelhoff "recruit the thief to protect the jewels"?

"implies periods of contemplation and deliberation, and working through a moral calculus," says one ethics expert. But who has time for this when operating at Internet speed? It seems as if many companies today are created, hyped, and sold with less concern for attracting real customers than for lining one's pockets with investors' money.[7]

How Do Businesses and Employees Make Ethical Choices?

Determining what's right in any given situation can be difficult. One approach is to measure each act against certain absolute standards. In the United States, these standards are often grounded in religious teachings, such as "Do not lie" and "Do not steal." Another place to look for ethical guidance is the law. If saying, writing, or doing something is clearly illegal, you have no decision to make; you obey the law. Nevertheless, telephone companies continually break the law when they switch someone's long distance service without their consent (a practice known as slamming) or slip unauthorized charges into phone bills (a practice known as cramming). Penalties against offenders for such unethical behavior have reached millions of dollars.[8]

Even though legal considerations will resolve some ethical questions, you'll often have to rely on your own judgment and principles. When trying to decide the most ethical course of action, you might apply the Golden Rule: Do unto others as you would have them do unto you. Or you might examine your motives: If your intent is honest, the decision is ethical, even though it may be factually or technically incorrect; however, if your intent is to mislead or manipulate, your

LEARNING
OBJECTIVE   *2*
List four questions you might ask
yourself when trying to make an
ethical decision

decision is unethical, regardless of whether it is factually or technically correct. You might also consider asking yourself a series of questions:

1. Is the decision legal? (Does it break any laws?)

2. Is it balanced? (Is it fair to all concerned?)

3. Can you live with it? (Does it make you feel good about yourself?)

4. Is it feasible? (Will it actually work in the real world?)

When you need to determine the ethics of any situation, these questions will get you started. You may also want to consider the needs of stakeholders, and you may want to investigate one or more philosophical approaches (see Exhibit 2.1).

These approaches are not mutually exclusive alternatives. On the contrary, most businesspeople combine them to reach decisions that will satisfy as many stakeholders as possible without violating anyone's rights or treating anyone unjustly. In any case, wanting to be an ethical corporate citizen isn't enough; people in business must actively practice ethical behavior.

How Can Companies Become More Ethical?

Many companies are concerned about ethical issues and are trying to develop approaches for improving their ethics. Boeing requires all employees to undergo at least one hour of ethical training a year, and the company's senior managers must undergo five hours. Lockheed Martin has created a newspaper called *Ethics Daily* that runs articles based on ethical problems employees have faced and how they resolved them.[9]

code of ethics
Written statement setting forth the principles that guide an organization's decisions

Additionally, more than 80 percent of large companies have adopted a written **code of ethics,** which defines the values and principles that should be used to guide decisions (see Exhibit 2.2). By

IS THE DECISION ETHICAL?	DOES IT RESPECT STAKEHOLDERS?	DOES IT FOLLOW A PHILOSOPHICAL APPROACH?
IS IT LEGAL?	WILL OUTSIDERS APPROVE?	IS IT A UTILITARIAN DECISION?
☐ Does it violate civil law?	☐ Does it benefit customers, suppliers, investors, public officials, media representatives, and community members?	☐ Does it produce the greatest good for the greatest number of people?
☐ Does it violate company policy?		DOES IT UPHOLD INDIVIDUAL, LEGAL, AND HUMAN RIGHTS?
IS IT BALANCED?	WILL SUPERVISORS APPROVE?	☐ Does it protect people's own interests?
☐ Is it fair to all concerned, in both the short and the long term?	☐ Did you provide management with information that is honest and accurate?	☐ Does it respect the privacy of others and their right to express their opinion?
CAN YOU LIVE WITH IT?	WILL EMPLOYEES APPROVE?	☐ Does it allow people to act in a way that conforms to their religious or moral beliefs?
☐ Does it make you feel good about yourself?	☐ Will it affect employees in a positive way?	
☐ Would you feel good reading about it in a newspaper?	☐ Does it handle personal information about employees discreetly?	DOES IT UPHOLD THE PRINCIPLES OF JUSTICE?
IS IT FEASIBLE?	☐ Did you give proper credit for work performed by others?	☐ Does it treat people fairly and impartially?
☐ Does it work in the real world?		☐ Does it apply rules consistently?
☐ Will it improve your competitive position?		☐ Does it ensure that people who harm others are held responsible and make restitution?
☐ Is it affordable?		
☐ Can it be accomplished in the time available?		

EXHIBIT 2.1

ITEMIZED LIST FOR MAKING ETHICAL DECISIONS
Companies with the most success in establishing an ethical structure are those that balance their approach to making decisions.

itself, however, a code of ethics can't accomplish much. "You can have grand motives, but if your employees don't see them, they aren't going to mean anything," says one ethics manager at accounting firm Arthur Andersen.[10] To be effective, a code must be supported by employee communications efforts, a formal training program, employee commitment to follow it, and a system through which employees can get help with ethically difficult situations.[11]

Codes of ethics are so important that according to the Federal Sentencing Guidelines (1991), a company found to be violating federal law might not be prosecuted if it has the proper ethics policies and procedures in place. As one ethics expert explains, "If you have an active ethics program in place ahead of time, then bad things shouldn't happen; but if they do happen, it won't hurt you as badly."[12] Perhaps inspired by these guidelines, some companies have created an official position—the ethics officer—to guard morality. Originally hired to oversee corporate conduct—from pilfering company pens to endangering the environment to selling company secrets—many ethics officers today function as corporate coaches for ethical decision making.

Keep in mind, however, that ethical behavior starts at the top. The CEO and other senior managers must set the tone for people throughout the company. At Aveda, a cosmetics company, the corporate mission is to bring about positive effects through responsible business methods. "We do this, quite frankly, out of self-preservation," says founder and chairman Horst Rechebecher.[13]

Another way companies support ethical behavior is by establishing ethics hot lines that encourage *whistle-blowing*—an employee's disclosure of illegal, unethical, wasteful, or harmful practices by the company. Whistle-blowing can bring with it high costs: Public accusation of wrongdoing hurts the business's reputation, requires attention from managers who must investigate the accusations, and damages employee morale. Moreover, whistle-blowers risk being fired or demoted, and they often suffer career setbacks, financial strain, and emotional stress. The fear of such negative repercussions may allow unethical or illegal practices to go unreported. Still, all things considered, many employees do the right thing as Exhibit 2.3 suggests.

LEARNING OBJECTIVE **3**
Identify three steps that businesses are taking to encourage ethical behavior

---

THE INSTITUTE OF ELECTRICAL AND ELECTRONICS ENGINEERS, INC.

CODE OF ETHICS

We, the members of the IEEE, in recognition of the importance of our technologies affecting the quality of life throughout the world, and in accepting a personal obligation to our profession, its members and the communities we serve, do hereby commit ourselves to the highest ethical and professional conduct and agree:

1. to accept responsibility in making engineering decisions consistent with the safety, health and welfare of the public, and to disclose promptly factors that might endanger the public or the environment;

2. to avoid real or perceived conflicts of interest whenever possible, and to disclose them to affected parties when they do exist;

3. to be honest and realistic in stating claims or estimates based on available data;

4. to reject bribery in all its forms;

5. to improve the understanding of technology, its appropriate application, and potential consequences;

6. to maintain and improve our technical competence and to undertake technological tasks for others only if qualified by training or experience, or after full disclosure of pertinent limitations;

7. to seek, accept, and offer honest criticism of technical work, to acknowledge and correct errors, and to credit properly the contributions of others;

8. to treat fairly all persons regardless of such factors as race, religion, gender, disability, age, or national origin;

9. to avoid injuring others, their property, reputation, or employment by false or malicious action;

10. to assist colleagues and co-workers in their professional development and to support them in following this code of ethics.

EXHIBIT 2.2

IEEE CODE OF ETHICS

The Institute of Electrical and Electronics Engineers promotes the public policy interests of its U.S. members. The organization's code of ethics serves as a model for members to adopt.

EXHIBIT 2.3

DOING THE RIGHT THING

According to a recent survey of 1,002 randomly selected adults, when it comes to ethics in the workplace most employees try to do the right thing.

If you found out your employer was doing something contrary to your ethical standards, you would:

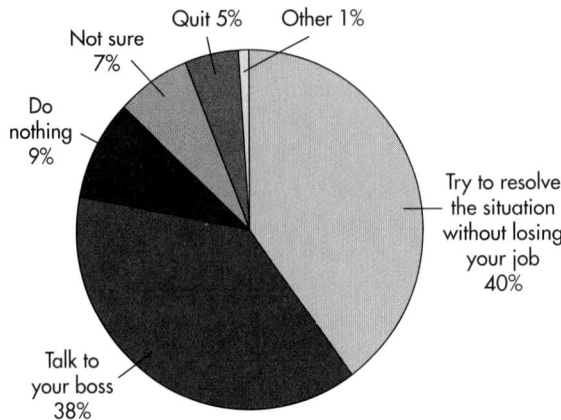

Other 1%
Quit 5%
Not sure 7%
Do nothing 9%
Try to resolve the situation without losing your job 40%
Talk to your boss 38%

SOCIAL RESPONSIBILITY IN BUSINESS

In addition to practicing ethics in the workplace, companies such as Patagonia strive to create organizations that encourage social responsibility in their policies and among their employees. Of course, the ideal relationship between business and society is a matter of debate. Supporters of the concept of **social responsibility** argue that a company has an obligation to society beyond the pursuit of profits.

social responsibility
The idea that business has certain obligations to society beyond the pursuit of profits

A recent Business Week/Harris poll found that 95 percent of adults reject the notion that a corporation's only role is to make money. In fact, 76 percent of respondents said that if price and quality were equal, they would be likely to switch brands and retailers to support socially responsible companies.[14] Some companies link the pursuit of socially responsible goals with their overall growth strategies, such as Ben & Jerry's, Tom's of Maine (which produces natural personal-care products), and Working Assets (which provides long-distance telephone service).[15] Still, many other managers believe that their primary obligation is to the company's shareholders and that social responsibility is a secondary concern. Finding the right balance is challenging.

Ben & Jerry's: Social Responsibility versus Profits

Ben & Jerry's founders Ben Cohen and Jerry Greenfield have long struggled to balance the company's social initiative with shareholder demands for better profits. Since its inception in 1978, Ben & Jerry's Homemade Ice Cream has donated 7.5 percent of pretax profits to various causes (including saving the family farm, promoting world peace, saving the world's rain forests, and keeping French nuclear testing out of the South Pacific). Unfortunately, the company fell on hard times in the 1990s, nearly confirming the view that socially responsible companies would ultimately go out of business. But Perry D. Odak became CEO in 1997 and proved the skeptics wrong.[16]

Best of the Web Best of the Web Best of

BUILD A BETTER BUSINESS

One way to distinguish your business as an ethical organization is to join the Better Business Bureau (BBB). Members of this private, not-for-profit business group agree to maintain specific standards for operating ethically and addressing customer complaints. The BBB Web site is packed with information about the organization, member businesses, and programs that benefit businesses and consumers alike. You can find reports on companies, register complaints, get help with consumer problems, and access publications on all kinds of consumer issues, such as avoiding business scams and investigating charitable organizations. www.bbb.org/

When Odak took over, sales were down, and so was company morale. Employees didn't want to abandon Ben & Jerry's social mission in a search for profits. Many of them regretted the cancellation of efforts such as the Peace Pop program and its "One Percent for Peace." But as colorful as some of those programs were, they had also been inefficient. Nevertheless, things changed under Odak. By focusing on the balance sheet, CEO Odak managed not only to tighten Ben & Jerry's business practices and improve its bottom line but also to enhance its ability to contribute to worthy causes.[17]

In 1999, Ben & Jerry's was sold to Unilever, a $45 billion global giant that owns Breyer's and Good Humor ice cream brands, for $325 million in cash. Protestors were concerned that the new owner would not preserve the company's commitment to social causes. But Unilever assured them that Ben & Jerry's social mission would be encouraged and well-funded. Unilever agreed to donate an initial $5 million and 7.5 percent of Ben & Jerry's annual profits to the Ben & Jerry's Foundation. Moreover, it promised not to reduce jobs or alter the way the ice cream is made. In spite of strong resistance from Vermont residents and loyal customers, some saw the sale as an opportunity to project social consciousness onto a large multinational corporation.[18]

When word spread that the founders of Ben & Jerry's were interested in selling the company, protesters gathered to voice their concerns. Many worried that buyers would not carry forward the social responsibility programs that are the core of Ben & Jerry's existence.

The Evolution of Social Responsibility

Social responsibility is a concept with decades-old roots. In the nineteenth and early twentieth centuries, the prevailing view among U.S. industrialists was that business had only one responsibility: to make a profit. "The public be damned," said railroad tycoon William Vanderbilt, "I'm working for the shareholders."[19] *Caveat emptor* was the rule of the day—"Let the buyer beware." If you bought a product, you paid the price and took the consequences. No consumer groups or government agencies would help you if the product was defective or caused harm.

By the early twentieth century, however, reformers were beginning to push politicians and government regulators to protect citizens from the abuses of big business. Their efforts paid off. Laws were passed to ensure the purity of food and drugs, limit the power of monopolies, and prevent unfair business practices, among other reforms. (See Component Chapter B for a list of early government regulations pertaining to business.)

During the Great Depression, which started in 1929, 25 percent of the workforce was unemployed. Many people lost their faith in capitalism, and pressure mounted for government to fix the system. At the urging of President Franklin D. Roosevelt, Congress passed laws in the 1930s and 1940s that established the Social Security system, allowed employees to join unions and bargain collectively, set a minimum hourly wage, and limited the length of the workweek. New laws prevented unfair competition and false advertising and started the Securities and Exchange Commission (SEC) to protect investors.

Public confidence in U.S. business revived during World War II, and throughout the 1950s the relationship between business, government, and society was relatively tranquil. However, the climate shifted in the 1960s, as activism exploded on four fronts: environmental protection, national defense, consumerism, and civil rights. These movements have drastically altered the way business is conducted in the United States. Many of the changes have been made willingly by socially responsible companies such as Patagonia and Ben & Jerry's, others have been forced by government action, and still others have come about because of pressure from citizen groups.

Efforts to Increase Social Responsibility

Today's businesses are about more than just making products or profits. As Ben & Jerry's and Patagonia show, socially responsible businesses can indeed make a difference in the world. *Industry Week*'s 100 Best Managed Companies all actively engage in socially responsible activities. Some work to curb child abuse or domestic violence. Others provide the best benefits packages for employees. Still others have strong recycling programs to keep the environment

LEARNING OBJECTIVE   4
Discuss three activities in which socially responsible companies might engage

social audit
Assessment of a company's performance in the area of social responsibility

David Lubetzky, the founder of Peaceworks, is helping the Middle East peace process on two fronts: by encouraging cooperative business ventures between Jews and Arabs and by increasing awareness among American consumers.

clean. In the past five years, General Mills has provided some $155 million in donations and contributions to help combat hunger, to provide education to students, and to ensure the safety of the neighborhoods where the company operates.[20] Those that give back to society are finding that their efforts can lead to a more favorable public image and stronger employee morale. Thus, more and more organizations are attempting to be socially responsible citizens by conducting a *social audit*, by engaging in *cause-related marketing,* or by being *philanthropic.*

A **social audit** is a systematic evaluation and reporting of the company's social performance. The report typically includes objective information about how the company's activities affect its various stakeholders. For example, once a year Ben & Jerry's Homemade Ice Cream asks an outsider to conduct a social audit that assesses the impact of the company's operations on its employees, customers, communities, suppliers, and shareholders. The company announces the results of the audit in its annual report to shareholders.

Companies can also engage in *cause-related marketing,* in which a portion of product sales helps support worthy causes. For example, Johnson & Johnson gives the World Wildlife fund a cut from sales of a special line of children's toiletries. Similarly, Peaceworks encourages joint business ventures among people of different backgrounds who live in volatile regions of the world. One of the company's product lines is *spraté,* uniquely flavored spreads produced in Israel by a Jewish-owned company that buys all its ingredients from Israeli Arabs and Palestinians. When consumers buy a jar of spraté, they not only get a tasty spread, but they also support the peace process in the Middle East.[21]

Some companies choose to be socially responsible corporate citizens by being **philanthropic;** that is, they donate money, time, goods, or services to charitable, humanitarian, or educational institutions (see Exhibit 2.4). Corporations such as Microsoft, General Electric, Dell, and Wal-Mart donate billions of dollars in cash and products to charity each year. American Express employees in Phoenix, Arizona, donate time to repair the houses of elderly, disabled, and low-income residents.[22] And Wendy's founder, Dave Thomas, travels around the country urging large companies to help employees with the costs associated with adopting children. "Writing a check is not

EXHIBIT 2.4

CIVIC RESPONSIBILITIES

Executives generally support the notion that companies should serve their communities and act in philanthropic ways.

PERCENTAGE OF EXECUTIVES WHO "STRONGLY AGREE" OR "AGREE" THAT COMPANIES SHOULD:	PERCENTAGE
Be environmentally responsible	100
Be ethical in operations	100
Earn profits	96
Employ local residents	94
Pay taxes	94
Encourage and support employee volunteering	89
Contribute money and leadership to charities	85
Be involved in economic development	75
Be involved in public education	73
Involve community representatives in business decisions that impact community	62
Target a proportion of purchasing toward local vendors	61
Help improve quality of life for low-income populations	54

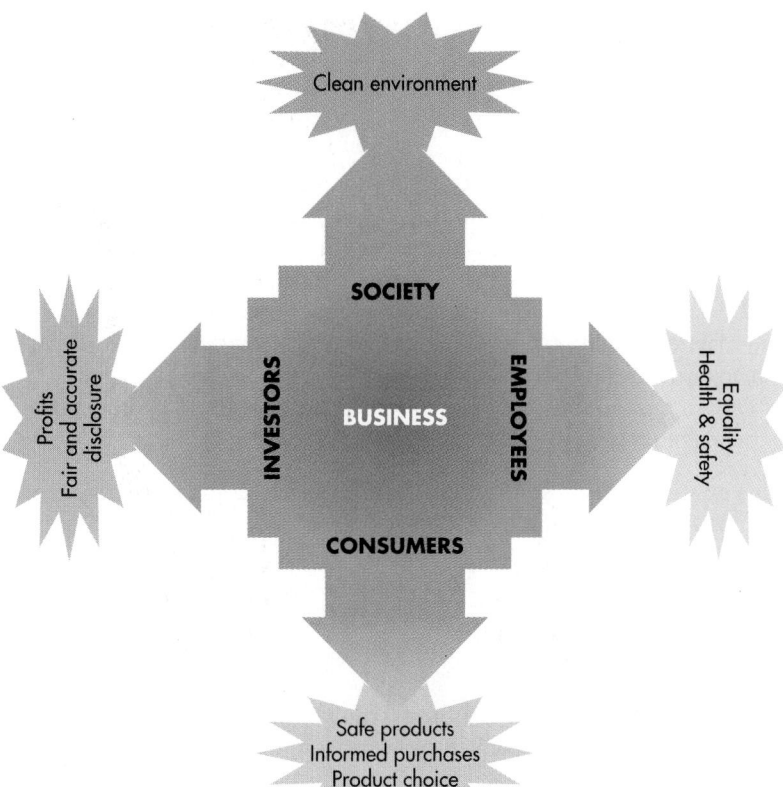

EXHIBIT 2.5

BALANCING BUSINESS AND STAKEHOLDERS' RIGHTS

Balancing the individual needs and interests of a company's stakeholders is one of management's most difficult tasks.

enough," says Thomas. "You have to let people know that you are putting money where your heart is by giving your time, too."[23]

In short, businesspeople are doing whatever they can—donating computers, taking kids on field trips, supporting basketball teams, building houses for people, or helping people find jobs. "We try to function as though we live next door to everybody in our community," says the director of the Socially Responsible Banking Fund at Vermont National Bank.[24]

philanthropic
Descriptive term for altruistic actions such as donating money, time, goods, or services to charitable, humanitarian, or educational institutions

■ BUSINESS'S RESPONSE TO THE NEEDS OF SOCIETY

Exactly how much can businesses contribute to social concerns? This is a difficult decision for most companies because they have limited resources. Thus, they must allocate their resources to a number of goals, such as upgrading facilities and equipment, developing new products, marketing existing products, and rewarding employee efforts, in addition to contributing to social causes. This juggling act is a challenge that every business faces. For example, if a company consistently ignores its stakeholders, its business will suffer and eventually fold. If the company disregards society's needs (such as environmental concerns), voters will clamor for laws to limit the offensive business activities, consumers who feel their needs and values are being ignored will spend their money on a competitor's products, investors who are unhappy with the company's performance will invest elsewhere, and employees whose needs are not met will become unproductive or will quit and find other jobs. As Exhibit 2.5 shows, stakeholders' needs sometimes conflict. In such cases, which stakeholders should be served first—society, consumers, investors, or employees?

Responsibility Toward Society and the Environment

Environmental issues exemplify the difficulty that businesses encounter when they try to reconcile conflicting interests: Society needs as little pollution as possible from businesses. But producing quality products to satisfy customers' needs can cause pollution to some degree. Business executives such as Patagonia's Yvon Chouinard try to strike a balance by making environmental management a formal part of their business strategy—along with quality, profits, safety, and other daily business operations.[25] Still, merging industrialism with environmentalism is not an easy task, says William Clay Ford Jr., chairman of Ford Motor Company. In an unprecedented step toward that goal, Ford recently admitted that SUVs foul the air more than cars and pledged to engineer breakthroughs to make SUVs cleaner.[26]

pollution
Damage to or destruction of the natural environment caused by the discharge of harmful substances

The Pervasiveness of Pollution Our air, water, and land can easily be tainted by **pollution** (the contamination of the natural environment by the discharge of harmful substances). Moreover, the pollution in any one element can easily taint the others. Environmental pollution pervades industrialized and developing nations alike. The emerging economies of Asia and Latin America have based much of their growth on loose environmental standards. However, Mexico, Malaysia, and other developing countries realize that their prosperity can be sustained only if their citizens can enjoy the quality of life that comes with a clean environment. At the same time, the countries of Eastern Europe are scrambling to reverse the decades of environmental neglect that occurred under communism.[27]

LEARNING OBJECTIVE 5
Name three kinds of pollution and outline activities to control them

Air Pollution The most noticeable form of air pollution is smog, which is produced by the interaction of sunlight and hydrocarbons (gases released when fossil fuels are burned). Another kind of air pollution causes acid rain, which is created when emissions from coal-burning factories and electric utility plants react with air. Acid rain has been blamed for damaging lakes and forests in the northeastern United States and southeastern Canada.

Experts also worry about airborne toxins emitted during some manufacturing processes. Large and small companies together release millions of pounds of chemical wastes into the air each year. Although the effects of many of these substances are unknown, some are carcinogenic (cancer-causing).[28] Emissions from factories and cars also contribute to global warming. The greenhouse effect occurs when heated gases form a layer of unusually warm air around the earth, trapping the sun's heat and preventing the earth's surface from cooling. Some scientists estimate that global warming will cause worldwide temperatures to rise by 1 to 3.5 degrees Celsius in the next century. This could lead to increases in both droughts and floods in some regions and raise the sea level about 50 centimeters (20 inches) by 2100.[29]

Water Pollution Our air is not the only part of our environment to suffer. Water pollution has damaged many U.S. lakes, rivers, streams, harbors, and coastal waters. Contamination comes from a variety of sources: manufacturing facilities, mining and construction sites, farms, and city sewage systems. Although dramatic accidents are widely publicized (such as the Exxon *Valdez* oil spill in Alaskan waters), the main threat is the careless day-to-day disposal of wastes from thousands of individual sources.

Land Pollution Even if all wastewater were purified before being discharged, our groundwater would still be endangered by leakage from the millions of tons of hazardous substances that have been buried underground or dumped in improper storage sites. Much of this pollution was created years ago by companies that carelessly—but legally—disposed of substances (now known to be unhealthy) in landfills, where few (if any) protective barriers could be counted on to prevent dangerous chemicals from leaking into the soil and the water supply. Cleaning up these wastes is extremely difficult and expensive.

In addition, companies and individuals alike generate enormous amounts of solid waste—more than 200 million tons in the United States each year. Much of this waste ends up in landfills. A large part of the landfill problem comes from consumer demands for convenience and fashion. Fortunately, recent efforts to conserve and recycle resources are helping to combat the land pollution problem.[30]

ecology
Study of the relationships between living things in the water, air, and soil, their environments, and the nutrients that support them

The Government Effort to Reduce Pollution Widespread concern for the environment has been growing since the 1960s with the popularization of **ecology,** or the study of the balance of nature. In 1963 federal, state, and local governments began enacting laws and regulations to reduce pollution. (See Component Chapter B for a brief summary of major federal environmental legislation.) In December 1970 the federal government established the Environmental Protection Agency (EPA) to regulate air and water pollution by manufacturers and utilities, supervise the control of automobile pollution, license pesticides, control toxic substances, and safeguard the purity of drinking water. Congress is currently attempting to reform the EPA, because critics contend that the agency's tough restrictions actually prohibit companies from finding the most cost-effective ways to reduce pollution.

Many individual states have also passed their own tough clean air laws. For example, California requires that 10 percent of all new vehicles sold in the state be pollution-free by 2003. In response, both large and small car manufacturers are working to produce electric vehicles. General Motors and Honda have already begun selling their first models.[31]

Progress has also been made in reducing water pollution. Both government and private business have made major expenditures to treat and reuse wastewater, as well as to upgrade sewage systems. Unfortunately, the war on toxic waste has not been quite as successful. Government attempts to force businesses to clean up these sites have yielded many lawsuits and much expense but disappointing results. At some sites, the groundwater may never be restored to drinking-water purity.

Although many companies do a good job of regulating themselves, it is often pressure from the public and the government that causes businesses to clean up their acts. Companies that pollute excessively not only risk being charged with violating federal laws but also risk being sued by private citizens. Of course, such after-the-fact costs are ultimately passed on to consumers. Clearly, society benefits most when companies take it upon themselves to find cost-effective ways of reducing pollution.

3M's decision to discontinue Scotchguard fabric protector is a noteworthy example of company self-regulation. 3M was under no government mandate to stop manufacturing products with perfluorooctane sulfonate (PFOs). Moreover, evidence that PFOs harmed humans did not exist. But when traces of the chemical showed up in humans, 3M decided to pull the plug on the product and not wait until scientific evidence might someday link PFOs to a disease. This decision cost 3M $500 million in annual sales because the company did not have a substitute product to fill Scotchguard's void.[32]

In response to EPA pressure for a cleaner environment, automobile manufacturers are experimenting with several gas alternatives referred to as zero-emission vehicles. DaimlerChrysler recently unveiled one prototype called NECAR 4. Powered by a liquid hydrogen fuel cell, this four-passenger Mercedes A-Class can go 280 miles before refueling and can attain a speed of 90 miles per hour. Future revisions of this prototype will use methane for fuel.

The Business Effort to Reduce Pollution Today's managers are learning from the mistakes of their predecessors and are taking steps to reduce and prevent pollution. Some use high-temperature incineration to destroy hazardous wastes, some recycle wastes, some give their wastes to other companies that can use them, some neutralize wastes biologically, and some have redesigned their manufacturing processes so that they don't produce the wastes in the first place. In Kahlundborg, Denmark, some companies practice what they call *industrial symbiosis*, which means that they work together in a mutually advantageous relationship. Manufacturers as diverse as a pharmaceutical company, an oil refinery, a farm, a building materials company, and a power plant are linked via pipes and ground transportation systems so that each can use the waste products from the others as fuel and raw materials for themselves. The idea started among the managers of the companies as a way to lower costs and boost profits. But the reduction of waste and pollution has been so substantial that the EPA has taken notice. It is now supporting the development of similar ecoindustrial parks in the United States.[33]

Another innovative approach to reducing pollution is based on free-market principles. In certain cities, companies can buy and sell pollution rights. Each company is given an allowable "pollution quota" based on such factors as its size and industry. If a company voluntarily reduces pollution below its limit, it can sell its "credits" to another company. This system provides an incentive for companies to find efficient ways of reducing pollution. Evidence so far suggests that the plan is effective in reducing overall levels of pollutants such as sulfur dioxide.[34]

Companies are also reducing the amount of solid waste they send to landfills by implementing companywide recycling programs. The EPA reports that over 20 percent of the solid waste generated in the United States is now recycled.[35] In addition, hundreds of thousands of tons of waste have been eliminated through conservation and more efficient production.[36]

LEARNING OBJECTIVE 6

Highlight at least five actions that some businesses are taking to address environmental problems

Many businesses such as Patagonia are recognizing the link between environmental performance and financial well-being and are addressing environmental problems by:[37]

■ Considering them a part of everyday business and operating decisions

■ Accepting environmental staff members as full-fledged partners in improving the company's competitiveness

■ Measuring environmental performance

■ Tying compensation to environmental performance

■ Determining the long-term environmental costs *before* such costs occur

■ Considering environmental impact in the product-development process

■ Challenging suppliers to improve environmental performance

■ Conducting training and awareness programs

More and more companies are discovering that spending now to prevent pollution can end up saving more money down the road (by reducing cleanup costs, litigation expense, and production costs). From building ecoindustrial parks to improving production efficiency, these activities are a part of the *green marketing* movement, in which companies distinguish themselves by using less packaging materials, recycling more waste, and developing new products that are easier on the environment.

Responsibility Toward Consumers

consumerism
Movement that pressures businesses to consider consumer needs and interests

The 1960s activism that awakened business to its environmental responsibilities also gave rise to **consumerism,** a movement that put pressure on businesses to consider consumer needs and interests. Consumerism prompted many businesses to create consumer-affairs departments to handle customer complaints. It also prompted state and local agencies to set up bureaus to offer consumer information and assistance. At the federal level, President John F. Kennedy announced a "bill of rights" for consumers, laying the foundation for a wave of consumer-oriented legislation. (See Component Chapter B for a list of major federal consumer legislation.) These rights include the right to safety, the right to be informed, the right to choose, and the right to be heard.

LEARNING OBJECTIVE 7

Discuss the four rights of consumers

The Right to Safe Products In the 1970s, household clothes irons could overheat into a melted mess, mower blades could continue turning even after users let go of the machine, over-the-counter drugs didn't come in childproof containers, and cars had so many problems that consumers expected to have trouble with them. Of course, today's irons turn off automatically, mowers shut off when the operator lets go, childproof caps are commonplace, and car quality has risen sharply.[38]

The U.S. government imposes many safety standards that are enforced by the Consumer Product Safety Commission (CPSC), as well as by other federal and state agencies. Theoretically, companies that don't comply with these rules are forced to take corrective action. Moreover, the threat of product-liability suits and declining sales motivates many companies to meet safety

Best of the Web Best of the Web Best of

GO FOR THE GREEN

Maybe you want to lead more of a green lifestyle, but you're not sure where to begin. The Web site of the Sustainable Business Network (SBN) is a good starting point. This site has valuable information on environmental business issues ranging from recycling and renewable energy to organic products, social investing, and certified forestry. You can also access databases of information on environmentally conscious companies, locate green business opportunities, and find jobs that let you put your business skills to work to help the environment. Then follow the link to the EnviroLink Network to learn even more about the latest environmental issues.

sbn.envirolink.org/

standards. After all, a poor safety record can damage a company's reputation. But with or without government action, many consumer advocates complain that some unsafe products still slip through the cracks.

Consider Firestone tires, for example. Critics claim that Ford and Firestone didn't act fast enough once they suspected problems with Firestone Wilderness AT and ATX tires (see "Firestone and Ford: Failure to Yield . . . or Asleep at the Wheel?"). Not only did Ford and Firestone handle the recall of 6.5 million tires poorly, but they waited much too long before they removed the defective tires from the marketplace.[39]

The Right to Be Informed Consumers have a right to know what is in a product and how to use it. They also have a right to know the sales price of goods or services and the details of any purchase contracts. The Food and Drug Administration, the Federal Trade Commission, and the Agriculture Department are the federal agencies responsible for regulating product labels to make sure no false claims are made. These agencies are concerned not only with safety but also with accurate information. Research shows that nearly three-quarters of shoppers read labels when deciding whether to buy a food product the first time, so labels are an important element in informing consumers.[40]

If a product is sufficiently dangerous, a warning label is required by law, as in the case of cigarettes. However, warning labels can be a mixed blessing for consumers. To some extent, the presence of a warning protects the manufacturer from product-liability suits, but the label may not deter people from using the product or from using it incorrectly. The billions of dollars a year still spent on cigarettes in the United States illustrate this point. Moreover, as the world economy becomes more and more service-oriented, consumers are buying items that don't necessarily carry a label. Therefore, consumers must take it upon themselves to ensure that they are getting what they pay for.

The Right to Choose Which Products to Buy Especially in the United States, the number of products available to consumers is truly amazing. But how far should the right to choose extend? Are we entitled to choose products that are potentially harmful, such as cigarettes, liquor, or guns? To what extent are we entitled to learn about these products? Should beer and wine ads be eliminated from television, just as ads for other types of alcoholic beverages have been? Should advertising aimed at children be banned altogether?

Consumer groups are concerned about these questions, but no clear answers have emerged. In general, however, business is sensitive to these issues. Recent public concern about drunk driving, for example, has led the liquor industry to encourage responsible drinking. Coors now runs advertisements designed to discourage underage drinking and drinking on the job.[41] Similarly, several major broadcast television networks have implemented a rating system

By the time Bridgestone/Firestone finally admitted that it made "bad tires," the company had been aware of peeling tire tread problems for at least three years. Most of the recalled tires were 15-inch Wilderness AT and ATX tires that were sold with Ford Explorer vehicles.

Best of the Web Best of the Web Best of

SURF SAFELY

Although the majority of telemarketing and online businesses are legitimate, unethical businesses bilk consumers out of billions of dollars every year. Fortunately, the National Fraud Information Center (NFIC) can help consumers fight back. The center was established by the National Consumers League (NCL) to safeguard consumers against telemarketing and Internet fraud. Resources on the center's Web site include reports about current online and telephone scams, tips for online safety, advice on how to file a fraud report, statistics about telemarketing fraud, and special advice for seniors, who are targeted by con artists. Even if you consider yourself a savvy consumer, the site contains a lot of valuable information to help you avoid being ripped off.
www.fraud.org/

THINKING ABOUT ETHICS

FIRESTONE AND FORD: FAILURE TO YIELD . . . OR ASLEEP AT THE WHEEL?

For nearly a decade, lawsuits claimed that treads on tires manufactured by Bridgestone/Firestone were peeling off without warning, causing Ford Explorers to flip over. Mounting consumer complaints and damaging media reports led to a federal investigation in 2000, putting pressure on Firestone to recall 6.5 million defective tires. But the public soon learned that trouble had started long before the massive tire recall.

As early as 1998, Ford Motor Company received reports of Firestone tire tread separations on Ford Explorers in countries with hot climates, such as Saudi Arabia and Venezuela. Ford took the complaints to Firestone because it didn't have enough information to investigate the problem itself. (Tires are the only significant part of the car that is guaranteed by the tire supplier, not the automaker.) Firestone reassured Ford that the tire problems resulted from a combination of variables: hot climate, fast drivers, and improper tire care by consumers. Meanwhile, Ford was getting an early warning about tire safety problems from its own warranty data. Still, Firestone refused to recall the tires.

Convinced that its tire supplier was not owning up to problems, Ford stepped in and unilaterally replaced Firestone tires on nearly 50,000 vehicles in 16 foreign countries. Problem is, neither Ford nor Firestone bothered to inform U.S. authorities about the overseas tire recall. Soon similiar tire failures began to occur in the United States at unusually high rates, and Ford initiated its own investigation in early 2000. About that same time, the federal government entered the scene.

Meanwhile, simmering tensions between the longtime partners burst into open hostilities as Ford and Firestone engaged in bitter finger-pointing over who was responsible for the tire problems and why they didn't come to light sooner. Convinced that tread separations were related to inadequate tire pressures, Firestone claimed Ford had ignored the tire maker's warnings to boost the recommended tire pressure for Explorers. But Ford pinned the blame on Firestone, claiming the company stalled in analyzing and sharing its warranty-claims data. Firestone executives, in turn, argued that Explorers had been involved in 16,000 rollover accidents within the past decade—but fewer than 10 percent had involved tread separation of Firestone tires.

In spite of over 100 deaths from accidents involving Explorers with Firestone radials, Firestone and Ford admitted they didn't realize the extent of the lethal tire problems until just before the recall. But one U.S. congressman claimed both companies had been asleep at the wheel. "What does it take to put a company . . . on notice that perhaps they've got a defective product out there?" the congressman challenged. "You've got a lawsuit, you've got people killed . . . Doesn't that tell you that something is probably wrong with your product?"

■ QUESTIONS FOR CRITICAL THINKING

1. Why did Bridgestone/Firestone wait so long to recall the defective tires?

2. What lesson(s) can other companies learn from the Ford/Firestone debacle?

to help the public gauge whether a show is appropriate for a young audience. Most U.S. businesspeople prefer to help consumers make informed choices—rather than be told what choices to offer.

Still, some consumer groups say that government does not do enough. For example, when a product has been proven to be dangerous, does the fact that it is legal justify its sale? Should the government take measures to make the product illegal, or should consumers be allowed to decide for themselves what they buy? Consider cigarettes, for example. Scientists determined long ago that the tar and nicotine in tobacco are both harmful and addictive. In 1965 the Federal Cigarette Labeling and Advertising Act was passed, requiring all cigarette packs to carry the now-famous Surgeon General's warnings. Over the years, tobacco companies have spent billions of dollars to defend themselves in lawsuits brought by smokers suffering from cancer and respiratory diseases. As recently as 1996, the Liggett Group (a major U.S. tobacco company) admitted publicly that cigarettes cause cancer, are addictive, and have been promoted to encourage smoking among minors. And in 1997 the tobacco industry agreed to pay $368.5 billion over 25 years and an additional $15 billion per year after that to settle lawsuits brought by smoking victims and 40 state governments. Even so, consumers can still purchase cigarettes in the marketplace. RJR Nabisco chairman Steve Goldstone reminds us that "behind all the allegations . . . is the simple truth that we sell a legal product."[42]

The Right to Be Heard Many companies have established toll-free numbers for consumer information and feedback, and these numbers are often printed on product packages. In addition, more and more companies are establishing Web sites that provide product information and access for customer feedback. Of course, businesses benefit from gathering as much information about their customers as possible. Customer information allows companies to make informed decisions about changing current products and offering new ones. However, as this chapter's "Focusing on E-Business Today" highlights, the pursuit of information and the growth of e-commerce have given rise to a new ethical concern—maintaining customer privacy.

Recent media blitzes by antismoking organizations have appeared in magazines, on billboards, and in television commercials. The hope is that ads such as this one will elevate consumer awareness about the health problems cigarette smoking causes.

The right to be heard also covers a broad range of complaints about discrimination against customers. More than 4,000 African American customers complained to the U.S. Justice Department about racial discrimination by some Denny's restaurants. Among their complaints: They were asked to pay for meals in advance (although other customers weren't asked to do so), and they received slower service than other customers did. Flagstar, the chain's owner, responded by making a public apology and paying $46 million to settle the claims. In addition, the number of African American–owned Denny's franchises has risen from 1 to 27 in three years, and 12 percent of the company's supplies are now purchased from minority-owned vendors.[43]

Responsibility Toward Investors

In addition to their other responsibilities, businesses are responsible to those who have invested in the company. Historically, investors have been primarily interested in a company's financial performance. Clearly, a business can fail its investors by depriving them of their fair share of the profits. But a business can also fail its shareholders by being too concerned about profits. Today a growing number of investors are concerned about the ethics and social responsibility of the companies in which they invest. One study found that 26 percent of investors consider social responsibility to be extremely important.[44]

The job of looking out for a company's investors falls to its board of directors. Lately, more investors are turning up the heat on the individuals who sit on those boards (as discussed in Chapter 5). Concerned investors are targeting board members who fail to attend meetings, who sit on the boards of too many companies, who are underinvested (own very little stock in the companies they direct), and who sit on boards of companies with which their own firms do business. Looking out for investors is no easy task, but investors are finding that holding individual directors more accountable improves overall performance.[45] Of course, any action that cheats the investors out of their rightful profits is unethical.

Misrepresenting the Investment Every year tens of thousands of people are the victims of investment scams. Lured by promises of high returns, people sink more than a billion dollars per year into nonexistent oil wells, gold mines, and other fraudulent operations touted by complete strangers over the telephone and the Internet. Shady companies use other types of scams to take people's money, too. For example, con artists can dupe unwary investors by offering shares in start-up companies that don't exist. Investors should be especially careful of opportunities advertised over the Internet because it's so difficult for regulators to control online scams.[46] Other ways of misrepresenting the potential of an investment fall within the law. For example, with a little "creative accounting," a business that is in financial trouble can be made to look reasonably good to all but the most astute investors. Companies have some latitude in their reports to shareholders, and some firms are more conscientious than others in representing their financial performance.

Diverting Earnings or Assets Business executives may also take advantage of the investor by using the company's earnings or resources for personal gain. Managers have many opportunities to indirectly take money that rightfully belongs to the shareholders. Perhaps the most common approach is to cheat on expense accounts. Padding invoices and then splitting the overcharge with the supplier is another common ploy. Other tactics include selling company secrets to competitors or using confidential, nonpublic information gained from one's position in a company to benefit from the purchase and sale of stocks. Such **insider trading** is illegal and is closely watched by the Securities and Exchange Commission (SEC).

insider trading
The attempt to benefit from stock market fluctuations by using unpublicized information gained on the job

Overdoing the Quest for Profits Even though few companies knowingly break laws in an attempt to gain a competitive advantage, companies have taken questionable steps in their zeal to maximize profits. In order to protect earnings, some companies have used questionable methods to get bankrupt customers to sign repayment agreements. And to get ahead of the competition, some companies have engaged in corporate spying. Although businesses need to gather as much strategic information as they can, ethical companies steer clear of stealing patents, searching rivals' trash bins for sensitive information, accessing telephone records, hiring employees from competitors to gain trade secrets, and electronically eavesdropping.

Responsibility Toward Employees

Patagonia's Yvon Chouinard has always emphasized employee relationships that are ethical and supportive. For some companies, the past 30 years have brought dramatic changes in the attitudes and composition of the workforce. These changes have forced businesses to modify their recruiting, training, and promotion practices, as well as their overall corporate values and behaviors. (Consult Chapter 10 for an in-depth discussion of the staffing and demographic challenges employers are facing in today's workplace.)

The Push for Equality in Employment The United States has always stood for economic freedom and the individual's right to pursue opportunity. Unfortunately, until the past few decades many people were targets of economic **discrimination,** relegated to low-paying, menial jobs and prevented from taking advantage of many opportunities solely on the basis of their race, gender, disability, or religion.

discrimination
In a social and economic sense, denial of opportunities to individuals on the basis of some characteristic that has no bearing on their ability to perform in a job

The Civil Rights Act of 1964 established the Equal Employment Opportunity Commission (EEOC)—the regulatory agency that battles job discrimination. The EEOC is responsible for monitoring the hiring practices of companies and for investigating complaints of job-related discrimination. It has the power to file legal charges against companies that discriminate and to force them to compensate individuals or groups who have been victimized by unfair practices. The Civil Rights Act of 1991 extended the original act by allowing workers to sue companies for discrimination and by granting women powerful legal tools against job bias.

affirmative action
Activities undertaken by businesses to recruit and promote women and minorities, based on an analysis of the workforce and the available labor pool

Affirmative Action In the 1960s, **affirmative action** programs were developed to encourage organizations to recruit and promote members of minority groups. Proponents of the programs believe that minorities deserve and require preferential treatment to boost opportunities and to make up for years of discrimination. Opponents of affirmative action believe that creating special opportunities for women and minorities creates a double standard that infringes on the rights of other workers and forces companies to hire, promote, and retain people who are not necessarily the best choice from a business standpoint. Regardless, any company that does business with the federal government must have an affirmative action program.

Still, studies show that affirmative action has not been entirely successful. For one thing, efforts to hire more minorities do not necessarily change negative attitudes about differences among individuals. To combat this problem, about 75 percent of U.S. companies have established **diversity initiatives.** These initiatives often involve increasing minority employment and promotion, contracting with more minority vendors, including more minorities on boards of directors, and targeting a more diverse customer base. In addition, diversity initiatives use diversity training to promote understanding of the unique cultures, customs, and talents of all employees.

diversity initiatives
Company policies designed to enhance opportunities for minorities and to promote understanding of diverse cultures, customs, and talents

What killed men and women on the job last year; fatal injuries caused by:

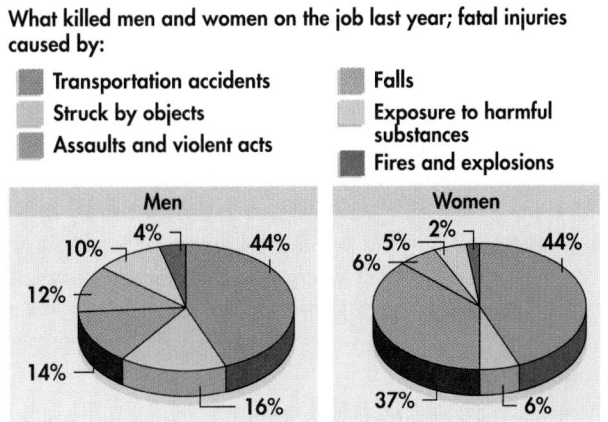

EXHIBIT 2.6

Transportation accidents are the leading workplace killer.

People with Disabilities In 1990 people with a wide range of physical and mental difficulties got a boost from the passage of the federal Americans with Disabilities Act (ADA), which guarantees equal opportunities for an estimated 50 million to 75 million people who have or have had a condition that might handicap them. As defined by the 1990 law, *disability* is a broad term that protects not only those with obvious physical handicaps but also those with less-visible conditions, such as cancer, heart disease, diabetes, epilepsy, AIDS, drug addiction, alcoholism, and emotional illness. In most situations, employers cannot legally require job applicants to pass a physical examination as a condition of employment. The law also forbids firing people who have serious drinking or drug problems unless their chemical dependency prevents them from performing their essential job functions.

Businesses serving the public are required to make their services and facilities accessible to people with disabilities. This requirement means that restaurants, hotels, stores, airports, buses, taxis, banks, sports stadiums, and so forth must try to accommodate people who have disabilities. A hotel, for example, must equip 5 percent of its rooms with flashing lights or other "visual alarms" for people with hearing impairments.[47]

Occupational Safety and Health Each day 17 workers lose their lives on the job while another 24,000 are injured in the workplace (see Exhibit 2.6).[48] During the activist 1960s, mounting concern about workplace hazards resulted in passage of the Occupational Safety and Health Act of 1970, which set mandatory standards for safety and health and which established the Occupational Safety and Health Administration (OSHA) to enforce them.

OSHA's new ergonomic safety regulations, for example, will protect millions of workers from *ergonomic* or repetitive stress injuries such as carpal tunnel syndrome (from repetitive keyboarding) and back injuries (from repetitive lifting). The rules will grant workers up to 90 days of employer-paid sick leave for people injured on the job as a result of repetitive actions. Studies show that about 1.8 million U.S. workers each year suffer musculoskeletal injuries at work from performing repetitive actions, and that about one-third of the cases are serious enough to require time off. Nonetheless, the rules have generated a firestorm of protests from businesses who view them as vague, confusing, onerous, and very expensive.[49]

Concerns for employee safety have also been raised by the international expansion of businesses. Many U.S. companies subcontract production to companies in foreign countries, making it more difficult to maintain proper standards of safety and compensation. For example, when a local labor advocacy group inspected a Nike factory in Vietnam, members discovered violations of minimum wage and overtime laws, as well as physical abuse of workers. Nike has been criticized in recent years for similar conditions in its other Southeast Asian and Chinese factories. Many other companies, including the Gap, Guess, and the Body Shop have come under similar criticism. In 1997 a presidential task force composed of apparel industry representatives, labor unions, and human rights groups drafted a code of conduct to uphold the rights of foreign workers of U.S. manufacturing companies. Among the provisions of the code are minimum wage requirements and limits on the number of hours employees work in a week.[50]

ETHICS AND SOCIAL RESPONSIBILITY AROUND THE WORLD

As complicated as ethics and social responsibility can be for U.S. businesses, these issues grow even more complex when cultural influences are applied in the global business environment. There, corporate executives may face simple questions regarding the appropriate amount of money to spend on a business gift or the legitimacy of payment to "expedite" business. Or they may encounter out-and-out bribery, environmental abuse, and unscrupulous business practices. What does it mean for a business to do the right thing in Thailand? In Africa? In Norway? What may be considered unethical in the United States may be an accepted practice in another culture. Several areas of corruption are being addressed by international agreements: bribes, air pollution, and corporate behavior.

- *Bribes.* In the United States, bribing officials is illegal, but Kenyans consider paying such bribes a part of life. To get something done right, they pay *kitu kidogo* (or "something small"). In China businesses pay *huilu*. In Russia they pay *vzyatka*, in the Middle East it's *baksheesh*, and in Mexico it's *una mordida* ("a small bite"). The United States has lobbied other nations for 20 years to outlaw bribery, and at last the industrialized nations have signed a treaty that makes payoffs to foreign officials a criminal offense. The ban on bribes came after a string of high-level scandals around the world: Two South Korean presidents went to prison for accepting bribes. French cabinet ministers and mayors resigned during an investigation of kickbacks. The late dictator of Zaire (now Congo) actually merged his family's finances with those of the state. Moreover, corruption is such an obstacle in the Ukraine and Russia that some U.S. companies quit trying to do business there. Of course, bribery won't end just because a treaty has been signed, but supporters are optimistic that countries will ratify the treaty, pass legislation, and enforce the new laws stringently.[51]

- *Air pollution.* In a similar pact, 150 nations recently signed an agreement in Kyoto, Japan, to reduce worldwide emissions of carbon dioxide and other pollutants thought to be contributing to global warming. To comply with the agreement, countries around the world will be turning to energy from renewable sources, such as sun and wind—good news for companies like Houston-based Enron, which markets natural gas and oversees solar and wind projects.[52] The European Union (EU) had proposed a huge 15 percent cut in three of the best-known greenhouse gases by the year 2015, but the Kyoto compromise requires an 8 percent cut in six gases. Will Europe stand by its original offer? Europe would need to drop carbon dioxide emissions by 800 million tons at a cost of $15 billion to $21 billion.[53]

- *Corporate behavior.* Espionage is another issue on the U.S. agenda for global ethics. FBI Director Louis Freeh recently testified that U.S. companies are under economic attack from 23 countries trying to steal trade secrets and other intellectual property in the most severe threat to national security since the Cold War.[54] For instance, when Disney released its animated film *Mulan* in Hong Kong, the city's shopping arcades had already been selling the illegal video compact disc (VCD) for a week—complete with Chinese subtitles. Asian pirates are active not only in Hollywood but also in Silicon Valley and in the music business. In the Philippines, according to the Software Publishers Association, 83 percent of business software is pirated; even government offices openly use illegally copied programs. Laws against such piracy exist, but enforcing them is as difficult for Asian countries as it was for the United States to enforce Prohibition in the 1920s. As soon as one operation is shut down, another pops up in its place.[55] Meanwhile, the Organization for Economic Cooperation and Development (OECD) has drawn up a 22-page world standard for "good corporate behavior." The OECD's 29 members include most of the world's richest countries, and they hope world agencies will get nonmembers to adopt the standards and put them into law.[56]

As you can see, the issue of global business ethics is the ultimate dilemma for many U.S. businesses. As companies do more and more business around the globe, their assumptions about ethical codes of conduct are indeed put to the test.

FOCUSING ON E-BUSINESS TODAY

Who Will Win the Great E-Commerce Privacy Debate?

Most people have long accepted the need to provide some information about themselves in order to vote, work, shop, or even borrow a library book. But as they go from site to site, few Web surfers realize they're being tracked by companies they've never heard of.

CYBERSPIES

In the background, companies are building ever-expanding profiles of where people browse, what they buy, how they think, and who they are. They're stockpiling this information to send surfers targeted advertising or to sell or trade it with other sites. The trackers are a growing breed of online advertising companies such as DoubleClick. Using the banner ads that appear across the tops of Web pages, the ad companies drop tiny ID tags on users' hard drives (called cookies). Even if a surfer doesn't click on a single ad, these cookies allow ad companies to compile detailed profiles as they follow surfers through the thousands of linked Web sites that each ad company services.

PUBLIC OUTCRY

Although cookies alone can't divulge your name or address, they can reveal how long you stay at a page and which products you like. Moreover, recent advances in computing and in data-analysis techniques now make it possible to link a surfer's name to anonymous information collected online. DoubleClick planned to link its anonymous online profiles to the real-world databases it acquired when it purchased Abacus Direct in 1999. Abacus's databases contain information on millions of consumers that was gathered by major direct-mail catalog marketers. But public outcry forced DoubleClick to drop its controversial plan—which set off heated debates between privacy advocates and companies collecting such online information.

A RISING TIDE OF CONCERN

Under current U.S. law, everything a Web company knows about you can be sold to the highest bidder. Only voluntary privacy policies designed to put customers at ease keep companies from doing so. But advocates of privacy laws point out that so far self-regulation has failed. A recent Federal Trade Commission survey of 1,400 U.S. Internet sites found that only 2 percent posted a privacy policy in line with that advocated by the commission.

Pressure for privacy laws is also mounting from Europe, where privacy is recognized as a right. European companies must clearly spell out what they intend to do with the information they solicit from people, and

Europeans have the right to find out what companies know about them. Such privacy policies create all sorts of problems for U.S. companies conducting global e-commerce, forcing many of them to extend greater privacy protections in Germany or France than they do at home. E-commerce giants Amazon.com and eBay have set up separate Web sites in some European countries so that they can keep customer data from the two continents separate.

Meanwhile, responding to a growing chorus of privacy-related complaints, many states have drafted legislation curtailing the sale of personal information. But this piecemeal approach creates even more confusion in a global economy. So privacy advocates want the U.S. government to get involved.

BUSINESS WEEK'S FOUR-POINT PLAN

LEARNING OBJECTIVE

Discuss four governing principles proposed by *Business Week* to address privacy concerns of individuals conducting e-commerce

A recent Business Week/Harris poll reports that 57 percent of consumers want the U.S. government to pass laws on how personal information is collected. One proposal outlined by *Business Week* includes these four governing principles:

1. *Display your practices.* Companies conducting business online should be required by law to disclose clearly how they collect and use information. Privacy policies should be mandatory, easy to find, and written in plain English. Companies should clearly state why they are collecting information and collect no more data than they need for that purpose.

2. *Give people a choice.* Upon site registration it is often unclear whether you need to *"opt out"* to stop the site from sharing information with others or to *"opt in"* by granting the site your permission to pass information on to another site. Because opting in is a stricter measure, it should only be used to ask surfers permission to collect data if the company wants to resell personal data or share it with advertising networks. In all other situations, users should be given the option to opt out.

3. *Show me the data.* Web surfers should have the right to inspect the data collected on them and to correct any errors they discover. This principle is also known as "subject access" rights.

4. *Play fair or pay.* The U.S. government must have the power to impose penalties on those companies that break the rules. An agency, such as the FTC, should enforce and interpret the law according to the Fair Information Practices.

**How should government approach
Internet privacy issues?**

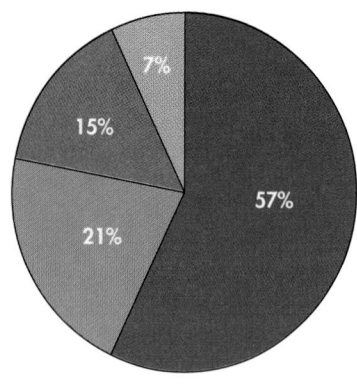

■ Pass laws regulating how personal
information can be collected and used

■ Recommend Internet privacy standards
but not pass laws currently

■ Let groups develop voluntary privacy
standards; take action only if necessary

■ Don't know, or none of the above

TARGETED ADS: CONSUMER TRAP OR NET NECESSITY?

Of course, most companies disagree with these proposals. They say that collecting customer data allows them to target ads to consumers who are most likely interested in the products, thus slashing wasteful marketing costs. Such profiling, they say, provides the foundation of the new Internet economy, and laws that require businesses to seek users' permission before collecting or using data about Web-surfing habits could weaken this foundation. Without profiles, advertising revenues might suffer, and the millions of dollars' worth of free content that Web users take for granted would be impossible. Moreover, bringing in the feds could mine the Net in bureaucratic layers that would undercut the very promise of efficiency that many online business are counting on. The Internet, they say, is supposed to draw companies closer to customers, allowing them to anticipate their desires.

Privacy advocates, on the other hand, don't think companies should take personal information when consumers aren't looking. They say that consumers should have more control over what is collected about them and how it can be used. Privacy advocates also worry that online profiles that attach real-world identities to surfers could be easily abused. If "subject access" becomes law, privacy advocates predict that U.S. Web users will be stunned by how much data large corporations have on them. Moreover, there is no guarantee that consumers won't willingly hand over some personal data—especially if motivated by financial incentives. And, if more consumers can be assured that their personal information is safe, more of them will flock to the Net.

Who will win the great e-commerce privacy debate? Stay tuned, the outcome of this issue will have a tremendous impact on the future of e-commerce.[57] (For additional coverage of Internet privacy and safety topics, consult Part 1 of this text's online supplement, E-Business in Action, at www.prenhall.com/mescon.)

SUMMARY OF LEARNING OBJECTIVES

1. **Explain the difference between an ethical dilemma and an ethical lapse.**
   An ethical dilemma is an issue with two conflicting but arguably valid sides. An ethical lapse occurs when an individual makes a decision that is illegal, immoral, or unethical.

2. **List four questions you might ask yourself when trying to make an ethical decision.**
   When making ethical decisions ask yourself: (1) Is the decision legal? (Does it break any law?), (2) Is it balanced? (Is it fair to all concerned?), (3) Can you live with it? (Does it make you feel good about yourself?), (4) Is it feasible? (Will it work in the real world?).

3. **Identify three steps that businesses are taking to encourage ethical behavior.**
   Businesses are adopting codes of ethics, appointing ethics officers, and establishing ethics hot lines to encourage whistle-blowing.

4. **Discuss three activities in which socially responsible companies might engage.**
   Companies can conduct social audits to assess whether their performance is socially responsible, engage in cause-related marketing by using a portion of product sales to help support worthy causes, and engage in philanthropy by donating their money, time, goods, or services to charitable, humanitarian, or educational institutions.

5. **Name three kinds of pollution and outline activities to control them.**
   Air, water, and land pollution are all significant problems. In 1970 the government set up the Environmental Protection Agency to regulate the disposal of hazardous wastes and to clean up polluted areas. Many individual states have also passed their own tough clean air laws. Companies are also taking steps to reduce and prevent pollution by practicing industrial symbiosis, recycling waste materials, and safely disposing of hazardous wastes.

6. **Highlight at least five actions that some businesses are taking to address environmental problems.**

The eight actions discussed are (1) making environmental problems part of everyday decisions, (2) making environmental staff members full-fledged partners in improving competitiveness, (3) measuring environmental performance, (4) tying compensation to environmental performance, (5) determining environmental costs *before* they occur, (6) considering the environmental impact of the product-development process, (7) helping suppliers improve their environmental performance, and (8) conducting training and awareness programs.

7. **Discuss the four rights of consumers.**

Consumers have the right to safe products; the right to be informed—which includes the right to know a product's contents, use, price, and dangers; the right to choose which products to buy; and the right to be heard, such as the right to voice a complaint or concern.

8. @ **Discuss four governing principles proposed by *Business Week* to address privacy concerns of individuals conducting e-commerce.**

The four governing principles of the proposal are (1) Companies should clearly disclose how they collect and use information; (2) companies should ask Web surfers to "opt in" if they want to resell personal data or share it with advertising networks and give consumers the right to "opt out" in all other privacy situations; (3) Web surfers should have the right to inspect data collected on them and correct erroneous data; and (4) the U.S. government should have the right to impose penalties on companies that break the privacy rules.

KEY TERMS

affirmative action (58)

code of ethics (46)

consumerism (54)

discrimination (58)

diversity initiatives (58)

ecology (52)

ethical dilemma (44)

ethical lapse (44)

ethics (44)

insider trading (58)

philanthropic (50)

pollution (52)

social audit (50)

social responsibility (48)

stakeholders (44)

TEST YOUR KNOWLEDGE

QUESTIONS FOR REVIEW

1. Who shapes a company's ethics?

2. How do companies support ethical behavior?

3. How has business's sense of social responsibility evolved since the turn of the century?

4. How are businesses responding to the environmental issues facing society?

5. What can a company do to assure customers that its products are safe?

QUESTIONS FOR ANALYSIS

6. Why can't legal considerations resolve every ethical question?

7. How do individuals employ philosophical principles in making ethical business decisions?

8. Why does a company need more than a code of ethics to be ethical?

9. Explain how Ben & Jerry's managed to balance its social responsibility efforts with its need to make profits.

10. If you discovered that a company initiated ethics programs only to avoid prosecution under the Federal Sentencing Guidelines of 1991, would you conclude that its actions were unethical because its motives were self-serving? Would you consider the company's actions manipulative or misleading? Explain your answer.

11. @ Why are business scams more prevalent in the Internet Age?

QUESTIONS FOR APPLICATION

12. You sell musical gifts on the Web and in quarterly catalogs. Your two-person partnership has quickly grown into a 27-person company, and you spend all your time on quality matters. You're losing control of important environmental choices about materials suppliers, product packaging, and even the paper used in your catalogs. What steps can you take to be sure your employees continue making choices that protect the environment?

13. At quitting time, you see your new colleague filling a briefcase with expensive software programs that aren't supposed to leave the premises. What do you do? Explain your answer.

14. In Chapter 1 we identified knowledge workers as the key economic resource of the twenty-first century. If an employee leaves a company to work for a competitor, what types of knowledge would be ethical for the employee to share with the new employer and what types of knowledge would be unethical to share?

15. Is it ethical for state and city governments to entice businesses to relocate their operations to that state or city by offering them special tax breaks that are not extended to other businesses operating in that area?

PRACTICE YOUR KNOWLEDGE

SHARPENING YOUR COMMUNICATION SKILLS

In one page or less, explain why you think each of the following is or is not ethical.

- De-emphasizing negative test results in a report on your product idea

- Taking a computer home to finish a work-related assignment

- Telling associates who are close friends that they had better pay more attention to their work responsibilities or management will fire them

- Recommending the purchase of excess equipment to use up your allocated funds before the end of the year so that your budget won't be cut next year

HANDLING DIFFICULT SITUATIONS ON THE JOB: TRUTH AND CONSEQUENCES

Choosing to blow the whistle on your employees or co-workers can create all kinds of legal, ethical, and career complications. Here are five common workplace scenarios that might cause you to search your soul about whether or not to go public with potentially damaging charges. Read them carefully and decide what you would do in each situation.[58]

1. You believe your company is overcharging or otherwise defrauding a customer or client.

2. With all of the headlines generated by sexual harassment cases lately, you'd think employees wouldn't dare break the law. But it's happening right under your company's nose.

3. You discover that your company, or one of its divisions, products, or processes, presents a physical danger to workers or to the public.

4. An employee is padding overtime statements, taking home some of the company's inventory, or stealing equipment.

5. You smell alcohol on a co-worker's breath and notice that individual's work hasn't been up to standard lately.

BUILDING YOUR TEAM SKILLS

All organizations, not just corporations, can benefit from having a code of ethics to guide decision making. But who should a code of ethics protect, and what should it cover? In this exercise, you and your team are going to draft a code of ethics for your school.

Start by brainstorming about who will be protected by this code of ethics. What stakeholders should the school consider when making decisions? What negative effects might decisions have on these stakeholders?

Then think about the kinds of situations you want your school's code of ethics to cover. One example might be employment decisions; another might be disclosure of confidential student information.

Next, using Exhibit 2.2 as a model, draft your school's code of ethics. Write a general introduction explaining the purpose of the code and who is being protected. Next, write a positive statement to guide ethical decisions in each situation you identified earlier in this exercise. Your statement about promotion decisions, for example, might read: "School officials will encourage equal access to job promotions for all qualified candidates, with every applicant receiving fair consideration."

Compare your code of ethics with the codes drafted by other teams. Did all the teams' codes seek to protect the same stakeholders? What differences and similarities do you see in the statements guiding ethical decisions?

EXPAND YOUR KNOWLEDGE

KEEPING CURRENT USING *THE WALL STREET JOURNAL*

Articles on corporate ethics and social responsibility regularly appear in *The Wall Street Journal* (print or online editions). Look in recent issues (or search the online edition at www. wsj.com, go to the "Select a Page" drop-down menu in the upper left-hand corner of the screen and select "Search"). Find one or more articles discussing one of the following ethics or social responsibility challenges faced by a business:

- Environmental issues, such as pollution, acid rain, and hazardous-waste disposal

- Employee or consumer safety measures

- Consumer information or education

- Employment discrimination or diversity initiatives

- Investment ethics

- Industrial spying and theft of trade secrets

- Fraud, bribery, and overcharging

- Company codes of ethics

1. What was the nature of the ethical challenge or social responsibility issue presented in the article? Does the article report any wrongdoing by a company or agency official? Was the action illegal, unethical, or questionable? What course of action would you recommend the company or agency take to correct or improve matters now?

2. What stakeholder group(s) are affected? What lasting effects will be felt by (a) the company and (b) these stakeholder group(s)?

3. Writing a letter to the editor is one way consumers can speak their mind. Review some of the Letters to the Editor in past issues of the *Wall Street Journal* (in the interactive edition, click on Editorial Page, and then on Letters). Why are letters to the editor an important feature of a newspaper or journal?

DISCOVERING CAREER OPPORTUNITIES

Businesses, government agencies, and not-for-profit organizations offer numerous career opportunities related to ethics and social responsibility. How can you learn more about these careers?

1. Search through Component Chapter D to identify jobs related to ethics and social responsibility. One example is Occupational Health and Safety Manager, a job concerned with a company's responsibility toward its employees. What are the duties and qualifications of the jobs you have identified? Are the salaries and future outlooks attractive for all of these jobs?

2. Select one job for further consideration. Following the suggestions in Component Chapter D, what sources of employment information might provide more details about this job? Which of these sources are available in your school or public library? What additional sources can you consult for more information about the daily activities of this job and for ideas about locating potential employers?

3. What skills, educational background, and work experience do you think employers are seeking in applicants for the specific job you are researching? What key words do you think employers would search for when scanning electronic résumés submitted for this position?

EXPLORING THE BEST OF THE WEB

URLs for all Internet exercises are provided at the Web site for this book, www.prenhall.com/mescon. *When you log on to the text Web site, select Chapter 2, then select "Student Resources," click on the name of the featured Web site, and follow the detailed navigational directions to complete these exercises.*

Build a Better Business, page 48

The Better Business Bureau Web site has a lot of useful information for businesses and consumers alike. Log on and learn.

1. What are "BBB Reliability Reports"? What does it mean when the BBB does not have a report on a particular company? How are these reports related to the consumer's right to be informed?

2. What is BBB Auto Line? What kind of disputes are handled by the program? What right does a consumer forfeit when accepting the decision of an Auto Line arbitrator? As a consumer, what primary benefits would you expect from this program?

3. According to the BBB Code of Advertising, when is it acceptable for BBB members to use the word *sale* in advertising? How should BBB members handle "extra charges" in their advertising? Why is it in the best interest of advertisers to comply with the ethical principles of the BBB's guidelines, even if they are not BBB members?

Go for the Green, page 54

The Sustainable Business Network makes it easier for businesses and consumers to find the information that will enable them to make environmentally responsible choices. Visit the site and make the right choice.

1. What is the mission of the Business for Social Responsibility (BSR)? What products and services does BSR provide its members? As a future businessperson, do you support the goals of BSR? Would you want to work for a company that supports those goals? Why or why not?

2. What is Green Seal, and how does it help protect the environment? Why would a business want to have the Green Seal label on its products? Why might a business not want to be associated with Green Seal?

3. Browse through the internships that interest you at the SBN Job Center. What skills or experience would help you obtain these positions? What can you do to develop such skills while you are a student?

Surf Safely, page 55

Visit the Web site of the National Fraud Information Center (NFIC) and learn how to protect yourself from telephone and Internet scams.

1. What percentage of U.S. adults have reported receiving fraudulent telephone offers? According to FBI estimates, how many illegal telephone sales companies are operating in the United States? Why should legitimate businesses be concerned about these high rates of telephone fraud?

2. What do you think are the three most important Internet tips for staying safe in cyberspace? Given the increase in the number of Internet businesses, how easy or difficult is it for consumers to follow these guidelines?

3. What two ways can you report fraud to the NFIC? What information should you supply in your report? How does the government benefit from consumers' taking action against fraudulent businesses? How does this action indirectly affect all consumers?

Explore on Your Own

Review these chapter-related Web sites on your own to learn more about ethics and social responsibility in the workplace.

1. Lawoffice.com, www.lawoffice.com, provides legal information that helps consumers.

2. The *Online Journal of Ethics*, www.depaul.edu/ethics/ethg1.html, provides reports on cutting-edge research into business and professional ethical questions.

3. The United States Environmental Protection Agency, www.epa.gov/, has the latest information on today's environmental issues. Helpful articles and links make this site a must for all businesses.

A CASE FOR CRITICAL THINKING

■ *The Shady Side of the Olympics*

Cities around the world pursue the Olympic Games for many reasons. Some want the millions of dollars the extravaganza brings in tourism. Others want the new highways, hotels, skating rinks, and sports arenas. The people of Salt Lake City, Utah, just wanted a little respect.

TARNISHED GOLD

Tired of being viewed as Mormon country with some good skiing, Salt Lake yearned to show the world that it was a booming, high-tech city. In 1985, the city was shut out by Anchorage, Alaska, as a U.S. finalist for the 1992 Winter Games. Shock turned to anger when Salt Lake officials discovered that Anchorage gave U.S. Olympic committee members fishing trips, hunting trips, helicopter rides, and more. Anchorage schmoozed. Salt Lake played by the rules—and lost.

Salt Lake got a second chance in 1991 when it won the U.S. endorsement for the 1998 Winter Games. Still, its fate rested with the International Olympic Committee (IOC), which makes the final Olympic site selection. City officials were confident that the IOC would select Salt Lake over rival Nagano, Japan, because Japan's proposal was based on plans and sketches, while Salt Lake was ready to go. But Nagano won by a four-vote margin, and Salt Lake was stunned—

for the second time. "You can't believe the crap they [Nagano] were pulling," says Kim Warren, international relations coordinator for the Salt Lake bid committee. "We were giving out saltwater taffy and cowboy hats; they were giving out computers"—and more.

THE WIDE WORLD OF PAYOLA

IOC committee members were among the most courted humans on the planet. For years, bidding cities would lavish IOC members with first-class plane tickets, accommodations in five-star hotels, gourmet dinners, and expensive gifts. Some members even cashed in their first-class tickets, bought coach seats, and pocketed the difference. To curb the abuse, in 1986 the committee put a $150 limit on gifts. But the bribes continued.

CITY OF LATTER-DAY SCANDAL

The decision to award the Winter Olympics to Nagano, with its lousy facilities and mediocre snow, was Salt Lake's turning point. In 1995 Salt Lake got the U.S. nomination again. This time Salt Lake Olympic committee members would do whatever it would take to secure the necessary IOC votes for the 2002 Winter Olympics. Between 1992 and 1995 they doled out some $800,000 in gifts to IOC members. The gifts included $400,000 in various scholarships, free medical care, expensive firearms and skis, trips in state-owned planes, tips on lucrative real estate deals, a $10,000 contribution to the mayoral campaign of a Chilean delegate, and a $50,000 gift to a Congolese IOC member to establish sports programs for poor children (so they thought).

Of course, such bribery had been going on for years. Australia (host of the 2000 Summer Games) offered $35,000 each to IOC members from Kenya and Uganda for their countries' sports organizations and catered a $1.9 million lunch for East Berliners. Atlanta, Georgia (host of the 1996 Summer Olympics) treated IOC members to trips to Disney World and expensive golf outings. Meanwhile, officials in Toronto (which lost the 1996 bid to Atlanta) spent some $700,000 on travel for IOC members. The list goes on. But it was the extent of the corruption in Salt Lake that surprised just about everyone.

NO MORE FUN AND GAMES

When the news involving Salt Lake's bribes broke in February 1999, residents were stunned that this could happen to a city with such high moral standards. "It tarnished our reputation," said Salt Lake's mayor. "Obviously, we did break the rules," says Ken Bullock, one of Salt Lake's organizers. "The Games are an aphrodisiac. If you want something bad enough, you stretch the boundaries."

Separate investigations are still sorting out who's to blame. Some blame the IOC because they allowed the "sucking up." Others note that just because someone is available to be bribed doesn't mean you bribe them. Still others think the reports will depict a system so systematically corrupt that it might easily have blinded the good folk of Salt Lake. To begin with, the 115 unpaid delegates from all over the world serve on the IOC committee until they are 80 years old or die. New members are not elected but are sponsored by existing committee members during a murky process in which senior members wield great influence.

As a result of the Salt Lake City investigation, the IOC has implicated one-fifth of its 115 members and 10 others have either resigned or have been expelled. About 20 local, national, and international Olympics officials have lost their jobs or are under suspicion. And an ethics commission has drawn up new guidelines for IOC members. Meanwhile, visits from IOC members to bid cities and vice versa are no longer allowed. And only eight IOC members, along with a few athletes and members of sports groups, will decide which city is to get the Games in the future.

CRITICAL THINKING QUESTIONS

1. Why did Salt Lake City relax its ethical standards?

2. Why did Salt Lake City suffer the most harm of all the offenders?

3. Why were organizing committees willing to spend so much money to get the Olympic Games?

4. Go to Chapter 2 of this text's Web site at http://www.prenhall.com/mescon and click on the hot link to the International Olympic Committee Web site. Follow the online instructions to answer these questions: How have the Host City Election Procedures changed? Read the IOC Code of Ethics. Why doesn't Section 2, Integrity, give explicit parameters?

VIDEO CASE AND EXERCISES

■ *Putting People Before Profits at Madison Park Greetings*

SYNOPSIS

Judi Jacobsen wanted to learn to paint—and, in the process, founded a successful greeting card company. She and a partner, also interested in crafts, started Madison Park Greetings (www.madpark.com) in 1997 with just $400. Based in Seattle, Washington, the company has grown to $3 million in annual sales, with 25 employees and 8,000 customers. The company has been honored by the U.S. Small Business Administration for its commitment to social responsibility. For example, Jacobsen improved her urban neighborhood by transforming a run-down building into modern offices to house her business. She also helps middle school and high school students learn sales skills and earn scholarship money by selling her cards. In this entrepreneur's view, people come first, not profits.

EXERCISES
Analysis

1. If Madison Park Greetings decided to sell stock to the public, how might this change in ownership affect Jacobsen's inclination to put people ahead of profits?

2. In using business funds to renovate her company's inner-city building, has Jacobsen diverted money that rightfully belonged to Madison Park Greetings?

3. How would you characterize Jacobsen's attitude toward equality in employment?

4. How can Madison Park Greetings be socially responsible if it makes products that deplete natural resources such as timber?

5. Do you agree with Jacobsen's decision to put employees before profits?

Application
Choose a local business (such as a restaurant, factory, farm, or service business) and describe how it could be more socially responsible.

Decision
Assume that a huge greeting card company wants to buy out Madison Park Greetings. If Jacobsen sells, she can remain in charge but she will have to follow the employment policies of the new owner. Should she sell?

Communication
Draft a two-minute speech to all Madison Park Greetings employees to explain the decision you recommended in the preceding question (making up any details you may need).

Integration
Refer to the discussion of competitive advantage in Chapter 1. How does Madison Park Greetings gain a competitive advantage over its many rivals in the greeting card industry?

Ethics
Imagine that Madison Park Greetings is getting ready to promote one of two artists to a new position. Is it ethical for the company to promote an employee who does not believe in the company's social responsibility agenda, when the other employee (equally qualified) is a strong supporter of the agenda?

Debate
Is it ethical for Judi Jacobsen to personally profit from the operation of a business that she sees as putting people before profits? Choose one side of this question and prepare for a classroom debate by outlining your arguments.

Teamwork
With three other students, identify a cause or group that could benefit from a helping hand from Madison Park Greetings. How might the company support this cause or group?

Online Research
Using Internet sources, find out how Madison Park Greetings has grown and what products it is now offering. How is the company's growth likely to affect its workforce? See Component Chapter A, Exhibit A.1, for search engines to use in doing your research.

 **MYPHLIP COMPANION WEB SITE**

Learning Interactively

Visit the myPHLIP Web site at www.prenhall.com/mescon. For Chapter 2, take advantage of the interactive "Study Guide" to test your chapter knowledge. Get instant feedback on whether you need additional studying. Read the "Current Events" articles to get the latest on chapter topics, and complete the exercises as specified by your instructor. Expand your learning with a visit to the "Research Area." There you will find a wealth of information you can use to complete your course assignments.

 **MASTERING BUSINESS ESSENTIALS**

Go to "The Goal of the Firm and Social Responsibility" and "Ethical Issues" episodes on the Mastering Business Essentials interactive, video-enhanced CD-ROM. View the management team at CanGo (an e-business start-up) debate the potentially adverse effects of violent online games. Help CanGo's management team search for a way to balance the company's reputation with market demands.

Next, learn about an ethical dilemma faced by Andrew, the director of marketing, and assist him with his difficult decision.

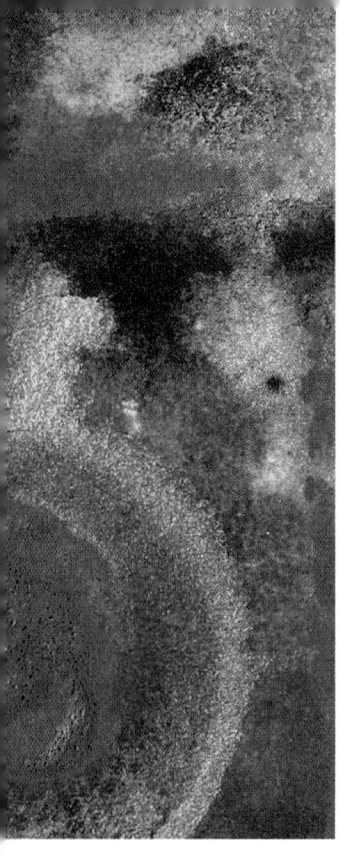

GLOBAL BUSINESS

3

LEARNING OBJECTIVES

After studying this chapter, you will be able to

1. Highlight the opportunities and challenges of conducting business in other countries

2. List five ways to improve communication in an international business relationship

3. Identify five forms of international business activity

4. Discuss why nations trade

5. Explain why nations restrict international trade and list four forms of trade restrictions

6. Highlight three protectionist tactics nations use to give their domestic industries a competitive edge

7. Outline the causes of the global economic crisis at the end of the twentieth century and summarize the lesson learned by this example

@ 8. Summarize the challenges European and Asian countries are facing as they attempt to narrow the U.S. lead in global e-commerce

Inside Business

Lance Armstrong, winner of the 1999 and 2000 Tour de France, boldly displays his affiliation.

TREK BIKES:
TREKKING AROUND THE GLOBE
w w w . t r e k b i k e s . c o m

It's a world away from the bright lights of Paris. But the little town of Waterloo, Wisconsin, captured the world's attention during the 1999 Tour de France. When Lance Armstrong zoomed across the finish line on Paris's Champs-Elysées, the American cycler raced to victory on an American bike—a bike made by Trek Bicycle Corporation of Waterloo.

At first glance, Waterloo seems an unlikely place for the headquarters of an international business. Dairy farms dominate the rural landscape. And when Green Bay Packers' fans support their favorite team, they also promote the state's most famous commodity by wearing foam cheese wedges on their heads. Even so, Waterloo is where Trek opened for business in 1976 with five workers assembling bicycle frames by hand in an old wooden barn.

During the company's first few years, Trek sold its bicycles exclusively in the United States. But all that changed in 1985 when Joyce Keehn, now Trek's worldwide sales director, received several inquiries about exporting Treks to Canada. A novice in international trade, Keehn consulted the state's export agency and sought advice from local exporters at state-sponsored trade seminars. After considering Trek's close proximity to Canada, Keehn decided that selling directly to Canadian bicycle shops was the company's best option for international expansion.

As more exporting opportunities opened up, Keehn experimented with other foreign distribution methods. For instance, to minimize cultural and language barriers, she relied on the expertise and knowledge of local distributors instead of approaching retailers directly. In other countries, she advised Trek to create wholly owned subsidiaries for handling sales, inventory, warranties, customer service, and direct distribution to retail outlets. Such subsidiary offices allowed Trek to maintain higher profits and more control over its products.

Still, Keehn hit some bumps in the road as she ventured into the global marketplace. For example, customs delays created frequent insurance and financial problems; some shipments even disappeared during customs clearances in Mexico. On one occasion, Trek halted distribution of its catalog after discovering that a featured cartoon character was offensive to Germans. And customizing bikes for the European markets increased Trek's production costs.

Cyberspace presented even more challenges for Keehn. Trek's international dealers must charge higher prices than those charged by U.S. sellers to cover such costs as shipping and tariffs. Moreover, international prices must allow for fluctuating foreign exchange rates. To avoid this confusion and to protect its international sellers, Trek does not sell bicycles or reveal prices on its Web site. Instead, it refers customers to authorized dealers in their area.

Today, whether you're in cyberspace, Cincinnati, or Cyprus, you won't have to travel far to find a Trek. Keehn has established a network of 65 distributors on six continents and seven wholly owned subsidiaries in Europe and Japan. From its humble beginnings in Waterloo, Trek is now the world's largest maker of racing bikes, mountain bikes, and other types of specialty bikes. The company sells more than a half million bikes in more than 70 countries every year. In 10 years, annual revenues have grown from $18 million to over $400 million, of which 40 percent now come from international business.[1]

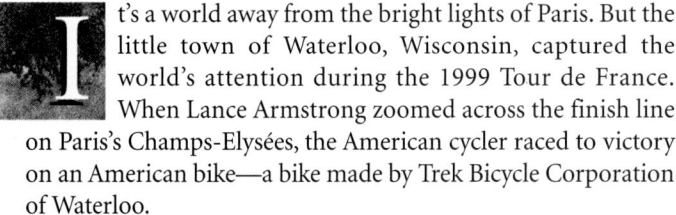

■ THE GLOBAL BUSINESS ENVIRONMENT

LEARNING OBJECTIVE 1

Highlight the opportunities and challenges of conducting business in other countries

Like Trek, more and more enterprises are experiencing the excitement of conducting business in the global marketplace. Although selling goods and services in foreign markets can generate increased sales, produce operational efficiencies, expose companies to new technologies, and provide greater consumer choices, venturing abroad also exposes companies to many new challenges, as Joyce Keehn discovered. For instance, each country has unique ways of doing business, which must be learned: Laws, customs, consumer preferences, ethical standards, labor skill, and political and economic stability vary from country to country, and all have the potential to affect a firm's international prospects. Furthermore, volatile currencies and international trade relationships can indeed make global expansion a risky proposition.

Still, in most cases the opportunities of the global marketplace greatly outweigh the risks. Consider UPS. When this company began its rapid global expansion program in the 1980s, it had to attain air rights into each country, unravel a patchwork of customs laws, learn how to deal with varying work ethics and employment policies, and so on. But the company's efforts paid off. Today UPS delivers over 13 million packages annually in more than 200 countries. Over 13 percent of the company's revenue now comes from international package deliveries.[2]

Cultural Differences in the Global Business Environment

Cultural differences present a number of challenges in the global marketplace, as Joyce Keehn's experience shows. For one thing, companies must recognize and respect differences in social values, ideas of status, decision-making habits, attitudes toward time, use of space, body language, manners, and ethical standards. Otherwise such differences can lead to misunderstandings in international business relationships, particularly if language differences also exist (see Exhibit 3.1). Furthermore, companies that sell their products overseas must often adapt the products to meet the unique needs of international customers, just as Trek does.

The best way to prepare yourself to do business with people from another culture is to study that culture in advance. Learn everything you can about the culture's history, religion, politics, and customs—especially its business customs. Who makes decisions? How are negotiations usually conducted? Is gift giving expected? What is the proper attire for a business meeting? In addition to the suggestion that you learn about the culture, seasoned international businesspeople offer the following tips for improving intercultural communication:

LEARNING OBJECTIVE 2

List five ways to improve communication in an international business relationship

■ *Be alert to the other person's customs.* Expect the other person to have values, beliefs, expectations, and mannerisms different from yours. For instance, don't be surprised when businesspeople in Pakistan excuse themselves in the middle of a meeting to conduct prayers. Moslems pray five times a day.

EXHIBIT 3.1

GOING GLOBAL HAS ITS BARRIERS

Learning a country's business customs and cultural differences is the first step in going global.

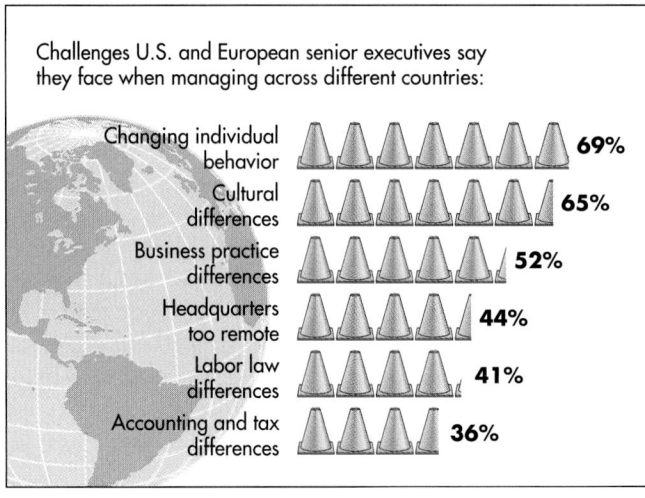

Challenges U.S. and European senior executives say they face when managing across different countries:

Changing individual behavior	69%
Cultural differences	65%
Business practice differences	52%
Headquarters too remote	44%
Labor law differences	41%
Accounting and tax differences	36%

COMPETING IN THE GLOBAL MARKETPLACE

WHEN WILL CHINA GET REAL?

Welcome to the People's Republic of China, where everything from soap to software is pirated. China produces more fakes than any other nation—everything from autos to aircraft parts, beer to razor blades, soap to shampoo, TVs to toilets. China produces nearly half of the world's 14 billion batteries. But most of them are fake versions of Panasonic, Gillette, and other big brands. Moreover, it is estimated that a quarter of the world's watch production (perhaps a third of which is counterfeit) is concentrated in Guangdong—China's richest and fastest-growing region.

Fake-making has infiltrated nearly every sector of China's economy. Most counterfeiters work at small to mid-sized factories, but many stay at home, doing things like filling Head & Shoulders bottles from large vats in their living rooms. Overall, the amount of China's manufacturing base that is dependent on fakes and other illegal knockoffs is estimated to be 10 percent to 30 percent—and growing. The simple reason for the explosion in counterfeits is the potential for big money at low risk. Chinese counterfeiters know they'll get only a slap on the wrist if caught.

Raids do occur daily, but even the government's crackdown isn't real. Local officials are hesitant to crack down on pirates because they create millions of jobs. "Entire villages live off counterfeiting. If you suddenly throw these people out of work, you'll have riots," says one spokesperson for a leading private anti-counterfeiting agency. Yiwu is China's largest wholesale distribution center, where it is estimated that 80 percent of the consumer goods sold are counterfeits. Shutting down the fakes in Yiwu would cripple the city's economy, because many hotels, restaurants, and businesses cater to the trade.

Worse still, the fakes are exported everywhere—to Europe, Russia, the Middle East. Unilever says that fake Dove soap is making its way from China into Europe. Bose (a maker of highend audio systems), is finding Chinese fakes in overseas markets. Indeed, the pirates have moved to a whole new level of sophistication. Ten years ago, China's knockoffs were below Western standards. Today, many fake Duracells look so genuine that Gillette has to send them to a forensics lab to analyze them. Fake watches even contain full-sized Swiss movements and real gems.

So what are pirated brand owners to do? For the most part, companies are trying to boost government enforcement, a tough task. For example, U.S. sunglasses maker Oakley has gotten Chinese authorities to close counterfeiters' factories, but new ones pop up in their place. Many multinationals are shutting or shrinking some product lines in China because these products are overrun by counterfeits. But China's market is so vast and promising, few companies are willing to pull out entirely.

When will China get real? Moreover, why hasn't China enacted the tough laws and rigid enforcement needed to get the job done? For one thing, China's legal system is riddled with loopholes. There isn't even a clear definition of counterfeiting—which is so ingrained in China's culture that many Chinese view it as harmless. For another, few offenders ever go to prison because a real crackdown on counterfeiting could create serious social turmoil and cost the central government dearly. So endless raids are all China has to offer—for now.

■ QUESTIONS FOR CRITICAL THINKING

1. Why doesn't China use its manufacturing skills to make its own products?

2. Why doesn't the Chinese government stop the counterfeiting?

■ *Deal with the individual.* Don't stereotype the other person or react with preconceived ideas. Regard the person as an individual first, not as a representative of another culture.

■ *Clarify your intent and meaning.* The other person's body language may not mean what you think, and the person may read unintentional meanings into your message. Clarify your true intent by repetition and examples. Ask questions and listen carefully. The Japanese are generally appreciative when foreigners ask what is proper behavior, because it shows respect for the Japanese way of doing things.[3]

■ *Adapt your style to the other person's.* If the other person appears to be direct and straightforward, follow suit. If not, adjust your behavior to match. In many African countries, for example, people are suspicious of others who seem to be in a hurry. Therefore, you should allow plenty of time to get to know the people you are dealing with.

■ *Show respect.* Learn how respect is communicated in various cultures—through gestures, eye contact, and so on. For example, in Spain let a handshake last five to seven strokes; pulling away too soon may be interpreted as a rejection. In France, however, the preferred handshake is a single stroke.

Legal Differences in the Global Business Environment

All U.S. companies that conduct business in other countries must be familiar with U.S. law, international law, and the laws of the specific countries where they plan to trade or do business. For example, all companies doing international business must comply with the 1978 Foreign Corrupt Practices Act. This U.S. law outlaws actions such as bribing government officials in other nations to approve deals. It does, however, allow certain payments, including small payments to officials for expediting routine government actions.

Critics of this U.S. law complain that payoffs are a routine part of world trade, so forbidding U.S. companies to follow suit cripples their ability to compete. Others counter that U.S. exports haven't been affected by this law and that companies can conduct business abroad without violating antibribery rules. Regardless of whether they agree or disagree with the law, some companies have had to forgo opportunities as a result of it. For example, a U.S. power-generation company recently walked away from a $320 million contract in the Middle East because government officials demanded a $3 million bribe. The contract went to a Japanese company instead.[4]

Forms of International Business Activity

LEARNING OBJECTIVE *3*

Identify five forms of international business activity

importing
Purchasing goods or services from another country and bringing them into one's own country

exporting
Selling and shipping goods or services to another country

Once a company decides to operate in the global marketplace, it must decide on the level of involvement it is willing to undertake. Five common forms of international business activities are *importing and exporting, licensing, franchising, strategic alliances and joint ventures,* and *foreign direct investment.* Each has a varying degree of ownership, financial commitment, and risk.

Importing and Exporting **Importing,** the buying of goods or services from a supplier in another country, and **exporting,** the selling of products outside the country in which they are produced, have existed for centuries. In the last few decades, however, the increased level of these activities has caused the economies of the world to become tightly linked.

Exporting, one of the least risky forms of international business activity, permits a firm to enter a foreign market gradually, assess local conditions, and then fine tune its product to meet the needs of foreign consumers. In most cases the firm's financial exposure is limited to market research costs, advertising costs, and the costs of either establishing a direct sales and distribution system or hiring intermediaries. Such intermediaries include *export management companies,* domestic firms that specialize in performing international marketing services on a commission basis, and *export trading companies,* general trading firms that will buy your products for resale overseas as well as perform a variety of importing, exporting, and manufacturing functions. Still another alternative is to use foreign distributors.

Best of the Web Best of the Web Best of

NAVIGATING GLOBAL BUSINESS DIFFERENCES

In today's global marketplace, knowing as much as possible about your international customers' business practices and customs could give you a strategic advantage. To help you successfully conduct business around the globe, navigate the resources at USA Trade.gov. Begin with the Country Commercial Guides. Prepared by U.S. Embassy staff, these guides contain helpful information on foreign marketing practices, trade regulations, investment climate, and business travel for a number of countries. And if your international plans include a business trip, begin your journey here. You'll be glad you did.

www.usatrade.gov/

Working through a foreign distributor with connections in the target country is often helpful to both large and small companies because such intermediaries can provide you with the connections, expertise, and market knowledge you will need to conduct business in a foreign country.[5] In addition, many countries now have foreign trade offices to help importers and exporters interested in doing business within their borders. Other helpful resources include professional agents, local businesspeople, and the International Trade Administration of the U.S. Department of Commerce. This trade organization offers a variety of services, including political and credit risk analysis, advice on entering foreign markets, and financing tips.

International Licensing Licensing is another popular approach to international business. License agreements entitle one company to use some or all of another firm's intellectual property (patents, trademarks, brand names, copyrights, or trade secrets) in return for a royalty payment. Underwear manufacturer Jockey licenses the rights to use the Jockey name to certain foreign manufacturers of women's active wear, sleepwear, and slippers. Jockey licenses its products in more than 120 countries but is careful that all such arrangements add value to the Jockey name.[6]

Many firms choose licensing as an approach to international markets because it involves little out-of-pocket costs. A firm has already incurred the costs of developing the intellectual property to be licensed. Pharmaceutical firms, for instance, routinely use licensing to enter foreign markets. Once a pharmaceutical firm has developed and patented a new drug, it is often more efficient to grant existing local firms the right to manufacture and distribute the patented drug in return for royalty payments. Israel's Teva Pharmaceutical Industries, for example, has a license to manufacture and market Merck's pharmaceutical products in Israel. This arrangement saves Merck the expense of establishing its own Israeli salesforce.[7] Of course, licensing agreements are not restricted to international business. A company can also license its products or technology to other companies in its domestic market.

licensing
Agreement to produce and market another company's product in exchange for a royalty or fee

International Franchising Some companies choose to expand into foreign markets by *franchising* their operation. International franchising is among the fastest-growing forms of international business activity today. Under this arrangement, a franchisor enters into an agreement whereby the franchisee obtains the rights to duplicate a specific product or service—perhaps a restaurant, photocopy shop, or a video rental store—and the franchisor obtains a royalty fee in exchange. Holiday Inn Worldwide has used this approach to reach customers in over 65 countries. Smaller companies have also found that franchising is a good way for them to enter the global marketplace.[8] By franchising its operations, a firm can minimize the costs and risks of global expansion and bypass certain trade restrictions. (The advantages and disadvantages of franchising in general will be discussed in detail in Chapter 4.)

International Strategic Alliances and Joint Ventures A **strategic alliance** is a long-term partnership between two or more companies to jointly develop, produce, or sell products in the global marketplace. To reach their individual but complimentary goals, the companies typically share ideas, expertise, resources, technologies, investment costs, risks, management, and profits.

strategic alliance
Long-term relationship in which two or more companies share ideas, resources, and technologies in order to establish competitive advantages

Best of the Web Best of the Web Best of

GOING GLOBAL

Have you ever thought about getting into the world of exporting? Where would you go for information and help? Many small and large companies have gotten valuable export assistance from online material such as the *Basic Guide to Exporting*. This joint publication by the U.S. Department of Commerce and Unz & Company has a wealth of information about export procedures; foreign markets, industries, companies, and products; export financing; unfair trade practices; trade statistics; and more.

www.unzco.com/basicguide/index.html

Strategic alliances are a popular way to expand one's business globally. The benefits of this form of international expansion include ease of market entry, shared risk, shared knowledge and expertise, and synergy. In other words, companies that form a strategic alliance with a foreign partner can often compete more effectively than if they entered the foreign market alone. Consider the strategic alliance established by American Airlines, British Airways, Cathay Pacific Airways, Quantas, and others. Named *oneworld*, this partnership makes global travel easier for consumers. Benefits include integrated frequent flyer programs, common airport lounges, and more efficient ticketing among member carriers so that a change of airlines is transparent when booking international flights.[9]

A **joint venture** is a special type of strategic alliance in which two or more firms join together to create a new business entity that is legally separate and distinct from its parents. In some countries, foreign companies are prohibited from owning facilities outright or from investing in local business. Thus, establishing a joint venture with a local partner may be the only way to do

joint venture
Cooperative partnership in which organizations share investment costs, risks, management, and profits in the development, production, or selling of products

COMPETING IN THE GLOBAL MARKETPLACE

HOW TO AVOID BUSINESS BLUNDERS ABROAD

Doing business in another country can be extremely tricky. Here are some issues to consider when you conduct business abroad.

The Importance of Packaging
Numerous problems result from the failure to adapt packaging for other cultures. Sometimes only the color of the package needs to be altered to enhance a product's sales. For instance, white symbolizes death in Japan and much of Asia; green represents danger or disease in Malaysia. Obviously, using the wrong color in these countries might produce negative reactions.

The Language Barrier
Some product names travel poorly. For instance, the gasoline company Esso found out that its name means "stalled car" in Japan. However, some company names have traveled well. Kodak may be the most famous example. A research team deliberately developed this name after searching for a word that was pronounceable everywhere but had no specific meaning anywhere.

Problems with Promotions
In its U.S. promotion, one company had effectively used this sentence: "You can use no finer napkin at your dinner table." The U.S. company decided to use the same commercials in England because, after all, the British do speak English. To the British, however, the word napkin or nappy actually means "diaper." The ad could hardly be expected to boost sales of dinner napkins in England.

Local Customs
Social norms vary greatly from country to country and it is difficult for any outsider to be knowledgeable about all

of them, so local input is vital. For example, one firm promoted eyeglasses in Thailand with commercials featuring animals wearing glasses. However, in Thailand animals are considered a low form of life; humans would never wear anything worn by an animal.

Translation Problems
The best translations of an advertising message convey the concept of the original but do not precisely duplicate the original. PepsiCo learned this lesson when it reportedly discovered that its slogan "Come alive with Pepsi" was translated into German as "Come alive out of the grave with Pepsi." In Asia, the slogan was once translated as "Bring your ancestors back from the dead."

The Need for Research
Proper market research may reduce or eliminate most international business blunders. Market researchers can uncover needs for product adaptations, potential name problems, promotional requirements, and useful market strategies. Good research may even uncover potential translation problems.

As you can see, doing business in other cultures can be risky if you're unprepared. However, awareness of differences, consultation with local people, and concern for host-country feelings can reduce problems and save money.

■ QUESTIONS FOR CRITICAL THINKING

1. If you were thinking of selling a breakfast cereal in Japan, what issues might you want to consider?

2. What steps can companies take to avoid business blunders abroad?

1999 Rank	Company	Foreign Revenue (in millions)	Total Revenue (in millions)	Foreign as Percent of Total
1	ExxonMobil	$115,464	$160,883	72
2	IBM	50,377	87,548	58
3	Ford Motor	50,138	162,558	31
4	General Motors	46,485	176,558	26
5	General Electric	35,350	111,630	31
6	Texaco	32,700	42,433	77
7	Citigroup	28,749	82,005	35
8	Hewlett-Packard	23,398	42,370	55
9	Wal-Mart Stores	22,728	165,013	14
10	Compac Computer	21,174	38,525	55
11	American Intl Group	20,311	40,656	50
12	Chevron	20,020	45,198	44
13	Philip Morris Cos.	19,670	61,751	32
14	Procter & Gamble	18,351	38,125	48
15	Motorola	17,760	30,931	58
	TOTAL	$522,675	$1,286,184	41

EXHIBIT 3.2

FIFTEEN LARGEST U.S. MULTINATIONALS

On average, the 15 largest U.S. multinational corporations earn about 41 percent of their revenue from foreign sales.

business in that country. In other cases, foreigners may be required to move some of their production facilities to the country to earn the right to sell their products there. For instance, the Chinese government would not allow Boeing to sell airplanes in China until the company agreed to move half of the tail-section production for its 737s to Xian.[10]

Foreign Direct Investment Exporting, licensing, franchising, and strategic alliances allow a firm to enter the global marketplace without investing in foreign factories or facilities. However, many firms prefer to enter international markets through ownership and control of assets in foreign countries.

The most comprehensive form of international business is a wholly owned operation run in another country, without the financial participation of a local partner. Many U.S. firms conduct business this way, as do companies based in other countries. These operations vary in form, size, and purpose. Some are started from scratch; others are acquired from local owners. Some are small sales offices; others are full-scale manufacturing facilities. Some are set up to exploit the availability of raw materials; others take advantage of low wage rates; still others minimize transportation costs by choosing locations that give them direct access to markets in other countries. In almost all cases, at least part of the workforce is drawn from the local population.

Companies with a physical presence in numerous countries are called **multinational corporations (MNCs).** Because they operate on such a worldwide scale, at times it's difficult to determine exactly where home is (see Exhibit 3.2). Since 1969, the number of multinational corporations in the world's 14 richest countries has more than tripled, from 7,000 to 24,000.[11] Some multinational corporations increase their involvement in foreign countries by establishing **foreign direct investment (FDI).** That is, they either establish production and marketing facilities in the countries where they operate or purchase existing foreign firms, as Wal-Mart did in the late 1990s, when it acquired large retail stores in Germany and Great Britain and later converted them into Wal-Mart supercenters. Such

multinational corporations (MNCs)
Companies with operations in more than one country

foreign direct investment (FDI)
Investment of money by foreign companies in domestic business enterprises

China is becoming too big a PC market for anyone to ignore. Dell, which recently opened its fourth PC factory in the world on China's southeastern coast, can now deliver PCs to Chinese customers as fast as it does to North American ones.

EXHIBIT 3.3

THE WORLD'S BIG EMERGING MARKETS

The countries that hold the greatest potential for U.S. exports in the coming two decades are not our traditional trading partners.

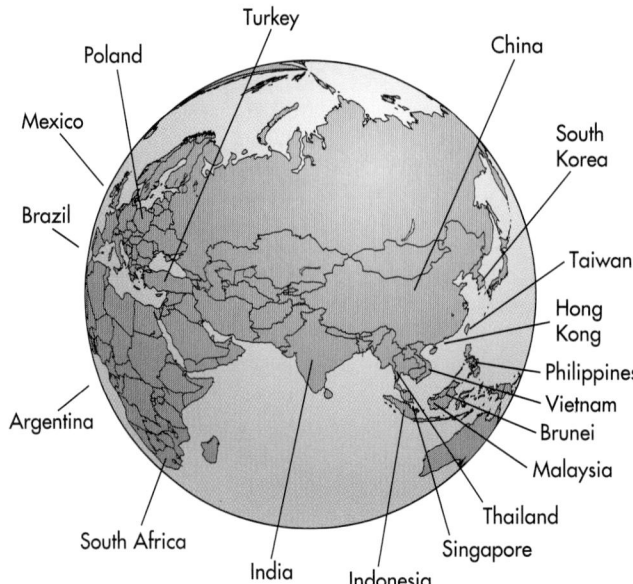

foreign direct investment constitutes the highest level of international involvement. Moreover, it carries much greater economic and political risk and is more complex than any other form of entry in the global marketplace.[12]

The U.S. Commerce Department reports that foreign direct investment in the United States has been rising steadily over the past few years.[13] For example, Daimler-Benz's $40 billion acquisition of Chrysler and British Petroleum's $48 billion acquisition of Amoco propelled Germany and the United Kingdom to the top two foreign countries investing in the United States.[14]

In addition to the United States, areas such as the Chinese Economic Area (China, Hong Kong, and Taiwan), South Korea, Singapore, Thailand, Malaysia, Indonesia, Vietnam, India, South Africa, Turkey, and Brazil are becoming attractive spots for foreign investment. Labeled *big emerging markets,* these countries make up 70 percent of the world's land, 85 percent of the world's population, and 99 percent of the anticipated growth in the world's labor force.[15] As such, they have been identified by the U.S. International Trade Administration as having the greatest potential for large increase in U.S. exports over the next two decades (see Exhibit 3.3).

■ FUNDAMENTALS OF INTERNATIONAL TRADE

The success of U.S. businesses such as Trek, Wal-Mart, UPS, and others that operate in the global marketplace depends, in part, on the international economic relationships the United States maintains with other countries. Basically, the objective of the United States is to devise policies that balance the interests of U.S. companies, U.S. workers, and U.S. consumers. Other countries, of course, are trying to do the same thing. As you might expect, the many players in world trade sometimes have conflicting goals.

Why Nations Trade

No single country has the resources to produce everything its citizens want or need. Countries specialize in the production of certain goods and trade with other countries to obtain raw materials and goods that are unavailable to them or too costly for them to produce. Moreover, international trade has many benefits: it increases a country's total output, it offers lower prices and greater variety to consumers, it subjects domestic oligopolies and monopolies to competition, and it allows companies to expand their markets and achieve production and distribution efficiencies.[16]

How does a country know what to produce and what to trade for? In some cases the answer is easy: a nation may have an **absolute advantage,** which means it can produce a particular item more efficiently than *all* other nations, or it is virtually the only country producing that product. Absolute advantages rarely last, however, unless they are based on the availability of natural re-

LEARNING OBJECTIVE 4
Discuss why nations trade

absolute advantage
A nation's ability to produce a particular product with fewer resources per unit of output than any other nation

sources. Saudi Arabia, for example, has an absolute advantage in crude oil production because of its huge, developed reserves. Thus, it makes sense for Saudi Arabia to specialize in providing the world with oil, and to trade for other items its country needs.

In most cases, a country can produce many of the same items that other countries can produce. The **comparative advantage theory** explains how a country chooses which items to produce and which items to trade for. The theory states that a country should produce and sell to other countries those items it produces more efficiently or at a lower cost, and trade for those it can't produce as economically. To see how the theory works, consider the United States and Brazil. Each can produce both steel and coffee, but the United States is more efficient at producing steel than coffee, while Brazil is more efficient at producing coffee than steel. According to the comparative advantage theory, the two countries will be better off if each specializes in the industry where it is more efficient and if the two trade with each other—the United States sells steel to Brazil and Brazil sells coffee to the United States.[17] The basic argument behind the comparative advantage theory is that such specialization and exchange will increase a country's total output and allow both trading partners to enjoy a higher standard of living.

How International Trade Is Measured

In Chapter 1 we discussed how economists monitor certain key economic indicators to evaluate how well their country's economic system is performing. One trend that economists watch carefully is the level of a nation's imports and exports. For instance, at any given time, a country may be importing more than it is exporting. As Exhibit 3.4 illustrates, the United States imports more consumer goods than it exports, but it exports more services than it imports. Two key measurements of a nation's level of international trade are the *balance of trade* and the *balance of payments*.

The total value of a country's exports *minus* the total value of its imports, over some period of time, determines its **balance of trade.** In years when the value of goods and services exported by the United States exceeds the value of goods and services it imports, the U.S. balance of trade is said to be positive: People in other countries buy more goods and services from the United States than the United States buys from them, creating a **trade surplus.** Conversely, when the people of the United States buy more from foreign countries than the foreign countries buy from the United States, the U.S. balance of trade is said to be negative. That is, imports exceed exports, creating a **trade deficit.** As Exhibit 3.5 shows, in 1999 the U.S. trade deficit soared to a record $267 billion (produced by a $347 billion trade deficit in goods and an $80 billion trade surplus in services). Economists attribute this deficit to a falloff in U.S. exports rather than a surge in foreign imports.[18]

Bear in mind that the excess of imports over exports does not necessarily mean that U.S. companies are not competitive in the world market. The balance of trade is obscured by several factors. One such factor is the change in the value of the dollar compared with the value of other currencies. When the dollar is strong, products from other countries seem relatively inexpensive in the United States, and U.S. products seem relatively expensive overseas. As U.S. consumers buy more of the relatively inexpensive imported goods and consumers overseas buy less of the relatively expensive U.S. goods, the U.S. trade deficit grows. When the situation is reversed and U.S. consumers buy fewer imported goods while people in other countries buy more U.S. exports, the U.S. trade deficit narrows and may even turn into a trade surplus. (Currency valuations and their impact on global trade will be discussed later in this chapter.)

Another reason that the balance of trade can be misleading is **intrafirm trade,** which is trade between the various units of a multinational corporation. In fact, intrafirm trade now accounts for one-third of all the goods traded around the world.[19] Multinational corporations such as Whirlpool, AT&T, Texas Instruments, and General Electric set up factories to make components in countries where wage rates are low, then ship the components back to the United States for assembly. These shipments to the United States are counted as imports even though they are used by the same company. By contrast, products produced by subsidiaries of foreign companies in the United States for the U.S. market are not considered imports. As you can see, by itself, the balance of trade does not paint a complete picture of a nation's global competitiveness.

The **balance of payments** is the broadest indicator of international trade. It is the total flow of money into the country *minus* the total flow of money out of the country over some period of time. The balance of payments includes the balance of trade plus the net dollars received and

---

comparative advantage theory
Theory that states that a country should produce and sell to other countries those items it produces more efficiently

balance of trade
Total value of the products a nation exports minus the total value of the products it imports, over some period of time

trade surplus
Favorable trade balance created when a country exports more than it imports

trade deficit
Unfavorable trade balance created when a country imports more than it exports

intrafirm trade
Trade between global units of a multinational corporation

balance of payments
Sum of all payments one nation receives from other nations minus the sum of all payments it makes to other nations, over some specified period of time

EXHIBIT 3.4

U.S. EXPORTS AND IMPORTS

The United States actively participates in global trade by exporting and importing goods and services.

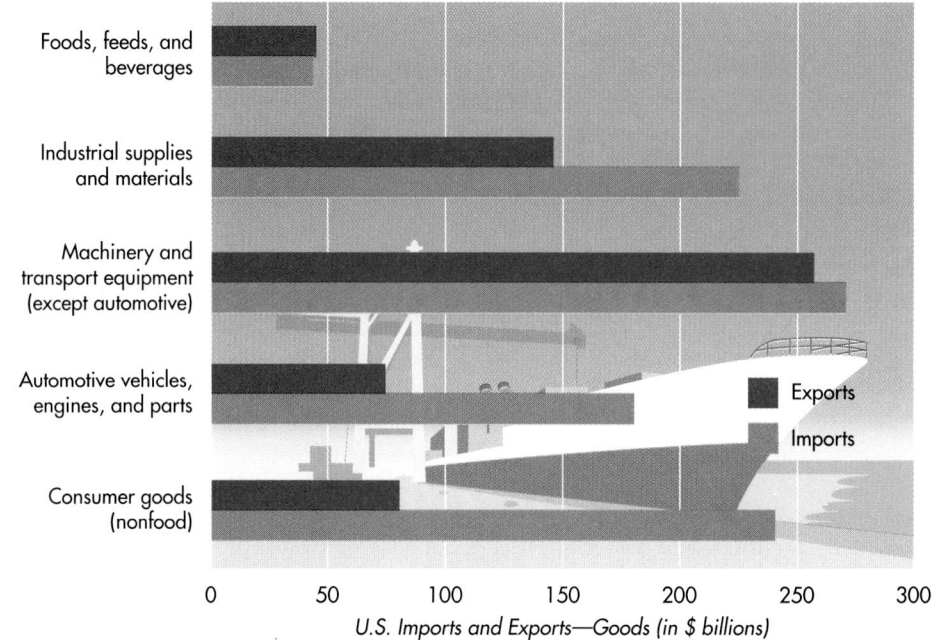

U.S. Imports and Exports—Goods (in $ billions)

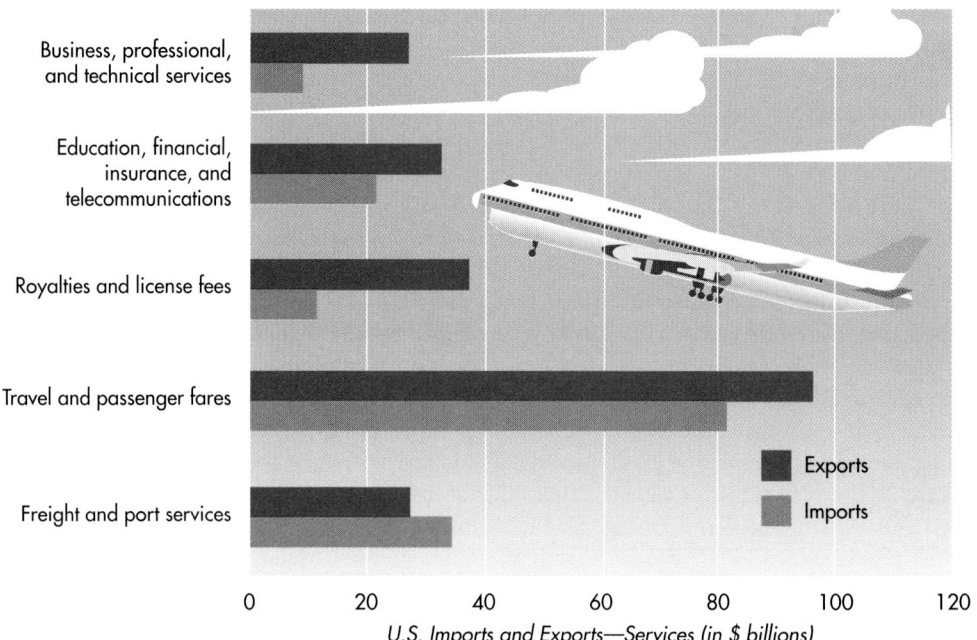

U.S. Imports and Exports—Services (in $ billions)

spent on foreign investment, military expenditures, tourism, foreign aid, and other international transactions. For example, when a U.S. company such as Whirlpool buys all or part of a company based in another country, that investment is counted in the balance of payments but not in the balance of trade. Similarly, when a foreign company such as Daimler-Benz buys a U.S. company such as Chrysler or purchases U.S. stocks, bonds, or real estate, those transactions are part of the balance of payments. The U.S. government, like all governments, desires a favorable balance of payments. That means more money is coming into the country than is flowing out. In 1999 the U.S. balance of payments amounted to a deficit of $339 billion, of which 79 percent was attributable to the country's trade deficit.[20]

protectionism
Government policies aimed at shielding a country's industries from foreign competition

Trade Restrictions

Even though international trade has many economic advantages, sometimes countries practice **protectionism**; that is, they restrict international trade for one reason or another. Sometimes

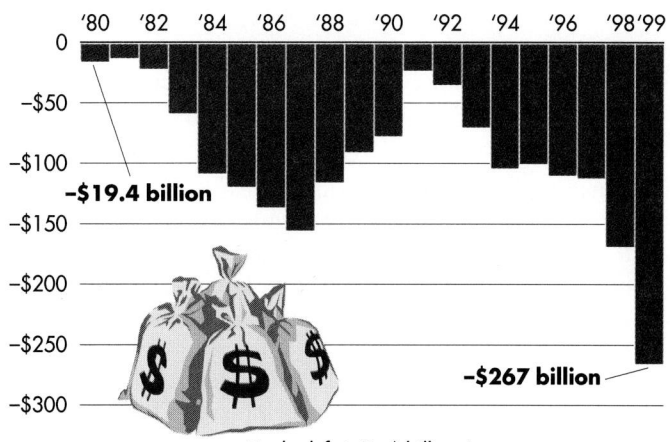

Trade deficit (in $ billions)

EXHIBIT 3.5

TRADE DEFICIT ON THE RISE

U.S. officials say the exploding trade deficit is evidence that the United States maintains the world's most open markets.

they restrict trade to shield specific industries from foreign competition and the possible loss of jobs in these industries. Sometimes they try to protect certain industries that are key to their national defense and the health and safety of their citizens. Or, in the case of emerging economies such as China, they engage in protectionist measures to give new or weak industries an opportunity to grow and strengthen.[21]

Are trade restrictions a good idea or a bad idea? Study after study has shown that in the long run, they hurt a country because they remove competition, stifle innovation, and allow domestic producers to charge more for their goods. The most commonly used forms of trade restrictions include:

■ *Tariffs.* **Tariffs** are taxes, surcharges, or duties levied against imported goods. Sometimes tariffs are levied to generate revenue for the government, but more often they are imposed to restrict trade or to punish other countries for disobeying international trade laws.

■ *Quotas.* **Quotas** limit the amount of a particular good that countries can import during a year. The United States puts ceilings on foreign sugar, peanuts, and dairy products. Limits may be set in quantities, such as pounds of sugar, or in values, such as total dollars' worth of peanuts. In some cases, a product faces stiff tariffs once it reaches its quota. After foreign tobacco products hit their quotas, for example, additional shipments face 350 percent tariffs.[22]

■ *Embargoes.* In its most extreme form, a quota becomes an **embargo,** a complete ban on the import or export of certain products. For example, Canada forbids the importation of oleomargarine in order to protect its dairy industry, and the U.S. bans the importation of toys with lead paint because of health concerns.

■ *Sanctions.* Sanctions are politically motivated embargoes that revoke a country's normal trade relations status: They are often used as forceful alternatives short of war. Sanctions can include arms embargoes, foreign-assistance reductions and cutoffs, trade limitations, tariff increases, import-quota decreases, visa denials, air-link cancellations, and more. About two dozen countries are now subject to U.S. sanctions, including Iraq (for its invasion of Kuwait) and India (for conducting nuclear tests). Still, most governments today (including the United States) use sanctions sparingly, because studies show that sanctions are ineffective at getting countries to change.[23]

In addition to restricting foreign trade, sometimes governments give their domestic producers a competitive edge by using these protectionist tactics:

■ *Restrictive import standards.* Countries can assist their domestic producers by establishing restrictive import standards, such as requiring special licenses for doing certain kinds of business and then making it difficult for foreign companies to obtain such a license. For example, Saudi Arabia restricts import licenses for a variety of products, including chemicals, pasteurized milk, and information technology products.[24] Other countries restrict imports by requiring goods to pass special tests.

■ *Subsidies.* Rather than restrict imports, some countries subsidize domestic producers so that their prices can compete favorably in the global marketplace. Airbus, originally an alliance of

LEARNING OBJECTIVE **5**

Explain why nations restrict international trade and list four forms of trade restrictions

tariffs
Taxes levied on imports

quotas
Fixed limits on the quantity of imports a nation will allow for a specific product

embargo
Total ban on trade with a particular nation (a sanction) or of a particular product

LEARNING OBJECTIVE **6**

Highlight three protectionist tactics nations use to give their domestic industries a competitive edge

state companies from Germany, France, England, and Spain, was subsidized for years to help the company compete against rival Boeing. Now that Airbus is a strong competitor the complex alliance has been sold to a joint venture composed of two private companies—the French-German-Spanish European Aeronautic Defense and Space Company NV (EADS), and Britain's BAE Systems PLC.[25]

dumping
Charging less than the actual cost or less than the home-country price for goods sold in other countries

■ *Dumping.* The practice of selling large quantities of a product at a price lower than the cost of production or below what the company would charge in its home market is **dumping.** This tactic is often used to try to win foreign customers or to reduce product surpluses. Most industrialized countries have antidumping regulations. Section 301 of the U.S. Trade Act of 1988, for instance, obligates the U.S. president to retaliate against foreign producers that dump products on the U.S. market. So when reports showed that Japan was dumping coated steel, which is used primarily in metal containers, cans, bakeware, and home builders' hardware, on the U.S. market, the United States imposed a 95 percent antidumping penalty on the coated steel to prevent Japan from materially injuring the U.S. steel industry.[26]

Agreements and Organizations Promoting International Trade

free trade
International trade unencumbered by restrictive measures

To prevent trade disputes from escalating into full-blown trade wars, and to ensure that international business is conducted in a fair and orderly fashion, countries worldwide have created trade agreements and organizations. Philosophically, most of these agreements and organizations support the basic principles of **free trade;** that is, each nation will ultimately benefit by freely exchanging the goods and services it produces most efficiently for the goods and services it produces less efficiently. The major trade agreements and organizations include the GATT, the WTO, the APEC, the IMF, and the World Bank.

The General Agreement on Tariffs and Trade (GATT) The General Agreement on Tariffs and Trade (GATT) is a worldwide pact that was first established in the aftermath of World War II. The pact's guiding principle—most favored nation (MFN)—is one of nondiscrimination: Any trade advantage a GATT member gives to one country must be given to all GATT members, and no GATT nation can be singled out for punishment. In 1995 GATT established the World Trade Organization (WTO), which has now replaced GATT as the world forum for trade negotiations.

The World Trade Organization (WTO) The World Trade Organization (WTO) is a permanent forum for negotiating, implementing, and monitoring international trade procedures and for mediating trade disputes among its 138 member countries. The organization's goals include facilitating free trade, lowering the costs of doing business, enhancing the international investment environment, simplifying customs, and promoting technical and economic cooperation. Experts believe that the WTO should ultimately prove to be more effective than the GATT because the WTO has a formal legal structure for settling disputes.

Admission to the organization is by application process and requires approval by two-thirds of the members. All WTO members enjoy "favored" access to foreign markets in exchange for adhering to a long list of fair-trading rules and laws governing patents, copyrights, and trademarks. China, for example, was required to eliminate many tariffs and quotas on a wide range of products and open its market of 1.4 billion people to foreign goods as conditions to its membership in the WTO. One group that spoke out strongly against China's admission to the WTO was U.S. textile workers, who feared that lifting U.S. quotas on foreign textiles by 2005 would increase textile imports and severely affect the U.S. textile industry.[27]

The WTO's third international conference was met by massive numbers of protestors in the host city of Seattle. The WTO has become a target of grievance for everything that has gone wrong in the world. Protestors who lined the Seattle streets represented steelworkers, textile workers, environmentalist, concerned senior citizens, and many others who wanted to voice their diverse viewpoints.

The Asia Pacific Economic Cooperation Council (APEC) The Asia Pacific Economic Cooperation Council (APEC) is an organization of 18 countries that are making efforts to liberalize trade in the Pacific Rim (the land areas that surround

Best of the Web Best of the Web Best of

BANKING ON THE WORLD BANK

The World Bank plays an important role in today's fast-changing, closely meshed global economy. Do you know what this organization of five closely associated institutions does? Do you know who runs the bank, where the bank gets its money, and where the money goes? Learn how this organization's programs and financial assistance help poorer nations as well as affluent ones. Log on to the World Bank Web site and find out why global development is everyone's challenge.

www.worldbank.org

the Pacific Ocean). Among the member nations are the United States, Japan, China, Mexico, Australia, South Korea, and Canada. In 1994 the members agreed to eliminate all tariffs and trade barriers among industrialized countries of the Pacific Rim by 2010 and among developing countries by 2020.[28]

The International Monetary Fund (IMF) The International Monetary Fund (IMF) was founded in 1945 and is now affiliated with the United Nations. Its primary function is to provide short-term loans to countries that are unable to meet their budgetary expenses. As such, the IMF is often looked upon as a lender of last resort. For example, the IMF has provided well over a combined total of $150 billion in loans to South Korea, Indonesia, Brazil, Thailand, and other countries to help rescue them from a global financial crisis at the end of the twentieth century.[29]

The World Bank Officially known as the International Bank for Reconstruction and Development, the World Bank was founded to finance reconstruction after World War II. It now provides low-interest loans to developing nations for the improvement of transportation, telecommunications, health, and education. Currently, the World Bank is focused on bringing the Internet to the less-developed regions of the world, such as Africa. World Bank officials and telecommunication executives hope that Internet connections will attract more companies to the region, and thus lead to more rapid economic development.[30] Both the IMF and the World Bank are funded by deposits from its 182 member nations. The bulk of the funds come from the United States, western Europe, and Japan.

Trading Blocs

Trading blocs are another type of organization that promotes international trade. Generally comprising neighboring countries, trading blocs promote free trade among regional members. Although specific rules vary from group to group, their primary objective is to ensure the economic growth and benefit of members. As such, trading blocs generally promote trade inside the region while creating uniform barriers against goods and services entering the region from nonmember countries. Trading blocs are becoming a significant force in the global marketplace.[31]

Trading blocs can be advantageous or disadvantageous in promoting world trade, depending on one's perspective. Some economists are apprehensive about the growing importance of regional trading blocs. They fear that the world is splitting into three camps, revolving around the Americas, Europe, and Asia. Any nation that does not fall into one of these economic regions could suffer, they say, because members of the trading blocs could place severe restrictions on trade with nonmember countries. The critics fear that overall world trade could decline as members become more protective of their own regions. As a result, consumers could find themselves with fewer choices, and many producers could lose sales in lucrative foreign markets.

Others claim, however, that trading blocs could improve world trade. For one thing, the growth of commerce and the availability of customers and suppliers within a trading bloc could be a boon to smaller or younger nations that are trying to build strong economies. For another, the lack of trade barriers within the bloc could help their industries compete with producers in

trading blocs
Organizations of nations that remove barriers to trade among their members and that establish uniform barriers to trade with nonmember nations

An average of $65 million in goods funnel through Laredo, Texas (the busiest U.S.–Mexico crossing point) *each* day. Honking lines of trucks choke the town with traffic jams.

more developed nations, and, in some cases, member countries could reach a wider market than before.[32] Furthermore, close ties to more stable economies could help shield emerging nations from fluctuations in the global economy and could promote a greater sharing of knowledge and technology; both outcomes could aid future economic development.

The four most powerful trading blocs today are the Association of Southeast Asian Nations (ASEAN), South America's Mercosur, the NAFTA (North American Free Trade Agreement) countries, and the European Union (EU), with the latter two being the largest and most powerful organizations (see Exhibit 3.6). Because many trading nations see Latin America as an area for large-scale economic growth in the future, they are eager to establish ties with Mercosur, which links Argentina, Brazil, Paraguay, and Uruguay, and registers a population of 210 million people that produces more than $1 trillion in goods and services.[33] Like other trading blocs, the Mercosur's objectives include the free movement of goods and services across the borders of its members. Furthermore, the group seeks an economic integration which it hopes will make the four countries more competitive in the global marketplace.[34] Some U.S. officials hope that Mercosur will eventually join the North American Free Trade Agreement (NAFTA) to form a Free Trade Area of the Americas (FTAA).[35]

NAFTA   In 1994 the United States, Canada, and Mexico formed a powerful trading bloc, the North American Free Trade Agreement (NAFTA). The agreement paves the way for the free flow of goods, services, and capital within the bloc by eliminating all tariffs and quotas on trades between the three nations.[36] Talks are currently under way to expand NAFTA to include Chile. Ultimately, NAFTA's supporters would like to see the agreement expanded to include all of Central and South America by 2005.

NAFTA has always been controversial. Debate still continues about whether the agreement is helping or hurting the U.S. economy. One primary concern is NAFTA's effect on U.S. jobs. Critics contend that many jobs have been lost because U.S. manufacturers have moved production to Mexico and Canada. Supporters, on the other hand, say that U.S. jobs have multiplied as a result of increased exports. Which side is right? It's still too early to tell whether NAFTA's overall impact on the U.S. economy will be positive or negative.[37] Over the coming years, U.S. trade policy and NAFTA will certainly continue to be watched closely.

The European Union   One of the largest trading blocs is the European Union (EU), which combines 15 countries and more than 370 million people. Talks are under way to admit more countries, including the Czech Republic, Estonia, Hungary, Slovenia, and Poland.[38] EU nations are working to eliminate hundreds of local regulations, variations in product standards, and protectionist measures that limit trade between member countries. Eliminating barriers enables the nations of the EU to function as a single market, with trade flowing between member countries as it does between states in the United States.

In 1999, 11 of the 15 countries formed the economic and monetary union (EMU) and turned over control of their individual monetary policies to the newly created European Central Bank. With a combined population of about 300 million people, these 11 countries account for 19.4 percent of the world's gross domestic product (GDP), making them a commanding force in the world economy.[39] The four countries that did not join the EMU are Greece, which did not meet the strict qualification requirements, and Britain, Denmark, and Sweden, which chose not to participate initially.

euro
A planned unified currency used by European nations that meet certain strict requirements

One of the driving forces behind the decision to join forces was the anticipated advantages these 11 countries would enjoy by creating a unified currency called the **euro.** Officially launched in 1999 (with notes and coins available in 2002), the euro could wipe out some $65 billion annually in

EXHIBIT 3.6

MEMBERS OF MAJOR TRADE
BLOCS

As the economies of the world
become increasingly linked, many
countries have formed powerful
regional trade blocs that trade freely
with one another and limit foreign
competition.

European Union (EU)*	North American Free Trade Agreement (NAFTA)	Association of Southeast Asian Nations (ASEAN)	Mercosur
Austria	Canada	Brunei	Argentina
Belgium	Mexico	Indonesia	Brazil
Finland	United States	Malaysia	Paraguay
France		Philippines	Uruguay
Germany		Singapore	
Ireland		Thailand	
Italy			
Luxembourg			
Netherlands			
Portugal			
Spain			
Denmark			
Great Britain			
Greece			
Sweden			

*Boxed countries are members of the Economic and Monetary Union (EMU).

currency exchange costs among participants and cut the middleman out of trillions of dollars' worth of foreign exchange transactions. U.S. businesses and travelers alone could save as much as 50 percent of the costs they now pay to convert dollars into multiple European currencies. Moreover, with prices in these 11 nations now in one currency, consumers can compare prices on similar items whether they are sold in Lisbon or Vienna.[40]

Heralded by some as a possible rival to the dollar or yen as the international currency of trade, the euro got off to a rocky start. Confidence in the new currency eroded when its value plunged to 83 U.S. cents—losing more than 28 percent of its original value. Nevertheless, the euro's weak start wasn't all bad for Europe. A decline in the value of the euro lowered the prices of goods sold by the 11 nations and fueled a boom in European exports—a plus for many European manufacturers.[41] In the next section we will discuss how a currency's value affects a country's economy—especially in the global marketplace.

INTERDEPENDENCE OF ECONOMIES IN THE GLOBAL MARKETPLACE

As more and more companies such as Trek seek international markets for their goods and services, or search for the most cost-effective locations to produce their goods or to transact business, they become even more tangled in the global marketplace. The opportunities in the global marketplace are many, but these opportunities are not without risks. A worldwide economic crisis at the end of the twentieth century showed, in dramatic fashion, just how risky the global marketplace could be. In this section, we'll show how one small country's decision to *float* its currency set a spark that ignited a regional economic crisis that sent shock waves throughout the world. But we must first explain some important concepts about foreign exchange rates and currency valuations so that you can understand how the change in value of one country's currency could cause such global economic turmoil.

Foreign Exchange Rates and Currency Valuations

When companies buy and sell goods and services in the global marketplace, they complete the transaction by exchanging currencies. For instance, if a Japanese company borrows money from a U.S. bank to build a manufacturing plant in Japan, it must repay the loan in U.S. dollars. Or if a South Korean car manufacturer imports engine parts from Japan, it must pay for them in yen

foreign exchange
Trading one currency for the equivalent value of another currency

exchange rate
Rate at which the money of one country is traded for the money of another

floating exchange rate system
World economic system in which the values of all currencies are determined by supply and demand

(Japan's currency). To do so, companies exchange their currency at any international bank that handles **foreign exchange,** the conversion of one currency into an equivalent amount of another currency. The number of yen, francs, or pounds that must be exchanged for every dollar, mark, or won is known as the **exchange rate** between currencies.

Most international currencies operate under a **floating exchange rate system;** thus, a currency's value or price fluctuates in response to the forces of global supply and demand (as we discussed in Chapter 1). The supply and demand of a country's currency are determined in part by what is happening in the country's own economy (as we'll see in the next section). Moreover, because supply and demand for a currency are always changing, the rate at which it is exchanged for other currencies may change a little each day. For example, Japanese currency might be trading at 137.6 yen to the dollar on one day and 136.8 on the next.

Even though most governments let the value of their currency respond to the forces of supply and demand, sometimes a government will intervene and adjust the exchange rate of its country's currency. Why would a government do this? One reason is to keep the price of a nation's goods and services more affordable in the global marketplace and to protect the nation's economy against trade imbalances. Another is to boost or slow down the country's economy.

Devaluation, or the drop in the value of a nation's currency relative to the value of other currencies, can at times boost a country's economy because it makes the country's products and services more affordable in foreign markets while it increases the price of imports. Because fewer units of foreign currency are required to purchase the devalued currency, such situations tend to raise a country's exports and lower its imports. Conversely, a strong currency boosts imports and dampens exports.

Some countries fix, or peg, the value of their currencies to the value of more stable currencies, such as the dollar or the yen, instead of letting it float freely. Hong Kong, for example, pegs its currency to the U.S. dollar. If a currency is pegged, its value fluctuates proportionally with the value of the foreign currency to which it is linked. So if the U.S. dollar declines, so will the Japanese yen and other currencies that are pegged to it. Of course, this system works well as long as the proportionate relationship between the two currencies remains valid. But if one partner suffers economic hardship, demand for its currency will decline significantly and the exchange rate at which the two are pegged will become unrealistic. Such was the case with many of the Southeast Asian currencies in the late 1990s.

The global economic crisis drove down prices on the foreign stock markets. Two traders at the Tokyo Stock Exchange react to the plunge of the benchmark Nikkei index.

The Global Economic Crisis at the End of the Twentieth Century

From the early 1980s until 1997, Southeast Asian countries wooed foreign investment. By the early 1990s, their economies were booming, export sectors were growing, cities were flush with money, and the people enjoyed some of the fastest-rising standards of living in the world. But the Southeast Asian economies soon overheated as consumers spent their newly acquired riches and inflation picked up.[42]

The bubble burst in July 1997 when Thailand unpegged its currency (the baht) from the U.S. dollar to allow the currency to float and gradually seek its true value. Anticipating that its currency would drop somewhat in value, Thailand was caught off guard when the currency went into a free fall. At about the same time, Indonesia unpegged the rupiah from the U.S. dollar to let the currency seek its true value, and the currency fell from 2,500 to 7,900 to the dollar, a devaluation of 300 percent in about 6 months.[43] Subsequent currency devaluations by other countries that felt pressured to keep the price of their exports competitive soon ignited an economic crisis that spread and infected nations as far flung as Guyana, Lebanon, Zimbabwe, Brazil, and Russia.

One by one the crisis struck economies that were already weak as a result of internal economic problems. Currencies plunged, commodity prices fell, stock markets crashed, and investors panicked and fled—taking with them the capital these emerging countries needed to fund their growth.[44] What caused the crisis, and why did the contagion spread? Economists now cite a combination of factors that contributed to the global economic turmoil.

What Caused the Global Economic Crisis? As the currencies plunged, foreign investors, who had poured over $100 billion a year into the world's emerging markets, panicked. Overnight, they pulled their money out of these countries, and economic growth hit the brakes. Without this growth, the supply of local currencies exceeded their demand, forcing these currencies to fall even lower.[45]

LEARNING
OBJECTIVE 7
Outline the causes of the global economic crisis at the end of the twentieth century and summarize the lesson learned by this example

As currencies devalued, consumers in the Southeast Asian countries were hit hard. Many could not afford to pay back their loans. Others lost their businesses. Still others watched their investments shrink in value overnight. As a result, Southeast Asia's demand for commodities such as oil, copper, aluminum, and gold tailed off, depressing world commodity prices to 10-year lows. This plunge in commodity prices transferred the economic crisis to other emerging markets and to Russia, because a large share of their exports are commodity-based. Meanwhile, to bail these countries out, the IMF and the World Bank lent them large sums of money: $17.2 billion to Thailand, $42 billion to Indonesia, $58.4 billion to South Korea, and $41.5 billion to Brazil.[46]

Although these loans were intended to stabilize the failing economies, some contend that the IMF's strict conditions for loan recipients made matters worse. By imposing tight fiscal and monetary requirements on the recipients, the IMF forced loan recipients to slash budget deficits.[47] To accomplish this goal, governments had to raise taxes and cut government spending; both actions hurt consumers even more. Another condition required recipients to privatize inefficient state-owned industries. This pressure resulted in massive worker layoffs and further depressed economies that were already plagued by internal problems:[48]

- *Excessive amounts of foreign-denominated debt.* Because most emerging nations could not finance their own growth, they had borrowed large sums of money from the United States and Japan to build new roads, dams, and industries. This practice seemed safe as long as the exchange rate for their local currencies remained stable. But once the value of these currencies plummeted, the borrowers could not afford to pay back their dollar- or yen-denominated debts. For example, a $1 million U.S. loan (equivalent to 26 million baht) doubled after the currency's free fall to 52 baht to the dollar. This meant that borrowers would have to exchange 52 million baht to pay back the $1 million loan to U.S. banks.

- *Bad loans.* Many Southeast Asian and Japanese banks worked on a buddy system (called croney capitalism) and made risky loans to friends who were poor credit risks and whose businesses were not financially sound. This practice kept profitless enterprises alive and led to the misallocation of resources. South Korean chaebol (giant family-controlled conglomerates) with the right connections, for example, were granted loans by local banks often in return for under-the-table payoffs.[49]

- *Plunging real estate prices.* Global economic turmoil hit while Japan was experiencing a severe real estate recession. At its peak, the land beneath the Imperial palace in downtown Tokyo was said to be worth as much as all of California, and a parking space in Hong Kong sold for $517,000. Many Japanese banks relied on the overvalued real estate as collateral for loans. When real estate prices plunged—some falling to 10 percent of their peak values—banks were reluctant to call their loans in hopes that real estate values would rebound. With few good lending opportunities at home, Japanese banks began lending elsewhere in Southeast Asia, adding to the banks' own troubles.[50]

Southeast Asia's Road to Recovery Today, many Southeast Asian economies have made a significant recovery: Currencies have stabilized; interest rates (which were boosted to attract foreign investors) have declined; and stock markets have recovered to near precrisis levels. Several factors have driven the recovery at a faster pace than originally expected:[51]

▪ *Increased exports.* Substantial currency devaluations have made the crisis countries more competitive and their exports more attractive. A booming U.S. economy provided a bottomless market for Southeast Asian goods such as semiconductors and telecommunications equipment.

▪ *Aid from Japan.* Historically the largest investor in the region, Japan slashed its investments in Southeast Asia during the 1990s as its own economy stagnated. But when the crisis hit, Japan offered the region over $35 billion in aid.

▪ *Rise in oil prices.* A steep rise in oil prices and some of the best weather in the region also helped bail out the crisis-hit economies.

▪ *Bank and corporate reforms.* The Southeast Asian countries have closed or restructured insolvent banks and removed the corrupt bank officials. Several Southeast Asian countries have passed bankruptcy and foreclosure laws. Meanwhile, many investors have shifted their resources into factories, Internet start-ups, and telecommunications as a source of future prosperity. Such investments will help long-term recovery.

Some experts contend that if these countries continue to restructure their economic systems as a result of the crisis, they could emerge as much stronger nations.[52] Still, recovery is far from assured. Some worry whether recovery is sustainable. Others fear swift recoveries and restored optimism could sideline many of the meaningful reforms that are getting under way and cause Asia to suffer a relapse.[53]

Russians line up outside a Moscow currency exchange to convert their devalued rubles into more stable currencies.

Recovery in Russia Foreign direct investment has picked up some in Russia. When the ruble's value plunged against the dollar after the August 1998 crisis, dollar-denominated imports became too expensive for most Russians. So foreign companies concluded that the best way to thrive in Russia was to begin manufacturing there. Nevertheless, big problems loom. Tarnished by scandals and corruption, most of Russia's largest banks have gone bankrupt, defaulting on loans to Western creditors and confiscating the deposits of their domestic clients. Lack of confidence in the Russian economy has prompted Russians to convert their rubles to other stable currencies.[54]

Effect of the Crisis on the United States

Ironically, the world's financial troubles had little negative impact on the United States economy. Although some businesses such as Boeing faced a slew of cancelled orders from Asian carriers, others prospered.[55] In fact, U.S. businesses thrived during a period of global economic malaise for several reasons: The U.S. government lowered interest rates on several occasions to boost the U.S. economy. (Lower interest rates make it more affordable for companies and consumers to borrow money and purchase more goods.) Plunging commodity prices kept U.S. inflation low and saved U.S. businesses billions of dollars, while the strong dollar made imports cheaper. Meanwhile, U.S. manufacturers found other markets for their goods.[56]

Still, some economists warn that the United States cannot expect to remain "an oasis of prosperity" if global economic turmoil were to reignite.[57] As the Asian crisis demonstrates, in the global marketplace—where economies of the world are entangled—problems in one country can indeed send shock waves around the globe.

Roadblocks on the European and Asian Superhighways

Late to the Internet and electronic commerce, Europe and Asia have trailed the United States in its use and enthusiasm for the Web. But now they are trying to catch up. Young firms in Europe and Asia are bursting through the gates at lightning pace, taking ideas originally conceived and launched in the United States and adapting them for the local market. But many roadblocks exist for these foreign companies.

E-COMMERCE IN EUROPE

The Internet in Europe is still in its infancy. Though rapidly growing, only 10 percent of Europeans currently use the Web. The pattern of e-commerce development varies country by country. Scandinavians are early adopters, driven partly by the excellence of local telecommunications manufacturers such as Ericsson of Sweden and Nokia of Finland. France, on the other hand, has been slow to take to the Web, partly because of cultural resistance and partly because of high telecommunications prices and tariffs, as well as inefficient phone systems.

LEARNING OBJECTIVE 8

Summarize the challenges European and Asian countries are facing as they attempt to narrow the U.S. lead in global e-commerce

---

Improvements to the European Highway

In spite of these obstacles, recent advancements in Europe's digital, cable, and satellite services are vastly improving the continent's telecommunications infrastructure. Europe is building on its strength in mobile telephones and will likely lead the world in mobile e-commerce (as Chapter 8 points out). Moreover, Europe's transition to the new economy is being fueled by a shift in career preferences from big traditional corporations to smaller start-ups due to a growing acceptance of entrepreneurship, as the exhibit on Bootstrap Capitalism suggests. Experts predict that e-commerce sales in Europe will skyrocket from a mere $5.6 billion in 1998 to $430 billion by 2003. Still, roadblocks exist.

Surfing a Web of Red Tape

European leaders say they support the rise of the Internet economy. Nonetheless, their governments burden e-commerce with a maze of rules, regulations, and tax laws from another era. For instance, to protect neighborhood stores, German regulations prohibit most price discounting on consumer goods. The same laws keep airlines from dumping unsold seats at the last minute with fire-sale fares. Online auctions run into legal tangles because laws require the physical display of goods to be sold at the auction. And legislative mazes turn the simple act of registering a Web address into a long and complex process. Moreover, they discourage e-commerce entrepreneurs.

E-COMMERCE IN ASIA

Asia is home to half the world's population but is even further behind Europe. Like Europe, Asia is not a homogeneous market. It varies widely by language, culture, literacy, and wealth. For instance, Singapore's and Hong Kong's wired societies have little in common with Sumatran villages of Indonesia or the rusting industrial ports of mainland China. In order to develop and thrive, e-commerce must jump several hurdles in Asia.

Hurdles on the Asian Highway

Lack of access to investment capital and expensive, uneven telecommunications service contribute to the Internet's lag in Asia. Getting a decent phone connection, let alone a net linkup, is a challenge in some parts of Asia. Worse, most commercial transactions in Asia still require cash and written receipts. A lack of comprehensive credit services also means that each e-marketplace buyer and seller must be painstakingly screened, which can take weeks. "It's difficult enough in the real world, but on the Internet, it can be even harder," says one Asian e-business owner.

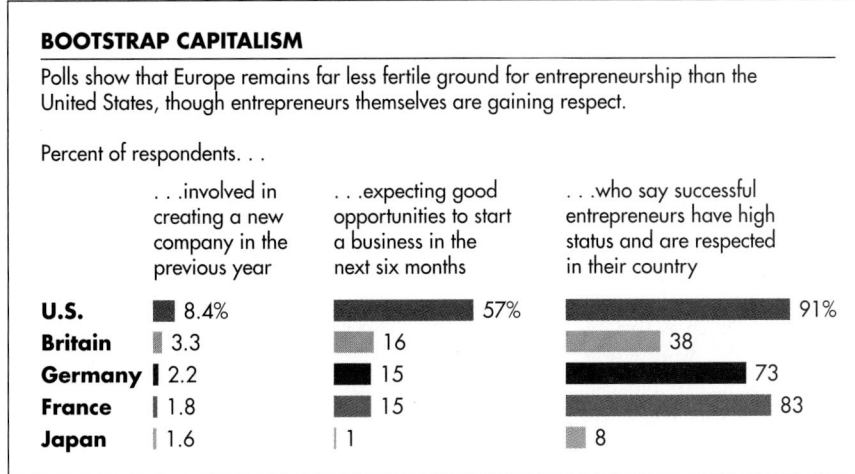

BOOTSTRAP CAPITALISM

Polls show that Europe remains far less fertile ground for entrepreneurship than the United States, though entrepreneurs themselves are gaining respect.

Percent of respondents. . .

	. . .involved in creating a new company in the previous year	. . .expecting good opportunities to start a business in the next six months	. . .who say successful entrepreneurs have high status and are respected in their country
U.S.	8.4%	57%	91%
Britain	3.3	16	38
Germany	2.2	15	73
France	1.8	15	83
Japan	1.6	1	8

Cultural differences also play a role. Shopping in Asia is a revered family outing. Thus, getting Asian consumers to shop online has been an arduous task. Those who do make online purchases face delivery problems because there is no local ground delivery equivalent to UPS or FedEx. Qualified shippers, warehouses, insurers, credit agencies, and finance companies are in great demand to move the goods.

China

Dot-coms highlight the central contradiction of China today—the drive to modernize without giving up one-party rule. The government wants the economic benefits of the Internet without the freedom it gives: the information revolution, minus the revolution. The question is not whether the Chinese government will pull the plug on the Internet, but whether it will regulate it in a way that will make it commercially viable.

Nevertheless, signs of advancement in China do exist. For instance, Net entrepreneurs are becoming role models for a new generation who see that they can get ahead on their own initiative, without relying on official connections. "People used to think you could only get rich with stocks or smuggling," says one Chinese CEO. "Now, with the Internet, they know they can get rich using their intelligence."

Japan

Fostering start-ups in leading-edge businesses has only recently become a priority in Japan, whose culture favors lifelong employment, consensus decision making, and conformity. In the hyper-paced e-commerce environment, companies have to innovate and change quickly—not one of Japan's strengths. Home to world-class multinationals and a highly educated workforce, Japan has been slow to free up the resources needed for promising start-ups. Moreover, Japan's top-down management style does not embrace technologies such as e-mail (which transfer decision making to middle managers). But Japan is changing. Despite its entrenched conservatism and regulated economy, Japan is undergoing a corporate revolution that will radically remake Japan's business culture—mostly in America's image.

A new generation of English-speaking, keyboard-literate college graduates is hitting the streets in Japan. Fujitsu is a $50 billion company with 190,000 employees, and it dominates the Japanese computer industry. Recently, Fujitsu declared that every facet of the company will now focus on the Internet. Companies such as Sony and Mitsubishi are cutting jobs and gutting the notion of lifelong employment. This creates incentives for people to start new, small companies. Still, churning out entrepreneurs has never been Japan's strength, especially since Japanese society tends to frown on displays of individual excellence.

Nonetheless, with e-commerce projected to increase in Japan from $3.2 billion to $63.4 billion by 2004, some think Japan may be on the brink of its next revolution: e-commerce. Japan could even catch the United States by surprise—just as it did in the 1980s when Japan's manufacturing excellence left the rest of the world in its wake.[58]

SUMMARY OF LEARNING OBJECTIVES

1. **Highlight the opportunities and challenges of conducting business in other countries.**
   Conducting business in other countries can provide such opportunities as increased sales, operational efficiencies, exposure to new technologies, and consumer choices. At the same time, it poses challenges such as the need to learn unique laws, customs, and ethical standards. Furthermore, it exposes companies to the risks of political and economic instabilities.

2. **List five ways to improve communication in an international business relationship.**
   To improve international communication, learn as much as you can about the culture and customs of the people you are working with; keep an open mind and avoid stereotyping; anticipate misunderstandings and guard against them by clarifying your intent; adapt your style to match the style of others; and learn how to show respect in other cultures.

3. **Identify five forms of international business activity.**
   Importing and exporting, licensing, franchising, strategic alliances and joint ventures, and foreign direct investment are five of the most common forms of international business activity. Each provides a company with varying degrees of control and entails different levels of risk and financial commitment.

4. **Discuss why nations trade.**
   Nations trade to obtain raw materials and goods that are unavailable to them or too costly to produce. International trade benefits nations by increasing a country's total output, offering lower prices and greater variety to its consumers, subjecting domestic oligopolies and monopolies to competition, and allowing companies to expand their markets and achieve production and distribution efficiencies.

5. **Explain why nations restrict international trade and list four forms of trade restrictions.**

Nations restrict international trade to boost local economies, to shield domestic industries from head-to-head competition with overseas rivals, to save specific jobs, to give weak or new industries a chance to grow strong, and to protect a nation's security. The four most commonly used forms of trade restrictions are tariffs (taxes, surcharges, or duties levied against imported goods), quotas (limitations on the amount of a particular good that can be imported), embargoes (the banning of imports and exports of certain goods), and sanctions (politically motivated embargoes).

6. **Highlight three protectionist tactics nations use to give their domestic industries a competitive edge.**

From time to time countries give their domestic producers a competitive edge by imposing restrictive import standards such as requiring special licenses or unusually high product standards, by subsidizing certain domestic producers so they can compete more favorably in the global marketplace, and by dumping or selling large quantities of a product at a lower price than it costs to produce the good or at a lower price than the good is sold for in its home market.

7. **Outline the causes of the global economic crisis at the end of the twentieth century and summarize the lesson learned by this example.**

The global economic crisis was the result of a combination of factors. Fueled by investor speculation, foreign currency devaluations, falling global commodity prices, and IMF interference, the crisis hit countries whose internal economies were suffering from excessive amounts of foreign denominated debt, bad loans, and plunging real estate prices. The global crisis demonstrated that in the global marketplace economies of the world are entangled. Thus, economic problems in one country can impact the economies of others—especially if they are plagued by their own internal problems.

8. **Summarize the challenges European and Asian countries are facing as they attempt to narrow the U.S. lead in global e-commerce.**

European roadblocks to e-commerce include cultural resistance, restrictive government regulations, high telecommunications prices, inefficient phone systems, and slow acceptance of entrepreneurship. Asian roadblocks include inadequate and inefficient infrastructures, cultural differences, reluctance to use credit cards, government resistance, bureaucratic and hierarchical management structures, and inadequate support for entrepreneurs.

KEY TERMS

absolute advantage (76)
balance of payments (77)
balance of trade (77)
comparative advantage theory (77)
dumping (80)
embargo (79)
euro (82)
exchange rate (84)
exporting (72)

floating exchange rate system (84)
foreign direct investment (FDI) (75)
foreign exchange (84)
free trade (80)
importing (72)
intrafirm trade (77)
joint venture (74)
licensing (73)
multinational corporations (MNCs) (75)

protectionism (78)
quotas (79)
strategic alliance (73)
tariffs (79)
trade deficit (77)
trade surplus (77)
trading blocs (81)

TEST YOUR KNOWLEDGE

QUESTIONS FOR REVIEW

1. How can a company use a licensing agreement to enter world markets?
2. What is the balance of trade, and how is it related to the balance of payments?
3. What is intrafirm trade?
4. What is dumping, and how does the United States respond to this practice?
5. What is a floating exchange rate?

QUESTIONS FOR ANALYSIS

6. Why would a company choose to work through intermediaries when selling products in a foreign country?
7. How do companies benefit from forming international joint ventures and strategic alliances?

8. What types of situations might cause the U.S. government to implement protectionist measures?
9. How do tariffs and quotas protect a country's own industries?
10. Why is it important to understand other cultures when designing an e-commerce Web site?
11. Should the U.S. government more closely regulate the practice of giving trips and other incentives to foreign managers to win their business? Is this bribery?

QUESTIONS FOR APPLICATION

12. Suppose you own a small company that manufactures baseball equipment. You are aware that Russia is a large market, and you are considering exporting your products there. What steps should you take? Who might be able to give you assistance?
13. Because your Brazilian restaurant caters to Western businesspeople and tourists, much of the food you buy is imported from the

United States. Lately, the value of the real (Brazil's currency) has been falling relative to the dollar. This change makes your food imports much more costly, and it negatively affects your profitability. You have three options: Which one will you choose? (a) Raise menu prices across the board. (b) Accept only U.S. dollars from customers. (c) Try to purchase more of your food items locally. Please explain your selection.

14. Review the theory of supply and demand discussed in Chapter 1. Using this theory, explain how a country's currency is valued and why governments sometimes adjust the values of their currency.

15. You just received notice that a large shipment of manufacturing supplies you have been waiting for has been held up in customs for two weeks. A local business associate tells you that you are expected to give customs agents some "incentive money" to see that everything clears easily. How will you handle this situation? Evaluate the ethical merits of your decision by answering the questions outlined in Exhibit 2.1 on page 46.

PRACTICE YOUR KNOWLEDGE

SHARPENING YOUR COMMUNICATION SKILLS

Languages never translate on a word-for-word basis. When doing business in the global marketplace, choose words that convey only their most specific denotative meaning. Avoid using slang or idioms (words that can have meanings far different from their individual components when translated literally). For example, if a U.S. executive tells an Egyptian executive that a certain product "doesn't cut the mustard," chances are that communication will fail.

Team up with two other students and list 10 examples of slang (in your own language) that would probably be misinterpreted or misunderstood during a business conversation with someone from another culture. Next to each example, suggest other words you might use to convey the same message. Make sure the alternatives mean exactly the same as the original slang or idiom. Compare your list with those of your classmates.

HANDLING DIFFICULT SITUATIONS ON THE JOB: SHOULD COMPANIES STRESS ENGLISH ONLY ON THE JOB?

When Frances Arreola read the memo announcing that employees should speak only English on the job, she was outraged. Arreola, a lens inspector for Signet Amoralite, a lens-manufacturing firm in southern California, is fluent in both English and Spanish but feels that the English-only rules constitute discrimination.

More than half of Signet's 900 employees are Asian, Filipino, or Hispanic. The company defends its English-only rule on the ground that "speaking in another language that associates cannot fully understand can lead to misunderstandings, is impolite, and can even be unsafe." While the policy carries no punishment, it is considered by some critics to violate federal discrimination laws.[59]

1. If you were a manager at Signet Amoralite, how would you defend the company's English-only policy?

2. If a company knowingly hires an employee who is not fluent in English, should the company have a right to require English only on the job?

3. If you took a job in another country where you weren't fluent in the native language, would you feel compelled to learn the language even if your employer did not require you to?

BUILDING YOUR TEAM SKILLS

In today's interdependent global economy, fluctuations in a country's currency can have a profound effect on the flow of products across borders. The U.S. steel industry, for example, has been feeling intense competition from an influx of Korean, Brazilian, and Russian steel imports. After the currencies of those countries plummeted in value, the price of steel products exported to the United States dropped as well, making U.S. steel much more expensive by comparison.

Fueled by low prices, steel flooded into the United States, hurting sales of U.S. steel. Over the course of several months, the volume of steel imports nearly doubled. Stung, U.S. steelmakers slashed production and laid off more than 10,000 U.S. workers. U.S. trade officials charge that the cheap imported steel is being dumped, and they are considering protectionist measures such as imposing quotas on steel imports.[60]

With your team, brainstorm a list of at least four additional ways the United States might handle this situation. Once you have your list, consider the probable effect of each option on these stakeholders:

- U.S. businesses that buy steel
- U.S. steel manufacturers
- U.S. businesses that export to Korea, Brazil, or Russia
- Employees of U.S. steel manufacturers

On the basis of your analysis and discussion, which option will your team recommend? Select a spokesperson to explain your selection and your team's reasoning to the other teams. Compare your recommendation with those of your classmates.

EXPAND YOUR KNOWLEDGE

KEEPING CURRENT USING *THE WALL STREET JOURNAL*

Find a *Wall Street Journal* article describing an experience of a U.S. company or division that conducts business in a foreign country. As an alternative, look for an article describing how a company or division based in another country has started doing business in the United States. If you are using *The Wall Street Journal* online edition on the Web (www.wsj.com), search past editions (click on Past

Editions and Articles) using key terms such as "joint venture," "licensing," or "strategic alliance."

1. Describe in your own words the company's experience. Was it positive, negative, or mixed? Why?

2. What legal or political barriers did the company have to overcome? What cultural or business differences did the

company encounter? What problems did these difference create for the company? What did the company do to overcome the obstacles?

3. Companies involved in international trade have to watch the foreign exchange rates of the countries in which they do business. Find yesterday's foreign exchange rates for the euro, Japanese yen, Brazilian real, and Russian ruble relative to the U.S. dollar. If you were a U.S. exporter, how might a stronger dollar affect demand for your products? How might a weaker dollar affect demand? (Note: one Internet source for foreign exchange rates is www.x-rates.com/.)

DISCOVERING CAREER OPPORTUNITIES

If global business interests you, consider working for a U.S. government agency that supports or regulates international trade. For example, here are the duties performed by an international trade specialist at the International Trade Administration of the U.S. Department of Commerce: "The incumbent will assist senior specialists in coordination and support of government trade programs and events; perform research and analysis of trade data and information on specific topics or issues within a larger project or assignment; and disseminate trade information and materials on government products/services to U.S. businesses and associations. Incumbent will attend meetings and engage in other activities for developmental purposes. As a condition of employment, applicants must be available for reassignment and relocation within the United States."[61]

1. On the basis of this description, what education and skills (personal and professional) would you need to succeed as an international trade specialist? Why? How does this job description fit your qualifications and interests?

2. Given their duties, where would you expect international trade specialists to be situated or transferred? Would you be willing to move to another city or state for this type of position?

3. What sources would you contact to locate trade-related jobs with government agencies such as the International Trade Administration?

EXPLORING THE BEST OF THE WEB

URLs for all Internet exercises are provided at the Web site for this book, www.prenhall.com/mescon. When you log on to the text Web site, select Chapter 3, then select "Student Resources," click on the name of the featured Web site, and follow the detailed navigational directions to complete these exercises.

Navigating Global Business Differences, page 72

The resources available at USA Trade.gov will start your journey into the world of global business on the right foot. Log on to this

site, and access the Country Commercial Guide for a specific country you would like to learn more about.

1. What are the economic trends and future outlook for that country?

2. What role does the government play in the country's economy?

3. How do the business customs of that country differ from those of the United States? What is the country's official language?

Going Global, page 73

Many factors must be considered before exporting a product. The information in the *Basic Guide to Exporting,* available online, can help you make sense of it all. Explore the publication to increase your knowledge about export procedures, foreign markets, and more.

1. Describe the general factors you should examine before reaching a decision to enter the global marketplace.

2. What kinds of information can you find at U.S. Export Assistance Centers?

3. What questions should a company consider before preparing a product for export? Why do governments impose foreign product regulations on imported goods?

Banking on the World Bank, page 81

Log on to the World Bank Web site and learn about the important role this organization plays in today's global economy.

1. What is the goal of the World Bank? What does the World Bank do?

2. Who runs the World Bank? Where does it get its money? Where does the money go?

3. What are the World Bank's latest environmental initiatives?

Explore on Your Own

Review these chapter-related Web sites on your own to learn more about doing business in the global marketplace.

1. World Trade Markets, www.wtm.com/, provides trade leads by date, country, or product type.

2. World Trade Organization, www.wto.org, lists the rules that pertain to international security, cooperation, economic growth, trade restrictions, human rights, and dispute settlement. Log on and learn more about these rules, international economic relations, and a variety of trade topics.

3. Foreign Currency Exchange Rates, www.x-rates.com/, provides foreign exchange rates and history of performance in table and graph format.

A CASE FOR CRITICAL THINKING

■ *Doing Everybody's Wash— Whirlpool's Global Lesson*

Everybody is talking about going global these days, but most people don't understand what that really means. David Whitwam, chairman and CEO of Whirlpool, does. When he first began eyeing the global marketplace, this Michigan-based appliance maker was

concentrating only on the U.S. market, producing and marketing washers, refrigerators, and other household appliances under the Whirlpool, KitchenAid, Roper, and Kenmore brand names.

THE RIGHT WAY TO GO GLOBAL

Determined to convert Whirlpool from essentially a U.S. company to a major global player, Whitwam purchased N. V. Philips's floundering European appliance business in 1989. The CEO's first challenge was to integrate and coordinate the many European operations with the U.S. operation. Some companies accomplish this task by imposing the parent's systems on the acquired companies, but Whitwam started down a more ambitious path. He created cross-cultural teams with members from the European and North American operations, and together they designed a program to ensure quality and productivity throughout Whirlpool's worldwide operation. In the eyes of other corporate leaders, Whirlpool was doing everything right. The company was even featured in a 1994 *Harvard Business Review* article titled "The Right Way to Go Global."

SPINNING OUT OF CONTROL

Whitwam soon discovered, however, that developing global strategies was far easier than executing them. Whirlpool had not counted on the difficulty in marketing appliances—a largely homogeneous process in the United States—to the fragmented cultures of Europe, Asia, and Latin America. For instance, clothes washers sold in northern European countries such as Denmark must spin-dry clothes much better than in southern Italy, where consumers often line-dry clothes in warmer weather. And consumers in India and southern China prefer small refrigerators because they must fit in tight kitchens.

Despite these challenges, Whitwam was convinced that he could remake Whirlpool into a truly global company. But Whirlpool's timing couldn't have been worse. Just as the company was planting its feet in international markets, economic turmoil hit Asia and Europe. Wildly fluctuating foreign exchange rates wreaked havoc in Asia, where Whirlpool had participated in several joint ventures. Fortunately, less than 5 percent of Whirlpool's sales came from Asia, so the company was not seriously hurt. Still, ongoing global economic woes contributed to Whirlpool's multimillion-dollar losses overseas.

REARRANGING THE GLOBAL LOAD

The global economic crisis forced Whitwam to fine-tune his expansion plans. Whirlpool dropped one joint venture in China (costing the company $350 million) and rearranged others as intense competition and weak economic conditions drove appliance prices down and sapped profits. "The thing we misjudged was how rapidly Chinese manufacturers could improve their quality," notes Whitwam.

In Brazil, where Whirlpool had long been profitable, a currency crisis slowed appliance sales to a trickle. Still, Whitwam remained committed to the market. Anticipating future growth opportunities in this emerging market, Whirlpool invested hundreds of millions of dollars to modernize operations, cut costs, and solidify its position as the country's market leader in refrigerators, room air conditioners, and washers.

To expedite its entry into foreign markets, Whirlpool kept things simple. The company used licensing arrangements and formed strategic alliances with others. It also developed standardized products, which it could modify to meet specific market needs. For instance, front-loading washing machines were scaled down for European homes as were refrigerators for India. Despite their widely different exteriors and sizes, the appliances had plenty of common "innards."

ULTIMATE REWARD

In less than a decade, Whitwam transformed Whirlpool from essentially a U.S. company into the world's leading manufacturer of major home appliances. With 11 major brands sold in 170 countries, international sales now account for about 45 percent of the company's $10 billion annual revenue. Moreover, the outlook for growth in the global appliance industry looks promising. Still, Whitwam understands that doing business in the global marketplace is fraught with risk; conditions can change at the drop of a baht, ruble, or dollar.

CRITICAL THINKING QUESTIONS

1. What did Whirlpool find to be the advantages and disadvantages of doing business around the world?

2. How did global expansion affect Whirlpool's products?

3. Should Whirlpool be concerned about a currency devaluation in a country where it sells few appliances?

4. Find out how Whirlpool is faring with its global strategy. Go to Chapter 3 of this text's Web site at www.prenhall.com/mescon. Follow the online instructions to read the latest news releases about Whirlpool's financial performance, international operations, and plans for expansion. How are Whirlpool's sales doing outside the United States? Where is the company strongest? Where is it struggling? What changes, if any, is the company making to its global strategy?

VIDEO CASE AND EXERCISES

■ *Yahoo! and Lands' End: Think Global, Act Local*

SYNOPSIS

Although Internet media pioneer Yahoo! (www.yahoo.com) is headquartered in California, and apparel retailer Lands' End (www.landsend.com) is based in Wisconsin, both see international business activity as a way to fuel growth. Lands' End, founded in 1963, started its global expansion in 1987 by sending catalogs to customers in Canada. Soon the company was selling by

mail in 175 countries. As global sales increased, the company opened offices in the United Kingdom and Japan and learned, through trial and error, how to navigate cultural differences. For its part, Yahoo! moved into global markets just two years after it was founded in 1994, starting with a Web site with language and content customized for Japan. Yahoo! has continued opening several new international Web sites every year, carefully tailoring the offerings on each site to fit local customs and culture.

EXERCISES
Analysis

1. What forms of international business activity have Lands' End and Yahoo! used to enter global markets?

2. Why do Lands' End managers say that "the United States and the United Kingdom are two countries divided by a common language"?

3. How do the sales made by U.S. companies offering products on international Yahoo! sites affect the U.S. balance of trade?

4. If a country in which Lands' End operates decides to devalue its currency, what is the likely effect on Lands' End?

5. Managers at Yahoo! say that services such as their Web sites are "apolitical," yet they are careful to abide by each country's customs. Why?

Application

Companies choosing among the five types of international business activities must consider the degree of risk, ownership, and financial commitment they find acceptable. What risks might Lands' End encounter in opening facilities in South Africa to handle local customers' orders? How might the company research these risks in more detail?

Decision

Assume that an Egyptian entrepreneur has asked to license the Yahoo! name for a local Web site. What are the advantages and disadvantages of licensing the Yahoo! brand? What decision would you recommend to the top management of Yahoo!—and why?

Communication

Write a one-page memo to Jasmine Kem, international marketing manager for Yahoo!, explaining the decision you recommend concerning whether Yahoo! should license its name to the entrepreneur in Egypt.

Integration

Turn back to the discussion of labor-intensive and capital-intensive businesses in Chapter 1. How would you categorize Yahoo! and Lands' End? Why?

Ethics

Does Yahoo! have an ethical obligation to prevent its users in Japan, China, and other countries from falling victim to Internet scams such as fraudulent sales offers?

Debate

Many successful e-businesses have been founded in the United States, especially in and around Silicon Valley. Does the United States have a comparative advantage in e-business? Use this question as the subject of a debate, offering evidence to support your stand for or against.

Teamwork

In a team of three students, consider how Lands' End would be affected if Japan decided to pursue a protectionist strategy. What kinds of trade restrictions would hurt Lands' End? Could any restrictions help Lands' End?

Online Research

Using Internet sources, identify all the countries and languages in which Yahoo! sites are available. Also research the company's plans for opening new international sites in the coming year. Summarize your findings in a paragraph or two.

 **MYPHLIP COMPANION WEB SITE**

Learning Interactively

Visit the myPHLIP Web site at www.prenhall.com/mescon. For Chapter 3, take advantage of the interactive "Study Guide" to test your chapter knowledge. Get instant feedback on whether you need additional studying. Read the "Current Events" articles to get the latest on chapter topics, and complete the exercises as specified by your instructor. Expand your learning with a visit to the "Research Area." There you will find a wealth of information you can use to complete your course assignments.

PART   1

MASTERING GLOBAL AND GEOGRAPHICAL SKILLS: ADIOS, ARGENTINA—HELLO, BRAZIL

"Love thy neighbor" is not an easy commandment to live by for Argentina. The 35 percent slide of the Brazilian real against the Argentine peso at the end of the twentieth century made Argentine products comparatively more expensive both at home and abroad. Worse, the cost of doing business became far cheaper in Brazil than in Argentina, spurring some two dozen companies to jump the border. One manufacturer after another moved north to Brazil. At least 15 auto-parts companies have left, taking with them 7,000 jobs, or one-fifth of the industry's workforce. And the stampede isn't limited to the auto industry.

You are the owner of a U.S.-based home security equipment manufacturing company with a local operation in Argentina, and your Argentine workers have been bolting for Brazil like everyone else. So now you're thinking of packing it up and moving your Argentine operation to São Paulo, Brazil. Not only is the cost of doing business more affordable there, but with all the people migrating north, you'll have no trouble finding customers and employees.[62]

You heard (unofficially) that the market for home security equipment is good in Brazil. But you know very little about the Brazilian laws, culture, and infrastructure. You speak fluent Spanish, but not a word of Portuguese. And you think it would be a good idea to research the Brazilian marketplace before making such an important decision. Fortunately, many good Internet resources can provide you with information on countries and markets around the world. These sites include:

- CIA World Factbook

- U.S. State Department Background Notes

- Big Emerging Markets Resource Page

Log on to this text's Web site, Chapter 3—Mastering Global and Geographic Skills, for current links to these resources and navigational directions. Use these resources and others you may find on the Internet or at the library to answer the following questions:

1. Briefly describe Brazil's infrastructure. How do most products reach Brazil? Is internal transportation primarily by air or truck? Which state in Brazil has the best highways? Which transportation-related industries have been privatized or are scheduled to be privatized? In which area of Brazil does the majority of the population live? How does the size of Brazil compare to that of the United States? Which countries border Brazil.

2. How does the size of Brazil's economy compare to other nations in the world? What industries are strongest in Brazil?

3. Briefly outline the typical steps required for importing products into Brazil.

4. Discuss the overall economic outlook for sales of security and safety equipment in Brazil.

Business PlanPro

CONDUCTING BUSINESS IN THE GLOBAL ECONOMY

Review the Appendix, "Getting Started with Business PlanPro Software," to learn how to use Business PlanPro Software so that you can complete these exercises.

Think Like a Pro

Objective: By completing these exercises, you will become acquainted with the sections of a business plan that address forms of competition, company and product/service descriptions, and the economic outlook for the related industry. For these exercises, you will use the sample business plan for Adventure Travel International (ATI).

Open the BPP software and explore the sample business plan Travel Agency.spd. Click on the Plan Outline icon to access the plan's Task Manager. Find the headings What You're Selling and The Business You're In and double click on each of the sections under these headings to read the text portion of the business plan that discusses these topics.

1. What products and services does ATI provide? Will ATI compete on price, speed, quality, service, or innovation to gain a competitive advantage?

2. What is the economic outlook for the travel industry? What are the principal categories of this industry? What percentage of the industry involves international travel?

3. How has the Internet affected this industry?

Find the heading What You're Selling. Double click on Product and Service Description. The text view of BPP software provides helpful instructions for each section of a business plan. Click on the Instructions Tab located at the top of your screen.

4. What information should you include about a company's product and service in a business plan?

Now return to the Task Manager and double click on Competitive Comparison. Click on the Instructions Tab.

5. What are some of the things you should discuss about your competition in a business plan?

Create Your Own Business Plan

Think about your own business. Describe in detail the product or service your company will provide. Indicate whether you will compete on price, speed, quality, service, or innovation. In what industry will you compete? What is the economic outlook for that industry? What kinds of competition do you expect to face?

The Match

FedEx is the leader in overnight air delivery. Arch-rival United Parcel Service (UPS), also known as "Big Brown," practically owns the business of moving packages by truck and delivering them to any address in the United States. Both companies compete in the same transportation industry sector—air delivery, freight, and parcel services. Several years ago UPS began going after FedEx's profitable core business—next day air express, with surprising success. Acknowledging that it is losing ground to UPS, FedEx is counterattacking.

1999 Revenue

$17.5 billion $27.2 billion

- International operations
- U.S. ground
- U.S. two-day air
- U.S. overnight
- Other

FedEx Hits the Ground

In 1997 FedEx acquired RPS, a trucking company, to wage a ground turf war against UPS. But FedEx feared that combining the two companies could tarnish the FedEx image, so it kept RPS at arm's length. Meanwhile, poor integration of the FedEx air and RPS ground units made things tough for corporate customers who wanted to ship by both truck and overnight air. They had to deal with two salespeople, call two numbers, and so on. By contrast, UPS offers both services seamlessly. So UPS captured the lion's share of e-commerce delivery traffic.

Realizing that customers wanted integrated ground and air services, FedEx combined the two operations in early 2000, renamed RPS to FedEx Ground, and changed RPS's focus to business-to-business deliveries. Then it developed FedEx Home to beef up deliveries to residential neighborhoods—going right after the heart of UPS. Later that year, FedEx increased its aggressive counterattack against UPS by acquiring American Freightways, a large U.S. ground shipper.

UPS Flexes Its Muscle

Even though FedEx is making inroads with its acquisition of RPS and American Freightways, UPS still has the ground advantage. With three times the number of trucks of FedEx, UPS delivers to virtually every U.S. address. Moreover, UPS's massive volume of ground-based shipments keeps its residential package delivery costs low. So UPS can pass the savings on to customers and still make money. Furthermore, UPS has poured a stunning $11 billion into technology to improve its package-tracking systems and on-time delivery performance. Like FedEx, UPS customers can track the exact location of their packages.

Fighting a Battle in the Sky and on the Ground!

	FedEx www.fedex.com	UPS www.ups.com
Sales (annual)	$17.5 billion	$27.2 billion
Daily Packages	4.5 million	13 million
Delivered Market Share	25% of package delivery market	55% of package delivery market
Employees	149,000	344,000
Equipment	43,500 trucks; 637 planes	150,000 trucks; 610 planes

The Fight Goes Airborne

For years UPS's air-express business lagged far behind FedEx's, and UPS could not match FedEx's reputation for reliability. But UPS has improved its air delivery service and is gradually chipping away at FedEx's lead. Furthermore, when possible, UPS shifts packages from expensive airplane delivery to less-expensive truck delivery, then passes the savings on to the customer.

Duking It Out in China

Both UPS and FedEx are major players in the global marketplace, but their approach in China differs significantly. FedEx has poured money into an all-out China blitz in advance of market demand. Since 1995, the company has flown its own jets to and from China's mainland. Moreover, FedEx boasts its American identity with brightly-painted FedEx trucks and promotes its service with U.S.-style, and at times abrasive, advertising.

UPS, by contrast, has taken a more conservative approach to China, waiting for China's market to develop before investing there. UPS delivers cargo to China, but until recently, the company was required to turn over the cargo to another airline in Hong Kong for delivery to the mainland, a process that hurt UPS's reliability and lengthened its delivery time. Compared to rival FedEx, UPS's advertising in China is understated and old-fashioned. In fact, UPS keeps a low profile and hopes Chinese customers won't even notice that it is a U.S. company.

During the Asian economic crisis, UPS's go-slow strategy made economic sense. But now UPS would like to be in FedEx's shoes. China, with 1.4 billion people, is the fastest-growing freight market in the world. To catch up, UPS recently acquired its own air routes into Beijing and Shanghai, stripping FedEx of what UPS claims is a monopoly. With six new China routes, UPS hopes to make a bigger dent in rival FedEx's 13 percent share of China's express delivery market.

Betting on the Future of E-Commerce

FedEx thinks the Internet will drive demand for business-to-business shipping services and is placing bets that businesses will increasingly need parts and supplies shipped overnight. Thus, FedEx is focusing on the business-to-business side of e-commerce. By contrast, UPS thinks the Internet will continue to drive delivery traffic to homes. With 80 percent of its revenue already coming from deliveries between businesses, UPS is placing bets on the business-to-consumer side of e-commerce. UPS is aware of the fact that delivery to homes is less profitable than delivery to businesses because homes are more scattered. To boost its home-delivery service, in 2001 UPS purchased

the largest shipping retail outlet in the country, Mail Boxes Etc. (MBE), and will operate the 4,300 retail stores in 29 countries as an independent company, This could give UPS an advantage over FedEx, should UPS decide to price its services at MBE lower than the prices charged by competitors.

Double Trouble for UPS

The U.S. Postal Service, while currently not much of a threat to these companies will be firing its guns once it completes construction of its competitive package-tracking system. U.S. mail trucks already deliver letters to virtually every address in the country, so the added cost of delivering packages via mail trucks will be low. Furthermore, by law, FedEx and UPS must set their package delivery prices twice as high as those charged by the U.S. Post Office.

Recognizing this potential threat, FedEx is not sitting still. Instead it negotiated an alliance with the U.S. Post Office whereby FedEx would deliver most U.S. Priority Mail and Express Mail shipments and be allowed to place its purple-and-white express-delivery boxes at U.S. post offices. UPS and other carriers, of course, will eventually be allowed to place their delivery boxes at postal locations too. Nonetheless, the FedEx-U.S. Postal Service delivery alliance is a big setback for rival UPS.

QUESTIONS FOR CRITICAL THINKING

1. Are the barriers to entry in the package delivery service industry high or low? Explain your answer.

2. What economies of scale did FedEx hope to gain by folding RPS ground delivery services into a single FedEx operation?

3. What are the pros and cons of each company's approach in China?

4. How is the U.S. Postal Service a threat to both UPS and FedEx? Should a government agency which is funded by U.S. tax dollars, be allowed to form an alliance with privately-funded enterprise?

5. If UPS and FedEx had the opportunity to "do it all over again," what changes do you think they would make in their competitive approaches? Why?

6. Explore the UPS and FedEx Web sites to learn more about each company. How is the Internet changing the way these companies do business?

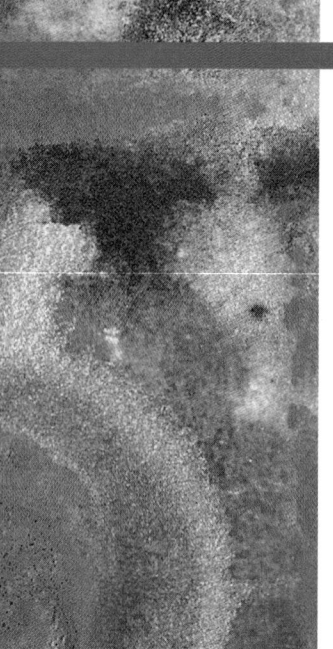

SMALL BUSINESS, NEW VENTURES, AND FRANCHISES

LEARNING OBJECTIVES

After studying this chapter, you will be able to

1. Identify the key characteristics (other than size) that differentiate small businesses from larger ones

2. Highlight the major contributions small businesses make to the U.S. economy

3. Discuss three factors contributing to the increase in the number of small businesses

4. Cite the key characteristics common to most entrepreneurs

5. List three ways of getting into business for yourself

6. Identify three sources of small-business assistance

7. Discuss the principal sources of small-business private financing

@ 8. Explain why many dot-com businesses failed at the beginning of the twenty-first century

TODAY

Inside Business

Since founding idealab! in 1996, Bill Gross (top) has had a hand in launching CarsDirect.com, Free-PC, GoTo.com, e-Machines, and a number of other ventures.

IDEAS BY THE DOZEN: HATCHING INTERNET COMPANIES AT IDEALAB!
www.idealab.com

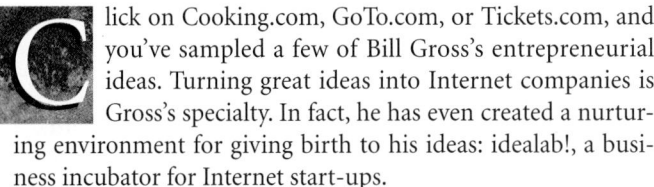

Click on Cooking.com, GoTo.com, or Tickets.com, and you've sampled a few of Bill Gross's entrepreneurial ideas. Turning great ideas into Internet companies is Gross's specialty. In fact, he has even created a nurturing environment for giving birth to his ideas: idealab!, a business incubator for Internet start-ups.

Seasoned entrepreneurs like Gross know that starting a business from scratch takes more than a great idea. An entrepreneur since the age of 12, Gross realized that building a successful Internet company required enormous investments of time and resources. Moreover, he knew that Internet ventures needed a jump start on the competition in the vast world of cyberspace. So how could he turn his great ideas into great Internet companies at lightning-fast speeds?

First Gross assessed his own strengths and weaknesses. Although he thrived on creative challenges, Gross disliked the details of managing the daily operations of a business. So he envisioned creating an outlet for his wealth of ideas that would allow his creativity to reign supreme.

Then he assessed ways to speed up the basic steps of starting an e-business. Every Internet start-up required such basic necessities as office space, telephone systems, and computer equipment. But Gross reasoned that start-ups could save valuable time and reduce expenses by pooling resources. If Internet entrepreneurs could draw on a central resource for basic business services, they could devote their time and energy to developing strategies for their new ventures instead of contending with personnel or accounting problems.

Confident that he could devise a strategy for streamlining the process of starting Internet companies, Gross focused on creating a model business incubator for Internet start-ups. After rounding up $5 million in initial financing from his own resources and from such notable investors as director Stephen Spielberg and actor Michael Douglas, Gross launched idealab! in 1996. Thirteen months later, Gross's new roost had hatched 23 Internet companies from scratch.

Idealab!'s most recognized e-businesses include CarsDirect.com, Petsmart.com, and CitySearch. But Gross's bright ideas are not always foolproof. Idealab! has canned several start-up ventures, such as the Web broadcast site, EntertainNet.com, and Homelink.com, a search site for real estate, and like other entrepreneurs, Gross got caught up in the early Internet mania and invested in some bad Internet start-ups. Still, Gross contends that the experiences were valuable learning lessons for idealab! "Although the companies failed, we learned a tremendous amount from those experiences, which we now use to benefit our networks of other companies," he insists.

Today Gross's brood of e-commerce chicklings consists of more than 40 Internet businesses, including 7 publicly traded companies. Idealab! supplies the start-ups with ideas, office space, administrative staff and services, and seed money of $250,000 to $500,000 (which Gross obtains from a variety of investors in exchange for a share of ownership in each new venture). In other words, like a busy mother hen, Gross provides his newborns with everything they need to make their way into the world of e-commerce.[1]

▉ UNDERSTANDING THE WORLD OF SMALL BUSINESS

Small businesses such as idealab! are the cornerstone of the U.S. economic system. The country was originally founded by people involved in small businesses—the family farmer, the shopkeeper, the craftsperson. Successive waves of immigrants carried on the tradition, launching restaurants and laundries, providing repair and delivery services, and opening newsstands and bakeries.

This trend continued for many years, until improvements in transportation and communication enabled large producers to manufacture goods at low costs and pass the savings on to consumers. As a result, many small, independent businesses could not compete. Scores of them closed their doors, and big business emerged as the primary economic force. The trend toward bigness continued for several decades, then it reversed.

The 1990s were a golden decade for entrepreneurship in the United States. Small companies have, in fact, turned the U.S. economy into the growth engine for the world (see Exhibit 4.1). Today, being a small business is equated with being nimble and dynamic.[2] Even so, defining what constitutes a small business is surprisingly tricky, because *small* is a relative term. For example, a manufacturing firm with 500 employees might be considered small if it competes against much larger companies, but a retail establishment with 500 employees might be classified as big when compared with its competitors.

One reliable source of information for small businesses is the Small Business Administration (SBA). This government agency serves as a resource and advocate for small firms, providing them with financial assistance, training, and a variety of helpful programs. The SBA defines a **small business** as a firm that (a) is independently owned and operated, (b) is not dominant in its field, (c) is relatively small in terms of annual sales, and (d) has fewer than 500 employees. According to SBA figures, 80 percent of all U.S. companies have annual sales of less than $1 million.[3]

small business
Company that is independently owned and operated, is not dominant in its field, and meets certain criteria for the number of employees and annual sales revenue

Characteristics of Small Businesses

Small businesses are of two distinct types: lifestyle businesses and high-growth ventures. Roughly 80 to 90 percent are modest operations with little growth potential (although some have attractive income potential for the solo businessperson). The self-employed consultant working part-

EXHIBIT 4.1

NEW SMALL BUSINESSES

The growth in the number of small-business start-ups is fueling today's economy.

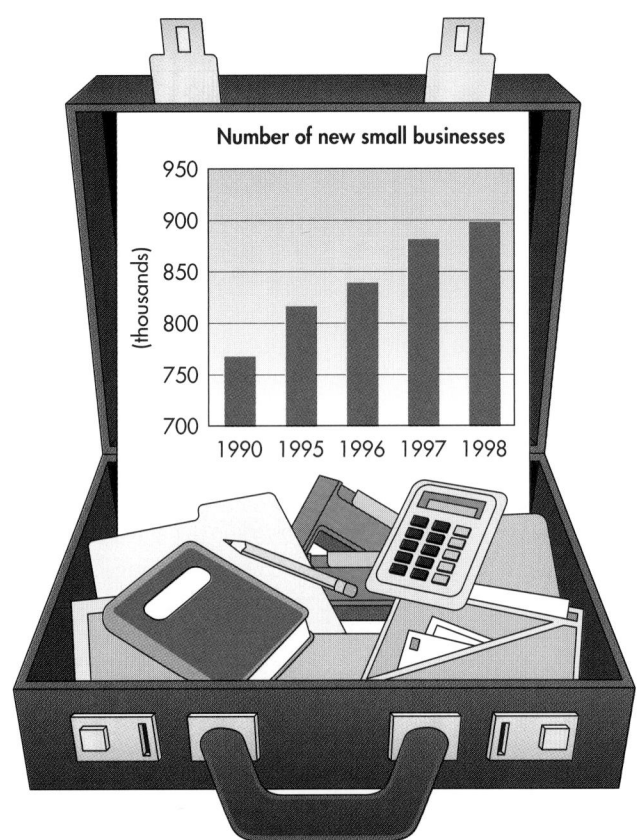

Number of new small businesses

(thousands)

950
900
850
800
750
700

1990 1995 1996 1997 1998

time from a home office, the corner florist, and the neighborhood pizza parlor fall into the category of *lifestyle businesses*—firms built around the personal and financial needs of an individual or a family.[4] Lifestyle businesses aren't designed to grow into large enterprises.

In contrast to lifestyle businesses, some firms are small simply because they are new. Many companies—such as FedEx, Microsoft, and E*Trade—start out as small entrepreneurial firms but quickly outgrow their small-business status. These *high-growth ventures* are usually run by a team rather than by one individual, and they expand rapidly by obtaining a sizable supply of investment capital and by introducing new products or services to a large market. But expanding from a small firm into a large enterprise is no easy task; there's a world of difference between the two.

The typical small business has few products or services, focuses on a narrow group of customers, and remains in close contact with its markets. In addition, small businesses tend to be more open-minded and willing to try new things, whereas big companies tend to say *no* more often than *yes*. Midwest Express, the nation's 17th-largest airline, is a good example of the small-business difference. The airline is reporting high-flying profits in an era when most big airlines are struggling. What's Midwest's secret? The company focuses on serving the growing needs of business travelers. All 34 Midwest routes make direct flights between small cities. Fares match those of the big airlines, but the company offers only business-class service with such amenities as wide leather seats, free coffee and newspapers at terminals, and fresh-baked gooey chocolate chip cookies in flight. Midwest earns high marks from its customers for going that extra mile.[5]

Innovation in Small Business Another characteristic of small businesses is that they tend to be more innovative than larger firms. Case studies show that (1) small businesses can make decisions faster, (2) the owners are more accessible, and (3) employees have a greater opportunity for individual expression. Putting an idea into action in big companies often means filing formal proposals, preparing research reports, and attending lots of meetings. This process could kill an idea before it has a chance to take off. Consider Microsoft, for example. One manager quit out of frustration with the company's snail's pace for decision making. It took 10 meetings and three months to act on his suggestion to add a feature to Hot Mail (the company's freebie Internet e-mail service) that would quickly take 40 million users to Microsoft's MSN Web site. In contrast, it took only 30 minutes to write the code for this feature.[6]

To stimulate innovation, many big companies are now dividing their organizations into smaller work units. Xerox, AT&T, du Pont, Motorola, Hewlett-Packard, and others have launched their own small enterprises to keep new ideas from falling through the cracks. Run by *intrapreneurs*—people who create innovation of any kind *within* an organization (not to be confused with *entrepreneurs*—risk takers in the private enterprise system)—these ventures get funding and support from the parent organization. Nevertheless, some intrapreneurial ventures continue to face giant obstacles because the parent corporation burdens them with strict reporting requirements and formal procedures.[7]

LEARNING
OBJECTIVE 1
Identify the key characteristics (other than size) that differentiate small businesses from larger ones

Is it the cookies or the direct flights? Some think big airlines should follow Midwest Express's recipe for customer service.

Limited Resources and Hard Work Because most small companies have limited resources, owners and employees must perform a variety of job functions in order to get the work done. Being a jack-of-all-trades, however, is not for everyone (see Exhibit 4.2). Unfortunately, some owners learn this the hard way. They discover that running a small business takes a lot of hard work and that being a successful corporate employee doesn't necessarily translate into being a successful small-business owner.

When Bob Hammer and Sue Crowe purchased Blue Jacket Ship Crafters, a mail-order model-ship-kit manufacturer, they quickly learned that running a small company was not like running Motorola, where the two had been senior managers for the better part of their careers. It took a lot more work and time than they had imagined. Even Crowe admits, "You will put in more money than you thought you would, you will take out a lot less, and you will work harder

EXHIBIT 4.2

HOW ENTREPRENEURS SPEND THEIR TIME

The men and women who start their own companies are jacks-of-all-trades, but they devote the lion's share of their time to selling and producing the product.

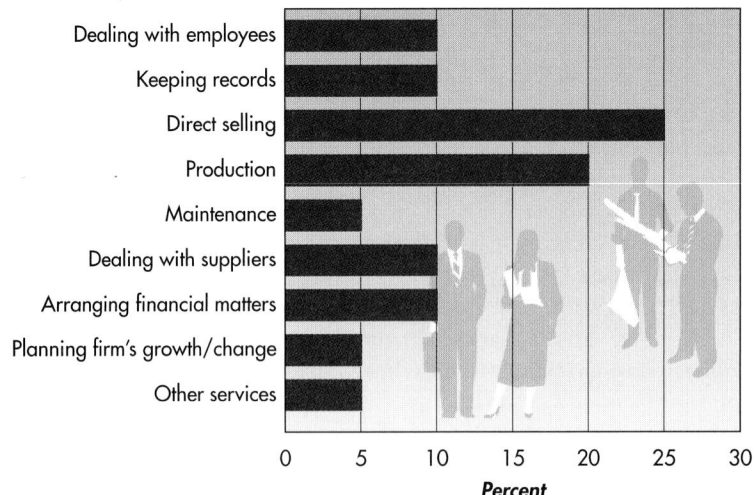

Percent

than you did when you were making a six-figure salary at your large corporation."[8] Many executives who leave the corporate world to start a small business have trouble adjusting to the unglamorous details of daily life in a small business. They miss the support services and fringe benefits they enjoyed in large corporations.[9]

Economic Role of Small Businesses

Small businesses play a number of important roles in the economy:

LEARNING OBJECTIVE *2*

Highlight the major contributions small businesses make to the U.S. economy

- *They provide jobs.* Small businesses create about 70 percent of new jobs. Moreover, some 24 million small businesses employ 53 percent of the private nonfarm U.S. workforce and generate more than half of the private U.S. gross domestic product.[10]

- *They introduce new products.* The National Science Foundation estimates that 98 percent of the nation's "radical" new-product developments spring from small firms, a staggering percentage given the fact that small companies spend less than 5 percent of the nation's research-and-development money.[11]

- *They supply the needs of large corporations.* Many small businesses act as distributors, servicing agents, and suppliers to large corporations. Consider Parallax. This 160-employee firm inspects nuclear power plants, implements safety procedures, and cleans up hazardous and nuclear waste at power plants and weapons complexes across the nation. Seventy percent of Parallax's business comes from large corporations such as Westinghouse and Lockheed Martin. Not bad for a company launched out of the founder's home with $10,000 in personal savings.[12]

- *They provide specialized goods and services.* When Mike Woods tried to teach his son how to read he couldn't find any toys on the market that helped teach phonics. So he left his job as a partner in a big law firm and started LeapFrog. The company's initial product was the Phonics Disk, a $50 toy that teaches children shapes, sounds, and pronunciation of letters and words. Today LeapFrog, a division of Knowledge Universe, produces 17 toys geared toward teaching children to read and write.[13]

In addition to these roles, small businesses spend $2.2 trillion annually in the U.S. economy, just a bit less than the $2.6 trillion spent by big companies.[14]

Factors Contributing to the Increase in the Number of Small Businesses

LEARNING OBJECTIVE *3*

Discuss three factors contributing to the increase in the number of small businesses

Three factors are contributing to the increase in the number of small businesses today: technological advances, an increase in the number of women and minority business owners, and corporate downsizing and outsourcing.

Technology and the Internet   The Internet together with e-commerce has spawned thousands of new business ventures, as this chapter's Focusing on E-Business Today feature shows. Some

548 companies went public in 1999, of which 290 were Internet-related.[15] It is estimated that over 38 percent of small businesses now have a Web site.[16] While the Internet makes it easier to launch or expand your business, there's a twist. If it's so easy for you to start an online business, then it's just as easy for everyone else. No company understands this better than drkoop.com, the Internet-based consumer health care network. Shortly after founder Dr. Everett Koop (former U.S. Surgeon General) launched his innovative concept, a startling number of "me-toos" copied his idea.

Not only does the Internet make it easier to start a business, but it allows small companies to compete on a level playing field with larger ones. Small businesses can use the Internet to communicate with customers and suppliers all over the world—any time of the day—and to access the types of resources and information that were previously available only to larger firms. (For additional coverage of how small businesses can use the Internet to compete against corporate giants, consult Part 2 of this text's online supplement, E-Business in Action, at www.prenhall.com/mescon.)

Besides the Internet, technological advances such as computer-aided manufacturing equipment and affordable data processing systems enable small companies to customize their products and deliver them as efficiently as their larger rivals. One small company that is successful because of technology is Isis, a pharmaceutical company. Being first to introduce a new drug in the market is critical in the pharmaceutical industry. But it takes years of research and data analysis to get the required agency approvals. In the past, small companies could not afford to spend millions of dollars on data-crunching systems to process the information efficiently. But today, less expensive versions of these sophisticated systems are available. As a result, a small firm like Isis can file its 40,000-page reports with the U.S. Food and Drug Administration in one-third the time by compressing the information onto one CD-ROM.[17]

Technology also makes it easier start a small home-based business. With the Internet and online resources accountants, writers, lawyers, and consultants can set up shop at home. According to one study, about 24 million home-based businesses exist in the United States, and an additional 11 million people telecommute.[18] Some predict that as much as half the workforce soon may be involved in full- or part-time home-based businesses.[19]

Rise in Number of Women and Minority Small-Business Owners The number of women-owned small businesses has increased sharply over the past three decades—from 5 percent to 38 percent of all small businesses. These businesses now employ more than 18.5 million people and ring up more than $3.1 trillion in annual sales.[20]

As Exhibit 4.3 shows, women are starting small businesses for a number of reasons. Some choose to run their own companies so they can enjoy a more flexible work arrangement; others leave the corporate world because of advancement barriers—known as the glass ceiling. Take Josie Natori, for a perfect example. By her late twenties, Natori was earning six figures as the first female vice president of investment banking at Merrill Lynch. Where could she go from there? Today Natori is the owner of a $33 million fashion empire that sells elegant lingerie and evening wear.[21] Nevertheless, going solo does not guarantee success. Many women business owners still struggle to be taken seriously.

Similar advances are also showing up in minority segments of the population. Data from the U.S. Small Business Administration show that between 1987 and 1997, the number of minority-owned firms grew 168 percent— more than triple the 47 percent rate of U.S. businesses overall. Minority-owned firms now employ an estimated 3.9 million people.[22]

Downsizing and Outsourcing Beginning in the late 1980s and continuing through the 1990s, many big corporations dramatically reduced their number of employees to improve their profits. Such downsizing ushered in an age in which "small became beautiful." Some companies, such as Procter & Gamble, were able to function with fewer people once they redesigned their

Sue Calloway is among the growing number of women starting a small business. Calloway started S.C.R.U.B.S. to provide carefree hospital clothing to doctors and nurses. Her whimsical designs help brighten hospital settings, easing patients' anxieties.

EXHIBIT 4.3

WOMEN STARTING BUSINESSES

More than half of all women business owners started their own businesses because they had an entrepreneurial idea or wished to further advance their careers.

What women with companies less than a decade old say is the main reason they started a business:

Entrepreneurial idea	35%
Glass ceiling	22%
Bored in job	14%
Downsized	10%
Fell into it	10%
Family event	5%
Born entrepreneur	3%
Reenter workforce	1%

outsourcing
Subcontracting work to outside companies

business systems to operate more efficiently.[23] Others made up for the layoffs of permanent staff by **outsourcing** or subcontracting special projects and secondary business functions to experts outside the organization. Still others turned to outsourcing as a way to permanently eliminate entire company departments.

Regardless of the reason, the increased use of outsourcing provides opportunities for smaller businesses to service the needs of larger enterprises. Many employees who leave big corporations find it more fulfilling to work as independent contractors or to join smaller firms. Some, like Harold Jackson, are even wooing their former employers as customers. After working several years as Coca-Cola's manager of media relations in Atlanta, Jackson left to found JacksonHeath Public Relations International, taking Coke with him as his most valuable client.[24]

Recuperating from a broken ankle while vacationing in Lake Tahoe, Perry Klebahn decided to try out a pair of snowshoes he found in a friend's closet. Today his company, Atlas Snowshoe, sells high-end snowshoes in more than 1,000 stores across the United States ringing in annual sales of about $12 million.

STARTING AND EXPANDING A SMALL BUSINESS

People in the United States are starting new businesses at dizzying rates. Could you or should you join the thousands of entrepreneurs like Josie Natori, Bill Gross, and Harold Jackson who start new businesses every year? What qualities would you need?

Characteristics of Entrepreneurs

Contrary to what you might expect, most entrepreneurs are not glamorous adventurers; instead, they are often ordinary people like Bill Gross who have a good idea. But even Gross knows it takes more than a good idea to launch a successful business. Most entrepreneurs have these qualities in common: They prefer excitement, are highly disciplined, like to control their destiny, listen to their intuitive sense, relate well to others, are eager to learn whatever skills are necessary to reach their goal, learn from their mistakes, stay abreast of market changes, are willing to exploit new opportunities, seldom follow trends (rather, they spot and interpret trends), are driven by ambition, think positively, and prefer the excitement and potential rewards of risk taking over security.[25] Moreover, while many are anxious to become their own boss, surprisingly they cite making money as the secondary reason for starting their own business.[26] Exhibit 4.4 lists some successful entrepreneurs and the key factor contributing to their success.

Many entrepreneurs start with relatively small sums of money and operate informally from their homes, at least for a while.[27] Most have diverse backgrounds in terms of education and business experience. Some come from companies unlike the ones they start; oth-

EXHIBIT 4.4

ENTREPRENEURIAL
SUCCESS
If you like a product, chances are
an entrepreneur is behind it.

KEY SUCCESS FACTOR	COMPANY
Persistence	*Breed Technologies:* It took Allen Breed over 10 years to convince carmakers that air bags could save several thousand lives a year. Today Breed Technologies is one of the most profitable suppliers in the automotive industry—his company makes the sensors that trigger the air-bag system. With more than 5,000 employees and branches in eight countries, this company's sales went from zero to nearly half a billion dollars in less than a decade.
Skill	*La Tempesta:* Using Aunt Isa's recipe for biscotti (twice-baked Italian cookies), Bonnie Tempesta baked them and sold them at a fancy San Francisco chocolate shop. While attending a fancy-foods trade show one day, she noticed that she was the only one there with biscotti. Today she sells over $9 million worth through 65 separate regional distributors to 5,000 stores, including Starbucks, Nordstrom, and Neiman Marcus.
Passion	*Transmissions by Lucille:* Lucille Treganowan didn't grow up yearning to repair cars. In fact, she didn't know a transmission from a turnip. So she began asking mechanics questions, reading, and working on cars. In 1973 she started her business. Today, transmissions are more than a business; they are a passion.
Hobby	*Rusty Cos:* Russell Preisendorfer is an avid surfer. To support his habit he began shaping surfboards. Last year his privately owned Rusty Cos grossed $57 million from sales of surfboards and royalties from a line of surfing apparel he helps design.
Common Sense	*Auntie Anne's:* To bring in some extra cash, Anne Beiler managed a food stand at a farmer's market in Maryland. She noticed that the fastest-selling items at the stand were hand-rolled pretzels that sold for 55 cents each. Not bad for 7 cents worth of ingredients. So Beiler decided to try the pretzel business herself. Today Beiler's mini-empire consists of over 300 franchised pretzel shops in about 35 states.
Talent	*S.C.R.U.B.S.:* Sue Callaway's colorful, carefree, handmade scrubs were admired by more than the children in the neonatal intensive-care unit where she worked. Callaway's creations are graced with playful dogs, happy dolphins, smiling teddy bears, and other whimsical designs. When Callaway began getting orders from other hospital care professionals, this creative seamstress quit her nursing job and went into business for herself. Within two years, her business was bursting at the seams with orders. To attract new customers, Callaway's company mails over 18 million catalogs each year and has opened a small number of retail stores in shopping malls across the country.

ers use their prior knowledge and skills—such as editing, telemarketing, public relations, or selling—to start their own businesses. Still others have less experience but an innovative idea or a better way of doing something. Like Bill Gross, they find an overlooked corner of the market, exploit a demographic trend unnoticed by others, or meet an unsatisfied consumer need through better service or a higher-quality product. Moreover, they often plan and develop their product quickly, while the rest of the business world ponders whether a market for the product exists.

LEARNING
OBJECTIVE   4
Cite the key characteristics
common to most entrepreneurs

Importance of Preparing a Business Plan

Although many successful entrepreneurs claim to have done little formal planning, even the most intuitive of them have *some* idea of what they're trying to accomplish and how they hope to do it. No amount of hard work can turn a bad idea into a profitable one: The health-food store in a meat-and-potatoes neighborhood and the child-care center in a retirement community are probably doomed from the beginning. Before you rush in to supply a product, you need to be sure that a market exists.

You must also try to foresee some of the problems that might arise and figure out how you will cope with them. For instance, what will you do if one of your suppliers suddenly goes out of business? Can you locate another supplier quickly? What if he neighborhood starts to change—even for the better? An influx of wealthier neighbors may cause such a steep increase in rent that your business must move. Also, tough competition may move into the neighborhood along with

MANAGING IN THE 21ST CENTURY

CREATE A WINNING BUSINESS PLAN

Although the business plan has a simple, straight-forward purpose, it still requires a great deal of thought. For example, before you open your doors, you have to make important decisions about personnel, marketing, facilities, suppliers, and distribution. A written business plan forces you to think about those issues and develop programs that will help you succeed. If you are starting out on a small scale and using your own money, your business plan may be relatively informal. But at a minimum, you should describe the basic concept of the business and outline its specific goals, objectives, and resource requirements. A formal plan, suitable for use with banks or investors, should cover these points:

- *Summary.* In one or two pages, summarize your business concept. Describe your product or service and its market potential. Highlight some things about your company and its owners that will distinguish your firm from competition. Summarize your financial projections and the amount of money investors can expect to make on their investment. Be sure to indicate how much money you will need and for what purpose.

- *Mission and objectives.* Explain the purpose of your business and what you hope to accomplish.

- *Company and industry.* Give full background information on the origins and structure of your venture and the characteristics of its industry.

- *Products or services.* Give a complete but concise description of your product or service, focusing on its unique attributes. Explain how customers will benefit from using your product or service instead of those of your competitors.

- *Market and competition.* Provide data that will persuade the investor that you understand your target market and can achieve your sales goals. Be sure to identify the strengths and weaknesses of your competitors.

- *Management.* Summarize the background and qualifications of the principals, directors, and key manage-

ment personnel in your company. Include résumés in the appendix.

- *Marketing strategy.* Provide projections of sales and market share, and outline a strategy for identifying and contacting customers, setting prices, providing customer services, advertising, and so forth. Whenever possible, include evidence of customer acceptance, such as advance product orders.

- *Design and development plans.* If your product requires design or development, describe the nature and extent of what needs to be done, including costs and possible problems.

- *Operations plan.* Provide information on the facilities, equipment, and labor needed.

- *Overall schedule.* Forecast development of the company in terms of completion dates for major aspects of the business plan.

- *Critical risks and problems.* Identify all negative factors and discuss them honestly.

- *Financial projections and requirements.* Include a detailed budget of start-up and operating costs, as well as projections for income, expenses, and cash flow for the first three years of business. Identify the company's financing needs and potential sources.

- *Exit strategy.* Explain how investors will be able to cash out or sell their investment, such as through a public stock offering, sale of the company, or a buyback of the investors' interest. When covering these points, keep in mind that your audience wants short, concise information—not lengthy volumes—and realistic projections for growth.

■ QUESTIONS FOR CRITICAL THINKING

1. What details should you know about your business before writing a business plan?

2. Why is it important to identify critical risks and problems in a business plan?

the fatter pocketbooks. Do you have an alternative location staked out? What if styles suddenly change? Can you switch quickly from, say, hand-painted crafts to some other kind of artwork?

One of the first steps you should take toward starting a new business is to develop a **business plan,** a written document that summarizes an entrepreneur's proposed business venture, communicates the company's goals, highlights how management intends to achieve those goals, and shows how consumers will benefit from the company's products or services. Preparing a

business plan
A written document that provides an orderly statement of a company's goals and how it intends to achieve those goals

COMPETING IN THE GLOBAL MARKETPLACE

ARE YOU CRAZY?

If you've ever thought about quitting your job and starting a business, it's almost certain that someone—a spouse, a co-worker, a friend—uttered these three words: "Are you crazy?" The reason is that risk taking, an essential quality of entrepreneurship, scares most people. But you're different. You're forging ahead because you have a dream. And you're not afraid, because, after all, you're about to embark on the greatest voyage of your life—just as the following entrepreneurs did.

Edward DuCoin: $100 was more than enough for this entrepreneur when, at 18, he launched Impact Telemarketing. Inspired by his telemarketing job for a lawn-care company, DuCoin found a used desk, bought an inexpensive, old answering machine, and set up shop in his bedroom. He began drumming up business by answering help-wanted ads for telephone salespeople in the local newspaper. He pointed out to companies that it would be more economical for them to use his services than to hire and train a new employee. Soon he had a team of telemarketers working for him out of their homes. With gross revenues near $12 million, in 1997 DuCoin merged his company with four other collection firms and mailing services and took the company public as Compass International.

Kelly Dunn: In 1996 this single mother and Pillsbury secretary scoured Minneapolis for a concierge who might relieve her of household chores. She couldn't find one. So after attending a one-day seminar on the concierge business, Dunn quit her job and started her own concierge company, Consider It Dunn. She knocked on doors for months at downtown offices, asking whether they needed a concierge. Nobody did. Meanwhile, she combed Minneapolis for topflight vendors—shoe repair shops, jewelers, and so on—comparing prices, quality, and speed. Her big break came when Pillsbury (her former employer) hired her as its first concierge. Today she employs 10 workers and is projecting a gross profit of $80,000 on revenues of $237,000.

Kate Spade: When Spade quit her job as accessories editor for *Mademoiselle* and launched her own handbag company in 1991, even her mother said she had gotten cocky. Priced at $100 to $400, Spade's nylon bags weren't cheap, and she had a tough time getting them into trade shows because she didn't "do leather." But Spade's instincts were better than the stylemakers[1]. On an impulse the night before her first trade show, Spade ripped the labels "kate spade new york" from the inside of her bags and stitched them on the outside, sewing until her fingers got puffy. Good move. Barneys ordered 18 of her bags, and *Vogue* decided to feature them on the glossy's accessories page. It wasn't long before Julia Roberts and Gwyneth Paltrow (who saw the bags in fashion magazines) had them on their shoulders. Nevertheless, the company didn't become profitable until 1996, when Saks and Neiman Marcus each ordered 3,000 bags for all their stores. Today Kate Spade, Inc. has its own retail outlets with a new line of clothing. Sales are projected to top $30 million.

■ QUESTIONS FOR CRITICAL THINKING

1. What key entrepreneurial characteristics did each of these individuals exhibit?

2. Which of these businesses would be considered lifestyle businesses and which, if any, would be considered high-growth ventures? Why?

business plan serves two important functions: First, it guides the company operations and outlines a strategy for turning an idea into reality; Second, it helps persuade lenders and investors to finance your business. In fact, without a business plan, many investors won't even grant you an interview. Keep in mind that sometimes the greatest service a business plan can provide an entrepreneur is the realization that "the concept just won't work." Discovering this on paper can save you considerable time and money. (See the Appendix, "Getting Started With Business PlanPro Software," and the end-of-text part Business PlanPro Exercises for a more in-depth discussion of business plans.)

Small-Business Ownership Options

Once you've done your research and planning, if you decide to take the risk, you can get into business for yourself in three ways: Start from scratch, buy an existing business, or obtain a franchise. Roughly two-thirds of business founders begin **start-up companies;** that is, they start from scratch rather than buying an existing operation or inheriting the family business. Starting a

start-up companies
New ventures

EXHIBIT 4.5

WEIGHING THE ADVANTAGES AND DISADVANTAGES OF STARTING A NEW BUSINESS

Owning a business has many advantages, but you must also consider the potential drawbacks.

Advantages	Disadvantages
+ Control over your own destiny	− Uncertainty of income
+ Ability to reach your full potential	− Risk of losing your entire investment
+ Unlimited profits	− Long hours and hard work
+ Recognition for your efforts	− Complete responsibility
+ Doing what you enjoy	− High levels of stress

LEARNING OBJECTIVE   5

List three ways of getting into business for yourself

business from scratch has many advantages and disadvantages, as Exhibit 4.5 points out. Of the three options for going into business for yourself, starting a new business is the most common route, and in many cases, the most difficult. Exhibit 4.6 provides a checklist of some of the many tasks involved in starting a new business.

Another way to go into business for yourself is to buy an existing business. This approach tends to reduce the risks—provided, of course, that you check out the company carefully. When you buy a business, you generally purchase an established customer base, functioning business systems, a proven product or service, and a known location. You don't have to go through the painful period of building a reputation, establishing a clientele, finding suppliers, and hiring and training employees. In addition, financing an existing business is often much easier than financ-

EXHIBIT 4.6

BUSINESS START-UP CHECKLIST

You have many tasks to perform before you start your business. Here are just a few.

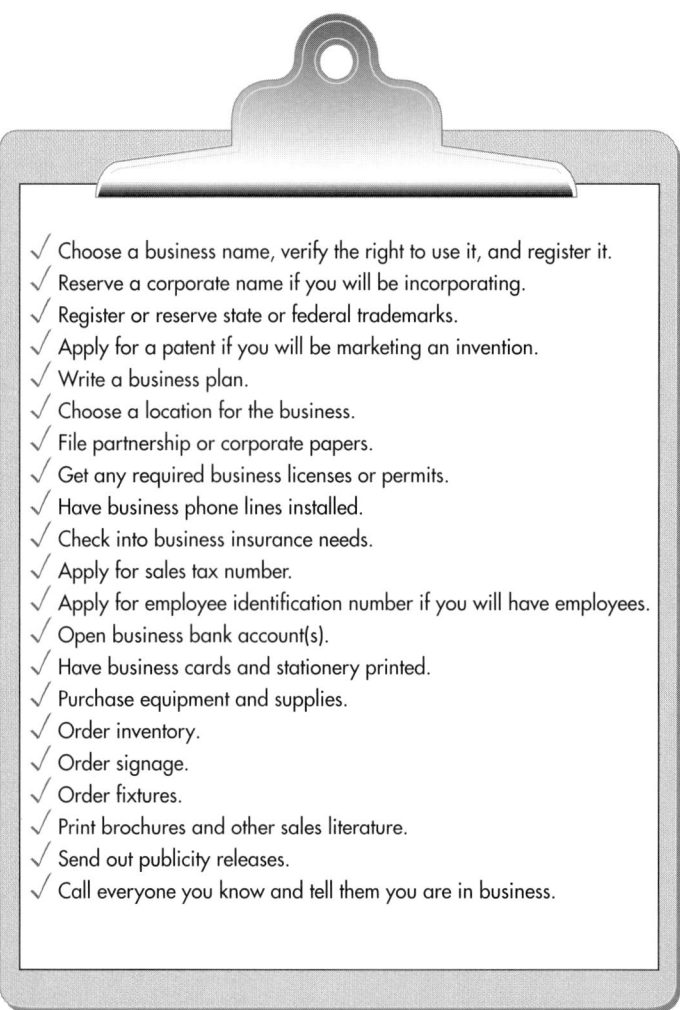

√ Choose a business name, verify the right to use it, and register it.
√ Reserve a corporate name if you will be incorporating.
√ Register or reserve state or federal trademarks.
√ Apply for a patent if you will be marketing an invention.
√ Write a business plan.
√ Choose a location for the business.
√ File partnership or corporate papers.
√ Get any required business licenses or permits.
√ Have business phone lines installed.
√ Check into business insurance needs.
√ Apply for sales tax number.
√ Apply for employee identification number if you will have employees.
√ Open business bank account(s).
√ Have business cards and stationery printed.
√ Purchase equipment and supplies.
√ Order inventory.
√ Order signage.
√ Order fixtures.
√ Print brochures and other sales literature.
√ Send out publicity releases.
√ Call everyone you know and tell them you are in business.

ing a new one; lenders are reassured by the company's history and existing assets and customer base. With these major details already settled, you can concentrate on making improvements.

Still, buying an existing business is not without disadvantages. For one thing, the business may be overpriced. For another, inventories and equipment may be obsolete. Furthermore, the location may no longer be satisfactory, the previous owner may have created ill will, your personality may clash with those of existing managers and employees, and outstanding bills owed by customers may be difficult to collect. Keep in mind that no matter how fast you learn and how much investigating you do, you're likely to find that the challenges of running an existing business are far greater than you anticipated.[28]

The Franchise Alternative

An alternative to buying an existing business is to buy a **franchise** in somebody else's business. This approach enables the buyer to use a larger company's trade name and sell its products or services in a specific territory. In exchange for this right, the **franchisee** (the small-business owner who contracts to sell the goods or services) pays the **franchisor** (the supplier) an initial fee (and often monthly royalties as well). Franchises are a factor of rising importance in the U.S. economy. Franchising now accounts for roughly $1 trillion, or about 50 percent of all U.S. retail sales.[29]

Types of Franchises Franchises are of three basic types. A *product franchise* gives you the right to sell trademarked goods, which are purchased from the franchisor and resold. Car dealers and gasoline stations fall into this category. A *manufacturing franchise,* such as a soft-drink bottling plant, gives you the right to produce and distribute the manufacturer's products, using supplies purchased from the franchisor. A *business-format franchise* gives you the right to open a business using a franchisor's name and format for doing business. Fast-food chains such as KFC, Taco Bell, and Pizza Hut typify this form of franchising.

How to Evaluate a Franchise How do you protect yourself from a poor franchise investment? The best way is to study the opportunity carefully before you commit. Since 1978 the Federal Trade Commission has required franchisors to disclose information about their operations to prospective franchisees. By studying this information, you can determine the financial condition of the franchisor and ascertain whether the company has been involved in lawsuits with franchisees. Before signing a franchise agreement, it's also wise to consult an attorney. Exhibit 4.7 suggests some points to consider as you study the package of information on the franchise.

Nevertheless, some people find out too late that franchising isn't the best choice for them. They make a mistake common among prospective franchisees—buying without really understanding the day-to-day business. Often, prospects simply don't get beyond the allure of the successful name or concept—or the mistaken notion that a franchise brings instant success. "People go into a sub shop at the noon hour and see the cash register opening and closing," says the president of Franchise Solutions. "What they don't see is having to get there at 4 A.M. to bake the

franchise
Business arrangement in which a small business obtains rights to sell the goods or services of the supplier (franchisor)

franchisee
Small-business owner who contracts for the right to sell goods or services of the supplier (franchisor) in exchange for some payment

franchisor
Supplier that grants a franchise to an individual or group (franchisee) in exchange for payments

---

Best of the Web Best of the Web Best of

GET SMART

It seems as if one-stop shopping is the way to go these days—everything under one roof, or on one page if you're on the Net. Smartbiz puts the world of business resources at your fingertips with business articles, resources, hot tips, franchise information, home office ideas, Internet links, and more. Thinking about buying an existing franchise? Better check out the franchisor first. Perhaps starting a home business sounds more appealing. Where should you begin? What are some of the advantages or disadvantages? Be sure to Browse SBS for some answers. Do you have a Web site? It takes only five minutes to build one. Find out how by visiting Smartbiz, click on Business on the Net, and scroll down to the hot link The Home Page Maker. Don't forget to e-mail us your URL.

www.smartbiz.com

EXHIBIT 4.7

TEN QUESTIONS TO ASK BEFORE SIGNING A FRANCHISE AGREEMENT

A franchise agreement is a legally binding contract that defines the relationship between the franchisee and the franchisor. Because the agreement is drawn up by the franchisor, the terms and conditions generally favor the franchisor. Before signing the franchise agreement, be sure to consult an attorney.

1. What does the initial franchise fee cover? Does it include a starting inventory of supplies and products?

2. How are the periodic royalties calculated and when are they paid?

3. Are all trademarks and names legally protected?

4. Who provides and pays for advertising and promotional items?

5. Who selects the location of the business?

6. Is the franchise assigned an exclusive territory?

7. If the territory is not exclusive, does the franchisee have the right of first refusal on additional franchises established in nearby locations?

8. Is the franchisee required to purchase equipment and supplies from the franchisor or other suppliers?

9. Under what conditions can the franchisor and/or the franchisee terminate the franchise agreement?

10. Can the franchise be assigned to heirs?

bread." Buying a franchise is much like buying any other business: It requires analyzing the market, finding capital, choosing a site, hiring employees, and buying equipment. The process also includes an element not found in other businesses—evaluating the franchisor.[30]

One of the best ways to evaluate a prospective franchisor is by talking to other franchisees. At a minimum, you should find out what other franchisees think of the opportunity. If they had it to do over again, would they still invest? You might even want to spend a few months working for someone who already owns a franchise you're interested in. Fabiola Garcia did. She worked at a 7-Eleven evenings and swing shifts, learning all aspects of the business as part of the screening and training process for prospective 7-Eleven franchise owners. This was in addition to a two-week special session at headquarters, where Garcia learned the franchisor's paperwork procedures.[31]

Nevertheless, as Jim and Laura White discovered, evaluating a franchise means more than assessing the current operation. What the market will be like tomorrow is just as important an issue to address. For example, when the Whites opened their Body Shop franchise in 1994, they expected to earn a comfortable living on their $300,000 investment. Instead, the outlet lost money every year. What they hadn't taken into account was that less than a year after the Whites' Body Shop opened, Bath & Body would come into the same mall. So did Crabtree & Evelyn, followed a year later by Garden Botanika (these chains sell products that compete directly with Body Shop's, and each of the stores was bigger than the Whites').[32]

Advantages of Franchising Why is franchising so popular? For one thing, when you invest in a franchise, you know you are getting a viable business, one that has "worked" many times before. If the franchise is well established, you get the added benefit of instant name recognition, national advertising programs, standardized quality of goods and services, and a proven formula for success. Buying a franchise also gives you instant access to a support network, and in many cases a ready-made blueprint for building a business. For an initial investment (from a few thousand dollars to upward of a million, depending on the franchise), you get services such as site-location studies, market research, training, and technical assistance, as well as assistance with building or leasing your structure, decorating

For 23 years, the Body Shop, a high-quality skin and hair care manufacturer and retailer with nearly $1 billion in sales and more than 1,700 outlets in 48 countries, has served consumers for whom natural, no-frills cosmetics products have been both beneficial and culturally relevant. But competition from savvy, better-looking, and in some cases, lower-priced competitors has seriously eroded the Body Shop's market share. To shake things up, the Body Shop has reduced the number of franchisees in favor of company-owned stores and has begun an extensive store renovation campaign.

the building, purchasing supplies, and operating the business for 6 to 12 months. Because few franchisees are able to write a check for the amount of the total investment, some franchisors also provide financial assistance.

Disadvantages of Franchising Although franchising offers many advantages, it is not the ideal vehicle for everyone. First, owning a franchise is no guarantee of wealth. Even though it may be a relatively easy way to get into business, not all franchises are hugely profitable. Some franchisees barely survive, in fact. One of the biggest disadvantages of franchising is the monthly payment, or royalty, that must be turned over to the franchisor. This fee varies from nothing at all to 20 percent of sales. High royalties are not necessarily bad as long as the franchisee gets ongoing assistance in return.

Another drawback of franchises is that many allow individual operators little independence. Franchisors can prescribe virtually every aspect of the business, down to the details of employee uniforms and the color of the walls. Furthermore, when a chain loses its cutting edge in the marketplace, being stuck with a franchise can be painful. By contrast, if independent retailers run into trouble with their product lines, they can change suppliers or perhaps switch rapidly to a whole new line of business. Franchisees can't. They're usually bound by contracts to sell only authorized goods, often supplied by the franchisor itself at whatever price the franchisor wants to charge.

Although franchisors can make important decisions without consulting franchisees, the days of franchisors' exercising such control are ending. In many cases the relationship between franchisor and franchisee is becoming more of a joint venture. Some franchisors are rewriting contracts to become less dictatorial, says the CEO of U.S. Franchise Systems. Newer contracts offer stock options, automatic contract renewals, and empowerment through franchise advisory boards. Great Harvest Bread, for instance, promotes innovation among its franchisees. Owners are free to run their bakeries as they see fit—on just one condition: they must share what they learn along the way with other franchise owners.[33] Some franchisors are giving franchisees a voice in how advertising funds are used. Moreover, legislative proposals are being considered that would require franchisors to meet certain criteria (something like an accreditation) before they can sell a franchise in the United States.[34]

Why New Businesses Fail

Even if you carefully evaluate a prospective franchisor or write a winning business plan, you have no guarantee for success. In fact, you may have heard some depressing statistics about the number of new businesses that fail. Some reports say your chances of succeeding are only one in three; others claim that the odds are even worse, stating that 85 percent of all new business ventures fail within 10 years. Actual statistics, however, show otherwise. Of the 857,000 small businesses that closed their doors in 1997, only 16 percent closed because they failed or went bankrupt.[35] Moreover, the true failure rate is much lower if you remove those operations that Dun & Bradstreet (D&B) business analysts say aren't "genuine businesses." For instance, a freelancer who writes one article for a magazine and then stops writing would be counted as a failed business under the traditional measurement (which is based on tax returns).[36]

Most new businesses fail for a number of reasons, as Exhibit 4.8 suggests. Moreover, once the signs of failure begin to surface, some entrepreneurs don't pull the plug fast enough. Jeff Schwarz worked three years without drawing a salary and used up $100,000 of his personal savings before closing his photography business, Remarkable Moments.[37]

1. Management incompetence
2. Lack of industry experience
3. Inadequate financing
4. Poor business planning
5. Unclear or unrealistic goals
6. Failure to attract and keep target customers
7. Uncontrolled growth
8. Inappropriate location
9. Poor inventory and financial controls
10. Inability to make the entrepreneurial transition

EXHIBIT 4.8

WHY NEW BUSINESSES FAIL

Experts have identified these 10 reasons as the most likely causes of new business failure.

Another thing to keep in mind is that failure isn't always the end of the world. Many presidents of big, successful companies, including Fred Smith of FedEx, can spin long tales about how failure got them where they are today or how failure was a valuable learning experience.[38] Still, not everybody bounces back. Experts advise that you can increase your chances for success by thinking about these important points before embarking on your entrepreneurial journey:[39]

■ *Know yourself and what you want to accomplish.* Ask yourself whether you have what it takes to start and operate a business. Consider whether you like dealing with people, enjoy the intricacies of making or selling the product or service, and get satisfaction from meeting the needs of your customers. Find out whether you have the technical knowledge and business management skills to do a better job than your competitors.

■ *Know how to find the money you need.* Financing is one of the biggest challenges small businesses face. Many banks shy away from lending money to new businesses because they consider new businesses risky investments. (Financing the enterprise will be discussed later in this chapter.)

■ *Know how to register and insure your business.* Having all the proper registrations, certifications, licenses, and insurance protects you from violations that could eventually shut down your business. In Component Chapter D we will discuss insurance and risk management.

■ *Know who your customers are and how to reach them.* One of the most important parts of preparing a business plan is to learn who your customers are and to develop strategies for reaching those customers. Nonetheless, most businesspeople make the mistake of assuming that all you need is a good idea and that as soon as you open your doors, customers will come rushing in.

■ *Know where to go for help.* Experts advise that you always seek professional assistance before beginning your entrepreneurial journey. For instance, you should pull together a team of professionals and consultants to whom you can turn for advice on a regular basis. These professionals include a good lawyer, accountant, bookkeeper, banker, insurance agent, and marketing expert. Besides using these professionals, a number of business resources exist that can help you with your undertaking, as the next section shows.

LEARNING
OBJECTIVE 6
Identify three sources of small-business assistance

Sources of Small-Business Assistance

Many local business professionals are willing to serve as mentors and can help you avoid the pitfalls of business. As a small-business owner, you may turn to small-business resources such as the Service Corps of Retired Executives (SCORE—a resource partner of the SBA), incubators, and the Internet. These resources can help you evaluate your business idea, develop a business plan, locate start-up funding sources, and show you how to package your business image professionally.

SCORE Some of the best advice available to small businesses costs little or nothing. It's delivered by SCORE's 12,000 volunteers. These men and women are working and retired executives and active small-business owners who offer advice and one-to-one counseling sessions on topics such as developing a business plan, securing financing, and managing business growth. To date, more than 3.5 million clients, such as New York Bagel, have been helped by SCORE counselors.[40]

Whether you use a SCORE counselor or find a private mentor, having someone to bounce your ideas off of or help you create a five-year financial forecast can increase the chances of your business's survival, as Lynelle and John Lawrence discovered. Owners of the Mudhouse Café in Charlottesville, Virginia, the

After a friend referred John and Lynelle Lawrence to SCORE, counselor Joe Geller (right) helped the couple through each stage of preparation for their Mudhouse Café in Charlottesville, Virginia.

Lawrences used a SCORE representative to help them prepare a detailed business plan and obtain financing. "There's no way we would be here without SCORE," confesses the couple.[41]

Incubators As this chapter's opening vignette highlights, **incubators** are centers that provide "new-born" businesses with just about everything a company needs to get started—office space, expert advice, legal and accounting services, clerical services, marketing support, contacts, and more.[42]

incubators
Facilities that house small businesses during their early growth phase

Some incubators are open to businesses of all types; others specialize, such as Bill Gross's idealab! Regardless, the goal is to convert "tenant" firms into "graduates," so most incubators set limits—from 18 months to five years—on how long a company can stay in the nest. Most Internet fledglings, however, are up and running within 90 days.[43]

Incubators, of course, are not a new idea. Thousands of them hatch successful businesses each year. Create-A-Saurus, producer of a line of playground equipment assembled from recycled and reconditioned tires, was hatched from the Oakland (California) Small Business Growth Center. Similarly, a Milwaukee, Wisconsin, business incubator gave Yolanda Cross the chance to move her catering-related business from her home into a more professional setting, where it has flourished.[44] Studies show that firms that start out in incubators typically increase sales by more than 400 percent from the time they enter until the time they leave.[45] Furthermore, 8 out of 10 businesses nurtured in incubators succeed. "Our companies are like children—we will do anything to make them succeed," says Gross.[46]

The Internet The Internet is another source of small-business assistance. Sonja Edmond, owner of Heavenly Bounty Giftbaskets, a hand-crafted gift-basket business, had to look no farther than her computer screen when she needed help. Although she enjoyed making gift baskets as a hobby, she wasn't sure whether a viable market existed to support a home-based business. So she posted a price-setting question on CompuServe's Working from Home and Handcrafts forum. Within 24 hours, her e-mail box was flooded with answers from forum members, who "convinced me I could do this," she says. Edmond struck a resource gold mine: Not only did she find the encouragement she needed to plunge into entrepreneurship; she also got valuable business leads and advice on licensing her product.[47]

Importance of Managing Growth

Growing from start-up enterprise into a professionally managed organization creates a number of challenges for most small businesses. While the benefits of growth are many—it creates jobs, provides a stimulating and exciting environment to work in, and offers a potential for new wealth—growth has its drawbacks too. Growth forces change throughout the organization, affecting every aspect of the business operation. When growth is too rapid, it can force so much change that things spin out of control. And nothing can kill a successful business faster than chaos.[48]

Doug and Jill Smith learned this the hard way. With a 50 percent increase in sales—in one year alone—their company, Buckeye Beans & Herbs, was spinning out of control. They needed more people to take the orders, fill them, package the product, and so on. It took them a while to realize they weren't running a little mom-and-pop operation anymore. "We just couldn't do it all, and we didn't have the people in place yet," note the Smiths, who eventually got things back on the right track.[49]

Like the Smiths, many small-business owners find they know little about managing a larger company. "There are times I have moments of sheer panic," notes the president of Creedon Controls, an electrical contractor. "Where am I going to get the money? How am I going to cover the payroll? How am I going to get the job done?"[50] These are just a few of the challenges owners of a growing business must face. In general, growing companies need to install more sophisticated systems and processes. They must staff positions that never existed and learn how to delegate responsibilities and control. And they must hire experienced managers. For some owners, managing a larger company means losing what they like most about being small—the ability to work closely with employees in a hands-on environment.

As you move from one level to the next in a growing company, experts advise that you take these steps:[51]

■ *Get help.* Although some entrepreneurs are good at launching companies, they sometimes lack the skills needed to manage companies over the long term. The person who excels during the start-up phase might know the industry and the product or service very well but may have problems figuring out how to run the expanded business. Therefore, as a company grows, you need to hire advisers with good business expertise.

■ *Prepare to change your role.* As a company grows, the owner's role must change. The leader of a growing concern needs to become the strategic thinker and the planner—and must learn to delegate day-to-day responsibilities. The CEO needs to be in charge of tomorrow while other people are in charge of today.

■ *Modify your systems.* A growing company usually needs new technology, more inventory, new product-ordering systems, and new communication systems. Growth means there will be many more vendors, more bills, and more checks to write. "If you double the size of the company, the number of bills you have to pay goes up by a factor of six," notes one entrepreneur.[52]

■ *Stay focused.* One of the biggest mistakes entrepreneurs make is straying too far from the original product or market. Take Lifeline Systems, a provider of personal-response systems for the elderly. Fewer than 10 years after it was founded, the company went public and was distributing its monitoring devices in more than 700 hospitals across the United States. Fearing that its focus was too small, the company diversified by introducing a new version of its monitoring device that could be used by children and college students in emergencies. It sold these devices to drug, electronics, and department stores at roughly half the price of the original model. But the mass-market strategy found few buyers. Worse, it alienated the company's hospital customers, whose demand for the original product was already falling as a result of slashed hospital budgets. Lifeline began reporting losses. When a new CEO was hired to turn things around, one of the first things he did was undo the company's diversification efforts and restore the company's original focus.[53]

■ FINANCING A NEW BUSINESS

LEARNING
OBJECTIVE   7
Discuss the principal sources of
small-business private financing

Once you've decided to go into business for yourself, you will probably need some money to get started. Choosing the right sources of capital can be just as important as choosing the right location. Your decision will affect your company forever. Moreover, undercapitalization is a leading factor of small-business failure, as shown in this chapter's Focusing on E-Business Today feature.

Private Financing Sources

Most new companies must borrow money from private sources. Obtaining money from family and friends is, of course, one possibility for financing a new enterprise. Bank loans are another. Keep in mind that obtaining a bank loan can be a challenge because many banks shy away from lending money to new businesses. For one thing, banks consider start-ups risky. For another, the risk inherent in some start-ups justifies higher interest rates than banks are allowed to charge by law. Thus, most banks will finance a start-up only if they can obtain payment guarantees from other financially sound parties or to the extent that the business has marketable collateral, such as buildings and equipment, to back the loan.[54] (In Chapter 17, we'll discuss the advantages, the disadvantages, and the risk of financing with borrowed money or debt versus financing with equity by selling shares of stock in your firm to the public.) In addition to friends and bank loans, other sources of private financing assistance include venture capitalists, angel investors, credit cards, and the SBA.

venture capitalists
Investment specialists who provide money to finance new businesses or turnarounds in exchange for a portion of the ownership, with the objective of making a considerable profit on the investment; also called VCs

Venture Capitalists **Venture capitalists** are investment specialists who raise pools of capital from large private and institutional sources (such as pension funds) to fund ventures that have a high, rapid growth potential and a need for large amounts of capital. Venture capitalists, or VCs as they're called in entrepreneurial circles, do not simply lend money to a small business as a bank would. Instead they provide money and management expertise in return for a sizable ownership interest in the business. Once the business becomes profitable, venture capitalists reap the reward by selling their interest to other long-term investors for a sizable profit.

Overwhelmed by the number of potential start-ups and a flood of investment funds, most venture capitalist firms will only finance firms that need $10 million or more.[55] Moreover, because it takes the same commitment to watch a small company as a large one, most VCs limit their investments to companies that have the capability of generating $100 million in revenues within a three-year time frame.[56] Thus, if you're looking for only $1 or $2 million of financing, you might want to find an angel instead.

Angel Investors Comfortable with risks that scare off many banks, *angel investors* put their own money into start-ups with the goal of eventually selling their interest for a large profit. These wealthy individuals are willing to loan smaller amounts of money than are VCs and to stay involved with the company for a longer period of time.

In 1999, some 400,000 angels invested about $30 billion in 40,000 U.S. companies.[57] Start-ups that seek out angels typically have spent their first $50,000 to $100,000 and are now looking for the next $250,000 to grow their business.[58] In addition to providing financing, angels can be a great source of business expertise and credibility. High-profile angels include such experts as Bill Gates (chairman of Microsoft), Marc Andresseen (founder of Netscape), and others.[59]

Credit Cards According to a recent study by Arthur Andersen Company, one-third of businesses with 19 or fewer employees use credit cards to finance their new business ventures.[60] Many people turn to credit cards because credit card companies don't care how borrowers spend the money just as long as they pay the bill. Others use credit cards because they are the only source of funding available to them. But with high interest rates, credit cards are a risky way to finance a business, as Jorge de la Riva discovered. He used personal credit cards to start up his industrial wholesale business—an experience he calls "playing with the tiger." As de la Riva put it, "You can make it work only if you have a definite plan to pay back the debt."[61] Unfortunately, many do not. (Credit cards are discussed in greater detail in Chapter 17.)

Small Business Administration Assistance

If your business doesn't fit the profile of high-powered venture-capital start-ups, or you can't find an angel, you might be able to qualify for a bank loan backed by the SBA. To get an SBA-backed loan, you apply to a regular bank, which actually provides the money; the SBA guarantees to repay up to 80 percent of the loan if you fail to do so. The average SBA-backed loan is about $100,000; the upper limit is $1 million with a 75 percent guarantee.[62] Guaranteed loans provided by the SBA launched FedEx, Intel, and Apple Computer. These three now pay more annual taxes to the federal government than the entire yearly cost of running the SBA.[63] In addition to operating its loan guarantee program, the SBA provides a limited number of direct loans to minorities, women, and veterans.[64]

From the businessperson's standpoint, SBA-backed loans are especially attractive because most have longer repayment terms than conventional bank loans—nine years as opposed to two

The partners in a start-up called WebTaggers.com, a computer application provider, recently spent an anxious day and a half preparing to present their business plan to venture capitalists. "In that 10-minute pitch I've got to give the whole story and ask for $10 million," says CEO David Chevalier.

Best of the Web Best of the Web Best of

START A SMALL BUSINESS

Thinking about starting your own business? The U.S. Small Business Administration (SBA) Web site puts you in touch with a wealth of resources to assist you in your start-up. Perhaps you would like some professional business counseling, financial assistance, or advice on developing a business plan. Starting a new business or buying an existing one can be an overwhelming process. But you can increase your chances of success by taking your first steps with the SBA's Start-up Kit. So log on to find out if entrepreneurship is for you. Then do your research and discover some of the secrets of success.

www.sba.gov

Aspiring entrepreneurs like Karla Brown, who might not qualify for regular bank loans, can apply for SBA microloans to make their dreams come true.

or three. A longer repayment term translates into lower monthly payments. Unfortunately, demand for SBA loans vastly outstrips the agency's budget.[65] Nevertheless, Karla Brown is one of the lucky ones. With plenty of perseverance and a $19,000 microloan from the SBA, Brown was able to start her business, Ashmont Flowers Plus. The SBA microloan program began in 1992 to help people realize the American dream—to own a business and be self-sufficient. Microloans range from $100 to $25,000, with the average loan of $10,000 paid back over four years.[66]

Another option for raising money is one of the investment firms created by the Small Business Administration. Small Business Investment Companies (SBICs) and Minority Enterprise Small Business Investment Companies (MESBICs), which finance minority-owned businesses, are similar in operation to venture-capital firms, but they tend to make smaller investments and are willing to consider businesses that VCs may not want to finance.[67]

Going Public

stock
Shares of ownership in a corporation

initial public offering (IPO)
Corporation's first offering of stock to the public

direct public offering (DPO)
Sale of shares of a company's stock directly to investors instead of going through underwriters

prospectus
Formal written offer to sell securities that sets forth the facts that an investor needs to make an informed decision

Whenever a corporation offers its shares of ownership, or **stock,** to the public for the first time, the company is said to be *going public.* The initial shares offered for sale are the company's **initial public offering (IPO).** Going public is an effective method of raising needed capital, but it can be an expensive and time-consuming process filled with regulatory nightmares. Before deciding to finance your company by selling stock, you should weigh the advantages and disadvantages of financing with stock, bonds, and bank loans, as Chapter 17 discusses in detail. Keep in mind that going public is one of the most difficult transactions a business can undertake. For one thing, it requires years of advance planning—sometimes as long as five years before the target date. For another, IPO candidates must have audited financial reports and a solid management team in place.[68] (For information on Internet IPOs, consult Part 6 of this text's online supplement, E-Business in Action, at www.prenhall.com/mescon.)

Because of the high costs and complexity of an IPO, some companies choose to sell their stock directly to the public—a practice known as a **direct public offering (DPO).**[69] The number of DPOs is steadily growing, thanks to the Internet, and DPOs are expected to become an increasingly popular financing option.

The biggest advantage of a DPO is cost savings. DPOs provide businesses with fresh capital at less than half the cost of an IPO. Electronic printing and distribution of a firm's **prospectus,** a preliminary printed statement that is distributed to prospective investors, and the use of virtual

Best of the Web Best of the Web Best of

LEARN THE ABCS OF IPOS

Taking a company public is not for the faint of heart. But like a Broadway opening, a successful debut can launch a relatively unknown company into stardom—or allow it to quietly disappear from the public eye. Even today's largest corporations were at some point small start-ups looking for public financing. Which company is the next AOL, Xerox, or Microsoft? How do IPOs work? How does a young company play the IPO game? You can find the answers to these questions and more by checking out the Beginners Guide to IPOs at Hoover's IPO Central.

www.hoovers.com/ipo

sales presentations instead of live ones can save a company hundreds of thousands of dollars in travel, printing, and distribution costs.[70] In spite of these savings, most companies still go the traditional IPO route. For one thing, DPO shares are not traded on public security exchanges, making it difficult for shareholders to find subsequent buyers for their shares. (Security exchanges are discussed in Chapter 18.) For another, lack of security coverage and support before, after, and during the offering make it difficult to find investors.[71] Even Spring Street Brewing, one of the most highly publicized DPOs, admits that reaching out directly to investors on the Internet will not be as easy for others as it was for Spring Street Brewing, as the company benefited from unusually high levels of publicity because it was the first Internet DPO.[72]

If a company chooses to go the DPO route, it must still follow rules and regulations for selling securities privately. For example, Rule 504 of Regulation D of the Securities and Exchange Commission (also known as "504 offerings" or "Regulation D" offerings) allows companies to raise up to $1 million every 12 months by selling stock, provided they register the securities with the state. Regulation A extends the size of the offering to $5 million but requires a registration with the Small Business Office of the SEC.[73]

 # FOCUSING ON E-BUSINESS TODAY

Why Are the Dot-Coms Falling to Earth?

On April 8, 1999, Craig Winn became a dot-com billionaire. Investors flocked to Value America, his idea of a "Wal-Mart" of the Internet, where shoppers could order jars of caviar along with their gas barbecues or desktop computers. The company would transmit customer orders immediately to manufacturers, who would ship their merchandise directly to customers. Value America's IPO was a success. The stock closed the first day at $55 a share, valuing the three-year-old profitless company at $2.4 billion.

RUNNING ON EMPTY

Twelve months later, Value America filed for Chapter 11 bankruptcy protection, and the price of the company's stock fell to 72 cents. The cyberstore was supposed to harness every efficiency promised by the Net: no inventory, no shipping costs, no warehouse, no physical store. But like many Internet entrepreneurs, Winn tried to do too much too soon. Company computers crashed, customers waited for their orders to be filled, returned merchandise piled up in the halls of the company's offices, and discounting and advertising drained the company's cash, wiping out any chance of profitability.

LEARNING OBJECTIVE

Explain why many dot-com businesses failed at the beginning of the twenty-first century

INSTANT PAPER MILLIONS

Value America's rise and fall is emblematic of an era of unbridled optimism. In the late 1990s just about any dot-com company that wanted to hawk wares over the Net found plenty of eager investors hoping to reap huge profits from the dot-com craze. The Web was like a vast, underdeveloped prairie. Young entrepreneurs with a good idea and a half-baked business plan could make a couple of phone calls to venture capitalists (VCs) and raise millions. Enthusiastic investors raced to claim a stake in the new frontier at Internet speed. Most went in with their eyes wide shut.

THE PARTY'S OVER

Amid the popping of champagne corks, troubles soon began to brew. Entrepreneurs learned the hard way that successfully launching a public company was much different from successfully running one. Cyberspace got crowded. New dot-coms went unnoticed. And desperate to get consumers' attention and business, e-tailers spent lavishly on

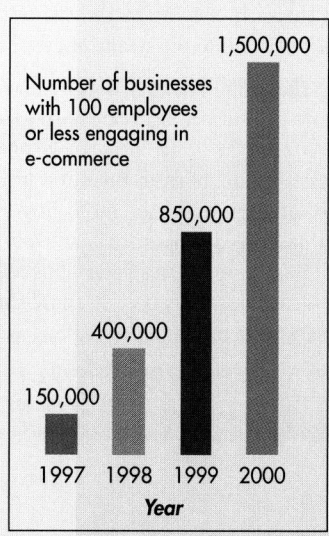

Number of businesses with 100 employees or less engaging in e-commerce

1,500,000
850,000
400,000
150,000
1997 1998 1999 2000
Year

advertising. Some pumped out discount offers and free-shipping promises—hemorrhaging cash and piling up losses. This prompted investors to take a second look and change their minds—overnight. Profits, it seemed, mattered after all.

Of course, some had predicted the fallout, saying that history would repeat itself. After all, from 1855 to 1861, the number of start-up telegraph companies in the United States shrank by 87 percent—from 50 to 6. Many believed the Internet could not escape a shakeout of its own. Still, many investors were caught by surprise when their stock prices fell through the floor. Why did the dot-coms run out of steam? Experts now cite these reasons for the dot-com shakeout:

- **Poor management.** Many dot-coms were founded by people with cool ideas but no business sense. Some entrepreneurs were attracted by the potential to get rich rather than to create a company that was "built to last." Craig Winn's business background, for instance, consisted mainly of leading another public company into bankruptcy. His technology experience was nil. Only during an apparent suspension of the "rules of business" could someone with Winn's background amass the funds to launch such a risky venture.

- **Unrealistic goals.** Many dot-com start-ups were dedicated to achieving the impossible—launching companies in weeks, and attracting millions of customers in months.

- **Going public too soon.** Venture capitalists (VCs), eager to back the next AOL or Amazon.com, tossed huge sums of money at companies that had barely a prayer of prospering. In many cases the VCs took the dot-coms public way too soon. Instead of waiting the customary four to five years, dot-coms were taken public in two years or less—long before the company or its management could prove consistent performance. Meanwhile, investors overlooked business fundamentals and threw money at these businesses—driving their stock prices into the stratosphere.

- **Fighting the laws of supply and demand.** Demand-driven start-ups such as Cisco are born to fulfill existing needs of consumers or businesses. By contrast, supply-driven start-ups are born in the mind of the entrepreneur with little more than a gut feeling that someone will eventually need or want the company's product or service. Thus, supply-driven start-ups leave the company with the enormous task of establishing a market rather than participating in one. Moreover, with rela-

tively low barriers to entry, other dot-coms can easily copy a good idea. At the turn of the twenty-first century, the supply of start-ups greatly exceeded their demand.

- **Extravagant spending.** Companies spent recklessly to lure customers with special promotions and silly marketing campaigns—no matter the cost. In less than one year online health site drkoop.com used up three-quarters of the $84 million it raised in an IPO. Losses were excused as a necessary evil in the pursuit of new customers. To compete, some dot-coms even began to act like conventional retailers—building costly warehouses and adding staff.

- **Locked out of cash.** Most dot-coms were started with venture capital. When they used up that money, they had to find new funding or go public. For many, neither happened. As more and more dot-coms began to fail, investors forced companies to cut costs vigorously, look for merger candidates, postpone or scrap their plans to go public, find a buyer at any price, or close up shop.

As a result of the shakeout, some dot-coms have postponed their plans to go public. Techies.com, an Internet exchange for technology professionals and the businesses seeking to recruit them, was one such company. With sales skyrocketing from $1 million in 1998 to $5 million in the first quarter of 2000, the stage was set for the company's IPO. But less than 24 hours before the IPO presentation team was scheduled to begin its pre-IPO road show, company officials postponed the offering—and then scrapped it altogether. Data showed that prices and trading ranges of the latest IPOs had sharply deteriorated. It simply was not a good time to take a company public.

RETURN TO YESTERYEAR

Today's Internet start-ups must work harder to make a convincing case before going public. Venture capitalists and investors now want companies with proven businesses, the ability to manage costs, and a clear sign of profitability (old-economy rules). Of course, there's always room for new killer ideas, but the IPO window of opportunity has closed for many. As the shakeout continues, some dot-coms will look for a buyer. Some may even be picked up by big traditional companies that stood on the sidelines during the initial dot-com craze. After all, Commodore Vanderbilt never built a railroad in his life. Instead, he bought badly run ones, restructured them, merged them into efficient operations, and managed them superbly.[74]

SUMMARY OF LEARNING OBJECTIVES

1. **Identify the key characteristics (other than size) that differentiate small businesses from larger ones.**
   Small businesses tend to sell fewer products and services to a more targeted group of customers. They have closer contact with their customers and tend to be more open-minded and innovative. Because they have limited resources, the owners must work harder and perform a variety of job functions.

2. **Highlight the major contributions small businesses make to the U.S. economy.**
   Small businesses provide about 70 percent of all new jobs, employ over half of the private nonfarm U.S. workforce, and generate more than half of the private U.S. gross domestic product. They introduce new goods and services, provide specialized products, and supply the needs of large corporations. Additionally, they spend almost as much as big businesses in the economy each year.

3. **Discuss three factors contributing to the increase in the number of small businesses.**
   One factor is the advancement of technology and the Internet, which makes it easier to start a small business, compete with larger firms, or work from home. A second factor is the increase in the number of women and minority entrepreneurs entering the workforce. Finally, corporate downsizing and outsourcing have made self-employment or small-business ownership an attractive and viable option.

4. **Cite the key characteristics common to most entrepreneurs.**
   Entrepreneurs are highly disciplined, intuitive, innovative, ambitious individuals who are eager to learn, like to set trends, and are willing to take risks.

5. **List three ways of getting into business for yourself.**
   You can start a new company from scratch, you can buy a going concern, or you can invest in a franchise.

6. **Identify three sources of small-business assistance.**
   One source for small-business assistance is SCORE—an organization staffed by retired executives and active small-business owners who provide counseling and mentoring for free. Incubators are another source. They provide facilities, business resources, and all types of start-up support. Finally, the Internet is an excellent resource for product and market research, business leads, advice, and contacts.

7. **Discuss the principal sources of small-business private financing.**
   Bank loans are a principal source of private financing. Family and friends are another. Other alternatives include venture capitalists, angel investors, and credit cards. Finally, the Small Business Administration, though not an actual source, can assist entrepreneurs by guaranteeing small bank loans up to 80 percent of the amount borrowed.

8. **Explain why many dot-com businesses failed at the beginning of the twenty-first century.**
   When e-commerce first became popular, new dot-coms had little competition. Entrepreneurs with new ideas got financial backing based on their potential to carve out a niche and gain new online customers. Then competition heated up. Many dot-coms spent excessive amounts of money to acquire customers—at any cost. Most rushed to the Web without solid business plans, realistic goals, and strong management teams. Once dot-comes began to fail, investors decided that profits indeed mattered and began evaluating dot-coms under old-economy rules. Locked out of cash, many dot-coms closed up shop; others postponed, scrapped, or slowed their IPO plans; still others cut costs in hopes of paving their way to profitability.

KEY TERMS

business plan (106)
direct public offering (DPO) (116)
franchise (109)
franchisee (109)
franchisor (109)

incubators (113)
initial public offering (IPO) (116)
outsourcing (104)
prospectus (116)

small business (100)
start-up companies (107)
stock (116)
venture capitalists (114)

TEST YOUR KNOWLEDGE

QUESTIONS FOR REVIEW

1. What are two essential functions of a business plan?

2. What are the key reasons for most small-business failures?

3. What is a business incubator?

4. What are the advantages of buying a business rather than starting one from scratch?

5. What are the advantages and disadvantages of owning a franchise?

QUESTIONS FOR ANALYSIS

6. Why is writing a business plan an important step in starting a new business?

7. Just about anyone can launch a Web site and start a business on the Internet these days. Why is this both good and bad?

8. Take the ServiceMaster Entrepreneur Test at www.ownafranchise.com/self_test.html to assess your entrepreneurial skills. What did you learn about yourself from this test? How can tests like these help you fine-tune your business skills?

9. What things should you consider when evaluating a franchise agreement?

10. Why would a company seek financing from an angel investor instead of using a venture capitalist or going public?

11. You're thinking about starting your own hot dog and burger stand. You've got the perfect site in mind, and you've analyzed

the industry and all the important statistics. It looks as if all systems are go. Uncle Pete is even going to back you on this one. You really understand the fast-food market. In fact, you've become a regular at a competitor's operation (down the road) for over a month. The owner thinks you're his best customer. He even wants to name a sandwich creation after you. But you're not there because you love Frannie's fancy fries. No, you're actually spying. You're learning everything you can about the competition so you can outsmart them. Is this behavior ethical? Explain your answer.

QUESTIONS FOR APPLICATION

12. Briefly describe an incident in your life pertaining to a particular failure. What was it and what did you learn from this experience?

13. If you were starting a new business, how would you go about finding a mentor or an adviser?

14. Entrepreneurs are one of the five factors of production as discussed in Chapter 1. Review that material plus Exhibit 1.3 (Rags to Riches; see page 9), and explain why entrepreneurs are an important factor for economic success.

15. Pick a local small business or franchise that you visit frequently and discuss whether that business competes on price, speed, innovation, convenience, quality, or any combination of those factors. Be sure to provide some examples.

PRACTICE YOUR KNOWLEDGE

SHARPENING YOUR COMMUNICATION SKILLS

Effective communication begins with identifying your primary audience and adapting your message to your audience's needs. This is true even for business plans. One of the primary reasons for writing a business plan is to obtain financing. With that in mind, what do you think are the most important things investors will want to know? How can you convince them that the information you are providing is accurate? What should you assume investors know about your specific business or industry?

HANDLING DIFFICULT SITUATIONS ON THE JOB: DECIDING TO MOVE FROM A LARGE TO A SMALL BUSINESS

Your brother, Ruben N. Rodriguez Jr., started the family-owned Los Amigos Tortilla Manufacturing, Inc., in 1969 with only $12,000. While Los Amigos developed, you were able to help support the family with your income from your job at IBM. Today, the Atlanta-based tortilla business enjoys annual sales of about $4.5 million—and its prospects look bright.

Ruben has asked you to leave your position as head of marketing for IBM's Latin American Division to join the family business. Before answering, you conduct some research into the matter. You find that Hispanic-owned businesses have outstripped U.S. business growth in general. You know that many Hispanic corporate executives are leaving big companies and starting their own businesses. Now you're excited about becoming part of this amazing trend, not only because of the profit potential but also because you love your family and want to help your brother expand the company. Maybe someday your children will join the business as well.

Still, resigning from a key position at IBM is a major step. Are you ready to give up the responsibilities and respect that come with your corporate position? On the other hand, can you disappoint your brother and your entire family when they are asking for your help?[75]

1. What are some of the advantages you see in moving from IBM, a giant corporation, to Los Amigos Tortilla Manufacturing? What are some of the disadvantages?

2. How do you think your IBM experience might help you address the problems of managing small-business growth in the family business?

3. What kinds of questions should you ask your brother before making your final decision? What kinds of questions should you ask yourself?

BUILDING YOUR TEAM SKILLS

The 10 questions shown in Exhibit 4.7 cover major legal issues you should explore before plunking down money for a franchise. In addition, however, there are many more questions you should ask in the process of deciding whether to buy a particular franchise.

With your team, think about how to investigate the possibility of buying a 7-Eleven convenience store franchise. Franchisees operate roughly 3,000 7-Eleven stores in the Midwest, in the Northeast, and on the West Coast. If you or your teammates have shopped in a 7-Eleven store or have seen 7-Eleven advertising, you may already know something about this company. Now is your chance to dig deeper and find out whether buying a 7-Eleven franchise might make sense for you.

First, brainstorm with your team to draw up a list of sources (such as printed sources, Internet sources, and any other suitable sources) where you can locate basic background information about the franchisor. Also list at least two sources you might consult for detailed information about buying and operating a 7-Eleven franchise. Next, generate a list of at least 10 questions any interested buyer should ask about this potential business opportunity.

Choose a spokesperson to present your team's ideas to the class. After all the teams have reported, hold a class discussion to analyze the lists of questions generated by all the teams. Which questions were on most teams' lists? Why do you think those questions are so important? Can your class think of any additional questions that were not on any teams' lists but seem important?

EXPAND YOUR KNOWLEDGE

KEEPING CURRENT USING *THE WALL STREET JOURNAL*

Scan issues of *The Wall Street Journal* (print or online editions) for articles describing problems or successes faced by small businesses in the United States. Clip or copy three or more articles that interest you and then answer the following questions.

1. What problem or opportunity does each article present? Is it an issue faced by many businesses, or is it specific to one industry or region?

2. What could a potential small-business owner learn about the risks and rewards of business ownership from reading these articles?

3. How might these articles affect is someone who is thinking about starting a small business?

DISCOVERING CAREER OPPORTUNITIES

Would you like to own and operate your own business? Whether you plan to start a new business from scratch or buy an existing business or a franchise, you will need certain qualities to be successful. Start your journey to entrepreneurship by reviewing this chapter's section on entrepreneurs and by studying Exhibit 4.4. Now you are ready to delve deeper into the career opportunities of owning and running a small business.

1. Which of the entrepreneurial characteristics mentioned in the chapter and in Exhibit 4.4 describe you? Which of those characteristics can you develop more fully in advance of running your own business?

2. Using library sources, find a self-test on entrepreneurial qualities or use the entrepreneurial test at the Web site www.onlinewbc. org/docs/starting/test.html. Analyze the test's questions. Which of the characteristics discussed in this chapter are mentioned or suggested by the questions included in the test?

3. Answer all the questions in the self-test you have selected. Which questions seem the most critical for entrepreneurial success? How did you score on this self-test—and on the questions you think are most critical? Before you go into business for yourself, which characteristics will you need to work on?

EXPLORING THE BEST OF THE WEB

URLs for all Internet exercises are provided at the Web site for this book, www.prenhall.com/mescon. When you log on to this text's Web site, select Chapter 4, then select "Student Resources," click on the name of the featured Web site, and follow the detailed navigational directions to complete Internet exercises.

Get Smart, page 109

Buying a franchise is sometimes easier than starting from scratch—provided, of course, that you understand what you're getting into. Visit the Smartbiz Web site to help in your investigation.

1. Find the Checklist for Evaluating Your Suitability as a Franchisee. Explain why the following items appear on this checklist: (a) Are you prepared to give up some independence of action in exchange for the advantages the franchise offers you? (b) Is it possible for either you or your spouse to become employed in the type of business you seek to buy before any purchase?

2. Find the Checklist of Information to Secure from a Franchisor. Why is it important to know whether you will have the right of first refusal to adjacent areas?

3. Visit a related Web site, Fran Info, and take Self-Test 1 to determine whether you are suited to become a franchise owner. What did you learn by taking this test?

Increase Your Chances for Success, page 115

Starting a new business or buying an existing one can be an overwhelming process. But you can increase your chances of success if you do your research and plan ahead. Go to the SBA Web site and explore the site's wealth of information for small-business owners.

1. Take the quiz for success. After you've worked through the entire quiz, go back and add up your points. Then compare your total with the Success Quotient table to see how you compare with some of California's most successful businesspeople.

2. Review the Startup Kit. Then decide whether entrepreneurship is for you by answering the questions about entrepreneurs. Would you classify yourself as an entrepreneur? Why or why not?

3. Review the SBA Business Plan Outline. What information should you include in a business plan when describing your business or products? What information should you provide about your competitors? What questions should you answer about your management team?

Learn the ABCs of IPOs, page 116

Thinking about taking your company public? Check out Hoover's IPO Central and learn how to walk, talk, and speak the IPO language before you play the game.

1. When is an IPO a done deal? What is a lockup period? What is the difference between an offering price and opening price?

2. In your own words, briefly summarize the IPO process.

3. What general information does a prospectus contain? What are some warning signs prospective IPO investors might be looking for?

Explore on Your Own

Review these chapter-related Web sites on your own to learn more about entrepreneurship and small business.

1. The Small Business Advisor, www.isquare.com, is packed with tips, online guides, and articles designed to assist individuals who are considering starting a business or who are operating a small business.

2. *Inc. Magazine* maintains a Web site Inc.com, www.inc.com, that is full of advice and information for entrepreneurs. Click on the research tab, and read the articles under Growing Your Business.

3. Entrepreneur.com's Franchise Zone, www.entrepenuer.com/ Franchise_Zone/FZ_FrontDoor, claims to be the online frachising authority. The site offers news and advice for those looking to buy a franchise, an expert advice column, an "Entrepreneur's Guide to Franchising," interactive discussions, over 900 franchise opportunities by category, and much more.

A CASE FOR CRITICAL THINKING

■ *Why is Papa John's Rolling in Dough?*

Every success seems to roll down a road littered with skeptics. And that skeptic was very close to John Schnatter's home. In 1984, when Schnatter installed a pizza oven in a converted tavern closet in his hometown of Jeffersonville, Indiana, his mom said "Why don't you do something else to be successful?" Schnatter reminds her of that at least once a year. Today Papa John's has more than 2,388 stores in 47 states and five international markets. Annual sales have mushroomed to about $1.4 billion.

LOVE AT FIRST SAUCE

It was love at first sauce for Schnatter, the company's founder and CEO. "I liked everything about the pizza business," he says. "I liked making the dough; I liked kneading the dough; I liked putting the sauce on; I liked putting the toppings on; I liked running the oven. From the get-go, I fell in love with the business." Working his way through college by making pizzas, Schnatter was no novice. He knew the grass roots of the business, had an intuitive grasp on what customers wanted, and knew how to make his pizza taste a little bit better than the competition's.

PIPING-HOT PERFORMANCE

Papa John's has done a great job of emerging out of nowhere. It's an incredible entrepreneurial success story of a visionary and capable man. Competitive in nature, Schnatter doesn't sit around and wait for things to happen. Instead, he makes them happen. So it's no surprise that Papa John's has been winning the pizza war—grabbing business from giants such as Pizza Hut, Little Caesars, and delivery king, Dominos. Now the fourth-largest pizza chain and the fastest growing, Papa John's consistently reports double-digit growth in an industry that is expanding at a rate of only 2 to 3 percent a year—even though Americans consume pizza at the rate of 350 slices per second.

EXPANDING THE PIE CHART

Acquisitions play an increasingly important role in Papa John's growth strategy—especially abroad. In 1999 Papa John's made its European debut by acquiring Perfect Pizza Holdings, a 205-unit delivery and carryout pizza chain in the United Kingdom. The acquisition gave Papa John's instant access to proven sites that would have been difficult to obtain. Besides the real estate, Perfect Pizza had a good management team that Schnatter could fold into his organization. If one strength rises above the others in Schnatter's path to success, it's his ability to recruit and retain the right people. "There's nothing special about John Schnatter except the people around me," Schnatter says. "They make me look better and make Papa John's what it is."

THE PERFECT CRUST

Good people are indeed an important part of Schnatter's success. But his secret recipe is quality control. Before a single pizza hits the ovens, franchisees spend six months to a year assessing an area's potential. Papa John's doesn't just move into an area and open up 200 stores. It does it one store at a time. Once a store is up and running, the company puts enormous effort into forecasting product demand. Franchisees project demand one to two weeks in advance. They factor in anything from forthcoming promotions to community events to the next big high-school football game. If a big game is on TV, store owners are ready for the surge in deliveries.

To ensure a high-quality product, Papa John's keeps things simple. The stores have no seating, offer just two types of pizza—thin crust or regular—and have no salads, sandwiches, or buffalo wings. Owners are trained to remake any pies that rate less then 8 on the company's 10-point scale. If the cheese shows a single air bubble or the crust is not golden brown, out the offender goes. To make sure everything is in order, Schnatter visits four to five stores a week, often unannounced. His attention to detail has helped earn Papa John's the title of best U.S. pizza chain according to surveys. Which is why Papa John's customers keep coming back for more.

CRITICAL THINKING QUESTIONS

1. What factors have contributed to Papa John's success?

2. If you were drafting Papa John's initial business plan, what would you need to know about competition?

3. What type of franchise is Papa John's? Why did Papa John's purchase Perfect Pizza Holdings instead of establishing new franchisees in the United Kingdom?

4. Go to Chapter 4 of this text's Web site at www.prenhall. com/mescon. Click on the Papa John's link to get the latest pizza industry facts from Pizzaware. How many pizzerias exist in the United States? How big is the pizza industry (in dollars)? What is the long-term outlook for the industry? How much pizza does each person eat on average per year? What is America's favorite pizza topping?

VIDEO CASE AND EXERCISES

■ *Booting Up Computer Friendly Stuff*

SYNOPSIS

Chris Cole became an entrepreneur in 1997. With his sister and a team of entrepreneurial friends with diverse talents, Cole started Computer Friendly Stuff (www.computerbug.com), a Chicago-based small business that makes computer toys and software products. He originally planned to finance the new business using credit cards, but then he found investors and raised $70,000 in exchange for giving investors an ownership stake in the company. What he and his friends lacked in business know-how and resources, they made up in hard work and enthusiasm. More than a year after the company was founded, its products finally began to catch on. Now Computer Friendly Stuff has a licensing agreement with Warner Brothers and sells its toys and software in 11 countries.

EXERCISES

Analysis

1. What are the advantages and disadvantages of Chris Cole's use of credit cards and angel investors to finance his business?

2. Do you think franchising would be a good way for Computer Friendly Stuff to expand internationally?

3. Which of the success factors shown in Exhibit 4.4 do Chris Cole and his colleagues seem to possess?

4. Can Computer Friendly Stuff be classified as a lifestyle business or a high-growth venture? Why?

5. Would you give Computer Friendly Stuff a better chance of survival if its management had more experience with financial management and other key functions?

Application

A solid business plan can guide a start-up through some difficult periods. If you were helping to write the business plan for Computer Friendly Stuff, how would you describe its mission? What critical risks and problems would you identify in your plan, and why?

Decision

If Computer Friendly Stuff received a rush order from a giant U.S. retailer for $1,000,000 worth of computer toys, it would face a diffi-cult decision. It might have to turn down the order because the company lacks the manufacturing capacity to produce that volume in short time. However, if it said no, the retailer might never place another order. On the other hand, if it accepted the order and could not fill it completely and on time, the retailer would also be upset. What should Computer Friendly Stuff do in such a situation?

Communication

Select one of Computer Friendly Stuff's products. Based on the descriptions of this product in the video and on the company Web site (www.computerbug.com), write a 30-second oral description to use in selling this product to a large retail chain.

Integration

Review the information on responsibility toward investors, as discussed in Chapter 2. As a privately held company, what are Computer Friendly Stuff's responsibilities?

Ethics

Is it ethical for Chris Cole to approach investors for funding for new products and additional promotions, even though Computer Friendly Stuff has not yet made a profit?

Debate

Should Chris Cole plan to take Computer Friendly Stuff public? Choose one side of this question to debate and prepare a two-minute statement summarizing your main arguments and reasoning.

Teamwork

No business plan is complete without an analysis of the competition. Working with two other students, identify one or more products that compete with Computer Friendly Stuff's products. Develop a table comparing the strengths and weaknesses of each product with those of Computer Friendly Stuff. Overall, what do you think of Computer Friendly Stuff's competitive situation?

Online Research

Use Internet sources to research Computer Friendly Stuff's latest products and initiatives. How is the company doing? What opportunities and challenges has it faced in recent months? See Component Chapter A, Exhibit A.1, for search engines to use in doing your research. Write a one-page report on the findings of your research.

MYPHLIP COMPANION WEB SITE

Learning Interactively

Visit the myPHLIP Web site at www.prenhall.com/mescon. For Chapter 4, take advantage of the interactive "Study Guide" to test your chapter knowledge. Get instant feedback on whether you need additional studying. Read the "Current Events" articles to get the latest on chapter topics, and complete the exercises as specified by your instructor. Expand your learning with a visit to the "Research Area." There you will find a wealth of information you can use to complete your course assignments.

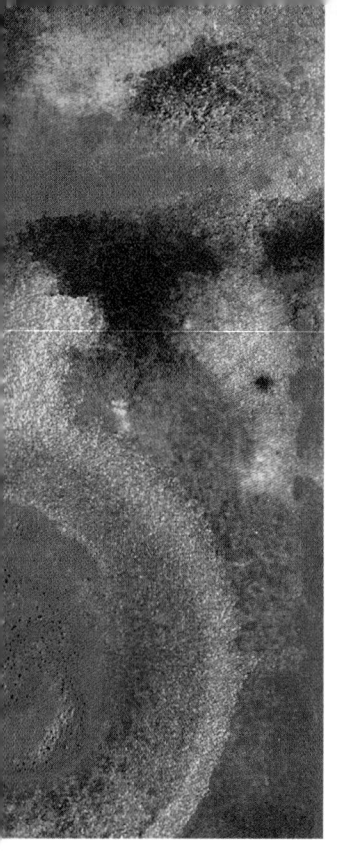

FORMS OF BUSINESS OWNERSHIP AND BUSINESS COMBINATIONS

5

LEARNING OBJECTIVES

After studying this chapter, you will be able to

1. List five advantages and four disadvantages of sole proprietorships

2. List five advantages and two disadvantages of partnerships

3. Explain the differences between common and preferred stock from a shareholder's perspective

4. Highlight the advantages and disadvantages of public stock ownership

5. Cite four advantages and three disadvantages of corporations

6. Delineate the three groups that govern a corporation and describe the role of each

7. Identify six main synergies companies hope to achieve by combining their operations

@ 8. Explain how the role of dot-com directors differs from the role played by directors of traditional corporations

RESTRUCTURING KINKO'S PARTNERSHIPS TO DUPLICATE SUCCESS

www.kinkos.com

Kinko's, once known simply as the leading chain of printing and copy shops, has recast itself for the work-obsessed digital age.

Paul Orfalea knew he would run a big company someday. He just never envisioned Kinko's as that dream. At 22 Orfalea borrowed enough money to open a copying service near the University of California, Santa Barbara. The store was so small that he had to wheel the single copier onto the sidewalk to make room for customers. Nevertheless, it serviced the needs of local college students.

By 1995 (some 25 years later), Kinko's—named after Orfalea's reddish, curly hair—had grown into a chain of 815 stores operating in five countries. But Kinko's wasn't managed as a single entity. Instead, the business consisted of 130 separate partnerships, each operating groups of stores. Even though Orfalea retained a majority interest in each partnership, the partners were free to operate their stores as they saw fit. Therefore, not all Kinko's were the same, and that was a problem. Some partners reinvested their earnings in high-tech equipment; others cashed in their profits. This meant that traveling customers would find varing equipment and services from store to store: from color copiers and high-speed Internet access at spruced-up outlets in one city to dilapidated storefronts with little more than black-and-white copy machines in another.

Orfalea knew that to succeed in a high-tech marketplace, all Kinko's stores would have to look alike and offer comparable services. Moreover, with more and more people working from home and other remote locations, the stores would have to invest in expensive equipment such as digital printers, high-speed copiers, fast Internet connections, and even videoconferencing equipment to service growing customer needs. Orfalea also knew that such changes would require additional financing and the help of experts. So in 1997 Orfalea selected private investors Clayton, Dublier & Rice (CD&R) to help turn things around.

Paying out $220 million in exchange for a 33 percent share of Kinko's, CD&R rolled the 130 individual partnerships into a single privately held corporation, giving each partner shares of stock in the newly formed organization. It took the original partners some time to adjust to the new corporate structure, but eventually they came around. Besides, the partners knew that having a private equity stake in Kinko's could be worth a sizable fortune if the company went public.

As a corporate entity, everyone was now working in the same direction. The store managers lobbied aggressively for new equipment and expanded their services to include on-site computer rentals, document binding and finishing, custom printing, passport photos, mailing services, videoconference facilities, and more. In addition, the company launched KinkonetSM, a proprietary document distribution and print network that allows customers to submit projects at one Kinko's site and pick up finished projects at another.

With annual sales now topping $1 billion, Kinko's is indeed the leader in the $7 billion copy-services market. Today customers can go into any of the 1,000 Kinko's in such far-flung places as Australia, Japan, South Korea, and the United Kingdom and find the same equipment, supplies, and services, making it possible for small-business owners and travelers to rely on Kinko's as their office away from home.[1]

■ CHOOSING A FORM OF BUSINESS OWNERSHIP

As Paul Orfalea knows, one of the most fundamental decisions you must make when starting a business is selecting a form of business ownership. This decision can be complex and have far-reaching consequences for your business. Furthermore, as your business grows, chances are you may change the original form you selected, as Orfalea did.

The three most common forms of business ownership are sole proprietorship, partnership, and corporation. Each form has its own characteristic internal structure, legal status, size, and fields to which it is best suited. Each has key advantages and disadvantages for the owners. Exhibit 5.1 contrasts the characteristics of the three forms of business ownership.

Sole Proprietorships

A **sole proprietorship** is a business owned by one person (although it may have many employees), and it is the easiest and least expensive form of business to start. Many farms, retail establishments, and small service businesses are sole proprietorships, as are many home-based businesses (such as caterers, consultants, and computer programmers).

LEARNING OBJECTIVE 1
List five advantages and four disadvantages of sole proprietorships

sole proprietorship
Business owned by a single individual

CORPORATE STRUCTURE	OWNERSHIP RULES AND CONTROL	TAX CONSIDERATIONS	LIABILITY EXPOSURE	EASE OF ESTABLISHMENT AND TERMINATION
Sole proprietorship	One owner has complete control.	Profits and losses flow directly to the owners and are taxed at individual rates.	Owner has unlimited personal liability for business debts.	Easy to set up but leaves owner's personal finances at risk. Owner must generally sell the business to get his or her investment out.
General partnership	Two or more owners; each partner is entitled to equal control unless agreement specifies otherwise.	Profits and losses flow directly to the partners and are taxed at individual rates. Partners share income and losses equally unless the partnership agreement specifies otherwise.	Personal assets of any operating partner are at risk from business creditors.	Easy to set up. Partnership agreement recommended but not required. Partners must generally sell their share in the business to recoup their investment.
Limited partnership	Two or more owners; the general partner controls the business; limited partners don'the participate in the management.	Same as for general partnership.	Limited partners are liable only for the amount of their investment.	Same as for general partnership.
Corporation	Unlimited number of shareholders; no limits on stock classes or voting arrangements. Ownership and management of the business are separate. Shareholders in public corporations are not involving in daily management decisions; in private or closely held corporations, owners are more likely to participate in managing the business.	Profits and losses are taxed at corporate rates. Profits are taxed again at individual rates when they are distributed to the investors as dividends.	Investor's liability is limited to the amount of their investment.	Expense and complexity of incorporation vary from state to state; can be costly from a tax perspective. In a public corporation, shareholders may trade their shares on the open market; in a private corporation, shareholders must find a buyer for their shares to recoup their investment.

EXHIBIT 5.1

CHARACTERISTICS OF THE FORMS OF BUSINESS OWNERSHIP

The "best" form of ownership depends on the objectives of the people involved in the business.

Advantages of Sole Proprietorships A sole proprietorship has many advantages. One is ease of establishment. All you have to do to launch a sole proprietorship is obtain necessary licenses, start a checking account for the business, and open your doors. Another advantage is the satisfaction of working for yourself. As a sole proprietor, you can make your own decisions, such as which hours to work, whom to hire, what prices to charge, whether to expand, and whether to shut down. Best of all, you can keep all the after-tax profits, and profits are taxed at individual income tax rates not at the higher corporate rates.

As a sole proprietor, you also have the advantage of privacy; you do not have to reveal your performance or plans to anyone. Although you may need to provide financial information to a banker if you need a loan, and you must provide certain financial information when you file tax returns, you do not have to prepare any reports for outsiders as you would if the company were a public corporation.

Disadvantages of Sole Proprietorships One major drawback of a sole proprietorship is the proprietor's **unlimited liability**. From a legal standpoint, the owner and the business are one and the same. Any legal damages or debts incurred by the business are the owner's responsibility. As a sole proprietor, you might have to sell personal assets, such as your home, to satisfy a business debt. And if someone sues you over a business matter, you might lose everything you own if you do not have the proper types and amount of business insurance (see Component Chapter C).

In some cases, the sole proprietor's independence can also be a drawback because it means that the business depends on the talents and managerial skills of one person. If problems crop up, the sole proprietor may not recognize them or may be too proud to seek help, especially given the high cost of hiring experienced managers and professional consultants. Other disadvantages include the difficulty of a single-person operation obtaining large sums of capital and the limited life of a sole proprietorship. Although some sole proprietors pass their business on to their heirs as part of their estate, the owner's death may mean the demise of the business. And even if the business does transfer to an heir, the founder's unique skills may have been crucial to the successful operation of the business.

Partnerships

If starting a business on your own seems a little intimidating, you might decide to share the risks and rewards of going into business with a partner. In that case, you would form a **partnership**—a legal association of two or more people as co-owners of a business for profit. You and your partners would share the profits and losses of the business and perhaps the management responsibilities. Your partnership might remain a small, two-person operation or it might have multiple partners, like Kinko's did.

Partnerships are of two basic types. In a **general partnership**, all partners are considered equal by law, and all are liable for the business's debts. In a **limited partnership**, one or more people

unlimited liability
Legal condition under which any damages or debts attributable to the business can also be attached to the owner because the two have no separate legal existence

partnership
Unincorporated business owned and operated by two or more persons under a voluntary legal association

general partnership
Partnership in which all partners have the right to participate as co-owners and are individually liable for the business's debts

limited partnership
Partnership composed of one or more general partners and one or more partners whose liability is usually limited to the amount of their capital investment

Best of the Web Best of the Web Best of

PLANNING YOUR ONLINE BUSINESS

Thinking about launching your own e-commerce business? Planning and running an online business could involve more work than you think. Actium Publishing's Internet Business Start-Ups lists several things you must consider. Among them are finding the best Internet connection and server provider, deciding whether to join an online mall, selecting someone to design and maintain your Web site, and developing appropriate advertising. Have you thought about these important decisions? Moreover, do you know how much setting up a business on the Internet costs? Which products sell well on the Internet and which don't? Find the answers to these questions and more by logging on to Internet Business Start-Ups. Be sure to check out the tips Internet entrepreneurs have for you.

www.actium1.com

act as *general partners* who run the business, while the remaining partners are passive investors (that is, they are not involved in managing the business). These partners are called *limited partners* because their liability (the amount of money they can lose) is limited to the amount of their capital contribution. Many states now recognize *limited liability partnerships* (LLPs) in which all partners in the business are limited partners and have only limited liability for the debts and obligations of the partnership. Most states restrict LLPs to certain types of professionals such as attorneys, physicians, dentists, and accountants.[2] Of the three forms of business ownership, partnerships are the least-common form (see Exhibit 5.2).

LEARNING
OBJECTIVE   *2*
List five advantages and two
disadvantages of partnerships

Advantages of Partnerships Proprietorships and partnerships have some of the same advantages. Like proprietorships, partnerships are easy to form. Partnerships also provide the same tax advantages as proprietorships, because profits are taxed at individual income-tax rates rather than at corporate rates.

However, in a couple of respects, partnerships are superior to sole proprietorships, largely because there's strength in numbers. When you have several people putting up their money, you can start a more ambitious enterprise. In addition, the diversity of skills that good partners bring to an organization leads to innovation in products, services, and processes, which improves your chances of success.[3] The partnership form of ownership also broadens the pool of capital available to the business. Not only do the partners' personal assets support a larger borrowing capacity, but the ability to obtain financing increases because general partners are legally responsible for paying off the debts of the group. Finally, by forming a partnership you increase the chances that the organization will endure, because new partners can be drawn into the business to replace those who die or retire. For example, even though the original partners of the accounting firm KPMG Peat Marwick (founded in 1897) died many years ago, the company continues.

Disadvantages of Partnerships Except in limited liability partnerships, at least one member of every partnership must be a general partner. All general partners have unlimited liability. Thus, if one of the firm's partners makes a serious business or professional mistake and is sued by a disgruntled client, all general partners are financially accountable. At the same time, general partners are responsible for any debts incurred by the partnership. Of course, malpractice insurance or business-risk insurance offers some financial protection (see Component Chapter C), but these types of insurance are costly.

Another disadvantage of partnerships is the potential for interpersonal problems. Difficulties often arise because each partner wants to be responsible for managing the organization. Electing a managing partner to lead the organization may diminish the conflicts, but disagreements are still likely to arise. Moreover, the partnership may have to face the question of what to do with unproductive partners. And if a partner wants to leave the firm, conflicts can arise over claims on the firm's profits and on capital the partner invested. Provisions for handling the departure and addition of partners are usually covered in the partnership agreement.

EXHIBIT 5.2

POPULAR FORMS OF BUSINESS OWNERSHIP

The most popular form of business ownership is a sole proprietorship, followed by a corporation and then a partnership.

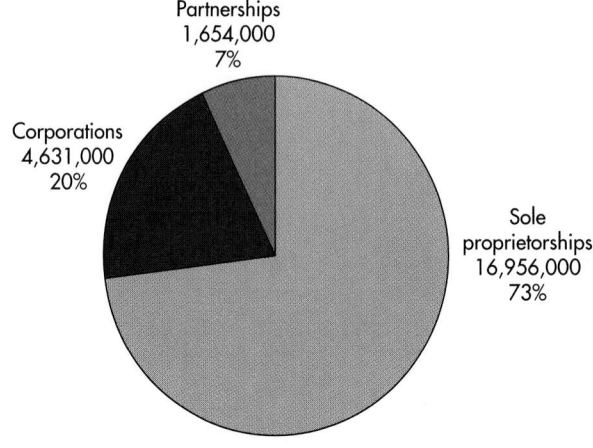

Approximate number and percentages of existing firms in the United States

Partnership Agreement A *partnership agreement* is a written document that states all the terms of operating the partnership by spelling out the partners' rights and responsibilities. Although the law does not require a written partnership agreement, it is wise to work with a lawyer to develop one. One of the most important features of the agreement is that it addresses in advance sources of conflict that could result in battles between partners. To avoid disagreements later on, begin by spelling out such details as the division of profits, decision-making authority, expected contributions, and dispute resolution. Moreover, a key element of this document is the buy/sell agreement, which defines the steps a partner must take to sell his or her partnership interest or what will happen if one of the partners dies.

Corporations

A **corporation** is a legal entity with the power to own property and conduct business. The modern corporation evolved in the nineteenth century when large sums of capital were needed to build railroads, coal mines, and steel mills. Such endeavors required so much money that no single individual or group of partners could hope to raise it all. The solution was to sell shares in the business to numerous investors, who would get a cut of the profits in exchange for their money. These investors got a chance to vote on certain issues that might affect the value of their investment, but they were not involved in managing day-to-day operations. The investors were protected from the risks associated with such large undertakings by having their liability limited to the amount of their investment.

It was a good solution, and the corporation quickly became a vital force in the nation's economy. As rules and regulations developed to define what corporations could and could not do, corporations acquired the legal attributes of people. Like you, a corporation can receive, own, and transfer property; make contracts; sue; and be sued. Unlike the case with sole proprietorships and partnerships, a corporation's legal status and obligations exist independently of its owners.

Tom and Kate Chappell are partners in Tom's of Maine, a manufacturer of all-natural health and beauty products.

corporation
Legally chartered enterprise having most of the legal rights of a person, including the right to conduct business, to own and sell property, to borrow money, and to sue or be sued; owners of the corporation enjoy limited liability

Ownership The corporation is owned by its **shareholders,** who are issued shares of stock in return for their investments. These shares are evidenced by a **stock certificate,** and they may be bequeathed or sold to someone else. As a result, the company's ownership may change drastically over time while the company and its management remain intact (as long as the company is economically sound). The corporation's unlimited life span, combined with its ability to raise capital, gives it the potential for significant growth.

shareholders
Owners of a corporation

stock certificate
Document that proves stock ownership

Common Stock Most stock issued by corporations is **common stock.** Owners of common stock have voting rights and get one vote for each share of stock they own. They can elect the company's board of directors in addition to voting on major policies that will affect ownership—such as mergers, acquisitions, and takeovers. Besides conferring voting privileges, common stock

common stock
Shares whose owners have voting rights and have the last claim on distributed profits and assets

Best of the Web Best of the Web Best of

CHOOSING A FORM OF OWNERSHIP

Which legal form of ownership is best suited for a new business? Answering this question can be a challenge—especially if you're not familiar with the attributes of sole proprietorships, partnerships, and corporations. That's where Nolo Self-Help Centers can help. Because there's no right or wrong choice for everyone, your job is to understand how each legal structure works and then pick the one that best meets your needs. Start your research by browsing the small business law center at Nolo. Be sure to check out the FAQs and Legal Encyclopedia.
www.nolo.com

dividends
Distributions of corporate assets to shareholders in the form of cash or other assets

frequently pays **dividends,** payments to shareholders from the company's profits. Dividends can be paid in cash or stock (called *stock dividends*). They are declared by the board of directors but their payment is not mandatory. For example, some companies, especially young or rapidly growing ones, pay no dividends. Instead, they reinvest their profits in new product research and development, equipment, buildings, and other assets so they can grow and earn future profits.

LEARNING
OBJECTIVE   3
Explain the differences between common and preferred stock from a shareholder's perspective

In addition to dividends, common shareholders can earn a return on their investment. If shareholders sell their stock in good times for more than they paid for it, they stand to pocket a handsome gain. But because the value or price of a company's common stock is subject to many economic variables besides the company's own performance, common-stock investments are risky and shareholders may not get any profit at all. In fact, if investors sell shares of common stock for less than they paid for it, they could incur a sizable financial loss. Common stock, risk, and financial investments are discussed in detail in Chapter 18.

Avis has never paid cash dividends to shareholders. The company believes that shareholders are best served by reinvesting profits back into the company to foster long-term growth.

Preferred Stock In contrast to common stock, **preferred stock** does not usually carry voting rights. It does, however, give preferred shareholders the right of first claim on the corporation's assets (in the form of dividends) after all the company's debts have been paid. This right is especially important if the company ever goes out of business. Moreover, preferred shareholders get their dividends before common shareholders do. The amount of preferred dividend is usually set (or fixed) at the time the preferred stock is issued and can provide investors with a source of steady income. Like common stock, however, dividends on preferred stock may be omitted in times of financial hardship. Still, most preferred stock is *cumulative preferred stock,* which means that any unpaid dividends must be paid before dividends are paid to common shareholders.

Public versus Private Ownership The stock of a **private corporation** such as Kinko's is held by only a few individuals or companies and is *not publicly traded.* By withholding their stock from public sale, the owners retain complete control over their opera-

preferred stock
Shares that give their owners first claim on a company's dividends and assets after all debts have been paid and whose owners do not have voting rights

private corporation
Company owned by private individuals or companies

public corporation
Corporation that actively sells stock on the open market

tions and ownership. Such famous companies as Hallmark and Hyatt Hotels have opted to remain private corporations (also referred to as *closed corporations* or *closely held companies*). These companies finance their operating costs and growth from either company earnings or other sources, such as bank loans. By contrast, the stock of a **public corporation** is held by and available for sale to the general public; thus the company is said to be *publicly traded.*

In Chapter 4 we discussed the concept of going public in the context of financing the enterprise. Bear in mind that in addition to providing a ready supply of capital, public ownership has other advantages and disadvantages. Among the advantages are increased liquidity, enhanced visibility, and the establishment of an independent market value for the company. Moreover, having a publicly traded stock gives companies flexibility to use such stock to acquire other firms. This was one of the primary reasons UPS decided to sell 10 percent of its stock to the public in 1999, after nearly a century of remaining a privately held organization.[4] Nevertheless, selling your stock to the public has distinct disadvantages: (1) the cost of going public is high (ranging from $50,000 to $500,000), (2) the filing requirements with the SEC (Securities and Exchange Commission) are burdensome, (3) you lose ownership control, (4) management must be ready to handle the administrative and legal demands of heightened public exposure, and (5) it subjects the value of the company's stock to external forces that are beyond the company's control.

LEARNING
OBJECTIVE   4
Highlight the advantages and disadvantages of public stock ownership

Advantages of Corporations No other form of business ownership can match the success of the corporation in bringing together money, resources, and talent; in accumulating assets; and in creating wealth. As it grows, a corporation gains from a diverse labor pool, greater financing options, and expanded research-and-development capabilities. The corporation has certain inherent qualities that make it the best vehicle for reaching those objectives. One such quality is limited liability. Although a corporate entity can assume tremendous liabilities, it is the corporation that is liable and not the private shareholders. Take Johannes Schwartlander, who ran his San Francisco marble and granite business as a sole proprietorship for seven years. When the company began to grow, Schwartlander decided to incorporate to protect himself. "When we had so many employees and started installing marble panels ten stories up, I realized that if five years later something fell down, I would be responsible," he says.[5] Incorporation also protects him from personal liability should his business go bankrupt.

In addition to limited liability, corporations that sell stock to the general public have the advantage of **liquidity,** which means that investors can easily convert their stock into cash by selling it on the open market. This option makes buying stock in a corporation attractive to many investors. In contrast, liquidating the assets of a sole proprietorship or a partnership can be difficult. Moreover, shareholders of public corporations can easily transfer their ownership by selling their shares to someone else. Thus, corporations tend to be in a better position than proprietorships and partnerships to make long-term plans as a result of their unlimited life span and the funding available through the sale of stock. As they grow, corporations can benefit from the diverse talents and experience of a large pool of employees and managers. Moreover, large corporations are often able to finance projects internally.

Keep in mind that a company need not be large to incorporate. Most corporations, like most businesses, are relatively small, and most small corporations are privately held. The big ones, however, are *really* big. The 500 largest corporations in the United States, as listed by *Fortune* magazine, have combined sales of over $6.3 trillion. Wal-Mart stores alone employ 1,400,000 people, which is greater than the population of Detroit, Michigan.[6]

Hyatt's owners, the Pritzker family, have opted to retain control of their enterprise because they appreciate the long-term value of doing so. That status also has a profound effect on the way Hyatt runs its 190 hotels and resorts worldwide. Public companies, which have an eye trained on the stock price, tend to overlook the long-term effects of decision in favor of short-term gains. But Hyatt general managers have the freedom from concern about quarterly earning reports and stock prices. This gives them a certain entrepreneurial attitude that other hotel managers might not enjoy.

Disadvantages of Corporations Corporations are not without some disadvantages. As mentioned earlier, publicly owned companies are required by the government to publish information about their finances and operations. These reporting requirements increase the pressure on corporate managers to achieve short-term growth and earnings targets in order to satisfy shareholders and to attract potential investors. In addition, having to disclose financial information increases the company's vulnerability to competitors and to those who might want to take over control of the company against the wishes of the existing management.

LEARNING OBJECTIVE 5

Cite four advantages and three disadvantages of corporations

liquidity
The level of ease with which an asset can be converted to cash

Best of the Web Best of the Web Best of

FOLLOWING THE FORTUNES OF THE FORTUNE 500

Quick! Name the largest corporation in the United States, as measured by annual revenues. Give up? Just check *Fortune* magazine's yearly ranking of the 500 largest U.S. companies. For years, General Motors has topped the list with its $160 billion-plus in annual revenues, but Ford, Wal-Mart, General Electric, and other giants have also been strong contenders in recent years. The Fortune 500 not only ranks corporations by size but also offers brief company descriptions along with industry statistics and additional measures of corporate performance. You can search the list by ranking, by industry, by company name, or by CEO. And to help you identify the largest international corporations, there's a special Global 500 list as well.
www.pathfinder.com/fortune/fortune500/500list.html

The paperwork and costs associated with incorporation can also be burdensome, particularly if you plan to sell stock. The complexity varies from state to state, but regardless of where you live, it is wise to consult an attorney and an accountant before incorporating. In addition, corporations are taxed twice. They must pay federal and state corporate income tax on the company's profits, and individual shareholders must pay income taxes on their share of the company's profits received as dividends.

Special Types of Corporations Certain types of corporations enjoy special privileges provided they adhere to strict guidelines and rules. One special type of corporation is known as the **S corporation** (or subchapter S corporation). An S corporation is a distinction that is made only for federal income tax purposes and is, in terms of legal characteristics, no different from any other corporation. Basically, the owners receive the tax advantages of a partnership while they raise money through the sale of stock. In addition, income and tax deductions from the business flow directly to the owners, who are taxed at individual income-tax rates, just as they are in a partnership. Corporations seeking "S" status must meet certain criteria: (1) they must have no more than 75 investors, none of whom may be nonresident aliens; (2) they must be a domestic (U.S.) corporation; and (3) they can only issue one class of common stock, which means that all stock must share the same dividend and liquidation rights (but may have different voting rights).[7]

Limited liability companies (LLCs) are another special type of corporation. These flexible business entities combine the tax advantages of a partnership with the personal liability protection of a corporation. Furthermore, LLCs are not restricted in the number of shareholders they can have, and members' participation in management is not restricted as it is in limited partnerships. Members of an LLC normally adopt an operating agreement (similar to a partnership agreement) to govern the entity's operation and management. These agreements generally are flexible and permit owners to structure the allocation of income and losses any way they desire, so long as certain tax rules are followed. In addition, the agreements can be designed to meet the special needs of owners, such as special voting rights, management controls, and buyout options. The only limit to what can be done is the owners' imagination.[8]

Some corporations are not independent entities; that is, they are owned by a single entity. **Subsidiary corporations,** for instance, are partially or wholly owned by another corporation known as a **parent company,** which supervises the operations of the subsidiary. A **holding company** is a special type of parent company that owns other companies for investment reasons and usually exercises little operating control over those subsidiaries.

Corporations can also be classified according to where they do business. An *alien corporation* operates in the United States but is incorporated in another country. A *foreign corporation,* sometimes called an *out-of-state corporation,* is incorporated in one state (frequently the state of Delaware, where incorporation laws are lenient) but does business in several other states where it is registered. And a *domestic corporation* does business only in the state where it is chartered (incorporated).

Corporate Governance Although a corporation's common shareholders own the business, they are rarely involved in managing it, particularly if the corporation is publicly traded. Instead, the common shareholders elect a board of directors to represent them, and the directors, in turn, select the corporation's top officers, who actually run the company (see Exhibit 5.3).

The center of power in a corporation often lies with the **chief executive officer,** or **CEO.** Together with the chief financial officer (CFO) and the chief operating officer (COO), the CEO is responsible for establishing company policies, managing corporate direction, and making the big decisions that will affect the company's growth and competitive position. In Chapter 6, we'll discuss in detail the functions and roles of management. Keep in mind that the chief executive officer may also be the chairman of the board, the president of the corporation, or both. Moreover, because corporate ownership and management are separate, the owners may get rid of the managers (in theory, at least) if the owners vote to do so.

Shareholders Shareholders of a corporation can be individuals, other companies, not-for-profit organizations, pension funds, and mutual funds. All shareholders who own voting shares are invited to an annual meeting to choose directors, select an independent accountant to audit the company's financial statements, and attend to other business. Those who cannot attend the annual meeting in

---

S corporation
Corporations with no more than 75 shareholders that may be taxed as a partnership; also known as a subchapter S corporation

limited liability companies (LLCs)
Organizations that combine the benefits of S corporations and limited partnerships without the drawbacks of either

subsidiary corporations
Corporations whose stock is owned entirely or almost entirely by another corporation

parent company
Company that owns most, or all, of another company's stock and that takes an active part in managing that other company

holding company
Company that owns most, or all, of another company's stock but that does not actively participate in the management of that other company

chief executive officer (CEO)
Person appointed by a corporation's board of directors to carry out the board's policies and supervise the activities of the corporation

LEARNING OBJECTIVE 6
Delineate the three groups that govern a corporation and describe the role of each

EXHIBIT 5.3

CORPORATE GOVERNANCE
In theory the shareholders of a corporation own the business, but in practice they elect others to run it.

person vote by **proxy,** signing and returning a slip of paper that authorizes management to vote on their behalf. Because shareholders elect the directors, in theory they are the ultimate governing body of the corporation. In practice, however, most individual shareholders in large corporations—where the shareholders may number in the millions—accept the recommendations of management.

Typically, the more shareholders a company has, the less tangible the influence each shareholder has on the corporation. However, some shareholders have more influence than others. In recent years, *institutional investors,* such as pension funds, insurance companies, mutual funds, and college endowment funds, have accumulated an increasing number of shares of stock in U.S. corporations. As a result, these large institutional investors are playing a more powerful role in governing the corporations in which they own substantial shares, especially with regard to the election of a company's board of directors.[9] Furthermore, at companies such as Avis and United Airlines, employees are major shareholders and so have a significant voice in how the company is run. For example, when United Airlines employees did not endorse management's decision to promote company president John Edwardson to the CEO position, Edwardson resigned.[10]

Board of Directors Representing the shareholders, the **board of directors** is responsible for declaring dividends, guiding corporate affairs, reviewing long-term strategic plans, selecting corporate officers, and overseeing financial performance. The board has the power to vote on major management decisions, such as building a new factory, hiring a new president, or buying a new subsidiary. Depending on the size of the company, the board might have anywhere from 3 to 35 directors, although 15 to 25 is the typical range for traditional corporations, with a smaller number for e-businesses. At most large corporations, boards are composed exclusively of directors from outside the company, with only the CEO and a senior executive or two from inside the organization. This helps ensure that the board provides diligent and independent oversight. Still, outside directors may be large company shareholders, and many serve on the boards of several companies.[11]

The board's actual involvement in running a corporation varies from one company to another. Some boards are strong and independent and serve as a check on the company's management. Others act as a "rubber stamp," simply approving management's recommendations. Hands-on boards are becoming far more common these days, as this chapter's Focusing on E-Business Today feature shows. Every Home Depot director, for instance, must make formal visits to at least 20 stores each year to gain a hands-on perspective of the company's operation.[12]

To compensate directors for their time and contributions, most large companies pay their directors a sizable fee and issue them stock options, the right to purchase a set number of shares of stock at a specific price (see Chapter 11). Some think compensation in the form of company stock aligns the directors' interests with those of other stockholders. But, critics of this practice claim it could compromise the directors' independence, nevertheless evidence shows that companies in which directors own large amounts of stock and take an active role in guiding the company usually outperform those with more passive boards.

proxy
Document authorizing another person to vote on behalf of a shareholder in a corporation

board of directors
Group of people, elected by the shareholders, who have the ultimate authority in guiding the affairs of a corporation

■ UNDERSTANDING BUSINESS COMBINATIONS

Companies have been combining in various configurations since the early days of business. Joining two companies is a complex process because it involves every aspect of both companies. For instance, executives have to agree on how the combination will be financed and how the power will be transferred and shared. Marketing departments often need to figure out how to blend advertising campaigns and sales forces. Data processing and information systems, which seldom mesh, must be joined together seamlessly. And companies must deal with layoffs, transfers, and changes in job titles and work assignments.

KEEPING PACE WITH TECHNOLOGY AND ELECTRONIC COMMERCE

HOW CISCO BOUGHT ITS WAY TO THE TOP

In an industry where buying companies for their technology is routine, Cisco Systems has turned that strategy into a successful way of life. Armed with over $12 billion in annual revenue, this San Jose supplier of computer networking equipment for the Internet and corporations knows how to spot a good company when it sees one. In fact, its masterly buying methods have spurred the company's success.

Cisco, which has bought 55 companies over the past decade, plans to make 10 to 15 new acquisitions each year. Why? Cisco recognizes that it can't build everything it needs to grow, so it swallows innovative start-up firms to enhance its high-tech arsenal and, in doing so, obtains some highly talented people. Still, few companies can integrate acquired firms into their existing operation as smoothly as Cisco does. What's the company's secret?

According to Mike Volpi, vice president of business development, Cisco looks for five things in an acquisition candidate: "We look at a company's vision; its short-term success with customers; its long-term strategy; the chemistry of the people with ours; and its geographic proximity." Then there's one final test: "We pick companies that are old enough to have finished and tested their product, yet young enough to be privately held and flexible in their ways."

Even though Cisco leaves much of the acquired firm's infrastructure in place, it makes sure the acquired employees know who their new employer is. "I don't believe a merger of equals works," notes CEO John Chambers. "In a merger you can't blend resources and cultures—only one can survive." Which is why Cisco prefers to focus on smaller start-up firms. These companies are easier to integrate. "You know exactly what everybody does," says Volpi. Big firms can result in duplicate functions and culture clashes. "Acquire a business that's too mature, and risk soars," Volpi explains. Moreover, figuring out how to integrate a company with existing customers, product flaws, and entrenched systems could take nine months—and that's a lifetime in the high-tech industry. After all, as Volpi puts it: "When you adopt a very young child, they become your kid pretty quickly. But if you adopt a 16-year-old who is set in their ways, it's pretty hard to get them to be your son or daughter."

■ QUESTIONS FOR CRITICAL THINKING

1. When Cisco absorbs a company, it usually makes a no-layoffs pledge. Why would the company promise to keep the acquired firm's employees?

2. Why does Cisco prefer to buy start-up companies?

LEARNING OBJECTIVE   7

Identify six main synergies companies hope to achieve by combining their operations

merger
Combination of two companies in which one purchases the other, assuming control of all property and liabilities

consolidation
Combination of two or more companies in which the old companies cease to exist and a new enterprise is created

acquisition
Form of business combination in which one company buys another company's voting stock

Mergers, Consolidations, and Acquisitions

Two of the most popular forms of business combinations are mergers and consolidations. The difference between a merger and a consolidation is fairly technical, having to do with how the financial and legal transaction is structured. Basically, in a **merger,** one company buys another company, or parts of another company, and emerges as the controlling corporation. The controlling company assumes all the debts and contractual obligations of the company it acquires, which then ceases to exist. A **consolidation** is similar to a merger except that an entirely new firm is created by two or more companies that pool their interests. In a consolidation, both firms terminate their previous legal existence and become part of the new firm.

A third way that a company may acquire another firm is by purchasing that firm's voting stock. This transaction is generally referred to as an **acquisition** and is completed when the shareholders of the acquired firm tender their stock for either cash or shares of stock in the acquiring company. Keep in mind that the purpose and outcome of these three business combinations are basically the same, which is why you will often hear these terms used interchangeably.

Advantages of Mergers, Consolidations, and Acquisitions   Business combinations provide several financial and operational advantages. Combined entities hope to eliminate expenditures for redundant resources; increase their buying power as a result of their larger size; increase revenue by cross-selling products to each other's customers; increase market share by combining product lines to provide more comprehensive offerings; eliminate manufacturing overcapacity; and gain access to new expertise, systems, and teams of employees who already know how to work together.

Often these advantages are grouped under umbrella terms such as *economies of scale, efficiencies,* or *synergies,* which generally mean that the benefits of working together will be greater than if each company continued to operate independently. For instance, when Daimler-Benz and Chrysler merged, they expected to gain competitive advantages that were unavailable to either before the merger, as this chapter's case study explains.

Disadvantages of Mergers, Consolidations, and Acquisitions Despite the promise of economies of scale, studies of merged companies show that 65 to 85 percent of these deals fail to actually achieve promised efficiencies.[13] One such study even found that the profitability of acquired companies on average declined.[14] Keep in mind that "bigger" does not always equate to "better." Honda is only a fraction of GM's size, yet it has consistently outperformed GM for the past 20 years. Moreover, a recent study by Accenture found that, since 1995, small banks have consistently operated more efficiently per customer than their much larger competitors.[15] As one expert put it, if you combine two lumbering companies, you get one that runs worse, not better.[16]

Part of the problem with mergers is that companies often borrow immense amounts of money to acquire a firm, and the loan payments on this corporate debt use cash that is needed to run the business. Moreover, managers must help combine the operations of the two entities and this pulls them away from their normal day-to-day responsibilities. Another obstacle that companies face when combining forces is *culture clash.*

In Chapter 6 we discuss organizational culture in detail. A company's culture is the way people in the organization do things. Culture clash occurs when two joining companies have different beliefs about what is really important, how to make decisions, how to supervise people, how to communicate, and so on. Experts note that in too many deals the acquiring company imposes its values and management systems on the acquired company without any regard to what worked well there. When Quaker Oats acquired Snapple, for example, it immediately dismantled Snapple's distribution system, a key factor in Snapple's success. Ultimately, Quaker Oats paid the price by discovering that if you destroy another company's systems, you often end up buying nothing.[17]

Keep in mind that culture includes not only management style and practices but also the way people dress, how they communicate, or whether they punch a time clock. Recent studies have shown that underestimating the difficulties of merging two cultures was the major factor in failed mergers, and experts contend that the increasing number of worldwide mergers, consolidations, and acquisitions will make culture clash an even bigger challenge.[18] When Ford acquired Volvo, for example, Swedish autoworkers were nervous that they might lose their health club benefits and other perks that Swedish companies give to workers to compensate them for the high income taxes they pay the government.[19] Similarly, culture clash has been an issue at DaimlerChrysler as this chapter's case study will show.

Types of Mergers Mergers tend to happen in waves, in response to changes in the economy. One of the biggest waves of merger activity occurred between 1881 and 1911, when capitalists created giant monopolistic trusts, buying enough stock of competing companies in basic industries such as oil and steel to control the market. These trusts were **horizontal mergers,** or combinations of competing companies performing the same function. The purposes of a horizontal merger are to achieve the benefits of economies of scale and to fend off competition. The rise of a government antitrust movement and the dissolution of Standard Oil in 1911 marked the end of this wave.

A second great wave occurred in the boom decade of the 1920s. This era was marked by the emergence of **vertical mergers,** in which a company involved in one phase of an industry absorbs or joins a company involved in another phase of the same industry. The aim of a vertical merger is often to guarantee access to supplies or to markets. For example, until fairly recently, both Ford and General Motors owned the companies that supplied most of the parts for their cars.

A third wave of mergers occurred in the late 1960s and early 1970s, when corporations acquired strings of unrelated businesses, often in an attempt to moderate the risks of a volatile economy. These **conglomerate mergers** were designed to augment a company's growth and to diversify its risks. Theoretically, when one business was down, another would be up, thus creating a balanced performance picture for the company as a whole. At their peaks, some of these conglomerates had hundreds of companies. TLC Beatrice (formerly Beatrice Foods Company), for example, at one time owned companies as diverse as Tropicana (juice), Samsonite (luggage),

horizontal mergers
Combinations of companies that are direct competitors in the same industry

vertical mergers
Combinations of companies that participate in different phases of the same industry (e.g., materials, production, distribution)

conglomerate mergers
Combinations of companies that are in unrelated businesses, designed to augment a company's growth and to diversify risk

THINKING ABOUT ETHICS

DO MERGERS FULFILL MANAGEMENT'S RESPONSIBILITY TO SHAREHOLDERS?

For over a century, mergers and acquisitions have continually changed the face of business in the United States. Today a wave of strategic mergers is changing it all over again as corporations merge to create more competitive organizations that will increase shareholder value. But do shareholders really benefit from mergers? Strong evidence suggests that they often do not.

A recent study by accounting and consulting firm KPMG shows that 83 percent of mergers failed to produce any benefits for shareholders—who are supposed to be the key beneficiaries. And, over half actually diminished shareholder value. In fact, the only winners appear to be the shareholders of the acquired firm who sell their company stock for more than it's really worth.

Why do such a high percentage of mergers and acquisitions fail? While no one answer applies to every situation, experts cite these common mistakes:

- Companies often rush into deals in search of synergies but then fail to develop them. Once the merger is done, management simply assumes that the computer programmers, sales managers, and engineers will cut costs and boost revenues according to plan.

- Companies pay excessively high premiums for the companies they acquire. According to one expert, any time an acquiring company pays a premium of 25 percent or more over the trading price of the acquired company's stock, the acquiring company is exposing itself and its shareholders to substantial risk.

- Companies are unable to reconcile differences in corporate cultures. A successful merger requires more than respecting each partner's differences. Procedures must be established to settle disputes and to integrate workforces and product lines strategically.

Without question, some mergers and acquisitions are beneficial to companies and shareholders in both the short term and the long term. Synergies can be realized. However, managers need to approach mergers and acquisitions with caution by answering these questions: Will the regulatory environment change? How will competitors respond? Do the expected gains justify the up-front costs? Will the cultures of the two companies blend well? Without seeking honest answers to these questions, management may find it difficult to fulfill its obligation to the company's shareholders.

■ QUESTIONS FOR CRITICAL THINKING

1. If you were on the board of directors at a company and the CEO announced plans to merge with a competitor, what types of questions would you want answered before you gave your approval?

2. If a CEO has the opportunity to merge with or acquire another company and is reasonably certain that the transaction will benefit shareholders, is the CEO obligated to pursue the deal? Why or why not?

Stiffle (lamps), and Eckrich (meats). Since the late 1960s, many of the superconglomerates have been dismantled or slimmed down to streamline operations, to build up capital for other endeavors, or to get rid of unprofitable subsidiaries.

leveraged buyout (LBO)
Situation in which individuals or a group of investors purchase a company primarily with debt secured by the company's assets

In the 1980s, a wave of **leveraged buyouts (LBOs)** also occurred. In an LBO, one or more individuals purchase a company's publicly traded stock by using borrowed funds. The debt is expected to be repaid with funds generated by the company's operations and, often, by the sale of some of its assets. For an LBO to be successful, a company must have a reasonably priced stock and easy access to borrowed funds. Unfortunately, in many cases, the acquiring company must make huge interest and principle payments on the debt; this depletes the amount of cash that the company has for operations and growth.

Also during the 1980s, some investors purchased large companies because they were actually worth more by the piece than by the whole. These purchasers, often referred to as "corporate raiders," would buy undervalued companies and quickly sell off divisions to realize a quick and handsome gain.[20] Consider Beatrice. In 1986 investors Kohlberg Kravis Roberts bought the giant conglomerate and shortly thereafter broke it into pieces by selling off the subsidiaries.[21]

In the 1990s, a new wave of mergers, consolidations, and acquisitions began that were motivated by long-term strategies. Instead of using debt to take over and dismantle a company for a quick profit, corporate buyers used cash and stock to selectively acquire businesses to enhance their position in the marketplace. From 1992 through 2000, 71,811 corporate mergers, consolidations, and acquisitions at a combined value of $6.66 trillion were completed.[22]

Current Trends in Mergers, Consolidations, and Acquisitions Today "corporate mergers have grown so frequent and so large," says Robert Pitofsky, chairman of the Federal Trade Commission (FTC), that "there's not a week that goes by that we're not called upon to review a big merger that has significant implications in the marketplace."[23] Some even predict that mergers that looked like

earthquakes in the past may look like mere tremors years from now.[24] Consider, for instance, the $160 billion merger of America Online (the world's biggest Internet provider) and Time Warner (the world's biggest media company). This megadeal, announced only 10 days into the new millennium, linked AOL's twenty-some million subscribers and unmatched e-commerce capabilities with Time Warner's sprawling cache of world-class media, entertainment, news brands, and broadband delivery systems to produce the world's first fully integrated media and communications company.[25]

The AOL Time Warner merger has potential synergies that make some competitors drool. The merged company promises to offer consumers a soup-to-nuts menu of media and information products. Moreover, it offers AOL a potentially powerful tool for distributing its services.

One key factor contributing to this merger frenzy is fierce global competition. In today's global environment, large domestic companies must compete with foreign competitors even in their home markets. Tough competitive conditions have prompted the U.S. government to relax its regulatory standards. Rather than opposing any merger that might allow a company to develop a dominant position in the market, the FTC and the Anti-Trust Division of the Justice Department are stepping back to ensure that industries remain competitive in the global marketplace.

As Chapter 1 and Component Chapter B discuss, the relaxation of existing industry regulations is designed to make industries more competitive and to provide consumers with improved products and lower prices. But some think industry deregulation has backfired by spurring mass consolidation instead. Take the telecommunications industry, for example. Some see the 1999 consolidation of SBC and Ameritech as nothing more than a reassembly of the Ma Bell monopoly splintered by the Justice Department in 1984. As one naysayer put it: "First there were seven Baby Bells, then six, then five, and now four."[26] Moreover, Bell Atlantic's recent merger with GTE (to form Verizon) has reduced the number of Baby Bells to three, and they aren't babies.

The airline industry is also flirting with consolidation. Merger talks between UAL (United's parent) and US Airways in 2000 set off a raft of merger proposals between major airline carriers that could end with United, American, and Delta controlling 85 percent of U.S. air traffic. U.S. airlines now say that the only viable way to get significantly larger is to acquire competitors. "There's no other industry where consolidation and mergers probably makes more sense," says one U.S. airline board member. "But there's also no other industry where it's more difficult." Critics of such megamergers say that there's a limit on how far mergers and consolidations should go. They point out that the promise of deregulation—some 20 years ago—was lots of new competitors, not mergers and consolidations.[27]

Like the telecommunications and airline industries, the banking industry is also undergoing mass consolidation as a result of relaxed industry regulation. Since 1990 over 3,300 banks have been gobbled up by larger ones. Furthermore, the 1998 acquisition of Travelers by Citicorp (valued at $83 billion) spliced together a global bank, an insurance company, a brokerage firm, a credit-card operation, and some 100 million customers in 100 countries.[28] As Chapter 17 points out, the repeal of the Glass-Steagall Act now paves the way for banking, securities, and insurance industries to expand into one another's businesses and sets the stage for another wave of consolidations.[29]

Jüergen Schrempp (left) and Robert Eaton show off official DaimlerChrysler NYSE stock certificates on the company's first day of business as a merged entity.

hostile takeover
Situation in which an outside party buys enough stock in a corporation to take control against the wishes of the board of directors and corporate officers

This megamerger trend is also occurring in the oil and automobile industries. The $81 billion marriage of Exxon and Mobil in 1999 created the world's largest oil company, whereas the $36 billion combination of Daimler-Benz and Chrysler in 1998 was the biggest acquisition of any U.S. company by a foreign buyer—and one that is destined to transform the way the auto industry operates worldwide. Some believe that by combining product and sales networks, DaimlerChrysler has set the pace for the global car wars to come. As one economist put it, "If you don't play the game as a global company, you're going to wind up a niche player."[30]

Merger, Consolidation, and Acquisition Defenses About 95 percent of all business combinations are friendly deals, as opposed to **hostile takeovers,** where one party fights to gain control of a company against the wishes of the existing management.[31] But not all hostile takeovers are bad. In November 1999 pharmaceutical giants Warner-Lambert and American Home Products (AHP) announced a $54.5 billion merger. The two were caught off guard when that same day rival Pfizer launched an unfriendly takeover bid for Warner-Lambert and eventually sweetened its bid as an inducement to wrap things up quickly. In February 2000, Pfizer succeeded in its hostile bid to buy Warner-Lambert for $90 billion. Warner-Lambert conceded that Pfizer's hostile bid was better for shareholders than its planned merger with AHP.[32]

As mentioned earlier, every corporation that sells stock to the general public is potentially vulnerable to takeover by any individual or company that buys enough shares to gain a controlling interest. Basically, a hostile takeover can be launched in one of two ways: by tender offer or by proxy fight. In a *tender offer,* the raider offers to buy a certain number of shares of stock in the corporation at a specific price. The price offered is generally more than the current stock price so that shareholders are motivated to sell. The raider hopes to get enough shares to take control of the corporation and to replace the existing board of directors and management. In a *proxy fight,* the raider launches a public relations battle for shareholder votes, hoping to enlist enough votes to oust the board and management. Proxy fights sound easy enough, but they are tough to win. The insiders have certain advantages: They can get in touch with shareholders, and they can use money from the corporate treasury in their campaign.

During the 1980s, when many takeovers were uninvited and even openly hostile, corporate boards and executives devised a number of schemes to defend themselves against unwanted takeovers:

▪ *The poison pill.* This plan, triggered by a takeover attempt, makes the company less valuable in some way to the potential raider; the idea is to discourage the takeover from actually happening. A good example is a special sale of newly issued stock to current stockholders at prices below the market value of the company's existing stock. Such action increases the number of shares the raider has to buy, making the takeover more expensive. Many shareholders believe that poison pills are bad for a company because they can entrench weak management and discourage takeover attempts that would improve company value.[33]

▪ *The golden parachute.* This method is designed to benefit a company's top executives by guaranteeing them generous compensation packages if they ever leave or are forced out after a takeover. These packages often total millions of dollars for each executive and therefore make the takeover much more expensive for the acquiring company. In this way, a golden parachute has an effect similar to that of a poison pill.

▪ *The shark repellent.* This tactic is more direct; it is simply a requirement that stockholders representing a large majority of shares approve of any takeover attempt. Of course, such a plan is viable only if the management team has the support of the majority of shareholders.

■ *The white knight.* This tactic uses a friendly buyer to take over the company before a raider can. White knights usually agree to leave the current management team in place and to let the company continue to operate in an independent fashion. Starwood Lodging Trust, a large hotel investment firm, used this tactic to block the hostile takeover attempt of ITT by Hilton Hotels.[34]

Sometimes a group of investors is able to take a publicly traded company off the open market by purchasing all of the company's stock. This tactic is known as "taking the company private." Descendants of Levi Strauss, for example, borrowed $3 billion to buy back all the shares of Levi's stock so that the family could maintain control of the company.[35]

Companies sometimes go private to thwart unwanted takeovers. But this is a radical action. First of all, stockholders must be willing to sell, and second, buyers must have enough cash on hand to repurchase all the company's stock. Moreover, going private eliminates the firm's ability to raise future capital by selling authorized shares to the public, so it's not a move that many corporations make.

Strategic Alliances and Joint Ventures

In Chapter 3 we discussed strategic alliances and joint ventures from the perspective of international expansion. We defined a strategic alliance as a long-term partnership between companies to jointly develop, produce, or sell products, and we defined a joint venture as a special type of strategic alliance in which two or more firms jointly create a new business entity that is legally separate and distinct from its parents. In this chapter we will look at these forms of business combinations as an alternative to a merger, consolidation, or acquisition.

Strategic alliances can accomplish many of the same goals as a merger, consolidation, or acquisition without requiring a painstaking process of integration.[36] One of the biggest benefits of a strategic alliance is that the companies involved need not become fast friends for life. Pharmaceutical companies, for example, typically form strategic alliances to jointly develop products, but they go their separate ways once the patents on the drugs expire.

Many strategic alliances are driven by the realization that no single company can offer customers everything they need. Consider the alliance between Pacific Bell (a San Francisco–based local telecommunications provider) and Orconet (an Orange County, California, Internet service provider). Pacific Bell refers its telephone customers to Orconet for Internet connections, and Orconet promotes Pacific Bell's speedy DSL data-dedicated lines. Each company brings its pool of traditional customers to the other, expanding the potential markets for both.[37]

Companies can also form joint ventures to accomplish the same growth objectives. Joint ventures are similar to partnerships except that they are formed for a specific, limited purpose. America Online, Philips Electronics, and Direct TV recently formed a joint venture to develop and offer an interactive service that lets customers access the Internet via their TV sets. Joint ventures have many advantages. They allow companies to use each other's complementary strengths that might otherwise take too long to develop on their own, and they allow companies to share what may be the substantial cost and risk of starting a new operation.[38]

 FOCUSING ON E-BUSINESS TODAY

The New Breed of Dot-Com Directors

Traditionally, a board of directors sets corporate policy, provides an independent perspective, elects officers, and lets them do their job. But the Internet is spawning a new breed of board member. Today's e-commerce start-ups are headed by younger, less-experienced executives, who know little about corporate governance. To compensate for this deficiency, entrepreneurs rely on board members to help them build the e-business from the ground up. Being a dot-com board member is often a hands-on job.

DIFFERENT RULES, ROLES, AND GOVERNING STYLES

Today's dot-com directors are an extension of management. Many are brought in for their connections or their specific technical knowledge rather than for their independent perspective. They become active participants and

LEARNING
OBJECTIVE @8

Explain how the role of dot-com directors differs from the role played by directors of traditional corporations

help create and shape strategies, define markets, and build senior management teams. They work on Internet time, which means they have months, not years to make an impact. Some use their connections to facilitate financing and other business deals. Most provide the company with much sought after e-commerce expertise.

Because e-commerce is relatively new, only a handful of experts exist. Thus most dot-com directors sit on multiple boards. Such cross-sitting means that directors know the forecasts, marketing plans, corporate strategies, and secrets of many companies. That's not all bad, say some. Sitting on one another's boards means entrepreneurs can network and exchange ideas. Asked if they are worried about revealing too much to competitors, most reply that if you don't give, you don't get back. Put differently, if you remain insular in the e-world, you'll get eaten alive.

SMALLER IN SIZE

While traditional boards tend to be large and diverse, most dot-coms have small boards. A recent study of 39 Internet companies found that dot-com boards average about 7 directors versus 11 for most traditional public companies. EBay's board has just five members. Amazon and Yahoo! each have six. Having a micro board is an advantage for a company that has to move at an Internet pace. "When you're starting a business from scratch, speed is everything," says Yahoo!'s Tim Koogle. "Keeping the board small and concentrated means you don't have to manage the interrelationships between board members." Nonetheless, small boards could make a company vulnerable to disruption. The absence of just one member could have a huge impact.

THE INDEPENDENCE DILEMMA

A typical dot-com board consists of two or three company insiders, two representatives of the venture capital firm that helped launch the company, and a couple of independent directors who may also have close business ties to the company. Having such a high ratio of insiders to outsiders has always been frowned upon at large public companies because outsiders provide independent oversight. To prevent potential conflicts, governance experts

BOARD	E-COMMERCE COMPANY	TRADITIONAL COMPANY
Attitude	Proactive	Defensive
Role	Works closely with CEO	Less contact with management
Involvement	Hands-on	Little day-to-day involvement
Direction	Board-driven	CEO-driven
Commitment	Huge in terms of directors' time and energy	Only at a maximum during a crisis
Rewards	Potential equity stake; satisfaction of building something new	Prestige—and an average annual retainer of $130,000

recommend that the majority of board seats be held by outsiders.

Still, many e-commerce boards ignore such advice. They disagree that high insider representation poses a conflict of interests. As they see it, small boards consisting of insiders and well-connected outsiders can create a strategic advantage by providing the company with much-needed expertise.

Most start-ups cannot afford to pay their directors salaries, so they pay their dot-com directors with stock and stock options. At Yahoo! the six board members control 14.5 percent of the stock. Some see this form of compensation as a good thing. They argue that high stock ownership aligns directors more closely with shareholders' interests. However, critics argue that large stock-ownership interests could taint the board's independent perspective. That's because the "right" decision for the company could have a negative short-term impact on the company's financial performance, which could lower the market value of the company's stock.

In short, some see the relaxation of dot-com board standards as a dangerous trend. "It's really not until something goes wrong that people focus on governance," says one expert. Furthermore, you can bet that the minute a high-profile tech company blows up, the question long asked of traditional companies—"Where was the board?"—is sure to be raised.[39]

SUMMARY OF LEARNING OBJECTIVES

1. List five advantages and four disadvantages of sole proprietorships.
Sole proprietorships have five advantages: (1) They are easy to establish, (2) they provide the owner with control and independence, (3) the owner reaps all the profits, (4) profits are taxed at individual rates, and (5) the company's plans and financial performance remain private. The four main disadvantages of a sole proprietorship are (1) the company's financial resources are usually limited, (2) management talent may be thin, (3) the owner is liable for the debts and damages incurred by the business, and (4) the business may cease when the owner dies.

2. List five advantages and two disadvantages of partnerships.
In addition to being easy to establish and having profits taxed at individual rates, partnerships offer a greater ability to obtain financing, longevity, and a broader base of skills. The two main disadvantages of partnerships are unlimited liability for general partners and the potential for personality and authority conflicts.

3. Explain the differences between common and preferred stock from a shareholder's perspective.
Common shareholders can vote and can share in the company's profits through discretionary dividends and adjustments in the market value of their stock. In other words, they can profit from their investment if the value of the stock rises above the price they paid for it, or they can lose money if the value of the stock falls below the price they paid for it. In contrast, preferred shareholders cannot vote, but they can get a fixed return (dividend) on their investment and a priority claim on assets after creditors.

4. Highlight the advantages and disadvantages of public stock ownership.
Public stock ownership offers a company increased liquidity, enhanced visibility, financial flexibility, and an independently established market value for the stock. The disadvantages of public stock ownership are high costs, burdensome filing requirements, loss of ownership control, heightened public exposure, and loss of direct control over the market value of the company's stock.

5. Cite four advantages and three disadvantages of corporations.
Corporations are a separate legal entity; they have the power to raise large sums of capital; they offer the shareholders protection

from liability; they provide liquidity for investors; and they have an unlimited life span. In exchange for these advantages, they pay large fees to incorporate, and they are taxed twice on company profits—corporations pay tax on profits and individuals pay tax on dividends (distributed corporate profits). Finally, if publicly owned, corporations must adhere to strict government reporting requirements.

6. Delineate the three groups that govern a corporation and describe the role of each.
Shareholders are the basis of the corporate structure. They elect the board of directors, who in turn elect the officers of the corporation. The corporate officers carry out the policies and decisions of the board. In practice, the shareholders and board members have often followed the lead of the chief executive officer. However, some board members are becoming increasingly active in corporate governance. This is especially true of young dot-com corporations that appoint directors for their management expertise and industry connections.

7. Identify six main synergies companies hope to achieve by combining their operations.
By combining their operations, companies hope to eliminate redundant costs, increase their buying power, increase their revenue, improve their market share, eliminate manufacturing overcapacity and gain access to new expertise and personnel.

8. Explain how the role of dot-com directors differs from the role played by directors of traditional corporations.
Dot-com directors play a more active role in the organization's management because of the pressing need for e-commerce expertise. In addition to providing such expertise, they use their connections to facilitate financing and corporate deals. Dot-com boards tend to be smaller, more cohesive, and they have significant financial and equity interests in the company. Most dot-com directors are compensated with stock, which some think could jeopardize their independent judgment. That's because the "right" decision could have a negative short-term effect on the company's financial performance and thus lower the market value of the company's stock.

KEY TERMS

acquisition (134)

board of directors (133)

chief executive officer (CEO) (132)

common stock (129)

conglomerate mergers (135)

consolidation (134)

corporation (129)

dividends (130)

general partnership (127)

holding company (132)

horizontal mergers (135)

hostile takeover (138)

leveraged buyout (LBO) (136)

limited liability companies (LLCs) (132)

limited partnership (127)

liquidity (131)

merger (134)

parent company (132)

partnership (127)

preferred stock (130)

private corporation (130)

proxy (133)

public corporation (130)

S corporation (132)

shareholders (129)

sole proprietorship (126)

stock certificate (129)

subsidiary corporations (132)

unlimited liability (127)

vertical mergers (135)

TEST YOUR KNOWLEDGE

QUESTIONS FOR REVIEW

1. What are the three basic forms of business ownership?

2. What is the difference between a general and a limited partnership?

3. What is a closely held corporation, and why do some companies choose this form of ownership?

4. What is the role of a company's board of directors? How is this role changing?

5. What is culture clash?

QUESTIONS FOR ANALYSIS

6. Why is it advisable for partners to enter into a formal partnership agreement?

7. To what extent do shareholders control the activities of a corporation?

8. How might a company benefit from having a diverse board of directors that includes representatives of several industries, countries, and cultures?

9. @ Selling antiques on the Internet has become more successful than you imagined. Overnight your Web site has grown into a full-fledged business—now generating some $200,000 in annual revenue. It's time to think about the future. Several competing online antique dealers have approached you with a proposal to merge their Web site with yours to create the premier online antique store. The money sounds good, but you have some concerns about joining forces. What might they be? What other growth options should you consider before joining forces with another e-business?

10. Why do so many mergers fail?

11. ▣ Your father sits on the board of directors of a large, well-admired, public company. Yesterday, while looking for an envelope in his home office, you stumbled on a confidential memorandum. Unable to resist the temptation to read the memo, you discovered that your father's company is talking with another publicly traded company about the possibility of a merger, with Dad's company being the survivor. Dollar signs flashed in your mind. Should the merger occur, the value of the other company's stock is likely to soar. You're tempted to log on to your E*Trade account in the morning and place an order for 1,000 shares of that company's stock. Better still, maybe you'll give a hot tip to your best friend in exchange for the four Dave Matthews Band tickets your friend has been flashing in your face all week. Would either of those actions be unethical? Explain your answer.

QUESTIONS FOR APPLICATION

12. Suppose you and some friends want to start a business to take tourists on wilderness backpacking expeditions. None of you has much extra money, so your plan is to start small. However, if you are successful, you would like to expand into other types of outdoor tours and perhaps even open up branches in other locations. What form of ownership should your new enterprise take, and why?

13. Carco, the leading automobile parts manufacturer, is considering acquiring Parts Plus, the nation's third-largest automobile parts retailer. Both companies are financially solid, and both have dedicated employees, strong management, and good reputations in their industries. Carco expects to offer Parts Plus shareholders a 20 to 25 percent premium over the company's current stock price. What do you think the chances of success will be if the acquisition goes through? What issues might arise that could limit the transaction's success?

14. ⌇ In Chapter 3 we discussed international strategic alliances and joint ventures. Why might a U.S. company want to enter into those types of arrangements instead of merging with a foreign concern?

15. ⌇ Review the Chapter 3 discussion of "How International Trade is Measured." Briefly discuss how the Daimler Chrysler merger affects the U.S. balance of trade and the U.S. balance of payments.

PRACTICE YOUR KNOWLEDGE

SHARPENING YOUR COMMUNICATION SKILLS

You have just been informed that your employer is going to merge with a firm in Germany. Since you know very little about the German culture and business practices, you think it might be a good idea do some preliminary research—just in case you have to make a quick trip overseas. Using the Internet or library sources, find information on the German culture and customs and prepare a short report discussing such cultural differences as German social values, decision-making customs, concepts of time, use of body language, social behavior and manners, and legal and ethical behavior.

HANDLING DIFFICULT SITUATIONS ON THE JOB: FINDING THE RIGHT BOARD OF DIRECTORS

Robert Hedin, the owner of Paradise Sportswear in Hawaii, has finally hit "pay dirt." His first business, silk-screening and airbrushing T-shirts, was all but destroyed in 1992 by Hurricane Iniki. When he set up the company again, Hawaii's red dirt started seeping into his warehouse and ruining his inventory. Finally, a friend suggested that Hedin stop fighting Mother Nature. So the entrepreneur mortgaged his condo and began producing Red Dirt Shirts with dye created from the troublesome local dirt. "You can make 500 shirts with a bucket of dirt," says Hedin.

All the Red Dirt Sportswear designs were quickly snapped up by locals and tourists in Hedin's eight Paradise Sportswear retail outlets. Soon the company was selling Red Dirt clothing in every Kmart in the Hawaiian Islands, as well. Then Hedin added a new line of clothing he called Lava Blues because the colors come from local lava rock.

With the growing popularity of Red Dirt, Hedin had his hands full managing the entire operation and selling his apparel throughout the islands. Nevertheless, with local sales at over $2 million, the owner has decided to expand to the mainland.[40] As part of his expansion, Hedin is searching for four people to enlarge his board of directors from six to ten members. He has approached your recruiting firm to help identify suitable candidates. You don't know whether the entrepreneur really wants the guidance and challenge of a strong, independent board or whether he is putting together a rubber-stamp board that will simply approve his plans.

1. What are some of the decisions Hedin's board might have to make in the near future?

2. When Hedin asks for your professional advice, will you recommend all outsiders or a mix of employees and outsiders to fill the director positions? Why?

3. What kinds of expertise would you suggest Hedin seek in outside directors to make the board an even more valuable resource as Red Dirt expands? Why?

BUILDING YOUR TEAM SKILLS

Directors often have to ask tough questions and make difficult decisions, as you will see in this exercise. Imagine that the president of your college or university has just announced plans to retire. Your team, playing the role of the school's board of directors, must decide how to choose a new president to fill this vacancy next semester.

First, generate a list of the qualities and qualifications you think the school should seek in a new president. What background and experience would prepare someone for this key position? What personal characteristics should the new president have? What questions would you ask to find out how each candidate measures up against the list of credentials you have prepared?

Now list all the stakeholders that your team, as directors, must consider before deciding on a replacement for the retiring president. Of these stakeholders, whose opinions do you think are most important? Whose are least important? Who will be directly and indirectly affected by the choice of a new president? Of these stakeholders, which should be represented as participants in the decision-making process?

Select a spokesperson to deliver a brief presentation to the class summarizing your team's ideas and the reasoning behind your suggestions. After all the teams have completed their presentations, discuss the differences and similarities among credentials proposed by all the teams for evaluating candidates for the presidency. Then compare the teams' conclusions about stakeholders. Do all teams agree on the stakeholders who should participate in the decision-making process? Lead a classroom discussion on a board's responsibility to its stakeholders.

EXPAND YOUR KNOWLEDGE

KEEPING CURRENT USING *THE WALL STREET JOURNAL*

In recent issues of *The Wall Street Journal* (print or online editions) find an article or series of articles illustrating one of the following business developments: merger, acquisition, consolidation, hostile takeover, or leveraged buyout.

1. Explain in your own words what steps or events led to this development.

2. What results do you expect this development to have on (a) the company itself, (b) consumers, (c) the industry the company is part of? Write down and date your answers.

3. Follow your story in *The Wall Street Journal* over the next month (or longer, as your instructor requests). What problems, opportunities, or other results are reported? Were these developments anticipated at the time of the initial story, or did they seem to catch industry analysts by surprise? How well did your answers to question 2 predict the results?

DISCOVERING CAREER OPPORTUNITIES

Are you best suited to working as a sole proprietor, as a partner in a business, or in a different role within a corporation? For this exercise, select three businesses with which you are familiar: one run by a single person, such as a dentist's practice or a local landscaping firm; one run by two or three partners, such as a small accounting firm; and one that operates as a corporation, such as Target.

1. Write down what you think you would like about being the sole proprietor, one of the partners, and the corporate manager or an employee in the businesses you have selected. For example, would you like having full responsibility for the sole proprietorship? Would you like being able to consult with other partners in the partnership before making decisions? Would you like having limited responsibility when you work for other people in the corporation?

2. Now write down what you might dislike about each form of business. For example, would you dislike the risk of bearing all legal responsibility in a sole proprietorship? Would you dislike having to talk with your partners before spending the partner-ship's money? Would you dislike having to write reports for top managers and shareholders of the corporation?

3. Weigh the pluses and minuses you have identified in this exercise. In comparison, which form of business most appeals to you?

EXPLORING THE BEST OF THE WEB

URLs for all Internet exercises are provided at the Web site for this book, www.prenhall.com/mescon. When you log on to this text's Web site, select Chapter 5, then select "Student Resources," click on the name of the featured Web site, and follow the detailed navigational directions to complete Internet exercises.

Planning Your Online Business, page 127

Planning and running an online business involve more work than you might imagine. Visit Actium Publishing's Internet Business Start-Ups and find out what it takes to plane, promote, market, and run a business online.

1. What are some points you should consider when choosing an Internet server provider?

2. What are the five most important things to remember about running a business online?

3. What is the biggest mistake Internet entrepreneurs make? What are the advantages and disadvantages of hiring an expert to design your Web site? What advantages does an online business have over a conventional one?

Choosing a Form of Ownership, page 129

Browse the Nolo small-business law center to review the advantages and disadvantages of the different legal forms of business ownership.

1. What are the main advantages of a limited liability company (LLC)?

2. Which key issues should you cover in a partnership agreement?

3. What is a buy/sell agreement and under what circumstances is it normally used?

Following the Fortunes of the Fortune 500, page 131
Review the latest Fortune 500 lists to see who the titans of the U.S. corporate world are, how much revenue they generate, and more.

1. What corporation heads the current Fortune 500 list? What corporation is number 500 on the list?

2. What are some of the most significant changes in the current list compared with the previous year's list?

3. Which listed company had the biggest increase in revenues? Which one had the highest profits?

Explore on Your Own
Review these chapter-related Web sites on your own to learn more about small business ownership and expansion.

1. The Idea Café, www.ideacafe.com, is a terrific resource for entrepreneurs looking to expand their business. Bounce your idea off others and learn from their experiences. Find the latest technology and business book reviews. Have some fun and be sure to cyberschmooze!

2. Find out which companies are joining forces. Tech Web News, www.techweb.com/wire/finance/mergers, has the latest news on the 15 most recent mergers and acquisitions.

3. Learn more about running a small e-business at ZDNet E-Commerce, www.zdnet.com/enterprise/e-business. As a sole proprietor you'll be looking for as much e-commerce advice as you can get. Check out this site's case studies, classes, products, news, best practices, tips, and advice.

A CASE FOR CRITICAL THINKING

■ *DaimlerChrysler: Merger of Equals or Global Fender Bender?*

The champagne was on ice when Chrysler and Daimler-Benz announced a stunning $36 billion merger in May 1998. Headquartered in Germany, DaimlerChrysler would be the world's third-largest automaker. On paper, the companies were a perfect fit—one was strong where the other was weak. Daimler's engineering was legendary, and it was strong in technology. Chrysler excelled at new product design and development. Complementary products and geographical mix would allow them to challenge rivals around the world. Moreover, anticipated synergies would save the combined operation $3 billion annually.

ENGINEERING A DEAL
To keep things equal both Daimler's chairman Jürgen Schrempp and Chrysler's chairman Robert Eaton agreed to share the power for three years—until Eaton retired. Together they would co-manage the 440,000-employee colossus. It was the most unusual union of two chief executives anywhere in the world. Charged with excitement and curious about each other's cars and culture, the two companies began the integration process by holding marathon meetings in Switzerland. As weeks went by, the Americans learned more about their new German partners and vice versa. At first it was intriguing. But then the novelty wore off. Indeed, there were many differences to iron out.

TRAVELING ALONG A BUMPY ROAD
Being six time zones apart complicated the postmarriage adjustment period, of course. By the time the Americans started their day, the Germans had already had lunch. Thus, Stuttgart, Germany, always seemed to have a head start on Auburn Hills, Michigan. Even Schrempp seemed to be one step ahead, planning his next move while everyone was still trying to figure out his last one.

Moreover, fundamental differences in management, operational, and decision-making styles made matters even worse. German management-board members had executive assistants who prepared detailed position papers on any number of issues. The Americans didn't. They formulated their decisions by talking directly to engineers or other specialists. A German decision worked its way through the bureaucracy for final approval at the top. Then it was set in stone. The Americans valued consensus building and shared decision making. Moreover, they allowed mid-level employees to proceed on their own initiative, sometimes without waiting for executive-level approval.

FIGHTING THE CULTURE WARS
Once the Germans and Americans began the nitty-gritty of melding the two companies, turf battles bogged down the combination process. Managers from both sides spent more time defending their way of doing things than promoting the integration of systems. The Germans wanted to expedite the integration of the two companies. They wanted to put the unpopular issues on the table right from the start. The Americans preferred to edge into changes. So the infighting began.

Issues that should have been resolved by managers were bumped up to the company's board of directors. The travel policy alone took six months to settle. Daimler-Benz employees were accustomed to flying first class to preserve the company's image—a perk reserved for only top officers at Chrysler. Worse yet, the financial results of the merged entity were a monumental letdown. Revenues rose indeed, but profits remained stagnant. As a result, the value of DaimlerChrysler's stock plummeted.

Cultural integration and disappointing results fueled an undercurrent of tension. So did the gap in pay scales. The Americans earned two, three, and in some cases four times as much as their German counterparts. But the expenses of U.S. workers were tightly controlled compared with the German system. Daimler-Benz employees thought nothing of flying to Paris or New York for a half-day meeting, then capping the visit with a fancy dinner and a night in an expensive hotel. The Americans blanched at the extravagance.

THE GERMANS TAKE CHARGE
Meanwhile, the public view of DaimlerChrysler as a merger of equals had begun to crack. The stock was banished from the S&P 500 index because the company wasn't incorporated in America. As a result, the percentage of U.S. shareholders fell from 43 percent on the day of the merger announcement to 25 percent. But the number of U.S. shareholders wasn't the only thing shrinking.

Frictions led to the departure of talented Chrysler midlevel managers, and several top Chrysler executives—including Chrysler's president Thomas Stallkamp, who had played an instrumental role in orchestrating the merger. And the management board was scaled down from 17 members to 13—8 Germans and 5 Americans. Soon the reality became clear. Daimler executives were indeed running the show. DaimlerChrysler wasn't a merger of equals. Instead, Daimler-Benz had acquired Chrysler, and an American icon had lost its independence.

CRITICAL THINKING QUESTIONS

1. What prevented DaimlerChrysler from achieving the promised synergies?

2. Why would Eaton and Schrempp agree to share the top position of the merged entity?

3. Which of these stakeholders benefited the most from the merger: the original Chrysler shareholders or the new DaimlerChrysler shareholders? Explain your answer.

4. Visit DaimlerChrysler's Web site. Follow the navigational directions provided at this text's Web site, www.prenhall.com/mescon to learn about the company's shared beliefs and values. Which beliefs and values seem to be more characteristic of German business culture and practices? Which ones seem more American? Why?

VIDEO CASE AND EXERCISES

■ *Amy's Ice Creams Serves Up Texas-Sized Expansion*

SYNOPSIS

Amy Miller was a premed student at Tufts University in the early 1980s when she got her first taste of the ice cream business. Working for Steve's Ice Cream, she helped to open stores in New York City and Miami, Florida. After Steve's was sold, Miller teamed up with a partner to start a new ice cream business, which they structured as a corporation to limit liability and allow the business to continue even if the founders moved on (as Miller's co-founder did). Now Amy's Ice Creams (www.amysicecreams.com) has nine locations in and around Austin, Houston, and San Antonio, Texas, ringing up sales of nearly $3.5 million by selling close to 100,000 gallons of such flavors as Mexican Vanilla, Belgian Chocolate, Egg Nog, and Macadamia every year.

EXERCISES
Analysis

1. Why would Amy Miller choose to form a corporation rather than a partnership when starting her business with a partner?

2. What are the tax implications of making Amy's Ice Creams a corporation rather than a partnership?

3. If Amy's Ice Creams agreed to be acquired by Procter & Gamble, would this combination be considered a horizontal merger, vertical merger, or conglomerate merger?

4. If Amy's Ice Creams went public, under what circumstances might top management decide to take the company private later on?

5. How do techniques such as the paper bag job application help Amy Miller manage her growing ice cream empire?

Application

What kinds of people would you suggest that Amy Miller invite to serve on her board of directors—and why?

Decision

Assume that Unilever, the corporation that owns Ben & Jerry's Homemade, wants to acquire Amy's Ice Creams. How could Amy Miller evaluate the advantages and disadvantages of agreeing to be acquired by this corporation?

Communication

If you were considering becoming a shareholder of Amy's Ice Creams, what questions would you ask Amy Miller so you could determine whether this would be a good investment for you? Draft a brief letter outlining at least five questions you would want answered before investing in Miller's business.

Integration

Review the discussion of international strategic alliances and joint ventures in Chapter 3. If Amy Miller wanted to open new ice cream stores across the border in Mexico, would you recommend a strategic alliance or a joint venture? Explain your answer.

Ethics

Is it ethical for Amy Miller to share certain proprietary information about the business with some shareholders but not with others?

Debate

Many owners of private companies see going public as a way to improve liquidity. Should Amy's Ice Creams go public or remain privately held? Choose one side of this debate and prepare your arguments, using information from the chapter and the video to support your points.

Teamwork

Form a team of four students to brainstorm a list of five or more questions that Amy Miller would want to ask before acquiring a two-store ice cream parlor chain in Dallas. Be sure to cover important details such as financial results and obligations.

Online Research

Using Internet sources, research trends in U.S. ice cream consumption. What are the implications for the future growth of Amy's Ice Creams? How are these trends likely to affect shareholders who have invested in Amy's Ice Creams? See Component Chapter A, Exhibit A.1, for search engines to use in doing your research.

MYPHLIP COMPANION WEB SITE

Learning Interactively

Visit the myPHLIP Web site at www.prenhall.com/mescon. For Chapter 5, take advantage of the interactive "Study Guide" to test your chapter knowledge. Get instant feedback on whether you need additional studying. Read the "Current Events" articles to get the latest on chapter topics, and complete the exercises as specified by your instructor. Expand your learning with a visit to the "Research Area." There you will find a wealth of information you can use to complete your course assignments.

P A R T   2

MASTERING GLOBAL AND GEOGRAPHICAL SKILLS: COMMUNICATING WITH INTERNATIONAL SUPPLIERS

With 95 percent of the world's population living outside the United States, more and more U.S. businesses today are purchasing and selling their products globally. Chances are, even if you own a small business in a strip mall, you're purchasing merchandise or supplies from somewhere else in the world. Take a moment to think about just how international your own daily life is becoming. Look at your clothes, your car, the food you eat, the movies you see, the materials that built and decorated your home. How many of these items came, in whole or in part, from another country? As a new business owner, you will be communicating with many international businesses and customers. In preparation, visit several local small stores and learn how they do business in the global marketplace.

1. Look at 10 products sold in the store and note where they are made. How many of the products can you easily identify as coming from outside the United States?

2. Arrange to meet with the stores' owners or managers. Find out how they order these international products. Do they submit their orders by mail? telephone? fax machine? Internet? Find out whether these local stores sell any of their products overseas. How do their international customers purchase products from them? Do they have a Web site? Do they send out international mailings or catalogs?

3. Although it's easier today, doing business around the globe increases your need to understand world geography. Consider time differences, for example. Your U.S. business hours certainly won't coincide with the store hours of your suppliers in Europe or Asia. How will you adjust for these differences? The Internet, of course, is one way. But what if you really need to talk to the store manager? When should you place the call? Visit your local library, search the Web, or use resources such as the *World Almanac* to learn more about international time.

   a. How many time zones are there in the United States (including possessions)?

   b. If it's noon in New York City, what time is it in Cape Town, South Africa? Copenhagen, Denmark? Sydney, Australia? Tokyo, Japan? Athens, Greece? Honolulu, Hawaii? Moscow, Russia?

4. As a new business owner, you will be communicating with people who speak many different languages. Log on to this text's Web site, Chapter 5—Mastering Global and Geographical Skills, for a current link to the Alta Vista Translation Service. Use this resource to answer these questions: How do you say "inventory" in Italian? Portuguese? German? French? Chinese?

BUSINESS PLANPRO EXERCISES: STARTING A SMALL BUSINESS

Review the Appendix, Getting Started with Business PlanPro Software, to learn how to use Business PlanPro Software so that you can complete these exercises.

Think Like a Pro

Objective: By completing these exercises, you will become acquainted with the sections of a business plan that address forms of ownership, financing the enterprise, and the franchising alternative. For these exercises you will use the sample business plan for Golf Masters Pro Shops.

Open the BPP software and explore the sample business plan Golf Pro Shop.spd. Click on the Plan Outline icon to access the plan's Task Manager.

Find the heading What You're Selling. Double-click on the sections Product and Service Description and Competitive Comparison and read those sections of the business plan. Using the Task Manager, find the heading The Business You're In and read Industry Participants.

1. What products and services does Golf Master Pro Shops provide? How will the company differentiate its products and services from those of its competitors?

Find the heading Your Company and read the section Company Ownership.

2. What form of ownership will Golf Master Pro Shops use? What are the advantages of selecting that form of ownership?

Read the company's financial plan summary under the Task Manager heading Financial Plan.

3. How will Golf Master Pro Shops finance its start-up expenses and its growth?

Find the heading Finish and Polish and read the Strategy Pyramid section. Now read the company's Pricing Strategy under the heading Your Sales Forecast.

4. Explain the company's master franchise strategy. How will Golf Master Pro Shops use franchising to grow their business? What fees will master franchises pay? What commissions and royalties will master franchises earn? What fees will store franchises pay? As a potential franchise owner, what might you want to know about the required advertising contribution?

Access the Company Ownership section of the business plan and in text view click on the Instructions Tab located at the top of your screen.

5. What information should you include about company ownership in a business plan? Which outside resources might you use to help you select the best form of ownership?

Create Your Own Business Plan

Think about your own business. What form of ownership will you choose? Why? How much start-up money will you need? How will you finance your start-up costs? Where will you obtain the money that you will need to grow your business?

BARNESANDNOBLE.COM VS. AMAZON

Amazon Writes a New Chapter

The Internet was barely a blip on the world's business radar when Jeffrey Bezos read a report predicting that World Wide Web usage would grow 2,300 percent per year. Bezos wasted no time. In 1994, he quit his job on Wall Street, drafted a business plan for a completely automated bookstore on the Web, and moved to Seattle to launch his dream. Amazon opened its electronic doors in 1995, ushering in a new era of electronic retailing.

Barnes & Noble Tiptoes into the Internet Arena

In 1994 Stephen Riggio, vice chairman of Barnes & Noble (and brother of the chain's CEO, Leonard Riggio), told company executives that the Internet was the future of bookselling. But Barnes & Noble had just completed the debut of its supersized bookstores—with innovative cafes, music shops, and more. Worried that an Internet bookstore would steal sales from the superstores, executives of the nation's largest bookseller decided to invest company resources in the expansion of Barnes & Noble's physical stores.

Two years after Amazon opened its doors, Barnes & Noble halfheartedly launched its online sibling, Barnesandnoble.com. But the delay proved damaging. By then Amazon had built a loyal customer base, raised millions of dollars in an IPO, claimed the title of the earth's largest bookstore, and captured the lion's share of the online market. Barnes & Noble became a textbook example of letting an Internet upstart gain a decisive advantage. And its online sibling, Barnesandnoble.com, has spent its entire life trying to catch up.

"There was a period at the beginning of the Internet where I didn't get it," admits Leonard Riggio." Now Barnesandnoble.com wants to be the Internet bookshelf's bestseller. But with only a 15 percent market share, it's a distant second behind Amazon.

To free the Internet start-up from Barnes & Noble's corporate bureaucracy, Barnes & Noble spun off the online venture into a separate Internet company, but retained all ownership shares. As a separate company with only a handful of warehouses, Barnesandnoble.com could avoid charging sales tax in most states and match Amazon's low Internet book prices. (Internet and mail-order companies are only required to collect sales tax in states where they have a physical presence, such as a warehouse.)

Stacking up the Amazon Advantage

	Amazon.com www.amazon.com	Barnesandnoble.com www.barnesandnoble.com
Sales (annual)	$1,649 million	$202.6 million
Net loss (annual)	($643 million)	($20.6 million)
Customers	16.9 million	4 million
Employees	7,600	1,237
Market Share	80 percent	15 percent

Barnesandnoble.com Launches a Surprise Attack

Once Barnesandnoble.com was up and running, it went after Amazon's throat. First, the challenger strengthened its competitive arsenal in 1998 when Bertelsmann AG, Europe's largest media company, invested $200 million in the upstart for a 40 percent ownership interest (Barnes & Noble retained the remaining 60 percent). Then, one year later, Barnes & Noble sold 20 percent of its shares to public investors in a highly publicized IPO. The upstart used the cash to add innovative services at a blistering rate. Same-day delivery to Manhattan customers, free online courses, downloadable manuscripts, thousands of out-of-print books, an unprecedented one million titles, an online music store, a prints and poster gallery, and a free eCards service were just some of the services Barnesandnoble.com introduced to grab market share from the king of the bookselling hill.

A failed attempt by Barnes & Noble to purchase Ingram Book Group, the nation's leading book supplier, was a big setback for the Riggio brothers, but in 2000 Barnesandnoble.com rebounded and purchased Fatbrain, the nation's third largest online technical bookseller for $64 million, buying its way into the market for online professional and business-related materials, such as computer textbooks and corporate-training manuals.

The Riggios Revise Their Strategy

It didn't take long for the Riggio brothers to realize that their strategy to operate Barnesandnoble.com independently from its parent was flawed. Customers didn't differentiate between Barnes & Noble physical stores and Barnesandnoble.com. Nor did they care that the two were separate companies. In fact, they became angry when they could not return books they purchased from Barnesandnoble.com at a Barnes & Noble superstore. Moreover, as separate entities they did not combine their marketing programs, share their management teams, or take advantage of the benefits of working together.

So in 2000, Barnes & Noble entered into a partnership with its online sibling to integrate their operations. Now customers could pick up or return items they purchased from Barnesandnoble.com at any of the 551 Barnes & Noble superstores, and Barnes & Noble could use its physical stores to promote the Web site—something Amazon could not do.

Amazon Takes on the World

While Barnesandnoble.com attacked Amazon, the reigning online book king decided to fight a different battle. With an eye on the Internet universe, "more markets" became Amazon's battle cry. Bezos expanded Amazon's product offerings to include consumer electronics, games, toys, tools, electronic greeting cards, sporting gear, luxury gifts, table saws, and more. He introduced an online auction service and a low-cost hosting service called zShops, which enabled online merchants to set up shop under Amazon's banner for a small monthly fee and a small percentage of sales revenues.

And he entered into a joint venture with Toys "R" Us to develop a toy and video Web site. To handle this wide range of merchandise, Amazon built state-of-the-art distribution centers and filled the warehouses with merchandise. But the warehouses were expensive to operate and stock.

Barnesandnoble.com Sticks with Books

Barnesandnoble.com, on the other hand, stayed its course. "We're not going to be the Sears of the Web," says Stephen Riggio. "I don't think customers would accept Barnesandnoble.com selling televisions and refrigerators." Instead, Barnesandnoble.com would continue to focus on the kinds of products that helped expand its brick-and-mortar sibling into a $4 billion business: books. And if you ask Stephen Riggio where Barnesandnoble.com is going next, he'll flat out tell you: digital content—the kind of stuff you download over the Internet and print on demand.

The Literary Titans Duke It Out in Cyberspace

Critics, of course, have chastised Barnes & Noble for arriving late to the Internet scene and for initially failing to use its physical stores to drive traffic to Barnesandnoble.com Nonetheless, in the online bookselling arena, Barnesandnoble.com has two key advantages: its operating partnership with the physical stores, and the financial and promotional backing from Barnes & Noble and Bertelsmann, who each own 40 percent of Barnesandnoble.com's stock. In fact, Bertelsmann has set aside a whopping $13.2 billion to spend on future e-commerce acquisitions and initiatives, which means Bertelsmann could help Barnesandnoble.com grab market share from Amazon by financing a price war, should it choose that path. As one securities analyst put it, all Barnesandnoble.com needs to do to knock out Amazon is "to discount it to death for three Christmases in a row."

Bezos, of course, is not losing sight of his challenger or his core business—books. In 2001 Amazon formed an alliance with Borders to take over Borders' online bookselling operation.

Furthermore, Amazon will focus on electronic books and digital music while Bezos pursues loftier goals. He wants Amazon to become the king of the e-commerce universe—even though some fear that doing so could jeopardize the company's lead in the cyber book battle.

With over 20 million customers, Amazon has a commanding lead in the battle of the literary titans. But as Amazon grows, so do its troubles (see charts). To remain in the lead, Amazon must become profitable. It can't continue to lose money on every transaction, as analysts claim it is doing. After all, Barnesandnoble.com is getting stronger. And even though it is still well behind Amazon in sales, it is losing much less money than its rival.

QUESTIONS FOR CRITICAL THINKING

1. How did Amazon's and Barnes & Noble's initial approach to the Internet differ? How did their initial approach impact their ability to compete in the future?

2. Why did Barnes and Noble create a separate entity for its online business?

3. Why do you think Amazon decided to expand beyond books and music?

4. If Amazon and Barnesandnoble.com had the opportunity to "do it all over again," what changes do you think they would make in their competitive strategies and why?

5. What are the advantages and disadvantages of combining the operations of Barnesandnoble.com with those of Barnes & Noble's physical stores?

6. Explore the Amazon.com and Barnesandnoble.com Web sites to learn more about each company. From a consumer's perspective, what notable differences exist between the content and usability of each Web site?

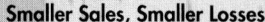

Smaller Sales, Smaller Losses

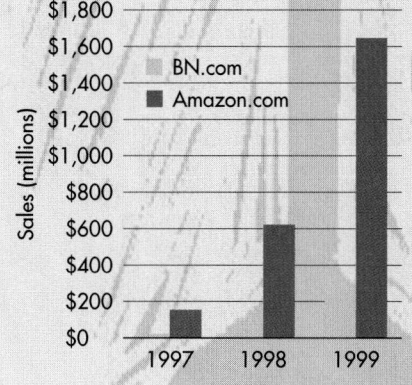

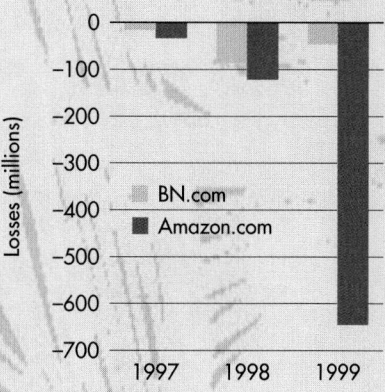

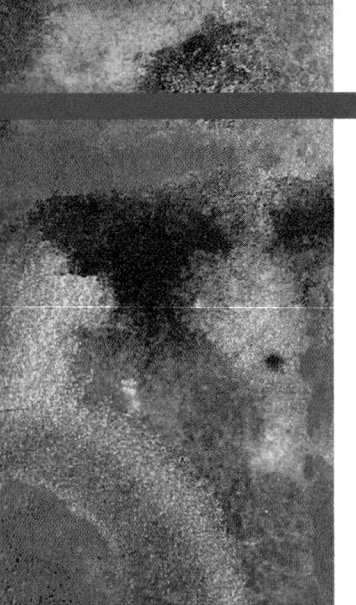

FUNCTIONS AND SKILLS OF MANAGEMENT

LEARNING OBJECTIVES

After studying this chapter, you will be able to

1. Define the four basic management functions

2. Outline the seven tasks of the strategic planning process

3. Explain the purpose of a mission statement

4. List the benefits of setting long-term goals and objectives

5. Cite three leadership styles and explain why no one style is best

6. Clarify how total quality management (TQM) is changing the way organizations are managed

7. Identify and explain the three types of managerial skills

@ 8. Highlight the seven habits of highly effective e-managers

TRANSFORMING THE WORLD: STEVE CASE'S VISION FOR AOL TIME WARNER

www.aol.com

When the Federal Communications Commission approved the merger of AOL and Time Warner, Steve Case became the chairman of the world's biggest media business.

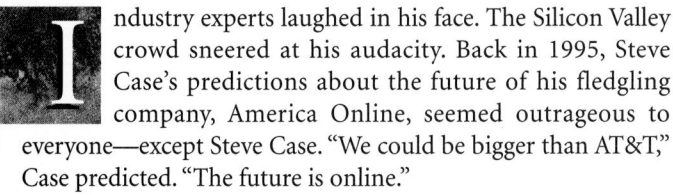

Industry experts laughed in his face. The Silicon Valley crowd sneered at his audacity. Back in 1995, Steve Case's predictions about the future of his fledgling company, America Online, seemed outrageous to everyone—except Steve Case. "We could be bigger than AT&T," Case predicted. "The future is online."

It was a vision that Case refused to abandon, in spite of the odds against him. Long before others dreamed of connecting the world through digital networks, Case saw infinite possibilities in cyberspace. A brief experiment with some online services during the early 1980s was the spark that ignited his imagination. "There was something magical about being able to sit at home . . . and talk to people over the world," he recalled. "It wasn't a great leap of faith to think that if you made it affordable and easy to use, people would want it."

Determined to turn his vision into reality, Case took the reins of an unsuccessful online business in 1985. Although the techies scoffed at his strategy of building a simple service for ordinary people, Case doggedly pursued his dream. He continuously assessed the needs of his customers, and he responded to their desires for an easier way to access information over the Internet by replacing arcane codes with simple graphics.

By 1992 Case had given his company a catchy name— America Online (AOL)—and had taken the company public. All the while, he continued analyzing other online services to understand the competitive and constantly changing world of cyberspace. He reacted to the intense competition by developing and executing a strategy for dominating the online market. To attract more customers, Case introduced a flat monthly rate for unlimited Internet access and blanketed the country with millions of free AOL disks. Millions of customers signed up for

AOL's services—far more than the company's communication networks could handle. But Case moved quickly and decisively to resolve the immediate crisis, regaining customer confidence by expanding the network's capacity.

Still, crisis after crisis threatened to topple Case's online kingdom. By 1995 AOL was losing money, agitating customers, and fighting intense competition. Although critics predicted the company's demise, Case remained focused on his original vision, to establish a global communications medium that would change people's lives. He knew where he was headed and why. Ignoring his detractors, Case concentrated on long-range goals. He examined AOL's existing resources and determined which outside resources he needed to help push AOL to the top. Then he expanded his customer base by acquiring such existing businesses as Netscape Communications and rival CompuServe.

By millennium's end, AOL was a profitable Internet powerhouse, serving more than 22 million customers around the globe. Case continued to look toward the future. He examined the changing technological environment and decided that AOL needed high-speed cable lines to build the Web's infrastructure for the new century. Determined to strengthen AOL as a global communications company, Case orchestrated the largest merger in history by joining forces with Time Warner, the world's largest media company.

Case's stunning move silenced the mockery of his critics. Driven by a vision that never wavered, he defied odds that seemed insurmountable to create the world's first fully integrated media and communications company. AOL Time Warner can change the way people live, work, learn, and communicate throughout the twenty-first century.[1]

WHAT IS MANAGEMENT?

management
Process of coordinating resources to meet organizational goals

Much of Steve Case's success comes from on his ability to envision the future and find the best managers to help him turn his vision into reality and run his organization. But as Case knows, not everyone is equipped to be an effective manager. **Management** entails four basic functions: planning, organizing, leading, and controlling resources (land, labor, capital, and information) to efficiently reach a company's goals.[2] Managers are the employees responsible for performing these four functions in addition to a number of other duties to coordinate the organization's work. These duties, or **roles,** fall into three main categories:

roles
Behavioral patterns associated with or expected of certain positions

- *Interpersonal roles.* Managers perform ceremonial obligations; provide leadership to employees; build a network of relationships with bosses, peers, and employees; and act as liaison to groups and individuals both inside and outside the company (such as suppliers, competitors, government agencies, consumers, special-interest groups, and interrelated work groups).

- *Informational roles.* Managers spend a fair amount of time gathering information by questioning people both inside and outside the organization. They also distribute information to employees, other managers, and outsiders.

- *Decisional roles.* Managers use the information they gather to encourage innovation, to resolve unexpected problems that threaten organizational goals (such as reacting to an economic crisis), and to decide how organizational resources will be used to meet planned objectives. They also negotiate with many individuals and groups, including suppliers, employees, and unions.[3]

Being able to move among these roles while performing the four basic management functions is just one of the many skills that managers must possess.

THE FOUR BASIC FUNCTIONS OF MANAGEMENT

LEARNING OBJECTIVE *1*

Define the four basic management functions

Steve Case demonstrates that when managers possess the right combination of vision, skill, experience, and determination, they can lead an organization to success. To do this, however, they must perform the four basic functions of management: (1) planning, (2) organizing, (3) leading, and (4) controlling (see Exhibit 6.1). These functions are not discrete; they overlap and influence one another. Let's examine these four functions in detail.

The Planning Function

planning
Establishing objectives and goals for an organization and determining the best ways to accomplish them

Planning is the primary management function, the one on which all others depend. Managers engaged in **planning** develop strategies for success, establish goals and objectives for the organization, and translate their strategies and goals into action plans. To develop long-term strategies and goals, managers must be well informed on a number of key issues and topics that could influence their decisions. A closer look at the strategic planning process will give you a clearer idea of the types of information managers need to help them plan for the company's future.

Best of the Web Best of the Web Best of

CATCH THE BUZZ!

Buzzwords. You may hear them often in your business classes, but they will come at you from all sides when you enter the business world. You can stay on top of all of these management terms by looking them up in the Management and Technology Dictionary. This online dictionary of management terms includes definitions of both established terms and trendy buzzwords. The site's emerging technology glossary keeps track of the jargon of the digital age, and is expanded and updated on a daily basis. In addition, a handy finance dictionary provides definitions of the many financial terms you will need to know as a manager. So log on now and add these dictionaries to your collection of business resources.
www.strategyweb.net/reference/index.html

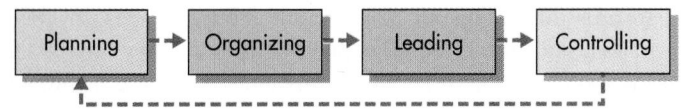

EXHIBIT 6.1

THE FOUR BASIC FUNCTIONS OF MANAGEMENT

Some managers, especially those in smaller organizations, perform all four managerial functions. Although these functions tend to occur in a somewhat progressive order, sometimes they occur simultaneously, and often the process is ongoing.

Understanding the Strategic Planning Process **Strategic plans** outline the firm's long-range (two to five years) organizational goals and set a course of action the firm will pursue to reach its goals. These long-term goals encompass eight major areas of concern: market standing, innovation, human resources, financial resources, physical resources, productivity, social responsibility, and financial performance.[4] A good strategic plan answers: Where are we going? What is the environment? How do we get there?

To answer these questions and establish effective long-term goals, managers require extensive amounts of information. For instance, managers must study budgets, production schedules, industry and economic data, customer preferences, internal and external data, competition, and so on. Managers use this information to set a firm's long-term course of direction during a process called strategic planning. Consisting of seven interrelated critical tasks, the strategic planning process is an ongoing event as Exhibit 6.2 suggests.[5]

Develop a Clear Vision Most organizations are formed in order to realize a **vision,** a realistic, credible, and attainable view of the future that grows out of and improves on the present.[6] Henry Ford envisioned making affordable transportation available to every person. Fred Smith (founder of FedEx) envisioned making FedEx an information company (besides being a transportation company). Bill Gates (chairman of Microsoft) envisioned empowering people through great software, anytime, anyplace, and on any device. And Steve Case was able to see, before others, a global medium that would change the way people live, learn, and work. Case envisioned a world where everyone was connected by computers.[7] Without such visionaries, who knows how the world would be different. Thus, developing a clear vision is a critical task in the strategic planning process. But having a vision alone is no guarantee of success; it must also be communicated to others, executed, and modified as conditions change.

Translate the Vision into a Meaningful Mission Statement To transform vision into reality, managers must define specific organizational goals, objectives, and philosophies. A starting point

strategic plans
Plans that establish the actions and the resource allocation required to accomplish strategic goals; usually defined for periods of two to five years and developed by top managers

LEARNING OBJECTIVE 2

Outline the seven tasks of the strategic planning process

vision
A viable view of the future that is rooted in but improves on the present

LEARNING OBJECTIVE 3

Explain the purpose of a mission statement

EXHIBIT 6.2

SEVEN TASKS OF THE STRATEGIC PLANNING PROCESS

In today's rapidly changing economy, strategic planning is an ongoing process comprising these seven tasks.

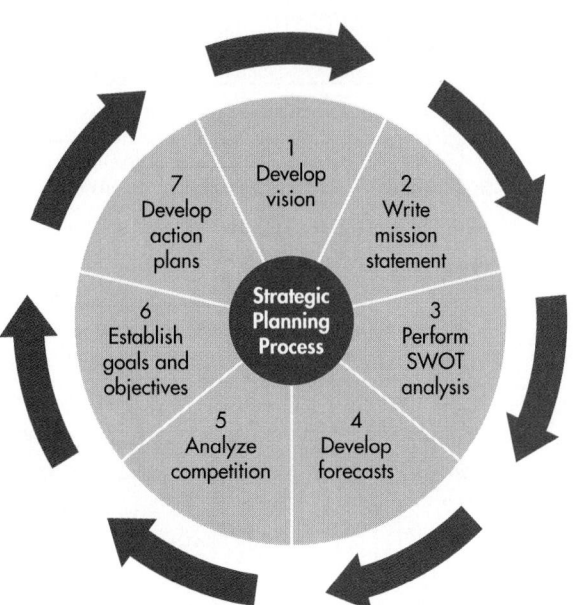

mission statement
A statement of the organization's purpose, basic goals, and philosophies

is to write a company **mission statement,** a brief document that defines why the organization exists, what it seeks to accomplish, and the principles that the company will adhere to as it tries to reach its goals (see Exhibit 6.3). Put differently, a mission statement communicates who we are, what we do, and where we're headed. Typical components of a mission statement include the company's product or service; primary market; fundamental concern for survival, growth, and profitability; managerial philosophy; and commitment to quality and social responsibility.

Another important function of a mission statement is to bring clarity of focus to members of the organization. A mission statement helps employees understand how their role is tied to the organization's greater purpose. Thus, it should inspire and guide employees and managers in a way that they can understand the firm's vision and identify with it. Furthermore, the statement must be congruent with the organization's core values. Managers should refer to it to assess whether new project proposals are within the scope of the company's mission.[8]

Consider Edge Learning Institute, an employee-training firm based in Tempe, Arizona. Edge executives were considering mass-marketing their training videos through television "infomercials." However, they realized that this was contrary to the company's mission of using "the human touch when providing individuals and organizations with information." So they decided instead to expand Edge's reach by developing a network of franchises that follow the company's training methods.[9]

Assess the Company's Strengths, Weaknesses, Opportunities, and Threats Before establishing long-term goals, a firm must have a clear assessment of its strengths and weaknesses compared with the opportunities and threats it faces. Such analysis is commonly referred to as SWOT, which stands for strengths, weaknesses, opportunities, and threats.

Strengths are positive internal factors that contribute to a company's success such as having a steady supply of knowledgeable employees or having a dynamic leader such as Steve Case at the helm. *Weaknesses* are negative internal factors that inhibit the company's success such as obsolete facilities, inadequate financial resources to fund the company's growth, or lack of managerial depth and talent. Identifying a firm's internal strengths and weaknesses helps management understand its abilities and current operating position. Management uses this internal analysis as a guide when establishing future goals.

One particular strength worth noting is a firm's *core competence.* A **core competence** is a bundle of skills and technologies that enable a company to provide a particular benefit to customers. A firm's core competence sets the company apart from its competitors and is difficult for competitors to duplicate. Sony's core competence, for example, is miniaturization. Federal

core competence
Distinct skills and capabilities that a firm has or does especially well so that it sets the firm apart from its competitors

EXHIBIT 6.3

MISSION STATEMENT

The mission statement for Dell Computer embodies the firm's high standards for quality and customer service

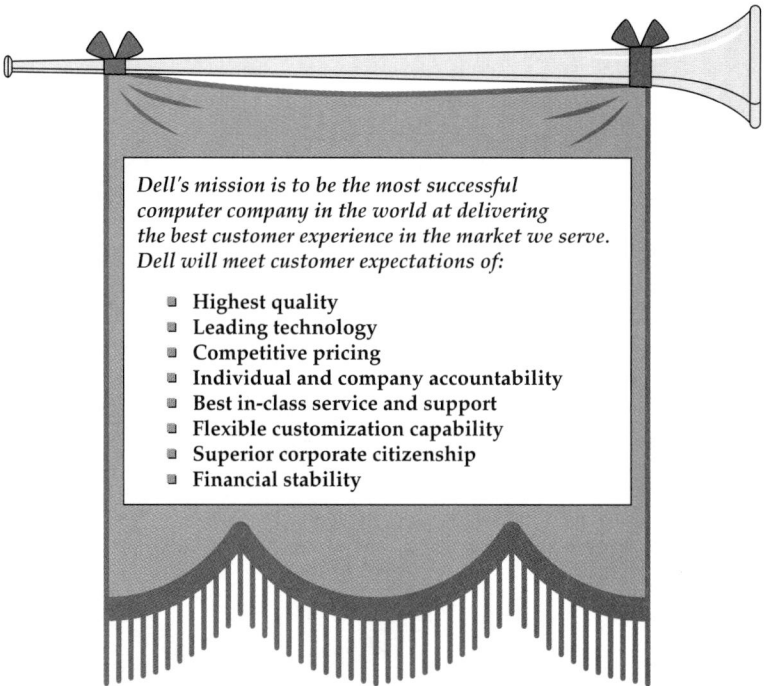

Dell's mission is to be the most successful computer company in the world at delivering the best customer experience in the market we serve. Dell will meet customer expectations of:

- **Highest quality**
- **Leading technology**
- **Competitive pricing**
- **Individual and company accountability**
- **Best in-class service and support**
- **Flexible customization capability**
- **Superior corporate citizenship**
- **Financial stability**

Express's core competence is its efficient delivery process. America Online's core competence is the simplicity of its software. In most cases a core competence represents the sum of knowledge across the organization. Thus, it lasts even though individual employees may leave the firm.

Once managers have taken inventory of a company's internal strengths and weaknesses, they must next identify the external opportunities and threats that might significantly affect their ability to attain certain goals. *Opportunities* are positive external factors, such as new potential markets or customers. *Threats* are negative external forces that could inhibit the firm's ability to achieve its objectives. Threats include new competitors or entrants into the market, new government regulations, economic recession, increase in interest rates, technological advances that could make a company's product obsolete, and so on. Harvard Business School Professor Clayton Christensen notes that graveyards are full of big firms that ignored the competitive threats from start-ups.[10] (Threats and external analysis will be discussed in detail in Chapter 12 in the context of developing a strategic marketing plan.)

Webvan's core competence is its efficient order processing and delivery systems. The company relies on its core competence to promote itself as the most convenient way for consumers to purchase groceries.

Develop Forecasts To plan for the future, managers must make a number of educated assumptions about future trends and events and modify those assumptions once new information becomes available. But as Steve Case knows, forecasting is not an exact science. In fact, Case once told a reporter, "What I've figured out is that I can predict the future. I just can't predict when."[11] To predict the future managers rely on expert forecasts that can be found in publications such as *Industry Week*'s "Trends and Forecasts," *Business Week*'s "Survey of Corporate Performance," and Standard & Poor's *Earnings Forecast*. However, these sources may not always include key variables specific to an individual company or industry. Therefore, managers must also develop their own forecasts.

Managerial forecasts fall under two broad categories: *quantitative forecasts,* which are typically based on historical data or tests and which involve complex statistical computations; and *qualitative forecasts,* which are based on intuitive judgments or consumer research. Statistically analyzing the cycles of economic growth and recession over several decades to predict when the economy will take a downward turn is an example of quantitative forecasting. Making predictions about sales of a new product on the basis of experience and consumer responses to a survey is an example of qualitative forecasting. Neither method is foolproof, but both are valuable tools, enabling managers to fill in the unknown variables that inevitably crop up in the planning process.

Best of the Web Best of the Web Best of

BECOME A BETTER MANAGER

ManagementFirst.com can help you become a better manager. Focused on management theory and practice, this Web site is a management portal that explores in-depth management issues including leadership, time management, training, strategy, knowledge management, personal development, customer relationship management, and more. Each channel provides lengthy articles, advice, and a collection of carefully annotated links. Log on today and join ManagementFirst.com to become information rich and well organized. Learn why knowledge management is important. Discover what emotional intelligence is all about. And find out why companies form stategic alliances.

www.managementfirst.com

Analyze the Competition   "Business is like any battlefield. If you want to win the war, you have to know who you're up against," says one management consultant.[12] Thus, sizing up the competition is another important task in planning for a company's future. It gives management a realistic view of the market, the company's position in it, and its ability to attain certain goals.

Managers begin the competitive analysis process by identifying existing and potential competitors. Next they determine the competencies, strengths, and weaknesses of their major competitors—just as they did for their own organization. Armed with competitive information, they look for ways to capitalize on a competitor's weaknesses or match or surpass their strengths to gain a competitive edge.

A company can gain a competitive edge through at least one of three competitive strategies:

- *Differentiation.* A company using differentiation develops a level of service, a product image, unique product features (including quality), or new technologies that distinguish its product from competitors' products. Volvo, for instance, stresses the safety of its cars. Caterpillar Tractor emphasizes product durability.

- *Cost leadership.* Businesses that pursue this strategy aim to become the low-cost leader in an industry by producing or selling products more efficiently and economically than competitors. Cost leaders have a competitive advantage by reaching buyers whose primary purchase criterion is price. Wal-Mart is a typical industry cost leader.

- *Focus.* When using a focus strategy, companies concentrate on a specific regional market or consumer group, such as the Southwest United States or economy car drivers. This type of strategy enables organizations to develop a better understanding of their customers and to tailor their products specifically to customer needs.[13] Examples of focused strategies include Abercrombie and Fitch (high-end apparel for young adults) and Williams Sonoma (quality cookware and appliances for serious cooks).

Establish Company Goals and Objectives   As mentioned earlier, establishing goals and objectives is the key task in the planning process. Although these terms are often used interchangeably, a **goal** is a broad, long-range accomplishment that the organization wishes to attain in typically five or more years, whereas an **objective** is a specific, short-range target designed to help reach that goal. For AOL, a goal might be to become the number-one Internet service provider in the Brazilian marketplace, and an objective might be to add 100,000 new Brazilian subscribers by year-end.

To be effective, organizational goals and objectives should be specific, measurable, relevant, challenging, attainable, and time-limited. For example it is better to state "increase our customer base by 10 percent over the next three years" than "substantially increase our customer base."

Setting appropriate goals has many benefits: it increases employee motivation, establishes standards for measuring individual and group performance, guides employee activity, and clarifies management's expectations. By establishing organizational goals, managers set the stage for the actions needed to achieve those goals. If actions aren't planned, the chances of reaching company goals are slim.

Develop Action Plans   Once managers have established a firm's long-term strategic goals and objectives, it must then develop a plan of execution. **Tactical plans** lay out the actions and the allocation of resources necessary to achieve specific, short-term objectives that support the company's broader strategic plan. Tactical plans typically focus on departmental goals and cover a period of one to three years. Their limited scope permits them to be changed more easily than strategic plans. **Operational plans** designate the actions and resources required to achieve the objectives of tactical plans. Operational plans usually define actions for less than one year and focus on accomplishing a firm's specific objectives such as increasing the number of new subscribers by 5 percent over the next six months.

Keep in mind that many highly admired CEOs have stumbled, not because they didn't have strategies for success, but because they didn't execute their strategies or deliver on their commitments. That's because developing a strategy or vision is less than half the battle. It's executing it that counts. In today's information age, strategies quickly become public property. Everyone knows Dell's direct business model, for example, yet few companies, if any, have successfully copied its execution.

---

goal
Broad, long-range target or aim

objective
Specific, short-range target or aim

LEARNING
OBJECTIVE   4

List the benefits of setting long-term goals and objectives

---

tactical plans
Plans that define the actions and the resource allocation necessary to achieve tactical objectives and to support strategic plans; usually defined for a period of one to three years and developed by middle managers

operational plans
Plans that lay out the actions and the resource allocation needed to achieve operational objectives and to support tactical plans; usually defined for less than one year and developed by first-line managers.

Planning for a Crisis No matter how well a company plans for its future, any number of problems can arise to threaten its existence. An ugly fight for control of a company, a product failure, a breakdown in routine operations (as a result of fire, for example), or an environmental accident could develop into a serious and crippling crisis. Managers can help a company survive these setbacks through **crisis management,** a plan for handling such unusual and serious problems.

The goal of crisis management is to keep the company functioning smoothly both during and after a crisis. Successful crisis management requires comprehensive contingency plans in addition to speedy, open communication with all who are affected by the crisis. Experts suggest selecting in advance a communications team and a knowledgeable spokesperson to handle the many requests for information that arise during a crisis. The individuals selected should be able to remain honest and calm when a crisis hits. Moreover, top managers should be visible in the hours immediately following the crisis to demonstrate that the company will do whatever is necessary to control the situation as best it can, find the cause, and prevent a future occurrence.[14]

Ford and Bridgestone/Firestone were criticized for not taking these actions when reports started surfacing about the faulty tires manufactured by Bridgestone/Firestone and fitted on Ford Explorer sports utility vehicles. When the vehicles were driven at high speed, the treads separated from the tires, causing the car to roll over and injuring—even killing—passengers. Although both Ford and Firestone eventually recalled 6.5 million tires, both companies are paying the price for making serious mistakes in handling the crisis. Some say that Firestone's reputation may even be damaged beyond repair.[15]

Responding to a crisis, of course, is much easier when management has prepared for problems by actively looking for signs of a disaster in the making. When Belgian and French consumers became ill after drinking cans of Coke produced with substandard carbon dioxide, Coca-Cola officials were caught off guard. "No one would have thought that this would happen to Coke. But they should have planned for it," notes one beverage industry expert. Instead, Coca-Cola's officials made the situation worse by denying that Coke could have been the problem. Company officials eventually issued an apology, but even today Coca-Cola suffers the consequences of its delayed response. The company has had far higher marketing costs in Europe because of the incident.[16]

Keep in mind that crisis planning is not only for large corporations, as Rocket USA will attest. Ready for takeoff in 1997, this five-person manufacturer of collectible windup toys had planned for everything—except a UPS strike. The company found itself with orders streaming in and inventory stacked high in the warehouse, yet no way to fill orders. "We were totally in the dark about how we were going to ship," confesses the company president. The company had no backup plan.[17]

The Organizing Function

Organizing, the process of arranging resources to carry out the organization's plans, is the second major function of managers. During the organizing stage, managers think through all the activities that employees carry out (from programming the organization's computers to mailing its letters), as well as all the facilities and equipment employees need in order to complete those activities. They also give people the ability to work toward organizational goals by determining who will have the authority to make decisions, to perform or supervise activities, and to distribute resources.

The organizing function is particularly challenging because most organizations undergo constant change. Long-time employees leave, and new employees arrive. Equipment breaks down or becomes obsolete, and replacements are needed. The public's tastes and interests change, and the organization has to reevaluate its plans and activities. Shifting political and economic trends can lead to employee cutbacks—or perhaps expansion. Long-time competitors take unexpected actions, and new competitors enter the market. Every week the organization faces new situations, so management's organizing tasks are never finished. Consider Microsoft. The company continually challenges itself by asking: "Are we making what customers want and working on products

crisis management
System for minimizing the harm that might result from some unusually threatening situations

Cans of banned Coke were dumped at Coca-Cola depot in Evere, Belgium, as part of the largest recall in the company's history.

organizing
Process of arranging resources to carry out the organization's plans

and technologies they'll want in the future? Are we staying ahead of all our competitors? What don't our customers like about what we do, and what are we doing about it? Are we organized most effectively to achieve our goals?"[18]

The organizing function will be discussed in detail in Chapter 7. In this chapter, however, we will discuss the three levels of a corporate hierarchy—top, middle, bottom—commonly known as the **management pyramid.** In general, **top managers** are the upper-level managers who have the most power and who take overall responsibility for the organization. An example is the chief executive officer (CEO). Top managers establish the structure for the organization as a whole, and they select the people who fill the upper-level positions. Top managers also make long-range plans, establish major policies, and represent the company to the outside world at official functions and fund-raisers.

Middle managers have similar responsibilities, but usually for just one division or unit. They develop plans for implementing the broad goals set by top managers, and they coordinate the work of first-line managers. In traditional organizations, managers at the middle level are plant managers, division managers, branch managers, and other similar positions—reporting to top-level managers. But in more innovative management structures, middle managers often function as team leaders who are expected to supervise and lead small groups of employees in a variety of job functions. Similar to consultants, they must understand every department's function, not just their own area of expertise. Furthermore, they are granted decision-making authority previously reserved for only high-ranking executives.[19]

At the bottom of the management pyramid are **first-line managers** (or *supervisory managers*). They oversee the work of operating employees, and they put into action the plans developed at higher levels. Positions at this level include supervisor, department head, and office manager.[20] Even though more managers are at the bottom level than at the top, as illustrated in Exhibit 6.4, today's leaner companies tend to have fewer levels, flattening the organizational structure, as Chapter 7 points out.

The Leading Function

Leading—the process of influencing and motivating people to work effectively and willingly toward company goals—is the third basic function of management. Leading becomes even more challenging in today's business environment, where individuals who have different backgrounds and unique interests, ambitions, and personal goals are melded into a productive work team. Managers with good leadership skills have greater success in influencing the attitudes and actions of others, both through the demonstration of specific tasks and through the manager's own behavior and spirit. Furthermore, effective leaders are good at *motivating,* or giving employees a reason to do the job and to put forth their best performance (see Chapter 10).

What makes a good leader? When early researchers studied leadership, they looked for specific characteristics, or *traits*, common to all good leaders. At the time, they were unable to prove any link between particular traits and leadership ability. However, researchers found that leaders who have specific traits, such as decisiveness and self-confidence, are likely to be more effective.[21] Additional studies have shown that managers with strong interpersonal skills and high emotional quotients (EQs) tend to be more effective leaders. The characteristics of a high EQ include:[22]

---

management pyramid
Organizational structure comprising top, middle, and lower management

top managers
Those at the highest level of the organization's management hierarchy; they are responsible for setting strategic goals, and they have the most power and responsibility in the organization

middle managers
Those in the middle of the management hierarchy; they develop plans to implement the goals of top managers and coordinate the work of first-line managers

first-line managers
Those at the lowest level of the management hierarchy; they supervise the operating employees and implement the plans set at the higher management levels; also called supervisory managers

leading
Process of guiding and motivating people to work toward organizational goals

---

EXHIBIT 6.4

THE MANAGEMENT PYRAMID

Separate job titles are used to designate the three basic levels in the management pyramid.

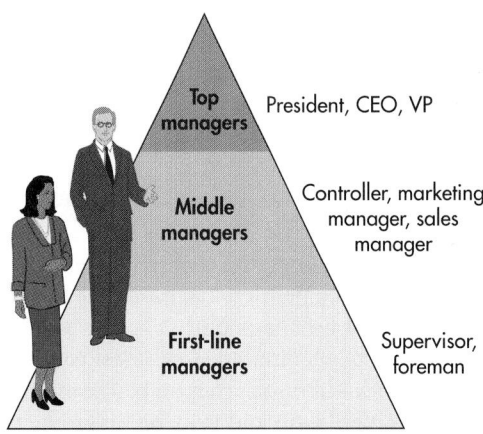

▨ *Self-awareness.* Self-aware managers have the ability to recognize their own feelings and how they, their job performance, and other people are affected by those feelings. Moreover, managers who are highly self-aware know where they are headed and why.

▨ *Self-regulation.* Self-regulated managers have the ability to control or reduce disruptive impulses and moods. They can suspend judgment and think before acting. Moreover, they know how to utilize the appropriate emotion at the right time and in the right amount.

▨ *Motivation.* Motivated managers are driven to achieve beyond expectations—their own and everyone else's.

▨ *Empathy.* Empathetic managers thoughtfully consider employees' feelings, along with other factors, in the process of making intelligent decisions.

▨ *Social skill.* Socially skilled managers tend to have a wide circle of acquaintances, and they have a knack for finding common ground with people of all kinds. They assume that nothing important gets done by one person alone and have a network in place when the time for action comes.

Keep in mind that these traits alone do not define a leader. Different leadership traits are appropriate under different leadership situations.[23]

Adopting an Effective Leadership Style *Leadership style* is the way a manager uses authority to lead others. Every manager, from the baseball coach to the university chancellor, has a definite style. The three broad categories of leadership style are *autocratic, democratic,* and *laissez-faire.*

LEARNING OBJECTIVE 5

Cite three leadership styles and explain why no one style is best

Autocratic leaders make decisions without consulting others. "My way or the highway" summarizes this style, which tends to go with traditional, hierarchical organizational structures. Although autocratic leadership can be highly effective when quick decisions are necessary, it does little to empower employees or encourage innovation. Al Dunlop, past CEO of Sunbeam, used an autocratic leadership style to try to turn the failing household appliance maker around, as this chapter's Case for Critical Thinking shows.

In contrast, **democratic leaders** delegate authority and involve employees in decision making. Even though their approach can lead to slower decisions, soliciting input from people familiar with particular situations or issues may result in better decisions. As more companies adopt the principles of teamwork, democratic leadership continues to gain in popularity. For example, managers at Rhone-Poulenc, the U.S. subsidiary of France's leading chemical and pharmaceutical manufacturer, gradually made the transition from autocratic to democratic leadership as the organization moved from a hierarchical structure to a team-based environment. CEO Peter Neff says, "I don't look over people's shoulders anymore. . . . My role now is to enable people to do the best they know how to do." For Neff, this means acting as an opportunity seeker, coach, facilitator, motivator, and mentor rather than as a controller or problem solver.[24]

Richard Branson's brash, ambitious, and flamboyant leadership style has often put him at odds with the business establishment. Nevertheless, under his leadership, Virgin Group has launched several successful businesses. Among them are Virgin Atlantic Airways (a high-quality, low-fare, trans-Atlantic carrier competing against British Airways) and Virgin Megastore (a chain of music superstores).

The third leadership style, laissez-faire, is sometimes referred to as free-rein leadership. The French term *laissez faire* can be translated as "leave it alone," or more roughly as "hands off." **Laissez-faire leaders** take the role of consultant, encouraging employees' ideas and offering insights or opinions when asked. The laissez-faire style may fail if workers pursue goals that do not match the organization's. However, the style has proven effective in some situations. Managers at Hewlett-Packard's North American distribution organization adopted a laissez-faire style when they were given nine months to reorganize their order-fulfillment process. The managers eliminated all titles,

autocratic leaders
Leaders who do not involve others in decision making

democratic leaders
Leaders who delegate authority and involve employees in decision making

laissez-faire leaders
Leaders who leave the actual decision making up to employees

supervision, job descriptions, and plans, and they made employees entirely responsible for the project. At first there was chaos. However, employees soon began to try new things, make mistakes, and learn as they went. In the end, the team finished the reorganization ahead of schedule, reduced product delivery times from 26 days to 8 days, and cut inventory by 20 percent. Moreover, the employees experienced a renewed sense of challenge, commitment, and enjoyment in their work.[25]

More and more businesses are adopting democratic and laissez-faire leadership as they reduce the number of management layers in their corporate hierarchies and increase the use of teamwork. However, experienced managers know that no one leadership style works every time. In fact, new research shows that leaders with the best results do not rely on only one leadership style; instead they adapt their approach to match the requirements of the particular situation.[26] Adapting leadership style to current business circumstances is called **contingency leadership.** You can think of leadership styles as existing along a continuum of possible leadership behaviors, as suggested by Exhibit 6.5.

Coaching and Mentoring Managers can provide effective leadership by coaching and mentoring their employees. On a winning sports team, the coach focuses on helping all team members perform at their highest potential. In a similar way, *coaching* managers strive to bring out the best in their employees.

Coaching involves taking the time to meet with employees, discussing any problems that may hinder their ability to work effectively, and offering suggestions and encouragement to help them find their own solutions to work-related challenges. This process requires keen powers of observation, sensible judgment, and both a willingness and an ability to take appropriate action. However, just as a sports coach cannot play the game for team members, a coaching manager must step back and let employees perform when it's "game time." Coaching managers develop a solid game plan and empower their team to carry it out. If the team gets behind, the manager offers encouragement to boost morale. And when team members are victorious, the manager recognizes and praises their outstanding achievement.[27] Tom Gegax, co-founder of Tires Plus stores, has been using internal coaches in his organization for years. "People are more willing to take feedback from a coach than from a boss because so many of us have been coached before," says Gegax.[28]

Acting as a mentor is similar to coaching, but mentoring also emphasizes helping employees understand how the organization works. A **mentor** is usually an experienced manager or employee who can help guide other employees through the corporate maze. Mentors have a deep knowledge of the business and a useful network of industry colleagues. In addition, they can explain office politics, serve as a role model for appropriate business behavior, and provide valuable advice about how to succeed within the organization.

contingency leadership
Adapting the leadership style to what is most appropriate, given current business conditions

coaching
Helping employees reach their highest potential by meeting with them, discussing problems that hinder their ability to work effectively, and offering suggestions and encouragement to overcome these problems

mentor
Experienced manager or employee with a wide network of industry colleagues who can explain office politics, serve as a role model for appropriate business behavior, and help other employees negotiate the corporate structure

Boss-centered leadership						Employee-centered leadership
Use of authority by the manager						Area of freedom for workers
Manager makes decision, announces it.	Manager "sells" decision.	Manager presents ideas, invites questions.	Manager presents tentative decision subject to change.	Manager presents problems, gets suggestions, makes decisions.	Manager defines limits, asks group to make decision.	Manager permits workers to function within defined limits.

EXHIBIT 6.5

CONTINUUM OF LEADERSHIP BEHAVIOR

Leadership style occurs along a continuum, ranging from boss-centered to employee-centered. Situations that require managers to exercise greater authority fall toward the boss-centered end of the continuum. Other situations call for a manager to give workers leeway to function more independently.

MANAGING IN THE 21ST CENTURY

HOW MICHAEL DELL WORKS HIS MAGIC

Michael Dell wasn't *Industry Week*'s CEO of the Year just because of Dell Computer's resounding financial success or because of his contributions to the community where he and his family live. He was chosen because of the way he keeps Dell Computer one step ahead of its competitors by constantly pushing the envelope of change. Dell has the ability to visualize and then capitalize on changes in the business world before they occur. As a result, he has propelled Dell Computer to the top with an unconventional business model for selling and manufacturing, which his competitors are now scrambling to copy.

"You have to be self-critical to succeed," says Dell. "If you sat in on our management meetings, you would find that we are a remarkably self-critical bunch with a disdain for complacency that motivates us. We are always looking to do things more efficiently. We are 99 percent focused on what is going to happen and what could change the business in the future. We ask ourselves, what are the risks to the business, what could go wrong."

From day one, the company's mission has been the same: Build better computers and sell them at lower prices. And it is this simple mission that has kept the company's management focused on doing what it does best. Furthermore, it drives management to continually ask, "What is the most efficient way to do things?" Pretty basic stuff for an $18 billion global corporation. Nevertheless it keeps Dell Computer on track. When the company has deviated from the direct-sales model in the past, business has suffered. So if you ask Michael Dell whether the company would consider taking some of his billions and branching out beyond the computer business today, he'll flat out tell you no. "You have to be careful about expanding into new businesses, because if you get into too many too quickly, you won't have the experience or the infrastructure to succeed," he explains.

So what drives the fourth-richest person in the country, whose company stock has increased 29,600 percent in one decade, to go to work each day? "Not money," says Dell. "Do you have any idea how much fun it is to run a billion-dollar company?" In fact, walk into his executive suite and chances are you'll see a man standing behind a podium desk, both absorbed in and invigorated by his work. Michael Dell's office has chairs, of course, but they are only for visitors. Dell works standing up.

■ QUESTIONS FOR CRITICAL THINKING

1. What leadership style do you think Michael Dell practices, and why?

2. How does Michael Dell successfully manage change?

Your mentor won't necessarily be your boss. Relationships with mentors often develop informally between the individuals involved. However, some companies have established formal mentoring programs. In the program at Xerox, women employees can spend a few hours every month discussing work or career issues with any of the participating women executives.[29] Mentoring offers benefits for both parties: The less-experienced employee gains from the mentor's advice and ideas; the mentor gains new networking contacts, in addition to personal satisfaction.

Managing Change Another important function of leaders is to manage the process of change. As competitive pressures get worse, the pace of change accelerates while companies search for even higher levels of quality, service, and overall speed. Sometimes managers initiate change; other times change imposes itself from outside the company. Nonetheless, effective leaders refrain from launching new initiatives until current ones are embedded in the company's DNA. Take GE's Jack Welch, for example. He has introduced just five major initiatives in his 18 years as CEO.[30] Leaders such as Welch provide a powerful vision to pull people in a desired direction.[31] Then they work with employees to ensure that the change process goes smoothly.

According to one recent study, about 70 percent of all change initiatives fail.[32] Resistance to change often arises because people don't understand how it will affect them. Mention change and most people automatically feel victimized. Some worry that they may have to master new skills—ones that might be difficult. Others fear that their jobs will be in jeopardy. Experts advise that if

Best of the Web Best of the Web Best of

LINKING TO ORGANIZATIONAL CHANGE

Looking for more information on every aspect of organizational change management? You'll find a comprehensive collection of links on the Web site of the Management Assistance Program for Nonprofits. This is the place to access articles, discussion groups, and other resources related to organizational change in businesses and in not-for-profit organizations. Start with the overview, which sets the stage for browsing the many links devoted to exploring management and employee perspectives on the challenges and goals of managing change.

www.mapnp.org/library/mgmnt/orgchnge.htm

CEO Carly Fiorina is driving the change effort to reconnect Hewlett-Packard's (HP) employees with the spirit of invention that started HP over 60 years ago. "We have to get rid of some bad habits. Instead of being slow, we have to be fast. Instead of being indecisive, we have to be focused. We have to lead instead of follow. We have to be bold," says Fiorina, whose vision for HP centers on a world where everything will be connected electronically.

managers want less resistance to change, they should build trust with employees long before the change arrives and, when it does, explain to them how it will affect their jobs. Moreover, cultivating constant change on a small scale can prepare employees for even larger changes; it's the difference between asking someone to run a race who has never even practiced before versus asking someone to run a race who jogs every day.[33]

Building a Strong Organizational Culture Strong leadership is a key element in establishing a productive **organizational culture**—the set of underlying values, norms, and practices shared by members of an organization. When you visit an organization, observe how the employees work, dress, communicate, address each other, and conduct business. Each organization has a special way of doing things. In corporations, this force is often referred to as *corporate culture.*

A company's culture influences the way people treat and react to each other. It shapes the way employees feel about the company and the work they do; the way they interpret and perceive the actions

organizational culture
A set of shared values and norms that support the management system and that guide management and employee behavior

taken by others; the expectations they have regarding changes in their work or in the business; and how they view those changes.[34] Look at Southwest Airlines. As one manager puts it, "Our whole culture drives everything. So many companies, while they don't put it in writing, create a culture that says, 'Leave your personality at home; all we want you to do is work.' At Southwest, we say, 'Bring your personality and your sense of humor to work.' Our ads, our recruitment techniques, and our interview process—all of it attracts a certain type of individual who values hard work, family, and, yes, fun."[35]

The Controlling Function

Controlling is the fourth basic managerial function. In management, **controlling** means monitoring a firm's progress toward meeting its organizational goals and objectives, resetting the course if goals or objectives change in response to shifting conditions, and correcting deviations if goals or objectives are not being attained.

controlling
Process of measuring progress against goals and objectives and correcting deviations if results are not as expected

The Control Cycle Managers strive to maintain a high level of **quality**—a measure of how closely goods or services conform to predetermined standards and customer expectations. Many firms control for quality through a four-step cycle that involves all levels of management and all employees. In the first step, top managers set **standards,** or criteria for measuring the performance of the organization as a whole. At the same time, middle and first-line managers set departmen-

quality
A measure of how closely a product conforms to predetermined standards and customer expectations

standards
Criteria against which performance is measured

COMPETING IN THE GLOBAL MARKETPLACE

HOW MUCH DO YOU KNOW ABOUT THE COMPANY'S CULTURE?

Before you accept a job at a new company, try to learn as much as possible about the company's culture. Use this list of questions to guide you in your investigation.

Company Values

- Is there a compelling vision for the company?
- Is there a mission statement supporting the vision that employees understand and can implement?
- Do employees know how their work relates to this vision?
- Is there a common set of values that bind the organization together?
- Do officers/owners follow these values, or is there a gap between what they say and what they do?

People

- How are people treated?
- Is there an atmosphere of civility and respect?
- Is teamwork valued and encouraged, with all ideas welcomed?
- Are employee ideas acknowledged, encouraged, and acted upon?
- Are employees given credit for their ideas?
- Is there a positive commitment to a balance between work and life?
- Is there a commitment from top management to support working parents?

Community Involvement

- Is the company involved in the community?

- Is there a corporate culture of service?
- Is there a stated policy of community involvement by the company and its employees?

Communication

- Is there open communication?
- Do officers/owners regularly communicate with all levels?
- Are the customer service and financial results widely distributed?
- Is there meaningful two-way communication throughout the organization?
- Are employee surveys on workplace issues conducted and published? Are employees asked for input on solutions?
- Is there an open-door policy for access to management?

Employee Performance

- How are personnel issues handled?
- Is employee feedback given regularly?
- Are employee valuations based on agreed upon objectives that have been clearly communicated?
- Are employees asked to provide a summary of their accomplishments for placement into their evaluations?

◼ QUESTIONS FOR CRITICAL THINKING

1. How might a job candidate find the answers to these questions?

2. Why is it important to learn about the company's culture before accepting a job?

---

tal quality standards so they can meet or exceed company standards. Establishing control standards is closely tied to the planning function and depends on information supplied by employees, customers, and other external sources. Examples of specific standards might be "Produce 1,500 circuit boards monthly with less than 1 percent failures."

In the second step of the control cycle, managers assess performance, using both quantitative (specific, numerical) and qualitative (subjective) performance measures. In the third step, managers compare performance with the established standards and search for the cause of any discrepancies. If the performance falls short of standards, the fourth step is to take corrective action, which may be done by either adjusting performance or reevaluating the standards. If performance meets or exceeds standards, no corrective action is taken. As Exhibit 6.6 shows, if everything is operating smoothly, controls permit managers to repeat acceptable performance. If results are below expectations, controls help managers take any necessary action.

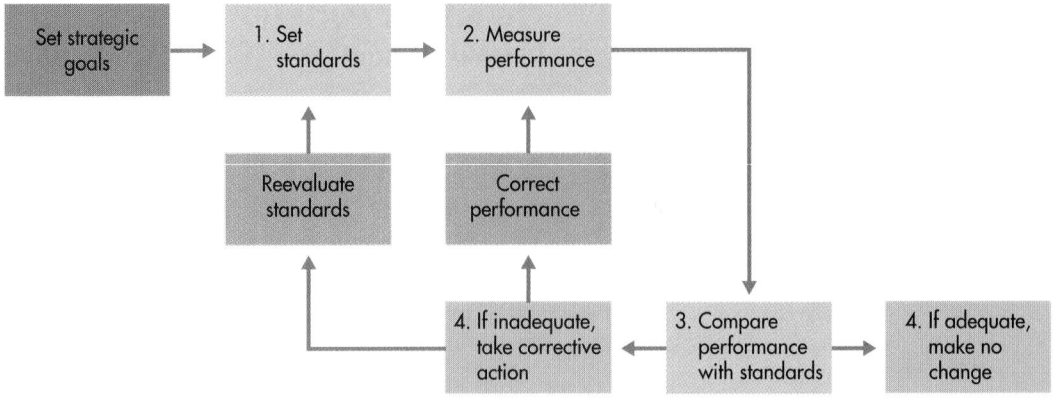

EXHIBIT 6.6

THE CONTROL CYCLE

The control cycle has four basic steps: (1) On the basis of strategic goals, top managers set the standards by which the organization's overall performance will be measured. (2) Managers at all levels measure performance. (3) Actual performance is compared with the standards. (4) Appropriate corrective action is taken (if performance meets standards, nothing other than encouragement is needed; if performance falls below standards, corrective action may include improving performance, establishing new standards, changing plans, reorganizing, or redirecting efforts).

Take America Online. Suppose the company does not reach its objectives of adding 100,000 new Brazilian customers by year-end. With proper control systems in place, managers will evaluate why these objectives were not reached. Perhaps they will find that a shortage of phone lines prevented expansion. Or perhaps the market where expansion was targeted became saturated with new Internet service providers. Regardless, management will search for the cause of the discrepancies before modifying the company's objectives or trying a different approach to achieve the company's long-term goals. Control methods are examined in greater detail in Chapter 9.

LEARNING
OBJECTIVE   6

Clarify how total quality management (TQM) is changing the way organizations are managed

Total Quality Management The controlling function is an important part of total quality management, which is sometimes referred to as *total quality control*. In the past, *control* often meant those little sticky tags attached to new items that say, "inspected by #47." Companies would inspect finished products and rework or discard items that didn't meet quality standards. Today, this inspection step is only one small part of the total control process.

total quality management (TQM)
Comprehensive, strategic management approach that builds quality into every organizational process as a way of improving customer satisfaction

Total quality management (TQM) is both a management philosophy and a strategic management process that focuses on delivering the optimum level of quality to customers by building quality into every organizational activity (see Exhibit 6.7). Total quality management draws its ideas, principles, and tools from psychology, sociology, statistics, management, and marketing. The goal of TQM is to create an environment that encourages people to grow as individuals and to learn to bring about continuous and breakthrough improvements. Companies that adopt TQM create a value for all stakeholders—customers, employees, owners, suppliers, and the community.[36] The four key elements of TQM are employee involvement, customer focus, benchmarking, and continuous improvement.

participative management
Sharing information with employees and involving them in decision making

■ *Employee involvement.* Total quality management involves every employee in quality assurance. Workers are trained in quality methods and are empowered to stop a work process if they feel that products or services are not meeting quality standards. Managers also encourage employees to speak up when they think of better ways of doing things. This approach exemplifies a **participative management** style, the sharing of information at all levels of the organization (also known as *open-book management*). By directly involving employees in decision making, companies increase employees' power in an organization and improve the flow of information between employees and managers. At Borg-Warner Automotive (BWA), manufacturer of highly engineered components and systems for vehicle engines and transmissions, participatory management is ingrained in the company's culture. The product emphasis there

EXHIBIT 6.7

TOTAL QUALITY
MANAGEMENT

These 14 points, based on the work
of W. Edwards Deming, can help
managers improve their goods and
services through total quality
management.

1. **Create constancy of purpose for the improvement of goods and services.**
   The organization should constantly strive to improve quality, productivity, and consumer satisfaction to improve performance today and tomorrow.

2. **Adopt a new philosophy to reject mistakes and negativism.**
   Customers, managers, and employees all need to change their attitudes toward unacceptable work quality and sullen service.

3. **Cease dependence on mass inspection.**
   Instead of inspecting products after production to weed out bad quality, improve the process to build in good quality.

4. **End the practice of awarding business on price alone.**
   Create long-term relationships with suppliers who can deliver the best quality.

5. **Improve constantly and forever the system of production and service.**
   Improvement is not a one-time effort; managers must lead the way to continuous improvement of quality, productivity, and customer satisfaction.

6. **Institute training.**
   Train all organization members to do their jobs consistently well.

7. **Institute leadership.**
   Managers must provide the leadership to help employees do a better job.

8. **Drive out fear.**
   Create an atmosphere in which employees are not afraid to ask questions or to point out problems.

9. **Break down barriers between units.**
   Ensure that people in organizational departments or units do not have conflicting goals and are able to work as a team to achieve overall goals.

10. **Eliminate slogans, exhortations, and targets for the workforce.**
    These alone cannot help anyone do a better job, and they imply that employees could do better if they tried harder; instead, management should provide methods for improvement.

11. **Eliminate numerical quotas.**
    Quotas count only finished units, not quality or methods, and they generally lead to defective goods, wasted resources, and demoralized employees.

12. **Remove barriers to pride in work.**
    Most people want to do a good job but are prevented from doing so by misguided management, poor communication, faulty equipment, defective materials, and other barriers that managers must remove to improve quality.

13. **Institute a vigorous program of education and retraining.**
    Both managers and employees have to be educated in the new quality methods.

14. **Take action to accomplish the transformation.**
    With top-management commitment, have the courage to make the changes throughout the organization that will improve quality.

is high-tech and the workforce emphasis is high-involvement. Management understands that people are the true drivers of improvement.[37]

■ *Customer focus.* Focusing on the customer simply means finding out what customers really want and then providing it. This approach requires casting aside assumptions about customers and relying instead on accurate research. It also requires developing long-term relationships with customers, as Chapter 12 discusses in detail.

■ *Benchmarking.* This element of TQM involves comparing your company's processes and products against the standards of the world's best companies and then working to match or exceed those standards. This process entails rating the manufacturing process, product development, distribution, and other key functions against those of acknowledged leaders; analyzing how

Computer Discount Warehouse's (CDW) Customer Service Web page is dedicated to finding out what customers want so the company can provide it.

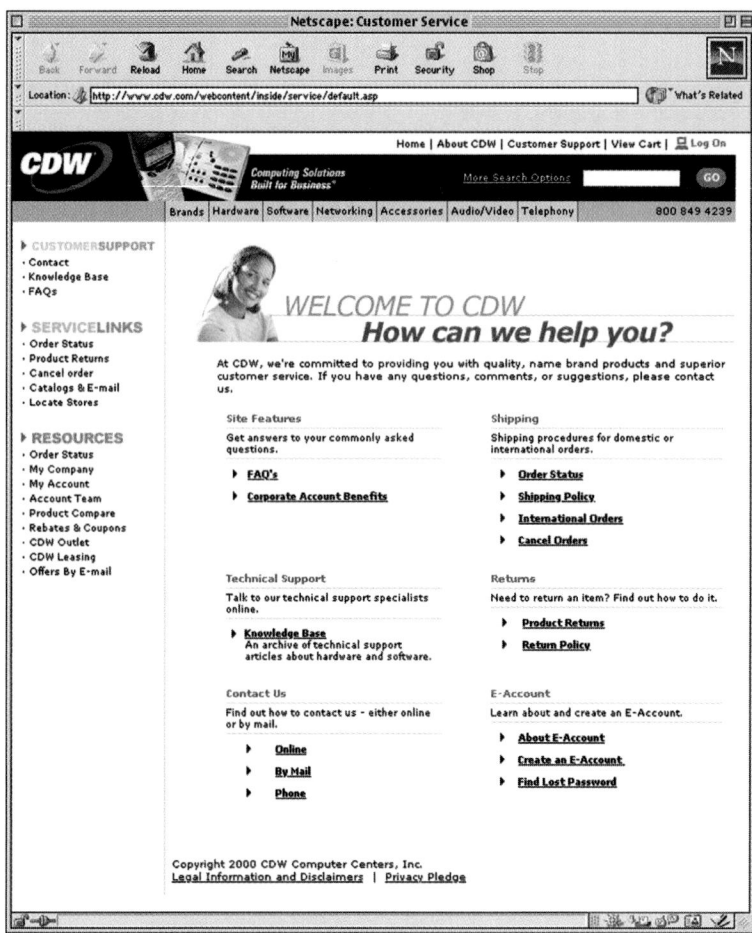

those role models achieve their outstanding results; and then applying that knowledge to make quality improvements. Among the world-class organizations frequently cited as benchmarks for production are Toyota, IBM, and Hewlett-Packard; for distribution, L.L. Bean and FedEx; and for customer service, American Express and Nordstrom.[38]

◼ *Continuous improvement.* This key feature of TQM requires an ongoing effort to reduce defects, cut costs, slash production and delivery times, and offer customers innovative products. Improvements are often small, incremental changes that add up to greater competitiveness over the long run. Because responsibility for such improvement often falls on employees, it becomes management's job to provide employee incentives that will motivate them to want to improve. Geon, a manufacturer of polyvinyl chloride (PVC) resins, motivates its employees through two programs. The first links employee bonuses to improvements in productivity, quality, and manufacturing. In recent years, employees have received an average bonus of 11 percent of their annual salaries through the program. The second program is a success-sharing plan tied to sales gains and stock price. This plan pays out millions of dollars in stock each year. Both initiatives have helped Geon produce 20 percent more PVC resin with 25 percent less manufacturing capacity, putting the company in a much better financial position.[39]

Although many U.S. companies are enjoying greater success as a result of total quality initiatives, a recent study of the largest U.S. companies indicates that such initiatives have fallen short of expectations in a large number of companies. However, the fact that total quality principles played a significant role in propelling Japanese businesses from postwar ruins to pillars of innovation and productivity suggests that much can be gained from the process. What may be lacking in the United States is a firm commitment to TQM. Many companies have jumped on the

TQM bandwagon hoping for a quick boost in performance without really thinking about how to make total quality a part of their long-term strategy. Such companies often fail to provide the necessary managerial and financial support for the programs. In about half of the firms studied, less than 40 percent of workers and less than 80 percent of management teams were sufficiently knowledgeable about TQM philosophy, concepts, and tools.[40] Experts agree that the entire organization—from the bottom all the way up to the CEO—must be actively and visibly involved for TQM to work. Companies that make a halfhearted commitment should not expect dramatic improvements.[41]

At the same time, pursuing TQM is not necessarily a prerequisite for success. Many successful companies do not have TQM programs.[42] However, no business that operates in a competitive environment can expect long-term success unless managers strive to meet customers' needs, improve processes, lower costs, and empower employees in one way or another.

■ MANAGEMENT SKILLS

Managers rely on a number of skills to perform their functions and maintain a high level of quality in their organizations. These skills can be classified into three basic categories: *interpersonal, technical,* and *conceptual.* As managers rise through the organization's hierarchy, they may need to strengthen their abilities in one or more of these skills; fortunately, managerial skills can usually be learned.[43]

LEARNING
OBJECTIVE 7
Identify and explain the three types of managerial skills

Interpersonal Skills

The various skills required to communicate with other people, work effectively with them, motivate them, and lead them are **interpersonal skills.** Because they mainly get things done through people, managers at all levels of the organization use interpersonal skills in countless situations. Encouraging employees to work together toward common goals, interacting with employees and other managers, negotiating with partners and suppliers, developing employee trust and loyalty, and fostering innovation—all these activities require interpersonal skills.

Communication, or exchanging information, is the most important and pervasive interpersonal skill that managers use. Effective communication not only increases the manager's and the organization's productivity but also shapes the impressions made on colleagues, employees, supervisors, investors, and customers. Communication allows you to perceive the needs of these stakeholders (your first step toward satisfying them), and it helps you respond to those needs.[44] Moreover, as the workforce becomes more and more diverse, managers will need to adjust their interactions with others, communicating in a way that considers the different needs, backgrounds, and experiences of people.

interpersonal skills
Skills required to understand other people and to interact effectively with them

Technical Skills

A person who knows how to operate a machine, prepare a financial statement, program a computer, or pass a football has **technical skills;** that is, the individual has the knowledge and ability to perform the mechanics of a particular job. Technical skills are most important at lower organizational levels because managers at these levels work directly with employees who are using the tools and techniques of a particular specialty, such as automotive assembly or computer programming. Still, twenty-first-century managers must have a strong technology background. They must find new computer applications that can complete daily work routines faster or provide more accurate information sooner.

Managers at all levels use **administrative skills,** which are the technical skills necessary to manage an organization. Administrative skills include the abilities to make schedules, gather information, analyze data, plan, and organize. Managers often develop such skills through education and then improve them by working in one or more functional areas of an organization, such as accounting or marketing.[45] Project management skills are becoming an increasingly important administrative skill. Managers must know how to start a project or work assignment from scratch, map out each step in the process to its successful completion, develop project costs and timelines, and establish checkpoints at key project intervals.

technical skills
Ability and knowledge to perform the mechanics of a particular job

administrative skills
Technical skills in information gathering, data analysis, planning, organizing, and other aspects of managerial work

Conceptual Skills

conceptual skills
Ability to understand the relationship of parts to the whole

Managers need **conceptual skills** to see the organization as a whole, in the context of its environment, and to understand how the various parts interrelate. Conceptual skills are especially important to top managers. These managers are the strategists who develop the plans that guide the organization toward its goals. Entrepreneurs such as Steve Case use their conceptual skills to acquire and analyze information, identify both problems and opportunities, understand the competitive environment in which their companies operate, develop strategies, and make decisions.

decision making
Process of identifying a decision situation, analyzing the problem, weighing the alternatives, choosing an alternative and implementing it, and evaluating the results

A key managerial activity requiring conceptual skills is **decision making,** a process that has five distinct steps: (1) recognizing the need for a decision, (2) identifying, analyzing, and defining the problem or opportunity, (3) generating alternatives, (4) selecting an alternative and implementing it, and (5) evaluating the results. Managers monitor the results of decisions over time to see whether the chosen alternative works, whether any new problem or opportunity arises because of the decision, and whether a new decision must be made (see Exhibit 6.8).[46]

Keep in mind that a company's managerial structure defines the way decisions are made. Today's flatter organizations, for example, allow information to flow more freely among all levels of the organization, and they push decision making down to lower organizational levels. As Chapter 7 discusses in detail, more and more organizations are empowering their employees and teams by giving them increasing discretion over work-related issues.[47] This is especially true for e-businesses whose organizational and management structures must facilitate independent decision-making flexibility, risk taking, and open communication.

EXHIBIT 6.8

GREATEST MANAGEMENT DECISIONS EVER MADE

Great decisions change things. Here are some of the greatest management decisions made in the twentieth century.

Coca-Cola
During WWII, Robert Woodruff, president of Coca-Cola, committed to selling bottles of Coke to members of the armed services for a nickel a bottle. Customer loyalty never came cheaper.

Diners Club
In 1950, when Frank McNamara found himself in a restaurant with no money, he came up with the idea of the Diners Club Card. The first credit card changed the nature of buying and selling throughout the world.

Holiday Inn
When the Wilson family of Memphis went on a motoring vacation, they discovered it was not much fun staying in motels that were either too expensive or too slovenly. So Kemmons Wilson built his own. The first Holiday Inn opened in Memphis in 1952.

Honda
When Honda arrived in America in 1959 to launch its big motor bikes, customers weren't keen on their problematic performance. However, they did admire the little Supercub bikes Honda's managers used. So Honda bravely changed direction and transformed the motorbike business overnight.

Weight Watchers
When Jean Nidetch was put on a diet by the Obesity Clinic at New York Department of Health, she invited six dieting friends to meet in her apartment every week. In 1961 she created Weight Watchers and launched the slimming industry.

CNN
Ignoring market research, Ted Turner launched the Cable News Network in 1980. No one thought a 24-hour news network would work.

Sony
Sony chief Akito Morita noticed that young people liked listening to music wherever they went. So in 1980 he and the company developed what became the Walkman. There was no need for market research, because according to Morita, "The public does not know what is possible. We do."

Tylenol
When Johnson & Johnson pulled Tylenol from store shelves in 1982 after capsules were found to be poisoned, the company put customer safety before corporate profit. And it provided a lesson in media openness.

Dell
In 1984 Michael Dell decided to sell PCs direct and built to order. Now everybody in the industry is trying to imitate Dell Computer's strategy.

FOCUSING ON E-BUSINESS TODAY

Seven Habits of Highly Effective E-Managers

Think fast. The pace of the Web is breathless. To gain a competitive edge, e-managers must be more entrepreneurial, spontaneous, and team oriented than yesterday's managers. They must be willing to make fast decisions with far less data and analysis than they had in the old economy. And they must rely on their instincts to process information quickly—because in the e-world, there simply isn't time for day-to-day decisions to go up and down a traditional corporate hierarchy.

LEARNING OBJECTIVE @ 8

Highlight the seven habits of highly effective e-managers

What does it take to be an effective e-manager? In addition to the traditional managerial skills, e-managers must practice seven habits to succeed in the e-world.

1. MAKE CUSTOMER OBSESSION A TOP PRIORITY

In the old economy, businesses could comfortably take three to six months to conduct customer surveys and perform other types of marketing research. In the e-world, this process must accelerate because customers change their minds with a click of the mouse. Companies must quickly learn what their customers want so that they can make their Web sites more productive and engaging to the people who use them daily. E-leaders must focus on improving the customer's total experience with the company, whether customers do business by e-mail, via Web site, by phone, via automated teller machine, by kiosk, by pager, via smart card, or in person.

2. FLATTEN THE ORGANIZATIONAL STRUCTURE

The traditional command-and-control style of management that worked in the old economy is no longer effective for conducting e-business. Successful e-businesses turn the corporate hierarchy upside down. Senior people learn from their juniors, old-timers learn from newcomers, and orders issued from the top are replaced by ideas spreading from any part of the organization. A flatter, more flexible organizational structure allows employees to receive the information they need to make fast decisions. "We don't want any employee to be more than three levels away from any other," says Jeffrey Killeen, CEO of Forbes.com. (Corporate organizational structures are discussed in detail in Chapter 7.)

3. PLAN OFTEN

In the old economy, strategic planning was an annual event. But in the fast-paced e-world, strategic planning must be an ongoing event. Otherwise, by the time you've gotten through the annual strategic planning process, your competitor will have gained the upper hand. The task of creating an e-strategy begins with a series of questions. E-managers must continually ask: What is the Internet doing to our industry and customers? Should we enter new businesses? Exit existing ones? Are acquisitions necessary? Possible? How can we increase the value we deliver to customers? How are people, products, and services going to change? Which core competencies will be most valuable in the e-business environment? What Internet opportunities and threats exist?

4. COMMUNICATE THE E-VISION

All effective leaders have a vision. But leaders blazing the Internet trail are faced with the perpetual challenge of selling their vision both internally (to employees) and externally (to customers). Moreover, they must communicate the e-vision throughout the entire organization to keep all its parts aligned. You have to make people *really* understand, emotionally and logically, that transforming into an

E-BUSINESS OPPORTUNITIES AND THREATS MANAGERS SAY ARE MOST IMPORTANT

OPPORTUNITIES	RANK
Improving customer service	1
Gaining access to new customers	2
Enhancing brand awareness	3
Creating new revenue sources	4
Reducing operating costs	5
Introducing innovative pricing	6
THREATS AND CHALLENGES	**RANK**
Data integrity and security	1
Intensified competition	2
Loss of key personnel to others	3
Downward pressure on prices	4
Cannibalizing their main business	5
Increased customer turnover	6

e-business is different from all other company initiatives, as David S. Pottruck, co-CEO of Charles Schwab can attest.

Faced with employee resistance to converting more of the discount brokerage's business to the Net, Pottruck took dramatic action: He assembled nearly 100 of his senior managers at the base of the Golden Gate Bridge in San Francisco in October 1997, handed them jackets emblazoned with the phrase, "Crossing the Chasm," then led them in a march across the bridge—and, symbolically, into the Internet Age. "We wanted to do something dramatic to help people understand what a big deal this was," said Pottruck. "This was not a new product or a new Web site. This was the beginning of the reinvention of our company. There was no turning back." Schwab's Net strategy has paid off big time. The company now ranks number one among online trading companies in stock trading volume.

5. BE WILLING TO TAKE RISKS

Successful e-businesses have innovative leaders who are willing to take risks. They invent new approaches and constantly try new things to stay ahead. George Sheehan, CEO of online grocer Webvan, is pumping millions of dollars into building a network of large automated warehouses—all on the unproven premise that vast groups of shoppers will point and click their way through weekly grocery lists.

However, according to author and management guru Gary Hamel, only 15 percent of U.S. CEOs are currently taking full advantage of the Web to reinvent their companies. Most are either experimenting with the Internet or contemplating using it in some way for their business. At some point, e-managers must stop kicking the tires and start driving. They must stop worrying about making a mistake, because in the e-world it's better to be unsafe than sorry.

6. WORK HARD AND COMMIT

Every manager must work hard these days, regardless of organization type. But e-managers typically tally 80 to 100 hours each week, and they must learn how to do more with less. Many e-business "failures" are a result of leaders who only pay lip service to Internet initiatives. To be successful, "you've got to have your CEO behind the Web effort 100 percent," says one Dell spokesperson. "Michael Dell is our strongest online advocate . . . His commitment to the Web has been complete and total. He feels that the Web is our most strategic weapon—our strongest differentiation point."

7. LEARN NEW TECHNOLOGICAL SKILLS

E-business leaders must master the new technological skills that are crucial for survival in today's competitive environment. They must by Web-savvy. And they must understand the possibilities of the Web and of other forms of technology from both a business and consumer perspective.

Still, integrating these new technologies into an organization is no easy task. Today, even the most successful e-businesses are just beginning to grapple with the challenges that the Internet, e-business, and new technologies create for their organizations.[48]

SUMMARY OF LEARNING OBJECTIVES

1. **Define the four basic management functions.**
   The four management functions are (1) planning—establishing objectives and goals for the organization and translating them into action plans; (2) organizing—arranging resources to carry out the organization's plans; (3) leading—influencing and motivating people to work effectively and willingly toward company goals; and (4) controlling—monitoring progress toward organizational goals, resetting the course if goals or objectives change in response to shifting conditions, and correcting deviations if goals or objectives are not being attained.

2. **Outline the seven tasks of the strategic planning process.**
   The strategic planning process begins with a clear vision for the company's future. This vision is then translated into a mission statement so it can be shared with all members of the organization. Next, managers assess the company's strengths, weaknesses, opportunities, and threats; develop forecasts; and analyze the competition. Then they use this information to establish goals and objectives. Finally they translate these goals and objectives into action plans.

3. **Explain the purpose of a mission statement.**
   A mission statement defines why the organization exists, what it does, what it hopes to achieve, and the principles it will abide by to meet its goals. It is used to bring clarity of focus to members of the organization and to provide guidelines for the adoption of future projects.

4. **List the benefits of setting long-term goals and objectives.**
   Goals and objectives establish long- and short-range targets that help managers fulfill the company's mission. Setting appropriate goals increases employee motivation, establishes standards by which individual and group performance can be measured, guides employee activity, and clarifies management's expectations.

5. **Cite three leadership styles and explain why no one style is best.**
   Three leadership styles are autocratic, democratic, and laissez-faire (also called free-rein). Each may work best in a different situation: autocratic when quick decisions are needed, democratic when employee participation in decision making is desirable, and laissez-faire when fostering creativity is a priority. Good

leaders are flexible enough to respond with the best approach for the situation.

6. **Clarify how total quality management (TQM) is changing the way organizations are managed.**
Total quality management is both a management philosophy and a management process that focuses on delivering quality to customers. TQM redirects management to focus on four key elements: (1) Employee involvement includes team building and soliciting employee input on decisions. (2) Customer focus involves gathering customer feedback and then acting on that feedback to better serve customers. (3) Benchmarking involves measuring the company's standards against the standards of industry leaders. (4) Continuous improvement requires an ongoing commitment to reducing defects, cutting costs, slashing production and delivery times, and offering customers innovative products.

7. **Identify and explain the three types of managerial skills.**
Managers use (1) interpersonal skills to communicate with other people, work effectively with them, and lead them; (2) technical skills to perform the mechanics of a particular job; and (3) conceptual skills (including decision making) to see the organization as a whole, to see it in the context of its environment, and to understand how the various parts interrelate.

8. **Highlight the seven habits of highly effective e-managers.**
Successful managers of e-businesses make customer obsession a top priority, reduce the number of levels in the organizational structure to encourage communication and allow for faster decision making, plan on a continual basis, communicate the e-vision throughout the organization, take risks, work hard and commit fully to Internet initiatives, and learn new technological skills, which include a firm knowledge of the Internet's potential.

KEY TERMS

administrative skills (167)
autocratic leaders (159)
coaching (160)
conceptual skills (168)
contingency leadership (160)
controlling (162)
core competence (154)
crisis management (157)
decision making (168)
democratic leaders (159)
first-line managers (158)
goal (156)

interpersonal skills (167)
laissez-faire leaders (159)
leading (158)
management (152)
management pyramid (158)
mentor (160)
middle managers (158)
mission statement (154)
objective (156)
operational plans (156)
organizational culture (162)
organizing (157)

participative management (164)
planning (152)
quality (162)
roles (152)
standards (162)
strategic plans (153)
tactical plans (156)
technical skills (167)
top managers (158)
total quality management (TQM) (164)
vision (153)

TEST YOUR KNOWLEDGE

QUESTIONS FOR REVIEW

1. What is management? Why is it so important?
2. What is forecasting, and how is it related to the planning function?
3. What is the goal of crisis management?
4. What are some common characteristics of effective leaders?
5. Why are interpersonal skills important to managers at all levels?

QUESTIONS FOR ANALYSIS

6. Is the following statement an example of a strategic goal or an objective? "To become the number-one retailer of computers and computer accessories in terms of revenue, growth, and customer satisfaction." Explain your answer
7. How do the three levels of management differ?
8. Why are coaching and mentoring effective leadership techniques?
9. How are the four main elements of total quality management related to the goal of delivering quality to customers?
10. Select an e-business you are familiar with. From a consumer's perspective, what do you think the company's core competence is? Explain your answer.

11. When an organization learns about a threat that could place the safety of its workers or its customers at risk, is management obligated to immediately inform these parties of the threat? Explain your answer.
12. What are your long-term goals? Develop a set of long-term career goals for yourself and several short-term objectives that will help you reach those goals. Make sure your goals are specific, measurable, and time-limited.
13. Do you have the skills it takes to be an effective manager? Find out by taking two online skills tests. Start with the interpersonal Communication Skills Test offered at www.queendom.com/tests/eng/commun_frm.html. Next take the Meyer-Briggs Personality Type Test at the Keirsey Temperament Sorter www.keirsey.com/cgi-bin/newkts.cgi.
14. Using Dell Computer's mission statement in Exhibit 6.3 as a model and the material you learned in Chapter 3, develop a mission statement for a socially responsible company such as Patagonia or Ben & Jerry's.
15. What is the principal difference between a business plan (as discussed in Chapter 4) and a strategic plan?

PRACTICE YOUR KNOWLEDGE

SHARPENING YOUR COMMUNICATION SKILLS

Interview the owner or manager of a local business to learn about the organization's culture, and summarize your findings in a brief memo to your instructor. Some of the questions you might want to ask include:

- How does the company define success?
- How is the company organized, and how do people report to each other?
- How are decisions made? Is the emphasis on individual or group responsibility?
- How do people dress and address each other?
- How are goals and objectives established?
- How are employee learning and innovation encouraged?

HANDLING DIFFICULT SITUATIONS ON THE JOB: COOKING UP PLANS FOR THE UNEXPECTED

A few months ago you landed the most exciting job you could imagine, as a production assistant for Meg McComb, one of the best-known movie food stylists in Hollywood. But some days it's just a little too exciting. Like today. McComb has just been hired to concoct a twelfth-century feast for a period costume drama directed by Kenneth Branagh. That means food for 150 actors that must look authentic and be on the movie set by 1 P.M. tomorrow. McComb is a pro, and you have full confidence in her as she races around the office handing out assignments. You've seen her juggle all kinds of unforeseen problems, such as what to do with a banquet for 150 when shooting is canceled at the last minute (feed it to friends).[49]

Now McComb tosses you a catalog of food suppliers and shouts "asparagus" as she zips onto the next food item in the feast. You know she means asparagus for 150. Luckily, most produce suppliers are here in California, so you are pretty sure you can get fresh, jumbo spears overnight. Aside from worrying about the cost, which you'll just have to pass on to Branagh, you are nervous about what the asparagus will look like and whether it will arrive on time. Failure is definitely not an option. You know that Branagh is depending on your company—and may very well hire another firm for his next movie if things don't work out. All this pressure starts you thinking: Is there a better way the company can prepare for the unexpected?

1. What can you say to convince McComb that the company needs to do a better job of planning? Do you think organizing, leading, and controlling should be taken into consideration as part of this planning process? Why?
2. Do you consider rush projects (like this last-minute order) a crisis? Is crisis management appropriate for such situations? Explain your answers.
3. Knowing that directors are likely to want anything at a moment's notice, what can you, in your role as McComb's assistant, do to better prepare the company for the unexpected?

BUILDING YOUR TEAM SKILLS

A good mission statement should define the organization's purpose and ultimate goals and outline the principles that are to guide managers and employees in working toward those goals. Using library sources such as annual reports or Internet sources such as organizational Web sites, locate mission statements from one not-for-profit organization, such as a school or a charity, and one company with which you are familiar.

Bring these statements to class and, with your team, select four mission statements to evaluate. How many of the mission statements contain all five of the typical components (product or service; primary market; concern for survival, growth, and profitability; managerial philosophy; commitment to quality and social responsibility)? Which components are most often absent from the mission statements you are evaluating? Which components are most often included? Of the mission statements your team is analyzing, which is the most inspiring? Why?

Now assume that you and your teammates are the top management team at each organization or company. How would you improve these mission statements? Rewrite the four mission statements so that they cover the five typical components, show all organization members how their roles are related to the vision, and inspire commitment among employees and managers.

Summarize your team's work in a written or oral report to the class. Compare the mission statement that your team found the most inspiring with the statements that other teams found the most inspiring. What do these mission statements have in common? How do they differ? Of all the inspiring mission statements reported to the class, which do you think is the best? Why? Does this mission statement inspire you to consider working for or doing business with this organization?

EXPAND YOUR KNOWLEDGE

KEEPING CURRENT USING *THE WALL STREET JOURNAL*

Find two articles in *The Wall Street Journal* (print or online editions) that profile two senior managers who lead business or not-for-profit organizations.

1. What experience, skills, and business background do the two leaders have? Do you see any striking similarities or differences in their backgrounds?
2. What kinds of business challenges have these two leaders faced? What actions did they take to deal with those challenges? Did they establish any long-term goals or objectives for their company? Did the article mention a new change initiative?

3. Describe the leadership strengths of each person as they are presented in the articles you selected. Is either leader known as a team builder? Long-term strategist? Shrewd negotiator? What are each leader's greatest areas of strength?

DISCOVERING CAREER OPPORTUNITIES

If you become a manager, how much of your day will be spent performing each of the four basic functions of management? This is your opportunity to find out. Arrange to shadow a manager (such as a department head, a store manager, or a shift supervisor) for a few hours. As you observe, categorize the manager's activities in terms of the four management functions and note how much time each activity takes. If observation is not possible, interview a manager in order to complete this exercise.

1. How much of the manager's time is spent on each of the four management functions? Is this the allocation you expected?

2. Ask whether this is a typical work day for this manager. If it isn't, what does the manager usually do differently? During a typical day, does this manager tend to spend most of the time on one particular function?

3. Of the four management functions, which does the manager believe is most important for good organizational performance? Do you agree?

EXPLORING THE BEST OF THE WEB

URLs for all Internet exercises are provided at the Web site for this book, www.prenhall.com/mescon. When you log on to the text Web site, select Chapter 6, then select "Student Resources," click on the name of the featured Web site, and follow the detailed navigational directions to complete these exercises.

Catch the Buzz, page 152

The online Management and Technology Dictionary can help you identify business terms that are unfamiliar to you and can keep you current on management buzzwords. Explore the dictionary to answer the following questions.

1. What is the definition of *dependent demand?* Give an example.

2. What are *knowledge workers,* and what challenges do they present to managers?

3. What is outsourcing, and what are some of its benefits?

Become a Better Manager, page 155

Becoming a good manager involves learning about leadership, time management, knowledge management, and more. Information at ManagementFirst.com provides you with in-depth information on a variety of important management issues.

1. What is knowledge management, and why is it important? What are two common types of knowledge?

2. Why is emotional intelligence important? Can emotional intelligence be learned?

3. What are the two main types of strategic alliance, and why do companies form strategic alliances?

Linking to Organizational Change, page 162

Leaders in all kinds of organizations must be able to effectively handle change management. Luckily, help is available at the Web site of the Management Assistance Program for Nonprofits. Read the Basic Context for Organizational Change and then explore some of the links before answering these questions.

1. What is the distinction between organizational change and smaller-scale change in an organization? What are some examples of organization-wide change?

2. Why do employees and managers often resist change? What can top management do to address such resistance to organizational change?

3. What mistakes do managers frequently make in their attempts to sell managing change? What three positive steps can management take to facilitate change?

Explore on Your Own

Review these chapter-related Web sites on your own to learn more about management.

1. The MBA Program Information site, www.mbainfo.com, offers details on more than 2,250 MBA programs from 1,160 universities, business schools, and management colleges in 126 countries.

2. Women's Studies Section: Women and Business, www.csulb.edu/~sbsluss/Women_and_Business.html, is a resource for women in business with links to associations, directories, discussion forums, journals, and statistical sources.

3. Links to America's Most Admired Companies are provided by *Fortune* magazine, www.fortune.com/fortune/mostadmired. Find out who's hot, who's not, and how the list was created.

A CASE FOR CRITICAL THINKING

■ *The Ax Falls on Sunbeam's Chainsaw Al*

It seemed like the perfect match: a self-confident CEO with a successful history of saving troubled companies, and one of America's largest household appliance makers in desperate need of restructuring. That was the case when Al Dunlap arrived at Sunbeam back in 1996, vowing to turn around the company within a year. True to his word, Dunlap turned Sunbeam inside out and upside down—and nearly destroyed the company with his autocratic, "chainsaw" management style.

RAMBO IN PINSTRIPES

Dunlap had garnered high praise from corporate America by restructuring and selling such companies as Scott Paper Company and Crown-Zellerbach. In every case, Dunlap engineered the turnarounds by axing thousands of jobs, slashing costs, and setting up

the company for a quick sale. Confident and boastful, Dunlap called himself "Rambo in Pinstripes." Everyone else called him "Chainsaw Al."

Banking on Dunlap's successful track record, Sunbeam recruited the experienced CEO to jump-start its sagging sales and to reverse its declining profits on such products as electric blankets and barbecue gear. Within days after arriving at Sunbeam, Dunlap developed an ambitious tactical plan for a company turnaround.

ON THE CHOPPING BLOCK

The first step of Dunlap's strategy focused on cutting costs. He axed half of the company's 12,000 employees and outsourced as many functions as possible. Then he eliminated 87 percent of Sunbeam's products and closed or sold two-thirds of the company's 18 manufacturing facilities. Hoping to increase sales of new products, Dunlap expanded Sunbeam's product mix by acquiring Coleman, the camping-gear maker; First Alert, the smoke alarm producer; and Signature Brands, the maker of Mr. Coffee.

SLICED AND DICED

At first, Dunlap's strategy seemed to be on track. Sunbeam reduced overall annual expenses by $225 million and racked up big sales and profits during 1997. But Dunlap's chainsaw had sliced deep into the company, leaving shortages of experienced employees and wreaking havoc on day-to-day operations. Factories suffered from a lack of parts for production and a shortage of workers to produce goods and fulfill orders. Furthermore, his downsizing efforts often backfired, creating additional costs. After firing the entire computer staff, for example, Dunlap hired contract workers who demanded higher pay rates—including some workers who had just been fired. Moreover, Dunlap's ax fell just as Sunbeam was upgrading its computer system. No backups existed, and Sunbeam couldn't track shipments or orders. Computers were down for months, forcing employees to manually invoice such major customers as Wal-Mart and Sears Roebuck.

CRUSHING PRESSURE

To make matters worse, Sunbeam executives recognized that Dunlap had set unrealistic goals for the company. Chances were slim that Sunbeam could meet Dunlap's goal of boosting profit margins to 20 percent, considering the current 2.5 percent margin on household appliances. Moreover, to meet Dunlap's goal of doubling revenues to $2 billion within the next year, Sunbeam needed to increase sales five times faster than the competition. And the chief executive's aim of generating $600 million in new product sales would require extraordinary sales of every new product.

Still, Chainsaw Al refused to acknowledge any weakness in his tactical plans. Instead of motivating employees to meet his goals, he threatened to place their jobs on the chopping block if they failed to perform. Managers, in turn, passed that intimidation down the line. Although his actions crushed morale and created unbearable stress on employees, Dunlap continued to exert excruciating pressure on his staff. "I don't get heart attacks; I give them," he boasted.

THE AX FALLS

But Dunlap's boastful ways halted when Sunbeam reported a first-quarter loss for 1998. Then Sunbeam's board of directors made an alarming discovery: Dunlap hadn't executed a turnaround at all. Sunbeam had persuaded retailers to buy seasonal goods like gas grills before the normal selling season by offering hefty discounts, easy payment terms, and the promise to hold the goods in Sunbeam's warehouses for later delivery. Although the "bill-and-hold" strategy allowed Dunlap to show an impressive sales jump for 1997, the gimmick backfired in the subsequent year. Stocked to the max, retailers crushed any prospects of future sales.

So Sunbeam's board of directors turned the chainsaw on Dunlap, immediately firing the CEO. Although Dunlap's strategy of axing jobs and selling assets had worked at other companies, his autocratic management style and chainsaw approach almost destroyed Sunbeam. In fact, Chainsaw Al left Sunbeam in shambles. With $898 million in losses for 1998, the household appliance maker continues its struggle to rebuild the business that Dunlap's chainsaw nearly shattered.

CRITICAL THINKING QUESTIONS

1. Why were Dunlap's goals unrealistic for Sunbeam?

2. Was Dunlap's slice-and-dice plan a long-term or short-term strategy? Please explain.

3. Review the four key elements of TQM and comment on each of these elements with respect to Dunlap's turnaround strategy.

4. Go to Chapter 6 of this text's Web site at www.prenhall.com/mescon and click on the hot link to get to the Sunbeam Web site. Follow the online instructions to answer the following questions: Why would Sunbeam post information about the company's past performance on its Web site? How is Sunbeam correcting its past mistakes? How does Sunbeam plan to drive future growth?

VIDEO CASE AND EXERCISES

■ *Managing Mad Dogs and Englishmen*

SYNOPSIS

When Nick Cohen and a friend entered some of their creative work in industry contests, they called their nonexistent advertising agency Mad Dogs and Englishmen (www.maddogsandenglishmen.com). Cohen used the name when he started his own agency not long afterward. Although the company had just 2 employees when it first opened, the workforce grew to 7 in the first year and 14 in the second year. Today, 30 managers and employees work for Cohen and his partners, paying close attention to the needs of consumers so they can develop innovative and effective advertising campaigns for MovieFone and other clients. Company managers pay attention to all four management functions, but they leave some leeway in their planning to allow for spur-of-the-moment changes and creativity. Despite differences in leadership styles between the founder and the company president, both share a com-

mitment to total quality management, which keeps Mad Dogs and Englishmen operating at peak performance.

EXERCISES
Analysis

1. Which of the three leadership styles does Nick Cohen appear to have adopted? Which does Robin Danielson appear to have adopted?

2. Why do the creative directors who manage the writing of advertisements at Mad Dogs and Englishmen need interpersonal skills as well as conceptual skills?

3. Which of the management skills does Nick Cohen seem to be emphasizing, and why?

4. Why is the controlling function essential for an advertising agency such as Mad Dogs and Englishmen?

5. How does Mad Dogs and Englishmen's mission provide a foundation for day-to-day management?

Application

How does Mad Dogs and Englishmen combine the four elements of total quality management to encourage the development of innovative and attention-getting advertising campaigns for its clients?

Decision

Imagine that Nick Cohen finds himself in disagreement with the creative department regarding the tone of a new television commercial. He believes the tone is too strong and would be less appealing to viewers than a more subtle approach. However, he doesn't want to cause long-term friction by simply overriding the decisions of the creative team. What should he do?

Communication

As a creative director for Mad Dogs and Englishmen, you think that your client would see a significant sales increase if it boosted its advertising budget to allow you to make a much splashier commercial. Draft a one-page memo to the client in which you make a case for your recommendation.

Integration

Chapter 1 identified three general types of competition. Which of these apply to Man Dogs and Englishmen? Who are the company's competitors?

Ethics

If a client did not want Mad Dogs and Englishmen to submit its advertisements to industry contests, would it be ethical for Cohen to submit the materials using a fictitious agency name?

Debate

Most managers seek to grow their companies year after year, but Mad Dogs and Englishmen is not most companies. Form a team of four students, with two students debating in favor of planned growth at Mad Dogs and Englishmen and two students taking the opposing view. Hold a brief classroom debate and then ask the class to vote on which side presented the most persuasive arguments.

Teamwork

In a team of three students, devise an idea for advertising a product of your team's choice. How would your team assess the product's strengths, weaknesses, opportunities, and threats? How would you organize to write and produce this advertisement? What standards would you set for the control cycle? As a team, prepare a brief report or presentation to explain your ideas to the class.

Online Research

Use Internet sources to find out about Mad Dogs and Englishmen's latest clients and awards. Has the company continued to grow? How do the current activities embody Nick Cohen's vision for the company? See Component Chapter A, Exhibit A.1, for search engines to use in doing your research.

M Y P H L I P   C O M P A N I O N   W E B   S I T E

Learning Interactively

Visit the myPHLIP Web site at www.prenhall.com/mescon. For Chapter 6, take advantage of the interactive "Study Guide" to test your chapter knowledge. Get instant feedback on whether you need additional studying. Read the "Current Events" articles to get the latest on chapter topics, and complete the exercises as specified by your instructor. Expand your learning with a visit to the "Research Area." There you will find a wealth of information you can use to complete your course assignments.

M A S T E R I N G   B U S I N E S S   E S S E N T I A L S

Go to the "Leadership" and "Concepts of Strategic Management" episodes on the Mastering Business Essentials interactive, video-enhanced CD-ROM. Assist the management team at CanGo (an e-business start-up) with its strategic planning process. Then, witness how Liz, the company's founder, meets the challenge of leading two very different groups.

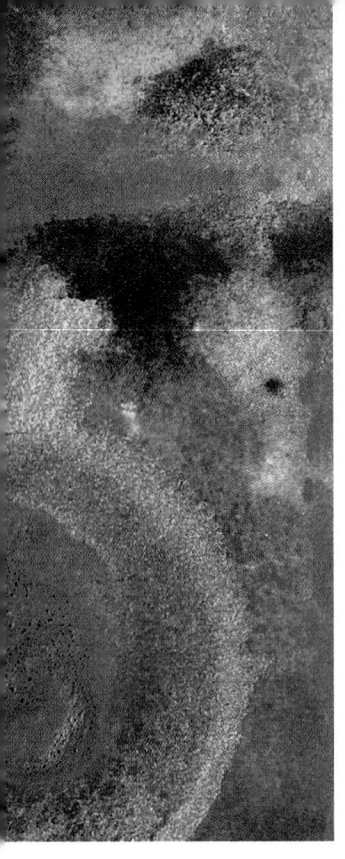

ORGANIZATION, TEAMWORK, AND COMMUNICATION

7

LEARNING OBJECTIVES

After studying this chapter, you will be able to

1. Discuss the function of a company's organization structure
2. Explain the concepts of accountability, authority, and delegation
3. Define four types of departmentalization
4. Describe the five most common forms of teams
5. Highlight the advantages and disadvantages of working in teams
6. List the characteristics of effective teams
7. Review the five stages of team development
@ 8. Highlight 10 strategies for smart Web writing

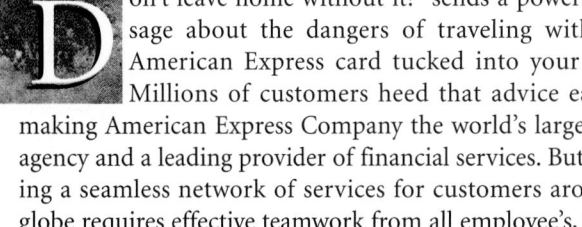

Inside Business
TODAY

American Express has continuously transformed itself to become a leading global travel, financial, and network services provider.

DON'T LEAVE HOME TO GO TO WORK: AMERICAN EXPRESS COMPANY'S VIRTUAL ENVIRONMENT
w w w . a m e r i c a n e x p r e s s . c o m

Don't leave home without it!" sends a powerful message about the dangers of traveling without an American Express card tucked into your pocket. Millions of customers heed that advice each day, making American Express Company the world's largest travel agency and a leading provider of financial services. But providing a seamless network of services for customers around the globe requires effective teamwork from all employee's, whether they're working from the New York headquarters or telecommuting from home in Los Angeles. David House makes sure that his employees have everything they need to work together and contribute to the company's success—even if they don't leave home to go to work.

As president of American Express Global Establishment Services, the division that recruits new American Express merchants, House encourages his staff members to work together to achieve their goals. But uniting employees in sales offices across the country demands more than a few rousing pep talks. To build a successful team, House uses technology to promote communication within his division. He provides every employee with access to the company's highly efficient computer network. He offers employees the opportunity to work from home, eliminating the time, expense, and stress of daily commutes to the office. Furthermore, he contracts with outside sources to set up the home offices, arranging for everything from installation of phone lines to home safety checks for such things as carbon monoxide levels and availability of fire extinguishers. He even provides employees with computer training, software and hardware setup, and selection and delivery of office furniture to complete their virtual office environment.

Nevertheless, House knows that effective teams need more than equipment to produce quality work. They need to communicate. House's telecommuters conduct virtual meetings with colleagues around the world, taking advantage of e-mail and videoconferencing to brainstorm and collaborate on projects. Several units in House's division use a buddy system that requires remote workers to chat with on-site colleagues by phone every morning, covering topics from new customers to office politics. Other telecommuters report to a local or regional office several times each week, meeting with co-workers for specific purposes. Office meetings have predetermined agendas and follow regular schedules to reduce wasted meeting time and to allow team members to communicate face-to-face.

To encourage team members to work together, House commends outstanding team efforts. Each year, he awards lavish prizes to the top 75 sales reps for their contributions, and he makes a special point to recognize team members who share information with their peers. For example, House acknowledged one outstanding rep who focused on her team's regional sales objectives instead of her own quotas. She not only accompanied other reps on sales calls in her region, but made an effort to share her sales strategies by distributing copies of her winning presentations to every rep in the country.

House's knack for developing and using virtual teams at American Express has indeed paid off. Not only do virtual teams save the company time and travel costs, but they have increased employee productivity and improved customer satisfaction rates. Moreover, by using virtual teams, House has reduced the number of field offices from 85 to 7, resulting in additional cost savings for the company.[1]

LEARNING OBJECTIVE 1

Discuss the function of a company's organization structure

organization structure
Framework enabling managers to divide responsibilities, ensure employee accountability, and distribute decision-making authority

organization chart
Diagram showing how employees and tasks are grouped and where the lines of communication and authority flow

informal organization
Network of informal employee interactions that are not defined by the formal structure

DESIGNING AN EFFECTIVE ORGANIZATION STRUCTURE

Whether you're working from home as a member of David House's virtual team or in a traditional office setting, the decision-making authority of employees and managers is supported by the company's **organization structure.** This structure helps the company achieve its goals by providing a framework for managers to divide responsibilities, effectively distribute the authority to make decisions, coordinate and control the organization's work, and hold employees accountable for their work. In some organizations, this structure is a relatively rigid, vertical hierarchy like the management pyramid described in Chapter 6. In other organizations, such as American Express, teams of employees and managers from across levels and functions work together to make decisions and achieve the organization's goals.[2]

When managers design the organization's structure, they use an **organization chart** to provide a visual representation of how employees and tasks are grouped and how the lines of communication and authority flow. Exhibit 7.1 shows the organization chart for a grocery store chain. An organization chart depicts the official design for accomplishing tasks that lead to achieving the organization's goals, a framework known as the *formal organization*. Every company also has an **informal organization**—the network of interactions that develop on a personal level among workers. Sometimes the interactions among people in the informal organization parallel their relationships in the formal organization, but often interactions transcend formal boundaries. Crossing formal boundaries can help establish a more pleasant work environment, but it can also undermine formal work processes and hinder a company's ability to get things done.[3]

How do companies design an organization structure, and which organization structure is the most effective? As management guru Peter Drucker sees it, "There is no such thing as one right organization. Each has distinct strengths, distinct limitations, and specific applications." Drucker further notes that managers of the future will require a toolbox full of organization structures and will have to select the right tool for each specific task: on some tasks employees will be working in teams; on others, under a traditional command-and-control hierarchy.[4] Nevertheless, four factors must be taken into consideration when designing an effective organization structure: work specialization, chain of command, vertical organization, and horizontal organization and coordination.

EXHIBIT 7.1

ORGANIZATION CHART FOR FOOD LION GROCERY STORE CHAIN

At first look, organization charts may appear very similar. In fact, the traditional model of an organization is a pyramid in which numerous boxes form the base and lead up to fewer and fewer boxes on higher levels, ultimately arriving at one box at the top. A glance at Food Lion's organization chart reveals who has authority over whom, who is responsible for whose work, and who is accountable to whom.

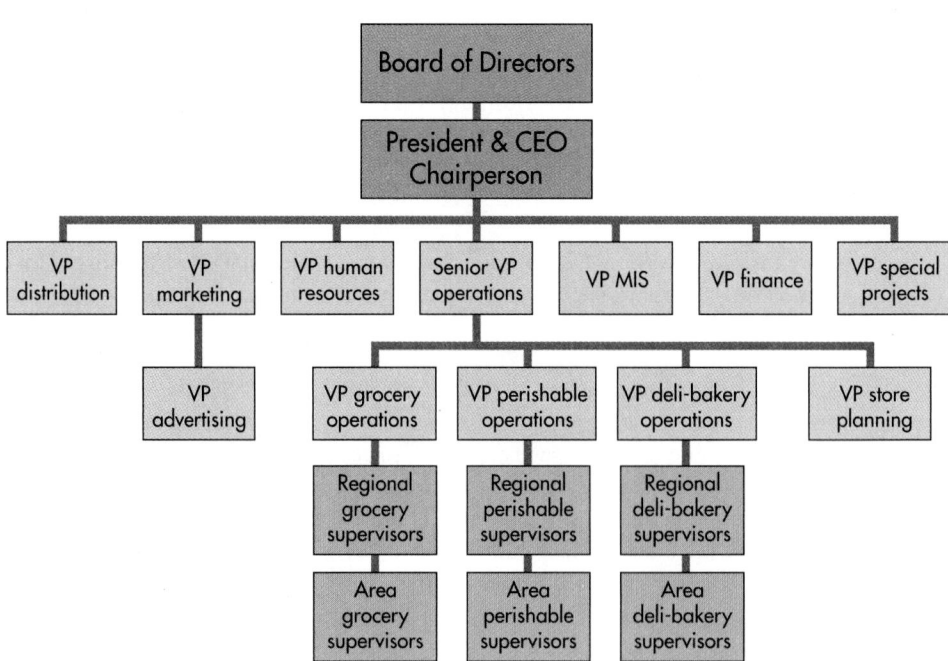

Work Specialization

Before designing an organizational structure, management must first decide on the optimal level of **work specialization**—the degree to which organizational tasks are broken down into separate jobs.[5] Few employees have the skills to perform every task a company needs. Therefore, work specialization can improve organizational efficiency by enabling each worker to perform tasks that are well defined and that require specific skills. For example, in 1776 Scottish economist Adam Smith found that if each of 10 workers went through every step needed to make a pin, the entire group could make 200 pins a day. However, if each worker performed only a few steps and no one made a pin from start to finish, the same 10 workers could make 48,000 pins a day. When employees concentrate on the same specialized tasks, they can perfect their skills and perform their tasks more quickly. A classic example of work specialization is the automobile assembly line.

However, organizations can overdo specialization. If a task is defined too narrowly, employees may become bored with performing the same tiny, repetitive job over and over. They may also feel unchallenged and alienated. Managers must think carefully about how specialized or how broad each task should be. In fact, a growing number of companies are balancing specialization and employee motivation through teamwork. This approach enables group members to decide how to break down a complex task, and it allows employees to rotate among the jobs that the team is collectively responsible for. The team then shares credit for the results, and workers feel that they have created something of value. The team approach to organization is discussed in more depth later in this chapter.

Chain of Command

Besides incorporating work specialization into an organizational structure, companies must also establish a **chain of command,** the unbroken line of authority that connects each level of management with the next level. The chain of command helps organizations function smoothly by making two things clear: who is responsible for each task, and who has the authority to make official decisions.

All employees have a certain amount of **responsibility**—the obligation to perform the duties and achieve the goals and objectives associated with their jobs. As they work toward the organization's goals, employees must also maintain their **accountability,** their obligation to report the results of their work to supervisors or team members and to justify any outcomes that fall below expectations. Managers ensure that tasks are accomplished by exercising **authority,** the power to make decisions, issue orders, carry out actions, and allocate resources to achieve the organization's goals. Authority is vested in the positions that managers hold, and it flows down through the management pyramid. **Delegation** is the assignment of work and the transfer of authority and responsibility to complete that work.[6]

Look again at Exhibit 7.1. The senior vice president of operations delegates responsibilities to the vice presidents of grocery operations, perishable operations, deli-bakery operations, and store planning. These department heads have the authority to make certain decisions necessary to fulfill their roles, and they are accountable to the senior VP for the performance of their respective divisions. In turn, the senior VP is accountable to the company CEO.

The simplest and most common chain-of-command system is known as **line organization** because it establishes a clear line of authority flowing from the top down, as Exhibit 7.1 depicts. Everyone knows who is accountable to whom, as well as which tasks and decisions each is responsible for. However, line organization sometimes falls short because the technical complexity of a firm's activities may require specialized knowledge that individual managers don't have and can't easily acquire. A more elaborate system called **line-and-staff organization** was developed out of the need to combine specialization with management control. In such an organization, managers in the chain of command are supplemented by functional groupings of people known as *staff,* who provide advice and specialized services but who are not in the line organization's chain of command (see Exhibit 7.2).

Span of Management The number of people a manager directly supervises is called the **span of management** or *span of control.* When a large number of people report directly to one person, that person has a wide span of management. This situation is common in **flat organizations** with relatively few levels in the management hierarchy. Sun Microsystems, Visa, and Oticon (a hearing-aid

work specialization
Specialization in or responsibility for some portion of an organization's overall work tasks; also called division of labor

LEARNING OBJECTIVE 2

Explain the concepts of accountability, authority, and delegation

chain of command
Pathway for the flow of authority from one management level to the next

responsibility
Obligation to perform the duties and achieve the goals and objectives associated with a particular position

accountability
Obligation to report results to supervisors or team members and to justify outcomes that fall below expectations

authority
Power granted by the organization to make decisions, take actions, and allocate resources to accomplish goals

delegation
Assignment of work and the authority and responsibility required to complete it

line organization
Chain-of-command system that establishes a clear line of authority flowing from the top down

line-and-staff organization
Organization system that has a clear chain of command but that also includes functional groups of people who provide advice and specialized services

span of management
Number of people under one manager's control; also known as span of control

flat organizations
Organizations with a wide span of management and few hierarchical levels

EXHIBIT 7.2

SIMPLIFIED LINE-AND-STAFF STRUCTURE

A line-and-staff organization divides employees into those who are in the direct line of command (from the top level of the hierarchy to the bottom) and those who provide staff (or support) services to line managers at various levels. Staff reports directly to top management.

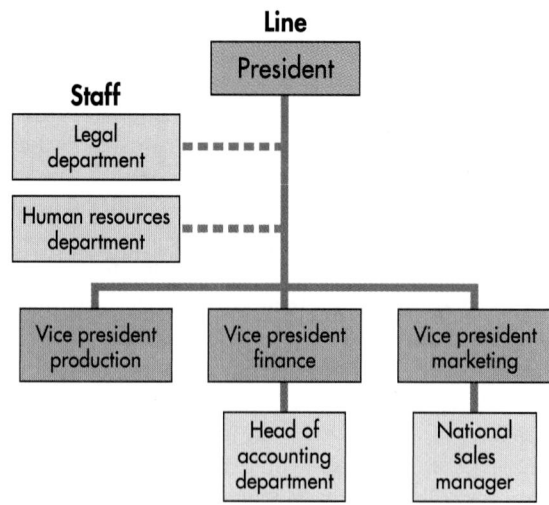

manufacturer in Denmark) are all companies that have flat organizations. British Petroleum (BP) is also amazingly flat and lean for an organization with $70 billion in revenues, 53,000 employees, and 90 business units that span the globe. At BP there is no level between the general managers of the business units and the group of nine operating executives who oversee the businesses.[7]

tall organizations
Organizations with a narrow span of management and many hierarchical levels

In contrast, **tall organizations** have many hierarchical levels, usually with only a few people reporting to each manager. In such cases, the span of management is narrow (see Exhibit 7.3). General Motors has traditionally had a tall organization structure with as many as 22 layers of management. However, as are many companies, GM is flattening its organization structure by delegating some middle management responsibilities to work teams.[8]

No formula exists for determining the ideal span of management. How well people work together is more important than the number of people reporting to one person. Still, several factors affect the number of people a manager can effectively supervise, including the manager's personal skill and leadership ability, the skill of the workers, the motivation of the workers, and the nature of the job. In general, employees who are highly skilled or who are trained in many work tasks don't require as much supervision as employees who are less skilled.

centralization
Concentration of decision-making authority at the top of the organization

decentralization
Delegation of decision-making authority to employees in lower-level positions

Centralization Versus Decentralization   Organizations that focus decision-making authority near the top of the chain of command are said to be centralized. **Centralization** benefits a company by utilizing top management's rich experience and broad view of organizational goals. Both line organizations and line-and-staff organizations tend to be centralized.

However, the trend in business today is to decentralize. **Decentralization** pushes decision-making authority down to lower organizational levels—such as department heads—while control over essential companywide matters remains with top management. Implemented properly, decentralization can stimulate responsiveness because decisions don't have to be referred up the hierarchy.[9] Consider General Electric. Managers at each of GE's 13 independent businesses have $25 million they can spend as they see fit without having to get the approval of the board of directors or the CEO. Giving each core business more decision-making authority has helped GE achieve tremendous growth in sales and profits.[10]

However, decentralization does not work in every situation or in every company. At times, strong authority from the top of the chain of command may be needed to keep the organization focused on immediate goals. Managers should select the level of decision making that will most effectively serve the organization's needs given the individual circumstances.[11]

Vertical Organization

vertical organization
Structure linking activities at the top of the organization with those at the middle and lower levels

Choosing between a vertical and a horizontal model is one of the most critical decisions a company can make. Many organizations use a traditional vertical structure to define formal relationships and the division of tasks among employees and managers. **Vertical organization** links the activities at the top of the organization with those at the middle and lower levels.[12] This structure also helps managers delegate authority to positions throughout the organization's hierarchy.

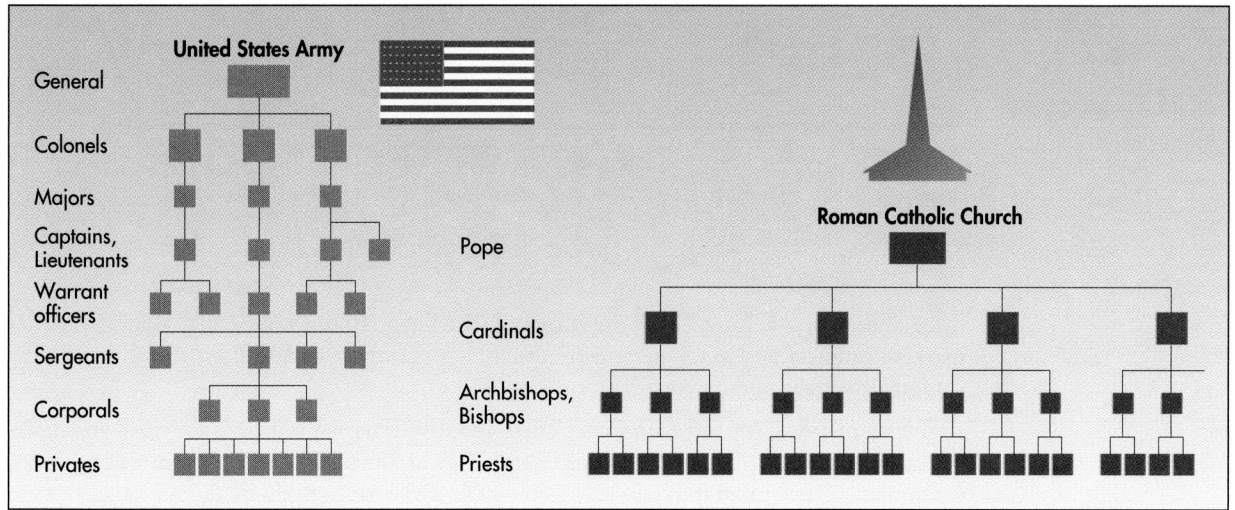

EXHIBIT 7.3

TALL VERSUS FLAT ORGANIZATIONS

A tall organization has many levels with a narrow span of management at each level so that relatively few people report to each manager on the level above them. In contrast, a flat organization has relatively few levels with a wide span of management so that more people report to each manager.

Besides authority, the structure defines specific jobs and activities across vertical levels. In a vertical organization, companies define jobs and activities by using **departmentalization**—the arrangement of activities into logical groups that are then clustered into larger departments and units that form the total organization.[13] Four common ways of departmentalizing are by function, division, matrix, and network. An organization may use more than one method of departmentalization, depending on its particular needs.

Departmentalization by Function **Departmentalization by function** groups employees according to their skills, resource use, and expertise. Common functional departments include marketing, human resources, operations, finance, research and development, and accounting, with each department working independently of the others.[14] As depicted in Exhibit 7.1, functional departmentalization is highly centralized. In this structure, work doesn't flow through the company, it bounces around from department to department.

Splitting the organization into separate functional departments offers several advantages: (1) Grouping employees by specialization allows for the efficient use of resources and encourages the development of in-depth skills; (2) centralized decision making enables unified direction by top management; and (3) centralized operations enhance communication and the coordination of activities within departments. Despite these advantages, functional departmentalization can create communication barriers between departments, thereby slowing response to environmental change, hindering effective planning for products and markets, and overemphasizing work specialization (which alienates employees).[15] For these reasons, most large companies have abandoned the functional structure in the past decade or so.

Departmentalization by Division **Departmentalization by division** establishes self-contained departments that encompass all the major functional resources required to achieve their goals—such as research and design, manufacturing, finance, and marketing. These departments are typically formed according to similarities in product, process, customer, or geography.

■ *Product divisions.* Many organizations use a structure based on **product divisions**—grouping around each of the company's products or family of products. The logic behind this organizational structure is that each department can manage all the activities needed to develop, manufacture, and sell a particular product or product line.

■ *Process divisions.* **Process divisions,** also called *process-complete* departments, are based on the major steps of a production process. For example, a table-manufacturing company might have

departmentalization
Grouping people within an organization according to function, division, matrix, or network

LEARNING OBJECTIVE 3
Define four types of departmentalization

departmentalization by function
Grouping workers according to their similar skills, resource use, and expertise

departmentalization by division
Grouping departments according to similarities in product, process, customer, or geography

product divisions
Divisional structure based on products

process divisions
Divisional structure based on the major steps of a production process

EXHIBIT 7.4

CUSTOMER DIVISIONS

Acer America's organizational structure supports the company's mission to be more customer focused.

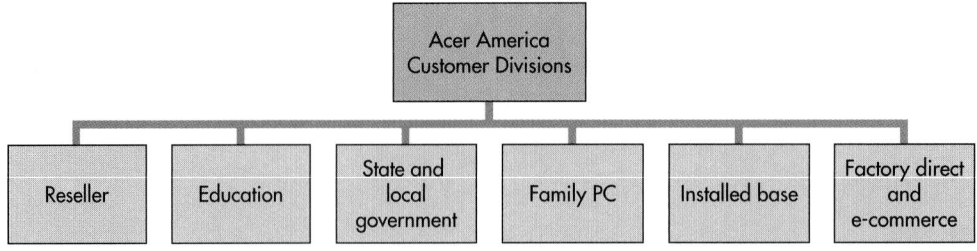

customer divisions
Divisional structure that focuses on customers or clients

geographic divisions
Divisional structure based on location of operations

three divisions, one for each phase of manufacturing a table. Astra/Merck, a company that markets antiulcer and antihypertension drugs, is organized around six process divisions, including drug development and distribution.[16]

■ *Customer divisions.* The third approach, **customer divisions,** concentrates activities on satisfying specific groups of customers. For example, Acer America, manufacturer of computer equipment, restructured into six customer-centric divisions to facilitate the fulfillment of the company's mission—to provide customers with the highest level of quality, reliability, and support (see Exhibit 7.4).[17]

■ *Geographic divisions.* **Geographic divisions** enable companies spread over a national or an international area to respond more easily to local customs, styles, and product preferences. For example, Quaker Oats has two main geographic divisions: (1) U.S. and Canadian Grocery Products and (2) International Grocery Products. Each division is further subdivided to allow the company to focus on the needs of customers in specific regions.

Divisional departmentalization offers both advantages and disadvantages. First, because divisions are self-contained, they can react quickly to change, thus making the organization more flexible. In addition, because each division focuses on a limited number of products, processes, customers, or locations, divisions can offer better service to customers. Moreover, top managers can focus on problem areas more easily, and managers can gain valuable experience by dealing with the various functions in their divisions. However, divisional departmentalization can also increase costs by duplicating the use of resources such as facilities and personnel. Furthermore, poor coordination between divisions may cause them to focus too narrowly on divisional goals and neglect the organization's overall goals. Finally, divisions may compete with one another for employees, money, and other resources, causing rivalries that hurt the organization as a whole.[18]

departmentalization by matrix
Assigning employees to both a functional group and a project team (thus using functional and divisional patterns simultaneously)

Departmentalization by Matrix **Departmentalization by matrix** is a structural design in which employees from functional departments form teams to combine their specialized skills (see Exhibit 7.5). This structure allows the company to pool and share resources across divisions and functional groups. The matrix may be a permanent feature of the organization's design, or it may be established to complete a specific project. Consider Black & Decker, which formed a matrix organization in the early 1990s. Departments such as mechanical design, electrical engineering, and model shop assigned employees with specific technical skills to work on product-development projects in such categories as saws, cordless appliances, and woodworking.[19]

EXHIBIT 7.5

DEPARTMENTALIZATION BY MATRIX

In a matrix structure, each employee is assigned to both a functional group (with a defined set of basic functions, such as production manager) and a project team (which consists of members of various functional groups working together on a project, such as bringing out a new consumer product).

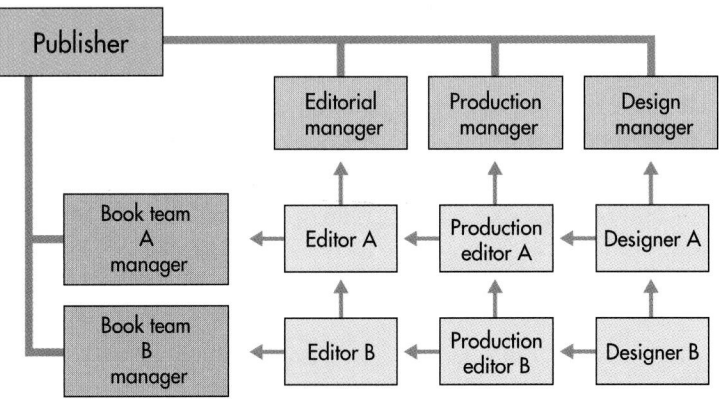

Best of the Web Best of the Web Best of

GETTING ORGANIZED

Want an inside peek at how real organizations are structured? A growing number of government agencies and companies are posting their organization charts on the Web for the world to see. Some show no names, just listing job titles in the individual boxes. Others, including the City of Sacramento, name names as well as positions. Looking at Sacramento's organization chart will show you the chain of command, the span of management, and the departmentalization method. And clicking on any name will lead you to detailed contact information for that part of the organization. In short, this chart is a virtual who's who for Sacramento government.
www.sacto.org/cityorg.htm

Matrix departmentalization can help big companies function like smaller ones by allowing teams to devote their attention to specific projects or customers without permanently reorganizing the company's structure. But matrix structures are not without drawbacks. One problem of a matrix structure is that team members usually continue to report to their functional department heads as well as to a project team leader. Another drawback is that authority tends to be more ambiguous and up for grabs, creating power struggles and other interpersonal conflicts. Black & Decker realized this soon after it implemented the matrix organization. The manager with the most authority was always the functional department head, and the project team did not really hold any control. The company has since redesigned its organization structure, which is now based on product divisions that employ teams of people from many functional areas.[20]

In a matrix organization, excellent communication and coordination are necessary to avoid conflicts. In addition, companies may find it difficult to coordinate the tasks of diverse functional specialists so that projects are completed efficiently.[21] However, because it facilitates the pooling of resources across departments, a matrix organization can also enable a company to respond better to changes in the business environment.

Departmentalization by Network **Departmentalization by network** is a method of electronically connecting separate companies that perform selected tasks for a headquarters organization. Also called a *virtual organization,* the network organization *outsources* engineering, marketing, research, accounting, production, distribution, or other functions. This means that the organization hires other organizations under contracts to handle one or more of those functions. In fact, companies such as Nike, Liz Claiborne, and Dell Computer sell hundreds of millions of dollars' worth of products even though they outsource most of their manufacturing. As these companies have learned, the network approach is especially appropriate for international operations, allowing every part of the business to draw on resources no matter where in the world they may be.[22]

A network structure can also enable small companies to compete on a large scale. For example, Barbara Schrager operates Attainment Marketing Partners with only one employee. By using a virtual staff of designers and copywriters who work under contract on specific projects, she is able to create marketing, advertising, and public relations campaigns for major clients in New York.[23]

As Barbara Schrager knows, a network structure is extremely flexible because it gives companies the ability to hire whatever services are needed and then change them after a short time. The limited hierarchy required to manage a network organization also permits the company to make decisions and react to change quickly. Additional advantages are that the organization can continually redefine itself, and a lean structure usually means employees have greater job variety and satisfaction. However, the network approach lacks hands-on control, because the functions are not in one location or company. Also, if one company in the network fails to deliver, the headquarters organization could suffer or even go out of business. Finally, strong employee loyalty and team spirit are less likely to develop, because the emotional connection between the employee and the organization is weak.[24]

departmentalization by network
Electronically connecting separate companies that perform selected tasks for a small headquarters organization

Horizontal Organization

More and more businesses are transforming their traditional bureaucratic and hierarchical vertical structure into a horizontal organization.[25] The horizontal organization rejects the separation of people and work into functional departments by using the team concept to flatten hierarchies and integrate the many tasks of a business into a few smooth-flowing operations. The biggest benefit of horizontal organization is that everyone works together. Employees from various departments or functions are grouped around a few organization-wide, cross-functional core processes, and they are responsible for an entire core process from beginning to end. Employees who create new product designs, for instance, work with engineers and marketing personnel to make sure the designs can be manufactured and marketed.

A typical core process group might include staff from finance, research and development, manufacturing, and customer service. All core processes lead to one objective: creating and delivering something of value to the customer. The Occupational Safety and Health Administration (OSHA), the U.S. agency charged with protecting the safety of workers, recently organized its 1,400 field employees around two basic core processes to benefit customers: (1) preventing workplace accidents and (2) responding to accidents and complaints.[26]

While some companies completely dismantle their vertical structure to create horizontal organizations, others prefer a hybrid organization—one that combines vertical and horizontal functions. In these firms, core processes are supported by organization-wide functional departments such as human resources and finance. The Xerox corporation, for example, organized its business operations around five core processes based on five types of products. The core processes are supported by two companywide vertical operations: technology management and customer service. This way researchers are not constrained by specific markets, and customers face only one customer service representative even if they buy different product types.[27]

By now you can see that whether it uses a traditional vertical or an innovative horizontal organization structure, every organization must coordinate activities and communication among its employees. **Horizontal coordination** facilitates communication across departments without the need to go up and down the vertical chain of command. Horizontal coordination also gives employees the opportunity to share their views, which strengthens their willingness to understand, support, and implement innovative ideas. Without horizontal coordination, functional departments would be isolated from one another, and they would be unable to align their objectives.[28] Of course, one way to inject horizontal coordination into a vertical structure is by working in teams.

A modular office layout such as this one at Continental Packaging Products encourages an open communication climate and the sharing of information among employees.

horizontal coordination
Coordinating communication and activities across departments

■ WORKING IN TEAMS

While the vertical chain of command is a tried-and-true method of organizing for business, it is limited by the fact that decision-making authority is often located high up the management hierarchy. Companies that organize vertically may become slow to react to change, and high-level managers may overlook many great ideas for improvement that originate in the lower levels of the organization. As this section will show, the value of involving employees from all levels and functions of the organization in the decision-making process can not be overstated. As a result, most companies today use a variety of team formats in day-to-day operations.

According to a recent survey of Fortune 1,000 executives, 83 percent said their firms are working in teams or moving in that direction.[29] Even though this approach has many advantages, shifting to a team structure often requires a fundamental shift in the organization's culture. For one thing, management must show strong support for team concepts by empowering teams to make important decisions about the work they do. For another, teams must have clear goals that are tied to the company's strategic goals, and their outcomes need to be measured and compared with benchmarks. Moreover, employees must be motivated to work together in teams. Such motivation requires extensive training and a compensation system that is based, at least in part, on team performance.

Earth and Environmental Services in San Francisco encourages its employees to work collaboratively so they can benefit from the knowledge of other team members.

What Is a Team?

A **team** is a unit of two or more people who work together to achieve a goal. Teams differ from work groups in that work groups interact primarily to share information and to make decisions to help one another perform within each member's area of responsibility. In other words, the performance of a work group is merely the summation of all group members' individual contributions.[30] By contrast team members have a shared mission and are collectively responsible for their work. By coordinating their efforts, team members generate a positive synergy and achieve a level of performance that exceeds what would have been accomplished if members had worked individually.[31]

team
A unit of two or more people who share a mission and collective responsibility as they work together to achieve a goal

At Microsoft, almost all work is completed in teams. Two factors that have made Microsoft teams so successful are clear goals and strong leadership.[32] Although the team's goals may be set either by the team or by upper management, it is the job of the team leader to make sure the team stays on track to achieve those goals. Team leaders are often appointed by senior managers, but sometimes they emerge naturally as the team develops. Westinghouse Hanford, an electric power company, also uses teams. As one employee notes, by using teams, "we come up with better ideas, work more cohesively and find better ways to solve problems." All of these factors help companies become more flexible and respond more quickly to the challenges of the competitive global workplace.[33]

Types of Teams

The type, structure, and composition of individual teams within an organization all depend on the organization's strategic goals and the objective for forming the team. The five most common forms of teams are *problem-solving teams, self-managed teams, functional teams, cross-functional teams,* and *virtual teams.* Such classifications are not unique. For example, a problem-solving team may also be self-managed and cross-functional. Similarly, some teams are established on an informal basis. That is, they are designed to encourage employee participation but do not become part of the formal organization structure.

LEARNING OBJECTIVE 4

Describe the five most common forms of teams

Problem-Solving Teams The most common type of informal team is the **problem-solving team.** Also referred to as *quality circles,* problem-solving teams usually consist of 5 to 12 employees from the same department who meet voluntarily to find ways of improving quality, efficiency, and the work environment. Any recommendations they come up with are then submitted to management for approval.[34] Land Rover, a manufacturer of luxury sport-utility vehicles, was able to save millions of dollars, improve productivity, and sell more vehicles by using problem-solving teams.[35] If such teams are able to successfully contribute to the organization, as Land Rover's were, they may evolve into formal teams, a change that represents a fundamental shift in the way the organization is structured.

problem-solving team
Informal team of 5 to 12 employees from the same department who meet voluntarily to find ways of improving quality, efficiency, and the work environment

Self-Managed Teams Self-managed teams take problem-solving teams to the next level. As the name implies, **self-managed teams** manage their own activities and require minimum supervision. Typically they control the pace of work and determination of work assignments. Fully

self-managed teams
Teams in which members are responsible for an entire process or operation

COMPETING IN THE GLOBAL MARKETPLACE

MERVYN'S CALLS SWAT TEAM TO THE RESCUE

The situation is tense. The stakes are high. Time is short. So who do you call for help if you're an executive at Mervyn's California facing the Christmas rush or the loss of a key manager? You call the company's SWAT team, of course.

Mervyn's is a department store chain with 32,000 employees and 270 locations in 14 states. Its SWAT team consists of 19 managers who race from division to division, usually at a moment's notice, to help with the kinds of crises that inevitably erupt in a high-pressure retail environment. SWAT team members must have experience in at least one specific discipline: buying, merchandising, or advertising. Assignments are as short as a week or as long as six months. Even though SWAT team members don't travel around in armored vehicles, life on the team can be pretty hectic.

This group of highly trained people can be deployed anywhere in the company's buying divisions, at any time, wherever they are needed. They can perform jobs quickly and efficiently, without a long learning curve. They help the company manage its unpredictable staffing needs, meet the requirements of its erratic markets, and seize unanticipated opportunities.

Originally created as an experiment to fill in for vacancies created by managers working flextime or on fam-ily leave, Mervyn's SWAT team has become something bigger. It has become an effective vehicle for moving talent around the company. SWAT team members aren't just good at learning fast; they're good at sharing what they've learned in other departments. And because team members have had a lot of exposure to various areas in the company, they're the most valued and highly sought after employees in the organization.

It's no surprise that the team's biggest problem is turnover: Members are frequently hired away for full-time positions by managers whom they've impressed. In fact, joining the SWAT team has become a high-priority career tactic for young people who want to move up or for veterans who want a change of pace.

■ QUESTIONS FOR CRITICAL THINKING

1. How could Mervyn's parent company, Target, use the SWAT team concept to benefit all its stores—Target, Dayton's, Hudson's, and Marshall Fields? (Hint: Think about the benefits of cross-functional teams.)

2. How does Mervyn's benefit from using the SWAT team concept on both a short-term and a long-term basis?

self-managed teams select their own members. As you might imagine, many managers are reluctant to embrace self-managed teams because it requires them to give up significant control.

At SEI Investments, administrator for $121 billion in investor assets, the defining unit of operation is the self-managed team. Finding itself indistinguishable from other competitors, SEI took a wrecking ball to the traditional corporate pyramid and formed 140 self-managed teams to speed up reaction time, innovate more quickly, and get closer to the customer. Some SEI teams are permanent, designed to serve big customers or important markets; others are temporary—they come together to solve a problem and disband when their work is done. This flexible team structure is supported by having all office furniture on wheels so that teams can easily create their own work areas. In fact, employees move their desks so often that SEI has created software to map every employee's location.[36]

functional teams
Teams whose members come from a single functional department and that are based on the organization's vertical structure

Functional Teams **Functional teams,** or *command teams,* are organized along the lines of the organization's vertical structure and thus may be referred to as vertical teams. They are composed of managers and employees within a single functional department. For example, look again at Exhibit 7.1. Functional teams could be formed in Food Lion's marketing, human resources, and finance departments. The structure of a vertical team typically follows the formal chain of command. In some cases, the team may include several levels of the organizational hierarchy within the same functional department.[37]

cross-functional teams
Teams that draw together employees from different functional areas

Cross-Functional Teams In contrast to functional teams, **cross-functional teams,** or horizontal teams, draw together employees from various functional areas and expertise. In many cross-

Best of the Web Best of the Web Best of

BUILDING TEAMS IN THE CYBER AGE

If you want to learn more about building effective teams, you can read many excellent books on the subject. But you might be surprised by just how much information on team building you can find on the Internet. One good starting point is the Self Directed Work Teams page. This site's designers are passionate about teamwork, and they want to make it easier for people to work effectively in teams. Read the Frequently Asked Questions (FAQs) to better understand the site's purpose. Then explore some of the links to discover more about teams and teamwork.

www.users.ids.net/~brim/sdwth.html

functional teams, employees are cross-trained to perform a variety of tasks. At Pillsbury the most experienced workers can handle 23 different jobs.[38] Cross-functional teams inject horizontal coordination into a typical vertical organization structure in several ways: (1) they facilitate the exchange of information between employees, (2) they generate ideas for how to best coordinate the organizational units that are represented, (3) they encourage new solutions for organizational problems, and (4) they aid the development of new organizational policies and procedures.[39]

Boeing, for instance, used hundreds of "design-build" teams that integrated design engineers and production workers to develop its 777 airplane.[40] Cross-functional teams have also become a way of life at Chrysler (now DaimlerChrysler). Under the old setup, the company relied on functional departmentalization in which each function (such as design, engineering, manufacturing, and so on) handed the results of its work to the next function in essentially a sequential process that was time-consuming, costly, and prone to errors. Now team members from various functions work simultaneously and communicate frequently to ensure that the shape of a particular body part will accommodate adjacent components. As a result, the company has reduced the time it takes to bring a new vehicle to market from five years to less than three years.[41] Cross-functional teams such as the ones used at Boeing and DaimlerChrysler can take on a number of formats:

■ *Task forces.* A **task force** is a type of cross-functional team formed to work on a specific activity with a completion point. Several departments are usually involved so that all parties who have a stake in the outcome of the task are able to provide input. However, once the goal has been accomplished, the task force is disbanded.[42] Saint Francis Hospital in Tulsa, Oklahoma, established a task force to find ways to reduce the cost of supplies. The team members came from many departments, including surgery, laboratory, nursing, financial planning, administration, and food service. The team not only helped the hospital save money by curbing supply waste but also generated excitement among hospital employees about working together for common goals.[43]

task force
Team of people from several departments who are temporarily brought together to address a specific issue

■ *Special-purpose teams.* Like task forces, **special-purpose teams** are created as temporary entities to achieve specific goals. However, special-purpose teams are different because they exist outside the formal organization hierarchy. Such teams remain a part of the organization but they have their own reporting structures, and members view themselves as separate from the normal functions of the organization. A special-purpose team might be used to develop a new product when complete creative freedom is needed. By operating outside the formal organization, the team would be able to test new ideas and new ways of accomplishing tasks.[44]

special-purpose teams
Temporary teams that exist outside the formal organization hierarchy and are created to achieve a specific goal

■ *Committees.* In contrast to a task force, a **committee** usually has a long life span and may become a permanent part of the organization structure. Committees typically deal with regularly recurring tasks. For example, a grievance committee may be formed as a permanent resource for handling employee complaints and concerns. Because many committees require official representation in order to achieve their goals, committee members are usually selected on the basis of their titles or positions rather than their personal expertise.

committee
Team that may become a permanent part of the organization and is designed to deal with regularly recurring tasks

Virtual Teams **Virtual teams,** such as those used by David House's division, are groups of physically dispersed members who work together to achieve a common goal. Virtual team members

virtual teams
Teams that use communication technology to bring geographically distant employees together to achieve goals

Managing a virtual team involves training team members to communicate effectively using different types of technology.

communicate using a variety of technological formats and devices such as company intranets, e-mail, electronic meeting software, and telephones. Occasionally, they may meet face-to-face. The biggest advantage of virtual teams is that members are able to work together even if they are thousands of miles and time zones apart. At Texas Instruments, for instance, microchip engineers in India, Texas, and Japan are able to pool ideas, design new chips, and collaboratively debug them—even though they're 8,000 miles and 12 time zones apart.[45]

The three primary factors that differentiate virtual teams from face-to-face teams are the absence of nonverbal cues, limited social context, and the ability to overcome time and space constraints. Because virtual teams must function with less direct interaction among members, team members require certain competencies. Among these are project-management skills, time management skills, ability to use electronic communication and collaboration technologies, ability to work across cultures, and heightened interpersonal awareness.[46]

In many cases, virtual teams are as effective as teams that function under a single roof. At British Petroleum, for example, virtual teams link workers in the Gulf of Mexico with teams working in the eastern Atlantic and around the globe. By using a virtual team network, the company has decreased the number of helicopter trips to offshore oil platforms, has avoided refinery shutdowns because technical experts at other locations were able to handle problems remotely, and has experienced a significant reduction in construction rework, among other benefits.[47] (For additional discussion of virtual teams and organizations, consult Part 3 of this text's online supplement, E-Business in Action, at www.prenhall.com/mescon.)

ADVANTAGES AND DISADVANTAGES OF WORKING IN TEAMS

LEARNING OBJECTIVE   5

Highlight the advantages and disadvantages of working in teams

Even though teams can play a vital role in helping an organization reach its goals, they are not appropriate for every situation. Managers must weigh both the advantages and the disadvantages of teams when deciding whether to use them.[48]

One of the biggest advantages of teams is that the interaction of the participants leads to higher-quality decisions based on the combined intelligence of the group. Moreover, teams lead to increased acceptance of a solution. Team members who participate in making a decision are more likely to enthusiastically support the decision and encourage others to accept it.[49] Another big advantage is that teams have the potential to unleash vast amounts of creativity and energy in workers. Motivation and performance are often increased as workers share a sense of purpose and mutual accountability. Teams can also fill the individual worker's need to belong to a group. Furthermore, they can reduce boredom, increase feelings of dignity and self-worth, and reduce stress and tension between workers. Finally, teams empower employees to bring more knowledge and skill to the tasks they perform and thereby often lead to greater efficiency and cost reduction. Organizational flexibility is another key benefit of using teams in the workplace. Such flexibility means employees are able to exchange jobs, workers can be reallocated as needed, managers can delegate more authority and responsibility to lower-level employees, and the company can meet changing customer needs more effectively.

In short, using teams can add up to more satisfied employees performing higher-quality work that helps the organization achieve its goals. Studies of individual industries show that companies using teamwork to organize, plan, and control activities enjoy greater productivity, increased profits, fewer defects, lower employee turnover, less waste, and even increased market value.[50] Consider the results these companies achieved by using employee teams: Kodak has halved the amount of time it takes to move a new product from the drawing board to store shelves; Tennessee Eastman, a division of Eastman Chemical, increased labor productivity by 70 percent; Texas Instruments increased revenues per employee by over 50 percent; and Ritz-Carlton Hotels jumped to the top of the J. D. Power and Associates consumer survey of luxury hotels.[51]

Although teamwork has many advantages, it also has a number of potential disadvantages. For one thing, power within the organization sometimes becomes realigned with teams. Successful teams mean that fewer supervisors are needed, and usually fewer middle and front-line managers. Adjusting to their changing job roles, or even to the loss of their jobs, is understandably difficult for many people. Another potential disadvantage is **free riders**—team members who don't contribute their fair share to the group's activities because they aren't being held individually accountable for their work. The free-ride attitude can lead to the nonfulfillment of certain tasks. Still another drawback to teamwork is the high cost of coordinating group activities. Aligning schedules, arranging meetings, and coordinating individual parts of a project can eat up a lot of time and money. Moreover, a team may develop *groupthink,* a situation in which pressures to conform to the norms of the group cause members to withhold contrary or unpopular opinions. Groupthink can hinder effective decision making because some possibilities will be overlooked.[52]

free riders
Team members who do not contribute sufficiently to the group's activities because members are not being held individually accountable for their work

◼ CHARACTERISTICS OF EFFECTIVE TEAMS

Team size is one factor that contributes to a team's overall effectiveness. The optimal size for teams is generally thought to be between 5 and 12 members. Teams smaller than 5 may be lacking in skill diversity and may, therefore, be less effective at solving problems. Teams of more than 12 may be too large for group members to bond properly and may discourage some members from sharing their ideas. Larger groups are also prone to disagreements and factionalism because so many opinions must be considered, thus making the team leader's job more difficult. Moreover, studies have shown that turnover and absenteeism are higher in larger teams because members tend to feel that their presence makes less of a difference.

LEARNING
OBJECTIVE   6
List the characteristics of effective teams

For a team to be successful over time, it must also be structured to accomplish its task and to satisfy its members' needs for social well-being. Effective teams usually fulfill both requirements with a combination of members who assume one of four roles: task specialist, socioemotional role, dual role, or nonparticipator. People who assume the *task-specialist role* focus on helping the team reach its goals. In contrast, members who take on the *socioemotional role* focus on supporting the team's emotional needs and strengthening the team's social unity. Some team members are able to assume *dual roles,* contributing to the task and still meeting members' emotional needs. These members often make effective team leaders. At the other end of the spectrum are members who are *nonparticipators,* contributing little to reaching the team's goals or to meeting members' emotional needs. Exhibit 7.6 outlines the behavior patterns associated with each of these roles.

Other characteristics of effective teams include the following:[53]

◼ *Clear sense of purpose.* Team members clearly understand the task at hand, what is expected of them, and their role on the team.

◼ *Open and honest communication.* The team culture encourages discussion and debate. Team members speak openly and honestly, without the threat of anger, resentment, or retribution. They listen to and value feedback from others. As a result, all team members participate.

◼ *Creative thinking.* Effective teams encourage original thinking, considering options beyond the usual.

◼ *Focused.* Team members get to the core issues of the problem and stay focused on key issues.

◼ *Decision by consensus.* All decisions are arrived at by consensus. No easy, quick votes are taken.

Of course, learning effective team skills takes time and practice, so many companies now offer employees training in building their team skills. At Saturn, for example, every team member goes through a minimum of 92 hours of training in problem solving and people skills. Saturn teaches team members how to reach a consensus point they call "70 percent comfortable but 100

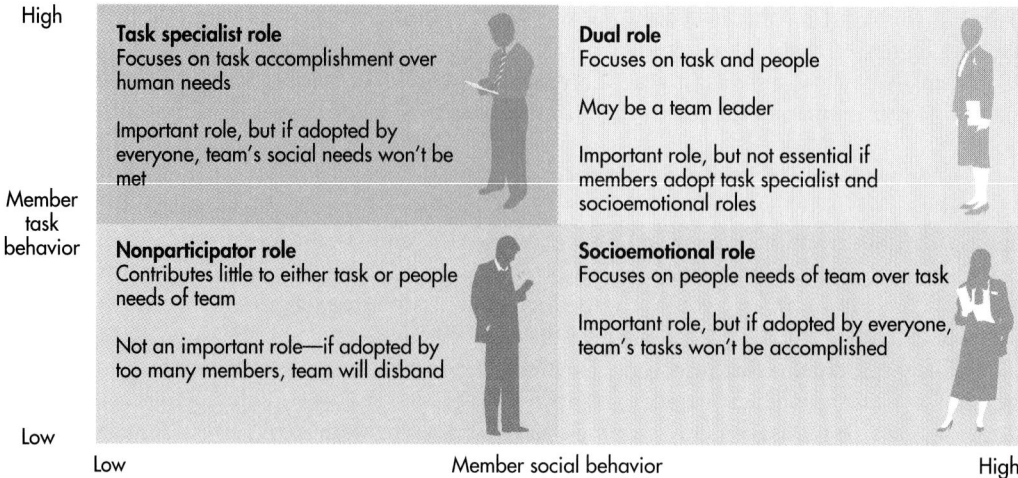

EXHIBIT 7.6

TEAM MEMBER ROLES

Team members assume one of these four roles. Members who assume a dual role often make effective team leaders.

percent supportive." At that level of consensus, everybody supports the solution.[54] For a brief review of characteristics of effective teams, see Exhibit 7.7.

Five Stages of Team Development

LEARNING OBJECTIVE 7
Review the five stages of team development

Developing an effective team is an ongoing process. Like the members who form them, teams grow and change as time goes by. You may think that each team evolves in its own way. However, research shows that teams typically go through five definitive stages of development: forming, storming, norming, performing, and adjourning.[55]

- *Forming.* The forming stage is a period of orientation and breaking the ice. Members get to know each other, determine what types of behaviors are appropriate within the group, identify what is expected of them, and become acquainted with each other's task orientation.

- *Storming.* In the storming stage, members show more of their personalities and become more assertive in establishing their roles. Conflict and disagreement often arise during the storming stage as members jockey for position or form coalitions to promote their own perceptions of the group's mission.

- *Norming.* During the norming stage, these conflicts are resolved, and team harmony develops. Members come to understand and accept one another, reach a consensus on who the leader is, and reach agreement on what each member's roles are.

- *Performing.* In the performing stage, members are really committed to the team's goals. Problems are solved, and disagreements are handled with maturity in the interest of task accomplishment.

- *Adjourning.* Finally, if the team has a limited task to perform, it goes through the adjourning stage after the task has been completed. In this stage, issues are wrapped up and the team is dissolved.

cohesiveness
A measure of how committed the team members are to their team's goals

As the team moves through the various stages of development, two things happen. First, the team develops a certain level of **cohesiveness,** a measure of how committed the members are to the team's goals. The team's cohesiveness is reflected in meeting attendance, team interaction, work quality, and goal achievement. Cohesiveness is influenced by many factors. Two primary factors are competition and evaluation. If a team is in competition with other teams, cohesiveness increases as the team strives to win. In addition, if a team's efforts and accomplishments are recognized by the organization, members tend to be more committed to the team's goals. Strong team cohesiveness generally results in high morale. Moreover, when cohesiveness is coupled with strong management support for team objectives, teams tend to be more productive.

EXHIBIT 7.7

CHARACTERISTICS OF EFFECTIVE TEAMS

Effective teams practice these good habits.

Build a sense of fairness in decision making
√ Encourage debate and disagreement without fear of reprisal
√ Allow members to communicate openly and honestly
√ Consider all proposals
√ Build consensus by allowing team members to examine, compare, and reconcile differences
√ Avoid quick votes
√ Keep everyone informed
√ Present all the facts

Select team members wisely
√ Involve stakeholders
√ Limit size to no more the 12 to 15 members
√ Select members with a diversity of views
√ Select creative thinkers

Make working in teams a top management priority
√ Recognize and reward individual and group performance
√ Provide ample training opportunities for employees to develop interpersonal, decision-making, and problem-solving skills
√ Allow enough time for the team to develop and learn how to work together

Manage conflict constructively
√ Share leadership
√ Encourage equal participation
√ Discuss disagreements
√ Focus on the issues, not the people
√ Keep things under control

Stay on track
√ Make sure everyone understands the team's purpose
√ Communicate what is expected of team members
√ Stay focused on the core assignment
√ Develop and adhere to a schedule
√ Develop rules and obey norms

The second thing that happens as teams develop is the emergence of **norms**—informal standards of conduct that members share and that guide their behavior. Norms define what is acceptable behavior. They also set limits, identify values, clarify what is expected of members, and facilitate team survival. Norms can be established in various ways: from early behaviors that set precedents for future actions, from significant events in the team's history, from behaviors that come to the team through outside influences, and from a leader's or member's explicit statements that have an impact on other members.[56]

norms
Informal standards of conduct that guide team behavior

Team Conflict

By now you can see that being an effective team member requires many skills. However, none is more important than the ability to handle *conflict*—the antagonistic interactions resulting from differences in ideas, opinions, goals, or ways of doing things. Conflict can be both constructive and destructive to a team's effectiveness. Conflict is constructive if it increases the involvement of team members and results in the solution to a problem. Conflict is destructive if it diverts energy from more important issues, destroys the morale of teams or individual team members, or polarizes or divides the team.[57]

The important thing to remember about resolving conflict is that people can usually get what they want if they are willing to work together. In many cases, the resolution process is an exchange of opinions and information that gradually leads to a mutually acceptable solution.

THINKING ABOUT ETHICS

OFFICE ETHICS: TEAMS MAKE IT HARD TO TATTLE

A co-worker fakes a document, steals from petty cash, or sneaks trade secrets to the competition. Do you tell the boss? That may depend on whether you work alone or on a team.

The rise in the use of employee teams has some experts worried that unethical behavior is going unreported. Members of a team often forge close ties. "You know them, and you're more dependent on one another," says the executive director of the Ethics Officer Association. Experts say that reluctance to blow the whistle on co-workers makes sense. It's truth versus loyalty. Is it right to tell the truth and risk losing friendships? Apparently not. At least that's what the statistics show.

A recent study found that 21 percent of workers did not report misconduct by a colleague. Furthermore, 96 percent of those who failed to turn in a co-worker for unethical behavior did so because they feared they would be accused of "not being a team player." Even people who want to do the right thing worry that turning in a team member reflects badly on the whole group.

So what's a manager to do? Experts suggest managers begin by fostering an open environment where workers feel safe voicing concerns. Managers should also

(1) draft ethics policies and share them with all employees; (2) give team members a way to provide confidential information without fear of retribution; (3) encourage workers to tell if something is amiss by assuring confidentiality; and (4) follow up with employees who do report unethical behavior so they will know their input was taken seriously. Finally, managers should keep their eyes and ears open. A recent study found that 48 percent of employees admitted to illegal or unethical actions in one year.

■ QUESTIONS FOR CRITICAL THINKING

1. One of your teammates, Jenny Carnes, just informed you that she has accepted a new job with your company's chief competitor. The project you're both working on is confidential, and you're concerned that by staying on the team, Jenny may learn some trade secrets to take to her new employer. What should you do?

2. Last month you reported to the human resources department that two of your teammates called in sick when they were really on vacation. Now all of your teammates are giving you the cold shoulder. How should you handle this situation?

Causes of Team Conflict Team conflicts can arise for a number of reasons. First, teams and individuals may feel they are in competition for scarce or declining resources, such as money, information, and supplies. Second, team members may disagree about who is responsible for a specific task; this type of disagreement is usually the result of poorly defined responsibilities and job boundaries. Third, poor communication can lead to misunderstandings and misperceptions about other team members or other teams. In addition, intentionally withholding information can undermine trust among members. Fourth, basic differences in values, attitudes, and personalities may lead to clashes. Fifth, power struggles may result when one party questions the authority of another or when people or teams with limited authority attempt to increase their power or exert more influence. Sixth, conflicts can arise because individuals or teams are pursuing different goals.[58] For example, a British cardboard-manufacturing company switched from a hierarchical, functionally oriented organization to a team-based structure with the hope of empowering employees and reducing scrap. However, once they got started, the teams realized that the company had many problems to solve. Conflicts resulted when team members couldn't agree on which problems to tackle first.[59]

How to Resolve Team Conflict Each team member has a unique style of dealing with conflict, but the members' styles are primarily based on how competitive or cooperative team members are when a conflict arises. Depending on the particular situation, the same individual may use one of several styles, which include avoidance, defusion, and confrontation.[60] *Avoidance* may involve ignoring the conflict in the hope that it will subside on its own, or it may even involve physically separating the conflicting parties. *Defusion* may involve several actions, including downplaying differences and focusing on similarities between team members or teams, compromising on the disputed issue, taking a vote, appealing to a neutral party or higher authority, or redesigning the team. *Confrontation* is an attempt to work through the conflict by getting it out in the open, which may be accomplished by organizing a meeting between the conflicting parties.

These three styles of conflict resolution come into play after a conflict has developed, but team members and team leaders can take several steps to prevent conflicts. First, by establishing clear goals that require the efforts of every member, the team reduces the chance that members will battle over their objectives or roles. Second, by developing well-defined tasks for each member, the team leader ensures that all parties are aware of their responsibilities and the limits of their authority. And finally, by facilitating open communication, the team leader can ensure that all members understand their own tasks and objectives as well as those of their teammates. Keep in mind that communication builds respect and tolerance, and it provides a forum for bringing misunderstandings into the open before they turn into full-blown conflicts.

MANAGING THE FLOW OF INFORMATION IN THE ORGANIZATION

Whether an organization has a vertical or horizontal structure or is made up of functional or cross-functional teams, communication provides the crucial link between individuals, teams, departments, and divisions. The sharing of information among the parts of an organization, as well as between the organization and the outside world, is the glue that binds the organization together. In a large organization, transmitting the right information to the right people at the right time is a real challenge. To meet this challenge, organizations depend on both formal and informal communication channels.

Formal and Informal Communication Channels

The **formal communication network** is aligned with the official structure of the organization. As we have seen, this structure is illustrated by an organization chart such as the one in Exhibit 7.1. Each box in the chart represents a link in the chain of command, and each line represents a formal channel for the transmission of official messages. Information may travel down, up, and across channels in the organization's formal hierarchy.

When managers depend too heavily on formal channels for communicating, they risk encountering **distortion,** or misunderstanding. Every link in the communication chain opens up a chance for error. So by the time a message makes its way all the way up or down the chain, it may bear little resemblance to the original idea. As a consequence, people at lower levels may have only a vague idea of what top management expects of them, and executives may get an imperfect picture of what's happening lower down the chain. This is less of a problem in flat organizations than it is in tall organizations, as fewer levels means fewer links in the communication chain.

Formal organization charts illustrate how information is supposed to flow; in actual practice lines and boxes on a piece of paper cannot prevent people from developing other communication channels. The **informal communication network,** or grapevine, is the invisible side of the organization: It consists of who talks to whom, who listens to whom, and who is really making the decisions and moving the work forward. This informal network isn't reflected in the formal chart. The formal and informal organizations coexist in the same space and time, but they are often independent entities, operating sometimes in concert and sometimes at cross-purposes.[61] Exhibit 7.8 illustrates a typical informal communication network, which is often a very powerful structure within the company.

Barriers to Communication

Many individual and organizational barriers to effective communication exist within firms. Perhaps the most common barrier to communication is simply a lack of attention on the receiver's part. We all let our minds wander now and then, regardless of how hard we try to concentrate, especially if we are tired or if we feel that the information is too difficult or is unimportant. Communication can also break down if either the sender or the receiver has strong emotions about a subject.

formal communication network
Communication network that follows the official structure of the organization

distortion
Misunderstanding that results when a message passes through too many links in the organization

informal communication network
Communication network that follows the organization's unofficial lines of activity and power

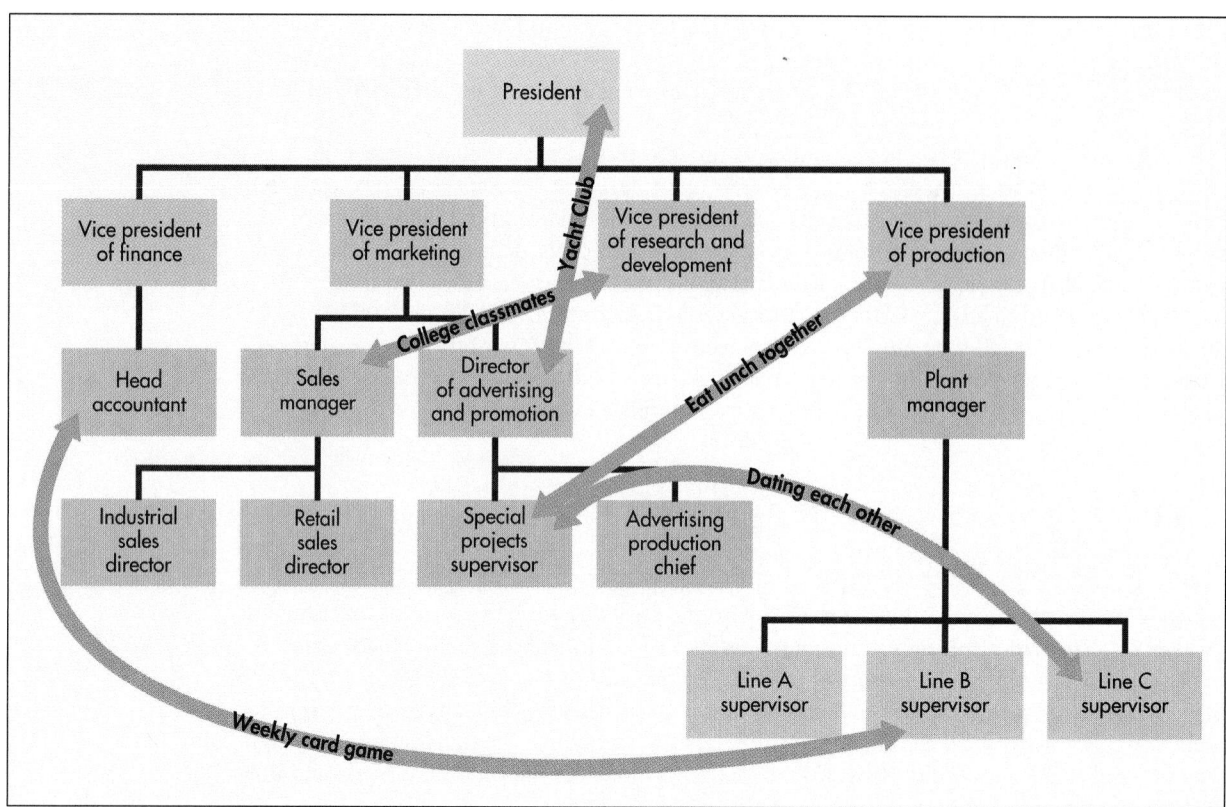

EXHIBIT 7.8

INFORMAL COMMUNICATION NETWORK

In addition to its formal channels of communication, every company has an informal communication network. This network is often formed without regard for hierarchy or departmentalization.

Other persuasive barriers to communication include:

- *Perceptual differences.* How people perceive meanings of words, gestures, tone of voice, and other symbols is affected by their background, including age, culture, education, gender, economic position, religion, or political views.

- *Incorrect filtering.* People often screen out or abbreviate information before passing a message on to someone else. In business, secretaries, assistants, associates, and voice mail are just a few of the filters that exist between you and your receiver.

- *Language.* Even among people of the same culture, language can become a barrier to communication. If you have ever tried to read a legal contract, you know the problem. Lawyers, doctors, accountants, and computer programmers all use specialized vocabularies that affect their ability to communicate ideas.

Of course, many other factors can distort both the messages you send and those you receive in an organization. In fact, executives say that 14 percent of each 40-hour workweek is wasted because of poor communication between staff and management. [62] Nonetheless, as this chapter shows, such barriers can be reduced by designing an effective organization structure, by providing opportunities for employees to communicate, and by encouraging employees to work together in teams.

Learning as much as possible about another culture will enhance your ability to communicate with its members.

Best of the Web Best of the Web Best of

ATTENDING A COMMUNICATIONS MASTER CLASS ONLINE

With a click of your mouse, you can delve deeper into the topic of organizational communication. Spotlight Communications, a U.K. firm, offers an Online Masterclass with many valuable tips about becoming a good communicator. From planning to audience analysis to effective listening, this cyberclass covers all the basics. So click your way to better communication by browsing the lessons at this informative site.
www.spotlight communications.co.uk/frameset.htm

FOCUSING ON E-BUSINESS TODAY

Strategies for Smart Web Writing

One of the most common errors found on company Web sites is poor communication. What people think of you is determined to a great extent by the way you present information on your Web site. How your Web site looks and works is very important, as Chapter 15 points out. But on the Internet the lowly word reigns supreme.

As with any medium, writing for the Web is unique. Studies show that unlike with newspapers and magazines, people who read material on the Web typically focus on the text first, looking at photos and other graphics afterward. Even so, dumping screenful upon screenful of text on a page is reader abuse. People go to the Web because they want to get information efficiently and will zip through content until they spot key words. For most people, reading on the Web is more difficult than reading from a printed page.

WRITE FOR SCANNABILITY

Effective writing for the Web applies most of the lessons taught in a college business communication course, but

LEARNING OBJECTIVE @8

Highlight 10 strategies for smart Web writing

there's a twist. On the Internet, most readers scan Web pages and have far less patience than they have with printed materials. Keep in mind that whenever readers visit a Web site, they have more than 5 million other cybersites they could log on to. Many businesses make the mistake of assuming that Web site visitors want to read rather than just skim the content. So here are some strategies to help guide your readers along.

- *Get to the point.* Stories on the Web should contain half the word count or less than they would in print. Put your

most important concept in the first 50 words, in case search engines pick up those words to describe your site.

- *Be concise.* Write shorter sentences and paragraphs to ease the reading process and to fit your text in narrow columns.

- *Break information into chunks.* Include only one idea per paragraph. Users will skip over any additional ideas if they are not hooked by the first few words in the paragraph.

- *Use hyperlinks.* Successful online documents split information into pages and connect these pages with hyperlinks. This way, each separate page is brief while all pages together can cover extensive and detailed information.

- *Adopt a conversational tone.* Adopt a lighter, less formal writing style. Infuse as much of your organizational or individual personality into your text as you wish, but don't be chatty.

- *Be audience-centered.* Too many messages have an "I" or "we" attitude, which causes the sender to sound self-centered and uninterested in the audience's needs. On the simplest level, you can adopt an audience-centered

KEEP THESE STATISTICS IN MIND WHEN WRITING FOR THE WEB

- 79 percent of users scan the page instead of reading it word for word.

- Reading from computer screens is 25 percent slower than from paper.

- Web content should have 50 percent of the word count of its paper equivalent.

approach by replacing terms that refer to yourself and your company with terms that refer to your audience. In other words, use *you, yours, we, us,* and *ours* instead of *I, me,* and *mine.*

- *Use plain English.* One of the worst mistakes you can make is to include bureaucratic-sounding text from printed sources. Plain English is a way of writing and arranging technical materials so that your audience can understand your meaning. It's close to the way people normally speak.

- *Avoid self-congratulatory puffery.* Web users are skeptical. The more you exaggerate, the more they'll ignore you.

- *Avoid slang and idioms.* The Web is an international medium. When speaking to people less fluent in your native language, try to choose words carefully so that they won't be misunderstood by readers from other cultures. Avoid slang, idioms, and corporate jargon. For example, the phrase "big bucks" to some may mean a great deal of money, but to others it could mean large male deer or physically large currency. Keep in mind that abbreviations and acronyms (such as CAD/CAM) may also lead to confusion.

- *Highlight key words.* Hypertext links serve as one form of highlighting; typeface variations and color are others. Other options are pullout quotes and captions. Avoid highlighting entire sentences or long phrases, since a scanning eye can only pick up two (or at most three) words at a time.

  Use headings and subheadings. Headline text has to stand on its own and make sense because oftentimes

the underlying content is on a different Web page. Keep headings informative (rather than cute and meaningless).

- *Use bulleted and numbered lists.* Lists are easy to skim because they slow down the scanning eye and draw attention to important points. They facilitate the skimming process for busy readers, simplify complex subjects, highlight the main point, break up the page visually, and give the reader a breather. Use numbered lists when the order of entries is important. Use bulleted lists whenever the sequence of the entries is not important.

WRITE THE CONCLUSION FIRST, DETAILS LATER

Journalists have long adhered to an inverse approach to writing: They start the article by telling the reader the conclusion first, follow with the most important supporting information, and end by giving the background. This style is known as the inverted pyramid and is useful in newspapers because readers can stop at any time and will still get the most important parts of the article. Because readers scroll on the Web, the inverted pyramid becomes even more important. Some will only read the top part of an article. So put the most important information at the top, then link to supporting details. A good example of this approach is the Ziff-Davis Anchor Desk on the Web at www.zdnet.com/anchordesk. The first Web page contains a paragraph-long summary of each story. Readers can then click on a link to get a page-long story, and click again (if interested) to get extensive background articles.[63]

SUMMARY OF LEARNING OBJECTIVES

1. **Discuss the function of a company's organization structure.**
   An organization structure provides a framework through which a company can coordinate and control the work, divide responsibilities, distribute authority, and hold employees accountable.

2. **Explain the concepts of accountability, authority, and delegation.**
   Accountability is the obligation to report work results to supervisors or team members and to justify any outcomes that fall below expectations. Authority is the power to make decisions, issue orders, carry out actions, and allocate resources to achieve the organization's goals. Delegation is the assignment of work and the transfer of authority and responsibility to complete that work.

3. **Define four types of departmentalization.**
   Companies may departmentalize in any combination of four ways: (1) by function, which groups employees according to their skills, resource use, and expertise; (2) by division, which establishes self-contained departments formed according to similarities in product, process, customer, or geography; (3) by matrix, which assigns employees from functional departments to interdisciplinary project

teams and requires them to report to both a department head and a team leader; and (4) by network, which connects separate companies that perform selected tasks for a headquarters organization.

4. **Describe the five most common forms of teams.**
   The five most common forms of teams are (1) problem-solving teams, which seek ways to improve a situation and then submit their recommendation to management; (2) self-managed teams, which manage their own activities and seldom require supervision; (3) functional teams, which are composed of employees within a single functional department; (4) cross-functional teams, which draw together employees from various departments and expertise in a number of formats such as task forces, special-purpose teams, and committees; and (5) virtual teams, which bring together employees from distant locations.

5. **Highlight the advantages and disadvantages of working in teams.**
   Teamwork has the potential to increase creativity, motivation, performance, and satisfaction of workers and thereby can lead to greater company efficiency, flexibility, and cost savings. The po-

tential disadvantages of working in teams include the difficulties of managing employees' changing roles, the possibilities of free riders and groupthink, and the costs and time needed to coordinate members' schedules and project parts.

6. List the characteristics of effective teams.
Effective teams have a clear sense of purpose, communicate openly and honestly, build a sense of fairness in decision making, think creatively, stay focused on key issues, manage conflict constructively, and select team members wisely by involving stakeholders, creative thinkers, and members with a diversity of views. Moreover, effective teams have an optimal size of between 5 and 12 members.

7. Review the five stages of team development.
Teams typically go through five stages of development. In the forming stage, team members become acquainted with each other and with the group's purpose. In the storming stage, conflict often arises as coalitions and power struggles develop. In the norming stage, conflicts are resolved and harmony develops. In the performing stage, members focus on achieving the team's goals. In the adjourning stage, the team dissolves upon completion of its task.

8. Highlight 10 strategies for smart Web writing.
Because most Web users scan pages instead of reading them, when writing for the Web you should be brief, break information into chunks, use hyperlinks, adopt a conversational tone, be audience-centered, use plain English, not brag, avoid slang and idioms, discuss the most important information first, and provide links to supporting information and background material.

KEY TERMS

accountability (179)

authority (179)

centralization (180)

chain of command (179)

cohesiveness (190)

committee (187)

cross-functional teams (186)

customer divisions (182)

decentralization (180)

delegation (179)

departmentalization (181)

departmentalization by division (181)

departmentalization by function (181)

departmentalization by matrix (182)

departmentalization by network (183)

distortion (193)

flat organizations (179)

formal communication network (193)

free riders (189)

functional teams (186)

geographic divisions (182)

horizontal coordination (184)

informal communication network (193)

informal organization (178)

line organization (179)

line-and-staff organization (179)

norms (191)

organization chart (178)

organization structure (178)

problem-solving team (185)

process divisions (181)

product divisions (181)

responsibility (179)

self-managed teams (185)

span of management (179)

special-purpose teams (187)

tall organizations (180)

task force (187)

team (185)

vertical organization (180)

virtual teams (187)

work specialization (179)

TEST YOUR KNOWLEDGE

QUESTIONS FOR REVIEW

1. Why is organization structure important?

2. What are the characteristics of tall organizations and flat organizations?

3. What are the advantages and disadvantages of work specialization?

4. What are the advantages and disadvantages of functional departmentalization?

5. How can using the informal communication network help a manager be more effective?

QUESTIONS FOR ANALYSIS

6. Why would you expect a manager of a group of nuclear physicists to have a wide span of management?

7. How does horizontal organization promote innovation?

8. What can managers do to help teams work more effectively?

9. How can companies benefit from using virtual teams?

10. What type of organization structure would you expect a start-up e-business selling gourmet food baskets to have? Explain your answer.

11. You were honored that you were selected to serve on the salary committee of the employee negotiations task force. As a member of that committee, you reviewed confidential company documents listing the salaries of all department managers. You discovered that managers at your level are earning $5,000 more than you, even though you've been at the company the same amount of time. You feel that a raise is justified on the basis of this confidential information. How will you handle this situation?

QUESTIONS FOR APPLICATION

12. You are the leader of a cross-functional work team whose goal is to find ways of lowering production costs. Your team of eight employees has become mired in the storming stage. They disagree on how to approach the task, and they are starting to splinter into factions. What can you do to help the team move forward?

13. Your warehouse operation is currently functioning at capacity. To accommodate anticipated new business, your company must either build a major addition to your current warehouse operation or build a new warehouse that would be located at a distant site. As director of warehouse operations, you would like several people to

participate in this decision. Should you form a task force, a committee, or a special-purpose team? Explain your choice.

14. One of your competitors has approached you with an intriguing proposition. The company would like to merge with your company. The economies of scale are terrific. So are the growth possibilities. There's just one issue to be resolved. Your competitor is organized under a horizontal structure and uses lots of cross-functional teams. Your company is organized under a traditional vertical structure that is departmentalized by function.

Using your knowledge about culture clash, what are the likely issues you will encounter if these two organizations are merged?

15. In Chapter 6 we discussed three styles of leadership: autocratic, democratic, and laissez-faire. Using your knowledge about the differences in these leadership styles, which style would you expect to find under the following organization structures? (a) vertical organization—departmentalization by function; (b) vertical organization—departmentalization by matrix; (c) horizontal organization; (d) self-directed teams.

PRACTICE YOUR KNOWLEDGE

SHARPENING YOUR COMMUNICATION SKILLS

Write a brief memo to your instructor describing a recent conflict you had with a peer at work or at school. Be sure to highlight the cause of the conflict and steps you took to resolve it. Which of the three conflict resolution styles discussed in this chapter did you use? Did you find a solution that both of you could accept?

HANDLING DIFFICULT SITUATIONS ON THE JOB: GOING THE DISTANCE WITH TEAMWORK

Dettmers Industries was cruising at an altitude of $3 million in annual sales when co-founder Michael Dettmers introduced self-directed teams. Employees at the Florida-based firm, which makes furnishings for private planes, were initially skeptical. So Dettmers started small, setting up one experimental self-directed team with the authority to hire new members, schedule work, handle customer service, supervise quality, and manage cash flow. As an incentive, Dettmers promised to pay members 25 percent of the revenues from sales of products made by the team—and guaranteed that members' incomes wouldn't be less than the previous year's earnings.

Dettmers required team members to attend 13 hours of quarterly training in teamwork, communication, and business skills. And to help teams get up to speed, Dettmers walked the shop floor for hours, coaching team leaders, facilitating meetings, and resolving conflicts.

By the end of the first year, members' earnings were averaging $45,000, compared with $32,000 the year before. Skepticism gave way to enthusiasm, once people could see that by working together effectively as a team they would make more money.

Even though teamwork is now a way of life, disputes still pop up. The members of your team are grumbling about one member who has become a free rider and is no longer contributing a fair share to the production output. As team leader, you want to quickly resolve this conflict, before it threatens cohesiveness. But how?[64]

1. To defuse the conflict, should you suggest first asking other teams about their experience with free riders, or should you immediately call a team meeting to confront the free rider?

2. As a last resort, should you ask Dettmers how to handle the free-rider conflict? Why or why not?

3. To avoid this kind of conflict in the future, should you work as a team to draft rules for publicly reporting each member's output every week, or should you suggest delegating the process of tracking weekly member output to a few team members?

BUILDING YOUR TEAM SKILLS

What's the most effective organization structure for your college or university? With your team, obtain a copy of your school's organization chart. If this chart is not readily available, gather information by talking with people in administration, and then draw your own chart of the organization structure.

Analyze the chart in terms of span of management. Is your school a flat or a tall organization? Is this organization structure appropriate for your school? Does decision making tend to be centralized or decentralized in your school? Do you agree with this approach to decision making?

Finally, investigate the use of formal and informal teams in your school. Are there any problem-solving teams, task forces, or committees at work in your school? Are any teams self-directed or virtual? How much authority do these teams have to make decisions? What is the purpose of teamwork in your school—what kinds of goals do these teams have?

Share your team's findings during a brief classroom presentation, and then compare the findings of all teams. Is there agreement on the appropriate organization structure for your school?

EXPAND YOUR KNOWLEDGE

KEEPING CURRENT USING *THE WALL STREET JOURNAL*

Although teamwork can benefit many organizations, introducing and managing team structures can be a real challenge. Search past issues of *The Wall Street Journal* (print or online editions) to locate articles about how an organization has overcome problems with teams.

1. Why did the organization originally introduce teams? What types of teams are being used?

2. What problems did each organization encounter in trying to implement teams? How did the organization deal with these problems?

3. Have the teams been successful from management's perspective? From the employees' perspective? What effect has teamwork had on the company, its customers, and its products?

DISCOVERING CAREER OPPORTUNITIES

Because every employee is a vital link in the organization's information chain, good communication skills are essential to your career—especially when you choose a career path in business communication. What do professional communicators do for their organizations? This is your opportunity to find out.

1. Visit your school's career center or use printed or online sources to research a list of at least three organizational jobs directly related to communication, such as webmaster and media relations specialist. Do these positions deal with internal or external communications?

2. Locate someone in your area who holds one of the jobs you have researched, and arrange a brief telephone interview. What are the duties and goals of this position? What training, education, and skills are needed for this job?

3. What about this job interests you? What else would you need to do or learn to be qualified for this kind of position?

EXPLORING THE BEST OF THE WEB

URLs for all Internet exercises are provided at the Web site for this book, www.prenhall.com/mescon. *When you log on to the text Web site, select Chapter 7, then select "Student Resources," click on the name of the featured Web site, and follow the detailed navigational directions to complete these exercises.*

Getting Organized, page 183

The organization chart is your road map to who does what in any organization. A good case in point is the organization chart of the City of Sacramento, which you can access on the Internet to answer the following questions.

1. Who is the city manager of Sacramento, and what is this person's span of management? Why do you think there are so many deputy city managers? What is the span of management for the deputy city manager in charge of neighborhoods?

2. What departmentalization method does Sacramento seem to be using for positions that report to the city manager? Why is this departmentalization method appropriate?

3. How many levels in the hierarchy separate the fire chief and the mayor? Do you consider this a flat or a tall organization? Why?

Building Teams in the Cyber Age, page 187

The wealth of information on the Internet makes it convenient to learn more about almost any topic, and teamwork is no exception.

Visit the Self-Directed Work Teams page and click through the links to get a feel for the many resources available. Then answer the following questions.

1. Do high-performing teams prefer dialogue or debate?

2. Which three major issues facing teams are most important to the assigned in-class teams in which you've participated? Which three do you think are most important to a team of production workers looking for ways to cut costs and production time?

3. What aspects of teamwork are the team assessment questions measuring? Take this test (using your experience on a school or work team) and submit your answers. What response do you get? Which areas do you think are most important for your team to focus on?

Attending a Communications Master Class Online, page 195

Sharing information through communication is the glue that binds together all the employees of an organization. An easy way to learn more about good communication is to take Spotlight Communications' Online Masterclass.

1. What are the three questions of planning stages one and two? What activities make up planning stage three? Why is this last stage important? Should you follow this planning process in all communications situations?

2. What may differ from one audience to another? In the example in which the restaurant owner communicates about longer hours, what three audiences are identified? How does the message differ for each audience?

3. What are the four stages of effective listening? What can you do to set the scene for effective listening? Why should you ask questions?

Explore on Your Own

Review these chapter-related Web sites on your own to learn more about organizational structures and teamwork.

1. The Malcolm Baldrige Award Web site, www.baldrige.org/show.htm, has profiles of recent winners who have improved quality through better teamwork and communication.

2. Teamworks: The Virtual Team Assistant, www.vta.spcomm.uiuc.edu/, is a Web site dedicated to providing support for group communication processes and teams.

3. The Center for the Study of Work Teams, www.workteams.unt.edu/, has many links, articles, and research reports on the subject matter of teams.

A CASE FOR CRITICAL THINKING

■ *Harley-Davidson—from Dysfunctional to Cross-Functional*

Richard Teerlink knows what it's like being at the bottom looking up. When he joined Harley-Davidson in 1981 as Chief Financial Officer, the motorcycle manufacturer was as low as it could go. Harley was indeed an American icon, but it wasn't having much success in the marketplace. The company had a poor reputation for quality and reliability. It was behind the curve on product design and development. And its big-iron cruisers and long-distance touring bikes were heavy, chrome laden, and ex-

pensive. Moreover, they leaked oil and they vibrated excessively. Some even joked that customers should buy two Harleys—one to ride and one for parts.

HARLEY GOES FULL THROTTLE

Facing some of the toughest competitors in the world from such companies as Honda, Suzuki, and Yamaha, Harley-Davidson had to make some changes. So Teerlink began by successfully lobbying Congress in 1983 for tariff protection against Japanese bike manufacturers. This protection gave Harley the breathing room it needed to improve quality, introduce new products, and cut costs.

Then Harley's management team set out to rebuild the company's production processes from the ground up.

By 1986 the company's future looked bright. New products were coming to market, quality had improved, and the company was turning a profit. In fact, product demand rebounded so strongly that dealers reported long waiting lists of riders eager to climb on a Harley. Moreover, the Harley Owners Group (HOG), which was launched by the company to communicate more effectively with customers, soon turned into the world's largest motorcycle club. Some fiercely loyal fans even tattooed the company's logo on their chests.

Harley-Davidson's inspiring comeback was a cheering symbol of American industrial renaissance. To make a public statement of confidence, Harley's management asked Congress to repeal the tariffs against heavyweight bike imports one year before their 1988 expiration date. By the time Teerlink climbed into the CEO saddle in 1989, the hard work of saving the company was behind him. Harley had survived several arduous years of crisis and had overcome its obstacles under the direction of a very strong hierarchical, centralized leadership group.

MORE POTHOLES AHEAD

Back in the U.S. market, the Japanese fumbled at first, emphasizing sport bikes and introducing cruisers with sleek, modern designs. But eventually they caught on. In 1995 they introduced Harley clones. The bikes were spitting images of Harleys with one exception—they had many technical improvements. Once again, Harley faced a daunting challenge. In spite of its many improvements, Harley's quality standards were not on par with those of its foreign competitors. Moreover, Harley's cost structure was among the highest in the industry. Teerlink had his work cut out for him—again.

HARLEY REVS UP ITS ENGINES

Teerlink knew that the best way to improve quality and reliability and lower production costs was to create an environment where everyone took responsibility for the company's present and future. Of course, such an approach would not come naturally to Harley. The previous crisis had been managed with an unmistakable top-down approach, as is so often the case with turnarounds. But times had changed. Employees could no longer be privates, taking orders and operating within strict limits.

So Teerlink flattened the corporate hierarchy and established teams of cross-functional leaders to work collaboratively and provide senior leadership with direction. This is the structure under which Harley currently operates. At the heart of the organizational structure are three cross-functional teams called Circles—the Create Demand Circle, the Produce Product Circle, and the Provide Support Circle. Each Circle includes design engineers, purchasing professionals, manufacturing personnel, marketing personnel, and others. The cross-functional teams are responsible for every motorcycle produced by Harley—from product conception to final design. Within each team, the leadership role moves from person to person, depending on the issue being addressed.

Recognizing that suppliers' input is crucial to Harley's new-product development, all cross-functional teams include key suppliers who work elbow-to-elbow with Harley personnel. "Suppliers are the experts. They have expertise in not only what they're developing today but also what's going on in their industry," says one Harley purchasing director. "The more input we have up front, the better our products will be."

MAKING A U-TURN

Cross-functional teamwork has indeed paid off for Harley. With record profits and a good chance of soon reaching their annual production goal of 200,000 bikes, the company's 6,000-plus employees have much to celebrate these days. In fact, employee satisfaction is at record levels, and customer satisfaction with the Harley-Davidson Sportster has improved by 200 percent. Moreover, the 16-to-24 month waiting period for a new Sportster has been reduced to about two weeks.

Teerlink attributes much of Harley's success to its move from a top-down hierarchy to one based on cross-functional teams. Everyone must now add value to the organization. Still, "the work is not done," says Teerlink (who retired as CEO in 1999 and is now a member of the board of directors). "Transforming a culture takes time . . . It's a journey that will never end unless we let it."

CRITICAL THINKING QUESTIONS

1. During Teerlink's tenure as Harley's CFO, was the organization structure flat or tall? Centralized or decentralized? Explain your answers.

2. As CEO, how did Teerlink change the organization structure?

3. Why does Harley-Davidson include outside suppliers on its cross-functional teams?

4. Go to Chapter 7 of this text's Web site at www.prenhall.com/mescon and click on the hot link to get to the Harley-Davidson Web site. Follow the online instructions to answer the following questions: How many motorcycles did Harley produce in the most recent quarter? What is the output trend? What is the trend in Harley's worldwide sales?

VIDEO CASE AND EXERCISES

■ *Nantucket Nectars Juices Up Organization, Teamwork, and Communication*

SYNOPSIS

In 1989, Tom Scott and Tom First whipped up a tasty peach nectar drink to start Nantucket Nectars (www.juiceguys.com). In those early days, the two Toms—also known as the juice guys—ran the entire operation from their boat. Now the company's drinks, in 48 flavors, are shipped to thirsty customers in 40 states and a number of other countries. Nantucket Nectars is no longer a one-boat operation, with 130 employees split between headquarters in Cambridge, Massachusetts, and several field offices. As a result, management has developed a more formalized organization structure and communication channels to keep the business running smoothly and ensure that information reaches the right people at the right time. For example, headquarters employees gather every Tuesday morning for updates on company activities. The company also relies on cross-functional teams to handle special projects such as the implementation of new accounting software. These strategies have helped Nantucket Nectars successfully manage its rapid growth.

EXERCISES
Analysis

1. What type of organization is in place at Nantucket Nectars?

2. How would you describe th top-level span of management at Nantucket Nectars?

3. Why did Nantucket Nectars use a cross-functional team for its software implementation project?

4. What contributed to the cohesiveness of this cross-functional team?

5. How does the company's regular Tuesday morning meeting support both the formal and informal communication networks?

Application

As Nantucket Nectars expands into new products and new markets, it may need to change its current organization structure. Under what circumstances would some form of divisional departmentalization be appropriate for the company?

Decision

Assume that top management at Nantucket Nectars has decided to purchase a well-established specialty beverage company. The company being acquired has a tall organization structure that emphasizes top-down control rather than teamwork. Identify some of the problems that management might face in integrating the acquired company with the existing organization.

Communication

Communicating praise for a job well done is important in any organization. Write a one-minute presentation acknowledging the accomplishments of the cross-functional team that worked on implement-

ing the new accounting software at Nantucket Nectars. Be specific about what the team achieved and why it is being recognized.

Integration

Which of three broad leadership styles described in Chapter 6 seems to be the norm at Nantucket Nectars?

Ethics

It can be hard for individual accomplishments to stand out in a cross-functional team setting. Is a strong emphasis on this type of teamwork really fair to unusually outstanding and ambitious employees?

Debate

If Nantucket Nectars shifted to a team structure, would self-managed teams or functional teams be more effective? Prepare to debate one side of this question in class, supporting your stand with information from the chapter and from the video.

Teamwork

With another student, consider what managers at Nantucket Nectars can do to encourage a cross-functional team to move through the forming, storming, and norming stages so team members can perform as expected. As your instructor directs, write a brief report about your team's ideas or prepare a presentation to the class.

Online Research

Using Internet sources, find out how sales of Nantucket Nectars have grown in recent years. Also investigate where the company is currently distributing its products. See Component Chapter A, Exhibit A.1, for search engines to use in doing your research. Report your findings in a brief class presentation and prepare to lead a discussion about the implications for the company's organization and communication.

MY PHLIP COMPANION WEB SITE

Learning Interactively

Visit the myPHLIP Web site at www.prenhall.com/mescon. For Chapter 7, take advantage of the interactive "Study Guide" to test your chapter knowledge. Get instant feedback on whether you need additional studying. Read the "Current Events" articles to get the latest on chapter topics, and complete the exercises as specified by your instructor. Expand your learning with a visit to the "Research Area." There you will find a wealth of information you can use to complete your course assignments.

MASTERING BUSINESS ESSENTIALS

Go to the "Groups and Teams" episode on the Mastering Business Essentials interactive, video-enhanced CD-ROM. Witness how Maria, director of human resources at CanGo (an e-business start-up) faces the challenge of getting a team to act in an organized and effective manner. Observe the team as it moves through various developmental stages.

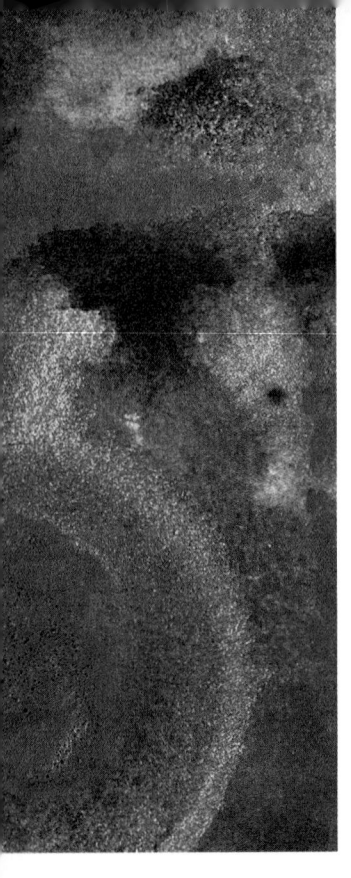

TECHNOLOGY AND INFORMATION MANAGEMENT

8

LEARNING OBJECTIVES

After studying this chapter, you will be able to

1. Explain the importance of information and the characteristics of useful information

2. Distinguish between data and information, and identify the principal sources of data

3. Discuss the responsibilities of the chief information officer

4. Differentiate between operations information systems, management information systems, and decision support systems

5. Describe the four classes of computers

6. Describe the primary hardware components and transmission media of a computer network

7. Discuss four technology issues affecting today's workplace

@ 8. Explain how advances in wireless technology will change the way we conduct e-business and list the challenges that must be overcome before these changes can take place

MEET MR. INTERNET:
JOHN CHAMBERS—CISCO'S LIVE WIRE
w w w . c i s c o . c o m

John Chambers, CEO of Cisco, has turned the company into the world's most comprehensive end-to-end supplier of networking equipment.

Nobody is more responsible for fueling the Internet revolution than John Chambers, CEO of Cisco Systems. His company makes routers—souped-up computers that act as traffic cops—converting, sorting, and directing data throughout the Internet. Pretty basic stuff, but considering that about 70 percent of all Internet traffic passes through a Cisco router before it reaches its final destination, it's a very big business. So with Internet usage projected to grow exponentially, why is Chambers looking for new territory to conquer?

Chambers believes that the Internet is about to undergo a dramatic change, merging with the telephone and cable TV businesses and creating one mammoth voice-video-data network worldwide. As he sees it, tomorrow's homes will become much like today's offices—networks of linked devices and appliances connected to a server. And Chambers wants Cisco to play a key role in that transformation, putting the company squarely into competition with telecom equipment suppliers Lucent Technologies and Northern Telecom, both of whom are many times Cisco's size. Chambers is also stepping up efforts in two booming markets—wireless and optical—and going after leaders Nokia, Motorola, and Ericsson. "I want Cisco to be a dynasty," he says. "I think it can be the company that changes the world."

Chambers's confidence seems particularly astounding considering that Cisco is probably the most faceless dynasty-in-training ever. Popular as Cisco is with technology gurus its products are boring and invisible to most. "The joke around here," says one Cisco staffer, "is that we're the most important company no one's ever heard of." But Chambers is working hard to put an end to that joke. He wants people to think of Cisco as a communications company, not a mere router company.

Part of Chambers's drive comes from his past experience. Before joining Cisco Systems in January 1991, he spent six years at IBM and eight years at minicomputer maker Wang Laboratories watching both companies get hammered by the PC revolution. He learned the hard way that selling all technology products to all people doesn't work. He got a chance to put his experience to work when he was appointed Cisco's CEO in 1994. It was an unconventional appointment because Chambers was a salesman—not a technology visionary like Microsoft's Bill Gates or Apple's Steve Jobs. But it turned out to be a wise move for Cisco.

As CEO, Chambers has orchestrated a series of acquisitions and developed critical partnerships to turn Cisco into the world's must comprehensive end-to-end supplier of networking equipment. Moreover, he reorganized Cisco's entire operation so that all business functions—from finance to employee communications—are Internet based. Some 90 percent of the company's sales and 80 percent of customer inquiries are transacted over the Web. "We provide the majority of company information and communications via the Web, which empowers employees to make decisions at all levels of the organization and to move at an Internet pace," says Chambers.

Since going public in 1990, Cisco has increased revenues by 30 to 40 percent each year. But in 2001, that pattern changed. Growing disarray among telecom customers, a sharp economic slowdown, and stepped up heat from Juniper, its major competitor, stalled Cisco's hypergrowth, and the company was forced to trim its workforce by 17 percent. Even though Cisco's annual sales top $13 billion, some believe that its glory days are history. Chambers, of course, disagrees. Cisco has the leading product in the marketplace, and with Internet traffic doubling every 100 days or so, Chambers insists that Cisco can keep up the pace. Based on his track record, few would bet against him.[1]

LEARNING
OBJECTIVE   1

Explain the importance of
information and the characteristics
of useful information

WHAT IS EFFECTIVE INFORMATION MANAGEMENT?

As John Chambers knows, all businesses rely on the fast distribution of information for just about everything they do. Businesspeople need information to increase organizational efficiencies, stay ahead of competitors, find new customers, keep existing customers, develop new products, and so on. Fortunately, we live in the Information Age, where information is easily accessible and readily available. But having too much information can be overwhelming and at times counterproductive.

It has been estimated that humans have produced more information in the past 30 years than in the previous 5,000 and that most of it has been added in the past few years thanks to the Internet and other electronic media.[2] As the amount of information continues to increase, employees must learn how to discriminate between useful and useless information and between what is truly important and what is routine. Technology, of course, plays a key role in managing a company's information. Computers, computer networks, and telecommunication devices enable organizations to track, store, retrieve, process, and share information that can be leveraged to achieve competitive advantages. But in addition to using technology to gather and manage information, companies must develop strategies and systems for analyzing and presenting information so managers and employees can use it in their daily decision making.

According to Bill Gates, "The most meaningful way to differentiate your company from your competition is to do an outstanding job with information."[3] But what exactly does this involve? For one thing, information is most useful to those people who can act on it. A computer technician, for example, doesn't need to know the costs of office supplies, and the advertising manager doesn't need to know the repair schedules for the company's fleet of delivery equipment. Therefore, a key element of an effective information management system is the ability to *filter* information: making sure that the *right information* reaches the *right people* at the *right time*, and in the *right form*.[4] Moreover, for information to be useful, it must be accurate, timely, complete, relevant, and concise.[5] The closer information comes to meeting these five criteria, the more it will facilitate the company's decision-making process.

Of course, information in the real world is rarely perfect, and managers must often make do with whatever data they can get. So another key element of effective information management is understanding the difference between data and information and learning how to turn data into information.

Turning Data into Information

LEARNING
OBJECTIVE   2

Distinguish between data and
information, and identify the
principal sources of data

Each day companies collect, generate, and store vast quantities of *data* (recorded facts and statistics) that are relevant to a particular decision or problem. For example, the accounting department may have price and sales data for hundreds of different products, the marketing department may have customer data, the purchasing department may have inventory data, and so on (see Exhibit 8.1). These data are stored in *databases,* centralized collections of data that can be used by people throughout an organization. However, these data do not become information until they are used to solve a problem, answer a question, or make a decision.

When managers want to know the average monthly sales of products X, Y, and Z, they must cross-reference the data. Through a process known as **data warehousing,** data are moved from separate databases into a well-organized central database where they are sorted, summarized, and stored. Managers from the different functional areas can then make complex *queries,* or ask questions of the central database to review the data, analyze it, solve problems, answer questions, or make decisions (see Exhibit 8.2). Such multidepartmental queries are not possible when data are stored in separate databases throughout the organization.[6]

When a query is made, the computer software sifts through huge amounts of data, identifying what is valuable to the specific query and what is not. This process, known as **data mining,** allows computers to look for patterns and turn mountains of data into useful information.[7] For example, MCI WorldCom has marketing records on 140 million households, each of which may have as many as 10,000 separate attributes. By mining these data, the company can detect patterns that indicate which customers are most likely to switch to a different long-distance provider. Marketing personnel can use this information to decide which customers to target for special promotions and which incentives to offer current customers.[8]

data warehousing
Building an organized central database out of files and databases gathered from various functional areas, such as marketing, operations, and accounting

data mining
Sifting through huge amounts of data to identify what is valuable to a specific question or problem

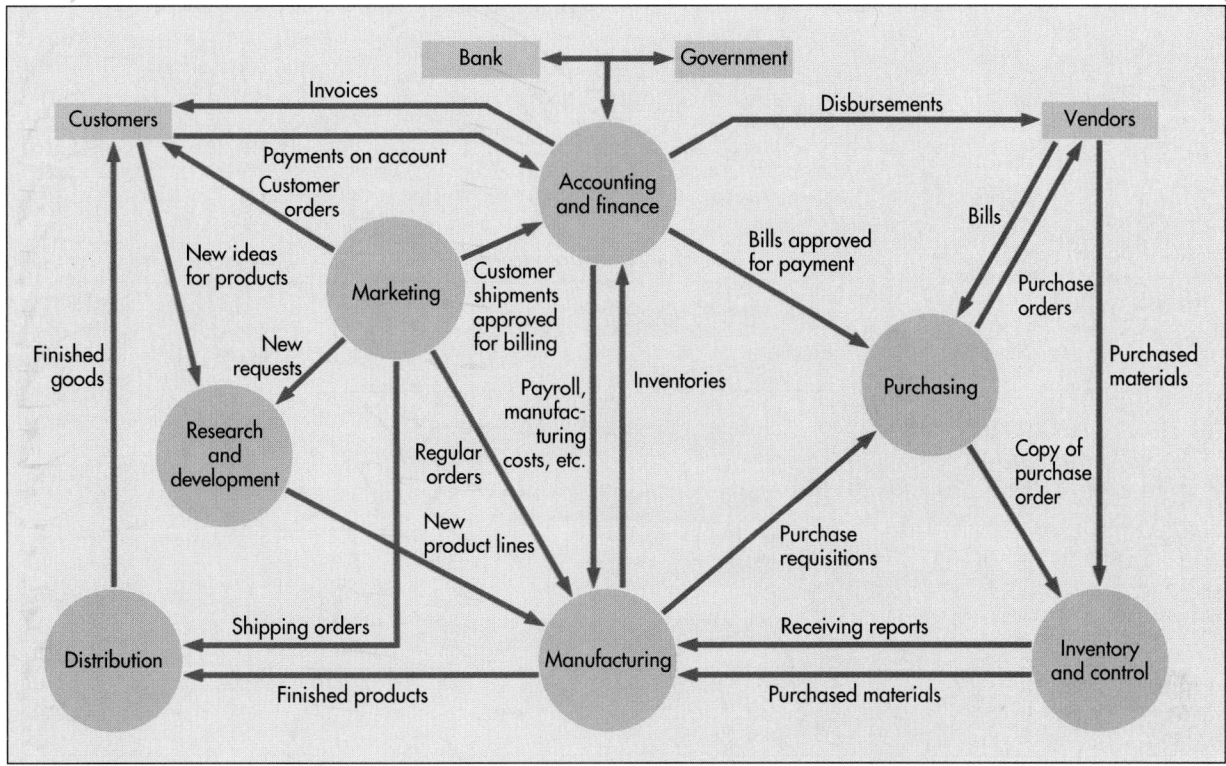

EXHIBIT 8.1

INFORMATION FLOW IN A TYPICAL MANUFACTURING COMPANY

Many kinds of manipulations and transfers of information support daily operations and decision making in a manufacturing company.

Gathering Data Before you can turn data into meaningful information, however, you must first know where and how to obtain data. Data are frequently classified in two main ways: (1) according to where they are located, and (2) according to the purpose for which they were gathered.

Data grouped according to location are either internal data or external data. **Internal data** are those available in the company's own records—invoices, purchase orders, personnel files, and the like. **External data** are those obtained from outside sources. These include government agencies, such as the Census Bureau, and nongovernment sources, such as trade associations and trade periodicals. Internal data are sometimes easier to obtain and more specific to the company, but outside sources often have better resources for gathering data on broad economic and social trends.

Data grouped by purpose are either primary or secondary. **Primary data** are facts, statistics, and information not previously published that you gather on your own for the study of a specific problem. **Secondary data** consist of facts, statistics, and information previously published or collected by others. Sometimes the collection of secondary data is characterized as "library research." In business research, government and trade organizations are the major sources of secondary data.

Businesspeople usually examine secondary data first because these data often have three advantages over primary data:

■ *Speed.* Secondary data sources provide information at a moment's notice.

■ *Cost.* Collecting primary data may be an expensive process.

■ *Availability.* The owner of a business can hardly expect the owner of a competing firm to make information available. Trade associations and the government, on the other hand, collect information from all firms and make it available to everyone.

internal data
Data acquired from company sources such as internal records and documents

external data
Data acquired from sources outside the company

primary data
Data gathered for the study of a specific problem

secondary data
Data previously produced or collected for a different purpose

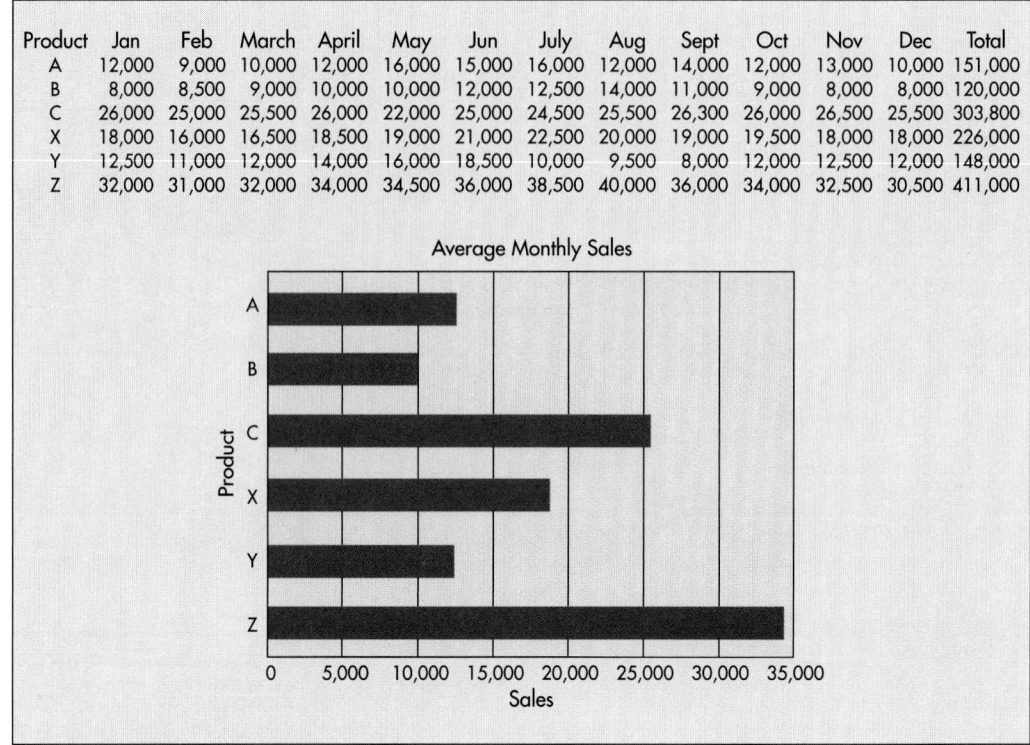

Product	Jan	Feb	March	April	May	Jun	July	Aug	Sept	Oct	Nov	Dec	Total
A	12,000	9,000	10,000	12,000	16,000	15,000	16,000	12,000	14,000	12,000	13,000	10,000	151,000
B	8,000	8,500	9,000	10,000	10,000	12,000	12,500	14,000	11,000	9,000	8,000	8,000	120,000
C	26,000	25,000	25,500	26,000	22,000	25,000	24,500	25,500	26,300	26,000	26,500	25,500	303,800
X	18,000	16,000	16,500	18,500	19,000	21,000	22,500	20,000	19,000	19,500	18,000	18,000	226,000
Y	12,500	11,000	12,000	14,000	16,000	18,500	10,000	9,500	8,000	12,000	12,500	12,000	148,000
Z	32,000	31,000	32,000	34,000	34,500	36,000	38,500	40,000	36,000	34,000	32,500	30,500	411,000

EXHIBIT 8.2

DATA VERSUS INFORMATION

The table at the top represents sales data for a small company's six products. In this form, the data are just statistics that answer no particular question and solve no particular problem. Therefore, they are not considered information. But when a manager queries the database to identify the average monthly sales for each product, specific information is required. The sales data are used to generate the graph that illustrates the requested information.

Secondary data do have some drawbacks, however. The information may be out of date, or it may not be as relevant as it first seems. The company or agency that collected the data may not be as impartial as it should be. Furthermore, the source may lack expertise. The best way to overcome the disadvantages of secondary data may be to collect primary data through original research.

Some data obtained through primary and secondary research pertain to people's likes and dislikes, their opinions and feelings; other data are of a more factual nature. Factual data presented in numerical form are referred to as **statistics.** Examples of statistics include the batting averages of ballplayers, the number of highway deaths in a year, and the number of ice cream cones eaten in August. Statistics are often expressed as percentages—an inflation rate of 7 percent, for instance.

Businesspeople rely on statistical information because of its relative precision and analytical value. Although they must be able to understand such statistics, they do not really need to be statisticians. Today many microcomputer software packages are available that allow even those who have little experience with statistics to analyze and interpret data.

Analyzing Data   Once you have gathered enough data, you must analyze it so that you can turn the data into meaningful information. In other words, raw data—lists and tables of numbers—are of little practical value by themselves. Instead, they must be manipulated to bring forward certain key numbers, such as averages, index numbers, and trends.

Averages   One way to present data in an easily understood way is to find an *average,* a number typical of a group of numbers or quantities. A marketing manager, for example, may want to know the average age of potential consumers of a new product in order to slant advertising toward that age group. The most widely used averages are the *mean,* the *median,* and the *mode.*

statistics
Factual data that can be presented in numerical form

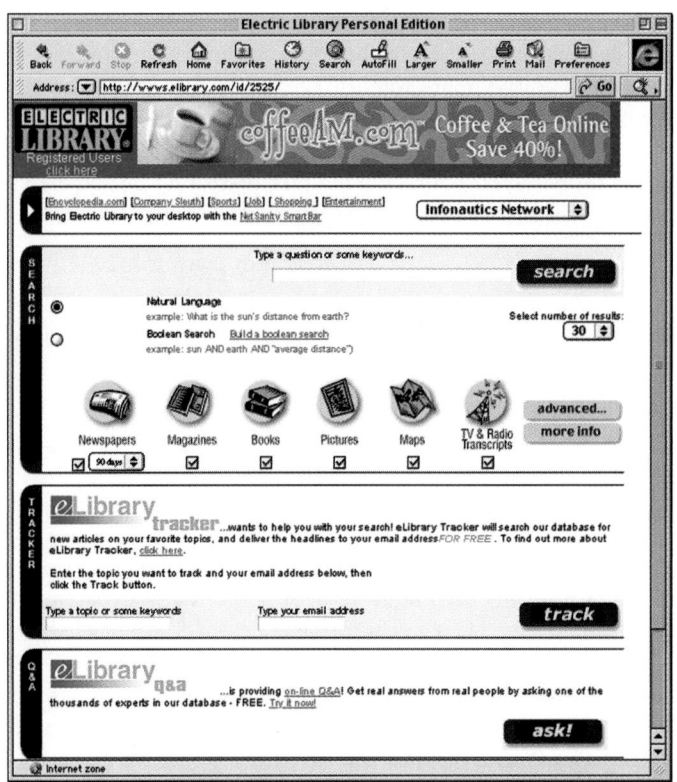

Electric Library is one of the many Internet resources for secondary data. This Web site contains the latest newspaper and magazine articles on a variety of topics.

■ *The Mean.* The statistic most often thought of as an average is the **mean,** the sum of all the items in a group divided by the number of items in the group. The mean is invaluable when comparing one item or individual with a group.

■ *The Median.* When items or numbers are arranged from lowest to highest, as in Exhibit 8.3, it is possible to find the **median**—the midpoint, or the point at which half the numbers are above and half are below.

■ *The Mode.* The **mode** is the number that occurs most often in any series of data or observations. The mode answers the question, How frequently? or What is the usual size or amount? One important use of the mode is to supply marketing information about common sizes of shoes and clothing. If you were the owner of a shoe store, you would not want to stock 4 pairs of every shoe size in each style. You might find that for every 40 pairs of size 8 sold, only 2 of size 12 were sold.

As Exhibit 8.3 demonstrates, a single set of data may be used to produce all three averages.

Index Numbers In business, it is often important to know how results in one period compare with those of another. To express this comparison conveniently, an index number is used. An

mean
Sum of all items in a group, divided by the number of items in the group

median
Midpoint, or the point in a group of numbers at which half are higher and half are lower

mode
Number that occurs the most often in any series of data

EXHIBIT 8.3

MEAN, MEDIAN, AND MODE

The same set of data can be used to produce three kinds of averages, each of which has important business applications.

Salesperson	Sales	
Wilson	$3,000	
Green	5,000	
Carrick	6,000	
Wimper	7,000	— Mean
Keeble	7,500	— Median
Kemble	8,500	
O'Toole	8,500	— Mode
Mannix	8,500	
Caruso	9,000	
Total	$63,000	

index number
Percentage used to compare such figures as prices or costs in one period with those in a base or standard period

index number is a percentage that represents the amount of fluctuation between a base figure, such as a price or cost at one period, and the current figure.

Say an oil company wants to keep an index on the number of workers it employs. It chooses as a base year 1999, when it employed 5,000 workers. In 2000 employment slipped to 4,900 workers. In 2001 it surged to 5,300. The index numbers for the years 2000 and 2001 are obtained by dividing the base-year figure into the current-year figure and then multiplying by 100 to change the resulting decimal to a percentage:

$$\frac{Current\text{-}year\ employment\ (2000)}{Base\text{-}year\ employment} = \frac{4,900}{5,000}$$

$$= 0.98,\ or\ 98\%$$

$$\frac{Current\text{-}year\ employment\ (2001)}{Base\text{-}year\ employment} = \frac{5,300}{5,000}$$

$$= 1.06,\ or\ 106\%$$

These figures tell us that employment was off 2 percent in 2000 but up 6 percent in 2001.

Trends Managers must often determine whether the variations in business activity indicated by statistics have any regular pattern. Suppose that a department store's monthly index of sales shows an increase of 6 percent for June. Before deciding whether to increase the number of salesclerks and the amount of inventory, the manager must know whether the increase in sales will continue into July and August and beyond. **Trend analysis** is the examination of data over a sufficiently long time so that regularities and relationships can be detected, interpreted, and used as the basis for forecasts of business activity.

trend analysis
Examination of data over a sufficiently long period so that regularities and relationships may be detected, analyzed, and used as the basis for forecasts

Presenting Information

Even the most carefully planned and painstakingly prepared data analysis may be a waste of time if your analysis is poorly presented. Presentations of information must be clear and easy to follow. Tables and graphs help, and such visual aids may even be crucial to giving readers a clear picture of the situation.

With all the graphics software available for computers, there is little reason not to present information in a form that has visual impact. Several types of diagrams are used to display relationships among data so that they are turned into meaningful information (see Exhibit 8.4):

- A *line graph* is a line connecting points. Line graphs show trends, such as an increase in profits or a decrease in sales.

- A *bar chart* uses either vertical or horizontal bars to compare information. Because of its simplicity, the bar chart is frequently used in business reports.

- A *pictograph* is a variation of the bar chart, with symbols or pictures instead of bars used to represent data. Pictographs are good attention-getters, but using them can often mean sacrificing some accuracy.

- A *pie chart* is a circle divided into slices. The slices are labeled as percentages of the whole circle, or 100 percent. A pie chart provides a vivid picture of relationships, but it is not good for showing precise data.

- A *statistical map* shows both locations and quantities by variations in color, texture, or shading or by a concentration of dots. Like the pie chart, it shows general relationships better than it shows specifics.

table
Grid for displaying relationships between words and numbers, particularly many precise numbers

A **table,** a grid of words and numbers, is commonly used to present data when there is a large amount of precise numerical information to convey. Exhibit 8.5 shows the standard parts of a table.

Designing Effective Information Systems

As you can see, turning data into useful information requires a lot of work and analysis. Organizations depend on quality information to make good decisions and to help them accomplish their goals. Imagine how much harder it would be for Cisco Systems to offer new products

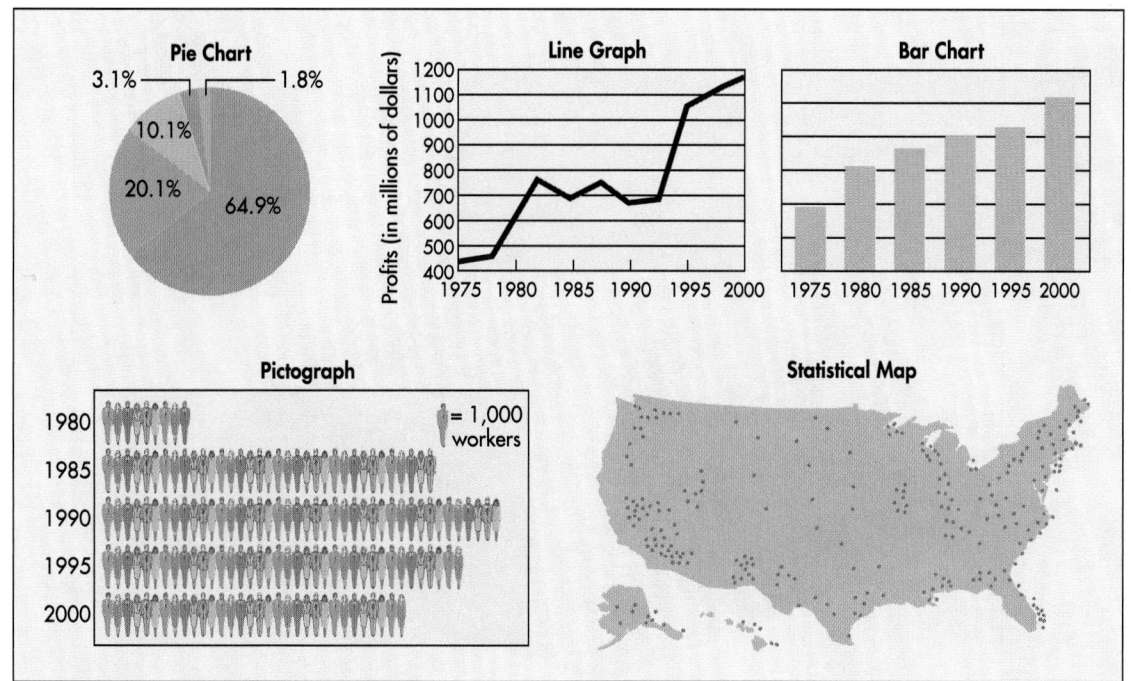

EXHIBIT 8.4

DIAGRAMS USED IN BUSINESS REPORTS

These types of diagrams—pie chart, line graph, bar chart, pictograph, and statistical map—are most often used to present business data.

without knowing sales trends and other vital statistics. Think of how much longer it would take Chambers to respond to customer requests if employees were not able to share their information with management. In fact, the design and development of effective information systems is of such vital importance to a company that some companies hire a top-level manager, called a **chief information officer (CIO)**, to oversee the management of a company's information systems.

The CIO's responsibilities include finding out who in the organization needs what types of information, how these individuals will use this information, how often they will need it, and how they will share it with others. Once the company's information needs have been assessed, the CIO plans what types of data to track and develops systems to collect, track, store, process, retrieve, and distribute the data. Additionally, the CIO oversees the purchase and installation of computer hardware and software and other technologies to facilitate the collection and distribution of information. The types of information systems the CIO designs generally fall into two major categories: operations information systems and management support systems.[9] As Exhibit 8.6 illustrates, each category typically corresponds to business operations at specific levels of the organization.

chief information officer (CIO)
Top corporate executive with responsibility for managing information and information systems

LEARNING
OBJECTIVE   3

Discuss the responsibilities of the chief information officer

EXHIBIT 8.5

THE PARTS OF A TABLE

All tables, whether long or short, simple or complicated, contain a title, column heads (across the top), line heads (down the left side), and entries to complete the matrix. They may also include footnotes and a source note.

GROSS REVENUES BY SOURCE (IN THOUSANDS OF DOLLARS)				
SOURCE OF REVENUE	1998[*]	1999	2000	2001
Entertainment and recreation	445,165	508,444	571,079	643,380
Motion pictures	118,058	152,135	134,785	161,400
Consumer products and other	66,602	80,564	90,909	109,725
TOTAL REVENUES	629,825	741,143	796,773	914,505

[*]Reclassified for comparative purposes and to comply with reporting requirements adopted in 1996.
Source: Company Annual Reports, 1998, 1999, 2000, 2001.

EXHIBIT 8.6

INFORMATION SYSTEMS AND ORGANIZATIONAL LEVELS

Managers and employees at the various levels of an organization rely on different types of information systems to help them accomplish their goals.

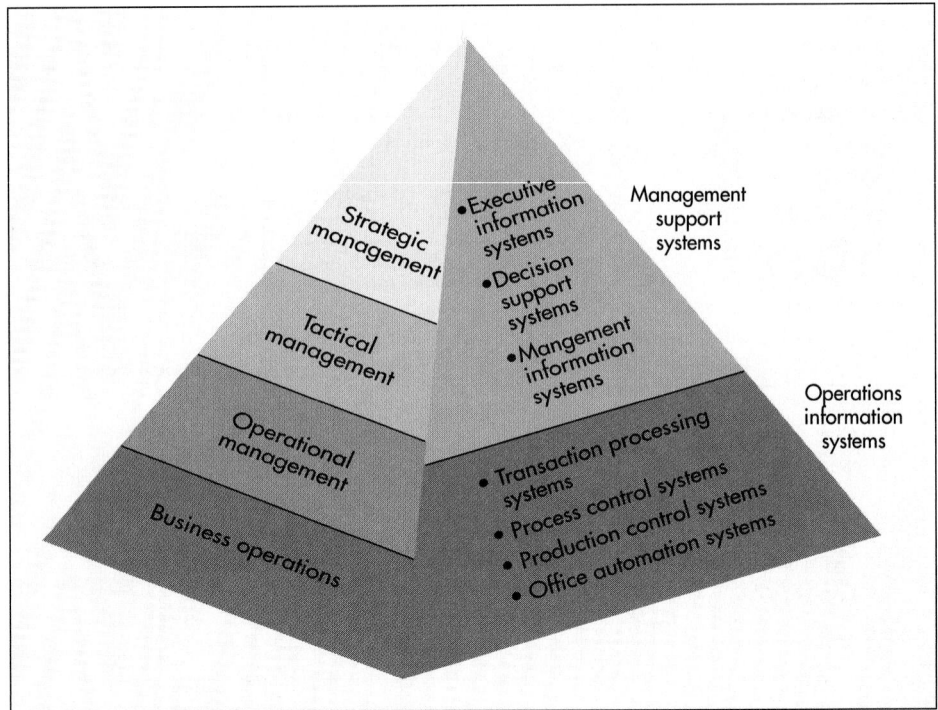

LEARNING OBJECTIVE   4

Differentiate between operations information systems, management information systems, and decision support systems

transaction processing system (TPS) Computerized information system that processes the daily flow of customer, supplier, and employee transactions, including inventory, sales, and payroll records

electronic data interchange (EDI) Information systems that transmit documents such as invoices and purchase orders between computers, thereby lowering ordering costs and paperwork

process control systems Computer systems that use special sensing devices to monitor conditions in a physical process and make necessary adjustments to the process

Operations Information Systems   Operations information systems include transaction processing systems, process and production control systems, and office automation systems. These systems typically support daily operations and decision making for lower-level managers and supervisors.

Much of the daily flow of data into and out of the typical business organization is handled by a **transaction processing system (TPS),** which captures and organizes raw data and converts these data into information. Common transaction processing systems take care of customer orders, billing, employee payroll, inventory changes, and other essential transactions. For example, credit card companies use TPSs to accept charges and to bill cardholders. Another example is the computer that an airline representative uses to assign you a seat on your flight. These TPSs interact with human beings. However, sometimes a TPS interacts directly with another computer system, as when a drugstore's computer senses the need for more products and transmits orders to a drug wholesaler's computers via **electronic data interchange (EDI).** EDI systems transmit specially formatted documents (such as invoices and purchase orders) from one company's computers to another's. This can greatly reduce the time, paperwork, and cost associated with placing and processing orders, thereby making it easier and more profitable for a customer to do business with the company. Nevertheless, EDI systems are costly and complex. As a result, many companies are now moving EDI transactions to the Internet, as Chapter 9 points out.

Operations information systems are also used to make routine decisions that control operational processes. **Process control systems** monitor conditions such as temperature or pressure

Best of the Web Best of the Web Best of

STAY INFORMED WITH CIO

How do chief information officers make smart business decisions? Find out by reading CIO Online, a leading resource for information managers. Log on and research critical information topics, listen to industry experts, receive career advice, get the latest Internet survey information, visit the reading room, join a discussion forum, and more. Don't worry if you missed an issue or two—access to the archives is as easy as a click of the mouse.

www.cio.com

KEEPING PACE WITH TECHNOLOGY AND ELECTRONIC COMMERCE

USING INFORMATION TO MAKE A SCRUBADUB DIFFERENCE

You don't have to be a dot-com company to be on the cutting edge. Consider ScrubaDub, one of the largest car-wash operators in the Northeast. Founded in 1968, the company owns 10 outlets in Massachusettes and Rhode Island, where it has earned a reputation as one of the top innovators in the car-wash business—thanks in part to its savvy use of technology.

In an industry where many companies don't even know the names of their best customers, owners Bob and Dan Paisner have made masterful use of computer databases to develop lasting relationships with thousands of car owners. Customers are encouraged to enroll each of their cars in ScrubaDub's CarCare Club and earn points toward free washes and discounts. A windshield-mounted bar code identifies member cars. When the car pulls into a ScrubaDub location, a scanner, linked to a central database via the Internet, recognizes it and flashes the customer's name and other information on a computer screen so that attendants can greet the driver by name and recommend specific services, such as waxing, based on past purchases.

"Using the Internet for updating our database has saved us hundreds of hours of office work," says the owners, who explain that the system also provides vital operations information. There's a four-day guarantee, for example. If anything dirties your car during that time, you can return it for a free rewash. But first the computer must scan your car's bar code to verify the original wash date.

Cost control is another big benefit of ScrubaDub's technology. Although computers can't vacuum or squeegee, they can make sure there are enough workers on hand to do those jobs. "Our mangers have information on what is happening throughout the chain, giving them the opportunity to make timely changes," says the owners. Moreover, the database helps the company market more effectively by telling the company who its best customers are, what kind of cars they drive, and where they come from. This accountability gives the company a major competitive advantage and is a contributing factor to the company's ongoing success.

■ QUESTIONS FOR CRITICAL THINKING

1. What could a manager learn about ScrubaDub's customers by querying the company's database?

2. What kinds of customer and company information could ScrubaDub communicate by using graphs?

---

change in physical processes. These systems use special sensing devices that take measurements, enabling a computer to make any necessary adjustments to the process.[10]

Production control systems are used to manage the production of goods and services by controlling production lines, robots, and other machinery and equipment. In Chapter 9 we will discuss how computer-aided manufacturing can increase efficiency and improve quality by automating production processes. In some cases, manufacturing software is linked with design software to automate the entire design-and-production cycle. For instance, an engineer designing a new component for a car engine can electronically transfer the design to the production department, which will then control a milling machine that automatically carves the part from a block of steel.

production control systems
Computer systems that manage production by controlling production lines, robots, and other machinery and equipment

Office automation systems (OAS) include any type of operations information system that helps you execute typical office tasks. Whether the job is producing a report or calculating next year's budget, an OAS allows you to complete the task more efficiently by converting the process into an electronic format. Office automation systems range from a single personal computer with word-processing software to networks of computers that allow people to send electronic mail and share work among computers.

office automation systems (OAS)
Computer systems that assist with the tasks that people in a typical business office face regularly, such as drawing graphs or processing documents

Management Support Systems Management support systems are designed to help managers make decisions. A variety of such systems exist, which allow users to analyze data, identify business trends, and make forecasts. A **management information system (MIS)** provides managers with information and support for making effective routine decisions. An MIS takes data from a database and summarizes or restates the data into useful information such as monthly sales figures, daily inventory levels, product manufacturing schedules, employee earnings, and so

management information system (MIS)
Computer system that supplies information to assist in managerial decision making

on. This information is generally organized in a report or graphical format, making it easier for managers to read and interpret.

Whereas a management information system provides structured, routine information for managerial decision making, a **decision support system (DSS)** assists managers in solving highly unstructured and nonroutine problems with the use of decision models and specialized databases. Compared with an MIS, a DSS is more interactive (allowing the user to interact with the system instead of simply receiving information), and it usually relies on both internal and external information.[11] Similar in concept to a DSS is an **executive information system (EIS),** which helps executives make the necessary decisions to keep the organization moving forward. An EIS usually has a more strategic focus than a DSS, and it is used by higher management to plan for the future.

Perhaps the greatest potential for computers to aid decision making and problem solving lies in the development of **artificial intelligence**—the ability of computers to solve problems through reasoning and learning and to simulate human sensory perceptions.[12] One type of computer system that can simulate human reasoning by responding to questions, asking for more information, and making recommendations is the **expert system.**[13] As its name implies, an expert system essentially takes the place of a human expert by helping less knowledgeable individuals make critical decisions. For instance, the troubleshooting methods used by an experienced auto mechanic could be programmed into an expert system. A beginning mechanic could describe a sick engine's symptoms to the system, which would then apply the expert mechanic's facts and rules to suggest which troubleshooting methods might reveal the cause of the problem.

Several software companies have taken expert systems a step further by giving them the ability to suggest innovative solutions for problem solving. Drawing on their preprogrammed knowledge of inventive principles, physics, chemistry, and geometry, such systems often come up with solutions to problems that lead to new-product inventions. One example is a flash for pocket cameras that eliminates "red eye."[14]

A second advance in artificial intelligence to make its way into business is the **speech-recognition system.** Using computer software, a generic vocabulary database, and a microphone, speech-recognition systems enable the user to interact with the computer verbally. Today the average microcomputer can accept spoken words at speeds of up to 125 words per minute. Artificial intelligence techniques enable the computer to learn the user's speech patterns and update its vocabulary database continually. In this way, the system evolves, becoming more intelligent, versatile, and easy to use. Although most systems are still limited to a single user, some systems are able to recognize words spoken by anyone. Business uses for this technology include both navigation, which uses voice commands in place of a mouse to open files, launch programs, and move around in document, and dictation, which enables the user to enter data verbally rather than through the keyboard.[15]

THE ROLE OF COMPUTERS IN INFORMATION MANAGEMENT

Now that you have an idea of what is involved in effective information management, it's time to take a closer look at the role computers play in the information management process. To understand what makes computers tick, we must first distinguish hardware from software and discuss the types of computers that are used in today's workplace. **Hardware** represents the tangible equipment used in a computer system, such as disk drives, keyboards, modems, and *integrated circuits* (small pieces of silicon containing thousands of transistors and electronic circuits). **Software,** on the other hand, encompasses the programmed instructions, or applications, that direct the activity of the hardware.

Types of Computers

Computers can be found in a variety of shapes and sizes. However, the most distinguishing characteristic of any computer is its computing capacity, or the amount of processing that it can accomplish in a unit of time. Four popular classifications of computers by capacity are mainframes, microcomputers, workstations, and supercomputers.

---

decision support system (DSS)
Information system that uses decision models, specialized databases, and artificial intelligence to assist managers in solving highly unstructured and nonroutine problems

executive information system (EIS)
Similar to decision support system but customized to strategic needs of executives

artificial intelligence
Ability of computers to reason, to learn, and to simulate human sensory perceptions

expert system
Computer system that simulates the thought processes of a human expert who is adept at solving particular problems

speech-recognition system
Computer system that recognizes human speech, enabling users to enter data and give commands vocally

hardware
Physical components of a computer system, including integrated circuits, keyboards, and disk drives

software
Programmed instructions that drive the activity of computer hardware

LEARNING OBJECTIVE 5

Describe the four classes of computers

■ *Mainframe computers.* A **mainframe computer** is a large and powerful system capable of handling vast amounts of data. Smaller mainframes are commonly referred to as *midsize computers.*[16] Mainframes are especially useful when large-scale number crunching is involved, as with finance and accounting activities. Other common uses include controlling a manufacturing process in a factory, managing a company's payroll, and maintaining very large databases. As you'll read later in the chapter, many mainframes are being replaced by *client/server systems* composed of groups of smaller computers. However, an estimated 70 to 80 percent of the world's corporate data are still stored on mainframes. Moreover, organizations are discovering that their mainframe computers make excellent "Web servers." This means that the companies are able to use their existing mainframes to support the Internet applications that are becoming an increasingly important part of their business. These applications include sharing documents, sending and receiving e-mail, taking customer orders, and processing transactions.[17]

mainframe computer
A large and powerful computer, capable of storing and processing vast amounts of data

■ *Microcomputers.* A **microcomputer,** often referred to generically as a *personal computer* or *PC,* represents the smallest and least-expensive class of computers. Unlike large mainframes, a microcomputer is built around a single microprocessor. Computers in this category are now available in several sizes, designated by *desktop, laptop, notebook,* and even *palmtop* (for computers that fit in your hand). Because of their versatility, made possible by a huge variety of software applications, microcomputers are now common in homes as well as in both large and small businesses.

microcomputer
Smallest and least-expensive class of computers; often referred to as a personal computer

■ *Workstations.* A **workstation** marries the speed of a midsize computer with the desktop convenience of microcomputers. Workstations are used primarily by designers, engineers, scientists, and other power users who need fast computing and powerful graphics capabilities to solve mathematically challenging problems. Workstations look like microcomputers and are just as "personal" because they are typically used by one person. But they are distinguished from microcomputers by their speed and input/output devices. A typical workstation will have a high-resolution (high-clarity) monitor and other devices that enable the user to create precision drawings and perform other specialized functions.

workstation
Class of computers with the basic size and shape of microcomputers but with the speed of traditional midsize computers; often used for design, engineering, and scientific applications

■ *Supercomputers.* While mainframes are capable of processing huge amounts of data quickly, they are limited in the complexity of calculations they can perform. A scientific calculation, for example, might tie up a university's mainframe for days at a time.[18] **Supercomputers** represent the leading edge in computer performance. They are capable of handling the most complex processing tasks with speeds in excess of 12 trillion calculations per second (a measure of computer speed known as teraflops).[19] Seismic analysis, weather forecasting, complex engineering modeling, and genetic research are among the common uses of supercomputers. Virtual reality design simulators are another application. For instance, Caterpillar designs new tractors and earth movers using virtual reality that lets engineers see how the machines will look and operate before they build physical prototypes.[20]

supercomputers
Computers with the highest level of performance, often boasting speeds greater than 12 trillion calculations per second

Delta Airlines relies on supercomputers to handle massive amounts of data at its Operations Control Center in Atlanta.

Hardware Components

Whether it's a palmtop computer keeping track of your appointment schedule or a supercomputer modeling the structure of a DNA molecule, every computer is made up of a basic set of hardware components. Of course, the hardware in a supercomputer differs greatly from the hardware in a handheld unit, but the concepts are similar. Hardware can be divided into four basic groups: input devices, the central processing unit, output devices, and storage (see Exhibit 8.7).

Input Devices Before it can perform any calculations, a computer needs data. Such data can be entered through a keyboard, mouse, computerized pen, microphone (for speech-recognition systems), or optical scanner. With the growth of the Internet and *multimedia* computer applications, video cameras and digital cameras have also become increasingly important input devices.

EXHIBIT 8.7

HARDWARE ELEMENTS IN A COMPUTER SYSTEM

The primary elements of computer hardware are input devices, the central processing unit, output devices, and storage.

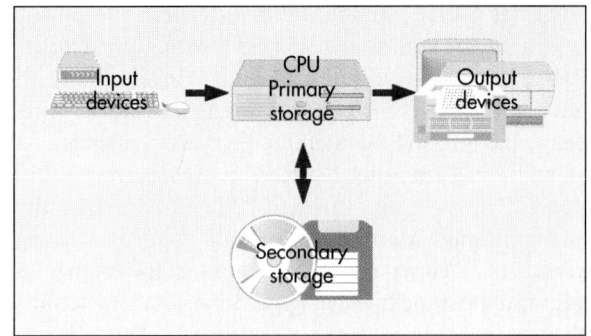

central processing unit (CPU)
Core of the computer, performing the three basic functions of arithmetic (addition, etc.), logic (comparing numbers), and control/communication (managing the computer)

microprocessor
Advanced integrated circuit that combines most of the basic functions of a computer onto a single chip

parallel processing
Use of multiple processors in a single computer unit, with the intention of increasing the speed at which complex calculations can be completed

primary storage device
Storage for data and programs while they are being processed by the computer

random-access memory (RAM)
Primary storage devices allowing a computer to access any piece of data in such memory at random

read-only memory (ROM)
Special circuits that store data and programs permanently but don't allow users to record their own data or programs; a common use of ROM is for the programs that activate start-up routines when the computer is turned on

secondary storage
Computer storage for data and programs that aren't needed at the moment

disk drive
Most common mechanism for secondary storage; includes both hard disk drives and floppy disk (diskette) drives

CD-ROMs
Storage devices that use the same technology as music CDs; popular because of their low cost and large storage capacity

Central Processing Unit A computer's calculations are made in the **central processing unit (CPU),** which interprets and executes program instructions. The CPU performs the three basic functions of arithmetic, logic, and control/communication.[21] In microcomputers the CPU consists of a single integrated circuit, known as a **microprocessor,** and some associated support circuitry. In workstations, mainframes, and supercomputers, the CPU can be either a single processing unit made of multiple integrated circuits or multiple processing units operating in parallel, a scheme known as **parallel processing.** In such a setup, each processor takes one part of the problem—rather like 10 students working on 10 parts of an assignment at the same time.

Output Devices Once the data have been successfully entered and the CPU has processed them, they won't be of any use unless they are sent back to the outside world. The first place a computer's output usually goes is the *display,* or monitor. The display acts in the same basic manner as a television, providing the user with text, graphics, or a combination of both. However, when you need a permanent record or when you need to share hard copy with someone, you will probably use a printer. Engineers and scientists also use *plotters,* output devices that use pens to reproduce a displayed image by drawing it on paper.

In addition, as with input devices, specialized equipment can provide output for particular applications. For example, a *projection panel* is a special display device that connects to your computer and sits on top of a regular overhead projector. These panels can display everything from regular computer screens to videotape from a VCR. When combined with presentation and multimedia software that use graphics, projection panels enable computer users to develop unique and impressive business presentations.

Storage Input, processing, and output complete the basic computing cycle, but this cycle can't happen without some form of storage for the data being processed and for the software that is in charge of the operation. A **primary storage device** stores data and programs while they are being used in the computer. This device usually involves a set of semiconductor components known as **random-access memory (RAM),** so called because the computer can access any piece of data in such memory at random. Computers use RAM for temporary storage of programs and data during input, processing, and output operations. Unless it is provided with special backup circuitry, RAM is erased when electrical power is removed from the computer. RAM's counterpart is called **read-only memory (ROM),** which uses special circuits for permanent storage. ROM keeps its contents even when power is cut off, and it cannot be accessed by the user for everyday data storage. ROM typically stores programs such as the start-up routines that computers go through when they are first turned on, which involves checking for problems and getting ready to go to work.

Secondary storage takes care of data and programs that aren't needed at the moment and provides a permanent record of those data and programs. For instance, if you've finished working on a report that you might need to modify in a month, you put it in secondary storage. The most common mechanism for secondary storage is the **disk drive,** which can be of three types: a hard disk drive, a floppy disk drive, or a CD-ROM drive. *Hard disk drives* are usually enclosed inside the computer and can store data internally on rigid magnetic disks. *Floppy disk drives,* on the other hand, store data on removable magnetic disks. Although they are easily portable, floppy disks, (also called *diskettes*) can store far less information than hard disks. **CD-ROMs** are based on the same technology as music compact discs (CDs) and can store the equivalent of about 477 floppy diskettes. Run on *CD-ROM drives,* they are a key component in multimedia computing, which combines regular computer data with audio, computer animation, photography, and full-motion video.[22] The rapid and universal acceptance of the CD-ROM has given rise to another technology: CD-Re-Writable (CD-RW), which allows you to write and rewrite to a CD just as you do to a diskette.[23]

Computer Software

Computer applications in today's business world are almost limitless. Companies use them to set goals, hire employees, order supplies, manage inventory, sell products, store data, communicate with employees, and perform countless other tasks. The term *application* refers both to an actual task, such as preparing reports and memos, and to the *software* that is used to complete the task.

Systems Software Systems software is perhaps the most important software category because it includes **operating systems,** which control such fundamental actions as storing data on disk drives and displaying text or graphics on monitors. Commonly used operating systems include MS-DOS, Windows (which increases the usability of MS-DOS by incorporating a graphical user interface), UNIX, IBM's OS/2, and Apple's Macintosh system. When you first turn on a computer, the operating system begins to direct the actions that enable the various computer hardware devices and software applications to interact in ways that are useful to you. A word-processing program, for instance, can't read the disk or write text to the display by itself; it relies on the operating system to direct the computer's hardware and to manage the flow of data into, around, and out of the system.

operating systems
Class of software that controls the computer's hardware components

Application Software **Application software** encompasses programs that perform specific user functions, such as word processing, database management, desktop publishing, and so on. Application software can be either *custom* (developed specifically for a single user or set of users and not sold to others) or *general purpose* (developed with the goal of selling it to multiple users). Commercially available general-purpose software products are commonly referred to as *packages,* as in a *word-processing package.* In today's business-software market, the array of software packages is vast, including products that can prepare books and newspapers, monitor the stock market, locate potential customers on a map, track employee records, and produce sales reports, to name just a few. Exhibit 8.8 highlights the features of fundamental business software applications. Keep in mind that many of these individual programs are sold bundled together as integrated software programs such as Microsoft Office or Claris Works, making it easier to incorporate the work from one program into another.

application software
Programs that perform specific functions for users, such as word processing or spreadsheet analysis

Communications Software Today computers play a central role in business communications. A computer can exchange information with other computers through communications software, which opens up an entirely new spectrum of business capabilities: *electronic mail,* or *e-mail,* enables users to transmit written messages in electronic format between computers; *bulletin board systems (BBS)* and *newsgroups* are electronic versions of traditional bulletin boards that allow users to exchange ideas, news, and other information; file transfer software enables the transfer of digital files—including data, programs, text, images, sounds, and videos—from one computer to another; and EDI systems permit computers to communicate with each other to handle transactions that used to require human intervention.[24] Computers can also send and receive faxes as easily as a fax machine if they have the right software and hardware. Furthermore, computers enable people in different locations to communicate face-to-face through videoconferencing and

Equitel, a division of Siemens Corp., in São Paulo, Brazil, uses videoconferencing to communicate and collaborate with its customers, suppliers, and employees who are thousands of miles apart.

Software Application Programs

Word processing: Word processing programs enable users to type, store, edit, format, and print documents for almost any purpose. Text and graphics can be added, deleted, and moved without retyping the entire document. Special word-processing features include spelling checkers, grammar checkers, automatic text entry, mail merge (a feature that allows you to insert names into a generic form letter, giving the appearance that the letter is personalized), and automatic page numbering. Repetitive keystrokes or tasks can be recorded in a *macro*, a customized program you create to handle the typing or task automatically.

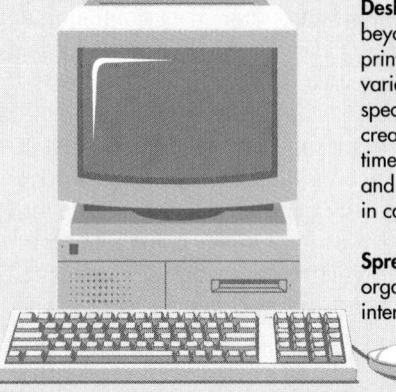

Desktop publishing (DTP): Desktop publishing software goes a step beyond typical word processors by allowing designers to lay out printer-ready pages that incorporate artwork, photos, and a large variety of typographic elements. Together with scanners and other specialized input devices, publishing programs let businesspeople create sophisticated documents on their computers in a fraction of the time it once took. Flyers, brochures, user manuals, annual reports, and newsletters are just a few of the documents that can be produced in camera-ready formats that go directly to the print shop.

Spreadsheets: A spreadsheet is a program designed to let users organize and manipulate data in a row-column matrix. The intersection of each row-and-column pair is called a *cell*, and every cell can contain a number, a mathematical formula, or text used as a label. Among the spreadsheet's biggest strengths is the ability to quickly update masses of calculations when conditions change. This is possible because a spreadsheet will automatically update a record if one of the records to which it is linked is changed. Businesspeople use spreadsheets to solve a wide variety of problems, ranging from statistical analysis to simulation models used in decision support systems.

Databases: Database management software allows users to create, store, maintain, rearrange, and retrieve contents of databases. Almost anywhere you find a sizable amount of data in electronic format, you'll find a database management program at work. Such programs help users produce useful information by allowing users to look at data from various perspectives.

Graphics: Graphic programs allow users to create and modify charts, graphs, tables, and diagrams. Together with specialized output devices such as plotters and color printers, business graphics software can produce overhead transparencies, 35 mm slides, posters, and signs. The graphic images created with these software packages can be imported in publishing and word-processing programs for incorporation into documents and presentations.

EXHIBIT 8.8

BUSINESS SOFTWARE APPLICATIONS

Software applications have been developed to satisfy almost every business need. Here's a quick review of their features.

other telecommunication devices. In fact, new developments in communications software and computer languages promise even more exciting possibilities.

For years, programmers all over the world have been quietly developing XML, short for Extensible Markup Language. Simply put, XML provides a standard way for computer applications and Web sites to understand each other and pass data—such as text, spreadsheet numbers, pricing lists, employee records, and so on—back and forth.[25] Today, to check your finances on the Internet, you use your PC to access the Web site of each financial institution you do business with. But with XML and any kind of digital device, in the future you will soon be able to ask a single "Web service" to give you a composite picture by combining the information from multiple Web sites. With a few keystrokes, you might even be able to transfer money from your Schwab account to your Chase checking account. Moreover, users will be able to excerpt text or numerical tables directly from a Web page, paste them into a word-processing or spreadsheet application on a PC, and then edit or annotate the text or manipulate the numbers. (In the past, when using the cut-and-paste feature on a Web site, text lost its formatting and spreadsheets become impossible to manipulate.)[26]

Telecommunications and Computer Networks

It used to be that each piece of equipment in an office was self-contained. Even in the early years of business computing, the computer was used for word and data processing, the fax machine was used for transmitting data, the telephone was a device for communicating verbally, and the pager was for contacting people when they weren't near a telephone. Similarly, at home the computer, the television, the radio, and the telephone were all separate appliances that served individual purposes. However, all of these distinctions are now becoming blurred, thanks to advances in telecommunications and computer technology.

This linking of computers and communication devices is creating new opportunities for companies to accomplish their goals more efficiently and more effectively. For one thing, businesspeople can now easily stay in touch with their offices, their computers, their associates, and their families while they travel the world. It is also much easier for workers in remote locations to share work, ideas, and resources. What makes all of this possible are complex networks of linked computers and communication devices such as those manufactured by Cisco.

Types of Networks The brief discussion of communications earlier in this chapter hinted at one of the most important issues in business computing: connecting multiple computers in one way or another and allowing them to exchange data, a process known as **data communications.** Data communications systems connect users to all sorts of information both inside and outside the organization, as well as to expensive resources such as supercomputers and high-speed laser printers. However, computers are not limited to data communications only; audio and video communications between computers are also becoming increasingly common. How do they do it? Through networks.

As defined in Component Chapter A, a *network* is a collection of hardware, software, and communications media that are linked so they can share data and expensive hardware. Networks are classified by the size of their geographic area. In a **wide area network (WAN),** computers at different geographic locations are linked through one of several transmission media. In contrast, a **local area network (LAN),** as its name implies, meets data communications needs within a small area, such as an office or a university campus. As we discussed in Component Chapter A, intranets are wide area private corporate networks that allow employees to communicate with each other quickly, regardless of their location.

In the past, computer networks were highly centralized, usually consisting of a number of terminals connected to a mainframe host. However, the affordability and power of today's microcomputers has led to the emergence of client/server networks as the new standard. In a **client/server system,** a server computer—which can be anything from a microcomputer to a supercomputer—performs certain functions for its clients, such as data and applications software storage. The client computer, which is typically a microcomputer or workstation, relies on the server for processing support, but it also runs certain applications and performs certain functions on its own. By sharing processing duties, the client and server optimize application efficiency. For example, the server might store and maintain a centralized corporate database. Using *front-end software,* the client user downloads part of the database from the server to the client. The user can then process the data on the client computer without burdening the server. When finished, the user uploads the processed data to the server's *back-end software* for processing and storage.

Network Hardware Any computer can be part of a network, provided it has the right hardware, software, and transmission media. To communicate over standard telephone lines, a computer must be equipped with a **modem** (modulator-demodulator), which can be either a stand-alone unit or a circuit board that is plugged into the computer. The transmitting computer's modem converts digital computer signals to analog signals so that they can be transmitted over telephone lines. The receiving computer's modem converts the signals from analog back to digital. Modems are always required for data transmission via telephone lines, but are not necessarily required for other transmission media. For instance, some Internet-ready digital phones, pagers, computers, and other wireless communication devices transmit digital information over networks through antennas, satellites, cables, and special phone lines.[27]

In addition to modems, networks may depend on several other components to keep the network running smoothly. Front-end processors, multiplexers, and routers all work behind the scenes to help the network operate efficiently, and to enable different networks to communicate with each other. Exhibit 8.9 explains the role that each of these components plays in a network.

Network Transmission Media When people speak of a computer as being "online," they mean that it is part of a network. The "lines" that link the computers in the network may actually be one of several different transmission media. Currently the most common medium is telephone lines.

data communications
Process of connecting computers and allowing them to send data back and forth

wide area network (WAN)
Computer network that encompasses a large geographic area

local area network (LAN)
Computer network that encompasses a small area, such as an office or a university campus

client/server system
Computer system design in which one computer (the server) contains software and data used by a number of attached computers (the clients); the clients also have their own processing capabilities, and they share certain tasks with the server, enabling the system to run at optimum efficiency

modem
Hardware device that allows a computer to communicate over a regular telephone line

LEARNING
OBJECTIVE   6

Describe the primary hardware components and transmission media of a computer network

EXHIBIT 8.9

HARDWARE COMPONENTS IN COMPUTER NETWORKS

Computer networks often rely on several hardware components to help them transmit data more efficiently. The *front-end processor* establishes a link between the source of the transmission and the destination, thereby freeing up the host to take care of other processing duties. The *multiplexer's* job is to gather data from several low-speed devices, such as terminals and printers, and concentrate it for transmission over a single communications channel, saving both time and expense. *Routers* link networks that use different operating systems and communications protocols. When a message is sent from a computer in one network to a computer in an incompatible network, the router converts the message to the necessary protocol and routes it to its final destination.

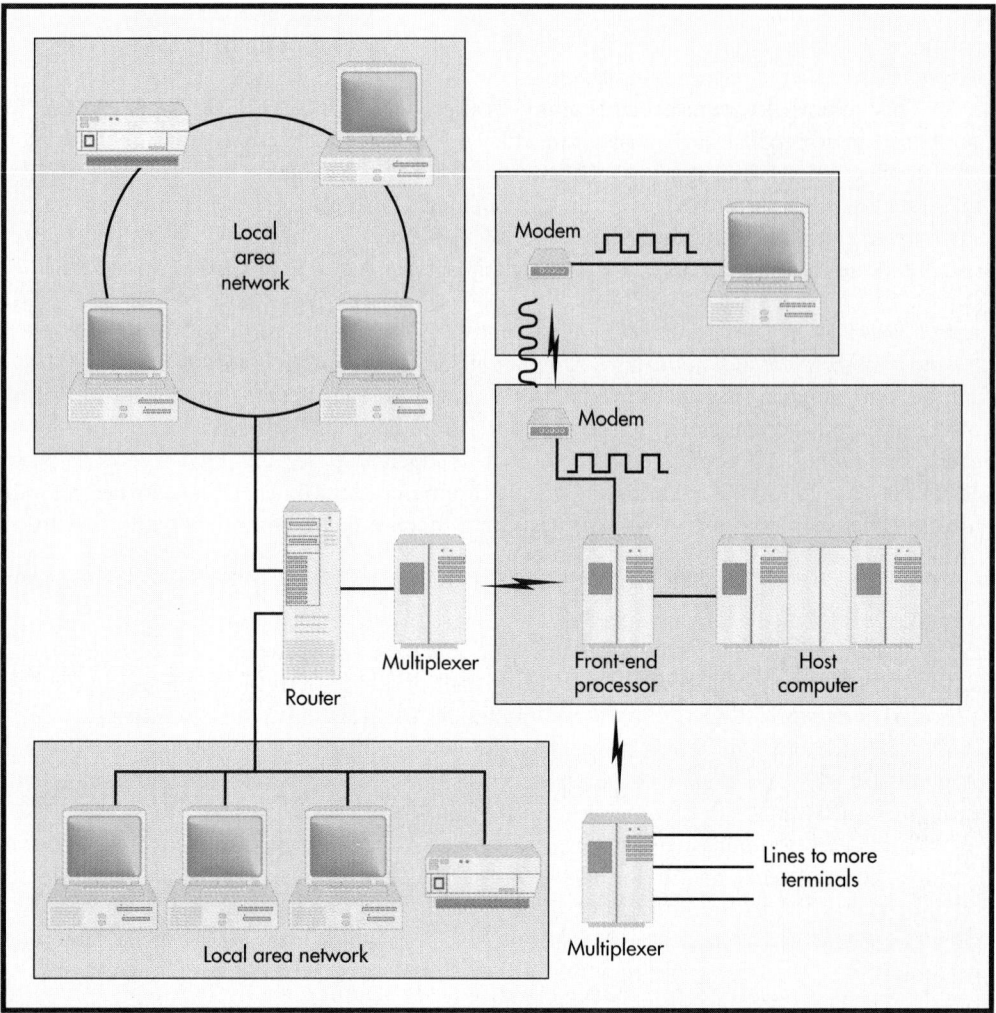

These lines consist of two insulated copper wires bundled in pairs. Because virtually all homes and businesses in the United States are wired for telephones, these lines have been the natural choice for wide area networks and the Internet.

Cable The speed at which standard telephone lines can transmit data is limited. Therefore, many LANs use *coaxial cable* to achieve high-speed data transmission. Coaxial cable is the same type of wire used to bring cable channels to your television. Many cable television companies now offer Internet access over their coaxial lines, which requires using a specially designed *cable modem.*[28]

Standard telephone lines and coaxial cable transmit data as electrical signals. In contrast, **fiber optic cable** transmits data as laser-generated pulses of light at incredibly fast speeds. Transmitted data is measured in bits; a standard phone line can transmit up to 56,000 bits per second. However, researchers at Lucent Bell Labs recently transmitted 3.28 terabits per second of data over a 180-mile stretch of fiber optic cable—that's roughly 20 million times faster than the speed of today's phone lines. Put differently, a 3.28 terabit capacity would be capable of moving three times today's global Internet traffic every second.[29]

Fiber optic cable now links the major countries and cities of the world for both voice and data transmission. However, because of the high cost involved, it will probably be quite a while before homes and businesses are linked by a universal fiber optic network. Instead, telephone companies are developing technologies to increase the data transmission capacity, or **bandwidth**, of common telephone lines.

Wireless Communication Wireless communication offers an alternative to standard telephone, coaxial, and fiber optic lines. Just as humans can now communicate without wires via

fiber optic cable
Cable that transmits data as laser-generated pulses of light; capable of transmitting data at very fast speeds

bandwidth
Maximum capacity of a data transmission medium

Best of the Web Best of the Web Best of

RIDE THE TECHNOLOGY WAVE

Computer technology advances at a dizzying pace. Today's industry standards in hardware and software can become dinosaurs almost overnight. This can be especially problematic for businesses that spend thousands, or even millions, of dollars on computer systems intended to improve productivity. Fortunately, a number of excellent resources are available on the Internet to help both businesspeople and home computer users stay on top of the advancing waves of technology. *PC Magazine Online* is one such resource. This Web site offers news on future technologies, reviews of current hot products, and hints for effective information and technology management, as well as hundreds of free software downloads. Take some time to explore this resource. In business today, any extra information you can get about technology trends may become a competitive advantage.
www.zdnet.com/pcmag

cellular telephones and pagers, so can computers send and receive data without being "hardwired" to a network. This feat is accomplished by transmitting data as microwave signals or radio signals to the receiving computer via stations located on mountains, towers, or tall buildings or by satellites orbiting the earth. **Wireless transceivers** are small devices attached to the computer that transmit and receive data. The mobility offered by this configuration is ideal for many applications.

wireless transceivers
Small hardware attachments that enable a computer to transmit and receive data

At Wal-Mart Stores, for example, customers no longer pace the aisles while an employee checks whether an item missing from the shelf is available. With a few keystrokes on a wireless handheld computer, employees can find out on the spot whether merchandise is in the stockroom or at a nearby store. Similarly, handheld wireless computers do double duty as order pads and cash registers at some restaurants. Orders can be transmitted and credit cards electronically billed, right at tables.[30]

Wireless technology is also changing the traditional office setup. At Postnet, the Swedish postal service's Internet subsidiary, for example, wireless technology is a part of the company's culture. There are no desks at Postnet, just tables with electrical and data-connection cables. Few people work at the same table from one day to the next. Most simply pick any free table, plug in a laptop, and get down to business. "When people go home, the only thing left on the table is cables," says Lisbeth Gustafsson, Postnet's CEO. Gustafsson spends most of her day walking around the office carrying her mobile phone, which is connected to the company's main switchboard. "If I had a fixed phone, I would have to be in a fixed place, and that's not part of our concept. The concept here is mobility." And it's a concept that promises to change the way people shop, work, and go about their daily lives.[31]

TECHNOLOGY ISSUES AFFECTING TODAY'S WORKPLACE

Computers are machines, and most machines can be used either well or poorly. Just as automobiles are both convenient and dangerous, computers can be both a help and a hindrance. A computer can greatly improve an employee's productivity, but it can also create new ways for employees to shirk responsibility, such as playing computer games and surfing the Internet. Computers can be a terrific source of customer information, but if put in the hands of a wrongdoer, serious damage can be inflicted on a person's privacy or on a company's ability to operate. As you can imagine, the use of technology in the workplace is continually challenged with a variety of issues.

An employee at the Electronic Boutique in Schaumburg, Illinois, scans a shopper's selections, charges his card, and prints a receipt using a portable check-out station.

KEEPING PACE WITH TECHNOLOGY AND ELECTRONIC COMMERCE

WAIT, DON'T PUNCH THAT COMPUTER MONITOR!

In offices around the nation, tech glitches have tempers flaring. Workers everywhere are mad at their modem, mad at the Internet. Technology failures seem to cause more headaches than summertime road construction. Copiers, cell phones, modems—nothing seems to work the way it should.

Few deny that technology has been a boon to time-starved workers, but glitches mean newfangled equipment can sometimes do more to raise blood pressure than productivity. In the old days, fixing problems was often as easy as changing a typewriter ribbon. Now, employees must wait for an army of trained technicians to get them back to work. Some are finding that the slightest technology snag is all it takes to set them off.

More than 80 percent of network managers report that users have become abusive—smashing monitors, breaking keyboards, or kicking hard drives—when faced with computer woes. "One guy ripped out a keyboard. Another guy punched out a screen, he was so frustrated," recalls the owner of one computer consulting and repair firm. "He was actually relieved because he'd gotten even. I just went outside, chuckled, and came in and did my job."

When technology fails, what causes workers to feel like a shaken up can of soda ready to explode? Experts say they feel this way for several reasons:

- *We expect instant fixes.* In an age of microwave lunches, videoconferencing, and instant e-mail, employees aren't used to delays.

- *We don't have time for technology woes.* Companies have shed excess fat by getting rid of employees and piling extra work on fewer individuals. With so much to do, workers don't have the spare time to fritter away on technology woes.

- *We're taking out anger about other issues on technology.* The wrath workers exhibit toward their equipment can be a sign of deeper problems. Employees may vent at their equipment even though they're really steamed about a boss, job responsibilities, or an organization.

So if your computer screen is struck by the dreaded "blue screen of death," what should you do? Putting a fist through the monitor certainly won't make things better, warn experts. Instead, take a deep breath or take a walk around the block. Remember, technology troubles probably will always be around, so learning how to cope with them is a necessity in today's workplace.

■ QUESTIONS FOR CRITICAL THINKING

1. What can a company do to help prevent such employee demonstrations of anger?

2. What can employees do to minimize technology failures?

LEARNING OBJECTIVE *7*

Discuss four technology issues affecting today's workplace

Data Security

Before computers, a typical company conducted the vast majority of its business on paper. Important files and documents were kept under lock and key, and when something was sent to someone across the office or in another part of the country, security precautions were almost always used. Furthermore, only a limited number of people had access to vital company data. But today's move from paper-based systems to electronic data management poses a real threat to corporate security.[32]

Global networks increase the possibility that crucial information sent over an intranet or the Internet can fall into the wrong hands. Of course, cyberterrorism—orchestrated attacks on a company's information systems for political or economic purposes—is a very real threat. But an even greater security threat is a network without proper safeguards. Vulnerable networks can become a high-tech sieve that lets crooks steal or destroy sensitive data. That's because digital data are far easier to duplicate and disseminate. Furthermore, a PC without the proper password protections can easily become a fountain of insider information.

For these reasons, experts advise companies to install proper security systems and take these security measures: (1) Provide ongoing security education; (2) conduct background checks on all new employees; and (3) maintain clearly defined security policies that at a minimum encourage employees to use passwords, turn computer systems off when not in use, and rely on encryption when sending sensitive e-mail. Taking these measures, will of course, deter potential offenders, but it will not guarantee the security of your information. Systems protected by some of the world's foremost computer engineers can be vulnerable to attack, a lesson Microsoft learned after hackers broke into the company's computer network and viewed confidential data.[33]

Information Privacy

Information privacy in today's workplace is another hot issue. Employers must find the right balance between protecting valuable company information and respecting employees' privacy rights. For instance, many employees erroneously believe that their e-mail and voice mail messages are private, and they're surprised when e-mail ends up in places they did not intend it to go. But employers have the legal right to monitor everything from an employee's Web access to the content of their company e-mail or voice mail messages. According to a survey by the American Management Association, about 35 percent of major U.S. companies keep tabs on workers by recording phone calls or voice mail and by checking employees' computer files and e-mail.[34] Moreover, both e-mail and voice mail can be used as evidence in court cases.[35] Therefore, a good rule of thumb is not to say anything in e-mail or voice mail that you would not want to see published in a newspaper.

Employee Productivity

Maintaining a high level of employee productivity is another challenge companies are facing. E-mail, voice mail, conference calls, and faxes interrupt employees while they work. Chat or real-time conversation windows can pop up on computer screens and demand immediate conversation. And the percentage of employees who use company resources for personal business is astounding (see Exhibit 8.10). Sending personal e-mail and faxes and surfing the Net are the three most common employee abuses.[36] Still, it's hard to be productive if you can't use the Internet when you need it, so restricting employees' access may be counterproductive.

Sabotage and Theft

Today, criminals are doing everything from stealing intellectual property and committing fraud to committing pranks or, worse yet, acts of cyberterrorism in which political groups or unfriendly governments nab crucial information. For all the sophisticated work on firewalls, intrusion-detection systems, encryption, and computer security, it takes a relatively simple

Many businesspeople on the road today are not being nearly as mindful as they should be about protecting sensitive company information in public. Using laptops and cell phones in public places, for example, could allow competitors to learn about a company's top-secret marketing plan or other confidential information.

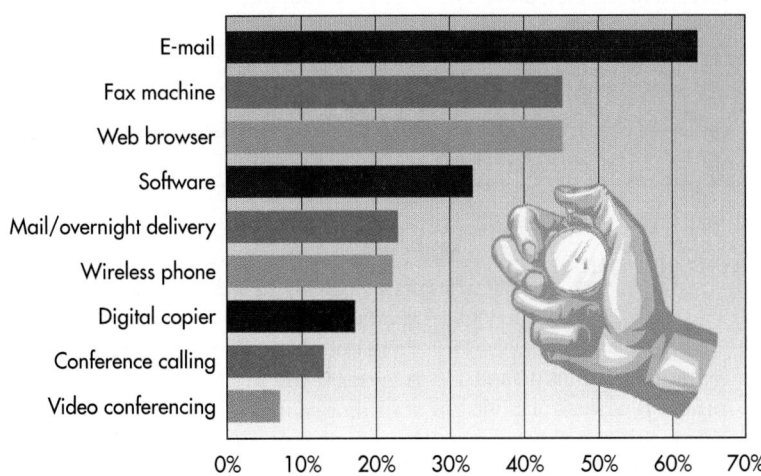

EXHIBIT 8.10

PERCENTAGE OF EMPLOYEES WHO USE OFFICE RESOURCES FOR PERSONAL BUSINESS

Everyone's doing it: Photocopying tax returns on the office copier, faxing a loan application, slipping personal mail into an overnight delivery envelope. According to a recent Ziff Davis survey, the Net is still the top company resource most workers use for personal business.

Best of the Web Best of the Web Best of

LEARN THE RULES OF THE ROAD

Business owners, managers, and employees who use technology in the workplace should be familiar with rules of technology and e-commerce before they cruise on the superhighway. Do you know the laws involving privacy, security, fraud, and intellectual property? Find out what the legal experts have to say about these hot topics by logging on to the Electronic Commerce Resource Center and checking out the legal issues. Need to brush up on your netiquette? Read what Emily Postnews has to say in a satirical Q & A. Finally, stop by Cookie Central to learn what your options are next time you catch someone leaving a trail of crumbs on your hard drive. www.becrc.org/index.html

technique (like dialing a telephone number repeatedly) to tie up some of the biggest e-commerce sites. EBay, Yahoo!, Amazon.com, CNN, and others discovered this fact the hard way when traffic to their sites was virtually choked off in February 2000 by a prankster. It was a huge wake-up call for businesses as they realized that they need to spend as much time protecting their Web sites and networks as they do linking them with customers, suppliers, and contractors.[37]

Computer viruses, hidden programs that can work their way into computer systems and erase or corrupt data and programs, are the most common form of computer sabotage. Computer viruses behave much like human viruses by invisibly attaching themselves to computer data and programs that come into contact with them. They can be spread by diskettes, electronic bulletin boards, or computer networks, including the Internet. The "love bug" virus, which shut down the e-mail systems of the Pentagon, Congress, Ford Motor, British Parliament, the Danish government, and thousands of others in May 2000, was spread via e-mail. The virus originated in Asia and swept across Europe and throughout North and South America as quickly as the morning sun moved around the globe.[38]

There is no way to entirely stop the spread of computer viruses, as new ones are created all the time. However, a number of excellent "vaccine" software programs exist that search for and destroy viruses and prevent new ones from infecting your computer system. You can reduce the chances of your system becoming infected by using such software to periodically scan your hardware and software for viruses and by being very cautious about what programs and files you load onto your hard drive.

Regardless of the type of sabotage, the FBI now estimates that reported computer losses add up to $10 billion a year, and the biggest threat comes from within. Up to 60 percent of computer break-ins are from employees. Still, most attacks go unreported because corporate victims want to avoid bad publicity.[39] And the situation could get worse. The United States will soon be awash in Web-browsing televisions, networked game consoles, smart refrigerators, and all kinds of wireless telecommunication devices—all of which have powerful processors, all of which are connected to the Net, and all of which are vulnerable to attacks.

 FOCUSING ON E-BUSINESS TODAY

Going Mobile: The Exciting Future of M-Commerce

Move over big color monitors, ergonomic keyboards, and multigigabyte disk drives. The Internet is downsizing. If it hasn't already, wireless technology will soon put the Internet in your pocket, replace fixed-line phones, and render many offices superfluous. It will extend the electronic marketplace into hundreds of millions (even billions) of pockets, purses, and cars. Instead of waiting patiently for you to sit down and log on, the mobile Net will be riding shotgun through your life, flashing, beeping, and vibrating with buying opportunities.

DON'T CALL US, WE'LL CALL YOU

Consider a scenario from the near future. Customers entering a butcher shop are offered a discount for waving their cell phone through an infrared sensor that records the telephone's number. Business at the store is brisk throughout the day. But near closing time, the butcher is anxious to get rid of some prime cuts of Argentine beef. So he sends out a special offer to the cell phones of customers who have ordered Argentine beef recently—and who happen to be near the store. The mobile network finds these customers and charges the store a few cents for each message delivered (although an advertiser might pick up half the tab). Customers who buy the Argentine beef online get a discount, and the cost of their purchase is charged to the debit card inside their phone.

LEARNING OBJECTIVE 8

Explain how advances in wireless technology will change the way we conduct e-business and list the challenges that must be overcome before these changes can take place

Of course, several hurdles must be cleared before this type of m-commerce (mobile electronic commerce) can happen. Currently most mobile Internet users can get lines of text, without graphic, video, or sound. Now companies must develop media content that fits on matchbox-size display screens, slips through narrow bandwidths, and requires no keyboards or heavy disk drives. Also, wireless connection speeds must improve significantly. We haven't solved these problems yet, but technological advancements are in the works. After struggling with the failure of early mobile-Internet software, called WAP (wireless application protocol), a new communications standard for the wireless Web is being developed to allow users to see on a tiny screen a mini-version of what is displayed on a PC. Called 3G (for Third Generation), the protocol is complex because it must ensure that m-commerce services work as uniformly as possible across all leading wireless communications technologies and on all end-user operating systems. Nonetheless, 3G has a long way to go before it turns phones into replacements for the PC—especially if you live in the United States.

UNITED STATES LAGS IN M-COMMERCE

In Europe and Asia, people are using mobile phones to send text messages to other users (instead of calling them), to exchange e-mail, to read the morning news, to surf certain Web sites, and to make purchases (such as movie tickets, flowers, or items from a vending machine) and charge them to their monthly phone bill. But it may be some time before that kind of m-commerce takes off in the United States.

The biggest reason for the U.S. lag in m-commerce is the lack of a uniform standard for digital communica-

CUTTING THE CORD: WIRELESS INTERNET SUBSCRIBERS

	1999	2003
United States	560,000	73.1 million
Western Europe	91,000	72.0 million
Asia Pacific	460,000	143.4 million
Japan	3.8 million	40.9 million

tions. In Europe, bureaucrats have mandated one standard (called the Global System for Mobile Communications, or GSM). Japan has endorsed GSM too. But in the United States, the FCC caved in to intensive lobbying efforts by various corporate interests and adopted several wireless standards. So now it struggles under the weight of a regional (as opposed to a national) licensing system. This regional system adds layers of complexity to any m-commerce effort and makes it expensive for companies to develop new products (because they must adhere to multiple communication standards).

KEEP YOUR EYES ON FINLAND

Despite its small size and relative isolation in the Arctic Circle, Finland leads the pack in mobile phone technology and its applications. The country is a laboratory of eager users and will soon pioneer the use of so-called third-generation mobile phones that boast lightning-quick access to the Internet. Part of the reason for Finland's advancement is its geography. When telecommunications developed in the 1970s, Finns were more inclined to pursue wireless options because the costs of running cable to isolated pockets of a vast and frozen nation were daunting. Thus, wireless technology became a priority for the government and the private sector.

Today the wireless mentality is so ingrained in Finland that many new homeowners don't bother ordering fixed-line service. An astonishing 70 percent of Finns own mobile phones, compared with about 25 percent of Americans. Even Finland's kids are hooked. Some have become so talented at creating text messages with a single thumb punching a phone keypad that retailers stage promotions in which the fastest finger in Finland wins a free phone.

MOBILE E-COMMERCE IS DIFFERENT

Make no mistake, however, m-commerce is radically different from its plugged-in kin. It is not for shopping for books or browsing Web sites for ski weekends. Instead, m-commerce has everything to do with speed and location, with short requests for information and prompt, relevant replies. In other words, don't think of it as a miniature version of the Web we already know. Instead, think of it as a Web-on-the-go—one that will find you when necessary (as the butcher shop scenario suggests). Locating you is possible because mobile-phone services communicate via base stations whose precise locations are known.

Of course, being logged on to the Net 24 hours a day has many advantages. But for many, having their whereabouts known day and night is a growing concern. Some fear that the marriage of cell phones and the Net will increase the trend toward a never-ending workday.

Others worry that it might turn their cell phone into a remote device controlling their life. Still others worry about the security of wireless transactions. For instance, when users send a bit of information from their cell phone to their wireless carrier, there is a vulnerable moment in the journey when the information is unsecured. Regardless of all these concerns, m-commerce is the next wave of technological growth. And with more and more wireless devices being developed daily, m-commerce promises to change the way companies do business—again![40]

SUMMARY OF LEARNING OBJECTIVES

1. Explain the importance of information and the characteristics of useful information.

Employees and managers need information to make better decisions and to do their jobs. For information to be useful, it must be accurate, timely, complete, relevant, and concise, and it must reach the right people at the right time and in the right form.

2. Distinguish between data and information, and identify the principal sources of data.

Data are recorded facts and statistics; information is created when data are arranged in such a manner as to be meaningful for a particular problem or situation. The principal sources of data are internal data, which consist mainly of company records and documents, and external data, which are documents and records that are obtained from outside sources. Both internal and external data may be primary data or secondary data. Primary data do not already exist; instead you must gather primary data on your own. Secondary data do exist; they consist of information that was previously gathered by other people to meet their needs.

3. Discuss the responsibilities of the chief information officer.

The chief information officer (CIO) is responsible for designing and developing the company's information systems. This task involves assessing the company's needs, deciding on what data to track, and developing systems to track, store, process, retrieve, and distribute the data. Additionally, the CIO is responsible for installing computer hardware and software and other technologies to assist with the collection and distribution of information.

4. Differentiate between operations information systems, management information systems, and decision support systems.

Operations information systems include transaction processing systems, process control systems, and office automation systems. These systems support daily operations and provide the information lower-level managers and supervisors need in order to make decisions that affect the operations of a company. By contrast, management information systems provide managers with information they need to make effective routine decisions, whereas decision support systems assist managers in solving nonroutine problems.

5. Describe the four classes of computers.

Mainframes are large, powerful computers capable of processing and storing huge amounts of data. Microcomputers or PCs are the smallest and least-expensive computers and their processing capabilities are limited. Workstations are similar in size and shape to microcomputers, but they have much greater power and additional devices that enable them to perform specialized functions. Supercomputers are the fastest and most expensive computers. They are capable of handling the most complex processing tasks.

6. Describe the primary hardware components and transmission media of a computer network.

Network hardware components include modems, front-end processors, multiplexers, and routers. Network transmission media include telephone lines, coaxial cable, fiber optic cable, microwave stations, and satellites.

7. Discuss four technology issues affecting today's workplace.

Computers enhance productivity in many ways, but they can also create new workplace challenges. These include maintaining data security, drawing the line between protecting the organization and invading an employee's privacy, maintaining a high level of employee productivity, and protecting against computer sabotage and theft.

8. Explain how advances in wireless technology will change the way we conduct e-business and list the challenges that must be overcome before these changes can take place.

Wireless technology will expand the electronic marketplace to an anywhere, anytime event by allowing consumers to access the Internet and e-merchants via cell phones and other small wireless devices. Advancements in wireless technology will allow storekeepers to keep targeted customers informed of last-minute special deals. Customers will use the same technology to get prompt answers to their information requests. But before this can effectively happen, several advancements must occur: (1) companies must develop Web sites with media content that fits on small screens and does not require huge bandwidths, (2) wireless Internet transmissions and access speeds must become significantly faster, and (3) a uniform standard for digital communications must be enforced.

KEY TERMS

application software (215)

artificial intelligence (212)

bandwidth (218)

CD-ROMs (214)

central processing unit (CPU) (214)

chief information officer (CIO) (209)

client/server system (217)

data communications (217)

data mining (204)

data warehousing (204)

decision support system (DSS) (212)

disk drive (214)

electronic data interchange (EDI) (210)

executive information system (EIS) (212)

expert system (212)

external data (205)

fiber optic cable (218)

hardware (212)

index number (208)

internal data (205)

local area network (LAN) (217)

mainframe computer (213)

management information system (MIS) (211)

mean (207)

median (207)

microcomputer (213)

microprocessor (214)

mode (207)

modem (217)

office automation systems (OAS) (211)

operating systems (215)

parallel processing (214)

primary data (205)

primary storage device (214)

process control systems (210)

production control systems (211)

random-access memory (RAM) (214)

read-only memory (ROM) (214)

secondary data (205)

secondary storage (214)

software (212)

speech-recognition system (212)

statistics (206)

supercomputers (213)

table (208)

transaction processing system (TPS) (210)

trend analysis (208)

wide area network (WAN) (217)

wireless transceivers (219)

workstation (213)

TEST YOUR KNOWLEDGE

QUESTIONS FOR REVIEW

1. Would employee records be considered data or information? Explain your answer.

2. What are the functions of a central processing unit?

3. What is the purpose of data warehousing and data mining?

4. What advantages do secondary data have over primary data?

5. What are the differences among the mean, median, and mode of a set of data?

QUESTIONS FOR ANALYSIS

6. How do graphics facilitate the presentation of data?

7. How has artificial intelligence been applied to business?

8. How are common computer software applications used by businesspeople?

9. Why do companies need information and information management systems?

10. How will Extensible Markup Language make it easier to use Web site data?

11. You finally saved enough money to buy a CD recorder so that you can burn your own CDs and save lots of money. You log on to the Internet, but before you can download your favorite tunes you must first agree to all those WARNING messages.

Of course, you're in too much of a hurry to actually read them, so you simply check "agree" and begin downloading songs. What do you think the purpose of these warning messages is? Is it ethical for you to agree to them without understanding what you are agreeing to? What happens if you disagree?

QUESTIONS FOR APPLICATION

12. Are you tech savvy? Find out just how much you know by taking a series of interactive technology quizzes prepared by the Manassas City Schools at www.manassas.k12.va.us/round/Technology/quizes.htm.

13. It appears that more and more job listings are requiring knowledge of the latest software packages and excellent computer skills. Your computer skills are just average. You especially struggle with spreadsheets and databases. What are some of the ways you can learn new software programs and update your computer skills?

14. Most small businesses can't afford to hire a chief information officer. If you owned a small business, how would you go about setting up effective information systems? (Hint: think about using both internal and external resources.)

15. Virtual teams communicate using a variety of technological devices. Your boss has asked you to serve on a global virtual team. What kinds of technology will you request from the company so that you can be an effective virtual team member?

PRACTICE YOUR KNOWLEDGE

SHARPEN YOUR COMMUNICATION SKILLS

Telephone answering machines and voice mail messages can be both a curse and a blessing. For one thing, people leave the strangest incoming messages. For another, some of the outgoing recordings are unprofessional and hard to understand. Your office has recently installed a new voice mail system and you must record a short greeting for your personal mailbox. On a piece of paper, compose an effective greeting you might use for your voice mailbox. What specific things should you include in that message?

HANDLING DIFFICULT SITUATIONS ON THE JOB: CONVINCING YOUR BOSS TO ASSIGN YOU HOMEWORK

You have been seriously thinking about the possibility of working from home three days a week and going to the office on the remaining two days. You could easily do your work from home using your laptop, the Internet, and, of course, the company intranet. But first you must sell this idea to your boss and get department approval. Prepare for a meeting with your boss by making a list of the questions you think might be asked about this arrangement. Next think about how you will answer those questions. Jot down key points that you will want to bring up during your meeting. Besides preparing questions and answers in advance, what additional steps could you take to help sell your idea to your boss?

BUILDING YOUR TEAM SKILLS

A computer virus shut down the computer system of your major competitor last month, and you heard from a friend that they are still experiencing serious problems. So you decide to learn from this unfortunate incident. As manager of the data processing department you have assembled your team of data processors to brainstorm a list of precautions and steps your department should take to protect the company's data against computer viruses. Using teams of students, generate this list of recommendations and then group the recommendations into logical categories. Compare your team's recommendations with those generated by the other teams in your class.

EXPAND YOUR KNOWLEDGE

KEEPING CURRENT USING *THE WALL STREET JOURNAL*

Scan recent issues of *The Wall Street Journal* (print or online edition) for an article showing how computers or other new technology helped a company gain a competitive advantage or improve its profitability.

1. What new technology did the company acquire and how did they use it to gain a competitive advantage or improve profitability?
2. Did the article mention any problems the company had implementing its new technology? What were they? Do you think the problems could have been avoided? How?
3. Did the technology require employees to learn new skills? If so, what were they?

DISCOVERING CAREER OPPORTUNITIES

Do you love technology but cringe at the thought of sitting in front of the computer all day, writing miles of code for new programs or designing complicated networks? Perhaps you should consider a career in technology sales. Learn about the different job positions in technology sales by reading the online article "Are You Cut Out for a Job in Tech Sales," by Jack Falvey. Then answer the article questions and decide whether a high-tech sales career is for you. To access this article, log on to the online Career Journal sponsored by *The Wall Street Journal* at careerjournal.com/, and click on Salaries by Industry. Under Industry and Job Functions, click on Computers and Information Technology. Find the article.

EXPLORING THE BEST OF THE WEB

URLs for all Internet exercises are provided at the Web site for this book, www.prenhall.com/mescon. When you log on to this text's Web site, select Chapter 8, then select "Student Resources," click on the name of the featured Web site, and follow the detailed navigational directions to complete these exercises.

Stay Informed with CIO, page 211

Chief information officers make smart business decisions by staying current in the field of information technology. Resources like CIO Online provide them with expert advice and links to many industry-related resources. Review this Web site and then answer these questions.

1. Which of the site's contents did you find most informative? Why might a small-business owner want to read CIO?
2. Read any article under the subject heading CIO Role that gives advice. What advice does the article offer and how might a CIO use that advice on the job?
3. What is a cyber résumé? How does it differ from a standard résumé and when should you use it?

Ride the Technology Wave, page 219

PC Magazine Online can be a valuable resource for businesspeople who want to stay on top of the latest advances in computer technology. Take some time to explore the many resources at this Web site and then answer the following questions.

1. Choose a product of interest to you and review what the critics say about that product. Describe the product and its uses in your own words. How might the information supplied in this article be of use to a small-business owner who is looking to improve productivity, manage data more effectively, enhance employee communications, or establish a presence on the Internet?
2. Review a new product on the market. Is this product a hardware or software product? What are the implications of this new product for business? What benefits does it offer? What are its limitations?
3. Explore the Web site in more detail and write a short summary of the site's contents. If you were a corporate CIO or a small-business owner, how might you use *PC Magazine Online*?

Learn the Rules of the Road, page 222

Electronic Commerce Resource Center offers a collection of news, research, and helpful information you should become familiar with before you cruise the superhighway. Read what the experts have to say on the hot topics in electronic commerce and then answer these questions.

1. What ten points should a company consider when developing a privacy policy?
2. What are some things you can do to guard against Internet fraud?
3. What are cookies used for and why were they developed in the first place?

Explore on Your Own

Review these chapter-related Web sites on your own to learn more about technology and information management.

1. Discover what the latest handheld personal digital assistants can do by logging on to 3Com's Palm site at www.palm.com.
2. Keep your tech vocabulary up to date by logging on to the TechEncyclopedia at www.techweb.com/encyclopedia. Search the database of over 14,000 definitions of computer terms and concepts.
3. Need some more hi-tech advice? You'll find expert advice on e-business and technology in addition to the latest information on software programs at Advisor.com, www.advisor.com.

A CASE FOR CRITICAL THINKING

■ *How Nokia Rings Up Profits*

Founded in 1865, the Finnish corporation Nokia produced everything from diapers and toilet paper to tires and rubber boots for more than a century. But all that changed during the early 1990s when a global recession threw the company into a tailspin. To avoid disaster, Nokia concentrated its efforts on wireless communications. And by the end of the twentieth century, the Finnish conglomerate had turned cell phones into a necessity around the globe.

BAD SIGNALS

More than 125 years of profitable operations came to a sudden standstill when Nokia's rubber, paper, and chemical divisions stopped churning cash in the early 1990s. Hit hard by a global recession, Nokia's customers stopped buying products. The collapse of the Soviet Union, Finland's chief trading partner, made matters worse. Moreover, Nokia's struggling mobile phone division couldn't keep up with the mass-production techniques used by competitors. By the time Nokia appointed Jorma Ollila as CEO in 1992, the company was floundering for survival.

STRONG CONNECTIONS

Told to come up with a survival plan, Ollila ditched the conglomerate's other interests in favor of a new focus: wireless telecom. Ollila's "hands-off" management style inspired innovation and creativity, and employees worked together in teams to turn the company around. Furthermore, Nokia beefed up its research-and-development efforts and designed a new line of phones with stylish features to meet the moods of the market. By the time Nokia shipped the new 2100 series in late 1993, the goal was to sell 400,000 phones. Instead, Nokia sold 20 million.

THE RIGHT NUMBERS

Although the company's operating profits soared to $1 billion in 1995, Nokia was determined to stay one step ahead of the competition. So the company began introducing different models of phones that appealed to specific market segments, such as user-friendly phones that required only one hand to operate and models with such innovative features as switchable covers and changeable ringing tones. Nokia also developed more appealing and more innovative products than its competitors throughout the 1990s. It

even surpassed Motorola to become the world's leading maker of mobile phones in 1998, capturing nearly 30 percent of the global market and more than one-third of the U.S. market. Competitors began to worry that Nokia had a secret code.

NOKIA'S SECRET CODE

From the beginning of Nokia's dramatic turnaround, the company realized that teamwork, focus, and innovation were key elements for future success. So Nokia began hosting a series of annual meetings known as the Nokia Way, giving employees the opportunity to determine Nokia's priorities. Nokia executives would then translate these priorities into a strategic vision for the company and make sure that Nokia stayed on track with its innovations by monitoring annual revenue growth. If annual growth of a product line falls below 25 percent, for example, employees shift their focus to other products with more growth potential.

Another element of Nokia's success is the company's ability to innovate with an eye on the future. With 13,000 employees in research and development, Nokia encourages workers to turn good ideas into reality and to develop business models from laboratory projects. Nokia not only concentrates on inventing products, but shapes entire markets for its merchandise by staying in touch with consumer needs. Like clothing designers and car manufacturers, Nokia introduces new and more sophisticated products every year. Currently Nokia is focusing on developing such new products as videophones, and the company is working with wireless local area networks (LANs) to create high bandwidth "hot spots" in hotels and airports so business travelers can log on to the Internet without wires. This constant stream of new products encourages consumers to upgrade their phones and to take advantage of soaring bandwidth and new voice and data devices.

To get the right quantity of mobile phones to retailers and cellular operators at the right time, Nokia makes sure that everything is in place for the release of its new products. This means the company must coordinate the efforts of everyone from researchers and designers to such outside sources as network operators and local start-ups. Of course, such attention to detail has paid off for Nokai.

Today the company makes nearly one-third of all phones sold, and reaps $4 billion in annual operating profits. But as competition heats up in the mobile phone industry, even Nokia knows it must work hard to stay on top.

CRITICAL THINKING QUESTIONS

1. Why did Nokia shift its focus to wireless communications?

2. How does Nokia stay ahead of its competitors?

3. How does Nokia encourage innovation and keep it from spinning out of control?

4. Go to Chapter 8 of this text's Web site at www.prenhall.com/mescon and click on the hot link to get the Nokia Web site. Follow the online instructions to answer these questions: How has Nokia achieved global success? What is Nokia's everyday goal? How is Nokia paving the way for a mobile information society?

VIDEO CASE AND EXERCISES

■ Voice, Video, and Data Join Hands Electronically at Vivid Group

SYNOPSIS

Convergence—the integration of communications and computer technologies—is making the world smaller but opening up new worlds of possibilities. Thanks to technology and innovative information management techniques, people can now access data through their television sets, hold conversations over the Internet, and get radio and television programming via computer. Companies like Vivid Group (www.vividgroup.com) are harnessing the power of convergence to create interactive virtual environments for museums and science centers, where participants can learn while being entertained. As another example, Sun Microsystems of Canada (www.sun.ca) is using convergence to find new and better ways of serving its customers through high-tech call centers. However, critics fear that overemphasis on technology will make employees into human extensions of corporate systems.

EXERCISES
Analysis

1. What type of network would Sun Microsystems be likely to use for data communications within an individual call center? For linking computers at several call centers?

2. What do experts mean when they talk about needing more bandwidth to handle the new technologies that arise from convergence?

3. What kind of data would you expect Sun Microsystems to have available to call center representatives who speak with customers?

4. Why would Sun Microsystems be concerned about data security at its call centers?

5. Should Sun Microsystems put the chief information officer or the head of marketing in charge of its call centers? Explain your answer.

Application

Imagine that Sun Microsystems invited customers to click on a link at its Web site and speak online with a customer service representative about any products shown on the site. From the customer's perspective, what are the benefits of using this technology compared with placing a regular telephone call to Sun?

Decision

What should Mike Walsh of Sun Microsystems consider in making a decision about updating his company's call centers with wireless communication techonology?

Communication

You're the head of programming for a local science museum, and you want to convince your board of directors to allocate money for Vivid Group to install a virtual environment system. Prepare a two-minute oral presentation explaining how museum visitors will benefit from using this system.

Integration

Referring to what you learned about management in Chapter 6, identify the management skills that are most important for supervisors who manage customer service representatives working at Sun Microsystems' call centers.

Ethics

The issue of replacing employees with technology (or machinery of any kind) has long troubled some observers of the business world and remains a key issue as companies struggle to continue improving productivity. Is it fair to replace a good employee with technology?

Debate

Should Sun Microsystems monitor the voice and data transmissions of customer service representatives who work at its call centers? As your instructor directs, choose one side and prepare your arguments for a classroom debate or submit a written summary of your main points.

Teamwork

In a team of four students, outline a plan for applying the convergence of video, voice, and data to a job that one of you now holds or has held in the past. One student should server as "devil's advocate" when the plan is finished, searching for flaws.

Online Research

Using Internet sources, do the research necessary to uncover trends in Internet-based telephone calls, also known as Internet telephony. How many calls are being made annually over the Internet? Why is this an increasingly popular technology? See Component Chapter A, Exhibit A.1, for search engines to use in doing your research.

MYPHLIP COMPANION WEB SITE

Learning Interactively

Visit the myPHLIP Web site at www.prenhall.com/mescon. For Chapter 8, take advantage of the interactive "Study Guide" to test your chapter knowledge. Get instant feedback on whether you need additional studying. Read the "Current Events" articles to get the latest on chapter topics, and complete the exercises as specified by your instructor. Expand your learning with a visit to the "Research Area." There you will find a wealth of information you can use to complete your course assignments.

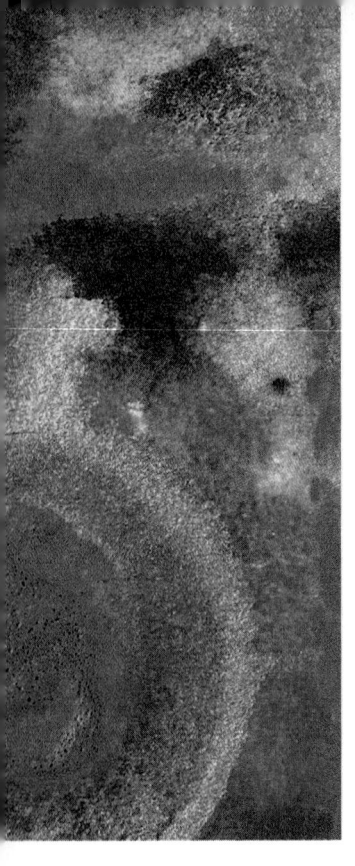

PRODUCTION OF QUALITY GOODS AND SERVICES

9

LEARNING OBJECTIVES

After studying this chapter, you will be able to

1. Explain what production and operations managers do

2. Identify key tasks involved in designing a production process

3. Discuss the role of computers and automation technology in production

4. Explain the strategic importance of managing inventory

5. Distinguish among JIT, MRP, and MRP II inventory management systems

6. Highlight the differences between quality control and quality assurance

7. Describe the supply chain and explain how companies today are managing their supply chains

@ 8. Explain what business-to-business e-commerce is, the economic benefits it promises, and the challenges that must be overcome before it can take off

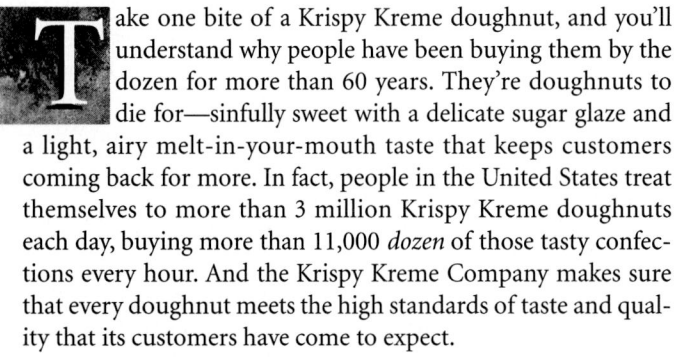

TODAY

Inside Business

With such a strong customer following, it's not uncommon to hear tales of driving several hours just to have a Krispy Kreme doughnut.

SWEET SUCCESS: PRODUCING PERFECT KRISPY KREME DOUGHNUTS

www.krispykreme.com

Take one bite of a Krispy Kreme doughnut, and you'll understand why people have been buying them by the dozen for more than 60 years. They're doughnuts to die for—sinfully sweet with a delicate sugar glaze and a light, airy melt-in-your-mouth taste that keeps customers coming back for more. In fact, people in the United States treat themselves to more than 3 million Krispy Kreme doughnuts each day, buying more than 11,000 *dozen* of those tasty confections every hour. And the Krispy Kreme Company makes sure that every doughnut meets the high standards of taste and quality that its customers have come to expect.

More than 150 Krispy Kreme stores across the country produce and sell about 20 different types of doughnuts, ranging from dunking sticks to the popular glazed variety. Stores feature glass walls that allow customers to view the automated doughnut-making process in action. Between mixing the dough with water and sugar-glazing the finished product, the procedure for making Krispy Kreme doughnuts takes about an hour. But the manufacturing process begins long before stores in Arizona or Nebraska crank up their doughnut production lines. Every Krispy Kreme doughnut starts from a special mix created at the company's headquarters in Winston-Salem, North Carolina.

Whether you're indulging in a doughnut in New York or California, Krispy Kreme wants you to enjoy the same delicious taste with every bite. So the company maintains consistent product quality by carefully controlling each step of the production process. First, Krispy Kreme tests all raw ingredients—such as shortening, sugars, and flours—against established quality standards. For instance, every delivery of wheat flour is sampled and measured for such characteristics as moisture content and protein levels. If a sample from a 25-ton delivery fails to meet Krispy Kreme's quality standards, the entire delivery is rejected.

After blending the approved ingredients, the company seasons the mix in its warehouse for at least a week. Then Krispy Kreme tests the doughnut mix for quality. Technicians in the company's test kitchen make doughnuts from every 2,500-pound batch of mix to make sure that all ingredients have been blended correctly. Since the characteristics of the flour produced from different crops of wheat may require adjustments in the mixing time or the amount of water added to the dough mix, the technicians note such differences and pass the information along to the stores.

But it takes more than a quality mix to produce perfect Krispy Kreme doughnuts all the time. To ensure consistent quality, Krispy Kreme supplies its stores with everything they need to produce premium doughnuts. The company produces all of its own icings and fillings, shipping the goods by truck from its North Carolina warehouse to stores across the country. Krispy Kreme even makes the production machinery and equipment for its retail sites, following the tradition established by founder Vernon Rudolph, who invented and built the world's first doughnut-making equipment. Today, the company continues to craft everything from conveyors to fryers in its own metal shop. These high standards of product quality have created sweet success for Krispy Kreme. With a loyal customer base that extends far beyond the company's Southern roots, Krispy Kreme sells more than $238 million of doughnuts every year.[1]

231

UNDERSTANDING PRODUCTION AND OPERATIONS MANAGEMENT

As managers of Krispy Kreme know, the extremely competitive nature of the global business environment requires companies to produce high-quality goods and services in the most efficient way possible. Few defects, fast production, low costs, excellent customer service, broad market reach, innovative products and processes, less waste, and high flexibility are all objectives that improve quality by adding value to the good or service being produced. Companies pursue these objectives to maintain a competitive advantage.[2] Moreover, managers understand that the level of quality that a company aspires to in the production of goods and services affects its long-term ability to address the needs of its customers.

What Is Production?

What exactly is production and what does it involve? To many people, the term *production* suggests images of factories, machines, and assembly lines staffed with employees making automobiles, computers, furniture, Krispy Kreme doughnuts, or other tangible goods. That's because in the past people used the terms *production* and *manufacturing* interchangeably. With the growth in the number of service-based businesses and their increasing importance to the economy, however, the term **production** is now used to describe the transformation of resources into goods and services that people need or want. The broader term **production and operations management (POM),** or simply *operations management,* refers to all the activities involved in producing a firm's goods and services.

Like other types of management, POM involves the basic functions of planning, organizing, leading, and controlling. It also requires careful consideration of a company's goals, the strategies for attaining those goals, and the standards against which results will be measured. In both manufacturing and service organizations, the production and operations manager is the person responsible for performing these functions. One of the principal responsibilities of the production and operations manager is to design and oversee an efficient conversion process—one which lowers costs by optimizing output from each resource used in the process. These resources include money, materials, inventories, people, buildings, and time.

What Is the Conversion Process?

At the core of production is the *conversion process,* the sequence of events that convert resources (or inputs) into products and services. This process applies to both intangible services and tangible goods. For an airline to serve its customers, for example, it transforms tangible and intangible inputs such as the plane, pilot's skill, fuel, time, and passengers through processes such as booking flights, flying airplanes, maintaining equipment, and training crews. The output of this process is the arrival of customers at their destinations. For a clothing manufacturer to produce a jacket, inputs such as cloth, thread, and buttons are transformed by the seamstress into the finished product (see Exhibit 9.1).

Conversion is of two basic types. An **analytic system** breaks raw materials into one or more distinct products, which may or may not resemble the original material in form and function. In meatpacking, for example, a steer is divided into hide, bone, steaks, and so on. A

LEARNING OBJECTIVE 1

Explain what production and operations managers do

production
Transformation of resources into goods or services that people need or want

production and operations management (POM)
Coordination of an organization's resources for the manufacture of goods or the delivery of services

analytic system
Production process that breaks incoming materials into various component products and divisional patterns simultaneously

EXHIBIT 9.1

THE CONVERSION PROCESS

Production of goods or services is basically a process of conversion. Inputs (the basic ingredients) are transformed (by the application of labor, equipment, and capital) into outputs (the desired product or service).

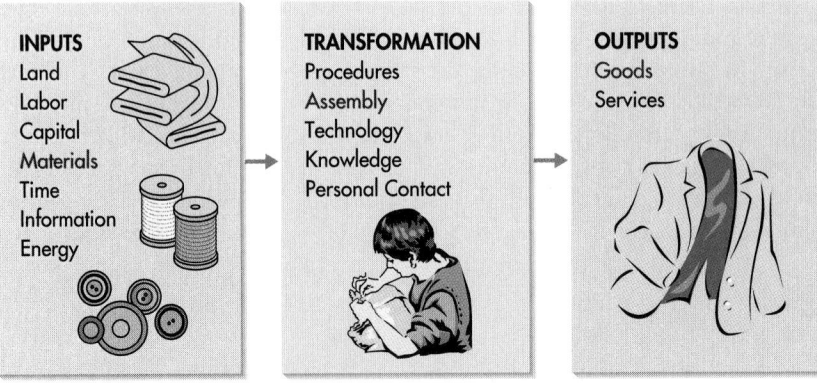

INPUTS	TRANSFORMATION	OUTPUTS
Land	Procedures	Goods
Labor	Assembly	Services
Capital	Technology	
Materials	Knowledge	
Time	Personal Contact	
Information		
Energy		

SYSTEM	INPUTS	TRANSFORMATION COMPONENTS	TRANSFORMATION FUNCTION	TYPICAL DESIRED OUTPUT
Hospital	Patients, medical supplies	Physicians, nurses, equipment	Health care	Healthy individuals
Restaurant	Hungry customers, food	Chef, waitress, environment	Well-prepared and well-served food	Satisfied customers
Automobile factory	Sheet steel, engine parts	Tools, equipment, workers	Fabrication and assembly of cars	High-quality cars
College or university	High school graduates, books	Teachers, classrooms	Impart knowledge and skills	Educated individuals
Department store	Shoppers, stock of goods	Displays, salesclerks	Attract shoppers, promote products, fill orders	Sales to satisfied customers

EXHIBIT 9.2

INPUT-TRANSFORMATION-OUTPUT RELATIONSHIPS FOR TYPICAL SYSTEMS

Both goods and services undergo a conversion process, but the components of the process vary to accommodate the differences between tangible and intangible outputs.

synthetic system combines two or more materials to form a single product. For example, in steel manufacturing, iron is combined with small quantities of other minerals at high temperatures to make steel.

Another thing to keep in mind is that the conversion process for a service operation and goods-production operation is similar in terms of *what* is done—that is, inputs are transformed into outputs. But the two differ in how the processes are performed (see Exhibit 9.2). That's because the production of goods results in a tangible output—something you can see or touch, such as a jacket, doughnut, desk, or bicycle—and the production of a service results in an intangible act. As such, the production of services involves a much higher degree of customer contact, is subject to greater variability, is more labor intensive, and results in a lower uniformity of output than the production of goods.

> **synthetic system**
> Production process that combines two or more materials or components to create finished products; the reverse of an analytic system

Mass Production versus Mass Customization

Mass production—manufacturing goods in large quantities—means little or no customization. Because of the high volume of similar goods produced, this process reduces production costs per unit and makes products available to more people. Even though mass production has economic advantages, the competitive pressures of the global economy often require production techniques that are flexible, customer-focused, and quality-oriented.

Consider Andersen Windows. Throughout most of its long history, Andersen mass-produced a range of standard windows in large batches. However, in the early 1990s customer demands and an increasing error rate caused Andersen to rethink the way it built windows. To better meet customer needs, the company developed an interactive computer catalog that allows customers to add, change, and remove features of Andersen's standard windows until they've designed the exact windows they want. Once the customers select their design, the computer automatically generates a price quote and sends the order to the factory, where standardized parts are tailored to customer specifications. Today the company offers close to 200,000 different products that are virtually error-free. Andersen's current production system is known as **mass customization**— using mass production techniques to produce customized goods. The company also uses *batch-of-one manufacturing*, in which every product is made to order from scratch.[3] The basic idea behind mass customization is that consumers have individual needs and are best served by products that can be easily customized for them.

Like Andersen Windows, many companies are adopting manufacturing techniques that let them tailor goods to individuals on a large scale. The key to customizing on a mass scale is digital technology—a combination of hardware, software, and new machines that fine-tune the production process. Levi Strauss & Company and Brooks Brothers are among those offering machine-customized clothing, thanks to new technologies that handle single items on the assembly line, or

> **mass production**
> Manufacture of uniform products in great quantities

> **mass customization**
> Producing customized goods and services through mass production techniques

Best of the Web Best of the Web Best of

LEARN WHAT IT TAKES TO MANAGE A CD OPERATION

Are you up for a career in operations management? Find out by taking the online challenge. Get some real-world experience making some important decisions as the operations manager of a CD production company. Learn more about jobs in operations management and purchasing. Find out what inventory controllers, production planners, and materials controllers do on the job. Finally, decide whether you have the right skills to pursue a career in operations management.
www.scicareers.org.uk/index.htm

LEARNING
OBJECTIVE 2

Identify key tasks involved in designing a production process

take body measurements that are then zapped to a manufacturing plant through the Web. Nike has Nike ID, which allows customers to alter the color, design, and even the construction of their shoes. Meanwhile, Mattel is hawking "My Design" dolls, customized "friends" of Barbie with clothing, skin color, hair styles, and even personalities picked by each owner.[4]

production forecasts
Estimates of how much of a company's goods and services must be produced in order to meet future demand

■ DESIGNING THE PRODUCTION PROCESS

Designing an effective production process is one of the key responsibilities of production and operations managers. It involves five important tasks: forecasting demand, planning for capacity, choosing a facility location, designing a facility layout, and scheduling work.

Forecasting Demand

The first step in designing an effective production process for a manufacturing operation is to determine how much product the company will need to produce in a certain time span. Using customer feedback, market research, past sales figures, industry analyses, and educated guesses about the future behavior of the economy and competitors, operations managers prepare **production forecasts,** estimates of future demand for the company's products. These estimates are then used to plan, budget, and schedule the use of resources. Of course, many factors in the business environment cannot be predicted or controlled with certainty. For this reason, managers must regularly review and adjust their forecasts to account for these uncertainties.

Service companies must also forecast demand. For example, dentists must be able to project approximately how many patients they will treat in a given time period so they can staff their offices properly and have enough dental supplies on hand. Without such forecasts, dentists can't run their production process (treating patients) efficiently. Similarly, cruise ship operators must forecast exactly how much food and supplies to stock for one week's journey, because once the ship sets sail, there are no last-minute deliveries. On the basis of years of experience, operation managers for Carnival's Elation Cruise Line can now forecast that a one-week Caribbean cruise will require some 10,000 pounds of meat, 10,080 bananas, and 41,600 eggs.[5]

Planning for Capacity

Once product demand has been estimated, management must determine the company's capacity to produce the goods or services. The term *capacity* refers to the volume of manufacturing or service capability that an organization can handle. For example, a doctor's office with only one examining room limits the number of patients the doctor can see each day. And a cruise ship with 750 staterooms limits the number of passengers that the ship can accommodate in any given week. Similarly, a beverage bottling plant with

Many of the newer, larger cruise ships have elegant restaurants, boutiques, luxury spas, high-tech fitness rooms, conference and meeting rooms, theaters, playrooms, ice-skating rinks, and even rock-climbing walls. With passenger counts of 2,600 and upward, managing an operation this large is like running a small village and every component in it.

only one conveyor belt and one local warehouse limits the company's ability to manufacture beverage products.

Capacity planning is a long-term strategic decision that establishes the overall level of resources needed to meet customer demand. The neighborhood convenience store needs to consider traffic volume throughout the day and night in order to plan staffing levels appropriately. At the other extreme of complexity, when managers at Boeing plan for the production of an airliner, they have to consider not only the staffing of thousands of people but also factory floor space, material flows from hundreds of suppliers, internal deliveries, cash flow, tools and equipment, and dozens of other factors. Because of the potential impact on finances, customers, and employees, capacity planning involves some of the most difficult decisions that managers have to make.

Top management uses long-term capacity planning to make significant decisions about an organization's ability to produce goods and services, such as expanding existing facilities, constructing new facilities, or phasing out unneeded ones. Such decisions entail a great deal of risk, for two reasons: (1) large shifts in demand are difficult to predict accurately, and (2) long-term capacity decisions can be difficult to undo. For example, if a new facility is built to produce a new product that then fails, or if demand for a popular product suddenly declines, the company will find itself with expensive excess capacity. Managers must decide what they should do with this excess capacity. If they keep it, they might try to find an alternate use for this space. If they eliminate it and demand picks up again, the company will have to forgo profits because it is unable to meet customer demand.[6]

capacity planning
A long-term strategic decision that determines the level of resources available to an organization to meet customer demand

Choosing a Facility Location

One long-term issue that management must resolve early when designing the production process for goods and services is the location of production facilities. The goal is to choose a location that minimizes costs while increasing operational efficiencies and product quality. To accomplish this goal, management must consider such regional costs as land, construction, labor, local taxes, energy, and local living standards. In addition, management must consider whether the local labor pool has the skills that the firm needs. For example, firms that need highly trained accountants, engineers, or computer scientists often locate in areas near university communities, such as Boston. On the other hand, if most of the jobs can be filled by unskilled or semiskilled employees, firms can choose locations where such labor is available at a relatively low cost. The search for low-cost labor has led many U.S. companies to locate their manufacturing operations in countries such as Mexico, Taiwan, and Indonesia, where wages are relatively lower. However, companies that fail to compensate foreign workers fairly are risking strong consumer backlash in the United States.

Also affecting location decisions are transportation costs, which cover the shipping of supplies and finished goods. Almost every company needs easy, low-cost access to ground transportation such as highways and rail lines. Moreover, companies that sell a lot of products overseas must be able to arrange for efficient air or water transportation. Finally, companies must consider raw materials costs. For example, the location of a coal-based power plant must be chosen to minimize the cost of distributing electrical power to customers and to minimize the cost and *lead time* of shipping coal to the plant.

Location considerations may be different for some service organizations. Although they may also take regional costs into consideration, the main objective for many service firms is to locate where profit potential is greatest. Unlike manufacturing operations, in which low production costs are an important consideration, services tend to focus on more customer-driven factors.[7] Because they often require one-on-one contact with customers, service organizations such as gas stations, restaurants, department stores, and charities must locate where their target market is large and sustainable. Therefore, market research often plays a central role in site selection. However, for service companies that reach customers primarily by telephone, mail, or the Internet, proximity to customers is less of a consideration.

Designing a Facility Layout

Once a site has been selected, managers must turn their attention to *facility layout*, the arrangement of production work centers and other elements (such as materials, equipment, and support departments) needed to process goods and services. Layout includes the efforts involved in selecting specific locations for each department, process, machine, support function, and other activity required for the operation or service. The need for a new layout design can occur for a number of reasons besides new construction; for instance, a new process or method might become available, the volume of business might change, a new product or service may be offered, an outdated facility may be remodeled, the mix of goods or services offered may change, or an existing product or service may be redesigned.[8]

Facility layout affects the amount of on-hand inventory, the efficiency of materials handling, the utilization of equipment, and the productivity and morale of employees. In goods manufacturing, the primary concern is the efficient movement of resources and inventory. In the production of services, facility layout controls the flow of customers through the system and influences the customer's satisfaction with the service.[9] In both services and goods operations, the major goals of a good layout design are to minimize materials-handling costs, reduce bottlenecks in moving material or people, provide flexibility, provide ease of supervision, use available space effectively and efficiently, reduce hazards, and facilitate coordination and communications wherever appropriate.[10] Four typical facility layouts are the *process layout, product layout, cellular layout,* and *fixed-position layout* (see Exhibit 9.3).[11]

A **process layout** is also called a *functional layout* because it concentrates everything needed to complete one phase of the production process in one place. Specific functions, such as drilling or welding, are performed in one location for different products or customers (see Exhibit 9.3A). The process layout is often used in machine shops as well as in service industries. For example, a medical clinic might dedicate one room to X-rays, another room to routine examinations, and still another to outpatient surgery.

An alternative to the process layout is the **product layout,** also called the assembly-line layout, in which the main production process occurs along a line, and products in progress move from one workstation to the next. Materials and subassemblies of component parts may feed into the main line at several points, but the flow of production is continuous. Electronics and personal-computer manufacturers are just two of many industries that typically use this layout (see Exhibit 9.3B).

Some production of services is also organized by product. For example, when you go to your local department of motor vehicles to get a driver's license, you usually go through a series of steps administered by several people: registering, taking a written or computerized test, having an eye exam, paying a cashier, and getting your picture taken. You emerge from this system a licensed driver (unless, of course, you fail one of the tests).

A **cellular layout** groups dissimilar machines into work centers (or cells) to process parts that have similar shapes and processing requirements (see Exhibit 9.3C). Arranging work flow by cells can improve the efficiency of a process layout while maintaining its flexibility. At the same time, grouping smaller numbers of workers in cells facilitates teamwork and joint problem solving. Employees are also able to work on a product from start to finish, and they can move between machines within their cells, thus increasing the flexibility of the team. Cellular layouts are commonly used in computer chip manufacture and metal fabricating.[12]

Finally, the **fixed-position layout** is a facility layout in which labor, materials, and equipment are brought to the location where the good is being produced or the customer is being served. Buildings, roads, bridges, airplanes, and ships are examples of the types of large products that are typically constructed using a fixed-position layout (see Exhibit 9.3D). Service companies also use fixed-position layouts; for example, a plumber goes to a job site bringing the tools, material, and expertise needed to repair a broken pipe.

Routing is the task of specifying the sequence of operations and the path through the facility that the work will take. The way production is routed depends on the type of product and the layout of the plant. A table-manufacturing company, for instance, uses a process layout because it has three departments, each handling a different phase of the table's manufacture and each equipped with specialized tools, machines, and employees. Department 1 cuts wood into tabletops and legs. These pieces are then sent to department 2, where holes are drilled and rough finishing is done. Finally, the individual pieces are routed to department 3, where the tables are assembled and painted.

Scheduling Work

In any production process, managers must use **scheduling**—determining how long each operation takes and setting a starting and ending time for each. A master schedule, often called a *mas-*

---

process layout
Method of arranging a facility so that production tasks are carried out in separate departments containing specialized equipment and personnel

product layout
Method of arranging a facility so that production proceeds along a line of workstations

cellular layout
Method of arranging a facility so that parts with similar shapes or processing requirements are processed together in work centers

fixed-position layout
Method of arranging a facility so that the product is stationary and equipment and personnel come to it

routing
Specifying the sequence of operations and the path the work will take through the production facility

scheduling
Process of determining how long each production operation takes and then setting a starting and ending time for each

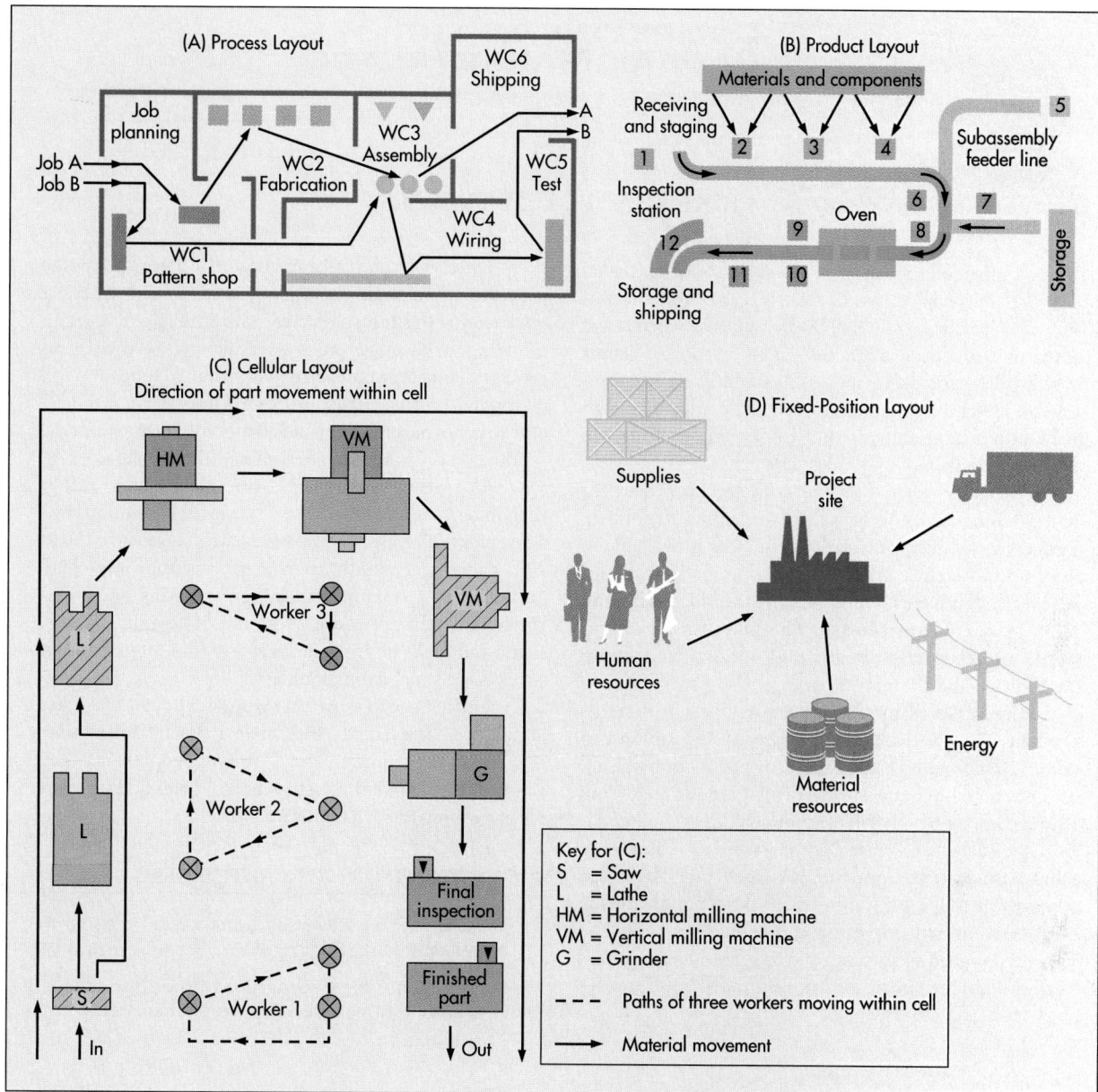

EXHIBIT 9.3

TYPES OF FACILITY LAYOUTS

Facility layout is often determined by the type of product an organization is producing.
(A) Process layout: Typically, a process layout is used for an organization producing made-to-order products. A process layout is arranged according to the specialized employees and materials involved in various phases of the production process.
(B) Product layout: A product layout is used when an organization is producing large quantities of just a few products. In a product or assembly-line layout, the developing product moves in a continuous sequence from one workstation to the next.
(C) Cellular layout: A cellular layout works well in organizations that practice mass customization. In a cellular layout, parts with similar shapes or processing requirements are processed together in work centers, an arrangement that facilitates teamwork and flexibility.
(D) Fixed-position layout: A fixed-position layout requires employees and materials to be brought to the product and is used when the product is too large to move.

ter production schedule (MPS), is a schedule of planned completion of items. In services such as a doctor's office, the appointment book serves as the master schedule.

When a job has relatively few activities and relationships, many production managers keep the process on schedule with a **Gantt chart.** Developed by Henry L. Gantt in the early 1900s, the Gantt chart is a bar chart showing the amount of time required to accomplish each part of a

Gantt chart
Bar chart used to control schedules by showing how long each part of a production process should take and when it should take place

COMPETING IN THE GLOBAL MARKETPLACE

A BIKE THAT REALLY TRAVELS

When bike industry veteran Hanz Scholz decided to pedal across Europe in 1987, his vision of packing a folding bike in a suitcase when it was time to board a plane or train soon began to fade. Scholz was very disappointed by the quality of folding bikes available. So he set out to build his own: one compact enough to fit into a large suitcase, but high quality enough to tackle steep hills and long, rugged stretches.

Five years later, the first commercial orders for Scholz's Bike Friday were rolling in. Unlike its fold-up predecessors—often one-size-fits-all models available in retail stores—all Bike Friday's are custom made by manufacturer Green Gear Cycling to meet the rider's size and component/color preference. The bike fits into a car trunk, a tight storage space, or an optional suitcase to travel on a plane like regular baggage.

Green Gear's operations are as distinctive as its product. The relatively small company ($3 million in sales, 30 employees, 17,000 sq. ft. of production space), uses advanced manufacturing principles adopted from Toyota Motor and other large manufacturers. Built individually, each Bike Friday begins its life as a bundle of tubes, components, and other structures. These are processed through a build-to-order, flow-manufacturing configuration that is organized in a series of cells. The cells are designed so that any one cell can do some of the work of the previous or next cell if production runs behind or ahead.

Once work on a bike has begun, it flows though the process without hesitation at any point. "It works like a track relay with a transition area," says Scholz. "We've set up everything with single-process-specific tools so there is no process changeover time. The flow motto is "touch it once, do it now." When a quality problem is discovered, the operator switches on a red light and all procedures stop until the production cell is adjusted to eliminate the problem.

Operating in a one-at-a-time flow system rather than in batches maximizes the chances for continuous improvement. "For us, every bike is a batch, so we have 150 to 200 chances per month to make process improvements," says Scholz. "A small manufacturer operating in a large-batch mode can be put out of business if he ruins just one. If you can make improvements as you find them, you can survive as a small manufacturer."

Today Green Gear Cycling builds about 2,000 bikes annually. At an average selling price of $1,700, Bike Friday commands a premium price. "We give people what they want, when they want it," says Scholz. "If you do that, people are willing to pay you for it."

■ QUESTIONS FOR CRITICAL THINKING

1. What are the advantages of using a cellular layout to manufacture Bike Friday?

2. Does Green Gear Cycling mass-produce or mass-customize folding bikes? Explain your answer.

---

program evaluation and review technique (PERT)
A planning tool that managers of complex projects use to determine the optimal order of activities, the expected time for project completion, and the best use of resources

critical path
In a PERT network diagram, the sequence of operations that requires the longest time to complete

process. It allows managers to see at a glance whether the process is in line with the schedule they had planned (see Exhibit 9.4).

For more complex jobs, the **program evaluation and review technique (PERT)** is helpful. It is a planning tool that helps managers identify the optimal sequencing of activities, the expected time for project completion, and the best use of resources within a complex project. To use PERT, the manager must (1) identify the activities to be performed, (2) determine the sequence of activities, (3) establish the time needed to complete each activity, (4) diagram the network of activities, (5) calculate the longest path through the network that leads to project completion, and (6) refine the network's timing or use of resources as activities are completed. The longest path through the network is known as the **critical path** because it represents the minimum amount of time needed to complete the project.

In place of a single time projection for each task, PERT uses four figures: an *optimistic* estimate (if things go well), a *pessimistic* estimate (if they don't go well), a *most likely* estimate (how long the task usually takes), and an *expected* time estimate, an average of the other three estimates.[13] The expected time is used to diagram the network of activities and determine the length of the critical path.

Consider the manufacture of shoes in Exhibit 9.5. At the beginning of the process, three paths deal with heels, soles, and tops. All three processes must be finished before the next phase

ID	Task Name	Start Date	End Date	Duration	2001
1	Make legs	8/1/01	8/28/01	20d	
2	Cut tops	8/22/01	8/28/01	5d	
3	Drill	8/29/01	9/4/01	5d	
4	Sand	9/5/01	9/11/01	5d	
5	Assemble	9/12/01	9/25/01	10d	
6	Paint	9/19/01	9/25/01	5d	

EXHIBIT 9.4

A GANTT CHART

A chart like this one enables a production manager to see immediately the dates on which production steps must be started and completed if goods are to be delivered on schedule. Some steps may overlap to save time. For instance, after three weeks of cutting table legs, cutting tabletops begins. This overlap ensures that the necessary legs and tops are completed at the same time and can move on together to the next stage in the manufacturing process.

(sewing tops to soles and heels) can be started. However, one of the three paths—the tops—takes 33 days, whereas the other two take only 18 and 12 days. The shoe tops, then, are on the critical path because they will delay the entire operation if they fall behind schedule. In contrast, soles can be started up to 21 days after starting the tops without slowing down production. This free time in the soles schedule is called *slack time* because managers can choose to produce the soles anytime during the 33-day period required by the tops.

Included in the scheduling process is the **dispatching** function, or the issuing of work orders to department supervisors. These orders specify the work to be done and the schedule for its completion. Work orders also inform department supervisors of their operational priorities and the schedule they must maintain.

Of course, once the schedule has been set and the orders dispatched, a production manager cannot just sit back and assume that the work will get done correctly and on time. Even the best scheduler may misjudge the time needed to complete an operation, and production may be delayed by accidents, mechanical breakdowns, or supplier problems. Therefore, the production manager needs a system for handling delays and preventing a minor disruption from growing into chaos. A successful system is based on good communication between the employees and the production manager.

Suppose a machine breakdown causes department 2 of a manufacturing company to lose half a day of drilling time. If the schedule is not altered to direct other work to department 3 (the next department), the employees and equipment in department 3 will sit idle for some time. However, if department 2 informs the production manager of its machine problem right away, the production manager can immediately reschedule some fill-in work for department 3.

dispatching
Issuing work orders and schedules to department heads and supervisors

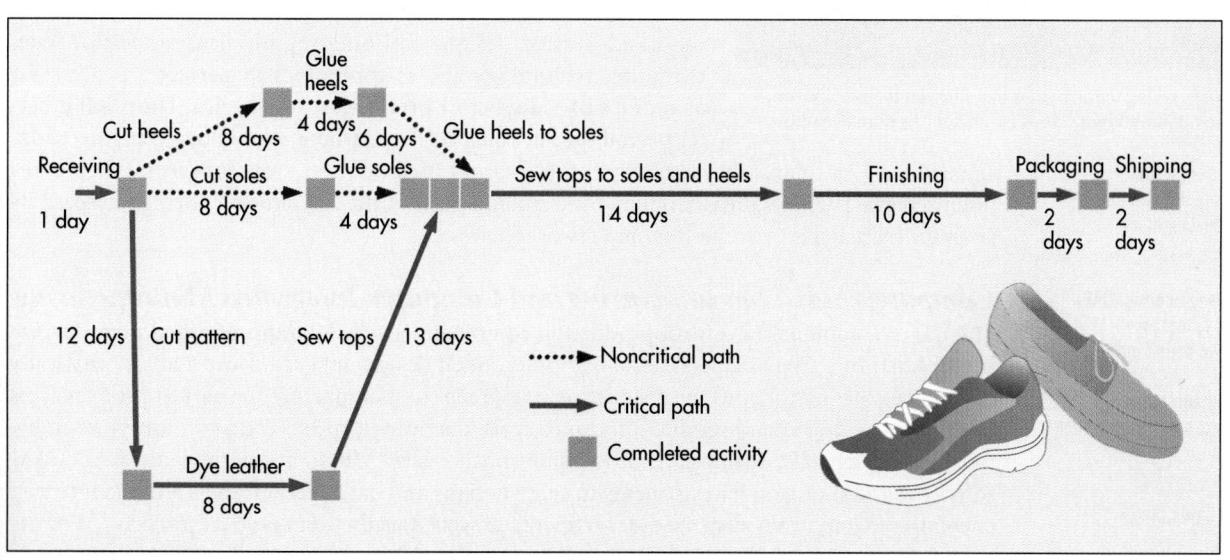

EXHIBIT 9.5

PERT DIAGRAM FOR MANUFACTURING SHOES

In the manufacture of shoes, the critical path involves receiving, cutting the pattern, dyeing the leather, sewing the tops, sewing the tops to soles and heels, finishing, packaging, and shipping—a total of 61 days.

LEARNING
OBJECTIVE   3
Discuss the role of computers and
automation technology in
production

robots
Programmable machines that can complete a variety of tasks by working with tools and materials

IMPROVING PRODUCTION THROUGH TECHNOLOGY

Today more and more companies are taking advantage of new production technologies to improve their efficiency and productivity. Alliant Food Services, for example, ships about 1 million cases of food and supplies daily. Historically, the shipping process was fraught with errors. But by using the Internet and wireless technology, the company has reduced shipping errors by more than 60 percent.[14]

Two of the most visible advances in production technology are computers and **robots**— programmable machines that work with tools and materials to perform various tasks. Although industrial robots may seem exotic, like some science fiction creation, they are quite common and are really nothing more than smart tools. Industrial robots can easily perform precision functions as well as repetitive, strenuous, or hazardous tasks.[15] When equipped with machine vision, or electronic eyes, robots can place doors on cars in precise locations, cull blemished vegetables from frozen-food processing lines, check the wings of aircraft for dangerous ice buildup, make sure that drug capsules of the right color go into the correct packages before they are shipped to pharmacies, and even assist with surgery.[16]

In addition to robots, other major developments in manufacturing automation include computer-aided design and engineering, computer-aided manufacturing, computer-integrated manufacturing, flexible manufacturing systems, and electronic information systems. Let's look a little closer at each of these.

Computer-Aided Design and Computer-Aided Engineering

Widely used today is **computer-aided design (CAD)**, the application of computer graphics and mathematical modeling to the design of products. A related process is **computer-aided engineering (CAE)**, in which engineers use computer-generated three-dimensional images and computerized calculations to test products. With CAE, engineers can subject proposed products to changing temperatures, various stresses, and even simulated accidents without ever building preliminary models. Moreover, the *virtual reality* capability of today's computers allows designers to see how finished products will look and operate before physical prototypes are built.

Using computers to aid design and engineering saves time and money because revising computer designs is much faster than revising hand-drafted designs and building physical models. In fact, computer technology allows companies to perfect a product or abandon a bad idea before production even begins. The result is better overall product quality. For example, when Boeing engineers de-

Robots don't do everything these days. At this Chrysler plant in Detroit, polishing a limited-edition Viper GTS-R is still done by human hands.

computer-aided design (CAD)
Use of computer graphics and mathematical modeling in the development of products

computer-aided engineering (CAE)
Use of computers to test products without building an actual model

computer-aided manufacturing (CAM)
Use of computers to control production equipment

signed the 777 airplane, they corrected problems and tried out new ideas entirely on their computer screens. Digitally preassembling the 3 million parts of the 777 allowed Boeing to exceed its goals for reducing errors, changes, and rework.[17]

Computer-Aided Manufacturing and Computer-Integrated Manufacturing

The use of computers to control production equipment is called **computer-aided manufacturing (CAM)**. In a CAD/CAM system, computer-aided design data are converted automatically into processing instructions for production equipment to manufacture the part or product. This integration of design and production can increase the output, speed, and precision of assembly lines, as well as make customized production much easier.[18] In addition, the latest CAD/CAM software allows company departments to share designs and data over intranets and the Internet, enabling geographically dispersed departments to work together on complex projects.[19] For example, Ford uses a CAD/CAM/CAE system it calls C3P to develop new vehicle prototypes. Whereas it once took two to three months to build, assemble, and test a car chassis prototype, with C3P the entire process can now be completed in less than two weeks. Although the program is still quite new, Ford expects it to improve engineering efficiency by 35 percent and reduce prototype costs by up to 40 percent.[20]

The highest level of computerization in operations management is **computer-integrated manufacturing (CIM),** in which all the elements of production—design, engineering, testing, production, inspection, and materials handling—are integrated into one automated system. Computer-integrated manufacturing is not a specific technology but rather a strategy that uses technology for organizing and controlling a factory. Its role is to link the people, machines, databases, and decisions involved in each step of producing a good.[21]

Flexible Manufacturing Systems

Advances in design technology have been accompanied by changes in the way the production process is organized. Traditional automated manufacturing equipment is *fixed* or *hard-wired,* meaning it is capable of handling only one specific task. Although fixed automation is efficient when one type or model of good is mass produced, a change in product design requires extensive equipment changes. Such adjustments may involve high **setup costs,** the expenses incurred each time a manufacturer begins a production run of a different type of item. In addition, the initial investment for fixed automation equipment is high because specialized equipment is required for each of the operations involved in making a single item. Only after much production on a massive scale can a company recoup the cost of that specialized equipment.

An alternative to a fixed manufacturing system is a **flexible manufacturing system (FMS).** Such systems link numerous programmable machine tools by an automated materials-handling system of conveyors known as automatic guided vehicles (AGVs). These driverless computer-controlled vehicles move materials from any location on the factory floor to any other location. Changing from one product design to another requires only a few signals from a central computer. Each machine changes tools automatically, making appropriate selections from built-in storage carousels that can hold more than 100 tools. In addition, the sequence of events involved in building an item can be completely rearranged.[22] This flexibility saves both time and setup costs. Moreover, producers can outmaneuver less agile competitors by moving swiftly into profitable new fields. Flexible manufacturing also allows producers to adapt their products quickly to changing customer needs.[23] Such systems are particularly suited for *job shops,* such as small machine shops, which make dissimilar items or produce at so irregular a rate that repetitive operations won't help.

As a $10 million manufacturer of precision metal parts, Cook Specialty is one small company able to compete with larger manufacturers through flexible manufacturing. Cook used to make only certain products, such as basketball hoops and display racks. However, the company has transformed its production facilities so that it is now capable of manufacturing custom-engineered medical instruments and precision parts for high-tech equipment. Technical innovations for these devices advance rapidly, but Cook is able to adapt its production facilities to keep up with the changes. In fact, almost one-third of the products Cook manufactures each year are new.[24]

Wise Use of Technology

Of course, none of the production technologies mentioned so far will increase profits unless the company designs products to fit customer needs. As Chapter 8 discussed, today, many companies recognized for their quality link themselves with their customers through information systems. These systems enable companies to respond immediately to customer issues, support rapid changes in customer needs, and offer "made-to-order" products. Moreover, information technology allows customers to track their products and obtain status reports throughout the production cycle. It can also promote better communication within the company, thereby improving the way a company designs, manufacturers, and delivers goods and services.

While the benefits of using technology in the manufacturing process are many, one of the worst mistakes a company can make is to automate a series of tasks without first examining the underlying process. If the basic process creates the wrong products or involves needless steps, nothing is gained by automating it without first cleaning it up. Otherwise a business runs the risk of simply doing the wrong things faster. Problems can also result from installing production technology without properly preparing the workforce to implement and use the technology.

TRW is a global manufacturing and service company that targets the automotive, space, and defense industries. TRW regularly and carefully checks its automated production systems to make sure it is improving the production process without wasting capital. One employee focuses

computer-integrated manufacturing (CIM)
Computer-based systems, including CAD and CAM, that coordinate and control all the elements of design and production

setup costs
Expenses incurred each time a producer organizes resources to begin producing goods or services

flexible manufacturing system (FMS)
Production system using computer-controlled machines that can adapt to various versions of the same operation

full-time on auditing machines for output mistakes, developing strategies for error reduction, and training other employees. Rather than automating for speed, the company focuses its efforts on designing "mistake-proofing" technology into its equipment, ensuring that it uses technology to work smarter as well as faster.[25]

MANAGING AND CONTROLLING THE PRODUCTION PROCESS

During the production design phase, operations managers forecast demand, plan for capacity, choose facility locations, design facility layouts and configurations, and develop production schedules and sequences. Once the design of the production process has been completed, operations managers are responsible for managing and controlling these processes and systems. In this section, we will discuss two important management and control concepts: inventory management and quality assurance.

Inventory Management

Forward-thinking companies have realized that maintaining a competitive advantage requires continuously seeking ways to reduce costs, increase manufacturing efficiency, and improve customer value. They know how wasteful it is to tie up large sums of money in **inventory**—the goods and materials kept in stock for production or sale. On the other hand, not having an adequate supply of inventory can delay production and result in unhappy customers. That's why more and more companies are changing the way they purchase and handle the materials they use to produce goods and services.

Purchasing is the acquisition of the raw materials, parts, components, supplies, and finished products required to produce goods and services. The goal of purchasing is to make sure that the company has all of the materials it needs, when it needs them, at the lowest possible cost. To accomplish this goal, a company must always have enough supplies on hand to cover a product's **lead time**—the period that elapses between placing the supply order and receiving materials.

In the past, companies would buy large enough supply inventories to make sure they would not run out of parts during peak production times. As soon as inventory levels dropped to a predetermined level, the purchasing department would order new parts. Many companies continue to operate this way, which does offer certain benefits. For example, companies typically get a better price when they buy inventory in bulk, and having a large supply on hand enables them to meet customer demand quickly. Unfortunately, carrying a large inventory also ties up the company's money and increases the risk that products will become obsolete.

To minimize this risk and cost, and to increase manufacturing efficiency, many companies establish a system of **inventory control**—some way of (1) determining the right quantities of supplies and products to have on hand and (2) tracking where those items are. Three methods that companies use to control inventory and manage the production process are *just-in-time systems, material requirements planning,* and *manufacturing resource planning.*

Just-in-Time Systems An increasingly popular method of managing operations, including inventory control and production planning, is the **just-in-time (JIT) system.** The goal of just-in-time systems is to have only the right amounts of materials arrive at precisely the times they are needed. Because supplies arrive just as they are needed, and no sooner, inventories are eliminated and waste is reduced.

The maintenance of a "zero inventory" under JIT does have some indirect benefits. For instance, reducing stocks of parts to practically nothing encourages factories to keep production flowing smoothly, from beginning to end, without any holdups. And a constant production flow requires good teamwork. On the other hand, JIT exposes a company to greater risks, as a disruption in the flow of raw materials from suppliers can slow or stop the production process. A JIT system also places a heavy burden on suppliers because they must be able to meet the production schedules of their customers. For instance, an increasingly strong demand for electronic and computer components at the beginning of the twenty-first century left many electronic equip-

LEARNING
OBJECTIVE   4

Explain the strategic importance of managing inventory

inventory
Goods kept in stock for the production process or for sales to final customers

purchasing
Acquiring the raw materials, parts, components, supplies, and finished products needed to produce goods and services

lead time
Period that elapses between the ordering of materials and their arrival from the supplier

inventory control
System for determining the right quantity of various items to have on hand and keeping track of their location, use, and condition

just-in-time (JIT) system
Continuous system that pulls materials through the production process, making sure that all materials arrive just when they are needed with minimal inventory and waste

LEARNING
OBJECTIVE   5

Distinguish among JIT, MRP, and MRP II inventory management systems

ment manufacturers battling one another for computer chips and other components. "Just-in-time has become just-in-trouble," says the chief financial officer of one electronics company.[26]

Thus, to be effective, JIT systems must be designed to include multifunctional teamwork, flexible manufacturing, small-batch production, strict production control, quick setups, consistent production levels, preventive maintenance, and reliable supplier networks. Furthermore, poor quality simply cannot be tolerated in a stockless manufacturing environment because one defective part can bring production to a grinding halt. In other words, JIT cannot be implemented without a commitment to total quality control.[27] When all of these factors work together in sync, the manufacturer achieves *lean production;* that is, it can do more with less.[28]

In those cases where it is difficult for manufacturers and suppliers to coordinate their schedules, JIT may not work. For example, shoemaker Allen-Edmonds cannot get its principal raw material whenever it wants because calfskin hides come on the market only at certain times each year.[29] Additional factors can also affect JIT: whether a product is seasonal or promotional or perishable; whether it has unusual handling characteristics; its size; its weight; and the volatility of the sales cycle.[30]

Keep in mind that JIT concepts can also be used to reduce inventory and cycle time for service organizations. Consider Koley's Medical Supply, which manages inventory for hospitals using what it calls "stockless distribution." Rather than making large, general deliveries to the stockroom, the company delivers specific items in just the right quantities to the various floors and rooms in the hospital. Doing so isn't always easy: At one hospital, Koley's has to make deliveries to 168 individual receiving points. But the system creates value for Koley's customers. For example, in Omaha, Nebraska, Bishop Clarkson Memorial Hospital reduced its annual inventory costs from $500,000 to just $7,000.

Material Requirements Planning (MRP) **Material requirements planning** (MRP) is another inventory-control technique that helps a manufacturer get the correct materials where they are needed, when they are needed, and without unnecessary stockpiling. Managers use computer programs to calculate when certain materials will be required, when they should be ordered, and when they should be delivered so that storage costs will be minimal. These systems are so effective at reducing inventory levels that they are used almost universally in both large and small manufacturing firms.

A more automated form of material requirements planning is the **perpetual inventory** system, in which computers monitor inventory levels and automatically generate purchase orders when supplies fall below a certain level. The price scanners found at the checkout counters of many stores are part of perpetual inventory systems. Every time a product is purchased, the scanner deletes that particular item from the computer system's inventory data. When inventory of the product reaches a predetermined level, the system generates an order for more. Often the store's system is linked to the supplier's own computer system, which enables the order to be placed with virtually no human involvement.

Manufacturing Resource Planning (MRP II) The MRP systems on the market today are made up of various modules, including inventory control, purchasing, customer order entry, production planning, shop-floor control, and accounting. With the addition of more and more modules that focus on capacity planning, marketing, and finance, an MRP system evolves into a **manufacturing resource planning (MRP II)** system.

Because it draws together all departments, an MRP II system produces a companywide game plan that allows everyone to work with the same numbers (see Exhibit 9.6). Employees can now draw on data, such as inventory levels, back orders, and unpaid bills, once reserved for only top executives. Moreover, the system can track each step of production, allowing managers throughout the company to consult other managers' inventories, schedules, and plans. In addition, MRP II systems are capable of running simulations (models of possible operations systems) that enable managers to plan and test alternative strategies.[31] An extension of MRP II is **enterprise resource planning (ERP),** which expands the scope of the production planning process to include customer and supplier information. ERP is based on software developed by SAP AG, a German software company. Using this software and ERP, manufacturers can tap into huge databases of company information to improve production processes.

material requirements planning (MRP)
Method of getting the correct materials where they are needed, on time, and without carrying unnecessary inventory

perpetual inventory
System that uses computers to monitor inventory levels and automatically generate purchase orders when supplies are needed

manufacturing resource planning (MRP II)
Computer-based system that integrates data from all departments to manage inventory and production planning and control

enterprise resource planning (ERP)
A comprehensive database system that includes information about the firm's suppliers and customers as well as data generated internally

EXHIBIT 9.6

MRP II

An MRP II computer system gives managers and workers in every department easy access to data from all other departments, which in turn makes it easier to generate—and adhere to—the organization's overall plans, forecasts, and schedules.

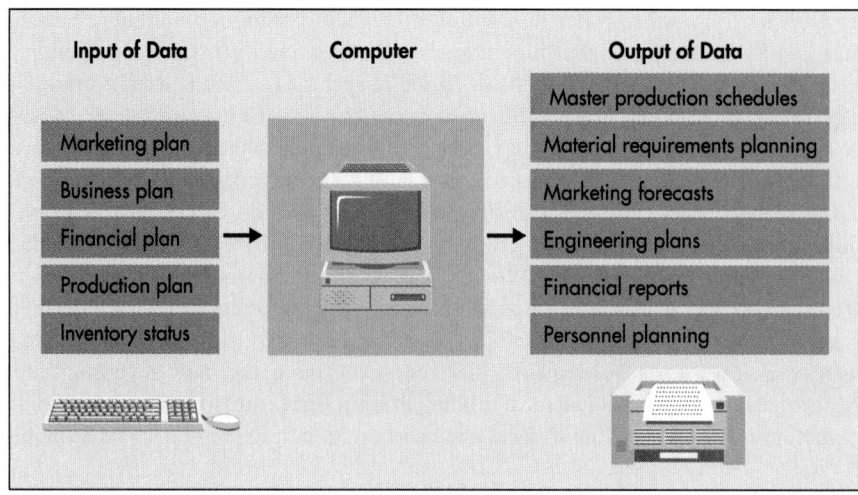

LEARNING OBJECTIVE **6**

Highlight the differences between quality control and quality assurance

quality control
Routine checking and testing of a finished product for quality against an established standard

quality assurance
System of policies, practices, and procedures implemented throughout the company to create and produce quality goods and services

statistical quality control (SQC)
Monitoring all aspects of the production process to see whether the process is operating as it should

statistical process control (SPC)
Use of random sampling and control charts to monitor the production process

Quality Assurance

Besides maintaining optimal inventory levels, companies today must produce high-quality goods as efficiently as possible. In almost every industry you can name, this global challenge has caused companies to reexamine their definition of quality and reengineer their production processes. Still, adopting high quality standards is not an easy task, because the manufacture of complex goods is not simply a matter of adding part A to part B to part C and so forth until a product emerges ready to ship. For example, the Mercedes M-Class sport-utility vehicle is assembled from subunits built by 65 major suppliers and many other smaller ones.[32] Making sure that all the pieces are put together in the proper sequence and at the proper time requires large-scale planning and scheduling. The same is true for the production of complex services.

The traditional means of maintaining quality is called **quality control**—measuring quality against established standards after the good or service has been produced and weeding out any defects. A more comprehensive approach is **quality assurance,** a system of companywide policies, practices, and procedures to ensure that every product meets preset quality standards. Quality assurance includes quality control as well as doing the job right the first time by designing tools and machinery properly, demanding quality parts from suppliers, encouraging customer feedback, training employees, empowering them, and encouraging them to take pride in their work. As discussed in Chapter 6, total quality management takes things to even a higher level by building quality into every activity within an organization.

Companies approach quality assurance in various ways. As a builder of sheet-metal components and electromechanical assemblies, Trident Precision Manufacturing empowers workers to make decisions on the shop floor, and it spends 4.7 percent of payroll on employee training.[33] High-end computer maker Sequent Computer Systems has a "customer process engineering manager" whose primary responsibility is to continually communicate with customers and identify any recurring problems. These companies know that eliminating only one inefficiency, such as a defect or an excessively complex process, can reduce total product costs because less money is spent on inspection, complaints, and product service.[34]

Statistical Quality Control and Continuous Improvement Quality assurance also includes the now widely used concept of **statistical quality control (SQC),** in which all aspects of the production process are monitored so that managers can see whether the process is operating as it should. The primary tool of SQC is **statistical process control (SPC),** which involves taking samples from the process periodically and plotting observations of the samples on a *control chart*. A large enough sample provides a reasonable estimate of the entire process. By observing the random fluctuations graphed on the chart, managers and workers can identify whether such changes are normal or whether they indicate that some corrective action is required in the process. In this way SPC can prevent poor quality.[35]

Statistical quality control is not limited to goods-producing industries. For example, financial services provider GE Capital uses statistical control methods to make sure the bills it sends to customers are correct. The company's use of SQC lowers the cost of making adjustments while improving customer satisfaction.[36]

KEEPING PACE WITH TECHNOLOGY AND ELECTRONIC COMMERCE

CHEK LAP KOK'S TURBULENT TAKEOFF

Opening day at Chek Lap Kok, Hong Kong's new airport, was a monumental disaster. The state-of-the-art facility, designed to handle 80 million passengers annually, was promoted as a symbol of Swiss-watch efficiency. But on the airport's first day of operations, every single thing broke down—or so it seemed (see photo, p. 246).

The airport lurched from crisis to crisis. Planes were stranded on the tarmac with no directions to parking gates. Passengers missed flights because of malfunctions in the Flight Information Display system. Some planes left without food for their passengers; others went without passengers altogether. Arriving passengers were imprisoned in the aircraft while mechanics repaired broken jetway doors. And baggage systems (designed to handle 13,700 pieces of luggage an hour) crashed, leaving passengers without luggage and loading luggage on planes without passengers—a serious security breach.

Then, just as the chaos in the passenger terminal seemed under control, computer glitches all but paralyzed air-cargo operations. A software bug disabled the computer system running the new $1.2 billion on-site automated cargo handling facilities—one of the largest in the world. Thousands of air freight containers were strewn across the tarmac. And perishable goods rotted in state-of-the-art warehouses while new shipments were rerouted.

Poor communications, overconfidence, and lack of system testing and contingency planning—even incompetence—are just a few of the reasons why the July 6, 1998, debut of Hong Kong's international airport at Chek Lap Kok turned into a nightmare. For example, communications systems and software on which the modern airport depended had not been thoroughly tested. Sample tests of 10,000 transactions had produced some minor problems, but when 70,000 actual transactions hit the systems on opening day, the systems were pushed to the breaking point. For another, political pressure forced officials to open the airport months before it should have been.

Chek Lap Kok is a good example of what can happen without sufficient quality control. Besides inflicting serious damage on Hong Kong's image, the airport's poor opening cost all parties involved over $5 billion—one-fifth of the airport's $25 billion construction cost. The government wanted Chek Lap Kok to be world famous, and it was—but for all the wrong reasons.

■ QUESTIONS FOR CRITICAL THINKING

1. What steps might airport managers have taken to prevent Chek Lap Kok's disastrous opening?

2. Why did statistical quality-control tests fail to produce the serious problems that occurred on opening day?

In addition to using SQC, companies can empower each employee to continuously improve the quality of goods production or service delivery. The Japanese word for continuous improvement is *kaizen.* Japanese manufacturers learned long before many U.S. manufacturers that continuous improvement is not something that can be delegated to one or a few people. Instead it requires the full participation of every employee. This means encouraging all workers to spot quality problems, halt production when necessary, generate ideas for improvement, and adjust work routines as needed.[37]

Global Quality Standards Companies that do business in Europe have to leap an extra quality hurdle. Many manufacturers and service providers in Europe require that suppliers comply with **ISO 9000,** a set of international quality standards that establishes a minimum level of acceptable quality. Set by the International Organization for Standardization, a nongovernment entity based in Geneva, Switzerland, ISO 9000 focuses on internal production and process issues that affect quality, but it doesn't measure quality in terms of customer satisfaction or business results. Usually the standards are applied to products that have health- and safety-related features. However, even companies that manufacture products not covered by ISO 9000 standards are being forced to gain accreditation by customers seeking quality assurance. The standards are now recognized in over 100 countries, and one-fourth of all of the world's corporations insist that all their suppliers be ISO 9000 certified. Even the U.S. Navy requires its suppliers to meet ISO 9000 standards.[38]

ISO 9000
Global standards set by the International Organization for Standardization establishing a minimum level of acceptable quality

Best of the Web Best of the Web Best of

STEP INSIDE ISO ONLINE

The International Organization for Standardization (ISO) is a worldwide federation of national standards bodies from some 130 countries, one from each country. Established in 1947, ISO is a nongovernmental organization with the following mission: to promote the development of standardization and related activities in the world with a view to facilitating the international exchange of goods and services, and to developing cooperation in the spheres of intellectual, scientific, technological and economic activity. Step inside ISO Online and take a closer look at how ISO standards are developed and why international standardization is needed.
www.iso.ch/

Computer failures at Hong Kong's huge new airport, Chek Lap Kok, left cargo, including perishables, sitting on the tarmac for days.

ISO 9000 helps companies develop *world-class manufacturing,* a term used to describe the level of quality and operational effectiveness that puts a company among the top performers in the world. Companies seeking world-class quality can use as benchmarks those companies that are globally recognized quality leaders. They can also follow the guidelines of various national quality awards. In Japan, the Deming Prize is a highly regarded industrial quality award, and in the United States, the Malcolm Baldrige National Quality Award honors the quality achievements of U.S. companies. Of course, even if an organization doesn't want to actually apply for an award, it can improve quality by measuring its performance against the award's standards and working to overcome any problems uncovered by this process (see Exhibit 9.7).

MANAGING THE SUPPLY CHAIN

A company's ability to deliver quality products and services is often tied to the dynamics of its suppliers. One faulty part, one late shipment, can send rippling effects through the production system and can even bring operations to a grinding halt. When a surge of orders for new Boeing 747s stepped up demand for parts, for instance, Boeing's suppliers were caught flat-footed. "We had $25,000 engine mounts that couldn't be finished because we were waiting for $40 nuts and bolts," noted one Boeing supplier. As a result, promised aircraft delivery dates were delayed and Boeing suffered huge losses. To avoid such problems in the future, Boeing now works hand in hand with its suppliers to refine products and delivery schedules.[39]

The group of firms that provide all the various processes required to make a finished product is called the *supply chain.* The chain begins with the provider of raw materials and ends with the company that produces the finished product that is delivered to the final customer. The members of the supply chain vary according to the nature of the operation and type of product but typically include suppliers, manufacturers, distributors, and retailers. For example, if the finished product is a wood table, the supply chain going backward would include the retail store where it was sold, the shipping company that delivered it to the retail store, the furniture manufacturer, the hardware manufacturer, and the lumber company that acquired the wood from the forest.[40]

Through a process known as **supply-chain management,** many companies now integrate all of the facilities, functions, and activities involved in the production of goods and services going from suppliers to customers.[41] The process is based on the belief that because one company's

LEARNING OBJECTIVE *7*

Describe the supply chain and explain how companies today are managing their supply chains

supply-chain management
Integrating all of the facilities, functions, and processes associated with the production of goods and services, from suppliers to customers

- LEADERSHIP. Have senior leaders clearly defined the company's values, goals and ways to achieve the goals? Is the company a model "corporate citizen"?

- INFORMATION AND ANALYSIS. Does the company effectively use data and information to support customer-driven performance excellence and marketplace success?

- STRATEGIC PLANNING. How does the company develop strategies and business plans to stengthen its performance and competitive position?

- HUMAN RESOURCES DEVELOPMENT AND MANAGEMENT. How does the company develop the full potential of its work force? How are its human resource capabilities and work systems aligned with its strategic and business plans?

- PROCESS MANAGEMENT. How does the company design, manage, and improve key processes, such as customer-focused design and product and service delivery?

- BUSINESS RESULTS. How does the company address performance and improvement in key business areas—product and service quality, productivity and operational effectiveness, supply quality, and financial performance indicators linked to these areas?

- CUSTOMER FOCUS AND SATISFACTION. How does the company determine requirements, expectations, and preferences of customers? What are its customer satisfaction results?

EXHIBIT 9.7

CRITERIA FOR THE MALCOLM BALDRIGE NATIONAL QUALITY AWARD

The Malcolm Baldrige National Quality Award is given annually to companies that demonstrate an outstanding commitment to quality. Named after former Secretary of Commerce Malcolm Baldrige, the awards are given to companies in each of four categories: manufacturing, services, small businesses, and universities and hospitals. This chart lists the criteria on which companies are judged for the award.

output is another company's (or consumer's) input, all companies involved will benefit from working together more closely.[42] Building high-trust relationships was once thought possible only with internal suppliers. But today more and more companies are reducing the number of outside suppliers they use, working collaboratively with them, sharing information with them, and even involving them in the production and design processes.

Honda, for example, has developed a process called Design In, which focuses directly on early supplier involvement. Honda will invite suppliers to work side by side with Honda's engineers, designers, and technologists in the very early stages of a new project. In addition, Honda believes in maintaining a frank, open, and collaborative relationship with its suppliers and even extends this philosophy to sharing cost data. "We show our suppliers our logic in coming up with the cost, and they show us theirs," notes Honda's senior purchasing manager.[43] This sharing of information with members of the supply chain has many benefits. Among them are increased sales, cost savings, inventory reductions, improved quality, accelerated delivery time, and improved customer service.[44]

Some companies are taking things one step further and actually involving suppliers in the manufacturing of their product. For example, at Volkswagen's factory in Resende, Brazil, seven main suppliers build components and assemble them onto vehicles inside the Volkswagen factory, using the suppliers' own equipment and workers. Volkswagen figures that integrating the suppliers so deeply into the production process is a strong incentive for the suppliers to deliver high-quality components in unprecedented time.[45]

Best of the Web Best of the Web Best of

MAKE QUALITY COUNT

In today's competitive business environment, companies have to be concerned about the quality of their goods and services. For information and advice, many turn to the American Society for Quality (ASQ). There you can find out about ISO 9000 and the Malcolm Baldrige Award. Find out why the award was established, how winning companies are selected, which companies have won the award, and how the award differs from ISO 9000. Follow the links to other quality-related Web sites. At the ASQ, quality is only a click away.

www.asq.org/

■ OUTSOURCING THE MANUFACTURING FUNCTION

As companies strive to find better ways to produce goods, some are learning that outsourcing the manufacturing function can provide tremendous cost efficiencies. For one thing, outsourcing allows companies to redirect the capital and resources spent on manufacturing to new product research, marketing, and customer service. As a result, some manufacturers today don't really "manufacture" products at all. Instead, they design them, market them, and support them. This is especially true with high-tech products. Cisco Systems, for instance, owns only two of the 34 plants that produce its products. Cisco outsources its production to contract electronic manufacturers (CEMs).[46]

Solectron is part of a new breed of U.S. supercontractors that make dozens of brand-name electronics at the same factory.

Solectron is a California CEM. The company has 24 production lines, which simultaneously assemble everything from pagers to printers to television decoding boxes for some of the biggest brand names in electronics. With sales topping $13 billion, Solectron is the only company that has twice won the Malcolm Baldrige Award for manufacturing excellence.[47] Similarly, Ingram Micro, the world's largest wholesale distributor of computers, does assembly work for archrivals that together control more than one-third of the U.S. computer market. In some cases these supercontractors even manage their customers' entire product lines by offering an array of services from design to inventory management and by providing delivery and after-sales service.[48]

Companies that outsource their manufacturing operations, of course, claim that their products are differentiated from those of their competitors (even if they are all assembled by the same contractor) because unique features and levels of quality are designed into a company's products. As one Hewlett-Packard vice president commented, "We own all the intellectual property; we farm out the direct labor; we don't need to screw the motherboard into the metal box and attach the ribbon cable." Still, others fear that outsourcing the manufacturing function could jeopardize a company's control over the product's intellectual property or quality. Intel, National Semiconductor, and Merck are among the corporate giants that have chosen to keep manufacturing in-house to protect their competitive edge.[49]

An Airbus A300-600 ST Beluga cargo plane has the biggest transportation volume of any plane.

Besides outsourcing, another trend sweeping manufacturing organizations is relegating more work to suppliers. In some companies, in-house manufacturing operations consist of nothing more than bolting together fabricated chunks that have been manufactured by suppliers. Consider Airbus's jetliner factory in Toulouse, France, for example. Large sections of Airbus jets manufactured at factories throughout Europe are flown to Toulouse in giant modified cargo jets called Belugas. There, small teams "snap together" the largely complete components, attach the landing gear, and drill holes to fasten wings to fuselages. The result is a much more modern and efficient production system than the one used by the industry leader, Boeing. In fact, Airbus now produces more revenue per employee than Boeing's commercial airplane division and is narrowing the gap between the number one and two spots of this industry duopoly. As competition heats up, Airbus recognizes that the company's competitor is not the Boeing of today, but rather "the Boeing that will be."[50]

FOCUSING ON E-BUSINESS TODAY

What's All the Buzz About B2B?

Whether you call it B2B, e-marketplaces, electronic exchanges, or network hubs, business-to-business e-commerce spells opportunity—and it promises to fundamentally change the way organizations conduct business with each other in the future. For years manufacturing giants such as Wal-Mart, General Motors, Eastman Kodak, Boeing, and others have used private computer networks to link with their suppliers so that they could order inventory automatically and squeeze costs and time out of inefficient supply chains. But thanks to the Internet, many companies are now joining forces and expanding such networks into e-businesses.

UNDERSTANDING B2B BASICS

Called B2B for short, business-to-business e-commerce is the transaction of e-commerce between companies that are linked directly or through a hub known as an electronic market or exchange. Compared with traditional electronic data interchange (EDI) systems, Internet-based networks are easier and more cost-effective to implement because the Internet allows a large number of buyers and sellers to transact business on a common Internet-based platform.

LEARNING OBJECTIVE @ 8

Explain what business-to-business e-commerce is, the economic benefits it promises, and the challenges that must be overcome before it can take off

The two most common types of B2B exchanges are *buyer exchanges* and *supplier exchanges*. Buyer exchanges are marketplaces formed by large groups of buyers who purchase similar items. By joining forces they can achieve economies of scale that are not possible individually. *Supplier exchanges* are formed by suppliers who band together to create marketplaces to sell their goods online. These groups of suppliers typically offer buyers one-stop shopping for most of their needs. Highly standardized products such as steel, chemicals, office supplies, electronic and mechanical components, auto parts, and medical and laboratory supplies are most suitable for B2B marketplaces. Heavy products that cost more to ship than manufacture and highly customized products such as prefabricated steel beams are not good e-commerce candidates.

Business-to-business exchanges can be run by third-party independent dot-coms or they can be run by existing industry players who join forces to form a new venture. They can be as basic as a manufacturer putting up a bare-bones Web site to let distributors securely order a handful of products; or they can be as complex as a marketplace where buyers, sellers, creditors, distributors, and shippers share all kinds of information about inventory, prices, markets, purchase orders, invoices, payments, credit approvals, and so on.

PROMISES, PROMISES

By all estimates the potential economic benefits of B2B e-commerce are enormous. B2B exchanges make it easier for geographically scattered buyers and sellers to find one another. Moreover, they expand the choices available to buyers and increase economies of scale for all parties involved. Exchanges can save members billions of dollars annually by reducing their transaction costs, and in some cases, they can earn money by charging users commissions and subscription fees. As one Hewlett-Packard spokesperson put it, "The savings are so compelling we can't afford to screw this up."

ESTIMATED SAVINGS FROM B2B E-COMMERCE	
Aerospace machining	11%
Chemicals	10%
Communications	5–15%
Computing	11–20%
Electronic components	29–39%
Food ingredients	3–5%
Forest products	15–25%
Freight transport	15–20%
Health care	5%
Life sciences	12–19%
Machining (metals)	22%
Media and advertising	10–15%
Oil and gas	5–15%
Paper	10%
Steel	11%

STRICTLY BUSINESS-TO-BUSINESS

Anticipating these economic benefits, hundreds of online marketplaces in many different industries have been launched, and more are announced each day. Consider the auto industry, for example. Historically, automakers have consumed vast amounts of time and money lining up suppliers for each of the thousands of parts that go into creating cars and trucks. This process involves a hurricane of blueprints, specifications, and bids along with endless meetings, phone calls and conferences. Now General Motors, Ford, and DaimlerChrysler, the three biggest competitors in the automobile-manufacturing industry, are joining forces with Nissan and other carmakers to form Covisint—a giant online marketplace where automakers can purchase one-half trillion dollars' worth of raw materials, parts, office supplies, and other goods they need each year. By turning the mounds of paperwork into electronic transmissions, automating processes, and providing a convenient one-stop shop for many supplies, automakers hope to save more than $1,000 per car—and that's only the beginning. If the exchange is successful, it could lead to the ability to link a customer to a car long before it leaves the factory floor.

B2B arrangements are popping up in other industries too. Hotels, for instance, have traditionally bought supplies from thousands of manufacturers, suppliers, and intermediaries, each focusing on its special product—soap, food, restaurant equipment, furnishings, and so on. Like the automobile industry, the purchasing process is time consuming and expensive. Which is why rivals Marriott, Hyatt, Bass Hotels and Resorts, and ClubCorp are joining forces to form a separate Internet company, Avendra LLC, to supply the hotel industry, restaurants, and even hospitals with everything from bath soap to electricity.

Other promising B2B exchanges are a Worldwide Retail exchange led by Safeway and Kmart, a giant marketplace for high-tech firms overseen by Hewlett-Packard and Compaq Computer, and a collaboration between technology maker Commerce One and the four largest participants in the aerospace and defense industry—Boeing, Lockheed Martin, Raytheon, and BAE Systems (whose purchases total $70 to $100 billion annually and involve 37,000 suppliers, hundreds of airlines, and multitudes of governments).

MAJOR ROADBLOCKS EXIST

While B2B digital marketplaces sound intriguing on paper, it might be years before such exchanges reap any benefits. Getting these ambitious B2B exchanges off the drawing board takes a lot of hard work. Companies are learning quickly that there's more to launching an online exchange than simply designing a cool Internet site. Many B2B marketplaces are facing major roadblocks:

- *Member rivalry.* For such exchanges to work effectively, decades-old rivals such as the Big Three automakers must be willing to share their pricing, inventory, and design policies with each other. As one naysayer put it, "The single biggest problem is that joint ventures are hard, joint ventures with many players are twice as hard, and joint ventures with many players who've been competitors for 80 years are nearly impossible."

- *Government concern.* When competitors get together, it almost always raises antitrust questions. Even though many of these B2B exchanges are forming independent entities and hiring separate management teams and independent boards, some think their true motives are suspect. Of particular government concern is the information sharing among competitors, which could raise suspicions about collusion.

- *Supplier resistance.* Many suppliers worry that online marketplaces, auction-like pricing, and easy access to cheaper goods, will drive down the prices of their goods. Although it's easy to see the benefits for manufacturers, suppliers are unsure how they will benefit from such exchanges. If these exchanges are to succeed, there has to be a superior value opportunity for all parties involved.

- *Customer resistance.* Many companies are unwilling to dump the network of suppliers they've built up over the years and make all their purchases through a new, unfamiliar medium.

- *Incompatible systems.* One of the biggest challenges facing B2B exchanges is the seamless blending of dozens of software packages, accounting systems, data-management systems, and manufacturing schedules. Furthermore, different customs, languages, and laws complicate such endeavors.

Despite these stumbling blocks, ideas for new B2B exchanges are sprouting like weeds. But only a handful of exchanges are actually up and running, and very few are profitable. In fact, most are still in the planning stages and are years away from reaching their true potential. Still the B2B buzz in boardrooms continues as companies grapple with these questions: Do we spin out a new company to attack this opportunity? Do we just take a stake in an existing company? Do we partner with our competitors? If so, does it give us a competitive advantage? Who will control the exchange? Who will run it? Who will build the technology? How will it connect with our current systems? The questions are many and the stakes are high. Especially since experts predict that only one or two big electronic marketplaces will survive in each industry.[51]

SUMMARY OF LEARNING OBJECTIVES

1. **Explain what production and operations managers do.**
Production and operations managers design and oversee an efficient conversion process—the sequence of events that convert resources into goods and services. To do this, they must coordinate a firm's resources and optimize output from each resource. Additionally, production and operations managers perform the four basic functions of planning, organizing, leading, and controlling, but the focus of these activities is the production of a company's goods and services.

2. **Identify key tasks involved in designing a production process.**
Managers must first prepare production forecasts, or estimates of future demand for the company's products. Next they must consider capacity, which is a business's volume of manufacturing or service delivery. The next step is to find a facility location that minimizes regional costs (land, construction, labor, local taxes, leasing, energy), transportation costs, and raw materials costs. Once a location has been selected, managers need to consider facility layout—the arrangement of production work centers and other facilities (such as material, equipment, and support departments) needed for the processing of goods and services. Finally, managers must develop a master production schedule.

3. **Discuss the role of computers and automation technology in production.** Computers and automation technology improve the production process in several ways:
(1) Robots perform repetitive or mundane tasks quickly and with great precision; (2) CAD and CAE systems allow engineers to design and test virtual models of products; (3) CAM systems easily translate CAD data into production instructions; (4) CIM systems link the people, machines, databases, and decisions involved in each step of producing a good; and (5) flexible manufacturing systems (FMSs) reduce setup costs and time by linking programmable, multifunctional machine tools through a computer network and an automated materials-handling system.

4. **Explain the strategic importance of managing inventory.**
The goods and materials kept in stock for production or sale make up inventory, which must be managed to minimize costs and ensure that the right supplies are in the right place at the right time. Having too much inventory is costly and increases the risk that products will become obsolete. Having too little inventory can result in production delays and unfilled orders.

5. **Distinguish among JIT, MRP, and MRP II inventory management systems.**
Just-in-time (JIT) systems reduce waste and improve quality by producing only enough to fill orders when they are due, thus eliminating finished-goods inventory. Furthermore, under the JIT system, parts or materials are ordered only when they are needed, thus eliminating supplies inventories. Material requirements planning (MRP) and perpetual inventory systems are used to determine when materials are needed, when they should be ordered, and when they should be delivered. A more advanced system is manufacturing resource planning (MRP II), which brings together data from all parts of a company (including financial, design, and engineering departments) to better manage inventory and production planning and control.

6. **Highlight the differences between quality control and quality assurance.**
Quality control focuses on measuring finished products against a preset standard and weeding out any defects. On the other hand, quality assurance is a system of companywide policies, practices, and procedures that build quality into a product and ensure that each product meets quality standards.

7. **Describe the supply chain and explain how companies today are managing their supply chains.**
The supply chain consists of all companies involved in making a finished product. The members of the chain vary according to the nature of the operation and the type of product but typically include suppliers, manufacturers, distributors, and retail outlets. Today more and more companies are working closely with their supply chains to be more responsive to the changing needs of their customers. To do this, companies are reducing the number of firms in their supply chain, developing long-term relationships with remaining members, and sharing information with them. Some companies are even involving members of their supply chain in the design and production processes.

8. **Explain what business-to-business e-commerce is, the economic benefits it promises, and the challenges that must be overcome before it can take off.**
Business-to-business e-commerce, or B2B, is the transaction of e-commerce between companies that are linked via an electronic network to form an electronic market or exchange. The two most common types of exchanges are buyer exchanges and supplier exchanges. These exchanges are run by independent third parties or by existing industry players who form a joint venture. The economic benefits of B2B e-commerce include expanded markets, increased product choices, reduced transaction and processing costs, substantial savings in time and labor, and increased economies of scale. Before B2B exchanges can realize these benefits, members must overcome such challenges as existing industry rivalries, government concern over antitrust issues, supplier resistance, customer resistance, and incompatible software and processing systems.

KEY TERMS

TEST YOUR KNOWLEDGE

QUESTIONS FOR REVIEW

1. What is the conversion process?

2. What is mass customization?

3. What factors need to be considered when selecting a site for a production facility?

4. Why is an effective system of inventory control important to every manufacturer?

5. Why might a company want to outsource its manufacturing function?

QUESTIONS FOR ANALYSIS

6. Why is capacity planning an important part of designing operations?

7. How do JIT systems go beyond simply controlling inventory?

8. Why have companies moved beyond quality control to quality assurance?

9. How can supply-chain management help a company establish a competitive advantage?

10. Select an e-business you are familiar with and visit that company's Web site. Using your knowledge about that company and production and operations management, answer these questions:

   a. What is the coversion process for this e-business?

   b. What types of information might you expect to see in the company's production forecasts?

   c. What factors do you think the company took into consideration when choosing a facility location?

   d. Who are the members of the company's supply chain?

11. How does society's concern for the environment affect a company's decisions about facility location and layout?

QUESTIONS FOR APPLICATION

12. Assume you are the production manager for a small machine shop that manufactures precision parts for industrial equipment. How can you use CAD, CAE, CAM, CIM, and FMS to manufacture better parts more easily?

13. If your final product requires several unique subunits that are all produced with different machinery and in differing lengths of time, what facility layout will you choose and why?

14. Review the discussion of franchises in Chapter 4. From an operational perspective, why is purchasing a franchise such as Wendy's or Jiffy Lube an attractive alternative for starting a business?

15. Review the discussion of corporate cultures in Chapter 6. What things could you learn about a company's culture by observing the layout and design of its production facility? Discuss both goods and services operations.

PRACTICE YOUR KNOWLEDGE

SHARPENING YOUR COMMUNICATION SKILLS

As the newly hired manager of Campus Athletics—a shop featuring athletic wear bearing logos of colleges and universities—you are responsible for selecting the store's suppliers. Merchandise with team logos and brands can be very trendy. When a college team is hot, you've got to have merchandise. You know that selecting the right supplier is a task that requires careful consideration, so you have decided to host a series of selection interviews. Think about all the qualities you would want in a supplier, and develop a list of interview questions that will help you assess whether that supplier possesses those qualities.

HANDLING DIFFICULT SITUATIONS ON THE JOB: GIVING SUPPLIERS A REPORT CARD

Just when you thought there was nothing left to measure and evaluate, your boss at Microsoft, Roxanna Frost, suggested something new. Frost, who is the program manager for Microsoft's Executive Management and Development Group, recently led a discussion emphasizing the importance of employee performance reviews. "It's all about improving clarity in terms of goals and expectations," noted one manager. Frost agreed: "Right—so everyone can talk about accomplishments and improvements." Then Frost suggested that the same should go for suppliers.

"There's a gap between what we want our suppliers to do and the feedback they're getting."

Thinking about this observation, you realize that 60 percent of the employee services your group monitors (travel assistance, retirement plans, the library at Microsoft's Redmond, Washington, campus) are outsourced to independent suppliers. This is nothing unusual at Microsoft, where many departments outsource both goods and services. What is new is Frost's idea of providing suppliers with feedback about their performance.

As the discussion continues, Frost points out that it would be a good idea to periodically evaluate *all* the outside suppliers that serve the company. When she asks for a volunteer to coordinate this new project, you raise your hand. This is just the kind of challenge you relish. Now, how will you get the project under way?[52]

1. You know that on-time delivery is important; what additional criteria should Microsoft departments use for supplier evaluation? Identify at least four but no more than six criteria.

2. Frost wants Microsoft to evaluate its suppliers more than once. How often would you recommend gathering feedback to send to suppliers? Why?

3. When Microsoft provides feedback, how might suppliers be expected to respond?

BUILDING YOUR TEAM SKILLS

Facility layout is one of the most critical decisions production managers must make. In this exercise, you and your team are playing the role of production managers for the following companies, some producing a specific good and some producing a specific service:

- Mountain Dew—soft drinks
- H & R Block—tax consultation
- Bob Mackie—custom-made clothing
- Burger King—fast food
- Boeing—commercial jets
- Massachusetts General Hospital—medical services
- Hewlett-Packard—fax machines
- Toyota—sport-utility vehicles

For each company on the list, discuss and recommend a specific facility layout, referring to Exhibit 9.3 for an overview of the four layouts. Why does your team believe the recommended layout is best suited to the product or service each company produces? How would the recommended layouts affect the movement of resources and inventory for the manufacturers on the list? How would the layouts affect customer interaction for the service providers on the list?

EXPAND YOUR KNOWLEDGE

KEEPING CURRENT USING *THE WALL STREET JOURNAL*

Seeking increased efficiency and productivity, a growing number of producers of goods and services are applying technology to improve the production process. Find an article in *The Wall Street Journal* (print or online edition) that discusses how one company used CAD, CAE, robots, electronic information systems, or other technological innovations to refit or reorganize its production operations.

1. What problems led the company to rethink its production process? What kind of technology did it choose to address these problems? What goals did the company set for applying technology in this way?

2. Before adding the new technology, what did the company do to analyze its existing production process? What changes, if any, were made as a result of this analysis?

3. How did technology-enhanced production help the company achieve its goals for financial performance? For customer service? For growth or expansion?

DISCOVERING CAREER OPPORTUNITIES

Whether you prefer to work with products or services, many possible careers await you in production and operations. From input to transformation to output, companies are looking for resourceful, results-oriented employees able to meet the demands of ever-changing schedules and specifications. Start your research by scanning the help-wanted classified and display ads in your local newspaper and in *The Wall Street Journal;* also check help-wanted ads in business magazines such as *Industry Week.* If you have Internet access, search the production and manufacturing jobs listed on America's Job Bank at www.ajb.dni.us.

1. As you read through these want ads, note all the production-related job titles you find. How many of these jobs include quality or technology (or both) among the duties and responsibilities?

2. Select two job openings that interest you. Reread the ads for those jobs to find out what kind of work experience and educational background are required. What further preparation will you need to qualify for these jobs?

3. Assume you have the qualifications for the two jobs you have selected. What key words should you include on your electronic résumé to show the employers that you are a good job candidate?

EXPLORING THE BEST OF THE WEB

URLs for all Internet exercises are provided at the Web site for this book, www.prenhall.com/mescon. *When you log on to the text Web site, select Chapter 9, then select "Student Resources," click on the name of the featured Web site, and follow the detailed navigational directions to complete these exercises.*

Learn What It Takes to Manage a CD Operation, page 234

Find out if a career in operations management is right for you. Discover the skills you will need and the types of management positions available in the supply chain.

1. Is operations management the right career for you? Take the test. As manager of the CD production company, what kinds of decisions will you have to make?

2. What skills do you need to be an operations manager?

3. What are the job responsibilities of inventory controllers and production planners?

Step Inside ISO Online, page 246

The International Organization for Standardization (ISO) promotes standards to facilitate the international exchange of goods and services. Browse ISO Online to become more familiar with the types of standards and how they are developed.

1. Why is international standardization needed?

2. How are ISO standards developed?

3. What fields are covered by ISO standards?

Make Quality Count, page 247

Stop by the American Society for Quality (ASQ) to learn more about ISO 9000 and the Malcolm Baldrige Award.

1. What steps are involved in a quality improvement process?

2. Who was Malcolm Baldrige? Why was the Malcolm Baldrige award created?

3. How does the Malcolm Baldrige Award differ from Japan's Deming Prize?

Explore on Your Own

Review these chapter-related Web sites on your own to learn more about production and operations management

1. Solectron Corporation, www.solectron.com, is the world's largest electronics manufacturing services company. Visit this Web site to learn more about supply chain management and the benefits of outsourcing.

2. Visit the Operations Management Center at www.mhhe.com/business/opsci/pom/index.htm, and take a closer look at topics in operations management by checking out the OM resources.

3. Airbus Industrie, www.airbus.com/about/assembly.html, has some interesting information on how the consortium assembles plans. View the videos to see how components from the four partners are transported to Tolouse, France, for modular assembly.

A CASE FOR CRITICAL THINKING

■ *Porsche—Back in the Fast Lane*

The German automaker Porsche enjoyed a long ride of success with its sleek, high-performance sports cars, cruising straight into the hearts of both consumers and racing fans with the introduction of its first model back in 1948. Producing such classics as the 356, the 550 Spyder, and the legendary 911, Porsche garnered a winning reputation for engineering excellence and for its victories in the racing world. Owning a Porsche became the ultimate fantasy of car lovers around the world, and the company's annual sales grew to more than 50,000 cars by the mid-1980s. Then everything changed, driving Porsche toward a collision course with disaster.

HEADED FOR A CRASH

Faced with a global recession during the early 1990s, consumers postponed buying cars—especially expensive sports cars. Demand dropped sharply for Porsche's 911 model, and sales plummeted by nearly 75 percent. By the time Wendelin Wiedeking took over the company's production and materials management, Porsche was racing toward record losses of $150 million.

Few people believed Wiedeking could get Porsche back on track. After all, the German engineer was the fourth person in five years to manage the company. But Wiedeking was determined to save Porsche from bankruptcy. "It was a question of 'to be or not to be'—as simple as that," Wiedeking recalls.

STEERING AWAY FROM DISASTER

To start the process of implementing changes, Wiedeking obtained benchmarks on every aspect of production by measuring the amount of time, money, and effort that was being spent on making a Porsche. Then he compared Porsche's production methods to those of Japanese automakers. After touring the production facilities of Honda, Toyota, and Nissan, Wiedeking and his managers were convinced they could apply the Japanese's lean, efficient production system at Porsche and turn the company around by slash-ing production costs and increasing productivity. Back at home, Wiedeking launched an improvement program to eliminate waste and to establish standards for quality and efficiency. Moreover, he paved the way for change by simplifying the management structure and assigning new responsibilities to every employee.

MEETING CHALLENGES HEAD-ON

But in spite of Wiedeking's efforts, Porsche's losses continued to mount. Drastic measures were needed to save the company, and Wiedeking had to act fast. He needed to overhaul the entire production system, and he needed the full cooperation of every worker to implement the changes. So he consulted a team of former Toyota managers who were experts in the concept of *kaizen*, a system developed by Toyota that emphasized continuous improvement in the quality of production.

The consultants quickly pointed out ways to save time and effort in Porsche's production assembly process. Under the current system, for example, workers searched through shelves crammed with 30 days of inventory to find the components for assembling an engine. To save time and distance, the consultants replaced the shelves with robotic carts that carried the necessary parts for one engine straight to workers on the assembly line.

A NEW SENSE OF DIRECTION

Wiedeking worked swiftly to implement the new production methods throughout the entire assembly process. Employees received intensive training in the principles of lean production, and Porsche worked hand in hand with its suppliers to improve products and delivery schedules. Within a week of implementing the changes, productivity increased dramatically.

As the company began to recover, Wiedeking instructed Porsche's engineers to apply the concepts of lean production to the development process. Instead of building expensive prototypes, the engineers used computer simulation to revamp the 911 model and to design a new two-seat roadster, the Boxster. They also incorporated the 911's basic engine and parts into the new

Boxster and created a common assembly line to produce the two cars, eliminating waste and saving time and money. As a result, Porsche's profits leaped into high gear, totaling $50 million on sales of $2.2 billion in 1996.

DRIVING THE FUTURE

Thanks to Wiedeking's dramatic turnaround of the company, Porsche was back in the fast lane at the close of the twentieth century. After implementing the production changes, the company slashed its production time for each 911 from 120 to 60 hours, built more engines with half the space, decreased the number of manufacturing defects, and cut its stockpiles of inventory from seven days to one. The company even established a new division, Porsche Consulting, to advise other businesses on how to improve productivity. By 1999, Porsche's pretax profits had zoomed to $368 million, sales had increased by 25.5 percent over the previous year—and the company was enjoying the highest profit margins of any manufacturer in the automobile industry.

CRITICAL THINKING QUESTIONS

1. Why did Porsche run into problems during the early 1990s?

2. What initial steps did Wiedeking take to overhaul Porsche's production methods?

3. What additional production improvements did the former Toyota managers recommend?

4. Go to Chapter 9 of this text's Web site at www.prenhall. com/mescon and click on the hot link to get the Porsche Web site. Follow the online instructions to answer these questions: What has Porsche learned from its past mistakes? Is Porsche prepared to meet the competitive and business challenges of the future? Does Porsche actively promote the *kaizen* method of production?

VIDEO CASE AND EXERCISES

■ *Whirlpool Puts a New Spin on Productivity and Quality*

Synopsis

Whirlpool (www.whirlpool.com) knows that better productivity and quality can provide a world-class competitive advantage. The 3,000 employees in the two-million-square-foot Whirlpool plant in Clyde, Ohio, turn out 14,000 automatic washing machines every working day—one-half of all such appliances sold in the United States. Still, Whirlpool is being squeezed by the dual pressures of global competition and prices that ignore inflation. To cope, Whirlpool has consolidated the U.S. production of automated washing machines at the Clyde facility; invested in developing innovative technology for its washing machines; sought customer feedback about features and benefits; taken the long view of overall costs; encouraged employee involvement in production improvements; and added corporate support for benchmarking, continuous improvement, and other techniques. Not only do employees share pride in the accomplishments of their teams, they share in the financial rewards of cost savings achieved through productivity improvements at the Clyde facility.

EXERCISES
Analysis

1. Describe the inputs, outputs, and transformation function of Whirlpool's Clyde plant.

2. Because Whirlpool makes appliances under five different brands, is it using mass customization?

3. What kind of information would Whirlpool look at when preparing production forecasts for automatic washing machines?

4. Why would Whirlpool locate its automatic washing machine production facility in Ohio rather than near Miami, Florida, or Seattle, Washington?

5. Does the Clyde plant appear to be using a process, product, cellular, or fixed-position layout?

Application

When an employee team at the Clyde facility finds a way to fasten control panels onto washing machines in half the time, how is this improvement likely to affect the critical path? When the team finds a way to use gravity to move washer baskets from the point of fabrication to a location where they can be retrieved for installation into washing machines, how is this improvement likely to affect the critical path?

Decision

Now that the Clyde facility has been reorganized and the equipment maintenance function has been integrated into the product assembly organization, should corporate headquarters maintain control of the dispatching function responsible for scheduling required maintenance procedures? Why or why not?

Communication

Assume you are the executive assistant to J. C. Anderson, Whirlpool's corporate vice president. Anderson wants to explain to Clyde plant employees why the company is promoting its ISO 9000 compliance in consumer advertising. Draft a one-page memo for Anderson to send to the employees.

Integration

Reviewing the discussion of organization structure in Chapter 7, does the new organization at Whirlpool's Clyde plant represent departmentalization by function, division, matrix, or network?

Ethics

Is it ethical for Whirlpool to consolidate its entire washing machine production into one huge plant at Clyde, which might aggravate emissions, increase waste output, and intensify other strains on the environment in that location?

Debate

Should Whirlpool's Clyde facility apply for the Baldrige award to demonstrate its quality achievements? Prepare for a classroom debate by creating a list of arguments to support one side of this question.

Teamwork

Working with another student, consider how Sears might explain to its sales staff the differences between Kenmore washing machines and Whirlpool washing machines—both made in Whirlpool's Clyde plant. What can Sears say to help the sales staff use their understanding of the differences in selling appliances to consumers?

Online Research

Using Internet sources, research how well Whirlpool is doing in the appliance industry. Is it selling as many appliances as in previous years? How is the industry doing overall? What are the implications for Whirlpool's production strategy? See Component Chapter A, Exhibit A.1, for search engines to use in doing your research.

MY PHLIP COMPANION WEB SITE

Learning Interactively

Visit the myPHLIP Web site at www.prenhall.com/mescon. For Chapter 9, take advantage of the interactive "Study Guide" to test your chapter knowledge. Get instant feedback on whether you need additional studying. Read the "Current Events" articles to get the latest on chapter topics, and complete the exercises as specified by your instructor. Expand your learning with a visit to the "Research Area." There you will find a wealth of information you can use to complete your course assignments.

MASTERING BUSINESS ESSENTIALS

Go to the "Strategy and Operations" episode on the Mastering Business Essentials interactive, video-enhanced CD-ROM. Participate in a brainstorming session with the managers of CanGo (an e-business start-up). Help Elizabeth, the company's founder, develop solutions to a variety of operational problems that are adversely affecting the company's performance.

P A R T   III

MASTERING GLOBAL AND GEOGRAPHICAL SKILLS: WHY IS THE SILICON VALLEY IN CALIFORNIA RATHER THAN COLORADO OR KENTUCKY?

Comparing geographic information about companies and industries can lead to some interesting questions. For instance, why are so many high-tech companies located in California's Silicon Valley (an area encompassing San Jose, Santa Clara, Palo Alto, and surrounding cities south of San Francisco)? For some industries, patterns of location and development seem fairly obvious. Florida has an ideal climate for citrus trees. Various cities along the East, West, and Gulf coasts have excellent natural harbors, which aided the development of a healthy shipping industry in those areas. Sometimes studying physical geography leads you to answers fairly quickly.

In other industries, however, the geographic connection seems weaker. For instance, why is so much of the insurance industry centered in Hartford, Connecticut? Why is Washington's manufacturing output (measured in dollar value) more than twice as high as Maryland's even though the two states have similar populations?[53] Why are the three largest U.S. steel producers headquartered in Ohio and Pennsylvania when most iron ore (source of the primary ingredient in steel) is mined in Minnesota, Michigan, Utah, and Missouri?

Exploring these geographic patterns helps you understand how industries develop and how they affect local and regional economies and societies. Choose one of the following five industries:

- Computer software
- Automobiles
- Carpeting
- Commercial passenger aircraft
- Poultry processing

Using the research tools in your library and on the Internet, answer the questions that follow.

1. Where did the industry start in the United States?

2. Who are the biggest competitors today?

3. Where are they located?

4. What influence has geography had on the industry's growth?

5. How strong is the influence of physical geography compared with the influence of other factors (such as where an industry pioneer happened to be living or where the cost for labor happened to be less expensive)?

6. Search the World Wide Web for specific companies in the industry you are researching. Visit the companies' Web sites, and find out in how many different geographic locations each company now operates. Based on your research and on what you have learned from the text, what are some of the factors that have influenced the geographic expansion of these particular companies?

Business PlanPro

MANAGING A BUSINESS

Review the Appendix, "Getting Started with Business PlanPro Software" to learn how to use Business PlanPro Software so that you can complete these exercises.

Think Like a Pro

Objective: By completing these exercises, you will become acquainted with the sections of a business plan that address a company's mission, goals and objectives, and management team. For these exercises use the sample business plan for Salvador's.

Open the BPP software and explore the sample business plan Salvador's Sauces Food Dis.spd. Click on the "Plan Outline" icon to access the plan's Task Manager and use it to navigate the company's business plan. Find the sections titled "Your Company" and "What You're Selling" to acquaint yourself with Salvador's product and goals.

1. What products does Salvador's sell? How does the company compete? What is the outlook for the Hispanic food industry?

Find the section titled "Initial Assessment" and read the company's mission statement.

2. Evaluate Salvador's mission statement. Does it summarize why the organization exists, what it seeks to accomplish, and the principles that the company will adhere to as it tries to reach its goals? How might you improve Salvador's mission statement?

Find the section titled "Initial Assessment" and review the company's objectives.

3. Evaluate Salvador's objectives. Are they clearly stated? Are they measurable? Do they seem realistic? Which objectives might need some refining?

Locate the section titled "Your Management Team" and review each of the sections under that heading.

4. Evaluate the strengths and weaknesses of the company's management team. What important management skills are the team lacking? How will the company address these gaps?

Now click on the "Instructions" tab (in text view).

5. What information should you include about your management team in a business plan? Should you mention the team's weaknesses in addition to its strengths? Why?

Create Your Own Business Plan

Make a list of your company's goals and objectives. Be sure they are clearly stated and measurable. What accomplishments do they assume? How will you reach these goals and objectives? What might prevent you from doing so?

AIRBUS VS. BOEING

A Wing-and-Wing Race

Boeing has been defined by its sheer technical bravado—and at times by its almost willful disregard for financial realities. The Seattle company designed the B-52 in a single weekend and launched the 747 jumbo jet in spite of the many observers who declared it financial suicide. Boeing is the world's largest aerospace company and the largest U.S. exporter. It has built some 85 percent of the world's jetliners and has dominated commercial aviation since the 1950s. But in 1999, the once unthinkable happened: rival Airbus sold twice as many planes as Boeing.

Airbus was founded in 1970 as a consortium of four European partners with homes in Great Britain, Germany, France, and Spain. Airbus would never have gotten off the ground without subsidies from the partners' governments. In 2001, confident that Airbus could finally stand on its own, the partners turned it into a single private company. Like Boeing, Airbus manufactures a full fleet of planes. Unlike Boeing, it has no jumbo jet. As a result, when it approaches an airline with a package deal, it has no big plane to clinch the sale.

A Different Approach

Airbus and Boeing build their planes differently. At Airbus, large airplane components, such as wings, cockpits, engines, and landing gear, are produced by suppliers all over the world and flown in giant cargo jets to a final assembly building in Toulouse, France. There, a handful of employees operating giant machines snap the large plane sections together. The finished aircraft are sold by Airbus Industrie, a sales and marketing joint venture owned by the partners. Many once-loyal Boeing customers now find innovative Airbus designs to be technologically superior and more comfort-

able for passengers. Besides offering wider planes that accommodate wider passenger seats, more overhead bin space, and more aisle space, all Airbus jets share the same cockpit design. This uniformity allows pilots to easily shift from flying one model to the next, which can slash pilot training from 30 days to less than eight and save airlines millions of dollars annually.

Until recently, Boeing customized a cockpit for every model and built airplanes like customized houses: Airlines could select from 109 shades of white paint or 20,000 galley and lavatory configurations. Worse yet, Boeing relied on a manual numbering system to track the four million parts and 170 miles of wiring needed for any one airplane. Compared to Airbus, Boeing's assembly lines were a beehive of activity, and its systems were woefully inefficient. Boeing is now rebuilding its operations and systems, but only after learning its lesson the hard way.

Sleepless in Seattle

With Airbus gaining ground in the mid 1990s, Boeing decided to deal this challenger a crippling blow. Banking on its ability to overhaul operations, cut production costs by 25 percent, and double production of its profitable 747 line, Boeing offered customers deep discounts on smaller jets to win multi-aircraft orders. But its plan backfired. The company was besieged with more orders than it could deliver on time. Production problems, management turmoil, and a market slowdown (spurred by the Asian economic crisis) collided head-on with Boeing's planned system upgrades, sending the aerospace giant into a tailspin. The company took years to recover, and the crisis triggered a massive reengineering attempt. Boeing is now following its rival's footsteps by outsourcing the manufacturing of more components. "The goal is to transform Boeing into a company focused on design, marketing, and assembly while letting others build the parts," says one Boeing spokesperson.

Boeing and Airbus Take Off in Different Directions

Boeing and Airbus have very different visions of the future of aviation. Airbus believes that the number of people traveling between the world's biggest airports will grow faster than airport capacity, boosting demand for a new generation of gigantic planes. Airbus projects that the market potential for a superjumbo is about 1,500 planes. So it is spending $12 billion to develop the world's biggest passenger jet, which it claims will revolutionize air travel just as the 747 did. The wide A380 superjumbo double-decker will seat 555 passengers (and can be configured to seat 800), surpassing Boeing's 416-seat 747-400. The A380 will showcase the latest technology and use light-weight composite materials currently found in military aircraft, making the A380 cheaper to operate per seat-mile than Boeing's 747-400. But the superjumbo will fly no faster than today's jets.

The Race for Orders

AIRBUS HOPES BIGGER WILL BE BETTER

	BOEING 747-400	AIRBUS A380
	www.boeing.com	www.airbus.com
Aircraft length	225 ft.	239 ft.
Aircraft height	63 ft.	79 ft.
Seats	416	555–650
Flight range	8,380 miles	8,798 miles
Fuel capacity	57,285 gallons	85,900 gallons
Cost per seat mile	3.46 cents	3.25 cents (based on 555 seats)
Maximum takeoff weight	875,000 pounds	1,190,000 pounds

"Not worth it," says Boeing chairman Phil Condit. After taking a close look at the superjumbo, Boeing concluded that it couldn't make the plane pay. Boeing sees demand for new jets in the 400 plus category ranging between 400 and 1,000 units over the next 20 years. The company plans on servicing this growth with its current 747 model and a new longer-range version that could fly an additional 775 miles without sacrificing airspeed or cargo capacity. In fact, Boeing thinks the Europeans "have gotten themselves in a terrible jam. They just won't be able to meet their commitments," says Joe Sutter, the engineer who led the design team that produced the original 747. Airports would need to spend hundreds of millions of dollars to upgrade terminals and taxiways to service the A380 and its two levels of jetways. Furthermore, the superjumbo's huge capacity limits its use to only the most densely traveled routes.

In contrast, Boeing is betting that airlines will begin using moderately smaller planes to fly passengers directly between smaller cities, bypassing congested hub airports. The company anticipates that new airports will be developed to accommodate passenger needs—especially in trans-Pacific and intra-Asian markets. So instead of building a superjumbo, Boeing will spend about $10 billion to develop a near-supersonic plane that will be able to fly 20 percent faster than today's conventional planes without breaking the sound barrier and without increasing operating costs. The Sonic Cruiser 20XX will save one hour of flying time for every 3,000 miles flown, which could change the way the world flies (perhaps as dramatically as the introduction of the jet engine).

The Point of No Return

If the Airbus vision is right, the newcomer will likely steal some of the most lucrative sales from big markets such as Japan, where Boeing holds a commanding market share. For instance, if the Japanese buy the A380, Airbus could become the undisputed world leader in the market for big jets, ending Boeing's 30-year jumbo-jet monopoly. Furthermore, if customers like the A380 better than Boeing's current 747 or its planned long-range version, they may be tempted to buy their smaller jets from Airbus as well. On the other hand, if Airbus has misjudged the market demand for super-jumbos, the company and its backers would be facing a financial catastrophe. For one thing, developing the proposed A380 could zap resources from existing lines, which would hurt the company's overall competitiveness at a time when Boeing is devoting its engineering efforts to squeezing costs out of planes and manufacturing processes while developing a smaller plane for faster travel.

If Boeing is on target with its vision for the future of air travel, it will head off the serious Airbus challenge that has already upset the U.S. producer's market dominance. But if Boeing has miscalculated, it will sacrifice large profits, as well as the huge jumbo-jet market that, until now, it had controlled entirely. In good years, roughly half of Boeing's profits came from sales of Boeing's 747, the uncontested queen of the skies and flagship of most of the world's major airlines. Designing a new superjumbo would take years, so if it turns out that Boeing's vision is wrong, the company would be hard pressed to catch up.

Both Boeing and Airbus are making one of those bet-your-company decisions. Airlines buy planes well in advance of market demand, and then they fly them for decades. "You make decisions and then you don't find out whether they make sense until ten years later," says Boeing's Sutter. But "that's what life's about in the airplane business."

QUESTIONS FOR CRITICAL THINKING

1. How does Boeing's vision of its industry's future differ from the Airbus vision?

2. How might the Airbus A380 and the Boeing Sonic Cruiser 20XX change the future of air travel? What risk is each company taking by developing these new planes?

3. What are the competitive advantages of each company?

4. Why are management decisions in the aircraft industry *especially* challenging?

5. If Boeing and Airbus had the opportunity to "do it all over again," what changes do you think they would make in their competitive strategies? Why?

6. Learn more about Boeing and Airbus by visiting their Web sites. At the Boeing site, click on "About Boeing and Vision." At the Airbus site, click on "About Airbus and Our Philosophy." Which company does a better job of communicating its long-term vision? Explain your answer.

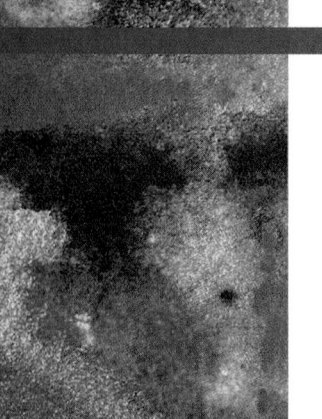

MOTIVATION, TODAY'S WORKFORCE, AND EMPLOYEE-MANAGEMENT RELATIONS

10

LEARNING OBJECTIVES

After studying this chapter, you will be able to

1. Identify and explain three important theories of employee motivation

2. Discuss three staffing challenges employers are facing in today's workplace

3. Highlight two trends contributing to the diversity of the U.S. workforce

4. Discuss three popular alternative work arrangements companies are offering their employees

5. Explain the two steps unions take to become the bargaining agent for a group of employees

6. Cite three options unions can exercise when negotiations with management break down

7. Cite three options management can exercise when negotiations with a union break down

@ 8. Identify the advantages and disadvantages of working for a start-up e-business from an employee's perspective

Inside Business

SAS Institute CEO Jim Goodnight takes a snack break with children at the company's on-site day care center.

CREATING COMPANY LOYALTY: TRUE BLUE EMPLOYEES AT SAS INSTITUTE

w w w . s a s . c o m

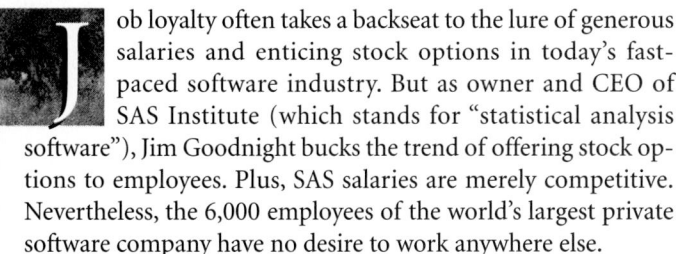

Job loyalty often takes a backseat to the lure of generous salaries and enticing stock options in today's fast-paced software industry. But as owner and CEO of SAS Institute (which stands for "statistical analysis software"), Jim Goodnight bucks the trend of offering stock options to employees. Plus, SAS salaries are merely competitive. Nevertheless, the 6,000 employees of the world's largest private software company have no desire to work anywhere else.

What's Goodnight's secret? Basically he does everything he can to create a corporate culture that respects employees and their needs for balancing work with their personal lives. Goodnight manages and motivates his workforce by relying on the philosophy that some things are more important to employees than money or stock offerings. The result? SAS employees are loyal. The company boasts a turnover rate of less than 5 percent—five times lower than the industry average.

It all began in 1981 when Goodnight realized that his small software company couldn't afford to lose talented workers. So he persuaded female employees to return to work after their maternity leaves by offering a powerful motivator: on-site day care. Today, the Cary, North Carolina, company operates the state's largest in-house day care operation, with a capacity of 700 children.

But child care is only part of Goodnight's approach to keeping his staff happy and productive. Goodnight believes employees are more creative when they aren't preoccupied with worries about their families or outside responsibilities. So he gives workers everything they need to do a good job—a rare bonanza of benefits, including peace of mind about their personal lives and an enjoyable work environment.

SAS encourages employees to take care of their personal health and the health of their loved ones. The company provides everything from free health insurance and unlimited sick days to the services of a full-time elder-care consultant and an on-site health clinic staffed by doctors and nurse practitioners. Employees also have free access to a country-club-style haven of sports and exercise facilities at corporate headquarters. An on-site gym, for example, includes basketball courts, workout areas, space for aerobics classes, a dance studio, and meditation rooms. SAS even provides employees with such luxuries as a putting green, massage services, free juice and soda, three subsidized cafeterias, and overnight laundering of sweaty gym clothes at no cost.

To encourage employees to spend more time with their families, the company closes its doors promptly at six o'clock each evening. And SAS supplies baby seats and highchairs in company cafeterias so that children can eat lunch with their parents. Moreover, flexible work hours and a standard 35-hour workweek are the norm, along with three weeks of annual vacation and an additional week off with pay during Christmas.

In return for the lavish benefits, Goodnight expects performance from his employees. And they deliver in a big way. Not only are employees motivated to do their best, but such motivation gives SAS a competitive edge against giants like Oracle, Microsoft, and IBM. Furthermore, it shows up in the company's bottom line. With customers in more than 115 countries around the world, SAS maintains a 30 percent profit margin on $1 billion in annual sales. As Jim Goodnight puts it "Doing the right thing—treating people right—is also the right thing to do for the company."[1]

■ UNDERSTANDING HUMAN RELATIONS

As Jim Goodnight knows, organizations need human resources to run their businesses. In fact, employees are a company's most valuable asset. "Ninety-five percent of our assets drive out the gate every afternoon at five," says Goodnight. "I want them to come back in the morning. I need them to come back in the morning."[2] But like most companies today, SAS faces an increasing need for qualified, skilled employees in an environment plagued by labor shortages and annual employee turnover rates that average about 20 percent. So Goodnight must offer employees benefits and reasons to return to SAS each morning.

Employee turnover, unscheduled absenteeism, and waning morale cost companies an estimated $200 billion or more annually, says one report—and that does not include the impact on a company's productivity.[3] For instance, if you have employees managing territories that generate from $1 to $2 million in company sales and one of them leaves, it might take you three to four months to find a replacement—and another three to four months before that individual becomes productive.[4] Which is why companies today can't afford to ignore the needs of their workforce. "If you do, it will have a significantly negative impact on the bottom line, and also be reflected in more lost workdays, more tardiness, poor morale, and low productivity," says one DaimlerChrysler director.[5]

In organizations, the goal of **human relations**—interactions among people within the organization—is to balance the diverse needs of employees with those of management. For instance, employers must motivate employees and keep them satisfied. But they must also remain competitive in the marketplace to ensure the organization's long-term success. Of course, achieving this balance becomes increasingly difficult because companies today face many staffing and demographic challenges. In this chapter we'll explore these challenges, and we'll discuss the role that labor unions play in the human relations function. Then in Chapter 11 we'll take a close look at what human resources managers do, as we explain the details of the hiring process, employee compensation, and specific employee benefits.

human relations
Interaction among people within an organization for the purpose of achieving organizational and personal goals

■ MOTIVATING EMPLOYEES

Every employee, by human nature, needs to feel valued, challenged, and respected. But when it comes to attracting and keeping talented people, even Jim Goodnight knows that money alone won't do it. Although compensation and employee benefits are indeed important, research shows that employees who maintain a high **morale** or a positive attitude toward both their job and organization perform better.[6]

Employees, regardless of their status, want and expect their employers to treat them fairly. They want more than a good paycheck and satisfying work. They want to balance their careers and their family lives. "There's an increasing interest in people finding meaning in their lives and in their work," notes Don Kuhn, the executive director of the International University Consortium for Executive Education. "People are no longer content with income and acquisition alone, but are looking for personal satisfaction."[7] They want to be part of something they can believe in, something that confers meaning on their work and on their lives. They want to be motivated.[8]

morale
Attitude individuals have toward their job and employer

What Is Motivation?

Motivation is an inner force that moves individuals to take action. In some cases, fear of management or of losing a job may move an employee to take action, but such negative motivation is much less effective than encouraging an individual's own sense of direction, creativity, and pride in doing a good job. Some managers rely on various kinds of rewards to motivate and reinforce the behavior of hardworking employees. These rewards include gifts, certificates, medals, dinners, trips, and so forth. Others, such as Jim Goodnight, motivate their employees by providing a culture that makes it enjoyable to come to work. Still others use positive and negative reinforcement to motivate their employees.

motivation
Force that moves someone to take action

Positive and Negative Reinforcement Some companies try to control or change employee actions by using **behavior modification.** They systematically encourage those actions that are desirable and discourage those that are not. A manager can encourage or discourage employee behavior

behavior modification
Systematic use of rewards and punishments to change human behavior

through the use of *reinforcement.* If an action results in pleasant consequences, the employee is likely to repeat the action; if the consequences are unpleasant, the employee is unlikely to repeat the action.

Positive reinforcement offers pleasant consequences (such as a gift or praise) for completing or repeating a desired action. Experts recommend the use of positive reinforcement because it emphasizes the desired behavior rather than the unwanted behavior. In contrast, *negative reinforcement* allows people to avoid unpleasant consequences by behaving in the desired way. Imagine, for example, that employees know they will have to work late if they don't finish a project on time. In this case, employees can avoid working late (unpleasant consequences) by finishing on time (desired behavior).

Management by Objectives Another proven motivation technique used by many organizations is **management by objectives (MBO),** a companywide process that empowers employees and involves them in goal setting and decision making. The process consists of four steps: setting goals, planning actions, implementing plans, and reviewing performance (see Exhibit 10.1). Because employees at all levels are involved in all four steps, they learn more about company objectives and feel that they are an important part of the companywide team. Furthermore, they understand how even their small job function contributes to the organization's long-term success.

One of the key elements of MBO is a collaborative goal-setting process. Together, a manager and employee define the employee's goals, the responsibilities for achieving those goals, and the means of evaluating individual and group performance so that the employee's activities are directly linked to achieving the organization's long-term goals. Jointly setting clear and challenging—but achievable—goals can encourage employees to reach higher levels of performance. At Aptar Group, a manufacturer of aerosol valves, finger pumps, and other caps for bottles, employee work teams set their own goals and report on their progress to senior management. Rob Revak, director of human resources at one of Aptar's divisions, finds that employees who set their own goals strive hard to reach them.[9]

management by objectives (MBO)
A motivational tool whereby managers and employees work together to structure personal goals and objectives for every individual, department, and project to mesh with the organization's goals

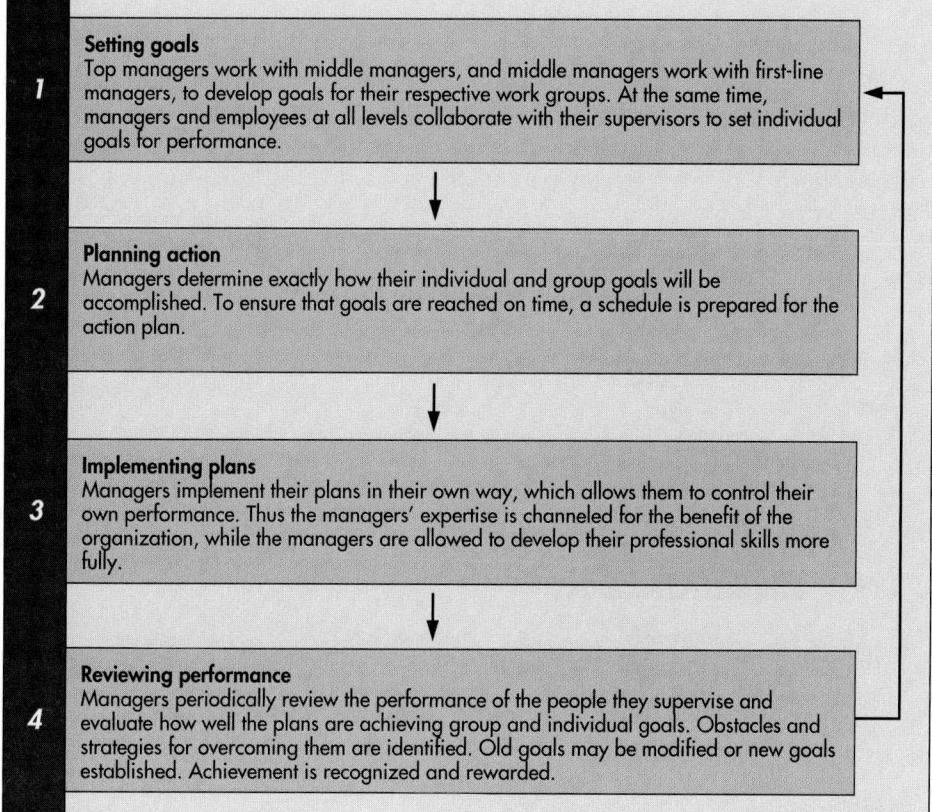

EXHIBIT 10.1

MANAGEMENT BY OBJECTIVES

The MBO process has four steps. This cycle is refined and repeated as managers and employees at all levels work toward establishing goals and objectives, thereby accomplishing the organization's strategic goals.

1 Setting goals
Top managers work with middle managers, and middle managers work with first-line managers, to develop goals for their respective work groups. At the same time, managers and employees at all levels collaborate with their supervisors to set individual goals for performance.

2 Planning action
Managers determine exactly how their individual and group goals will be accomplished. To ensure that goals are reached on time, a schedule is prepared for the action plan.

3 Implementing plans
Managers implement their plans in their own way, which allows them to control their own performance. Thus the managers' expertise is channeled for the benefit of the organization, while the managers are allowed to develop their professional skills more fully.

4 Reviewing performance
Managers periodically review the performance of the people they supervise and evaluate how well the plans are achieving group and individual goals. Obstacles and strategies for overcoming them are identified. Old goals may be modified or new goals established. Achievement is recognized and rewarded.

MBO, of course, is just one of the ways companies motivate employees to perform. As you can imagine, humans are motivated by many factors. Thus, the challenge for managers is to select motivators that will inspire employees to achieve organizational goals. But which ones are the most effective? Several theories of motivation have attempted to answer that question.

Theories of Motivation

LEARNING
OBJECTIVE 1

Identify and explain three
important theories of employee
motivation.

scientific management
Management approach designed to
improve employees' efficiency by
scientifically studying their work

Motivation has been a topic of interest to managers for more than a hundred years. Frederick W. Taylor was a machinist and engineer from Philadelphia who became interested in employee efficiency and motivation late in the nineteenth century. Taylor developed **scientific management,** an approach that seeks to improve employee efficiency through the scientific study of work. In Taylor's view, people were motivated almost exclusively by money, so he set up pay systems that rewarded employees when they were productive.

Under Taylor's piecework system, for example, employees who just met or fell short of the quota were paid a certain amount for each unit produced. Those who produced more were paid a higher rate for *all* units produced, not just for those that exceeded the quota; this pay system gave employees a strong incentive to boost productivity.

Although money has always been a powerful motivator, scientific management fails to take into account other motivational elements, such as opportunities for personal satisfaction or individual initiative. Thus, scientific management can't explain why a person still wants to work even though that person's spouse already makes a good living or why a Wall Street lawyer will take a hefty pay cut to serve in government. Therefore, other researchers have looked beyond money to discover what else motivates people.

Maslow's Hierarchy of Needs In 1943 psychologist Abraham Maslow proposed the theory that behavior is determined by a variety of needs. He organized these needs into five categories and then arranged the categories in a hierarchy. As Exhibit 10.2 shows, the most basic needs are at the bottom of this hierarchy, and the more advanced needs are toward the top. In Maslow's hierarchy, all of the requirements for basic survival—food, clothing, shelter, and the like—fall into the category of *physiological needs*. These basic needs must be satisfied before the person can consider higher-level needs such as *safety needs, social needs* (the need to give and receive love and to feel a sense of belonging), and *esteem needs* (the need for a sense of self-worth and integrity).

At the top of Maslow's hierarchy is *self-actualization*—the need to become everything one can become. This need is also the most difficult to fulfill. Employees who reach this point work not only to make money or to impress others but also because they feel their work is worthwhile and satisfying in itself. Self-actualization needs partially explain why some people make radical career changes or strike out on their own as entrepreneurs.

Although Maslow's hierarchy is a convenient way to classify human needs, it would be a mistake to view it as a rigid sequence. A person need not completely satisfy each level of needs before being motivated by a higher need. Indeed, at any one time, most people are motivated by a combination of needs.

EXHIBIT 10.2

MASLOW'S HIERARCHY OF NEEDS

According to Maslow, needs on the lower levels of the hierarchy must be satisfied before higher-level needs can be addressed.

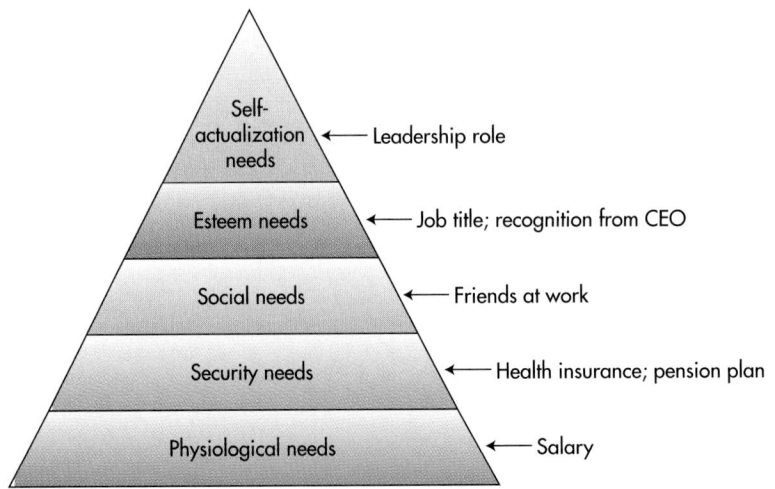

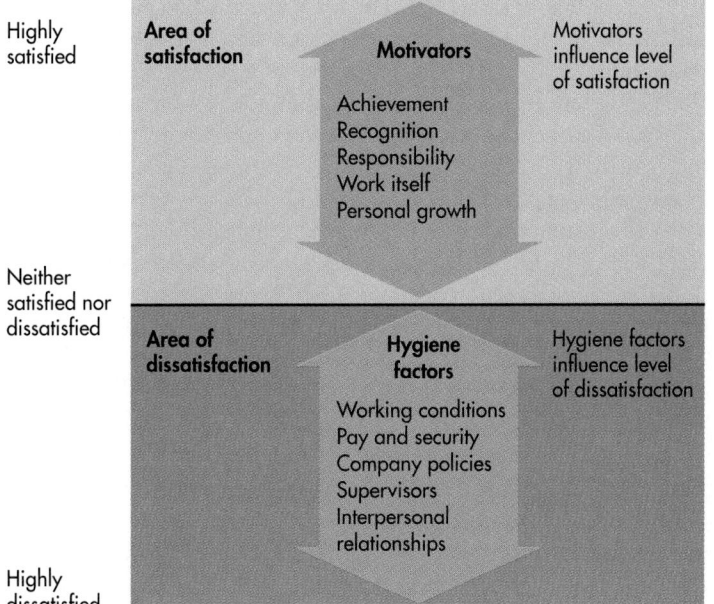

EXHIBIT 10.3

TWO-FACTOR THEORY

Hygiene factors such as working conditions and company policies can influence employee dissatisfaction. On the other hand, motivators such as opportunities for achievement and recognition can influence employee satisfaction.

Two-Factor Theory In the 1960s, Frederick Herzberg and his associates undertook their own study of human needs. They asked accountants and engineers to describe specific aspects of their jobs that made them feel satisfied or dissatisfied. Upon analyzing the results, they found that two entirely different sets of factors were associated with satisfying and dissatisfying work experiences: *hygiene factors* and *motivators* (see Exhibit 10.3).

What Herzberg called **hygiene factors** are associated with dissatisfying experiences. The potential sources of dissatisfaction include working conditions, company policies, and job security. Management can lessen worker dissatisfaction by improving hygiene factors that concern employees, but such improvements seldom influence satisfaction. On the other hand, managers can help employees feel more motivated and, ultimately, more satisfied, by paying attention to **motivators** such as achievement, recognition, responsibility, and other personally rewarding factors. Herzberg's theory is related to Maslow's hierarchy of needs: The motivators closely resemble the higher-level needs, and the hygiene factors resemble the lower-level needs.

Should managers concentrate on motivators or on hygiene factors? It depends. A skilled, well-paid, middle-class, middle-aged employee may be motivated to perform better if motivators are supplied. However, a young, unskilled worker who earns low wages, or an employee who is insecure, will probably still need the support of strong hygiene factors to reduce dissatisfaction before the motivators can be effective.[10]

hygiene factors
Aspects of the work environment that are associated with dissatisfaction

motivators
Factors of human relations in business that may increase motivation

Theory X and Theory Y In the 1960s, psychologist Douglas McGregor identified two radically different sets of assumptions that underlie most management thinking. He classified these sets of assumptions into two categories: *Theory X* and *Theory Y* (see Exhibit 10.4).

THEORY X	THEORY Y
1. Employees inherently dislike work and will avoid it whenever possible.	1. Employees like work and consider it as natural as play and rest.
2. Because employees dislike work, they must be threatened with punishment to achieve goals.	2. People naturally work toward goals they are committed to.
3. Employees will avoid responsibilities whenever possible.	3. The average person can learn to accept and even seek responsibility.
4. Employees value security above all other job factors.	4. The average person's intellectual potential is only partially realized.

EXHIBIT 10.4

THEORY X AND THEORY Y

McGregor proposed two distinct views of human beings: The assumptions of Theory X are basically negative, whereas those of Theory Y are basically positive.

Theory X
Managerial assumption that employees are irresponsible, unambitious, and distasteful of work and that managers must use force, control, or threats to motivate them

Theory Y
Managerial assumption that employees like work, are naturally committed to certain goals, are capable of creativity, and seek out responsibility under the right conditions

According to McGregor, **Theory X**–oriented managers believe that employees dislike work and can be motivated only by the fear of losing their jobs or by *extrinsic rewards* such as money, promotions, and tenure. This management style emphasizes physiological and safety needs and tends to ignore the higher-level needs in Maslow's hierarchy. In contrast, **Theory Y**–oriented managers believe that employees like work and can be motivated by working for goals that promote creativity or for causes they believe in. Thus, Theory Y-oriented managers seek to motivate employees through *intrinsic rewards.*

The assumptions behind Theory X emphasize authority; the assumptions behind Theory Y emphasize growth and self-direction. It was McGregor's belief that, although some employees need the strong direction demanded by Theory X, those who are ready to realize their social, esteem, and self-actualization needs will not work well under Theory X assumptions.[11]

■ KEEPING PACE WITH TODAY'S WORKFORCE

Although motivational theories shed some light on what managers can do to motivate employees to work efficiently and effectively toward achieving the organization's goals, managers must also address the needs of today's workforce. They must manage a diverse group of individuals and recognize that all employees have interests and obligations outside of work, such as family, volunteer activities, and hobbies. Addressing employees' many needs becomes even more critical in a work environment plagued with a number of staffing challenges.

Staffing Challenges

LEARNING OBJECTIVE   2
Discuss three staffing challenges employers are facing in today's workplace.

If you ask business leaders what their biggest challenges are today, you will most likely get these answers: finding, attracting, and keeping talented people; rightsizing their workforces; and satisfying employees' desire for a work–life balance.[12] Finding and keeping good workers is especially hard for small-company owners, who often trail bigger companies in salary, benefits, job security, and other criteria that lead workers to choose one company over another. Larger companies can woo top job applicants with hiring bonuses, flexible work schedules, job training, and other incentives. But because such enticements are costly, they are not feasible for smaller concerns.

Shortage of Skilled Labor   A close look at Component Chapter D confirms that many of today's growing occupations require specialized skills or training, whereas the shrinking occupations involve activities that require fewer skills or ones that are increasingly being automated. In fact, nearly all jobs today require computer literacy. Machinists, for example, need computer skills to operate chip-controlled equipment. Telemarketers must know how to keyboard. Even package delivery involves data entry. But finding technology-literate employees is a dilemma for most companies today.

By one estimate there are already 190,000 unfilled high-tech jobs, and the demand for people with engineering, computer, and other technical skills is mushrooming. An additional 1 million such jobs are expected to be created in this decade, with virtually no increase in supply.[13] Furthermore, the gap is widening between what employers will require of new employees in the years ahead and the actual skills of these employees.

One factor contributing to the skilled-labor shortage is the robust U.S. economy. An increasing demand for U.S. goods and services has put pressure on U.S. companies to operate at breakneck speeds. But with unemployment hovering at around 4 to 5 percent, the economy is considered to be at full employment.[14] So companies are exploring different options to attract and keep employees in their organizations.

Some companies are revamping rigid pay systems to make it easier for employees to move laterally and enhance their skills. Others are installing new career-development programs to help employees plan their career moves. Managers at International Paper, for example, sit down with every employee once a year to discuss their career desires, separate from their annual performance reviews.[15] Still others are instituting educational programs to attract and keep skilled employees. Cisco Systems, a manufacturer of computer network routers, runs its own Networking Academy. This in-house vocational program teaches students how to build and manage the computer-server networks the company sells. Cisco hopes that eventually the students will return to the company for permanent jobs.[16]

UPS took a particularly creative approach with its staffing dilemma when Louisville, Kentucky, could not supply the 6,000 additional employees the company needed to staff its growing $6 billion air-freight business. Rather than moving its main U.S. air hub from Louisville to another location, UPS partnered with the city of Louisville to attract new employees to the area. Together they built "UPS University," and special dormitories so student-workers could sleep during the day, attend classes taught by professors from the University of Louisville at night, and then work the UPS graveyard shift (from 11:30 P.M. to 3:30 A.M.) and still have time to study. With over 15,000 employees in Louisville alone, UPS is now Kentucky's largest employer.[17]

Rightsizing The increasing demand for educated workers and the continuing conversion from a manufacturing-based economy to a service-based economy (as discussed in Chapter 1) are also forcing companies to pull apart their workforce and then piece it back together differently. More than 4.6 million job cuts were announced in the 1990s. Factors contributing to *downsizing* decisions included company reorganizations, business downturns, elimination of unprofitable product lines, outsourcing, mergers and acquisitions, and a general mismatch between employee job skills and job demands. Even though corporate downsizing continues today, what is puzzling is a concurrent trend toward "upsizing," or massive hiring—and often within the same firm.[18]

This phenomenon can best be explained by the needs of companies to *rightsize*, or realign their workforces into business growth areas. For example, employees from Department A are let go while new hires are sought to keep up with the growth demands of Department B. Such was the case with defense electronics giant Raytheon. Even though the company slashed 8,700 defense jobs, or 10 percent of its workforce, it redeployed 5,000 engineers to its booming commercial units.[19]

Declining Employee Loyalty As you can imagine, rightsizing is a contributing factor to declining employee loyalty. Devastated by the lack of job security, as Exhibit 10.5 shows, employees quickly learn to "do what's best for me." In fact, today's employees are cautious. They recognize that the old idea of a paternal company taking care of employees has, for the most part, died. Employee expectations are now more realistic. Hardworking, loyal employees no longer expect to move up the organizational hierarchy. They realize that companies are going to do whatever they have to do to succeed and to survive. And this may mean manufacturing in South America, eliminating three layers of management, or closing down plants.[20] Even the Japanese tradition of lifetime employment is under attack. After years of severe economic recession and intense global competition, the Japanese are realizing that unconditional loyalty is becoming too expensive to justify. To remain competitive, Japanese companies are chipping away at their seniority-based management system and are forcing executives to perform or go—bringing Japan a little closer to the U.S. model.[21]

Increasing Employee Burnout Rightsizing is also putting pressure on remaining employees to work longer hours. When 3M spun off its data-storage and medical-imaging divisions, for example, some employees began putting in 80-hour weeks. One 3M customer service consultant summed up the feelings of many employees when he said, "I always perceived work to be a means to an end, but not *the* end."[22] Others are working longer hours just to keep up. "It seems like you work, work, work," says one Michigan chemist.[23]

CHARACTERISTIC	THEN	NOW
Attachment to employer	Long-term	Near-term
Readiness to change jobs	Not interested	Not looking (but will listen)
Priorities on the job	The firm and its goals	Personal life and career
Devotion to employer goals	Follows orders	Buys in (usually)
Effort on the job	100 percent	110 percent
Motto	Always faithful	Seize the day

EXHIBIT 10.5

THE COMMITTED EMPLOYEE—THEN AND NOW

Employee loyalty isn't what it used to be. A recent survey confirms that even today's most valuable committed workers often put career development and life and family issues ahead of company goals. This chart illustrates this shift in workforce commitment.

Best of the Web Best of the Web Best of

WORKING HARD ON THE WEB

Frustrated workers and managers now have a place to go to voice their opinions, commiserate with others, and get advice on how to motivate employees. The place is Hard@Work, a Web site created "to reduce the oversupply of fear and alienation in the workplace by meeting the pent-up demand for constructive communication about what's happening on the job." Visitors can hang around the "Water Cooler" to chat with others about work issues; play "Stump the Mentor," which offers suggestions for handling sticky work situations; or dig into the "Rock Pile," which features realistic case studies. Hard@Work offers something for workers and job seekers alike.
www.hardatwork.com/

On average, workers are putting in 260 more hours a year than a decade ago—many without overtime pay.[24] Moreover, the Bureau of Labor Statistics says the proportion of professionals and managers working extremely long hours—49 or more a week—has risen by as much as 37 percent since 1985.[25] Such long hours can lead to employee *burnout,* which is characterized by emotional exhaustion, depersonalization, and lower levels of achievement. Severe burnout or stress may even lead to clinical depression.[26] Other causes of employee burnout are job insecurity, technological advancements, and information overload:

■ *Job insecurity.* Workers anxious about job security feel they have to give 150 percent (or more) or risk being seen as expendable. What once were considered crises-mode workloads have now become business as usual. These extra hours, which don't always bring extra pay, can leave employees feeling burned out and resentful.[27]

GeniusBabies.com, seller of educational toys, allows workers such as Michelle Donahue-Arpas to telecommute so she can spend more time with her daughter.

■ *Technological advancements.* New technology allows employees to work from home, but being wired to the office 24 hours a day can add extra pressure. Employees feel compelled to answer that voice mail or e-mail whatever the hour. "We have all these great tools to save our time," notes one career expert. "Instead, it just extends our week. We're never out of touch anymore."[28]

■ *Information overload.* Managers claim they're unable to handle the vast amounts of information they now receive. In fact, more information has been produced in the last 30 years than the previous 5,000, and the total quantity of printed material is doubling every 5 years, and accelerating.[29]

How does burnout affect the ability of workers to do their jobs? "When you feel under stress, you find your mental wheels spinning and you work mechanically rather than creatively," says one human resources expert. "The tasks that normally would take a few minutes sit unfinished for days because you lose the capacity to prioritize and you put off larger, important projects that take more energy and concentration."[30]

Quality of Work Life   A recent survey by jobtrack.com found that 42 percent of all job seekers identified work–life issues as the most important consideration in their choice of a new job. For some employees the primary work–life issue is caring for an elder parent; for others it's child care, rising college tuition costs, or a desire to return to school part-time.[31] Regardless, achieving a work–life balance is especially difficult when both parents work or in situations

COMPETING IN THE GLOBAL MARKETPLACE

CHUCKLE WHILE YOU WORK

Lighten up. Let loose. Laugh a little. Experts are now advising managers to make company-sponsored fun a fundamental part of work. That's because after experiencing a decade of restructuring, downsizing, and reengineering, employees could use a laugh or two. In fact, a recent survey of 1,300 corporate managers showed that more than 60 percent disagreed with the statement "I have fun at work these days."

"Because we spend more of our waking hours working than doing anything else, fun should be a very fundamental part of work," notes one expert on human behavior. In fact, workplace fun is increasingly important because today's jobs are more insecure and more competitive than they once were. Furthermore, camaraderie is diminishing as employees spend more and more time relating to machines rather than each other, eating lunch at their desks, or working from home.

Although traditional business wisdom says that people having fun on the job are probably slacking off, studies show that a happy workforce is also a productive one. For one thing, a little wisecracking and side-splitting laughter can go a long way toward relieving stress. Moreover, it can raise a company's bottom line by improving health, reducing absenteeism, boosting morale, building teamwork, releasing creativity, improving productiv-

ity, and increasing enthusiasm. So while the pursuit of fun may seem frivolous to the serious-minded, more and more companies are beginning to see the value of a good hearty laugh or a little giggle now and then.

Take Sprint, for example. Recent company-sponsored fun days encouraged employees to wear clothes backward and to go on a photo safari with disposable cameras, taking candid photos of employees. Similarly, hospital employees at Charleton Memorial Hospital spent their fun day matching pictures of employees' pets to owners. Other companies have organized employee costume parties, hosted goofy birthday celebrations, and sponsored fun-filled weekends at hotels. Still others are lifting the workplace spirit by hanging funny signs and posters in offices, holding a messiest desk contest with prizes, and posting comic strips and snapshots on company bulletin boards. These companies and others recognize that if work is fun, people will want to come to work.

■ QUESTIONS FOR CRITICAL THINKING

1. Under which level of Maslow's hierarchy of needs would you place having fun at work?

2. When can having fun at work get out of hand?

---

where downsizing and restructuring have left remaining employees with heavier workloads than in the past.

To help employees balance the demands of work and family, businesses are offering child care assistance, family leave, flexible work schedules, telecommuting, and other solutions that are explored later in this chapter and in Chapter 11. Many, such as SAS, are also focusing on improving the **quality of work life (QWL),** the environment created by work and job conditions.[32] An improved QWL benefits both the individual and the organization. Employees gain the chance to use their specialized abilities, improve their skills, and balance their lives. The organization gains a more motivated and loyal employee.

Two common ways of improving QWL are through **job enrichment,** which reduces specialization and makes work more meaningful by expanding each job's responsibilities, and through **job redesign,** which restructures work to provide a better fit between employees' skills and their jobs. As this chapter's opening vignette shows, quality of work life can be improved in other ways, too. Like SAS, many organizations are providing their employees with a number of benefits designed to help them balance their work with personal responsibilities. Accenture (formerly Andersen Consulting), for instance, will send someone to pick up an employee's car from the repair shop; Pepsi has an on-site dry cleaning drop-off at its New York headquarters; and American Banker's Insurance Group and Hewlett-Packard have sponsored schools at company sites that allow employees to visit their children during lunchtime and after school. All of these measures can improve employees' lives by freeing up their time and by making work a more enjoyable place to be.[33]

quality of work life (QWL)
Overall environment that results from job and work conditions

job enrichment
Reducing work specialization and making work more meaningful by adding to the responsibilities of each job

job redesign
Designing a better fit between employees' skills and their work to increase job satisfaction

Demographic Challenges

The U.S. workforce is undergoing significant changes that require major alterations in how managers keep employees happy and productive. One of the most significant demographic trends facing companies today is increasing workforce diversity.

Workforce Diversity The U.S. workforce is diverse in race, gender, age, culture, family structures, religion, and educational backgrounds—and will become even more so in the years ahead. Although nearly three-fourths of the U.S. population is still classified as white, that's changing fast. By 2050 whites will represent only 53 percent of the U.S. population. Hispanics will make up about 24 percent, African Americans 14 percent, Asian Americans 8 percent, and Native Americans 1 percent.[34]

Managing this changing mixture of ages, faces, values, and views is, of course, increasingly difficult. Not only does a diverse workforce bring with it a wide range of skills, traditions, backgrounds, experiences, outlooks, and attitudes toward work that can affect individuals' behavior on the job, but managers must be able to communicate with and motivate this diverse workforce while fostering cooperation and harmony among employees. Two trends contributing to the diversity of the U.S. workforce are the influx of immigrants and the aging population.

LEARNING OBJECTIVE 3

Highlight two trends contributing to the diversity of the U.S. workforce.

Influx of Immigrants Today foreign-born engineers jam the corridors of the U.S. Silicon Valley, hoping to reap the benefits of the nation's information technology boom. Meanwhile tens of thousands of Mexicans slip across the border each year. At the same time employers are clamoring for more foreign-born workers to fill their critical labor shortages, and they are pressuring Congress to enact legislation that would admit hundreds of thousands of additional immigrants each year. As a result, the percentage of immigrant workers in the U.S. labor force has climbed to its highest level in seven decades.[35] This trend is having profound effects on the economy—helping to hold down wages in unskilled jobs and giving many companies the employees they need to expand.

Aging Population The population in the United States is aging, a situation that creates new challenges and concerns for employers and employees alike. The general aging of the population and the declining number of young people entering the workforce is largely due to the decisions of baby boomers (born 1946–1960) to marry later, to postpone or forgo starting a family, and to have fewer children. About 84 percent of baby boomers participate in today's labor market.[36] Experts predict that because of inadequate pensions, high medical costs, and a general desire to stay active, baby boomers will put off retirement until they are in their seventies.

Widespread delayed retirement will indeed present challenges for all parties involved. For one thing, even though the 1967 Age Discrimination in Employment Act (ADEA) makes workers over 40 a protected class, many suspect that age discrimination is widespread.[37] For another, older, more experienced employees command higher salaries. "For my salary, the company could hire two twenty somethings," says a 41-year-old. "I'm good at what I do. But am I better than two people? Even I know that's not true." Not only do older employees earn more, but the costs of employee benefits such as medical insurance and pensions rise with age as well.[38] Furthermore, as the speed of change gets faster, it can be difficult for older employees to keep up unless they have the stamina of a 25-year-old.

Age has its advantages, of course. According to one recent study, older employees have more experience, better judgment, and a greater commitment to quality. They are also more likely to show up on time and less likely to quit. But these traits pale by comparison with the highly desired traits characteristic of younger workers, who appear more flexible, more adaptable, more accepting of new technology, and better at learning new skills. Studies also show that the difference in job performance between someone with 20 years experience and someone with just 5 years does not always justify the higher costs of maintaining a senior workforce.[39]

Putting more people of various ethnicities on the floor—and in executive positions—is a no-brainer for Wal-Mart, which was recently ranked by *Fortune* magazine as one of America's 50 best companies for Asian, black, and Hispanic Americans. This group, for instance, includes two senior vice presidents, four vice presidents, and two corporate counsels.

Diversity Initiatives To cope with increasing workforce diversity, many companies offer employees sensitivity or awareness training to help them understand the different attitudes and beliefs that women, minorities, and immigrants bring to their jobs.[40] At Allstate Insurance, for example, all nonagent employees with service of more than one year are expected to complete diversity training—a company investment in excess of 540,000 hours of classroom time.[41] And at the Marriott Marquis Hotel in New York, mandatory diversity-training classes teach managers how to avoid defining problems in terms of gender, culture, or race. These classes also help managers become more sensitive to the behavior and communication patterns of employees with diverse backgrounds.

The number of U.S. workers over 65 has edged up during the past decade from 3 million to 3.8 million and is expected to rise to 4.3 million by 2005. In the meantime, the number of workers aged 25 to 44 is falling.

Although encouraging sensitivity to employee differences is important, a company stands to benefit most when it incorporates its employees' diverse perspectives into the organization's work. This assimilation enables the company to uncover new opportunities by rethinking primary tasks and redefining markets, products, strategies, missions, business practices, and even cultures. Consider the small public-interest law firm of Dewey & Levin. In the mid-1980s the firm had an all-white legal staff. Concerned about its ability to serve ethnically diverse populations, the firm hired a Hispanic female attorney. She introduced Dewey & Levin to new ideas about what kinds of cases to take on, and many of her ideas were pursued with great success. Hiring more women of color brought even more fresh perspectives. The firm now pursues cases that the original staff members would never have considered because they would not have understood the link between the issues involved in the cases and the firm's mission.[42] In short, diversity is an asset, and one of the challenges of corporate human relations is to make the most of this asset.

Gender-Related Issues Another demographic challenge companies have been grappling with for years is the gender gap in compensation. Women today earn about 76 percent of men's median pay.[43] Moreover, even though women now hold 46 percent of executive, administrative, and managerial positions (up from 34 percent in 1983), only 10 percent of the top managerial positions at the nation's 500 largest companies are held by women. At levels of vice president or higher, the figure is only 2.4 percent.[44] Some attribute this inequality to the *glass ceiling*.

The Glass Ceiling The **glass ceiling** is an invisible barrier that keeps women and minorities from reaching the highest-level positions. One theory about the glass ceiling suggests that top management has long been dominated by white males who tend to hire and promote employees who look, act, and think as they do. Another theory states that stereotyping by male middle managers leads them to believe that family life will interfere with a woman's work. As a result, women are relegated to less visible assignments in the company, so their work goes unnoticed by top executives and their careers stagnate.[45]

glass ceiling
Invisible barrier attributable to subtle discrimination that keeps women out of the top positions in business

In recent years, women have made significant strides toward overcoming job discrimination on the basis of gender, or **sexism,** thanks to a combination of changing societal attitudes and company commitments to workplace diversity. Such initiatives include long-term commitments to hiring more women, company-sponsored networking and career planning for women, diversity training and workshops, and mentoring programs designed to help female employees move more quickly through the ranks.

sexism
Discrimination on the basis of gender

Pitney Bowes's long-term commitment to diversity, for instance, has resulted in women holding 5 of the top 11 jobs at the company. Patagonia boasts that women now hold more than half of the company's top-paying jobs and almost 60 percent of managerial jobs. And the appointment of Carly Fiorina to CEO of Hewlett-Packard (HP) was hailed by many as a milestone for women. With more than a quarter of HP's managers being women, it seems that the glass ceiling at this company has been shattered.[46]

sexual harassment
Unwelcome sexual advances, request for sexual favors, or other verbal or physical conduct of a sexual nature within the workplace

Sexual Harassment Another sensitive issue that women often face in the workplace is sexual harassment. As defined by the EEOC, **sexual harassment** takes two forms: the obvious request for sexual favors with an implicit reward or punishment related to work and the more subtle creation of a sexist environment in which employees are made to feel uncomfortable by off-color jokes, lewd remarks, and posturing. Even though male employees may also be targets of sexual harassment, and both male and female employees may experience same-sex harassment, sexual harassment of female employees by male colleagues continues to make up the majority of reported cases.

To put an end to sexual harassment, many companies are now enforcing strict harassment policies. Recent Supreme Court rulings explain (for the first time) how all employers—both large and small—can insulate themselves from potential sexual harassment lawsuits. In short, a company can defend itself successfully if it can prove that it had an effective policy against sexual harassment in place and that the employee alleging harassment failed to take advantage of this policy. To be effective, the policy must be in writing, communicated to all employees, and enforced.[47] This means that the company must train all employees on the policy, and the company must have clear procedures for reporting such behavior—including allowing employees access to management other than their supervisors. Without such policies, companies can be held indirectly responsible for a harasser's actions even when top managers had no idea that such practices were going on.[48]

Alternative Work Arrangements

To meet today's staffing and demographic challenges, many companies are adopting alternative work arrangements. Three of the most popular arrangements are flextime, telecommuting, and job sharing. Many organizations find that a mix of these arrangements and other employee benefits works better than a one-size-fits-all approach.[49]

Flextime An increasingly important alternative work arrangement, **flextime** is a scheduling system that allows employees to choose their own hours within certain limits. Approximately 66 percent of all companies now offer some form of flextime.[50] For instance, a company may require everyone to be at work between 10:00 A.M. and 2:00 P.M., but employees may arrive or depart whenever they want as long as they work a total of 8 hours every day. Another popular flextime schedule is to work four 10-hour days each week, taking one prearranged day off (see Exhibit 10.6).

Should women be allowed to wear whatever they want to work? For every Erin Brockovich who can make gains by wearing low-cut tops and short skirts, it's more common for a woman in such outfits to not be taken seriously in today's workplace.

At SAS Institute, for instance, every white-collar employee has the opportunity to create a flexible schedule.[51] Other companies nationally recognized for having superior flextime policies are Pillsbury, Deloitte & Touche, and Aetna Life & Casualty.[52] Of course, flextime is more feasible in white-collar businesses that do not have to maintain standard customer-service hours. For this reason, it is not usually an option for employees on production teams, in retail stores, or in many offices where employees have to be on hand to wait on customers or answer calls.

The sense of control employees get from arranging their own work schedules is motivating for many. Companies have found that flextime reduces turnover, enables the company to adapt to business cycles, allows operation of a round-the-clock business, and helps maintain morale and performance after reengineering or downsizing. Still, flextime is not without drawbacks. They include supervisors who feel uncomfortable and less in control when employees are coming and going, and co-workers who resent flextimers because they assume that people who work flexible hours don't take their jobs seriously enough.[53]

Telecommuting Related to flexible schedules is **telecommuting**—working from home or another location using computers and telecommunications equipment to stay in touch with the employer's offices. Depending on which study you read, between 20 and 58 percent of employers now offer telecommuting arrangements for their employees. In fact, current estimates now put the number of U.S. telecommuters at about 16 million.[54]

LEARNING
OBJECTIVE   4

Discuss three popular alternative work arrangements companies are offering their employees.

flextime
Scheduling system in which employees are allowed certain options regarding time of arrival and departure

telecommuting
Working from home and communicating with the company's main office via computer and communication devices

Full-time, permanent employees and independent contractors who say these are "extremely important" in job satisfaction	Full-time	Independent
Ability to work from home	15%	44%
Flexible work schedule	40%	62%
Freedom from office politics	44%	60%
Believing in what they do	72%	83%
Making right amount of money	50%	46%
Work they find challenging	55%	59%

EXHIBIT 10.6

9-TO-5 NOT FOR EVERYONE

For many full-time employees and independent contractors, their degree of job satisfaction is closely linked to the availability of these job conditions or attributes.

Of course, some company operations clearly are not designed for telecommuting. For example, a printer who runs giant color presses can't run the presses from home. But for the kinds of jobs that can be performed from remote sites, telecommuting helps meet employees' needs for flexibility while boosting their productivity as much as 20 percent. Half of AT&T's 50,000 managers worldwide now telecommute.[55] Companies such as AT&T, IBM, and Lucent Technologies provide employees with laptops, dedicated phone lines, software support, fax-printer units, help lines, and full technical backup at the nearest corporate facility. Some even provide employees who work at home with a generous allowance for furnishings and equipment to be used at their discretion.[56]

Telecommuting offers many advantages. For one thing, it can save the company money by eliminating offices people don't need, consolidating others, and reducing related overhead costs.[57] Telecommuting also enables a company to hire talented people in distant areas without requiring them to relocate. This option expands the company's pool of potential job candidates while benefiting employees who have an employed spouse, children in school, or elderly parents to care for.[58] Employees also like telecommuting because they can set their own hours, reduce job-related expenses such as commuting costs, and spend more time with their families.

Telecommuting does have its limitations. The challenges of managing the cultural changes required by telecommuting are substantial. In telecommuting situations, midlevel managers relinquish direct, visual employee supervision. Some find it scary to be in the position of managing people they can't see. Others are concerned that people working at home will slack off or that telecommuting could cause resentment among office-bound colleagues or weaken company loyalty.[59] Regardless, companies are learning that you can't just give people computers, send them home, and call them telecommuters. You have to teach an employee how to think like a telecommuter.

Merrill Lynch recognizes this fact. Prospective telecommuters at Merrill Lynch must submit a detailed proposal that covers when and how they're going to work at home, and even what their

Best of the Web Best of the Web Best of

TELECOMMUTING YOUR WAY TO SUCCESS

Does telecommuting reality match the hype? Follow the links at this Web site and decide for yourself. Read the guidelines and articles. Then test your knowledge of basic telecommuting issues by taking the quiz and shooting for a virtual million. Learn what skills and qualifications are required to succeed in telecommuting. Log on to the telecommuting forum and ask questions, share ideas and experiences, or just have fun. Next explore other alternative working arrangements. Which ones are suited for you?

www.telecommuting.about.com/smallbusiness/telecommuting

KEEPING PACE WITH TECHNOLOGY AND ELECTRONIC COMMERCE

IS TELECOMMUTING RIGHT FOR YOU?

Telecommuting sounds like the perfect life. No commute. No morning rush to get ready for. No expensive wardrobe. No day care for kids. But for many people, telecommuting also means no social life.

Many home-based workers soon find that they miss interacting with colleagues. Some worry that if they're not in the office—if they're not seen—they'll be forgotten. Others find that they actually put in longer hours or they encounter too many distractions, such as young children requiring attention. Still others discover that it takes a lot of willpower and self-discipline to be productive when the refrigerator and a nice warm bed are just a few feet away.

Is telecommuting right for you? Here's a checklist to help you determine whether you'd be a good candidate. If you answer yes to all the questions, go for it. But if you answer no to any of them, you need to think the issue through carefully before taking the leap.

√ Have you worked at your company long enough to thoroughly understand its culture and expectations?

√ Can others perform their jobs without your being physically available?

√ Are you content to work in isolation?

√ Can you perform your job, complete projects, and meet your deadlines without supervision?

√ Can you physically take your work home with you in a briefcase?

√ Can you communicate everything you need for your daily workload via phone or e-mail?

√ Does your home have a separate room in which to work, with a door that shuts?

√ Does your home work space have a separate phone line for a fax, modem, computer, and other equipment?

√ If you have a child, will you have day care available while you work?

√ If you live with someone else who works at home, will this situation pose any problems?

√ Are you disciplined enough to stop working at the end of the day?

√ If you were your boss, would you let you telecommute?

■ QUESTIONS FOR CRITICAL THINKING

1. What can companies do to prepare employees for the challenges of telecommuting?

2. Why is it important to understand a company's culture before you begin telecommuting?

---

home office will look like. Next they participate in a series of meetings. Finally, they spend two weeks in a simulation lab that lets employees and their managers experience the change. Once at home, telecommuters are required to document their at-home working hours and submit weekly progress reports.[60] But even for those companies that provide support, some telecommuters are finding that this "ideal setup" is not for everyone.

job sharing
Splitting a single full-time job between two employees for their convenience

Job Sharing Job sharing, which lets two employees share a single full-time job and split the salary and benefits, has been slowly gaining acceptance as a way to work part-time in a full-time position. According to a recent survey by Hewitt Associates (a firm specializing in employee benefits), 37 percent of employers offer job-sharing arrangements to their employees.[61] But such arrangements are usually offered to people who already work for the company and who need to cut back their hours. Rather than lose a good employee or have to find and train someone new, the company finds a way to split responsibilities.

Consider UnumProvident, a leading provider of insurance products. When two of its employees approached the company about sharing a job, the company decided to let them do it. Now one employee works all day Monday and Tuesday, the other works all day Thursday and Friday, and the two overlap on Wednesday. The personal benefits are exactly what the employees hoped for—more time at home. The company benefits because the position is rarely left uncovered during times of vacation or illness and because two people, instead of just one person, bring their ideas and creativity to the job.[62]

▮ WORKING WITH LABOR UNIONS

Not only do today's employees want alternative work arrangements, but they want safe and comfortable working conditions and pay that rewards their contributions to the organization. At the same time, however, business owners must focus on using company resources to increase productivity and profits. In the best of times and in the most enlightened companies, these two sets of needs can often be met simultaneously. However, when the economy slows down and competition speeds up, balancing the needs of employees with those of management can be a challenge.

Because of this potential for conflict, many employees join **labor unions,** organizations that seek to protect employee interests by negotiating with employers for better wages and benefits, improved working conditions, and increased job security. (See Exhibit 10.7 for a summary of the most significant laws relating to labor unions.) Employees are most likely to turn to unions if they are deeply dissatisfied with their current job and employment conditions, if they believe that unionization can be helpful in improving those job conditions, and if they are willing to overlook negative stereotypes that have surrounded unions in recent years.[63]

One advantage of joining labor unions is that it gives employees stronger bargaining power. By combined forces, union employees can put more pressure on management than they could as individuals. For instance, in August 1997, the International Brotherhood of Teamsters called a national strike against United Parcel Service (UPS) to fight for better pay for part-time workers, more full-time jobs, and better pension benefits. UPS finally agreed to most of the union's demands but only after the U.S. public supported the strike and began taking their business elsewhere. The 15-day labor dispute cost UPS about $1 billion in lost revenues.[64]

Not all employees support labor unions, of course. Many believe that unions stifle individual initiative and are not necessary to ensure fair treatment from employers. Moreover, companies that have most successfully resisted unionization seem to have adopted participative management styles and an enhanced sense of responsibility toward employees. Consider Marriott International. Marriott has recognized that the primary reasons employees consider unionizing is because they feel they are not treated well by management. In order to demonstrate to workers

labor unions
Organizations of employees formed to protect and advance their members' interests

LEGISLATION	PROVISION
Norris–La Guardia Act of 1932	Limits companies' ability to obtain injunctions against union strikes, picketing, membership drives, and other activities.
National Labor Relations Act of 1935 (Wagner Act)	Gives employees the right to form, join, or assist labor organizations; the right to bargain collectively with employers through elected union representatives; and the right to engage in strikes, pickets, and boycotts. Prohibits certain unfair labor practices by the employer and union. Establishes the National Labor Relations Board to supervise union elections and to investigate charges of unfair labor practices by management.
Labor-Management Relations Act of 1947 (Taft-Hartley Act)	Amends Wagner Act to reaffirm employees' rights to organize and bargain collectively over working conditions. Establishes specific unfair labor practices both for management and for unions, and prohibits strikes in the public sector.
Landrum-Griffin Act of 1959	Amends Taft-Hartley Act and Wagner Act to control union corruption and to add the secondary boycott as an unfair labor practice. A secondary boycott occurs when a union appeals to firms or other unions to stop doing business with an employer who sells or handles goods of a company whose employees are on strike. The act requires all unions to file annual financial reports with the U.S. Department of Labor, making union officials more personally responsible for the union's financial affairs. The act guarantees individual member rights such as the right to vote in union elections, the right to sue unions, and the right to attend and participate in union meetings.
Plant-Closing Notification Act of 1988	Requires employers to give employees and local elected officials 60 days advance notice of plant shutdowns or massive layoffs.

EXHIBIT 10.7

KEY LEGISLATION RELATING TO UNIONS

Most major labor legislation was enacted in the 1930s and 1940s. However, some more recent legislation has also been passed to protect organized labor.

that they are valued, Marriott offers its employees stock options, social-service referral networks, day care, training classes, and opportunities for advancement. As a result, Marriott's employee turnover is well below that of most companies, and its employees' enthusiasm is high.[65]

Still, even the best working conditions are no guarantee that employees won't seek union representation. For instance, although Starbucks is renowned for its generous employee benefit programs and supportive work environment, employees of stores in Vancouver, British Columbia, organized and successfully bargained for higher wages.[66]

How Unions Are Structured

locals
Relatively small union groups, usually part of a national union or a labor federation, that represent members who work in a single facility or in a certain geographic area

Many unions are organized at local, national, and international levels. **Locals,** or local unions, represent employees in a specific geographic area or facility; an example is Local 1853, which represents GM's Saturn employees. Each local union is a hierarchy with a broad base of *rank-and-file* members, the employees the union represents. These members pay an initiation fee, pay regular dues, and vote to elect union officials. Each department or facility also has or elects a **shop steward,** who works in the facility as a regular employee and serves as a go-between with supervisors when a problem arises. In large locals and in locals that represent employees at several locations, an elected full-time **business agent** visits the various work sites to negotiate with management and enforce the union's agreements with those companies.

shop steward
Union member and employee who is elected to represent other union members and who attempts to resolve employee grievances with management

business agent
Full-time union staffer who negotiates with management and enforces the union's agreements with companies

By comparison, a **national union** is a nationwide organization composed of many local unions that represent employees in specific locations; examples are the United Auto Workers (UAW) of America and the United Steelworkers of America. *International unions* have members in more than one country, such as the Union of Needletrades, Industrial, and Textile Employees (UNITE). A national union is responsible for such activities as organizing new areas or industries, negotiating industrywide contracts, assisting locals with negotiations, administering benefits, lobbying Congress, and lending assistance in the event of a strike. Local unions send representatives to the national delegate convention, submit negotiated contracts to the national union for approval, and provide financial support in the form of dues. They have the power to negotiate with individual companies or plants and to undertake their own membership activities.

national union
Nationwide organization made up of local unions that represent employees in locations around the country

labor federation
Umbrella organization of national unions and unaffiliated local unions that undertakes large-scale activities on behalf of their members and that resolves conflicts between unions

The AFL-CIO is a **labor federation** consisting of a variety of national unions and of local unions that are not associated with any other national union. The AFL-CIO's two primary roles are to promote the political objectives of the labor movement and to provide assistance to member unions in their collective bargaining efforts.[67] In recent years, the AFL-CIO has also become much more active in recruiting new members, organizing new locals, and publicizing unions in general.

LEARNING OBJECTIVE 5

Explain the two steps unions take to become the bargaining agent for a group of employees.

How Unions Organize

Union organizers, whether professional or rank-and-file, generally start by visiting with employees, although dissatisfied employees may also approach the union (see Exhibit 10.8). The organizers survey employees by asking questions such as "Have you ever been treated unfairly by your supervisor?" Employees who express interest are sent information about the union

Best of the Web Best of the Web Best of

SPREADING THE UNION MESSAGE

Of all the Web sites devoted to union causes, the AFL-CIO's site offers perhaps the most extensive collection of statistics, information, and commentaries on union issues and programs. The site is designed to educate members and prospective members about union activities and campaigns. Topics include union membership campaigns, safety and family issues, and much more. The AFL-CIO also maintains online directories with the e-mail addresses of members of Congress plus sample letters to encourage communication with legislators. Browse this site to get the latest on union initiatives as well as information about trends in the labor movement today.

www.aflcio.org/

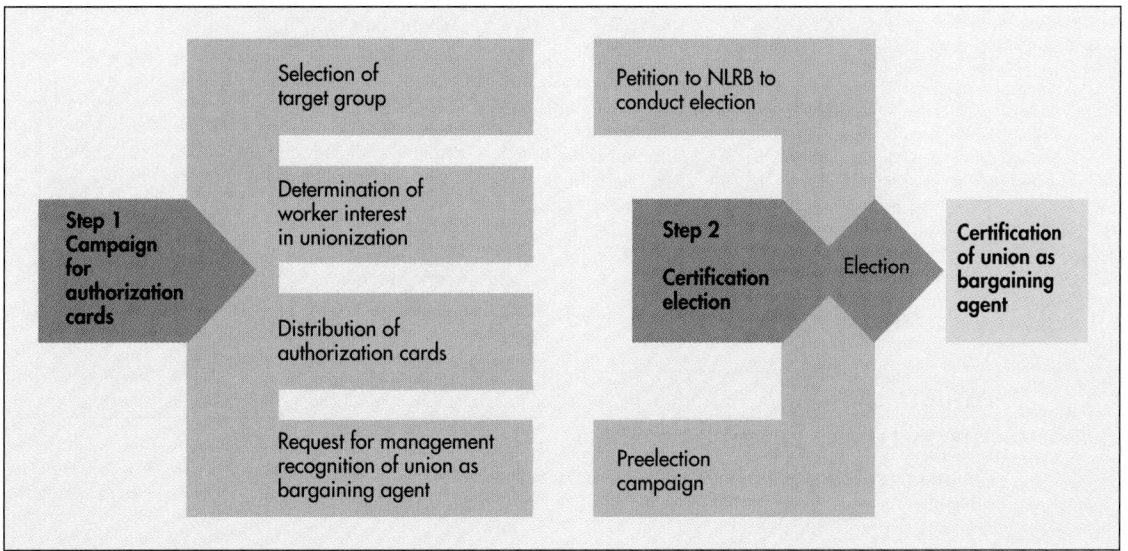

EXHIBIT 10.8

THE UNION-ORGANIZING PROCESS

This diagram summarizes the steps a labor union takes when organizing a group of employees and becoming certified to represent them in negotiations with management. The certification election is necessary only if management is unwilling to recognize the union.

along with **authorization cards**—sign-up cards used to designate the union as their bargaining agent. If 30 percent or more of the employees in the group sign the union's authorization cards, the union may ask management to recognize it. Usually, however, unions do not seek to become the group's bargaining agent unless a majority of the employees sign.

Often the company's management is unwilling to recognize the union at this stage. The union can then ask the National Labor Relations Board (NLRB), an independent federal agency created in 1935 to administer and enforce the National Labor Relations Act, to supervise a **certification** election, the process by which a union becomes the official bargaining agent for a company's employees. If a majority of the affected employees choose to make the union their bargaining agent, the union becomes certified. If not, that union and all other unions have to wait a year before trying again.

Once a company becomes aware that a union is seeking a certification election, management may mount an active campaign to point out the disadvantages of unionization. A company is not allowed, however, to make specific threats or promises about how it will respond to the outcome of the election, and it is not allowed to change general wages or working conditions until the election has been concluded.

Even when a union wins a certification election, there's no guarantee that it will represent a particular group of employees forever. Sometimes employees become dissatisfied with their union and no longer wish to be represented by it. When this happens, the union members can take a **decertification** vote to take away the union's right to represent them. If the majority votes for decertification, the union is removed as bargaining agent.

The Collective Bargaining Process

As long as a union has been recognized as the exclusive bargaining agent for a group of employees, its main job is to negotiate employment contracts with management. In a process known as **collective bargaining,** union and management negotiators work together to forge the human resources policies that will apply to the unionized employees—and other employees covered by the contract—for a certain period, usually three years.

authorization cards
Sign-up cards designating a union as the signer's preferred bargaining agent

Maurice Miller, a meat cutter at Wal-Mart in Jacksonville, Texas, got the unionizing ball rolling when he was promised management training that didn't materialize, as this chapter's Case for Critical Thinking explains.

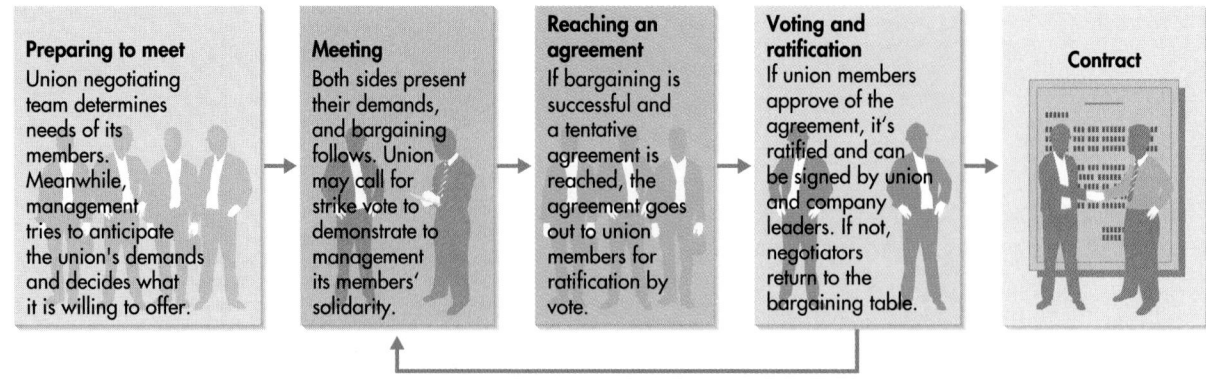

EXHIBIT 10.9

THE COLLECTIVE BARGAINING PROCESS

Contract negotiations go through the four basic steps shown here.

certification
Process by which a union is officially recognized by the National Labor Relations Board as the bargaining agent for a group of employees

decertification
Process employees use to take away a union's official right to represent them

collective bargaining
Process used by unions and management to negotiate work contracts

mediation
Process for resolving a labor-contract dispute in which a neutral third party meets with both sides and attempts to steer them toward a solution

arbitration
Process for resolving a labor-contract dispute in which an impartial third party studies the issues and makes a binding decision

Most labor contracts are a compromise between the desires of union members and those of management. The union pushes for the best possible deal for its members, and management tries to negotiate agreements that are best for the company (and the shareholders, if a corporation is publicly held). Exhibit 10.9 illustrates the collective bargaining process.

Meeting and Reaching an Agreement   When the negotiating teams made up of representatives of the union and management actually sit down together, they state their opening positions and each side discusses its position point by point. Labor usually wants additions to the current contract. In a cooperative atmosphere, the real issues behind the demands gradually come to light. For example, management may begin by demanding the right to determine the sizes of work crews when all it really wants is smaller work crews; the union, however, wants to protect the jobs of its members and keep crew sizes as large as possible but may agree to certain reductions in exchange for, say, higher pay. After many stages of bargaining, each party presents its package of terms, and any gaps between labor and management demands are then dealt with.

If negotiations reach an impasse, outside help may be needed. The most common alternative is **mediation**—bringing in an impartial third party to study the situation and make recommendations for resolution of the differences. Mediators are generally well-respected community leaders whom both sides will listen to. However, mediators can only offer suggestions, and their solutions are not binding. When a legally binding settlement is needed, the negotiators may submit to **arbitration**—a process in which an impartial referee listens to both sides and then makes a judgment by accepting one side's view. In *compulsory arbitration,* the parties are required by a government agency to submit to arbitration; in *voluntary arbitration,* the parties agree on their own to use arbitration to settle their differences.

Exercising Options When Negotiations Break Down   The vast majority of management–union negotiations are settled quickly, easily, and in a businesslike manner. Nevertheless, sometimes negotiations reach an impasse, and neither side is willing to compromise. Both labor and management are able to draw on many powerful options when negotiations or mediation procedures break down.

Labor's Options   Strikes and picket lines are perhaps labor's best-known tactics, but other options are also used.

LEARNING
OBJECTIVE   6

Cite three options unions can exercise when negotiations with management break down.

strike
Temporary work stoppage by employees who want management to accept their union's demands

■ *Strike.* The most powerful weapon that organized labor can use is the **strike,** a temporary work stoppage aimed at forcing management to accept union demands. The basic idea behind the strike is that, in the long run, it costs management more in lost earnings to resist union demands than to give in. A 54-day strike at General Motors (GM) in 1998, for instance, cost the automaker over $2 billion in lost production revenues. Even though the union eventually won temporary reprieves on the closing of unprofitable plants, the settlement agreement failed to directly address important national issues, such as GM's push to open new factories overseas and trim its U.S. workforce. As a result, some observers pegged this costliest strike in decades as a lose-lose situation for both the company and the union.[68] An essential part of any strike is

picketing, in which union members positioned at entrances to company premises march back and forth with signs and leaflets, trying to persuade nonstriking employees to join them and to persuade customers and others to stop doing business with the company.

■ *Boycott.* A less direct union weapon is the **boycott,** in which union members and sympathizers refuse to buy or handle the product of a target company. Millions of union members form an enormous bloc of purchasing power, which may be able to pressure management into making concessions. One of the best-known boycotts was the grape boycott organized by Cesar Chavez in the early 1970s. To pressure California growers into accepting the United Farm Workers (UFW) as the bargaining agent for previously unorganized farm laborers, he and his colleagues persuaded an estimated 17 million people in the United States to stop buying grapes. Eventually, the California legislature passed the country's first law guaranteeing farmworkers the right to hold union elections.[69]

■ *Publicity.* Increasingly, labor is pressing its case by launching publicity campaigns, often called *corporate campaigns,* against the target company and companies affiliated with it. These campaigns might include sending investors alerts that question the firm's solvency, staging rallies during peak business hours, sending letters to charitable groups questioning executives' motives, handing out leaflets that allege safety and health-code violations, and stimulating negative stories in the press.

Labor's other options include *slowdowns,* in which employers continue to do their jobs but at a snail's pace, and *sickouts,* in which employees feign illness and stay home. Both can cripple a company. For instance, in 2000 United Airlines was forced to cancel more than 20,000 flights during the peak summer travel months because company pilots refused to fly overtime hours and called in sick to protest the slow pace of contract negotiations.[70] Similarly, American Airlines was forced to cancel more than 6,600 flights when its pilots staged a sickout in 1999 to protest a lower wage scale for pilots of newly acquired Reno Air. A federal judge later ordered the pilots' union at American Airlines to pay the carrier $45.5 million to compensate the company for the costs it incurred and the business it lost as a result of the sickout.[71]

Management's Options As powerful as the union's tactics are, companies are not helpless when it comes to fighting back. Management can use a number of legal methods to pressure unions when negotiations stall:

■ *Strikebreakers.* When union members walk off their jobs, management can legally replace them with **strikebreakers,** nonunion workers hired to do the jobs of striking workers. (Union members brand them as "scabs.") For example, when over 2,000 union workers struck at the *Detroit News* and *Detroit Free Press* newspapers, management kept the presses rolling by hiring 1,400 replacement workers. Although the strike caused both papers to lose customers, advertisers, and profits, the papers persevered for 19 months until the union gave in. By that time, many temporary replacements had been hired permanently, an action that management is legally permitted to take if it's necessary to keep a business going.[72]

■ *Lockouts.* The U.S. Supreme Court has upheld the use of **lockouts,** in which management prevents union employees from entering the workplace in order to pressure the union to accept a contract proposal. A lockout is management's counterpart to a strike. It is a preemptive measure designed to force a union to accede to management's demands. Lockouts are legal only if the union and management have come to an impasse in negotiations and the employer is defending a legitimate bargaining position. During a lockout, the company may hire temporary replacements as long as it has no antiunion motivation and negotiations have been amicable.[73]

■ *Injunctions.* An **injunction** is a court order prohibiting union workers from taking certain actions. Management used this weapon without restriction in the early days of unionism, when companies typically sought injunctions to order striking employees back to work on the grounds that the strikers were interfering with business. Today injunctions are legal only in certain cases. For example, the president of the United States has the right, under the Taft-Hartley Act, to obtain a temporary injunction to halt a strike deemed harmful to the national interest. In 1997 Bill Clinton used that power to intervene in American Airlines' labor dispute with its pilots' union. The president designated a 60-day period during which a

picketing
Strike activity in which union members march at company entrances to persuade nonstriking employees to walk off the job and to persuade customers and others to cease doing business with the company

boycott
Union activity in which members and sympathizers refuse to buy or handle the product of a target company

LEARNING OBJECTIVE 7
Cite three options management can exercise when negotiations with a union break down.

strikebreakers
Nonunion workers hired to replace striking workers

lockout
Management tactic in which union members are prevented from entering a business during a strike in order to force union acceptance of management's last contract proposal

injunction
Court order prohibiting certain actions by striking workers

specially appointed arbitration panel was to help the two sides reach an agreement. Although the workers were free to strike after 60 days, an agreement was reached and the strike was avoided.[74]

The Labor Movement Today

Unions remain a significant force in employee-management relations in the United States. But their membership continues to decline. Unions now represent only 14 percent (16.4 million) of workers in the United States (down from 20 percent in 1983).[75] One key reason for the decrease in union membership is the shift from a manufacturing-based economy to one dominated by service industries, which tend to appeal less to unions. Another factor contributing to the decline is the changing nature of the labor force. Women, young workers, and highly skilled workers have been harder to organize with traditional methods, as have workers in less hierarchical organizations.[76]

Dynamic labor leaders have recognized that their own inertia is partly to blame for the unions' decline, and they are taking corrective measures. Even though unions are sticking to their traditional causes—good wages, safe conditions, and benefits—progressive labor leaders are pursuing new workplace issues such as job security, increasing health care costs, labor involvement in decisions, child care, and more job training.[77] In the United States, AFL-CIO president John Sweeney has beefed up recruiting efforts, especially among low-wage service workers, minorities, and women. In addition, new industries are being targeted, including high technology and health care. Sweeney has also launched a highly visible public relations campaign and has begun to target people in smaller businesses and self-employed workers to bring them into the union fold. Some unions have already begun to show increases in membership as a result.[78]

What does the future hold for employee-management relations? It is difficult to make predictions. Although John Sweeney's leadership is boosting enthusiasm and political action among union members, as well as generating a new wave of recruiting and organizing, many experts agree that today's global economic conditions severely limit the ability of unions to regain the strength they once had. This is the case both in the United States and in other countries.

 ## FOCUSING ON E-BUSINESS TODAY

The Reality of Working for an E-Business Start-Up

If you're like many, the glamour of working in the technology industry and especially for an e-commerce company carries a powerful mystique. The myth goes something like this: acquire computer skills, join an aggressive Internet start-up, and when the company goes public, cash in and make millions of dollars. It worked for the employees of Amazon, Yahoo!, eBay, and scores of others. But will it work for you?

LEARNING OBJECTIVE

Identify the advantages and disadvantages of working for a start-up e-business from an employee's perspective.

LIVING THE LATE SHIFT

Seeking to cash in on the Internet, thousands of young workers have migrated to one coast or the other to pursue the silicon dream. But once there, they soon discover that cyberspace is rife with sweatshops. For all the glamorous images of being a dot-com CEO or future dot-com manager, the time spent in the office typically adds up to between 80 and 100 hours each week, and sometimes as many as 125. It's a slap of cold reality for most who actually do it. "I see so many dawns it is ridiculous," says one systems architect for an e-commerce-solutions company. Moreover, the working conditions are less than ideal. Cramped, cluttered offices, severe stress, meager employee benefits, and financial peril can quickly morph the cyber fantasy of boundless potential into an unexpected nightmare.

MORE GRIND THAN GLAMOUR

To keep people at their terminals longer, CEOs persuade their employees to look beyond the low pay and long hours. They liken their e-businesses to wars and their workers to zealous warriors. "There's a revolution going on," says one e-commerce CEO, "and we're handing out rifles"—and pillows. E-companies intentionally blur the line between work and play, office and home. Bring your dog to work. Drink all the Mountain Dew you can stomach. It's the job of executives at the top of the Internet food chain to convert the low-cost enthusiasm and work-is-play lifestyle into publicly traded companies worth millions of dollars. A number have succeeded, but most don't.

BANKING ON STOCK OPTIONS

Salaries in the e-world, while decent, are hardly stratospheric. According to one recent study, high-tech jobs pay an average annual salary of about $37,000. Moreover, very few e-business start-ups pay overtime or bonuses. That's because during the pre-IPO phase, precious capital must be allocated to marketing and sales, rather than rent and salaries. So e-companies lure cyber talent with stock options, or the ability to cash in on shares of newly minted stock at some time in the future and earn a handsome profit.

But for the crew in the engine rooms of these Internet start-ups setting sail for IPO land, the reality is that many of them will never see stock-option millions. Some won't be able to sustain the grueling hours. They'll become cyberspaced out and declare e-nough! Others won't stay at the company for the four years it takes the typical options package to vest (that is, for the shares to become sellable). Moreover, for every 10 companies that offer employees options packages, only one actually goes public. And, the only people who really get wealthy are the VPs and higher. Which is why more and more disenchanted employees are bolting from dot-coms and rushing back to U.S. corporations.

COMPENSATING TODAY'S EMPLOYEES

COMPENSATION	TRADITIONAL COMPANY	INTERNET COMPANY
Salary	37%	8%
Bonus	15%	2%
Long-term incentives	36%	62%
Other compensation	12%	28%

WELCOMING BACK ALUMNI

Larry Clink, a highly sought-after Web site developer, was one defector. Clink left Freddie Mac, the Washington mortgage investor, "to see what was out there." He joined National Electronics Warranty, where great stories were spun about the company going public and the potential windfall that he could reap. "They told me I would be the lead Web developer," says Clink. "But it turned out I was the *only* Web developer." Frustrated by endless budgetary restrictions, the loss of generous benefits, serious overtime, and the lack of stability, Clink returned to Freddie Mac where he got a promotion and a 20 percent raise.

Although the reasons for dot-com defections vary widely, thanks to the worst labor shortage in recent history, employers who once shied away from hiring "defectors" like Clink are now aggressively recruiting these "alumni" back. In fact, so many employees have returned to Freddie Mac that the company keys in its own name when searching the Web for electronic résumés. After scouting out the alumni, the company courts them, hoping that they're disenchanted enough to return. Similarly, accounting firm Deloitte & Touche sends departing employees a survey asking if they'd ever consider returning; the company hired back over 800 alumni in 1999. Still, hiring back alumni is not a long-term staffing solution.

OLD-ECONOMY COMPANIES WAKE UP

To compete in today's tight labor market, many old-economy companies have made themselves over in the image of their high-tech competitors. They've revamped their employee benefits to match their worker-snatching Internet rivals, doled out signing bonuses, offered stock options to secretaries, flattened organizational structures, and instituted everyday casual dress. As a result, employees who once scoffed at the security, stability, and seasoned management of brick-and-mortar companies are now finding these qualities more and more attractive. "A tremendous number of people thought the [e-business] grass was greener, and it wasn't," says the president of one executive search firm.[79]

SUMMARY OF LEARNING OBJECTIVES

1. Identify and explain three important theories of employee motivation.

Malsow's hierarchy organizes individual needs into five categories and proposes that the individual must satisfy the most basic needs before being able to address higher-level needs. Herzberg's two-factor theory suggests that hygiene factors—such as working conditions, company policies, and job security—can influence employee dissatisfaction, but an improvement in these factors will not motivate employees. Only motivational factors such as recognition and responsibility can improve employee performance. McGregor's theory proposes two distinct views of individuals: Theory X–oriented managers believe that people dislike work and can be motivated only by fear, whereas Theory Y–oriented managers believe that people like work and are motivated by exposure to opportunities and challenges.

2. **Discuss three staffing challenges employers are facing in today's workplace.**

A shortage of skilled labor, rightsizing the workforce, and an increasing employee desire to balance work and life responsibilities are making it difficult for employers to find and keep talented people. The factors contributing to these staffing challenges are the increasing use of technology in the workplace, a robust U.S. economy, the conversion of a manufacturing-based economy to a service-based economy, a general mismatch between employee job skills and job demands, declining employee loyalty, and increasing employee burnout.

3. **Highlight two trends contributing to the diversity of the U.S. workforce.**

The influx of immigrants and the aging population are two trends contributing to the diversity of the U.S. workforce. The percentage of immigrant workers in the U.S. workforce is climbing as employers clamor to fill their critical labor shortages and pressure Congress to admit additional immigrants each year. The aging workforce is a result of the decline in the number of young people entering the workforce and the decision of baby boomers to delay retirement for a number of reasons.

4. **Discuss three popular alternative work arrangements companies are offering their employees.**

To meet today's staffing and demographic challenges, companies are offering their employees flextime (the ability to vary their work hours), telecommuting (the ability to work from home or another location), and job sharing (the ability to share a single full-time job with a co-worker).

5. **Explain the two steps unions take to become the bargaining agent for a group of employees.**

First, unions distribute authorization cards to employees, which designate the union as the bargaining agent, and if at least 30 percent (but usually a majority) of the target group sign the cards, the union asks management to recognize it. Second, if management is unwilling to do so, the union asks the National Labor Relations Board to sponsor a certification election. If a majority of the employees vote in favor of being represented by the union, the union becomes the official bargaining agent for the employees.

6. **Cite three options unions can exercise when negotiations with management break down.**

Unions can conduct strikes, organize boycotts, and use publicity to pressure management into complying with union proposals. A strike is a temporary work stoppage, which the union hopes will cost management enough in lost earning so that management will be forced to accept union demands. A boycott is a union tactic designed to pressure management into making concessions by convincing sympathizers to refuse to buy or handle the product of the target company. A negative publicity campaign against the target company is a pressure tactic designed to smear the reputation of the company in hopes of gaining management's attention.

7. **Cite three options management can exercise when negotiations with a union break down.**

To pressure a union into accepting its proposals, management may continue running the business with strikebreakers (nonunion workers hired to do the jobs of striking workers), institute a lockout of union members by preventing union employees from entering the workplace, or seek an injunction against a strike or other union activity.

8. **Identify the advantages and disadvantages of working for a start-up e-business from an employee's perspective.**

Many employees are lured by the glamour of working for a start-up dot-com. They want to be part of the digital revolution and enjoy such advantages as getting in on the ground floor of something big, contributing to a new e-company's success, and ultimately getting rich by cashing in on stock options after the company goes public. However, they are finding that working for a start-up e-business is not without disadvantages. For one thing, the working hours are long and the working conditions are less than ideal. For another, only a handful are making millions and the road to riches is not guaranteed. Furthermore, as more and more traditional corporations revamp their employee benefits to match those of Internet rivals, dot-com employees are finding these old-economy companies are becoming a more attractive place to work. As a result, some dot-com defectors are returning to U.S. corporations.

KEY TERMS

arbitration (278)

authorization cards (277)

behavior modification (262)

boycott (279)

business agent (276)

certification (277)

collective bargaining (277)

decertification (277)

flextime (272)

glass ceiling (271)

human relations (262)

hygiene factors (265)

injunction (279)

job enrichment (269)

job redesign (269)

job sharing (274)

labor federation (276)

labor unions (275)

locals (276)

lockouts (279)

management by objectives (MBO) (263)

mediation (278)

morale (262)

motivation (262)

motivators (265)

national union (276)

picketing (279)

quality of work life (QWL) (269)

scientific management (264)

sexism (271)

sexual harassment (272)

shop steward (276)

strike (278)

strikebreakers (279)

telecommuting (272)

Theory X (266)

Theory Y (266)

TEST YOUR KNOWLEDGE

QUESTIONS FOR REVIEW

1. What is the goal of human relations?

2. What is rightsizing?

3. What are the principal causes of employee burnout?

4. What is the glass ceiling?

5. What is quality of work life, and how does it influence employee motivation?

QUESTIONS FOR ANALYSIS

6. Why do managers often find it difficult to motivate employees who remain after downsizing?

7. How can diversity initiatives benefit a company?

8. What are some of the advantages and disadvantages of alternative work arrangements?

9. @ What kinds of staffing challenges should a company prepare for when launching a Web site or increasing the amount of e-commerce it transacts?

10. Why do employees choose to join labor unions? Why do they not join labor unions?

11. ◻ You've got a golf game scheduled for Sunday afternoon, and you've worked all weekend to write a proposal to be pre-sented Monday morning. The proposal is more or less finished, but a few more hours of work would make it polished and persuasive. Do you cancel the game?[80]

QUESTIONS FOR APPLICATION

12. Some of your talented and hardworking employees come to you one day and say they do not feel challenged. They expected to be able to diversify their skills more and take on greater responsibility than they now have. How do you respond?

13. Assume you are the plant manager for a company that manufactures tires for cars and light trucks. To compete more economically in the global market, the company is seriously considering closing the plant within the next year and moving manufacturing operations to Southeast Asia. Upon hearing about the possible plant closing, the union votes to launch a strike in one week if its demands for job security aren't met. Because of a recent surge in orders, the company is not in a position to close the plant yet. What are your options as you continue to negotiate with union representatives? Which option would you choose and why?

14. 〰 How do economic concepts such as profit motive and competitive advantage (see Chapter 1) affect today's workforce?

15. 〰 Why is it difficult for small businesses to allow employees to telecommute, share jobs, and work flexible hours?

PRACTICE YOUR KNOWLEDGE

SHARPENING YOUR COMMUNICATION SKILLS

As the director of public relations for a major airline your job is to prepare news releases should the pilots decide to strike. This is a challenging task because many people will be affected by the strike. Being a good communicator, you know that one of the first things you must do before preparing a message is to analyze the audience. Think about an airline strike and answer these questions briefly to practice this important communication technique:

1. What groups of people do you think would be interested in the information about the airline strike?

2. What do you think each of these groups would want to know about most?

3. How might they react to the information you will provide?

Summarize your answers to these three questions in a short memo to your instructor.

HANDLING DIFFICULT SITUATIONS ON THE JOB: SERVING UP STAFF SATISFACTION

This is the second summer you've worked as a food server at Ed's, a health-conscious eatery on Old Highway 101 in Cardiff, California. Normally, beach crowds cross the highway in the late afternoons for Ed's $4 smoothies and gourmet organic dinners. But with beach erosion, there haven't been as many sunbathers this year. Still, as far as you can tell, people are lining up in healthy numbers to order the sunset dinner specials and watch the dolphins play in the surf.

To save on overhead, Ed has cut back on the number of servers and kitchen staff. This means that during busy periods, customers wait longer for their food and for their tables (or leave in anger) while orders back up in the kitchen. You're working twice as hard and making fewer tips, since your customers now have to wait up to half an hour for their dinners. You've even lost some regulars you remember from last year, people who brought in all of their out-of-town guests and left you hefty tips.

Clearly, being short-staffed is as bad for the long-term health of the business as it is for the satisfaction and motivation of the servers—including yourself. Rumors are flying that a new restaurant is going to open down the street, so you may yet be able to salvage some tips for the season. As the restaurant empties out, the manager heads your way. This is your chance to speak up.[81]

1. Should you tell your manager what angry customers have said or mention how many customers have left without ordering? If you decide to tell the manager, what should you say—and how?

2. Think about the hygiene factors and motivators that influence your job as a server. How are these affecting your motivation and your satisfaction with the policies at Ed's?

3. Assuming that Ed's wants Theory Y employees, can you offer a suggestion for keeping costs down while improving the motivation of the servers and kitchen staff?

BUILDING YOUR TEAM SKILLS

Debate the pros and cons of union membership within a group of four students (two students take the pro side, and the other two take the con side). As you prepare for this debate, consider the relevance of unions at a time when legislation is becoming more protective of employees' rights and companies are staying lean to compete more effectively. Are unions necessary now that participatory management and employee involvement in organizational decision making are more commonplace? What about the role of unions in professions such as medicine? Are unions more relevant in some industries or businesses than in others?

During your team's debate, let one side present its arguments while the other side takes notes on the major points. After both sides have completed their presentations, discuss all the supporting points and come to an agreement about the relevance of unions. Draft a one-page statement outlining your team's conclusion and reasoning, and then share it during a class discussion.

Compare your team's conclusion and reasoning with those of other teams. Do most teams believe that unions are relevant or not? What issues do most teams agree on? What issues do they disagree on?

EXPAND YOUR KNOWLEDGE

KEEPING CURRENT USING *THE WALL STREET JOURNAL*

Select one or two articles from recent issues of *The Wall Street Journal* (print or online editions) that relate to employee motivation or morale.

1. What is the problem or trend discussed in the article(s) and how is it influencing employee attitudes or motivation?

2. Is this problem unique to this company, or does it have broader implications? Who is affected by it now, and who do you think might be affected by it in the future?

3. What challenges and opportunities does this situation present to the company or industry? The employees? Management?

DISCOVERING CAREER OPPORTUNITIES

Is an alternative work arrangement such as telecommuting or flextime in your career future? This exercise will help you think about whether these work arrangements fit into your career plans.

1. Look at the list of possible business careers in Component Chapter D. Of the careers that interest you, which seem best suited to telecommuting? To flextime?

2. Select one of the careers that seems suited to telecommuting. With this career in mind, answer the questions in this chapter's box "Is Telecommuting Right for You?" Did you answer no to any questions? Is there any way to turn that no into a yes?

3. Thinking about the same career, do you think it would be possible to split the job's responsibilities with a co-worker under a job-sharing arrangement? What issues, if any, might you need to resolve first?

EXPLORING THE BEST OF THE WEB

URLs for all Internet exercises are provided at the Web site for this book, www.prenhall.com/mescon. When you log on to the text Web site, select Chapter 10, then select "Student Resources," click on the name of the featured Web site, and follow the detailed navigational directions to complete these exercises.

Working Hard on the Web, page 268

Visitors to the Hard@Work Web site can get help with difficult work situations and chat with others about work and careers. Browse the site and then answer the questions below.

1. Select a case to review and draft a paragraph in response to your selected case. Then compare your response with those suggested by other students who selected the same case. How do your responses differ? What does this difference say

about the challenges of managing and motivating various employees?

2. Look at the issues posted in the section Stump the Mentor. Have you or any of your classmates faced these types of situations at work? Select one case and read through the mentor's comments. Do you agree with the mentor? Why or why not?

3. Explore the Water Cooler and other links on the site. How would managers, employees, or job seekers benefit from visiting this Web site? Do you find the information on this site valuable? Why?

Telecommuting Your Way to Success, page 273

Does telecommuting reality match the hype? Follow the links at this Web site and decide for yourself.

1. Read the 1999 Survey of Teleworkers and Managers. Where do telecommuters work? What equipment do telecommuters use? How can companies improve the telecommuting experience?

2. Who wants to be a telecommuter? Take the quiz and earn a possible virtual million.

3. What are some reasons for telecommuting? What skills and qualifications are required for telecommuting?

Spreading the Union Message, page 276

The AFL-CIO maintains one of the most comprehensive Web sites dedicated to union activities and issues. Explore the site and then respond to these questions.

1. Read The Union Difference and the Work in Progress weekly e-letter. What worker issues and advantages of union membership are being highlighted?

2. Follow the link to Safety and Health on the Job. Are any new legislative initiatives being tracked? If so, what issues are these bills addressing? What is the AFL-CIO's position on these bills? Do you agree with its position?

3. Under the Executive PayWatch link, read about AFL-CIO's comments on executive compensation. What actions does the union suggest to limit executive pay? As a business student, what is your reaction to the union's stand? What are some of the positive and negative effects that might result from union activities on this issue?

Explore on Your Own

Review these chapter-related Web sites on your own to learn more about motivation, today's workforce, and employee-management relations.

1. You Can Work From Anywhere, www.youcanworkfromanywhere. com is full of information, tips, tools, articles, ideas, and other resources to help improve the productivity of telecommuters, mobile workers, and home-based workers.

2. The Equal Employment Opportunity Commission, www. eeoc.gov, created by the 1964 Civil Rights Act, investigates and

resolves charges of discrimination. Read about federal laws prohibiting job discrimination and how to file a charge of employment discrimination.

3. The Society of Human Resource Management, www.shrm.org, provides education and information services for the human resource profession.

A CASE FOR CRITICAL THINKING

■ *Delivering Better Employee-Management Relations at UPS*

For more than 80 years, United Parcel Service (UPS) enjoyed generally good relations with the International Brotherhood of Teamsters. But in the 1990s, conflicts erupted over a number of workplace issues. And when the majority of UPS workers joined a national strike against the company, managers at the world's largest package delivery service were caught by surprise.

WEIGHING THE ISSUES

Despite economic and competitive pressures, UPS and Teamster officials had usually worked collaboratively to keep the Atlanta-based company running smoothly and profitably. Handling over 12 million parcels every day, UPS employees enjoyed good pay and rarely left the company. In fact, turnover was less than half the industry average.

But the company's growing reliance on part-time employees concerned Teamsters officials during the mid-1990s. Over 50 percent of all UPS jobs were part-time, paying half the hourly rate of full-time positions. To fight for better pay for part-timers, more full-time jobs, and better pension benefits, the union called a national strike against UPS in August 1997.

A BUMPY RIDE

UPS managers—including many ex-Teamsters who had risen through the ranks—were convinced that the strike would be short-lived because most employees would cross the picket lines. They were wrong. The vast majority of UPS employees joined the strike. And for the first time in 20 years, a nationwide poll found that the U.S. public overwhelmingly supported the strike, even though it caused major inconveniences for millions of people. For one thing, many UPS customers knew their UPS drivers personally and supported their concerns. For another, unequal pay and benefits to part-time employees were hot issues at many companies.

As the days passed and customers took their business elsewhere, UPS laid off drivers to keep their operating costs down. Finally forced back to the negotiating table to settle the 15-day labor dispute, management agreed to nearly every union demand, including the creation of 2,000 full-time positions annually for the duration of the five-year contract.

As UPS employees returned to work, managers faced the challenge of renewing the spirit of cooperation among employees, management, and union officials. They strategized how to win back customers who had defected to other carriers during the strike. "All of us on the management team communicated that we

were going to look forward, that we don't look back, and that what we should be focusing on is not this aberration, but what the future can hold for us working together," said Lea Soupata, senior vice president for human resources at UPS.

A DIFFERENT ROUTE

Eager to repair working relationships and to make up the $1 billion in lost revenues during the strike, UPS distributed a videotaped message from the CEO that urged all 330,000 employees to get back to business as usual. Then senior managers met with workers in the 60 UPS regional districts, answering questions and soliciting comments. UPS also set up a special toll-free hotline so that employees could anonymously report problems, and the company unveiled a program to reward drivers and supervisors for wooing customers back to UPS.

Still, some employees and union personnel claimed that tensions remained high because UPS supervisors were "riding the drivers constantly" to get even for the walkout. Nevertheless, UPS insisted that such claims were unfounded, noting that hotline complaint calls had not increased significantly. Furthermore, union officials were heartened to hear that top management would straighten out managers who continued to hold grudges. Two months after the strike, a companywide survey of employee attitudes indicated that in spite of declining morale, employees were still committed to UPS.

SEALED AND DELIVERED

While the fires smoldered, UPS managers diffused another tense labor situation—this one with company pilots. After nearly two years of wrangling with UPS managers over pay, hours, and conditions, UPS pilots (who were members of the Independent Pilots Association) wanted an agreement similar to the contract between FedEx and its pilots' union. The union and UPS quickly settled the dispute with 30 hours of nonstop talks under the supervision of the National Mediation Board. They agreed on terms that were comparable to the FedEx pilots' contract, keeping UPS flying high without interruption.

Back on the ground, however, Teamster union officials were fuming when UPS resisted its pledge to hire 2,000 full-time workers under the first year of the new labor contract. In fact, the company reduced the number of full-time positions by roughly 6 percent, claiming that UPS was not contractually obligated to create more full-time jobs because sales volume had not surpassed pre-strike levels. But when an independent arbitrator ordered UPS to create the full-time jobs, management complied—even though it would cost the company back pay and employee benefits for the new hires.

CRITICAL THINKING QUESTIONS

1. Why did UPS drivers go on strike?

2. Why was UPS management caught by surprise?

3. What did UPS gain, if anything, from initially resisting the Teamsters' demands? What did they lose?

4. Go to Chapter 10 of this text's Web site at www.prenhall. com/mescon. Click on the Teamsters' link to answer these questions: What kinds of issues are the Teamsters fighting for? What is the current status of relations between UPS and the union? What other industries are represented by the Teamsters?

VIDEO CASE AND EXERCISES

■ *Putting Motivation to Work in a Service Business: Ritz Carlton*

SYNOPSIS

The Ritz Carlton hotel chain (www.ritzcarlton.com) operates in an industry traditionally known for low wages, high turnover, and competitive pressure. Yet this upscale chain has achieved an extremely high 97 percent customer satisfaction rating and enjoys strong customer loyalty, thanks to a diverse and motivated workforce. The company is very selective in its recruiting, hiring only one out of every 100 applicants. It also provides two days of orientation plus on-the-job training for all new employees. Self-directed teams work on quality-improvement projects, and management empowers employees at all levels to make decisions and take actions that will satisfy customers and encourage them to stay at Ritz Carlton hotels whenever they travel.

EXERCISES
Analysis

1. Is Ritz Carlton applying Theory X or Theory Y in its dealings with employees?

2. Under Herzberg's two-factor theory, what motivators is Ritz Carlton offering its employees?

3. What effect does workforce diversity have on the hotel chain's ability to motivate employees?

4. How does Ritz Carlton's motto of "ladies and gentlemen serving ladies and gentlemen" reflect its approach to motivation?

5. How might the hotel chain use management by objectives to implement its quality improvement program?

Application

Could Ritz Carlton's management apply Taylor's scientific management principles to increase the efficiency of any jobs in the hotel?

Decision

Many Ritz Carlton employees feel the pressure of trying to balance work and home obligations. Of the alternative work arrangements discussed in the chapter, which would you recommend that the hotel chain implement to help employees better balance their personal and professional lives?

Communication

Assume that you are the manager of the Ritz Carlton in Phoenix, Arizona. Should you use e-mail, a written memo, a phone call, or some other communication technique to explain the decision you made (on the above question) to the chain's senior management?

Integration

Refer back to the discussion of goals and objectives in Chapter 6. What two goals can you suggest that Ritz Carlton management set for improving service quality in the hotel chain?

Ethics

Ritz Carlton management is striving for near-perfect service quality. Is it ethical for the hotel chain to push employees to ever-higher performance despite the possibility of increasing employee burnout?

Debate

If Ritz Carlton can achieve a 99 percent customer satisfaction rating, should it give out bonuses, or would this put too much reliance on monetary rewards to motivate employees?

Teamwork

Working with another student, identify ways that Ritz Carlton can help satisfy its employees at all five levels of Maslow's hierarchy.

Online Research

Use Internet sources to find out how Ritz Carlton's sales have grown over the past year and how many hotels are in the chain today. What are the implications for the hotel chain's relations with employees? See Component Chapter A, Exhibit A.1, for search engines to use in doing your research.

MY PHLIP COMPANION WEB SITE

Learning Interactively

Visit the myPHLIP Web site at www.prenhall.com/mescon. For Chapter 10, take advantage of the interactive "Study Guide" to test your chapter knowledge. Get instant feedback on whether you need additional studying. Read the "Current Events" articles to get the latest on chapter topics, and complete the exercises as specified by your instructor. Expand your learning with a visit to the "Research Area." There you will find a wealth of information you can use to complete your course assignments.

MASTERING BUSINESS ESSENTIALS

Go to the "Work Motivation" episode on the Mastering Business Essentials interactive, video-enhanced CD-ROM. See how the management team at CanGo (an e-business start-up) motivated its employees to take on a set of new and challenging tasks.

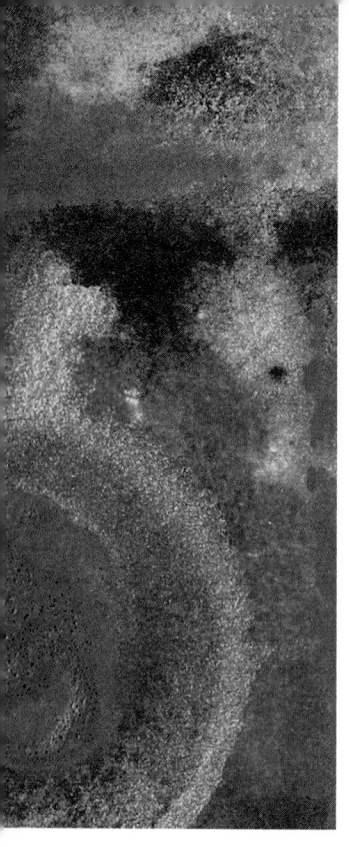

HUMAN RESOURCES MANAGEMENT

11

LEARNING OBJECTIVES

After studying this chapter, you will be able to

1. List six main functions of human resources departments

2. Cite eight methods recruiters use to find job candidates

3. Identify the six stages in the hiring process

4. Discuss how companies incorporate objectivity into employee performance appraisals

5. List seven popular types of employee incentive programs

6. Highlight five popular employee benefits

7. Describe five ways an employee's status may change

@ 8. Explain how job seekers and employers are using the Internet in the recruiting process, and highlight the benefits and drawbacks of Internet recruiting

TODAY
Inside Business

The Jamba Juice HR team conducts a thorough hiring process. Their goal is to get employees to stick around for the long term.

BLENDING A SUCCESSFUL WORKFORCE: JAMBA JUICE WHIPS UP CREATIVE RECRUITING STRATEGIES

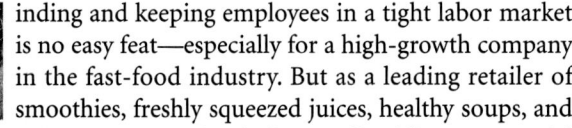
www.jambajuice.com

Finding and keeping employees in a tight labor market is no easy feat—especially for a high-growth company in the fast-food industry. But as a leading retailer of smoothies, freshly squeezed juices, healthy soups, and breads, Jamba Juice meets the challenge of building a successful workforce with an appealing blend of savvy recruiting strategies and creative incentive tools.

Since founder Kirk Perron opened his first smoothie store in 1990, Jamba Juice has grown to 300 locations in 15 states. The majority of Jamba's 4,000 employees are part-time workers, primarily high school and college students who whip up healthy concoctions between classes and during school breaks. To attract part-time "team members," Perron promotes the key ingredients of the company's success: nutrition, fitness, and fun. And he quickly points out that the company's name reflects the enjoyable working environment. *Jamba* is a West African word meaning "to celebrate."

As Jamba Juice expands its operations, Perron and his human resources staff work closely with the company's real estate committee to forecast demand for the number of workers needed in specific locations. Human resources begins the search at least four months before an official store opening, allowing time for finding, interviewing, and training new employees.

Searches are conducted using a variety of resources, and they are customized for each market. For instance, to attract young, cyber-savvy candidates who fit the profile of a typical Jamba employee, human resources uses the Internet.

Jamba Juice lists job openings on recruiting Web sites such as restaurantrecruit.com, a popular site with managers in the food industry. These sites, in turn, provide a direct link to Jamba Juice's Web site so that job seekers can find out more about the company or send an e-mail requesting additional information.

Of course, Internet ads can generate responses from applicants who live as far away as Australia and France. So Perron and his staff must sift through the piles of applications and identify the strongest candidates to interview. Initial interviews are conducted by telephone. During 30-minute phone screenings, human resources looks for personable candidates with a strong work ethic—the type of candidate who wants to stick with the company.

But recruiting new staff is only one of the challenges that Jamba Juice faces. Perron must also retain current store managers. To do that, Perron offers incentives to reward store performance. Managers receive a percentage of their store's sales every eight weeks. Furthermore, managers accrue retention bonuses for building the store's business. After accumulating three years of retention bonuses, managers receive a cash payment for their efforts. And managers who sign up for three more years of employment are rewarded with a three-week paid sabbatical.

Indeed Jamba's aggressive recruiting strategies and management incentives have paid off. The company's turnover rate dipped by 8 percent in one year. That's pretty impressive considering that annual employee turnover for the restaurant industry can reach 100 percent.[1]

UNDERSTANDING WHAT HUMAN RESOURCES ▪ MANAGERS DO

human resources management (HRM)
Specialized function of planning how to obtain employees, oversee their training, evaluate them, and compensate them

As Kirk Perron knows, hiring the right people to help a company reach its goals and then overseeing their training and development, motivation, evaluation, and compensation is critical to a company's success. These activities are known as **human resources management (HRM),** which encompasses all the activities involved in acquiring, maintaining, and developing an organization's human resources. Because of the accelerating rate at which today's workforce, economy, and corporate cultures are being transformed, the role of HRM is increasingly viewed as a strategic one.

Human resources (HR) managers must figure out how to attract qualified employees from a shrinking pool of entry-level candidates; how to train less-educated, poorly skilled employees; how to keep experienced employees when they have few opportunities for advancement; and how to lay off employees equitably when downsizing is necessary. They must also retrain employees to enable them to cope with increasing automation and computerization, manage increasingly complex (and expensive) employee benefits programs, shape workplace policies to address changing workforce demographics and employee needs (as discussed in Chapter 10), and cope with the challenge of meeting government regulations in hiring practices and equal opportunity employment.

**LEARNING
OBJECTIVE** 1

List six main functions of human resources departments

In short, human resources managers and staff members keep the organization running smoothly at every level by planning for a company's staffing needs, recruiting and hiring employees, training and developing employees and managers, and appraising employee performance. The HR staff also administers compensation and employee benefits and oversees changes in employment status (promotion, reassignment, termination or resignation, and retirement). This chapter explores each of these human resources responsibilities, beginning with planning (see Exhibit 11.1).

▪ PLANNING FOR A COMPANY'S STAFFING NEEDS

One of the six functions of the human resources staff members is to plan for a company's staffing needs. Proper planning is critical because a miscalculation could leave a company without enough employees to keep up with demand, resulting in customer dissatisfaction and lost business. Yet if a company expands its staff too rapidly, profits may be eaten up by payroll, or the firm may have to lay off people who were just recruited and trained at considerable expense. The plan-

EXHIBIT 11.1

THE FUNCTIONS OF THE HUMAN RESOURCES DEPARTMENT

Human resources departments are responsible for these six important functions.

1. Planning for staffing needs
2. Recruiting and hiring
3. Training and development
4. Appraising performance
5. Administering compensation and benefits
6. Overseeing changes in employment status

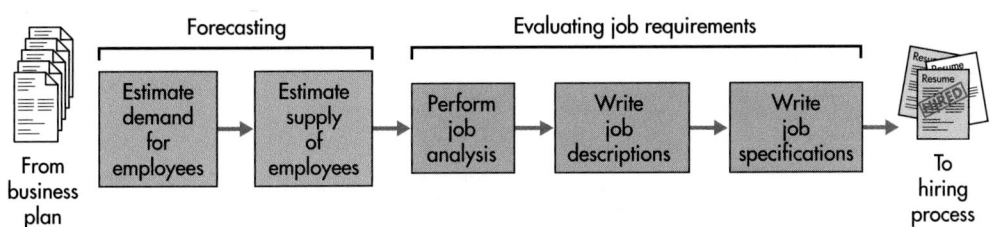

EXHIBIT 11.2

STEPS IN HUMAN RESOURCES PLANNING

Careful attention to each phase of this sequence helps ensure that a company will have the right human resources when it needs them.

ning function consists of two steps: (1) forecasting supply and demand and (2) evaluating job requirements (see Exhibit 11.2).

Forecasting Supply and Demand

Planning begins with forecasting *demand,* the numbers and kinds of employees that will be needed at various times. For example, suppose Jamba Juice is planning to open another store in San Francisco within six months. The HR department would forecast that the store will need a store manager and an assistant manager as well as part-time salespeople. Although Jamba Juice might start looking immediately for someone as highly placed as the manager, hiring salespeople might be postponed until just before the store opens.

The next task is to estimate the *supply* of available employees. In many cases, that supply is within the company already—perhaps just needing training to fill future requirements. Jamba Juice may well find that the assistant manager at an existing store can be promoted to manage the new store, and one of the current salespeople can be named assistant manager. If existing employees cannot be tapped for new positions, the human resources manager must determine how to find people outside the company who have the necessary skills. In some cases, managers will want to consider strategic staffing alternatives such as hiring part-time and temporary employees to avoid drastic overstaffing or understaffing.

Part-Time and Temporary Employees More and more businesses try to save money and increase flexibility by building their workforces around part-time and temporary employees, or "temps," whose schedules can be rearranged to suit the company's needs. As a result, this segment of the labor force has increased by leaps and bounds in recent years. The Bureau of Labor Statistics projects that the temp-agency workforce will reach 4 million by 2006 (an increase of over 200 percent since 1997).[2] The temporary ranks include computer systems analysts, human resources directors, accountants, doctors, and even CEOs, with technical fields making up the fastest-growing segment of temporary employment.[3] Of the 19,000 Microsoft employees in the Puget Sound area, for example, 5,000 to 6,000 are temporary workers.[4]

The use of temps is an excellent recruiting technique because it allows companies to try out employees before hiring them permanently. Thus, what often begins as a temp assignment can turn into multiyear employment. Some 29 percent of workers employed by temp agencies remain on the job assignment for one year or more, says the Bureau of Labor Statistics. Many of these "permatemps" hold high-prestige, high-skilled technology jobs at firms such as Microsoft. In fact, they often do the same work as the company's permanent employees, but because they are temps, they do not qualify for the benefits enjoyed by regular workers.

Of course, for many, using permatemps is a win-win situation. Companies get a steady, knowledgeable labor supply, and workers have the flexibility to work for six months and then take some time off. But a recent spate of lawsuits could undo this mutually beneficial work arrangement. Some permatemps are suing companies, saying that they are, in fact, full-time employees and as such deserve employee benefits.[5]

Outsourcing Outsourcing is another way that companies fulfill their human resources needs without hiring permanent employees. Companies may outsource for a variety of reasons. Chief among them are that the outside source can provide materials, parts, or services better, at a lower price, and more efficiently. Expertise and flexibility are other reasons for outsourcing. Of course, outsourcing has many advantages: It gives companies access to new resources and world-class capabilities; it shares the risk of getting the work done; and it frees company resources for other

MANAGING IN THE 21ST CENTURY

ARE TEMP WORKERS BECOMING A FULL-TIME HEADACHE?

They get no sick days or personal days. They don't get paid for holidays such as the day after Thanksgiving or Christmas. And the company on their paycheck doesn't read Microsoft or IBM but the name of the employment agency that places them. Still, many temporary workers are content with this arrangement—in the beginning, anyway.

Some see temporary work as a win-win situation for both the worker and the company. Temp workers (also known as noncore staff, the flexible workforce, contingent employees, and permatemps) can get challenging work at leading companies, earn top hourly rates, and job-hop at will, learning new skills at each stop. Companies can staff their workforce strategically, secure hard-to-find talent, move them from project to project, and save big dollars by not paying temporary workers employee benefits.

But with short-term projects turning into years of service, some temporary workers are rebelling. They want the same benefits as their full-time counterparts. And a recent ruling by the U.S. Court of Appeals for the Ninth Circuit concurs. Because Microsoft uses long-term temps in the same capacity as employees, the court ruled that these Microsoft temporary workers were "common-law employees" (even if they're signed up with a temp agency) and are entitled to the same benefits as permanent employees. This includes company stock options, of course. As a result of the ruling and the high number of temp employee complaints, Microsoft is now limiting the length of temporary workers' contracts to 365 days and is requiring workers to take 100 days off between assignments.

Although some permatemps are excited about the recent court decision and Microsoft's new policy, others are concerned. They fear that the Microsoft ruling could backfire and create fewer opportunities for workers who want to take time off or move freely from job to job. Some experts predict that the ruling could cause a major shakeout in the temporary services business and get rid of permatemps permanently.

■ QUESTIONS FOR CRITICAL THINKING

1. How might a decline in the use of temporary workers affect company staffing?

2. Besides employee benefits, what other human resources challenges might the use of permatemps create?

---

purposes. Still, outsourcing has its share of risks. Among them are loss of control, greater dependency on suppliers, and loss of in-house skills. Some companies have also experienced work delays, unhappy customers, and labor union battles as a result of outsourcing.[6]

Evaluating Job Requirements

The second step of the planning function is to evaluate job requirements. If you were the owner of a small business, you might have a good grasp of the requirements of all the jobs in your company. However, in large organizations where hundreds or thousands of employees are performing a wide variety of jobs, management needs a more formal and objective method of evaluating job requirements. That method is called **job analysis.**

To obtain the information needed for a job analysis, the human resources staff asks employees or supervisors several questions: What is the purpose of the job? What tasks are involved in the job? What qualifications and skills are needed to do it effectively? In what kind of setting does the job take place? Is there much public contact involved? Does the job entail much time pressure? Sometimes they obtain job information by observing employees directly. Other times they ask employees to keep daily diaries describing exactly what they do during the workday.

Once job analysis has been completed, the human resources staff develops a **job description,** a formal statement summarizing the tasks involved in the job and the conditions under which the employee will work. In most cases, the staff will also develop a **job specification,** a statement describing the skills, education, and previous experience that the job requires.

job analysis
Process by which jobs are studied to determine the tasks and dynamics involved in performing them

job description
Statement of the tasks involved in a given job and the conditions under which the holder of the job will work

job specification
Statement describing the kind of person who would be best for a given job—including the skills, education, and previous experience that the job requires

RECRUITING, HIRING, AND TRAINING
NEW EMPLOYEES

Having forecast a company's supply and demand for employees and evaluated job requirements, the next step is to match the job specification with an actual person or selection of people. This task is accomplished through **recruiting,** the process of attracting suitable candidates for an organization's jobs. Recruiters are specialists on the human resources staff who are responsible for locating job candidates. They use a variety of methods and resources, including internal searches, newspaper and Internet advertising, public and private employment agencies, union hiring halls, college campuses and career offices, trade shows, corporate "headhunters" (people who try to attract people at other companies), and referrals from employees or colleagues in the industry (see Exhibit 11.3). As this chapter's Focusing on E-Business Today feature discusses, one of the fastest-growing recruitment resources for both large and small businesses is the Internet. Today many companies recruit online through their Web sites in addition to using popular online recruiting services.

recruiting
Process of attracting appropriate applicants for an organization's jobs

LEARNING OBJECTIVE 2
Cite eight methods recruiters use to find job candidates

The Hiring Process

After exploring at least one—but usually more—of the available recruitment channels to assemble a pool of applicants, the human resources department may spend weeks and sometimes months on the hiring process. Most companies go through the same basic stages in the hiring process as they sift through applications to come up with the person (or persons) they want.

The first stage is to select a small number of qualified candidates from all of the applications received. Finalists may be chosen on the basis of a standard application form that all candidates fill out or on the basis of a résumé—a summary of education, experience, and personal data compiled by each applicant (see "Preparing Your Résumé" in Component Chapter D for further details). Sometimes both sources of information are used. Many organizations now use computer scanners to help them quickly sort through résumés and weed out those that don't match the requirements of the job.

The second stage in the hiring process is to interview each candidate to clarify qualifications and to fill in any missing information (see "Interviewing with Potential Employers" in Component Chapter D for further details). Another goal of the interview is to get an idea of the applicant's personality and ability to work well with others. Depending on the type of job at stake, candidates may also be asked to take a test or a series of tests.

After the initial prescreening interviews comes the third stage, when the best candidates may be asked to meet with someone in the human resources department who will conduct a more probing interview. For higher-level positions, candidates may go through a series of interviews with managers, potential co-workers, and the employees who will make up the successful candidate's staff. Sometimes this process can take weeks. Consider Southwest Airlines. To fill 4,200 job openings in one year, the company interviewed nearly 80,000 people. For many positions, candidates undergo a rigorous interview process that can take as long as six weeks before they are hired. Southwest wants to make sure that new employees will fit in with the company's culture. The payback: low turnover and high customer satisfaction.[7]

LEARNING OBJECTIVE 3
Identify the six stages in the hiring process

Employers

Look for someone inside the organization	Rely on networking contacts and personal recommendations	Hire an employment agency or search firm	Review/send unsolicited résumés	Place/read a newspaper or an Internet ad

Job Seekers

EXHIBIT 11.3

HOW EMPLOYERS AND JOB SEEKERS APPROACH THE RECRUITING PROCESS

Studies show that employers prefer to fill job openings with people from within their organization or from an employee's recommendation. Placing want ads is often viewed as a last resort. In contrast, typical job seekers begin their job-search process from the opposite direction (starting with reading a newspaper or Internet ads).

The way to handle an interview depends on what stage of the interview process you are in. For instance, in the screening stage, your main objective is to differentiate yourself from the other candidates. In later stages, your objective is to highlight your strengths and explain three or four of your best qualifications in depth.

After all the interviews have been completed, the process moves to the final stages. In the fourth stage, the position's supervisor evaluates the candidates, sometimes in consultation with a higher-level manager, the human resources department, and staff. During the fifth stage, the employer checks the references of the top few candidates. The employer may also research the candidates' education, previous employment, and motor vehicle records. A growing number of employers are also checking candidates' credit histories, a practice that is drawing criticism as a violation of privacy.[8] In the sixth stage, the supervisor selects the most suitable person for the job. Now the search is over—provided the candidate accepts the offer.

Background Checks Violence in the workplace is an increasing threat that can harm employees and customers, hurt productivity, and lead to expensive lawsuits and higher health care costs. More than 1 million physical assaults and thousands of homicides occur at work each year. If an employer fails to prevent "preventable violences," that employer will likely be found liable. This means that companies need to be especially careful about negligent hiring.[9] In one case, Saks Fifth Avenue hired an undercover security officer at its flagship store in New York without adequately checking his background. After he raped a young woman executive twice in her office, it was discovered that the security officer had been convicted of sexually abusing an 11-year-old girl in Kentucky.[10]

This and similar cases emphasize the need for employers to conduct thorough background checks on job applicants, including verifying all educational credentials and previous jobs, accounting for any large time gaps between jobs, and checking references (see Exhibit 11.4). Background checks are particularly important for jobs in which employees are in a position to possibly harm others. For example, a trucking company must check applicants' driving records to avoid hiring a new trucker with poor driving skills.

Hiring and the Law Federal and state laws and regulations govern many aspects of the hiring process. In particular, employers must be careful to avoid discrimination in the wording of their application forms, in interviewing, and in testing. Employers must also respect the privacy of applicants. Consider the dilemma this presents for employers.

On the one hand, asking questions about unrelated factors such as citizenship, marital status, age, and religion violates the Equal Employment Opportunity Commission's regulations be-

EXHIBIT 11.4

CHECKING OUT NEW HIRES

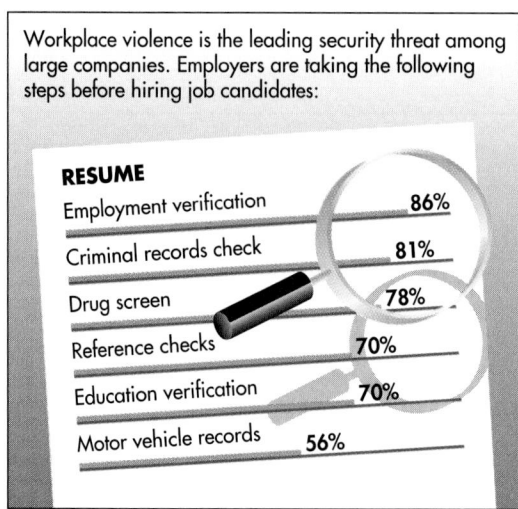

Workplace violence is the leading security threat among large companies. Employers are taking the following steps before hiring job candidates:

RESUME

Employment verification	86%
Criminal records check	81%
Drug screen	78%
Reference checks	70%
Education verification	70%
Motor vehicle records	56%

cause they may lead to discrimination. In addition, employers are not allowed to ask questions about whether a person has children, whether a person owns or rents a home, what caused a physical disability, whether a person belongs to a union, whether a person has ever been arrested, or when a person attended school. The exception is when such information is related to a bona fide occupational qualification for the specific job.

On the other hand, employers must also obtain sufficient information about employees to avoid becoming the target of a negligent-hiring lawsuit. Moreover, the Immigration Reform and Control Act (passed in 1986) forbids almost all U.S. companies from hiring illegal aliens. The act also prohibits discrimination in hiring on the basis of national origin or citizenship status. This results in a sticky situation for many employers who must try to determine their applicants' citizenship so they can verify that the newly hired are legally eligible to work without asking questions that violate the law. As you can imagine, striking the balance can be quite a challenge.

Testing One much-debated aspect of the hiring process is testing—using not only the tests that prospective employers give job applicants but any devices that can evaluate employees when making job decisions. Tests are used to gauge abilities, intelligence, interests, and sometimes even physical condition and personality.

Many companies rely on preemployment testing to determine whether applicants are suited to the job and whether they'll be worth the expense of hiring and training. Companies use three main procedures: job-skills testing, psychological testing, and drug testing. Job-skills tests are the most common type, designed to assess competency or specific abilities needed to perform a job. Psychological tests usually take the form of questionnaires. These tests can be used to assess overall intellectual ability, attitudes toward work, interests, managerial potential, or personality characteristics—including dependability, commitment, and motivation. People who favor psychological testing say that it can predict how well employees will actually perform on the job. However, critics say that such tests are ineffective and potentially discriminatory.

To avoid the increased costs and reduced productivity associated with drug abuse in the workplace (estimated to cost industry some $100 billion a year), many employers require applicants to be tested for drug use. Studies show that substance abusers have two to four times as many workplace accidents as people who do not use drugs. Moreover, drug use can be linked to over 40 percent of industry fatalities. Nevertheless, some employers prefer not to incur the extra expense to administer drug tests; others consider such tests an invasion of privacy.[11]

orientation
Session or procedure for acclimating a new employee to the organization

Training and Development

To make sure that all new employees understand the company's goals, policies, and procedures, most large organizations and many small ones have well-defined **orientation** programs. Although they vary, such programs usually include information about company background and structure, equal opportunity practices, safety regulations, standards of employee conduct, company culture, employee compensation and benefit plans, work times, and other topics that newly hired employees might have questions about.[12] Orientation programs help new employees understand their role in the organization and feel more comfortable.

At Intel, for instance, all new hires participate in a six-month "integration" curriculum. Day One begins when new hires receive a packet at their home. The packet contains material about the company's culture and values, along with some forms to fill out. During the first month, all new hires attend a class called "Working at Intel," a formal eight-hour introduction to the company's corporate culture. At the

At this employee orientation session, new employees review the company's mission statement, policies, procedures, benefits, and safety regulations before they meet with their department managers.

Best of the Web Best of the Web Best of

STAYING ON TOP OF THE HR WORLD

Like all areas of business, the world of human resources changes quickly. To stay informed about trends in recruiting, compensation, benefits, and employee satisfaction, turn to HR Live. This comprehensive online resource provides HR professionals with information about layoffs, employment markets and trends, labor statistics, recruiting methods, and much more. The site also offers convenient links to job fairs and conventions in a variety of industries so recruiters (and job seekers) can plan ahead.
www.hrlive.com/

end of the six-month period, each new hire participates in a two-hour structured question-and-answer session, in which an executive reviews the employee's transition into Intel and then asks a final long-term question: "What do you think it will take to succeed at Intel?"[13]

In addition to orientation programs, most companies offer training (and retraining), because employee competence has a direct effect on productivity and profits. Wal-Mart's senior vice president of human resources Coleman Peterson believes that training is the most important part of human resources management. As Peterson puts it, "Wal-Mart is in the business of keeping and growing talent."[14] Although some employers worry that employees who develop new or improved skills might leave them for higher-paying jobs, studies show that the contrary is true. The more training given to employees, the more likely they will want to stay, because training gives them a sense that they are going somewhere in their careers, even if they're not getting a promotion.[15]

In most companies, training takes place at the work site, where an experienced employee oversees the trainee's on-the-job efforts, or in a classroom, where an expert lectures groups of employees. Tires Plus is one of a growing number of companies that invests heavily in employee training to become more competitive. Some 1,700 employees spend a total of 60,000 hours annually attending formal training programs at Tires Plus University. Additionally, Tires Plus offers special training programs to develop inexperienced but promising workers into mechanics and managers. While training programs cost Tires Plus more than $3 million a year, they help the company retain talented workers and fill leadership positions—a small price to pay in today's tight labor market.[16] Southwest Airlines is another company that offers its employees training through its "University for People." Employees can choose courses that will help them to do their jobs more effectively and be more flexible in the tasks they can perform.[17]

Hoping to create a better workforce, appliance maker Whirlpool sends a group of new hires to live together in a large house, where during the course of their eight-week stay, they prepare more than 900 meals, wash more than 120 bags of laundry, and perform countless hours of loading and reloading of Whirlpool dishwashers and dryers. This group of recruits will then use their knowledge to train sales staffs at retailers such as Sears that sell the company's appliances.

Employee training may also involve a self-study component using training manuals, computers, tests, and interactive modules. For example, employees at Days Inn of America participate in interactive self-paced Web-based training to learn reservation operations, housekeeping duties, supervision, and even how to deal with surly guests.[18] (Consult Part 4 of this text's e-commerce online supplement at www.prenhall.com/mescon for a more extensive discussion of virtual training and employee development.)

APPRAISING EMPLOYEE PERFORMANCE

How do employees know whether they are doing a good job? How can they improve their performance? What new skills should they learn? Most human resources managers attempt to answer these questions by developing **performance appraisal** systems to objectively evaluate employees according to set criteria. Such systems promote fairness because their standards are usually job-related.

The ultimate goal of performance appraisals is not to judge employees but rather to improve their performance. Thus, experts recommend that performance reviews be an ongoing discipline—not just a once-a-year event linked to employee raises. Periodic performance evaluations are especially important in today's project-driven, results-oriented workplace. Employees need fast feedback so they can correct their deficiencies in a timely manner.[19]

Most companies require regular, written evaluations of each employee's work. To ensure objectivity and consistency, firms generally use a standard company performance appraisal form to evaluate employees (see Exhibit 11.5). The evaluation criteria are in writing so that both employee and supervisor understand what is expected and are therefore able to determine whether the work is being done adequately. Written evaluations also provide a record of the employee's performance, which may protect the company in cases of disputed terminations.

Many performance appraisal systems require the employee to be rated by several people (including more than one supervisor and perhaps several co-workers). This practice further promotes fairness by correcting for possible biases. One appraisal format that moves the review process from a one-dimensional perspective to a multidimensional format is the 360-degree review. Designed to provide employees with a broader range of perspectives, the 360-degree review solicits feedback from colleagues above, below, and around the employee to provide observations of the person's performance in several skill and behavioral categories. This means that employees rate the performance of their superiors as well as that of their peers.[20]

One of the biggest problems with any employee appraisal system is finding a way to measure productivity. In a production job, the person who types the most pages of acceptable copy or who assembles the most defect-free microprocessors in a given amount of time is clearly the most productive. But how does an employer evaluate the productivity of the registration clerk at a hotel or the middle manager at a large television station? Although the organization's overall productivity can be measured (number of rooms booked per night, number of viewers per hour), often the employer can't directly relate the results to any one employee's efforts.

Evaluating productivity becomes an even greater challenge in organizations where employees work in teams. Some companies, such as Con-Way Transportation Services, meet this challenge by having teams evaluate themselves. About every three months a neutral facilitator leads a discussion in which team members rate team performance on a 1 to 5 scale for 31 criteria, which can include customer satisfaction, the ability to meet goals, employee behavior toward co-workers and customers, job knowledge, motivation, and skills. During the meetings, members discuss the team's performance. Individual performance is also discussed but only in the context of the team. Each person creates two columns on a sheet of paper, one labeled "strengths" and the other, "something to work on." Team members self-assess and then pass the list around the room so other team members can add their comments.[21]

ADMINISTERING COMPENSATION AND EMPLOYEE BENEFITS

On what basis should employees be paid? How much should they be paid? When should they be paid? What benefits should they receive? Every day, company leaders confront these types of decisions. Administering **compensation,** a combination of payments in the form of wages or salaries, incentive payments, employee benefits, and employer services, is another major responsibility of a company's human resources department.

Wages and Salaries

Many blue-collar (production) and some white-collar (management and clerical) employees receive compensation in the form of **wages,** which are based on calculating the number of hours

LEARNING OBJECTIVE 4
Discuss how companies incorporate objectivity into employee performance appraisals

performance appraisal
Evaluation of an employee's work according to specific criteria

compensation
Money, benefits, and services paid to employees for their work

wages
Cash payment based on the number of hours the employee has worked or the number of units the employee has produced

Name _____	Title _____	Service Date _____	Date _____
Location _____	Division _____	Department _____	
Length of Time in Present Position	Period of Review	Appraised by _____	
_____	From: ___ To: ___	Title of Appraiser _____	

Area of Performance	Comment	Rating
Job Knowledge and Skill *Understands responsibilities and uses background for job. Adapts to new methods/techniques. Plans and organizes work. Recognizes errors and problems.*		5 4 3 2 1
Volume of Work *Amount of work output. Adherence to standards and schedules. Effective use of time.*		5 4 3 2 1
Quality of Work *Degree of accuracy–lack of errors. Thoroughness of work. Ability to exercise good judgment.*		5 4 3 2 1
Initiative and Creativity *Self-motivation in seeking responsibility and work that needs to be done. Ability to apply original ideas and concepts.*		5 4 3 2 1
Communication *Ability to exchange thoughts or information in a clear, concise manner. Dealing with different organizational levels of clientele.*		5 4 3 2 1
Dependability *Ability to follow instructions and directions correctly. Performs under pressure. Reliable work habits.*		5 4 3 2 1
Leadership Ability/Potential *Ability to guide others to the successful accomplishment of a given task. Potential for developing subordinate employees.*		5 4 3 2 1

5. Outstanding	*Employee who consistently exceeds established standards and expectations of the job.*
4. Above Average	*Employee who consistently meets established standards and expectations of the job. Often exceeds and rarely falls short of desired results.*
3. Satisfactory	*Generally qualified employee who meets job standards and expectations. Sometimes exceeds and may occasionally fall short of desired expectations. Performs duties in a normally expected manner.*
2. Improvement Needed	*Not quite meeting standards and expectations. An employee at this level of performance is not quite meeting all the standard job requirements.*
1. Unsatisfactory	*Employee who fails to meet the minimum standards and expectations of the job.*

I have had the opportunity to read this performance appraisal.

How long has this employee been under your supervision?

Signature   Date

Signature of Supervisor   Date

EXHIBIT 11.5

SAMPLE PERFORMANCE APPRAISAL FORM

Many companies use forms like this one to ensure performance appraisals are as objective as possible.

worked, the number of units produced, or a combination of both time and productivity. Wages provide a direct incentive to an employee: The more hours worked or the more pieces completed, the higher the employee's paycheck. Moreover, employers in the United States must comply with the Fair Labor Standards Act of 1938, which sets a minimum hourly wage for most employees and mandates overtime pay for employees who work longer than 40 hours a week. Most states also have minimum wage laws intended to protect employees not covered by federal laws or to set higher wage floors.[22]

Employees whose output is not always directly related to the number of hours worked or the number of pieces produced are paid **salaries.** As with wages, salaries base compensation on time, but the unit of time is a week, two weeks, a month, or a year. Salaried employees such as

salaries
Fixed weekly, monthly, or yearly cash compensation for work

Best of the Web Best of the Web Best of the

DIGGING DEEPER AT THE BUREAU OF LABOR STATISTICS

By now you're probably aware that the U.S. government has an agency for almost every purpose. Many of these agencies gather facts and statistics on trends in the United States, and the Bureau of Labor Statistics is no exception. When you need to research detailed information about national or regional employment conditions—such as wages, unemployment, productivity, and benefits—point your Web browser to this site.
www.bls.gov/

managers normally receive no pay for the extra hours they sometimes put in; overtime is simply part of their obligation. However, they do get a certain amount of leeway in their schedules.

Both wages and salaries are, in principle, based on the contribution of a particular job to the company. Thus, a sales manager, who is responsible for bringing in sales revenue, is paid more than a secretary, who handles administrative tasks but doesn't sell or supervise. However, as the tables in Component Chapter D show, pay varies widely by position, industry, and location. Among the best-paid employees in the world are chief executive officers of large U.S. corporations.

Incentive Programs

To encourage employees to be more productive, innovative, and committed to their work, many companies such as Jamba Juice provide managers and employees with **incentives,** cash payments that are linked to specific individual, group, and companywide goals; overall productivity; and company success. In other words, achievements, not just activities, are made the basis for payment. The success of these programs often depends on how closely incentives are linked to actions within the employee's control:

- *Bonuses.* For both salaried and wage-earning employees, one type of incentive compensation is the **bonus,** a payment in addition to the regular wage or salary. As an incentive to reduce turnover during the year, some firms pay an annual year-end bonus, amounting to a certain percentage of each employee's wages. Other cash bonuses are tied to company performance.

- *Commissions.* In contrast to bonuses, **commissions** are a form of compensation that pays employees a percentage of sales made. Used mainly for sales staff, they may be either the sole compensation or an incentive payment in addition to a regular salary.

- *Profit sharing.* Employees may be rewarded for staying with a company and encouraged to work harder through **profit sharing,** a system in which employees receive a portion of the company's profits. Depending on the company, profits may be distributed quarterly, semi-annually, or annually.

- *Gain sharing.* Similar to profit sharing, **gain sharing** ties rewards to profits (or cost savings) achieved by meeting specific goals such as quality and productivity improvement. For example, gain sharing is one tool that the city of College Station, Texas, uses to encourage savings and innovative ideas. In 1997, 520 full-time city employees each received $460 as a reward for helping to save the city $884,000.[23]

- *Pay for performance.* A variation of gain sharing, **pay for performance,** requires employees to accept a lower base pay but rewards them if they reach production targets or other goals. Experts estimate that 30 percent of U.S. companies have already adopted at least some pay-for-performance measures. Many have realized productivity gains as well as greater flexibility in keeping employees during hard times.[24] However, some critics point out that such incentives can actually lead to lower quality because employees become focused on working fast rather than working well.

- *Knowledge-based pay.* Another approach to compensation being explored by companies is **knowledge-based pay,** or skill-based pay, which is tied to employees' knowledge and abilities rather than to their job per se. Typically, the pay level at which a person is hired matches that

---

LEARNING OBJECTIVE 5

List seven popular types of employee incentive programs

incentives
Cash payments to employees who produce at a desired level or whose unit (often the company as a whole) produces at a desired level

bonus
Cash payment, in addition to the regular wage or salary, that serves as a reward for achievement

commissions
Payments to employees equal to a certain percentage of sales made

profit sharing
System for distributing a portion of the company's profits to employees

gain sharing
Plan for rewarding employees not on the basis of overall profits but in relation to achievement of goals such as cost savings from higher productivity

pay for performance
Accepting a lower base pay in exchange for bonuses based on meeting production or other goals

knowledge-based pay
Pay tied to an employee's acquisition of skills; also called skill-based pay

person's current level of skills; as the employee acquires new skills, the pay level goes up. Because employees do not compete with each other to increase their pay through promotions, knowledge-based pay enhances teamwork, flexibility, and motivation.[25]

■ *Broadbanding.* Like knowledge-based pay, **broadbanding** gives pay raises without promoting employees. Instead of having many narrow pay grades, the company has fewer, broader pay grades. For example, instead of a range of $30,000 to $40,000 for a particular job, a broadband range may be $20,000 to $50,000. This approach allows today's flatter organizations to reward employees without having to move them up a hierarchy. It also allows companies to move employees to different positions without being restricted by the pay grades normally associated with specific jobs.

broadbanding
Payment system that uses wide pay grades, enabling the company to give pay raises without promotions

Although these incentive programs are popular in today's workplace, some companies find it difficult to change the way workers think about pay. For a long time, businesses have trained their employees to associate higher job grades with status, titles, and eligibility for additional benefits. Furthermore, some critics say that broadbanding and other incentives don't really benefit employees, but are just another way for companies to keep labor costs down. One study by compensation consulting firm William M. Mercer reported that under broadbanding, employees' long-term career earnings actually decrease between 10 and 50 percent.[26]

Employee Benefits and Services

employee benefits
Compensation other than wages, salaries, and incentive programs

Companies also regularly provide **employee benefits**—financial benefits other than wages, salaries, and incentives. For example, Starbucks offers medical and dental insurance, vacation and holiday pay, stock options, discounts on Starbucks products, and a free pound of coffee every week. The benefits package is available to part-time as well as full-time employees, so Starbucks attracts and retains good people at every level.[27]

Some companies offer employee benefits as a preset package; that is, the employee gets whatever insurance, paid holidays, pension plan, and other benefits the company sets up. But a growing number of companies recognize that people have different priorities and needs at different stages of their lives. So they offer employees flexible benefits. Such plans allows employees to pick their benefits—up to a certain dollar amount—to create a benefits package that is tailored to their individual needs. Moreover, they smooth out imbalances in benefits received by single employees and workers with families.[28] An employee with a young family might want extra life or health insurance, for example, and might feel no need for a pension plan, whereas a single employee might choose to "buy" an extra week or two of vacation time by giving up some other benefit.

LEARNING OBJECTIVE 6

Highlight five popular employee benefits

By offering benefits to all employees (including part-timers), Starbucks attracts and keeps quality employees.

The benefits most commonly provided by employers are insurance, retirement benefits, employee stock-ownership plans, stock options, and family benefits. In the next sections, we will explore how these benefits and services are undergoing considerable change to meet the needs of today's workforce.

Insurance Although it is entirely optional, insurance is the most popular employee benefit. Many businesses offer substantial compensation in the form of life and health insurance, but dental and vision plans, disability insurance, and long-term-care insurance are also gaining in popularity (see Component Chapter C for a discussion of types of employee insurance coverage). Today only about 62 percent of employees are covered by a company health plan.[29]

Often a company will negotiate a group insurance plan for employees and pay most of the premium costs. However, faced with exploding health costs, many companies now require employees to pay part of their insurance premiums or more of the actual doctor bills.[30] In addition, more companies are hiring part-time and temporary workers, who typically receive very few company benefits. Nonetheless, some companies, such as Schlotzky's company-owned restaurants provide employees with fully paid health coverage because doing so discourages employee turnover. "The benefits plan is a positive incentive for people to come on board; it helps hire people who might have gone to Wendy's or Burger King," says Schlotzky's human resources director, Alice Klepac.[31]

Retirement Benefits In the past, few people were able to save enough money in the course of their working years for their retirement. The main purpose of the Social Security Act was to provide basic support to those who could not accumulate the retirement money they would need later in life. Today, nearly everyone who works regularly has become eligible for Social Security payments during retirement. This income is paid for by the Social Security tax, part of which is withheld by the employer from employees' wages and part of which is paid by the employer.

In addition to Social Security, many employees receive company-sponsored retirement benefits. Studies show that 72 percent of workers at large firms (more than 500 employees) have some form of company-sponsored retirement coverage.[32] The most popular type of retirement coverage is the **pension plan,** which is funded by company contributions. Each year, enough money is set aside in a separate pension account to cover employees' future retirement benefits. These plans are regulated by the Employees' Retirement Income Security Act of 1974 (ERISA), which established a federal agency to insure the assets of pension plans.

pension plan
Company-sponsored program for providing retirees with income

Three of the most popular types of company-sponsored pension plans are *defined contribution plans, defined benefit plans,* and *401(k) plans.* About 51 percent of company pension plans are defined contribution plans, which are similar to savings plans that provide a future benefit based on annual employer contributions, voluntary employee matching contributions, and accumulated investment earnings. Less popular are defined benefit plans, which are offered by only 27.4 percent of those companies offering pension plans.[33] Defined benefit plans are formula-based plans in which employers typically promise to pay their employees a benefit upon retirement based on the employee's retirement age, final average salary, and years of service.[34] Another popular type of retirement plan is the employer-sponsored 401(k) plan, which allows eligible participants to contribute pre-tax dollars to a tax-qualified retirement plan. One special feature of a 401(k) plan is the deferral of federal and state income taxes and Social Security taxes on contributions up to a maximum of $10,500 until the time of withdrawal.[35]

In addition to these three plans, a number of employers are now offering employees "hybrid" plans that combine the features of both defined benefit and defined contribution plans. One example is a cash-balance plan, which is a defined benefit plan that provides a defined-contribution–type lump sum distribution consisting of contributions and interest earnings for employees who leave before retirement age.[36]

Employee Stock-Ownership Plans Another employee benefit being offered by a number of companies is the **employee stock-ownership plan (ESOP),** under which a company places a certain amount of its stock in trust for some or all of its employees, with each employee entitled to a certain share. These plans allow employees to later purchase the shares at a fixed price. If the company does well, the ESOP may provide a substantial employee benefit.

employee stock-ownership plan (ESOP)
Program enabling employees to become partial owners of a company

Of course, linking the financial success of employees to the success of the company is indeed a worthy goal, but some say that in the long run ESOPs are not effective performance motivators. Consider United Airlines. In 1994, United Airlines' pilots made major wage concessions in exchange for receiving a 55 percent equity stake in the company via an ESOP. As a result of those concessions, United's pilots trailed the industry in pay. Nevertheless, the pilots hoped to recover the equivalence of their lost wages and more through increased market value of their ESOP shares, and the company hoped to gain enhanced employee morale and improved customer service by making the employees stockholders. Neither occurred. "I was one of the people who believed it [employee stock ownership] would make a difference and that life would be better than it has been," says one United pilot spokesperson. "But it doesn't seem to have made a great deal of difference in the way the company was run." Moreover, because ESOP rules bar employees from selling their shares until they retire or quit, the shares were useless for financing a mortgage or a college education. In short, the pilots felt they had been taken for a ride.[37] So after a summer of tense union negotiations and thousands of cancelled United flights, in September 2000 management finally agreed to give the pilots substantial wage hikes and to terminate the ESOP.[38]

Best of the Web Best of the Web Best of

In recent years, employee ownership through ESOPs and stock options has become a popular way for companies to reward and motivate employees. The National Center for Employee Ownership (NCEO) is a not-for-profit organization dedicated to improving awareness of and participation in employee ownership programs. The NCEO Web site contains free interactive educational activities and reports plus fee-based publications and services. Explore the site to learn more about the ownership programs covered in this chapter.
www.nceo.org/

stock options
Contract allowing the holder to purchase or sell a certain number of shares of a particular stock at a given price by a certain date

Stock Options   A related method for tying employee compensation to company performance is the stock option plan. The National Center for Employee Ownership estimates that between 7 to 10 million employees received stock options in 1999 (an increase of 20 percent from 1998). **Stock options** grant employees the right to purchase a set number of shares of the employer's stock at a specific price, called the *grant price*, during a certain time period. Options typically "vest" over five years, at a rate of 20 percent annually. This means that at the end of one year employees can purchase up to 20 percent of the shares in the original grant, at the end of two years 40 percent, and so on.

For example, in 1997 paper products maker Kimberly-Clark gave its 57,000 employees a grant of 25 to 125 options each at $52.125 a share (the grant price). The options could be exercised from January 2, 2000, to October 21, 2004. If the market price of Kimberly-Clark's stock climbs above the grant price during this exercise period, employees can purchase their set number of shares at the grant price, sell them at the market price, and pocket the profit. If the market price does not exceed $52.125, employees will let their options expire.[39]

Stock options can be a win-win situation for employers and employees. From the employer's perspective, stock options cost very little and provide long-term incentives for good people to stay with the company. From the employee's perspective, stock options can generate a handsome profit if the stock's market price exceeds the grant price. But stock options lose their appeal when the stock does not perform as expected. Employees could lose considerable profits if the stock's price falls below the option grant price.[40]

Family Benefits   The Family Medical and Leave Act (FMLA), signed into law in 1993, requires employers with 50 or more workers to provide them with up to 12 weeks of unpaid leave per year for childbirth, adoption, or the care of oneself, a child, a spouse, or a parent with serious illness.[41] Although the intent of the law is noble, the fact is that the average person can't afford to take extended periods of time off without pay.

Day care is another important family benefit, especially for two-career couples. Although only 10 percent of companies provide day care facilities on the premises, 86 percent of companies surveyed by Hewitt & Associates offer child-care assistance. Types of assistance include dependent-care spending accounts and resource and referral (R&R) services, which help employees find suitable child care. Firms estimate that they save anywhere from $2.00 to $6.75 in lost productivity and employee absenteeism for every $1.00 they spend on R&R programs.[42]

A related family issue is care for aging parents. An estimated 50 percent of employers offer some form of elder-care assistance, ranging from referral services that help find care providers to dependent-care allowances. Some companies will even agree to move elderly relatives when they transfer an employee to another location.[43]

Other Employee Benefits   Although sometimes overlooked, paid holidays, sick pay, premium pay for working overtime or unusual hours, and paid vacations are important benefits.[44] Companies handle holiday pay in various ways. To provide incentives for employee loyalty, most companies grant employees longer paid vacations after they've been with the organization for a prescribed number of years. Some companies let employees buy additional vacation time or sell unused days back to the employer. Sick-day allowances also vary from company to company and from industry to industry. Some U.S. companies, including Texas Instruments, have begun offering paid-time-off banks that combine vacation, personal use, and sick days into one package. Employees can then take a certain number of days off each year for whatever reason necessary, with no questions asked.[45]

Among the many other benefits that companies sometimes offer are sabbaticals, tuition loans and reimbursements, professional development opportunities, personal computers, financial counseling and legal services, assistance with buying a home, paid expenses for spouses who travel with employees, employee assistance programs, nap time, and wellness programs. Typical wellness programs include health screenings, health and wellness education programs, and fitness programs. Children's clothier Osh Kosh B'Gosh, for example, provides wellness education classes in nutrition, heart disease, cancer, diabetes, prescription medication, and others.[46] Wellness programs have been reported to reduce absenteeism, health care costs, sickness, and work-related accidents.[47]

According to the U.S. Labor Department, 48 percent of all employers with more than 100 workers now offer **employee assistance programs (EAPs).** EAPs offer private and confidential

employee assistance programs (EAPs)
Company-sponsored counseling or referral plans for employees with personal problems

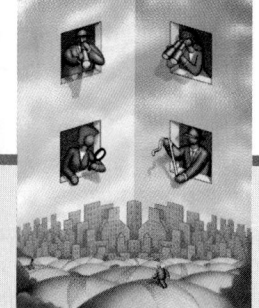

MANAGING IN THE 21ST CENTURY

IT'S OKAY TO FALL ASLEEP ON THE JOB

Nodding off at work? You're not alone. It is estimated that 70 to 80 million people in the United States are sleep-deprived—which means they just don't get enough of the stuff. But take heart. While afternoon siestas have long been the norm in many foreign countries, the nap is now slowly inching its way into the U.S. corporate culture. Skip the coffee or coke break, advise experts, and instead put your head down for 15 to 20 minutes.

Being sleepy impairs judgment and slows down reaction time. In fact, workforce fatigue is one of the key causes behind costly accidents, productivity lapses, and poor decision making. But a 20-minute snooze can earn you three to four hours more of peak alertness. Power napping, or napping for a short period of time, can help you quickly regain creativity and problem-solving skills "without the crash you suffer once the caffeine buzz wears off," says sleep expert Dr. Martin Moore-Ede. Furthermore, napping allows you to cope with a longer work day, and it increases productivity. Which is why experts are now advising companies to provide the ultimate employee benefit—the nap room.

Corporate nap rooms are popping up in the strangest places—and so are nappers. Take Russ Klettke, for example. Before he owned his own public relations firm, he used to try to hide his nap habit by sneaking siestas in his office cubicle. Now Klettke stretches out at

least once a day in the company's storage closet, which doubles as a napping nook. And he's not the only one. While getting some fax paper, he once stepped on a slumbering co-worker.

Some companies are even going all out in designing their sleep space. Gould Evens Goodman Associates, a Kansas City architectural firm, uses "spent tents" instead of a traditional nap room—which reminded company executives of a nurse's station. These one-person tents are equipped with blankets and alarm clocks. "It's like a little village," notes one employee. Others are building nap rooms outfitted with recliners, couches, cots, earplugs, relaxing music, alarm clocks, and phones—just in case you have to take a call.

So next time you find yourself dropping your eyelids for a couple of ZZZZZs, rather than crawl under your desk or hide in a bathroom stall, tell your boss about the hottest employee benefit—nap rooms. After all, sleeping on the job can indeed be a good thing.

■ QUESTIONS FOR CRITICAL THINKING

1. Should employees be paid for the time they spend napping in a company nap room? Why or why not?

2. How can companies minimize employee abuse of benefits such as nap rooms?

Studies show that workers who exercise have fewer sick days and job-related injuries. As a result, companies are bending in all directions to offer health and fitness programs to their employees, These Hewlett-Packard employees, for example, enjoy kickboxing at the company's on-site fitness center after a hard day's work.

counseling to employees who need help with issues related to drugs, alcohol, finances, stress, family, and other personal problems. Studies by the National Council on Alcoholism and Drug Dependence (NCADD) show that the average annual cost for EAP services run from $12 to $20 per employee. But, on average, these services save between $5 and $16 for each dollar spent as a result of improved safety and productivity, as well as reduced employee turnover.[48]

Benefits such as company cars, paid country club memberships, free parking, and expanded casual dress days are often referred to as perks. With today's tight job market, perks are being offered more frequently to attract the best managers (see Exhibit 11.6).[49] "But recruitment perks only go so far," says one compensation expert. "Organizations must offer the total work experience to attract talent." And to keep talent from leaving, they must offer workers challenging jobs and training, more family-related benefits, and better management supervision.[50]

■ OVERSEEING CHANGES IN EMPLOYMENT STATUS

Of course, providing competitive compensation and good employee benefits is no guarantee that employees will stay with the company. A recent survey shows that all things being equal, 25 percent would leave their current jobs for a pay increase of 10 percent or less, and more than 55 percent would leave for an increase of at least 20 percent.[51] Employees may also leave for reasons other than compensation. Some may decide to retire or may resign voluntarily to pursue a better opportunity. On the other hand, the company may take the initiative in making the change—by promoting, reassigning, or terminating employees. Whatever the reason, losing an employee usually means going to the trouble and expense of finding a replacement, whether from inside or outside the company. Overseeing changes in the employment status is another responsibility of the human resources department.

LEARNING OBJECTIVE *7*

Describe five ways an employee's status may change

Promoting and Reassigning Employees
When a person leaves or is promoted to a position of more responsibility, the company has to find someone else for the open job. As Exhibit 11.3 shows, many companies prefer to look within

EXHIBIT 11.6

LIFE IS NOT SHABBY AT THE TOP

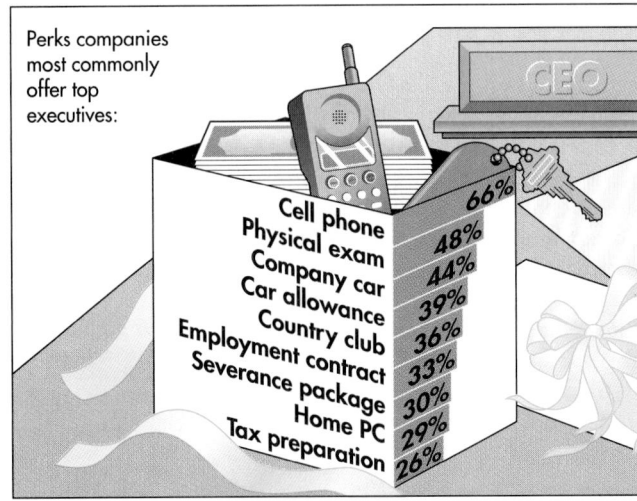

Perks companies most commonly offer top executives:

Cell phone 66%
Physical exam 48%
Company car 44%
Car allowance 39%
Country club 36%
Employment contract 33%
Severance package 30%
Home PC 29%
Tax preparation 26%

the organization for such candidates. In part, this "promote from within" policy allows a company to benefit from the training and experience of its own workforce. This policy also rewards employees who have worked hard and demonstrated the ability to handle more challenging tasks. In addition, morale is usually better when a company promotes from within because employees see that they can advance.

However, a potential pitfall of internal promotion is that a person may be given a job beyond that person's competence. A common practice is for someone who is good at one kind of job to be made a manager. Yet managing often requires a completely different set of skills. Someone who consistently racks up the most sales in the company, for example, is not necessarily a good candidate for sales manager. If the promotion is a mistake, the company not only loses its sales leader but also risks losing the employee altogether. People who can't perform well in a new job generally become demoralized and lose confidence in the abilities they do have. At the very least, support and training are needed to help promoted employees perform well.

One big issue these days is *relocation* of promoted and reassigned employees. In the past, companies transferred some employees fairly often, especially those being groomed for higher management positions. Now, however, fewer and fewer employees are willing to accept transfers. The reasons are many: disruption of a spouse's career; strong ties to family, friends, and community; disinterest in the proposed new location; the expense of relocating (buying and selling homes, planning around the reduction of a spouse's income, facing a higher cost of living in the new location); availability of good schools and child care; and the possibility that relocating won't be good for the employee's career.[52]

To encourage employee relocation, many employers today are covering the costs of house-hunting trips, moving, storage, transportation, and temporary living expenses. In addition, many employers are now helping spouses find good jobs in new locations, assisting transferees with home sales, providing school and day care referral services, and sometimes reimbursing employees for spouses' lost wages or for financial losses resulting from selling and buying houses. Many companies are also reconsidering their transfer policies and asking employees to transfer only when it is absolutely necessary.[53]

Terminating Employees

A company invests time, effort, and money in each new employee it recruits and trains. This investment is lost when an employee is removed by **termination**—permanently laying the employee off because of cutbacks or firing the employee for poor performance. Many companies facing a downturn in business have avoided large-scale layoffs by cutting administrative costs (curtailing travel, seminars, and so on), freezing wages, postponing new hiring, implementing job-sharing programs, or encouraging early retirement. However, sometimes a company has no alternative but to reduce the size of its workforce, leaving the human resources department to handle layoffs and their resulting effects on both the terminated and the remaining employees.

termination
Act of getting rid of an employee through layoffs or firing

Layoffs **Layoffs** are the termination of employees for economic or business reasons unrelated to employee performance. To help ease the pain of layoffs, many companies provide laid-off employees with job-hunting assistance. *Outplacement* aids such as résumé-writing courses, career counseling, office space, and secretarial help are offered to laid-off executives and blue-collar employees alike. Moreover, outplacement centers offer courses and tests to help employees decide what types of jobs are best suited for them.[54]

layoffs
Termination of employees for economic or business reasons

Some companies adopt no-layoff, or guaranteed-employment, policies. This means that in an economic downturn, employees may be shifted to other types of jobs, perhaps at reduced pay, or given the chance to participate in work-sharing programs. Such no-layoff policies help promote employee loyalty and motivation, which benefit the company over the long run. Rhino Foods realized the benefit of this policy when the company hit a downturn in the mid-1990s. Employees voluntarily took temporary jobs with other companies, which Rhino helped them find. If the new companies paid lower wages than the employees normally received, Rhino made up the difference. Employees also kept their Rhino seniority, benefits, and accrued vacation time. When business picked up again, the employees returned. As a result of the exchange program, Rhino enjoys much higher employee morale, loyalty, and trust than it would had it laid off workers.[55]

Firings and Employment at Will It has long been illegal for any U.S. company to fire employees because they are would-be union organizers, have filed a job-safety complaint, or are of a particular

employment at will
Employer's right to keep or terminate employees as it wishes

wrongful discharge
Firing an employee with inadequate advance notice or explanation

race, religion, gender, or age. Beyond those restrictions, the courts have traditionally held that any employee not covered by a contract may be fired "at will." **Employment at will** is the right of the employer to keep or terminate employees as it sees fit. Recently, however, a number of legal decisions have begun to alter this doctrine. The most far-reaching decisions have held that there may be an implied contract between employer and employee requiring that any firing be done "fairly." **Wrongful discharge** suits—lawsuits that contend the employee was fired without adequate advance notice or explanation—have been plentiful in light of the massive layoffs in recent years. Some fired employees have even argued that their being called "permanent" employees by the company should protect them from firing—or at least from unfair firing. To combat this problem, many companies require employees to sign an "employment at will" statement acknowledging that they may be fired at any time at the company's discretion.

Retiring Employees

As Chapter 10 discussed, the U.S. population is aging rapidly. For the business community, an aging population presents two challenges. The first is to give job opportunities to people who are willing and able to work but who happen to be past the traditional retirement age. Many older citizens are concerned about their ability to live comfortably on fixed retirement incomes. Others simply prefer to work. For several decades, many companies and industries had **mandatory retirement** policies that made it necessary for people to quit working as soon as they turned a certain age. Then in 1967 the federal Age Discrimination in Employment Act outlawed discrimination against anyone between the ages of 40 and 65. In 1986 Congress amended the act to prohibit mandatory retirement for most employees. As a corollary, employers are also forbidden to stop benefit contributions or accruals because of age.

mandatory retirement
Required dismissal of an employee who reaches a certain age

The second challenge posed by an aging workforce is to find ways to encourage older employees to retire early. One method a company may use is to offer older employees financial incentives to resign, such as enhanced retirement benefits or one-time cash payments. Inducing employees to depart by offering them financial incentives is known as a **worker buyout**. This method can be a lot more expensive than firing or laying off employees. However, the method has several advantages: The morale of the remaining employees is preserved because they feel less threatened about their own security, younger employees see a rise in their chances for promotion, and the risk of age-discrimination lawsuits is minimized.

worker buyout
Distribution of financial incentives to employees who voluntarily depart, usually undertaken in order to reduce the payroll

 FOCUSING ON E-BUSINESS TODAY

The Truth About Job Recruiting on the Internet

Whether a company is a start-up or an industry powerhouse, it must fill key positions and staff critical projects. However, in today's tight labor market, finding the best candidates for these jobs requires extraordinary speed and efficiency. As with so many other business functions, more and more companies are turning to the Internet to gain a competitive edge.

TAKING THE TRADITIONAL PATH

Before the advent of the Internet, recruiting followed a traditional path: A company "announced" a job opening to the marketplace (through a classified ad, an executive recruiter, employee referral incentives, a job fair, or other medium), and recruiters made endless rounds of cold telephone calls to identify potential job candidates. Then,

LEARNING OBJECTIVE 8
Explain how job seekers and employers are using the Internet in the recruiting process and the benefits and drawbacks of Internet recruiting

after a lengthy process of sorting through faxed and mailed résumés, someone from human resources called the most promising candidates and interviewed them.

But this process is inefficient and expensive. For one thing, communication by regular mail is slow. By the time a phone call is made or snail mail is received, some of the best candidates have accepted another job. Plus, the cost of placing classified ads in newspapers is high, so most ads contain brief job descriptions and appear for only days or weeks. Furthermore, the traditional process operates mostly in one direction. Traditionally, applicants generally would not place ads announcing their availability—although some job seekers would send unsolicited letters with résumés.

WHO'S USING INTERNET RECRUITING?

E-cruiting (recruiting over the Internet) is used by both job seekers and companies. Job seekers use the Internet not only to reply to employment ads but also to place résumés on their own Web pages or on popular recruiting and career Web sites such as Monster.com, Hotjobs.com, and CareerMosaic.com (also known as job boards). In addition, job seekers use the Internet to research companies and obtain career advice. A recent survey of 750 undergraduate students from 25 major universities reports that more than 90 percent of job applicants check out a company's Web site before taking a job, more than half seek career advice on the Internet, and nearly two-thirds use the Internet to look for articles about prospective employers.

Companies use the Internet to find qualified applicants for jobs from entry-level position to CEO and from truck driver to airline pilot. Apparently no job is outside the Internet's reach. Additionally, many companies now advertise job vacancies on their Web sites and on third-party job boards. The Internet is also used to search for résumés of promising candidates, take online applications, accept electronic résumés (via e-mail attachments), conduct interviews, and administer tests.

BENEFITS AND DRAWBACKS OF E-CRUITING

In comparison with other recruiting methods, the benefits of Internet recruiting are many:

- *Speed.* The Internet allows job seekers to search for jobs quickly, from any place and at any time, and to communicate via e-mail with potential employers. Companies can also save time in the hiring process by using the Internet to become a 24-hour, seven-days-a-week recruiter and give applicants quick responses to their queries. Determined nocturnal headhunters can snap up hot techie résumés posted on the Internet before dawn and contact candidates immediately by e-mail. Some companies report receiving responses and résumés only minutes after posting a job opening.

- *Reach.* The Internet allows employers to contact a broader selection of applicants more quickly, target specific types of applicants more easily, and reach highly skilled applicants more efficiently. Some company Web sites bring in as many as 7,000 résumés in one week, a volume that would be far too cumbersome to manage through traditional means. For the job seeker, the Internet is a convenient way to find information on a large number of jobs worldwide and to post résumés for large-volume distribution. Services such as Job Sleuth (www.jobsleuth.com) allow job seekers to search the Internet's top job sites and databases by using custom user profiles.

- *Cost savings.* The Internet saves companies the cost of advertising openings and processing applicants. Electronic ads typically cost less than traditional print, career fairs, and open houses. Moreover, processing electronic application forms is efficient. Intelligent automated search agents can filter or prescreen potential applicants and find résumés that match job descriptions and specific employer criteria.

Of course, e-cruiting is not without drawbacks. The biggest complaint voiced by companies is that the Internet produces more job applicants than ever before, and the increased volume of résumés makes it more difficult to cull promising candidates from unqualified ones. Another limitation is that not everyone has Internet access or uses the Internet to search for jobs, which makes it difficult to reach nontechnical people.

THE FUTURE OF E-CRUITING

In spite of these drawbacks, the future of e-cruiting looks more and more promising each day. Currently, only 5 percent of employment advertising takes place online, reports one recent survey. Of the remaining 95 percent, 48 percent of recruitment is still done by classified print ads, 13 percent by employee referrals, 12 percent by recruiting firms, 12 percent by self-referrals, and 10 percent by temp-to-hire opportunities.

But over time, more of the job market is expected to move to the Internet. This transfer will gradually occur as more good screening and matching tools are developed to manage the volume of résumés and to weed out inappropriate ones. "There is still a large window of opportunity for companies to leverage the Internet and other technologies as part of their recruiting strategies," notes Gordon Bingham, senior vice president at Olsten, a strategic staffing firm. The e-cruiting bandwagon is rolling. Its ultimate destination just isn't clear yet.[56]

WHO'S USING INTERNET RECRUITING?

Inc. 500 companies that say they find Internet recruiting useful, by business sector

Computer-related	60.2%
Business services	17.6%
Consumer goods	4.7%
Telecommunications	4.1%
Health care	3.5%
Industrial products	2.9%
Construction	2.3%
Finance	2.3%
Media	1.8%
Transportation	.6%

SUMMARY OF LEARNING OBJECTIVES

1. **List six main functions of human resources departments.**

   Human resources departments plan for a company's staffing needs, recruit and hire new employees, train and develop employees, appraise employee performance, administer compensation and employee benefits, and oversee changes in employment status.

2. **Cite eight methods recruiters use to find job candidates.**

   Recruiters find job candidates by (1) promoting internal candidates, (2) advertising in newspapers and on the Internet, (3) using public and private employment agencies, (4) contacting union hiring halls, (5) recruiting at college campuses and career placement offices, (6) attending trade shows, (7) hiring corporate "headhunters," and (8) soliciting referrals from employees or colleagues in the industry.

3. **Identify the six stages in the hiring process.**

   The stages in the hiring process are (1) narrowing down the number of qualified candidates, (2) performing initial screening interviews, (3) administering a series of follow-up interviews, (4) evaluating candidates, (5) conducting reference checks, and (6) selecting the right candidate.

4. **Discuss how companies incorporate objectivity into employee performance appraisals.**

   Employee performance appraisals are an effective way to inform employees if they are doing a good job and how they can improve their performance. To ensure objectivity and fairness, most firms use a standard, companywide format, provide a written record of appraisals for future reference, and solicit several perspectives by engaging superiors, peers, and colleagues at different levels in the organization in the review process.

5. **List seven popular types of employee incentive programs.**

   The most popular employee incentive programs are bonuses, commissions, profit sharing, gain sharing, pay for performance, knowledge-based pay, and broadbanding. In addition to these seven popular employee benefits, many companies offer paid holidays and vacations, sick pay, overtime pay, sabbaticals, tuition loans and reimbursements, professional development opportunities, wellness programs, and employee assistance programs.

6. **Highlight five popular employee benefits.**

   The two most popular employee benefits are insurance (health, life, disability, and long-term care) and retirement benefits, such as pension plans that help employees save for later years. Employee stock-ownership plans and stock options, two additional benefits, allow employees to receive or purchase shares of the company's stock, and thus obtain a stake in the company. Family benefits programs, also popular, include maternity and paternity leave, child-care assistance, and elder-care assistance.

7. **Describe five ways an employee's status may change.**

   An employee's status may change through promotion to a higher-level position, through reassignment to a similar or lower-level position, through termination (removal from the company's payroll), through voluntary resignation, or through retirement.

8. **Explain how job seekers and employers are using the Internet in the recruiting process, and highlight the benefits and drawbacks of Internet recruiting.**

   Companies are using the Internet in the recruitment process, or e-cruiting, to advertise job vacancies on their Web sites and on third-party job boards, to search for résumés of promising candidates, to take online applications and accept electronic résumés, and to conduct interviews and administer tests. Job seekers are using the Internet to obtain information about potential employers and communicate with them, to obtain career advice, to place résumés on their Web sites, to apply for jobs online, and to send résumés to companies or to the Web sites of searchable job boards. The Internet improves the recruiting process by making it faster, expanding the reach of potential employees and employers, and saving companies advertising and processing costs. The biggest drawback, however, is that the efficiency of the Internet produces an increased volume of résumés from job candidates, many of whom are not qualified for the position.

KEY TERMS

bonus (299)

broadbanding (300)

commissions (299)

compensation (297)

employee assistance programs (EAPs) (303)

employee benefits (300)

employee stock-ownership plan
(ESOP) (301)

employment at will (306)

gain sharing (299)

human resources management (HRM) (290)

incentives (299)

job analysis (292)

job description (292)

job specification (292)

knowledge-based pay (299)

layoffs (305)

mandatory retirement (306)

orientation (295)

pay for performance (299)

pension plan (301)

performance appraisal (297)

profit sharing (299)

recruiting (293)

salaries (298)

stock options (302)

termination (305)

wages (297)

worker buyout (306)

wrongful discharge (306)

TEST YOUR KNOWLEDGE

QUESTIONS FOR REVIEW

1. What are some strategic staffing alternatives that organizations use to avoid overstaffing and understaffing?

2. What is the purpose of conducting a job analysis? What are some of the techniques used for gathering information?

3. What are the three types of preemployment tests administered by companies, and how is each of these tests used to assist with the hiring decision?

4. What functions do orientation programs serve?

5. How do incentive programs encourage employees to be more productive, innovative, and committed to their work?

QUESTIONS FOR ANALYSIS

6. Why do some employers offer comprehensive benefits even though the costs of doing so have risen significantly in recent years?

7. Why do companies offer ESOPs and stock option plans?

8. Several smaller companies outsource their human resources functions to professional HR management companies. What are some of the advantages and disadvantages of doing so?

9. The 1986 Immigration Reform and Control Act forbids companies to hire illegal aliens but at the same time prohibits discrimination in hiring on the basis of national origin or citizenship status. How can companies satisfy both requirements of this law?

10. Review the employment ads section of your local newspaper. Which jobs can you identify as pertaining to e-commerce? What are the titles of these jobs? What skills are required?

11. Corporate headhunters have been known to raid other companies of their top talent to fill vacant or new positions for their clients. Is it ethical to contact the CEO of one company and lure him or her to join the management team of another company?

QUESTIONS FOR APPLICATION

12. If you were on the human resources staff at a large health care organization that was looking for a new manager of information systems, what recruiting method(s) would you use and why?

13. Assume you are the manager of human resources at a manufacturing company that employs about 500 people. A recent cyclical downturn in your industry has led to financial losses, and top management is talking about laying off workers. Several supervisors have come to you with creative ways of keeping employees on the payroll, such as exchanging workers with other local companies. Why might you want to consider this option?

14. Of the five levels in Maslow's hierarchy of needs, which is satisfied by offering salary? By offering health care benefits? By offering training opportunities? By developing flexible job descriptions?

15. What are some of the human resources issues managers are likely to encounter when two companies (in the same industry) merge?

PRACTICE YOUR KNOWLEDGE

SHARPENING YOUR COMMUNICATION SKILLS

Team up with a classmate to practice your responses to interview questions. Use the list of common interview questions provided in Component Chapter D, Exhibit D.9 (see p. 547) and take turns posing and responding to those questions. Which questions did you find most difficult to answer? What insights did you gain about your strengths and weaknesses by answering those questions? Why is it a good idea to rehearse your answers before going to an interview?

HANDLING DIFFICULT SITUATIONS ON THE JOB: BURGER MAKERS LEARN WHILE THEY EARN

Herb Schervish, owner of a Burger King in downtown Detroit, is worried about employee turnover. He needs to keep 50 people on his payroll to operate the outlet, but recruiting and retaining those people is tough. The average employee leaves after about seven months, which means that Schervish has to hire and train 90 people a year just to maintain a 50-person crew. At a cost of $1,500 per hire, the annual price tag for all that turnover is about $62,000.

Schervish knows that many employees quit because they think that flipping burgers is a dead-end job. But what if he offers to pay his employees' way through college if they remain with the store? Would that keep them behind the counter longer?

He's decided to give educational incentives a try. Employees who participate will earn their usual salary, but they will also get free books and college tuition, keyed to the number of hours they work each week. Those who work from 10 to 15 hours a week can take one free course at a nearby community college, those who work 16 to 25 hours can take two courses, and those who work 26 to 40 hours can take three courses. Schervish wants your advice about how to implement this voluntary program.[57]

1. Should Schervish pay only for employees who have worked at Burger King for six months or more to take courses? Why or why not?

2. Should Schervish publicize his educational program when recruiting? What effect do you think this program would have on his recruiting efforts?

3. How should Schervish handle payment for employees' tuition? If you recommend that he prepay for courses at the start of each semester, what should he do about employees who leave Burger King before the end of a course?

BUILDING YOUR TEAM SKILLS

How should the performance of a college or university instructor be evaluated? You and your team are going to design a performance appraisal form for this purpose. Working individually, generate a list of up to 10 areas of performance that you would apply to this job, such as "knowledge of course material" and "communication skills." Compare your list with those of your teammates;

discuss each item until your team has narrowed the focus to six basic criteria.

Now determine the rating system and period you will use. What would constitute an outstanding or unsatisfactory performance on the criteria you have set? How often do you think the performance of instructors should be evaluated?

In a presentation to the class, explain your team's ideas about areas of performance to be evaluated, performance ratings, and appraisal timing. What areas of performance were identified by other teams? Do you think all these areas are appropriate? Do you agree with the ratings and timing suggested by other teams? Why?

EXPAND YOUR KNOWLEDGE

KEEPING CURRENT USING *THE WALL STREET JOURNAL*

Locate one or more articles in *The Wall Street Journal* (print or online editions) that illustrate how a company or industry is adapting to changes in its workforce. (Examples include retraining, literacy or basic-skills training, flexible benefits, and benefits aimed at working parents or people who care for aging relatives.)

1. What changes in the workforce or employee needs caused the company to adapt? What did the company do to respond to these changes? Was the company's response voluntary or legally mandated?

2. Is the company alone in facing these changes, or is the entire industry trying to adapt? What are other companies in the industry doing to adapt to the changes?

3. What other changes in the workforce or in employee needs do you think this company is likely to face in the next few years? Why?

DISCOVERING CAREER OPPORTUNITIES

If you pursue a career in human resources, you'll be deeply involved in helping organizations find, select, train, evaluate, and retain employees. You have to like people and be a good communicator to succeed in HR. Is this field for you?

1. Using your local Sunday newspaper, the *Wall Street Journal*, or online sources such as Monster Board (www.monster.com), find ads seeking applicants for two or three of the HR jobs shown in Component Chapter D, Exhibit D.11 A–G (see pp. 549–555). What educational qualifications, technical knowledge, or specialized skills are applicants for these jobs expected to have? How do these requirements fit with your background and educational plans?

2. Next, look at the duties mentioned in the ad for each job. What do you think you would be doing on an average day in these jobs? Does the work in each job sound interesting and challenging?

3. Now think about how you might fit into one of these positions. Do you prefer to work alone, or do you enjoy teamwork? How much paperwork are you willing to do? Do you communicate better in person, on paper, or by phone? Considering your answers to these questions, which of the HR jobs seems to be the closest match for your personal style?

EXPLORING THE BEST OF THE WEB

URLs for all Internet exercises are provided at the Web site for this book, www.prenhall.com/mescon. When you log on to the text Web site, select Chapter 11, then select "Student Resources," click on the name of the featured Web site, and follow the detailed navigational directions to complete these exercises.

Staying on Top of the HR World, page 296

HR Live offers free online information about current human resources topics useful to more than just HR professionals. Visit the site and take a look around. Then respond to the following questions.

1. Browse through some of the top recruiting markets for occupations that interest you. How might an HR manager with a growing company use this information to recruit new employees in the future? How might this information figure in senior management's decision about where to locate new facilities?

2. Read one of the recent reports about a company that laid off employees. Why did the company lay off workers? How many were laid off, and over what time period?

3. Read the survey on the use of Internet recruiting. Read the executive summary for HR professionals. Are more HR professionals using the Internet to recruit this year than last year? What advantages and disadvantages are listed for this recruitment method?

Digging Deeper at the Bureau of Labor Statistics, page 299

The Bureau of Labor Statistics compiles data on workers, wages, employment, prices, and the economy in general. Explore the site to answer the following questions.

1. Review the unemployment rate, average hourly earnings, and productivity for the past several months. What do these numbers say about the health of the economy?

2. Read one of the recent employee benefits surveys. How might this report be of use to HR professionals?

3. Search the site using the search term "foreign labor statistics." When the results appear, scroll to the link Foreign Labor Statistics Home Page. What kind of reports are available? How could HR managers use these reports?

Understanding Employee Ownership, page 302

The National Center for Employee Ownership (NCEO) provides valuable information about employee ownership programs. Find out more about this growing trend by visiting the NCEO's Web site, checking out some of the links, and answering these questions.

1. What are two types of ESOPs? How do they differ?

2. Are ESOPs usually accomplished through employee purchases or employer contributions?

3. Who is eligible to participate? How does vesting work?

Explore on Your Own

Review these chapter-related Web sites on your own to learn more about the issues human resources departments are facing today.

1. *Workforce* magazine online, www.workforce.com, has the basics and the latest on HR issues such as recruiting, laws, managing the workforce, incentives, strategies, and more. Read the current edition online.

2. HR.com, www.hr.com, is the place to go to read about workplace trends, legislation affecting employers, recruiting, compensation, benefits, staffing, and more. Log on and learn.

3. Monster.com, www.monster.com/, has 2000 pages of career advice, résumés and salary information. Check out the job tip of the week. Get ahead in your choice of industry or profession by talking to career experts, top managers, and colleagues, and by researching different jobs that interest you.

A CASE FOR CRITICAL THINKING

■ *Brewing Up People Policies at Starbucks*

Hiring, training, and compensating a diverse workforce of 40,000 employees worldwide would be a difficult task for any company. But it was an especially daunting challenge in an industry whose annual employee turnover rate approached 300 percent. It was even more of a challenge for a company that was striving to open a new store every day, despite a tight labor market, an uncertain global economy, and increasingly intense competition.

GROUNDS FOR SUCCESS

This was the high-pressure situation facing Starbucks Coffee Company in the 1990s, when CEO Howard Schultz set a torrid pace for global expansion. Starbucks wanted to perk past $1 billion in yearly sales and spread its gourmet coffee cult across more continents. Already, the rich aroma of fresh-brewed espresso was wafting through neighborhoods all over North America, with new stores planned for the United Kingdom, Japan, even China. But Schultz and his management team knew that good locations and top-quality coffee were just part of the company's formula for success.

To keep up with this ambitious schedule of new store openings, Starbucks had to find, recruit, and train 700 new employees every month, no easy feat "when there is a shortage of labor and few people want to work behind a retail counter," as Schultz noted. Moreover, Starbucks' employees had to deliver consistently superior customer service in every store and every market. In other words Starbucks' employees (known internally as *partners*) had to do more than simply pour coffee—they had to believe passionately in the product and pay attention to all the details that can make or break the retail experience for the chain's 10 million weekly customers. In short, Starbucks' managers had to ensure that their stores provided the best service along with the best coffee—which meant attracting, training, and compensating a diverse and dedicated workforce.

PERKING UP BENEFITS

Schultz, of course, knew that attracting and motivating employees would take more than good pay and company declarations to "provide a great work environment and treat each other with respect and dignity." So guided by the company mission statement, the CEO and his managers designed a variety of human resources programs especially for Starbucks' partners (employees).

First they raised employees' base pay. "It's ironic that retailers and restaurants live or die on customer service," the CEO said, "yet their employees have some of the lowest pay in any industry. That's one reason so many retail experiences are mediocre for the public." Next, management bucked the trend in the industry by offering full medical, dental, life insurance, and disability insurance benefits to every partner who worked at least 20 hours per week. These partners were also eligible for paid vacation days and retirement savings plans, benefits not commonly available to part-time restaurant workers. Finally, to help partners better balance their work and family obligations—another priority for Starbucks—the human resources department designed a comprehensive work–life program. This program featured flexible work schedules, access to employee assistance specialists, referrals for child-care and elder-care support, and more.

A TASTE OF THE GOOD LIFE

Another Starbucks innovation was Bean Stock, a program offering stock options not just to upper-echelon managers but to all partners who worked 20 or more hours per week. "We established Bean Stock in 1991 as a way of investing in our partners and creating ownership across the company," explained Bradley Honeycutt, vice president of human resources. "It's been a key to retaining good people and building loyalty." For those who wanted to enlarge their financial stake in Starbucks, management devised a program that permitted partners to buy company stock at a discount. Owning a piece of the company motivated employees to take customer service to an even higher level of excellence.

THE PERFECT BLEND

Of course, Starbucks recognizes that good pay and benefits, while attractive, are not enough to meet the company's future growth plans. So to stay on schedule and on top, Starbucks continually invests in its workforce. Each new hire is provided with 24 hours of training about the finer points of coffee brewing as well as the company's culture and values. To encourage more and better feedback and communication, management holds a series of open forums in which company performance, results, and plans are openly discussed. Finally, Starbucks honors employees whose achievements exemplify the company's values.

In all, putting the focus on partners has helped Starbucks attract an energetic, committed workforce and keep turnover to a minimal 60 percent, much lower than the industry average.

CRITICAL THINKING QUESTIONS

1. Why do Starbucks' human resources managers need to be kept informed about any changes in the number and timing of new store openings planned for the coming year?

2. How does Starbucks benefit from using a part-time labor force?

3. How does Starbucks' liberal employee-benefits program help its employees balance their work and family obligations?

4. Go to Chapter 11 of this text's Web site at www.prenhall. com/mescon and click on the hot link to get to the Starbucks Web site. Follow the online instructions to see how Starbucks presents its HR policies to potential employees. Browse the pages that discuss working at Starbucks, reading about company culture, diversity, benefits, and learning and career devel-opment, to answer the following questions: Why would Starbucks post information about company culture in this sec-tion of the Web site? Why would job candidates be interested in learning about the culture as well as the employee benefits and training at Starbucks?

VIDEO CASE AND EXERCISES

▪ *Spotlight on Human Resources Management at Showtime*

SYNOPSIS

Human resources management is in the spotlight at Showtime Networks (www.showtimeonline.com). With four cable networks (Showtime, The Movie Channel, Flix, and Sundance) as well as a pay-per-view cable channel, Showtime operates across the United States and in several other countries. Its human resources manage-ment experts support corporate strategy by helping to determine what kinds of employees are needed to keep the company at peak performance. Showtime offers a variety of development and train-ing programs to improve the professional skills of its diverse work-force, and its open-door culture and mentoring programs allow employees to blaze rewarding career paths. Showtime's perform-ance management process, created with the direct involvement of employees, focuses on the work activities and results that further departmental goals, which in turn support corporate goals.

EXERCISES

Analysis

1. Why might Showtime Networks prefer to hire temporary and part-time employees in the course of making entertainment programs?

2. How do job descriptions and job specifications help Showtime's recruiters identify suitable candidates for open positions?

3. Why do Showtime executives say that the performance man-agement process is a two-way street?

4. How does Showtime use incentives to encourage good per-formance?

5. Why would Showtime be willing to rehire an employee who left for another job at an earlier time?

Application

What kinds of information might Showtime's human resources managers examine when forecasting the company's demand for new employees?

Decision

If Viacom, Showtime's parent company, mandates quarterly per-formance appraisals, should the same timing apply to appraisals at Showtime? Outline the pros and cons for consideration by Matthew Blank, Showtime's CEO.

Communication

Assume that Showtime is implementing a new employee assistance program. Write a brief memo to all employees explaining the ben-efits of this new program.

Integration

How could a manager at Showtime use the program evaluation and review technique (PERT), described in Chapter 9, to plan the writing, filming, and production of a new movie?

Ethics

If an employee is laid off from Showtime, is it ethical for that em-ployee to find a job at a direct competitor such as HBO and try to recruit former Showtime colleagues for the new employer?

Debate

Should Showtime outsource its training and development function so human resources management personnel can concentrate on plan-ning, recruiting, hiring, and other functions? Choose one side of this argument and list at least three arguments to support your position.

Teamwork

In a team of four students, brainstorm the various elements of an orientation program for new Showtime employees. Write a two-page report outlining your team's suggested orientation program.

Online Research

Use Internet sources to research how Viacom, Showtime's parent, is doing. What is the size of its workforce? What changes have oc-curred in recent months that would have affected demand for hu-man resources? See Component Chapter A, Exhibit A.1, for search engines to use in doing your research.

MYPHLIP COMPANION WEB SITE

Learning Interactively

Visit the myPHLIP Web site at www.prenhall.com/mescon. For Chapter 11, take advantage of the interactive "Study Guide" to test your chapter knowledge. Get instant feedback on whether you need additional studying. Read the "Current Events" articles to get the latest on chapter topics, and complete the exercises as specified by your instructor. Expand your learning with a visit to the "Research Area." There you will find a wealth of infor-mation you can use to complete your course assignments.

MASTERING GLOBAL AND GEOGRAPHICAL SKILLS: PEOPLE ARE THE SAME EVERYWHERE, AREN'T THEY?

Companies that expand across national or cultural borders sometimes run into barriers they don't expect in human resources management. For example, Japanese automakers were surprised when they tried to get workers in their new U.S. plants to join in for daily warm-up exercises. Even though the activity is commonplace in Japan, it simply didn't catch on in the United States. And DaimlerChrysler's U.S. managers were surprised by the German managers' extravagant travel and dining practices.

When companies operate across national and cultural borders, understanding cultural expectations and norms is crucial to effective management. Some of the concepts to consider involve personal space, conversational formalities (or lack thereof), friendliness, willingness to "job hop," respect for authority figures, and awareness of social class distinctions.

You can identify a number of potentially important workplace issues by exploring a country's general culture. Egyptians, for instance, address each other by first names only in informal, private settings. When in public, even good friends may add titles when addressing each other. Egyptians tend to be more conscious of social classes than are people in the United States. Moreover, they place great value on visiting friends and relatives.

Assume that you're the president of a financial-services firm based in Indianapolis and that you're ready to expand overseas. To ease your first attempt at international expansion, you're trying to find a country with workplace characteristics most similar to those in the United States. Gather as much relevant information as you can about the four countries that follow. Choose the one with work styles that feel most like those of the United States, and explain your choice. In addition to the resources in your library, explore the information available on the Internet. Possible Internet resources include the *Region and Country Information* of the International Trade Administration, *Background Notes* published by the U.S. Department of State, the Library of Congress's *Country Studies*, and the *CIA World Factbook*. Go to this text's Web site at www.prenhall.com/mescon for direct links to these resources. (Your instructor may want you to do this as a group exercise.)

- England
- France
- South Korea
- Mexico

Business PlanPro

MANAGING HUMAN RESOURCES AND LABOR RELATIONS

Review the Appendix, "Getting Started with Business PlanPro Software," to learn how to use Business PlanPro Software so that you can complete these exercises.

Think Like a Pro

Objective: By completing these exercises, you will become acquainted with the sections of a business plan that address staffing the enterprise and managing employees. For these exercises, use the sample business plan for Puddle Jumpers Airlines.

Open the BPP software and explore the sample business plan Puddle Jumpers Airline.spd. Click on the "Plan Outline" icon to access the plan's "Task Manager" and use it to navigate the company's business plan. Familiarize yourself with this firm's service and operation by reading the "Executive Summary" (see "Finish and Polish") and by reading the "Competitive Comparison" (see "What You're Selling").

1. According to the Competitive Comparison, Puddle Jumpers will achieve its low-cost operation by using fewer crew members and utilizing its flight crews 85 hours a month versus an industry average of 50 to 60 hours. How might this affect employee motivation and job stress? What programs might management implement to help pilots and flight crews achieve a work–life balance?

   Find the heading "What You're Selling" and read the business plan section titled "Fulfillment."

2. What services does Puddle Jumpers intend to outsource? Why does it make good sense to outsource these services?

   Find the heading "Your Company" and read about the "Company's Ownership."

3. What form of compensation will the company use to motivate and reward managers?

   Read about the company's Management Team. Consider the team's qualifications and experience.

4. What specific traits should you look for to evaluate whether the management team is capable of understanding and satisfying employees' needs?

   Review the company's "Personnel Plan" by double clicking on the "Personnel Table" under the "Your Management Team" heading.

5. Write a brief job description and job specification for three positions listed in the table.

   With the table displayed on your computer screen, click on the "Instructions Tab" and then on "Table Help." Play the Audio instructions.

6. How does BPP software use the information in this table in other segments of the business plan?

Create Your Own Business Plan

The success of your business depends on hiring, training, and motivating, the right employees. How many employees will your business require? Will you use part-time employees? How will you motivate your staff? Will you pay them a salary or a commission? Will you offer them alternative work arrangements? Benefits? If so, which ones?

WAL-MART VS. THE UNION

The Unshaken Warrior

Wal-Mart—America's largest private employer and the world's largest retailer—has long resisted unionization of its employees. Of its 885,000 U.S. employees, not one belongs to a union. Founder Sam Walton believed unions were divisive and unnecessary, especially in light of Wal-Mart's generous benefits and open-door policy.

All Wal-Mart employees are encouraged to voice their complaints and recommendations to management. Additionally, Wal-Mart keeps on top of workplace issues by conducting regular surveys to measure employee contentment. To keep employees motivated, store managers are given authority to solve problems, stock clerks are promoted to managerial positions, and all workers are encouraged to participate in the company's lucrative stock ownership plan. Nonetheless, one employee took a different view of Wal-Mart's participative management style. And he turned to a union organization for help, launching a battle against Wal-Mart that turned into a full-scale war.

A Raw Deal for the Butcher

With Wal-Mart's expansion into groceries at the end of the century, the company needed workers with more specialized skills than typical stock clerks and cashiers. To handle such tasks as meat cutting in its 200,000-square-foot supercenters, Wal-Mart hired workers like Maurice Miller, a butcher with 24 years of experience.

Miller's future seemed promising when he applied for work as a meat cutter at the Wal-Mart Supercenter in Jacksonville, Texas in 1999. Informed that he could quickly move into management, the butcher took a pay cut and accepted the job in hopes of working his way into a management trainee position.

But things didn't work out as Miller expected. First, Miller's management training classes were delayed. Then the store hired other meat cutters with less experience at higher pay. Furthermore, the high volume of meat deliveries often required Miller and his colleagues to work long past their 8-hour shifts. Instead of paying overtime for 10- and 12-hour days, management sent the meat cutters home as soon as they'd worked a total of 40 hours for the week.

Battling with Goliath

Dissatisfied with his treatment at Wal-Mart, Miller made a phone call to the United Food and Commercial Workers (UFCW), hoping that the UFCW could help his personal situation. The UFCW is one of the biggest U.S. unions—representing 1.4 million members, most of whom are store-level employees in the grocery industry. It consistently ranks as one of the most active unions in terms of organizing efforts. In fact, the UFCW manages to keep growing, even though

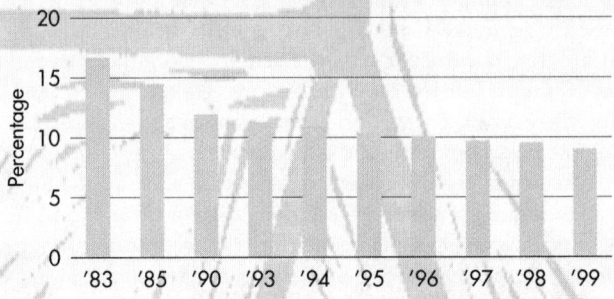

Percentage of private sector employees in labor unions

overall union membership in the United States has been on the decline for the past few decades. That's no small feat, because turnover in the grocery industry is high, which means that the UFCW has to organize 75,000 to 80,000 workers a year just to stay even.

The UFCW had been trying to organize Wal-Mart grocery workers for a decade. So when Miller contacted the union, it was like waving a red cape before a bull. The UFCW knew it would have a tough fight, but if any union could crack Wal-Mart, it was them. The battle began when Miller signed a union authorization card and started recruiting colleagues. Then Miller and nine other meat cutters at the Jacksonville, Texas, supercenter filed a petition with the National Labor Relations Board (NLRB) to hold a union certification election.

Wal-Mart's Beef

Wal-Mart was caught flat footed. But it didn't take long for the Bentonville, Arkansas, goliath to raise its sword. First, the company protested the meat cutters' petition, insisting to the NLRB that the election should include all 360 store employees. It lost that battle when the NLRB gave the go-ahead for a union vote by just the meat cutters. Next, Wal-Mart began conducting mandatory half-hour meetings with small groups of employees from other departments, explaining that a union contract could mean lower wages and fewer benefits for all employees. Finally, Wal-Mart obtained a temporary restraining order that prohibited the UFCW from soliciting Wal-Mart workers within its store—claiming that the union was violating Department of Agriculture guidelines by entering places where meat was kept, cut, and wrapped.

Wal-Mart indeed put up a good fight. But inspite of its efforts, on February 17, 2000, the Jacksonville meat cutters voted 7-3 to join the UFCW—marking the first successful vote to unionize workers in Wal-Mart's 38-year history. "These employees took on the giant and showed other Wal-Mart workers across the country that it could be done," boasted one UFCW organizer. Clearly, the union won its battle at the Jacksonville supercenter, but Wal-Mart was determined to win the war.

Butchers Win the Battle but Lose the War

Within a week after the meat cutters vote, Wal-Mart dealt the union a nasty blow. The company announced it would stop cutting meat in all its stores and start buying "case-ready" prepackaged beef and pork products from meatpackers. Wal-Mart denied the switch to prepackaged meat was in retaliation against the recent union vote. "This is the way the whole industry is going," said a company spokesperson. Wal-Mart insisted the change was made to push responsibility for meat safety and quality to outside meatpackers and to hold down retail costs by allowing meat-cutting space to be converted to selling space. Of course, for Wal-Mart's shoppers, the switch meant no more custom meat orders.

But Wal-Mart's announcement didn't cut it with the chain's 8,600 butchers, who were offered other Wal-Mart jobs with equal pay. After all, Wal-Mart had just invested $40,000 in a new meat-wrapping machine for the Jacksonville supercenter—a move that suggested meat cutting would continue in the store. Nonetheless, the company immediately introduced prepackaged beef in 80 stores throughout six states. And industry analysts predicted that other major supermarkets would soon follow Wal-Mart's lead.

The Real Union Battle Has Just Begun

With the meat cutters out of the picture, Wal-Mart returned to its non-union status. It was a big setback for the UFCW—but not for long, says the union. With over 888 supercenters and plans to open hundreds more, Wal-Mart will soon have to start locating stores in urban areas where unions are strongly represented. "We'll fight [Wal-Mart] everywhere we can," vows UFCW president Douglas H. Dority.

In fact, some industry analysts think that Wal-Mart's battle with the UFCW has just begun. Already the union has stepped up efforts to launch organizing campaigns at Wal-Marts around the country. And the union openly bad-mouths Wal-Mart to the public every chance it gets to discourage consumers from grocery shopping at the stores.

Like most union battles, the stakes are high for both sides. For one thing, the UFCW has more at stake than just Wal-Marts. Dority is especially concerned about union strongholds in California supermarkets, where the UFCW could take it on the chin if Wal-Mart builds supercenters there. An infiltration of non- union Wal-Mart supercenters in Southern California for example, could depress grocery industry wages and benefits for all California UFCW members because Wal-Mart's pay averages 47 percent less than competing unionized grocery chains. In fact, a recent spate of acquisitions and mergers involving Kroger, Safeway, and Albertson's in the California market was in part a defensive measure against the imminent encroachment of the non-union Wal-Mart goliath.

Wal-Mart, of course is determined to keep the union at bay. It has successfully challenged UFCW petitions filed by employees at other store locations across the country. And it vows to thwart the UFCW at every turn. As one Wal-Mart spokesperson puts it, "We're not saying unions aren't good for some companies; we're saying that they have no place in Wal-Mart."

QUESTIONS FOR CRITICAL THINKING

1. How has Wal-Mart managed to resist unionization of its employees for more than 38 years?

2. What factors prompted Miller to contact the UFCW?

3. Why did Wal-Mart conduct mandatory meetings with all store employees even though it was only the meat cutters who were attempting to organize?

4. Why did Wal-Mart decide to stop cutting meat in all its stores?

5. Why do some analysts think Wal-Mart's battle with labor unions has just begun? Why are unions such a threat to Wal-Mart?

6. Go to the United Food and Commercial Workers Web site at www.ufcw.org/ and read the Latest Issues and Information and Workers Actions to answer these questions: How does the UFCW encourage Wal-Mart workers to make their voices heard? Does the union advocate a boycott of Wal-Mart? What kinds of information does the union post on its Web site about Wal-Mart?

BUILDING UP WAL-MART
www.walmartstores.com/corporate

	Units 1/31/99	Units 1/31/00	Units 1/31/01
Supercenters	613	721	888
Discount Stores	1,388	1,801	1,738
Sam's Clubs	453	463	476
Neighborhood Markets	0	7	19
International units	729	1,003	1,062

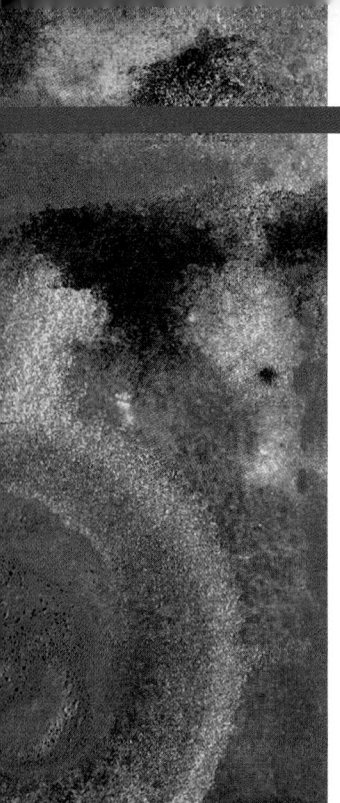

FUNDAMENTALS OF MARKETING AND CUSTOMER SERVICE

LEARNING OBJECTIVES

After studying this chapter, you will be able to

1. Explain what marketing is

2. Describe the four utilities created by marketing

3. Explain why and how companies learn about their customers

4. List five factors that influence the buyer's purchase decision

5. Discuss how marketing research helps the marketing effort, and highlight its limitations

6. Outline the three steps in the strategic marketing planning process

7. Define market segmentation and review five factors used to identify segments

@ 8. Explain why most e-tailers have lagged in providing effective customer service, and highlight five types of online customer support

DRIVEN BY DATA: BANKING ON INFORMATION AT CAPITAL ONE

www.capitalone.com

Capital One is winning big the cutthroat world of credit cards by analyzing customer information.

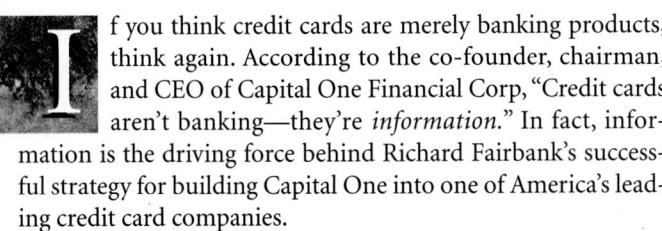f you think credit cards are merely banking products, think again. According to the co-founder, chairman, and CEO of Capital One Financial Corp, "Credit cards aren't banking—they're *information*." In fact, information is the driving force behind Richard Fairbank's successful strategy for building Capital One into one of America's leading credit card companies.

Fairbank collects extensive records on millions of consumers, maintaining massive databases on everything from customer demographics to individual card transactions. Then he uses that information not only to identify customers who would make good credit risks but also to develop customized marketing strategies for different customer segments.

First, Fairbank applies data mining techniques to his records of potential customers to find individuals who match the profile of the ideal credit card holder: the person who maintains a credit card balance but always makes a minimum monthly payment on time. And to build his customer base, he creates customized mailing lists by studying such demographics as educational levels and club memberships. For instance, Fairbank used data mining to develop his own profile of college students after he discovered that the credit card industry's mailing lists covered only one-third of the college population. Students overlooked by other credit card companies responded eagerly to Capital One's offers, returning 70 percent more applications than the industry's standard lists.

Next, Fairbank analyzes information about current Capital One customers to figure out how customers use their cards and to find meaningful patterns in consumer buying behavior. Finally, he conducts 40,000 tests each year, experimenting with everything from annual credit card fees to the color of the envelopes used for mailings. One of Fairbank's early experiments, featured the "teaser rate," offering low interest rates for an introductory period. When the experiment attracted millions of new customers, competitors launched similar programs.

With test results in hand, Fairbank produces and sells 7,000 types of customized credit cards—each with slightly different terms and conditions—aimed at different customer segments. Some customers pay $20 per year for a card with $200 worth of credit. Others carry no-fee cards with credit lines of $10,000 or $20,000. And many of the cards cater to customer preferences or interests, featuring images that range from Mt. Fuji to a Mercedes-Benz or a Canadian moose.

Fairbank even uses data mining to predict what customers might buy and how Capital One can sell those products and services to them. For example, after tests revealed that customers preferred to buy things when they call Capital One—rather than when Capital One calls them—Fairbank decided to offer additional products and services to incoming callers. He partnered with other businesses to sell callers such products as MCI long distance, Hartford insurance, and Damark International catalog club memberships. And he used an analysis of each customer's buying habits and demographics to develop a computer software system that recommends which products to sell specific customer types when they call Capital One.

Such aggressive marketing tactics have indeed paid off. Capital One sells more than 1 million non–credit card products annually. Furthermore, half of all new Capital One customers buy another product from the company within 12 months of signing up for their credit card. Meanwhile, Fairbank continues to bank on Capital One's extensive databases to identify new marketing opportunities—using the databases to test, produce, and sell a constant stream of new products to Capital One's 21 million customers.[1]

LEARNING
OBJECTIVE   1

Explain what marketing is

marketing
Process of planning and executing the conception, pricing, promotion, and distribution of ideas, goods, and services to create exchanges that satisfy individual and organizational objectives

customer service
Efforts a company makes to satisfy its customers to help them realize the greatest possible value from the products they are purchasing

place marketing
Marketing efforts to attract people and organizations to a particular geographical area

cause-related marketing
Identification and marketing of a social issue, cause, or idea to selected target markets

WHAT IS MARKETING?

Even though you are just beginning a formal classroom study of business, you probably already know quite a bit about marketing. Companies like Capital One have been trying to sell you things for years, and you've learned something about their techniques—contests, advertisements, tantalizing displays of merchandise, price markdowns, and product giveaways, to name but a few. However, marketing involves much more than a fancy display of merchandise, a clever commercial, or a special contest. In fact, a lot of planning and execution are needed to develop a new product, set its price, get it into stores, and convince people to buy it.

Think about all the decisions you would have to make if you worked for Richard Fairbank, for example. How many credit card customers would you need in order to be profitable? Which types of customers would you serve? How would you attract new customers? What fees would you charge for your service? What would you do if another credit card operation offered more attractive services or lower fees? These are just a few of the many marketing decisions that all companies make in order to be successful.

The American Marketing Association (AMA) defines **marketing** as planning and executing the conception, pricing, promotion, and distribution of ideas, goods, and services to create exchanges that satisfy individual and organizational objectives.[2] With respect to products, marketing involves all decisions related to determining a product's characteristics, price, production specifications, market-entry date, distribution, promotion, and sales. With respect to customers, marketing involves understanding customers' needs and their buying behavior, creating consumer awareness, providing **customer service**—which is everything a company does to satisfy its customers—and maintaining relationships with customers long after the sales transaction is complete (see Exhibit 12.1).

Most people, of course, think of marketing in connection with selling tangible goods for a profit (the term *product* refers to any "bundle of value" that can be exchanged in a marketing transaction). But marketing applies to services, not-for-profit organizations, people, places, and causes too. Politicians always market themselves. So do places (such as Paris or Poland) that want to attract residents, tourists, and business investment. **Place marketing** describes efforts to market geographical areas ranging from neighborhoods to entire countries. **Cause-related marketing** promotes a cause or a social issue—such as physical fitness, recycling, or highway safety.

EXHIBIT 12.1

WHAT IS MARKETING?

Each of the core marketing concepts—needs, wants, demands, products, services, values, satisfaction, quality, exchanges, transactions, relationships, and markets—building on the ones before it.

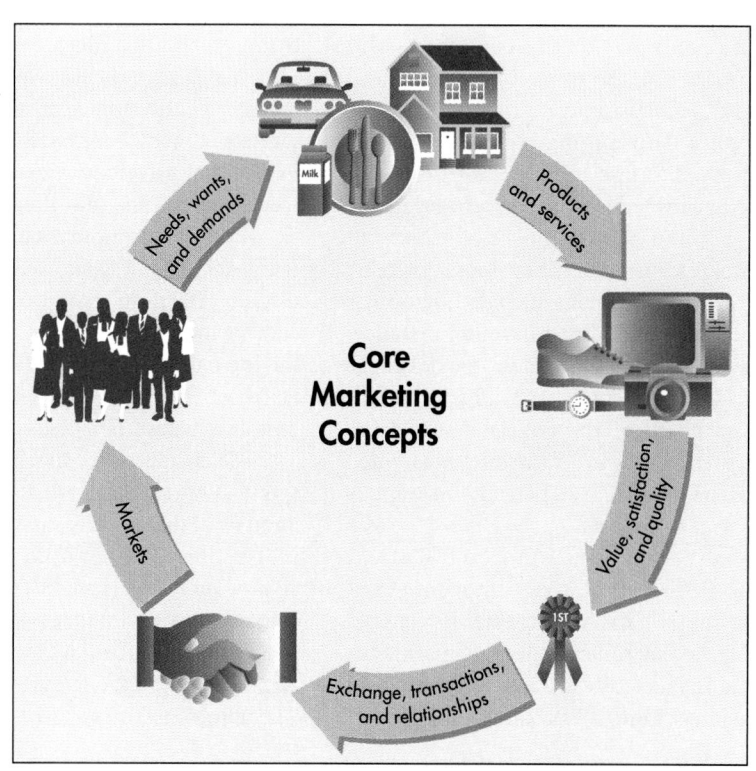

Permission marketing asks customers for permission before sending them marketing messages. American Airlines, for example, requests your permission before sending you weekly e-mail notices listing discounted air fares.

The Role of Marketing in Society

Take another look at the AMA definition of marketing. Notice that marketing involves an exchange between two parties—the buyer and the selling organization—both of whom must obtain satisfaction from the transaction. This definition suggests that marketing plays an important role in society by helping people satisfy their needs and wants and by helping organizations determine what to produce.

Needs and Wants To survive, people need food, water, air, shelter, and clothing. A **need** represents a difference between your actual state and your ideal state. You're hungry and you don't want to be hungry; you need to eat. Needs create the motivation to buy products and are therefore at the core of any discussion of marketing.

Your **wants** are based on your needs but are more specific. Producers do not create needs, but they do shape your wants by exposing you to alternatives. For instance, when you need some food, you may want a Snickers bar or an orange. A fundamental goal of marketing is to direct the customer's basic need for various products into the desire to purchase specific brands. Al Ries and Jack Trout, co-authors of *The 22 Immutable Laws of Marketing,* note that customers' wants are directed by changing people's perception of products.[3] After all, what's the real difference between Viva and Bounty paper towels? Is one actually more absorbent than the other, or do you only perceive it that way?

Exchanges and Transactions When you participate in the **exchange process,** you trade something of value (usually money) for something else of value, whether you're buying an airline ticket, a car, or a college education. When you make a purchase, you cast your vote for that item and encourage the producer of that item to make more of it. In this way, supply and demand are balanced, and society obtains the goods and services that are most satisfying.

When the exchange actually occurs, it takes the form of a **transaction.** Party A gives Party B $1.29 and gets a medium Coke in return. A trade of values takes place. Most transactions in today's society involve money, but money is not necessarily required. For example, when you were a child, you may have traded your peanut butter sandwich for a friend's bologna and cheese in a barter transaction that involved no money.

The Four Utilities To encourage the exchange process, marketers enhance the appeal of their products and services by adding **utility,** something of value to customers (see Exhibit 12.2). When organizations change raw materials into finished goods, they are creating **form utility** desired by consumers. For example, when Nokia combines plastic, computer chips, and other materials to make digital phones, the company is providing form utility. In other cases, marketers try to make their products available when and where customers want to buy them, creating **time utility** and **place utility.** Overnight couriers such as Airborne Express create time utility, whereas coffee carts in offices and ATM machines in shopping malls create place utility. The final form of utility is

Margin glossary

need
Difference between a person's actual and ideal states; provides the basic motivation to make a purchase

wants
Things that are desirable in light of a person's experiences, culture, and personality

exchange process
Act of obtaining a desired object from another party by offering something of value in return

transaction
Exchange between parties

LEARNING OBJECTIVE 2

Describe the four utilities created by marketing

utility
Power of a good or service to satisfy a human need

form utility
Consumer value created by converting raw materials and other inputs into finished goods and services

time utility
Consumer value added by making a product available at a convenient time

place utility
Consumer value added by making a product available in a convenient location

UTILITY	EXAMPLE
Form utility	Sunkist Funs Fruits are nutritious, bite-sized snacks that appeal to youngsters because of their shapes—numbers, letters, dinosaurs, spooks, and animals.
Time utility	LensCrafters has captured a big chunk of the market for eyeglasses by providing on-the-spot, one-hour service.
Place utility	By offering convenient home delivery of the latest fashion apparel and accessories, the Delia*s catalog and Web site have become favorites of teenaged girls.
Possession utility	RealNetworks, producer of software for listening to music from the Internet, allows customers to download and install its programs directly from the company's Web site.

EXHIBIT 12.2

EXAMPLES OF THE FOUR UTILITIES

The utility of a good or service has four aspects, each of which enhances the product's value to the consumer.

possession utility
Consumer value created when someone takes ownership of a product

possession utility—the satisfaction that buyers get when they actually possess a product, both legally and physically. First Union Mortgage, for example, creates possession utility by offering loans that allow people to buy homes they could otherwise not afford.

Technology and the Evolution of Marketing

Technology has always played a significant role in the evolution of the marketing function. Today, the Internet opens new channels for distributing tangible goods and intangible services worldwide, and it is changing the way marketers sell and advertise products, and communicate with customers. Moreover, the Internet provides customers with options they never had before—countless brands to choose from, searchable databases, personal attention, shipping and delivery options, built-to-order merchandise, instant access to information, and more.

Advances in other technologies are also changing today's marketing function. Mobil Speedpass, for example, is a tiny radio transmitter that attaches to a car window or a key chain and sends the user's credit card number to the gas station's computerized pump during a fuel stop.[4] Small free-standing electronic structures, called *kiosks*, vend products and services in convenient locations and introduce new products in dynamic ways. Located in showrooms or shopping areas, kiosks can inform customers about inventory, products, and store promotions; take and process orders; help people fill out applications; and sell small items such as entertainment and transportation tickets. Wild Oats, a chain of natural-foods grocery stores headquartered in Boulder, Colorado, for instance, uses kiosks to deliver health and nutritional information to customers.[5]

Not only do these new technologies improve the speed and convenience of customer transactions, but at the same time they provide marketers with information about customers' lifestyles, product preferences, and buying habits. Of course, without such technological advances, the world of marketing might resemble earlier eras.

sellers' market
Marketplace characterized by a shortage of products

Production Era and Sales Era During the *production era* (which lasted until the 1930s), many business executives viewed marketing simply as an offshoot of production. Product design was based more on the demands of mass-production techniques than on customers' wants and needs. This type of **sellers' market** existed in many industries where demand for products exceeded supply. Thus, manufacturers were generally able to sell all that they produced. They relied on a good, solid product to sell itself, and they comfortably limited their marketing efforts to taking orders and shipping goods.

Once technological advancements increased production capacity, however, the market for manufactured goods became more competitive. Business leaders, realizing that they would have to persuade people to buy all the goods they could make, expanded their marketing activities. To stimulate demand for their products, firms spent more on advertising, but they still focused on selling whatever the company produced. Consequently, this period (1930s to 1950s) was labeled the *sales era*. It lasted until companies began facing a new challenge: an overabundance of products, or **buyers' market**—that is, supply exceeded demand. Faced with excess product, companies shifted from pushing whatever they produced on all consumers to finding out what buyers wanted and then filling that specific need. They became more customer-centered. This shift in focus began the *marketing era* that continues to develop and evolve today (see Exhibit 12.3).

buyers' market
Marketplace characterized by an abundance of products

EXHIBIT 12.3

THE SELLING AND MARKETING ERAS CONTRASTED

During the sales era, firms sold what they made rather than focusing on what buyers wanted. But in today's marketing era, firms determine the needs and wants of a market and strive to deliver desired products or services more effectively and efficiently than their competitors do.

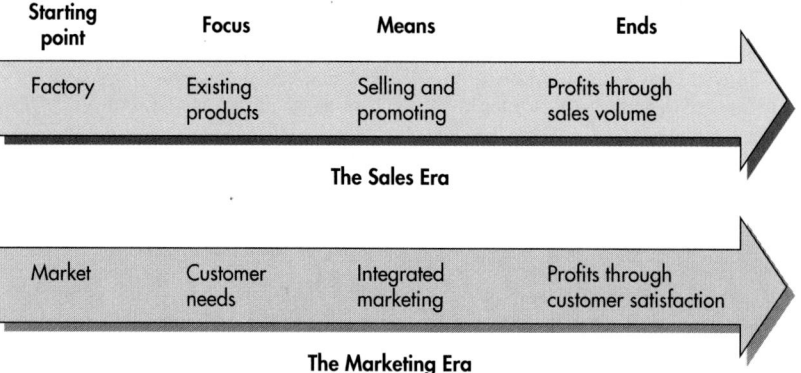

EXHIBIT 12.4

HOW THE INTERNET ENHANCES CUSTOMER RELATIONS

The Internet is a powerful tool for marketing research, establishing new markets, testing customer interest in emerging products, and conducting a dialogue with customers.

Internet capability →	Marketing and product research	Sales and distribution	Support and customer feedback
Benefits to company →	• Provides data for market research • Establishes consumer response to new products	• Reaches new customers • Provides a low-cost distribution method • Allows for electronic catalogs	• Improves customer access • Puts more staff in contact with customers • Allows immediate response to customer problems
Opportunities →	Increased market share	Lower costs	Enhanced customer satisfaction

Marketing Era and Relationship Era Although some companies still operate with sales- or production-era values, today most have adopted the **marketing concept,** stressing customer needs and wants, concentrating on specific target markets, seeking long-term profitability, and coordinating their own marketing efforts. Some organizations take the marketing concept to a higher level by maintaining long-term relationships with customers. Thus, the relationship between customer and company does not end with the sales transaction; instead it is viewed as an ongoing process.[6]

Relationship marketing is the process of building long-term satisfying relationships with key parties—customers, suppliers, distributors—to retain their long-term business. Frequently referred to as customer relationship management (CRM), relationship marketing focuses on establishing a learning relationship with each customer. The relationship gets smarter with each interaction—you learn something about your customer and you change your product or service to meet the customer's needs.

As Exhibit 12.4 shows, the Internet is a terrific vehicle for learning about and building relationships with customers. It brings the outside world closer and allows businesses to reach out and establish relationships with customers beyond their borders and market to the world. In addition, many companies are using the Internet to obtain information about customers, answer customers' questions, test their reaction to new products, sell products, obtain customer feedback, and better understand who their customers are and what they want.

marketing concept
Approach to business management that stresses customer needs and wants, seeks long-term profitability, and integrates marketing with other functional units within the organization

relationship marketing
A focus on developing and maintaining long-term relationships with customers, suppliers, and distributors for mutual benefit

◼ THE IMPORTANCE OF UNDERSTANDING CUSTOMERS

According to management consultant Peter Drucker, "The aim of marketing is to know and to understand the customer so well that the product or service fits him and sells itself."[7] This is a challenge because customers today are not very easy to understand. Consider SkyMall's experience. SkyMall, which sells gifts and other items through in-flight catalogs and the Web, got into trouble because it didn't really understand its customers. CEO Robert Worsley wanted to please customers by hand-delivering their in-flight purchases as soon as the airplane landed. This was a costly service, requiring large warehouses filled with inventory. As it turned out, however, customers, already burdened with luggage, were not eager to carry more packages. They enjoyed ordering from SkyMall while in the air, but they didn't want to pick up their packages once they arrived at the airport.[8] Worsley's mistake was to offer costly extra services his customers didn't want. Fortunately, the company discovered and corrected its mistake early. But it shows just how easy it is to lose touch with the needs of today's customers.

Focusing on Today's Customers

Today's customers are sophisticated, price sensitive, and demanding. They live time-compressed lifestyles and have little patience for retailers who do not understand them or will not adapt their business practices to meet their needs. They expect products and services to be delivered faster

LEARNING OBJECTIVE 3

Explain why and how companies learn about their customers

CarSmart has helped over 2 million consumers get a low competitive price without any hassles or haggling. Not only does the Web site provide consumers with free automobile price quotes and links to dealers, but it locates vehicles and arms consumers with just about everything they need to know before purchasing a car.

and more conveniently. And they have no qualms about switching to competitors if their demands are not met.

Armed with facts, prices, data, product reviews, advice, how-to guides, and databases, today's customers are informed, and this places them in an unprecedented position of control.[9] They walk into car dealerships reading spec sheets downloaded from such Web sites as CarSmart, Auto-by-Tel, or Edmunds.com that disclose the dealer's invoice cost, dealer rebates, and other purchasing incentives.[10] Prior to the Internet, of course, consumers had no way of knowing such detail—and many car dealers liked it this way. After all, ill-informed prospects are easily manipulated whereas educated buyers are not. But the Internet has changed all that. What does this mean for traditional car companies and dealers? As Robert Eaton, past co-chairman of DaimlerChrysler put it, "The customer is going to grab control of the process and we are all going to salute smartly and do exactly what the customer tells us if we want to stay in business."[11]

Of course, auto dealers aren't the only ones experiencing this power shift. "The realtor of yesterday was totally in control of basic information," notes George Stephens, chairman of the Houston Association of Realtors. Now home buyers use real estate Web sites to gain more control of the house-hunting process. Home descriptions, photographs, room dimensions, property tax information, and school and town information are all provided on Web sites—making it possible for customers to do their research online before setting foot in the real estate office.[12]

From travel agents to supermarkets to auto dealers to furniture stores to realtors—today's customers are indeed calling the shots. Which is why more and more businesses are striving to understand customers and satisfy their changing needs.

Satisfying Customers

How do you know whether your customers are satisfied? Better still, why do companies care if their customers return? Companies strive to satisfy their customers and keep them coming back for these reasons:[13]

- Acquiring a new customer can cost up to five times as much as keeping an existing one.
- Long-term customers buy more, take less of a company's time, bring in new customers, and are less price-sensitive.
- Satisfied customers are the best advertisement for a product.
- Firms perceived to offer superior customer service find that they can charge as much as 10 percent more than their competitors.
- Research shows that dissatisfied customers may tell as many as 20 other people about their bad experiences.

Best of the Web Best of the Web Best of

FASTEN YOUR SEATBELT

Technology such as the Internet is changing the way consumers research and make purchases. Buying a car used to be a consumer headache, but going car shopping on the Internet is a breeze. Fasten your seatbelt and log on to CarSmart to get smart about car purchases. Imagine what you'll do with all this information when you enter the dealer's showroom. Will the salespeople be ready for you?

www.carsmart.com

One of the best ways to measure customer satisfaction, of course, is to analyze your customer base: Are you getting new customers? Are good ones leaving? What is your customer retention rate? What are you doing to keep your customers loyal?

Look at Capital One. When a current customer calls the company to close his or her account, the customer is immediately transferred to a customer retention specialist, whose job is to offer the customer a better deal (interest rate, line of credit, and so on) to keep the customer's business. Some companies, of course, promote loyalty by offering extra-long product guarantees: Hewlett-Packard, for example, guarantees 99.999 percent product reliability and availability so that customers are loyal and are willing to buy additional goods and services;[14] A.T. Cross pens carry a lifetime guarantee; and Le Creuset cookware is guaranteed for 101 years.[15] Software maker Intuit is so focused on retaining customers that every employee—including the president—spends a few hours each month working the customer-service phone lines. This intense focus helps Intuit make its Quicken program so user-friendly that customers are fiercely loyal. As one marketing consultant put it: "People would rather change their bank than switch from Quicken."[16]

But such customer loyalty is the exception, not the norm. On average, U.S. companies lose half their customers every five years. Why are customers less loyal today? First, they have more choices; more styles, options, services, and products are available than ever before. Second, customers have more information from brochures, consumer publications, the Internet, and more, which empowers buyers and raises expectations. Third, when more and more products start to look the same, nothing stands out for customers to be loyal to. And fourth, time is scarce. If it's easier to buy gas at a different service station each week, customers will.[17] Furthermore, customer loyalty must be earned every day, because customer needs and buying habits change constantly (see Exhibit 12.5).

Keep in mind that not every customer is worth keeping. Some customers cost a great deal to service; others spend little but demand a lot. "We've gotten a lot smarter about separating the customers we do want from the customers we don't want," says C. Michael Armstrong,

Responding to customers' changing lifestyles, today's supermarkets offer more food options than ever before. Some stores are even transforming themselves into take-out centers.

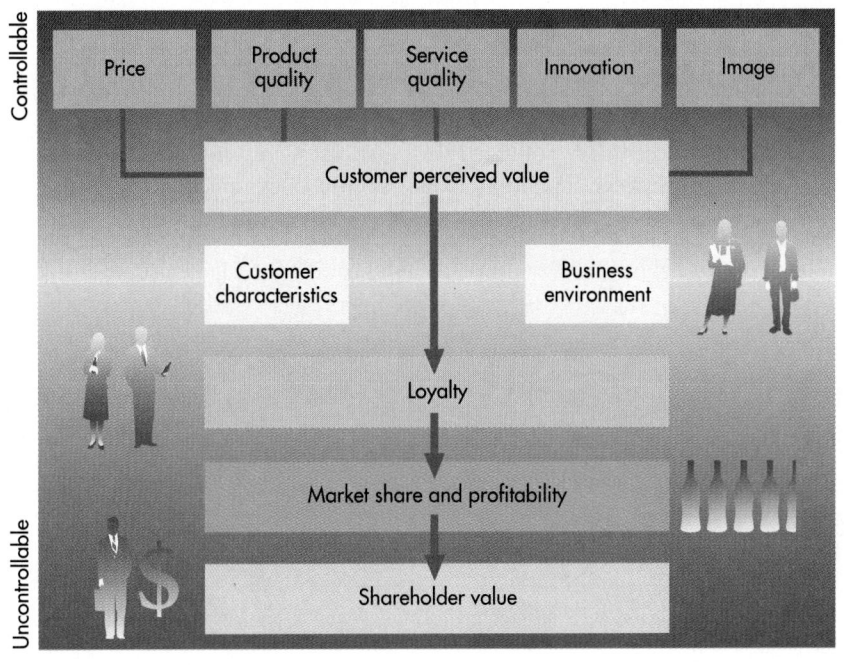

EXHIBIT 12.5

BEYOND CUSTOMER SATISFACTION

Satisfying the customer is no longer the ultimate business virtue. Companies today are looking for more and better ways of cementing customer loyalty to boost market share, profitability, and shareholder value.

Controllable

Price | Product quality | Service quality | Innovation | Image

Customer perceived value

Customer characteristics

Business environment

Loyalty

Market share and profitability

Shareholder value

Uncontrollable

CEO of AT&T. Facing $500 million in yearly losses on the millions of customers who make few long-distance calls, AT&T routes customer service calls from low spenders to automated systems and lavishes human attention on higher-spending customers.[18]

Learning About Customers

According to management expert Peter Drucker, the most important sources of information for strategic decision making come from customers.[19] Amazon.com, for example, uses the information it obtains from customers to make buying recommendations for them. But it also uses that information to, as CEO Jeff Bezos puts it, "invent things we suspect people will want."[20]

In the past, most companies obtained information about changing customer preferences, changing market trends, and new competitor products by utilizing a variety of marketing research techniques. But today, companies are tapping into this valuable source of information by using technology to engage in two-way, ongoing dialogues with customers through e-mail, Web pages, fax machines, and toll-free telephone numbers. Like Capital One, they are constructing and using customer databases to capture insights about customers in great detail, to remember customer preferences and priorities, and to make the customer experience more personal and compelling. Some are even using this data to serve up personalized marketing messages, create Web pages that display products and services that suit the customer's specific requirements, and present specific segments of a company's online catalog instead of requiring customers to click through multiple Web pages.

consumer buying behavior
Behavior exhibited by consumers as they consider and purchase various products

Consumer Buying Behavior   To learn what induces individuals to buy one product instead of another, companies study **consumer buying behavior.** For instance, when Israeli-based Sky Is the Ltd. needed to know where and how U.S. consumers buy crackers, its executives researched the behavior of U.S. shoppers. After conducting marketing research studies, they found that the firm's little-known brand would get lost among the sea of crackers on supermarket shelves but could attract some attention in gourmet food stores.[21]

Three things that companies must take into consideration when analyzing consumer buying behavior are the differences between organizational and consumer markets, the buyer's decision process, and factors that influence the buyer's decision process.

organizational market
Customers who buy goods or services for resale or for use in conducting their own operations

Organizational versus Consumer Buyers   The **organizational market** is made up of three main subgroups: the industrial/commercial market (companies that buy goods and services to produce their own goods and services, such as Toyota), the reseller market (wholesalers such as Ingram Micro, which wholesales computers, and retailers such as Ann Taylor, which sells women's clothing), and the government market (federal, state, and local agencies such as the state of Texas and the city of Dallas).

Organizations buy raw materials (grain, steel, fabric) and highly technical and complex products (printing presses, management consultation, buildings). They also buy many of the same products that consumers do—such as food, paper products, cleaning supplies, and landscaping services—but they generally purchase larger quantities and use a more complex buying process. By contrast, the **consumer market** consists of individuals or households that purchase goods and services for personal use. In most cases, consumers purchase smaller quantities of items and use a process similar to the one outlined in Exhibit 12.6.

consumer market
Individuals or households that buy goods or services for personal use

The Buyer's Decision Process   Suppose you want to buy a car. Do you rush to the dealer, plunk down money, and buy the first car you see? Of course not. Like most buyers, you go through a de-

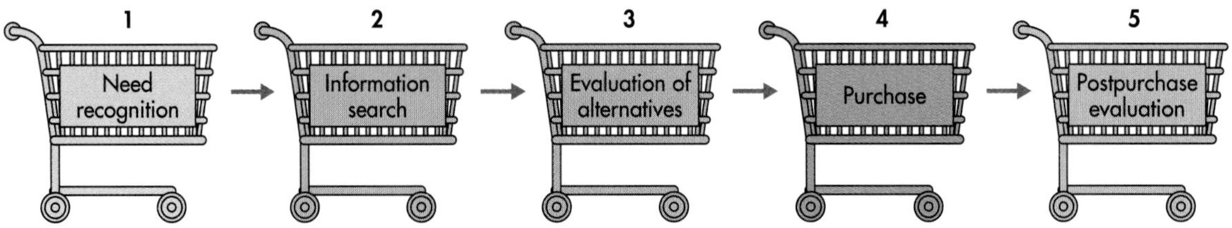

EXHIBIT 12.6

THE CONSUMER DECISION PROCESS
Consumers go through a decision-making process that can include up to five steps.

cision process, outlined in Exhibit 12.6, that begins with identifying a problem, which in this case is the need for a car. Your next step is to look for a solution to your problem. Possibilities occur to you on the basis of your experience (perhaps you recently drove a certain car) and on your exposure to marketing messages. If none of the obvious solutions seems satisfying, you gather additional information. The more complex the problem, the more information you are likely to seek from friends or relatives, magazines, salespeople, store displays, and sales literature.

Once you have all the information in hand, you are ready to make a choice. You may select one of the alternatives, such as a new Chevy Blazer or a used Ford Explorer. You might even postpone the decision or decide against making any purchase at all, depending on the magnitude of your desire, the outside pressure to buy, and your financial resources. If you decide to buy, you will evaluate the wisdom of your choice. If the item you bought is satisfying, you might buy the same product again under similar circumstances, thus developing a loyalty to the brand. If it is not satisfying, you will probably not repeat the purchase.

If the purchase was a major one, you will sometimes suffer from **cognitive dissonance,** commonly known as buyer's remorse. You will think about all the alternatives you rejected and wonder whether one of them might have been a better choice. At this stage, you're likely to seek reassurance that you have done the right thing. Realizing this tendency, many marketers try to reinforce their sales with guarantees, phone calls to check on the customer's satisfaction, user hot lines, follow-up letters, and so on. Such efforts help pave the way for repeat business.

cognitive dissonance
Anxiety following a purchase that prompts buyers to seek reassurance about the purchase; commonly known as *buyer's remorse*

Factors That Influence the Buyer's Decision Process Throughout the buying process, various factors may influence a buyer's purchase decision. An awareness of the following factors and consumer preferences enables companies to appeal to the group most likely to respond to its products and services:

■ *Culture.* The cultures and subcultures people belong to shape their values, attitudes, and beliefs and influence the way people respond to the world around them. Understanding culture is therefore an increasingly important step in international business and in marketing to diverse populations within a country such as the United States.

■ *Social class.* In addition to being members of a particular culture, people also belong to a certain social class—be it upper, middle, lower, or somewhere in between. In general, members of various classes pursue different activities, buy different goods, shop in different places, and react to different media.

■ *Reference groups.* A reference group consists of people who have a good deal in common: family members, friends, co-workers, sports enthusiasts, music lovers, computer buffs. Individuals are members of many such reference groups, and they use the opinions of the appropriate group as a benchmark when they buy certain types of goods or services.

■ *Self-image.* The tendency to believe that "you are what you buy" is especially prevalent among young people. Marketers capitalize on people's need to express their identity through their purchases by emphasizing the image value of goods and services. That's why professional athletes and musicians frequently appear as product endorsers—so that consumers will incorporate part of these celebrities' public image into their own self-image.

■ *Situational factors.* These factors include events or circumstances in people's lives that are more circumstantial but that can influence buying patterns. Such factors might include having a coupon, being in a hurry, celebrating a holiday, being in a bad mood, and so on.

LEARNING
OBJECTIVE 4
List five factors that influence the buyer's purchase decision

Marketing Research Conducting marketing research is another way companies learn about the needs and wants of their customers. **Marketing research** is the process of gathering and analyzing information about customers, markets, and related marketing issues. It is one of the tools used by managers to help understand the market. Companies rely on research when they set product goals, develop new products, and plan future marketing programs. They also use research to monitor a program's effectiveness by analyzing the number of consumers using a product or purchasing it more than once. In addition, they use marketing research to keep an eye on the competition, track industry trends, and measure customer satisfaction. Popular marketing research tools include personal observations, customer surveys and questionnaires, experiments, telephone or personal interviews, studies of small samples of the consumer population, and focused interviews of 6 to 10 people (called focus groups).

LEARNING
OBJECTIVE 5
Discuss how marketing research helps the marketing effort, and highlight its limitations

marketing research
The collection and analysis of information for making marketing decisions

Marketing surveys are a common way of gathering data directly from customers.

Limitations of Marketing Research Focus groups, consumer surveys, and other marketing research tools for probing customers wants and needs can indeed be useful, but they have limitations. In 1985 when Bell Labs first invented the cell phone, AT&T asked a big consulting firm to do a customer survey. The results convinced management that there was no market for the cell phone, and AT&T shelved the new product. Eight years later, AT&T ended up acquiring McCaw Cellular to catch up with the irreversible trend of cell phone usage.[22]

Part of the problem with surveys is that they are administered in artificial settings that do not accurately represent the marketplace. Moreover, surveys generally measure the level of service that the company currently provides instead of identifying ways to propel a company beyond its current state of service. Furthermore, if not carefully worded and administered, surveys can be misleading, as well as poor predictors of future buying behavior. For example, more than 90 percent of car buyers are either "satisfied" or "very satisfied" when they drive away from the dealer's showroom, but less than half wind up buying the same car the next time around.[23]

Keep in mind that marketing research can suggest, in a narrow way, what people might prefer or dislike today, but it is seldom a good predictor of what will excite consumers in the future.[24] Successful business people such as Barry Diller understand this. Diller forged ahead with Fox Broadcasting even though surveys said there was no need for another network. Sony is another classic example. The Walkman is one of the most successful consumer products ever introduced, yet it was greeted by skepticism during the prototype test.[25] FedEx and CNN were also met with public naysaying. So was the Chrysler minivan.[26]

Finally, marketing research is not a substitute for good judgment. When used inappropriately, research can be the source of expensive mistakes. Coca-Cola's experience with new Coke is a classic example of how marketing research can lead a company astray when data are not used correctly. In an effort to stem the growth of archcompetitor Pepsi, Coca-Cola conducted extensive taste tests to find a cola taste that consumers liked better than either Coke or Pepsi. On the basis of this research, the company launched New Coke, replacing the 100-year-old Coca-Cola formula. But New Coke simply did not sell, and Coca-Cola had to mount an expensive marketing effort to salvage the brand. At the same time, public outcry drove the company to bring back the original formula, renamed Coke Classic.

What went wrong? First researchers focused only on taste and failed to look at the emotional attachment consumers had to traditional Coke soft drink. Second, many of the people who participated in the test did not realize that old Coke would be taken off the shelf. If the company had asked the right questions, the rocky course of New Coke's introduction might have been smoother.[27]

Virtual Reality One especially effective marketing research tool is three-dimensional modeling (also known as virtual reality). Modeling allows the marketer to quickly and inexpensively re-create the atmosphere of an actual retail store on a computer screen. Consumers can view model shelves stocked with any kind of product, pick up the package from the shelf by touching its image on the monitor, turn the package to examine it from all sides, and move the product to the virtual shopping cart—as though it were an actual store. Meanwhile the computer records the amount of time the consumer spends shopping in each product category and examining the package, the quantity of products purchased, and the order in which they are purchased.

The advantages of virtual reality research over traditional marketing research methods include realistic settings; quick setup; easy reconfiguration of brands, pricing, and shelf space; fast and error-free data collection; low costs and flexibility; and the ability to test new concepts before incurring manufacturing or advertising costs. For instance, when Goodyear Tire wanted to expand its distribution to general merchandise outlets (previously the tires were only available in company-owned retails stores), Goodyear used a series of virtual reality simulations to assess consumer brand-name loyalty and pricing strategies. The simulations even identified which of Goodyear's competitors posed the greatest threat to its business.[28]

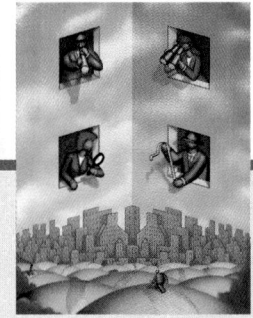

MANAGING IN THE 21ST CENTURY

MOVE OVER BOOMERS AND GEN XERS: HERE COMES GENERATION Y

Coca-Cola is out, Mountain Dew is in; Estee Lauder is out, Hard Candy is in; Levi Strauss is out, Tommy Hilfiger is in. That's the brand assessment of Generation Y, the 60 million people in the United States born between 1979 and 1994. Generation Y is a smaller segment than the 72 million baby boomers (their grandparents' generation) but triple the size of Generation X. And this gigantic market segment has enormous buying power: They spend a whopping $150 billion annually on their own and influence household spending by another $500 billion. Given such attractive demographics, it's not surprising that marketers are racing to identify opportunities for hooking these younger consumers while they are still making up their minds about brands.

But reaching these consumers can be a daunting challenge. Studies show that traditional marketing tactics that clicked with baby boomers and Generation Xers are not the way to reach Generation Y. This techno-savvy segment, also known as the Net Generation, relies on the Internet to keep up with the latest styles and fads and to find out about goods and services. "If a company can't communicate via e-mail, the attitude is, 'What's wrong with you?'" observes John R. Samuel, director of interactive marketing at American Airlines. Reaching out to the college market, American Airlines has begun a special e-mail-only program to communicate information about discounted airfares to students who register for the service.

Like American Airlines, more and more businesses are using updated marketing tactics that mesh much better with Generation Y attitudes and lifestyles. "As a brand, you need to go where they are, not just pick a fashion statement, put it on TV, and wait for them to come to you," says the president of the Lee Apparel brand. But because the buying behavior of this market segment changes at the blink of a cursor, Lee and other marketers keep a close watch on trends that signal new opportunities for reaching Generation Y consumers.

■ QUESTIONS FOR CRITICAL THINKING

1. What can marketers due to better understand the buying behavior of Generation Y consumers?

2. What factors do you think influence the buying behavior of Generation Y consumers? Give examples.

Database Marketing   Another way to learn about customer preferences—and more specifically about a customer's lifetime value—is to gather and analyze all kinds of customer-related data. As CEO Richard Fairbank knows, every credit card transaction, Internet sale, and frequent buyer purchase leaves behind a trail of information that retailers can use to their advantage. Frequent-shopper card programs, good for a wealth of discounts at checkout, have convinced customers to share some of the most intimate details about their lives. For instance, customer grocery purchases reveal preferences for everything from hygiene products to junk food to magazines.

Database marketing is the process of recording and analyzing customer interactions, preferences, and buying behavior for the purpose of contacting and transacting with customers. Although the terms *database marketing* and *relationship marketing* are sometimes used interchangeably, they are not the same. Database marketing is the act of gathering and analyzing customer information, whereas relationship marketing focuses on conducting two-way communication between the company and the customer in order to build long-term relationships. The underlying principle of database marketing is simple: All customers share some common needs and characteristics but each customer has his or her own twist. By analyzing data collected on each customer's key attributes, companies can determine which customers to target, which to avoid, and how to customize marketing offers for the best response (see Exhibit 12.7).[29]

Allstate, for example, uses database marketing to amass huge amounts of data about applicants (credit reports, driving records, claims histories) in order to swiftly price a customer's insurance policy.[30] Ritz Carlton records all customer requests, comments, and complaints in a worldwide database that now contains individual profiles of more than 500,000 guests. By accessing these profiles, employees at any Ritz Carlton hotel can accommodate the individual tastes of

database marketing
Process of building, maintaining, and using customer databases for the purpose of contacting customers and transacting business

EXHIBIT 12.7

TYPICAL DATABASE FOR CUSTOMERS' ORDERS

Designing a user-friendly database to record customer information is the key to building an effective database marketing program. The information from this simple order-entry screen will eventually be transferred to a customer history file so that the company can rank its customers by total dollars spent and other criteria.

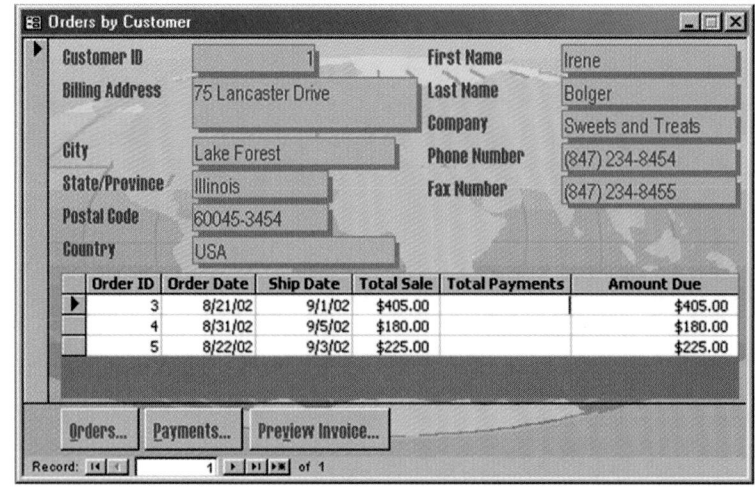

its customers from anywhere in the world.[31] And Capital One has enough customer information in its databases to fill the hard drives of more than 200,000 personal computers.[32]

As Chapter 8 explains, some companies take database marketing a step further by gathering details about customer transactions, requests, and preferences from every department. Using customer relationship management software, companies interact with customers, remember customer preferences and priorities, capture insights about customers in great detail, calculate customers' profitability and future potential, build sophisticated but easily accessible customer profiles, and share these data throughout the organization. As a result, salespeople, marketers, and service representatives all have access to a single, unified view of the customer.[33]

Companies store this information in computerized data warehouses. Through data mining, they analyze the data electronically and find meaningful patterns that lead the way to more effective, more targeted and individualized marketing. But as Chapter 2 points out, many companies are struggling to find a balance between satisfying their needs for customer information and respecting the customer's right to privacy (see "Who Will Win the Great E-Commerce Privacy Debate," pp. 61–62).

Treating Customers Individually

Companies used to rely primarily on differentiating their products and services to compete in the marketplace. But today many companies are gaining a competitive edge by differentiating the customer experience, making it more personal and compelling. Capital One, for instance, attracts millions of customers by presenting itself a little differently to each customer. The company offers more than 7000 variations of its credit card and up to 20,000 variations of other products, from phone cards to insurance.[34]

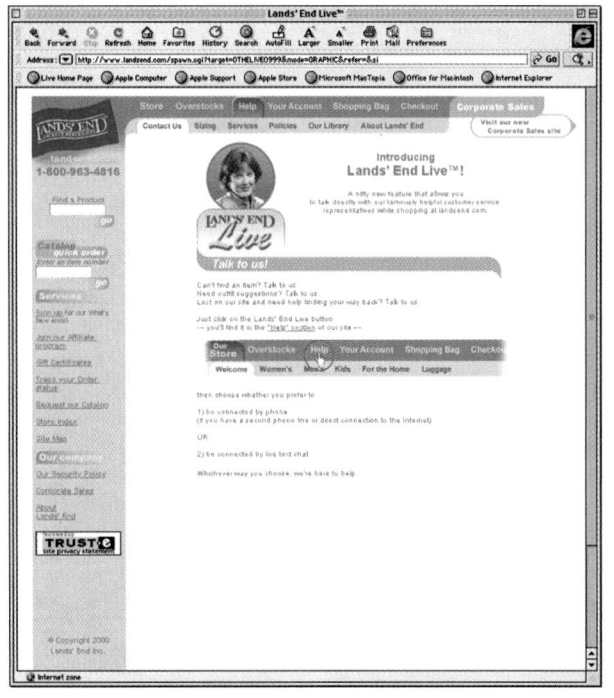

At the Lands' End Web site, customers can get more than answers to their questions. Personal shoppers can recommend additional products that match customers' preferences and even split the computer screen to display apparel combinations

One-to-one marketing involves individualizing a firm's marketing efforts for a single customer to accommodate the specific customer's needs. The four key steps to putting an effective one-to-one marketing program in place are: (1) identifying your customers, (2) differentiating among them, (3) interacting with them, and (4) customizing your product or service to fit each individual customer's needs.[35] Technology is, of course, a critical component of each of these steps. Here are some examples of successful one-to-one marketing programs:

■ Dell computer, which builds every computer according to customer specifications, designs a special ordering Web site, called Premier Pages, for customers with over 400 employees. Dell offers millions of computing configurations, but employees accessing Premier Pages may only be allowed to choose from 1,000, 100, or only 1 or 2 options (selected by the employee's organization). By placing customized limits on ordering options, Dell keeps its corporate customers' accounting departments happy. Of course, customers aren't the only ones benefiting from Premier Pages. They're also good for Dell. The program cuts Dell's costs by minimizing ordering errors and freeing up valuable sales staff.[36]

■ Nike's personalized shoe initiative, dubbed NikeID, allows customers to use the company's Web site to pick custom colors they want on their running shoes or cross trainers. Nike will even stitch a name (up to eight letters) next to the swoosh instead of having a celebrity name such as Michael Jordan.[37]

■ Levi's Original Spin is designed for customers who are not entirely satisfied with the roughly 130 styles of jeans sold off the shelf by Levis. Customers can order a custom-fitted pair, choosing from three basic models, 10 fabrics, five leg styles, and two types of fly.[38]

■ American Airlines displays a Web site that looks different to each of about one million registered AAdvantage flyers. Customers who log in are greeted by a name and sometimes by a direct marketing offer. The site is programmed to present a discount to any customer who has paid three visits without making a purchase.[39]

One-to-one marketing programs such as these require a thorough understanding of each customer's preferences and a detailed history of each customer's interactions with the company. But for companies the payoff can result in increased customer loyalty: The more time and energy a customer spends teaching a firm about that customer's own preferences, the more difficult it becomes for the customer to obtain the same level of individualized service from a competitor.[40]

■ HOW TO PLAN YOUR MARKETING STRATEGIES

By now you can see why successful marketing rarely happens without carefully analyzing and understanding your customers. Once you have learned about your customers, you're ready to begin planning your marketing strategies. *Strategic marketing planning* is a process that involves three steps: (1) examining your current marketing situation, (2) assessing your opportunities and setting your objectives, and (3) developing a marketing strategy to reach those objectives (see Exhibit 12.8). The purpose of strategic marketing planning is to help you identify and create a competitive advantage, something that sets you apart from your rivals and makes your product more appealing to customers.[41] Most companies record the results of their planning efforts in a document called the *marketing plan.* Here's a closer look at the three steps in the process.

LEARNING
OBJECTIVE   6
Outline the three steps in the strategic marketing planning process

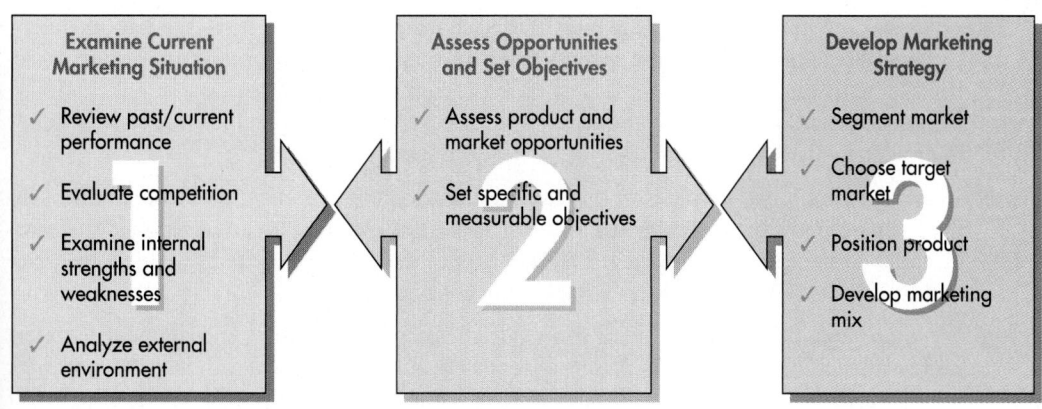

EXHIBIT 12.8

THE STRATEGIC MARKETING PLANNING PROCESS

Strategic marketing planning covers three steps: (1) examining your current marketing situation, (2) assessing your opportunities and setting objectives, and (3) developing your marketing strategy.

Step 1: Examining Your Current Marketing Situation

Examining your current marketing situation is the first step in the strategic marketing planning process; it includes reviewing your past performance (how well each product is doing in each market where you sell it), evaluating your competition, examining your internal strengths and weaknesses, and analyzing the external environment. The complexity of this step depends on the complexity of your business. Whereas giant multinational firms such as Xerox and Nestlé have to examine the current marketing situation for dozens of product lines and geographical divisions, smaller firms, such as individual Jiffy-Lube franchises, have far fewer products to think about.

Reviewing Performance Unless you're starting a new business, your company has a history of marketing performance. Maybe sales have slowed in the past year; maybe you've had to cut prices so much that you're barely earning a profit; or maybe sales are going quite well and you have money to invest in new marketing activities. Reviewing where you are and how you got there is critical, because you will want to repeat your successes and learn from your past mistakes.

Evaluating Competition In addition to reviewing past performance, you must also evaluate your competition. If you own a Burger King franchise, for example, you need to watch what McDonald's and Wendy's are doing. You also have to keep an eye on Taco Bell, KFC, Pizza Hut, and other restaurants in addition to paying attention to any number of ways your customers might satisfy their hunger—including fixing a sandwich at home. Furthermore, you need to watch the horizon for competitors that do not yet exist, such as the next big food craze.

Examining Internal Strengths and Weaknesses Besides reviewing past performance and evaluating competition, successful marketers identify and examine their internal strengths and weaknesses. In other words they look at such things as management, financial resources, production capabilities, distribution networks, managerial expertise, and promotional capabilities. Next, they try to identify sources of competitive advantage in addition to areas that need improvement. This step is important because you can't develop a successful marketing strategy if you don't know your strengths as well as your limitations. On the basis of your internal analysis, you will be able to decide whether your business should (1) limit itself to those opportunities for which it possesses the required strengths or (2) challenge itself to reach higher goals by acquiring and developing new strengths.

Understanding your strengths and weaknesses is especially important when evaluating the merits of global expansion. Selling products overseas requires not only managerial expertise and financial resources but also the ability to adjust your operation to different cultures, customs, legal requirements, and product specifications. Even selling on the Internet requires technological expertise and commitment as well as a thorough understanding of customer buying behavior.

Analyzing the External Environment Marketers must also analyze a number of external environment factors when planning their marketing strategies. These factors include:

- *Economic conditions.* Marketers are greatly affected by trends in interest rates, inflation, unemployment, personal income, and savings rates. In tough times, consumers put off buying expensive items such as major appliances, cars, and homes. They cut back on travel, entertainment, and luxury goods. When the economy is good, consumers open their wallets and satisfy their pent-up demand for higher-priced goods and services.

- *Natural environment.* Changes in the natural environment can affect marketers, both positively and negatively. Interruptions in the supply of raw materials can upset even the most carefully conceived marketing plans. Floods, droughts, and cold weather can affect the price and availability of many products as well as the behavior of target customers.

- *Social and cultural trends.* Planners also study the social and cultural environment to determine shifts in consumer values. If social trends are running against a product, the producer might need more advertising to educate consumers about the product's benefits. After Campbell Soup saw its sales of condensed soups slump, it began running commercials and posting Web pages about the benefits of soup as a cooking ingredient.[42] Alternatively, businesses may have to modify their products to respond to changing tastes. Shiseido, for example, changed its nail polish line after studying what Japanese teens were using.[43]

THINKING ABOUT ETHICS

...CTICS ON CAMPUS

A la...
th...
ta...
ning or re...

Col...
bombarde...
step on ca...
campuses...
cards in d...
into bags...
apply for c...
CDs, and p...
vacations. S...
follow them...
even get stu...
friends pres...

Colle...
the credit c...
loyal to thei...
students ofte...
sidered high-...
them out if...
63 percent o...
card in their ...
dents pay their bills in full each month, and the number
who usually make just the minimum payment is rising.

...ny young people can't even keep up with the min-
...yment. In fact, it is estimated that in one year
...eople younger than 25 will declare personal bank-
...at means for 150,000 young people, their first sig-
...nancial event as an adult will be to declare them-
...lure. And for each one who goes into bankruptcy,
...ozens just behind them, struggling with credit
... In one 4-month period, for instance, a Texas
...shman piled up $2,500 of charges on two Visa
...ur retail credit cards. The student couldn't afford
...$25 minimum a month on all of the cards so she
...d $150 in late fees and over-credit-limit fees.

...le some universities have banned credit card
... from campus to protect students from their
...tially destructive credit practices, many stu-
...'s paternalistic for schools to do so. After all,
...don't give up. They just move across the street
...r locations frequented by students, such as
...k vacation hot spots.

...IONS FOR CRITICAL THINKING

1. ...credit card companies be prohibited from so-
...ing on college campuses? Why or why not?

2. Why do credit card companies target students even
though they have little or no income?

■ *Laws and regulations.* As is every other function in business today, marketing is controlled by
laws at the local, state, national, and international levels. From product design to pricing to advertising, virtually every task you'll encounter in marketing is affected in some way by laws and
regulations. For example, the Nutritional Education and Labeling Act of 1990 forced marketers to put standardized nutritional labels on food products. Although this regulation cost
manufacturers millions of dollars, it was a bonanza for food-testing laboratories.

Best of the Web Best of the Web Best of

SIGN UP FOR ELECTRONIC COMMERCE 101

Think you may be interested in moving your business onto the Net but you don't know where to start? Study the
basics at Electronic Commerce 101 before you plan your marketing strategies. Find out how to succeed in electronic commerce. Read the beginners guide and the step-by-step process of becoming e-commerce enabled.
Learn how to process payments, credit cards, and e-cash. Still have a question? This site has free advice from
over 7,000 experts.

ecommerce.about.com/smallbusiness/ecommerce/library/bl101.htm

■ *Technology.* When technology changes, so must your marketing approaches. Look at Encyclopedia Britannica. It didn't take long for new computer technology to almost wreck this 230-year-old publishing company with annual sales of $650 million. After all, with books costing over $1,500, weighing 118 pounds, and taking 4.5 feet of shelf space, consumers opted for affordable CD-ROM and Internet versions offered by competitors. Today Encyclopedia Britannica delivers information via the Internet and CD-ROMs, as the "Case for Critical Thinking" in Chapter 15 will explain.[44]

Marketers must not only keep on top of today's external environment, they must also think about tomorrow's changes. Sprint, for example, is leading the race in wireless Web users even though the company trailed competitors in its market share for mobile phone subscribers. How? By continually pushing for the best technology—a key factor when it comes to accessing Web sites via mobile phones.[45]

Step 2: Assessing Your Opportunities and Setting Your Objectives

Once you've examined your current marketing situation, you're ready to assess your marketing opportunities and set your objectives. Successful companies are always on the lookout for new marketing opportunities, which can be classified into four options: selling more of your existing products in current markets (market penetration), creating new products for your current markets (new product development), selling your existing products in new markets (geographic expansion), and creating new products for new markets (diversification).[46] These four options are listed in order of increasing risk; trying new products in unfamiliar markets is usually the riskiest choice of all.

With opportunities in mind, you are ready to set your marketing objectives. A common marketing objective is to achieve a certain level of **market share**, which is a firm's portion of the total sales within a market. Objectives must be specific and measurable. Establishing a goal to "increase sales in the future" is not a good objective; it doesn't say by how much or by what date. On the other hand, a goal to "increase sales 25 percent by the end of next year" provides a clear target and a reference against which progress can be measured. Objectives should also be challenging enough to be motivating. As CEO Mitchell Leibovitz of the Pep Boys auto parts chain says: "If you want to have ho-hum performance, have ho-hum goals."[47] Whatever objectives you set, be sure all employees know and understand what the organization wants to accomplish. Every Ritz Carlton employee, for example, attends a daily 15-minute meeting in which managers reiterate the hotel chain's business goals and commitment to customer service.[48]

Step 3: Developing Your Marketing Strategy

Using your current marketing situation and your objectives as your guide, you're ready to move to the third step. This is where you develop your **marketing strategy,** which consists of dividing your market into *segments* and *niches,* choosing your *target markets* and the *position* you'd like to establish in those markets, and then developing a *marketing mix* to help you get there.

Dividing Markets into Segments A **market** contains all the customers or businesses that might be interested in a product and can pay for it. Most companies subdivide the market in an economical and feasible manner by identifying *market segments,* homogeneous groups of customers within a market that are significantly different from each other. This process is called **market segmentation;** its objective is to group customers with similar characteristics, behavior, and needs. Each of these market segments can then be targeted by offering products that are priced, distributed, and promoted differently.

Here are five factors marketers frequently use to identify market segments:

■ *Demographics.* When you segment a market using **demographics,** the statistical analysis of population, you subdivide your customers according to characteristics such as age, gender, income, race, occupation, and ethnic group. *People en Español,* for example, is targeted to the Hispanic American segment.[49] Be aware, however, that according to recent studies, demographic variables are poor predictors of behavior.[50]

■ *Geographics.* When differences in buying behavior are influenced by where people live, it makes sense to use **geographic segmentation.** Segmenting the market into different geographical units such as regions, cities, counties, or neighborhoods allows companies to customize and sell

---

market share
A firm's portion of the total sales in a market

marketing strategy
Overall plan for marketing a product

market
People or businesses who need or want a product and have the money to buy it

LEARNING
OBJECTIVE   7

Define market segmentation and review five factors used to identify segments

market segmentation
Division of total market into smaller, relatively homogeneous groups

demographics
Study of statistical characteristics of a population

geographic segmentation
Categorization of customers according to their geographical location

Best of the Web Best of the Web Best of

DEMOGRAPHICS FOR YOUR MARKETING TOOLBOX

How much does the typical family spend on food away from home? On entertainment? Are these consumer expenditures increasing each year? Find out by visiting the American Demographics Marketing Tools Web site and explore its toolbox of useful information. Read some of the current marketing articles. Follow the link to the Bureau of Labor Statistics (BLS) Web site. With all these sources, no wonder marketers today have more and better data about their customers.

www.marketingtools.com./

products that meet the needs of specific markets. For instance, car rental agencies stock more four-wheel-drive vehicles in mountainous and snowy regions than they do in the South.

- *Psychographics.* Whereas demographic segmentation is the study of people from the outside, **psychographics** is the analysis of people from the inside, focusing on their psychological makeup, including activities, attitudes, interests, opinions, and lifestyle. Psychographic analysis focuses on why people behave the way they do by examining such issues as brand preferences, media preferences, reading habits, values, and self-concept.

- *Geodemographics.* Dividing markets into distinct neighborhoods by combining geographical and demographic data is the goal of **geodemographics.** The geodemographic system developed by Claritas Corporation divides the United States into 40 neighborhood types, with labels such as "Blue Blood Estates" and "Old Yankee Rows." This system, known as PRIZM, uses postal ZIP codes for the geographic segmentation part, making it easy to use specialized marketing programs to reach people in targeted neighborhoods.[51]

- *Behavior.* Markets can also be segmented according to customers' knowledge of, attitude toward, use of, or response to products or product characteristics. This approach is known as **behavioral segmentation.** Web-based BizTravel knows that business travelers have definite preferences and attitudes toward airlines, hotels, pricing, and schedules. So when a customer logs on to plan a trip, BizTravel's automated system is set up to recommend a customized itinerary based on that customer's previous choices and purchases.[52]

When you segment your market, you end up with several customer groups, each representing a potentially productive focal point for marketing efforts. However, keep in mind that a single segment includes customers with a variety of needs. For example, people from the same neighborhood may purchase Colgate toothpaste, but some will buy it for its flavor, others because it prevents decay, and others because it has whiteners. One way to recognize such differing needs is to segment your market into smaller microsegments or niches.[53] Producing and marketing an all-purpose athletic shoe is an example of servicing a market segment, whereas producing and marketing specialized athletic shoes—running, walking, tennis, cross-training, biking, and so on—is an example of servicing a niche market.

Choosing Your Target Markets Once you have segmented your market, the next step is to find appropriate target segments or **target markets** to focus your efforts on. Deciding exactly which segment to target—and when—is not an easy task. Sometimes the answer will be obvious, such as when you lack the necessary technological skills or financial power to enter a particular market segment. At other times, you'll have the resources to compete in several segments but not enough resources to compete in all of them. In general, marketers use a variety of criteria to narrow their focus to a few

psychographics
Classification of customers on the basis of their psychological makeup

geodemographics
Method of combining geographical data with demographic data to develop profiles of neighborhood segments

behavioral segmentation
Categorization of customers according to their relationship with products or response to product characteristics

Health-conscious young adults are a highly sought-after target market for products such as bottled water.

target markets
Specific customer groups or segments to whom a company wants to sell a particular product

suitable market segments. These criteria can include size of segment, competition in the segment, sales and profit potential, compatibility with company resources and strengths, costs, growth potential, and risks.[54]

Targeting is such a critical part of strategic marketing that missteps can be costly, as Motorola found out. The company stayed focused on the traditional cell phone market segment long after rivals Nokia and Ericsson had expanded into the digital phone segment. Furthermore, Motorola didn't respond when it was asked to develop digital phones for AT&T's digital network. By the time Motorola began to work on digital phones, its competitors had grabbed market share and brand loyalty in that fast-growing segment.[55]

Exhibit 12.9 diagrams three popular strategies for reaching target market. Companies that practice *undifferentiated marketing* (or mass marketing) ignore differences among buyers and offer only one product or product line to satisfy the entire market. This strategy, which concludes that all buyers have similar needs that can be served with the same standardized product, was more popular in the past then it is today. Henry Ford, for instance, sold only one car type (the Model T Ford) and in one color (black) to the entire market.

By contrast, companies that manufacture or sell a variety of products to several target customer groups practice *differentiated marketing*. General Motors, for instance, manufactures a car for every personality, and Nike produces a shoe for every athlete. Differentiated marketing is a popular approach but it requires substantial resources because you have to tailor products, prices, promotional efforts, and distribution arrangements for each customer group.

When company resources are limited, *concentrated marketing* may be the best marketing strategy. You acknowledge that different market segments exist and you choose to target just one. Southwest Airlines, for instance, began its operation by originally concentrating on servicing the submarket of intrastate, no-frills commuters.[56] The biggest advantage of concentrated marketing is that it allows you to focus all your time and resources on a single type of customer. The strategy can be risky, however, since you've staked your company's fortune on just one segment.

EXHIBIT 12.9

MARKET-COVERAGE STRATEGIES

Three alternative market-coverage strategies are undifferentiated marketing, differentiated marketing, and concentrated marketing.

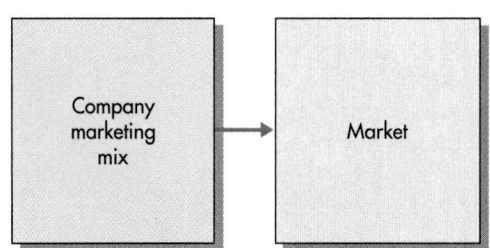

1. Undifferentiated marketing

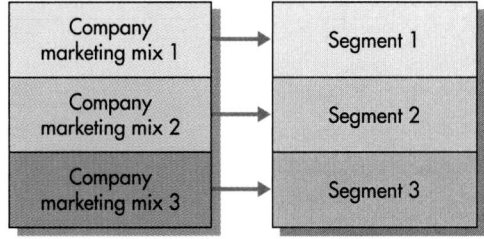

2. Differentiated marketing

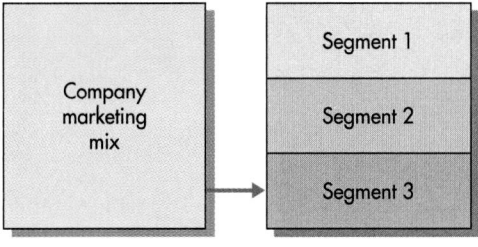

3. Concentrated marketing

Positioning Your Product Once a company has decided which segments of the market it will enter, it must then decide what position it wants to occupy in those segments. **Positioning** your product is the act of designing your company's offering and image so that it occupies a meaningful and distinct competitive position in your target customers' minds.

Most companies position their products by choosing among several differentiating product factors, including features, performance, quality, durability, reliability, style, design, and customer service such as ordering ease, delivery and installation methods, and customer support. For example, Colgate Total is positioned as a toothpaste to prevent gum disease, cavities, and plaque, whereas Rembrandt's Dazzling White is positioned as a toothpaste to whiten teeth. By contrast, Aquafresh Whitening is positioned as a toothpaste that whitens, fights cavities, and tastes good.[57] Chapter 13 explores some positioning strategies based on product factors and pricing. Keep in mind, however, that companies also differentiate their products on the basis distribution, and promotion—the other elements in the firm's *marketing mix*.[58]

Developing the Marketing Mix Once you've segmented your market, selected your target market, and positioned your product, your next task is to develop a marketing mix. A firm's **marketing mix** (often called the *four Ps*) consists of product, price, place (or distribution), and promotion (see Exhibit 12.10). The most basic marketing-mix element is *product,* which covers the product itself plus brand name, design, packaging, services, quality, and warranty. *Price,* the amount of money customers pay for the product (including any discounts) is the second marketing-mix element. *Place* (which is commonly referred to as *distribution*) is the third marketing-mix element. It covers the organized network of firms that move goods and services from the producer to the consumer. *Promotion,* the fourth marketing-mix element, includes all the activities the firm undertakes to communicate and promote its products to the target market. Among these activities are advertising, personal selling, public relations, and sales promotion.

We take a closer look at each of these four marketing-mix elements in the remaining chapters of this text part. Chapter 13 discusses product and pricing strategies, Chapter 14 focuses on distribution strategies, and Chapter 15 discusses promotional strategies.

positioning
Using promotion, product, distribution, and price to differentiate a good or service from those of competitors in the mind of the prospective buyer

marketing mix
The four key elements of marketing strategy: product, price, distribution (place), and promotion

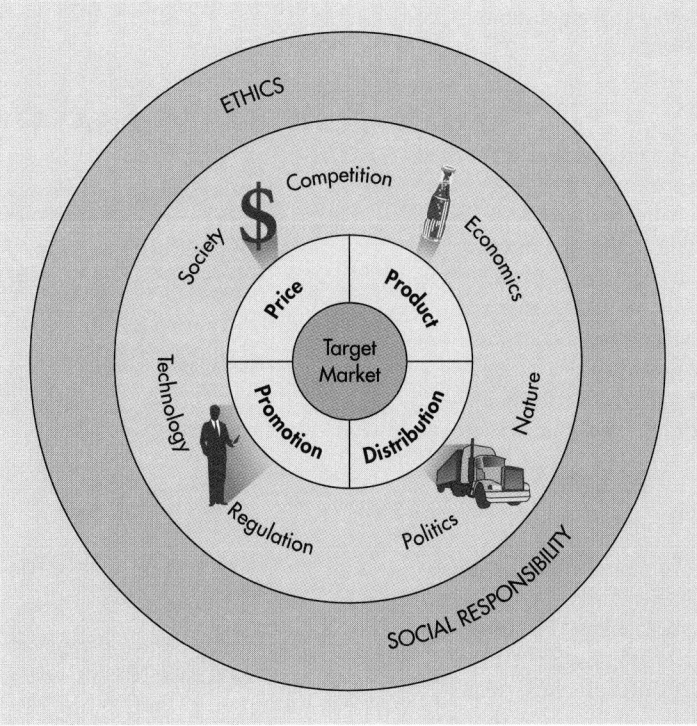

EXHIBIT 12.10

POSITIONING AND THE MARKETING ENVIRONMENT

When positioning products for target markets, you need to consider the four marketing-mix elements plus the external environment.

FOCUSING ON E-BUSINESS TODAY

It Takes More Than a Web Site

It seems like everyone is launching a Web site and selling over the Internet these days. After all, the case for shopping online is compelling. Customers like it for several reasons: they can help themselves, they can save time and money by scouring for products and discounts with their keyboards, they can avoid crowded malls, they have a greater selection of items to choose from; and best of all they can shop from home, day or night, in any state of

LEARNING OBJECTIVE @8

Explain why most e-tailers have lagged in providing effective customer service, and highlight five types of online customer support

dress or undress. Of course, e-tailers like online shopping be-cause it broadens their customer base, they don't have to invest in costly showrooms, and they don't have to hire salesclerks. In fact, all e-tailers have to do is put up a Web site and let customers click their way to the checkout counter. Right?

Many thought so initially. Dot-com companies were told that they could provide self-service as long they offered low prices. But it didn't take long for online retailers to discover that the very issues facing physical stores—order fulfillment, shipping errors, product returns, warranties, and so on—must be faced in the dot-com world as well. In both worlds, customers have questions, need help, and want personal attention.

IT'S THE SERVICE, STUPID

If anything, the world of e-commerce heightens the need for immediate attention to customer needs. For one thing, Web shoppers are less patient and more demand-ing. They've been sold on the idea that the Internet will improve their daily lives. So they have high expectations, such as around-the-clock service. Moreover, they want to know whether goods are actually in stock before they sub-mit a credit card number. And they want to know the e-tailer's shipping and return policies. Finally, they want to be treated as individuals, and they want immediate an-swers to their questions.

A WEB SITE ISN'T ENOUGH

In spite of rising customers' demands, many e-tailers don't take customer service seriously. Some of the hottest online retailers have yet to adopt the fundamen-tal customer service practices of physical stores. To them, self-service on the Net unfortunately means no service. Perhaps that's why two-thirds of e-shoppers abandon their virtual electronic "shopping cart" in the middle of a transaction or before checking out. They

terminate the transaction because they are confused, are concerned about security, have questions, can't find their way to the virtual checkout counter, and have no one to turn to for help.

Some e-tailers have discovered the hard way that having a Web site doesn't eliminate the need for human in-teraction. In fact, online vendors having a quality Internet-based customer support solution is just as critical as physi-cal stores having a customer service department. That's because many customers' questions and problems can't be handled by simply pointing and clicking. To be effective, online support should include a combination of services such as self-help Web pages, toll-free phone support, e-mail, online chat, and live support—when possible.

1-800-Call Us

Toll-free telephone support has been around for decades. Yet, fewer than half of commercial Web sites provide a toll-free phone number. And even if a toll-free number is listed, calls often go unanswered. Many call centers are staffed only during traditional working hours even though Web sites operate 24 hours a day. Moreover, phone-based ser-vice presents additional challenges for products sold on-line. For the average customer, calling the 800 number with a question means disconnecting from their Internet service first. Up to 40 percent of customers who are put in this po-sition fail to complete the sale, choosing instead to find a site that can answer their question.

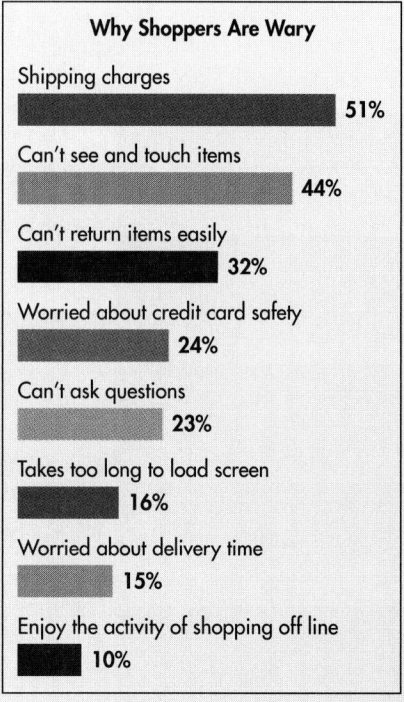

E-Mail Works—Sometimes

Every day Amazon.com hears from more than 20,000 customers with a problem: books ordered online haven't shown up yet, a cute new toy didn't turn out to be so cute after all, a first-time visitor to Amazon's Web site can't figure out how to place an order, and so on. Perched before computer terminals (the vast majority of complaints come in electronically), over 200 customer service reps write one e-mail after another, trying to put things right. As customers' complaints come up on representatives' screens, routine responses are rapidly assembled from a library of 1,400 prescripted remarks, or "blurbs." These responses address almost every conceivable issue, and they are customized with the customer's name and a few other details.

When things get ugly, the reps are authorized to waive shipping charges and placate shoppers with $10 gift certificates. Still, to do this job right, "you need a real passion for the consumer," says the head of Amazon's customer service. "At a company like this, we're the only heartbeat that customers ever hear." So far Amazon's efforts have paid off. The company is rated as the best overall online bookstore mostly because of its service-oriented culture.

Chat and Live Support

Chat is fast becoming a key ingredient in online customer support. Studies show that a text-based chat system can slash the costs of customer service because a single operator can handle multiple customer interactions simultaneously. Some forward-thinking e-tailers are using variations of chat and phone service to provide a Nordstrom-like experience on the Internet.

Customers of Landsend.com, for example, simply click on the Lands' End Live button to immediately engage a customer service representative in an electronic chat conversation. If customers would prefer to talk on the phone, they ask the representative to call them back. Called "personal shoppers," the online service reps can answer customer questions, solve problems, and make suggestions about appropriate merchandise—all in real time. They can even split the computer screen and display apparel combinations (such as a shirt and tie) to help the customer make a decision (see the picture on p. 328).

Live support worked for Eric Pegureo-Winters. Struggling to find a shirt he had previously seen in a Lands' End catalog, he logged on to Landsend.com, clicked the "help" icon, and watched as a sales rep took control of his browser and led him to a picture of the shirt. Then the rep used instant messaging to describe embroidery not visible on the screen. Pegureo-Winters eagerly bought the $50 garment. "I've never received that kind of service online," he says. "I felt like we were walking down the aisle in a store."

OUTSOURCING ONLINE SUPPORT

Because building and maintaining live, in-house Web-based customer support can cost millions of dollars and can take as long as a year to get off the ground, e-tailers are outsourcing online support. Companies such as LivePerson provide a skilled support staff to service millions of queries on a wide variety of products. The company charges e-tailers a one-time setup fee and a small monthly charge. In return, e-tailers get an outside team of customer service people who work "behind the scenes" to provide customers with immediate help when they have a question or problem. Because customers often ask similar questions, many of the answers are preformatted, so representatives can e-mail back what appears to be a personalized answer, just as Amazon.com does.

WHAT'S THE BOTTOM LINE?

The bottom line is this: E-tailers who don't offer good customer support risk losing customers to online competitors who do. The kings of e-commerce such as Amazon.com and Landsend.com are aware of this fact and have found innovative ways to address customers' needs. But plenty of Web retailers still need to get their act together. Which is why most online purchases are never completed, and less than 2 percent of visits to online retail sites result in purchases.[59]

SUMMARY OF LEARNING OBJECTIVES

1. Explain what marketing is.
Marketing is the process of planning and executing the conception, pricing, promotion, and distribution of ideas, goods, and services to create exchanges that satisfy individual and organizational objectives.

2. Describe the four utilities created by marketing.
Form utility is created when companies turn raw materials into finished goods desired by consumers. Time utility is created by making the product available when the consumer wants to buy it. Place utility is created when a product is made available at a location that is convenient for the consumer. Possession utility is created by facilitating the transfer of ownership from seller to buyer.

3. Explain why and how companies learn about their customers.
Companies learn about their customers so they can stay in touch with their current needs and wants, deliver quality products, and provide good customer service. Such attention tends

to keep customers satisfied and helps retain their long-term loyalty. Moreover, studies show that sales to repeat customers are more profitable. Most companies learn about their customers by studying consumer behavior, conducting marketing research, and using technology to capture and analyze customer data.

4. List five factors that influence the buyer's purchase decision.
The purchase decision is influenced by the buyer's culture, social class, reference groups, self-image, and situational factors.

5. Discuss how marketing research helps the marketing effort, and highlight its limitations.
Marketing research can help companies set goals, develop new products, segment markets, plan future marketing programs, evaluate the effectiveness of a marketing program, keep an eye on competition, and measure customer satisfaction. On the other hand, marketing research is a poor predictor of what will excite consumers in the future. It is sometimes ineffective because it is conducted in an artificial setting. And, it is not a substitute for good judgment.

6. Outline the three steps in the strategic marketing planning process.
The three steps in the strategic marketing planning process are (1) examining your current marketing situation, which includes reviewing your past performance, evaluating your competition, examining your internal strengths and weaknesses, and analyzing the external environment; (2) assessing your opportunities and setting your objectives; and (3) developing your marketing strategy, which covers segmenting your market, choosing your target markets, positioning your product, and creating a marketing mix to satisfy the target market.

7. Define market segmentation and review five factors used to identify segments.
Market segmentation is the process of subdividing a market into homogeneous groups to identify potential customers and to devise marketing approaches geared to their needs and interests. The five most common factors used to identify segments are demographics, geographics, psychographics, geodemographics, and behavior.

8. Explain why most e-tailers have lagged in providing effective customer service, and highlight five types of online customer support.
Many e-tailers are new to the retail game. They believed that all they had to do was build a Web site and let customers help themselves. But they soon learned that customers expect the same level of service they experience in brick-and-mortar stores, and more. They want product, shipping, and return information. They have questions, they want personal attention, and they need 24-hour help. Without proper support, customers will continue to abandon their electronic shopping carts. Effective online customer support should include a combination of self-help screens, toll-free phone support, e-mail, online chat, and live support—when possible. In some cases it may be more cost-effective to outsource the online customer support function than to build and maintain an internal customer service department.

KEY TERMS

behavioral segmentation (333)

buyers' market (320)

cause-related marketing (318)

cognitive dissonance (325)

consumer buying behavior (324)

consumer market (324)

customer service (318)

database marketing (327)

demographics (332)

exchange process (319)

form utility (319)

geodemographics (333)

geographic segmentation (332)

market (332)

market segmentation (332)

market share (332)

marketing (318)

marketing concept (321)

marketing mix (335)

marketing research (325)

marketing strategy (332)

need (319)

organizational market (324)

place marketing (318)

place utility (319)

positioning (335)

possession utility (320)

psychographics (333)

relationship marketing (321)

sellers' market (320)

target markets (333)

time utility (319)

transaction (319)

utility (319)

wants (319)

TEST YOUR KNOWLEDGE

QUESTIONS FOR REVIEW

1. What are some of the characteristics of today's customers?

2. How does the organizational market differ from the consumer market?

3. What is strategic marketing planning, and what is its purpose?

4. What external environmental factors affect strategic marketing decisions?

5. What are the four basic components of the marketing mix?

QUESTIONS FOR ANALYSIS

6. If relationship marketing is such a good idea, why don't more businesses do it?

7. How can data mining help companies better understand consumer buying behavior and improve their marketing efforts?

8. Why does a marketer need to consider its current marketing situation, including competitive trends, when setting objectives for market share?

9. Why do companies segment markets?

10. How has the Internet changed the marketing function?

11. When marketing researchers ask survey respondents to answer questions about family, friends, or neighbors, are they invading the respondents' privacy? Please explain.

QUESTIONS FOR APPLICATION

12. How might an airline use relationship and database marketing to improve customer loyalty?

13. How might a company use virtual realty simulations to test-market consumer acceptance of a new-age beverage such as Snapple or Fruitopia?

14. Why is it important to analyze a firm's marketing plan before designing the production process for a service or a good? What kinds of information are generally included in a marketing plan that might affect the design of the production process as discussed in Chapter 8?

15. How might these economic indicators impact a company's marketing decisions? (a) disposable income; (b) consumer price index; (c) inflation; (d) unemployment.

PRACTICE YOUR KNOWLEDGE

SHARPENING YOUR COMMUNICATION SKILLS

Collect some examples of mail communications you have received from companies trying to sell you something. How do these communications try to get your attention? Highlight all the instances in which these communications use the word *you* or even your personal name. How is using the word *you* an effective way to communicate with customers? Does the communication appeal to your emotion or to your logic? How does the company highlight the benefits of its product or services? How does the company talk about price? Finally, how does the company motivate you to act? Bring your samples to class and be prepared to present your analysis of these factors to your classmates.

HANDLING DIFFICULT SITUATIONS ON THE JOB: TURNAROUND AT TRAVELFEST

As a travel agent with Travelfest Inc., in Austin, Texas, you have been both amazed and troubled by recent changes in the travel industry. The upset started when airlines stopped paying a 10 percent commission on airline tickets and set a new limit of a flat $25 commission on one-way domestic flights and $50 on round-trip domestic flights. Your boss, Gary Hoover, has been working night and day to make up for declining revenues caused by the loss of airline commissions. He has tried everything, from direct-mail campaigns to discount coupons to drawings for cruises and weekend getaways. Still, revenues remain flat, and no solution is in sight.

After researching your target markets and your customers' buying behavior, you noticed that about 70 percent of Travelfest's revenues comes from corporate and business travel, and 30 percent comes from leisure travel—mainly trips taken by your corporate customers. Many of your customers are middle- to high-income sophisticated travelers who, according to your sales records, are doing more traveling overseas. This research sparked some ideas about how Travelfest can increase revenue from existing customers.

Given the growth in foreign travel, you'd like to sell videos and audiotape courses in Spanish and other languages. You'd like to offer a complete line of travel products, including luggage, maps, and travel guides, in addition to offering travel seminars led by experienced travelers. These new products might not generate much direct profit, but you believe they will effectively position Travelfest as a full-service agency and will attract customers interested in leisure travel to foreign destinations.[60]

1. What questions do you think your boss might have about your ideas for selling travel-related products?

2. How do your ideas build on Travelfest's internal strengths?

3. How will these new products help you establish better relationships with your customers?

BUILDING YOUR TEAM SKILLS

In the course of planning a marketing strategy, marketers need to analyze the external environment to consider how forces outside the firm may create new opportunities and challenges. One important environmental factor for buyers at Kmart, for example, is weather conditions. When Dennis Charles, head of Kmart's $1.3 billion lawn and garden division, thinks about the assortment and number of products he needs for the chain's stores, he doesn't place any orders without poring over long-range weather forecasts for each market.

In particular, temperature and precipitation predictions for the coming 12 months are critical to Charles's marketing plans, because they offer clues to consumer demand for barbecues, lawn furniture, gardening tools, and other merchandise. By keying product orders and offers to weather patterns, Charles was able to boost profit margins for Kmart's lawn and garden division for five consecutive years.[61]

What other products would benefit from examining weather forecasts? With your team, brainstorm to identify at least three types of products (in addition to lawn and garden items) for which Kmart should examine the weather as part of their analysis of the external environment. Then select one product from your list and come up with five or more questions the buyer at Kmart would be better equipped to answer after studying weather forecasts. Indicate which of the four marketing-mix elements each question is related to and how Kmart might use the answers to develop a more effective marketing plan.

Share your team's list and questions with the entire class. How many teams identified the same products your team did? What questions did the other teams suggest? What other marketing-mix variables were covered in the questions suggested by the rest of the teams?

EXPAND YOUR KNOWLEDGE

KEEPING CURRENT USING *THE WALL STREET JOURNAL*

From recent issues of *The Wall Street Journal* (print or online editions), select an article that describes in some detail a particular company's attempt to build relationships with its customers (either in general or for a particular product or product line).

1. Describe the company's market. What geographic, demographic, behavioral, or psychographic segments of the market is the company targeting?

2. How does the company hold a dialogue with its customers? Does the company maintain a customer database? If so, what kinds of information does it gather?

3. According to the article, how successful has the company been in understanding its customers?

DISCOVERING CAREER OPPORTUNITIES

Jobs in the four Ps of marketing cover a wide range of activities, including a variety of jobs such as personal selling, advertising, marketing research, product management, and public relations. You can get more information about various marketing positions by consulting the *Career Information Center* guide to jobs and careers, the U.S. Employment Service's *Dictionary of Occupational Titles,* and online job-search Web sites such as Headhunter.net, www.headhunter.net.

1. Select a specific marketing job that interests you. Using one or more of the preceding resources, find out more about this chosen job. What specific duties and responsibilities do people in this position typically handle?

2. Search through help-wanted ads in newspapers, specialized magazines, or Web sites to find two openings in the field you are researching. What educational background and work experience are employers seeking in candidates for this position? What kind of work assignments are mentioned in these ads?

3. Now think about your talents, interests, and goals. How do your strengths fit with the requirements, duties, and responsibilities of this job? Do you think you would find this field enjoyable and rewarding? Why?

EXPLORING THE BEST OF THE WEB

URLs for all Internet exercises are provided at the Web site for this book, www.prenhall.com/mescon. *When you log on to the text Web site, select Chapter 12, then select "Student Resources," click on the name of the featured Web site, and follow the detailed navigational directions to complete these exercises.*

Fasten Your Seatbelt, page 322

Today's consumers can use technology such as the Internet to locate a wealth of information about both goods and services. Take, for example, the process of shopping for a car or truck. Go to CarSmart to answer these questions.

1. Check out the Auto Buying Tips. How is this information useful to consumers?

2. Read How to Resolve a Dealer Service Complaint. Under what circumstances would consumers need this information? What part of the buying process does this section address?

3. Do you think car manufacturers and dealers like consumers' being armed with a great deal of information? Why or why not?

Sign Up for Electronic Commerce 101, page 331

Find out how to succeed in electronic commerce by reading the basics, step-by-step process, and beginners guide at Electronic Commerce 101.

1. Read the Beginners Guide to E-Commerce. What is a merchant account? Internet merchant account? What are merchant brokers? What are the advantages of having a merchant account?

2. Under Start-Up Ideas, read about the Amazon.com Associates Program. How does this program work? What are the advantages of this program?

3. Explore Some Model Sites by reviewing three of the Web sites listed. From a consumer's perspective, what do you like or dislike about these sites?

Demographics for Your Marketing Toolbox, page 333

Learning about consumer demographics is one of the first steps in developing an effective marketing plan. To answer these questions, visit the American Demographics Marketing Tools Web site.

1. Review the current issue of the publication *American Demographics.* Read some of the articles. How might this publication be helpful to marketers?

2. Follow the Links and Data and jump directly to the Bureau of Labor Statistics (BLS) Consumer Expenditure data and read the FAQs. What is the Consumer Expenditure Survey, and how is it used?

3. From the Consumer Expenditure homepage, find the Standard Tables and using the latest year of information, click on the Composition of Consumer Unit. Review the table. How much did the "husband and wife only" spend on food away from home? How much did they spend on entertainment? Go back and review some of the other tables. How do data like these help marketers?

Explore on Your Own

Review these chapter-related Web sites on your own to learn more about marketing and customer service.

1. Study demographic trends and other census-related data at the U.S. Census Bureau Web site, www.census.gov/population.

2. MOTI Market Research, iws.ohiolink.edu/moti/research.html, discusses how the Internet is impacting the way firms collect and analyze data about their customers and competitors.

3. Visit the American Marketing Association, www.ama.org, to find out more about this organization and careers in marketing. Be sure to explore the many marketing journals available online, and check out the daily news briefs.

A CASE FOR CRITICAL THINKING

■ *Is Levi Strauss Coming Apart at the Seams?*

Though Levi's has long been the denim darling of the baby boomer generation, young consumers formed a different perception of the famous brand during the 1990s. Teens and young adults found little appeal in the straight-leg Levi's that their parents loved, preferring more trendy, fashionable styles. But sticking with its "one brand fits all" marketing strategies that had worked successfully for years, Levi Strauss ignored the fashion statements of the younger generation. And losing touch with this youthful market created denim disaster for the company.

COMING APART AT THE SEAMS

Throughout the 1990s, Levi Strauss looked the other way as competitors such as the Gap, Lee, Faded Glory, and specialty retailers gained market share among consumers ages 14 to 19. After all, aging boomers still loved their Levi's, and the company's Dockers apparel line had been a solid hit with those core customers. But as the youth segment turned to competitors for jeans with baggier fits, wide pant legs, and bigger pockets, Levi's share of the denim jeans market plummeted from a healthy 31 percent to just 17 percent during the decade. Moreover, annual revenues plunged from nearly $7 billion to just under $6 billion.

To curb the losses, top management closed more than two dozen factories and laid off thousands of employees worldwide. But instead of focusing immediately on ways to regain market share, Levi Strauss launched an ambitious project for improving delivery to retailers. Distracted by the project, the company lost its focus on reaching out to younger customers. Moreover, the company executives, descendents of founder Levi Strauss, failed to encourage innovation of the company's core brand.

EXPANDING POCKETS

Still losing market share, the company finally scrambled to learn more about the perceptions and needs of two targeted consumer segments: youth, ages 13 to 25, and young adults, ages 25 to 35. After learning that younger buyers were interested in unique, uncommon styles, Levi Strauss launched several programs to attract younger consumers. First, it developed the Limited Edition product line, inspired by the movie *Mod Squad,* and restricted product availability to 60 days. In return for the film's featuring Levi's, the company promoted the movie in TV commercials and print ads. "We hear from kids that they want something different and exclusive, and this limited, short product offering is a new strategy for Levi's," explained the Levi Strauss communications manager.

Next, the company moved away from its traditional "one brand fits all" marketing strategy by creating a series of individual brands. For instance, Red Line jeans were positioned as more fash-

ionable and upscale. Nothing on the jeans indicated that they were related to Levi's, and distribution was limited to 25 trendy stores. To reach the youth segment, Levi Strauss introduced such new products as the Silver Tab brand with a baggier fit, Mobile Zip-Off pants with legs that unzipped to create shorts, and Engineered Jeans, a "reinvention" of the traditional five-pocket style with big pockets to hold such items as pagers and cell phones. The company even designed new brands specifically for the baby boomer segment—core customers that the company couldn't afford to lose. These new brands included Dockers Equipment for Legs and K-1 Khakis, a hipper version of the popular Dockers product line.

Going further, Levi Strauss created Original Spin, a high-tech program that allowed consumers to design their own jeans by accessing computerized kiosks at selected stores. And the company introduced more colorful packaging to give its products an exciting, youthful look.

FRAYED SEAMS

Despite its efforts, some of the company's early initiatives missed the mark. E-commerce, for example, was an integral part of the company's initial marketing plan. But its attempt at selling direct to consumers over the Internet failed to increase sales and even angered major retailers. So in early 2000, Levi's declared its e-commerce venture "unprofitable," halted direct sales from its Web site, and began referring customers to Macy's and J.C. Penney's Web sites for product purchases.

It's too soon to predict whether these changes will have an effect on the company's market share. And with the rapid and unpredictable changes in the fashion world, the question remains: Can Levi's be cool again? Can the company turn the brand around? Only time will tell whether the Levi's brand has really regained its cool.

CRITICAL THINKING QUESTIONS

1. Why did the company's market share decrease during the 1990s?

2. Why was Levi Strauss unresponsive to the demands of younger consumers?

3. What steps did Levi Strauss take to regain its market share?

4. Go to Chapter 12 of this text's Web site at www.prenhall. com/mescon. Click on the Levi's link to answer these questions: How is Levi Strauss using its Web site to attract younger consumers? How do the graphics and content reflect the needs and interests of the targeted segment? What points of differentiation are emphasized?

VIDEO CASE AND EXERCISES

■ Terra Chips Bites into the Snack Market

SYNOPSIS

Terra Chips (www.terrachips.com) was founded by Dana Sinkler and Alex Dzieduszycki, two chefs who were looking for a way to differentiate their business from the many catering firms in New York City. The chefs began making snack chips out of taro, parsnip, sweet potato, and other root vegetables. Customers liked the chips so much that the chefs decided to leave catering and start a chip-making business. After Saks Fifth Avenue placed an order for 50 cases—and sold the entire order within two weeks—the entrepreneurs began to realize that their unique chips had huge sales potential. Terra Chips are positioned as a high-quality but affordable luxury, a positioning supported by its higher price, sophisticated packaging, and high-end distribution. Sales have doubled year after year, and now the partners are wondering whether they should introduce Terra Chips to global markets.

EXERCISES

Analysis

1. What is the marketing mix for Terra Chips?

2. How does Terra Chips add form utility? Place utility?

3. How did the co-founders learn about customers' tastes and preferences prior to launching Terra Chips?

4. Which segment(s) of the organizational market did Terra Chips target to gain distribution?

5. Are buyers likely to feel cognitive dissonance after purchasing a bag of Terra Chips?

Application

Is Terra Chips using undifferentiated, differentiated, or concentrated marketing? Should it use the same approach to enter global markets? Explain your answer.

Decision

If Terra Chips wanted to sign a celebrity to endorse its products, who would you recommend? How would this celebrity help Terra Chips increase sales?

Communication

Prepare a two-minute presentation giving the creative experts at the advertising agency the background information they need to write a good commercial for Terra Chips.

Integration

Refer back to Exhibit 4.4 in Chapter 4, which shows key factors for entrepreneurial success. Which of these factors do the co-founders of Terra Chips appear to be demonstrating?

Ethics

Even though Terra Chips are considered snack foods, would it be ethical for the company to promote them as part of a healthy diet?

Debate

Should Terra Chips build a database of consumers who buy its products to use in marketing future products? Team up with another student to prepare a classroom debate on this topic, with one student arguing for and the other student arguing against. Ask the class which side was more persuasive, and why.

Teamwork

In a team of three students, brainstorm a list of six or more questions that Sinkler and Dzieduszycki might ask to uncover consumer reactions to a new product.

Online Research

Using Internet sources, learn more about any new products being introduced by Terra Chips. How do these products differ from the original products created by the co-founders? How do they work within the original positioning for Terra Chips? See Component Chapter A, Exhibit A.1, for search engines to use in doing your research.

MYPHLIP COMPANION WEB SITE

Learning Interactively

Visit the PHLIP Web site at www.prenhall.com/mescon. For Chapter 12, take advantage of the interactive "Study Guide" to test your chapter knowledge. Get instant feedback on whether you need additional studying. Read the "Current Events" articles to get the latest on chapter topics, and complete the exercises as specified by your instructor. Expand your learning with a visit to the "Research Area." There you will find a wealth of information you can use to complete your course assignments.

MASTERING BUSINESS ESSENTIALS

Go to the "Understanding Consumer Behavior" and "Marketing Concept/Strategy" episodes on the Mastering Business Essentials interactive, video-enhanced CD-ROM. Team up with Andrew, the director of marketing at Can Go (an e-business start-up), as he tries to understand customers' behavior by tracing their progress through the company's Web site. Discover how CanGo's Web site guides customers into a purchase, and observe how Andrew handles a mysterious surge of interest in the Web site by Japanese consumers. Finally, help Andrew define the company's competitive position, and develop a general marketing strategy for online gaming.

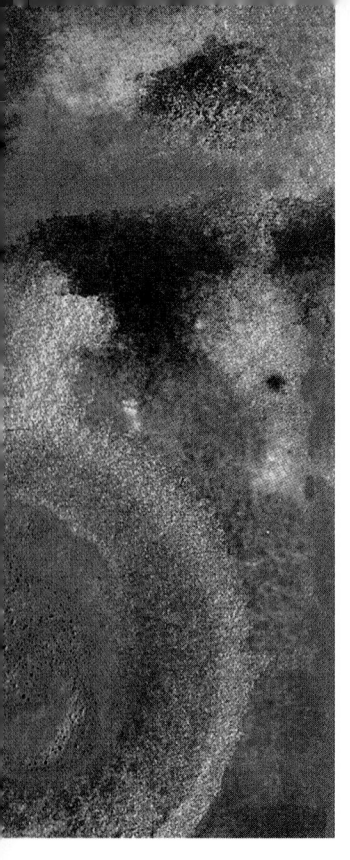

PRODUCT AND PRICING STRATEGIES

13

LEARNING OBJECTIVES

After studying this chapter, you will be able to

1. Describe the four stages in the life cycle of a product

2. Describe six stages of product development

3. Identify four ways of expanding a product line and discuss two risks that product-line extensions pose

4. Highlight several factors that should be considered when developing strategies for international markets

5. Cite three levels of brand loyalty

6. Discuss the functions of packaging

7. List seven factors that influence pricing decisions

@ 8. Explain what dynamic pricing is and discuss why dynamic pricing has been slow to catch on

A LIVING BRAND: MARTHA STEWART, AMERICA'S LIFESTYLE QUEEN

w w w . m a r t h a s t e w a r t . c o m

Martha Stewart and Chuck Conaway, Chairman and CEO of Kmart, celebrate the debut of Martha Stewart Everyday, an extensive line of housewares available at Kmart stores.

She wants to teach you how to create the good life—and sell you everything you need for it. Martha Stewart is the most famous U.S. homemaker, the living, human force behind a powerful personal brand that has become a household word.

Stewart established herself as a lifestyle expert during the 1980s by writing numerous books on such topics as entertaining, gardening, and cooking. By 1991 her popularity had snared the attention of Time, the publishing division of Time Warner. To capitalize on the public's recognition of Stewart's name, Time launched a magazine (*Martha Stewart Living*) featuring her image and advice, and it expanded her audience through a weekly syndicated television show, how-to books, and regular appearances on NBC's *Today* show.

As Stewart broadened her reach through a variety of media, she recognized the vast potential of supplying homemakers with affordable, quality products that they would need for tackling the projects featured in her magazine and on her TV show. So she made a lucrative deal with Kmart to provide consumers with a coordinated line of home products bearing her name. Her dominant image, already familiar to millions of fans, provided strong brand identity for the Kmart product line. Furthermore, the Kmart arrangement provided Stewart with the funds to purchase a controlling interest in *Martha Stewart Living* from Time in 1997.

The purchase gave Stewart complete control over the magazine's content—and the chance to refer readers to her brand-name products as she dispensed advice on everything from making beds to baking cakes. To introduce even more

consumers to the Martha Stewart brand name, Stewart developed new approaches for promoting her products. First, she featured her products in a mail-order catalog, Martha by Mail, and on her Web site, www.marthastewart.com. Then she expanded her relationships with such big retailers as Kmart and Sears, broadening her product mix to include paints, baby items, and garden tools. Moreover, she formed Martha Stewart Living Omnimedia as the parent company for her expanding empire. She also increased her media presence with daily radio features, a syndicated newspaper column, and additional television appearances. In 1999 Stewart took the empire public.

Today Stewart coordinates and integrates all communications and promotions efforts to maximize the impact of her name among consumers and to increase brand identity for her product mix. For instance, if Stewart features an article about rose gardening in *Martha Stewart Living*, she uses the same information as the basis for a segment on her television show and for how-to articles about rose gardening on her Web site. Moreover, each message directs consumers to Stewart's product line of garden tools. For example, the television program guide on Stewart's Web site links the rose-gardening segment with Stewart's garden products for sale at her Web store.

Stewart's savvy product and promotional strategies have transformed the former caterer into one of the nation's leading brands, which features a product mix of nearly 3,000 items. Annual sales of Martha Stewart products currently exceed $225 million, and analysts expect sales to approach $400 million in the near future.[1]

■ DEVELOPING PRODUCT STRATEGIES

product
Good or service used as the basis of commerce

Products such as ones bearing the Martha Stewart brand name are one of the four elements in a firm's marketing mix. From a marketing standpoint, a **product** is anything offered for the purpose of satisfying a want or a need in a marketing exchange. If you were asked to name three popular products off the top of your head, you might think of Doritos tortilla chips, the Volkswagen Beetle, and Gatorade drinks. You might not think of the Boston Celtics, Disney World, and the television show *60 Minutes*. That's because we tend to think of products as *tangible* objects, or things that we can actually touch and possess. Basketball teams, amusement parks, and television programs provide an *intangible* service for our use or enjoyment, not for our ownership; nevertheless, these and other services are products just the same.

Types of Products

Think again about Doritos tortilla chips and Disney World. You wouldn't market these two products in the same way because buyer behavior, product characteristics, market expectations, competition, and other elements of the equation are entirely different. Acknowledging these differences, marketers most commonly categorize products on the basis of tangibility and use.

Tangible and Intangible Products Although some products are predominantly tangible and others are mostly intangible, most products fall somewhere between those two extremes. When you buy software such as Norton Anti-Virus, for example, you get service features along with the product—such as virus updates, customer assistance, and so on. The *product continuum* indicates the relative amounts of tangible and intangible components in a product (see Exhibit 13.1). Education is a product at the intangible extreme, whereas salt and shoes are at the tangible extreme. TGI Friday's restaurants fall in the middle because they involve both tangible (food) and intangible (service) components.

Service products have some special characteristics that affect the way they are marketed. As we have seen, *intangibility* is one fundamental characteristic. You can't usually show a service in an ad, demonstrate it before customers buy, mass produce it, or give customers anything tangible to show for their purchase. Services marketers often compensate for intangibility by using tangible symbols or by adding tangible components to their products. Prudential Insurance, for example, uses the Rock of Gibraltar as a symbol of stability, and its ads invite you to get "your piece of the rock."

Another unique aspect of service products is *perishability*. Because services cannot usually be created in advance or held in storage until people are ready to buy, services are time sensitive. For instance, if airlines don't sell seats on a particular flight, once the flight takes off an unsold seat can never produce revenue. Hotel rooms and movie theatre seats are similar. For this reason, many services try to shift customer demand by offering discounts or promotions during slow periods. Movie theatres, for instance, offer discounted tickets before 6:00 P.M. and restaurants offer early-bird specials.

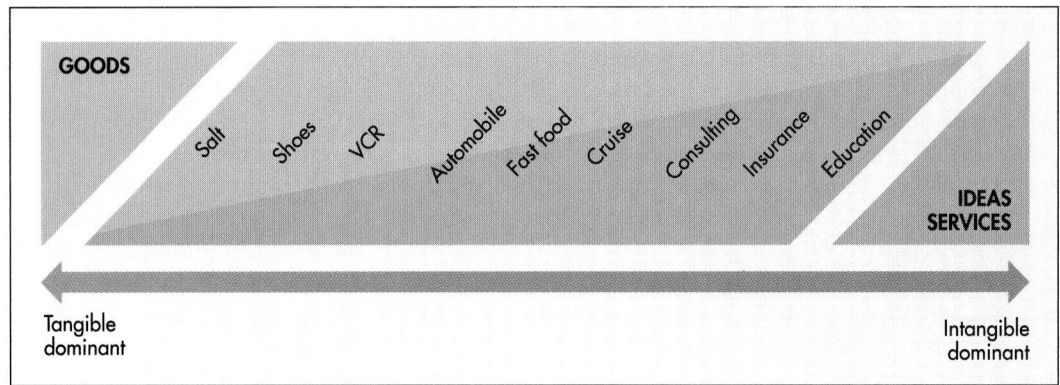

EXHIBIT 13.1

THE PRODUCT CONTINUUM

Products contain both tangible and intangible components; predominantly tangible products are categorized as goods, whereas predominantly intangible products are categorized as services.

Consumer Products As you saw in Chapter 12, organizational and consumer markets use many of the same products for different reasons and in different ways. Even though some products are sold to both markets, those known as *consumer products* are sold exclusively to consumers. Consumer products can be classified into four subgroups, depending on how people shop for them:

■ *Convenience products* are the goods and services that people buy frequently, without much conscious thought, such as toothpaste, dry cleaning, film developing, and photocopying.

■ *Shopping products* are fairly important goods and services that people buy less frequently: a stereo, a computer, a refrigerator, or a college education. Such purchases require more thought and comparison shopping to check on price, features, quality, and reputation.

■ *Specialty products* include CK perfume, Armani suits, and Suzuki violin lessons—particular brands that the buyer especially wants and will seek out, regardless of location or price. Specialty products are not necessarily expensive, but they are products that customers go out of their way to buy and rarely accept substitutes for.

Unsold seats at Yankee Stadium represent lost sales that can never be made up. Baseball teams, like many service businesses, rely on a variety of promotional tactics to pack the house.

■ *Unsought goods* are products that people do not normally think of buying, such as life insurance, cemetery plots, and new products they must be made aware of through promotion.[2]

Organizational Products *Organizational products,* or products sold to firms, are generally purchased in large quantities and are not for personal use. Two categories of organizational products are expense items and capital items. *Expense items* are relatively inexpensive goods and services that organizations generally use within a year of purchase. Examples are pencils and printer cartridges. *Capital items,* by contrast, are more expensive organizational products and have a longer useful life. Examples include desks, photocopiers, and computers.

Aside from dividing products into expense and capital items, organizational buyers and sellers often classify products according to their intended usage.

■ *Raw materials* like iron ore, crude petroleum, lumber, and chemicals are used in the production of final products.

■ *Components* like spark plugs and printer cartridges are similar to raw materials. They also become part of the manufacturers' final products.

■ *Supplies* such as pencils, nails, and lightbulbs that are used in a firm's daily operations are considered expense items.

■ *Installations* such as factories, power plants, airports, production lines, and semiconductor fabrication machinery are major capital projects.

■ *Equipment* includes less expensive capital items such as desks, telephones, and fax machines that are shorter lived than installations.

■ *Business services* range from simple and fairly risk-free services such as landscaping and cleaning to complex services such as management consulting and auditing.

The Product Life Cycle

Few products last forever. Most products go through a **product life cycle,** passing through four distinct stages in sales and profits: introduction, growth, maturity, and decline (see Exhibit 13.2). As the product passes from stage to stage, various marketing approaches become appropriate.

The product life cycle can describe a product class (gasoline-powered automobiles), a product form (sports utility vehicles), or a brand (Ford Explorer). Product classes and forms tend to

LEARNING
OBJECTIVE   1
Describe the four stages in the life cycle of a product

product life cycle
Four basic stages through which a product progresses: introduction, growth, maturity, and decline

EXHIBIT 13.2

THE PRODUCT LIFE CYCLE

Most products and product categories move through a life cycle similar to the one represented by the curve in this diagram. However, the duration of each stage varies widely from product to product.

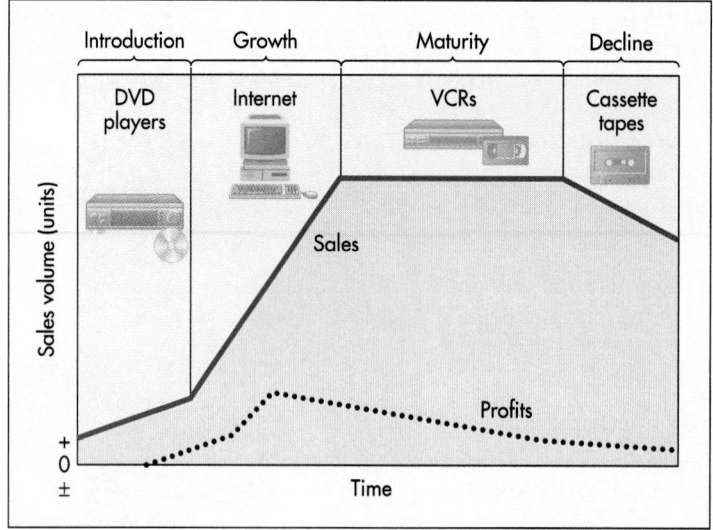

have the longest life cycles, whereas specific brands tend to have shorter life cycles. The amount of time that a product remains in any one stage depends on customer needs and preferences, economic conditions, the nature of the product, and the marketer's strategy. Still, the proliferation of new products, changing technology, globalization, and the ability to quickly imitate competitors is hurtling product forms and brands through their life cycles much faster today. The pace is so frenetic that in the words of GTE's president Kent Foster, "Companies are marketing products that are still evolving, delivered to a market that is still emerging, via technology that is changing on a daily basis."[3] Consider electronics, where product life is now a matter of months: Panasonic replaces its consumer electronic products with new models every 90 days.[4] Why? Smart companies know that if they don't keep innovating, competitors who do will capture the business.

Could Dryel be the next big hit? Procter & Gamble thinks so. The company expects Dryel's sales to reach $500 million, making it as big as Downy or Bounce. But in order to sell a new kind of home dry-cleaning product, P & G must first convince consumers that they need a product they've never heard of.

Introduction The first stage in the product life cycle is the *introductory stage*, during which producers launch a new product and stimulate demand. In this stage, companies typically spend heavily on conducting research-and-development efforts to create the new product, on developing promotions to build awareness of the product, and on establishing the distribution system to get the product into the marketplace. Every product—from personal computers to digital cameras—gets its start in this stage. The producer makes little profit during the introduction; however, these start-up costs are a necessary investment if the new product is to succeed. Procter & Gamble, for example, has spent millions to develop entirely new products such as Dryel, a home dry-cleaning product.[5]

Growth After the introductory stage comes the *growth stage*, marked by a rapid jump in sales and, usually, an increase in the number of competitors and distribution outlets. As competition increases, so does the struggle for market share. This situation creates pressure to introduce new product features and to maintain large promotional budgets and competitive prices. In fact, marketing in this stage is so expensive that it can drive out smaller, weaker firms. With enough growth, however, a firm can often produce and deliver its products more economically than in the introduction phase. Thus, the growth stage can reap handsome profits for those who survive.

Maturity During the *maturity stage*, the longest in the product life cycle, sales begin to level off or show a slight decline. Most products are in the maturity stage of the life cycle where competition increases and market share is maximized—making further expansion difficult. Because the costs of introduction and growth have diminished in this stage, most companies try to keep mature products alive so they can use the resulting profits to fund development of new products. Some companies extend the life of a mature product by modifying the product's characteristics to improve the product's quality and performance.

Consider Nike. Far and away the market leader in sales of athletic shoes, Nike is attempting to renew interest in this mature product form by making such improvements as boosting cushioning in the midsole, reducing shoe weight, and improving the heel.[6] Similarly Whirlpool keeps adding new styles and features to its dishwashers and washing machines, and Hewlett-Packard adds new performance features to its printers and computers to extend the life of these mature products.

Apple Computer's colorful iMac personal computers are another example of the kinds of improvements companies make as products approach the maturity stage. Introduced in the early maturity phase of personal computers, iMac helped Apple grab badly needed market share from competitors in addition to generating a healthy dose of higher revenues and profits. Looking ahead, the company plans to maintain sales momentum through ongoing upgrades, such as adding faster chips without increasing the price of future iMac computers.[7]

Decline Although maturity can be extended for many years, most products eventually enter the *decline stage,* when sales and profits slip and then fade away. Declines occur for several reasons: changing demographics, shifts in popular taste, product competition, and advances in technology. When a product reaches this point in the life cycle, the company must decide whether to keep it or discontinue it and focus on developing newer products. For instance, as digital photography moves ahead, some predict that the film business will dwindle into a small niche market. The challenge for Kodak will be to replace lost film sales with sales of newer products.[8]

Sometimes all a declining product needs is some innovation. The Dean Food Company, for example, decided to keep its chocolate milk product despite a long-term decline in milk consumption. By introducing new single-serving plastic bottles called Chugs, the company increased sales for the product and brought new life to the entire chocolate milk category.[9] Mattel faced a similar decision about declining Barbie sales not long ago. For years, the company had been able to bring Barbie products back from periodic sales dips by introducing innovations such as limited-edition collectible Barbie dolls, customizable Barbie dolls, and even Barbie software. One of Mattel's biggest hits of the 1990s was Holiday Barbie, a limited-edition line of dolls that generated more than $100 million in sales during its peak year. After nearly a decade, however, Holiday Barbie sales began to decline. Long after the holidays were over, some retailers resorted to deep discounts to move any leftover dolls. Finally, Mattel decided to discontinue the line—but not the technique. Limited-edition dolls such as Millennium Barbie remain a major marketing tool for Mattel.[10]

New-Product-Development Process

Suppose your company decides to develop a new product. Where do you begin? Many companies ask that question all the time. In fact, the possibility of developing a big winner is so alluring that U.S. companies spend billions of dollars a year trying to create new products or improve old ones.[11]

In reality, however, most new products are not really new at all; only about 5 percent are true innovations.[12] The rest are variations of familiar products, created by changing the packaging, improving the formula, or modifying the form or flavor. For example, when Kraft took its decade-old Crystal Light powdered fruit drink, added water, and packaged it in fancy plastic bottles, sales of the reinvented brand swiftly surpassed those of Coke's lavishly launched Fruitopia.[13]

Nevertheless, coming up with a winning product is not an easy task. That's because many competitors are likely to get the same idea at the same time. So the victory often goes to the company with the best *product-development process*—the series of stages through which a product idea passes (see Exhibit 13.3). As noted by MIT researcher and journalist Michael Schrage: Effective *prototyping* (or turning an idea into a working model) may be the most valuable competitive advantage an innovative organization can have.[14]

Consider Sony. The company's competitors can take 6 to 10 months to turn an idea into a prototype, but on average Sony takes only 5 days.[15] This faster development time is possible because innovative companies like Sony, Hewlett-Packard, and 3M use cross-functional teams to push new products through development and onto the market.

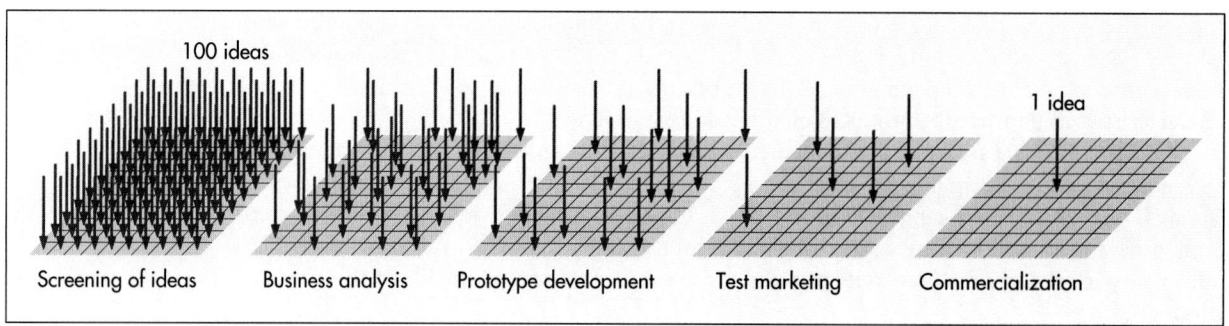

100 ideas

1 idea

Screening of ideas   Business analysis   Prototype development   Test marketing   Commercialization

EXHIBIT 13.3

THE PRODUCT-DEVELOPMENT PROCESS

For every hundred ideas generated, only one or two salable products may emerge from the lengthy and expensive process of product development.

How many of the new products created each year will endure? Nobody knows for sure, but the odds are that most new products will disappear within a few years. According to one authority, less than 1 percent of new product introductions will be around in five years; some will vanish within six months; others will never make it to market.[16] That's because not all ideas become new products. Some are killed midstream because they do not meet the exit criteria that specify what needs to be accomplished before a product moves from one stage into the next. Here are the six stages of the new-product-development process:

LEARNING OBJECTIVE 2

Describe six stages of product development

- *Idea generation.* The first step in the product-development process is to come up with ideas that will satisfy unmet needs. Customers, competitors, and employees are often the best source of new-product ideas. For instance, when Rubbermaid sent 15 two-person teams to willing consumers' homes to observe home-storage practices, the group returned with 300 new-product ideas in just three days.[17] Products such as Post-it notes and masking tape grew from 3M's 15 percent rule—which allows employees at 3M to spend up to 15 percent of their time working on a new-product idea without management's approval.[18]

- *Idea screening.* From the mass of ideas suggested, the company culls a few that appear to be worthy of further development, applying broad criteria such as whether the product can use existing production facilities and how much technical and marketing risk is involved. In the case of industrial or technical products, this phase is often referred to as a "feasibility study," in which the product's features are defined and its workability is tested. In the case of consumer products, marketing consultants and advertising agencies are often called in to help evaluate new ideas. In some cases, potential customers are asked what they think of a new product idea—a process known as concept testing.

- *Business analysis.* A product idea that survives the screening stage is subjected to a business analysis. During this stage the company reviews the sales, costs, and profit projections to see if they meet the company's objectives. For instance, one question the company must answer is whether the company can make enough money on the product to justify the investment. To answer this question, the company forecasts the probable sales of the product, assuming various pricing strategies. In addition, it estimates the costs associated with various levels of production. Given these projections, the company calculates the potential profit that will be achieved if the product is introduced. If the product meets the company's objectives, it can then move to the prototype-development stage.

- *Prototype development.* At this stage the firm actually develops the product concept into a physical product. The firm creates and tests a few samples, or *prototypes,* of the product, including its packaging.

After a long dry spell, Heinz is developing a number of new products. At this Heinz plant, workers sample prototypes of StarKist Tuna in a Pouch, the biggest innovation in tuna packaging since canned tuna was introduced 80 years ago. The company hopes the innovative package will make a big splash with consumers.

COMPETING IN THE GLOBAL MARKETPLACE

AFTER YOU: SOMETIMES IT PAYS TO BE SECOND

Coming in second seems downright un-American in a nation obsessed with firsts. But *not* being first to market can sometimes give companies the winning edge. In fact, countless companies have made their fortunes using what product experts call a "fast-follower" strategy.

Fast followers exist in virtually every industry. Although being a fast follower is no guarantee to success, being second to launch a new product can be a definite advantage. For one thing, you can wait until the first-to-market company has proven that product demand actually exists. For another, you can let the first-to-market educate consumers about the benefits of the new offering—a big task with any new product introduction. Finally, by being second you can improve the product to incorporate consumers' preferences. After all, most first-to-market companies are invaluable teachers. They show you what *not* to do, and basically do the market research for you.

The pattern of the second (or third or fourth) market entrant's prevailing over the early trailblazer shows up frequently. American Express, for example, dragged its feet about getting into the credit card business and introduced its first card eight years after the early leader, Diner's Club International. Where is Diner's Club today? Starbucks didn't pioneer the high-end coffee chain, Pete's of Seattle did. America Online lagged far behind Compuserve and Prodigy for years. Microsoft Word trailed WordPerfect word-processing software. And Wal-Mart didn't pioneer discount retailing.

Nonetheless, being a fast-follower is not without risks. For one thing, just because another company has successfully introduced a product doesn't guarantee that a similar product will also be successful. Plus the first-to-market product usually gets all the attention. Amazon.com, the first online bookseller did, and Barnesandnoble.com is still trying to catch up. Furthermore, the first-to-market may "brand" the product, both grabbing consumers' attention and positioning it as the best, or as the leader. Look at ibuprofen. Advil established such a strong brand early on that other products have had a hard time making inroads. Finally, customers may get comfortable with the first provider and find it too much of a hassle to move over to a better solution.

In short, deciding whether to be first or a fast-follower is a difficult decision indeed. Getting a new product to market first may give you an edge, but remember it takes hard work and enormous energy to stay on top.

■ QUESTIONS FOR CRITICAL THINKING

1. What kinds of risks do you think online grocer Peapod faced by being the first to introduce home-delivery grocery service?

2. What are some brands or products that benefited from being first to market? From being a fast-follower?

During this stage, the various elements of the marketing mix are put together. In addition, the company evaluates the feasibility of large-scale production and specifies the resources required to bring the product to market.

■ *Test marketing.* During **test marketing,** the firm introduces the product in selected areas of the country and monitors consumer reactions. Test marketing gives the marketer experience with marketing the product before going to the expense of a full introduction. It is most often used in cases where the cost of marketing a product far exceeds the cost of developing it. Still, test marketing is not without some risks. Testing a new product may give competitors a chance to find out about a company's newest ideas.[19]

test marketing
Product-development stage in which a product is sold on a limited basis—a trial introduction

■ *Commercialization.* The final stage of development is **commercialization,** the large-scale production and distribution of those products that have survived the testing process. This phase (also referred to as a *product launch*) requires the coordination of many activities—manufacturing, packaging, distribution, pricing, and promotion. A classic mistake is letting marketing get out of phase with production by promoting the product before the company can supply it in adequate quantity. Many companies roll out their new products gradually, going from one geographic area to the next. This plan enables them to spread the costs of launching the product over a longer period and to refine their strategy as the rollout proceeds.

commercialization
Large-scale production and distribution of a product

An estimated 50,000 new products are announced in the United States each year.[20] Sometimes companies launch new products because they have a terrific new concept, other times because they are following in the footsteps of their competitors. When a large organization develops a new product, it is often placed under the supervision of a product or brand manager. A **brand manager** is responsible for developing and implementing a strategic marketing plan for a specific brand and for creating a marketing mix for that brand's products as they move through the product life cycle.

brand manager
The person who develops and implements a complete strategy and marketing program for a specific product or brand

Product-Line and Product-Mix Decisions

To stay competitive, most companies continually add and drop products to ensure that declining items will be replaced by growth products. A **product line** is a group of products that are similar in terms of use or characteristics. The General Mills snack-food product line, for example, includes Bugles, Fruit Roll-Ups, Sweet Rewards Snack Bars, and Pop Secret Popcorn. Within each product line, a company confronts decisions about the number of goods and services to offer. Martha Stewart, for instance, must decide how many types of pie and cake tins the company should produce in its kitchenware line. Similarly, Home Depot must decide how many types of garden hoses it should sell in its retail stores.

product line
A series of related products offered by a firm

An organization with several product lines has a **product mix,** a collection of goods or services offered for sale. For example, the General Mills product mix consists of cereals, baking products, desserts, snack foods, main meals, and so on (see Exhibit 13.4). Three important dimensions of a company's product mix are *width, length,* and *depth.* A company's product mix is *wide* if it has several different product lines. General Mills' product mix, for instance, is fairly wide with five or more product lines. A company's product mix is long if it carries several items in its product lines as General Mills does. A product mix is deep if it has a number of versions of *each* product in a product line. General Mills, for example, produces several different versions of Cheerios—frosted, multigrain, and honey nut. The same is true for many other products in the company's other product lines.

product mix
Complete list of all products that a company offers for sale

When deciding on the dimensions of a product mix, a company must weigh the risks and rewards associated with various approaches. Some companies limit the number of product offerings and focus on selling a few selected items to be economical: Doing so keeps the production costs per unit down and limits selling expenses to a single sales force. Other companies adopt a full-line strategy as a protection against shifts in technology, taste, and economic conditions.

READY-TO-EAT CEREALS	SNACK FOODS AND BEVERAGES	BAKING PRODUCTS AND DESSERTS	MAIN MEALS AND SIDE DISHES	DAIRY PRODUCTS
Cheerios	Bugles Corn Snacks	Betty Crocker Cake Mixes	Bac*Os	Colombo Yogurt
Cinnamon Toast Crunch	Chex Snack Mix	Bisquick	Chicken Helper	Yoplait Yogurt
Cocoa Puffs	Fruit by the Foot	Creamy Deluxe Frosting	Hamburger Helper	
Kix	Fruit Roll-Ups	Gold Medal Flour	Potato Buds	
Nature Valley Granola	Nature Valley Granola Bars	Softasilk Cake Flour	Suddenly Salad	
Oatmeal Crisp	Pop Secret Popcorn		Tuna Helper	
Raisin Nut Bran	Sweet Rewards Snack Bars			
Total				
Wheaties				

EXHIBIT 13.4

THE PRODUCT MIX AT GENERAL MILLS

Selected products from General Mills show a product mix that is fairly wide but that varies in length and depth within each product line.

As Exhibit 13.5 shows, you can expand your product line in a number of ways. You can introduce additional items in a given product category under the same brand name—such as new flavors, forms, colors, ingredients, or package sizes.[21] Frito Lay, for example, extended the Doritos line in 1997 when it introduced its new zesty flavors Salsa Verde and Flamin' Hot Sabrositos to target the U.S. Hispanic market.[22] You can extend the brand to include new products. Crest toothpaste, for example, extended its brand to include dental floss, mouthwash, and brightening solutions. Keep in mind, however, that line extensions involve some risk. An overextended brand name might lose its specific meaning, and sales of an extension may come at the expense of other items in the line. A line extension works best when it takes sales away from competing brands, not when it cannibalizes the company's other items.[23]

LEARNING OBJECTIVE 3

Identify four ways of expanding a product line and discuss two risks that product-line extensions pose

Product Positioning Strategies

In Chapter 12 we defined a product's position as the place it occupies in the consumer's mind relative to competing products. For example, BMW and Porsche are associated with performance, Mercedes Benz with luxury, and Volvo with safety. By organizing products and services into categories based on the perceived position, consumers simplify the buying process. Instead of test-driving all cars, for instance, they may focus on those they perceive to be high-performance vehicles.

Even though consumers position products with or without the help of marketers, marketers do not want to leave their product's position to chance. Companies define the position they want to occupy in the consumer's mind before developing their marketing strategies. Then they choose positions that will give their products the greatest advantage in selected target markets.[24] Marketers can follow several positioning strategies. They can position their products on specific product features or attributes (such as size, ease of use, style), on the services that accompany the product (such as convenient delivery or lifetime customer support), on the product's image (such as reliability or sophistication), on price (such as low cost or premium), on category leadership (such as the leading online bookseller), and so forth.

When choosing the number of distinguishing variables to promote, companies try to avoid three major positioning errors: underpositioning (failing to ever really position the product at all), overpositioning (promoting too many benefits so that no one actually stands out), and confused positioning (mixing benefits that confuse the buyer such as sophisticated image and low cost). Consider McDonald's, for instance. To convince U.S. consumers that McDonald's McCafe coffee shops stand for premium, McDonald's decided to locate the cafes in a separate area of its fast-food franchises. The cafes have their own counter, sign, and coffeehouse-like furniture. Employees wear upscale outfits, beans are gourmet quality, and drinks are served in ceramic mugs—but prices are lower than those of competitors such as Starbucks.[25]

Product Strategies for International Markets

In the course of developing strategies for marketing products internationally, companies must consider a variety of important factors. First, they must decide on which products and services to

LEARNING OBJECTIVE 4

Highlight several factors that should be considered when developing strategies for international markets

METHOD OF EXPANSION	HOW IT WORKS	EXAMPLE
Line filling	Developing items to fill gaps in the market that have been overlooked by competitors or have emerged as consumers' tastes and needs shift	Alka-Seltzer Plus cold medicine
Line extension	Creating a new variation of a basic product	Tartar Control Crest toothpaste
Brand extension	Putting the brand for an existing product category into a new category	Virgin Cola
Line stretching	Adding higher- or lower-priced items at either end of the product line to extend its appeal to new economic groups	Marriott Marquis hotel

EXHIBIT 13.5

EXPANDING THE PRODUCT LINE

Knowing that no product or category has an unlimited life cycle, companies use one or more of these methods to keep sales strong by expanding their product lines.

Best of the Web Best of the Web Best of

BE A SHARP SHOPPER

Put your marketing knowledge to practice. Visit the Sharper Image Web site and think like a marketer. Evaluate the company's product mix. What types of consumer products does this company sell? Who is its target market? Do the products have recognizable brand names? Which other stores carry this type of product? Be sure to read about the company's mission. And don't leave without checking out the new products.
www.sharperimage.com

introduce in which countries. When selecting a country, they must take into consideration the type of government, market entry requirements, tariffs and other trade barriers, cultural and language differences, consumer preferences, foreign-exchange rates, and differing business customs. Then, they must decide whether to *standardize* the product, selling the same product everywhere, or to *customize* the product to accommodate the lifestyles and habits of local target markets. Keep in mind that the degree of customization can vary. At times, a company may change only the product's name or packaging; if it decides to customize, however, the company will be offering a completely different product in different markets.

Of course, understanding the country's culture and regulations will help a company make these important choices, as Chapter 3 discussed. But even the most successful U.S. companies sometimes blunder. Look at Disney. After losing $1 billion in Euro-Disney's first year of operation, the company realized that Paris was not Anaheim or Orlando. For example, French employees were insulted by the Disney dress code, and European customers were not accustomed to standing in line for rides or eating fast food standing up. So rather than continue alienating the Europeans, Disney switched from a standardized to a customized strategy by adjusting its marketing mix for Europeans. The company ditched its controversial dress code, authorized wine with meals, lowered admission prices, hired a French investor relations firm, and changed the name of the complex from Euro-Disney to Disneyland Paris to lure the French tourists.[26]

When Mars Incorporated designs and promotes its M&M candy products for the Russian market, it takes cultural context into account.

Like Disney, many U.S. manufacturers have customized their products after learning that international customers are not all alike. For instance, Heinz now varies its ketchup recipe in different countries—after having discovered that consumers in Belgium and Holland use ketchup as a pasta sauce. In China, Cheetos are cheeseless because the Chinese people don't really like cheese.[27] On the other hand, Kellogg sells the same Corn Flakes in Europe that it sells in the United States. Only recently, however, has Kellogg made significant inroads in European markets, thanks to television advertising and lifestyle changes that favor bigger breakfasts.[28] The latest twist is for companies to adapt non–U.S. products for U.S. markets. For example, Häägen-Dazs has successfully introduced a caramel ice cream from Argentina into U.S. markets.[29]

brand
A name, term, sign, symbol, design, or combination of those used to identify the products of a firm and to differentiate them from competing products

brand names
Portion of a brand that can be expressed orally, including letters, words, or numbers

brand mark
Portion of a brand that cannot be expressed verbally

■ DEVELOPING BRAND AND PACKAGING STRATEGIES

Regardless of what type of product a company sells, it usually wants to create a **brand** identity by using a unique name or design that sets the product apart from those offered by competitors. Jeep, Levi's 501, Apple, and Martha Stewart are **brand names,** the portion of a brand that can be spoken, including letters, words, or numbers. McDonald's golden arches symbol is an example of a **brand mark,** the portion of a brand that cannot be expressed verbally.

The choice of a brand name and any associated brand marks can be a critical success factor. A well-known brand name, for instance, can generate more sales than an unknown name. As a result, manufacturers zealously protect their names. Brand names and brand symbols may be registered with the Patent and Trademark Office as trademarks. As Component Chapter B explains, a **trademark** is a brand that has been given legal protection so that its owner has exclusive rights to its use. Keep in mind, however, that when a name becomes too widely used it no longer qualifies for production under trademark laws. Cellophane, kerosene, linoleum, escalator, zipper, shredded wheat, and raisin bran are just a few of the many brand names that have passed into public domain, much to their creators' dismay.

Sometimes companies, such as Warner Brothers, *license* or sell the rights to specific well-known names and symbols—such as Looney Tunes cartoon characters—and then manufacturers use these licensed labels to help sell products. In fact, 65 percent of Fortune 500 companies have

trademark
Brand that has been given legal protection so that its owner has exclusive rights to its use

COMPETING IN THE GLOBAL MARKETPLACE

WINNING AT THE NAME GAME

Across the United States each day, enterprises and businesses, large and small, are popping up like wildflowers after a spring rain. Eager to gain a competitive edge in these hyper-cutthroat times, owners are laboring to come up with a name for their products and companies. In fact, choosing a name may be the most important decision your company makes. It's everything. It's your calling card. It sets the tone for marketing and may shape your future opportunities. And, it's the one thing that your competition can't take away from you. So how do you make the right choice?

Elements of a Good Name

Great names create an image for the product, and they invoke visual images. Sunkist is one of the best names ever developed because it creates a warm, fresh image that works perfectly with the product. Another effective name is Lean Cuisine. It's memorable, and it says it all. On the Internet, a name should be easy to spell and translate well into other languages. For example, Dell Computer at www.dell.com is much easier than Hammacker Schlemmer (www.hammacker.com), the gift retailer.

In short, a good name should:

- Speak directly to the product's target customers.

- Motivate consumers to buy the product or service.

- Stick in the consumer's mind. (Think about your customers. What do you want the name to mean to them?)

- Be distinctive enough to prevent its unauthorized use.

- Be distinguishable from the competition.

Tips for Choosing Names

Selecting an effective name means looking hard at your company's strategy; it can be frustrating, time-consuming,

and fraught with legal difficulties. So when choosing a name be sure to

- *Find a flexible name for your company.* A good company name shouldn't simply describe what you do now. It should also describe what you hope to become in the future, and allow for a range of products and services to be rolled out over time.

- *Check for potential cultural conflicts.* Rolls-Royce Silver Mist is called Silver Shadow in Germany because *mist* in German means rubbish.

- *Keep it legible.* Is it easy to spell, pronounce, and read?

- *Keep it meaningful, friendly, and personalized.* Names like *Yahoo!*, the Internet search engine, create an immediate emotional bond between consumer and company.

- *Know the law.* The U.S. trademark system allows you to apply for and receive federal trademarks for names. But the law can be confusing so you may want to consult an attorney.

- *Get professional help.* Most global manufacturers use professional name-finding agencies before introducing a new product. Fees for naming consultants can range from $25,000 to as high as $100,000. But considering what's at stake, it can be a small price to pay. After all, a good name may not help sell a bad product, but a bad name can ruin the sales of a good one.

■ QUESTIONS FOR CRITICAL THINKING

1. Why is it important to choose a company name that is flexible?

2. What are the advantages of using professional agencies to assist you in naming your product or company?

Best of the Web Best of the Web Best of

PROTECT YOUR TRADEMARK

Got a winning idea for a new product? Don't forget to protect your trademark by registering it with the U.S. Patent and Trademark Office. Visit this government agency's Web site and learn the basic facts about registering a trademark. Find out how the process works and how much it costs. In fact, why not search its database now to see whether anyone has already registered your trademark?

www.uspto.gov/

national brands
Brands owned by the manufacturers and distributed nationally

private brands
Brands that carry the label of a retailer or a wholesaler rather than a manufacturer

generic products
Products characterized by a plain label, with no advertising and no brand name

---

LEARNING
OBJECTIVE   *5*

Cite three levels of brand loyalty

brand loyalty
Commitment to a particular brand

brand awareness
Level of brand loyalty at which people are familiar with a product; they recognize it

brand preference
Level of brand loyalty at which people habitually buy a product if it is available

brand insistence
Level of brand loyalty at which people will accept no substitute for a particular product

family branding
Using a brand name on a variety of related products

licensing agreements. Licensing can be a terrific source of revenue. General Mills alone has more than 1,200 licensing agreements that cover everything from clothes to cologne and generate annual revenues of $1.1 billion.[30]

Brand Categories

Brand names may be owned by manufacturers, retailers, wholesales, and a variety of business types. Brands offered and promoted by a national manufacturer, such as Procter & Gamble's Tide detergent and Pampers disposable diapers, are called **national brands. Private brands** are not linked to a manufacturer but instead carry a wholesaler's or a retailer's brand. DieHard batteries and Kenmore appliances are private brands sold by Sears. As an alternative to branded products, some retailers also offer **generic products,** which are packaged in plain containers that bear only the name of the product. Generic products can cost up to 40 percent less than brand-name products because of uneven quality, plain packaging, and lack of promotion. Yet generic goods have found a definite market niche, as a look at your local supermarket shelves will confirm.

Brand Equity and Loyalty

A brand name is often an organization's most valuable asset because it provides customers with a way of recognizing and specifying a particular product so that they can choose it again or recommend it to others. This notion of the value of a brand is also called *brand equity*. Strong brands often command a premium price in the marketplace, as Nike shoes, the North Face ski wear, Bobbie Brown cosmetics, and Evian water do.

Customers who buy the same brand again and again are evidence of the strength of **brand loyalty,** or commitment to a particular brand. Brand loyalty can be measured in degrees. The first level is **brand awareness,** which means that people are likely to buy a product because they are familiar with it. The next level is **brand preference,** which means people will purchase the product if it is available, although they may still be willing to experiment with alternatives if they cannot find the preferred brand. The third and ultimate level of brand loyalty is **brand insistence,** the stage at which buyers will accept no substitute.

Companies can take various approaches to building brands. One approach is to create separate brands for products targeted to different customer segments. For example, Second Cup Limited, a Canadian company, uses three distinct coffeehouse brands—Coffee Plantation, Gloria Jean's, and Coffee People—to target three geographical segments. The opposite approach is illustrated by Starbucks, which operates under one brand everywhere in the world.[31] Yet another approach is illustrated by the Gap. The $8 billion company has put its main brand on BabyGap and GapBody stores as well as its GapScents fragrances. Yet it has maintained separate brand identities for Banana Republic and Old Navy, two chains aimed at distinctly different customer segments.[32]

Family Branding   An increasing number of companies have been using **family branding** (using one brand on a variety of related products) to add to their product lines. Kraft, for example, has extended its Jell-O product line to include gelatin in a cup, pudding in a cup, and cheesecake snacks in a cup. These products build on the convenience-with-quality image of the Jell-O family brand.[33]

Building on the name recognition of an existing brand cuts the costs and risks of introducing new products. However, there are limits to how far a brand name can be stretched to accommodate new products and still fit the buyer's perception of what the brand stands for. Snickers ice cream bars and Dr. Scholl's socks and shoes worked as brand extensions, but Bic perfume and Rubbermaid computer accessories did not.

After years of being one of the coolest brands on the block, some think Tommy Hilfiger has overextended his brand. By plastering his name on everything from linens to infant clothes and pushing the brand into over 10,000 U.S. department stores and even discount outlets, Hilfiger alienated his loyal customers. As one customer put it, "Even cheap stores sell Tommy Hilfiger."[34] Richard Branson, founder of Virgin, has also been criticized of overextending the Virgin brand. Branson has slapped the Virgin name and logo on a chaotic jumble of hundreds of products—from airplanes to cola to financial services—putting it in danger of losing its identity. "Virgin makes no sense; it's completely unfocused," says the head of one New York communications firm.[35]

Co-Branding Co-branding is another way you can strengthen your brands and products. **Co-branding** occurs when two or more companies team up to closely link their names in a single product. Two examples of successful co-branding include Kellogg's Pop Tarts made with Smucker's jam and Nabisco Cranberry Newtons filled with Ocean Spray cranberries. Co-branding can help companies reach new audiences and tap the equity of particularly strong brands.[36] Moreover, it can help change a product's image. In an attempt to associate the Kodak brand with the output side of digital photography, the company has been co-branding its name with all things digital. The Kodak name sits above Lexmark's logo on an inkjet printer (one of the first to print photographic inkjet paper), and it's all over the Web sites of companies that trumpet their use of Kodak processing and papers.[37]

co-branding
Partnership between two or more companies to closely link their brand names together for a single product

Packaging and Labeling Your Products

Most products need some form of packaging to protect the product from damage or tampering and to make it convenient for customers to purchase. Packaging also makes products easier to display and facilitates the sale of smaller products. In addition, packaging can provide convenience, as with food products that are ready to eat right out of the wrapper. Quaker Oats, for example, has gained considerable market share by switching from bulky boxes to easy-open, lower-priced bags for its cereal products.[38] In some cases, packaging is an essential part of the product itself, such as microwave popcorn or toothpaste in pump dispensers.

Besides function, however, packaging plays an important role in a product's marketing strategy because most consumer buying decisions are made in the store. As a result, companies spend big bucks on packaging to attract consumer attention and to promote a product's benefits through the package's shape, composition, and design. Innovative packaging—such as Mentadent toothpaste's two-chamber package with pump—can give your product a powerful marketing boost, whereas a poorly designed package may drive consumers away.

Labeling is an integral part of packaging. Whether the label is a separate element attached to the package or a printed part of the container, it serves to identify a brand. Sometimes the label also gives grading information about the product or information about ingredients, operating procedures, shelf life, or risks. The labeling of foods, drugs, cosmetics, and many health products is regulated under various federal laws, which often require disclosures about potential dangers, benefits, and other issues consumers need to consider when making a buying decision.

Labels do more than communicate with consumers. They are also used by manufacturers and retailers as a tool for monitoring product performance and inventory. **Universal Product Codes (UPCs),** those black stripes on packages, give companies a cost-effective method of tracking the movement of goods. Store checkout scanners read UPC codes and relay the identity, sales, and prices of all products to the retailer's computer system. Such data can help retailers and manufacturers measure the effectiveness of promotions such as coupons and in-store displays.

LEARNING
OBJECTIVE 6
Discuss the functions of packaging

Universal Product Codes (UPCs)
A bar code on a product's package that provides information read by optical scanners

■ DEVELOPING PRICING STRATEGIES

Pricing, the second major component of a firm's marketing mix, is often one of the most critical decisions a company must make. Price is the only element in a company's marketing mix that produces revenue—all other elements represent cost. Thus, setting a product's price not only determines the amount of income your company will generate from sales of that product but it can differentiate the product from competition. As you can imagine, determining the right price is not an easy task. If a company charges too much, it will generate fewer sales; if it charges too little, it will sacrifice potential profits.

Break-Even Analysis

break-even analysis
Method of calculating the minimum volume of sales needed at a given price to cover all costs

variable costs
Business costs that increase with the number of units produced

fixed costs
Business costs that remain constant regardless of the number of units produced

break-even point
Sales volume at a given price that will cover all of a company's costs

How does a company determine the amount of profit it will earn by selling a certain product? **Break-even analysis** is a tool companies use to determine the number of units of a product they must sell at a given price to cover all manufacturing and selling costs, or to break even. In break-even analysis, you consider two types of costs. **Variable costs** change with the level of production. These include raw materials, shipping costs, and supplies consumed during production. **Fixed costs,** by contrast, remain stable regardless of the number of products produced. These costs include rent payments, insurance premiums, and real estate taxes. The total cost of operating the business is the sum of a firm's variable and fixed costs.

The **break-even point** is the minimum sales volume the company must achieve to avoid losing money. Sales volume above the break-even point will generate profits, whereas sales volume below the break-even amount will result in losses. You can determine the break-even point in number of units with this simple calculation:

$$Break\text{-}even\ point = \frac{Fixed\ costs}{Selling\ price\ per\ unit - Variable\ costs\ per\ unit}$$

For example, if you wanted to price haircuts at $20 and you had fixed costs of $60,000 and variable costs per haircut of $5, you would need to sell 4,000 haircuts to break even:

$$Break\text{-}even\ point\ (in\ units) = \frac{\$60,000}{\$20 - \$5} = 4,000\ units$$

Of course, $20 isn't your only pricing option. Why not charge $30 instead? When you charge the higher price, you need to give only 2,400 haircuts to break even (see Exhibit 13.6). However, before you raise your haircut prices to $30, bear in mind that a lower price may attract more customers and enable you to make more money in the long run.

Break-even analysis doesn't dictate what price you should charge; rather, it provides some insight into the number of units you have to sell at a given price to make a profit. This analysis is especially useful when you are trying to calculate the effect of running a special pricing promotion, and using spreadsheet software allows you to try different prices and see the results.

Factors Affecting Pricing Decisions

A company's pricing decisions are determined by manufacturing and selling costs, competition, and the needs of wholesalers and retailers who distribute the product to the final customer. In addition, pricing is influenced by a firm's marketing objectives, government regulations, consumers' perceptions, and consumer demand.

LEARNING
OBJECTIVE   7

List seven factors that influence pricing decisions

EXHIBIT 13.6

BREAK-EVEN ANALYSIS

The break-even point is the point at which revenues just cover costs. After fixed costs and variable costs have been met, any additional income represents profit. The graph shows that at $20 per haircut, the break-even point is 4,000 haircuts; charging $30 yields a break-even point at only 2,400 haircuts.

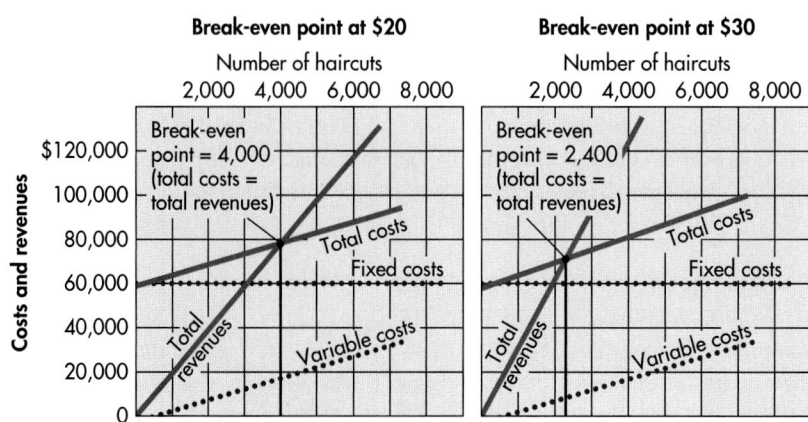

■ *Marketing objectives.* The first step in setting a price is to match it to the objectives you set in your strategic marketing plan. Is your goal to increase market share, increase sales, improve profits, project a particular image, or combat competition? Consider Intel. This Silicon Valley chipmaker slashed prices on its Pentium brand microprocessors to boost sales and fend off lower-priced rival brands.[39] Rolex takes a different approach, using premium pricing along with other marketing-mix elements to give its watches a luxury position.

■ *Government regulations.* Government plays a big role in pricing in many countries. To protect consumers and encourage fair competition, the U.S. government has enacted various price-related laws over the years. Three important classes of pricing are regulated: (1) *price fixing*— an agreement among two or more companies supplying the same type of products as to the prices they will charge, (2) *price discrimination*—the practice of unfairly offering attractive discounts to some customers but not to others, and (3) *deceptive pricing*—pricing schemes that are considered misleading.

■ *Consumer perceptions.* Another consideration is the perception of quality that your price will elicit from your customers. When people shop, they usually have a rough price range in mind. An unexpectedly low price triggers fear that the item is of low quality. South Korean carmaker Hyundai, for example, decided not to cut prices when the dollar gained strength against the Korean won, because the company did not want to reinforce an image of shoddy goods.[40] On the other hand, an unexpectedly high price makes buyers question whether the product is worth the money.

■ *Consumer demand.* Whereas a company's costs establish a floor for prices, demand for a product establishes a ceiling. Theoretically, if the price for an item is too high, demand falls and the producers reduce their prices to stimulate demand. Conversely, if the price for an item is too low, demand increases and the producers are motivated to raise prices. As prices climb and profits improve, producers boost their output until supply and demand are in balance and prices stabilize. Nonetheless, the relationship between price and demand isn't always this perfect. Some goods and services are relatively insensitive to changes in price; others are highly responsive. Marketers refer to sensitivity as **price elasticity**—how responsive demand will be to a change in price.

price elasticity
A measure of the sensitivity of demand to changes in price

Pricing Methods

Developing an effective price for your product is like a game of chess: Those who make their moves one at a time—seeking to minimize immediate losses or to exploit immediate opportunities—will be beaten by those who plan a few moves ahead. In other words, every element in the marketing mix must be carefully coordinated to support an overall marketing strategy. Here are a few methods that marketers use to set their prices.

Cost-Based and Priced-Based Pricing Many companies simplify the pricing task by using *cost-based pricing* (also known as cost plus pricing). They price by starting with the cost of producing a good or a service and then add a markup to the cost of the product. This form of pricing, while simple, makes little sense. First, any pricing that ignores demand and competitor prices is not likely to lead to the best price. Second, although cost-based pricing may ensure a certain profit, companies using this strategy tend to sacrifice profit opportunity.

Recent thinking holds that cost should be the last item analyzed in the pricing formula, not the first. Companies that use *priced-based pricing* can maximize their profit by first establishing an optimal price for a product or service. The product's price is based on an analysis of a product's competitive advantages, the users' perception of the item, and the market being targeted. Once the desired price has been established, the firm focuses its energies on keeping costs at a level that will allow a healthy profit. Keep in mind that although few businesses fail from overpricing their products, many more will fail from underpricing them.[41]

Price Skimming A product's price seldom remains constant and will vary depending on the product's stage in its life cycle. During the introductory phase, for example, the objective might be to recover product development costs as quickly as possible. To achieve this goal, the manufacturer might charge a high initial price—a practice known as **skimming**—and then drop the price later, when the product is no longer a novelty and competition heats up. Products such as HDTV and

skimming
Charging a high price for a new product during the introductory stage and lowering the price later

Best of the Web Best of the Web Best of

UNCOVERING HIDDEN COSTS

When you buy something online, the selling price is usually only part of your *total* cost. Factor in hidden costs such as shipping and sales tax, and the total cost can vary dramatically from one Web site to another. Using comparison-shopping sites can help you ferret out hidden costs. Take a look at Best Book Buys, which compares the total cost of buying a book from a variety of Internet sources. Check out one of the best-selling books or search for your favorite book. Click to see a table comparing the item price, shipping cost, and total cost at different retail Web sites. Then simply click to buy.

www.bestbookbuys.com/

flat-screen monitors are perfect examples of this practice. Price skimming makes sense under two conditions: if the product's quality and image support a higher price, and if competitors cannot easily enter the market with competing products and undercut the price.

Penetration Pricing Rather than setting a high initial price to skim off a small but profitable market segment, a company might try to build sales volume by charging a low initial price, a practice known as **penetration pricing.** This approach has the added advantage of discouraging competition, because the low price (which competitors would be pressured to match) limits the profit potential for everyone. America Online (AOL) used this strategy when it adopted the $19.95 monthly flat rate Internet access charge several years ago. AOL wanted every desktop it could get, even at a financial loss. The strategy worked. Today AOL is the world's largest Internet service provider.

Penetration pricing can also help you expand the entire product category by attracting customers who wouldn't have purchased at higher, skim-pricing levels. Furthermore, if your company is new to a category pioneered by another company, this strategy can help you take customers away from the pioneer.[42] Still, the strategy makes most sense when the market is highly price sensitive so that a low price generates additional sales and the company can maintain its low-price position long enough to keep out competition.

penetration pricing
Introducing a new product at a low price in hopes of building sales volume quickly

Price Adjustment Strategies

Once a company has set a product's price, it may choose to adjust that price from time to time to account for changing market situations or changing customer preferences. Three common price adjustment strategies are price discounts, bundling, and dynamic pricing.

discount pricing
Offering a reduction in price

Price Discounts When you use **discount pricing,** you offer various types of temporary price reductions, depending on the type of customer being targeted and the type of item being offered. You may decide to offer a trade discount to wholesalers or retailers as a way of encouraging orders, or you may offer cash discounts to reward customers who pay cash or pay promptly. You may offer a quantity discount to buyers who buy large volumes, or you may offer a seasonal discount to buyers who buy merchandise or services out of season.

Another way to discount products is by *value pricing* them, charging a fairly affordable price for a high-quality offering. Many restaurants, including Friendly's, offer value menus for certain times of the day or certain customer segments, such as seniors. This strategy builds loyalty among price-conscious customers without damaging a product's quality image.

Although discounts are a popular way to boost sales of a product, the downside is that they can touch off price wars between competitors. Price wars encourage customers to focus only on a product's pricing, and not on its value or benefits. Thus, they can hurt a business—even an entire industry—for years. Consider the price war that Web-based Amazon.com started when it began selling *New York Times* best-selling books at a 50 percent discount in an effort to bring more customers to its site. Online rivals Barnesandnoble.com and Borders.com quickly matched Amazon.com's prices, and smaller bookstores were forced to lower their prices on best-sellers. To offset the loss of revenue, some small bookstores stocked their shelves with more profitable book categories, such as specialty books. Others could not compete and eventually closed up shop.[43]

Bundling Sometimes sellers combine several of their products and sell them at one reduced price. This practice, called **bundling,** can promote sales of products consumers might not otherwise buy—especially when the combined price is low enough to entice them to purchase the bundle. Examples of bundled products are season tickets, vacation packages, sales of computer software with hardware, and wrapped packages of shampoo and conditioner. Bundling products and services can make it harder for consumers to make price comparisons.

bundling
Combining several products and offering the bundle at a reduced price

Dynamic Pricing **Dynamic pricing** is the opposite of fixed pricing. Using Internet technology, companies continually reprice their products and services to meet supply and demand. Dynamic pricing not only enables companies to move slow-selling merchandise instantly, but it also allows companies to experiment with different pricing levels. Because price changes are immediately posted to electronic catalogs or Web sites, customers always have the most current price information. Airlines and hotels are notorious for this type of continually adjusted pricing. In addition to posting current prices on their homepages and many travel Web sites, many major airlines and hotels send customers weekly e-mail notifications listing special discount fares.[44]

dynamic pricing
Charging different prices depending on individual customers and situations

Three popular dynamic pricing tactics are:

- *Auction pricing,* where buyers bid against each other and the highest bid buys the product
- *Group buying,* where buyers obtain volume discount prices by joining buying groups
- *Name-your-price,* where buyers specify how much they are willing to pay for a product and sellers can choose whether to sell at that price

All three are changing the way buyers and sellers conduct electronic business, as this chapter's Focusing on E-Business feature discusses. (For additional discussion of "Hot Online Pricing Strategies," consult Part 5 of this text's online supplement, E-Business in Action, at www.prenhall.com/mescon.)

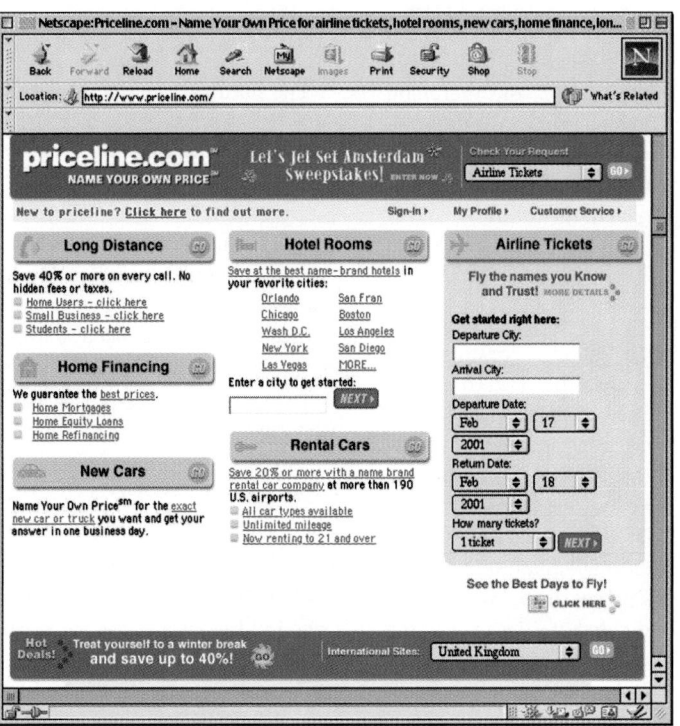

Thanks to the Internet, new pricing models such as name-your-own-price used by Priceline.com are becoming more and more popular. Priceline.com allows consumers to say what they're willing to pay for goods such as airline tickets, then tries to find sellers who will meet buyers' terms.

FOCUSING ON E-BUSINESS TODAY

A Revolution in Pricing? Not Yet

The Internet and its e-commerce ushered in a new era of dynamic pricing, in which prices are not fixed but change from transaction to transaction. However, dynamic pricing has not caused the pricing revolution that many thought it would. Despite years of experimenting with different strategies, e-merchants are still struggling to find ways of using dynamic pricing to attract as many customers as possible and fatten up razor-thin profit margins.

LEARNING OBJECTIVE @ 8

Explain what dynamic pricing is and discuss why dynamic pricing has been slow to catch on

PROMISES, PROMISES

Posting prices on the Internet was expected to offer online retailers a number of advantages. To begin with, e-tailers could change prices in response to demand with the click of a mouse, and they could do so as frequently as they desired, making it possible to fine-tune pricing strategies. However, the real payoff was supposed to be better information on exactly how price-sensitive customers are. For instance, by planting a cookie on a customer's hard drive, e-sellers could learn what kinds of prices a customer had or hadn't been willing to pay in the past. By mining this data, sellers could then reduce a price to spur the customer to buy, or they could raise a price if the purchasing pattern suggested the customer was not particularly price sensitive. If the customer didn't care whether a DVD cost $15.95 or $20.95, the merchant could charge that customer the higher price on the spot. Using that same cookie, e-businesses could also customize the prices that the customer would see when logging on to the company's Web site in the future.

EASIER SAID THAN DONE

Nonetheless, putting these pricing strategies into practice has turned out to be exceptionally difficult. For one thing, consumers are outraged when they discover they were charged more than someone else was for the same product. Online bookseller Amazon.com conducted a marketing test, varying prices to gauge the effect on demand. When customers learned they were paying different prices for the same DVD movies, they were irate. After receiving heated complaints, Amazon.com announced that it would refund the difference between the highest and lowest prices, and it promised consumers that it would never conduct such tests again.

Of course, catalog merchants have been charging customers different prices for years. Most catalog merchants print different catalogs—with different product selections and varying prices—for different parts of the country. When a customer calls to place an order, the sales rep first asks the customer for the number on the back of the catalog so that the rep knows which prices to charge the customer. But no one kicks up a fuss, because few catalog customers know what others are paying.

COMPLEX COMPARISONS

Unlike catalogs, the Internet allows consumers to compare prices and to find out whether other merchants are offering a better deal. Online pricing-comparison engines (shopbots) are supposed to make it easy for consumers to find the lowest price of any goods. Consumers can log on to sites such as Pricescan.com or Bottomdollar.com and use the engines to easily compare the prices and features of more than 10,000 products. But performing such price comparisons can be tedious.

Moreover, making effective use of competitive price information has been more difficult for consumers than e-tailers and economists originally thought. For one thing, price comparisons are far from straightforward. They must include a range of shipping options and fees, state-based sales taxes, and any special offers from individual merchants. Plus, the time it takes to look up the best prices for a collection of items, such as books or DVDs, can easily outweigh savings of a dollar or two. Besides, when it comes to e-commerce, not all consumers are price sensitive.

CUSTOMERS WANT CONVENIENCE

"The number one driver of purchases on the Internet is convenience," says Gartner Group consultants. "The drive for price is much lower." A shopper eager to get through the weekly grocery list has little time to bargain over every item on the list. In addition to convenience, many buyers place a value on—and are willing to pay for—reliable customer service, a familiar brand, or a trusted relationship with a particular product, merchant, or supplier. In fact, customers will pay up to $3 more for a book at Amazon than at other Web sites. Online grocer Webvan can charge prices similar to those charged by physical supermarkets because the company provides top-notch service, such as perfectly selected produce and groceries delivered right to your kitchen counter.

CATCH-22

It may be a while before online retailers can truly exploit the full theoretical pricing advantages of the Internet—if they ever do. Many e-businesses are still keeping prices low to attract price-sensitive consumers (see the accompanying graph). But low-price strategies haven't necessarily served online retailers well; in fact, they are part of the blame for the dot-com fallout at the turn of the century. Surviving e-tailers will continue to experiment with innovative pricing strategies. But if they push too hard to raise prices, they may risk alienating customers. Some e-sellers may decide to abandon dynamic pricing strategies altogether, using the Internet to set more effective fixed prices.[45]

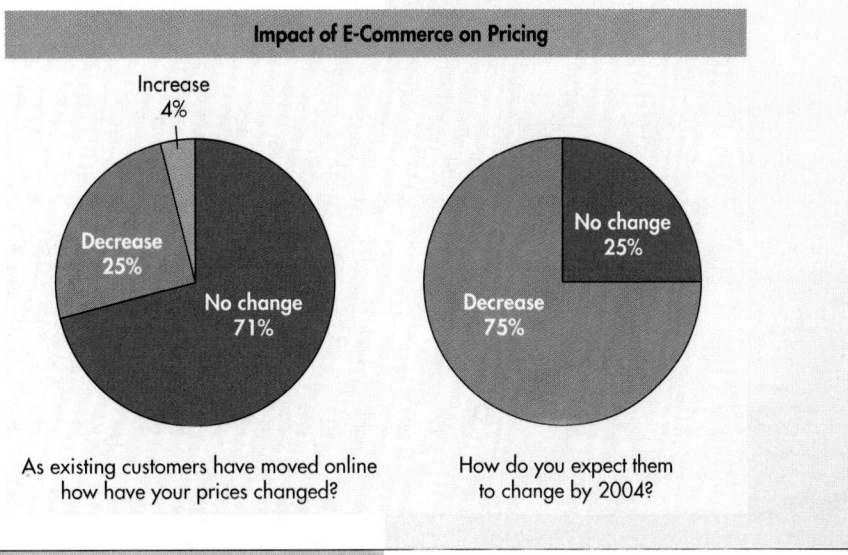

Impact of E-Commerce on Pricing

Increase 4%
Decrease 25%
No change 71%

As existing customers have moved online how have your prices changed?

No change 25%
Decrease 75%

How do you expect them to change by 2004?

SUMMARY OF LEARNING OBJECTIVES

1. Describe the four stages in the life cycle of a product.

Products start in the introductory stage and progress through a growth stage and a maturity stage before eventually moving into a decline stage.

2. Describe six stages of product development.

The first two stages of product development involve generating and screening ideas to isolate those with the most potential. In the third stage, promising ideas are analyzed to determine their likely profitability. Those that appear worthwhile enter the fourth, or prototype development stage, in which a limited number of the products are created. In the fifth stage, the product is test-marketed to determine buyer response. Products that survive the testing process are then commercialized, the final stage.

3. Identify four ways of expanding a product line and discuss two risks that product-line extensions pose.

A product line can be expanded by filling gaps in the market, extending the line to include new varieties of existing products, extending the brand to new product categories, and stretching the line to include lower- or higher-priced items. Two of the biggest risks with product-line extensions include a loss of brand identity (weakening of the brand's meaning), and cannibalization of sales of other products in the product line.

4. Highlight several factors that should be considered when developing strategies for international markets.

Before entering international markets, a company must consider the type of government, market entry requirements, tariffs and other trade barriers, cultural and language differences, consumer preferences, foreign-exchange rates, and business customs. Then the company must decide whether to standardize the product or customize it to meet the needs of individual markets.

5. Cite three levels of brand loyalty.

The first level of brand loyalty is brand awareness, in which the buyer is familiar with the product. The next level is brand preference, in which the buyer will select the product if it is available. The final level is brand insistence, in which the buyer will accept no substitute.

6. Discuss the functions of packaging.

Packaging provides protection for the product, makes products easier to display, and attracts attention. In addition, packaging enhances the convenience of the product and communicates its attributes to the buyer.

7. List seven factors that influence pricing decisions.

Pricing decisions are influenced by manufacturing and selling costs, competition, the needs of wholesalers and retailers who distribute the product to the final customer, a firm's marketing objectives, government regulations, consumer perceptions, and consumer demand.

8. Explain what dynamic pricing is and discuss why dynamic pricing has been slow to catch on.

Dynamic pricing is the opposite of fixed pricing; that is, sellers use the Internet to continually reprice their products and services to meet supply and demand. The Internet allows sellers to change prices on the fly, determine a customer's price sensitivity, and tailor prices to a specific customer by planting cookies on the customer's computer hard drives. Nonetheless, putting these pricing strategies into practice has been difficult. For one thing, customers resent being charged different prices for the same product. For another, not all e-commerce customers are price sensitive. Many want convenience and customer service, and are willing to pay a fixed price for such benefits.

KEY TERMS

brand (354)

brand awareness (356)

brand insistence (356)

brand loyalty (356)

brand manager (352)

brand mark (354)

brand names (354)

brand preference (356)

break-even analysis (358)

break-even point (358)

bundling (361)

co-branding (357)

commercialization (351)

discount pricing (360)

dynamic pricing (361)

family branding (356)

fixed costs (358)

generic products (356)

national brands (356)

penetration pricing (360)

price elasticity (359)

private brands (356)

product (346)

product life cycle (347)

product line (352)

product mix (352)

skimming (359)

test marketing (351)

trademark (355)

Universal Product Codes (UPCs) (357)

variable costs (358)

TEST YOUR KNOWLEDGE

QUESTIONS FOR REVIEW

1. What are the four main subgroups of consumer products?

2. Why are most services perishable?

3. What are the functions of packaging?

4. How many books will a publisher have to sell to break even if fixed costs are $100,000, the selling price per book is $60, and the variable costs per book are $40?

5. How does cost-based pricing differ from price-based pricing?

QUESTIONS FOR ANALYSIS

6. Why do businesses continually introduce new products, given the high costs of the introduction stage of the product life cycle?

7. How could a marketer confuse a consumer when developing a product's positioning strategies?

8. Why are brand names important?

9. Why is it important to review the objectives of a strategic marketing plan before setting a product's price?

10. How does dynamic pricing benefit companies? How does it benefit customers?

11. Why might an employee with high personal ethical standards act less ethically when developing packaging, labeling, or pricing strategies?

QUESTIONS FOR APPLICATION

12. In what ways might Mattel modify its pricing strategies during the life cycle of a toy product?

13. As the international marketing manager for Naya bottled water, you are responsible for investigating the possibility of selling bottled water overseas. What are some of the product-related issues you should consider during your study?

14. Review the theory of supply and demand in Chapter 1 (see pp. 11–12). How do skimming and penetration pricing strategies influence a product's supply and demand?

15. Review the discussion of cultural differences in international business in Chapter 3 (see pp. 70–72). Which cultural differences do you think Disney had to consider when planning its product strategies for Disneyland Paris? Originally the company offered a standardized product but was later forced to customize many of the park's operations. What might have been some of the cultural challenges Disney experienced under a standardized product strategy?

PRACTICE YOUR KNOWLEDGE

SHARPENING YOUR COMMUNICATION SKILLS

After scraping together enough money to purchase a new high-speed modem for your computer, you installed it, configured it, and were ready to cruise the Internet at high speed—or so you thought. But you've discovered that your apartment telephone line won't accommodate high-speed data transfer. Instead of 56 bps you're stuck at 28.8, and you're angry. For one thing, the store where you purchased the modem did not warn you that there might be a problem. For another, the only requirements listed on the product box or in the instructions were a computer and a phone line. Finally, the phone company has washed its hands of the problem altogether.

Getting your money back is not a problem, of course, but you think company authorities should be advised of your dissatisfaction. Whom should you advise: the store? the manufacturer? the telephone company? Would it be most effective to communicate your dissatisfaction by phone, e-mail, or a letter? Explain your answers.

HANDLING DIFFICULT SITUATIONS ON THE JOB: WHO PAYS THE BILL FOR FREDDY PUMPKIN?

Allen White had a bit of a shock when he opened his March phone bill a while back—and April's bill was no better. The statements for both months listed $40 worth of phone calls that White was sure he had not made. Finally, in May, when the mystery calls totaled $100, White figured out that his four-year-old son was placing calls to "Freddy Pumpkin"—a 900 telephone line advertised on children's television shows. The irate Mr. White paid the telephone bill but fired off a letter of protest to Robert H. Lorsch, president of Teleline, a company that operates children's phone-line services.

You are Mr. Lorsch's assistant, and you were in the office when White's letter arrived. Lorsch has asked you to draft a letter responding to this complaint. He believes that Teleline offers a legitimate service. Children who call the firm's 900 numbers hear a taped message featuring cartoon or fantasy characters. At $2.45 for the first minute and 45 cents for each additional minute, the calls aren't cheap; but they aren't a big problem unless a child develops a serious habit. Teleline receives fewer than 12 complaints a month. The company is careful to state its prices in its television ads for the phone lines, and it clearly warns children to ask their parents for permission before calling.[46]

1. Is pricing really the problem in this situation? What should you say about pricing in your letter to Mr. White?

2. What can you say in your letter about Teleline's promotional ethics?

3. What suggestions can you offer to Mr. Lorsch about changing Teleline's pricing or promotional strategies to minimize parents' complaints?

BUILDING YOUR TEAM SKILLS

When planning their pricing strategies, marketers need to understand their costs, both fixed and variable. Doing so is important not only for completing an accurate break-even analysis but also for setting prices that include sufficient profits. Consider pricing in the hotly competitive online brokerage industry, where Internet-based firms such as Ameritrade offer deeply discounted commissions on stock trades. At the higher end of the pricing spectrum are established brokerage firms such as Charles Schwab, which charges $29.95 per trade, whereas Ameritrade's pricing drops as low as $8 per buy or sell transaction.

Why are these companies' prices so different? Schwab has offices across the country and maintains a staff of registered brokers to work with customers who visit local branches or call to discuss trades. In contrast, Ameritrade operates only in cyberspace; its brokers are linked to customers by Internet or, when necessary, by phone. Both brokerage firms advertise heavily to attract and retain customers; both must factor taxes and stock exchange fees into their pricing. And thanks to its lower commission pricing, Ameritrade's profit margin is much thinner than Schwab's.[47]

With your team, brainstorm a listing of costs (such as paying brokers and buying computer equipment) that Ameritrade and Schwab must consider when pricing their trading services. Which of these costs are fixed, and which are variable? As the volume of online stock trading grows, which costs are likely to increase faster? Does Schwab have to bear certain costs that Ameritrade does not? What effect do you think these costs have on Schwab's pricing strategy?

Present your team's findings to your class. What additional costs did other teams identify? Did other teams categorize some costs as fixed that you thought were variable—or vice versa? Why did your categories differ? Why is it important to properly categorize costs when planning pricing?

EXPAND YOUR KNOWLEDGE

KEEPING CURRENT USING *THE WALL STREET JOURNAL*

Scan recent issues of *The Wall Street Journal* (print or online editions) for an article related to one of the following:

- New-product development
- The product life cycle
- Pricing strategies
- Packaging

1. Does this article report on a development in a particular company, several companies, or an entire industry? Which companies or industries are specifically mentioned?

2. If you were a marketing manager in this industry, what concerns would you have as a result of reading the article? What questions do you think companies in this industry (or related ones) should be asking? What would you want to know?

3. In what ways do you think this industry, other industries, or the public might be affected by this trend or development in the next five years? Why?

DISCOVERING CAREER OPPORTUNITIES

Being a brand manager for a leading product is a big responsibility, but it can be a lot of fun at the same time. Don't take our word for it, however. Read what the brand manager for Bounce fabric has to say at www.womenswire.com/work/go/brand/what.html. Explore this Web site. Take the reality check, and learn how to nail a job in brand management.

1. What does a brand manager do?

2. What are some key questions you might want to ask when interviewing for a job in brand management?

3. Which job skills and key personal traits should a brand manager have?

EXPLORING THE BEST OF THE WEB

URLs for all Internet exercises are provided at the Web site for this book, www.prenhall.com/mescon. When you log on to the text Web site, select Chapter 13, then select "Student Resources," click on the name of the featured Web site, and follow the detailed navigational directions to complete these exercises.

Be a Sharp Shopper, page 354

Now that you are a sharp marketer, go to the Sharper Image Web site and let's talk marketing.

1. What are the company's main product categories? Explore these categories. Is the product mix wide? Deep?

2. What is the company's target market? How does the company use product features and price to position its products?

3. Select any three Sharper Image products. In which of the four consumer product subgroups would you classify each product?

Protect Your Trademark, page 356

Visit the U.S. Patent and Trademark Office to learn about trademarks.

1. Review the Basic Facts About Registering a Trademark. How do you establish trademark rights? Are you required to conduct a search for conflicting marks before applying with the Patent and Trademark Office (PTO)? Who is allowed to use the ™ symbol?

2. How does a trademark differ from a service mark?

3. What are the four ways you can search this database?

Uncovering Hidden Costs, page 360

Point your Web browser to Best Book Buys to compare prices of a best-selling book and uncover the hidden costs at various online bookstores.

1. Go to Bestsellers, select the top-selling book on the list, and compare the prices. How do the item prices vary from store to store? How do the shipping costs, carrier, and delivery schedules vary?

2. In which states would a buyer pay sales tax from each store on the list? How does sales tax affect the total cost of the best-seller?

3. What is the lowest total cost for this book? What is the highest total cost? Why would a buyer choose to buy from an online store that does not have the lowest total cost?

Explore on Your Own

Review these chapter-related Web sites on your own to learn more about product and pricing strategies.

1. Private Label Manufacturers Association, www.plma.com, explains the growth, success, and importance of store brands sold under private labels.

2. Explore the Product "Hits and Misses" at The New Products Showcase and Learning Center, www.showlearn.com/index.html.

3. U.S. Business Reporter, www.activemedia-guide.com/index.htm, is a good place to start your marketing, company, and product research.

A CASE FOR CRITICAL THINKING

■ Saturn's Bumpy Ride

With the launch of Saturn in 1990, General Motors Corporation created a new star in the auto industry. Operating as an independent division of GM, Saturn found instant success with its no-haggle pricing, friendly service, and sporty compact cars. But Saturn veered off course during the last half of the 1990s, losing its popularity. And the "different kind of car company" discovered it needed a different kind of product strategy to drive Saturn sales.

A ROARING START

After three decades of declining market share, GM introduced Saturn as the first American-made alternative to compete with foreign compacts in the U.S. car market. And the strategy succeeded, luring young consumers and foreign car enthusiasts into Saturn's ring of owners. In fact, import owners purchased at least 60 percent of the 2 million Saturns sold during the 1990s. Moreover, Saturn's luxury-brand levels of quality and service inspired cultlike consumer devotion, earning some of the highest customer-satisfaction ratings in the auto industry.

SPUTTERING TO A HALT

Proud of Saturn's success, GM focused its resources on weaker divisions, pumping billions into new models to revive Oldsmobile and Buick. In 18 months alone, these GM divisions introduced 18 new car and minivan models, while Saturn remained stymied with only one lineup of compact cars. So when consumers began to eye sports utility vehicles and luxury cars, Saturn's sales slid by 19 percent. Although consumers loved their Saturns, its limited lineup forced many to defect.

Consumer research indicated a midsize Saturn would appeal to buyers on the strength of Saturn's brand equity. Moreover, expanding the brand into midsize models would also allow Saturn to compete in 41 percent of the U.S. market. But GM continued to withhold investments for new Saturn products, leaving Saturn stalled in a shrinking small-car market that accounted for only 17 percent of U.S. car sales.

WRONG TURNS

Finally GM agreed to launch Saturn's first new line of cars in a decade: a midsize sedan and station wagon known as the L-series (with the "L" standing for "larger"), designed to compete with Honda and Toyota. But Saturn ran into major roadblocks before the new line could get off the ground. To cut costs, Saturn agreed to share platforms with other GM brands, farm out production of key components, and move manufacturing to other GM locations outside of Saturn's primary facility in Spring Hill, Tennessee. Critics claimed Saturn had mortgaged its soul to compete. Union officials fumed and authorized a strike vote.

ROAD HAZARDS

In spite of a heavily promoted product launch, Saturn's L-series got off to a slow start. First, production delays created a shortage of cars, forcing potential buyers to turn to other brands. Then, Saturn's popular no-haggle pricing backfired when the company couldn't match year-end discounts offered by rivals. In fact, savvy customers with easy access to dealer invoices on the Internet were no longer impressed with Saturn's pricing policy.

The L-series sold at half its projected rate, marking the launch as one of the worst new-model debuts in recent history. Saturn not only discovered its sales forecasts had been far too optimistic, but underestimated the difficulties of expanding the brand into one of the most competitive segments in the U.S. market. "If I had to do it over again, we would have done a better job of predicting the fragmentation of the market and the strength of the other entrants," says Cynthia Trudell, Saturn's CEO.

Still, GM is determined to grow Saturn beyond its small-car niche and has committed $1.5 billion to launch a new Saturn SUV. "We have to get consumers to see Saturn as more than a small-car company," says one GM executive. In fact, GM is now counting on Saturn to help turn around GM's three decades of sliding market share. But Saturn is among the latecomers to the SUV market. And that means the company cannot make one more wrong turn. So stay tuned. Only time will tell whether Saturn and GM have truly learned their lesson from the L-series mishaps.

CRITICAL THINKING QUESTIONS

1. Why was Saturn billed as "a different kind of car company"?

2. Why did Saturn lose ground to competitors during the last half of the 1990s?

3. Why did Saturn's launch of the L-series fail?

4. Go to Chapter 13 of this text's Web site at www.prenhall.com/mescon and click on the hot link to get the Saturn Web site. Follow the online instructions to answer these questions:

How does Saturn's Web site introduce customers to the new SUV? How does Saturn promote the L-series on its Web site? What is Saturn's mission?

VIDEO CASE AND EXERCISES

■ *Prescribing Pricing for Watson Pharmaceuticals*

SYNOPSIS

Watson Pharmaceuticals (www.watsonpharm.com) specializes in developing new generic versions of pain-management drugs initially marketed by major pharmaceutical firms under brand names. The first company to get government approval to offer a generic version of a branded drug may price its product at 60 to 70 percent of the price of the branded drug and capture as much as 50 percent of the market by the end of its first year. When a second manufacturer gets approval for a generic version, however, the increased competition puts pricing pressure on the first company. Watson also builds its customer base using nonprice strategies such as changing payment terms and bundling products for purchase by distributors. Regardless of the specific pricing strategy used for a specific drug, Watson continuously monitors market conditions so it can adjust its pricing or other marketing-mix elements as needed.

EXERCISES
Analysis

1. Watson's management says its research-and-development costs are lower than those of branded drug manufacturers. Are these fixed or variable costs?

2. How do you think consumer perceptions affect the pricing of generic drugs?

3. What pricing method does Watson appear to be using when it markets the first generic version of a branded drug?

4. In addition to research-and-development costs, what other costs must Watson consider when setting prices for its generic drugs?

5. What factors are likely to affect demand for a particular generic drug?

Application

If the fixed costs of producing a generic drug are $150,000, the variable costs are $5 per bottle, and the price the manufacturer receives from wholesalers is $25, what is the manufacturer's break-even point?

Decision

Watson has just released its generic version of a branded pain management drug. Another manufacturer is about to release its generic version of the same drug. Should Watson reduce its price before the competing drug becomes available, or should it wait for pharmacies to ask Watson to match the competitor's lower price?

Communication

Consumers often complain about the high price of prescription drugs. Playing the role of a public relations specialist for a well-known pharmaceutical firm, draft a letter to a consumer who has written asking about the reasons underlying the pricing of a particular branded drug product.

Integration

Looking back at the discussion of need and want in Chapter 12, is demand for generic drugs based on need or want?

Ethics

Is it ethical for pharmaceutical firms to ring up high profits from selling drugs to treat the medical problems of consumers? Explain your response.

Debate

Should Watson Pharmaceuticals try to build its brand name to encourage loyalty to its generic drug products? List two arguments for and two arguments against this position.

Teamwork

With two other students, select a branded prescription drug and research its price at three local pharmacies. Also find out if any generic versions are available and research their price at the same pharmacies. Prepare a table showing the results of your research. What is the spread between the highest and lowest prices on the branded version? On the generic version?

Online Research

Using Internet sources, find out what generic drugs Watson Pharmaceuticals has recently introduced and look at recent trends in company sales. See Component Chapter A, Exhibit A.1, for search engines to use in doing your research.

MYPHLIP COMPANION WEB SITE

Learning Interactively

Visit the myPHLIP Web site at www.prenhall.com/mescon. For Chapter 13, take advantage of the interactive "Study Guide" to test your chapter knowledge. Get instant feedback on whether you need additional studying. Read the "Current Events" articles to get the latest on chapter topics, and complete the exercises as specified by your instructor. Expand your learning with a visit to the "Research Area." There you will find a wealth of information you can use to complete your course assignments.

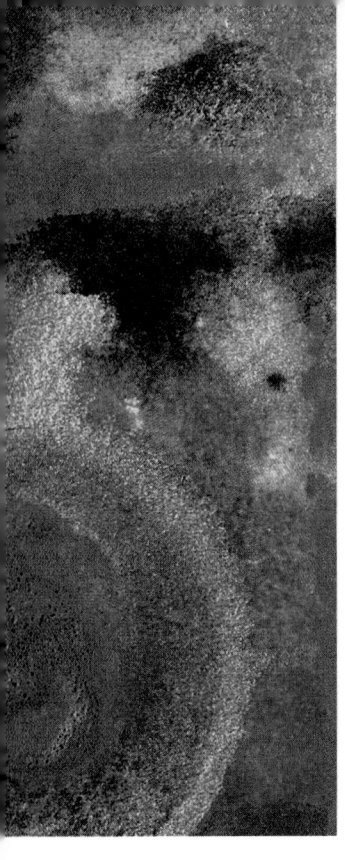

DISTRIBUTION STRATEGIES

14

LEARNING OBJECTIVES

After studying this chapter, you will be able to

1. Explain what marketing intermediaries do and list their seven primary functions

2. Discuss the key factors that influence channel design and selection

3. Differentiate between intensive, selective, and exclusive distribution strategies

4. Highlight the main advantage of a vertical marketing system and explain how it differs from a conventional marketing channel

5. Explain how wholesalers and retailers function as intermediaries

6. Identify at least six types of store retailers and four types of nonstore retailers

7. Highlight the key things to consider when choosing a form of transportation, and list the five major modes of transportation used in physical distribution

8. Discuss the Internet's effect on the distribution function

@ 9. Discuss how customers and traditional retailers benefit from a clicks-and-mortar distribution strategy

BUILDING A DISTRIBUTION STRATEGY: HOME DEPOT, THE ULTIMATE CATEGORY KILLER

w w w . h o m e d e p o t . c o m

Home Depot, the category killer that drove hundreds of mom-and-pop hardware stores out of business, is expanding its reach to the Internet.

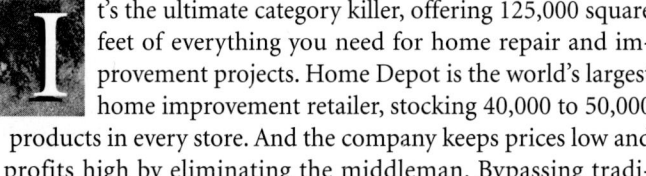

I t's the ultimate category killer, offering 125,000 square feet of everything you need for home repair and improvement projects. Home Depot is the world's largest home improvement retailer, stocking 40,000 to 50,000 products in every store. And the company keeps prices low and profits high by eliminating the middleman. Bypassing traditional retail distribution channels, Home Depot orders merchandise directly from manufacturers instead of purchasing from wholesale distributors. Furthermore, management negotiates deep discounts with producers for high-volume orders and passes the savings along to customers.

Today, with more than 1,000 stores, $40 billion in annual sales, and a huge traffic volume, Home Depot is an alluring distribution channel for producers. But first they must win Home Depot's business. And that's not easy. Home Depot's extensive store network and customer base give the retailer the upper hand in negotiating the best prices from suppliers. Keeping an eye on the bottom line, Home Depot conducts biannual reviews with every vendor. Hundreds of suppliers hawk their wares at the company's review sessions, vying to win, keep, or expand their shelf space at Home Depot. But management maintains a hard line with producers. Home Depot rarely agrees to price increases and constantly strives for additional discounts to improve the company's profit margins. "We've taken a lot of cost out of products through regular reviews with these vendors," says co-founder Arthur Blank.

Those who survive the ordeal get to sell their products to the legions of do-it-yourselfers who stuff their oversized shopping carts with every kind of home improvement product imaginable. Some producers are even willing to modify their traditional distribution channels for the chance to distribute their products through the retailing giant. Deere & Company, for example, has long distributed its riding mowers and heavy agricultural and construction equipment through established dealers. But those same dealers now face stiff competition from Home Depot's exclusive line of riding mowers produced by Deere under the brand name of Scotts. And that creates tension between Deere and its dealers.

Of course, the relationships between producers, dealers, and retailers have always been a bit tense. But now the Internet threatens to strain these connections more—even for giants such as Home Depot. Although the costs of shipping heavy or bulky goods prohibit many Home Depot suppliers from selling their wares directly to consumers, producers of smaller home improvement items are likely candidates for profitable e-commerce ventures. But not if Home Depot has anything to say about it. In fact, the company has no intention of competing against its suppliers for customers. And Blank indirectly told suppliers so in a letter which stated, "We realize that a vendor has a right to sell through whatever distribution channels it desires. However, we, too, have the right to be selective, . . . and we trust that you can understand that a company may be hesitant to do business with its competitors."

Will Home Depot have enough clout to prevent its suppliers from selling directly to customers on the Internet? Management thinks so. Home Depot plans to make its products available online in the future in addition to opening a new physical store every 53 hours. After all, as Arthur Blank sees it, "the Internet is really just another way that our customers are going to choose to shop with us."[1]

369

SELECTING THE MOST EFFECTIVE DISTRIBUTION ■ CHANNELS

distribution channels
Systems for moving goods and services from producers to customers; also known as marketing channels

distribution mix
Combination of intermediaries and channels a producer uses to get a product to end users

distribution strategy
Firm's overall plan for moving products to intermediaries and final customers

marketing intermediaries
Businesspeople and organizations that channel goods and services from producers to consumers

Home Depot is just one example of how producers use intermediaries to get their products to market. Getting products to consumers is the role of distribution, the fourth element of a firm's marketing mix—also known as *place*. **Distribution channels,** or *marketing channels,* are an organized network of firms that work together to get goods and services from producer to consumer. Distribution channels come in all shapes and sizes. Some channels are short and simple such as the direct model Home Depot uses; others are complex and involve many people and organizations. Nonetheless, as Arthur Blank knows, a company's decisions about which combination of channels to use—the **distribution mix**—and its overall plan for moving products to buyers—the **distribution strategy**—play a major role in the firm's success.

The Role of Marketing Intermediaries

Think of all the products you buy: food, toiletries, clothing, sports equipment, train tickets, haircuts, gasoline, stationery, appliances, CDs, videotapes, books, and all the rest. How many of these products do you buy directly from the producer? For most people, the answer is not many.

Most companies do not sell their goods directly to the final users, even though the Internet is making it easier to do so these days. Instead, producers in many industries work with **marketing intermediaries** (also called *middlemen*) to bring their products to market. In some cases, these "go-betweens" represent the producers but do not actually buy the products they sell; in others, the intermediaries buy and own what they sell.

Without marketing intermediaries, the buying and selling process would be expensive and time-consuming (see Exhibit 14.1). Intermediaries are instrumental in creating three of the four forms of utility mentioned in Chapter 12: place utility, time utility, and possession utility. By providing an efficient process for transferring products from the producer to the customer, intermediaries reduce the number of transactions and ensure that goods and services are available at a convenient time and place.

Overall, intermediaries perform a number of specific distribution functions that make life easier for both producers and customers. They

■ *Match buyers and sellers.* By making sellers' products available to multiple buyers, intermediaries reduce the number of transactions between producers and customers.

LEARNING OBJECTIVE 1

Explain what marketing intermediaries do and list their seven primary functions

EXHIBIT 14.1

HOW INTERMEDIARIES SIMPLIFY COMMERCE

Intermediaries actually reduce the price customers pay for many goods and services because they reduce the number of contacts between producers and consumers that would otherwise be necessary. They also create place, time, and possession utility.

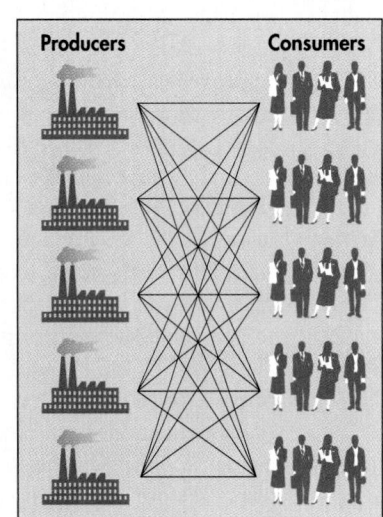
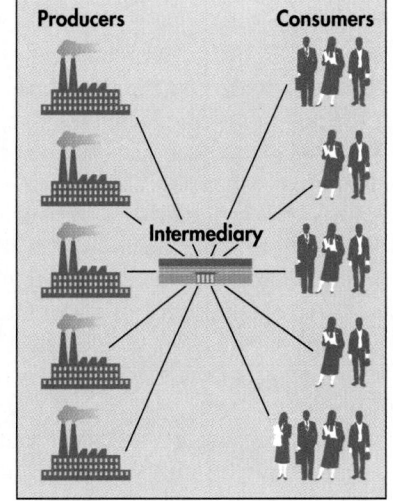

Number of transactions required when consumers buy directly from manufacturers

Number of transactions required when buying is conducted via intermediary

■ *Provide market information.* Intermediaries such as Home Depot collect valuable data about customer purchases: who buys, how often, and how much. Collecting these data allows them to spot buying patterns and to share marketplace information with producers.

■ *Provide promotional and sales support.* Many intermediaries create advertising, produce eye-catching displays, and use other promotional devices for some or all of the products they sell. Some employ a sales force, which can provide a number of selling functions, as illustrated in Chapter 15.

■ *Gather an assortment of goods.* Home Depot, Macy's, and other intermediaries receive bulk shipments from producers and break them into more convenient units by sorting, standardizing, and dividing bulk quantities into smaller packages.

■ *Transport and store the product.* Intermediaries such as retail stores maintain an inventory of merchandise that they acquire from producers so they can quickly fill customers' orders. In many cases retailers purchase this merchandise from wholesalers who, in addition to breaking bulk, may also transport the goods from the producer to the retail outlets.

■ *Assume risks.* When intermediaries accept goods from manufacturers, they take on the risks associated with damage, theft, product perishability, and obsolescence.

■ *Provide financing.* Large intermediaries sometimes provide loans to smaller producers.

Of course, the lines separating producers and their intermediaries are becoming fuzzier as some producers assume typical distribution functions. Producer S.C. Johnson Wax, for example, warehouses goods, stocks store shelves with Johnson Wax products, and even handles some retail functions for rival products as part of its contractual arrangement with Wal-Mart.[2] Similarly, Northern Telecom doesn't just send one gigantic shipment of telephones to Wal-Mart and other large intermediaries. Instead, the company has to inventory shipments, label boxes so they look like they come directly from the intermediaries, and perform other functions that minimize the intermediaries' inventory and handling costs.[3]

More and more intermediaries are performing functions once reserved exclusively for manufacturers. Computer wholesaler Ingram Micro, for instance, has been taking on such tasks as assembling PCs and handling inquiries from customers. Among the big-name producers that Ingram serves are Hewlett-Packard, Apple, and Compaq. Ingram also builds computers that dealers resell to consumers (and that bear the dealer's own name). Ingram is content to operate in the background and does not plan to enter the retail market with its own brand, says Ingram's CEO.[4]

Intermediaries such as Ingram Micro are expanding their functions to add value and to solidify their role within the distribution system. Ingram is responding to a dynamic environment filled with risks and opportunities. But some intermediaries feel threatened by the Internet. They worry that the Internet will allow manufacturers to bypass distributors and conduct business directly with end users. Others disagree. While they recognize that technology and the Internet are significantly changing the way intermediaries do business, they see the role intermediaries play as becoming more diverse and important now and in the future.

Types of Distribution Channels

The number and type of intermediaries in a distribution mix depend on the kind of product being sold and the marketing practices of the industry. An arrangement that works well for a power-tool and appliance manufacturer like Black & Decker or a book publisher like Prentice Hall would not necessarily work for an insurance company, a restaurant, a steel manufacturer, or a movie studio. In general, consumer products and business products tend to move through different channels (see Exhibit 14.2).

Channel Levels Most businesses purchase goods they use in their operations directly from producers, so the distribution channel is short. In contrast, the channels for consumer goods are usually longer and more complex than the channels for business goods. The four primary channels for consumer goods are:

■ *Producer to consumer.* Producers who sell directly to consumers through catalogs, telemarketing, infomercials, and the Internet are using the shortest, simplest distribution channel. Dell Computer and other companies that sell directly to consumers are seeking closer relationships

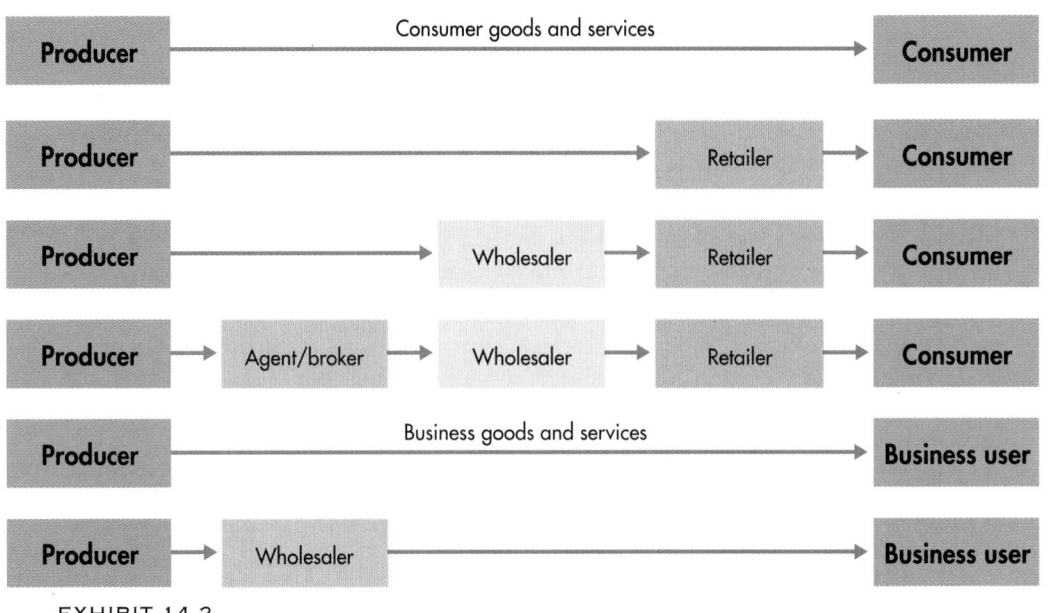

EXHIBIT 14.2

ALTERNATIVE CHANNELS OF DISTRIBUTION

Producers of consumer and business goods and services must analyze the alternative channels of distribution available for their products so they can select the channels that best meet their marketing objectives and their customers' needs.

with customers and more control over pricing, promotion, service, and delivery.[5] Although this approach eliminates payments to channel members, it also forces producers to handle distribution functions such as storing inventory and delivering products.

■ *Producer to retailer to consumer.* Some producers create longer channels by selling their products to retailers such as Home Depot, who then resell them to consumers. Ford vehicles, Benjamin Moore paint, and New Balance athletic shoes are typical of the many products distributed in this way.

■ *Producer to wholesaler to retailer to consumer.* Most manufacturers of supermarket and drugstore items rely on even longer channels. They sell their products to wholesalers, who in turn sell to the retailers. This approach works particularly well for small producers who lack the resources to sell or deliver merchandise to individual retail sites.

■ *Producer to agent/broker to wholesaler to retailer to consumer.* Additional channel levels are common in certain industries, such as agriculture, where specialists are required to negotiate transactions or to perform interim functions such as sorting, grading, or subdividing the goods.

Channels for Services So far we have examined how producers of tangible goods use various channels to reach consumers and businesses, but how do producers of intangible services reach their customers? Because delivery of a service requires direct contact between providers and users, most service marketers use a direct channel to reach their customers. Hairstylists and lawyers, for example, deal directly with their clients, as do accounting firms such as H&R Block.

Some service businesses, however, do use other distribution channels. For example, Air France and other airlines typically sell tickets and vacation packages through travel agents. Similarly, State Farm and many other insurance companies market their policies through insurance agents and brokers. Technology is also increasing the number of options for distributing services. Banks, for instance, distribute financial services to customers all over the globe using automated teller machines in shopping centers, airports, and many other locations.

Reverse Channels Although most marketing channels move products from producers to customers, *reverse channels* move them in the opposite direction. The two most common reverse channels are those used for recycling and for product recalls and repairs. Recycling channels continue to grow in importance as consumers and businesses become more sensitive to solid-waste-disposal problems. The channels for some recycled goods, like returnable soft drink bottles, use traditional intermediaries—which in this case are retailers and bottlers. In other cases, recycling collection centers have been established to funnel material from consumers back to producers.

Factors to Consider When Selecting Channels

Should you sell directly to end users or rely on intermediaries? Which intermediaries should you choose? Should you try to sell your product in every available outlet or limit its distribution to a few exclusive shops? Should you use more than one channel? These are some of the critical decisions that managers face when designing and selecting marketing channels for any product.

Keep in mind that building an effective channel system takes years and, like all marketing relationships, requires commitment. Once you commit to your intermediaries, changing your distribution arrangements may prove difficult. As Chris DeNove, a channel expert puts it, "It's much more difficult to modify an existing system than to start with a clean slate." Citing the automobile industry, for example, DeNove points out that "if an auto maker could start over now, none of them would create a franchise distribution system that looks like the existing one."[6]

Effective channel selection depends on a number of factors; some are related to the type of product and the target market, and others are related to the company—its strengths, weaknesses, and objectives. In general, however, choosing one channel over another is a matter of making trade-offs among four factors: the number of outlets that sell your product, the cost of distribution, the control of your product as it moves through the channel to the final customer, and the possibility of channel conflict.

Market Coverage The appropriate *market coverage*—the number of wholesalers or retailers that will carry your product—varies by type of product. Inexpensive convenience goods or organizational supplies such as Pilot pens sell best if they are available in as many outlets as possible. Such **intensive distribution** will require wholesalers and retailers of many types. In contrast, shopping

LEARNING OBJECTIVE 2

Discuss the key factors that influence channel design and selection

LEARNING OBJECTIVE 3

Differentiate between intensive, selective, and exclusive distribution strategies

intensive distribution
Market coverage strategy that tries to place a product in as many outlets as possible

Southwest Airlines uses a multi-channel sales approach. Customers can purchase travel tickets from intermediaries such as travel agents, or they may purchase tickets directly from the company's customer service reps or over the Internet.

selective distribution
Market coverage strategy that uses a limited number of outlets to distribute products

exclusive distribution
Market coverage strategy that gives intermediaries exclusive rights to sell a product in a specific geographical area

goods (goods that require some thought before being purchased) such as General Electric appliances require different market coverage, because customers shop for such products by comparing features and prices. For these items, the best strategy is usually **selective distribution,** selling through a limited number of outlets that can give the product adequate sales and service support.

If producers of expensive specialty or technical products do not sell directly to customers, they may choose **exclusive distribution,** offering products in only one outlet in each market area. Vehicle manufacturers have traditionally relied on exclusive distribution agreements to sell through one dealership in each local area. By contrast, other firms use multiple channels to increase their market coverage and reach several target markets. Apparel manufacturers such as Champion frequently sell through a combination of channels, including department stores, specialty stores, the Internet, and catalogs. Using multiple channels is becoming increasingly popular as explained in this chapters' special feature, Focusing on E-Business Today.

Cost Costs play a major role in determining a firm's channel selection. It takes money to perform all the functions that are handled by intermediaries. Small or new companies often cannot afford to hire a sales force large enough to sell directly to end users or to call on a host of retail outlets. Neither can they afford to build large warehouses and distribution centers or to buy trucks to transport their goods. These firms need the help of intermediaries who can spread the cost of such activities across a number of noncompeting products. With time and a larger sales base, a producer may build enough strength to take over some of these functions and reduce the length of the distribution channel.

Control A third issue to consider when selecting distribution channels is control of how, where, and when your product is sold. Remember, you can't force any intermediary to promote, service, sell, or deliver your product. Longer distribution channels mean less control for producers, who become increasingly distant from sellers and buyers as the number of intermediaries multiplies.

On the other hand, companies may not want to concentrate too many distribution functions in the hands of too few intermediaries. Control becomes critical when a firm's reputation is at stake. For instance, a designer of high-priced clothing might want to limit distribution to exclusive boutiques, because the brand could lose some of its appeal if the clothing were sold in discount stores. In addition, producers of complex technical products such as X-ray machines don't want their products handled by unqualified intermediaries who can't provide adequate customer service.

In a conventional marketing channel, wholesalers and retailers are independent of one another. Each firm essentially pursues its own objectives, although maximizing sales is usually a shared goal. In contrast, a **vertical marketing system (VMS)** is one in which the producer, wholesaler, and retailer act as a unified system to conduct distribution activities. One channel member owns the others, has contracts with them, or wields so much power that they must all cooperate. Thus, the main advantage of a VMS is channel control (see Exhibit 14.3).

LEARNING
OBJECTIVE   4

Highlight the main advantage of a vertical marketing system and explain how it differs from a conventional marketing channel

vertical marketing system (VMS)
Planned distribution channels in which members coordinate their efforts to optimize distribution activities

EXHIBIT 14.3

CONVENTIONAL CHANNELS VERSUS A VERTICAL MARKETING SYSTEM

In a conventional channel structure no channel member has control over the other members, but in a vertical marketing system, one channel member has significant control over the other members.

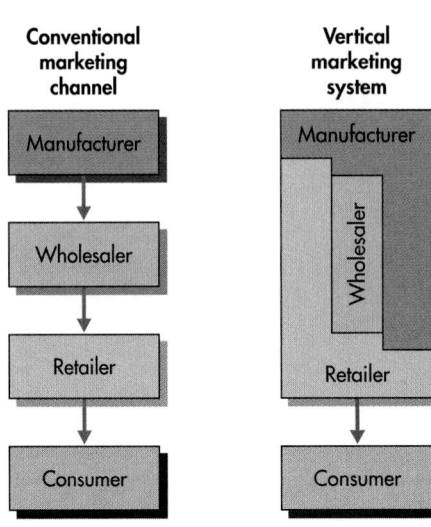

Vertical marketing systems vary in their level of formality:

■ *Corporate vertical marketing system.* This is the most controlled vertical marketing system, in which a single firm handles production, wholesaling, and retailing functions. An example of this arrangement would be a firm like Walt Disney that sells its merchandise through company-owned retail stores. In some cases, the entire distribution chain is controlled by a single firm, but often the channel contains a mix of corporate-controlled and independently owned operations.

■ *Administered vertical marketing system.* This is a less formal arrangement in which one member of the distribution chain has enough power to influence the behavior of the others, but there are no ownership ties. The dominant company, known as the **channel captain,** performs functions that work to the mutual benefit of the entire chain. The channel captain can be a large manufacturer such as Procter & Gamble, Kraft Foods, or Gillette who, by virtue of the volume of product sold through the channel, can command unusual cooperation from resellers regarding displays, shelf space, promotions, and price policies. Or they can be a retailer such as Home Depot or Wal-Mart who can use its power to exert a strong influence on suppliers. Wal-Mart, for example, pushes its 65,000 suppliers to become lean operations so they can meet Wal-Mart's strict pricing requirements. "I went there [to Wal-Mart] knowing we were going to get squeezed and wrung and twisted—all in positive ways," says the CEO of Liz Claiborne, which designs the Ross clothing brand exclusively for Wal-Mart.[7]

■ *Contractual vertical marketing system.* This system is a compromise between a corporate system and an administered system. With this approach, the members of the channel are legally bound by a contractual agreement that spells out their respective responsibilities. Franchising is the most common form of the contractual vertical marketing system. Many of the world's best-known retail outlets, from McDonald's to Radio Shack, rely on franchising to cover attractive markets.

channel captain
Channel member that is able to influence the activities of the other members of the distribution channel

Channel Conflict Because the success of individual channel members depends on the overall channel success, ideally all channel members should work together smoothly. However, individual channel members must also run their own businesses profitably. Which means that they often disagree on the roles each member should play. Such disagreements create *channel conflict.*[8]

Channel conflict may arise when suppliers provide inadequate support, when markets are oversaturated with intermediaries, or when companies sell products via multiple channels, each of which is competing for the same customers. For instance, Hallmark's decision to sell cards to mass-market outlets such as discount stores, supermarkets, and drugstores angered its 8,200 independent dealers who must now compete with large chains. To keep the peace, Hallmark launched a $175 million ad campaign and created new products exclusively for independents, but only time will tell whether these steps will be enough to save the card shops.[9]

Keep in mind that some channel conflict can be productive, especially when it leads to a more efficient channel system. Therefore, the challenge is not to eliminate channel conflict but rather to effectively manage it to avoid distribution system dysfunction and improve service to consumers. New channels, such as the Internet, are creating serious conflicts. Many producers are struggling for balance as they modify their channel arrangements to add Internet services while trying to maintain relationships with older, valued channel members.[10] Levi Strauss faced this challenge. In 1998 the jeans manufacturer announced that it was restricting online sales of Levis jeans to the manufacturer's Web site. Worried that they might lose jean sales, retail partners protested. Some even fought back by giving Levi's jeans less prominent display space in their stores. Eventually Levi Strauss caved in to retailer pressure and ceased selling merchandise directly to consumers via its company Web site.[11]

Other Factors In addition to market coverage, cost, control, and possible channel conflict, managers should consider several other factors when selecting distribution channels. These factors include the nature and price of the product, the market's growth rate, the geographical concentration of the customer base, customers' need for service, the importance of rapid delivery, the strengths and weaknesses of the various types of intermediaries within the channel, and international laws and customs when selling in other countries (see Exhibit 14.4).

KEEPING PACE WITH TECHNOLOGY AND ELECTRONIC COMMERCE

SMART CAR DEALERS SAY, "FOLLOW THAT MOUSE"

Change and innovation are the lifeblood of most retail businesses, but the automobile industry has been remarkably resistant to transformation—until recently. The 80-year-old automobile dealer system has persisted, largely because of existing state franchise laws that prevent manufacturers from selling cars directly to customers. Under state laws, "if you don't deliver the car in a licensed brick-and-mortar shop, you get arrested," says the president of Autobytel.com.

Manufacturers have tried (but failed) to bypass the dealers for years. So Internet companies such as Autobytel.com, Cars.com, MSN CarPoint, and others built their businesses by joining forces with existing dealers and functioning as referral services—for a fee, of course. They feasted off the inefficiencies of the traditional channel structure by providing customers with piles of helpful information, paperwork that's easy to understand, price quotes, automatic vehicle and dealer locators, financing, and more. And they revolutionized the way consumers shopped for and purchased their cars. Car dealers of course, worried that the Internet would soon drive them out of business. But Jack Fitzgerald didn't quite see it that way.

Fitzgerald, owner of nine car dealerships in three states, saw the Internet as a way to distinguish himself from competitors down the block. Tired of paying hefty online referral fees to Autobytel.com and others, Fitzgerald built his own company Web site, FitzMall.com. He uses the site to generate sales leads for his newly hired Internet sales staff and to post all kinds of helpful information for buyers, such as four different prices for each car in stock: the manufacturer's sticker price and the invoice price (the dealer's cost), and the dealer's two prices (one with service contracts and one without).

"The Internet is the greatest thing since sliced bread," says Fitzgerald. "Our sales are easier, and our customers are happier." And Fitzgerald isn't alone. According to the National Automobile Dealers Association 92 percent of new-car dealers now have Web sites and are using them to provide pricing and inventory information. In fact, car dealers are hogging the automotive e-commerce lane. And as more and more dealers follow Fitzgerald's footsteps and weave the Internet into their entire business processes, only one thing is for certain in this industry: The traditional way of buying a car is indeed automobile history.

■ QUESTIONS FOR CRITICAL THINKING

1. If a distribution channel is inefficient, why don't manufacturers just eliminate it?

2. Why do some car dealerships view the Internet as a threat to their existence?

EXHIBIT 14.4

FACTORS INVOLVED IN SELECTING DISTRIBUTION CHANNELS

The choice of distribution channel depends on the product, the customer, and the company's capabilities.

FACTOR	EXPLANATION
Number of transactions	When many transactions are likely, the channel should provide for many outlets, and several levels of intermediaries. If only a few transactions are likely, the number of outlets can be limited, and the channel can be relatively short.
Value of transactions	If the value of each transaction is high, the channel can be relatively short and direct, because the producer can better absorb the cost of making firsthand contact with each customer. If each transaction has a low value, a long channel is used to spread the cost of distribution over many products and outlets.
Market growth rate	In a rapidly growing market, many outlets and a long channel of distribution may be required to meet demand. In a shrinking market, fewer outlets are required.
Geographic concentration of market	If customers are clustered in a limited geographic area, the channel can be short, because the cost of reaching each account is relatively low. If customers are widely scattered, a multilevel channel with many outlets is preferable.
Need for service and sales support	Complex, innovative, or specialized products require sophisticated outlets where customers can receive information and service support; short, relatively direct channels are generally used. If the product is familiar and uncomplicated, the consumer requires little assistance; long channels with many self-serve outlets can be used.

■ SELLING PRODUCTS THROUGH INTERMEDIARIES

LEARNING
OBJECTIVE 5
Explain how wholesalers and
retailers function as intermediaries

Depending on the customer base and industry distribution patterns, products are normally distributed through two main types of intermediaries: wholesalers and retailers. **Wholesalers** sell primarily to retailers, to other wholesalers, and to organizational users such as government agencies, institutions, and commercial operations. In turn, the customers of wholesalers either resell the products or use them to make products of their own. Wholesalers that sell to organizational customers are often called **industrial distributors** to distinguish them from wholesalers that supply retail outlets.

Unlike wholesalers, **retailers** sell products to the final consumer for personal use. Retailers can operate out of a physical facility (supermarket or gas station), through vending equipment (soft drink machine, newspaper box, or automated teller), or from a virtual store (via telephone, catalog, or Web site). The form of contact affects the way intermediaries work with producers and customers, as explained in the following sections.

Selling Through Wholesalers

Because wholesalers seldom deal directly with consumers, you may not be familiar with this vital link in the distribution chain. Yet 453,000 U.S. wholesalers sell a whopping $4 trillion worth of goods every year.[12] Most U.S. wholesalers are independent, and they can be classified as *merchant wholesalers, agents,* or *brokers.*

The majority of wholesalers are **merchant wholesalers,** independently owned businesses that buy from producers, take legal title to the goods, then resell them to retailers or to organizational buyers. **Full-service merchant wholesalers** provide a wide variety of services, such as storage, selling, order processing, delivery, and promotional support. **Rack jobbers,** for example, are full-service merchant wholesalers that set up displays in retail outlets, stock inventory, and mark prices on merchandise displayed in a particular section of a store. **Limited-service merchant wholesalers,** on the other hand, provide fewer services. Natural resources such as lumber, grain, and coal are usually marketed through a class of limited-service wholesalers called **drop shippers,** which take ownership but not physical possession of the goods they handle.

In contrast to merchant wholesalers, **agents and brokers** never take title to the products they handle, and they perform fewer services. Their primary role is to bring buyers and sellers together, for which they are generally paid a commission (a percentage of the money received). Real estate agents, insurance brokers, and securities brokers, for example, match up buyers and sellers for a fee or a commission, but they don't own what they sell. Producers of commercial parts often sell to business customers through brokers. Georgia-based broker, Jerry Whitlock, has built a $1 million business by using the Internet to wholesale industrial seals made by nearly 100 producers to factories around the country.[13] Manufacturers' representatives, another type of agent, sell various noncompeting products to customers in a specific region and arrange for product delivery. By representing several manufacturers' products, these reps achieve enough volume to justify the cost of a direct sales call.

wholesalers
Firms that sell products to other firms for resale or for organizational use

industrial distributors
Wholesalers that sell to industrial customers rather than to retailers

retailers
Firms that sell goods and services to individuals for their own use rather than for resale

merchant wholesalers
Independent wholesalers that take legal title to goods they distribute

full-service merchant wholesalers
Merchant wholesalers that provide a wide variety of services to their customers, such as storage, delivery, and marketing support

rack jobbers
Merchant wholesalers that are responsible for setting up and maintaining displays in a particular section of a retail store

limited-service merchant wholesalers
Merchant wholesalers that offer fewer services than full-service merchant wholesalers; they often specialize in particular markets, such as agriculture

drop shippers
Limited-service merchant wholesalers that assume ownership of goods but don't take physical possession; commonly used to market agricultural and mineral products

agents and brokers
Independent wholesalers that do not take title to the goods they distribute but may or may not take possession of those goods

Best of the Web Best of the Web Best of

EXPLORE THE WORLD OF WHOLESALING

Thinking about a career as a wholesale sales representative? The Occupational Outlook Handbook is a terrific source for learning about careers in business. Read the online material discussing the functions wholesale sales reps perform, the skills and experience manufacturers look for in candidates, and how to acquire any necessary training. Find out what a typical day on the job involves. How will you be compensated? Will travel be required? Will you be required to work long hours? What types of reports will you be expected to submit? Log on and learn now. A career in wholesale sales may be just the thing for you.
stats.bls.gov/oco/ocos119.htm

LEARNING
OBJECTIVE 6

Identify at least six types of store retailers and four types of nonstore retailers

scrambled merchandising
Policy of carrying merchandise that is ordinarily sold in a different type of outlet

wheel of retailing
Evolutionary process by which stores that feature low prices gradually upgrade until they no longer appeal to price-sensitive shoppers and are replaced by new low-price competitors

specialty store
Store that carries only a particular type of goods

Selling Through Store Retailers

In contrast to wholesalers, retailers are a highly visible element in the distribution chain. More than 1.1 million retail intermediaries ring up merchandise worth $2.5 trillion every year.[14] Store retailers include department stores, discount stores, off-price stores, warehouse clubs, factory outlets, specialty stores, category killers, supermarkets, hypermarkets, convenience stores, and catalog stores (see Exhibit 14.5). They sell everything from rolling pins to Rolls-Royces and from hot dogs to haute cuisine.

Retail stores provide benefits to consumers in many ways. Retail stores like Home Depot save people time and money by providing an assortment of merchandise under one roof. Stores like Pier One Imports give shoppers access to goods and delicacies that they would have difficulty finding on their own. Still other retailers build traffic and add convenience by diversifying their product lines, a practice known as **scrambled merchandising.** For example, you can rent videos, eat pizza, and buy T-shirts at Grand Union supermarkets, and you can buy cosmetics, stationery, and toys at Walgreen's drugstores. Such mixed product assortments cut across retail classifications and blur store identities in the consumers' minds.

Many stores begin as discount operations and then upgrade their product offerings to become more like department stores in appearance, merchandise, and price. This process of store evolution, known as the **wheel of retailing,** follows a predictable pattern: An innovative retailer with low operating costs attracts a following by offering low prices and limited service. As this store adds more services over time to broaden its appeal, its prices creep upward, opening the door for lower-priced competitors. Eventually, these low-price competitors also upgrade their operations and are replaced by still other lower-priced stores that later follow the same upward pattern.

Specialty Stores, Category Killers, and Discount Stores Although department stores account for about 10 percent of overall U.S. retail sales, a much higher percentage of store sales are racked up by other types of retailers.[15] When you shop in a pet store, a shoe store, or a stationery store, you are in a **specialty store**—a store that carries only particular types of goods. The basic merchandising strategy of a specialty shop is to offer a limited number of product lines but an extensive

TYPE OF RETAILER	DESCRIPTION	EXAMPLES
Category killer	Type of specialty store focusing on specific products on giant scale and dominating retail sales in respective products categories	Office Depot Toys "R" Us
Convenience store	Offers staple convenience goods, long service hours, quick checkouts	7-Eleven
Department store	Offers a wide variety of merchandise under one roof in departmentalized sections and many customer services	Sears J.C. Penney Nordstrom
Discount store	Offers a wide variety of merchandise at low prices and few services	Kmart Wal-Mart
Factory/retail outlet	Large outlet store selling discontinued items, overruns, and factory seconds	Nordstrom Rack Nike outlet store
Hypermarket	Giant store offering food and general merchandise at discount prices	Super Kmart
Off-price store	Offers designer and brand-name merchandise at low prices and few services	T. J. Maxx Marshall's
Specialty store	Offers a complete selection in a narrow range of merchandise	Payless Shoes
Supermarket	Large, self-service store offering a wide selection of food and nonfood merchandise	Kroger
Warehouse club	Large, warehouse style store that sells food and general merchandise at discount prices; some require club membership	Sam's Club

EXHIBIT 14.5

TYPES OF RETAIL STORES

The definition of retailer covers many types of outlets. This table shows some of the most common types.

selection of brands, styles, sizes, models, colors, materials, and prices within each line stocked. Specialty shops are particularly strong in certain product categories: books, children's clothing, or sporting goods, for example.

At the other end of the retail spectrum are the **category killers**—superstores that dominate a particular product category by stocking every conceivable variety of merchandise in that category. Home Depot, Toys "R" Us, Office Depot, and Barnes & Noble are examples. Category killers ring up as much as one-third of all U.S. retail sales, a dominant position.[16] Still, experts predict that with increasing competition, category killers will eventually become a diminishing force. To increase their market share, some category killers such as Comp USA, Staples, and even Home Depot (using the Villager's Hardware name) are opening stores that are one-half to one-third the size of their other stores. Smaller stores help boost profits because they are less costly to run and stock only top-selling items.[17]

In contrast to category killers, **discount stores** offer a wider variety of merchandise, lower prices, and fewer services. Some experts predict that "the discount department segment is going to be the fastest-growing."[18] In fact, discount stores such as Wal-Mart and Target are stopping category killers like Toys "R" Us in their tracks. That's because a specific product category such as toys accounts for only a fraction of general discounters' sales, so the discounters can afford to cut prices on that category as a way to lure shoppers. But toys are the only category at Toys "R" Us, so lowering prices can hurt this category killer far more than it can hurt the multiproduct discount store.[19]

One of the newest categories of discounters are supercenters, large discount stores that offer large selections of groceries, toys, household items, and more. Since the early 1990s, Wal-Mart has opened over 800 U.S. supercenters with an average size of 182,000 square feet. The company continues to open 160 or more new supercenters each year, in addition to new supermarket-style Wal-Mart Neighborhood Markets. By combining a broad selection of products and services and everyday low prices, supercenters have made Wal-Mart one of the nation's largest food retailers. Lower prices are a major advantage: Wal-Mart admits that it can sell groceries below cost because it compensates by selling other profitable merchandise. But the world's largest retailer is also counting on its high-efficiency distribution system to put fresher produce on the shelves and keep popular items in stock at all times.[20]

Retail Industry Challenges One of the biggest challenges facing the retail industry today is an oversupply of physical retail stores. An estimated 21.5 square feet of retail space exists for every man, woman, and child in the United States today, a 46 percent increase from the 14.7 square feet per person in 1986. As one retail expert puts it, "We are absolutely overmalled."[21]

Some of this excess retail space is being transformed into office space. But the oversupply and changing consumer shopping habits have thrown the industry into a state of turmoil. Competition among retailers is more intense than ever, forcing continued mergers among store chains. Shoppers are tired of tramping from one store to another or are attracted by the convenience of shopping online. In fact, the average time consumers spend shopping has dropped 25 percent since 1982, and the average number of stores visited during a mall trip has dropped by 32 percent.[22] Furthermore, many retail locations are looking their age; nearly half of the more than 2,800 enclosed malls in the United States were built in the 1970s or earlier.[23]

To entice shoppers, some malls are being re-invented through extensive remodeling and the addition of newer stores, restaurants, and short-term shows and exhibits. New stores are also popping up everywhere—from airport terminals to tiny towns—offering anytime, anyplace shopping convenience to draw consumers back again and again.[24] Some retailers are trying to make their stores exciting, memorable, and fun. This trend toward "retail-tainment" is adding a touch of friendly theatrics to local outlets of giant chains. Customers who can attend a cooking

category killers
Discount chains that sell only one category of products

discount stores
Retailers that sell a variety of goods below the market price by keeping their overhead low

By leveraging its distribution and buying strengths, Wal-Mart is hoping that its Neighborhood Markets, about the same size as traditional supermarkets, will capture market share by offering shoppers everyday low prices.

Toys "R" Us sells over $11 billion in merchandise annually but is facing increasing competition from discounter Wal-Mart and online toy retailers. In 2000, the company formed a strategic alliance with Amazon. By sharing each other's strengths in toy retailing, the partners hope to become the world's leading seller of toys on the Internet.

class at Williams Sonoma or get tips from golf pros at the Sports Authority are likely to come back for the latest in-store event—and buy something when they do.[25]

Selling Through Nonstore Retailers

Nonstore retailing has its roots in the mail-order catalogs sent out by Sears and Montgomery Ward during the late 1800s, selling everything from household goods to ready-to-assemble housing materials. Today you can order clothing, electronics, flowers, and almost every other type of tangible and intangible product from anywhere in the world at any time of day without actually visiting a store. Nonstore retailing includes mail-order firms such as L. L. Bean, vending machines such as those selling candy bars and soft drinks, telemarketers such as those selling British Telecom services, door-to-door direct sellers, and a variety of electronic venues such as the Internet, television home shopping networks, and interactive kiosks (free-standing information and ordering machines).

Even though nonstore retailing has many venues, about 93 percent of goods and services are still sold through physical stores.[26] However, nonstore retailing is growing at a much faster rate than traditional store retailing, and it is estimated that one-third to one-half of all general merchandise could soon be sold through nonstore channels.[27] In many cases, producers are reaching shoppers through a carefully balanced blend of store and nonstore retail outlets, as this chapter's Focusing on E-Business Today feature highlights. Nike, for example, sells its products on its Web site, in addition to selling Nike products through store retailers. To encourage customers to purchase through store retailers, Nike lists the locations of its retailers on its Web site—and offers the products it sells on the Web at full price (no discounts).[28]

Despite the convenience of nonstore retailing, most people will continue to shop in stores because they like to see, feel, smell, and try out goods before they buy.[29] This was the line of thinking behind Gateway's decision to open Gateway Country stores. The company hopes that giving customers the opportunity to test-drive the computers and achieve a comfort level with the technology will eventually pay off.[30]

mail-order firms
Companies that sell products through catalogs and ship them directly to customers

Mail-Order Firms Among the most popular types of nonstore retailers are **mail-order firms.** These firms provide customers and businesses with a wide variety of goods ordered from catalogs and shipped by mail or private carrier. Catalog shopping is big business. In 1999, U.S. consumers spent more than $265 billion on mail-order goods and services, and businesses ordered another $190 billion worth through catalogs.[31] But this venue is facing stiff competition from the Internet and traditional stores. The annual growth rate for consumer catalog sales is expected to decline over the next few years from around 8 percent to 5 percent.[32]

To boost sales, catalog firms such as Harry and David, Delia*s, and L. L. Bean have developed Web sites to display their products and allow customers to place orders electronically. Some have even

Best of the Web Best of the Web Best of

EXPLORE THE WORLD OF RETAILING

Thinking about opening up a small store or building a career in retailing? Need some statistics? Find out what's hot in the retail industry by visiting the National Retail Federation Web site. Browse the FAQs and read the Washington Update. Learn which government proposals might affect your retail business and how to do something about them. Opening a retail store can be an exciting venture—especially if you're prepared.
www.nrf.com

MANAGING IN THE 21ST CENTURY

GATEWAY'S BIG GAMBLE

For all the out-of-the-box innovators the retail industry has seen, none has pushed the envelope quite as far as Ted Waitt, founder of Gateway computers. In the early 1990s Waitt's view of the personal computer market was simply that of a manufacturer trying to compete in a saturated market. But in 1995, when online sales were just a measly $150 million, Gateway became the first PC maker to sell its wares on the Net. By the end of the century, the company had launched a chain of Gateway Country retail stores and in one fell swoop repositioned itself as both a manufacturer and a retailer.

At first industry insiders scoffed. Why invest in bricks and mortar when the Internet was creating the most efficient channel possible? Now, nobody's laughing. The company has over 240 freestanding Gateway Country stores and 1,000 smaller Gateway stores-within-a-store located inside Office Max retail outlets. None of the stores carry inventory because all Gateway products are built-to-order. They allow customers to test-drive the machines, explore the different options, and then place a custom order. Furthermore, the freestanding stores have features such as couches, coffee, and small rooms where sales associates can talk to customers in a more private setting. "There's a kind of customer interaction that you're going to get at a Gateway Country store that you're not going to get at Best Buy or Circuit City," says one computer industry analyst.

Today, Gateway is the only PC manufacturer to effectively operate in three different channels of direct-to-consumer retailing. Consumers can buy Gateway products by phone, by Web, and by visiting its Gateway Country stores—which are driving big profits from e-commerce, Internet access, customer training, and other sources. And with plans to manufacture an array of Web appliances that some refer to as "beyond the box," Gateway is raising the ante again. Desktop net cruisers, touchpads for the kitchen, and wireless gadgets you can carry around the house are just a few of the future Gateway appliances the company plans to showcase in its stores. Gateway's vision of the future includes the networked home. And Gateway thinks the stores are a good way to show consumers how that will work.

■ QUESTIONS FOR CRITICAL THINKING

1. Why did Gateway open retail stores?

2. Why would Gateway locate smaller retail stores in Office Max outlets?

opened up small retail outlets in select cities. Why in this virtual age are catalogers opening physical stores? For one thing, retail stores soothe consumers' doubts about not seeing the product or gauging its quality. For another, some customers prefer to shop online versus paging through paper catalogs. As one retail expert put it, "the combination of bricks-and-mortar and the Internet is where we have to be."[33]

Automatic Vending For certain types of products, vending machines are an important nonstore retail outlet. In Japan, soda pop, coffee, candy, sandwiches, and cigarettes are all commonly sold this way. From the consumer's point of view, the chief attraction of vending machines is their convenience: They are open 24 hours a day and may be found in a variety of handy locations such as college dormitories. On the other hand, vending-machine prices are usually no bargain. The cost of servicing the machines is relatively high, and vandalism is a factor. So high prices are required in order to provide the vending-machine company and the product manufacturer with a reasonable profit.

While many computer sellers are either retreating from retail or pursuing direct sales strategies via the Web and catalogs, Gateway is taking a different path by establishing Gateway Country Stores.

Telemarketing and Door-to-Door Sales Telemarketing and door-to-door sales are also common forms of nonstore retailing. You have probably experienced telephone retailing, or *telemarketing*, in the form of calls from insurance agents, long-distance telephone companies, and assorted non-profit organizations, all trying to interest you in their products and causes. Every year, U.S. consumers buy more than $186 billion worth of goods and services over the telephone, and business purchases by phone top $239 billion.[34]

Door-to-door sales, in which a large sales force calls directly on customers in their homes or offices to demonstrate merchandise, take orders, and make deliveries, is becoming less popular. Two famous names in door-to-door selling—and its variant, the party plan—are Avon and Tupperware. However, both companies are launching initiatives to sell directly to the customer over the Internet. After 115 years of selling exclusively door-to-door, Avon is pushing into traditional retail by establishing Avon centers in Sears and J.C. Penney stores. Avon had always avoided such a move for fear of competing against its 500,000 U.S. sales representatives. So to keep the peace, the company is creating a separate line of "Avon Gold" products to sell at its store-within-a-store concept, and it is establishing kiosks in shopping malls that will be run by Avon sales representatives.[35]

Electronic Retailing Whether you call it electronic retailing, digital commerce, e-shopping, e-tailing, cybershopping, or virtual retail, the amount of money spent by consumers online is projected to increase exponentially each year.[36] Electronic retailing has many advantages. From the retailer's viewpoint, electronic retailing costs less (no expensive store rent and store payroll); from the customer's viewpoint, electronic retailing means being able to shop around the clock for products and information tailored to individual needs.

Some electronic retailers—known as *pure-plays*—sell goods only via the Internet. They have no physical stores and make the Internet the cornerstone of their distribution strategies. Amazon.com, for instance, is a pure-play electronic retailer. The company offers an online-only assortment of CDs, videos, and scores of other products besides its extensive book listings. Other electronic retailers, such as Barnes & Noble, operate both physical stores and Web stores—this approach is becoming more and more common.[37]

Dell Computer originally sold computers only through mail-order catalogs and telemarketing. But now it is moving business to the Internet—where it already generates an eye-popping $40 million in sales each day. "We're trying to transform the way Dell does business," explains the director of Dell Online. "We want the Net to become a core part of your experience with Dell."[38]

Nonetheless, hanging out a shingle on the Internet does not guarantee visitors, let alone sales (see Exhibit 14.6). Those products and selling approaches that best fit the Internet will succeed; less-appropriate products and selling approaches will fail.[39] Look at iPrint, an Internet-only printer of business cards, letterhead, and other stationery items. Although print-to-order products are commonly sold in person at Mail Boxes Etc. and many independent print shops, iPrint is thriving on a user-friendly, self-service approach. "The success of our Web site depends on the fact that it's as easy to use as a bank ATM," says Royal P. Farras, iPrint's

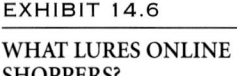

EXHIBIT 14.6

WHAT LURES ONLINE
SHOPPERS?

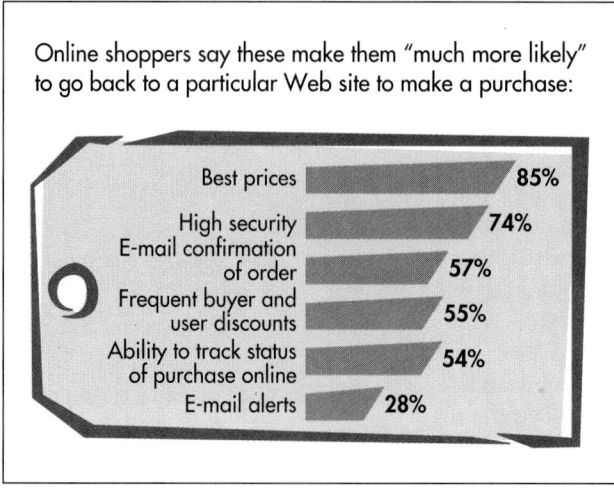

founder.[40] Among the ways you can sell your products online are through electronic catalogs and via cybermalls with virtual storefronts. (Consult Part II of the E-Business Online Supplement at www.prenhall.com/mescon for additional discussion of how iPrint pursues outsourcing, co-branding, and partnering.)

Electronic Catalogs Electronic catalogs (catalogs on computer disk or published over the Internet) have many advantages: they offer an easy way for customers to search for products, they allow businesses to reach an enormous number of potential customers at a relatively low cost, and they present timely information about a product's price and availability. Consider AMP, an electronics manufacturer in Harrisburg, Pennsylvania. The company was spending about $8 million to $10 million a year on its paper-based catalog, and some of the information was already out of date by the time the catalog was mailed. So, like many companies, AMP switched to electronic catalogs. W. W. Grainger, a 73-year-old industrial-parts supplier is another company that has moved its catalog, with over 80,000 items, to the Web. The company's annual Web sales now total about $400 million.[41]

Cybermalls A *cybermall* is a Web-based retail complex that houses dozens of *virtual storefronts,* or Internet-based stores. Consumers can buy everything from computer software to gourmet chocolates in cybermalls maintained by Yahoo!, America Online, and Microsoft. Like their physical counterparts, these Internet storefronts rely on a lot of "walk-in" traffic. For instance, cybermall shoppers interested in buying a CD might also click on the cyber shoe store. Besides exposure, another key advantage of a cybermall is that tenants do not have to create their own Web page or find a server to house it. Typically, the cybermall operator does all that for a sizable fee.[42]

Some cybermalls specialize. For example, MelaNet's African Marketplace specializes in goods and services provided by African Americans.[43] Other cybermalls feature a broader selection of retailers selling diverse goods and services. Yahoo!'s cybermall features well over 27,000 virtual storefronts, including big stores like J.C. Penney and smaller stores like the Amish Acres General Store. With cybermall sales increasing every day, Yahoo!'s chief operating officer predicts that online shopping will soon be bigger than catalog shopping.[44]

■ MANAGING PHYSICAL DISTRIBUTION

Besides selecting the most effective channels for selling a product, companies must decide on the best way to move their products and services through the channels so that they are available to the customers at the right place, at the right time, and in the right amount. **Physical distribution** encompasses all the activities required to move finished products from the producer to the consumer, including inventory control, order processing, warehousing, materials handling, and outbound transportation (see Exhibit 14.7).

The distribution process may not appear very glamorous or exciting, but it is vital to a company's success. To illustrate the importance of physical distribution, consider this: A typical box of breakfast cereal can spend as long as 104 days getting from factory to supermarket, moving haltingly through a series of wholesalers, distributors, brokers, diverters, and consolidators,

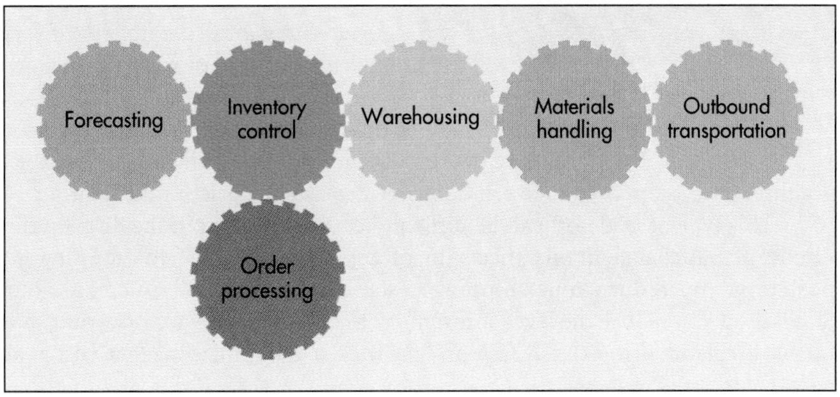

physical distribution
All the activities required to move finished products from the producer to the consumer

EXHIBIT 14.7

STEPS IN THE PHYSICAL DISTRIBUTION PROCESS

The phases of a distribution system should mesh as smoothly as the cogs in a machine. Because the steps are interrelated, a change in one phase can affect the other phases. The objective of the process is to provide a target level of customer service at the lowest overall cost.

logistics
The planning, movement, and flow of goods and related information throughout the supply chain

each of which has a warehouse. In fact, so many physical distribution systems are burdened with duplication and inefficiency that in industry after industry executives have been placing one item near the top of the corporate agenda: **logistics**—the planning and movement of goods and information throughout the supply chain.

Hard pressed to knock out competitors on quality or price, companies are trying to gain an edge through their ability to deliver the right stuff to the right place at the right time. For instance, PC Connection, a direct marketer selling computers and software, uses physical distribution to maintain an edge in customer service. Computer buyers who order as late as 2:45 A.M. can receive their purchases later that same day, nearly anywhere in the United States. PC Connection achieves this remarkable level of service by maintaining a warehouse at the Ohio airport used by its shipping partner, Airborne Express. When an order arrives by phone or fax, the merchandise can be loaded on the next Airborne flight. This dedication to customer service pays off for PC Connection in increased sales and a loyal customer base.[45] Plus, more skillful handling of logistics can put money back into a company's pocket by reducing inventory levels and holding time for finished goods.[46]

Keep in mind that streamlining processes that traverse companies and continents is not an easy task, but the payback can be enormous. Over a two-year period, National Semiconductor was able to cut its standard delivery time 47 percent, reduce distribution costs 2.5 percent, and increase sales 34 percent. How? By shutting down six warehouses around the globe and air-freighting its microchips to customers worldwide from a new distribution center in Singapore.[47]

Technology and Physical Distribution

Some of today's most advanced physical distribution systems employ satellite navigation and communication, voice-input computers, machine vision, robots, onboard computer logbooks, and planning software that relies on artificial intelligence. Kansas-based trucking firm OTR Express operates almost as if it were a giant computer system that just happens to use trucks to get the job done. By using custom software to track everything from the location of trucks to the best places in the country to buy tires, OTR racks up profits while keeping the firm's prices competitive.[48]

FedEx also fully exploits the benefits of technology to automate its services and provide superior customer service. The company's $180 million small-package sorting system processes over 400,000 packages an hour. Each parcel is scanned four times, weighed, and measured, and its digital image is recorded on computer. In addition, the company's world shipping software streamlines customer billing, reduces shipping paperwork, and allows customers to track their shipments over the Internet.[49]

Regardless of the technology you use, the key to success in managing physical distribution is to coordinate the activities of everyone involved, from the sales staff that is trying to satisfy demanding customers to the production staff that is trying to manage factory workloads. The overriding objective should be to achieve a competitive level of *customer-service standards* (the quality of service that a firm provides for its customers) at the lowest total cost. In general, as the level of service improves, the cost of distribution increases. A producer must analyze whether it is worthwhile to deliver the product in, say, three days as opposed to five, if doing so increases the price of the item.

FedEx founder Fred Smith believes that information about the package is almost as important as the package itself. FedEx relies on its elaborate package scanning and tracking systems to compete with UPS in the package delivery system.

This type of trade-off can be difficult because the steps in the distribution process are all interrelated. A change in one affects the others. For example, if you use slower forms of transportation, you reduce your shipping costs, but you probably increase your storage costs. Similarly, if you reduce the level of inventory to cut your storage costs, you run the risk of being unable to fill orders in a timely fashion. The trick is to optimize the *total* cost of achieving the desired level of service. This optimization requires a careful analysis of each step in the distribution process in relation to every other step.

In-House Operations

The steps in the distribution process can be divided into in-house operations and transportation. The in-house steps in the process include forecasting, order processing, inventory control, warehousing, and materials handling.

Forecasting To control the flow of products through the distribution system, a firm must have an accurate estimate of demand. To some degree, historical data can be used to project future sales; however, the firm must also consider the impact of unusual events (such as special promotions) that might temporarily boost demand. For example, if Home Depot decided to offer a special discount price on electric drills during September, management would need to purchase additional drills during the latter part of August to satisfy the extra demand.

Order Processing Order processing involves preparing orders for shipment and receiving orders when shipments arrive. It includes a number of activities, such as checking the customer's credit, recording the sale, making the appropriate accounting entries, arranging for the item to be shipped, adjusting the inventory records, and billing the customer. Because order processing involves direct interaction with the customer, it affects a company's reputation for customer service. Most companies establish standards for filling orders within a specific time period. PC Connection's guarantee of same-day shipping for orders received up to 2:45 A.M. is a good example.

Inventory Control As Chapter 9 discusses, in an ideal world, a company would always have just the right amount of goods on hand to fill the orders it receives. In reality, however, inventory and sales are seldom in perfect balance. Most firms like to build a supply of finished goods so that they can fill orders in a timely fashion. But how much inventory is enough? If your inventory is too large, you incur extra expenses for storage space, handling, insurance, and taxes; you also run the risk of product obsolescence. On the other hand, if your inventory is too low, you may lose sales when the product is not in stock. The objective of *inventory control* is to resolve these issues. Inventory managers decide how much product to keep on hand and when to replenish the supply of goods in inventory. They also decide how to allocate products to customers if orders exceed supply.

Warehousing Products held in inventory are physically stored in a **warehouse,** which may be owned by the manufacturer, by an intermediary, or by a private company that leases space to others. Some warehouses are almost purely holding facilities in which goods are stored for relatively long periods. Other warehouses, known as **distribution centers,** serve as command posts for moving products to customers. In a typical distribution center, goods produced at a company's various locations are collected, sorted, coded, and redistributed to fill customer orders.

Materials Handling An important part of warehousing activities is **materials handling,** the movement of goods within and between physical distribution facilities. One main area of concern is storage method—whether to keep supplies and finished goods in individual packages, in large boxes, or in sealed shipping containers. The choice of storage method depends on how the product is shipped, in what quantities, and to which locations. For example, a firm that typically sends small quantities of goods to widely scattered customers wouldn't want to use large containers. Materials handling also involves keeping track of inventory so that the company knows where in the distribution process its goods are located and when they need to be moved.

order processing
Functions involved in preparing and receiving an order

warehouse
Facility for storing inventory

distribution centers
Warehouse facilities that specialize in collecting and shipping merchandise

materials handling
Movement of goods within a firm's warehouse terminal, factory, or store

Today's distribution centers, such as this one for Amazon.com, are highly automated with advanced materials-handling systems controlled by a computer.

LEARNING OBJECTIVE 7

Highlight the key things to consider when choosing a form of transportation, and list the five major modes of transportation used in physical distribution

common carriers
Transportation companies that offer their services to the general public

contract carriers
Specialized freight haulers that serve selected companies under written contract

private carriers
Transportation operations owned by a company to move only its own products

Using technology in the materials-handling process can make a big difference. When customers place orders at Amazon.com, for example, workers known as pickers race around large distribution centers, pulling the items off the shelves and loading them onto a giant conveyor belt. The products move from belt to belt until they drop into one of the 2,000 chutelike assembly bins assigned to customers when they clicked the Web site's "buy it now" button. As the conveyer moves, other items for the same customer fall into the bin. When the order is complete, a light flashes below the bin, and a worker puts all the binned items into a box, which then travels down another series of belts through machines that pack it, tape it, weigh it, affix a mailing label, and load it onto a truck at one of the loading docks.[50]

Transportation Operations

Firms that move freight are called *carriers,* and they fall into three basic categories: **Common carriers** offer their services to the general public, **contract carriers** haul freight for selected companies under written contract, and **private carriers** are company-owned systems that move their own company's products. Some firms use a combination of carriers, relying on common or contract carriers to help out when their private carriers are running at capacity.

For any business, the cost of transportation is normally the largest single item in the overall cost of physical distribution. When choosing transportation, however, managers must also evaluate other marketing issues: storage, financing, sales, inventory size, speed, product perishability, dependability, flexibility, and convenience—to name a few. The goal is to maximize the efficiency of the entire distribution process while minimizing overall cost. Each of the five major modes of transportation described here has distinct advantages and disadvantages. By utilizing intermodal transportation (a combination of multiple modes), shippers can compound the benefits of each mode.

- *Rail.* Railroads can carry heavier and more diverse cargo and a larger volume of goods than any other mode of transportation. However, trains are constrained to tracks, so they can rarely deliver goods directly to customers.

- *Truck.* Trucks are a preferred form of transportation for two reasons: (1) the convenience of door-to-door delivery and (2) the ease and efficiency of travel on public highways, which does not require the use of expensive terminals or the execution of the right-of-way agreements (customary for air and rail transportation). However, trucks cannot carry all types of cargo cost effectively; for example, commodities such as steel and coal are too large and heavy.

- *Water.* The lowest-cost method of transportation is water, the preferred method for such low-cost bulk items as oil, coal, ore, cotton, and lumber. However, ships are slow, and service to any given location is infrequent. Furthermore, another form of transportation is usually needed to complete delivery to the final destination, like it is for rail.

- *Air.* Air transportation offers the advantage of speed, but at a price. Airports are not always convenient to customers; airplanes have size, shape, and weight limitations; and planes are the least dependable and most expensive form of transportation. Weather may cause flight cancel-

Best of the Web Best of the Web Best of

GET A MOVE ON

How much freight are companies moving around the United States? To find the answer, visit the Web site of the U.S. Department of Transportation's Commodity Flow Survey Program. Read the results of the latest survey to find out how many *billion* tons of raw materials and finished goods—worth *trillions* of dollars—are being shipped within the country. Surprisingly, more than half the shipments (as measured by tonnage) are headed to a destination less than 50 miles from their point of origin. So physical distribution is critical even when you are buying and selling locally.
www.bts.gov/ntda/cfs/

lations, and even minor repairs may lead to serious delays. But when speed is a priority, air is usually the only way to go.

■ *Pipeline.* For products such as gasoline, natural gas, and coal or wood chips (suspended in liquid), pipelines are an effective mode of transportation. Although they are expensive to build, they are extremely economical to operate and maintain. The downside is that transportation via pipeline is slow (three to four miles per hour), and routes are inflexible.

INCORPORATING THE INTERNET INTO YOUR ■ DISTRIBUTION STRATEGIES

LEARNING OBJECTIVE **8**

Discuss the Internet's effect on the distribution function

The Internet's efficient and effective global reach is revolutionizing the way goods and services are sold and distributed. Amazon.com's Jeff Bezos was a pioneer in recognizing the Internet's potential for making goods and services available to buyers. He reasoned that given a choice, many people would prefer the ease and convenience of online shopping to visiting a store every time they wanted to buy a book. He also believed that publishers would welcome Amazon.com as yet another way to get their books into the hands of readers.

Today, a growing number of businesses sell a huge selection of goods and services online. For some like Amazon, the Internet is their only marketing channel. For others like Recreational Equipment Inc. (REI), a sporting goods retailer, the Internet offers an additional way to sell to customers (see A Case For Critical Thinking, on p. 393). For an increasing number of businesses, the Internet represents an ideal way to communicate with customers, provide information, and promote their products or services. Funjet uses its Web site to advertise its charter vacations and provide potential customers with sufficient information to plan and price their trips. To book the trip, however, customers must still work through an authorized travel agent.[51]

Many intermediaries are using the Internet to improve the efficiency of their distribution systems and to expand their market reach. Herman Miller, an office furniture manufacturer, uses the Internet to target the home-office market, a segment that its traditional dealer network wasn't servicing. The company sees this as a terrific opportunity for the supplier and the distributor to reach new customers. An added benefit is that these home-office customers may eventually grow into corporate accounts (typically serviced by dealers).[52]

Some companies, of course, are using the Internet to eliminate the middleman entirely. After 110 years of offering medical insurance through 20,000 insurance agents, Provident American Life & Health Insurance Company dropped its agent network, changed its name to HealthAxis.com, and launched a Web site to sell a full line of insurance products directly to consumers. CEO Michael Ashker says that eliminating "costly middlemen in an industry where distribution is inefficient" allowed the company to cut its prices by 15 percent.[53]

The airline industry is another example of how some companies are using the Internet to eliminate intermediaries. For years, airlines have been encouraging fliers to bypass physical and online travel agencies and buy tickets direct from the carriers' own Web sites—a move that would save the airlines considerable commissions and fees. Orbitz.com, a joint venture owned by United Airlines, AMR (parent of American Airlines), Delta Airlines, Northwest Airlines, and Continental Airlines, now makes it easier for consumers to buy airline tickets direct from over 30 airlines. Critics of the joint venture claim that the purpose of Orbitz is to eliminate third-party travel agents and to transfer the ticketing business to the proprietary electronic channel. The airlines counter that Orbitz was established to create an additional channel for selling airline tickets and travel-related products such as hotel and car rental bookings, not clear the field of independent travel agents.[54]

As these examples show, the Internet is indeed a powerful force that is changing the role of traditional intermediaries. But jumping on the electronic-commerce bandwagon entails a variety of risks and costs that can complicate life for any company. Experts have, of course, recommended several strategies for incorporating the Internet into an existing channel structure. We explore these strategies in this chapter's special feature, Focusing on E-Business Today.

FOCUSING ON E-BUSINESS TODAY

Clicks and Mortar: Bridging the Physical and Virtual Worlds

In the mid-1990s, experts advised physical stores to keep their fledgling e-businesses separate. The thinking was that separate e-businesses could speed up decision making, be more flexible, be more entrepreneurial, act independently, and thus compete more effectively with pure-play e-businesses (those that exist only on the Internet, such as Amazon.com and E*Trade).

Barnes & Noble embraced this approach. To compete with Amazon.com, it established a completely separate division—Barnesandnoble.com—and later spun the division off as a stand-alone company. But unlike pure-plays, Barnes & Noble lacked a sense of urgency about the Web and let Amazon capture the lion's share of initial e-business and publicity. Other retailers debated whether to sell online at all. They worried about spreading their human and financial resources too thin. They worried about competing with their existing distributors, their competitors, and themselves (since their e-sales could cannibalize their physical-store sales).

MIXING IT UP

In hindsight, the experts may have been wrong. New studies of consumer Internet behavior indicate that the most effective way to attract and retain customers is a clicks-and-bricks approach. A *clicks-and-bricks* corporation (also

LEARNING
OBJECTIVE   9

Discuss how customers and traditional retailers benefit from a clicks-and-mortar distribution strategy

known as *clicks-and-mortar*) integrates its Web site (clicks) with its existing physical stores (bricks or mortar), and the two share logistics and marketing programs. Mixing clicks with bricks makes shopping simple and convenient for customers. Using multiple channels—Internet, phone, fax, mail, and physical stores—customers can purchase what they want, where they want, and when they want. The clicks-and-bricks strategy is not easy to adopt, but it has potential advantages. Chief among them are increased sales and improved customer service.

RETURN TO SENDER

Handling returned merchandise can be a huge advantage for clicks-and-mortar retailers in their battle with Internet pure-plays. It's a lot easier to drop something off at a nearby store than to find a box, wrap it up, and haul it somewhere for shipment. Of course, some e-commerce kings such as Amazon.com have found ways to streamline the return process by enclosing self-addressed return labels. But plenty of Web retailers still make merchandise returns a difficult process. After all, integrating Web returns with physical stores is no simple task. The two operations may have different computer systems, different management teams, and sometimes even different merchandise. Despite these hurdles, experts see this intermingling of operations as a necessity. And few companies have done it as well as Nordstrom and Macy's.

Every Nordstrom.com Web order arrives with a prepaid, addressed package for returns to be shipped (at the customer's expense unless the purchase was on a Nordstrom credit card). The physical Nordstrom stores grant full value on returns of anything bought on the Web site. Macys.com goes a step further. Web customers are allowed to return their purchases to any Macy's store, and Web customers in cities with Macy's stores have an additional option: They can call Macy's customer service department to have a store employee pick up a return. The service is free; the customer just has to be home when the Macy's employee arrives.

USING BRICKS TO WIN CLICKS

Customers aren't the only ones who benefit from the integrated clicks-and-mortar strategy. Existing stores are finding that one of the strongest assets for online selling is an offline store. As shown in the exhibit on page 389, multichannel retailers outperform pure e-tailers in the percentage of online sales in most product categories.

Consider Clinique. The cosmetic manufacturer was reluctant to sell its cosmetics brand via its Web site. But after much debate, the company managed to convince retailers who handled the Clinque brand that selling products online didn't present consumers with an either/or situation. Clinique now reports that at least 20 percent of its online buyers are new customers, and 41 percent of purchases are of products customers have never used before. Moreover, a recent study shows that 43 percent of online consumers are more comfortable purchasing from an online retailer that has a real-world store nearby.

As the Clinique example shows, extending a company's current brand to the Internet is a terrific way to increase sales (assuming, of course, that the brand is

E-Tailers vs. Retailers Percentage of Online Sales		
	Multichannel retailer	Pure e-tailer
Travel		
1998	45%	55%
1999	58%	42%
Computer hardware and software		
1998	77%	23%
1999	82%	18%
Books		
1998	13%	87%
1999	26%	74%
Apparel and sporting goods		
1998	85%	15%
1999	81%	19%
Flowers, cards, and gifts		
1998	80%	20%
1999	80%	20%
Event tickets		
1998	100%	0%
1999	97%	3%
Home and garden products		
1998	79%	21%
1999	76%	24%
Toys		
1998	63%	37%
1999	29%	71%

TAPPING INTO THE EXISTING CUSTOMER BASE

Getting new customers is one of the most costly activities for pure-play e-businesses. Boston Consulting Group reports that it costs Internet-only retailers $82 to acquire a new customer. But it costs only $38 for existing store-based Internet retailers to get an online customer and just $12 for catalog-based retailers. Existing name recognition and a proven reputation are the principal reasons for these cost differences. Moreover, catalog shoppers are among the fastest to shift to Internet purchases because they are already accustomed to buying goods without seeing or touching them.

CROSS-SELLING

An increasing number of e-businesses are using their Web sites and in-store technology such as kiosks to drive traffic to their physical stores and vice versa. Many Sears customers gather product information from Sears.com before heading to the outlet at their local mall. "We hear story after story about customers who go to the Web site, research what they want, print it out, and then bring it to the sales associate." By the time they talk to a salesperson, customers know what they want to buy. Salespeople can then add value by doing things the Web site can't: answering specific product questions, critically comparing features, and demonstrating products. Such cross-selling is paying off for Sears, Eddie Bauer, and scores of others. Eddie Bauer (which sells products through catalogs, 570 retail stores, and four Web sites) reports that shoppers who use all three methods spend five times more than those who shop only by catalog.

CREATING THE PERFECT BLEND

Of course, nobody can deny that the pure-play Internet companies can indeed shake up an industry. Just look at Amazon.com and E*Trade. But now even these e-tailers are getting physical. E*Trade is opening outposts in SuperTarget stores and Amazon.com has joined forces with Toys "R" Us to sell toys. "There isn't anyone who is a pure-play who will survive without a bricks-and-clicks play, and no retailer who will make it without an Internet strategy," says one retail consultant. In other words, success in the new economy will go to those who can execute clicks-and-mortar strategies that bridge the physical and virtual worlds so that customers can buy anytime and anywhere regardless of the channel.[55]

both well recognized and respected). But it takes tremendous time and money for a new pure-play business to build a brand from scratch and develop effective distribution systems. Unlike pure plays, most established retailers have existing supplier networks, well-tuned distribution systems, logistics expertise, available cash for marketing, a thorough knowledge of their business lines, and a good understanding of what customers want. In many cases, these systems can easily be expanded to accommodate Internet sales. By adopting a clicks-and-mortar strategy, existing retailers can use their years of experience and proven systems for the Internet. Furthermore, they have two huge advantages over new pure-play retailers: an existing customer base and the ability to cross-sell.

SUMMARY OF LEARNING OBJECTIVES

1. **Explain what marketing intermediaries do and list their seven primary functions.**

   Marketing intermediaries, or middlemen, bring producers' products to market and help ensure that the goods and services are available in the right time, place, and amount. More specifically, intermediaries match buyers and sellers; provide market information; provide promotional and sales support; sort, standardize, and divide merchandise; transport and store the product; assume risks; and provide financing.

2. **Discuss the key factors that influence channel design and selection.**

   Channel design and selection are influenced by the type of product; target market; company strengths, weaknesses, and objectives; desired market coverage; distribution costs; the desire for control; and the potential for channel conflict.

3. **Differentiate between intensive, selective, and exclusive distribution strategies.**

   With an intensive distribution strategy, a company attempts to saturate the market with its products by offering them in every available outlet. Companies that use a more selective approach to distribution choose a limited number of retailers that can adequately support the product. Firms that use exclusive distribution grant a single wholesaler or retailer the exclusive right to sell the product within a given geographic area.

4. **Highlight the main advantage of a vertical marketing system and explain how it differs from a conventional marketing channel.**

   The main advantage of a vertical marketing system (VMS) is channel control. In a VMS, the producer, wholesaler, and retailer act as a unified system to conduct distribution activities. By contrast, in a conventional marketing channel, wholesalers and retailers are independent. Each firm pursues its own objectives.

5. **Explain how wholesalers and retailers function as intermediaries.**

   Wholesalers buy from producers and sell to retailers, to other wholesalers, and to organizational customers such as businesses, government agencies, and institutions. Retailers buy from producers or wholesalers and sell the products to the final consumers.

6. **Identify at least six types of store retailers and four types of non-store retailers.**

   Some of the most common types of store retailers are department stores, discount stores, specialty stores, supermarkets, convenience stores, category killers, and superstores. Common nonstore retailers are mail-order firms, vending machines, telemarketers, and electronic approaches (which include Web sites, electronic catalogs, and cybermalls).

7. **Highlight the key things to consider when choosing a form of transportation, and list the five major modes of transportation used in physical distribution.**

   When choosing a form of transportation, you should consider cost, storage, sales, inventory size, speed, product perishability, dependability, flexibility, and convenience. The five most common methods of transporting goods are by truck, rail, ship, airplane, and pipeline.

8. **Discuss the Internet's effect on the distribution function.**

   Companies are using the Internet to enhance their existing channel structures, expand their market reach, and add efficiencies to their channel structures. Some are eliminating layers of intermediaries from a marketing channel and transferring the eliminated intermediary functions to the Internet. In many cases these changes—especially the bypassing of a channel—are causing channel conflict.

9. **Discuss how customers and traditional retailers benefit from a clicks-and-mortar distribution strategy.**

   Clicks and mortar, or the integration of e-commerce with physical retail in a multiple-channel strategy, provides customers with multiple shopping options. Essentially, customers can get what they want, where they want it, and when they want it. In some cases they can even return unwanted Internet purchases to physical stores. Traditional retailers benefit from a clicks-and-mortar strategy by using their existing name recognition and customer loyalty to attract e-commerce customers. Moreover, they can use their expertise and existing distribution systems to transact e-commerce more efficiently than pure-play e-tailers—who must start from scratch. And they can cross-sell—that is, use their physical stores to promote their e-business and use their e-business to promote their physical stores.

KEY TERMS

agents and brokers (377)

category killers (379)

channel captain (375)

common carriers (386)

contract carriers (386)

discount stores (379)

distribution centers (385)

distribution channels (370)

distribution mix (370)

distribution strategy (370)

drop shippers (377)

exclusive distribution (374)

full-service merchant wholesalers (377)

industrial distributors (377)

intensive distribution (373)

limited-service merchant wholesalers (377)

logistics (384)

mail-order firms (380)

marketing intermediaries (370)

materials handling (385)

merchant wholesalers (377)

order processing (385)

physical distribution (383)

private carriers (386)

rack jobbers (377)

retailers (377)

scrambled merchandising (378)

selective distribution (374)

specialty store (378)

vertical marketing system (VMS) (374)

warehouse (385)

wheel of retailing (378)

wholesalers (377)

TEST YOUR KNOWLEDGE

QUESTIONS FOR REVIEW

1. What is a distribution channel?

2. What forms of utility do intermediaries create?

3. What are some of the main causes of channel conflict?

4. How does a specialty store differ from a category killer and a discount store?

5. What is meant by the wheel of retailing?

QUESTIONS FOR ANALYSIS

6. How does the presence of intermediaries in the distribution channel affect the price of products?

7. What are some of the challenges facing retailers today?

8. What are the benefits of electronic catalogs and cybermalls?

9. What trade-offs must you consider when adopting a physical distribution system?

10. **@** If a manufacturer starts to sell its goods on its company Web site, why might this arouse channel conflict?

11. **▣** Direct-mail marketers often publish different prices in different catalogs targeted at different market segments. When you call to order, the sales representative first asks for your customer or catalog number so that the rep knows which price to charge you.[56] Is this practice ethical?

QUESTIONS FOR APPLICATION

12. Imagine that you own a small specialty store selling handcrafted clothing and jewelry. What are some of the nonstore retail options you might explore to increase sales? What are the advantages and disadvantages of each option?

13. Compare the prices of three products offered at a retail outlet with the prices charged if you purchase those products by mail order (catalog or phone) or over the Internet. Be sure to include hidden costs such as handling and delivery charges. Which purchasing format produced the lowest price for each of your products?

14. **〰** In Chapter 9 we discussed the fact that supply chain management integrates all the activities involved in the production of goods and services from suppliers to customers. What are the benefits of involving distributors in the design, manufacturing, or sale of a company's product or service?

15. **〰** Which of the four basic functions of management discussed in Chapter 6 would be involved in decisions that establish or change a company's channels of distribution? Explain your answer.

PRACTICE YOUR KNOWLEDGE

SHARPENING YOUR COMMUNICATION SKILLS

Select a consumer product with which you are familiar, and trace its channel of distribution. The product might be fresh foods, cosmetics, clothing, or manufactured goods (ranging from something as simple as a fork to something as complex as a personal computer). For information you might contact a business involved in the manufacture or distribution of the product, either by letter or by telephone. Examine the various factors involved in the distribution of the product, and prepare a brief summary of your findings. Consider the following:

- The role of the intermediary in distribution

- The type of distribution: intensive, selective, or exclusive

- The amount of control the manufacturer has over the distribution process

- The type of channel used in the distribution process and its influence on the cost of the product

HANDLING DIFFICULT SITUATIONS ON THE JOB: MERCEDES-BENZ STEERS INTO CATALOG SALES

Nearly every automobile company offers branded clothing and accessories for proud vehicle owners or wanna-be's: ties, T-shirts, watches, shoes, hats, jackets, sweaters. Most are sold right in the showrooms, and they're extremely popular, whether they be Saturn sneakers or Land Rover tweeds. Some of the upscale auto manufacturers have been developing logo-bearing clothing and gadgets that meet their customers' higher-class budgets as well as their tastes. But pricing can be tricky because customers object to

paying a lot more for an ordinary shirt dressed up with only a carmaker's trademark.

Steve Beaty, vice president of accessories marketing for Mercedes-Benz, is reaching out to car owners with a 55-page, glossy, full-color *Mercedes-Benz Personal & Automotive Accessories* catalog loaded with expensive logoed items. Mercedes-Benz has recruited world-class, top-of-the-line manufacturers and designers to produce merchandise worthy of the company's highly refined clientele. The new catalog presents Wittnauer watches, Caran D'Ache ballpoints, Bally bomber jackets, and silk boxers designed by artist Nicole Miller—all emblazoned with the triangle logo or images of Mercedes-Benz models, past and present. The catalog even features a $3,300 collapsible aluminum mountain bike for slipping into the trunk of your 500SL.[57] As Beaty's assistant, you wonder whether mail-order retailing is the best—or the only—way to sell these items.

1. What are the advantages and disadvantages of using mail-order catalogs to sell Mercedes-Benz clothing and accessories?

2. Should Mercedes-Benz sell these accessories in its car showrooms? What challenges and opportunities do you see with this retail approach?

3. What nonstore retail options would you recommend for these logo products? What are the advantages and disadvantages of each?

BUILDING YOUR TEAM SKILLS

In managing the transportation side of physical distribution, companies have to look at more than cost. Paying less to ship products is certainly an important consideration, but dependability—knowing that carriers can be counted on to deliver products—is equally vital. Smaller businesses such as Noah's Ark Original Deli in Teaneck, New Jersey, can't afford to maintain their own fleet of delivery vans, instead they rely on FedEx and other common carriers to whisk their products to customers around the United States.

Noah's Ark is one of thousands of businesses that contract with FedEx to fulfill customer orders that come in via the Internet. But what can the deli do if FedEx employees go on strike? David Sokolow, the deli's manager, is especially concerned about disrupting deliveries during the crucial year-end holiday gift-giving season, when orders for knishes and other specialty foods come from as far away as Puerto Rico and Hawaii.[58]

With your team, identify at least four transportation options that Noah's Ark might consider if FedEx is not able to make deliveries during the holidays. Next to each option, list both advantages and disadvantages. Then assess FedEx in the same way.

Now think about the way transportation will affect the deli's products during the delivery period. What product characteristics must Sokolow consider when he makes plans to deal with a possible FedEx strike? What additional information should he obtain about each transportation option before making a decision? What criteria should he use to choose among the many options? And what can he do in advance to be better prepared before any delivery disruptions occur?

Summarize and share your team's listing of options, advantages, and disadvantages with the class. Also share your team's thinking about additional information needed and criteria for deciding among the various options. Did other teams identify the same options and criteria as your team? Which option do most teams recommend for Noah's Ark? Why?

EXPAND YOUR KNOWLEDGE

KEEPING CURRENT USING *THE WALL STREET JOURNAL*

Find an article in *The Wall Street Journal* (online or print edition) discussing changes a company is making to its distribution strategy or channels. For example, is a manufacturer selling products direct to consumers? Is a physical retailer offering goods via a company Web site? Is a company eliminating the middleman? Has a nonstore retailer decided to open a physical store? Is a category killer opening smaller stores? Has a major retail tenant closed its stores in a mall?

1. What changes in the company's distribution structure or strategy have taken place? What additional changes, if any, are planned?

2. What were the reasons for the changes? What role, if any, did electronic commerce play in the changes?

3. If you were a stockholder in this company, would you view these changes as positive or negative? What, if anything, might you do differently?

DISCOVERING CAREER OPPORTUNITIES

Retailing is a dynamic, fast-paced field with many career opportunities in both store and nonstore settings. In addition to hiring full-time employees when needed, retailers of all types often hire extra employees on a temporary basis for peak selling periods, such as the year-end holidays. You can find out about seasonal and year-round job openings by checking newspaper classified ads, looking for signs in store windows, and browsing the Web sites of online retailers.

1. Select a major retailer, such as a chain store in your area or a retailer on the Internet. Is this a specialty store, discount store, department store, or another type of retailer?

2. Contact the store manager or the human resources department of the retailer you have selected. What are this company's hiring procedures? What qualifications are needed for seasonal positions? For full-time positions? When is the best time to apply?

3. Research your chosen retailer using library sources, the company's annual report (if available), or online resources. Is this retailer expanding? Is it profitable? Has it recently acquired or been acquired by another firm? What are the implications of this acquisition for job opportunities?

EXPLORING THE BEST OF THE WEB

URLs for all Internet exercises are provided at the Web site for this book, www.prenhall.com/mescon. When you log on to the text Web site, select Chapter 14, then select "Student Resources," click on the name of the featured Web site, and follow the detailed navigational directions to complete these exercises.

Explore the World of Wholesaling, page 377

Read what the Occupational Outlook Handbook has to say about a career as a wholesale sales representative.

1. What important functions do sales representatives perform? What does a sales rep typically do during a sales call?

2. What are the typical working conditions for a sale representative? What personal skills are desired?

3. How do sales reps learn about their customers' changing needs?

Explore the World of Retailing, page 380

Visit the National Retail Federation Web site to explore the world of retailing.

1. Read about NRF. What does this organization do? Why should a retailer join this organization?

2. What qualities should the ideal retail job seeker possess? What does a buyer do?

3. Why must small retailers stay on top of current retailing issues on the government agenda?

Get a Move On, page 386

Point your Internet browser to the U.S. Department of Transportation's Commodity Flow Survey Program Web page and learn about moving freight around the United States.

1. What transportation modes are covered in this survey?

2. How much freight was transported in 1997? Did the movement of freight within the United States increase or decrease compared with the 1993 results?

3. Check out some reports at the National Transportation Library on the trucking industry and rail transportation. How would these reports be helpful to Home Depot and other major companies that move merchandise within the United States?

Explore on Your Own

Review these chapter-related Web sites on your own to learn more about developing and executing distribution strategies.

1. Find out who the top 100 retailers, specialty stores, Internet retailers, and global retailers are from Stores Magazine at www.stores.org.

2. Get the latest Internet facts and figures—including online sales—at the Internet Economy Indicators, www.internetindicators.com/.

3. Learn about Wal-Mart's tough supplier requirements by reading the company's Supplier Standards at www.walmartstores.com/supplier.

A CASE FOR CRITICAL THINKING

■ REI's Perfect Blend of Retail and E-Tail Channels

During the mid-1990s, many bricks-and-mortar companies were reluctant to establish an online presence for fear of competing against existing distribution channels. But Recreational Equipment Inc. (REI) viewed the Web as an exciting new channel that could reach markets far beyond the limits of its physical stores and paper catalogs. And the outdoor gear retailer quickly developed a winning multichannel approach that successfully blended its online store with its off line businesses.

ON SOLID GROUND

Established in 1938, REI was formed as a consumer cooperative to provide its members with high-quality sports equipment at reasonable prices. Though REI welcomed the business of nonmembers, the co-op shared its profits with members each year, awarding dividends that averaged 10 percent of purchases. Offering everything from canoes to hiking gear through a thriving catalog business and more than 50 retail stores, REI had grown into the nation's largest consumer co-op by the mid-1990s.

GEARING UP

In spite of its success, REI wanted to reach new markets beyond its current customer base and established distribution channels. Moreover, REI needed a way to inform customers and employees about the increasingly sophisticated array of products in the outdoor gear industry. Though the Internet seemed like the perfect channel for accomplishing both objectives, REI carefully considered the impact of an online business on its existing distribution channels. "We knew it was going to cannibalize our catalog, and it might have an impact at retail as well," recalls Wally Smith, REI's president and chief executive officer.

But the advantages of venturing into the world of e-tailing outweighed the risks for REI. Start-up costs for REI's Web site—$500,000 for all computers and programming—paled in comparison to building and equipping the typical $6 million REI store. And six decades of experience, powerful name recognition, and a loyal customer base placed REI in a strong position to move into cyberspace. "My philosophy . . . was 'we'd better do it ourselves or somebody will do it to us,'" Smith says.

THE FIRST STEP

So REI pressed ahead with its Web store in 1996. Launching www.rei.com in five languages to attract customers around the world, REI made every effort to integrate the online store with its established channels. Unlike pure-play retailers that must start from scratch, REI called upon its existing retail and catalog distribution systems for processing e-tail orders. The co-op also extended its Web strategy into its retail channels by placing Internet kiosks in stores. With in-store access to REI's Web site, retail shoppers can place online orders, interact with experts, or download customized items such as topographic hiking maps. Furthermore, store cash registers are Web-linked, so clerks can look up product information or sell items that are out of stock at one store but available at another. Moreover, because REI's online and offline channels offer the same merchandise and use the same computer system, customers can return Web purchases to REI's physical stores without any hassles.

With the success of www.rei.com, REI then launched a second site to attract bargain hunters: www.rei-outlet.com. Featuring items that are not available at REI's stores, in its catalog, or on its main Web site, the online outlet store carries limited quantities of manufacturers' overstocks, seconds, and product closeouts at rock-bottom prices. Links connect the discount store with the main site, allowing REI to tailor messages to each audience segment.

FLYING HIGH

Offering more than 10,000 items—more than any physical REI store—the Web stores operate around the clock, seven days per week. REI's first-rate service appeals to e-tail shoppers, who place nearly one-third of online orders after regular retail hours. "Our value proposition for rei.com is to deliver any product, at any time, to any place, and to answer any question," says an REI executive.

And the strategy works. With more than $50 million in annual Internet sales, www.rei.com ranks as the largest online seller of outdoor gear. Web sales are equivalent to one of REI's top five retail stores, and a typical Internet order is twice the amount of an average retail purchase. Moreover, REI continues to scale new heights in physical and virtual retailing, breaking into new markets with its effective blend of clicks and mortar. The rapid growth of REI's Japanese site, for instance, convinced the co-op to open a retail store in Tokyo.

REI credits its multichannel approach to serving customers as one of the key reasons for the company's success. "We've recognized that we can't choose how our customers want to shop, but we can make it easier for them to access us and provide the same high-quality shopping experience however they interact with REI," says a company spokesperson.

CRITICAL THINKING QUESTIONS

1. Why did REI venture into e-commerce?

2. How has REI's success as a traditional retailer benefited its online business?

3. How does REI blend its online and off line channels?

4. Go to Chapter 14 of this text's Web site at www.prenhall.com/mescon and click on the hot link to get the REI Web site. Follow the online instructions to answer these questions: How does REI promote its physical stores? What are REI's return policies for online customers? What outdoor information does this site offer?

VIDEO CASE AND EXERCISES

Distribution at Hain Foods: The Natural Way

SYNOPSIS

Hain Foods (www.albafoods.com) manufactures natural food products under a variety of brands, including Estee, Kineret, and its own Hain Foods label. The company uses five indirect distribution channels, including supermarkets, natural food stores, specialty grocery stores, warehouse clubs, and vending machines. Hain sells through 50 food brokers who, in turn, sell to the 500 distributors who get the food products into the natural foods sections of 20,000 supermarkets throughout the United States, including the Kroger and Food Lion chains. Hain has found that consumers in Western states buy more natural foods, so it concentrates its warehouses in that area to ensure a steady flow of goods in line with demand at local stores. Now the company is looking at expanding internationally, starting with the United Kingdom, as one way to fuel future growth.

EXERCISES

Analysis

1. Why would Hain Foods work through food brokers rather than directly with retail chains and individual stores?

2. How many channel levels does Hain Foods work through in getting its products to consumers?

3. How can the market coverage of Hain Foods be characterized?

4. What is the likely effect of the number of channel levels on the price that consumers pay for Hain Foods products?

5. Why are the natural food stores that carry Hain Foods products considered specialty stores?

Application

How does selling Hain Foods through vending machines support the company's relationships with retailers and other resellers?

Decision

Assume that Hain Foods is thinking about changing its distribution strategy. Instead of selling through brokers and distributors, it is considering selling directly to supermarket chains. How would this decision affect its physical distribution operations?

Communication

Ellen B. Deutsch, the senior vice president of global marketing for Hain Foods, has asked you to write a brief article for the company newsletter explaining why Hain decided to sell through warehouse clubs such as Sam's, which does not have a reputation for offering natural food products.

Integration

Referring to Figure 12.2 in Chapter 12, explain how Hain Foods creates form, time, and place utility for its channel customers.

Ethics

A growing number of small stores in remote locations are approaching wholesalers asking to carry Hain Foods. Although these stores don't buy much and cost a great deal to serve, they are seeking access to the Hain Foods products that their customers want. Do the wholesalers who handle Hain Foods have a social obligation to serve these retailers, even if they earn little or no profit?

Debate

Should Hain Foods issue a natural foods catalog to sell directly to consumers? Choose either the pro or the con side of this issue and list at least two arguments that support your position. As your instructor directs, either submit your arguments in writing or participate in a classroom debate on this issue.

Teamwork

In a team of three students, pick two types of stores in which Hain Foods products are sold and list some of the services that a wholesaler could offer to enhance that channel relationship. If feasible, visit representative stores to get more ideas.

Online Research

Using Internet sources, learn more about Hain Foods and its product lines. What brands have been acquired in the last few years? How is the company doing financially? See Component Chapter A, Exhibit A.1, for search engines to use in doing your research.

MYPHLIP COMPANION WEB SITE

Learning Interactively

Visit the myPHLIP Web site at www.prenhall.com/mescon. For Chapter 14, take advantage of the interactive "Study Guide" to test your chapter knowledge. Get instant feedback on whether you need additional studying. Read the "Current Events" articles to get the latest on chapter topics, and complete the exercises as specified by your instructor. Expand your learning with a visit to the "Research Area." There you will find a wealth of information you can use to complete your course assignments.

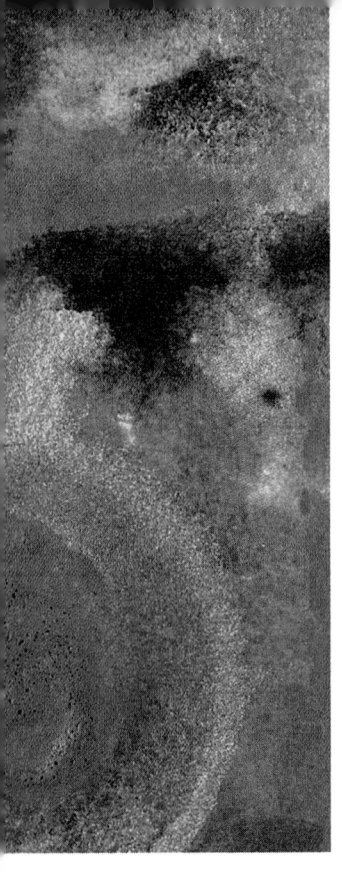

15
PROMOTIONAL STRATEGIES

LEARNING OBJECTIVES

After studying this chapter, you will be able to

1. Identify the five basic categories of promotion
2. List the seven steps in the personal-selling process
3. Explain the difference between logical and emotional advertising appeals
4. Define interactive advertising and discuss the challenge it presents to marketers
5. Name five popular direct marketing vehicles
6. Distinguish between the two main types of sales promotion, and give at least two examples of each
7. Explain the role of public relations in marketing
8. Discuss the use of integrated marketing communications
@ 9. Highlight the important elements of a winning Web site

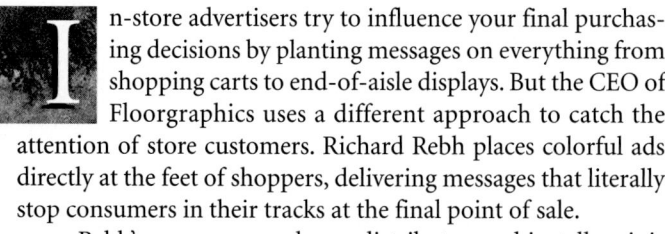

TODAY
Inside Business

Richard Rebh, founder of Floorgraphics, wants customers to walk all over his products.

FLOORING IT: MINI-BILLBOARDS AT YOUR FEET FROM FLOORGRAPHICS
w w w . f l o o r g r a p h i c s . c o m

In-store advertisers try to influence your final purchasing decisions by planting messages on everything from shopping carts to end-of-aisle displays. But the CEO of Floorgraphics uses a different approach to catch the attention of store customers. Richard Rebh places colorful ads directly at the feet of shoppers, delivering messages that literally stop consumers in their tracks at the final point of sale.

Rebh's company produces, distributes, and installs mini-billboards on the floors of major retailers across the country, carefully positioning each advertiser's message directly below the shelf location of the featured product. Since studies show that 70 percent of brand decisions are made in the store, Rebh insists that floor ads make a powerful impact on final buying decisions. "We believe we have the most crucial piece of real estate in the media world—right where every manufacturer wants to be, right in front of their product, right at the moment of decision," Rebh contends.

Rebh paves the way for Floorgraphics ads by leasing advertising floor space from stores for periods of three to five years. Then he sells the space to advertisers for 4-, 8-, or 12-week cycles and oversees every detail necessary for properly producing and installing each ad. After transforming an advertiser's digital photographs into six square feet of colorful, laminated decals, Floorgraphics' technicians affix the mini-billboards to the floors of participating merchants. Advertisers can promote their products with a single floor ad or divide their allotted space into smaller, separate components. Campbell Soup, for instance, uses a trail of small floor ads in the shape of Os to lead customers directly to the shelf location for SpaghettiOs.

Rebh of course avoids cluttering up every square inch of floor tile with splashy ads. To maintain the effectiveness of each message, he limits the number of floor ads to two per store aisle. Furthermore, he grants advertisers exclusive coverage in their brand categories. Floor ads for such competing brands as Pepsi and Coca-Cola, for example, do not appear in the same store.

To entice merchants to sign on with Floorgraphics, Rebh offers participating retailers a cut of ad revenue, usually about 25 percent of sales. And he provides advertisers a showcase for their advertising dollars that is economical, especially when compared to the costs of advertising on outdoor billboards, in TV commercials, and in other traditional media. For each mini-billboard, the cost-per-thousand impressions averages about $1 a day for advertisers, including production and installation charges.

Since the launch of Floorgraphics in 1998, Rebh has installed floor ads for more than 100 national advertisers in over 16,000 grocery, mass-merchandise, drug, and auto retail stores, including such retailing giants as Kmart and Food Lion. The unique promotional medium not only stimulates immediate sales but also reminds consumers of brand names and increases impulse purchases. Surveys commissioned by Floorgraphics reveal that floor ads increase brand sales by 25 to 27 percent, more than doubling the effect of advertising products such as shopping cart ads.

Rebh's future plans call for creating animated and electronic floor ads—complete with voice, sound, music, and full-motion images—that can be changed by remote control. And he envisions interactive floor displays that will allow customers to alter messages or register preferences by stepping on the ads. As far as Rebh is concerned, the floor's the limit for in-store consumer promotions.[1]

▪ THE PROMOTIONAL MIX

promotion
Wide variety of persuasive techniques used by companies to communicate with their target markets and the general public

Richard Rebh knows that promotions such as floor ads can increase brand awareness and stimulate customers to buy. Although **promotion** is defined in many ways, it is basically persuasive communication that motivates people to buy whatever an organization is selling—goods, services, or ideas. Promotion may take the form of direct, face-to-face communication or indirect communication through such media as television, radio, magazines, newspapers, direct mail, billboards, the Internet, floor ads, and other channels.

Of the four ingredients in the marketing mix (product, price, distribution, and promotion), promotion is perhaps the one most often associated with marketing. Although it is no guarantee of success, promotion does have a profound impact on a product's performance in the marketplace. Moreover, your **promotional strategy** defines the direction and scope of the promotional activities you implement to meet your marketing objectives.

promotional strategy
Statement or document that defines the direction and scope of the promotional activities that a company will use to meet its marketing objectives

Promotional Goals

You can use promotion to achieve three basic goals: to inform, to persuade, and to remind. *Informing* is the first promotional priority, because people cannot buy something until they are aware of it and know what it can do for them. Potential customers need to know where the item can be purchased, how much it costs, and how to use it. *Persuading* is also an important priority, because most people need to be encouraged to purchase something new or switch brands. Advertising that meets this goal is classified as **persuasive advertising.** *Reminding* the customer of the product's availability and benefits is also important, because such reminders stimulate additional purchases. The term for such promotional efforts is **reminder advertising.**

persuasive advertising
Advertising designed to encourage product sampling and brand switching

reminder advertising
Advertising intended to remind existing customers of a product's availability and benefits

Beyond these general objectives, your promotional strategy should accomplish specific objectives: They should attract new customers, increase usage among existing customers, aid distributors, stabilize sales, boost brand-name recognition, create sales leads, differentiate the product, and influence decision makers.

Promotional Ethics and Regulations

Although promotion serves many useful functions, critics argue that its goals are self-serving. Some contend that sellers use promotional tools to persuade people to buy unnecessary or potentially harmful goods like antiaging creams, baldness "cures," sweetened cereals, liquor, and cigarettes. Others argue that promotion encourages materialism at the expense of more worthwhile values, that it exploits stereotypes, and that it manipulates the consumer on a subconscious level. Still others argue that the money spent on promotion could be put to better use inventing new products or improving the quality of existing items.

Although abuses do occur, some of those charges are not justified. Take the charge about *subliminal advertising,* the notion that advertisers hide manipulative visual or audio cues in ads. Critics claim that flashing brief targeted messages across a movie screen (although too short to be recognized at the conscious level) can induce consumers to purchase the promoted products. However, there is no objective evidence of the existence of this sort of trickery and little psychological evidence to suggest that it would work even if anyone were doing it.[2]

Public concern about potential misuse of promotion has led the Federal Trade Commission (FTC) and other government agencies to pass strict rules and regulations that limit promotional abuses. One rule is that *all statements of fact must be supported by evidence.* For example, the Food and Drug Administration ordered Glaxo Wellcome PLC, makers of flu drug Relenza, to stop showing a widely aired commercial because it suggested that Relenza was "more effective than had been demonstrated."[3] Another rule is that *sellers must not create an overall impression that is incorrect.* So they cannot claim that doctors recommend a product if doctors do not; nor can they dress an actor in a doctor's white jacket to deliver the message; nor can they use whipped cream in a shaving-cream commercial to create an impression

Crackers so yummy, they'll tickle your tummy.

The goal of this advertisement is to inform or remind consumers of Sesame Street Snacks and to stimulate them to buy the product by associating the product with fun times.

Best of the Web Best of the Web Best of

LEARN THE CONSUMER MARKETING LAWS

Thinking about advertising or marketing your product? There are some laws you'll need to obey. Visit the Federal Trade Commission (FTC) Web site to learn how this agency protects consumers against unfair and deceptive marketing practices. Do you know what the FTC's policies are on deceptive pricing, use of the word *free,* or use of endorsements and testimonials? Find out what it means to substantiate product claims such as "tests prove," or "studies show." Learn what the rules are for unsolicited telephone calls and telephone slamming before you telemarket your product. Tune in to the FTC now and avoid making some serious mistakes later.
www.ftc.gov

of a firm, heavy lather. Most states also regulate promotional practices by certain businesses, such as liquor stores, stock brokerages, employment agencies, and loan companies.

Many individual companies and industries also practice self-regulation to restrain false and misleading promotion. The National Advertising Review Board, whose members include advertisers, agencies and the general public, has a full-time professional staff that investigates complaints of deceptive advertising. If the complaint appears justified, the board tries to get the offending company to stop—even if it means referring the offender to proper government enforcement agencies.

Five Elements of Promotion

Within the framework of these guidelines, marketers use a mix of five activities to achieve their promotional objectives: personal selling, advertising, direct marketing, sales promotion, and public relations. These elements can be combined in various ways to create a **promotional mix** for a particular product or idea (see Exhibit 15.1).

■ *Personal selling.* **Personal selling** is the interpersonal arm of the promotional mix. It involves person-to-person presentation—either face-to-face, by phone, or by interactive media such as Web TV's video conferencing or customized Web sites—for the purpose of making sales and building customer relationships. Personal selling allows for immediate interaction between the buyer and seller. It also enables the seller to adjust the message to the specific needs, interests,

---

LEARNING OBJECTIVE   **1**

Identify the five basic categories of promotion

promotional mix
Particular blend of personal selling, advertising, direct marketing, sales promotion, and public relations that a company uses to reach potential customers

personal selling
In-person communication between a seller and one or more potential buyers

---

ACTIVITY	REACH	TIMING	COST FLEXIBILITY	EXPOSURE
Personal selling	Direct personal interaction with limited reach	Regular, recurrent contact	Message tailored to customer and adjusted to reflect feedback	Relatively high
Advertising	Indirect interaction with large reach	Regular, recurrent contact	Standard, unvarying message	Low to moderate
Direct marketing	Direct personal interaction with large reach	Intermittent, based on short-term sales objectives	Customized, varying message	Relatively high
Sales promotion	Indirect interaction with large reach	Intermittent, based on short-term sales objectives	Standard, unvarying message	Varies
Public relations	Indirect interaction with large reach	Intermittent, as newsworthy events occur	Standard, unvarying message	No direct cost

EXHIBIT 15.1

THE FIVE ELEMENTS OF PROMOTION

The promotional mix typically includes a blend of various elements. The most effective mix depends on the nature of the market and the characteristics of the good or service being marketed. Over time the mix for a particular product may change.

and reactions of the individual customer. The chief disadvantage of face-to-face personal selling is its relatively high cost—about $170 per sales call according to one recent study.[4]

advertising
Paid, nonpersonal communication to a target market from an identified sponsor using mass communications channels

direct marketing
Direct communication other than personal sales contacts designed to effect a measurable response

sales promotion
Wide range of events and activities (including coupons, rebates, contests, in-store demonstrations, free samples, trade shows, and point-of-purchase displays) designed to stimulate interest in a product

public relations
Nonsales communication that businesses have with their various audiences (includes both communication with the general public and press relations)

■ *Advertising.* **Advertising** consists of messages paid for by an identified sponsor and transmitted through a mass-communication medium such as television, radio, or newspapers. The primary role of advertising is to create product awareness and stimulate demand by bringing a consistent message to a large targeted consumer group economically. As we shall see later in the chapter, advertising can take many forms—each with its own advantages and disadvantages.

■ *Direct marketing.* **Direct marketing** is defined by the Direct Marketing Association as distributing one or more promotional materials directly to a consumer or business recipient for the purpose of generating (1) a response in the form of an order, (2) a request for further information, or (3) a visit to a store or other place of business for purchase of a specific product or service.[5] As this definition shows, direct marketing is both a distribution method and a form of promotion. This chapter covers the promotion side, and Chapter 14 discusses the distribution side.

■ *Sales promotion.* **Sales promotion** includes a wide range of events and activities designed to stimulate immediate interest in and encourage the purchase of your product or service. The impact of sales promotion activities is often short-term; thus, sales promotions are not as effective as advertising or personal selling in building long-term brand preference.[6]

■ *Public relations.* **Public relations** encompasses all the nonsales communications that businesses have with their many audiences—communities, investors, industry analysts, government agencies and officials, and the news media. Companies rely on public relations to build a favorable corporate image and foster positive relations with these groups.

In the next sections we'll explore the unique characteristics, tools, advantages, and disadvantages of each of these five elements of the promotional mix.

■ PERSONAL SELLING

By almost any measure, personal selling is the dominant form of promotional activity. Most companies spend twice as much on personal selling as they do on all other marketing activities combined, even as technology is drastically changing the entire selling process.

Today's sales reps are plugged in—to headquarters and their customers. Many are walking electronic wonders, virtual offices with laptop computer, cell phone, and pager.[7] These new technologies provide online proposal-generation and order-management systems to relieve salespeople of nonproductive tasks, freeing them to spend more time attending to customers' specific needs. Consider the sales reps at Owens-Corning, for example. The company's newly developed Field Automation Sales Team system (FAST) has fundamentally changed the way salespeople do their jobs. Now they use laptops to learn about customers' backgrounds and sales histories, resolve customer service issues on the spot, modify pricing information as needed, print customized sales material, and more. By using the latest technology, Owens-Corning reps have become more empowered. "They become the real managers of their own business and their own territories," says Owens-Corning's regional general manager.[8]

Types of Sales Personnel

The people who do personal selling go by many names: salespeople, account executives, marketing representatives, sales representatives, and sales consultants, to cite only a few. Regardless of their title, salespeople can be categorized according to three broad areas of responsibility: order getting, order taking, and sales support services. Although some salespeople focus primarily on one area of responsibility, others may have broader responsibilities that span all three.

Owens-Corning's FAST sales force automation system makes working directly with customers easier than ever.

Order Getters **Order getters** are responsible for generating new sales and for increasing sales to existing customers. Order getters can range from telemarketers selling home security systems and stockbrokers selling securities to engineers selling computers and nuclear physicists selling consulting services. Order getting is sometimes referred to as **creative selling,** particularly if the salesperson must invest a significant amount of time in determining what the customer needs, devising a strategy to explain how the product can meet those needs, and persuading the customer to buy. This type of creative selling requires a high degree of empathy, and the salesperson focuses on building in a long-term relationship with the customer.

Order Takers **Order takers** do little creative selling; they primarily process orders. Unfortunately, the term *order taker* has assumed negative overtones in recent years because salespeople often use it to refer to someone too lazy to work for new customers or actively close orders, or they use it to refer to someone whose territory is so attractive that the individual can just sit by the phone and wait for orders to roll in. Regardless of how salespeople use the term, order takers in the true sense play an important role in the sales function.

With the aim of generating additional sales, many companies are beginning to train their order takers to think more like order getters. You've probably noticed that nearly every time you order a meal at McDonald's and don't ask for French fries, the person at the counter will ask, "Would you like an order of fries to go with that?" Such suggestions can prompt customers to buy something they may not otherwise order.

Sales Support Personnel **Sales support personnel** generally don't sell products, but they facilitate the overall selling effort by providing a variety of services. Their responsibilities can include looking for new customers, educating potential and current customers, building goodwill, and providing service to customers after the sale. The three most common types of sales support personnel are missionary, technical, and trade salespeople.

Missionary salespeople are employed by manufacturers to disseminate information about new products to existing customers (usually wholesalers and retailers) and to motivate them to sell the product to their customers. Manufacturers of pharmaceuticals and medical supplies use missionary salespeople to call on doctors and pharmacists. They leave samples and information, answer questions, and persuade doctors to prescribe their products.

Technical salespeople contribute technical expertise and assistance to the selling function. They are usually engineers and scientists or have received specialized technical training. In addition to providing support services to existing customers, they may also participate in sales calls to prospective customers. Companies that manufacture computers, industrial equipment, and sophisticated medical equipment use technical salespeople to sell their products as well as to provide support services to existing customers.

Trade salespeople sell to and support marketing intermediaries. Producers such as Hormel, Nabisco, and Sara Lee use trade salespeople to give in-store demonstrations, offer samples to customers, set up displays, restock shelves, and work with retailers to obtain more shelf space. Increasingly, producers work to establish lasting, mutually beneficial relationships with their channel partners, and trade salespeople are responsible for building those relationships.

The Personal Selling Process

Although it may look easy, personal selling is not a simple task. Some sales, of course, are made in a matter of minutes. However, other sales, particularly for large organizational purchases, can take months to complete. Many salespeople follow a carefully planned process from start to finish as Exhibit 15.2 suggests. But personal selling involves much more than performing a series of steps. Successful salespeople help customers understand their problems and show them new and better solutions to those problems. Moreover, they're willing to invest the time and effort to build a long-term relationship with customers both before and after the sale.[9]

order getters
Salespeople who are responsible for generating new sales and for increasing sales to existing customers

creative selling
Selling process used by order getters, which involves determining customer needs, devising strategies to explain product benefits, and persuading customers to buy

order takers
Salespeople who generally process incoming orders without engaging in creative selling

sales support personnel
Salespeople who facilitate the selling effort by providing such services as prospecting, customer education, and customer service

missionary salespeople
Salespeople who support existing customers, usually wholesalers and retailers

technical salespeople
Specialists who contribute technical expertise and other sales assistance

trade salespeople
Salespeople who sell to and support marketing intermediaries by giving in-store demonstrations, offering samples, and so on

Today's professional salespeople are as much problem solvers and consultants as they are "salespeople" in the traditional sense.

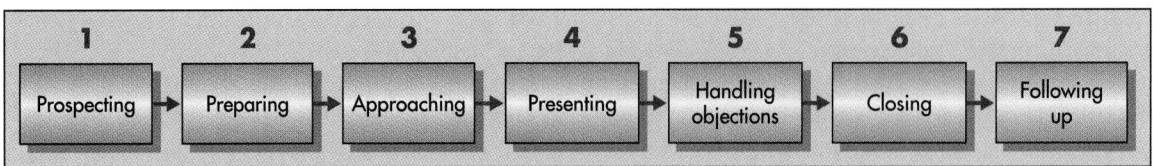

1	2	3	4	5	6	7
Prospecting	Preparing	Approaching	Presenting	Handling objections	Closing	Following up

EXHIBIT 15.2

THE PERSONAL SELLING PROCESS

The personal selling process can involve up to seven steps, starting with prospecting for sales leads and ending with following up after the sale has been closed.

LEARNING
OBJECTIVE   2

List the seven steps in the personal-selling process

prospecting
Process of finding and qualifying potential customers

qualified prospects
Potential buyers who have both the money needed to make the purchase and the authority to make the purchase decision

Step 1: Prospecting **Prospecting** is the process of finding and qualifying potential customers. This step involves three activities: (1) *generating sales leads*—names of individuals and organizations that *might* be likely prospects for the company's product; (2) *identifying prospects*—potential customers who indicate a need or a desire for the seller's product; and (3) *qualifying prospects*—the process of figuring out which prospects have both the authority and the available money to buy. Those who pass the test are called **qualified prospects.**

Step 2: Preparing With a list of hot prospects in hand, the salesperson's next step is to prepare for the sales call. Without this preparation, the chances of success are greatly reduced. Preparation starts with creating a prospect profile, which includes the names of key people, their role in the decision-making process, and other relevant information, such as the prospect's buying needs, motive for buying, current suppliers, income/revenue level, and so on.

Next, the salesperson decides how to approach the prospect. Possible options for a first contact include sending a letter or making a cold call in person or by telephone. For an existing customer, the salesperson can either drop by unannounced or call ahead for an appointment, which is generally preferred.

Before meeting with the prospect, the salesperson establishes specific objectives to achieve during the sales call. Depending on the situation, objectives can range anywhere from "getting the order today" to simply "persuading prospects to accept the company as a potential supplier." After establishing the objectives, the salesperson prepares the actual presentation, which can be as basic as a list of points to discuss or as elaborate as a product demonstration or multimedia presentation.

Step 3: Approaching the Prospect Whether the approach is by telephone, by letter, or in person, a positive first impression results from three elements. The first is an appropriate *appearance*—you wouldn't wear blue jeans to call on a banker, and you probably wouldn't wear a business suit to call on a farmer. Appearance also covers the things that represent you, including business cards, letters, and automobiles. Second, a salesperson's *attitude and behavior* can make or break a sale. A salesperson should come across as professional, courteous, and considerate. Third, a salesperson's *opening lines* should include a brief greeting and introduction, followed by a few carefully chosen words that get the prospect's attention and generate interest. The best way to get a prospect's attention is to focus on a benefit to the customer rather than on the product itself.

canned approach
Selling method based on a fixed, memorized presentation

need-satisfaction approach
Selling method that starts with identifying the customer's needs and then creating a presentation that addresses those needs; this is the approach used by most professional salespeople

Step 4: Making the Presentation The most crucial step in the selling process is the presentation. It can take many forms, but its purpose never varies: to personally communicate a product message that will persuade a prospect to buy. Most sellers use one of two methods: The **canned approach** is a memorized presentation (easier for inexperienced sellers, but inefficient for complex products or for sellers who don't know the customer's needs). The **need-satisfaction approach** (now used by most professionals) identifies the customer's needs and creates a presentation to specifically address them.

Step 5: Handling Objections No matter how well a presentation is delivered, it doesn't always conclude with an immediate offer that might move the prospect to buy. Often the prospect will express various types of objections and concerns throughout the presentation. In fact, the absence of objections is often an indication that the prospect is not all that interested. Many successful salespeople look at objections as a sign of the prospect's interest and as an opportunity to develop new ideas that will strengthen future presentations. Smart salespeople know that objec-

Best of the Web Best of the Web Best of

TAKE AN IDEA JOURNEY

Looking for a way to market your product or service? Perhaps what you really need is a new marketing idea. How about hundreds of them—many of which are quite unusual? Start your idea journey now by visiting the Sales and Marketing Management Web site. Learn some creative strategies for increasing your sales. Check out the tip of the week. Help solve a sticky management situation. Explore the list of resources for the sales and marketing professional. Follow the hot links. This journey never ends.

www.salesandmarketing.com/

tions to price are often a mask for some other issue. They also know *not* to argue with the customer. If you do, you may prove how smart you are by winning the argument, but you will probably lose the sale.

Step 6: Closing So far, you have invested considerable time and effort, but you haven't made a dime. You may have spent weeks or months to bring the customer to this point, but you don't make any money until the prospect decides to buy. This stage of the selling process, when you persuade the customer to place an order, is referred to as **closing.** How should you ask for the order? Closing techniques are numerous; among the more popular are the alternative proposal close, the assumptive close, the silent close, and the direct close. The *alternative proposal close* asks the prospect to choose between some minor details, such as method of shipment. Example: "Should we ship this standard freight or overnight?" With the *assumptive close,* you simply proceed with processing the order, assuming that the prospect has already decided to buy. Another alternative is the *silent close,* in which you finish your presentation and sit quietly, waiting for the customer to respond with a buying decision. Finally, many salespeople prefer the *direct close,* where you just come right out and ask for the order.

closing
Point at which a sale is completed

These closing techniques might strike you as tricks, and in the hands of unethical salespeople, some closing approaches certainly can be. However, the professional salesperson uses these techniques to make the selling process effective, and efficient, and as painless for the customer as possible—not to trick people into buying when they aren't ready.

Step 7: Following Up Most salespeople depend on repeat sales and referrals from satisfied customers, so it's important that they follow up on all sales and not ignore the customer once the first sale is made. During this follow-up stage of the selling process, you need to make sure that the product has been delivered properly and that the customer is satisfied. Inexperienced salespeople may avoid the follow-up stage because they fear facing an unhappy customer. However, an important part of a salesperson's job is to ensure customer satisfaction and to build goodwill.

ADVERTISING AND DIRECT MARKETING

Advertising and direct marketing are the two elements of a firm's promotional mix with which consumers are most familiar. The average U.S. resident is exposed to roughly 250 ads every day.[10] In addition to television, radio, and Internet ads, you receive phone calls from telemarketers, direct marketing letters, and a variety of communications—including floor ads—that try to sell you something.

All forms of advertising and direct marketing have three objectives: to create product awareness, to create and maintain the image of a product, and to stimulate consumer demand. Advertising and direct marketing are the promotional approaches that best reach mass audiences quickly at a relatively low per-person cost. Additionally, you have more control over these forms of promotion than over the others. For instance, you can say whatever you want, as long as you stay within the boundaries of the law and conform to the moral and ethical standards of the advertising medium and trade associations. Still, to be effective, your messages must be persuasive, stand out from competition, and motivate your target audience.

COMPETING IN THE GLOBAL MARKETPLACE

THREE STEPS TO AN EFFECTIVE SALES PRESENTATION

The sales presentation is a chance to show and tell, but it's not all show and tell. Successful sales reps know their audience's needs and concerns, goals and objectives, and hot buttons. They know what motivates them and how they make decisions. And they use this knowledge to perform these three important steps.

1. Establish a Bond
Prospects are much more inclined to buy from people who make them feel good and with whom they have developed a personal bond. Don't plunge into the presentation immediately. First build rapport—a sense of psychological connection—with the prospect. Build a feeling of agreement by discussing items of mutual interest or concern with the audience. These can range from industry issues, current events, sports, or even the weather—anything you and your audience will agree on.

2. Focus on Buyer's Benefits
After you've established a bond, use a "probing" period to find out the prospect's real needs and problems. Then describe and demonstrate the product in a way that the prospect can easily see and comprehend. Most important, focus on the buyer's benefits—showing how the product or service will meet the buyer's needs or solve a problem.

3. Make an Artful Close
The most striking characteristic of a great sales rep is the ability to close the sale and walk away with the prospect's signature on an order blank. Here are some proven closing techniques:

- *Summarize the presentation.* Use a simple anecdotal statement that clearly positions the need for the product in the buyer's mind.

- *Make the offer available for a limited time only.* This approach often gets immediate action.

- *Ask for a small "trial" order.* This can reduce the customer's risk.

- *Turn the buyer's last objection into a close.* By saying, "then you'd order if I could guarantee a one-year warranty in writing?" you leave the buyer in the position of having run out of valid objections.

Remember, some sales reps botch the sale because they can't stop talking—they effectively sell the product and then buy it back. So be sure that when you go for the final close you are able to keep quiet while the customer orders.

■ QUESTIONS FOR CRITICAL THINKING

1. Why is it important to understand your audience before giving a sales presentation?

2. Why are closing techniques necessary?

LEARNING OBJECTIVE 3

Explain the difference between logical and emotional advertising appeals

Advertising Appeals

Well-designed ads make a carefully planned appeal to whatever motivates the audience. The specific motivator depends largely on the target audience. By segmenting along age, ethnic group, lifestyles, and other variables, advertisers try to identify which groups of people can be reached with various kinds of appeals. Nonetheless, all appeals fall into one of two general categories: logical or emotional.

Some ads use a logical appeal to persuade you with data; others target your emotions to get their point across. When selling technical products, some industrial and high-tech marketers assume that logic is the only reasonable approach. However, even with the most unemotional sort of product, emotions can be a significant factor in the decision process because all people have hopes, fears, desires, and dreams, regardless of the products they're buying.

Emotional appeals range from the most syrupy and sentimental to the downright terrifying. Fear appeals cover a broad range: personal and family safety, financial security, social acceptance, and business success or failure. Appeals to fear have to be managed carefully, however. Laying it on too thick can anger the audience or even cause them to block out the message entirely.[11] On the lighter side, some companies try to convince you of how good it will feel to use their products. Flowers, greeting cards, and gifts are among the products usually sold with a positive emotional appeal.

Price or Value Appeal Promising to give buyers more for their money is one of the most effective appeals you can use, particularly in terms of audience recall.[12] A value appeal can be accomplished in several ways: lowering the price and making people aware of the new bargain price, keeping the price the same but adding value, or keeping the price and the product the same and trying to convince people that the product is worth whatever price you are charging.

Celebrity Appeal A popular ad theme is celebrity attribution. The theory behind using celebrities in ads is that people will be more inclined to use products endorsed by celebrities and that some of the stars' image will rub off on the products. After Tiger Woods won the 2000 PGA golf championship, his annual income increased by an estimated $50 to $200 million from celebrity product endorsements.[13] American Express chose Woods because he characterizes traits such as discipline, hard work, and preparation—the pillars of American Express. "It's hard to visualize anyone he wouldn't appeal to," says the company president.[14]

Similarly, Salton, a $500 million designer and seller of kitchen products, struck a deal with heavyweight champ George Foreman to promote a countertop grill. The promotion was such a success that the company eventually bought the rights to use George Foreman's name in perpetuity in association with its food preparation appliances.[15]

Nonetheless, celebrity ads are not always successful. Consumers don't always find them convincing (or at least don't claim to find them convincing). In one survey on the power of various advertising appeals, 70 percent of the respondents ranked celebrity endorsements as the least convincing. Another danger is that linking the celebrity to the product also links the celebrity's behavior (both good and bad) to the product. Madonna, Mike Tyson, O. J. Simpson, Michael Jackson, and Jennifer Capriati are among celebrities who have lost endorsement contracts when aspects of their private lives became public news.

Sales of Salton's countertop grill soared when it signed on former heavyweight champ George Foreman as the product's spokesperson. The success of the grill can be attributed to both a good product and the credibility Foreman has with the public.

Sex Appeal A tenant of advertising is, "sex sells." The classic technique is to have an attractive, scantily attired model share the page or TV screen with the product. The model may bring nothing to the ad beyond a visual focus point. The goal is to have the audience associate the product with pleasure. Guess Jeans and Calvin Klein's Obsession perfume are well-known examples of this approach. The sex appeal has to be used with some caution, however. At the extreme, using sex as the appeal can keep an ad from running, when print or electronic media refuse to accept it for publication or broadcast. In addition, attempts to present a sexy image may cross the line, offending some readers and viewers as simply sexist, not sexy.

Advertising Categories

Despite the type of appeal used, advertising can be classified by type. **Product advertising** is the most common type, designed to sell specific goods or services, such as Kellogg's cereals, Sega video games, or Esteé Lauder cosmetics. Product advertising generally describes the product's features and may mention its price. Other advertising classifications include institutional, advocacy, competitive, and comparative advertising.

Institutional Advertising **Institutional advertising** is designed to create goodwill and build a desired image for a company rather than to sell specific products. As discussed in Chapter 2, many companies are now spending large sums for institutional advertising that focuses on *green marketing*, creating an image of companies as corporate conservationists. Institutional advertisers tout their actions, contributions, and philosophies not only as supporting the environmental movement but as leading the way. When utilized as *corporate advertising*, institutional advertising often promotes an entire line of a company's products. Institutional ads can also be used to remind investors that the company is doing well.

product advertising
Advertising that tries to sell specific goods or services, generally by describing features, benefits, and, occasionally, price

institutional advertising
Advertising that seeks to create goodwill and to build a desired image for a company rather than to sell specific products

advocacy advertising
Ads that present a company's opinions on public issues such as education and health

Institutional ads that address public issues are called **advocacy advertising.** Mobil and W. R. Grace are well known for running ads that deal with taxation, environmental regulation, and other issues. Advocacy advertising has recently expanded beyond issues in which the organization has a stake. Some companies now run advocacy ads that don't directly benefit their business, such as ads to project opinions and attitudes that support those of their target audiences.

competitive advertising
Ads that specifically highlight how a product is better than its competitors

comparative advertising
Advertising technique in which two or more products are explicitly compared

Competitive versus Comparative Advertising You can argue that all advertising is competitive in nature, but the term **competitive advertising** is applied to those ads that specifically highlight how a product is better than its competitors. When two or more products are directly contrasted in an ad, the technique being used is **comparative advertising.** In some countries, comparative ads are tightly regulated and sometimes banned; that is clearly not the case in the United States. Indeed, the Federal Trade Commission encourages advertisers to use direct product comparisons with the intent of better informing customers.

Comparative advertising is frequently used by competitors vying with the market leader, but it is useful whenever you believe you have some specific product strengths that are important to customers. Burger King used it on McDonald's, Pepsi used it on Coke, and car manufacturers from Ford to Toyota use it. This approach is bare-knuckle marketing, and, when done well, is effective. However, comparative advertising sometimes ends up getting neutralized by look-alike campaigns from the competition. Analgesics (painkillers) is one category cited as an example of comparative advertising taken too far. There are so many claims and counterclaims in this "ad war" that consumers can't keep it all straight anymore.[16]

national advertising
Advertising sponsored by companies that sell products on a nationwide basis; refers to the geographic reach of the advertiser, not the geographic coverage of the ad

local advertising
Advertising sponsored by a local merchant

cooperative advertising
Joint efforts between local and national advertisers, in which producers of nationally sold products share the costs of local advertising with local merchants and wholesalers

National versus Local Advertising Finally, advertising can be classified according to the sponsor. **National advertising** is sponsored by companies that sell products on a nationwide basis. The term *national* refers to the level of the advertiser, not the geographic coverage of the ad. If a national manufacturer places an ad in only one city, the ad is still classified as a national ad. As Exhibit 15.3 shows, national advertisers spend over $215 billion annually.[17]

By contrast, **local advertising** is sponsored by a local merchant. Grocery store ads in the local newspaper are a good example. **Cooperative advertising** is a financial arrangement whereby companies with products sold nationally share the costs of local advertising with local merchants and wholesalers. As a result, it is a cross between local and national advertising.

Interactive Advertising For years advertisers produced a standard commercial and distributed it to the masses via TV, magazines, or newspapers. But the Internet, interactive TV, video screens on shopping carts, and freestanding kiosks have expanded the advertiser's choices from one-way passive to two-way active marketing communication.

Interactive advertising is the two-way exchange between a merchant and a potential customer. With interactive advertising, the consumer uses a TV remote control, computer mouse, or

EXHIBIT 15.3

U.S. NATIONAL ADVERTISING EXPENDITURES BY MEDIA TYPE

Despite downsizing, restructuring, and many changes in competitive marketing strategies, advertising is still being employed extensively by most marketers. U.S. national advertisers spent some $215.3 billion on a variety of media types for 1999.

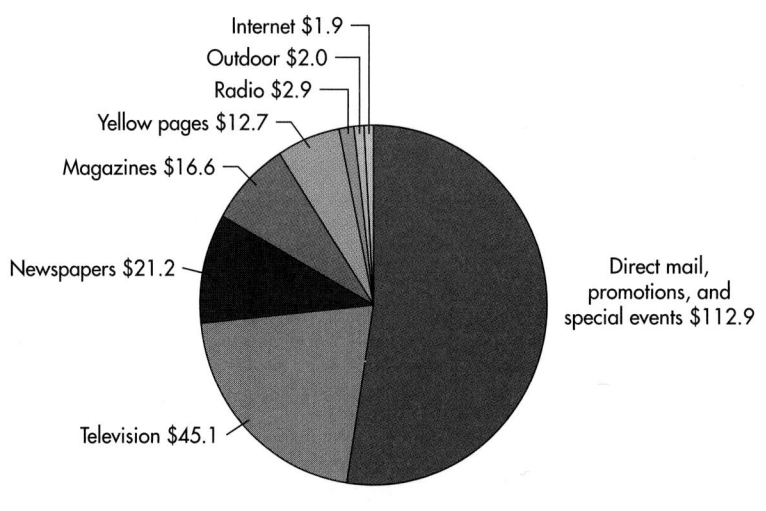

Internet $1.9
Outdoor $2.0
Radio $2.9
Yellow pages $12.7
Magazines $16.6
Newspapers $21.2
Television $45.1
Direct mail, promotions, and special events $112.9

**Total Advertising $215.3
($ billions)**

other electronic device to communicate with the advertiser. For example, a consumer can click on a device to participate in a television poll, purchase an item, or obtain additional product information. Interactive ads generally include more information than can possibly be packed into a 30-second commercial, but they have a major drawback: the consumer can control the amount of information received and can even decide not to participate in the ad's interactive features. Those who choose to participate in the ad, however, tend to be interested in the message—making it more effective.

Media Categories Advertising media fall into six major categories, each with its own strengths and weaknesses as highlighted in Exhibit 15.4. However, imaginative marketers are constrained only by their creativity. Free movie magazines are distributed in theater lobbies, commercial airlines carry in-flight advertising, and supermarkets run ads on their shopping bags, shopping carts, and now on their floors thanks to Floorgraphics. The most dramatic change in advertising is explored in the next section as we look at the opportunities afforded by marketing products through the Internet.

Direct and Internet Marketing

Direct marketing has become the promotion tool of choice for many companies because it enables them to more precisely target and personalize messages to specific consumer and business segments and build long-term customer relationships.[18] The most popular direct marketing vehicles are direct mail, targeted e-mail, telemarketing, direct response television, and the Internet.

Direct Mail and Targeted E-Mail The principal vehicle for direct marketing is **direct mail,** which includes catalogs and other materials delivered through the U.S. Postal Service and private carriers. Mailing out letters, brochures, videotapes, disks, and other promotional items to customers and prospects can be an effective way to increase sales, although companies must take into account the cost of printing and postage.

Increasingly, companies are sending complex e-mails to highly targeted lists of prospects. This technique works much the same way as offline direct marketing campaigns. Companies build databases of e-mail addresses by enticing customers to register on a Web site in exchange

LEARNING OBJECTIVE 4

Define interactive advertising and discuss the challenge it presents to marketers

interactive advertising
Customer–seller communication in which the customer controls the amount and type of information received

LEARNING OBJECTIVE 5

Name five popular direct marketing vehicles

direct mail
Advertising sent directly to potential customers, usually through the U.S. Postal Service

MEDIUM	ADVANTAGES	DISADVANTAGES
Newspapers	Extensive market coverage; low cost; short lead time for placing ads; good local market coverage; geographic selectivity	Poor graphic quality; short life span; cluttered pages; visual competition from other ads
Television	Great impact; broad reach; appealing to senses of sight, sound, and motion; creative opportunities for demonstration; high attention; entertainment carryover	High cost for production and air time; less audience selectivity; long preparation time; commercial clutter; short life for message; vulnerability to remote controls
Direct mail	Can deliver large amounts of information to narrowly selected audiences; excellent control over quality of message; personalization	High cost per contact; delivery delays; difficulty of obtaining desired mailing list; consumer resistance; generally poor image (junk mail)
Radio	Low cost; high frequency; immediacy; highly portable; high geographic and demographic selectivity	No visual possibilities; short life for message; commercial clutter; lower attention than television; easy to switch stations
Magazines	Good reproduction; long life; local and regional market selectivity; authority and credibility; multiple readers	Limited demonstration possibilities; long lead time between placing and publishing ads; high cost; less compelling than other major media
Internet	Fast-growing reach; low cost; ability to personalize; can appeal to senses of sight, sound, and motion	Difficulty in measuring audiences; consumer resistance; increasing clutter

EXHIBIT 15.4

ADVANTAGES AND DISADVANTAGES OF MAJOR ADVERTISING MEDIA

When selecting the media mix, companies attempt to match the characteristics of the media audiences with the characteristics of the customer segments being targeted. A typical advertising campaign involves the use of several media.

for information or access to a special offer.[19] For example, when Jive Records wanted to push 'NSync's album *No Strings Attached,* it sent e-mails to thousands of the band's fans. The e-mail featured a click-and-play video message from band members, encouraging fans to spread the word about the album. As you can imagine, this form of direct marketing has many advantages. Besides impressive response rates, targeted e-mail campaigns allow marketers to gauge how many people open and forward the e-mail, as well as track how long the user views the message and whether or not they click through to the Web site.[20]

telemarketing
Selling or supporting the sales process over the telephone

Telemarketing Another popular form of direct marketing is **telemarketing,** or selling over the telephone, a low-cost way to efficiently reach many people. Time-pressed customers often appreciate the convenience of buying by phone.[21] With *outbound telemarketing,* companies place *cold calls* to potential customers who have not requested a sales call; *inbound telemarketing* establishes phone lines for customers to call in to place orders or request information. However, because outbound telemarketing has been criticized as being intrusive, several states have enacted legislation that (1) gives consumers the right to place their names on "do not call" lists, (2) restricts telemarketers from calling during certain hours, and (3) prohibits telemarketers from blocking caller ID technology.[22]

Direct Response Television and Infomercials Direct marketers use print, TV, and radio advertising much as mass advertisers do but with one critical difference. With direct response advertising, an offer is made and a response vehicle such as an 800 number is provided. Direct response television, for example, allows customers who view an ad to communicate directly with sellers using a computer keyboard, a television, and a modem. Customers can use their keyboards to ask questions or to place product orders. Experts predict that direct response or interactive TV will be available in 24 million households by 2004.[23]

Television *infomercials* are another widely used direct marketing technique. These longer forms of advertisement—approximately 30 minutes in length—have the appearance of regular TV programs but provide viewers with a toll-free number to place an order. Infomercials are useful selling tools for new products that need some form of demonstration or technical explanation. Tae-Bo infomercials, for example, sold more than $75 million worth of product videos in one year by demonstrating the grueling combination of punches and kicks that can help you lose weight, and free your spirit.[24] Still, only 10 percent of infomercials sell between $5 million and $120 million of products in one year.[25]

Internet Advertising Look back at Exhibit 15.3. Even though 95 percent of direct marketers use the Internet for sales or marketing applications, it still plays only a minor role in the overall media mix.[26] Nonetheless, the use of Internet advertising is expected to increase exponentially.[27]

The principal advantages of Internet advertising include:[28]

■ *Timeliness.* Internet ads can be updated any time at a minimal cost.

■ *Reach.* Internet ads can reach very large numbers of potential buyers globally.

■ *Cost.* Internet ads can be less expensive than television, newspaper, or radio ads.[29]

■ *Interactive options.* Chat, e-mail, and instant messaging can be incorporated in the ad at a reasonable cost.

Moreover, just like targeted e-mail, Internet ads can be sent to specific interest groups or individuals. Advertisers can tailor a unique pitch to the individual and use interactive options to gather information about each interaction. For example, companies can (1) track the exact information accessed by any particular visitor to their Web site, (2) develop a profile for each of their regular visitors, (3) present information that may be of special interest to a particular visitor, and (4) alert customers to special savings or remind them of past purchases.

banner ads
A rectangular graphic display on a Web page that is used for advertising and linked to an advertiser's Web page

Banner ads are one of the most popular forms of Internet advertising. Called banners because of their long, thin shape, the ads generally appear at the top and bottom of Web sites and contain a short text or graphical message that can be customized for target audiences. In addition to clicking on the ad to go to the advertiser's Web site, *rich media,* a combination of high-grade graphics with audio and interactive capabilities, allows users to interact with the

KEEPING PACE WITH TECHNOLOGY AND ELECTRONIC COMMERCE

SHOULD MARKETERS TRASH THE BANNER?

In the early days of the Internet, advertisers thought they had found the magic bullet in banner ads. These horizontal ads, typically stripped across the top of Web pages, were a marketer's dream. Designed to stir a momentary impulse to buy a product, like a coupon in the mail, they became an advertising staple on the Internet. But recent studies show that banner ads are among the least productive advertising tools.

The proportion of viewers who actually click on the banners is steadily dropping. Initially, 30 percent of viewers responded to the ads by clicking on them, compared to a 1 percent to 3 percent response rate generated by traditional direct mail. But as the novelty wore off, banner ad clickthrough rates plunged. Today they're lower than 1 percent. Still, some say that clickthrough is only one way to measure a banner's effectiveness.

Expectations for banner ads are unreasonable, say some advertisers. People got caught up in clickthroughs and forgot that the key to advertising is to instill a subconsciously positive feeling about a company. Take Ford: They put ads in a magazine but they don't expect you to go out to buy their cars instantly. They want to make an impression so when you do go out and buy a car, Ford will be imprinted in your mind. Branding and product awareness are

an important part of banner ads too. But for some reason, advertisers threw the rules of traditional marketing out the window once the Web came—focusing solely on clickthroughs.

Disappointed with the percentage of clickthroughs, some advertisers say banners should be replaced by other forms of advertising. Others are beginning to embrace the notion that making a sale isn't necessarily the endgame—creating brand awareness is. Still others think banner ads should become more sophisticated—maybe a different shape, size, or format. Some are even experimenting with novelty items such as cursors that are shaped like a corporate logo that turn into banner ads when they rest on the desktop. Meanwhile, as experts debate the function and impact of banner advertising, chances are banners will not go away any time soon. A more likely outcome is that smart marketers will find new ways to make banners work.

■ QUESTIONS FOR CRITICAL THINKING

1. Why are expectations for banner ads unreasonable?
2. View three banner ads on the Internet. What do you like or dislike about this form of advertising?

banner ad by opening dropdown lists, selecting buttons, or performing other actions with a mouse inside the ad.

Another very important form of Internet advertising is a company's own Web site. This is the place where visitors can learn about your company, products, and services as demonstrated in this chapter's special feature, Focusing on E-Business Today. Sponsorships are another increasingly popular form of Internet advertising. Similar to co-branding, advertisers sponsor a Web site that provides content, while the advertiser gets to offer information about its own products. Hi-C, for example, sponsored a children's game area on the Web site MaMaMedia and cross-promoted the sponsorship on the back of Hi-C juice boxes.[30] For a list of Internet advertising terms, consult Exhibit 15.5.

Media Plans

Regardless of which form of advertising you use, you must get your message to your target audience by choosing suitable **media,** or channels of communication. Your **media plan** is a document that shows your advertising budget, how you will divide your money among various media, and when your ads will appear. The goal of your media plan is to make the most effective use of your advertising dollar.

The Media Mix The critical task in media planning is to select a **media mix,** the combination of print, broadcast, and other media for the advertising campaign. In Exhibit 15.4, we pointed out the advantages and disadvantages of popular advertising media types. When selecting the media

media
Communications channels, such as newspapers, radio, and television

media plan
Written plan that outlines how a company will spend its media budget, including how the money will be divided among the various media and when the advertisements will appear

media mix
Combination of various media options that a company uses in an advertising campaign

EXHIBIT 15.5

POPULAR CYBERMARKETING TERMS

New Internet marketing terms keep cropping up as marketers find creative ways to use Internet technology to communicate their messages.

TERM	EXPLANATION
Banner	Small, usually rectangular graphic display that appears on a Web site like a roadside billboard. Clicking on the banner will transfer you to the advertiser's Web site.
Click through	How often a viewer will respond to an ad by clicking on it.
Cost per click (CPC)	The ad rate charged only if the Web surfer responds to a displayed ad.
CPM (cost per thousand impressions)	The cost of delivering an impression to 1,000 people.
Impressions	The total number of times users call up a page with a banner during a specific time.
Interactive advertisement	Any advertisement that requires or allows the viewer/consumer to take some action.
Interstitials	Brief ad message that appears as a new Web page downloads. Intrusive style can create an impact but can also be annoying.
Pointcasting	Mass delivery of Internet information using push technology. Also known as Webcasting.
Pop-up windows	Linked ad messages that appear within a new browser window.
Splash screen	An initial Web page used as a promotion or lead-in to the site homepage and designed to capture the user's attention for a short time by using multimedia effects.

mix, the first step is to determine the characteristics of the target audience and the types of media that will reach the greatest audience at the lowest cost per exposure. The choice is also based on what the medium can do (show the product in use, list numerous sale items and prices, and so on). The second step in choosing the media mix is to pick specific vehicles in each of the chosen media categories, such as individual magazines (*Time, Rolling Stone, Sports Illustrated*) or individual radio stations (a rock station, a classical station).

Media Buying Sorting through all the media is a challenging task. In fact, many companies rely on professional media planners or *advertising agencies*—firms of marketing specialists who assist companies in planning and preparing advertisements—to find the best combinations of media and to negotiate attractive terms. These professionals use four important types of data in selecting their media buys. The first is **cost per thousand (CPM),** a standardized ratio that converts the total cost of advertising space to the more meaningful cost of reaching 1,000 people with the ad. CPM is especially useful for comparing media that reach similar audiences.

cost per thousand (CPM)
Cost of reaching 1,000 people with an ad

Two other decision tools are reach and frequency, which represent the trade-off between breadth and depth of communication. **Reach** refers to the total number of audience members who will be exposed to a message at least once in a given time period; it is usually expressed as a percentage of the total number of audience members in a particular population. **Frequency** is the average number of times that each audience member is exposed to the message; it is calculated by dividing the total number of exposures by the total audience population.

reach
Total number of audience members who will be exposed to a message at least once in a given period

frequency
Average number of times that each audience member is exposed to the message (equal to the total number of exposures divided by the total audience population)

The fourth decision tool is **continuity,** which refers to the period spanned by the media schedule and the timing of ad messages within the period evenly spread over the schedule or heavily concentrated in some periods. Obviously, within a fixed budget, a media plan cannot do everything: If it is important to reach a high percentage of a target group with significant frequency, the cost of doing so on a continuous basis may be prohibitive. Media planners often resort to airing messages in "waves" or "flights"—short periods of high reach and frequency that sacrifice continuity. This strategy is common in the travel industry, which crowds much of its annual media spending into the peak vacation seasons.

continuity
Pattern according to which an ad appears in the media; it can be spread evenly over time or concentrated during selected periods

SALES PROMOTION

The fourth element of promotion, sales promotion, consists of short-term incentives to encourage the purchase of a product or service. Over the past two decades, U.S. sales-promotion expenditures have grown so much they now exceed those for traditional forms of advertising.[31] Sales promotion can be broken down into two basic categories: consumer promotion and trade promotion.

Consumer Promotion Tools

Consumer promotion is aimed directly at final users of the product. Companies use a variety of promotional tools and incentives to stimulate repeat purchases and to entice new users:

- *Coupons.* The biggest category of consumer promotion—and the most popular with consumers—is **coupons,** certificates that spur sales by giving buyers a discount when they purchase specified products. Customers redeem their coupons at the time of purchase.[32] Companies offer coupons on packages, in print ads, in direct mail, at the checkout, and on the Internet to encourage trial of new products, reach out to nonusers of mature products, encourage repeat buying, and temporarily lower a product's price.[33] Ford and General Motors, for example, have mailed coupons to owners of older-model vehicles to induce them to buy new cars.[34] Couponing is a fairly inefficient technique, however: A lot of money is wasted on advertising and delivering coupons that are never redeemed. Also, critics say couponing instills a bargain-hunting mentality, leading some people to avoid buying unless they have a coupon.[35]

- *Rebates.* Similar to coupons, rebates are another popular promotional tool. Instead of receiving the discount at the time of purchase, buyers generally get reimbursement checks from the manufacturer by submitting proofs of purchase along with a prepared manufacturer's rebate form. Here again, many buyers neglect to redeem the rebates, making the costs of running such programs relatively low. Moreover, rebates allow the manufacturer to promote the reduced price even though customers pay the full price at checkout.[36]

- *Point-of-purchase.* Another widely used consumer promotion technique is the **point-of-purchase (POP) display,** a device for showing a product in a way that stimulates immediate sales. It may be simple, such as the end-of-aisle stacks of soda pop in a supermarket or the racks of gum and mints at checkout counters. Simple or elaborate, point-of-purchase displays really work: Studies show that in almost every instance, such displays significantly increase sales.[37]

- *Samples.* Studies repeatedly show that the most effective way to get someone to try a product—and subsequently buy it—is to give that person a sample. Neutrogena many years ago began placing sample sizes of its glycerine soap in hotel bathrooms. Butler and Procter & Gamble give dentists toothbrushes to pass on to their patients. Hall's puts bins heaped with cough drops in theatre lobbies. And Kellogg hands out single-serving packs of Smart Start cereal on street corners. Samples are an effective way to introduce a new product, encourage nonusers to try an existing product, encourage current buyers to use the product in a new way, or expand distribution into new areas.[38]

- *Special-event sponsorship.* Sponsoring special events has become one of the most popular sales-promotion tactics. Thousands of companies spend billions of dollars to sponsor events ranging from golf to opera. The 2000 Summer Olympic Games in Sydney drew over $315 million alone in sponsorship revenue. Coke, Visa, Panasonic, McDonald's, and General Motors were the games' largest sponsors.[39]

- *Cross-promotion.* Another popular sales promotion vehicle is **cross-promotion,** which involves using one brand to advertise another noncompeting brand. One example is PepsiCo's arrangement with Yahoo! to cross-promote each others' products. Pepsi promoted the Yahoo! Web site on 1.5 billion soft drink bottles and in-store displays, while Yahoo! promoted Pepsi products on its Web site.[40] Another example is "Intel Inside," one of the most successful cross-promotion campaigns ever. In just two years following the campaign's inception, awareness of the Intel chip went from roughly 22 percent of PC buyers to more than 80 percent.[41]

LEARNING OBJECTIVE 6
Distinguish between the two main types of sales promotion, and give at least two examples of each

consumer promotion
Sales promotion aimed at final consumers

coupons
Certificates that offer discounts on particular items and are redeemed at the time of purchase

point-of-purchase display
Advertising or other display materials set up at retail locations to promote products to potential customers as they are making their purchase decisions

cross-promotion
Jointly advertising two or more noncompeting brands

premiums
Free or bargain-priced items offered to encourage consumers to buy a product

specialty advertising
Advertising that appears on various items such as coffee mugs, pens, and calendars, designed to help keep a company's name in front of customers

Other popular consumer sales-promotion techniques include in-store demonstrations, loyalty and frequency programs such as frequent-flyer miles, and **premiums,** which are free or bargain-priced items offered to encourage the consumer to buy a product. Contests, sweepstakes, and games are also quite popular in some industries and can generate a great deal of public attention, particularly when valuable or unusual prizes are offered. **Specialty advertising** (on pens, calendars, T-shirts, and so on) helps keep a company's name in front of customers for a long period of time.

Many corporations promote their brands and products by placing advertising on everything from T-shirts to coffee mugs.

Trade Promotion Tools

Although shoppers are more aware of consumer promotion, trade promotion actually accounts for the largest share of promotional spending. **Trade promotions** are aimed at inducing distributors or retailers to sell a company's products by offering them a discount on the product's price, or a **trade allowance.** The distributor or retailer can pocket the savings and increase company profits or can pass the savings on to the consumer to generate additional sales. Besides discounts, other popular trade-allowance forms are display premiums, dealer contests or sweepstakes, and travel bonus programs. All are designed to motivate distributors or retailers to push particular merchandise.

Trade allowances can create the controversial practice of **forward buying,** in which the retailer takes advantage of a trade allowance by stocking up while the price is low. Say that the producer of Bumble Bee tuna offers retailers a 20 percent discount for a period of 6 weeks. A retailer might choose, however, to buy enough tuna to last 8 or 10 weeks. Purchasing this excessive amount at the lower price increases the retailer's profit, but at the expense of the producer's profit.

trade promotions
Sales-promotion efforts aimed at inducing distributors or retailers to push a producer's products

trade allowance
Discount offered by producers to wholesalers and retailers

forward buying
Retailers' taking advantage of trade allowances by buying more products at discounted prices than they hope to sell

trade shows
Gatherings where producers display their wares to potential buyers

Many companies targeting business buyers participate in **trade shows,** gatherings where producers display their wares to potential customers. According to one estimate, the average industrial exhibitor can reach 60 percent of all its prospects at a trade show, and some exhibitors do 25 percent or more of annual sales at a single show. Apart from attracting likely buyers, trade shows have the advantage of enabling a producer to demonstrate and explain the product and to compile information about prospects.[42]

■ PUBLIC RELATIONS

LEARNING OBJECTIVE 7

Explain the role of public relations in marketing

Public relations plays a vital role in the success of most companies, and that role applies to more than just the marketing of goods and services. Smart businesspeople know they need to maintain positive relations with their communities, investors, industry analysts, government agencies and officials, and the news media. All these activities fall under the umbrella of public relations. For many companies, public relations is the fastest growing element of the promotional mix.[43]

A good reputation is one of a business's most important assets. A recent study shows that companies with a good public image have a big edge over less-respected companies. Consumers are more than twice as likely to buy new products from companies they admire, which is why smart companies work hard to build and protect their reputations. Sometimes companies hire public relations firms to help them maintain or restore their public image. Tire maker Bridgestone/Firestone hired a public relations firm to help it restore its tattered image following the 2000 recall of 6.5 million Firestone tires that had been implicated to over 100 U.S. traffic deaths. A spokesperson for Bridgestone/Firestone acknowledged that the company had been slow to respond to public concerns. "We underestimated the intensity of the situation, and we have been too focused on internal details," he said. "We are determined to change all that."[44]

Best of the Web Best of the Web Best of

SAMPLE SUCCESS ON THE SALES MARKETING NETWORK

Want to know the fastest way to get the sales and marketing how-to and reference information you need? Tune in to the Sales Marketing Network (SMN), where you'll find over 100 how-to and reference articles, along with a wealth of sales and marketing trends, statistics, and legal issues. Check out the information on marketing strategies, promotions, trade shows, event marketing, direct marketing, and more. Learn how to incorporate the Internet into your promotional strategies. Discover the most effective sampling strategies. Find out how to attract and keep long-term customers using frequency marketing. And learn some tips for building customer profiles.
www.info-now.com/SMN

Another way that companies build and maintain good reputations is by maintaining good relations with both the general news media and specialized trade media. **Press relations** is the process of communicating with newspapers, magazines, and broadcast media. In the personal-computer industry, for example, manufacturers know that many people look to *ComputerWorld, PC, Byte,* and other computer publications as influential sources of information about new products. Editors and reporters often review new products and then make recommendations to their readers, pointing out both strengths and weaknesses. Companies roll out the proverbial red carpet for these media figures, treating them to hospitality suites at conventions, factory tours, and interviews with company leaders. When introducing products, manufacturers often send samples to reporters and editors for review, or they visit the media offices themselves.

Two standard public relations tools are the news release and the news conference. A **news release** is a short memo sent to the media covering topics that are of potential news interest; a *video news release* is a brief video clip sent to television stations. Companies use news releases to get favorable news coverage about themselves and their products. When a business has significant news to announce, it will often arrange a **news conference.** Both tools are used when the company's news is of widespread interest, when products need to be demonstrated, or when company officials want to be available to answer questions from the media.

press relations
Process of communicating with reporters and editors from newspapers, magazines, and radio and television networks and stations

news release
Brief statement or video program released to the press announcing new products, management changes, sales performance, and other potential news items; also called a *news release*

news conference
Gathering of media representatives at which companies announce new information; also called a *press briefing*

COORDINATING YOUR MARKETING EFFORTS

With five major promotional methods available—personal selling, advertising, direct marketing, sales promotion, and public relations—how do you decide on the right mix for your product? There are no easy answers, because you must take many factors into account. In fact, when you consider all the ways that audiences can receive marketing messages today, the potential for confusion is not all that surprising. Besides the traditional media—radio, television, billboards, print ads, and direct-mail promotions—marketers are using Web sites, e-mail, faxes, kiosks, sponsorships, and many other channels to deliver messages to targeted audiences. Coordinating these diverse vehicles is becoming vital if you are to send a consistent message and boost its effectiveness.

LEARNING
OBJECTIVE 8

Discuss the use of integrated marketing communications

Integrating Your Marketing Communications

Integrated marketing communications (IMC) is a strategy of coordinating and integrating all your communications and promotion efforts to provide customers with clarity, consistency, and maximum communications impact. "It's everything from running ads to developing new media, to creating custom media, licensing, promotion, sweepstakes—every aspect of communicating to consumers," says one media expert.[45] The basics of IMC are quite simple: communicating with one voice and one message to the marketplace, as Exhibit 15.6 suggests.

The need for communicating with one voice is even greater today. Consumers are exposed to a greater variety of marketing communications and don't necessarily distinguish between mes-

integrated marketing communications (IMC)
Strategy of coordinating and integrating communications and promotions efforts with customers to ensure greater efficiency and effectiveness

EXHIBIT 15.6

INTEGRATED MARKETING COMMUNICATIONS

Coordinating the five elements of promotion delivers a consistent message to the marketplace.

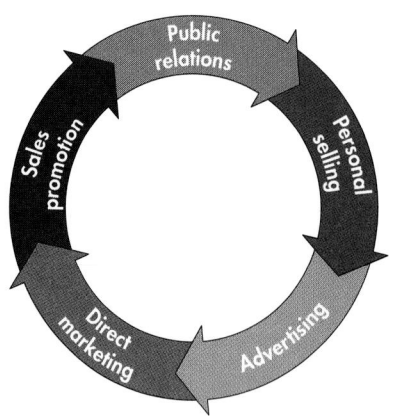

sage sources the way marketers do. In the consumer's mind, messages from different sources blur into one single message about the company. Thus, conflicting messages from different sources can result in confused company images and brand positions.[46]

Properly implemented, IMC increases marketing and promotional effectiveness. Look at Southwest Airlines. The company coordinates all marketing to establish and maintain a consistent image of low-fare, high-frequency service in new and existing markets. For example, when the Texas-based airline beefed up service on the East Coast, it used public relations, special events, and advertising to whip up excitement by promoting a special Thanksgiving Day cross-country flight from Baltimore, Maryland, to Oakland, California, at the bargain rate of $99. The resulting media coverage effectively communicated the airline's low-price, flyer-friendly position. "We always start out with the public relations side in announcing inaugural services. Then we integrate government relations, community affairs, service announcements, special events, advertising, and promotion," says the head of Southwest's ad agency. "We try to fire all guns at once so that by the time Southwest comes into the market, the airline already is part of the community."[47]

While integrating your communications and promotional efforts may seem logical and relatively simple, many organizations find IMC difficult to implement. They discover that over time their promotional mixes develop into collections of disconnected efforts. Organizational resistance is the primary cause for IMC failure. Many marketing departments are accustomed to autonomy and see IMC as a threat to their resources and decision-making power. Besides, moving to an IMC approach requires new ways of organizing, planning, and managing all marketing functions, and some marketing departments are not up to the task.[48]

Fine-Tuning Your Promotional Strategies

Besides integrating your marketing efforts, you must consider other factors when deciding on the right promotional mix. For one thing, most companies have limited resources, so establishing a promotional budget is often the first step in developing a promotional strategy. Next, you should consider the nature and appeal of the product, its position in the life cycle, the size and interests of its targeted segments, its competitive situation, any country and cultural differences, and its desired market position.

Product Considerations Various types of products lend themselves to differing forms of promotion. Simple, familiar items like laundry detergent can be explained adequately through advertising, but personal selling is generally required to communicate the features of unfamiliar and sophisticated goods and services such as office-automation equipment or municipal waste-treatment facilities. Direct, personal contact is particularly important in promoting customized services such as interior design, financial advice, or legal counsel. In general, consumer and organizational goods usually require differing promotional mixes.

The product's price is also a factor in the selection of the promotional mix. Inexpensive items sold to a mass market are well suited to advertising and sales promotion, which have a relatively low per-unit cost. At the other extreme, products with a high unit price lend themselves to personal selling because the high cost of a sales call is justified by the size of the order.

Furthermore, the nature of the selling process often demands face-to-face interaction between the buyer and seller.

Another factor that influences both the level and mix of promotional activity is the product's position in its life cycle. Early on, when the seller is trying to inform the customer about the product and build the distribution network, promotional efforts are in high gear. Selective advertising, sales promotion, and public relations are used to build awareness and to encourage early adopters to try the product; personal selling is used to gain the cooperation of intermediaries. For example, Gillette spent $300 million to promote the launch of the Mach3 razor during its first year—on top of $750 million-plus in development costs to accelerate the Mach3's transition from the costly introduction stage to the profitable growth stage faster than any previous Gillette razors. So far this strategy has paid off. In just 18 months after the Mach3 was launched, sales for the product hit $1 billion, making it the company's most successful new product ever.[49]

As the market expands during the growth phase, the seller broadens the advertising and sales-promotion activities to reach a wider audience and continues to use personal selling to expand the distribution network. When the product reaches maturity and competition is at its peak, the seller's primary goal is to differentiate the product from rival brands. Advertising generally dominates the promotional mix during this phase, but sales promotion is an important supplemental tool, particularly for low-priced consumer products. As the product begins to decline, the level of promotion generally tapers off. Advertising and selling efforts are carefully targeted toward loyal, steady customers.

Market Considerations To some extent, the promotional mix depends on whether the seller plans to focus the marketing effort on intermediaries or final customers. If the focus is on intermediaries, the producer uses a **push strategy** to persuade wholesalers and retailers to carry the item. Personal selling and sales promotions aimed at intermediaries dominate the promotional mix. If the marketing focus is on end users, the producer uses a **pull strategy** to appeal directly to the ultimate customer, using advertising, direct mail, contests, discount coupons, and so on. With this approach, consumers learn of the product through promotion and request it from retailers, who respond by asking their wholesalers for it or by going directly to the producer (see Exhibit 15.7).

Most companies use both push and pull tactics to increase the impact of their promotional efforts. For example, when Schering-Plough introduced Claritin antihistamine, it used push tactics to educate physicians about the prescription drug's use and efficacy while using pull tactics such as television and print advertising to increase market awareness and encourage consumers to ask for the new medication. This diverse, high-powered promotional mix helped Claritin capture a whopping 54 percent of the antihistamine drug market within a short time.[50]

push strategy
Promotional approach designed to motivate wholesalers and retailers to push a producer's products to end users

pull strategy
Promotional strategy that stimulates consumer demand, which then exerts pressure on wholesalers and retailers to carry a product

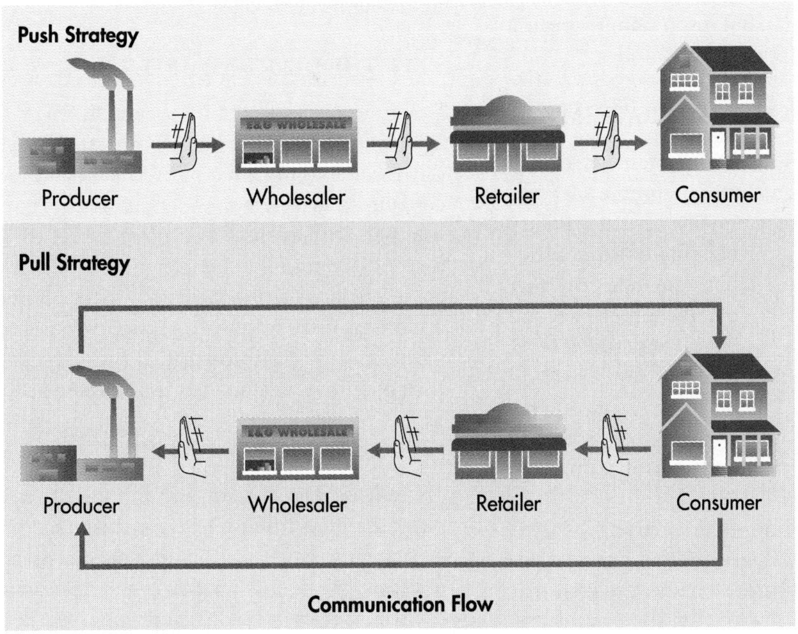

EXHIBIT 15.7

PUSH AND PULL STRATEGIES

Push strategies "push" products through distribution channels to final consumers by persuading wholesalers and retailers to carry the product. Pull strategies use consumer promotions and advertising to induce consumers to buy the product and "pull" the product through the distribution channels.

The promotional mix is also influenced by the size and concentration of the market. In markets with many widely dispersed buyers, advertising is generally the most economical way of communicating the product's features. In markets with relatively few customers, particularly when they are clustered in a limited area, personal selling is a practical promotional alternative. Many marketers use a combination of methods, often relying on advertising and public relations to build awareness and interest, following up with personal selling to complete the sale.

Positioning Considerations   The strategic importance of positioning is discussed in Chapter 13. Although promotion is just one aspect of the positioning process, it is certainly one of the most important. Consequently, positioning strategies should play a key role in the design of every company's promotional mix. The nature of a company's advertising, the type of salespeople it hires, its policy regarding coupons, its support for cultural events—decisions like these have a dramatic effect on the position that a company and its products will occupy in the minds of potential customers.

International Considerations   Businesses operating in international markets face another layer of strategic and tactical decisions when it comes to promotion. The *global* and *local* approaches to international advertising represent two extremes. With the global approach, the advertiser tries to keep the strategy and tactics identical in every country, with necessary exceptions made for local laws and media. With the local approach, the advertiser allows its divisions or representatives in each country to design and implement their own advertising. Most international campaigns fall somewhere between these two extremes. Advertisers who opt for the regional approach strike a compromise between the efficiency of the global approach and the cost and complexity of the local approach by grouping similar countries together under a single campaign. This grouping strategy is frequently adopted by e-businesses that created multiple Web sites to meet the language and cultural needs of international customers in the global marketplace.

FOCUSING ON E-BUSINESS TODAY

How to Create a Winning Web Site

These days anyone can learn to design and construct a Web site. All you need is the right Web-authoring software and a reasonably good PC to create pages with text, photos, and animated graphics. But if you want to create a winning Web site, here are a few tips to consider.

PRESENT A PROFESSIONAL CORPORATE IMAGE

A company's Web site is its most important advertisement. So be sure to provide a corporate profile that tells people a little bit about your company. Identify the key benefits of your product (include product details on a second page) and your services. But don't overkill on marketing hype. Include news releases or articles about your business so that customers can see how well known or dynamic you are in the industry.

LEARNING OBJECTIVE @9

Highlight the important elements of a winning Web site

Remember, users' online experience shapes their impression of your company. If viewers have a good experience at a Web site, they'll return. So make sure your ma-terial is accurate, interesting, and related to your products. If you're not sure what kinds of company information to include on your site, check out other Web sites for inspiration—especially your competitors' sites. Decide what you like or dislike about their appearance. Then think of ways to distinguish your site.

KEEP THE DESIGN SIMPLE

Don't overload your homepage with flashy graphics, images, colors, and different sizes of text. These features slow down the loading time of Web pages—especially when consumers use telephone modems to connect to the Internet. Studies show that users expect to wait no more than 13 seconds for a homepage to load. So if you must include any large, embedded graphics or photos, provide an option for users to select a text-only interface, or provide small images of photos (called thumbnails) for users to click on if they want to view larger, more detailed versions.

CREATE AN EASY-TO-NAVIGATE WEB SITE

Try to keep pages simple and the size of an average computer screen. Scrolling text and animated page elements constantly in motion irritate and distract users. So do pages that users must scroll up, down, and sideways to read.

Most Usable B2C Web Sites		
Company	**URL (assumes www)**	**Average Accessibility* (minutes)**
Amazon.com	amazon.com	2
Delta Air Lines	deltaairlines.com	2
Pacific Bell	pacbell.com	2.1
E*Trade	etrade.com	2.2
Half.com	half.com	2.2
Dell Computer	dell.com	2.3
eBay	ebay.com	2.3
JCP Media	jcpenney.com	2.3
Microsoft	microsoft.com	2.4
MP3.com	mp3.com	2.5
1-800-Flowers	1800flowers.com	2.5
Compaq	compaq.com	2.5

*Accessibility measures time and effort required to navigate to target pages and includes scan and load times.

Make sure all pages of your Web site have a consistent set of navigation links, including a link to your homepage. Place the navigational links at the top or bottom of each page. The links should guide users along. For example, a good Web site will pull consumers through the purchase process by transforming online visitors from being "mildly aware" to being "somewhat interested" to "truly considering" to "really evaluating whether to buy" to "making a decision," and finally by encouraging them to purchase something.

ANTICIPATE YOUR CUSTOMERS' NEEDS

Plan ahead. By including answers to frequently asked questions, chances are you'll cover about 90 percent of your customers' concerns. Remember, users tend to provide both frank and useful input, but only if you ask them for it. So be sure to include an active customer feedback mechanism such as e-mail, open feedback forms, or structured survey forms. But don't require users to register before they can see your site. You may drive them away.

MAKE YOUR WEB SITE INFORMATIVE

Most of today's online shoppers are time deprived and usually come to a Web site with a specific purpose in mind. This is true of both businesses and individual consumers. To them, visiting Web sites is about getting a job done—not cruising. Customers want companies to provide them with helpful product, service, and company information. They want engaging content—not propaganda.

When designing a Web site, be sure to include product information, comparative information, terms and conditions of purchases, delivery and return information, purchase confirmations, and easy access to technical support. Meanwhile, don't forget the basics. Always list your postal and e-mail addresses, phone and fax numbers, and the country where your company or its dealers are located. Remember, if the contents do not hold users' attention and empower them with useful information, they will "click away."

CUSTOMIZE YOUR WEB SITE FOR INTERNATIONAL AUDIENCES

Reaching an international audience on the Web involves more than simply offering translations of the English language. Successful global sites address the needs of international customers in five ways:

- *Consider the reader's viewpoint.* Assume your audience is unfamiliar with common American phrases and references. Provide both American units and metric equivalents for weights, measures, sizes, and temperatures. Express time in military format ("16:00" for 4 P.M.), and spell out dates, because Europeans read "10/04/2002" as April 10, 2002.

- *Avoid using slang and idioms.* Avoid phrases that aren't universally recognized, such as "putting all your eggs in one basket" or "jumping out of the frying pan into the fire."

- *Keep the message clear.* Use simple words and write in the active voice. Avoid complicated sentence structure to achieve a simple, straightforward tone. And don't forget to define abbreviations and acronyms.

- *Break through language barriers with graphics.* Clarify written concepts with graphics. But be careful, some images are more widely accepted than others. In some countries, for example, a mailbox doesn't necessarily convey the idea of sending mail. So an envelope might be a more appropriate symbol to reinforce the message, "Contact Us."

- *Consult local experts.* Work with local experts and Webmasters to develop native-language key words that will direct international customers to your site. Also seek the advice of local experts about customary phrases and references. Even simple terms like "homepage" differ from country to country. Spanish readers refer to the "first page," or "pagina inicial," whereas the French term is "welcome page," or "page d'accuei."

PROMOTE YOUR WEB SITE

Finally, don't just sit back and expect your Web site to perform magic. Promote your Web site. List it with numerous search engines—giant indexes that allow Web users to find information by entering key words. You may also want to place an ad in the newspaper and list your company in the Internet yellow pages. Finally, update and revise your Web site regularly. Keep it current so that viewers will keep coming back.[51]

SUMMARY OF LEARNING OBJECTIVES

1. **Identify the five basic categories of promotion.**
   The five basic categories of promotion are personal selling, advertising, direct marketing, sales promotion, and public relations.

2. **List the seven steps in the personal-selling process.**
   The seven steps are prospecting (finding prospects and qualifying them), preparing, approaching the prospects, making the sales presentation, handling objections, closing, and following up after the sale has been made.

3. **Explain the difference between logical and emotional advertising appeals.**
   You can view the difference between logical and emotional appeals as the difference between appealing to the head and appealing to the heart. Logical appeals try to convince the audience with facts, reasons, and rational conclusions. Emotional appeals, as the name implies, persuade through emotion—which can range from heart-warming tenderness to stark fear. It's important to remember, however, that nearly all ads contain a mixture of both logic and emotion; most just lean heavily in one direction or the other.

4. **Define interactive advertising and discuss the challenge it presents to marketers.**
   Interactive advertising is a two-way exchange between a merchant and a potential customer. The biggest challenge it presents is that marketers cannot control when the message is received and consumers must actively choose to participate.

5. **Name five popular direct marketing vehicles.**
   The most popular direct marketing vehicles are direct mailings of catalogs and other materials; targeted e-mail messages; telemarketing, or selling over the telephone; direct response television, which allows customers to place product orders using a computer keyboard, modem, and television; and Internet advertising, which includes banners, Web sites, and a variety of creative advertising formats.

6. **Distinguish between the two main types of sales promotion, and give at least two examples of each.**
   The two main types of sales promotion are consumer promotion and trade promotion. Consumer promotions are intended to motivate the final consumer to try new products or to experiment with the company's brands. Examples include coupons, cross-promotion, specialty advertising, premiums, point-of-purchase displays, and special events. Trade promotions are designed to induce wholesalers and retailers to stimulate sales of a producer's products. Examples include trade allowances, trade shows, display premiums, dealer contests, and travel bonus programs.

7. **Explain the role of public relations in marketing.**
   Because consumers and investors support companies with good reputations, smart companies use public relations to build and protect their reputations. They communicate with consumers, investors, industry analysts, and government officials through the media. They pursue and maintain press relations with representatives of newspapers, television, and other broadcast media so that they can give effective news releases and hold effective news conferences.

8. **Discuss the use of integrated marketing communications.**
   When companies use a greater variety of marketing communications, the likelihood of sending conflicting marketing messages to consumers increases. Integrated marketing communications (IMC) is a process of coordinating all of a company's communications and promotions efforts so that they present only one consistent message to the marketplace. Properly implemented, IMC increases marketing and promotional effectiveness.

9. **Highlight the important elements of a winning Web site.**
   A winning Web site presents a professional corporate image. It includes company contact information, general company information, and detailed but practical product information, such as pricing, purchase and delivery terms, and product specifications. The design of the site is simple to minimize loading time and it is easy to navigate. Moreover a winning Web site provides vehicles for customer feedback, and it anticipates customers' needs by including answers to frequently asked questions. Finally, because the Internet is global, companies design multiple Web sites to accommodate the language and cultural differences of international audiences.

KEY TERMS

advertising (400)

advocacy advertising (406)

banner ads (408)

canned approach (402)

closing (403)

comparative advertising (406)

competitive advertising (406)

consumer promotion (411)

continuity (410)

cooperative advertising (407)

cost per thousand (CPM) (410)

coupons (411)

creative selling (401)

cross-promotion (411)

direct mail (407)

direct marketing (400)

forward buying (412)

frequency (410)

institutional advertising (402)

integrated marketing communications (IMC) (413)

interactive advertising (406)

local advertising (407)

media (409)

media mix (409)

media plan (409)

missionary salespeople (401)

national advertising (406)

need-satisfaction approach (402)

news conference (413)

news release (413)

order getters (401)

order takers (401)

personal selling (399)

persuasive advertising (398)

point-of-purchase display (411)

premiums (412)

press relations (413)

product advertising (405)

promotion (398)

promotional mix (399)

promotional strategy (398)

prospecting (402)

public relations (400)

pull strategy (415)

TEST YOUR KNOWLEDGE

QUESTIONS FOR REVIEW

1. What are the three basic goals of promotion?

2. What is the biggest advantage of personal selling over other forms of promotion?

3. What techniques do skilled salespeople employ when closing a sale?

4. What are the four chief criteria used in media buying?

5. What are some common types of consumer promotion?

QUESTIONS FOR ANALYSIS

6. How is automation changing the function of sales personnel?

7. Why is it important to prepare for a sales call?

8. How do advertisers determine the type of appeal to use in designing an ad, and why must they execute caution when using celebrity appeals?

9. What is the biggest problem with trade allowances from the producer's perspective?

10. What are the principal advantages and disadvantages of Internet advertising?

11. Local Better Business Bureaus monitor thousands of small-business ads each year. If the agency determines an advertiser is using false or misleading ads and refuses to change the ads, the case is referred to the FTC. Scan your local papers and highlight or clip ads that could possibly mislead the public. What do you find misleading about the ad? How would you improve the ad?

QUESTIONS FOR APPLICATION

12. If you were a realtor, how would you determine whether it's worth investing a significant amount of time in a particular prospect?

13. Find three newspaper or magazine ads that you think are particularly effective and three more that you think are ineffective. What do you like about the effective ads? How might you improve the ineffective ads?

14. Should companies involve their marketing channels in the design of their promotional programs? What are the advantages and disadvantages of doing so?

15. Review the five forms of promotion discussed in this chapter. How can companies use each of these forms to build relationships with their customers?

PRACTICE YOUR KNOWLEDGE

SHARPENING YOUR COMMUNICATION SKILLS

Select a product you're familiar with, and examine the strategies used to advertise and promote that product. Identify the media (Web site, print, television, radio, billboards, and so on) used to advertise the product. Consider the following:

- Where do the ads appear?

- Who is the target audience? Does the company attempt to appeal to a wide variety of people with differing ads?

- What creative theme or appeal is being used?

- Does the company make a large financial investment in advertising? For information about advertising expenditures made by large companies, check the annual special issue of *Advertising Age*, "100 Leading National Advertisers."

- Is the company taking advantage of any Internet technologies for promotion?

In addition to your own observations, you might contact the manufacturer and interview a marketing representative regarding promotional strategies, or you might locate an article in a trade periodical that describes the promotional strategies for a specific product. Prepare a brief summary of your findings as directed by your instructor. Compare your findings with those of other students, and note any differences or similarities in the promotion of various products.

HANDLING DIFFICULT SITUATIONS ON THE JOB: PLEASE SMELL OUR CANDIE'S

Known for its flamboyant celebrity ads and its trendy shoes, Candie's is now setting its sights on the lucrative land of fragrance. The New York–based company has developed a full-scale, pricey line of fragrances to target teens. The company began its foray into the market with a splashy TV campaign featuring Alyssa Milano and buff young men frolicking on a big bed to the hit tune "Candy Man." The campaign is highly sexual but carefully walks the line between being risqué and appropriate for TV by adding a light touch of humor.[52]

You are the assistant public relations manager for Candie's. Since the ad appeared on television, both your e-mail and your snail mail have been flooded with complaints from angry parents who want the ad toned down or removed from television. Meanwhile, just last week you received reports from the ad agency responsible for creating the ad which showed that the ad is a huge success. Sales of Candie's fragrances have outperformed original projections. The agency strongly recommends that Candie's renew the ad for another three months. You will attend a cross-departmental meeting next week to discuss the ad's future. What will you recommend?

BUILDING YOUR TEAM SKILLS

In small groups discuss three or four recent ads or consumer promotions that you think were particularly effective. Using the knowledge you've gained from this chapter, try to come to consensus on what attributes contributed to the success of each ad or pro-

motion. For instance was it persuasive? Informative? Competitive? Creative? Did it have price or value appeal? Celebrity appeal? Did it stimulate you to buy the product? Why? Compare your results with those of other teams. Did you mention the same ads? Did you list the same attributes?

EXPAND YOUR KNOWLEDGE

KEEPING CURRENT USING *THE WALL STREET JOURNAL*

Choose an article from recent issues of *The Wall Street Journal* (print or online editions) that describe the advertising or promotion efforts of a particular company or trade association.

1. Who is the company or trade association targeting?
2. What specific marketing objectives is the organization trying to accomplish?
3. What role does advertising play in the promotion strategy? What other promotion techniques does the article mention? Are any of them unusual or noteworthy? Why?

DISCOVERING CAREER OPPORTUNITIES

Jobs in promotion—personal selling, advertising, direct marketing, sales promotion, and public relations—are among the most exciting and challenging in all of marketing. Choose a particular job in one of these five areas, such as public relations or media planning. Using personal contacts, local phone or Chamber of Commerce directories, or Internet resources such as company Web sites or search engines, arrange a brief phone, e-mail, or personal interview with a professional working in your chosen marketing field.

1. What are the daily activities of this professional? What tools and resources does this person use most often on the job? What does this professional like most and least about the job?
2. What talents and educational background does this professional bring to the job? How are the person's skills and knowledge applied to handle the job's daily activities?
3. What advice does the person you are interviewing have for newcomers entering this field? What can you do now to get yourself started on a career path toward this position?

EXPLORING THE BEST OF THE WEB

URLs for all Internet exercises are provided at the Web site for this book, www.prenhall.com/mescon. *When you log on to the text Web site, select Chapter 15, then select "Student Resources," click on the name of the featured Web site, and follow the detailed navigational directions to complete these exercises.*

Learn the Consumer Marketing Laws, page 399

Visit the Federal Trade Commission Web site to find out how this agency protects consumers.

1. What does the agency do and how does it serve the consumer?

2. Read the FTC Guides Against Deceptive Pricing. Can you recall any instance of these rules being violated by a retail store you visited?
3. How can consumers cut down on the number of unsolicited mailings, calls, and e-mails they receive?

Take an Idea Journey, page 403

Visit the Sales and Marketing Management Web site and read some articles that discuss creative strategies for increasing your sales.

1. What are some of the recurring article themes for this magazine, and how might marketers benefit from this information?
2. Review several of the idea groups discussed in Marketing Ideas. List five ideas that strike you as being innovative and ones that you might use as a future business owner. Compare your list to those of your fellow classmates.
3. Review several of the articles covered in past issues of *Sales and Marketing Management*. List five valuable marketing tips discussed in the articles you selected, and share your list with those of your fellow classmates.

Sample Success on the Sales Marketing Network, page 413

Check out the how-to and reference articles at the Sales Marketing Network (SMN). Learn how to maximize your product sampling programs and build customer profiles.

1. What steps can marketers take to maximize their product sampling programs?
2. What factors should direct marketers consider when building customer profiles?
3. What are the FTC requirements when using the word "free" in promotions?

Explore on Your Own

Review these chapter-related Web sites on your own to learn more about promotional strategies.

1. Tune into eCompany's guide to interactive TV at www.ecompany.com, and enter the search term "Interactive TV" to learn more about this hot topic.
2. Channel Seven bills itself as the "information source for Internet marketing and advertising decision makers." Find out why at www.channelseven.com.
3. Learn some aggressive marketing tactics from Guerrilla Marketing at www.gmarketing.com.

A CASE FOR CRITICAL THINKING

■ *Encyclopaedia Britannica Writes the Next Edition*

For over 200 years, Encyclopaedia Britannica was considered the ultimate reference source. Known for its accuracy and quality, the prestigious encyclopedia found a permanent spot on the shelves of libraries and homes across the United States. Then the digital age arrived, catching Britannica off-guard. And new technologies threatened to write the final chapter for Britannica—unless the oldest encyclopedia in the English language could find a way to survive in the face of change.

BY THE BOOK
Created by two Scottish printers in 1768, Encyclopaedia Britannica earned a sterling reputation for the high quality of its content. As generation after generation turned to Britannica, the encyclopedia not only became highly respected, but extremely profitable. Using effective personal selling techniques, an aggressive sales force of 2,300 persuaded thousands of households to fork over $1,500 to $2,000 for a 32-volume, hardbound set. By 1990, Britannica's annual sales reached an all-time high of $650 million.

LEFT ON THE SHELF
Basking in the success of its record year, the encyclopedia company failed to detect dramatic shifts in consumer behavior. The growing trend of two-income families meant that sales reps were knocking on the doors of empty houses, rarely finding both spouses at home. Moreover, households became reluctant to invite strangers into their homes for sales calls or product demonstrations. And as user-friendly, affordable computers arrived on the scene, parents chose personal computers over encyclopedias as an educational investment.

To make matters worse, Britannica looked the other way as competitors took advantage of new technologies and produced cheaper encyclopedias on CD-ROM. Competition from Microsoft's CD-ROM encyclopedia, Encarta, nearly devastated the company. Instead of thumbing through Britannica's massive, hardcover volumes, researchers could find instant answers with Encarta and one click of a mouse. Britannica's sales slumped as consumers snapped up Encarta for $50 to $70 or enjoyed the free version installed on new computers.

Scrambling to survive, Britannica fought back by offering its own CD-ROM for $1,000. Tied to its traditional sales channel, the company marketed the product exclusively through its sales force. But the stiff price tag attracted few buyers. Moreover, sales reps—accustomed to earning $500 to $600 commissions on each sale of the print version—balked at the idea of hawking the cheaper CD-ROMs.

REVISED EDITION
As sales plunged to $405 million in 1995, Britannica struggled to reinvent itself. First, the company reduced the cost of its sales force, the largest expense in its distribution chain. Britannica closed 70 of 90 regional offices, cut sales commissions, scaled back marketing, and dropped recruiting and training efforts. Then the company leaped into the electronic age by launching www.eb.com. To access the site's original Web articles and links, consumers paid an annual subscription fee of $150, while universities purchased site licenses. Although college licenses boomed, the site failed to attract consumers, who were accustomed to getting information for free on the Internet.

After six years of heavy losses, Britannica's owners—a trust controlled by the University of Chicago—sold the company to Swiss investors in 1996. Unable to maintain the expenses of commissions, administration, sales offices, and generating leads, the new owners immediately dumped the door-to-door sales force. "The revenues generated from our in-home sales efforts in North America no longer justify the costs," announced Britannica's management.

THE NEXT CHAPTER
Although Britannica tried to become more competitive by slashing the subscription price for its online service and the price of its CD-ROM, the efforts failed to rejuvenate the company. So Britannica mapped out an electronic blueprint for survival, basing its marketing and promotion strategy on the product's credibility and powerful brand name. Furthermore, Britannica decided to give away its content for free on the Internet.

In late 1999, Britannica launched a second site, www.britannica.com, a free online reference service that offers full access to the complete text of the 32-volume reference set and other sources. The site's search engine produces multiple results that include Britannica entries, articles from 70 magazines, pertinent news items, original Web content, and appropriate Web links.

Britannica plans to generate online revenue through a combination of Web advertising, subscription services to schools and other institutions, e-commerce sales to consumers, and sales of CD-ROM encyclopedias. "Our challenge is to take the brand name and redefine what Britannica can be," says Don Yannias, CEO of britannica.com. "We feel very confident we can turn the brand into a repository of trust and authority." Still, only time will tell whether Britannica can thrive in the digital age.

CRITICAL THINKING QUESTIONS

1. Why did Britannica's sales decline during the 1990s?

2. What challenges did Britannica face as it tried to reinvent itself?

3. How does Britannica plan to generate online revenue?

4. Go to Chapter 15 of this text's Web site at www.prenhall.com/mescon and click on the hot link to get the Britannica Web site. Follow the online instructions to answer these questions: What type of information appears on the homepage? How does the site blend information with e-commerce? How does Britannica promote its own products?

VIDEO CASE AND EXERCISES

■ Milk Becomes a Brand Through "Got Milk?" Campaign

SYNOPSIS

Milk consumption plummeted from 1980 into the early 1990s as U.S. consumers quaffed more soft drinks, bottled water, flavored teas, and sports drinks. To reverse this downward trend, the California Milk Processor Board worked with Goodby, Silverstein and Partners to create a humorous new advertising campaign that transformed milk from a boring commodity to a branded food product. Until that point, milk had been advertised on the basis of its health-enhancing qualities. Through research, the agency learned that consumers found milk indispensable as a complement to various foods—but they didn't realize it until they ran out of milk. As a result of this research, the agency created a new advertising campaign focusing on milk deprivation, ending each ad with the tag line "Got Milk?" (www.gotmilk.com).

EXERCISES
Analysis

1. Does the "Got Milk?" campaign use a logical or an emotional appeal?

2. Why was television chosen as the main medium for the "Got Milk?" campaign?

3. How could the California Milk Processor Board conveniently adapt the existing commericals for use in other major advertising media?

4. Do you think this campaign should aim for more reach or more frequency? Why?

5. How does this video segment act as public relations for the California Milk Processor Board and its message?

Application

Assume that the California Milk Processor Board wants to support the "Got Milk?" campaign with consumer promotion. Which one of the promotional tools would be most appropriate—and why?

Decision

No advertiser has an unlimited budget. Would you recommend that the California Milk Processor Board use a continuity schedule for the "Got Milk?" campaign or air messages in flights?

Communication

Imagine that Goodby, Silverstein and Partners has been asked to prepare a radio commercial to complement the "Got Milk?" television campaign. Write copy for a 15-second commercial to be read by a live announcer on a local radio station.

Integration

Review the section on the product life cycle in Chapter 13. Where in its life cycle does milk appear to be at present?

Ethics

In comparative advertising, advertisers show or discuss competing products. Would it be unethical to show or name a competing beverage such as Coca-Cola in a "Got Milk?" ad when the product is not given the opportunity to respond to the ad?

Debate

Should the California Milk Processor Board use comparative advertising to contrast milk with a soft drink such as Coca-Cola? Select one side of this question and list at least two arguments in preparation for a classroom debate.

Teamwork

Working with three other students, design a magazine advertisement that conveys the same kind of message as the "Got Milk?" television campaign. (Rough sketches and lettering will do.) List two or more publications where this advertisement should be placed.

Online Research

Using Internet sources, obtain the latest news on the "Got Milk?" campaign and investigate current trends in U.S. milk consumption. See Component Chapter A, Exhibit A.1, for search engines to use in doing your research.

MYPHLIP COMPANION WEB SITE

Learning Interactively

Visit the myPHLIP Web site at www.prenhall.com/mescon. For Chapter 15, take advantage of the interactive "Study Guide" to test your chapter knowledge. Get instant feedback on whether you need additional studying. Read the "Current Events" articles to get the latest on chapter topics, and complete the exercise as specified by your instructor. Expand your learning with a visit to the "Research Area." There you will find a wealth of information you can use to complete your course assignments.

MASTERING GLOBAL AND GEOGRAPHICAL SKILLS: WHAT'S THE BEST LOCATION FOR YOUR NEW STORE?

You've probably heard the remark that the three most important things to look for when buying real estate are location, location, and location. The same basic concern applies to businesses such as restaurants (although other factors certainly affect your chances of success).

Assume you're going to open a restaurant. Where would you put a restaurant in your city or town? Begin your decision process by outlining the type of restaurant you will open and the type of menu you will offer. Then determine who your target customers are. Next, using a street map, the yellow pages, and the Internet work through the following questions (if you're in a large city, you may want to restrict yourself to one particular section of the city):

1. Where do your target customers work, live, or travel regularly? For instance, if you've defined your business as an expensive restaurant, most of your customers are likely to come from business districts and affluent neighborhoods.

2. How will these people reach you? Can they walk? Will they have to drive? Will they use public transportation? Depending on the business you choose to start, you'll encounter different transportation needs. Think about how far people are willing to drive to eat at a special restaurant.

3. Where do your competitors seem to be? You can get a good idea from the yellow pages. Identify the restaurants you'll compete with and mark their locations on your map. (Again, you may want to restrict the geographic scope of this project; you don't want to track down a thousand restaurants!)

4. Using the Internet, find out more about your desired location. Use any of the search engines listed in Component Chapter A (see the Exhibit "Best of Internet Searching") to help you research these items:

   a. How is the area changing? Are any new buildings, offices, or residential properties scheduled for construction in the near future? (Hint: Local Chamber of Commerce Web sites frequently include this information.)

   b. Does the area offer forms of entertainment such as movies, plays, or sporting events that would help drive business to your restaurant? (Hint: Web sites such as Digital City home.digitalcity.com/ or City Search www.citysearch.com/ provide this information.)

   c. How easy will it be for customers to get to your restaurant? Log on to MapBlast at www.mapblast. com and check it out. Enter the location for your desired restaurant (as much information as you have) and generate the map. Now get *Driving Directions* from some main location points by entering their respective street locations and then clicking on *Drive.* Is your selected location near a major highway or thoroughfare?

Business PlanPro

DEVELOPING MARKETING STRATEGIES TO SATISFY CUSTOMERS

Review the Appendix, "Getting Started with Business PlanPro Software," to learn how to use Business PlanPro Software so that you can complete these exercises.

Think Like a Pro

Objective: By completing these exercises, you will become acquainted with the sections of a business plan that address a firm's target market and pricing, promotion, sales, and distribution strategies. For these exercises, use the sample business plan for Boulder Stop Gear.

Open the BPP software and explore the sample business plan Boulder Stop Gear.spd. Click on the "Plan Outline" icon to access the plan's Task Manager and use it to navigate the company's business plan. Familiarize yourself with this firm's service and operation by reading the "Executive Summary" (see "Finish and Polish") and by reading the sections listed under "Your Company," "What You're Selling," and "Your Sales Forecast."

1. Define the target market for Boulder Stop Gear. How will Boulder Stop Gear differentiate its products and services?

2. What are the company's pricing, promotion, sales, and distribution strategies?

Find "Your Market" and read the plan sections listed under this heading. View the market analysis graphic by double clicking on the "Market Analysis Summary" and then clicking on the "Chart" icon at the top of the screen. Click on the "Text" icon to return to the summary.

3. Rank the company's three market segmentation categories according to their importance.

Find the heading "Initial Assessment" and read the "Keys to Success" section.

4. What must Boulder Stop Gear do to be successful?

Use the BPP instructions to learn about this section of a business plan.

5. How do you benefit by preparing this section of a business plan?

Create Your Own Business Plan

Consider your own target market and customers. How will you segment your target market? Which customers are likely to buy your product or service? Describe your pricing, promotion, sales, and distribution strategies. Now make some preliminary sales forecasts. Review the BPP Task Manager. Under which section headings will you present this information?

Webvan's managers knew they would have a battle on their hands. Since Webvan's debut in 1999, the company was touted as the "efficient" cyber grocer that would finally make a dent in the $650 billion annual grocery market. Now Webvan had to prove it. Others, such as Peapod, Streamline, and HomeGrocer, had tried, but by the time Webvan entered the Internet fray these cyber-grocery pioneers were battling for their lives.

A Fresh Approach to Bringing Home the Bacon

Like its predecessors, Webvan believed that the convenience of pointing and clicking one's way through weekly shopping lists and having groceries delivered to customers' doorsteps would lead to big business. After all, grocery shopping is a task that most people dislike but still do once or twice a week, spending on average $4,600 per year. So Webvan set out to succeed where others had failed. It's strategy: build $40 million fully automated distribution centers in key markets across the nation, stock them with more than 18,000 items, and truck orders out to delivery stations situated like spokes throughout a metropolitan area. There, a fleet of high-tech refrigerated delivery vans would pick up the orders and deliver them to customers' homes at a conveniently scheduled time—give or take 30 minutes.

Starting in San Francisco, Webvan soon expanded its operations to Atlanta, Chicago, and a handful of other major cities such as Los Angeles, San Diego, and Seattle, using clever anti-grocery store advertising campaigns and a variety of promotional gimmicks. Wall Street analysts gushed over the company's potential, expecting Webvan to give the traditional supermarkets a run for their money. But the supermarkets were cautious warriors.

Supermarkets Nibble on the Net

For years, supermarket companies were e-commerce spectators, using the Web primarily to deliver corporate information. Unconvinced that anyone could earn a profit delivering groceries to homes, their boilerplate attitude seemed to be: Wait until online grocery retailing becomes profitable and then jump in. But that was before Webvan made its splashy debut. Webvan's managers had a reputation for being brilliant strategists and tough executers. And the supermarkets knew that if anyone could make online grocery shopping a success, Webvan could.

So rather than watch Webvan chip away at their market share, the traditional supermarkets made their initial cyber move. More than half the nation's major grocery chains began testing online shopping in at least one or two urban areas. Some forayed into e-commerce with a bricks-and-clicks strategy, launching Internet order-and-curbside pickup programs at local grocery stores, or using their existing stores as e-commerce fulfillment sites and linking up with independent companies to handle the home-delivery routine. Some, such as Safeway and Albertson's, established independent online grocery channels. But few promoted their online shopping alternatives aggressively.

Food Fight in the Cyber Grocery Aisles

While the supermarkets reluctantly dabbled in e-commerce, a food fight broke out in the cyber grocery aisles. Supermarkets watched closely as the cyber rivals feasted on each other's market share and battled over the right way to sell groceries via the Internet and deliver them to customers' doorsteps. Peapod, the oldest e-tailer in the business, provided ordering and home-delivery services to local grocers but used the local stores as fulfillment centers where Peapod employees picked and packed the pickles—a labor-intensive and costly approach. HomeGrocer's approach was similar to Peapod's, but it used small company-owned warehouses. Webvan, of course, had the most automated operation.

The lengthy battle ended with casualties. Cash-strapped Peapod was rescued in 2000 by Dutch grocer Royal Ahold NV, which shelled out $73 million for a majority interest in the cyber

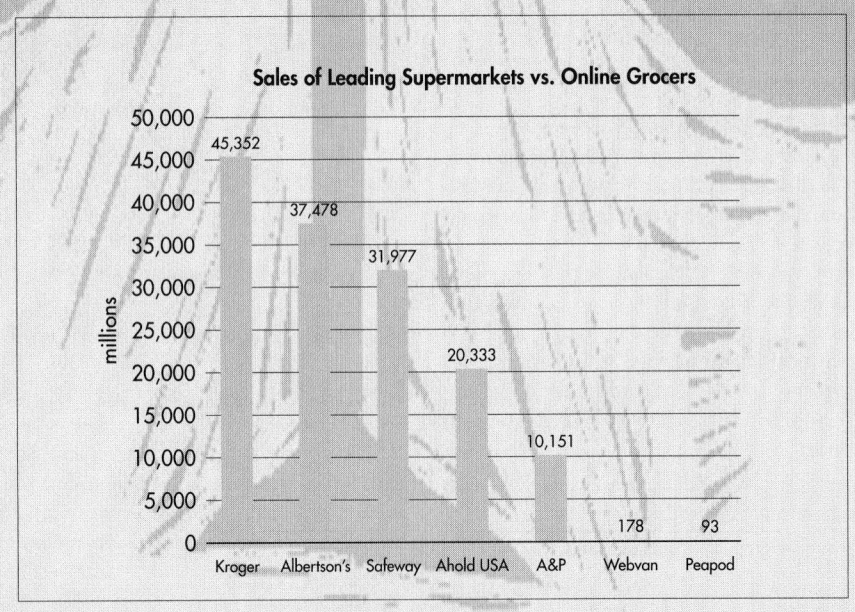

Sales of Leading Supermarkets vs. Online Grocers

	millions
Kroger	45,352
Albertson's	37,478
Safeway	31,977
Ahold USA	20,333
A&P	10,151
Webvan	178
Peapod	93

company. Ahold also scooped up the partial remains of failed Streamline and began building state-of-the-art distribution centers to launch a direct attack on Webvan. But Webvan bagged the number one spot by purchasing HomeGrocer.com, the number two online player, and incorporated HomeGrocer's leaner, less-automated warehouses in certain markets.

Meanwhile, the supermarkets stayed with their go-slow approach. After all, they did more business in a single busy afternoon than Webvan did in a year. Moreover, they had two aces up their sleeves: customers who were willing to pick and deliver the goods for free, and profits.

Why Customers Weren't Clicking

Moving food shoppers online was more of an uphill battle than Webvan had imagined. Although 41 percent of Americans admit they hate supermarket shopping, shoppers still want to squeeze the tomatoes. Moreover, consumers crave instant gratification and in most cases can drive to a traditional supermarket within minutes. In fact, 21 percent of Internet users said that nothing could make them more likely to buy groceries online—citing a number of key concerns (see table). And of those willing to buy groceries online, 43 percent said they would choose an online service offered by a local supermarket over a pure-play cyber grocer such as Webvan.

Webvan's managers acknowledge that "our single greatest challenge is to get customers out of the brick-and-mortar grocery stores." Put differently, for Webvan to be successful, it must not only offer consumers distinct advantages for shopping online, it must first convince them to change their decades-old consumer-shopping behavior.

Can Webvan Deliver the Goods?

Industry experts project that the online grocery market will grow exponentially—from $200 million in 1999 to $16.9 billion by 2004. But the reality so far is that cyber grocers have struggled gaining customer loyalty and securing the order volume and frequency needed

---

TOP TEN REASONS WHY CONSUMERS ARE NOT INTERESTED IN ONLINE GROCERY SHOPPING

Want to see and touch what they buy

Inconvenient delivery times and methods

Will miss social experience

Concern for quality of product that will be received

Products are overpriced

Too technical

Internet privacy concerns

Not interested in online shopping in general

Web sites are too difficult to navigate

No Internet access

---

to become profitable in a low-margin industry. Moreover, early claims that Internet grocers could turn around the razor-thin profits of the grocery business by building efficient warehouses, minimizing labor, and locating warehouses on non-prime real estate were, for the most part, overstated. In most cases the anticipated cyber advantages have been offset by huge startup and operational costs. Such costs include building and running high-tech distribution centers, packing shopping carts with customers' orders, maintaining a fleet of delivery trucks, and running a complex, private delivery service.

To boost order volume, Webvan expanded its product offerings to include nongrocery items such as office suppliers, books, flowers, and electrical appliances. Still, money has been gushing out of Webvan, and the cyber grocer has not yet turned a profit. So to conserve cash, Webvan temporarily scaled back its ambitious expansion plans and shifted into survival mode, countering weak consumer demand by cutting costs and focusing on its most profitable markets. Now some analysts are questioning whether Webvan can survive.

Will Supermarkets Pick and Pack the Produce?

The supermarkets are at a critical juncture. Providing store-to-door delivery service is an expensive service supermarkets would rather not offer. Doing so would require them to reconfigure warehouses to accommodate individual customer orders, create easy-to-use Web site storefronts, and set up home-delivery networks.

But Webvan thinks the supermarkets will take a pass. "If they [supermarkets] try to build a similar infrastructure, they will be layering on cost." Moreover, they will have to develop a way to pick and pack produce better than Webvan, while keeping their prices in line. On the other hand, if supermarkets don't take a more aggressive approach, and if Webvan succeeds, the supermarkets could find themselves in a real pickle. Catching the cyber grocery leader won't be easy if the supermarkets stay with their go-slow approach.

QUESTIONS FOR CRITICAL THINKING

1. Why have the traditional supermarkets chosen a go-slow approach to online grocery selling? What are the advantages and disadvantages of their doing so?

2. What competitive advantages does Webvan have over the supermarkets? What competitive advantages do the supermarkets have over Webvan?

3. What are Webvan's biggest challenges? How can it meet these challenges?

4. If you were to develop a marketing strategy for Webvan, what would you recommend?

5. What roadblocks will the traditional supermarkets likely face should they decide to launch a direct attack on Webvan and battle aggressively with the cyber warrior?

6. Explore Webvan's Web site at www.webvan.com. How could Webvan use its Web site to convince visitors to try its service?

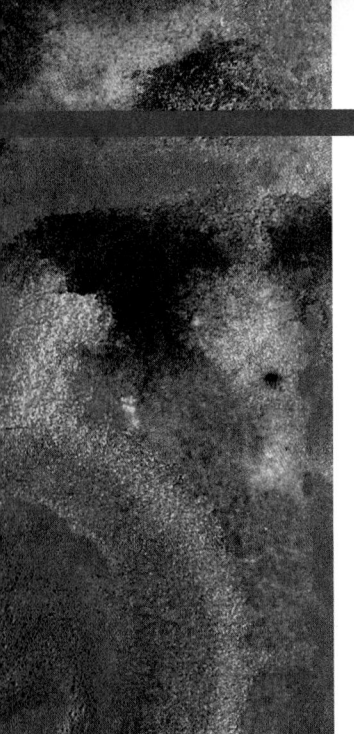

ACCOUNTING

16

LEARNING OBJECTIVES

After studying this chapter, you will be able to

1. Discuss how managers and outsiders use financial information

2. Describe what accountants do and explain how technology is changing their work

3. State the basic accounting equation and explain the purpose of double-entry bookkeeping

4. Differentiate between cash basis and accrual basis accounting

5. Explain the purpose of the balance sheet and identify its three main sections

6. Explain the purpose of the income statement

7. Explain the purpose of the statement of cash flows

8. Explain the purpose of ratio analysis and list the four main categories of financial ratios

@ 9. Discuss why and how some e-businesses record accounting transactions to inflate their sales

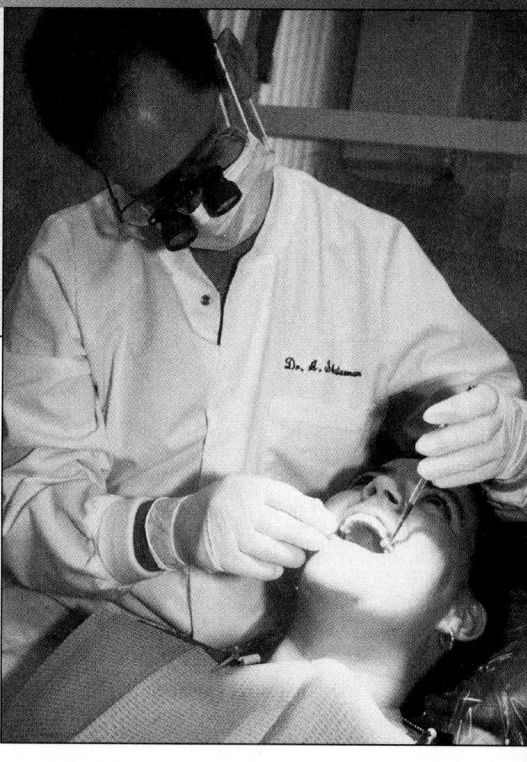

TODAY
Inside Business

DRILLING FOR DOLLARS AT DENTAL LIMITED
www.dentallimited.com

Dr. Arthur Schatzman, co-owner of Dental Limited, relies on his accountant for sound financial advice.

Most people don't think of their dentist's office as a business, but "running a dental practice is no different from running any other service business," says Dr. Arthur Schatzman, co-owner of Dental Limited in Wheeling, Illinois. "We have customers (patients), accounts receivable, accounts payable, depreciable equipment, employee profit-sharing plans, building insurance—and we face the same challenges that most small-business owners face." But there's a twist.

Unlike many small-business owners and professionals, dentists aren't trained to run a business. "We had one lecture in dental school about the cost of dental supplies," says Schatzman, "but that's about all the business we were taught. Everything I learned about running the business side of a dental practice I learned on my own—by reading business magazines, networking with other business owners, and talking with accountants and other business professionals." In fact, one of the first things Schatzman and his partner Dr. Robert Crane did when they established Dental Limited was to hire an independent accountant. The accountant helped the dentists set up their bookkeeping systems and taught them some accounting fundamentals.

Today, all bookkeeping and record processing at Dental Limited is automated. Patient records, routing slips, billing, insurance claims, and accounts receivable are processed electronically using a proprietary software package called Soft Dent. In addition to using Soft Dent, Dental Limited uses Intuit's Quick Books to pay bills and process patients' payments electronically. Quick Books generates cash receipts and disbursements journals along with a variety of financial reports and statements, which the dentists submit to their accountant. The accountant uses this information to prepare the company's quarterly payroll reports, compile the company's quarterly and annual finan-

cial statements, and prepare the company's tax return. But first the accountant reviews the daily computerized accounting transactions (to make sure they have been recorded properly) and prepares adjusted journal entries if errors are found.

Periodically the accountant meets with the dentists to advise them of changes in employment laws and tax laws or to assist them with important financial decisions. For example, several years ago Schatzman and Crane expanded Dental Limited by purchasing an existing dental practice from a retiring dentist. "Overnight we doubled the number of our patients and employees. We moved our existing practice into the larger space occupied by the retiring dentist, but we weren't thrilled about purchasing the entire office building—a requirement of the deal. We had to negotiate tenant leases and leasehold improvements, enter into building maintenance contracts, market vacant office space, and more" recalls Schatzman. "It was a big financial commitment."

To help them evaluate the merits of the acquisition, Schatzman and Crane relied on their accountant for financial advice. The accountant calculated a number of possible financial outcomes for the purchase of the practice and building using best-case and worst-case scenarios. For example, what if, say, 20 percent of the acquired patients decided not to stay with Dental Limited, or 30 percent of the current tenants decided not to renew their leases. "It's one thing to look at numbers on financial statements," says Schatzman, "but it takes a good accountant to teach you how to analyze the numbers and prepare for a possible range of financial outcomes."

Looking back, the dentists don't remember too many financial surprises—just some awfully big headaches. "We knew the upside and the downside of the deal," recalls Schatzman. "And thanks to our careful financial analysis, we were prepared."[1]

427

■ WHAT IS ACCOUNTING?

As Schatzman and Crane know, it's difficult to manage a business today without accurate and up-to-date financial information. **Accounting** is the system a business uses to identify, measure, and communicate financial information to others, inside and outside the organization. Financial information is important to businesses such as Dental Limited for two reasons: First, it helps managers and owners plan and control a company's operation and make informed business decisions. Second, it helps outsiders evaluate a business. Suppliers, banks, and other lenders want to know whether a business is creditworthy; investors and shareholders are concerned with a company's profit potential; government agencies are interested in a business's tax accounting.

Because outsiders and insiders use accounting information for different purposes, accounting has two distinct facets. **Financial accounting** is concerned with preparing financial statements and other information for outsiders such as stockholders and *creditors* (people or organizations that have lent a company money or have extended them credit); **management accounting** is concerned with preparing cost analyses, profitability reports, budgets, and other information for insiders such as management and other company decision makers. To be useful, all accounting information must be accurate, objective, consistent over time, and comparable to information supplied by other companies.

The Rules of Accounting

Much of accounting information is *proprietary,* which means it is not divulged to outsiders. Schatzman and Crane, for example, produce a variety of proprietary financial reports and analyses that help them run their dental practice more efficiently and profitably. But because they do not share these reports with outsiders, they are free to organize them in a format that suits their company's specific needs.

All U.S. public companies must prepare their published financial statements according to **generally accepted accounting principles (GAAP),** basic accounting standards and procedures that have been agreed on by the accounting profession. All U.S. public companies must publish their financial statements in accordance with GAAP. This requirement makes it possible for external users to compare the financial results of one company with those of another and to gain a general idea of a firm's relative effectiveness and its standing within a particular industry.

In the United States, the Financial Accounting Standards Board (FASB) is responsible for establishing GAAP. Other countries, of course, have similar governing boards, which means that foreign companies such as Nissan or Toyota may report accounting data using rules that are different from those used by U.S. companies such as Ford or General Motors. Nonetheless, foreign companies that list their securities on a U.S. stock exchange must publish a set of financial statements that conform to GAAP. Converting financial statements prepared under foreign accounting rules to GAAP puts all companies listed on U.S. stock exchanges on even ground. For example, when Toyota Motor Corporation listed its stock on the New York Stock Exchange the company's earnings dropped four percentage points because of a difference between Japanese accounting rules and U.S. accounting rules.[2]

To eliminate such confusion and simplify bookkeeping for multinational companies, the London-based International Accounting Standards Committee (IASC) is developing a uniform set of global rules for accounting. The committee hopes its proposed International Accounting Standards (IAS) will be adopted by all countries and accepted by all U.S and foreign stock exchanges. But such global rules are meeting strong resistance from the U.S. Securities and Exchange Commission (SEC) and FASB, which are concerned that many of the International Accounting Standards are not as strict as GAAP.[3]

Keep in mind that accounting rules set forth the principles and guidelines that companies and accountants must follow when preparing financial reports or recording accounting transactions (which we will discuss later in this chapter). But, as with any rules, they can be interpreted aggressively or conservatively. Furthermore, management and accountants often make estimates or financial projections in the course of their accounting work. Sometimes these numbers need to be adjusted because unexpected events happen or because the estimates were too optimistic or too conservative. In fact, pick up any newspaper business section and chances are you'll read about a company that is taking a "big charge against earnings" or is restating its financial reports

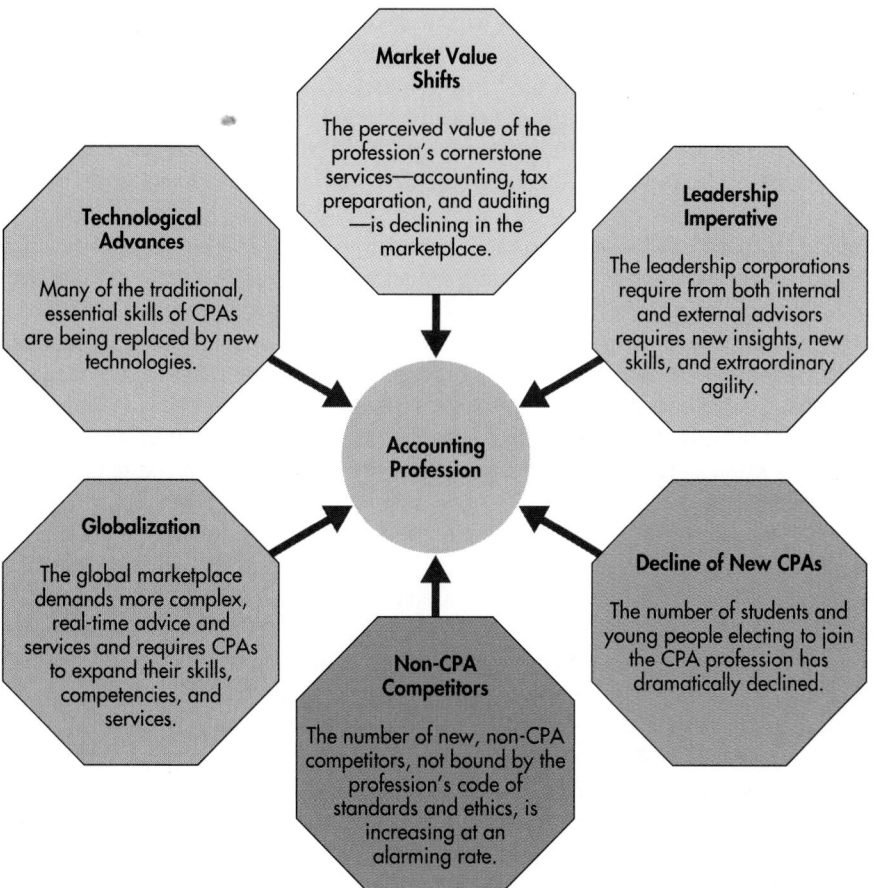

EXHIBIT 16.1

FORCES INFLUENCING THE ACCOUNTING PROFESSION

A number of forces are pressuring today's accountants to provide more value-added services.

because of revised projections. Interpreting accounting rules, establishing financial systems, preparing reports, and projecting the future are just some of the challenging tasks that accountants perform on the job.

What Accountants Do

Some people confuse the work accountants do with **bookkeeping,** which is the clerical function of recording the economic activities of a business. Although some accountants do perform some bookkeeping functions, their work generally goes well beyond the scope of this activity. Accountants design accounting systems, prepare financial statements, analyze and interpret financial information, prepare financial forecasts and budgets, prepare tax returns, interpret tax law, and do much more. In fact, the entire accounting profession is undergoing sweeping changes. As one spokesperson for the American Institute of Certified Public Accounts (AICPA) put it, "Users no longer want to look back—they want to look forward, and supplying forward-looking information is the kind of service businesses will be paying for in the future."[4]

Of course, one of the forces driving this change is the availability of new technology (see Exhibit 16.1). Today, financial data are produced, collected, analyzed, and distributed faster and in greater detail than ever before. New software programs, more powerful computers, and the ability to store vast amounts of data now make it possible to automate many accounting tasks. Thus, today's accountants have time to redirect their efforts to more important business functions, such as helping clients improve business processes, plan for the future, evaluate product performance, analyze profitability by customer and product groups, and design and install new computer systems. Not only are today's accountants involved in company decision making, but many assist clients such as Dental Limited in planning for the future.

Performing these functions, requires a strong business background and a variety of business skills beyond accounting (see Exhibit 16.2). For instance, many accountants work on

bookkeeping
Record keeping, clerical aspect of accounting

LEARNING OBJECTIVE 2

Describe what accountants do and explain how technology is changing their work

SKILLS
- Analytical
- Problem solving
- Interpersonal
- Listening
- Communication
- Leadership
- Decision making
- Time management
- Teamwork
- Computer

EXHIBIT 16.2

TEN MOST IMPORTANT SKILLS FOR ACCOUNTANTS

Besides having a thorough knowledge of accounting, today's accountants need the right mix of personal and business skills to increase their chances for a successful career.

certified public accountants (CPAs)
Professionally licensed accountants who meet certain requirements for education and experience and who pass a comprehensive examination

public accountants
Professionals who provide accounting services to other businesses and individuals for a fee

audit
Formal evaluation of the fairness and reliability of a client's financial statements

internal auditors
Employees who analyze and evaluate a company's operations and data to determine their accuracy

cross-functional teams so they must be able to convey technical messages to a nontechnical audience. In other words, accountants must be able to communicate effectively and relate comfortably to others outside their field.[5] To prepare accountants for these additional responsibilities, most U.S. states have increased the educational eligibility requirement to sit for the CPA examination from 120 to 150 semester hours.[6] This exam is prepared by the AICPA and is a requirement for accountants to become **certified public accountants (CPAs).**

Public Accountants **Public accountants,** such as the one hired by Dental Limited, are independent of the businesses, organizations, and individuals they serve. These accountants perform a variety of accounting functions for their clients. Perhaps the most widely recognized functions are compiling financial statements and preparing tax returns. Although all accountants can handle these tasks, only public accountants who have passed the CPA exam may ensure the integrity and reliability of a company's financial statements. They do this by conducting an **audit**—a formal evaluation of the fairness and reliability of financial statements. Companies whose stock (ownership shares) is publicly traded in the United States are required to file audited financial statements with the SEC.

During an audit, CPAs who work for an independent accounting firm (also known as *external* auditors) review a client's financial records to determine whether the statements that summarize these records have been prepared in accordance with GAAP and fairly present the financial position and operating results of the firm. Once the auditors have completed an audit, they attach a report summarizing their findings to the client's published financial statements. Sometimes these reports disclose information that might materially affect the client's financial position, such as the bankruptcy of a major supplier, a large obsolete inventory, costly environmental problems, or questionable accounting practices. For example, when auditors at Arthur Andersen discovered falsified shipping documents and purchase orders at Aviation Distributors, the auditors could no longer attest to the accuracy of the company's financial results.[7] Most companies, however, receive a clean audit report, which means that to the best of the auditors' knowledge the company's financial statements are accurate.

In addition to hiring external auditors, many large companies also have **internal auditors**—employees who investigate and evaluate a company's internal operations and data to determine whether they are accurate and whether they comply with GAAP, federal laws, and industry regulations. Although this self-checking process is vital to an organization's financial health, an internal audit is not a substitute for having an independent auditor look things over and render an unbiased opinion. Many people, such as creditors, shareholders, investors, and government agencies, rely on the integrity of a company's financial statements and place great trust and confidence in the independence of auditors whose detached position allows them to be objective and, when necessary, critical.

Today, 90 percent of all publicly held U.S. corporations are audited by the world's five largest accounting firms: PricewaterhouseCoopers, KPMG Peat Marwick, Arthur Andersen, Ernst & Young, and Deloitte & Touche.[8] In addition to auditing and accounting services, many accounting firms provide a variety of management consulting services for their clients. Some accounting firms have become multiline service organizations in which accounting and auditing are rapidly becoming secondary activities.[9] Others have established separate business con-

Best of the Web Best of the Web Best of

SIZE THEM UP

Exactly how big are the big accounting firms? Why not size one up. Log on to the Ernst & Young Web site and learn about the many services this large accounting firm has to offer. With global locations, thousands of clients, a commitment to industry specialization, and experts in just about everything, this firm is a powerhouse. If you thought accountants only prepared financial statements and tax returns, think again!

www.ey.com/global/gcr.nsf/US/US_Home

THINKING ABOUT ETHICS

AUDITORS AND CLIENTS: TOO CLOSE FOR COMFORT?

Are today's auditors independent enough? Should the same accounting firm that tallies the books, installs complex computer software, and delivers managerial expertise to clients also provide the essential "second look" at numbers? These are some of the questions that federal securities regulators are grappling with as more and more accounting firms become increasingly involved in the day-to-day operations of their audit clients.

Although no *major* problems have yet come to light in cases where the same firm provides both auditing and consulting functions, some experts say the double duties raise many uncertainties. For instance, will an accounting firm that is being paid $100 million to install complex software be willing to disagree with company executives on a controversial accounting issue if such actions might jeopardize the consulting job? Or, will an auditor who works for the same firm that installed a company's information system raise questions about flaws in that system? The accounting firms don't think there is a problem. In fact, most accounting firms maintain that the knowledge they gain about a client's operations and systems from a consulting engagement helps them perform a better audit.

But the SEC disagrees. Concerned that accounting firms might go easy on companies they audit in exchange for

consulting business, the SEC tried to limit the amount and types of consulting work that accountants could perform. But eventually the SEC backed down because it was unable to prove that wrongdoing had occurred. The SEC did, however, impose one new requirement. Companies are now required to disclose in their proxy statements the amounts they pay for consulting engagements performed by an audit firm.

But is this disclosure enough? Some think not. After all, in some cases consulting contributes more than half of an accounting firm's revenues, and the revenue from consulting is growing three times as fast as the revenue from auditing. There's a lot at stake—for everyone. One accounting professor summarizes the situation nicely: "As auditors, they will have to express an opinion on something that they did. That is a conflict, and that is a problem."

■ QUESTIONS FOR CRITICAL THINKING

1. What are the main advantages and disadvantages of hiring an auditor who is familiar with a client's operation and industry?

2. Why would an accounting firm perform consulting services for its clients, even if doing so means the firm might lose them as audit clients?

sulting units—many of which now rank among the world's leading consulting firms. Nonetheless, regulators are concerned that the increasing amount of work performed by public accountants for their clients places their independence at risk.[10]

Private Accountants Of the 1.9 million accountants worldwide, only 35 percent are in public practice. The remaining 65 percent are, for the most part, **private accountants** (sometimes called corporate accountants) working for a business, a government agency (such as the Internal Revenue Service, a school, or a local police department), or a nonprofit corporation (such as a church, charity, or hospital).[11] Although many private accountants are CPAs, a growing number are **certified management accountants (CMAs),** who earn certification by passing a two-day exam (given by the Institute of Management Accountants) that is comparable in difficulty to the CPA exam.[12]

Some accountants specialize in certain areas of accounting, such as **cost accounting** (computing

Accountants perform a variety of services for their clients beyond tax preparation and auditing. Many serve on strategic planning teams and help companies plan for the future.

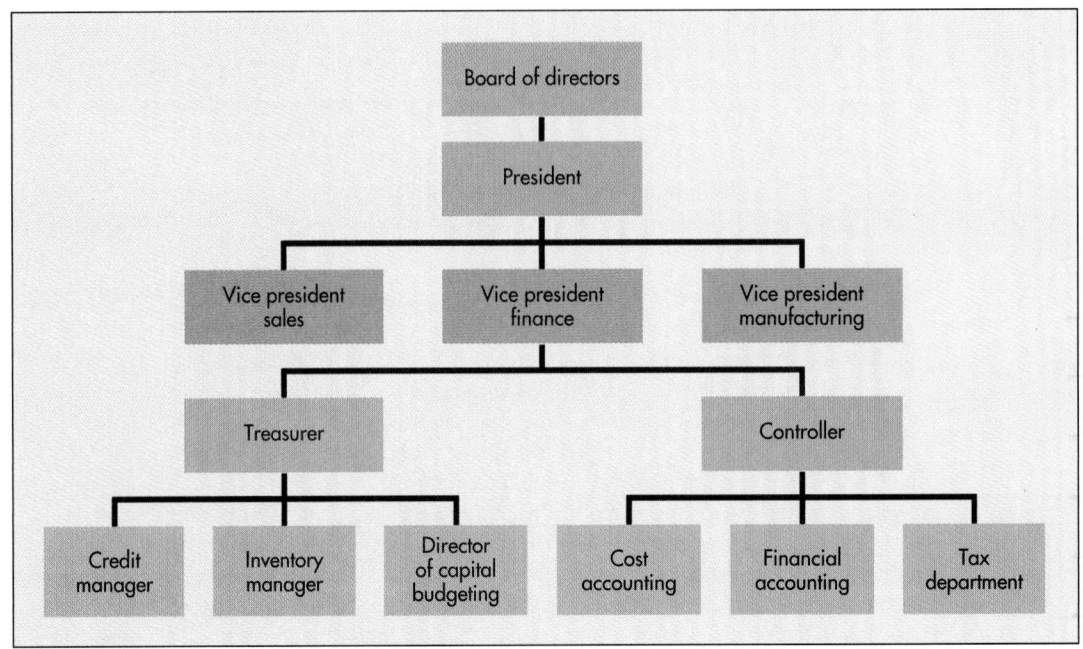

EXHIBIT 16.3

TYPICAL FINANCE DEPARTMENT

Here is a typical finance department of a large company. In smaller companies, the controller may be the highest ranking accountant and report directly to the president.

private accountants
In-house accountants employed by organizations and businesses other than a public accounting firm; also called *corporate accountants*

certified management accountants (CMAs)
Accountants who have fulfilled the requirements for certification as specialists in management accounting

cost accounting
Area of accounting focusing on the calculation of manufacturing and storage costs of products for use or sale in a business

tax accounting
Area of accounting focusing on tax preparation and tax planning

financial analysis
Process of evaluating a company's performance and analyzing the costs and benefits of a strategic action

controller
Highest-ranking accountant in a company, responsible for overseeing all accounting functions

assets
Any things of value owned or leased by a business

and analyzing production costs), **tax accounting** (preparing tax returns and tax planning), or **financial analysis** (evaluating a company's performance and the financial implications of strategic decisions such as product pricing, employee benefits, and business acquisitions). Most company accountants work together as a team under the supervision of the company **controller,** who reports to the vice president of finance. Exhibit 16.3 shows the typical finance department of a large company. In smaller organizations, the controller may be in charge of the company's entire finance operation and report directly to the president.

Of course, maintaining an accounting staff with the expertise businesses require to operate in today's competitive environment can be a costly proposition—even for large organizations. For this reason, more and more companies are assigning many of their accounting tasks and financial projects to outside accountants and consultants who specialize in an area of accounting or in an industry. Experts predict that outsourcing a company's accounting and finance functions will become even more widespread in the future.[13]

WHAT ARE THE FUNDAMENTAL ACCOUNTING CONCEPTS?

Regardless of who performs a company's accounting functions, all accountants must master the fundamental accounting concepts. Knowing the rules of accounting is critical to an organization's financial health. Without rules and standards, there would be no consistencies for comparisons. Moreover, assessing a company's performance or likelihood of continued success would be anyone's best guess.

In their work with financial data, accountants are guided by three basis concepts: the *fundamental accounting equation, double-entry bookkeeping,* and the *matching principle.*

The Accounting Equation

For thousands of years, businesses and governments have kept records of their **assets**—valuable items they own or lease, such as equipment, cash, land, buildings, inventory, and investments.

Claims against those assets are **liabilities,** or what the business owes to its creditors—such as banks and suppliers. For example, when a company borrows money to purchase a building, the lender or creditor has a claim against the company's assets. What remains after liabilities have been deducted from assets is **owners' equity:**

$$Assets - Liabilities = Owners'\ equity$$

Using the principles of algebra, this equation can be restated in a variety of formats. The most common is the simple **accounting equation,** which serves as the framework for the entire accounting process:

$$Assets = Liabilities + Owners'\ equity$$

This equation suggests that either creditors or owners provide all the assets in a corporation. Think of it this way: If you were starting a new business, you could contribute cash to the company to buy the assets you needed to run your business or you could borrow money from a bank (the creditor) or you could do both. The company's liabilities are placed before owners' equity in the accounting equation because creditors get paid first. After liabilities have been paid, anything left over belongs to the owners or, in the case of a corporation, to the shareholders. As a business engages in economic activity, the dollar amounts and composition of its assets, liabilities, and owners' equity change. However, the equation must always be in balance; in other words, one side of the equation must always equal the other side.

Double-Entry Bookkeeping

To keep the accounting equation in balance, companies use a **double-entry bookkeeping** system that records every transaction affecting assets, liabilities, or owners' equity. For example, if Dental Limited purchased a $6,000 dental chair on credit, assets would increase by $6,000 (the cost of the chair) and liabilities would also increase by $6,000 (the amount the company owes the vendor), keeping the accounting equation in balance. But if Dental Limited paid cash outright for the chair (instead of arranging for credit), then the company's total assets and total liabilities would not change because the $6,000 increase in equipment would be offset by an equal $6,000 reduction in cash. In fact, the company would just be switching assets—cash for equipment.

Even though software programs such as Quick Books do much of the tedious recording of accounting transactions such as the one just discussed, accountants must program the computer software so that all transactions are recorded properly. Furthermore, once these individual transactions are recorded and then summarized, accountants must review the resulting transaction summaries and adjust or correct all errors or discrepancies before they can **close the books,** or transfer net revenue and expense items to retained earnings.

The Matching Principle

The **matching principle** requires that expenses incurred in producing revenues be deducted from the revenue they generated during the same accounting period. This matching of expenses and revenue is necessary for the company's financial statements to present an accurate picture of the profitability of a business. Accountants match revenue to expenses by adopting the **accrual basis** of accounting, which states that revenue is recognized when you make a sale or provide a service, not when you get paid. Similarly, your expenses are recorded when you receive the benefit of a service or when you use an asset to produce revenue—not when you pay for it. Accrual accounting focuses on the economic substance of the event instead of on the movement of cash. It's a way of recognizing that revenue can be earned either before or after cash is received and that expenses can be incurred when you receive a benefit (such as a shipment of supplies) whether before or after you pay for it.

If a business runs on a **cash basis,** the company records revenue only when money from the sale is actually received. Your checkbook is an easy-to-understand cash-based accounting system: You record checks at the time of purchase and deposits at the time of receipt. Revenue thus equals cash received, and expenses equal cash paid. The trouble with cash-based accounting, however, is that it can be misleading. You can misrepresent expenses and income by the way you time payments. It's easy to inflate income, for example, by delaying the payment of bills. For that reason, public companies are required to keep their books on an accrual basis.

---

liabilities
Claims against a firm's assets by creditors

owners' equity
Portion of a company's assets that belongs to the owners after obligations to all creditors have been met

LEARNING OBJECTIVE   3
State the basic accounting equation and explain the purpose of double-entry bookkeeping

accounting equation
Basic accounting equation stating that assets equal liabilities plus owners' equity

double-entry bookkeeping
Way of recording financial transactions that requires two entries for every transaction so that the accounting equation is always kept in balance

close the books
The act of transferring net revenue and expense account balances to retained earnings for the period

LEARNING OBJECTIVE   4
Differentiate between cash basis and accrual basis accounting

matching principle
Fundamental principle requiring that expenses incurred in producing revenue be deducted from the revenues they generate during an accounting period

accrual basis
Accounting method in which revenue is recorded when a sale is made and expense is recorded when it is incurred

cash basis
Accounting method in which revenue is recorded when payment is received and expense is recorded when cash is paid

depreciation
Accounting procedure for systematically spreading the cost of a tangible asset over its estimated useful life

Depreciation, or the allocation of the cost of a tangible long-term asset over a period of time, is another way that companies match expenses with revenue. During the normal course of business, a company enters into many transactions that benefit more than one accounting period—such as the purchase of buildings, inventory, and equipment. When you buy a piece of real estate or equipment, instead of deducting the entire cost of the item at the time of purchase, you depreciate it, or spread its cost over the asset's useful life (because the asset will likely generate income for years to come). If the company were to expense long-term assets at the time of purchase, the financial performance of the company would be distorted in the year of purchase as well as in all future years when these assets generate revenue.

■ HOW ARE FINANCIAL STATEMENTS USED?

Because this building will be used by the owners to generate revenue for many years, its owners will depreciate the total cost of construction over the building's useful life.

An accounting system is made up of thousands of individual transactions—debits and credits to be exact. During the accounting process, sales, purchases, and other transactions are recorded and classified into individual accounts. Exhibit 16.4 presents the process for putting all of a company's financial data into standardized formats that can be used for decision making, analysis, and planning. To make sense of these individual transactions, accountants summarize them by preparing financial statements.

Understanding Financial Statements

Financial statements consist of three separate yet interrelated reports: the *balance sheet,* the *income statement,* and the *statement of cash flows.* Together these statements provide information about an organization's financial strength and ability to meet current obligations, the effectiveness of its sales and collection efforts, and its effectiveness in managing its assets. Organizations and individuals use financial statements to spot opportunities and problems, to make business decisions, and to evaluate a company's past performance, present condition, and future prospects. In sum, they're indispensable.

In the following sections we will examine the financial statements of Computer Central, a company engaged in direct sales and distribution of brand-name personal computers (such as Compaq, Toshiba, and Macintosh) and related computer products (such as software, printer cartridges, and scanners). The company conducts its primary business from a combined telemarketing, corporate office, warehouse, and showroom facility located in Denver, Colorado.

LEARNING OBJECTIVE 5

Explain the purpose of the balance sheet and identify its three main sections

balance sheet
Statement of a firm's financial position on a particular date; also known as a *statement of financial position*

There, Computer Central's 600-plus account executives service over 634,000 customers annually. In 2002 the company shipped over 2.3 million orders, amounting to more than $1.7 billion in sales—a 35 percent increase in sales from the prior year. The company's daily sales volume has grown exponentially over the last decade—from $232,000 to $6.8 million. Because of this tremendous growth and the increasing demand for new computer products, the company recently purchased a 276,000-square-foot building. Keep these points in mind as we discuss Computer Central's financial statements in the next sections.

Balance Sheet The **balance sheet,** also known as the statement of financial position, is a snapshot of a company's financial position on a particular date, such as December 31, 2002. In effect, it freezes all business actions and provides a baseline from which a company can measure change. This statement is called a balance sheet because it includes all elements in the accounting equation and shows the balance between assets on one side of the equation and liabilities and owners' equity on the other side. In other words, as in the accounting equation, a change on one side of the balance sheet means changes elsewhere. Exhibit 16.5 is the balance sheet for Computer Central as of December 31, 2002.

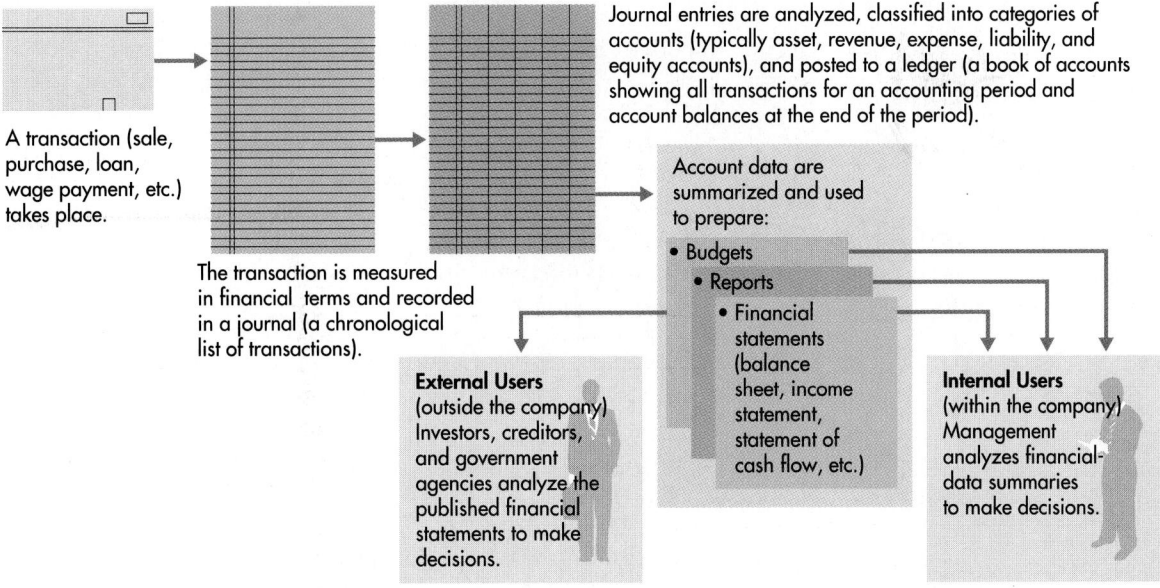

A transaction (sale, purchase, loan, wage payment, etc.) takes place.

The transaction is measured in financial terms and recorded in a journal (a chronological list of transactions).

Journal entries are analyzed, classified into categories of accounts (typically asset, revenue, expense, liability, and equity accounts), and posted to a ledger (a book of accounts showing all transactions for an accounting period and account balances at the end of the period).

Account data are summarized and used to prepare:
- Budgets
  - Reports
    - Financial statements (balance sheet, income statement, statement of cash flow, etc.)

External Users (outside the company) Investors, creditors, and government agencies analyze the published financial statements to make decisions.

Internal Users (within the company) Management analyzes financial-data summaries to make decisions.

EXHIBIT 16.4

THE ACCOUNTING PROCESS

The traditional printed accounting forms are shown here. Today, nearly all companies use the computer equivalents of these forms.

In reality, however, no business can stand still while its financial condition is being examined. A business may make hundreds of transactions of various kinds every working day. Even during a holiday, office fixtures grow older and decrease in value, and interest on savings accounts accumulates. Yet the accountant must set up a balance sheet so that managers and other interested parties can evaluate the business's financial position as if it were static, rather than ever-changing.

Every company prepares a balance sheet at least once a year, most often at the end of the **calendar year,** covering from January 1 to December 31. However, many business and government bodies use a **fiscal year,** which may be any 12 consecutive months. For example, a company may use a fiscal year of June 1 to May 31 because its peak selling season ends in May. Its fiscal year would then correspond to its full annual cycle of manufacturing and selling. Some companies prepare a balance sheet more often than once a year, perhaps at the end of each month or quarter. Thus, every balance sheet is dated to show the exact date when the financial snapshot was taken.

By reading a company's balance sheet you should be able to determine the size of the company, the major assets owned, any asset changes that occurred in recent periods, how the company's assets are financed, and any major changes that have occurred in the company's debt and equity in recent periods. Most companies classify assets, liabilities, and owners' equity into categories like those shown in the Computer Central balance sheet.

Assets As discussed earlier in this chapter, an asset is something owned by a company that will be used to generate income. Assets can consist of cash, things that can be converted into cash (such as investments), and equipment needed to make products or to provide services. For example, Computer Central needs a warehouse and a sizable inventory to sell computer products to its customers. Most often, the asset section of the balance sheet is divided into current assets and *fixed assets.* **Current assets** include cash and other items that will or can become cash within the following year. **Fixed assets** (sometimes referred to as property, plant, and equipment) are long-term investments in buildings, equipment, furniture and fixtures, transportation equipment, land, and other tangible property used in running the business. Fixed assets have a useful life of more than one year. Computer Central's principal fixed asset is the company's warehouse facility.

Assets are listed in descending order by *liquidity,* or the ease with which they can be converted into cash. Thus, current assets are listed before fixed assets. The balance sheet gives a subtotal for each type of asset and then a grand total for all assets. Computer Central's current assets consist primarily of cash, investments in short-term marketable securities such as

calendar year
Twelve-month accounting period that begins on January 1 and ends on December 31

fiscal year
Any 12 consecutive months used as an accounting period

current assets
Cash and items that can be turned into cash within one year

fixed assets
Assets retained for long-term use, such as land, buildings, machinery, and equipment; also referred to as property, plant, and equipment

Current Assets
Cash and other items that will or can be converted to cash within one year.

Fixed Assets
Long-term investments in buildings, equipment, furniture, and any other tangible property expected to be used in running the business for a period longer than one year.

Current Liabilities
Amounts owed by the company that are to be repaid within one year.

Long-Term Liabilities
Debts that are due a year or more after the date of the balance sheet.

Shareholders' Equity
Money contributed to the company for ownership interests, as well as the accumulation of profits that have not been paid out as dividends (retained earnings).

Computer Central
Balance Sheet
As of December 31, 2002
(in thousands)

ASSETS

Current Assets		
Cash	$4,230	
Marketable Securities	36,458	
Accounts Receivable	158,204	
Inventory	64,392	
Miscellaneous Prepaid and Deferred Items	6,504	
Total Current Assets		$269,788
Fixed Assets		
Property and Equipment	53,188	
Less: Accumulated Depreciation	−16,132	
Total Fixed Assets		37,056
Other Assets		4,977
Total Assets		**$311,821**

LIABILITIES AND SHAREHOLDERS' EQUITY

Current Liabilities		
Accounts Payable	$41,358	
Accrued Expenses	29,700	
Total Current Liabilities		$71,058
Long-Term Liabilities		
Loans Payable	$15,000	
Total Long-Term Liabilities		15,000
Total Liabilities		86,058
Shareholders' Equity		
Common Stock		
(21,571 shares @ $.01 par value)	$216	
Less: Treasury Stock (50,000 shares)	−2,089	
Paid-in Capital	81,352	
Retained Earnings	146,284	
Total Shareholders' Equity		225,763
Total Liabilities and Shareholders' Equity		**$311,821**

EXHIBIT 16.5

BALANCE SHEET FOR COMPUTER CENTRAL

The categories used on Computer Central's year-end balance sheet are typical.

money-market funds, accounts receivable (or amounts due from customers), and inventory (such as computers, software, and other items the company sells to customers).

current liabilities
Obligations that must be met within a year

long-term liabilities
Obligations that fall due more than a year from the date of the balance sheet

Liabilities   Liabilities come after assets because they represent claims against the company's assets, as shown in the basic accounting equation: *Assets = Liabilities + Owners' equity*. Liabilities may be current or long-term, and they are listed in the order in which they will come due. The balance sheet gives subtotals for **current liabilities** (obligations that will have to be met within one year of the date of the balance sheet) and **long-term liabilities** (obligations that are due one year or more after the date of the balance sheet), and then it gives a grand total for all liabilities.

Computer Central's current liabilities consist of accounts payable and accrued expenses. Accounts payable includes the money the company owes its suppliers (such as Compaq and Toshiba) as well as money it owes vendors for miscellaneous services (such as electricity and telephone charges). *Accrued expenses* are expenses that have been incurred but for which bills have not yet been received. According to the matching principle, Computer Central records its expenses when the company receives the benefit of the service, not when the company pays for it. For example, Computer Central's account executives earn commissions on computer sales to customers. The company has a liability to its account executives once the sale is made, regardless of when a check is issued to the employee. The company must record this liability because it represents a claim against company assets. If such expenses and their associated liabilities were not recorded, the company's financial statements would be misleading and would violate the matching principle (because the commission expenses that were earned at the time of sale would not be matched to the revenue generated from the sale).

Computer Central's long-term liabilities are relatively small for a company its size. In 2002, the company purchased a new $30 million warehouse facility with $15 million in cash it had saved over many years and a five-year, $15 million bank loan. The company invests its excess cash in short-term marketable securities so it can earn interest on these funds until they are needed for future projects.

Owners' Equity The owners' investment in a business is listed on the balance sheet under owners' equity (or shareholders' equity for a corporation such as Computer Central). Sole proprietorships list owner's equity under the owner's name with the amount (assets minus liabilities). Small partnerships list each partner's share of the business separately, and large partnerships list the total of all partners' shares. Shareholders' equity for a corporation is presented in terms of the amount of common stock that is outstanding, meaning the amount that is in the hands of the shareholders. The combined amount of the assigned or par value of the common stock plus the amount paid over the par value (paid-in capital) represents the shareholders' total investment. Roughly $81 million was paid into the corporation by Computer Central shareholders at the time the company's shares were issued. In 2002 the company repurchased 50,000 shares of the company's own stock in the open market for $948,000. The company will use this *treasury stock* for its employee stock option plan and other general corporate purposes.

Shareholders' equity also includes a corporation's **retained earnings**—the portion of shareholders' equity that is not distributed to its owners in the form of dividends. Computer Central's retained earnings amount to $146 million. The company did not pay dividends. Instead it is building its cash reserves for future asset purchases and to finance future growth.

Income Statement If the balance sheet is a snapshot, the income statement is a movie. The **income statement** shows how profitable the organization has been over a specific period of time, typically one year. It summarizes all **revenues** (or sales), the amounts that have been or are to be received from customers for goods or services delivered to them, and all **expenses,** the costs that have arisen in generating revenues. Expenses and income taxes are then subtracted from revenues

retained earnings
The portion of shareholders' equity earned by the company but not distributed to its owners in the form of dividends

LEARNING
OBJECTIVE 6
Explain the purpose of the income statement

income statement
Financial record of a company's revenues, expenses, and profits over a given period of time

revenues
Amount earned from sales of goods or services and inflow from miscellaneous sources such as interest, rent, and royalties

expenses
Costs created in the process of generating revenues

Best of the Web Best of the Web Best of

LINK YOUR WAY TO THE WORLD OF ACCOUNTING

Looking for one accounting supersite packed with information and links to financial resources? Check out the Electronic Accountant, an online launching point for accountants. This is the place to find answers to all kinds of questions about accounting, financial analysis, taxes, and more. Participate in one of the many focused discussion groups. Visit the niche sites for information on financial planning, practice management, technology consulting, or CPE requirements. Read the latest issues of *Accounting Technology* or the *Practical Accountant.* Don't leave without checking out the Career Center where you'll find information on the latest accounting hot jobs and opportunities.

www.electronicaccountant.com

net income
Profit earned or loss incurred by a firm, determined by subtracting expenses from revenues; also called the bottom line

to show the actual profit or loss of a company, a figure known as **net income**—profit, or the *bottom line.* By briefly reviewing a company's income statements you should have a general sense of the company's size, its trend in sales, its major expenses, and the resulting net income or loss. Owners, creditors, and investors can evaluate the company's past performance and future prospects by comparing net income for one year with net income for previous years. Exhibit 16.6 is the 2002 income statement for Computer Central, showing net income of almost $66 million. This is a 32 percent increase over the company's net income of $50 million for the previous year.

Expenses, the costs of doing business, include both the direct costs associated with creating or purchasing products for sale and the indirect costs associated with operating the business. Whether a company manufactures or purchases its inventory, the cost of storing the product for sale (such as heating the warehouse, paying the rent, and buying insurance on the storage facility) is added to the difference between the cost of the beginning inventory and the cost of the ending inventory in order to compute the actual cost of items that were sold during a period—or the **cost of goods sold.** The computation can be summarized as follows:

cost of goods sold
Cost of producing or acquiring a company's products for sale during a given period

gross profit
Amount remaining when the cost of goods sold is deducted from net sales; also known as *gross margin*

Cost of goods sold = Beginning inventory + Net purchases − Ending inventory

As shown in Exhibit 16.6, cost of goods sold is deducted from sales to obtain a company's **gross profit**—a key figure used in financial statement analysis. In addition to the costs directly associated with producing goods, companies deduct **operating expenses,** which include both *selling expenses* and *general expenses,* to compute a firm's *net operating income,* or the income that is

operating expenses
All costs of operation that are not included under cost of goods sold

---

Computer Central

Income Statement
Year ended December 31, 2002
(in thousands)

Revenues
Funds received from sales of goods and services to customers as well as other items such as rent, interest, and dividends. Net sales are gross sales less returns and allowances.

Revenues		
Gross Sales	$1,991,489	
Less Sales Returns and Allowances	−258,000	
Net Sales		$1,733,489

Cost of Goods Sold
Cost of merchandise or services that generate a company's income by adding purchases to beginning inventory and then subtracting ending inventory.

Cost of Goods Sold		
Beginning Inventory	$61,941	
Add: Purchases During the Year	1,515,765	
Cost of Goods Available for Sale	−1,577,706	
Less: Ending Inventory	64,392	
Total Cost of Goods Sold		−1,513,314
Gross Profit		$220,175

Operating Expenses
Generally classified as selling and general expenses. Selling expenses are those incurred through the marketing and distributing of the company's products. General expenses are operating expenses incurred in the overall administration of a business.

Operating Expenses		
Selling Expenses	$75,523	
General Expenses	40,014	
Total Operating Expenses		115,537
Net Operating Income (Gross Profit less Operating Expenses)		104,638
Other Income		4,373
Net Income Before Income Taxes		109,011
Less: Income Taxes		−43,170

Net Income After Taxes
Profit or loss over a specific period determined by subtracting all expenses and taxes from revenues.

Net Income After Taxes		**$65,841**

EXHIBIT 16.6

INCOME STATEMENT FOR COMPUTER CENTRAL

An income statement summarizes the company's financial operations over a particular accounting period, usually a year.

generated from business operations. **Selling expenses** are operating expenses incurred through marketing and distributing the product (such as wages or salaries of salespeople, advertising, supplies, insurance for the sales operation, depreciation for the store and sales equipment, and other sales department expenses such as telephone charges). **General expenses** are operating expenses incurred in the overall administration of a business. They include professional services (accounting and legal fees), office salaries, depreciation of office equipment, insurance for office operations, supplies, and so on.

A firm's net operating income is then adjusted by the amount of any nonoperating income or expense items such as the gain or loss on the sale of a building. The result is the firm's net income or loss before income taxes (losses are shown in parentheses), a key figure used in budgeting, cash flow analysis, and a variety of other financial computations. Finally, income taxes are deducted to compute the company's net income or loss for the period.

Statement of Cash Flows In addition to preparing a balance sheet and an income statement, all public companies and many privately owned companies prepare a **statement of cash flows** to show how much cash the company generated over time and where it went (see Exhibit 16.7). The statement of cash flows reveals not only the increase or decrease in the company's cash for the period but also the accounts (by category) that caused that change. From a brief review of this statement you should have a general sense of the amount of cash created or consumed by daily operations, the amount of cash invested in fixed or other assets, the amount of debt borrowed or repaid, and the proceeds from the sale of stock or payments for dividends. In addition,

selling expenses
All the operating expenses associated with marketing goods or services

general expenses
Operating expenses, such as office and administrative expenses, not directly associated with creating or marketing a good or a service

LEARNING OBJECTIVE 7

Explain the purpose of the statement of cash flows

statement of cash flows
Statement of a firm's cash receipts and cash payments that presents information on its sources and uses of cash

Computer Central		
Statement of Cash Flows **Year ended December 31, 2002** **(in thousands)**		
Cash flows from operating activities:*		
Net Income	$65,841	
Adjustments to reconcile net income to net cash provided by operating activities	–61,317	
Net cash provided by operations		$4,524
Cash flows from investing activities:		
Purchase of property and equipment	–30,110	
Purchase of securities	–114,932	
Redemptions of securities	112,463	
Net cash used in investment activities		–32,579
Cash flows from financing activities		
Loan proceeds	15,000	
Purchase of treasury stock	–2,089	
Proceeds from exercise of stock options	1,141	
Net cash used in financing activities		14,052
Net (decrease) increase in cash		–14,003
Cash and cash equivalents at beginning of year		$18,233
Cash and cash equivalents at end of year		$4,230

*Note: Numbers preceded by minus sign indicates cash outflows.

EXHIBIT 16.7

STATEMENT OF CASH FLOWS FOR COMPUTER CENTRAL

A statement of cash flows shows a firm's cash receipts and cash payments as a result of three main activities—operating, investing, and financing—for a period.

an analysis of cash flows provides a good idea of a company's ability to pay its short-term obligations when they become due. Computer Central's statement of cash flows shows that the company used $15 million of its cash reserves and the proceeds of a $15 million bank loan in 2002 to pay for its new facility.

Analyzing Financial Statements
Once financial statements have been prepared, managers and outsiders use these statements to evaluate the financial health of the organization, make business decisions, and spot opportunities for improvements by looking at the company's performance in relation to its past performance, the economy as a whole, and the performance of its competitors.

LEARNING OBJECTIVE 8

Explain the purpose of ratio analysis and list the four main categories of financial ratios

ratio analysis
Use of quantitative measures to evaluate a firm's financial performance

Trend Analysis The process of comparing financial data from year to year in order to see how they have changed is known as *trend analysis.* You can use trend analysis to uncover shifts in the nature of the business over time. Most large companies provide data for trend analysis in their annual reports. Their balance sheets and income statements typically show three to five years or more of data (making comparative statement analysis possible). Changes in other key items—such as revenues, income, earnings per share, and dividends per share—are usually presented in tables and graphs.

Of course, when you are comparing one period with another, it's important to take into account the effects of extraordinary or unusual items such as the sale of major assets, the purchase of a new line of products from another company, weather, or economic conditions that may have affected the company in one period but not the next. These extraordinary items are usually disclosed in the text portion of a company's annual report or in the notes to the financial statements.

Ratio Analysis Managers and others compute financial ratios to facilitate the comparison of one company's financial results with those of competing firms and with industry averages. **Ratio analysis** compares two elements from the same year's financial figures. They are called ratios because they are computed by dividing one element of a financial statement by another. The advantage of using ratios is that it puts companies on the same footing; that is, it makes it possible to compare different-size companies and changing dollar amounts. For example, by using ratios, you can easily compare a large supermarket's ability to generate profit out of sales with a similar statistic for a small grocery store.

The benefit of converting numbers into ratios can be explained by the following example: Suppose you wanted to know how well your favorite baseball player was performing this year. To find out, you would check the player's statistics—batting average, runs batted in (RBIs), hits, and home runs. In other

Bankers are particularly interested in the financial results of the companies that have borrowed money from them. They regularly meet with company owners and executives to assess the borrower's financial performance by reviewing key financial ratios.

Best of the Web Best of the Web Best of

SHARPEN YOUR PENCIL

You never know what you'll find at a gallery these days. How about annual reports—lots of them! Sharpen your pencil and start thinking like an accountant. Take a virtual field trip to the Report Gallery, where you can click to view the annual reports of Allstate, Boeing, and many other U.S. and international firms. Be sure to bring along your calculator; this is a good site for locating solid corporate data for trend analysis.
www.reportgallery.com/

words, you would look at data that have been arranged into meaningful statistics that allow you to compare present performance with past performance and with the performance of other players in the league. Financial ratios do the same thing. They convert the raw numbers from the current and prior years' financial statements into ratios that highlight important relationships or measures of performance.[14]

Just as baseball statistics focus on various aspects of performance (such as hitting or pitching), financial ratios help companies understand their current operations and answer key questions: Is inventory too large? Are credit customers paying too slowly? Can the company pay its bills? Ratios also set standards and benchmarks for gauging future business by comparing a company's scores with industry averages that show the performance of competition. Every industry tends to have its own "normal" ratios, which act as yardsticks for individual companies. Dun and Bradstreet, a credit rating firm, and Robert Morris Associates publish both average financial figures and ratios for a variety of industries and company sizes.

Before reviewing specific ratios, consider two rules of thumb: First, avoid drawing too strong a conclusion from any one ratio. For instance, even with a low batting average, a baseball player's RBIs may prove valuable in the team's lineup. Second, once ratios have presented a general indication, refer back to the specific data involved to see whether the numbers confirm what the ratios suggest. In other words do a little investigating, because statistics can be misleading. Remember, a baseball player who has been at bat only two times and has one hit has a batting average of .500.

Types of Financial Ratios Financial ratios can be organized into the following groups, as Exhibit 16.8 shows: profitability, liquidity, activity, and leverage (or debt).

Profitability Ratios You can analyze how well a company is conducting its ongoing operations by computing **profitability ratios,** which show the state of the company's financial performance or how well it's generating profits. Three of the most common profitability ratios are **return on sales,** or profit margin (the net income a business makes per unit of sales); **return on investment (ROI),** or return on equity (the income earned on the owner's investment); and **earnings per share** (the profit earned for each share of stock outstanding). Exhibit 16.8 shows how to compute these profitability ratios by using the financial information from Computer Central.

Liquidity Ratios **Liquidity ratios** measure the ability of the firm to pay its short-term obligations. As you might expect, lenders and creditors are keenly interested in liquidity measures. Liquidity can be judged on the basis of *working capital,* the *current ratio,* and the *quick ratio.* A company's **working capital** (current assets minus current liabilities) is an indicator of liquidity because it represents current assets remaining after the payment of all current liabilities. The dollar amount of working capital can be misleading, however. For example, it may include the value of slow-moving inventory items that cannot be used to help pay a company's short-term debts.

A different picture of the company's liquidity is provided by the **current ratio**—current assets divided by current liabilities. This figure compares the current debt owed with the current assets available to pay that debt. The **quick ratio,** also called the *acid-test ratio,* is computed by subtracting inventory from current assets and then dividing the result by current liabilities. This ratio is often a better indicator of a firm's ability to pay creditors than the current ratio because the quick ratio leaves out inventories—which at times can be difficult to sell. Analysts generally consider a quick ratio of 1.0 to be reasonable whereas a current ratio of 2.0 is considered a safe risk for short-term credit. Exhibit 16.8 shows that both the current and quick ratios of Computer Central are well above these benchmarks and industry averages.

Activity Ratios A number of **activity ratios** may be used to analyze how well a company is managing its assets. The most common is the **inventory turnover ratio,** which measures how fast a company's inventory is turned into sales; in general, the quicker the better, because holding excess inventory can be expensive. When inventory sits on the shelf, money is tied up without earning interest; furthermore, the company incurs expenses for its storage, handling, insurance, and taxes. In addition, there is always a risk that the inventory will become obsolete before it can be converted into finished goods and sold. The firm's goal is to maintain enough inventory to fill orders in a timely fashion at the lowest cost.

Keep in mind that it's difficult to judge a company by its inventory level. For example, lower inventories might mean one of many things: You're running an efficient operation; the

profitability ratios
Ratios that measure the overall financial performance of a firm

return on sales
Ratio between net income after taxes and net sales; also known as *profit margin*

return on investment (ROI)
Ratio between net income after taxes and total owners' equity; also known as *return on equity*

earnings per share
Measure of a firm's profitability for each share of outstanding stock, calculated by dividing net income after taxes by the average number of shares of common stock outstanding

liquidity ratios
Ratios that measure a firm's ability to meet its short-term obligations when they are due

working capital
Current assets minus current liabilities

current ratio
Measure of a firm's short-term liquidity, calculated by dividing current assets by current liabilities

quick ratio
Measure of a firm's short-term liquidity, calculated by adding cash, marketable securities, and receivables, then dividing that sum by current liabilities; also known as the *acid-test ratio*

activity ratios
Ratios that measure the effectiveness of the firm's use of its resources

inventory turnover ratio
Measure of the time a company takes to turn its inventory into sales, calculated by dividing cost of goods sold by the average value of inventory for a period

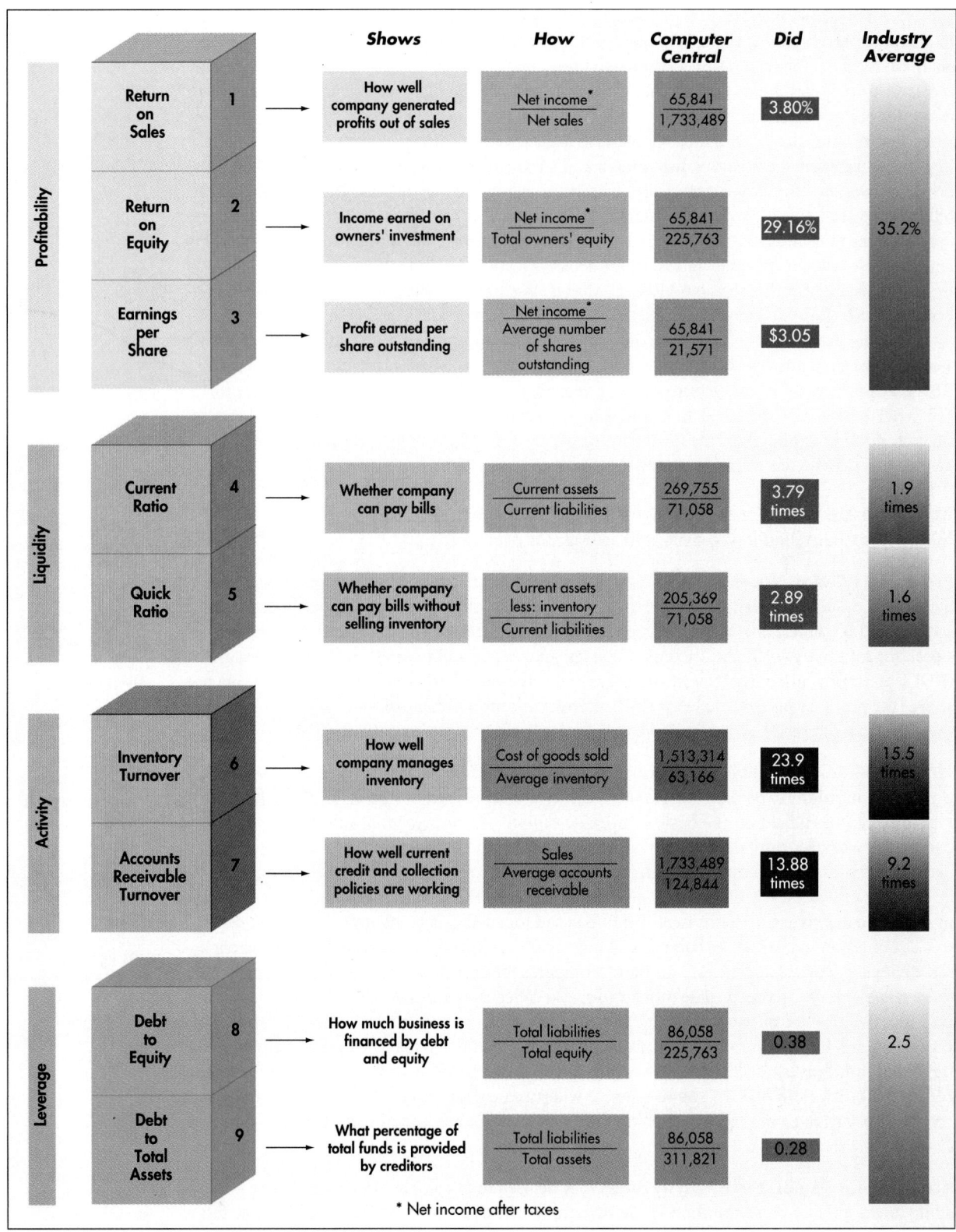

EXHIBIT 16.8

HOW WELL DOES THIS COMPANY STACK UP?

Nearly all companies use ratios to evaluate how well the company is performing in relation to prior performance, the economy as a whole, and the company's competitors.

right inventory is not being stocked; or sales are booming and you need to increase your orders. Likewise, higher inventories could signal a decline in sales, careless ordering, or stocking up because of favorable pricing. The "ideal" turnover ratio varies with the type of operation. In 2002 Computer Central turned its inventory 23.9 times (see Exhibit 16.8). This rate is unusually high when compared with industry averages, and it suggests that the company stocks only enough inventory to fill current orders and cover a product's reorder time, as discussed in Chapter 9.

Another popular activity ratio is the **accounts receivable turnover ratio,** which measures how well a company's credit and collection policies are working by indicating how frequently accounts receivable are converted to cash. The volume of receivables outstanding depends on the financial manager's decisions regarding several issues, such as who qualifies for credit and who does not, how long customers are given to pay their bills, and how aggressive the firm is in collecting its debts. Be careful here as well. If the ratio is going up, you need to determine whether the company is doing a better job of collecting or sales are rising. If the ratio is going down, it may be because sales are decreasing or because collection efforts are sagging. In 2002 Computer Central turned its accounts receivable 13.88 times—considerably higher than the industry average (see Exhibit 16.8).

Leverage, or Debt, Ratios You can measure a company's ability to pay its long-term debts by calculating its **debt ratios,** or leverage ratios. Lenders look at these ratios to determine whether the potential borrower has put enough money into the business to serve as a protective cushion for the loan. The **debt-to-equity ratio** (total liabilities divided by total equity) indicates the extent to which a business is financed by debt, as opposed to invested capital (equity). From the lender's standpoint, the lower this ratio, the safer the company, because the company has less existing debt and may be able to repay additional money it wants to borrow. However, a company that is conservative in its long-term borrowing is not necessarily well managed; often a low level of debt is associated with a low growth rate. Computer Central's low debt-to-equity ratio of 38 percent (as shown in Exhibit 16.8) reflects the company's practice of financing its growth by using excess cash flow from operations and by selling shares of common stock to the public.

The **debt-to-total-assets ratio** (total liabilities divided by total assets) also serves as a simple measure of a company's ability to carry long-term debt. As a rule of thumb, the amount of debt should not exceed 50 percent of the value of total assets. For Computer Central, this ratio is a very low 28 percent and again reflects the company's policy of using retained earnings to finance its growth (see Exhibit 16.8). However, this ratio, too, is not a magic formula. Like grades on a report card, ratios are clues to performance. Managers, creditors, lenders, and investors can use them to get a fairly accurate idea of how a company is doing. But remember, one ratio by itself doesn't tell the whole story.

Using Accounting Information to Make Financial Decisions

Suppose your company is considering changing the way it pays your sales force. Instead of paying them a fixed salary, the company would like to pay salespeople a base salary plus a commission, hoping that the commissions will motivate them to sell more product. How would you determine the best commission rate? Would this new pay structure cost the company more money? How could you guarantee that your sales force would benefit from this change? What if sales increased by 10 percent instead of the 20 percent you had projected? These are the types of questions accountants deal with daily. Sometimes questions are even more complex because there are more variables. Asking "what-if" questions is certainly not new. What is new, however, is the application of computing technology to the process.

By using electronic spreadsheet programs such as Microsoft Excel or Lotus 1-2-3, companies can analyze the financial costs and benefits of just about any

accounts receivable turnover ratio
Measure of the time a company takes to turn its accounts receivable into cash, calculated by dividing sales by the average value of accounts receivable for a period

debt ratios
Ratios that measure a firm's reliance on debt financing of its operations (sometimes called *leverage ratios*)

debt-to-equity ratio
Measure of the extent to which a business is financed by debt as opposed to invested capital, calculated by dividing the company's total liabilities by owners' equity

debt-to-total-assets ratio
Measure of a firm's ability to carry long-term debt, calculated by dividing total liabilities by total assets

In the cash-crazy world of professional sports, selling more food is one of the few ways teams can pad revenue after ticket prices and television royalties are set. At facilities with expanded concessions, food sales can account for 25 percent of annual team profit. Accountants project the amount of concession revenue a stadium will take in by performing a series of financial analyses using several different attendance scenarios.

MANAGING IN THE 21ST CENTURY

HOW TO READ AN ANNUAL REPORT

Whether you're thinking of investing in companies, becoming a supplier for them, or applying for a job with them, you'll need to know how to read annual reports in your career. Thus, it's worth your while to consider the advice of *Newsweek* columnist Jane Bryant Quinn, who provided these pointers.

Read the Letters
First, turn to the report of the certified public accountant. This third-party auditor will tell you right off the bat if the report conforms with generally accepted accounting principles. Now turn to the letter from the chairman. This letter should tell you how the company fared this year, but more important, the letter should tell you why. Keep an eye out for sentences that start with "Except for . . ." and "Despite the . . ." They're clues to problems. The chairman's letter should also give you insights into the company's future. For example, look for what's new in each line of business. Is management getting the company in good shape to weather the tough and competitive years ahead?

Dig into the Numbers
Check out the trend in the company's working capital (the difference between current assets and current liabilities). If working capital is shrinking, it could mean trouble. One possibility: The company may not be able to keep dividends growing rapidly.

Another important number to analyze is earnings per share. Management can boost earnings by selling off a plant or by cutting the budget for research and advertising. See the footnotes; they often tell the whole story. If earnings are down only because of a change in accounting, maybe that's good! The company owes less tax and has more money in its pocket. If earnings are up, maybe that's bad. They may be up because of a special windfall that won't happen again next year. One good indicator is the trend in net sales. If sales increases are starting to slow, the company may be in trouble.

Get Out Your Calculator and Compare
High and rising debt, relative to equity, may be no problem for a growing business. But it shows weakness in a company that's leveling out. So get out your calculator and divide long-term liabilities by shareholders' equity. That's the debt-to-equity ratio. A high ratio means the company borrows a lot of money to fund its growth. That's okay—if sales grow too, and if there's enough cash on hand to meet the payments. But if sales fall, watch out. The whole enterprise may slowly sink.

Remember, one ratio, one annual report, one chairman's letter won't tell you much. You have to compare. Is the company's debt-to-equity ratio better or worse than it used to be? Better or worse than the industry norms? In company-watching, comparisons are all. They tell you if management is staying on top of things.

■ QUESTIONS FOR CRITICAL THINKING

1. Why might a job seeker want to read a company's annual report before applying for a job with that company?

2. What types of valuable nonfinancial information might an annual report disclose to a potential supplier?

decision. For example, when Schatzman and Crane were deciding whether to purchase the retiring dentist's practice and building, their accountant analyzed the merits of the investment using a series of spreadsheet calculations.

Financial analysis begins with a firm's financial data. Typically, the accountant will enter these data into an electronic spreadsheet and manipulate the numbers by converting total costs to unit costs such as cost per passenger-mile (for airlines) or cost per package delivered (for companies such as FedEx). Next, the accountant will compute a range of outcomes using expected, best-case, and worst-case scenarios—such as unit costs will increase by 5 percent, 2 percent, or 10 percent. Armed with such information, management can make more educated decisions.

Building decision models with spreadsheet software is just one of the many tasks accountants perform, as this chapter demonstrates. In Chapter 17 we'll discuss other functions that accountants perform such as financial planning, budgeting, and managing a company's cash flow. But first we'll explore some accounting issues that are surfacing as more and more companies transact e-commerce.

FOCUSING ON E-BUSINESS TODAY

Are Those E-Business Revenues for Real?

Accountants have been fiddling with profit and loss statements for as long as there has been accounting. According to GAAP, you can bury sales discounts in other expenses, manipulate inventory values, and recognize revenue aggressively—and still remain within the letter of the law. That's because the rules that govern accounting for public companies are flexible so that they can accommodate a number of different scenarios. However, such flexibility can create disparities in the financial statements of similar companies.

Stretching the Limits of Sensible Accounting

Of course, transactions should be accounted for in the same way, whether a company is an e-business or a bricks-and-mortar business. But some think e-commerce is a magnet for accounting misbehavior. Most e-businesses aren't expected to produce a profit in their beginning years, so some investors have turned to other measures to determine the fair market value for Internet companies. Chief among the new yardsticks is a multiple of sales or revenues.

How companies recognize revenues for goods and services they offer has become an increasingly important

LEARNING OBJECTIVE @9

Discuss why and how some e-businesses record accounting transactions to inflate their sales

issue for e-businesses. Since e-commerce investors rely on revenue growth as a key benchmark, a tiny increase in reported revenues can translate into a huge increase in the market value of a company's stock. Moreover, fledgling e-businesses need booming stocks to raise capital at low costs and to attract and hold scarce stock-option-minded talent. Thus, Internet executives have considerable incentive to recognize revenue as soon as possible and to inflate sales by using a number of accounting gimmicks.

Are Those Revenues for Real?

Many Internet firms puff up their revenues by reporting the entire sales price a customer pays for a product even though the company keeps only a small percentage of that amount. Companies that act as brokers or travel agents, such as Priceline.com, often include the full amount customers pay for tickets, hotel rooms, and rental cars as revenues, instead of just their commission. Priceline justifies booking the entire amount to sales and treating the "product costs" or the amount it pays to airlines and hotels that supply the tickets and rooms as expenses because unlike a real-world travel agency, it assumes full risk of ownership as the "merchant of record." Real-world travel

agencies, on the other hand, have a fixed commission and do not own the tickets they sell. While some concur with Priceline's logic, many financial professionals find this tactic misleading. The following example shows the impact that different accounting methods can have on a company's sales even though both companies earn the same commission on the sale of a $250 airline ticket.

	Priceline	Real-World Travel
Sales	$250	$30
Product costs	$220	$0
Other costs	$10	$10
Profit	$20	$20

Disguising Discounts

Like many bricks-and-mortar companies, fledgling e-businesses attract potential customers with special introductory offers, discounts, coupons, rebates, and giveaways. But unlike their physical counterparts, some Net companies have discovered ways to hide the effect all the free stuff has on sales. For instance, say that a customer buys a $50 sweater using an electronic coupon worth 20 percent off. The customer pays only $40, but the company records the full $50 in revenues and records a $10 charge to "marketing expenses" instead of charging "sales discounts." Of course, there's no effect on the bottom line by doing it this way. Whichever way you record the entry you will still produce the same net income or loss, as the following example suggests. But hiding the impact of the discount in "marketing expense"—a figure investors believe will diminish once brand recognition has been established—and recording the full amount as sales pumps up net sales and makes the e-tailer look comparatively better.

	E-Tailer	Retailer
Sales	$50	$50
Sales discounts	$0	$10
Net sales	$50	$40
Cost of sales	$20	$20
Marketing expense	$10	$0
Profit	$20	$20

Fiddling with Fulfillment Costs

E-businesses also inflate sales by playing games with fulfillment costs—expenses associated with warehousing, packaging, and shipping products. Offline companies usually record such expenses on their income statements as cost of sales. But not dot-coms. Cost of sales cuts directly into a company's gross profit margin, another of the figures investors use to measure the future potential of fledgling e-businesses. Many e-businesses already operate with extremely narrow gross profit margins, so they have little interest in trimming them further. Amazon.com, 1-800-flowers, and others blend fulfillment costs with other marketing expenses for the same reasons that e-businesses charge discounts to marketing expenses. Textbook e-tailer Varsitybooks.com went so far as to dismiss auditor KPMG when it objected to lumping fulfillment costs under marketing expenses. The company's new auditor, PricewaterhouseCoopers, approved the practice.

SEC Clampdown

The SEC would like to see more uniformity in the way accounting transactions are recorded and is putting pressure on the accounting profession to tighten reporting standards. Fraudulent accounting has never been toler-

ated. "Cook the books, and you will go directly to jail without passing go," says SEC's director of enforcement Richard Walker. But it's difficult to keep pace with the creativity of accounting wizards who operate in the gray areas of the law.

To reverse the alarming trend in inflated revenue reports, the SEC is cracking down on the aggressive accounting practices that have become so popular among many dot-com firms, and it is forcing the companies that use such practices to restate their financial results. Still, the SEC knows that even though regulators and the accounting standards board may curb some practices, they will never be able to stop these practices entirely. As one accounting professor put it, "Clever accountants will always be able to bend the rules. But whether they do is a matter of ethics."[15]

SUMMARY OF LEARNING OBJECTIVES

1. **Discuss how managers and outsiders use financial information.**
   Managers use financial information to control a company's operation and to make informed business decisions. Outsiders use financial information to evaluate whether a business is creditworthy or a good investment. Specifically, banks want to know if a business is able to pay back a loan; investors want to know if the company is earning a profit; and governments want to be assured the company is paying the proper amount of taxes.

2. **Describe what accountants do and explain how technology is changing their work.**
   Accountants design accounting systems, prepare financial statements, analyze and interpret financial information, prepare financial forecasts and budgets, prepare tax returns, interpret tax law, and provide business expertise and consulting services. New technology is automating many traditional accounting tasks, so many accountants are using their freed-up time to help clients plan for the future by performing analytical tasks and other strategic business functions.

3. **State the basic accounting equation and explain the purpose of double-entry bookkeeping.**
   Assets = Liabilities + Owners' equity is the basic accounting equation. Double-entry bookkeeping is a system of recording financial transactions to keep the accounting equation in balance.

4. **Differentiate between cash basis and accrual basis accounting.**
   Cash basis accounting recognizes revenue at the time payment is received, whereas accrual basis accounting recognizes revenue at the time of sale, even if payment is not made.

5. **Explain the purpose of the balance sheet and identify its three main sections.**
   The balance sheet provides a snapshot of the business at a particular point in time. It shows the size of the company, the major assets owned, how the assets are financed, and the amount of owners' investment in the business. Its three main sections are assets, liabilities, and owners' equity.

6. **Explain the purpose of the income statement.**
   The income statement reflects the results of operations over a period of time. It gives a general sense of a company's size and performance.

7. **Explain the purpose of the statement of cash flows.**
   The statement of cash flows shows how a company's cash was received and spent in three areas: operations, investments, and financing. It gives a general sense of the amount of cash created or consumed by daily operations, fixed assets, investments, and debt over a period of time.

8. **Explain the purpose of ratio analysis and list the four main categories of financial ratios.**
   Financial ratios provide information for analyzing the health and future prospects of a business. Ratios facilitate financial comparisons between different-size companies and between a company and industry averages. Most of the important ratios fall into one of four categories: profitability ratios, which show how well the company generates profits; liquidity ratios, which measure the company's ability to pay its short-term obligations; activity ratios, which analyze how well a company is managing its assets; and debt ratios, which measure a company's ability to pay its long-term debt.

9. **Discuss why and how some e-businesses record accounting transactions to inflate their sales.**
   Fledgling e-businesses have considerable incentive to puff up their reported sales because most do not generate a profit; thus investors gauge the company's future potential by its ability to grow its sales. An increase in reported revenues can therefore boost investor confidence, which can translate into an increased market value for the company's stock. Because GAAP allows accountants to interpret the rules of accounting within certain parameters, companies can record accounting transactions in a number of ways. For example, two recorded transactions can

produce the same amount of company profit, but they can each produce different net sales figures depending on the amount assigned to sales, sales returns, and discounts, and the amount assigned to selling and general expenses. E-businesses who wish to inflate sales can do so by recording the entire price a customer pays for an item (even though the company keeps only a small amount) and by classifying sales discounts and fulfillment costs as marketing expenses.

KEY TERMS

accounting (428)
accounting equation (433)
accounts receivable turnover ratio (443)
accrual basis (433)
activity ratios (441)
assets (432)
audit (430)
balance sheet (434)
bookkeeping (429)
calendar year (435)
cash basis (433)
certified management accountants
   (CMAs) (432)
certified public accountants (CPAs) (430)
close the books (433)
controller (432)
cost accounting (432)
cost of goods sold (438)
current assets (435)
current liabilities (436)

current ratio (441)
debt ratios (443)
debt-to-equity ratio (443)
debt-to-total-assets ratio (443)
depreciation (434)
double-entry bookkeeping (433)
earnings per share (441)
expenses (437)
financial accounting (428)
financial analysis (432)
fiscal year (435)
fixed assets (435)
general expenses (439)
generally accepted accounting principles
   (GAAP) (428)
gross profit (438)
income statement (437)
internal auditors (430)
inventory turnover ratio (441)
liabilities (433)

liquidity ratios (441)
long-term liabilities (436)
management accounting (428)
matching principle (433)
net income (438)
operating expenses (438)
owners' equity (433)
private accountants (432)
profitability ratios (441)
public accountants (430)
quick ratio (441)
ratio analysis (440)
retained earnings (437)
return on investment (ROI) (441)
return on sales (441)
revenues (437)
selling expenses (439)
statement of cash flows (439)
tax accounting (432)
working capital (441)

TEST YOUR KNOWLEDGE

QUESTIONS FOR REVIEW

1. What is GAAP?
2. What is the primary difference between a public accountant and a private accountant?
3. What is an audit and why is it performed?
4. What is the matching principle?
5. What are the three main profitability ratios, and how is each calculated?

QUESTIONS FOR ANALYSIS

6. Why is accounting important to business?
7. Besides saving costs, how might a company benefit from outsourcing some of its accounting functions?
8. How has technology changed the jobs of accountants?
9. Why are the costs of fixed assets depreciated?
10. How might you expect the balance sheet of an e-tailer to differ from a physical toy store? (Hint: Think about the physical advantages many e-businesses have.)
11. In the process of closing the company books, you encounter a problematic transaction. One of the company's customers was charged twice for the same project materials, resulting in a $1,000 overcharge. You immediately notify the controller, whose response is, "Let it go, it happens often." What should you do now?

QUESTIONS FOR APPLICATION

12. The senior partner of an accounting firm is looking for ways to increase the firm's business. What other services besides traditional accounting can the firm offer to its clients?
13. Log on to Hoovers Web site at www.hoovers.com, and click on Companies and Industries. Find and print the annual financials for Ford Motor Company and General Motors Corporation. Using these financials, compute the working capital, current ratio, and quick ratio for each company. Does one company appear to be more liquid than the other? Why?
14. Review the material in Chapters 4 and 5 discussing the advantages and disadvantages of going public. What preliminary accounting steps might the controller of a company take to prepare the company for going public? Why?
15. Your appliance manufacturing company recently implemented a just-in-time inventory system (see Chapter 9) for all parts used in the manufacturing process. How might you expect this move to affect the company's inventory turnover rate, current ratio, and quick ratio?

PRACTICE YOUR KNOWLEDGE

SHARPENING YOUR COMMUNICATION SKILLS

Obtain a copy of the annual report of a business, and examine what the report shows about finances and current operations. In addition to other chapter material, use the information in "How to Read an Annual Report" on page 444 as a guideline for understanding the annual report's content.

- Consider the statements made by the CEO regarding the past year: Did the company do well, or are changes in operations necessary to its future well-being? What are the projections for future growth in sales and profits?

- Examine the financial summaries for information about the fiscal condition of the company: Did the company show a profit?

- If possible, obtain a copy of the company's annual report from the previous year, and compare it with the current report to determine whether past projections were accurate.

- Prepare a brief written summary of your conclusions.

HANDLING DIFFICULT SITUATIONS ON THE JOB: GIVING CREDIT WHERE CREDIT IS DUE

Selling music CDs, multimedia computers, stereo speakers, and other consumer electronics in a retail store on Saturday afternoons can create such loud and widely dispersed noise that no one can hear anything, including the sales pitch. Brown Innovations' virtual audio imager eliminates this problem by creating an "isolated" listening region directly beneath the speakers. This means that game arcade players can hear their own radical sound effects but no one else's. And consumer electronic stores can demo rap music on a boombox in one aisle while a salesperson explains the benefits of a laser printer in the next aisle—without shouting.

You work in the finance department of Brown Innovations, and you've been swamped with credit requests ever since a small item about the virtual audio imager appeared in *Newsweek*. Each day, Brown receives dozens of orders from music stores, arcades, and electronic equipment stores clamoring for your firm's noise-control equipment. Of course, none of these new customers expects to pay cash for the merchandise they are ordering; in this industry, it is common for commercial customers to obtain credit and pay 30 to 60 days after receiving the merchandise.

The head of finance at Brown has asked you to create a brief credit application and a process that will help the company screen out poor credit risks before the company sells them merchandise. This is your opportunity to save Brown Innovations a lot of money—and a lot of trouble.[16]

1. What basic customer information should you request on the credit application? Should you ask a new customer to provide the name and address of another vendor that has extended the business credit *or* the name of the company's public accountants so you can inquire about its creditworthiness?

2. Which financial statements should you ask each new customer to submit with the credit application? What do you expect to learn from these statements?

3. Of the various financial ratios, which ones do you think would be most helpful in gauging whether a music store will be able to pay in full and on time? Why?

BUILDING YOUR TEAM SKILLS

Divide into small groups and compute the following financial ratios for Alpine Manufacturing using the company's Balance Sheet and Income Statement. Compare your answers to those of your classmates:

- Profitability ratios: return on sales; return on equity; earning per share

- Liquidity ratios: current ratio; quick ratio

- Activity ratios: inventory turnover; accounts receivable turnover

- Leverage ratios: debt to equity; debt to total assets

ALPINE MANUFACTURING
Balance Sheet
December 31, 2000

Assets

Cash	$ 100
Accounts Receivable (beginning balance $350)	300
Inventory (beginning balance $250)	300
Current Assets	$ 700
Fixed Assets	2,300
Total Assets	**$3,000**

Liabilities and Shareholders' Equity

Current Liabilities (beginning balance $300)	$ 400
Long-Term Debts	1,600
Shareholders Equity (100 common shares outstanding valued at $12 each)	1,000
Total Liabilities and Shareholders' Equity	**$3,000**

ALPINE MANUFACTURING
Income Sheet
Year ended December 31, 2000

Sales	$1,800
Less: Cost of Goods Sold	1,000
Gross Profit	$ 800
Less: Total Operating Expenses	450
Net Operating Income Before Income Taxes	350
Less: Income Taxes	50
Net Income After Income Taxes	**$ 300**

EXPAND YOUR KNOWLEDGE

KEEPING CURRENT USING *THE WALL STREET JOURNAL*

Select an article from *The Wall Street Journal* (print or online editions) that discusses the quarterly or year-end performance of a company that industry analysts consider notable for either positive or negative reasons.

1. Did the company report a profit or a loss for this accounting period? What other performance indicators were reported? Did the company's performance improve or decline over previous accounting periods?

2. Did the company's performance match industry analysts' expectations, or was it a surprise? How did analysts or other experts respond to the firm's actual quarterly or year-end results?

3. What reasons were given for the company's improvement or decline in performance?

DISCOVERING CAREER OPPORTUNITIES

People interested in entering the field of accounting can choose among a wide variety of careers with diverse responsibilities and challenges. Select one of the occupations mentioned in this chapter or in Component Chapter D, under the section "Careers in Finance and Accounting." Using Component Chapter D, library sources, or Internet Web sites from one of the major accounting firms or the AICPA, dig deeper to learn more about your chosen occupation.

1. What are the day-to-day duties of this occupation? How would these duties contribute to the financial success of a company?

2. What skills and educational qualifications would you need to enter this occupation? How do these qualifications fit with your current plans, skills, and interests?

3. What kinds of employers hire people for this position? According to your research, does the number of employers seem to be increasing or decreasing? How do you think this trend will affect your employment possibilities if you choose this career?

EXPLORING THE BEST OF THE WEB

URLs for all Internet exercises are provided at the Web site for this book, www.prenhall.com/mescon. When you log on to the text Web site, select Chapter 16, then select "Student Resources," click on the name of the featured Web site, and follow the detailed navigational directions to complete these exercises.

Size Them Up, page 430

Dealing with the most complex accounting and financial management issues is all in a day's work for the experts at Ernst & Young. Visit the company's Web site to find the answers to these questions:

1. Why do you think a company would want to outsource its internal auditing function to an accounting firm?

2. What are some of the elements E&Y looks at when assessing a company's cash management system? How does a company benefit from better cash management?

3. What does E&Y look for in recruits? What are the different career paths E&Y offers?

Link Your Way to the World of Accounting, page 437

The Electronic Accountant is your launching pad for a wide variety of accounting-related Internet resources. Check out this Web site so you can answer these questions.

1. Which of the links listed at this Web site might you, as a business student, find useful in your studies? How?

2. When are business travel, business use of the home, and educational expenses deductible expenses?

3. What kind of records should individual taxpayers keep?

Sharpen Your Pencil, page 400

Learning about financial conditions and issues in various companies and industries is an important part of an accountant's job. Sharpen your pencil, go to the Report Gallery Web site, and click on Annual Reports to locate the latest annual report for a company of your choice. Now answer these questions:

1. Find the Chairman's Letter (also known as the *letter to shareholders*). Was it a good or a bad year for the company? Why?

2. Examine the company's Income Statement to find the company's annual revenues for the most recent year and the year before. By what percentage did revenues change from the prior year? (Hint: Use your calculator.) Does the chairman's letter explain this change?

3. Scan the financial section to find the Auditor's Report. Who are the company's auditors? Did the company get a clean audit report?

Explore on Your Own

Review these chapter-related Web sites on your own to learn more about accounting.

1. CPAnet, www.cpanet.com, promotes its Web site as the online community and complete resource for the accounting profession. Find out why.

2. Visit AccountingStudents, www.accountingstudents.com, to discover why the best time to start a career in accounting is now!

3. Learn about the ins and outs of the CPA exam at CPAExam.com, at www.cpaexam.com. Be sure to read the FAQs.

 A CASE FOR CRITICAL THINKING

■ *Perking Up Profits at Better Brew and Perfect Blend*

After years of dreaming about owning your own business, you decided that owning a coffee shop would be perfect. Rather than start from scratch, however, you and your partners decide to look at two existing establishments, Better Brew and Perfect Blend. The two are for sale at the same price, and they are located in equally attractive areas. You manage to get enough financial data to compare the year-end condition of the two companies, as shown in Exhibit 16.9. Study the numbers carefully; your livelihood depends on choosing wisely between the two establishments.

CRITICAL THINKING QUESTIONS

1. What factors should you consider before deciding which company to buy? What additional data might be helpful to you? (Note that net income is implied.)

2. What questions should you ask about the methods used to record revenues and expenses?

3. On the basis of the data provided, which company would you purchase? Detail the process you used to make your decision.

4. Visit the world's largest and most respected online coffee buying guide, Coffee Review. As an owner of a coffee shop, how might you use this resource?

	Better Brew	Perfect Blend
ASSETS	$10,000	$25,000
Cash	2,000	4,000
Accounts receivable	50,000	80,000
Coffee equipment	11,000	18,000
Supplies	22,000	34,000
TOTAL ASSETS	$95,000	$161,000
LIABILITIES AND OWNERS' EQUITY		
Accounts payable	$21,000	$38,000
Bank loans payable	49,000	68,000
Owners' equity	25,000	55,000
TOTAL LIABILITIES AND OWNERS' EQUITY	$95,000	$161,000
OTHER DATA		
Personal withdrawals from cash during 2000	$40,000	$38,000
Owners' investments in business during 2000	$16,000	$32,000
Capital balances for each business on January 1, 2000	$30,000	$12,000

EXHIBIT 16.9

FINANCIAL DATA FOR TWO COMPANIES

December 31, 2002, year-end balance sheets.

VIDEO CASE AND EXERCISES

■ *Accounting Counts at McDonald's*

SYNOPSIS

Collecting, analyzing, and reporting financial data from 27,000 restaurants in 119 countries is no easy task, as the accounting experts at McDonald's (www.mcdonalds.com) are well aware. Every month, the individual restaurants send their sales figures to be consolidated with data from other restaurants at the local or country level. From there, the figures are sent to country-group offices and then to one of three major regional offices before going to their final destination at the McDonald's headquarters in Oak Brook, Illinois. In the past, financial information arrived in Illinois in bits and pieces, sent by courier, mail, or fax. Today, local and regional offices log on to a special secure Web site and enter their figures, enabling the corporate controller to quickly produce financial statements for internal and external use.

EXERCISES
Analysis

1. How does McDonald's use of "constant currency" reporting for financial results benefit investors?

2. What types of assets might McDonald's list for depreciation in its financial statements?

3. What effect do the corporate income tax rates in the countries in which McDonald's does business have on the income statements prepared in local offices?

4. As an investor, would you prefer that McDonald's raise or lower its inventory turnover ratio on promotional products? As a customer?

5. Where on its income statement would you expect to see McDonald's list the cost of hamburger buns, patties, and other food items?

Application

Why do companies try to keep their debt levels as low as possible? What might happen if McDonald's financial statements showed unusually low debt?

Decision

Although McDonald's can now close its books four days after the end of a reporting period, assume that top management would like the information available even more quickly. Should individual restaurants be required to enter sales data directly on the company's centralized accounting Web site, instead of following the current procedure of sending it through country and regional channels?

Communication

Imagine that you're the CEO of McDonald's. Write a letter to shareholders explaining the use of constant currency in one of the financial statements contained in this year's annual report.

Integration

McDonald's franchises restaurants in many cities and countries. Referring back to the discussion of franchises in Chapter 4, what type of franchise does McDonald's offer?

Ethics

In terms of disclosing a company's financial health, how far is far enough? For instance, assume that McDonald's knows from past experience that its sales will suffer if a major hurricane or other severe weather hits several states. Is the company obligated to warn shareholders of possible sales dips whenever severe weather is in the forecast?

Debate

When people buy shares in a company, they are essentially betting that management will follow a sensible plan for reaching the company's goals. Should management have to reveal its strategic plans to all investors? Identify two or more arguments for or against this question.

Teamwork

Working with another student, obtain a recent annual report from McDonald's or another public corporation. Read what the chairman says in the letter to shareholders and review the financial data contained in the report. Does the letter completely and accurately reflect the performance shown in the financial data? As your instructor directs, prepare a brief written or oral report on your findings.

Online Research

Use Internet sources to research the current financial performance of McDonald's. Which regions are doing particularly well? Which are lagging? How does management explain this performance? See Component Chapter A, Exhibit A.1, for search engines to use in doing your research.

MYPHLIP COMPANION WEB SITE

Learning Interactively

Visit the myPHLIP Web site at www.prenhall.com/mescon. For Chapter 16, take advantage of the interactive "Study Guide" to test your chapter knowledge. Get instant feedback on whether you need additional studying. Read the "Current Events" articles to get the latest on chapter topics, and complete the exercises as specified by your instructor. Expand your learning with a visit to the "Research Area." There you will find a wealth of information you can use to complete your course assignments.

MASTERING BUSINESS ESSENTIALS

Go to the "Managerial Accounting and Cost Behavior" episode on the Mastering Business Essentials interactive, video-enhanced CD-ROM. Observe how the accounting and finance managers at CanGo (an e-business start-up) explain a new method of financial reporting to the company's management team. Witness how the team reacts to new standardized financial reporting procedures and prepares to adopt these required procedures.

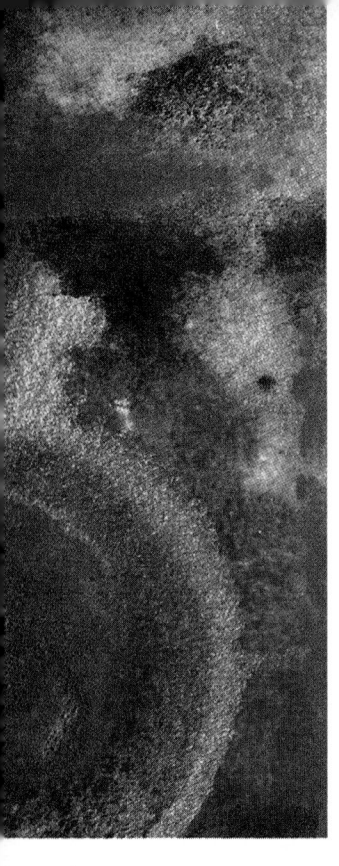

FINANCIAL MANAGEMENT AND BANKING

17

LEARNING OBJECTIVES

After studying this chapter, you will be able to

1. Identify the responsibilities of a financial manager

2. Discuss how financial managers improve a company's cash flow

3. Differentiate between a master budget and capital budget

4. Cite three things financial managers must consider when selecting an appropriate funding vehicle

5. Identify five common types of debt financing

6. Explain how consolidation is affecting the banking industry

7. Identify four ways the Federal Reserve System influences the U.S. money supply

@ 8. Identify the advantages of online banking and explain the challenges cyberbanks face in the competitive banking environment

Inside Business

Scott Cook, co-founder of Intuit, is betting the company's future on the Internet.

VIRTUAL FINANCIAL MANAGEMENT: INTUIT'S ONE-STOP MONEY SHOP
w w w . q u i c k e n . c o m

Balancing the family checkbook was a regular battle for Scott Cook's wife—until Cook came up with Quicken, an easy-to-use software program for managing personal finances. Today 12 million consumers and 3 million small-business owners track their finances with software developed and marketed by Intuit, under the Quicken brand name. And as co-founder of the world's largest maker of personal finance software, Cook is providing consumers with everything they need for money management through Quicken.com, Intuit's one-stop financial supermarket on the Web.

Ever since Cook developed the first edition of Quicken in 1984, Intuit has dominated the market for personal finance software with its three best-selling products—Quicken for personal financial management, QuickBooks for small-business accounting, and TurboTax for tax preparation. But the Internet boom in the mid-1990s convinced Cook that Intuit could no longer rely solely on sales of traditional software products. After all, computer manufacturers were offering free financial software with new computers, and Internet-savvy consumers had little desire to pay $50 for personal finance software when they could find financial tools on the Web for free. So Cook decided to transform the traditional software company into an Internet financial services provider.

Banking on the strength of the Quicken brand, Cook launched Quicken.com in 1997. Although the site initially offered stock quotes, financial planning advice, and online banking, Cook quickly expanded the scope of Intuit's online services. First, he integrated the site into Intuit's software products, allowing users of Quicken software programs to download data from Quicken.com with the click of a mouse. Then he part-nered with more than 50 banks and dozens of mortgage lenders and insurance carriers to turn the site into a full-service financial supermarket.

Today Quicken.com serves as a personal finance center, offering customers everything from bill payment to mortgages under one virtual roof. Using the "do-it-yourself" approach, consumers can download stock research, electronically file their tax returns, create a portfolio, or choose from an array of recommended mutual funds. Moreover, the site serves as a "virtual financial adviser" by directing consumers to the ideal financial instrument for their needs at the most reasonable price. Consumers in search of an auto loan, for example, can log on to Quicken.com to get quotes and compare rates from several different banks. But to complete the transactions, users will have to go to the bank's Web site. That's because Quicken.com doesn't actually sell financial products; rather, it acts as an intermediary—matching buyers and sellers and earning a commission for its services.

The site also attracts small-business owners by offering such services as CashFinder to entrepreneurs in search of capital and loans, and payroll services that work with QuickBooks. Furthermore, the site's online marketplace offers discounts on purchases of office supplies from such retailers as Office Depot and Gateway.

A firm believer that technology allows anyone to manage finances—even "people who think General Ledger is a World War II hero"—Cook continues to improve Intuit's range of online services. For example, Intuit became the first Internet provider to offer "pay anyone" capabilities by providing payment of electronic or traditional paper bills through Quicken's Web site. Another site feature consolidates bills, investments, credit card transactions,

453

and bank balances on one screen, permitting consumers to keep track of all their financial information in one place.

And Cook's vision for a one-stop money shop is paying off. Intuit now derives more than one-third of its revenue from Internet services, generating income through customer payments for such services as electronic tax filings and payroll services, through advertising and sponsorships, and through commissions on such transactions as loans and mortgages.[1]

■ WHAT DOES FINANCIAL MANAGEMENT INVOLVE?

LEARNING OBJECTIVE 1

Identify the responsibilities of a financial manager

As Intuit founder Scott Cook knows, all companies need to pay their bills and still have some money left over to improve the business. Furthermore, a key goal of any business is to increase the value to its owners (and other stakeholders) by making it grow. Maximizing the owner's wealth sounds simple enough: Just sell a good product for more than it costs to make. Before you can earn any revenue, however, you need money to get started. Once the business is off the ground, your need for money continues—whether it's to buy new road repair equipment or to build a new warehouse.

financial management
Effective acquisition and use of money

Planning for a firm's current and future money needs is the foundation of **financial management,** or finance. This area of concern involves making decisions about alternative sources and uses of funds with the goal of maximizing a company's value (see Exhibit 17.1). To achieve this goal, financial managers develop and implement a firm's financial plan; monitor a firm's cash flow and decide how to create or use excess funds; budget for current and future expenditures; recommend specific investments; develop a plan to finance the enterprise for future growth; and interact with banks and capital markets.

We begin this chapter by taking a close look at each of these activities. Next we discuss the banking environment in which financial managers operate. But first, keep in mind that in most smaller companies the owner is responsible for the firm's financial decisions, whereas in larger operations financial management is the responsibility of the finance department, which reports to a vice president of finance or a chief financial officer (CFO). This department includes the accounting function. In fact, most financial managers are accountants.

Developing and Implementing a Financial Plan

financial plan
A forecast of financial requirements and the financing sources to be used

One way companies make sure they have enough money is by developing a *financial plan.* Normally in the form of a budget, a **financial plan** is a document that shows the funds a firm will need for a period of time, as well as the sources and uses of those funds. When you prepare a financial plan for a company, you have two objectives: achieving a positive cash flow and efficiently investing excess cash flow to make your company grow. Financial planning requires looking beyond the four walls of the company to answer questions such as: Is the company introducing a new product in the near future or expanding its market? Is the industry growing? Is the national economy declining? Is inflation heating up? Would an investment in new technology improve productivity?[2]

EXHIBIT 17.1

SOURCES AND USES OF A COMPANY'S FUNDS

Financial management involves finding suitable sources of funds and deciding on the most appropriate uses for those funds.

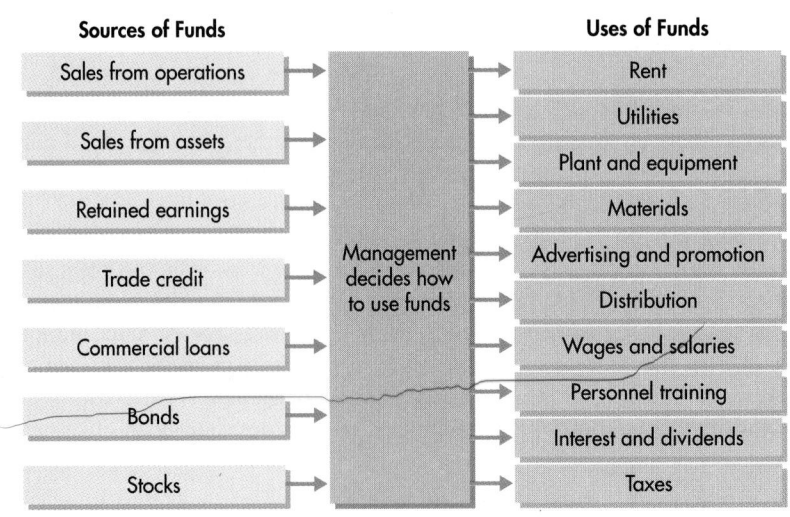

Monitoring Cash Flow An underlying concept of any financial plan is that all money should be used productively. This concept is important because without cash a company cannot purchase the assets and supplies it needs to operate or pay dividends to its shareholders. In accounting, we focused on the net income of a firm. Cash flows are generally related to net income; that is, companies with relatively high accounting profits generally have relatively high cash flows, but the relationship is not precise. That's because net income can be generated from a variety of accounting transactions that do not directly impact a firm's cash on hand.

One way financial mangers improve a company's cash flow is by monitoring its *working capital accounts:* cash, inventory, accounts receivable, and accounts payable. They use common-sense procedures such as shrinking accounts receivable collection periods, dispatching bills on a timely basis without paying bills earlier than necessary, controlling the level of inventory, and investing excess cash.

LEARNING
OBJECTIVE 2
Discuss how financial managers improve a company's cash flow

Managing Accounts Receivable and Accounts Payable Keeping an eye on accounts receivable—the money owed to the firm by its customers—is one way to manage cash flow effectively. The volume of receivables depends on the financial manager's decisions regarding several issues: who qualifies for credit and who does not; how long customers have to pay their bills; and how aggressive the firm is in collecting its debts. In addition to setting guidelines and policies to handle these issues, the financial manager analyzes the firm's outstanding receivables to identify patterns that might indicate problems and establishes procedures for collecting overdue accounts.

The flip side of managing receivables is managing payables—the bills that the company owes to its creditors. Here the objective is generally to postpone paying bills until the last moment, since accounts payable represent interest-free loans from suppliers. However, the financial manager also needs to weigh the advantages of paying promptly if doing so entitles the firm to cash discounts. In addition, paying on time is a good way to maintain the company's credit standing, which it turn influences a lender's decision to approve a loan. Of course, paying bills online with programs such as Intuit's Quicken and Microsoft Money is one way to manage cash aggressively and efficiently. As more and more companies deliver their bills electronically to customers via the Internet, and as such services become more reliable, online bill paying is expected to take off.[3]

Managing Inventory Inventory is another area where financial managers can fine-tune the firm's cash flow. In Chapter 9 we discussed that inventory sitting on the shelf represents capital that is tied up without earning interest. Furthermore, the firm incurs expenses for storage and handling, insurance, and taxes. Additionally, there is always the risk that inventory will become obsolete before it can be converted into finished goods and sold. Thus, the firm's goal is to maintain enough inventory to fill orders in a timely fashion at the lowest cost. To achieve this goal, financial managers work with operations managers and marketing managers to determine the economic order quantity (EOQ), or quantity of materials that, when ordered regularly, results in the lowest ordering and storage costs. (Inventory control techniques and efficient ordering systems are discussed in Chapter 9.)

Managing Cash Reserves Sometimes companies find themselves with more cash on hand than they need. A seasonal business may experience a quiet period between the time when revenues are collected from the last busy season and the time when suppliers' bills are due. Department stores, for example, may have excess cash during a few weeks in February and March. A firm may also accumulate cash to meet a large financial commitment in the future or to finance future growth. Using a company's own money instead of borrowing from an outside source such as a bank has one chief attraction: No interest payments are required. Finally, every firm keeps some surplus cash on hand as a cushion in case its needs are greater than expected.

Part of the financial manager's job is to make sure that excess cash is invested so that it earns as much interest as possible. Aggressive financial managers use electronic cash management (the ability to access bank account information online) to move cash between accounts and pay bills on a daily basis; they also invest excess cash on hand in short-term investments called **marketable securities.** These interest-bearing or dividend-paying investments include money-market funds or publicly traded stocks such as IBM or Sears. They are said to be "marketable" because they can be easily converted back to cash. Because marketable securities are

marketable securities
Stocks, bonds, and other investments that can be turned into cash quickly

LEARNING
OBJECTIVE   3
Differentiate between a master
budget and capital budget

budget
Planning and control tool that reflects
expected revenues, operating expenses,
and cash receipts and outlays

financial control
The process of analyzing and adjusting
the basic financial plan to correct for
forecasted events that do not
materialize

generally used as contingency funds, however, most financial managers invest these funds in securities of solid companies or the government—ones with the least amount of risk. (Securities are discussed in detail in Chapter 18.)

Budgeting

In addition to developing a financial plan and monitoring cash flow, financial managers are responsible for developing a **budget,** a financial blueprint for a given period (often one year). Master (or operating) budgets help financial managers estimate the flow of money into and out of the business by structuring financial plans in a framework of a firm's total estimated revenues, expenses, and cash flows. Accountants provide much of the data required for budgets and are important members of the budget development team because they have a complete understanding of the company's operating costs.

The master budget sets a standard for expenditures, provides guidelines for controlling costs, and offers an integrated and detailed plan for the future. For example, by reviewing the budget of any airline you can determine whether the company plans on increasing its fleet of aircraft, adding more routes, hiring more employees, increasing employees' pay, or continuing or abandoning any discounts for travelers. No wonder companies like to keep their budgets confidential. Once a budget has been developed, the finance manager compares actual results with projections to discover variances and then recommends corrective action—a process known as **financial control.**

Financial managers help their companies determine how much money they need for operations and for expansion. They're also responsible for identifying the right combination of funding sources at the lowest cost.

capital investments
Money paid to acquire something of
permanent value in a business

capital budgeting
Process for evaluating proposed
investments in select projects that
provide the best long-term financial
return

Capital Budgeting In contrast to operating budgets, capital budgets forecast and plan for a firm's **capital investments,** such as major expenditures in buildings or equipment. Capital investments generally cover a period of several years and help the company grow. Before investments can be made, however, a firm must decide on which of the many possible capital investments to make, how to finance those that are undertaken, and even whether to make any capital investments at all. This process is called **capital budgeting.**

The process generally begins by having all divisions within a company submit their capital requests—essentially, "wish lists" of investments that would make the company more profitable and thus more valuable to its owners over time. Next the financial manager decides which investments need evaluating and which don't. For example, the routine replacement of old equipment probably wouldn't need evaluating; however, the construction of a new manufacturing facility would. Finally, a financial evaluation is performed to determine whether the amount of money required for a particular investment will be greater than, equal to, or less than the amount of revenue it will generate. On the basis of this analysis, the financial manager can determine which projects to recommend to senior management for purchase approval.

Forecasting Capital Requirements Keep in mind that as with any major investment decision, an erroneous forecast of capital requirements can have serious consequences. If the firm invests too much in assets, it will incur unnecessarily heavy expenses. If it does not replace or upgrade existing assets on a regular basis, the assets will likely become obsolete. For example, old manufacturing equipment may be incapable of handling increasing capacities. This could even result in a loss of market share to competitors. For these important reasons, firms try to match capital investments with the company's goals. In other words, if the firm is growing, then projects that would produce the greatest growth rates would receive highest priority. However, if the company is trying to reduce costs, those projects that enhance the company's efficiency and productivity would be ranked toward the top. Because asset expansion frequently involves large sums of money and affects the company's productivity for an extended period of time, finance managers must carefully evaluate the best way to finance or pay for these investments, another major responsibility of financial managers.

Financing the Enterprise

Most companies can't operate and grow without a periodic infusion of money. Firms need money to cover the day-to-day expenses of running a business, such as paying employees and purchasing inventory. They also need money to acquire new assets such as land, production facilities, and equipment. Furthermore, as Chapter 4 pointed out, start-up companies need money to fund the costs involved in launching a new business.

Where can existing firms obtain the money they need to operate and grow? The most obvious source would be revenues: cash received from sales, rentals of property, interest on short-term investments, and so on. Another likely source would be suppliers who may be willing to do business on credit, thus enabling the company to postpone payment. Most firms also obtain money in the form of loans from banks, finance companies, or other commercial lenders. In addition, public companies can raise funds by selling shares of stock, and large corporations can sell bonds.

When Intel needs funds to purchase new equipment, management will weigh the advantages and disadvantages of using internal or external financing sources.

As you can imagine, financing an enterprise is a complex undertaking. The process begins by assessing the firm's financing needs and determining whether funds are needed for the short or long term. Next, the firm must assess the cost of obtaining those funds. Finally, it must weigh the advantages and disadvantages of financing through debt or equity, taking into consideration the firm's special needs and circumstances in addition to the advantages and disadvantages of public versus private ownership (as discussed in Chapter 5). The financing process is further complicated by the fact that many sources of long-term and short-term financing exist—each with their own special attributes, risks, and costs.

Length of Term Financing can be either short-term or long-term. **Short-term financing** is any financing that will be repaid within one year, whereas **long-term financing** is any financing that will be repaid in a period longer than one year. The primary purpose of short-term financing is to ensure that a company maintains its liquidity, or its ability to meet financial obligations (such as inventory payments) as they become due. By contrast, long-term financing is used to acquire long-term assets such as buildings and equipment or to fund expansion via any number of growth options. Long-term financing can come from both internal and external sources, as Exhibit 17.2 highlights.

LEARNING
OBJECTIVE 4

Cite three things financial managers must consider when selecting an appropriate funding vehicle

short-term financing
Financing used to cover current expenses (generally repaid within a year)

long-term financing
Financing used to cover long-term expenses such as assets (generally repaid over a period of more than one year)

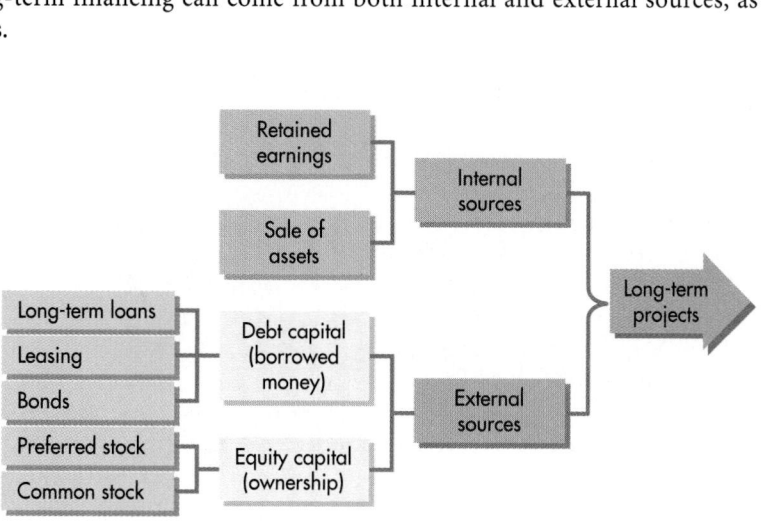

EXHIBIT 17.2

SOURCES OF LONG-TERM FINANCING

To finance long-term projects, financial managers rely on both internal and external sources of capital.

Cost of Capital In general, a company wants to obtain money at the lowest cost and least amount of risk. However, lenders and investors want to receive the highest possible return on their investment, also at the lowest risk. A company's **cost of capital,** the average rate of interest it must pay on its debt and equity financing, depends on three main factors: the risk associated with the company, the prevailing level of interest rates, and management's selection of funding vehicles.

Risk Lenders and investors who provide money to businesses expect their returns to be in proportion to the two types of risk they face: the quality and length of time of the venture. Obviously, the more financially solid a company is, the less risk investors face. However, time also plays a vital role. Because a dollar will be worth less tomorrow than it is today, lenders need to be compensated for waiting to be repaid. As a result, long-term financing generally costs a company more than short-term financing.

Interest Rates Regardless of how financially solid a company is, the cost of money will vary over time because interest rates fluctuate. The **prime interest rate (prime)** is the lowest interest rate offered on short-term bank loans to preferred borrowers. The prime changes irregularly and, at times, quite frequently—sometimes because of supply and demand and other times because the prime rate is closely tied to the **discount rate,** the interest rate Federal Reserve Banks charge on loans to commercial banks and other depository institutions. We will discuss the importance of the discount rate later in the chapter when we discuss the money supply.

Companies must take such interest rate fluctuations into account when making financing decisions. For instance, a company planning to finance a short-term project when the prime rate is 8.5 percent would want to reevaluate the project if the prime rose to 10 percent a few months later. Even though companies try to time their borrowing to take advantage of drops in interest rates, this option is not always possible. A firm's need for money doesn't always coincide with a period of favorable rates. At times, a company may be forced to borrow when rates are high and then renegotiate the loan when rates drop. Sometimes projects must be put on hold until interest rates become more affordable.

Opportunity Cost Using a company's own cash to finance its growth has one chief attraction: No interest payments are required. Nevertheless, such internal financing is not free; this money has an *opportunity cost.* That is, a company might be better off investing its excess cash in external opportunities, such as another company's projects or stocks of growing companies, and borrowing money to finance its own growth. Doing so makes sense as long as the company can earn a greater *rate of return,* the percentage increase in the value of an investment, on external investments than the rate of interest paid on borrowed money. This concept is called **leverage** because the loan acts like a lever: It magnifies the power of the borrower to generate profits (see Exhibit 17.3). However, leverage works both ways: Borrowing may magnify your losses as well as your gains. Because most companies require some degree of external financing from time to

---

cost of capital
Average rate of interest a firm pays on its combination of debt and equity

prime interest rate (prime)
Lowest rate of interest charged by banks for short-term loans to their most creditworthy customers

discount rate
Interest rate charged by the Federal Reserve on loans to commercial banks and other financial institutions

leverage
Technique of increasing the rate of return on an investment by financing it with borrowed funds

---

EXHIBIT 17.3

HOW LEVERAGE WORKS

If you invest $10,000 of your own money in a business venture and it yields 15 percent (or $1,500), your return on equity is 15 percent. However, if you borrow an additional $30,000 at 10 percent interest and invest a total of $40,000 with the same 15 percent yield, the ultimate return on your $10,000 equity is 30 percent (or $3,000). The key to using leverage successfully is to try to make sure that your profit on the total funds is greater than the interest you must pay on the portion of it that is borrowed.

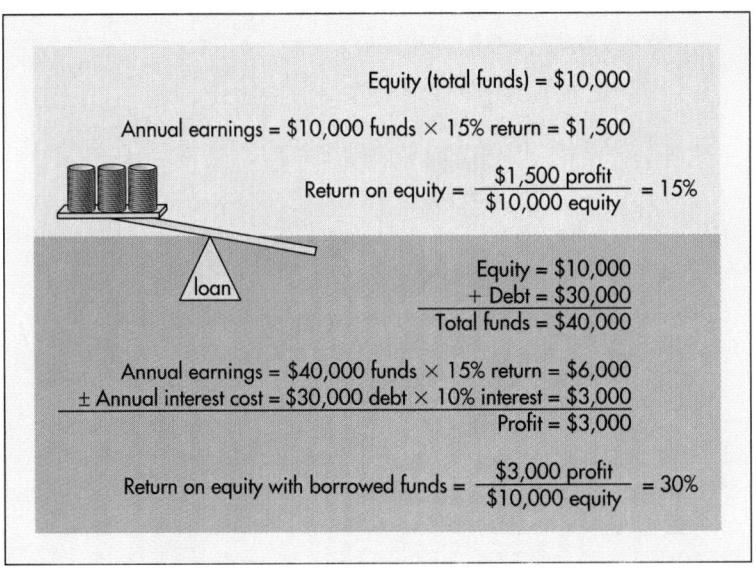

time, the issue is not so much whether to use outside money; rather, it's a question of how much should be raised, by what means, and when. The answers to such questions determine the firm's **capital structure,** the mix of debt and equity.

Debt Versus Equity Financing *Debt financing* refers to what we normally think of as a loan. A creditor agrees to lend money to a debtor in exchange for repayment, with accumulated interest, at some future date. *Equity financing* is achieved by selling shares of a company's stock. (The advantages and disadvantages of selling stock to the public are discussed in Chapter 5.) When choosing between debt and equity financing, companies consider a variety of issues, such as the cost of the financing, the claim on income, the claim on assets, and the desire for ownership control (see Exhibit 17.4)

Common Types of Debt Financing Two common types of short-term debt financing are **trade credit** (or open-account purchases) from suppliers—allowing purchasers to obtain products before paying for them; and **commercial paper**—short-term promissory notes of major corporations usually sold in denominations of $100,000 or more, with maturities of up to 270 days (the maximum allowed by the SEC without registration.

Loans, another common source of debt financing, can be long-term or short-term and secured or unsecured. **Secured loans** are those backed by something of value, known as **collateral,** which may be seized by the lender in the event that the borrower fails to repay the loan. The most common type of secured loan is a *mortgage,* in which a piece of property such as a building is used as collateral. Other types of loan collateral are accounts receivable, inventories, marketable securities, and other assets. **Unsecured loans** are ones that require no collateral. Instead, the lender relies on the general credit record and the earning power of the borrower. To increase the returns on such loans and to obtain some protection in case of default, most lenders insist that the borrower maintain some minimum amount of money on deposit at the bank—a **compensating balance**—while the loan is outstanding.

One example of an unsecured loan is a working capital **line of credit,** which is an agreed-on maximum amount of money a bank is willing to lend a business during a specific period of time, usually one year. Once a line of credit has been established, the business may obtain unsecured loans for any amount up to that limit, provided the bank has funds. The line of credit can be canceled at any time, so companies that want to be sure of obtaining credit when needed

capital structure
Financing mix of a firm

LEARNING
OBJECTIVE **5**

Identify five common types of debt financing

trade credit
Credit obtained by the purchaser directly from the supplier

commercial paper
An IOU, backed by the corporation's reputation, issued to raise short-term capital

secured loans
Loans backed up with something of value that the lender can claim in case of default, such as a piece of property

collateral
Tangible asset a lender can claim if a borrower defaults on a loan

unsecured loan
Loan requiring no collateral but a good credit rating

compensating balance
Portion of an unsecured loan that is kept on deposit at the lending institution to protect the lender and increase the lender's return

line of credit
Arrangement in which the financial institution makes money available for use at any time after the loan has been approved

EXHIBIT 17.4

DEBT VERSUS EQUITY

When choosing between debt and equity financing, companies evaluate the characteristics of both types of funding.

CHARACTERISTIC	DEBT	EQUITY
Maturity	**Specific:** Specifies a date by which it must be repaid.	**Nonspecific:** Specifies no maturity date.
Claim on income	**Fixed cost:** Company must pay interest on debt held by bondholders and lenders before paying any dividends to shareholders. Interest payments must be met regardless of operating results.	**Discretionary cost:** Shareholders may receive dividends after creditors have received interest payments; however, company is not required to pay dividends.
Claim on assets	**Priority:** Lenders have prior claims on assets.	**Residual:** Shareholders have claims only after the firm satisfies claims of lenders.
Influence over management	**Little:** Lenders are creditors, not owners. They can impose limits on management only if interest payments are not received.	**Varies:** As owners of the company, shareholders can vote on some aspects of corporate operations. Shareholder influence varies, depending on whether stock is widely distributed or closely held.

Best of the Web Best of the Web Best of

PLAN AHEAD

Start your personal financial planning now by using the tools at the Financenter. This Web site has loads of information on the best way to buy, finance or refinance major assets such as cars and houses. Use the calculators to compute what it will take to pay off your credit card balance. Find out whether you should consolidate your debts. Compute your available line of credit. Calculate how much money you can save by cutting your spending and investing the savings for 10 years. Better hurry. You may be losing interest.

www.financenter.com/

should arrange a revolving line of credit, which guarantees that the bank will honor the line of credit up to the stated amount.

Keep in mind that sometimes companies get into trouble by taking on too much debt. For example, when Quaker Oats unloaded Snapple for $300 million (after having plunked down a whopping $1.7 billion to purchase the brand from its creators less than three years earlier), the company recorded a $1.4 billion loss on the sale. Analysts estimate that Quaker lost $1.6 million for every day it owned Snapple because the net revenue generated from sales of the brand did not cover the costs of financing the acquisition.[4]

Rather than borrowing from a commercial lender to buy a piece of property or equipment, a firm may enter into a **lease,** under which the owner of an item allows another party to use it in exchange for regular payments. Leasing may be a good alternative for a company that has difficulty obtaining loans because of a poor credit rating. Creditors are more willing to provide a lease than a loan because, should the company fail, the lessor need not worry about a default on loan payments; it can simply repossess equipment it legally owns. Some firms use leases to finance up to 35 percent of their total assets, particularly in industries such as airlines, where assets are mostly large, expensive pieces of equipment.

When a company needs to borrow a large sum of money, it may not be able to get the entire amount from a single source. Under such circumstances, it may borrow from many individual investors by issuing *bonds*—certificates that obligate the company to repay a certain sum, plus interest, to the bondholder on a specific date. (Both bonds and stocks are traded on organized securities exchanges and are discussed in detail in Chapter 18.)

lease
Legal agreement that obligates the user of an asset to make payments to the owner of the asset in exchange for using it

THE U.S. FINANCIAL SYSTEM

Regardless of whether you finance your company's needs with debt, equity, or cash reserves, you will be interacting with financial institutions in a number of ways. The variety of financial institutions that operate within the U.S. banking environment can be classified into two broad categories: *deposit institutions* and *nondeposit institutions.* Deposit institutions accept deposits from customers or members and offer checking and savings accounts, loans, and other banking services. Among the many deposit institutions are the following:

- Commercial banks, which operate under state or national charters.

- Thrifts, including savings and loan associations (which use most of their deposits to make home mortgage loans) and mutual savings banks (which are owned by their depositors).

- Credit unions, which take deposits only from members, such as one company's employees or one union's members or another designated group.

Nondeposit institutions offer specific financial services but do not accept deposits. Among the many nondeposit institutions are the following:

- Insurance companies, which provide insurance coverage for life, property, and other potential losses; they invest the payments they receive in real estate, in construction projects, and in other ways.

- Pension funds, which are set up by companies to provide retirement benefits for employees; money contributed by the company and its employees is put into securities and other investments.

- Finance companies, which lend money to consumers and businesses for home improvements, expansion, purchases, and other purposes.

- Brokerage firms, which allow investors to buy and sell stocks, bonds, and other investments; many also offer checking accounts, high-paying savings accounts, and loans to buy securities. (Brokerage firms will be discussed more fully in Chapter 18.)

In the past, services such as checking, savings, and loans were not offered at all financial institutions; instead, each institution focused on offering a particular set of financial services for specific customer groups. However the competitive situation changed dramatically after the passage of the Depository Institutions Deregulation and Monetary Control Act of 1980. This law deregulated banking and made it possible for all financial institutions to offer a wider range of services—blurring the line between banks and other financial institutions and encouraging more competition between different types of institutions. Before we take a look at the changing U.S. banking environment, we must first discuss the types of traditional services offered by financial institutions.

Financial Services

No matter where in the world you live, work, or travel, today's businesses and individuals require a wide range of financial services. Banks of all sizes—from the largest multinational bank to the tiniest community bank—provide customers with a variety of financial services that include checking and savings accounts, loans, and credit, debit, and smart cards. Moreover, thanks to technological advances and Web sites such as Quicken.com, customers can now access their money and account information at any hour and from almost anywhere. Of course, the human touch is still a big part of banking. But in today's time-pressured world, more people want to handle banking transactions from different locations and at different times, not during traditional bankers' hours.

Checking and Savings Accounts Money you put into your checking account is a *demand deposit,* available immediately (on demand) through the use of **checks,** written orders that direct your bank to pay the stated amount of money to you or to someone else. Banks traditionally paid no interest on money in checking accounts. Since the laws changed in 1980, however, financial institutions have been allowed to offer interest-bearing NOW checking accounts. Most NOW accounts limit the number of checks customers can write and impose a fee if the account balance falls below a minimum level.

checks
Written orders that tell the customer's bank to pay a specific amount to a particular individual or business

You earn interest on the money you put away in savings accounts; credit unions typically pay slightly higher savings rates than commercial banks. Originally, these accounts were known as *passbook savings accounts* because customers received a small passbook in which the bank recorded all deposits, withdrawals, and interest. Today, banks send out statements instead of passbooks, so these accounts have become known as *statement savings accounts.* In general, money in savings accounts can be withdrawn at any time. Money in a *money-market deposit account* earns more interest, but you are allowed only a limited number of monthly withdrawals. Money held in a *certificate of deposit (CD)* earns an even higher interest rate, but you cannot withdraw the funds for a stated period, such as six months or more. If you want to make an early withdrawal from a CD, you will lose some or all of the interest you've earned.

Loans Banks are a major source of loans for customers who need money for a particular purpose. Individuals, for example, usually apply for mortgage loans when they want to buy a home. They also look to banks and financial services firms for auto loans, home-improvement loans, student loans, and many other types of loans. Businesses rely on banks to provide loans for expansion, purchases of new equipment, construction or renovation of plants and facilities, or other large-scale projects. Like consumers, businesses shop around to compare interest rates, fees, and repayment schedules before they take out a loan.

Credit, Debit, and Smart Cards For everyday access to short-term credit, banks issue **credit cards,** plastic cards that entitle customers to make purchases now and repay the loaned amount later. Many

credit cards
Plastic cards that allow the customer to buy now and pay back the loaned amount at a future date

banks charge an annual fee for Visa and MasterCard credit cards, and all charge interest on any unpaid credit card balance. Nondeposit institutions such as American Express also issue credit cards.

Credit cards have become immensely popular with consumers because they are convenient and allow people to make purchases without cash. They also help people manage their finances by either choosing to repay the full amount when they are billed or making small payments month by month until the debt has been repaid. Credit card companies make money by charging customers interest on their unpaid account balances and by charging businesses a processing fee, which can range from 2 to 5 percent of the value of each sales transaction paid by credit card. Nearly every store accepts credit cards, and mail-order merchants and Internet retailers are especially dependent on credit cards to facilitate purchases.

In addition to credit cards, many banks offer **debit cards,** plastic cards that function like checks in that the amount of a purchase is electronically deducted from the user's checking account and is transferred to the retailer's account at the time of the sale. Debit cards are ideal for customers who must control their spending or stick to a budget. **Smart cards** are plastic cards with tiny computer chips that can store amounts of money (from the user's bank account) and selected data (such as shipping address, credit card information, frequent-flyer account numbers, health and insurance details, or other personal information). When a purchase is made, the store's equipment electronically deducts the amount from the value stored on the smart card and

debit cards
Plastic cards that allow the bank to take money from the user's demand-deposit account and transfer it to a retailer's account

smart cards
Plastic cards that include an embedded chip to store money drawn from the user's demand-deposit account and information that can be used for purchases

THINKING ABOUT ETHICS

SURPRISE! YOU'VE BEEN SWIPED

Skimming. It's the fastest-growing area of credit card fraud. A skimmer is someone who steals customer account information by swiping a credit card through a handheld magnetic card reader—about the size of a pager. The reader copies the cardholder's name, account number, and even the card validation code—stored on the magnetic stripe—giving the counterfeiter all the data needed to create a perfect clone of the credit card. Readers can be purchased for as little as $100 over the Internet and are intended for legitimate use by banks, restaurants, retailers, and hotels. Unfortunately, some end up in the wrong hands.

Thieves, and increasingly organized crime groups, pay waiters and store clerks to steal information from credit cards using the concealed devices. By skimming 14 to 20 accounts, crooks can generate $50,000 to $60,000 worth of fraud that will probably go undiscovered until the victims get their bills—30 to 60 days after the crime. Moreover, skimmed data from say a customer in New York City or Washington can be e-mailed to Taiwan, Japan, or Europe and used for mail-order, telephone-order, or e-commerce overseas transactions within 24 to 48 hours of the theft. Professionals can even encode the stolen codes into a stripe and use equipment to produce an electronically indistinguishable counterfeit card.

While credit card issuers decline to say how much they are losing to skimmers—in part because they don't want to scare consumers out of using their plastic—industry analysts estimate skimmers reap over $125 million annually. To curb the fraud, major credit card issuers are cooperating with the U.S. Secret Service to pool information about fraudulent transactions. For example, issuers can generate computer analyses that flag locations where numerous cards may have been skimmed. Or if someone in Hong Kong tries to buy something with a credit card that was used two hours earlier in Chicago, the computer will reject the transaction.

What can you do to prevent your credit cards from getting skimmed? Not much, says experts besides reading your bills closely, checking your accounts on the Web or by phone during the month to make sure there are no surprises, and reporting improper charges promptly. Although you're not liable for fraudulent charges made to your accounts by skimmers or other scam artists, you do have to face the hassle of getting the unauthorized transactions removed from your bills. Of course, you can always pay with old-fashioned cash. But if you carry lots of that around, you may have to worry about the old-fashioned robber.

■ **QUESTIONS FOR CRITICAL THINKING**

1. To curb the abuse, why don't credit card issuers require customers to present additional personal validation data at the time of sale?

2. Why don't thieves skim debit cards too?

reads and verifies requisite customer information. Users reload money from their bank accounts to their smart cards as needed.

Although popular in Europe, smart cards have been slow to catch on in the United States for two reasons: Low U.S. telephone rates (compared to those of European countries) make it affordable to verify credit card transactions over the phone, and it is not cost-effective for most U.S. businesses to replace current credit card infrastructures with smart card readers and computer chip technology. Nevertheless, American Express has made inroads with its combination smart card and credit card, Blue. Designed to appeal to online shoppers, Blue comes with software and a small smart card reader that plugs into the user's serial port. Customers who purchase online simply insert Blue into the reader, type in a password, and the digital information stored on the smart card tells the vendor their credit card number, expiration date, and shipping address.[5]

Automated teller machines (ATMs) allow customers to perform certain bank transactions 24 hours a day in places other than a branch.

Electronic Banking Electronic banking includes various banking activities conducted from sites other than a physical bank location. For instance, all over the world, customers rely on **automated teller machines (ATMs)** to withdraw money from their demand-deposit accounts at any hour. In the United States, over 200,000 ATMs handle 11 billion electronic banking transactions every year. Look around: ATMs are everywhere, from banks, malls, and supermarkets to airports, resorts, and tourist attractions. By linking with regional, national, and international ATM networks, banks let customers withdraw cash far from home, make deposits, and handle other transactions. To compete, more banks are jazzing up their ATMs by allowing purchases of stamps, traveler's checks, movie tickets, ski lift tickets, and even foreign currency.[6]

Electronic funds transfer systems (EFTS) are another form of electronic banking. These computerized systems allow users to conduct financial transactions efficiently from remote locations. More than one-third of all U.S. workers take advantage of EFTS when their employers use *direct deposit* to transfer wages directly into employees' bank accounts. This procedure saves employers and employees the worry and headache of handling large amounts of cash.[7] Even the U.S. government uses EFTS for regular payments such as Social Security benefits.

In addition to automated teller machines and electronic funds transfer systems, most major banks and many thrifts and community banks now offer Internet or online banking to accommodate the growing number of individuals and businesses that want to transfer money between accounts, check account balances, pay bills, apply for loans, and handle other transactions at any hour. Online banking is not only fast and easy for customers but also extremely cost-efficient for banks (see Exhibit 17.5). But as discussed in this chapter's special feature, Focusing on E-Business Today, Internet banking has been slow to take off.[8]

automated teller machines (ATMs)
Electronic terminals that permit people with plastic cards to perform simple banking transactions 24 hours a day without the aid of a human teller

electronic funds transfer systems (EFTS)
Computerized systems for performing financial transactions

	Cost per transaction
Bank with live teller	$1.07
Bank through debit card	.29
Bank through ATM	.27
Bank on the Internet	.04

EXHIBIT 17.5

BANKING TRANSACTION COSTS

The average cost of having a teller handle a banking transaction is much higher than the cost for other ways of handling banking transactions. This is why banks want customers to bypass tellers whenever possible.

LEARNING
OBJECTIVE   6

Explain how consolidation is
affecting the banking industry

The Evolving U.S. Banking Environment

Since the deregulation of the banking industry in 1980, financial institutions have changed radically in response to deregulation, competitive pressures, and financial problems. The most obvious evidence: industry consolidation and the repeal of the Glass-Steagall Act.

In 1934, there were 14,146 main bank offices in the United States; by 1999, the number had plummeted to only 8,581.[9] Seeking strength, efficiency, and access to more customers and markets, U.S. banks underwent a series of mergers, acquisitions, and takeovers during the 1980s and 1990s. As banks and thrifts searched for higher profits in this competitive environment, some invested heavily in real estate and oil-drilling activities, loaned money to foreign governments, and financed company buyouts. Then the real estate market collapsed, oil prices plummeted, developers went bankrupt, and countries and companies hit hard by economic woes slowed or stopped payments on their loans. In many cases, failing institutions were taken over by stronger banks; in other cases, banks such as NationsBank and BankAmerica merged to cut costs and cover more territory with more services.

In 1999 Congress opened the floodgates for consolidation among banks, brokerage firms, and insurance companies by passing the 1999 Financial Services Modernization Act. This law repealed the Glass-Steagall Act (also known as the Banking Act of 1933) and portions of the 1956 Bank Holding Act, which for decades had kept banks out of the securities and insurance businesses. Originally enacted after the stock market crash of 1929 and the Great Depression, the Glass-Steagall Act was designed to restore confidence in U.S. financial houses by restricting investment banks and commercial banks from crossing into each others' businesses and potentially abusing their fiduciary duties at the expense of customers. Moreover, it ensured that a catastrophic failure in one part of the finance industry did not invade every other part, as it did in 1929. The 1956 Bank Holding Company Act restricted what banks could do in the insurance business.[10]

Integration of Financial Services The repeal of the Glass-Steagall Act and the lifting of other bank restrictions has fueled a raft of megamergers. Banks are combining with other banks and insurance companies to create financial supermarkets that offer customers a full range of services—from traditional loans to investment banking services to public stock offerings to insurance. The average U.S. resident now uses 15 banking and investment products (checking, credit cards, mortgage, mutual funds, life insurance, and so on) from five different companies. And financial supermarkets want to consolidate that scattered business into a single trusted brand name. For example, Merrill Lynch, a major brokerage firm, now offers federally insured interest-bearing savings and checking accounts among other bank products—in addition to securities trading. Similar offerings from other brokerage firms are expected.[11] Meanwhile, American Express has expanded beyond credit cards and now lends money to small businesses, Wal-Mart and E*Trade are purchasing banks, and tellers at Citibank are talking up mutual funds. Indeed, the line between brokers, bankers, and insurers is blurring beyond distinction.[12] And Scott Cook hopes that as competition heats up, customers will rely on Quicken.com for direction to the financial organization that will best match their particular needs at the most reasonable price.

Community Banks and Interstate Banking While consumer convenience, improved operating efficiencies, and integrated financial services are frequently cited as the chief benefits of industry consolidation, some worry that industry consolidation could concentrate too much power in large financial institutions. Others insist there will always be room for smaller, community banks.

Community banks are smaller banks that concentrate on serving the needs of local consumers and businesses. A number of factors are contributing to their increasing popularity. One is the void created by bank consolidations, which frequently lead to loan and other decisions being made by bank officials who are not local and don't know the applicants. Most community bankers, if they believe in a small business owner, will go out of their way to make a loan. They won't break the rules, but they might bend them a little. Moreover, community banks typically try to help their local customers by thinking creatively—offering customized

KEEPING PACE WITH TECHNOLOGY AND ELECTRONIC COMMERCE

HOW WILL YOU BE PAYING FOR THAT?

For years, companies and customers have been trying to figure out new and better ways to buy and sell goods online. Despite all the effort, credit cards seem to be working pretty well. An estimated 95 percent of Internet purchases are completed with a credit card. Yet there are problems with using a credit card online. One is security—although most credit card transactions are safe. Another is privacy. So, as electronic commerce grows, people are trying to find new ways to make money off of it.

E-money is one idea. Also known as *digital cash*, e-money is a way to store money for use on the Web that is the virtual equivalent of a phone card or a gift certificate. Here's how it works: A company creates a virtual currency that will be accepted only on the Internet. Retailers download the software that accepts the currency, and customers download the software that offers the currency. Customers buy the Internet currency using real money or a credit card and use the e-money to purchase online. Then retailers exchange the e-money for real currency. E-money, of course, limits fraud because even if the currency is stolen, it can only be used for e-purchases at online stores equipped with the software. Nonetheless, e-money faces one big hurdle. Retailers don't want to install new software unless they see a lot of customers using it. And customers don't want to download software unless they see a lot of retailers accepting it.

Digital wallets are another idea. Similar in concept to smart cards, digital or electronic wallets speed up online checkout by reading pertinent purchaser information from a customer's digital wallet. Customers download software that stores their credit card numbers, shipping and billing addresses, and other personal information. Participating sites download software that enables them to receive payment from the wallet. Yahoo! is the leader in electronic wallet use with a roster of more than 11,000 merchants, including Gap, Macy's, Barnes & Noble, Toys "R" Us, and Victoria's Secret. America Online's wallet is also making inroads. Here again, wallets can make transactions speedier and solve the problem of having to remember a different password and user name for each Web store. But this approach has the same flaw as e-cash—the difficulty of signing up retailers.

In spite of these challenges, e-money, digital wallets, and new online payment options are expected to gain ground as Internet shopping grows even more. So next time an online clerk asks you, "And how you will be paying for your purchase?" you may be surprised at the number of options you will have.

■ QUESTIONS FOR CRITICAL THINKING

1. What events might stimulate wider acceptance of e-money and digital wallets?

2. Why don't some consumers like to pay for online purchases with credit cards?

services "that maybe a large branching operation just simply does not have the flexibility to do," explains Robert J. Wingert of the Community Bankers Association of Illinois. Another reason for their increasing popularity is that consolidations have made considerable talent available to start community banks. Finally, favorable economic conditions have also contributed to their resurgence.[13]

As community banks continue to operate in smaller, well-defined areas, midsize and larger banks have been expanding into new markets by opening branch operations or merging with banks across state lines. Such interstate operations were made possible by the Riegle-Neal Interstate Banking and Branching Efficiency Act of 1994, a landmark law that reversed legislation dating back to 1927.[14] As a result, customers can now make deposits, cash checks, or handle any banking transaction in any branch of their bank, regardless of location. Of course, banks benefit too. BankAmerica, for example, had to operate separate banking systems in 10 states until the Riegle-Neal Act was passed. Now the company can combine its banks under a single operating system to maximize efficiencies.[15] Looking beyond U.S. borders, BankAmerica and other banks have gone global with branches in many countries—just as foreign banks such as Japan's Dai-Ichi Kangyo Bank have long done business in the United States and around the world.

Community bankers excel at personal service. They will meet with small-business owners and work with them on their business plan, and they will loan them money to help them grow their business to the next level.

Bank Safety and Regulation

Regardless of where or how you conduct your financial transactions, everyone (including Congress, regulators, and the financial community) worries about bank failure. As many as 9,000 U.S. banks failed during the Depression years from 1929 to 1934. In response to concerns about bank safety during that period, the government established the Federal Deposit Insurance Corporation (FDIC) to protect money in customer accounts. Today, money on deposit in U.S. banks is insured by the FDIC up to a maximum of $100,000 through the Savings Association Insurance Fund (for thrifts) and the Bank Insurance Fund (for commercial banks). Similarly, the National Credit Union Association protects deposits in credit unions.

In addition, a number of government agencies supervise and regulate banks. State-chartered banks come under the watchful eyes of each state's banking commission; nationally chartered banks are under the federal Office of the Comptroller of the Currency; and thrifts are under the federal Office of Thrift Supervision. The overall health of the country's banking system is, ultimately, the responsibility of the Federal Reserve System.

THE FUNCTIONS OF THE FEDERAL RESERVE SYSTEM

The Federal Reserve System was created in 1913. Commonly known as the Fed, it is the most powerful financial institution in the United States, serving as the central bank. The Fed's primary role is to manage the money supply so that the country avoids both recession and inflation. It also supervises and regulates banks and serves as a clearinghouse for checks.

The Fed is a network of 12 district banks that controls the nation's banking system. The overall policy of the Fed is established by a seven-member board of governors who meet in Washington, D.C. To preserve the board's political independence, the members are appointed by the president to 14-year terms, staggered at two-year intervals. Although all national banks are required to be members of the Federal Reserve System, membership for state-chartered banks is optional. Still, the Fed exercises regulatory power over all deposit institutions, members and nonmembers alike. The Federal Reserve System has three major functions: influencing the U.S. money supply, supplying currency, and clearing checks.

Best of the Web Best of the Web Best of

TAKE A FIELD TRIP TO THE FED

Visit the Fed. Find out what the Board of Governors of the Federal Reserve System does. Read summaries of their regulations. Learn what "Truth in Lending" means or how to file a consumer complaint against a bank. Brush up on your credit card knowledge. Do you know what a grace period is or how finance charges are calculated? Take a side trip to the Federal Reserve Banks. Don't leave without meeting Carmen Cents. She's at the FDIC and she has a wonderful tour planned for you.

www.federalreserve.gov/

Influencing the U.S. Money Supply

Money is anything generally accepted as a means of paying for goods and services. Before it was invented, people got what they needed by trading their services or possessions; in some societies, such as Russia, this system of trading, or bartering, still exists. However, barter is inconvenient and impractical in a global economy, where many of the things we want are intangible, come from places all over the world, and require the combined work of many people.

To be an effective medium of exchange, money must have these important characteristics: It must be divisible, portable (easy to carry), durable, and difficult to counterfeit; and it should have a stable value. In addition, money must perform three basic functions: First, it must serve as a medium of exchange—a tool for simplifying transactions between buyers and sellers. Second, it must serve as a measure of value so that you don't have to negotiate the relative worth of dissimilar items every time you buy something. Finally, money must serve as a temporary store of value—a way of accumulating your wealth until you need it.

The Fed's main job is to establish and implement *monetary policy,* guidelines for handling the nation's economy and the money supply. The U.S. money supply has three major components:

- **Currency:** Money in the form of coins, bills, traveler's checks, cashier's checks, and money orders
- **Demand deposit:** Money available immediately on demand, such as checking accounts
- **Time deposits:** Accounts that pay interest and restrict the owner's right to withdraw funds on short notice, such as savings accounts, certificates of deposit, and money-market deposit accounts

The Fed influences the money supply to make certain that enough money and credit are available to fuel a healthy economy. However, it must act carefully, because altering the money supply affects interest rates, inflation, and the economy. When the money supply is increased, more money is available for loans, so banks can charge lower interest rates to borrowers. On the other hand, an increased money supply can lead to more consumer spending and can result in the demand for goods exceeding supply. When demand exceeds supply, sellers may raise their prices, leading to inflation. In turn, inflation can slow economic growth—a situation the Fed wants to avoid. And, because so many companies now buy and sell across national borders, the Fed's changes may affect the interlinked economies of many countries, not just the United States.[16] That's why the Fed moves cautiously and keeps a close eye on the size of the money supply.

How the Money Supply Is Measured To get a rough idea of the size of the money supply, the Fed looks at various combinations of currency, demand deposits, and time deposits (see Exhibit 17.6). The narrowest measure, **M1,** consists of currency, demand deposits, and NOW accounts that are common forms of payment. **M2,** a broader measure of the money supply, includes M1 plus savings deposits, money-market funds, and time deposits under $100,000. **M3,** the broadest

money
Anything generally accepted as a means of paying for goods and services

currency
Bills and coins that make up the cash money of a society

demand deposit
Money in a checking account that can be used by the customer at any time

time deposits
Bank accounts that pay interest and require advance notice before money can be withdrawn

M1
That portion of the money supply consisting of currency and demand deposits

M2
That portion of the money supply consisting of currency, demand deposits, and small time deposits

M3
That portion of the money supply consisting of M1 and M2 plus large time deposits and other restrictive deposits

Best of the Web Best of the Web Best of

TOUR THE U.S. TREASURY

Take a virtual tour of the U.S. Treasury. Visit the Learning Vault and find out how much paper currency is printed in one day or one year. Click on the Site Map and explore this Department from the inside out. Learn about the benefits of electronic funds transfer. Take the link to the Bureau of Engraving and Printing where you can play money trivia and get some money production figures. Discover how money gets into circulation. Find out whose picture was on the $500 bill. Bet you wish you had one!

www.ustreas.gov

EXHIBIT 17.6

THE TOTAL MONEY SUPPLY

The U.S. money supply is measured at three levels: M1, M2, and M3. Here's a closer look at the size and composition of these three components.

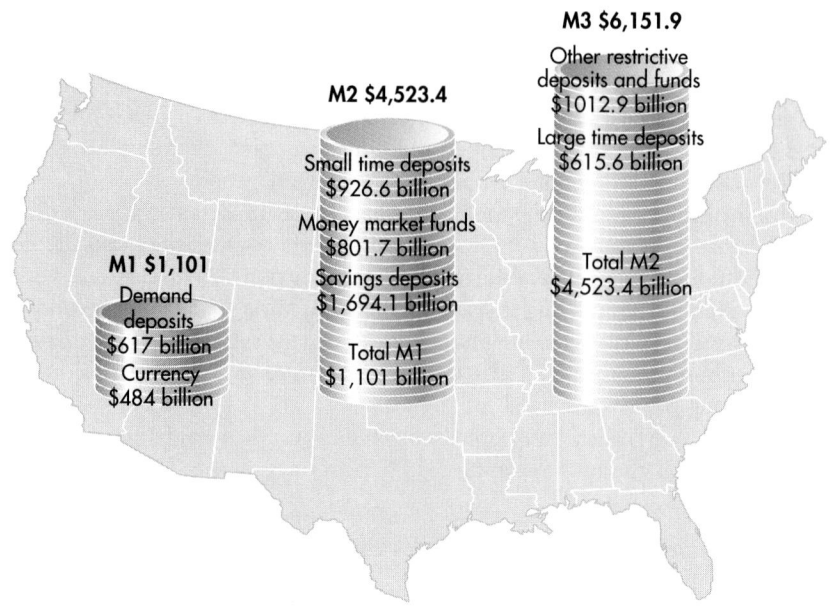

measure of the money supply, includes M2 plus time deposits of $100,000 and higher and other restricted deposits.

LEARNING OBJECTIVE *7*

Identify four ways the Federal Reserve System influences the U.S. money supply

reserve requirement
Percentage of a bank's deposit that must be set aside

Tools for Influencing the Money Supply The Fed can use four basic tools to influence the money supply:

■ *Changing the reserve requirement.* All financial institutions must set aside *reserves,* sums of money equal to a certain percentage of their deposits. The Fed can change the **reserve requirement,** the percentage of deposits that banks must set aside, to influence the money supply. However, the Fed rarely uses this technique because a small change can have a drastic effect. Increasing the reserve requirement slows down the economy: Banks have less money to lend, so businesses can't borrow to expand and consumers can't borrow to buy goods and services. Conversely, reducing this requirement boosts the economy, because banks have more money to lend to businesses and consumers (see Exhibit 17.7).

EXHIBIT 17.7

HOW BANKS CREATE MONEY

Banks stay in business by earning more on interest from loans than they pay out in the form of interest on deposits; they can increase their earnings by "creating" money. When customer A deposits $100, the bank must keep some in reserve but can lend, say, $80 to customer B (and earn interest on that loan). If customer B deposits the borrowed $80 in the same bank, the bank can lend 80 percent of *that* amount to borrower C. The initial $100 deposit therefore creates a much larger pool of funds from which customer loans may be made.

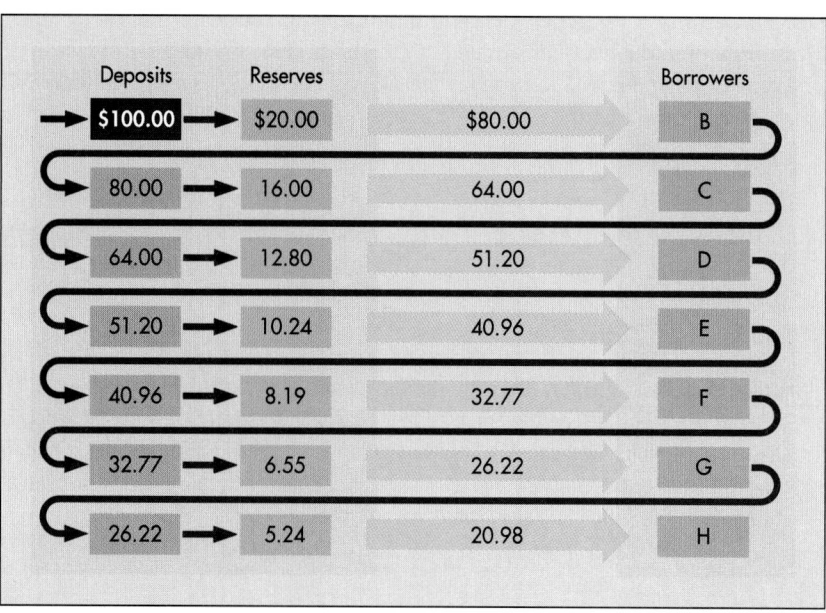

■ *Changing the discount rate.* The Fed can also change the discount rate, the interest rate it charges on loans to commercial banks and other depository institutions. When the Fed raises the discount rate, member banks generally raise the prime interest rate. Thus, raising the discount rate discourages loans, and in so doing tightens the money supply, which can slow down economic growth. By contrast, lowering the discount rate results in lower lending rates, which can encourage more borrowing and stimulate economic growth.

■ *Conducting open-market operations.* The tool the Fed uses most often to influence the money supply is the power to buy and sell U.S. government bonds. Because anyone can buy these bonds on the open market, this tool is known as **open-market operations.** If the Fed is concerned about inflation, it can reduce the money supply by selling U.S. government bonds, which takes cash out of circulation. And when the Fed wants to boost the economy, it can buy back government bonds, putting cash into circulation and increasing the money supply.

open-market operations
Activity of the Federal Reserve in buying and selling government bonds on the open market

■ *Establishing selective credit controls.* The Fed can also use **selective credit controls** to set the terms of credit for various kinds of loans. This tool includes the power to set *margin requirements,* the percentage of the purchase price that an investor must pay in cash when purchasing a stock or a bond on credit. By altering the margin requirements, the Fed is able to influence how much cash is tied up in stock market transactions.

selective credit controls
Federal Reserve's power to set credit terms on various types of loans

Exhibit 17.8 summarizes the effects of using these four tools.

Supplying Currency and Clearing Checks

The second function of the Fed is to supply currency to keep the U.S. financial system running smoothly. Regional Federal Reserve Banks are responsible for providing member banks with adequate amounts of currency throughout the year. For example, in preparation for potential disruptions due to year-2000 computer problems, the Fed was ready to provide U.S. banks with another $50 billion in cash.[17]

Another function of the Federal Reserve is to act as a clearinghouse for checks. Today, money on deposit in banks or other financial institutions is recorded in computerized ledger entries. When a customer deposits or cashes a check drawn on a bank in another city or town, the customer's bank uses the Fed's check-processing system to clear the check and receive payment. In clearing this check, the Fed's computer system charges and credits the appropriate accounts. Exhibit 17.9 shows the operation of this automated clearinghouse function, which is invisible yet indispensable to consumers and businesses. Keep in mind that a number of factors are contributing to the decline in check usage. These include increased use of electronic payments, direct payroll deposits, direct drafts from consumer bank accounts, credit and debit cards, and online banking.

To increase the money supply		To decrease the money supply
Decrease	**Reserve Requirements**	Increase
Lower	**Discount Rate**	Raise
Buy	**Open-Market Operations**	Sell
Fewer	**Selective Credit Controls**	More

EXHIBIT 17.8

INFLUENCING THE MONEY SUPPLY

The Federal Reserve uses four tools to influence the money supply as it attempts to stimulate economic growth while keeping inflation and interest rates at acceptable levels.

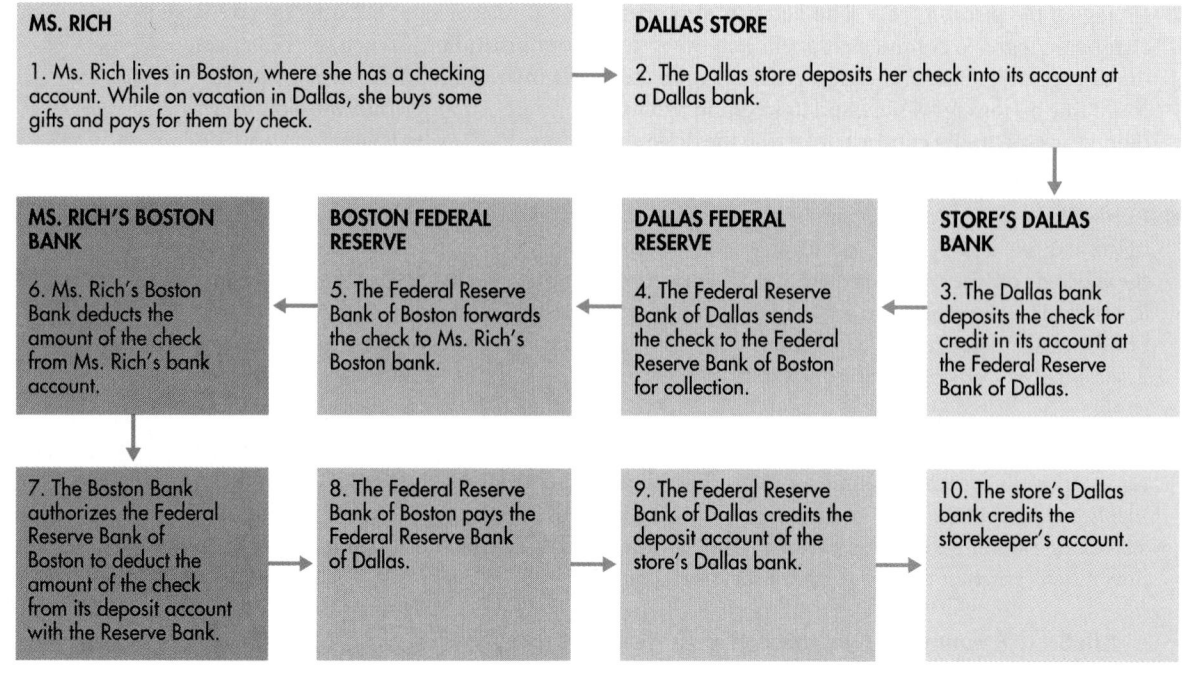

EXHIBIT 17.9

HOW THE FED CLEARS CHECKS

The Federal Reserve acts as a clearinghouse for checks in the United States. This example shows how the Fed clears a check that has been drawn on a bank in one city but deposited by a store into a bank in another city.

 FOCUSING ON E-BUSINESS TODAY

A Banking Revolution—On Hold!

When Internet-only banks began popping up in 1995, many believed they would revolutionize retail banking. Net banks, they said, would attract swarms of customers by offering higher interest rates on savings and lower-cost loans than traditional banks, little or no fees, and the convenience of banking at home, 24 hours a day, seven days a week. They can afford these benefits because electronic transactions cost less to process than paper transactions and because cyberbanks don't have to maintain and staff costly physical branch networks. But online banking has not caught on like online stock trading.

 LEARNING OBJECTIVE @8

Identify the advantages of online banking and explain the challenges cyberbanks face in the competitive banking environment

CYBERBANKS HIT A BRICK WALL

Why have cyberbanks been slow to catch on? To begin with, like most Internet-only start-ups, cyberbanks lack brand recognition. Thus, they have to launch their e-businesses with the same expensive marketing campaigns as the rest of the dot-com world—eliminating much of the Internet cost advantage. Moreover, touting customer advantages such as

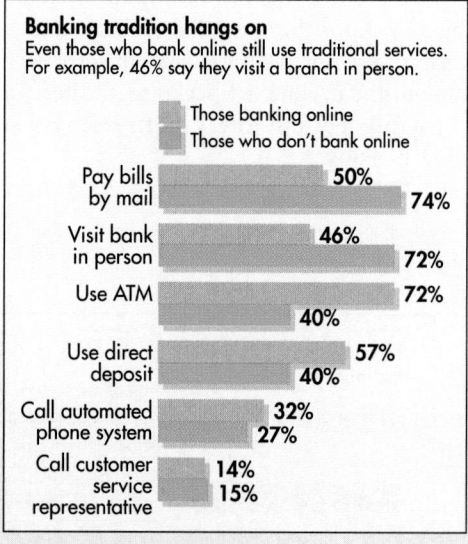

Banking tradition hangs on
Even those who bank online still use traditional services. For example, 46% say they visit a branch in person.

- Those banking online
- Those who don't bank online

	Those banking online	Those who don't bank online
Pay bills by mail	50%	74%
Visit bank in person	46%	72%
Use ATM	72%	40%
Use direct deposit	57%	40%
Call automated phone system	32%	27%
Call customer service representative	14%	15%

higher interest rates and access to account information at any time is nice, but customers also want customer service. Few are willing to switch to cyberbanks when faced with the following:

- *No friendly banker.* Without branches, many online banks lack a concrete place for customers to resolve problems. Getting things done at traditional banks can indeed take a long time, but reports from some online bank customers make the traditionals look speedy. Part of the problem is psychological. Customers want something tangible; they want to know someone is there (in person) if they need them.

- *Minimal cost savings.* In online securities trading, customers gain convenience and can save as much as $200 a trade by using an online discount broker such as E*Trade. In contrast, online banking, while convenient, does not save customers transaction fees. Internet-only banks don't have their own ATM networks so customers pay fees to use other banks' machines. In short, the opportunity for cost savings over what was available with traditional banks is not comparable to that experienced by online brokerage customers.

- *Limited services.* Cyberbanks can't replace local banks entirely. Few, if any, have ATMs, they can't handle daily cash deposits, they don't make local business loans, and they don't offer safe deposit boxes. Although some virtual banks provide postage-paid envelopes so that customers can deposit checks by mail, many customers find this cumbersome. Thus, cybercustomers must still venture into the physical world to get these banking services.

- *Complex Web sites.* Many customers find banking Web sites complicated and time consuming. Few sites provide adequate customer service, forcing customers to be their own bank clerks.

In spite of these challenges, new cyberbanks are coming online daily. Among them: VirtualBank, CompuBank, Everbank.com, JuniperBank, and Wingspan.com (Bank One's online venture). To attract customers, some are making forays into the real world. For example, JuniperBank allows customers to deposit checks at any of the thousands of MailBoxes Etc. outlets across the nation. Allfirst Financial allows customers to actually talk with bank staff through microphones and speakers that come with most newer computer models. Some are offering rebates on the ATM surcharges their customers pay to other banks. Others are moving to a clicks-and-bricks strategy by opening up phys-ical branches—making it harder and harder to differentiate virtual banks and traditional banks.

TRADITIONAL BANKS ARE FIGHTING BACK

But rather than give traditional banks a run for their money, cyberbanks have given them ideas. "We think bricks and clicks is a winning strategy," says First Boston's executive vice president. Many traditional banks now offer Web access as just another way to do business with them. Some even have far more Internet accounts than rival cyberbanks. Virtually all the nation's biggest lenders, including Citigroup, Chase Manhattan, Bank of America, and Wells Fargo have sought to keep pace with the cyberbanks by either developing or revamping their online offerings.

Some traditionals have not made an easy transition to the cyberworld. But at least they have been shaken out of their complacency. Most now offer customers new technologies and online services including electronic bill payment, access to account information, transfers between accounts, and online credit card applications, to name a few. Some are even hawking services that will combine a customer's financial and personal accounts in one convenient place. Others are swallowing up Internet start-up banks or scooping up prime partnership opportunities with existing Internet companies. Citigroup, for example, now provides online payment systems to America Online's 23 million users; Wells Fargo rolled out an online payment system for eBay's customers; and Bank of America took an ownership stake in the biggest online billing company, CheckFree Holdings. Still, others have set up separate virtual banks such as Bank One's WingspanBank.com.

INTERNET OR DIE

Still, a new report on e-banking confirms that cyberbanking has yet to reach mass appeal and may never be more than a tool for niche groups. Many banks have struggled with the Internet. They are finding it difficult and expensive to link existing legacy systems to the real-time personalized nature of the Web or to integrate Web sites with existing branch offices, ATMs, and telephone systems. Moreover, few banks are seeing profits from their online ventures, and Web customers still use branches. Nevertheless, most traditional banks believe they have no choice but to enter the Internet fray. Fail to offer a full online service, they say, and watch your customers gravitate toward rivals. "You're damned if you do, but you're even more damned if you don't," says one banking analyst.[18]

SUMMARY OF LEARNING OBJECTIVES

1. Identify the responsibilities of a financial manager.

The responsibilities of a financial manager include developing and implementing a firm's financial plan; monitoring a firm's cash flow and deciding how to create or use excess funds; budgeting for current and future expenditures; recommending specific investments; raising capital to finance the enterprise for future growth; and interacting with banks and capital markets.

2. Discuss how financial managers improve a company's cash flow.

Monitoring working capital accounts is one way financial managers improve a company's cash flow. This includes establishing effective accounts receivable credit and collection policies; establishing inventory procedures to maintain enough inventory to fill orders on time at the lowest purchase cost; and investing excess cash so it earns as much interest as possible.

3. Differentiate between a master budget and capital budget.

Master or operating budgets handle all revenues, expenses, and cash flows of the firm. Moreover, they provide guidelines for a firm's total expenditures. By contrast, capital budgets forecast and plan for a firm's capital investments such as buildings and equipment while matching a firm's capital investments with the company's overall long-term goals.

4. Cite three things financial managers must consider when selecting an appropriate funding vehicle.

Finance managers must determine whether the financing is for the short term or the long term. They must minimize the cost of capital by weighing the risk, interest costs, and opportunity costs of different financing alternatives. Finally, they must evaluate the merits of debt versus equity financing in light of their own needs.

5. Identify five common types of debt financing.

Five common types of debt financing are trade credit (paying for products after they are purchased); commercial paper (short-term promissory notes of major corporations); loans (money borrowed from the bank which is secured or unsecured, long-term or short-term); leases (paying for the use of someone else's property over a fixed term); and bonds (issuing corporate certificates to individual investors that obligate the company to repay a certain sum plus interest on a specific date).

6. Explain how consolidation is affecting the banking industry.

Aside from reducing the number of banks, consolidation in the banking industry is blurring the line between the types of financial services offered by banks, securities brokers, and insurance companies in addition to spurring the popularity of community banks. Passage of the 1999 Financial Services Modernization Act, which repealed the Glass-Steagall Act, is fueling a raft of megamergers among banks, insurance companies, and brokerage firms and increasing the competition among these institutions. Meanwhile community banks are stepping in to fill a void created by bank consolidations by focusing on the needs of local customers (generally smaller businesses).

7. Identify four ways the Federal Reserve System influences the U.S. money supply.

The Fed influences the U.S. money supply by changing reserve requirements (the percentage of deposits that banks must set aside), by changing the discount rate (the interest rate it charges on loans to commercial banks and other depository institutions), by carrying out open-market operations (selling and buying government bonds), and by setting selective credit controls (setting the amount of cash investors must pay when purchasing a stock or bond on credit).

8. Identify the advantages of online banking and explain the challenges cyberbanks face in the competitive banking environment.

Internet banking offers customers the convenience of anywhere, anytime services, higher interest rates, and lower transaction fees. Internet-only banks can save significant dollars thanks to lower processing costs and lower real property and payroll costs. Still, cyberbanks face many challenges in the competitive banking environment. They must provide adequate customer service to compensate for the lack of a physical presence (including a personal banker); they must provide more convenient access to ATM networks and be competitive with ATM transaction fees; they must make their Web sites more user friendly; finally, they must find a way to compete with traditional banks who offer similar financial services and more.

KEY TERMS

automated teller machines (ATMs) (463)

budget (456)

capital budgeting (456)

capital investments (456)

capital structure (459)

checks (461)

collateral (459)

commercial paper (459)

compensating balance (459)

cost of capital (458)

credit cards (461)

currency (467)

debit cards (462)

demand deposit (467)

discount rate (458)

electronic funds transfer systems (EFTS) (463)

financial control (456)

financial management (454)

financial plan (454)

lease (460)

leverage (458)

line of credit (459)

long-term financing (457)

M1 (467)

M2 (467)

M3 (467)

marketable securities (455)

money (467)

open-market operations (469)

prime interest rate (prime) (458)

reserve requirement (468)

secured loans (459)

selective credit controls (469)

short-term financing (457)

smart cards (462)

time deposits (467)

trade credit (459)

unsecured loan (459)

TEST YOUR KNOWLEDGE

QUESTIONS FOR REVIEW

1. What is the primary goal of financial management?

2. What types of projects are typically considered in the capital budgeting process?

3. What is the difference between a secured and an unsecured loan?

4. How do credit cards, debit cards, and smart cards work?

5. What is the main function of the Federal Reserve System?

QUESTIONS FOR ANALYSIS

6. Why do companies prepare budgets?

7. Why would a company lease a piece of property instead of purchasing it?

8. How can smaller community banks compete with large commercial banks?

9. What nontraditional locations might a growing community bank choose for its ATMs to better compete with larger banks that operate in the same city?

10. Besides shipping information and credit card information, what types of customer information might smart cards store in their chip that would be useful to e-businesses?

11. What issues regarding privacy of personal information must Citigroup and other financial supermarkets address to protect consumers?

QUESTIONS FOR APPLICATION

12. The financial manager for a small manufacturing firm wants to improve the company's cash flow position. What steps can this person take?

13. Why might a company's board of directors decide to lease a piece of property even though it is more economical to purchase it and finance it with a long-term loan?

14. Which of the four forms of utility discussed in Chapter 12 do electronic banking and Internet stock trading create?

15. How does the money supply affect the economy and inflation? (Hint: Think about the theory of supply and demand discussed in Chapter 1.)

PRACTICE YOUR KNOWLEDGE

SHARPENING YOUR COMMUNICATION SKILLS

The president of your vending machine company wants to expand your $20 million local operation nationwide. To start things rolling, your company will initially require about $50 million. But first management has to decide whether to finance this growth with debt or equity. Review the material in Chapter 4 on "Financing a New Business," the material in Chapter 5 on "Public versus Private Ownership," and the material in this chapter on "Financing the Enterprise." Then write a brief memo to the company president discussing the options the company has for financing its growth. Be sure to highlight the advantages and disadvantages of each option.

HANDLING DIFFICULT SITUATIONS ON THE JOB: BATTLING BESTBANK'S SCAMS

As a recent law school graduate working for the Denver Free Legal Clinic, you help clients resolve all kinds of problems. Today, Angelina Bigelow's story about BestBank has you riled.

Neither BestBank's owner, Edward P. Mattar, nor his associates have been accused of any crimes. But their "virtual bank," which advertised on the Internet, was seized by state regulators after they discovered $134 million in soured loans and only $23 million in BestBank reserves to cover them. One of BestBank's scams was to offer credit cards to people with poor credit histories. Bigelow had signed up but hadn't read the fine print, which said she was also agreeing to join a travel club—with a fee of $498 charged to her new card. An additional $45 fee used up nearly all of the elderly woman's $600 credit limit and put her in serious debt for her modest income level. When she couldn't make her high monthly payments, the bank added interest charges and $20 late fees that put her over the credit limit. Then the bank started adding an additional $20 per month "overlimit fee."

The state's seizure stopped the card billings. However, you've made a few calls and learned that these debts have been bought and new bills might show up again any day.[19] Angelina Bigelow is distraught and doesn't know how to get out of this seemingly endless debt trap. You are determined to help.

1. How can you find out which federal regulators to contact to follow up on BestBank's treatment of its credit card customers?

2. What specific actions will you ask regulators to take to solve Bigelow's problem?

3. What steps will you advise your clients to take to prevent similar credit card problems in the future?

BUILDING YOUR TEAM SKILLS

You and your team are going to build an operating expense budget worksheet for a neighborhood Domino's pizza franchise. Begin by brainstorming a list of expenses that are typical of a franchise/delivery restaurant. One way to do this is to think about the company's process—from making the pizza to delivering it. List the types of expenses and then group your list in categories such as delivery, marketing, manufacturing, financing, and so on. Leave the budget dollar amounts blank. Finally, develop a list of capital investments your company will make over the next three to five years. Compare your budget worksheets with those of the other teams in your class. Which operating and capital expenses did other teams have that your team did not? Which expenses did your team have that other teams omitted? Did all the teams categorize the expenses in a similar manner?

EXPAND YOUR KNOWLEDGE

KEEPING CURRENT USING *THE WALL STREET JOURNAL*

Choose a recent article from *The Wall Street Journal* (print or online editions) that discusses the financing arrangements or strategies of a particular company.

1. What form of financing did the company choose? Did the article indicate why the company selected this form of financing?

2. Who provided the financing for the company? Was this arrangement considered unusual, or was it routine?

3. What does the company intend to do with the arranged financing—purchase equipment or other assets, finance a construction project, finance growth and expansion, or do something else?

DISCOVERING CAREER OPPORTUNITIES

Is a career in branch banking for you? Bankers in local branch offices deal with a wide variety of customers, products, transactions, and inquiries every working day. To get a better idea of what branch bankers do, visit a local bank or a branch where you do business.

1. Talk with a customer service representative or an officer about the kinds of customers this branch serves. Does it handle a high volume of business banking transactions, or is it more geared to consumer banking needs? How does the mix of consumer and business customers affect the branch's staffing and working hours?

2. What banking services are offered by this branch? Does the branch have specialized experts on staff to service these customers? What kind of skills, experience, education, and licenses must these experts have?

3. What kinds of entry-level jobs in this branch are appropriate for your background? What are the advancement opportunities within the branch and within the bank organization? Now that you have a better idea of what branch banking is, how does this career fit with your interests and goals?

EXPLORING THE BEST OF THE WEB

URLs for all Internet exercises are provided at the Web site for this book, www.prenhall.com/mescon. When you log on to the text Web site, select Chapter 17, then select "Student Resources," click on the name of the featured Web site, and follow the detailed navigational directions to complete these exercises.

Plan Ahead, page 460

Start your personal financial planning now by using the tools at the Financenter. Evaluate whether you should pay cash, finance, or refinance major assets.

1. Calculate by how much you will need to increase your monthly payments in order to pay off your outstanding balance in 12 months. If you have no outstanding balance, use these numbers: amount now owed, $3,000; future monthly charges, $300; future monthly payments, $400; annual rate, 18%; annual fee, $50; desired months until pay off, 12.

2. Calculate how large a line of credit you can obtain if the appraised value of your home is $200,000 with a $125,000 mortgage.

3. Calculate whether you should finance or pay cash for your next car. Use either the numbers provided or enter your own numbers.

Take a Field Trip to the Fed, page 466

Visit the Fed to find out what the Board of Governors of the Federal Reserve System does, where the Federal Reserve Banks are located, and what FDIC is all about.

1. Who is the current chairperson of the Federal Reserve System? How is the chairperson appointed?

2. Where are the Federal Reserve Banks located?

3. What does it mean when a bank has a sign that says "Insured by FDIC"?

Tour the U.S. Treasury, page 467

Take a virtual tour of the U.S. Treasury. Discover how money gets into circulation and learn about electronic funds transfer.

1. Roughly how much currency is printed daily? What was the largest currency denomination ever produced?

2. What are some of the benefits of electronic funds transfer?

3. How much U.S. currency is in circulation? What is the life expectancy of a $1 bill?

Explore on Your Own

Review these chapter-related Web sites on your own to learn more about financial management and banking.

1. Follow the steps at 2020 green, www.2020green.com/index.jsp, to learn more about banking, credit, and savings. Be sure to rate your financial knowledge.

2. With over 5,000 definitions and 15,000 links between related terms, InvestorWords is the most comprehensive financial glossary you'll find anywhere. Log on at www.investorwords.com.

3. Learn how to manage your credit cards at Smart Money University, http://university.smartmoney.com/Departments/DebtManagement/CreditCards/. Remember, the key to getting a better credit card deal is figuring out how much a given card really costs you.

A CASE FOR CRITICAL THINKING

■ *Baking Up Millions at Top of the Tree*

Gordon Weinberger became an entrepreneur in his teens. During college, he founded a window washing company, and after college he co-founded a promotions agency. Following a stint in non-profit public relations, Weinberger joined a major Boston advertising agency. Then a pie recipe changed his life. Working from his great-grandmother's recipe, Weinberger baked apple pies that won blue ribbons in a New Hampshire contest two years in a row. These victories aroused his entrepreneurial instinct: Could an award-winning apple pie be his recipe for success?

Researching the pie industry, Weinberger identified a potential niche for fresh-tasting pies, a tiny slice of the market between the well-known brands sold in the freezer case and the store brands sold in the bakery department. Once Weinberger found his niche, he polished up his great-grandmother's recipe, drafted a detailed business plan, and talked with supermarket executives. But he needed money—$100,000 to be exact—to put his plan into action.

RAISING THE DOUGH

So Weinberger took to the phones, calling more than 70 friends, family members, and colleagues who might invest in his Top of the Tree Baking Company. Over the course of several months, he convinced 11 people to invest about $10,000 each—enough to get started. Then he scrounged up additional private financing once his operations got underway.

By the end of 1995, Weinberger's first year in business, Top of the Tree was churning out three-pound pies at the rate of 6,000 a week and had racked up about $1 million in gross sales. But in spite of increasing sales, the company was crumbling under debt. His great-grandmother's apple pie recipe had won him prizes at country fairs, but not profits at grocery counters. In fact, Weinberger's company was losing $1 on each pie sold. So he hatched a capital-raising plan that was outrageous, even by his standards.

SERVING PIE A LA ROAD

Weinberger turned to his primary marketing vehicle, a 44-foot refurbished school bus painted in a "piecadelic" motif. He took the "pie bus" on the road for a formal public offering to raise $1 million from investors in exchange for a piece of his pie company. Rather than wrestling with the big-league red tape associated with an initial public offering, Weinberger opted for private placement of his stock. His strategy: to park in front of some of the nation's finest hotels and hope for the best.

To everyone's amazement, including Weinberger's, it worked. He raised $950,000 in pledges to be delivered in four months. The remaining $50,000 to complete the offering was scrounged from friends and relatives.

Then disaster struck: A $300,000 investor reneged on his pledge. According to New Hampshire law, the entire private-placement offering was now void, and Weinberger could not collect a cent from anyone. In debt for $800,000, Weinberger needed a new recipe for success.

TRIMMING THE EXCESS WEIGHT

To begin with, Weinberger met with his creditors, promising them at least some payment in six months. Next, he closed his small pie factory and outsourced production to a local baker who could replicate his recipe at a lower cost. Finally, he began an exhausting but lucrative daily pie-bus tour—taking his marketing campaign to regional grocers and their customers and conducting in-store tastings and parking lot pie-eating contests. And it worked.

With about $1 million in new sales, Weinberger met with his creditors again. This time he offered them full payment over two to three years, or 50 cents on the dollar that day. Most opted for immediate cash. By reducing the liability to his creditors, Gordon's Top of the Tree Baking Company finally was able to turn a profit.

FOLLOWING THE "PIED" PIPER TO SUCCESS

To keep sales growing, Weinberger and a pie crew continued visiting two or three supermarkets a day. With disco music blasting from loudspeakers, the rangy "Pie Guy" greeted shoppers, handed out samples, and autographed pie boxes. Then the "Pied" Piper led them into the store to purchase Top of the Tree Pies—and anything else the local grocer might be promoting.

With a goal of becoming a $20 million company soon, Weinberger, will of course need more capital. Still, he's intent on raising the cash without giving up a significant amount of control of the company. "I don't want to give up half the company for $2 million," says Weinberger. The perfect investors, according to Weinberger, would have a lot of money in their wallets but be willing to step back and let him determine the company's course.

CRITICAL THINKING QUESTIONS

1. Why did Weinberger seek private investors instead of applying for a bank loan?

2. Why did Top of the Tree experience financial problems in spite of increasing sales?

3. Why did Weinberger decide to outsource production?

4. Go to Chapter 17 of this text's Web site and click on the hot link to Inc.com. Follow the online instructions to help Weinberger answer this question: What are the six Cs of credit?

VIDEO CASE AND EXERCISES

■ *IHOP Cooks Up Long-Term Financing*

SYNOPSIS

The International House of Pancakes (www.ihop.com), based in Glendale, California, can flip more pancakes and fry more hash browns these days, thanks to long-term financing arrangements. IHOP has 700 franchised family-style restaurants around the world, serving up more than 600,000 pancakes every day. When management bought the company from its previous owners in 1987, the transaction resulted in heavy debt. By 1991, CFO Frederick Silny and CEO Richard Herzer were looking for ways to finance more aggressive growth without adding to the debt burden. They could have refinanced the debt with new lenders at lower interest rates, or they could have waited for a better financial environment in which to go public. In the end, they decided on an IPO because restaurant stocks were popular and IHOP had high name recognition among potential investors.

EXERCISES

Analysis

1. Why would IHOP and other companies choose to sell stock to the public rather than finance growth through profits from current sales?

2. Beyond the initial rush of enthusiasm during the IPO, why would consumers who frequent IHOP restaurants maintain their investment in its stock?

3. Would you invest in a company that allows you little say in its decisions and operations?

4. Do you think investing in IHOP stock is more or less risky than putting your money into a time deposit?

5. How do changes in the prime interest rate affect IHOP's cost of capital?

Application

How did IHOP's IPO affect its capital structure?

Decision

Imagine that IHOP has excess cash for two weeks every month. How would you recommend that the company invest that money?

Communication

Assume that you own a restaurant that is about to sell shares to the public (use a real restaurant if you want). Write a letter to patrons explaining why you think this is a good investment for them.

Integration

Review the section on data security in Chapter 8. Why is this a vital issue for companies that use computerized financial management systems?

Ethics

No stock is a guaranteed investment, but does a publicly held company have an ethical obligation to protect its shareholders against possible losses?

Debate

If IHOP had not gone public in 1991, would it be a good move to launch an IPO today? Choose one side of this debate topic and outline two arguments to support your position.

Teamwork

Assume that IHOP brought in $10 million by selling more shares of stock. The firm plans to spend that money on new advertising and development of new menu items over the next 12 to 15 months. In a team of three students, decide how the company should invest the money.

Online Research

Using Internet sources, find out IHOP's ticker symbol and trace the progress of the stock's price over the past three months. What was the stock's highest and lowest closing price during that period? What was the closing price yesterday? See Component Chapter A, Exhibit A.1, for search engines to use in doing your research.

MYPHLIP COMPANION WEB SITE

Learning Interactively

Visit the myPHLIP Web site at www.prenhall.com/mescon. For Chapter 17, take advantage of the interactive "Study Guide" to test your chapter knowledge. Get instant feedback on whether you need additional studying. Read the "Current Events" articles to get the latest on chapter topics, and complete the exercises as specified by your instructor. Expand your learning with a visit to the "Research Area." There you will find a wealth of information you can use to complete your course assignments.

MASTERING BUSINESS ESSENTIALS

Go to the "Raising Capital" episode on the Mastering Business Essentials interactive, video-enhanced CD-ROM. Help the management team at CanGo (an e-business start-up) debate the advantages and disadvantages of financing alternatives. Help the team prepare for its meeting with investment bankers.

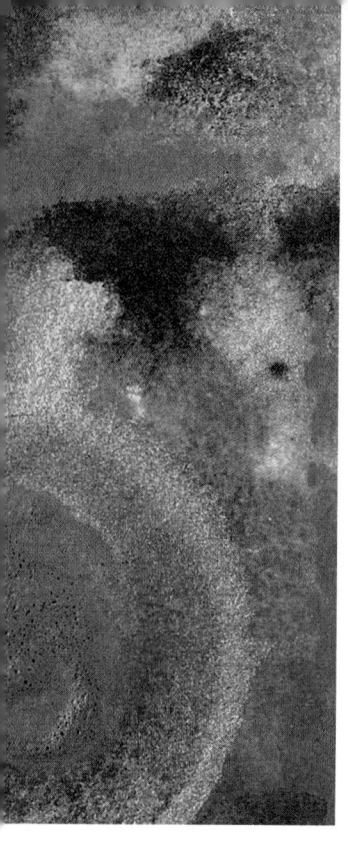

18

SECURITIES

LEARNING OBJECTIVES

After studying this chapter, you will be able to

1. Differentiate among a stock's par value, its market value, and its book value

2. Explain the safety and tax advantages of investing in U.S. government securities

3. Name five criteria to be considered when making investment decisions

4. Explain what mutual funds are and describe their main benefits

5. Describe the two types of securities exchanges

6. Identify two major challenges traditional securities exchanges are facing

7. Explain how government regulation of securities trading tries to protect investors

@ 8. List six major problems customers are experiencing when they trade online and identify the steps customers should take to resolve their differences with online securities brokers

To capture a large share of the fast-growing online trade market, E*Trade's CEO, Christos Cotsakos, has to juggle a variety of challenges.

TRICKS OF E*TRADE
www.etrade.com

In the early 1980s, Bill Porter was running a thriving business, providing Charles Schwab and other brokerage firms with electronic stock quotes and trading services. A physicist and inventor, Porter began to wonder why he and other individual investors had to pay brokers hundreds of dollars each time they bought or sold stocks, bonds, and mutual funds. Although personal computing was still in its infancy, he envisioned a more efficient, more direct method of placing trades directly from his PC keyboard. By 1992 Porter had translated his vision into E*Trade Securities, an all-electronic brokerage firm accessed through America Online and CompuServe. But E*Trade did not really take off until 1996, when the fledgling brokerage firm launched its multifaceted Web site, making online securities trading accessible and affordable for all Internet users.

E*Trade was at the forefront of a growing movement toward online investing, fueled in part by a healthy U.S. economy and by investors eager to participate in U.S. securities markets that were trending upward and setting record highs. Forecasts indicated that millions of investors would soon be trading online, and Porter wanted E*Trade to capture a large share of this fast-growing market.

Unlike traditional full-service brokers, E*Trade did not offer extensive research reports written by experts who investigated specific stocks and bonds in detail. And it did not offer the constant hand-holding of a personal broker. What it did offer was a quick, easy, and inexpensive way to buy and sell securities over the Internet. Investors who knew exactly what they wanted could simply go to the E*Trade Web site, then point and click to make trades—paying a fraction of the commissions charged by full-service brokers.

In 1996, to build E*Trade into a world-class brokerage firm, Porter brought in Christos Cotsakos, a former executive with Federal Express and A.C. Nielsen. Under Cotsakos's leadership, the company launched an aggressive multimillion-dollar ad campaign, using the tagline "Someday we'll all invest this way," and enhanced E*Trade's services by offering customers personalized Web screens, online securities research, and more. In just a few years, E*Trade became an online investing powerhouse with 1.9 million accounts. But it wasn't long before Schwab, TD Waterhouse, Merrill Lynch, and Morgan Stanley Dean Witter copied E*Trade's e-broker strategy.

So to keep a competitive edge, Cotsakos changed E*Trade's course. While the big guys were busy adding the clicks, E*Trade got physical. In 2000 E*Trade purchased thousands of ATMs from Credit Capture Services, opened the first of 200 planned bricks-and-mortar outlets called E*Trade Zone in a SuperTarget discount store, and announced plans to open an old-fashioned 30,000-square-foot New York retail outlet—one with helpful salesclerks, kiosks, and reams of marketing material.

"Pushing our brand into the real world is the next evolution for E*Trade," explains one E*Trade officer. And Cotsakos plans on doing just that by turning E*Trade into a financial supermarket—a place where people can handle all their personal financial needs. Still, big questions linger. With more competitors and financial-services companies saying, "If you want cheaper trading you can get it from us," Cotsakos will have to decide whether E*Trade should go it alone or merge with the kind of old-line financial services that have been the target of E*Trade's humorous ads.[1]

■ TYPES OF SECURITIES INVESTMENTS

securities
Instruments such as stocks, bonds, options, futures, and commodities

As Christos Cotsakos knows, **securities**—stocks, bonds, options, futures, commodities, and other investments—are much in the news these days. Look at the business section of any newspaper or magazine, and you'll read about a corporation selling stocks or bonds to finance operations or expansion. In the same way, governments and municipalities issue bonds to raise money for building or public expenses—from national defense to road improvements. These securities are traded in organized markets where investors (individuals and institutions) can buy and sell them to meet their investment goals.

Stocks

LEARNING OBJECTIVE 1

Differentiate among a stock's par value, its market value, and its book value

As you saw in Chapter 5, a share of stock represents ownership in a corporation; it is evidenced by a stock certificate. If you are a shareholder—someone who owns stock—you may vote on important issues but you have no say in day-to-day business activities. You and other shareholders have the advantage of limited liability if the corporation gets into trouble. At the same time, as part owners, you share in the fortunes of the business and are eligible to receive dividends as long as you hold the stock.

par value
Arbitrary value assigned to a stock that is shown on the stock certificate

Stock certificates issued to shareholders often include a **par value,** a dollar value assigned to the stock primarily for bookkeeping purposes and (for certain kinds of stock) for use in calculating dividends. Don't confuse par value with a stock's *market value,* the price at which a share currently sells, or its *book value,* the amount of net assets of a corporation represented by one share of common stock.

authorized stock
Shares that a corporation's board of directors has decided to sell eventually

The number of stock shares a company sells depends on the amount of equity capital the company will require and on the price of each share it sells. A corporation's board of directors sets a maximum number of shares into which the business can be divided. In theory, all these shares—called **authorized stock**—may be sold at once. In practice, however, the company sells only a part of its authorized stock. The part sold and held by shareholders is called **issued stock;** the unsold portion is called **unissued stock.** Common stock is one of two classes of stock an investor can buy; the other is preferred stock.

issued stock
Authorized shares that have been released to the market

unissued stock
Authorized shares that are to be released in the future

Common Stock Most investors buy common stock, which represents an ownership interest in a publicly traded corporation. As discussed in Chapter 5, shareholders of this class of stock vote to elect the company's board of directors, vote on other important corporate issues, and receive dividends—payments from the company's profits. In addition, they stand to make a profit if the stock price goes up and they sell their shares for more than the purchase price. The reverse is also true: shareholders of common stock can lose money if the market price drops and they sell the stock for less than they paid for it.

stock split
Increase in the number of shares of ownership that each stock certificate represents

From time to time a company may announce a **stock split,** in which it increases the number of shares that each stock certificate represents while proportionately lowering the value of each share. Companies generally use a stock split to make the share price more affordable. For instance, if a company with 1 million shares outstanding and a stock price of $50 per share announces a two-for-one split, it is doubling the number of shares. After the split, the company will have 2 million shares outstanding, and each original share will become two shares worth $25 each.

A special type of common stock is *tracking stock,* shares linked to the performance of a specific business unit of a public corporation. This type of stock allows a company to

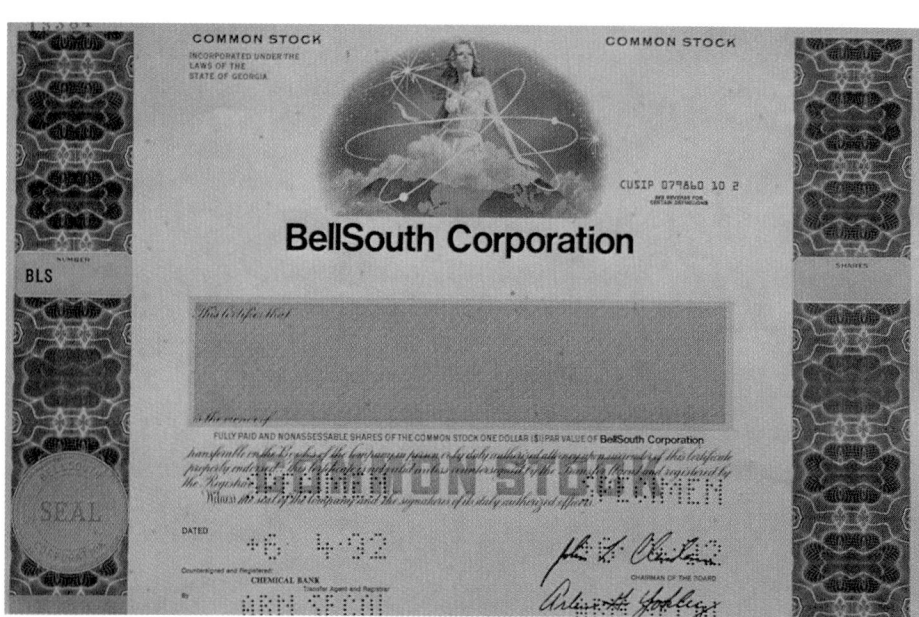

Stock certificates represent a share of ownership of a company.

wring top market value from an attractive business unit as if it were an independent company. From the investor's perspective, tracking stock is a convenient way to own part of this business unit while taking advantage of the parent's financial stability. But tracking stocks are risky, as "Are Tracking Stocks on Track?" points out. Conservative investors often prefer **blue-chip stock,** stock in a corporation such as General Electric that is well established and has a long record of solid earnings and dividends.

blue-chip stock
Equity issued by large, well-established companies with consistent records of stock price increases and dividend payments

Preferred Stock Investors who own preferred stock, the second major class of stock, enjoy higher dividends and a better claim (after creditors) on assets if the corporation fails. The amount of the dividend on preferred stock is printed on the stock certificate and set when the stock is first issued. If interest rates fluctuate, the market price of preferred stock will go up or down to adjust for the difference between the market interest rate and the stock's dividend.

Preferred stock often comes with special privileges. *Convertible preferred stock* can be exchanged, if the shareholder chooses, for a certain number of shares of common stock issued by the company. *Cumulative preferred stock* has an additional advantage: If the issuing company stops paying dividends for any reason, the dividends on these shares will be held (accumulate) until preferred shareholders have been paid in full—before common stockholders are paid.

bond
Method of funding in which the issuer borrows from an investor and provides a written promise to make regular interest payments and repay the borrowed amount in the future

Bonds

Unlike stock, which gives the investor an ownership stake in the corporation, bonds are debt financing. (See Chapter 17 for a detailed discussion of debt versus equity financing.) A **bond** is a

THINKING ABOUT ETHICS

ARE TRACKING STOCKS ON TRACK?

Tracking stocks are the latest rage on Wall Street. The oddball securities are a special class of common stock whose value is tied to the performance of a specific subsidiary, division, product, or business unit—usually the fastest-growing one. In other words, they "track" the performance of that specific unit. But there's a twist. Owners of tracking stocks have an equity claim on the cash flow of the tracked entity, but they do not legally own the assets of that business.

Tracking stocks have been issued by such companies as AT&T, General Motors, DuPont, Disney, Ziff-Davis, and many more for the past 15 years. But it's only in the past couple of years that they have gotten hot. One reason: they let the market judge the worth of a fast-growing part of a company independent of its slower-growing lines of business. With investors willing to pay more for growing concerns, tracking stocks can make it easier and more economical for companies to raise capital. Of course, instead of issuing a tracking stock, a company could simply spin off the line of business into a separate company. But keeping companies together allows management to take advantage of any synergies and efficiencies.

In spite of these alleged benefits, managing two classes of stock with one set of assets gives rise to hosts of conflicts for corporate managers and directors. Why?

Because you have one servant, the board, serving two or more masters (the separate shareholders). For instance, arguments can arise over how to allocate company expenses or available resources. In other words, should the company fund an operating system that specifically benefits the old shareholders or should it fund, say, an Internet portal that specifically benefits the new shareholders? Moreover, if the board decides that each business should stand on its own, then the fast-growing, but perhaps money-losing business (the tracking business) will starve. But if the board funds the tracking business with profits from the larger company, common shareholders could justifiably cry foul. And if one part of the company can't pay back its loans, the other part is on the hook.

Good or bad, the reality of investing in tracking stocks is that its shareholders have no rights. So even though Wall Street continues to peddle tracking stocks, investigate before you invest. After all, tracking stocks may wind up being just another investing fad.

■ QUESTIONS FOR CRITICAL THINKING

1. Why do tracking stocks pose an ethical dilemma for the issuing company's board of directors?

2. Why do companies issue tracking stocks? Why do investors purchase them?

method of raising money in which the issuing organization borrows from an investor and issues a written pledge to make regular interest payments and then repay the borrowed amount later. When you invest in this type of security, you are lending money to the company, municipality, or government agency that issued the bond. Bonds are usually issued in multiples of $1,000, such as $5,000, $10,000 and $50,000. Also like stocks, bonds are evidenced by a certificate, which shows the issuer's name, the amount borrowed (the **principal**), the date this principal amount will be repaid, and the annual interest rate investors receive.

principal
Amount of a debt, excluding any interest

The interest is stated in terms of an annual percentage rate but is usually paid at 6-month intervals. For example, the holder of a $1,000 bond that pays 8 percent interest due January 15 and July 15 could expect to receive $40 on each of those dates. A look at the financial section of any newspaper will show that some corporations sell new bonds at an interest rate two or three percentage points higher than that offered by other companies. Yet the terms of the bonds seem similar. Why? Because bonds are not guaranteed investments. The variations in interest rates reflect the degree of risk associated with the bond, which is closely tied to the financial stability of the issuing company. Agencies such as Standard & Poor's (S&P) and Moody's rate bonds on the basis of the issuers' financial strength. Exhibit 18.1 shows that the safest corporate bonds are rated AAA (S&P) and Aaa (Moody's). Low-rated bonds, known as *junk bonds,* pay higher interest rates to compensate investors for the higher risk.

Corporate Bonds *Corporate bonds*—those issued by companies—are big business. The New York Stock Exchange lists more corporate bonds than stocks, and the market value of all outstanding corporate bonds exceeds $2 trillion.[2]

secured bonds
Bonds backed by specific assets

debentures
Corporate bonds backed only by the reputation of the issuer

convertible bonds
Corporate bonds that can be exchanged at the owner's discretion into common stock of the issuing company

Corporate bonds are issued in a variety of types. **Secured bonds** are backed by company-owned property (such as airplanes or plant equipment) that will pass to the bondholders if the issuer does not repay the amount borrowed. *Mortgage bonds,* one type of secured bond, are backed by real property owned by the issuing corporation. **Debentures** are unsecured bonds, backed only by the corporation's promise to pay. Because debentures are riskier than other types of bonds, investors who buy these bonds receive higher interest rates. **Convertible bonds** can be exchanged at the investor's option for a certain number of shares of the corporation's common stock. Because of this feature, convertible bonds generally pay lower interest rates.

U.S. Government Securities and Municipal Bonds Just as corporations raise money by issuing bonds, so too do federal, state, city, and local governments and agencies. As an investor, you can buy a va-

EXHIBIT 18.1

CORPORATE BOND RATINGS

Standard & Poor's (S&P) and Moody's Investors Service are two companies that rate the safety of corporate bonds. When its bonds receive a low rating, a company must pay a higher interest rate to compensate investors for the higher risk.

S&P	INTERPRETATION	MOODY'S	INTERPRETATION
AAA	Highest rating	Aaa	Prime quality
AA	Very strong capacity to pay	Aa	High grade
A	Strong capacity to pay; somewhat susceptible to changing business conditions	A	Upper-medium grade
BBB	More susceptible than A rated bonds	Baa	Medium grade
BB	Somewhat speculative	Ba	Somewhat speculative
B	Speculative	B	Speculative
CCC	Vulnerable to nonpayment	Caa	Poor standing; may be in default
CC	Highly vulnerable to nonpayment	Ca	Highly speculative; often in default
C	Bankruptcy petition filed or similar action taken	C	Lowest rated; extremely poor chance of ever attaining real investment standing
D	In default		

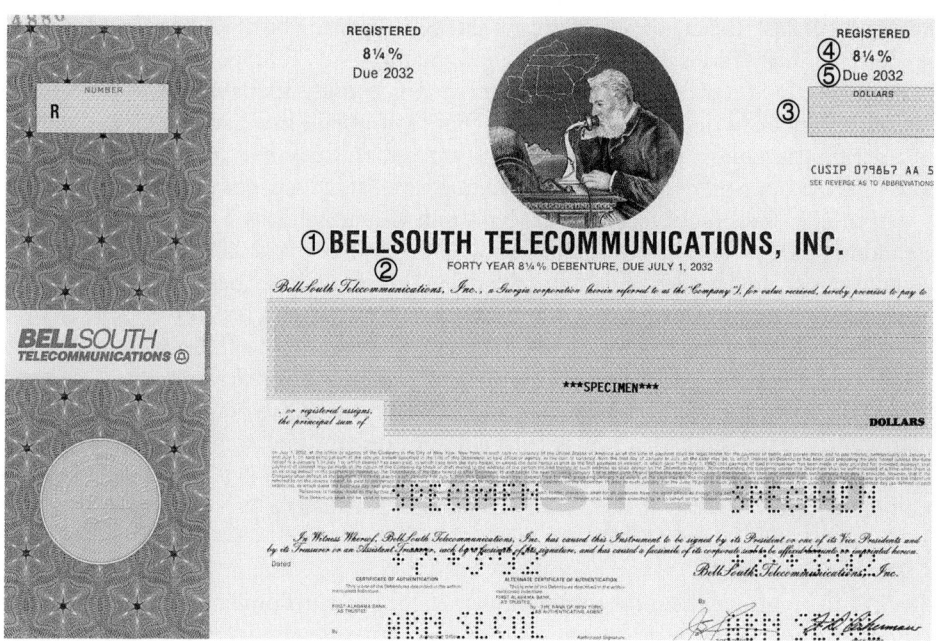

Bell South Telecommunications Bond Certificate. (1) name of corporation issuing bond; (2) type of bond (debenture); (3) face value of the bond; (4) annual interest rate (8.25%); (5) maturity date (due 2032).

riety of U.S. government securities, including three types of bonds issued by the U.S. Treasury, U.S. savings bonds, and bonds issued by various U.S. municipalities.

Treasury bills (also referred to as T-bills) are short-term U.S. government bonds that are repaid in less than one year. Treasury bills are sold at a discount and redeemed at face value. The difference between the purchase price and the redemption price is, in effect, the interest earned for the time periods. **Treasury notes** are intermediate-term U.S. government bonds that are repaid from 1 to 10 years after they were initially issued. **Treasury bonds** are long-term U.S. government bonds that are repaid more than 10 years after they were initially issued. In total, investors worldwide hold about $3.5 trillion in these three types of securities. Both treasury notes and treasury bonds pay a fixed amount of interest twice a year. But in general, U.S. government securities pay lower interest than corporate bonds because they are considered safer: There is very little risk that the government will fail to repay bondholders as promised. Another benefit is that investors pay no state or local income tax on interest earned on these bonds. Also, these bonds can easily be bought or sold through the Treasury or in organized securities markets.

A traditional choice for many individual investors, **U.S. savings bonds** are issued by the U.S. government in amounts ranging from $50 to $10,000. Investors who buy Series EE savings bonds pay just 50 percent of the stated value and receive the full face amount in as little as 17 years (the difference being earned interest). Once the bond's face value equals its redemption value, the bond continues to earn interest, but only until 30 years after the bonds were issued (the bond's final maturity date). Other savings bonds are Series HH, which can be bought only by exchanging Series EE bonds, and Series I, which pay interest indexed to the inflation rate.

Municipal bonds (often called *munis*) are issued by states, cities, and special government agencies to raise money for public services such as building schools, highways, and airports. Investors can buy two types of municipal bonds: general obligation bonds and revenue bonds. A **general obligation bond** is a municipal bond backed by the taxing power of the issuing government. When interest payments come due, the issuer makes payments out of its tax receipts. In contrast, a **revenue bond** is a municipal bond backed by the money to be generated by the project being financed. As an example, revenue bonds issued by a city airport are paid from revenues raised by the airport's operation. To encourage investment, the federal government doesn't tax the interest that investors receive from municipal bonds. Also exempt from state income tax is the interest earned on municipal bonds that are issued by the governments within the taxpayer's home state. However, **capital gains**—the return investors get from selling a security for more than its purchase price—are taxed at both the federal and state levels.

LEARNING OBJECTIVE 2

Explain the safety and tax advantages of investing in U.S. government securities

Treasury bills
Short-term debt issued by the federal government; also referred to as *T-bills*

Treasury notes
Debt securities issued by the federal government that mature within 1 to 10 years

Treasury bonds
Debt securities issued by the federal government that mature in 10 to 30 years

U.S. savings bonds
Debt instruments sold by the federal government in small denominations

municipal bonds
Debt issued by a state or a local agency; interest earned on municipal bonds is exempt from federal income tax and from taxes in the issuing jurisdiction

general obligation bond
Municipal bonds backed by the issuing agency's general taxing authority

revenue bond
Municipal bonds backed by revenue generated from the projects financed with the bonds

capital gains
Difference between the price at which a financial asset is sold and its original cost (assuming the price has gone up)

Retirement of Debt Issuers of bonds must eventually repay the borrowed amount to their bondholders. Normally, this is done when the bonds mature—say, 10, 15, or 20 years after the bond is issued. The cost of retiring the debt can be staggering because bonds are generally issued in large quantities—perhaps thousands of individual bonds in a single issue. To ease the cash flow burden of redeeming its bonds all at once, a company sometimes issues *serial bonds,* which mature at various times, as opposed to *term bonds,* which mature all at the same time.

Another way of relieving the financial strain of retiring many bonds all at once is to set up a **sinking fund.** When a corporation issues a bond payable by a sinking fund, it must set aside a certain sum of money each year to pay the debt. This money may be used to retire a few bonds each year, or it may be set aside to accumulate until the issue matures.

With most bond issues, a corporation retains the right to pay off the bonds before maturity. Bonds containing this provision are known as *callable bonds,* or *redeemable bonds.* If a company issues bonds when interest rates are high and interest rates fall later on, it may want to pay off its high-interest bonds and sell a new issue at a lower rate. However, this feature carries a price tag: Investors must be offered a higher interest rate to encourage them to buy callable bonds. The portion of the percentage rate that is above market rates is actually a "call premium."

Other Investments

Stocks and bonds are the most common marketable securities available for investors. However, other securities have been developed. For the most part, options, financial futures, commodities, and their variations are used by money managers and savvy traders. In recent years, some of these securities, particularly options, have been used more by individual investors.

Options and Financial Futures As Chapter 11 points out, a stock option is the purchased right—but not the obligation—to buy or sell a specified number of shares of a stock at a predetermined price during a specified period. Options can be used for wild speculation, or they can be used to **hedge** your positions—that is, partially protect against the risk of a sudden loss. By trading options, the investor doesn't have to own shares of stock in a company—only an option to buy or sell those shares. Investors who trade stock options are betting that the price of the stock will either rise or fall. The cost of buying an option on shares of stock is only the premium paid to the seller, or the price of the option.

All options fall into two broad categories: *puts* and *calls.* Exhibit 18.2 explains the rights acquired with each type of option. **Financial futures** are similar to options, but they are legally binding contracts to buy or sell a financial instrument (stocks, Treasury bonds, foreign currencies) for a set price at a future date.

Commodities For the investor who is comfortable with risky investments, nothing compares with speculating in **commodities**—raw materials and agricultural products, such as petroleum, gold, coffee beans, pork bellies, beef, and coconut oil. Commodities markets originally sprang up as a convenience for buyers and sellers interested in trading the actual commodities. A manufacturer of breakfast cereals, for example, must buy wheat, rye, oats, and sugar from hundreds of farmers. The easiest way to arrange these transactions is to meet in a forum where many buyers and sellers

Margin glossary

sinking fund
Account into which a company makes annual payments for use in redeeming its bonds in the future

hedge
To make an investment that protects the investor from suffering loss on another investment

financial futures
Legally binding agreements to buy or sell financial instruments at a future date

commodities
Raw materials used in producing other goods

EXHIBIT 18.2

OPTIONS

All options fall into two broad categories: puts and calls.

RIGHT	BUYER'S BELIEF	SELLER'S BELIEF
CALL OPTION		
The right to buy the stock at a fixed price until the expiration date.	Buyer believes price of underlying stock will increase. Buyer can buy stock at a set price and sell it at higher price for a capital gain.	Seller believes price of underlying stock will decline and that the option will not be exercised. Seller earns a premium.
PUT OPTION		
The right to sell the stock at a fixed price until the expiration date.	Buyer believes price of underlying stock will decline and wants to lock in a fixed profit. Buyer usually already owns shares of underlying stock.	Seller believes price of underlying stock will rise and that the option will not be exercised. Seller earns a premium.

come to trade. Because the commodities are too bulky to bring to the marketplace, the traders buy and sell contracts for delivery of a given amount of these raw materials at a given time.

Trading contracts for immediate delivery of a commodity is called *spot trading*, or *cash trading*. Most commodity trading is for future delivery, usually months in advance, sometimes a year or more; this is called *trading commodities futures*. The original purpose of futures trading was to allow producers and consumers of commodities to hedge their position, or protect themselves against violent price swings. For example, say you're a cattle rancher in Montana and each month you purchase 20,000 bushels of feed corn. A big rise in corn prices resulting from a flood in the Midwest could ruin you. To hedge against such risk, you purchase futures contracts guaranteeing you 20,000 bushels of corn at a given price when you need them at a later date. Now you know what you'll have to pay. But for every hedger, there must be a speculator—a person willing to take on the risk the hedger wants to shed. The per-

At the Chicago Mercantile Exchange (CME) orders stream in from customers trading futures and options from all over the world. Each CME trader acts as buyer and seller, communicating with hand signals and by shouting bids to buy and offers to sell.

son on the other end of your corn trade probably has no business interest in corn or cattle; the speculator simply wants to gamble on buying an offsetting corn contract at a lower price and thus make a profit on the deal.[3] But such speculation is risky—even seasoned veterans have been known to lose literally millions of dollars within a few days.

INVESTORS AND INVESTING

Whether you are a corporation or an individual, investing means putting your money to work to earn more money. Done wisely, it can help you meet your financial goals. But investing means you have to make decisions about how much you want to invest and where to invest it. To choose wisely, you need to know what options you have and what risks they entail.

Institutional and Private Investors

Two types of investors buy and sell marketable securities (investments that can easily be converted to cash): institutions and individuals. **Institutional investors**—such as pension funds, insurance companies, investment companies, banks, and colleges and universities—dominate U.S. securities markets. Institutional investors buy and sell securities in large quantities, often in blocks of at least 10,000 shares per transaction. Because institutions have such large pools of money to work with, their investment decisions have a major impact on the marketability of a company's shares as well as the overall behavior of the securities markets.

institutional investors
Companies that invest money entrusted to them by others

Investment Objectives

Many investors seek the highest **yield** or return to supplement their income. Yield on a stock is calculated by dividing the stock's dividends by its annualized market price. Some investors want to make a large profit in a short period of time. Others may be looking for a long-term steady return to fund retirement activities or provide money to send their children to college. In general, people make investment decisions on the basis of five criteria: *income, growth, safety, liquidity,* and *tax consequences.*

If an investor wants a steady, reasonably predictable flow of cash, he or she will seek an investment that provides fixed or dividend income. Fixed income investments include certificates of deposit, government securities, corporate bonds, and preferred stocks. A retired person wanting to supplement Social Security or pension benefits would be a customer for this type of investment.

Many investors are concerned with wealth accumulation, or growth. Their objective is to maximize capital gains. **Growth stocks** are issued by younger and smaller companies such as

yield
Income received from securities, calculated by dividing dividend or interest income by market price

LEARNING
OBJECTIVE   3

Name five criteria to be considered when making investment decisions

growth stocks
Equities issued by small companies with unproven products or services

E*Trade that have strong growth potential. These companies normally pay no dividends because they reinvest earnings in the company to expand operations. High-growth stocks attract a breed of investors who buy stocks with rapidly accelerating earnings and sell them on the tiniest of disappointments over a company's prospects. For this reason, they are considered the most *volatile* in the market—that is, their stock prices tend to rise more quickly, but they can fall just as quickly.

speculators
Investors who purchase securities in anticipation of making large profits quickly

Safety is another concern. Generally, the higher the potential for income or growth, the greater the risk of the investment. **Speculators** are investors who accept high risks in order to realize large capital gains. Of course, every investor must make some kind of trade-off. This is true for all investments. Government bonds are safer than corporate bonds, which are safer than common stocks, which are safer than futures contracts, which are safer than commodities.

Keep in mind that before you get too caught up in focusing on your own assessment of a specific security, you need to understand what other investors are thinking. You may see an abundance of value, or substantial growth potential, but if other investors don't share your view, your insights won't do you much good. The market is a voting machine, whereon countless individuals register choices—sometimes based on reason and sometimes based on emotion.[4]

Two additional investment objectives you should consider when selecting investments are liquidity and tax consequences. Liquidity is the measure of how quickly an investor can change an investment into cash. For example, common stock is more liquid than real estate; most financial assets can be changed into cash within a day. Some, like certificates of deposit, can be cashed in before maturity, but only after paying a penalty. All investors must consider the tax consequences of their decisions. Historically, dividend and interest income have been taxed heavily, and capital gains have been taxed relatively lightly. Also, as stated earlier in the discussion of municipal bonds, the income from most state and local municipal bonds is exempt from federal income tax.

Investment Portfolio

investment portfolios
Assortment of investment instruments

No single investment instrument will provide income, growth, and a high degree of safety. For this reason, all investors—whether institutions or individuals—build **investment portfolios,** or collections of various types of investments. Money managers and financial advisers are often asked to determine which investments should be in an investor's portfolio and to buy and sell securities and maintain the client's portfolio. Sometimes they must structure a portfolio to provide a desired **rate of return,** the percentage of gain or interest yield on investments.

rate of return
Percentage increase in the value of an investment

asset allocation
Method of shifting investments within a portfolio to adapt them to the current investment environment

Asset Allocation and Diversification Managing a portfolio to gain the highest rates of return while reducing risk as much as possible is known as **asset allocation.** A portion of the portfolio might be devoted to cash instruments such as money-market mutual funds, a portion to income instruments such as government and corporate bonds, and a portion to equities (mainly common stock). The money manager then determines how much each portion should be, on the basis of economic and market conditions—not an easy task. If the economy is booming and the stock market is performing well, the money manager might take advantage of the good environment by shifting 75 percent of the total portfolio into stocks, 20 percent into bonds, and 5 percent into cash. If the economy turns bad, the stock market heads downward, and inflation heats up, the

Best of the Web Best of the Web Best of

INVEST WISELY, DON'T BE A FOOL

Here's a fun securities Web site you can fool around at for a while. Visit the Motley Fool and don't be afraid to ask a foolish investment question or two. Roll up your sleeves and do a little work on your own. Discover the strategies, ideas, and information needed to make investment decisions at Fool's School. Learn the steps to investing foolishly and how to value stocks, plus much more. Take a journey through the balance sheet and find out why cash is king.

www.fool.com

money manager might readjust the portfolio and invest 30 percent in stocks, 40 percent in short-term government securities, and 30 percent in cash. This adjustment helps protect the value of the portfolio during poor investment conditions.[5]

Another major concern for these managers is **diversification**—reducing the risk of loss in a client's total portfolio by investing funds in several different securities so that a loss experienced by any one will not hurt the entire portfolio. One way to diversify is by investing in securities from unrelated industries and a variety of countries. Another way is by allocating your assets among different investment types. Both of these goals can be accomplished by investing in mutual funds.

diversification
Assembling investment portfolios in such a way that a loss in one investment won't cripple the value of the entire portfolio

Mutual Funds **Mutual funds** are financial organizations that pool money from many investors to buy a diversified mix of stocks, bonds, or other securities. These funds are particularly well suited for investors who wish to spread a fixed amount of money over a variety of investments and do not have the time or experience to search out and manage investment opportunities. *No-load* funds charge no fee to buy or sell shares, whereas *load funds* charge investors a commission to buy or sell shares. The most common types of loads are front end (assessed when you purchase the fund) and back end (assessed when you sell the fund).

Investment companies offer two types of mutual funds. An *open-end fund* issues additional shares as new investors ask to buy them. In essence, the fund's books never close. The number of shares outstanding changes daily as investors buy new shares or redeem old ones. These shares aren't traded in a separate market. *Closed-end funds,* on the other hand, raise all their money at once by distributing a fixed number of shares that trade much like stocks on major security exchanges. As soon as a certain number of shares are sold, the fund closes its books.

Various mutual funds have different investment priorities. Among the most popular mutual funds are **money-market funds,** which invest in short-term securities and other liquid investments. *Growth funds* invest in stocks of rapidly growing companies. *Income funds* invest in securities that pay high dividends and interest. *Balanced funds* invest in a carefully chosen mix of stocks and bonds. *Sector funds* (also known as specialty or industry funds) invest in companies within a particular industry. *Global funds* invest in foreign and U.S. securities, whereas *international funds* invest strictly in foreign securities. And *index funds* buy stocks in companies included in specific market averages, such as the Standard & Poor's 500. You can buy shares in mutual funds through your broker or directly from the mutual fund company.

LEARNING OBJECTIVE **4**
Explain what mutual funds are and describe their main benefits

mutual funds
Pools of money raised by investment companies and invested in stocks, bonds, or other marketable securities

money-market funds
Mutual funds that invest in short-term securities

■ SECURITIES MARKETS

Where can you purchase bonds, stocks, and other securities? Stocks and bonds are bought and sold in two kinds of marketplaces: primary markets and secondary markets. As discussed in Chapter 5, corporations sell their stock to the public to generate funds for expansion or other purposes. Newly issued shares or initial public offerings (IPOs) are sold in the **primary market.** Once these shares have been issued, subsequent investors can buy and sell them in the organized **secondary market** known as **stock exchanges** (or securities exchanges).

primary market
Market where firms sell new securities issued publicly for the first time

secondary market
Market where subsequent owners trade previously issued shares of stocks and bonds

Securities Exchanges
The New York Stock Exchange (NYSE), also known as the "Big Board," is the world's largest securities exchange. The stocks and bonds of about 2,900 companies, with a combined market value topping $12 trillion, are traded on the exchange's floor.[6] Options, futures, and closed-end funds are also traded there. After the NYSE, some of the largest stock exchanges are located in Tokyo, London, Frankfurt, Paris, Toronto, and Montreal. Many companies list their securities on more than one securities exchange. Thus, NYSE-listed stocks can also be bought and sold at one or more of the U.S. regional exchanges, such as the Pacific or Philadelphia exchanges, or in the *over-the-counter market.*

The **over-the-counter (OTC) market** consists of a network of registered stock and bond representatives who are spread out across the United States—and in some cases around the world. Most use a nationwide computer network owned by the National Association of Securities Dealers (NASD). This network is called **NASDAQ (National Association of Securities Dealers Automated Quotations).** NASDAQ, which now represents a total market value of about $4.8 tril-

stock exchanges
Location where traders buy and sell stocks and bonds

over-the-counter (OTC) market
Network of dealers who trade securities that are not listed on an exchange

NASDAQ (National Association of Securities Dealers Automated Quotations)
National over-the-counter securities trading network

Best of the Web Best of the Web Best of

STOCK UP AT THE NYSE

Tour the New York Stock Exchange. Visit the trading floor and learn about the hectic pace of trading. Find out why having a seat doesn't necessarily mean you'll have a chance to sit down. Listen in on a stock transaction and discover how a stock is bought and sold. Learn how investors are protected and how unusual stock transactions are spotted. Get the latest market information as well as a historical perspective of the Exchange. Don't leave without checking out your favorite stock price. Maybe it's time to sell.
www.nyse.com

lion, is home to many of the world's leading technology firms—Microsoft, Intel, Oracle, and a host of others. This chips-and-code crowd is largely responsible for NASDAQ's huge daily trading volume, which frequently surpasses the NYSE even though the total market value of the shares listed on the NYSE is about three times larger than the total market value of shares listed on the NASDAQ.[7] In 1998 NASD (owners of NASDAQ) acquired the American Stock Exchange (the world's third-largest auction exchange), making NASDAQ an even stronger competitor.[8]

Listing Requirements To have its stock traded on a securities exchange, a publicly held company must become a member of the exchange and meet certain listing requirements related to net income, the number of shares outstanding, and the total market value of all outstanding shares—its *market capitalization*. These listing requirements differ from exchange to exchange but generally increase as one moves from the NASDAQ to the regional exchanges to the larger New York Stock Exchange. For example, as of 2000, the minimum NASDAQ listing requirements were 1.1 million shares outstanding with a minimum bid price of $1.00 and net tangible assets valued at $6 million. By contrast the minimum listing requirements for the American Stock Exchange was 500,000 public shares with a total minimum capitalization value of $3 million, whereas a listing on the NYSE required 1.1 million shares with a total minimum capitalization value of $60 million.[9]

Over the years, NASDAQ has developed into a formidable challenger to the NYSE. In part, this growth came about because NASDAQ's listing requirements were less stringent than those of other exchanges, so younger companies with low market capitalizations could only be traded over the counter. But recently the NYSE loosened its standards a bit to attract fast-growth firms that once gravitated toward NASDAQ.[10]

Trading Systems The process for buying and selling securities varies according to the type of exchange. As Exhibit 18.3 depicts, in an **auction exchange,** such as the New York Stock exchange, all buy and sell orders (and all information concerning companies traded on that exchange) are funneled onto an auction floor. There, buyers and sellers are matched by a **stock specialist,** a broker who occupies a post on the trading floor and conducts all the trades in specific stocks via a central clearinghouse. If buying or selling imbalances occur in that stock, a specialist can halt trading to prevent the price from plunging without adequate cause. Specialists can also sell stock to customers out of their own inventory.[11] In contrast, a **dealer exchange,** such as NASDAQ, has no central marketplace exists for making transactions. Instead, all buy and sell orders are executed through computers by **market makers,** registered stock and bond representatives who sell securities out of their own inventories.

Electronic communication networks (ECNs) use the Internet to link buyers and sellers. Frequently referred to as a virtual stock market or cybermarket, ECNs have no exchange floors, specialists, or market makers. In fact, they are nothing more than computer networks with software programs that match buy and sell orders directly, cutting out the once dominant market makers and specialists. Like other securities marketplaces, ECNs aim to make money by providing a place where stocks can be traded and by collecting commissions on each trade. Most ECNs operate globally and economically—which is why they are becoming increasingly popular. All

LEARNING OBJECTIVE 5

Describe the two types of securities exchanges

auction exchange
Centralized marketplace where securities are traded by specialists on behalf of investors

stock specialist
Intermediary who trades in a particular security on the floor of an auction exchange; "buyer of last resort"

dealer exchange
Decentralized marketplace where securities are bought and sold by dealers out of their own inventories

market makers
Dealers in dealer exchanges who sell securities out of their own inventories so that a market is always available for buyers and sellers

Electronic communication networks (ECNs)
Internet-based networks that match up buy and sell orders without using a middleman

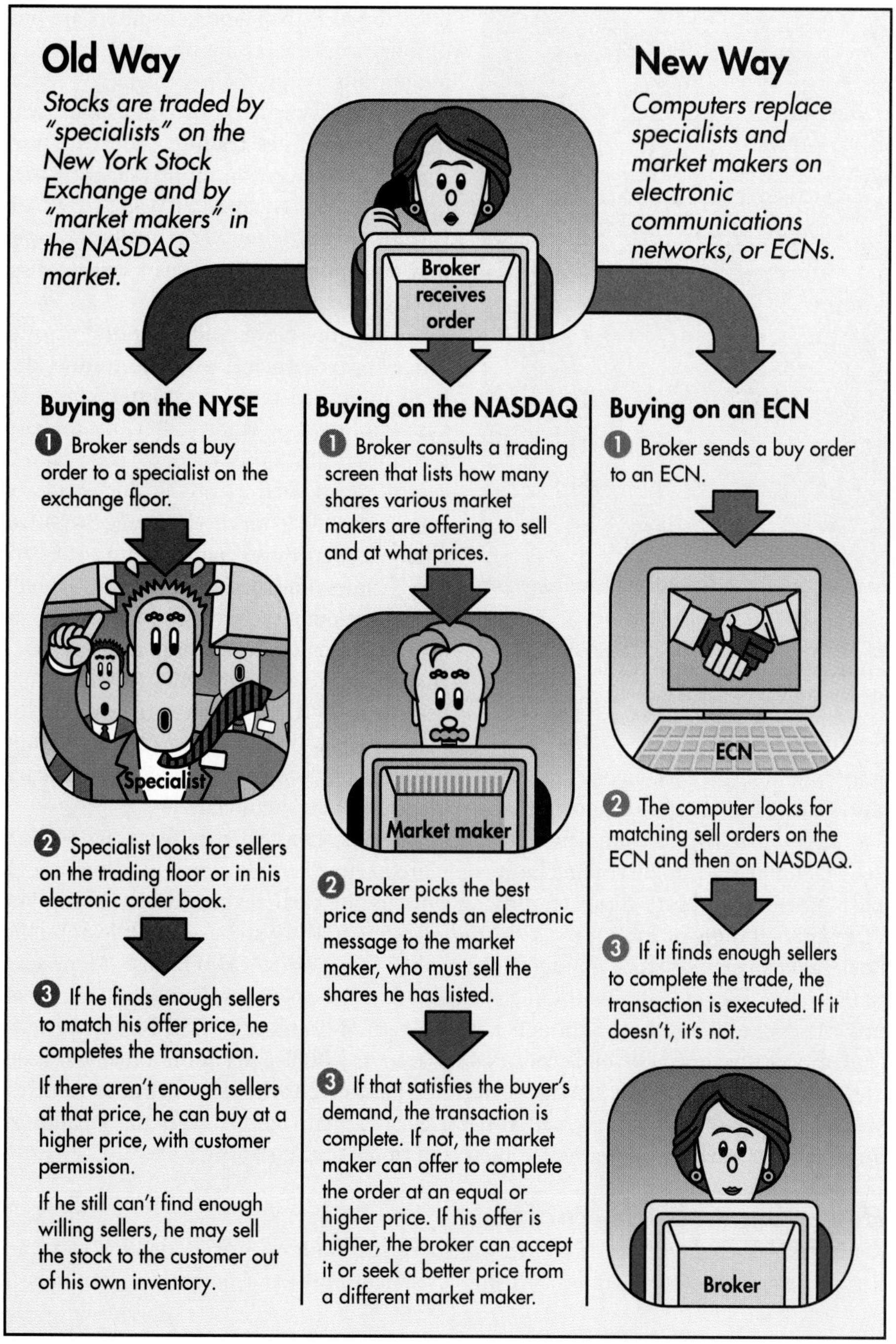

Old Way

Stocks are traded by "specialists" on the New York Stock Exchange and by "market makers" in the NASDAQ market.

New Way

Computers replace specialists and market makers on electronic communications networks, or ECNs.

Broker receives order

Buying on the NYSE

❶ Broker sends a buy order to a specialist on the exchange floor.

Specialist

❷ Specialist looks for sellers on the trading floor or in his electronic order book.

❸ If he finds enough sellers to match his offer price, he completes the transaction.

If there aren't enough sellers at that price, he can buy at a higher price, with customer permission.

If he still can't find enough willing sellers, he may sell the stock to the customer out of his own inventory.

Buying on the NASDAQ

❶ Broker consults a trading screen that lists how many shares various market makers are offering to sell and at what prices.

Market maker

❷ Broker picks the best price and sends an electronic message to the market maker, who must sell the shares he has listed.

❸ If that satisfies the buyer's demand, the transaction is complete. If not, the market maker can offer to complete the order at an equal or higher price. If his offer is higher, the broker can accept it or seek a better price from a different market maker.

Buying on an ECN

❶ Broker sends a buy order to an ECN.

ECN

❷ The computer looks for matching sell orders on the ECN and then on NASDAQ.

❸ If it finds enough sellers to complete the trade, the transaction is executed. If it doesn't, it's not.

Broker

EXHIBIT 18.3

OLD AND NEW WAYS TO BUY STOCKS

Some think that floor trading will become a thing of the past as electronic communication networks become increasingly popular.

told, the two biggest ECNs, Instinet and Island, together with seven others, now control nearly a third of all security trades.[12]

Keep in mind that even though a company's stock is listed on an auction or dealer exchange, its shares may also be traded on a ECN. For instance, many brokerage firms use a combination of auction exchanges, dealer exchanges, and ECNs to execute their trades. In fact, over 38 percent of NASDAQ shares are traded on ECNs, and new rules are letting ECNs take closer aim at the NYSE.[13]

The Changing Nature of Securities Exchanges Until recently, big Wall Street firms have lived with costly stock exchange floors, specialists, and market makers because the system worked well enough. But now these systems are under attack. As the Chairman of the NASD puts it, "the old methods of exchanging stocks no longer meet the needs of the investing consumer."[14] Discount brokers, ECNs, large securities institutions such as Merrill Lynch and Goldman Sachs (which are

LEARNING OBJECTIVE 6

Identify two major challenges traditional securities exchanges are facing

The New York Stock Exchange began under a buttonwood tree on Wall Street in 1792 when a group of brokers agreed to trade with one another. In 1817, the institution was established, with members taking seats in a room to trade stocks at designated times. For a long time, the floor was an important center of power in brokerage firms. Then came the Internet and ECNs. Today the NYSE is under competitive pressure to automate its trading systems.

investing in ECNs), and consumers are pushing traditional securities exchanges to offer electronic trading options within their exchanges.[15] As a result, the NYSE recently rolled out Direct Plus, which automatically executes trading orders for up to 2,099 shares—80 percent of all transactions—in five seconds.[16] Moreover, some of Wall Street's largest brokers are lobbying the SEC to adopt a sweeping new market system that includes a central display of all stock quotes.[17]

Like the NYSE and a handful or other "open-outcry" marketplaces—where traders do transactions in face-to-face—encounters, the 152-year-old Chicago Board of Trade (CBOT) is under assault by technologically superior new rivals. The CBOT recently surrendered its title as the world's busiest futures exchange to an all-electronic Swiss-German exchange called Eurex, which didn't exist three years ago.[18] Now some think that the CBOT's reluctance to adopt computer technology and its stubborn defense of face-to-face pit trading may be its undoing. Instead of investing heavily in technology, several years ago, the CBOT spent $182 million to build the giant trading floor it now occupies—a big mistake, according to some. Moreover, even if the exchange decides to adopt a fully electronic trading system—and it is inching in that direction—some fear it may be too late.[19]

The push toward round-the-clock trading is another challenge securities markets are facing. Extending traditional trading hours of 9:30 A.M. to 4 P.M. (Eastern U.S. time zone) by adding early-morning and late-night trading sessions is the next revolution sweeping Wall Street. *After-hours trading* or *extended-hours trading* refers to the purchase and sale of publicly traded stocks after the major stock markets, such as the NYSE and NASDAQ, close. Many securities exchanges now offer after-hours trading via ECNs that typically operate from 8:00 A.M. to 9:15 A.M. and 4:15 P.M. to 7 or 8 P.M., although some operate 24 hours a day. The biggest advantage to extended-hours trading is that it accommodates traders who live in regions outside the Eastern U.S. time zone. The biggest disadvantage, however, is lack of volume. Most institutional investors close up shop after the NYSE closing bell. Nonetheless, to remain competitive, many traditional securities exchanges have already extended their traditional trading hours.[20]

How to Buy and Sell Securities

Regardless of when you trade securities, where you trade securities, or how you trade securities, you must execute all trades by using a securities broker. Currently individuals cannot in-

EXHIBIT 18.4

STOCKBROKERS STILL NO. 1
WITH INVESTORS

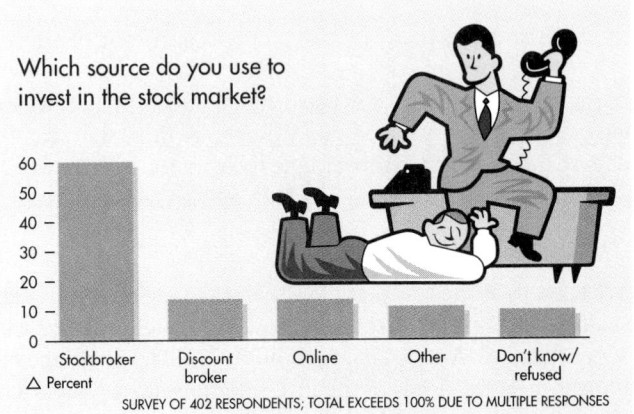

Which source do you use to invest in the stock market?

△ Percent

Stockbroker Discount broker Online Other Don't know/refused

SURVEY OF 402 RESPONDENTS; TOTAL EXCEEDS 100% DUE TO MULTIPLE RESPONSES

teract with securities marketplaces or ECNs directly; purchases must be made through traditional stock brokers—although some hope this will change soon.[21]

A **broker** is an expert who has passed a series of formal examinations and is legally registered to buy and sell securities on behalf of individual and institutional investors. As an investor, you pay *transaction costs* for every buy or sell order, to cover the broker's commission, which varies with the type of broker and the size of your trade: A *full-service broker* provides financial management services such as investment counseling and planning; a *discount broker* such as E*Trade provides fewer or limited services and generally charges lower commissions than a full-service broker.

For years, industry experts have been predicting the demise of the full-service broker. But as Exhibit 18.4 indicates, the traditional broker is not being erased by the click of a mouse just yet. Many customers still want and need personal financial advice that only an experienced professional can provide.

Trading Online E*Trade is part of the online trading phenomenon that has revolutionized the way investors buy and sell securities. Already, online trading is responsible for an estimated one-third of all stock trades made by individual investors.[22] Convenience, control, and cost are the main advantages of trading online. Rather than talk with your broker each time you want to trade, you can now visit your brokerage firm's or mutual fund's Web site, enter your buy or sell instructions, and pay a much lower broker's commission. In fact, full-service brokerages initially resisted online trading because they were concerned about losing their lucrative percentage commissions. But now even traditional firms like Merrill Lynch have jumped on the cyber-bandwagon, offering online trading with lower, flat-fee commissions in line with transaction charges levied by Schwab and others for Internet trades.[23]

Online trading is mostly about do-it-yourself investing; when you trade online, you trade alone, with no one to hold your hand, check for mistakes, or offer advice. Nonetheless, many online brokers, such as Charles Schwab's Internet site, offer a range of services and resources, including free or low-cost research, customized tracking of securities, e-mails confirming trades, electronic newsletters packed with investment tips, and more.[24] But online trading is far from perfect. Some sites have had problems that have prevented investors from placing online trades for minutes or even hours, as this chapter's Focusing on E-Business Today's special feature illustrates.

Using online brokers to trade securities is on the rise.

Trading Procedures Before you start to trade, take time to think about your objectives, both long term and short term. Next, look at how various securities match your objectives and your attitude toward risk, since investing in stocks and bonds can involve potential losses. Finally, consider the many ways you can have your broker buy or sell securities: A **market order** tells the broker to buy or sell at the best price that can be negotiated at the moment. A **limit order** specifies the highest price you are willing to pay when buying or the lowest price at which you are willing to sell. A **stop order** tells the broker to sell if the price of your security drops to or below the price you set, protecting you from losing more money if prices are dropping. You can also place a time limit on your orders. An **open order** instructs the broker to leave the order open until you cancel it. A **day order** is valid only on the day you place it, and should not be confused with a *day trader,* a stock trader who holds positions for a very short time (minutes to hours) and closes out these positions within the same day.

If you have special confidence in your broker's ability, you may place a **discretionary order,** which gives the broker the right to buy or sell your securities at the broker's discretion. In some cases, discretionary orders can save you from taking a loss, because the broker may have a better sense of when to sell a stock. If the broker's judgment proves wrong, however, you cannot hold the broker legally responsible for the consequences; so investigate your broker's background and think carefully before you give anyone the right to trade your securities.

broker
Individual registered to sell securities

market order
Authorization for a broker to buy or sell securities at the best price that can be negotiated at the moment

limit order
Market order that stipulates the highest or lowest price at which the customer is willing to trade securities

stop order
An order to sell a stock when its price falls to a particular point to limit an investor's losses

open order
Limit order that does not expire at the end of a trading day

day order
Any order to buy or sell a security that automatically expires if not executed on the day the order is placed

discretionary order
Market order that allows the broker to decide when to trade a security

First Charles Schwab grabbed huge chunks of market share from traditional brokers. Now it's cleaning up in the online trading market.

margin trading
Borrowing money from brokers to buy stock, paying interest on the borrowed money, and leaving the stock with the broker as collateral

short selling
Selling stock borrowed from a broker with the intention of buying it back later at a lower price, repaying the broker, and pocketing the profit

bull market
Rising stock market

bear market
Falling stock market

Investors sometimes borrow cash to buy stocks, a practice known as **margin trading.** Instead of paying for the stock in full, you borrow some of the money from your stockbroker, paying interest on the borrowed money and leaving the stock with the broker as collateral. As we mentioned in Chapter 17, the Federal Reserve Board establishes margin requirements. Be aware, however, that margin trading increases risk. If the price of a stock you bought on margin goes down, you will have to give your broker more money or the broker will sell your stock. Such forced sales can cause prices to fall even further, triggering a vicious cycle of sales and margin calls.[25]

If you believe that a stock's price is about to drop, you may choose a trading procedure known as **short selling.** With this procedure, you sell stock you borrow from a broker in the hope of buying it back later at a lower price. After you return the borrowed stock to the broker, you keep the price difference. For example, you might decide to borrow 25 shares that are selling for $30 per share and sell short because you think the share price is going to plummet. When the stock's price declines to $15, you buy 25 shares on the open market and make $15 profit on every share (minus transaction costs). Selling short is risky. If the stock had climbed to $32, you would have had to buy shares at that higher price, even though you would be losing money.

How to Analyze Financial News

Whether you trade online or off, you need to monitor financial news sources to see how your investments are doing. Start with daily newspaper reports on securities markets. Other sources include newspapers aimed specifically at investors (such as *Investor's Business Daily* and *Barron's*) and general-interest business publications that follow the corporate world and give hints about investing (such as the *Wall Street Journal, Forbes, Fortune,* and *Business Week*). Standard & Poor's, Moody's Investor Service, and Value Line also publish newsletters and special reports on securities. Online sources include your brokerage firm's Web site plus a growing number of excellent financial Web sites listed in "Put Your Money Where Your Mouse Is!"

What types of financial information should you be looking for? First, you want to determine the general direction of stock prices. If stock prices have been rising over a long period, the industry and the media will often describe this situation as a **bull market.** The reverse is a **bear market,** one characterized by a long-term trend of falling prices. You can see these broad market movements in Exhibit 18.5. Once you have the general picture, look at the timing. Has a bull market lasted for too long, suggesting that stocks are overvalued and a *correction* (tumbling prices) might be imminent? Also watch the volume of shares traded each day. If the stock market is down on heavy volume (that is, if prices are moving downward and a lot of trading is going on), investors may be trying to sell before prices go down further—a bearish sign.

Best of the Web Best of the Web Best of

MAKE A PILE OF MONEY

Do you want to learn about the stock market and investing but don't know where to turn? Try the Financial Info Centers at Investorama and get a head start on your investment education without wading through dense textbooks full of Wall Street jargon. Get the lowdown on the Dow. Learn some fundamental analysis techniques. Read some tips on choosing a broker. And find out which questions you should ask your broker before you invest. Aren't sure whether you should invest globally? Ask Investorama. You may discover a world of opportunity.
www.investorama.com/

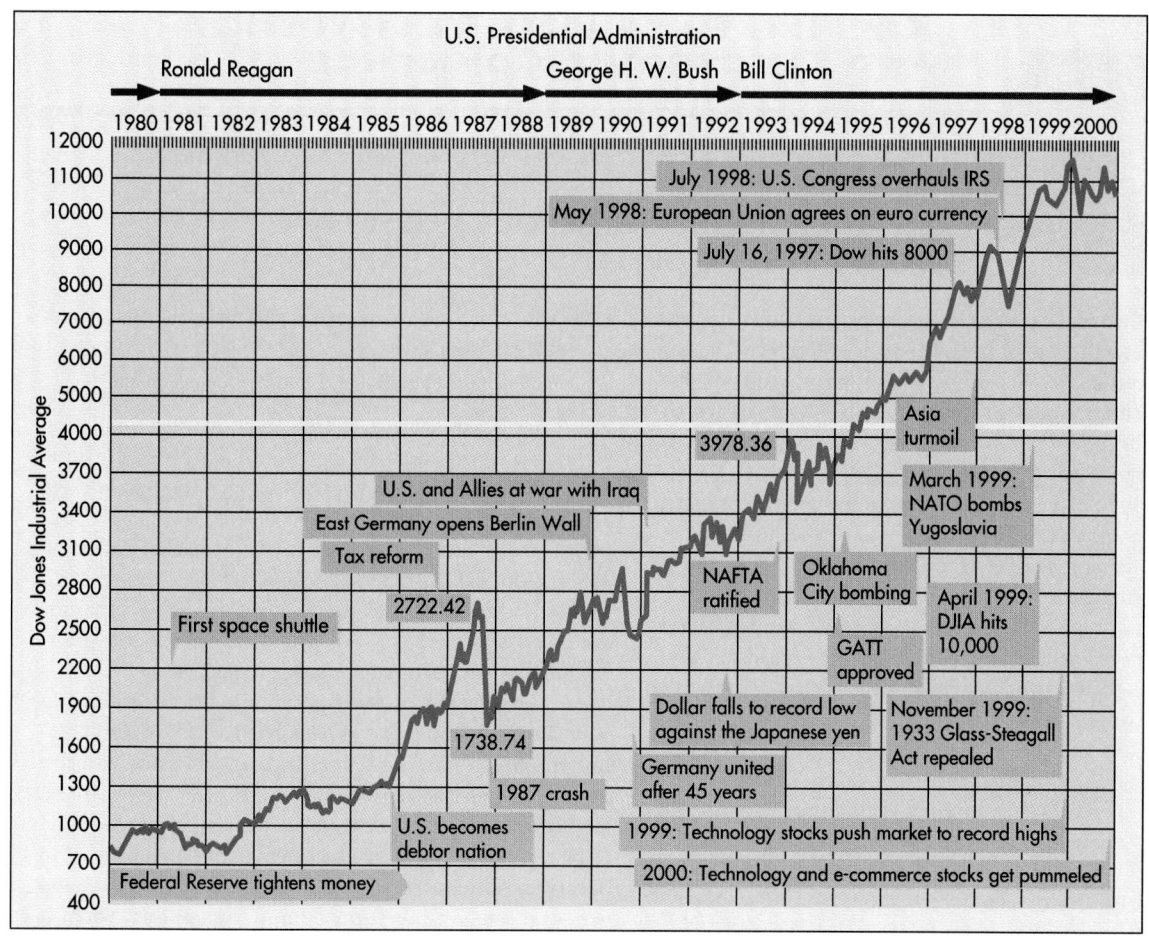

EXHIBIT 18.5

THE STOCK MARKET'S UPS AND DOWNS

The peaks and valleys on this chart represent swings in the Dow Jones Industrial Average, the most widely used indicator of U.S. stock prices.

Watching Market Indexes and Averages One way to determine whether the market is bullish or bearish is to watch **market indexes** and averages, which use the performance of a representative sampling of stocks, bonds, or commodities as a gauge of broader market activity. The most famous U.S. stock average is the Dow Jones Industrial Average (DJIA), which tracks the prices of 30 blue-chip stocks, each representing a particular sector of the U.S. economy. Critics say the Dow is too narrow and too susceptible to short-term swings, lacks the right stocks, and gives too much weight to higher-priced shares. But advocates say the Dow's 30 stocks serve as a general barometer of market conditions. Regardless, a recent shuffling of the index by the *Wall Street Journal* editors (guardians of the Dow) should make it more representative of the "new economy." In 1999 Microsoft, Intel, Home Depot, and SBC Communications replaced time-honored blue chips Chevron, Goodyear, Sears Roebuck, and Union Carbide.[26]

Another widely watched index is the Standard & Poor's 500 Stock Average (S&P 500), which tracks the performances of 500 corporate stocks, many more than the DJIA. This index is weighted by market value, not by stock price, so large companies carry far more weight than small companies.[27] The Wilshire 5000 Index, which actually covers some 7,000 stocks, is the broadest index measuring U.S. market performance. To get a sense of how technology stocks are doing, check the NASDAQ Composite Index, covering more than 3,000 over-the-counter stocks, including many high-tech firms. You can also look at indexes to learn about the performance of foreign markets, such as Japan's Nikkei 225 Index and the United Kingdom's FT-SE 100 Index.

Interpreting the Financial News In addition to watching market trends, you will want to follow the securities you own and others that look like promising investments. For stocks, you can turn to

market indexes
Measures of security markets calculated from the prices of a selection of securities

KEEPING PACE WITH TECHNOLOGY AND ELECTRONIC COMMERCE

PUT YOUR MONEY WHERE YOUR MOUSE IS!— INVESTMENT INFORMATION ON THE NET

The Internet has been hailed as the great equalizer between individual investors and Wall Street. Today's investors have access to a staggering amount of valuable information and investment tools—many of which are used by Wall Street professionals. But having access to information is one thing. Using it wisely is another. So before you put a dollar (or a franc) into any investment, learn as much as possible about the market, the security, its issuer, and its potential. Here are some tips to point you in the right direction.

For "how to" advice, try the Motley Fool (www.fool.com), Quicken's financial site (www.quicken.com/investments), or *Money*'s Web site (www.money.com). Also look at the economic trend sites linked to Dr. Ed Yardeni's Economics Network (www.yardeni.com/). Then research individual securities using Yahoo! (www.yahoo.com) or another Internet search tool. Plug in the company name and click to see the latest news. Go to Hoover's Online (www.hoovers.com) to read a little about the company's history and recent results. Be sure to stop by the company's Web site to read its press releases and financial statements. You can burrow even further into potential investments using these Web sites:

- Corporate financial data filed with the SEC (www.freeedgar.com)

- Morningstar mutual fund reports (www.morningstar.com)

- Bond prices and market performance (www.investinginbonds.com)

- Investorama links to research and analysis sites (www.investorama.com)

Try your hand at trading stocks before you actually invest hard cash, using CNNfn's stock market simulation (www.sandbox.com/cnnfn_finalbell/pub-doc/home.html). Also, construct a hypothetical portfolio on Quicken, Yahoo!, or another financial Web site and watch how your investments fare. Track your favorite market index on MSN MoneyCentral (http://moneycentral.msn.com/investor/home.asp) and compare it to your personal investment portfolio. Are your proposed investments meeting, missing, or beating the market index?

Now you're in a better position to buy securities, but your research shouldn't end here. Even after you start trading, you need to stay on top of the latest news and industry developments that can affect the securities in which you have invested. And if a potential investment seems too good to be true, point your Web browser to the North American Securities Administrators Association (www.nassa.org) and get some tips on investment fraud. Remember, when it comes to investments, your Web surfing can really pay off.

■ QUESTIONS FOR CRITICAL THINKING

1. Why is it important to learn about a company's financial results and background before buying its stock or bonds?

2. What are the disadvantages of searching for investment information on the Internet?

---

the stock exchange report in major daily newspapers. Exhibit 18.6 shows how to read this report, which includes high and low prices for the past 52 weeks, the number of shares traded (volume), and the change from the previous day's closing price. U.S. securities markets began quoting security prices in decimals (dollars and cents) in 2000. Prior to that year, prices were quoted in fractions as small as 1/16. Using decimals in trading makes stock prices easier for many investors to understand. Moreover, quoting shares down to the penny permits stocks to be priced in smaller increments.[28]

price-earnings ratio (p/e ratio)
Stock's current market price divided by issuer's annual earnings per share; also known as the price-earnings multiple

Included in the stock exchange report is the **price-earnings ratio,** or *p/e ratio* (also known as the price-earnings multiple), which is computed by dividing a stock's market price by its *prior* year's earnings per share. Some investors also calculate a forward p/e ratio using *expected* year earnings in the ratio's denominator. Bear in mind that if a stock's p/e ratio is well below the industry norm, either the company is in trouble or it's an undiscovered gem with a relatively low stock price. For more detailed data on a stock, consult the company's annual reports or documents filed with the Securities and Exchange Commission (SEC).

To follow specific bonds, check the bond quotation tables in major newspapers (see Exhibit 18.7). When reading these tables, remember that the price is quoted as a percentage of the bond's value. For example, a $1,000 bond shown closing at 65 actually sold at $650. Newspapers and

(1) 50-WEEK HIGH	52-WEEK LOW	(2) STOCK	(3) SYM	(4) DIV	(5) YLD %	(6) PE	(7) VOL 100S	(8) HI	LOW	(9) CLOSE	(10) NET CHG
55.25	26.20	NtlDataCp	NCD	.30	.8	20	3580	40.75	38.20	39.95	−.70
56.25	17.00	Navistar	NAV		...	9	2570	45.95	44.40	45.75	+1.30
33.75	15.00	NeimanMarc	NMG		...	11	888	24.70	23.65	23.80	−.80
22.90	**10.75**	**NoblDrill**	**NE**		...	**26**	**15762**	**24.00**	**22.75**	**24.00**	**+1.25**

1. **520-week high/low:** Indicates the highest and lowest trading price of the stock in the past 52 weeks plus the most recent week but not the most recent trading day (adjusted for splits). Stocks are quoted in decimals. In most newspapers, boldfaced entries indicate stocks whose price changed by 5% or more if the previous closing price was $2 or higher.

2. **Stock:** The company's name abbreviated. A capital letter usually means a new word. In this example, NtlDataCp is National Data Corporation, NeimanMarc is Neiman-Marcus Group, and NoblDrill is Noble Drill.

3. **Symbol:** Symbol under which this stock is traded on stock exchanges.

4. **Dividend:** Dividends are usually annual payments based on the last quarterly or semiannual declaration, although not all stocks pay dividends. Special or extra dividends or payments are identified in footnotes.

5. **Yield:** The percentage yield shows dividends as a percentage of the share price.

6. **PE:** Price-to-earnings ratio, calculated by dividing the stock's closing price by the earnings per share for the latest four quarters.

7. **Volume:** Daily total of shares traded, in hundreds. A listing of 888 indicates 88,800 shares were traded during that day.

8. **High/Low:** The stock's highest and lowest price for that day.

9. **Close:** Closing price of the stock that day.

10. **Net change:** Change in share price from the close of the previous trading day.

Common Stock Footnotes: d—new 52 week low; n—new; pf—preferred; s—stock split or stock dividend of 25 percent or more in previous 52 weeks; u—new 52 week high; v—trading halted on primary market; vi—in bankruptcy; x—ex dividend (the buyer won't receive a recently declared dividend, but the seller will)

EXHIBIT 18.6

HOW TO READ A NEWSPAPER STOCK QUOTATION

Even before you invest, you will want to follow the latest quotations for your stock. This table shows you how to read the newspaper stock quotation tables.

business publications also include tables of price quotations for investments such as mutual funds, commodities, options, and government securities (see Exhibit 18.8). These same publications also carry news about securities frauds and investor protection.

Regulation of Securities Markets

Whenever you buy and sell securities, your trades are governed by a network of state and federal laws. Combined with industry self-regulation, these laws are designed to ensure that you and all investors receive accurate information and that no one artificially manipulates the market price of a given security. Trading in stocks and bonds is monitored by the Securities and Exchange Commission. In addition, the SEC works closely with the stock exchanges and NASD to police securities transactions and maintain the system's integrity.

LEARNING OBJECTIVE 7

Explain how government regulation of securities trading tries to protect investors

SEC Filing Requirements As mentioned earlier, companies must meet certain requirements (which include filing a blizzard of registration papers and reports) to be listed on any exchange (see Exhibit 18.9). Similarly, brokers must operate according to the rules of the exchanges, rules that are largely designed to protect investors. (See Component Chapter B for a list of major federal legislation governing the securities industry.) Overseeing all these details keeps the SEC very busy indeed. Every year the SEC screens over 15,200 annual reports, 40,000 investor complaints, 14,000 prospectuses (a legal statement that describes the objectives of a specific investment), and 6,500 proxy statements (a shareholder's written authorization giving someone else

EXHIBIT 18.7

HOW TO READ A
NEWSPAPER BOND
QUOTATION

When newspapers carry bond
quotations, they show prices as a
percentage of the bond's value,
which is typically $1,000.

(1) COMPANY	(2) CUR YLD	(3) VOL	(4) CLOSE	(5) NET CHG
NYTel 6 1/8 10	6.6	11	93.40	−.25
PacBell 6 1/4 05	6.4	10	98.40	+.25
Safwy 9 7/8 07	8.4	20	117.50	+3.60
StoneC 11 1/4	11.1	24	103.50	−1.10
TimeWar 9 1/8 13	8.3	30	109.75	−.50

1. **Company:** Name of company issuing the bond, such as New York Telephone, and bond description, such as 6 ⅛ percent bond maturing in 2010.

2. **Current yield:** Annual interest on $1,000 bond divided by the closing price shown. The yield for New York Telephone is $61.25 ÷ $933.75 = 0.06559, or approximately 6.6 percent.

3. **Volume:** Number of bonds traded (in thousands) that day.

4. **Close:** Price of the bond at the close of the last day's business.

5. **Net change:** Change in bond price from the close of the previous trading day.

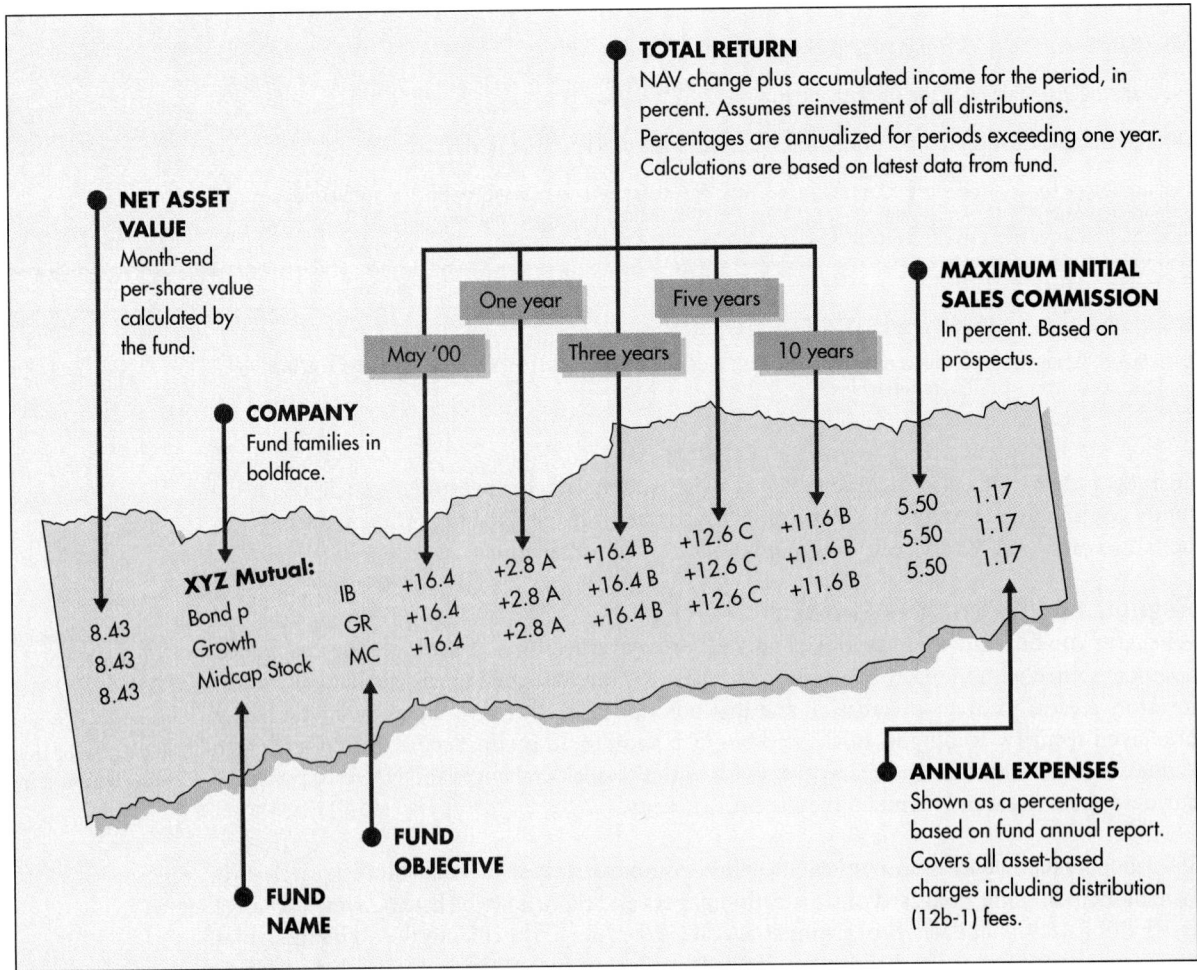

EXHIBIT 18.8

HOW TO READ A NEWSPAPER MUTUAL FUND QUOTATION

A mutual fund listing shows the new asset value of one share (the price at which one share is trading) and the change in trading price from one day to the next.

EXHIBIT 18.9

AN EDGAR SCORECARD

To successfully navigate the Securities and Exchange Commission's Edgar database of corporate filings, it helps to know the most common filings required of publicly traded companies and their content.

An Edgar Scorecard

10K ➡ The official version of a company's annual report, with a comprehensive overview of the business.

10Q ➡ An abridged version of the 10K, filed quarterly for the first three quarters of a company's fiscal year.

8K ➡ An interim report disclosing significant company events that occur before the company files its next 10Q or 10K.

12B-25 ➡ Request for a deadline extension to file a required report, like a 10K or 10Q. When the late report is ultimately filed, NT is appended to the report's name.

S1 ➡ Basic registration form for new securities, most often initial or secondary public offerings.

Proxy Statement ➡ Information and ballot materials for shareholder votes, including election of directors and approval of mergers and acquisitions when required.

Forms 3, 4, and 5 ➡ Directors, officers, and owners of more than 10 percent of a company's stock report their initial purchases on Form 3 and subsequent purchases or sales on Form 4; they file an annual statement of their holdings on Form 5.

the authority to cast his or her vote). The agency's Web site contains a mountain of public documents that investors can browse, download, or print to learn more about publicly traded companies.[29]

Insider Trading *Insider trading* occurs when people buy or sell a stock based on information that is not available to the general public. It comes in all flavors, from buying options in a company ahead of merger or earnings news to placing stock orders ahead of a big institution or group of retail investors (a practice called front-running). While insider trading can produce big profits for the unscrupulous, it also claims many victims. Acquisition companies, for example, are forced to pay higher-than-expected premiums to buy a target company when leaks trigger a run-up in the target's stock price. Most of the talk originates form loose-lipped company insiders.

One of the SEC's top priorities is to crack down on insider trading. But the SEC readily admits that success in the battle is about as likely as victory in the war against drugs. "As the volume of deals and the number of people involved in deals increases, it gets harder to enforce it," says SEC's associate enforcement director, William Baker. "People are getting access to information that they didn't have in the past." Moreover, the dizzying number of corporate mergers has given birth to a mountain of price-sensitive paperwork on Wall Street.

Regulation Fair Disclosure Regulation Fair Disclosure (FD) was adopted by the SEC in 2000 to create a level playing field for all investors. Specifically, the regulation mandates that any news with the potential to affect the price of a stock must be released to everyone simultaneously.

SEC Enforcement Director Richard H. Walker says his agency has the will and the means to stop online investment scams.

In other words, the regulation prohibits companies from "selectively disclosing" important information (such as earnings estimates) to big institutional shareholders and Wall Street analysts ahead of regular investors. Otherwise, early news recipients would be able to "make a profit or avoid a loss at the expense of those kept in the dark."[30]

In spite of its good intentions, the regulation could have unintended consequences, say critics. Some worry that instead of giving small and large investors equal access to market-sensitive information, the regulation could cut down on the amount of information received by everyone. Part of the problem stems from the fact that the SEC has not clearly defined what it means by *market-sensitive* information, so companies are opting to err on the side of silence. Moreover, some companies claim it's too difficult to give small investors the same level of information that they have selectively provided to investment analysts.[31]

Online Securities Fraud No longer do con artists need rooms full of cold-calling brokers. Today, with just an e-mail address list and a chat-board alias or two, penny-stock promoters can dupe tens of thousands (if not millions) of investors by making false claims about a company, watching investors eager to make a fast profit pump up the company's stock price, then selling or dump their penny shares at inflated prices and pocket a handsome profit.

The combination of a "get-rich" mindset and the huge number of people now investing online have made such cyber-scamming schemes common. Online and off, investors are getting ripped off to the tune of an estimated $10 billion a year—that's more than $1 million an hour. And the SEC's Internet complaint hotline gets up to 200 messages a day.[32] In fact, so pervasive has the problem become that it has drawn the attention of the Department of Justice, the FTC, the U.S. Attorney's offices, and even the FBI. To help curb Internet stock scams, NASD has developed an Internet search engine to find phrases such as "too good to be true," and it monitors securities chat forums for fraudulent or misleading information.[33] As an investor, your best defense against fraud is to carefully research securities before you buy and to steer clear of any investment that seems too good to be true (see Exhibit 18.10).

EXHIBIT 18.10

TEN QUESTIONS TO ASK BEFORE YOU INVEST

You can avoid getting taken in an online stock scam by asking yourself these 10 questions before you invest.

1. Is the investment registered with the SEC and your state's securities agency?
2. Have you read the company's audited financial statements?
3. Is the person recommending this investment a registered broker?
4. What does the person promoting the investment have to gain?
5. If the tip came from an online bulletin board or e-mail, is the author identifiable or using an alias? Is there any reason to trust that person?
6. Are you being pressured to act before you can evaluate the investment?
7. Does the investment promise you'll get rich quick, using words like "guaranteed," "high return," or "risk free"?
8. Does the investment match your objectives? Could you afford to lose all of the money you invest?
9. How easy would it be to sell the investment later? Remember, stocks with fewer shares are easy for promoters to manipulate and hard for investors to sell if the price starts falling.
10. Does the investment originate overseas? If yes, beware: It is tougher to track money sent abroad, and harder for burned investors to have recourse to justice.

FOCUSING ON E-BUSINESS TODAY

As Online Trading Rises, So Do the Number of Complaints

Morgan Roach thought he had made a small killing in the stock market. In August 1999, the software programmer logged on to online broker E*Trade and bought stock options worth 4,200 shares of America Online at an average price of $80 per share. A few hours later, he put in an order to sell his stake for $95 a share. The result: A tidy profit of $8,510. Except the trades never happened that way. Instead, complains Roach, E*Trade bought his shares for $8 a share more than his order called for, yielding a loss of $23,188.

Complaints such as Roach's are soaring—despite pledges from firms such as Ameritrade, E*Trade, and

LEARNING OBJECTIVE @8

List six major problems customers are experiencing when they trade online and identify the steps customers should take to resolve their differences with online securities brokers

Charles Schwab to make customer service Job One. A recent SEC study reveals that 4,258 complaints, including messed up trades like Roach's, were lodged against online brokers in 2000. Chief among the complaints were

failures to process orders on time, correctly, and at the price displayed on the company's Web site (see Exhibit). Moreover, when customers attempted to resolve these problems, they were frequently referred to inexperienced and unknowledgeable customer service representatives.

GETTING CUSTOMERS AT ALL COSTS

Rapid growth and limited resources are igniting many of the problems online brokers are facing. Today anywhere from 5 to 10 million people are trading stocks online. And Jupiter Communications projects that number to balloon to more than 20 million soon. "Anytime an industry grows this fast, you're bound to see problems," says one

Top Five Consumer Complaints Filed with the SEC Against Online Brokers
1. Failure to process orders or delays in executing orders
2. Difficulty in accessing account and contacting broker
3. Errors in processing orders
4. Execution of orders at higher prices than posted on Web site
5. Errors and omissions in account records and documents

Internet financial services analyst. Moreover, to beat stiff competition and lure traders, online brokers are spending wads of money on advertising and perks. But too few dollars are being spent to upgrade trading systems to handle the volume of customers that the companies have tried so hard to attract.

SEC filings show most online brokers spend far more on building their brand and acquiring new customers than on improving customer service operations. Ameritrade, for instance, spent some $157 million on advertising in 2000—an increase of 343 percent from the previous year. Some claim that online brokers remain far too willing to sacrifice customer service in favor of capturing new customer accounts or building their brands. "They're learning at the public's expense, and that's not right," says one securities expert. "They've got to slow down opening new accounts," says one securities expert. "It's unfair to clients, and it's not sound business practice." Even E*Trade's Cotsakos admits that "the best marketing tool is high-quality service."

BIG STEPS FOR EVERYONE

Of course, brokers say they're taking steps in the right direction to address these problems. But industry experts say those steps don't go far enough. And the government agrees. Ready to intervene, the SEC has put forth proposals that would require brokers to publish reports on how well they've executed trades and to tell customers (on request) where their orders were routed (so that they could track what went wrong). But if your online broker ticks you off before things get better, experts advise that you take these steps:

1. *Promptly file a written complaint (not an e-mail) with the broker.* Include as much supporting evidence as possible, such as details about the trade, the date, the amounts involved, and copies of any sales confirmation, monthly statements, or other correspondence. Then, if you don't get a response within two weeks, follow up with a second letter.

2. *File an online copy of your complaint with NASDR.* NASDR is the regulatory arm of the National Association of Securities Dealers (NASD). Use the online customer complaint form available on their Web site.

3. *Send a copy to your state securities regulator.* State securities regulators license brokers to do business in the state, and they try to investigate every complaint.

4. *Consider mediation.* If you still can't resolve the matter, or if you are seeking compensation or damages, the next step is mediation. This is an informal, voluntary

process in which a neutral party helps both sides negotiate a mutually acceptable outcome.

5. *Try arbitration.* If you're still at odds with your online broker, arbitration is your next option. An impartial person or panel (approved by both sides) studies the evidence, holds a hearing, and issues a binding resolution.

6. *Litigate as a last resort.* Keep in mind that getting your case heard by a judge or jury isn't easy because of the

arbitration clause in your account agreement. To open an account, customers must pledge to resolve disputes through mediation or arbitration panels, and not through courts.

Remember, Internet brokerage companies take different approaches to resolve client complaints. So don't give up. Although the deck may seem stacked against you, investors aren't powerless. The key is to follow the six steps and know when and where to apply the pressure.[34]

SUMMARY OF LEARNING OBJECTIVES

1. **Differentiate among a stock's par value, its market value, and its book value.**
Par value is the dollar value assigned to a stock for bookkeeping and for dividend calculations. Market value is the price at which a share of stock is currently selling. Book value is the portion of a corporation's net assets represented by a single share of common stock.

2. **Explain the safety and tax advantages of investing in U.S. government securities.**
U.S. Treasury securities are considered safe investments because the government is highly unlikely to fail to make payments as promised. Interest from Treasury bills, notes, and bonds is exempt from state and local income taxes, and investors can easily buy and sell these securities through the Treasury or organized markets.

3. **Name five criteria to be considered when making investment decisions.**
Investors should consider the income, growth, safety, liquidity, and tax consequences of alternative investments.

4. **Explain what mutual funds are and describe their main benefits.**
Mutual funds are pools of money drawn from many investors to buy diversified portfolios of stocks, bonds, and other marketable securities. The primary benefit is that investors gain greater diversification from buying a share in a mutual fund than from investing the same money in the stock of one company.

5. **Describe the two types of securities exchanges**
Auction exchanges such as the New York Stock Exchange funnel all buy and sell orders into one centralized location. Dealer exchanges such as NASDAQ are decentralized marketplaces in which dealers, known as market makers, are connected electronically to handle buy and sell orders without a single, centralized trading floor.

6. **Identify two major challenges traditional securities exchanges are facing.**
Electronic computerized networks (ECNs) are the biggest threat to the traditional ways of exchanging stocks. ECNs match buy and sell orders directly (cutting out the market makers and specialists), they operate globally, and they operate economically. The push toward extended trading hours is another key challenge. Some securities exchanges are meeting this challenge by using ECNs to offer limited after-hours trading.

7. **Explain how government regulation of securities trading tries to protect investors.**
The government tries to prevent fraud in the securities markets by requiring companies to file registration papers, fulfill certain requirements, and file periodic information reports so that investors receive accurate information. Regulations also try to monitor the use of insider information and police fraudulent manipulation of securities.

8. **List six major problems customers are experiencing when they trade online and identify the steps customers should take to resolve their differences with online securities brokers.**
The most common online broker complaints voiced by customers are (1) delays in executing trade orders, (2) difficulty in accessing their account or broker, (3) order processing errors, (4) order executions at prices higher than those displayed on the company's Web site, (5) account errors and omissions, and (6) inexperienced and unknowledgeable customer service representatives. To resolve problems that may occur during the online trading process, experts recommend that disgruntled customers take these steps: promptly file a written complaint with the broker and file copies of the complaint with NASDR and their state securities regulator. If the matter is still unresolved, customers should hire a mediator or arbitrator—reserving litigation as the last resort.

KEY TERMS

asset allocation (486)	growth stocks (485)	principal (482)
auction exchange (488)	hedge (484)	rate of return (486)
authorized stock (480)	institutional investors (485)	revenue bond (483)
bear market (492)	investment portfolios (486)	secondary market (487)
blue-chip stock (481)	issued stock (480)	securities (480)
bond (481)	limit order (491)	secured bonds (482)
broker (490)	margin trading (492)	short selling (492)
bull market (492)	market indexes (493)	sinking fund (483)
capital gains (483)	market makers (488)	speculators (486)
commodities (484)	market order (491)	stock exchanges (487)
convertible bonds (482)	money-market funds (487)	stock specialist (488)
day order (491)	municipal bonds (483)	stock split (480)
dealer exchange (488)	mutual funds (487)	stop order (491)
debentures (482)	NASDAQ (National Association of Securities	Treasury bills (483)
discretionary order (491)	Dealers Automated Quotations) (487)	Treasury bonds (483)
diversification (487)	open order (491)	Treasury notes (483)
electronic communication network	over-the-counter (OTC) market (487)	unissued stock (480)
(ECN) (488)	par value (480)	U.S. savings bonds (483)
financial futures (484)	price-earnings ratio (p/e ratio) (494)	yield (485)
general obligation bond (483)	primary market (487)	

TEST YOUR KNOWLEDGE

QUESTIONS FOR REVIEW

1. What are the differences between a Treasury bill, a Treasury note, and a U.S. savings bond?

2. What is the difference between a general obligation bond and a revenue bond?

3. What happens during a 2-for-1 stock split?

4. What is a p/e ratio, and what does it signify to an investor?

5. What is the function of the Securities and Exchange Commission?

QUESTIONS FOR ANALYSIS

6. What are some of the advantages of mutual funds?

7. What are some of the ways an investor can diversify investments to reduce risk of loss?

8. Why are debentures considered riskier than other types of bonds?

9. When might an investor sell a stock short? What risks are involved in selling short?

10. How are the Internet and e-commerce redefining the investment industry?

11. You work in the research and development department of a large corporation and have been involved in a discovery that could lead to a new, profitable product. News of the discovery has not been made public. Is it legal for you to buy stock in the company? Now assume the same scenario but you talk to your friend about your discovery while dining at a restaurant. The person at the next table overhears the conversation. Is it legal for the eavesdropper to buy the company's stock before the public announcement of the news?[35]

QUESTIONS FOR APPLICATION

12. If an investor wants a steady, predictable flow of cash, what types of investments should the investor seek and why?

13. If you were thinking about buying shares of AT&T, under what circumstances would you place a market order, a limit order, an open order, and a discretionary order?

14. Look back at Chapter 6 and review the discussion of mission statements. Suppose you were thinking about purchasing 100 shares of common stock in General Electric. Why might you want to first review the company's mission statement? What would you be looking for in the company's mission statement that could help you decide whether or not to invest?

15. In Chapter 5 we mentioned that one disadvantage of going public was the burdensome SEC filing requirements. Why do you think the SEC requires companies to file the documents listed in Exhibit 18.9, page 497?

PRACTICE YOUR KNOWLEDGE

SHARPENING YOUR COMMUNICATION SKILLS

One of the most important steps in preparing for an interview is developing a list of interview questions that are clear and concise. Practice your communication skills by developing two sets of questions:

1. Questions you might ask a stockbroker to help you decide whether you would use that stockbroker's services.

2. Questions you might pose to that broker to help you evaluate the merits of purchasing a specific security.

HANDLING DIFFICULT SITUATIONS ON THE JOB

You are a customer service representative for a popular online broker. One of the company's investors, Ian Stevens, placed an online market order for a hot new Internet stock, Theglobe.com, thinking it would cost between $15 and $25 a share. His order was filled for 2,300 shares, but at a price of $90 a share and a bill of $207,000—nearly $150,000 more than he expected. Stevens called E*Trade and was irate. Unfortunately, you were the lucky rep to get his call. Your company boldly posts statements on its Web site warning customers about possible delays and other potential problems with online trades. For example, it warns customers that high trading volume can delay the execution of an order, which may mean that a stock's price is significantly different from when the order was placed. It also informs customers of the difference between a market order and a limit order. Doesn't matter. Stevens is making all kinds of threats and he wants to speak to the president of the company NOW! You have been told to turn over situations such as these to your department manager, but only after you input all the facts in an electronic customer file. You need to ask Stevens a series of questions, but first you have to calm him down—without making any promises, of course. How will you accomplish this difficult task?[36]

BUILDING YOUR TEAM SKILLS

You and your team are going to pool your money and invest $5,000. Before you plunge into any investments, how can you prepare yourselves to be good investors? First, consider your group's goals. What will you and your teammates do with any profits generated by your investments? Once you have agreed on a goal for your team's profits, think about how much money you will need to achieve this goal and how soon you want to achieve it.

Next, think about how much risk you personally are willing to take to achieve the goal. Bear in mind that safer investments generally offer lower returns than riskier investments—and certain investments, such as stocks, can lose money. Now hold a group discussion to find a level of risk that feels comfortable for everyone on your team.

Once your team has decided how much risk to take, consider which investments are best suited to your group's goals and chosen risk level. Will you choose stocks, bonds, a combination of both, or other securities? What are the advantages and disadvantages of each type of investment for your team's situation? Then come to a decision about specific investment opportunities—particular stocks, for example—that your group would like to investigate further.

Compare your group's goal, risk level, and investment possibilities with those of the other teams in your class and discuss the differences and similarities you see.

EXPAND YOUR KNOWLEDGE

KEEPING CURRENT USING *THE WALL STREET JOURNAL*

You have $10,000 to invest. Using as much information as your instructor recommends, select a well-known company traded on the New York Stock Exchange, American Stock Exchange, or NASDAQ. Assignment: Begin a stock-transaction journal. On the first page, record the company's name, the stock exchange abbreviation, the exchange on which it is traded, the 52-week high and low, the price-earnings ratio, and your reasons for selecting this stock.

a. *Buying.* On the first day of the project, record the number of shares purchased (whole shares only), the price per share, the total purchase price (number of shares × price/share), the commission paid on your purchase (assume 1 percent of the purchase price), and today's Dow Jones Industrial Average. Now add the commission paid to the purchase price to get your *total purchase cost.*

b. *Monitoring.* Record and chart the closing price of your stock each day, and plot it on a graph. Scan *The Wall Street Journal* or other publications regularly for articles on your company to include in your journal. Note any major developments that may affect your stock.

c. *Selling.* In this exercise, you select the best time to sell as long as it meets two requirements: You must sell on or before the day designated by your instructor, and (if your instructor wishes) you must notify your instructor on the day you sell your stock. (This means that you'll probably need to sell on a day that your class meets—unless your instructor posts a sign-up sheet that you can use on other days.) On the day you sell your stock, record the following information: the selling price (the closing price/share that day), the number of shares sold, the total sales price (the number of shares × selling price/share), the commission paid on the sale (assume 1 percent of the total sales price), and that day's Dow Jones Industrial Average. Now subtract the commission paid from the total sales price to arrive at your *sales proceeds.*

d. *Analysis.* Subtract your total purchase cost from your sales proceeds to arrive at your *net gain* or *net loss.*

1. How well did your investment do? Use the articles you collected during this project to relate recent developments to the performance of your stock.

2. How did it compare with gains or losses in the Dow Jones Industrial Average during this period?

3. How close was the selling price to the stock's 52-week high or low?

DISCOVERING CAREER OPPORTUNITIES

Think you might be interested in a job in the securities and commodities industry? This industry has one of the most highly educated and skilled workforces of any industry. And the requirements for entry are high—most brokerage clerks have a college degree. Log on to the Bureau of Labor Statistics, Career Guide to Industries at, www.bls.gov/cghome.htm, and click on Financial and Insurance, then click on Securities and Commodities. Read the article, then answer these questions:

1. What are the licensing and continuing education requirements for securities brokers?

2. What is the typical starting position for many people in the securities industry?

3. What factors are expected to contribute to the projected long-term growth of this industry?

EXPLORING THE BEST OF THE WEB

URLs for all Internet exercises are provided at the Web site for this book, www.prenhall.com/mescon. When you log on to the text Web site, select Chapter 18, then select "Student Resources," click on the name of the featured Web site, and follow the detailed navigational directions to complete these exercises.

Invest Wisely, Don't Be a Fool, page 486

It's OK to fool around at this Web site for a while. In fact, you may learn a thing or two about investing in stocks by browsing the Motley Fool.

1. Get some answers to your not-so-foolish questions. Pick three items you would like to learn more about and review them. What did you learn? How helpful was this advice?

2. Go to Fool's School and read How to Value Stocks. Take A Journey Through the Balance Sheet and discover why cash is king. Because you learned about most of this stuff in Chapters 16 and 17, brush up on the components a bit and then jump to *working capital*. Why is working capital important?

3. What is market capitalization? What does the working capital to market capitalization ratio show you?

Stock Up at the New York Stock Exchange, page 488

Tour the New York Stock Exchange and learn how the exchange operates.

1. Why are specialists critical to the auction process?

2. What does regulation mean and why is the NYSE regulated?

3. What is Stock Watch? List some of the steps involved.

Make a Pile of Money, page 492

Get a headstart on your investment education without wading through dense textbooks full of Wall Street jargon. Log on to Investorama, browse around, and then answer these questions.

1. If you were to place an order for 100 shares of Coca-Cola, what steps occur behind the scenes between the time you place the order and the time the broker confirms the trade with you?

2. What are the five things you should consider when selecting an online broker?

3. Analysts' opinions mean different things to different people. What does it mean when Standard and Poor's recommends that you buy? Accumulate? Hold?

Explore on Your Own

Review these chapter-related Web sites on your own to learn more about securities.

1. Take a free online course in a variety of investing topics—stocks, mutual funds, and risk—at the GE Center for Financial Learning, www.financiallearning.com/. Click on Building a Financial Plan, scroll down to Courses, and click on Introduction to Financial Planning.

2. Discover the seven great reasons to buy treasury bonds at the U.S. Treasury's Bureau of the Public Debt Web site at www.publicdebt.treas.gov/. Click on Savings Bonds, scroll down and click on 7 Great Reasons.

3. Brush up on your investment and finance terms at Investopedia, www.investopedia.com. Each term entry provides a concise definition of the term and annotated related links.

A CASE FOR CRITICAL THINKING

■ *Floored by Technology at the New York Stock Exchange*

It boasts the biggest trading volume, the greatest liquidity, and the most impressive blue chip listings of any stock exchange in the world. But at the close of the twentieth century, the New York Stock Exchange (NYSE) and its established trading system were threatened by new technologies. The world's largest and most prestigious securities exchange was forced to change its services to keep pace with the demands of the electronic revolution.

TAKING STOCK OF BUSINESS

Ever since a group of brokers gathered on Wall Street to trade stocks in 1792, the NYSE has provided a central marketplace for buying and selling securities. Between the opening and closing bells of each business day, traders have scrambled to match buyers and sellers through face-to-face encounters on the auction floor. This floor-based auction system worked well for years, meeting the needs of large and small investors alike.

But the arrival of the computer age presented investors with an alternative to the NYSE's established trading system. The 1971 birth of NASDAQ, for example, allowed traders to transact business via computers for the first time. Moreover, the electronic revolution of the 1990s enabled investors to execute trades using electronic communication networks (ECNs) instead of using human traders on the auction floor.

TENSE EXCHANGE

As more and more customers bypassed the Big Board in favor of trading through electronic markets, NYSE chairman and CEO Richard Grasso acknowledged that the exchange could no longer cling to its old ways. "These are no longer the days of old, when we were the only game in town . . . Reinvention is absolutely essential," said Grasso in early 2000.

Still, Grasso had no desire to switch to an all-electronic market that could turn the NYSE into "a museum." After all, floor-based trading vanished in France soon after the country's futures exchange converted to electronic trading in the mid-1990s. And to complicate matters, specialists and traders at the NYSE were opposed to moves that threatened to replace their jobs with flashing screens. Furthermore, many customers still preferred human intervention on the trading floor, insisting that a broker's judgment often saved money for the consumer at the point of sale.

MOVES ON THE BIG BOARD

To meet demands for change without abolishing the existing auction system, the NYSE developed a strategy that offers a combination of electronic and human services. The exchange invested millions in new technology to maintain a competitive edge in the electronic market. Then it introduced Network NYSE, a portfolio of products and services that adopt ECN tech-niques. The network offers investors the benefits of trading instantly and electronically—and it retains the floor-based auction system. Direct Plus, for example, automatically executes orders for up to 2,099 shares on the NYSE without human intervention, enabling floor traders to preserve their roles for larger orders. On the other hand, Institutional Xpress allows big investors to bypass brokers and send orders to a specialist on the trading floor for automatic execution. Yet another new feature is MarkeTrac, which allows investors to navigate the trading floor in real time on the Web.

Indeed, the NYSE has no plans to eliminate the auction floor. In fact, the exchange proposes to construct a new facility across the street from its existing site, which will house the world's most technologically advanced center for the trading of equities. "In our vision, the trading floor continues to be the main mechanism for the exchange," a spokesperson said.

CRITICAL THINKING QUESTIONS

1. How does electronic trading threaten the NYSE's auction system?

2. Why does the NYSE want to maintain the existing auction system?

3. How did the NYSE respond to the demand for change?

4. Go to Chapter 18 of this text's Web site at www.prenhall.com/mescon and click on the hot link to get the New York Stock Exchange's Web site. Follow the online instructions to answer these questions: What is the mission of the NYSE? How does Network NYSE add a new dimension to the exchange? What makes the NYSE unique?

VIDEO CASE AND EXERCISES

■ *Up the Learning Curve: Investment Success Requires Homework*

SYNOPSIS

Investing in stock, bonds, and mutual funds requires a great deal of homework and a certain amount of risk. As an investor, you should be prepared to research the various investments before you plunk down your money. You should also think carefully about your investment goals and your appetite for risk. This video features investment and finance experts explaining the securities markets, answering common questions about securities and investments, and offering ideas about where to learn more about investments of all types.

EXERCISES
Analysis

1. Why would some investors choose to invest in preferred stock rather than in common stock?

2. What are the benefits of investing in mutual funds?

3. How do investments in financial futures work?

4. Why do U.S. government bonds pay lower interest rates than corporate bonds?

5. What are some reliable sources of information about securities such as stocks and bonds?

Application
If a friend's company is about to start selling stock, what questions would you ask before making a decision to buy shares?

Decision
You investigated the company mentioned in the previous question and believe it will be a good long-term investment, even though the industry is highly competitive and the company's immediate prospects are unclear. Should you recommend this stock to all your friends?

Communication
A growing number of investors are choosing to invest only in companies that are socially responsible. Select a publicly held company and draft a letter to the head of investment relations, asking about the company's position on a specific social-responsibility issue, such as anti-pollution measures or consumerism.

Integration
Review the section titled "Responsibility Toward Investors" in Chapter 2. Would you buy a stock if the only information you re-

ceived was from an online buddy in the chat room of a financial Web site?

Ethics

Many Internet companies go public and sell stock without knowing when (or if) they will report a profit. Is this ethical?

Debate

The Boston Celtics is one of several sports teams that have sold stock to investors. Does this team represent a good investment? Choose one side of this question and outline at least two arguments in support of your position.

Teamwork

Working with another student, research the services offered and the fees charged by E*Trade and by a full-service broker such as Morgan Stanley Dean Witter. Summarize your findings in a brief oral or written report and explain why you would choose to work with one of these two firms.

Online Research

Use Internet sources to compare volume on the New York Stock Exchange and NASDAQ over the past week. How many shares of stock changed hands through the NYSE and NASDAQ on each of the last five trading days? Why was volume heavier or lighter on these markets during the period you are investigating? See Component Chapter A, Exhibit A.1, for search engines to use in doing your research.

MYPHLIP COMPANION WEB SITE

Learning Interactively

Visit the myPHLIP Web site at www.prenhall.com/mescon. For Chapter 18, take advantage of the interactive "Study Guide" to test your chapter knowledge. Get instant feedback on whether you need additional studying. Read the "Current Events" articles to get the latest on chapter topics, and complete the exercises as specified by your instructor. Expand your learning with a visit to the "Research Area." There you will find a wealth of information you can use to complete your course assignments.

PART 6

MASTERING GLOBAL AND GEOGRAPHICAL SKILLS— MONITORING THE WORLD MARKETS

The Dow Jones Industrial Average (DJIA), the Standard & Poor's 500, the Wilshire Index—these and other such stock market indexes provide good indications of where U.S. markets are headed. Unfortunately, they aren't much help for markets in other countries. You can find similar indexes in all the other major industrialized countries of the world; perhaps the best known of these is Japan's Nikkei index.

Understanding the composition of a market index is vital to interpret the index's movement up or down and to compare it with the DJIA or other U.S. indexes. Select one of the following stock market indexes and use the Internet or financial newspapers to answer the questions that follow:

- Nikkei (Japan)

- XETRA-DAX (Germany)

- FSE (Britain)

- CAC (France)

- Hang Seng (Hong Kong)

1. Does the index have more or fewer companies than the DJIA? Than the S&P 500?

2. Over the last five or ten years, how has your chosen index performed, compared with the DJIA?

3. Does the index appear to represent the stock market as a whole or just one sector?

4. Go to the CNNfn Financial Network Web site to answer these questions:

   a. Do you spot any trends or patterns between the performance of the international stock market indexes and the U.S. market indexes?

   b. What explanation was provided in the CNNfn news capsules for Europe, Asia, and the U.S. that might have contributed to the performance of these world market indexes?

   c. Was the performance of either Europe's or Asia's markets linked in any way to U.S. news events?

MANAGING FINANCIAL INFORMATION AND RESOURCES

Review the Appendix, "Getting Started With Business PlanPro Software," to learn how to use Business PlanPro Software so that you can complete these exercises.

Think Like a Pro

Objective: By completing these exercises you will become acquainted with the sections of a business plan that address a company's financial and operational projections. For these exercises, use the sample business plan for Fantastic Florals.

Open the BPP software and explore the sample business plan Flower Importer.spd. Click on the Plan Outline icon to access the plan's Task Manager and use it to navigate the company's business plan. Familiarize yourself with this firm's products by reading the Executive Summary (see Finish and Polish) and by reading the sections listed under "Your Company," "What You're Selling," and "Your Sales Forecast."

Review the Start-up Summary and Start-up Table under the Your Company heading, and the Start-up Chart under the Financial Plan heading. Identify the two sources Fantastic Florals will use to fund its start-up costs.

1. Why is it important to indicate how much start-up money will be used to fund assets versus expenses?

2. Review the tables and graphs included in the Fantastic Florals business plan by double clicking on the table and graph icons in the Task Manager. (Note: When viewing financial statements in BPP software use the toolbar—accessible from the table view—to adjust your screen view. For example, to view detail by years only, select Years Only from the View menu. To view a larger portion of the table on your screen, select Hide Table Instructions from the Table menu.)

3. Assuming the financial projections included in the business plan are on target, would an investment of $75,000 for a 20 percent ownership stake in the company be prudent? Explain your answer. Which financial statement(s) did you use to make your decision?
Use the latest yearly financial figures from the company's projected profit and loss statement.

4. What is the company's most profitable product? (Hint: Which of the seven product types listed produces the most gross profit?) How did you arrive at your answer?
Graphs and tables are important features of a well-written business plan. They give the reader necessary detail and present data visually so they are easy to interpret and analyze.

5. Why is it a good idea to use only summary tables in the plan's body and place the detail in the plan's appendix?

Create Your Own Business Plan

Think about your own business. How will you categorize your revenue and expense items. Will you break down your sales by product type? By service? By location? What general operating and product-related expenses will you incur? Now take out a sheet of paper and list your revenue and expense categories and build the framework for your profit and loss statement without entering amounts. How do your categories compare to those used by Fantastic Florals?

Reinventing Schwab

Charles Schwab is a trendsetter. When the SEC ended fixed stock commissions in the 1970s, Schwab forged new ground by opening one of the nation's first discount brokerage houses. When mutual funds exploded in the 1980s, Schwab created a marketplace where investors could switch in and out of funds easily. And with the growing popularity of the Internet in the mid-1990s, Schwab saw the vast potential of online investing and took a giant leap of faith by becoming a full-fledged Internet brokerage.

Schwab didn't worry that moving to the Internet would cannibalize, even destroy, its brokers' traditional and lucrative businesses. Instead, the San Francisco discount broker leveraged the power of the Internet and its nationwide network of customer centers to provide a convenient way for investors to trade stocks. This clicks-and-bricks strategy helped Schwab bring in client assets faster than any other discount or full-service U.S. brokerage: $51 billion in new-client assets poured into Schwab within a six-month period in 1998, and total customer accounts soon climbed from 3 million to over 6 million. That jolted cross-country rival Merrill Lynch. Until that point Schwab had been little more than an annoyance to Merrill and other full-service Wall Street titans. But once Schwab began grabbing Merrill's high-asset customers, and Schwab's total stock valuation passed that of Merrill Lynch's, the nation's largest full-service brokerage firm knew that the moment of truth had arrived.

Merrill's E-Battle

For years, Merrill Lynch scoffed at the Internet. Worried that cheap Web trading would cannibalize the company's lucrative, full-priced brokerage service, Merrill was determined to fight the tide of online trading in order to protect its 17,000 brokers and their high commissions. But with one of every seven stock trades being executed online, and with Schwab going after its throat, Merrill Lynch could no longer turn the other cheek. Faced with defections among even its best customers to online discount trading firms such as Schwab, Merrill was at a critical juncture: Either put its brokers' commissions and fat profit margins at risk or lose a war of attrition to Internet-savvy providers. The stakes of either option were staggering. At risk was everything from the careers of Merrill's executives to the firm's ability to stay out of the arms of suitors such as Chase Manhattan Bank.

Slugfest Moves to the Web

On June 1, 1999, only 10 months after Merrill's executive vice president rallied in a speech that "the do-it-yourself model of investing, centered on Internet trading, should be regarded as a serious threat to America's financial lives," Merrill Lynch stunned the brokerage industry by being the first full-service brokerage to cave in to the Web. Six months later it launched Merrill Lynch Online, a trading Web site that rivaled the industry's best. Then it flexed its muscles and went head-to-head with online market leader Charles Schwab.

For the first time ever, the firm that virtually invented full-service, full-commission brokerage announced that it would now let its customers choose how to buy or sell stock: They could continue to place orders with Merrill's brokers and pay full commission, they could pay $29.95 for each trade they made on Merrill's Web site without a broker, or they could pay a flat fee, based on the size of their portfolios, for broker's advice and unlimited online stock and bond trading.

Broker Blues

As expected, Merrill's cyber move alienated some of its brokers even though the company promised to protect their six-figure incomes for a two-year period. Those who could not buy into Merrill's new program left. But Merrill knew the defectors would soon run into a wall at other brokerage houses because most full-service firms would likely follow Merrill's lead. As Merrill saw it, brokers would just have to find new ways of doing business. Rather than taking on fewer clients and encouraging frequent trading, brokers would have to bring more clients in the door and sell them more fee-based goodies. Moreover, because information that brokers hand out—historical stock charts, financial statements, news, and research—was now available on the Internet free or for a nominal fee, brokers would have to compete on the quality and breadth of the service they offered.

Merrill Turns Up the Heat

Merrill's plunge into cyber investing was more than an aggressive game of catch-up. It was a daring bid to get back on the cutting edge of the fast-changing brokerage industry. Even though the move would cost Merrill $1 billion in commis-

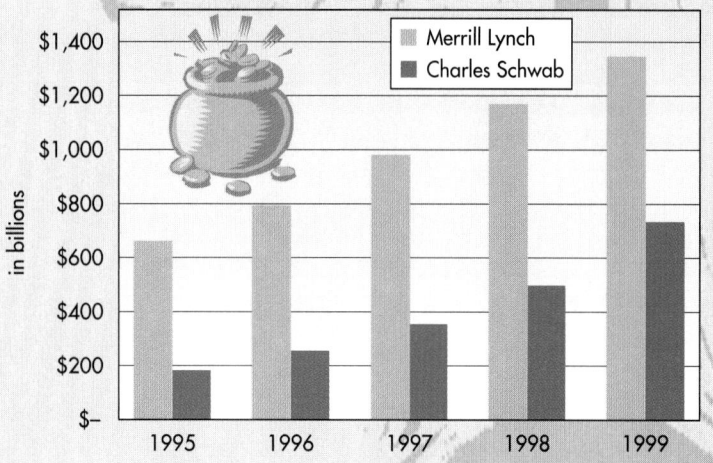

U.S. Client Assets

in billions

	Merrill Lynch	Charles Schwab
1995		
1996		
1997		
1998		
1999		

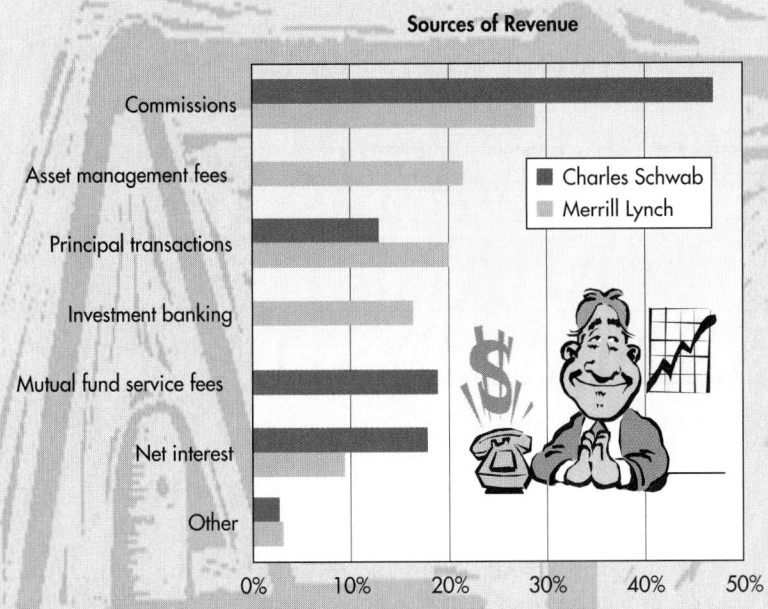

Sources of Revenue

- Commissions
- Asset management fees
- Principal transactions
- Investment banking
- Mutual fund service fees
- Net interest
- Other

■ Charles Schwab
■ Merrill Lynch

0% 10% 20% 30% 40% 50%

sions, the company was confident it could offset the losses by gaining additional client assets.

Determined to remain king of the financial hill, Merrill intensified its battle with rival Schwab—attacking Schwab in nearly every part of its business. For years, Schwab had quietly grabbed assets from its big rival. Now Merrill was grabbing back, turning Schwab from predator to prey. In fact, it didn't take Merrill long to reverse the trend in client-asset inflows and regain its edge over Schwab. But Schwab fought back.

Becoming a Pioneer—Again

Under attack by the country's biggest brokerage firm, Schwab began to offer more than just low prices and online trading. Schwab's co-CEO David Pottruck knew that investors wanted the best of both worlds: the convenience and flexibility of discount online trading with customer support that only people could provide. So to compete with Merrill and other industry rivals, Pottruck decided to develop a new strategy—one that differentiated Schwab from its rivals. "What we want is to be unlike anyone else," announced Pottruck, in *The Wall Street Journal*. "We're changing because customers' needs are changing."

Pottruck set out to turn Schwab into a *different* kind of full-service firm—one that emphasized quality while broadening the scope of its services. In 2000, Schwab acquired blue-chip asset-management firm U.S. Trust Corp, bringing the discount brokerage a step closer to offering a full-service menu of offerings to its investors. Then the company expanded its services to include wireless trading, account management, strategic investment advice, financial planning, portfolio evaluations, and new online research

tools that let customers take investment courses and hear live audio feeds of lectures. Finally, Schwab extended its human touch by expanding its phone centers, building more branch offices, and installing PC kiosks in its branches to provide customers with helpful investment information.

Never-Ending Broker Wars

With Merrill Lynch lowering its drawbridge to accept cheap Internet trades, the Schwab-Merrill war is now at ground-zero. Trade prices, are no longer a distinguishing factor—blurring the lines between full-service and discount brokers. Merrill has not only copied Schwab's multichannel strategy but taken advantage of the Glass-Steagall repeal to roll out new banking services and fight for customers' deposits. Many industry observers believe that if Merrill can stay on track, it will be difficult for Schwab to outrun the raging bull.

Pottruck, of course, sees it differently. He has made it clear that Schwab is not trying to become the traditional model of a full-service firm. Instead, Schwab is establishing a new model—one that will evolve over time. While that may sound vague for some, doomsayers are cautioned to remember that Schwab's Internet success did not occur by accident. Today some 81 percent of Schwab's trades are executed online (versus 36 percent in 1997). This happened because Schwab was willing to bet the company's future on the Web. And with some 7 million customers, $900 billion in assets, and over 20 percent of the online market, Schwab intends to stay ahead of Merrill and others. How? By giving customers what they want, when they want it, and how they want it, says Pottruck.[1]

QUESTIONS FOR CRITICAL THINKING

1. How and why has Schwab continually reinvented itself?

2. Why did Merrill Lynch executives initially scoff at the Internet? Why did they later change their minds?

3. What likely effect will Merrill's move have on its competitors and the brokerage industry as a whole?

4. What are the competitive advantages of both Schwab and Merrill?

5. If Schwab and Merrill had the opportunity to "do it all over again," what changes do you think they would make in their competitive strategies and why?

6. Review the Web sites of Schwab (www.schwab.com) and Merrill Lynch (www.ml.com) to learn more about the companies and their services. What noticeable differences exist between these two rivals?

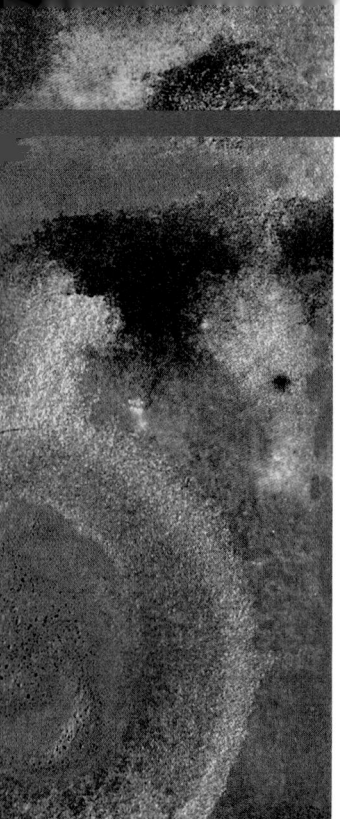

Component Chapter B Business Law, Taxes, and the U.S. Legal System
Component Chapter C Risk Management and Insurance
Component Chapter D Careers in Business and the Employment Search

COMPONENT CHAPTER B

BUSINESS LAW, TAXES, AND THE U.S. LEGAL SYSTEM

■ BUSINESS AND GOVERNMENT

Although the United States is philosophically committed to the free-market system, the government has often stepped in to enact laws and regulations that help resolve disputes between businesses, individuals, and communities. Two major areas in which the government regulates business activities are competition and stakeholder rights. Sometimes these areas overlap. For instance, laws designed to promote competition often have the ultimate goal of protecting consumers.

As you can imagine, keeping track of all these laws and regulations can be a costly and time-consuming undertaking. According to recent estimates, U.S. employers spend about $700 billion annually just to comply with federal laws and regulations.[1] Besides worrying about the federal government, businesses must also consider laws and regulations enacted by individual counties, states, and possibly foreign governments, many of which impose specific and sometimes conflicting restrictions. Of course, this abundance of laws makes it increasingly difficult to understand and stay current on what a business can or can't do. But it doesn't necessarily mean that businesses universally dislike regulation. Antitrust laws, for instance, make it possible for many small companies to compete with larger ones, while other laws encourage a safe, honest business environment. In addition, government regulation and deregulation of specific industries promote competition and protect consumers and other stakeholders.

Laws Promoting Competition
In most sectors of the economy, state and federal regulators work to ensure that all competitors have an equal chance of producing a product, reaching the market, and making a profit.

By setting ground rules and establishing basic standards of proper business behavior, government helps prevent conflicts and facilitates the workings of the economic system. Laws concerning competition make up a huge and complex body of government regulation.

When regulators determine that the public can be best served by limiting competition in certain industries, they will consider restricting entry into those markets. However, in most industries, the government prefers to set ground rules that enable many companies to compete. Over the last century or so, a number of regulations have been established to help prevent individual companies or groups of companies from gaining control of markets in ways that restrain competition or harm consumers. Some of the earliest government moves in this arena produced such landmark pieces of legislation as the Sherman Antitrust Act, the Clayton Antitrust Act, and the Federal Trade Commission Act, which generally sought to rein in the power of a few huge companies such as Standard Oil (see Exhibit B.1). These companies, usually referred to as *trusts* (hence the label *antitrust legislation,* discussed in Chapter 1), had financial and management control of a significant number of other companies in the same industry. The trusts thus controlled enough of the supply and distribution in their respective industries to muscle smaller competitors out of the way.

Whereas the Sherman Act got the regulatory ball rolling, the Clayton Act specifically prohibited **interlocking directorates,** or boards of directors made up of board members from competing firms; the practice of acquiring large blocks of competitors' stock; and discriminatory prices. The Clayton Act also restricted **tying contracts,** which attempt to force buyers to purchase unwanted goods along with goods actually desired. As Chapter 1 pointed out, the U.S. Justice Department

REGULATION	PURPOSE
Interstate Commerce Act (1887)	Regulates business practices, specifically railroad operations and shipping rates
Sherman Antitrust Act (1890)	Fosters competition by preventing monopolies and noncompetitive mergers; establishes competitive market environment as national policy
Pure Food and Drug Act (1906)	Prohibits misbranding and adulteration of food and drugs, specifically those transported across state lines
Meat Inspection Act (1906)	Encourages purity of meat and meat products, specifically those transported across state lines
Federal Trade Commission Act (1914)	Creates the Federal Trade Commission (FTC) to monitor activities that might be unfair and to control illegal trade practices (the FTC's authority was later expanded to cover practices that harmed the public, such as marketing unsafe products)
Clayton Antitrust Act (1914)	Restricts practices such as price discrimination, trying contracts, exclusive dealing, and interlocking boards of directors that give large businesses an advantage over smaller firms
Robinson-Patman Act (1936)	Prohibits price differentials that substantially weaken competition unless they can be justified by actual lower production and selling costs

EXHIBIT B.1

EARLY GOVERNMENT REGULATIONS PERTAINING TO BUSINESS

In response to public outcry against a few large and powerful companies, Congress passed a number of early laws to prevent monopolies and encourage competition.

Rebuffed by U.S. regulators, MCI WorldCom pulled the plug on its long-pending $129 billion megamerger with Sprint. The second- and third-largest U.S. telecom carriers maintained to the end that the deal would offer business and residential users more services, greater innovation, and lower prices. But the U.S. Department of Justice disagreed and filed suit to block the combination.

found Microsoft guilty of violating antitrust laws. In his historic decision, Judge Jackson concluded that Microsoft was guilty of bundling and used such tactics to thwart the challenge posed by Internet software makers, especially Netscape Communications. The judge concluded that "Web browsers and operating systems are indeed separate products" and that tying them together actually harmed consumers by making the Windows operating system more likely to crash. Microsoft, of course, appealed the judge's ruling, and the final outcome of the Microsoft case will eventually be resolved by the U.S. Supreme Court.[2]

Besides monopolies and tying contracts, another key area of concern to regulators is mergers and acquisitions. The government won't grant approval of a merger or an acquisition if regulators think it will restrain competition, as Chapter 5 pointed out. Regulators also keep an eye on changes in technology that might give companies an unfair advantage and on the ability of large companies to control technological development, as evidenced by the U.S. Justice Department's case against Microsoft.

Laws Protecting Stakeholders

As Chapter 2 discussed, businesses have many stakeholders, including employees, consumers, investors, and society as a whole. In the course of serving one or more of these stakeholders, the enterprise may sometimes neglect the interests of other stakeholders in the process. For example, managers who are too narrowly focused on generating wealth for shareholders might not spend the funds necessary to create a safe work environment for employees or to reduce waste. On the other hand, by withholding information about the company's financial performance, managers may hamper the ability of investors to make solid decisions, thereby possibly limiting investors' returns. As a result, government has passed many laws and has established several regulatory agencies that protect consumers, employees, shareholders, and the environment from the potentially harmful actions of business (see Exhibits B.2, B.3, B.4). The Occupational Safety and Health Administration (OSHA), the Equal Employment Opportunity Commission (EEOC), the Securities and Exchange Commission (SEC), and the Environmental Protection Agency (EPA) are just a few of the

LEGISLATION	PROVISION
National Environmental Policy Act (1999)	Establishes a structure for coordinating all federal environmental programs
Clear Air Act and amendments (1963, 1965, 1970, 1977, 1990)	Assists states and localities in formulating control programs; sets federal standards for auto-exhaust emissions; sets maximum permissible pollution levels; authorizes nationwide air-pollution standards and limitations to pollutant discharge; requires scrubbers in new coal-fired power plants; directs EPA to prevent deterioration of air quality in clean areas; sets schedule and standards for cutting smog, acid rain, hazardous factory fumes, and ozone-depleting chemicals
Solid Waste Disposal Act and amendments (1965, 1984)	Authorizes research and assistance to state and local control programs; regulates treatment, storage, transportation, and disposal of hazardous waste
Resource Recovery Act (1970)	Subsidizes pilot recycling plants; authorizes nationwide control programs
Federal Water Pollution Control Act and amendments (1972)	Authorizes grants to states for water-pollution control; gives federal government limited authority to correct pollution problems; authorizes EPA to set and enforce water-quality standards
Safe Drinking Water Act (1974, 1996)	Sets standards for drinking-water quality; requires municipal water systems to report on contaminant levels; establishes funding to upgrade water systems
Noise Control Act (1972)	Requires EPA to set standards for major sources of noise and to advise Federal Aviation Administration on standards for airplane noise
Toxic Substances Control Act (1976)	Requires chemicals testing; authorizes EPA to restrict the use of harmful substances
Oil Pollution Act (1990)	Sets up liability trust fund; extends operations for preventing and containing oil pollution

EXHIBIT B.2

MAJOR FEDERAL ENVIRONMENTAL LEGISLATION

Since the early 1960s, major federal legislation aimed at the environment has focused on providing cleaner air and water and reducing toxic waste.

federal regulatory agencies that most companies must deal with. In addition, the Nutrition Education and Labeling Act of 1990, the Fair Credit Reporting Act, the Americans with Disabilities Act, and the Clean Air Act represent only a fraction of the laws that most businesses must adhere to.

Industry Regulation and Deregulation

In addition to these agencies and laws, the government imposes another layer of regulations on specific industries. From mining to banking to advertising, government officials keep tabs on companies to ensure fair competition, safe working conditions, and generally ethical business practices. For instance, the Federal Aviation Administration (FAA) sets rules for the commercial airline industry; the Federal Reserve Board and the Treasury Department look after the banking industry; and the Federal Communications Commission (FCC) oversees telephone services and radio and television broadcasts.[3] Some lawmakers and citizens have recently called upon the FCC to also regulate Internet development and content more closely. However, top FCC officials have emphatically stated their belief that passing laws to regulate the Internet would be a mistake. Opponents of Internet regulation scored a huge victory in 1997 when the U.S. Supreme Court struck down the Communications Decency Act—a law signed in 1996 that prohibited the transmission of "indecent" material on the Internet—on the grounds that the act restricted the constitutional right to freedom of speech.[4]

In past years, some industries were under strict government control. In the most extreme cases, regulators decided who could enter an industry, what customers they had to serve, and how much they could charge. Consequently, companies that operated in heavily regulated industries had little or no competition. The telecommunications, airline, and banking industries fell under such control until the last few decades, when several waves of *deregulation*, the abandonment or relaxation of existing regulations, opened up competition.

When new competitors enter the market, they often drive down prices and create more choices for consumers. Consider the telecommunications industry, for example. In 1982 the federal government broke AT&T up into seven local telephone companies and one long-distance provider to allow smaller carriers such as MCI (now MCI Worldcom) to compete for long-distance telephone business. Some observers cite the AT&T breakup as the event that triggered the development of new technologies such as cellular networks and that facilitated the mainstreaming of the Internet.[5] The telecommunications industry was further deregulated with the passage of the Telecommunications Reform Act of 1996, which cleared the way for smaller telephone companies to compete in areas once dominated by large conglomerates. Although the act was intended to usher in a new and more competitive communications era, the debate is ongoing about whether it has achieved this goal. For example, the act allowed long-distance carriers to enter local telephone markets and ended the seven local tele-

LEGISLATION	PROVISION
Food, Drug, and Cosmetic Act (1938)	Puts cosmetics, foods, drugs, and therapeutic products under Food and Drug Administration's jurisdiction; outlaws false and misleading labeling
Wool Products Labeling Act (1939)	Requires manufacturers to identify the type and percentage of wool content in products
Flammable Fabrics Act (1953, 1967)	Prohibits interstate shipment of apparel or fabric made of flammable materials; sets stronger standards for clothing flammability
Automobile Information Disclosure Act (1958)	Requires automobile manufacturers to put suggested retail prices on all new passenger vehicles
Textile Fiber Products Identification Act (1958)	Requires labeling of fiber content on textile products
National Traffic Safety Act (1958)	Establishes safety standards for cars and tires
Federal Hazardous Substances Act (1960)	Requires warning labels on items with dangerous chemicals
Cigarette Labeling Act (1965)	Mandates warnings on cigarette packages and in ads
Child Protection Act (1966)	Prohibits the sale of hazardous toys; amended in 1969 to include products that pose electrical, mechanical, or thermal hazards
Fair Packaging and Labeling Act (1966, 1972)	Requires honest, informative package labeling; labels must show origin of product, quantity of contents, uses or applications
Truth-in-Lending Act (Consumer Protection Credit Act) (1968)	Requires creditors to disclose finance charge and annual percentage rate; limits cardholder liability for unauthorized use
Land Sales Disclosure Act (1968)	Protects consumers from unfair practices in sales of land conducted across state lines
Fair Credit Reporting Act (1970)	Requires credit-reporting agencies to set process for assuring accuracy; requires creditors who deny credit to tell consumers the source of information
Consumer Product Safety Act (1972)	Creates Consumer Product Safety Commission
Magnuson-Moss Warranty Act (1975)	Requires complete written warranties in ordinary language; requires warranties to be available before purchase
Alcohol Labeling Legislation (1988)	Requires warning labels on alcohol products, saying that alcohol impairs abilities and that women shouldn't drink when pregnant
Nutrition Education and Labeling Act (1990)	Requires specific, uniform product labels detailing nutritional information on every food regulated by the FDA
American Automobile Labeling Act (1992)	Requires carmakers to identify where cars are assembled and where their individual components are manufactured
Deceptive Mail Prevention and Enforcement Act (1999)	Establishes standards for sweepstakes mailings, skill contests, and facsimile checks to protect U.S. consumers against companies that use such tactics to deceive and exploit consumers

EXHIBIT B.3

MAJOR FEDERAL CONSUMER LEGISLATION

Major federal legislation aimed at consumer protection has focused on food and drugs, false advertising, product safety, and credit protection.

phone companies' monopolies. But some claim that recent mergers among these seven companies have in effect reassembled the original AT&T monopoly. The 1996 act also deregulated the cable television industry, enabling telephone companies and others to compete for cable television viewers, but large cable conglomerates still have a stronghold on most U.S. markets.[6]

Recent state initiatives to allow consumers to buy gas and electricity from several sources are spearheading the introduction of bills in Congress to deregulate the last of the major U.S.

LEGISLATION	PROVISION
Securities Act (1933)	Requires full disclosure of relevant financial information from companies that want to sell new stock or bond issues to the general public; also known as the Truth in Securities Act
Securities Exchange Act (1934)	Creates the Securities and Exchange Commission (SEC) to regulate the national stock exchanges and to establish trading rules
Maloney Act (1938)	Creates the National Association of Securities Dealers to regulate over-the-counter securities trading
Investment Company Act (1940)	Extends the SEC's authority to cover the regulation of mutual funds
Amendment to the Securities ExchangeAct (1964)	Extends the SEC's authority to cover the over-the-counter market
Securities Investor Protection Act (1970)	Creates the Securities Investor Protection Corporation (SIPC) to insure individual investors against losses in the event of dealer fraud or insolvency
Commodity Futures Trading Commission Act (1974)	Creates the Commodity Futures Trading Commission (CFTC) to establish and enforce regulations governing futures trading
Insider Trading and Securities Fraud Act (1988)	Toughens penalties, authorizes bounties for information, requires brokerages to establish written policies to prevent employee violations, and makes it easier for investors to bring legal action against violators
Securities Market Reform Act (1990)	Increases SEC market control by granting additional authority to suspend trading in any security for 10 days, to restore order in the event of a major disturbance, to establish a national system for settlement and clearance of securities transactions, to adapt rules for actions affecting market volatility, and to require more detailed record keeping and reporting of brokers and dealers
Private Securities Litigation Reform Act (1995)	Protects companies from frivolous lawsuits by investors: limits how many class-action suits can be filed by the same person in a 3-year period, and encourages judges to penalize plaintiffs that bring meritless cases

EXHIBIT B.4

MAJOR FEDERAL LEGISLATION GOVERNING THE SECURITIES INDUSTRY

Although you have no guarantee that you'll make money on your investments, you are protected by laws against unfair securities trading practices.

monopolies: the electric-power industry. Although many states have moved ahead with local power deregulation, some industry analysts cite public nervousness over too many unknowns as the reason that competition is getting off to a slow start.[7] Others are more optimistic, pointing out that overall deregulation is good for consumers. For instance, after adjustment for inflation, air fares have decreased by almost one-third since 1978 when Congress deregulated the airlines, and long-distance telephone rates have been cut by about 50 percent since the breakup of AT&T.[8]

Government as Tax Collector

Taxes have historically been used for two purposes in the United States. The most obvious purpose is to raise revenue for government. In addition, the government levies certain taxes and grants tax credits and deductions to provide incentives or disincentives for certain types of behavior.

A **tax credit** is a direct (dollar-for-dollar) reduction in the amount of income tax that an individual or corporate taxpayer owes. By contrast, a **tax deduction** is a reduction in the amount of income on which tax must be paid. For example, many state and local governments grant tax credits to businesses to encourage them to locate in their area. The U.S. government also grants tax credits for activities such as hiring people from selected population groups, increasing investments in research, or using alcohol for fuel.[9]

Like any typical regulatory structure, tax laws have developed in a hodgepodge fashion over many years. Entire segments of accounting and legal professions have sprung up to help companies and individuals cope with their interpretation and compliance. As you probably already know, filing a tax return can be a hair-pulling experience. Some corporations today file tax returns that are several feet thick or more.

The major taxes that affect businesses include those assessed to raise revenue for the operation of government—individual and corporate income taxes, property taxes, and sales taxes—and those assessed to restrict certain business activities such as *excise taxes* and *customs duties*.

■ *Individual and Corporate Income Taxes.* For decades, individual (personal) income taxes have been the federal government's largest single source of revenue and a major source of state revenue as well.[10] On the federal level, personal income is currently taxed at a graduated tax rate, which means that as your taxable income increases, so does the rate at which you pay tax. Some businesses—such as partnerships and sole proprietorships—include the profits generated from their operations in their personal income tax returns. These entities pay income tax at individual income tax rates. Only corporations pay federal income tax at corporate income tax rates. However, corporate profits distributed to individual shareholders (in the form of dividends) are taxed at individual income tax rates. In addition to federal income taxes, many state and local governments also levy income taxes on both corporations and individuals.

- *Property Taxes.* Both businesses and individual property owners pay property taxes on the land and structures they own. In some communities, taxes are assessed on the market value of this property. In addition, property owned by businesses (commercial property) is usually taxed at a higher rate than houses and farms. As a result, businesses often pay a larger portion of a community's property tax.

- *Sales Taxes.* In most states and in some cities, merchandise sold at the retail level is subject to a sales tax. Wholesale businesses, of course, are exempt from paying a sales tax on merchandise they buy for resale to other businesses. Nonetheless, all businesses are indirectly affected by the sales tax because such tax ultimately increases the price of a product to the consumer. Sales tax is collected by retail businesses on purchases made by their customers, and then forwarded to the government.

- *Excise Taxes.* A number of items, including gasoline, tobacco, and liquor, are subject to **excise taxes**—regulatory taxes intended to help control potentially harmful practices ("sin taxes") or to help pay for public services that are used by the taxpayers. For example, the gasoline tax is used to fund road-building projects. Federal excise taxes are also levied on certain services of national scope, such as air travel and telephone calls. Income from federal excise taxes must be used for a purpose related to the tax.

- *Customs Duties.* Products brought into this country are often subject to import taxes, or **customs duties.** These regulatory taxes are selective; they vary with the product and its country of origin. Designed to protect U.S. businesses against foreign competition, customs duties have the effect of raising the price of imports to a level comparable to the price of similar U.S.–made merchandise. Customs duties have been used with increasing frequency as a weapon in foreign policy; the products of friendly nations are often taxed at lower rates than those of indifferent or openly hostile countries.

Business's Influence on Government

Given the impact that government has on business, it is not surprising that business has responded by trying to influence government in various ways. One of the most common approaches is to create **lobbies,** groups of people who try to persuade legislators to vote according to the groups' interests. Industry associations such as the American Bankers Association and the American Medical Association are typically involved in lobbying. Although the members of such associations are competitors, they often have common objectives when it comes to government action. Consider the banking industry, which successfully lobbied Congress to block a bill that would have specified that credit card payments be considered paid as soon as they are postmarked, rather than when the banks receive them.[11] The nation's largest business lobbying group is the Chamber of Commerce of the United States, which spends

about $15 million a year on lobbying. Some of its pet causes include a balanced federal budget and lower corporate taxes.[12]

Businesses also try to influence government by donating money to politicians. Campaign laws strictly limit businesses' ability to donate money directly to candidates; however, they may funnel contributions through **political action committees (PACs).** Through a PAC, a company can solicit contributions from its employees and then allocate the money to various campaigns. In addition to operating company PACs, many companies also work through trade-association PACs. Opponents of PACs complain that these committees corrupt the democratic process, favor incumbents, and drive up the cost of campaigning for everyone. Some employees dislike PACs because they feel pressured to contribute, yet they have little say in how their money will be allocated.[13]

THE U.S. LEGAL SYSTEM

In addition to government agencies and regulations, one of the most pervasive ways that government affects business is through the U.S. legal system. The law protects both businesses and individuals against those who threaten society. It also spells out accepted ways of performing many essential business functions—along with the penalties for failing to comply. In other words, like the average person, companies must obey the law or face the consequences. Although this situation limits a company's freedom, it also provides protection from wrongdoers.

Types of Law

The U.S. Constitution, including the Bill of Rights, is the foundation for our laws. Because the Constitution is a general document, laws offering specific answers to specific problems are constantly embellishing its basic principles. However, law is not static; it develops in response to changing conditions and social standards. Individual laws originate in various ways: through legislative action (*statutory law*), through administrative rulings (*administrative law*), and through customs and judicial precedents (*common law*). To one degree or another, all three forms of law affect businesses. In addition, companies that conduct business overseas must be familiar with **international law,** the principles, customs, and rules that govern the affairs between nations and that regulate transactions between individuals and businesses of different countries.[14] Successful global business requires an understanding of the domestic laws of trading partners as well as of established international trading standards and legal guidelines.

Statutory Law **Statutory law** is law written by the U.S. Congress, state legislatures, and local governments. One very important part of statutory law affecting businesses is the **Uniform Commercial Code (UCC).** Designed to mitigate differences between state statutory laws and to simplify interstate commerce, this code is a comprehensive, systematic collection of statutes in a particular legal area.[15] For example, the UCC provides a nationwide standard in many issues of commercial law, such as sales contracts, bank deposits, and warranties. The UCC has been adopted in its entirety in 49 states and the District of Columbia, and about half of it has been adopted in Louisiana.

Administrative Law Once laws have been passed by a state legislature or Congress, an administrative agency or commission typically takes responsibility for enforcing them. That agency may be called on to clarify a regulation's intent, often by consulting representatives of the affected industry. The administrative agency may then write more specific regulations, which are considered **administrative law.**

Government agencies cannot, however, create regulations out of thin air; the agency's regulations must be linked to specific statutes to be legal. For example, the FTC (Federal Trade Commission) issues regulations and enforces statutory laws concerning such deceptive trade practices as unfair debt collection and false advertising. Recently the FTC cracked down on germ-fighting claims being made by Unilever, producer of Vaseline Intensive Care products. The FTC said that Unilever's claims that the lotion "stops germs for hours" lacked scientific proof and deceived consumers into thinking they would be shielded from disease-causing germs if they used the lotion. Unilever agreed to stop making such claims.[16]

Administrative agencies also have the power to investigate corporations suspected of breaking administrative laws. A corporation found to be misbehaving may agree to a **consent order,** which allows the company to promise to stop doing something without actually admitting to any illegal behavior. For example, Stone Container signed a 1998 consent order with the FTC settling the alleged charges that the company attempted to orchestrate an industrywide price increase in violation of federal antitrust laws. Admitting no guilt, Stone Container entered into the consent order to avoid costly and time-consuming litigation.[17]

As an alternative to entering into a consent order, the administrative agency may start legal proceedings against the company in a hearing presided over by an administrative law judge. For instance, the Securities and Exchange Commission required KPMG Peat Marwick to go before an administrative law judge to answer charges that the company violated the SEC's auditor independence rules when it audited the client of a former KPMG-affiliated company.[18] During such a hearing, witnesses are called and evidence is presented to determine the facts of the situation. The judge then issues a decision, which may impose corrective actions on the company. If either party objects to the decision, the party may file an appeal to the appropriate federal court.[19]

Common Law **Common law,** the type of law that comes out of courtrooms and judges' decisions, began in England many centuries ago and was transported to the United States by the colonists. It is applied in all states except Louisiana (which follows a French model). Common law is sometimes called the "unwritten law" to distinguish it from legislative acts and administrative-agency regulations, which are written documents. Instead, common law is established through custom and the precedents set in courtroom proceedings.

Despite its unwritten nature, common law has great continuity, which derives from the doctrine of *stare decisis* (Latin for "to stand by decisions"). What the *stare decisis* doctrine means is that judges' decisions establish a precedent for deciding future cases of a similar nature. Because common law is based on what has gone before, the legal framework develops gradually.

In the United States, common law is applied and interpreted in the system of courts (see Exhibit B.5). Common law thus develops through the decisions in trial courts, special

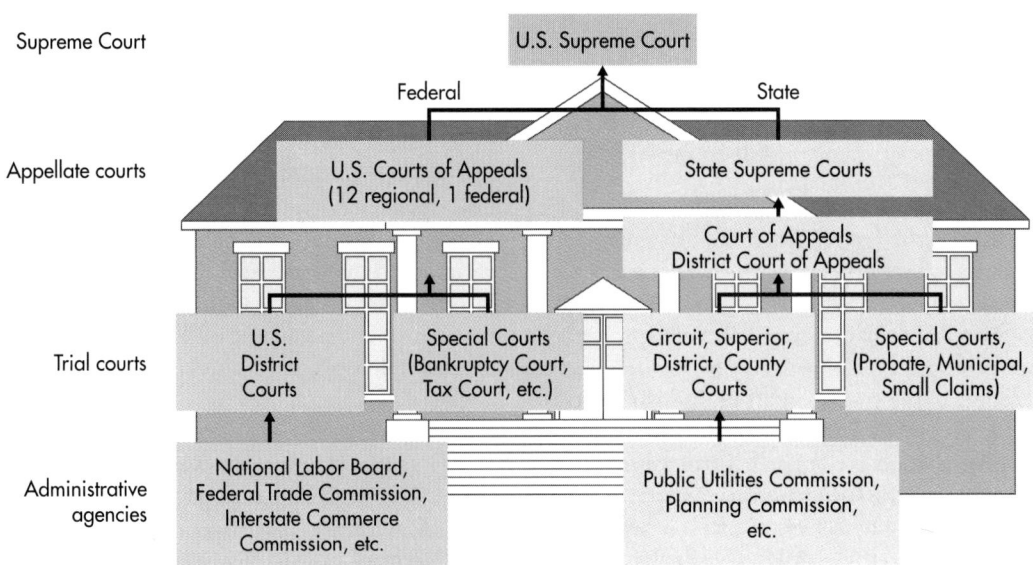

EXHIBIT B.5

THE U.S. COURT SYSTEM

A legal proceeding may begin in a trial court or an administrative agency (examples of each are given here). An unfavorable decision may be appealed to a higher court at the federal or state level. (The court of appeals is the highest court in states that have no state supreme court; some other states have no intermediate appellate court.) The U.S. Supreme Court, the country's highest court, is the court of final appeal.

courts, and appellate courts. The U.S. Supreme Court (or the highest court of a state when state laws are involved) sets precedents for entire legal systems. Lower courts must then abide by those precedents as they pertain to similar cases.

In all but six states, business cases are heard in standard trial courts. However, many corporations are pushing for the establishment of a network of special business courts. Advocates say that the special nature of business legal disputes requires experienced judges who understand business issues. They also feel that a system of business courts would go a long way toward reducing the expense and unpredictability of business litigation. However, opponents say that business courts are likely to favor local companies in disputes involving out-of-state litigants. Moreover, they say that the courts are likely to come under the influence of powerful business special-interest groups. It remains to be seen whether the states will continue to pursue the establishment of special business courts.[20]

In legal proceedings, common law, administrative law, and statutory law may all be applicable. If they conflict, statutory law generally prevails. However, the three forms of law overlap to such an extent that the differences between them are often indistinguishable. For instance, if you bought what you thought was a goose-down coat and then found out that the coat was actually filled with reprocessed polyester, you could sue the coat manufacturer for misrepresentation. Although the basis for this suit is an old concept in common law, it has also been incorporated in state and federal legislation against fraudulent and misleading advertising, which is further interpreted and enforced by the Federal Trade Commission.

Business Law

Although businesses must comply with the full body of laws that apply to individuals, a subset of laws can be defined more precisely as **business law.** This includes those elements of law that directly affect business activities. For example, laws pertaining to business licensing, employee safety, and corporate income taxes can all be considered business law. For the remainder of this chapter, we will examine some of the specific categories of laws affecting business, including torts; contracts; agency; property transactions; patents, trademarks, and copyrights; negotiable instruments; and bankruptcy.

Torts A **tort** is a noncriminal act (other than breach of contract) that results in injury to a person or to property.[21] A tort can be either intentional or the result of negligence. The victim of a tort is legally entitled to some form of financial compensation, or **damages,** for loss and suffering. This compensation is also known as a *compensatory damage award*. In some cases, the victim may also receive a *punitive damage award* to punish the wrongdoer if the misdeed was glaringly bad. You may have heard about cases of excessively high punitive damage awards, such as the $4 million punitive judgment against BMW for retouching a car that had paint damage and selling it as new or the $1.2 million awarded a former Home Depot worker after a jury found that she had been sexually harassed and unfairly terminated. However, a recent Cornell University study found that punitive damages are awarded in only about 6 percent of cases

Hope Larson, here with her son Jacob, paid $500 to an Internet seller for a camcorder, but it never arrived. An experienced Internet user, Larson thought she was the last person who would get cheated through an online auction. She was wrong. Only a fraction of similar fraud cases are tried in court because the amount of money involved is often small and the incidents cross state lines.

nationwide and that the majority of damages are commensurate with compensatory damage awards.[22]

Intentional Torts An **intentional tort** is a willful act that results in injury. For example, accidentally hitting a softball through someone's window is a tort, but purposely cutting down someone's tree because it obscures your view is an intentional tort. Note that *intent* in this case does not mean the intent to cause harm; it is the intent to commit a specific physical act. Some intentional torts involve communication of false statements that harm another's reputation. If the communication is in writing or on television, it is called *libel;* if it is spoken, it is *slander.*[23] For example, a group of Texas cattlemen sued television talk show host Oprah Winfrey for more than $12 million in damages because they said her disparaging remarks about beef in a 1996 television program caused beef prices to plummet. The jury found Winfrey not guilty of food-libel laws designed to protect perishable food products from disparagement or misinformation that could diminish their market value.[24]

Negligence and Product Liability In contrast to intentional torts, torts of **negligence** involve a failure to use a reasonable amount of care necessary to protect others from unreasonable risk of injury.[25] Cases of alleged negligence often involve **product liability,** which is a product's capacity to cause damages or injury for which the producer or seller is held responsible. Product liability lawsuits cost business owners as much as $150 billion every year.[26]

Consider American Home Products, for instance. In 1999 the company agreed to pay about $4 billion to thousands of individuals who contended they were injured by taking the company's popular diet pill combination fen-phen. The product, which had been hailed as a miracle weight-loss pill for the obese, was removed from the market at the request of the FDA after studies linked the drugs to heart valve damage. More than six million people took fen-phen, but only those who developed problems are eligible to collect an injury award; others will be reimbursed for out-of-pocket costs.[27]

A company may also be held liable for injury caused by a defective product even if the company used all reasonable care in the manufacture, distribution, or sale of its product. Such **strict product liability** makes it possible to assign liability without assigning fault. It must only be established that (1) the company is in the business of selling the product; (2) the product reached the customer or user without substantial change in its condition; (3) the product was defective; (4) the defective condition rendered the product unreasonably dangerous; and (5) the defective product caused the injury.[28]

Although few people would argue that individual victims of harmful products shouldn't be entitled to some sort of compensation, many people question whether such strict interpretation of product liability laws is good for society. Many individuals try to take advantage of the system by filing "frivolous" lawsuits. The large compensatory, and sometimes punitive, damages that plaintiffs are awarded make it difficult for many companies to obtain product liability insurance at a reasonable price. As a result, manufacturers have withheld products from the market that might otherwise benefit society. Although Congress passed a bill in 1996 that restricted the amounts of compensatory and punitive damages awarded in product liability suits, the bill was vetoed by President Clinton, who felt that it was too restrictive and would have a negative impact on consumers. Nonetheless, the issue continues to be a priority with lawmakers.[29]

Contracts   Broadly defined, a **contract** is an exchange of promises between two or more parties that is enforceable by law. Many business transactions—including buying and selling products, hiring employees, purchasing group insurance, and licensing technology—involve contracts. Contracts may be either express or implied. An **express contract** is derived from the words (either oral or written) of the parties; an **implied contract** stems from the actions or conduct of the parties.[30] Iris Kapustein learned the hard way how important written contracts can be in the business world. When she first started her trade show management and consulting firm, she operated on the principle of "my word is my bond." But after losing $15,000 to clients who didn't pay, she adopted a new principle: All clients must sign contracts, and all contracts supplied by clients must be reviewed by her attorney.[31]

Elements of a Contract   The law of contracts deals largely with identifying the exchanges that can be classified as contracts. The following factors must usually be present for a contract to be valid and enforceable:

- *An offer must be made.* One party must propose that an agreement be entered into. The offer may be oral or written, but it must be firm, definite, and specific enough to make it

clear that someone intends to be legally bound by the offer. Finally, the offer must be communicated to the intended party or parties.

- *An offer must be accepted.* For an offer to be accepted, there must be clear intent (spoken, written, or by action) to enter into the contract. An implied contract arises when a person requests or accepts something and the other party has indicated that payment is expected. If, for example, your car breaks down on the road and you call a mobile mechanic for repair service, you are obligated to pay the reasonable value for the services, even if you didn't agree to specific charges beforehand. However, when a specific offer is made, the acceptance must satisfy the terms of the offer. For example, if someone offers you a car for $18,000, and you say you would take it for $15,000, you have not accepted the offer. Your response is a *counteroffer,* which may or may not be accepted by the salesperson.

- *Both parties must give consideration.* A contract is legally binding only when the parties have bargained with each other and have exchanged something of value, which is called the **consideration.** The relative value of each party's consideration does not generally matter to the courts. In other words, if you make a deal with someone and later decide you didn't get enough in the deal, that result is not the court's concern. You entered into the deal with the original consideration in mind, and that fact is legally sufficient.[32]

- *Both parties must give genuine assent.* To have a legally enforceable contract, both parties must agree to it voluntarily. The contract must be free of fraud, duress, undue influence, and mutual mistake.[33] If only one party makes a mistake, it ordinarily does not affect the contract. On the other hand, if both parties made a mistake, the agreement would be void. For example, if both the buyer and the seller of a business believed the business was profitable, when in reality it was operating at a loss, their agreement would be void.

- *Both parties must be competent.* The law gives certain classes of people only a limited capacity to enter into contracts. Minors, people who are senile or insane, and in some cases those who are intoxicated cannot usually be bound by a contract for anything but the bare necessities: food, clothing, shelter, and medical care.

- *The contract must not involve an illegal act.* Courts will not enforce a promise that involves an illegal act. For example, a drug dealer cannot get help from the courts to enforce a contract to deliver illegal drugs at a prearranged price.

- *The contract must be in proper form.* Most contracts can be made orally, by an act, or by a casually written document; however, certain contracts are required by law to be in writing. For example, the transfer of goods worth $500 or more must be accompanied by a written document. The written form is also required for all real estate contracts.

A contract need not be long; all these elements of a contract may be contained in a simple document (see Exhibit B.6). In fact, a personal check is one type of simple contract.

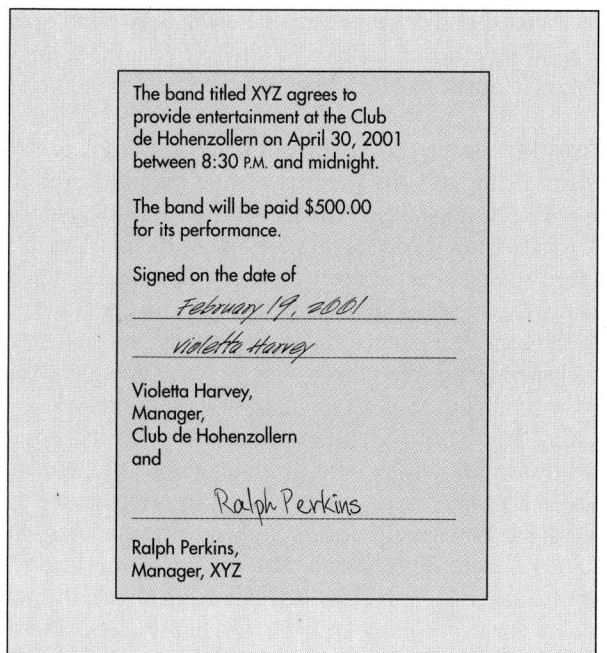

The band titled XYZ agrees to provide entertainment at the Club de Hohenzollern on April 30, 2001 between 8:30 P.M. and midnight.

The band will be paid $500.00 for its performance.

Signed on the date of

February 19, 2001

Violetta Harvey

Violetta Harvey,
Manager,
Club de Hohenzollern
and

Ralph Perkins

Ralph Perkins,
Manager, XYZ

EXHIBIT B.6

ELEMENTS OF A CONTRACT

This simple document contains all the essential elements of a valid contract.

Contract Performance Contracts normally expire when the agreed-to conditions have been met, called *performance* in legal terms. However, not all contracts run their expected course. Both parties involved can agree to back out of the contract, for instance. In other cases, one party fails to live up to the terms of the contract, a situation called **breach of contract.** The other party has several options at that point:

- *Discharge.* When one party violates the terms of the agreement, generally the other party is under no obligation to continue with the contract. In other words, the second party is discharged from the contract.

- *Damages.* A party has the right to sue in court for damages that were foreseeable at the time the contract was entered into and that result from the other party's failure to fulfill the contract. The amount of damages awarded usually reflects the amount of profit lost and often includes court costs as well.

- *Specific performance.* A party can be compelled to live up to the terms of the contract if money damages would not be adequate.

Jeffrey Katzenberg, former Walt Disney studio chief, recently settled a bitter breach-of-contract lawsuit after contending that he was owed as much as $581 million stemming from a unique contractual bonus arrangement with the Walt Disney Company. Katzenberg left the company on learning he would not be promoted to president but argued that he was due a lump sum equal to 2 percent of the projected future profits of films and television shows created during the 10 years he oversaw Disney's movie and television operations. The settlement

figure is private, but analysts speculate that Katzenberg received about $250 million.[34]

To control the increasing costs of litigation, more and more companies are now experimenting with alternatives to the courtroom. These include independent mediators, who sit down with the two parties and try to hammer out a satisfactory solution to contract problems, and mandatory arbitration, in which an impartial arbitrator or arbitration panel hears evidence from both sides and makes a legally binding decision. However, mandatory arbitration has come under fire by consumer groups because it can wipe out a customer's right to sue. For example, Gateway includes a clause in the purchase agreement documents it ships with every computer stating that any dispute or controversy arising from an agreement to purchase a Gateway product "shall be settled exclusively and finally by arbitration." Moreover, the courts have ruled that failure to read such documents constitutes acceptance of Gateway's terms. Although some consumers prefer to use alternative dispute resolution, those who do not wish to waive their right to sue are advised to read the fine print of all contracts and purchase agreements. The same advice applies to employment and service contracts. [35]

Warranties The Uniform Commercial Code specifies that everyday sales transactions are a special kind of contract (although this provision applies only to tangible goods, not to services), even though they may not meet all the exact requirements of regular contracts. Related to the sales contract is the notion of a **warranty,** which is a statement specifying what the producer of a product will do to compensate the buyer if the product is defective or if it malfunctions. Warranties come in several flavors. One important distinction is between *express warranties,* which are specific, written statements, and *implied warranties,* which are unwritten but involve certain protections under the law. Also, warranties are either *full* or *limited.* The former obligates the seller to repair or replace the product, without charge, in the event of any defect or malfunction, whereas the latter imposes restrictions on the defects or malfunctions that will be covered. Warranty laws also address a number of other details, including giving consumers instructions on how to exercise their rights under the warranty.[36]

Agency These days it seems that nearly every celebrity has an agent. Basketball players hire agents to get them athletic shoe commercials and handle their contract negotiations; authors' agents sell manuscripts to the publishers that offer the largest advances; actors' agents try to find choice movie and television roles for their clients. These relationships illustrate a common legal association known as **agency,** which exists when one party, known as the *principal,* authorizes another party, known as the *agent,* to act on the principal's behalf in contractual matters.[37]

All contractual obligations come into play in agency relationships. The principal usually creates this relationship by explicit authorization. In some cases—when a transfer of property is involved, for example—the authorization must be written in the form of a document called a **power of attorney,** which states that one person may legally act for another (to the extent authorized).

Usually, an agency relationship is terminated when the objective of the relationship has been met or at the end of a period specified in the contract between agent and principal. It may also be ended by a change of circumstances, by the agent's breach of duty or loyalty, or by the death of either party.

Property Transactions Anyone interested in business must know the basics of property law. Most people think of property as some object they own (a book, a car, a house). However, **property** is actually the relationship between the person having the rights to any tangible or intangible object and all other persons. The law recognizes two primary types of property: real and personal. **Real property** is land and everything permanently attached to it, such as trees, fences, or mineral deposits. **Personal property** is all property that is not real property; it may be tangible (cars, jewelry, or anything having a physical existence) or intangible (bank accounts, stocks, insurance policies, customer lists). A piece of marble in the earth is real property until it is cut and sold as a block, when it becomes personal property. Property rights are subject to various limitations and restrictions. For example, the government monitors the use of real property for the welfare of the public, to the point of explicitly prohibiting some property uses and abuses.[38]

Two types of documents are important in obtaining real property for factory, office, or store space: a deed and a lease. A **deed** is a legal document by which an owner transfers the *title*, or right of ownership, to real property to a new owner. A lease is used for a temporary transfer of interest in real property. The party that owns the property is commonly called the landlord; the party that occupies or gains the right to occupy the property is the tenant. The tenant pays the landlord, usually in periodic installments, for the use of the property. Generally, a lease may be granted for any length of time that the two parties agree on.

Patents, Trademarks, and Copyrights If you invent a product, write a book, develop some new software, or simply come up with a unique name for your business, you probably want to prevent other people from using or prospering from your **intellectual property** without fairly compensating you. Several forms of legal protection are available for your creations. They include patents, trademarks, and copyrights. Which one you should use depends on what you have created. Having a patent, copyright, or trademark still doesn't guarantee that your idea or product will not be copied. However, they do provide you with legal recourse if your creations are infringed upon.

Patents A patent protects the invention or discovery of a new and useful process, an article of manufacture, a machine, a chemical substance, or an improvement on any of these. Issued by the U.S. Patent Office, a patent grants the owner the right to exclude others from making, using, or selling the invention for 20 years.[39] After that time, the patented item becomes available for common use. On the one hand, patent law guarantees the originator the right to use the discovery exclusively for a relatively long period of time, thus encouraging people to devise new machines, gadgets, and processes. On the other hand, it

also ensures that rights to the new item will be released eventually, allowing other enterprises to discover even more innovative ways to use it.

Trademarks A trademark is any word, name, symbol, or device used to distinguish the product of one manufacturer from those made by others. A service mark is the same thing for services. McDonald's golden arches are one of the most visible of modern trademarks. Brand names can also be registered as trademarks. Examples are Exxon, Polaroid, and Chevrolet.

If properly registered and renewed every 20 years, a trademark generally belongs to its owner forever. Among the exceptions are popular brand names that have become generic terms, meaning that they describe a whole class of products. A brand-name trademark can become a generic term if the trademark has been allowed to expire, if it has been incorrectly used by its owner (as in the case of Borden's ReaLemon lemon juice, which the Federal Trade Commission ruled was being used by Borden to maintain a monopoly in bottled lemon juice), or if the public comes to equate the name with the class of products, as was the case with zipper, linoleum, aspirin, Xerox, and many other brand names.

Trade dress, defined as the general appearance or image of a product, has been easier to legally protect since 1992 when the U.S. Supreme Court extended trademark protection to products with "inherently distinctive" appearances. For instance, in 1999 Apple Computer filed suit against Future Power for allegedly infringing on the iMac trade dress with its lookalike E-Power PC and asked the court to prohibit the sale of E-Power in addition to an award of actual and punitive damages. The case was settled with Apple securing worldwide injunctions against Future Power from making, distributing, and selling their E-Power personal computers after the U.S. Federal Court barred the sale of E-Power computers that copied Apples' award-wining iMac computer.[40]

Copyrights Copyrights protect the creators of literary, dramatic, musical, artistic, scientific, and other intellectual works. Any printed, filmed, or recorded material can be copyrighted. The copyright gives its owner the exclusive right to reproduce (copy), sell, or adapt the work he or she has created. Copyright law covers reproduction by photocopying, videotape, and magnetic storage.

The Library of Congress Copyright Office will issue a copyright to the creator or to whomever the creator has granted the right to reproduce the work. (A book, for example, may be copyrighted by the author or the publisher.) Copyrights issued through 1977 are good for 75 years. Copyrights issued after 1977 are valid for the lifetime of the creator plus 50 years.

Copyright protection on the Internet has become an especially important topic as more businesses and individuals publish Web sites. Technically, copyright protection exists from the moment material is created. Therefore, anything you post on a Web site is protected by copyright law. However, loose Internet standards and a history of sharing information via the Net has made it difficult for some users to accept this situation.

Napster became an Internet phenomenon by allowing its 32 million users to download virtually any popular music for free. In 2000, major music labels went to court to try to force Napster to curb its music-transfer service, which the record industry regarded as a violation of copyright laws. Napster's inventor Shawn Fanning (pictured here), argued in court that noncommercial music downloading is indeed legal. In 2001, a U.S. Federal District judge ruled against Napster, shutting down the operation.

But the No Electronic Theft Act (enacted in 1998) makes it clear that the sanctity of the copyright extends into the area of cyberspace. This law makes it a crime to possess or distribute multiple copies of online copyrighted material for profit or not. Specifically, it closes the loophole that had allowed the distribution of copyrighted material as long as the offender didn't seek profit. Penalties include fines up to $250,000 and five years in prison.[41] To avoid potential copyright infringements, experts suggest that authors include copyright and trademark notices on Web pages that contain protected material, include a link on each page to a detailed copyright notice that explains what users can and cannot do, and place disclaimers on all pages that contain links to other sites.[42] (Consult "Emerging Legal Issues in E-Business at this text's online supplement, www.prenhall.com/mescon, for additional discussion of intellectual property issues in e-business.)

Negotiable Instruments Whenever you write a personal check, you are creating a **negotiable instrument,** a transferable document that represents a promise to pay a specified amount. (*Negotiable* in this sense means that it can be sold or used as payment of a debt; an *instrument* is simply a written document that expresses a legal agreement.) In addition to checks, negotiable instruments include certificates of deposit, promissory notes, and commercial paper. To be negotiable, an instrument must meet several criteria:[43]

■ It must be in writing and signed by the person who created it.

■ It must have an unconditional promise to pay a specified sum of money.

■ It must be payable either on demand or at a specified date in the future.

■ It must be payable either to some specified person or organization or to the person holding it (the bearer).

You can see how a personal check meets those criteria; when you write one, you are agreeing to pay the amount of the check to the person or organization to whom you're writing it.

Bankruptcy Even though the U.S. legal system establishes the rules of fair play and offers protection from the unscrupulous, it can't prevent most businesses from taking on too much debt. The legal system does, however, provide help for businesses that find themselves in deep financial trouble. **Bankruptcy** is the legal means of relief for debtors (either individuals or businesses) who are unable to meet their financial obligations.[44]

Voluntary bankruptcy is initiated by the debtor; *involuntary bankruptcy* is initiated by creditors. The law provides for several types of bankruptcy, which are commonly referred to by chapter number of the Bankruptcy Reform Act. In a Chapter 7 bankruptcy, the debtor's assets will be sold and the proceeds divided equitably among the creditors. Under Chapter 11 (which is usually aimed at businesses but does not exclude individuals other than stockbrokers), a business is allowed to get back on its feet and continue functioning while it arranges to pay its debts.[45] For the steps involved in a Chapter 11 bankruptcy, see Exhibit B.7. Keep in mind that filing for bankruptcy is an extremely risky venture and should not be pursued lightly. Bankruptcy can damage a company's or an individual's credit rating and reputation for a long time to come. Thus, it should never be used as a tactic to avoid paying creditors.

By entering Chapter 11, a company gains time to cut costs and streamline operations. Many companies emerge from Chapter 11 as leaner, healthier organizations. Creditors often benefit too. If the company can get back on its financial feet, creditors may be able to retrieve more of the money they are

Planet Hollywood, the movie-themed restaurant chain that has been financially bleeding despite backing from a star-studded roster of investors, filed for Chapter 11 bankruptcy reorganization to protect the company from creditors, bond owners, and especially leaseholders as it attempts to financially restructure. The restructuring is expected to end with most of the company's restaurants shattered.

Step 1: All current legal proceedings against the firm are halted. A decision is made to either liquidate or reorganize the firm, based on the value of the firm's assets. If liquidation is chosen, the firm's assets are transferred to a trustee, who sells them to pay the firm's debts. If reorganization is chosen, go to step 2.

Step 2: The courts may appoint a trustee to operate the firm, or current management may continue to operate it. A reorganization plan is developed either by current management, by the trustee, or by a committee of creditors. When plan is developed, go to step 3.

Step 3: Creditors and shareholders vote on the reorganization plan. Plan is ratified if (1) at least one-half of creditors vote in favor and if their claims against the company represent at least two-thirds of total claims; (2) at least two-thirds of shareholders approve the plan; and (3) the plan is confirmed by the court. When plan is ratified, go to step 4.

Step 4: The plan guarantees creditors new securities, and sometimes cash, in exchange for dismissal of their claims. With the firm discharged from its debts, it is free to start anew without the weight of past failures.

EXHIBIT B.7

STEPS IN CHAPTER 11 BANKRUPTCY PROCEEDINGS

Chapter 11 bankruptcy may buy a debtor time to reorganize finances and continue operating. However, using this device to evade financial obligations is extremely risky from a legal standpoint, and declaring bankruptcy may severely damage the reputation and credit rating of a firm or an individual.

owed. Consider Carson Pirie Scott & Company. The Milwaukee-based department store chain entered Chapter 11 in 1991 with an $800 million mountain of debt. Today the company is out of bankruptcy, is virtually debt-free, and brings in $1 billion a year in revenue.[46] However, some companies never recover.

Montgomery Ward was one such company. In 1997 GE Capital purchased the retailer for $650 million after Wards sank into bankruptcy. In 1999 Wards emerged from Chapter 11 bankruptcy protection with a new strategy that called for re-modeling stores and updating fashion. But the strategy failed to deliver the necessary financial results. So in December 2000, the 128-year-old retailer called it quits. Montgomery Ward filed for Chapter 11 bankruptcy again, this time closing its 250 stores and 10 distribution centers.[47]

TEST YOUR KNOWLEDGE

QUESTIONS FOR REVIEW

1. What are the major areas in which governments regulate business?

2. How did the deregulation of the telecommunications industry benefit consumers?

3. What are the three types of U.S. laws, and how do they differ? What additional laws must global companies consider?

4. What is the difference between negligence and intentional torts?

5. What are the seven elements of a valid contract?

QUESTIONS FOR ANALYSIS

6. What is precedent, and how does it affect common law?

7. What does the concept of strict product liability mean to businesses?

8. Why is agency important to business?

9. What is the advantage of declaring Chapter 11 bankruptcy? What is the disadvantage?

10. If you wrote a poem or a short story and published it on your own Web site, would your work be protected under copyright law? What steps should you take to make sure your work is not stolen or misused?

11. For a small investment, anyone can purchase a CD copier, called a CD burner, and record a free CD by downloading music off the Internet. If the 1998 Electronic Theft Act makes it a crime to possess or distribute multiple copies of online copy-righted material, whether for profit or not, why doesn't the government simply ban such copying devices?

CHAPTER GLOSSARY

administrative law
Rules, regulations, and interpretations of statutory law set forth by administrative agencies and commissions

agency
Business relationship that exists when one party (the principal) authorizes another party (the agent) to enter into contracts on the principal's behalf

bankruptcy
Legal procedure by which a person or a business that is unable to meet financial obligations is relieved of debt

breach of contract
Failure to live up to the terms of a contract, with no legal excuse

business law
Those elements of law that directly influence or control business activities

common law
Law based on the precedents established by judges' decisions

consent order
Settlement in which an individual or organization promises to discontinue some illegal activity without admitting guilt

consideration
Negotiated exchange necessary to make a contract legally binding

contract
Legally enforceable exchange of promises between two or more parties

customs duties
Fees imposed on goods brought into the country; also called import taxes

damages
Financial compensation to an injured party for loss and suffering

deed
Legal document by which an owner transfers the title, or ownership rights, to real property to a new owner

excise taxes
Taxes intended to help control potentially harmful practices or to help pay for government services used only by certain people or businesses

express contract
Contract derived from words, either oral or written

implied contract
Contract derived from actions or conduct

intellectual property
Intangible personal property, such as ideas, songs, trade secrets, and computer programs, that are protected by patents, trademarks, and copyrights

international law
Principles, customs, and rules that govern the international relationships between states, organizations, and persons

intentional tort
Willful act that results in injury

interlocking directorates
Situations in which members of the board of one firm sit on the board of a competing firm

lobbies
Groups that try to persuade legislators to vote according to the groups' interests

negligence
Tort in which a reasonable amount of care to protect others from risk of injury is not used

negotiable instrument
Transferable document that represents a promise to pay a specified amount

personal property
All property that is not real property

political action committees (PACs)
Groups formed under federal election laws to raise money for candidates through employee contributions

power of attorney
Written authorization for one party to legally act for another

product liability
The capacity of a product to cause harm or damage for which the producer or seller is held accountable.

property
Rights held regarding any tangible or intangible object

real property
Land and everything permanently attached to it

stare decisis
Concept of using previous judicial decisions as the basis for deciding similar court cases

statutory law
Statute, or law, created by a legislature

strict product liability
Liability for injury caused by a defective product when all reasonable care is used in its manufacture, distribution, or sale; no fault is assigned

tax credit
Direct reduction in the amount of income tax owed by a person or business; granted by a government body for engaging or not engaging in selected activities

tax deduction
Direct reduction in the amount of income on which a person or business pays taxes

tort
Noncriminal act (other than breach of contract) that results in injury to a person or to property

tying contracts
Contracts forcing buyers to purchase unwanted goods along with goods actually desired

Uniform Commercial Code (UCC)
Set of standardized laws, adopted by most states, that govern business transactions

warranty
Statement specifying what the producer of a product will do to compensate the buyer if the product is defective or if it malfunctions

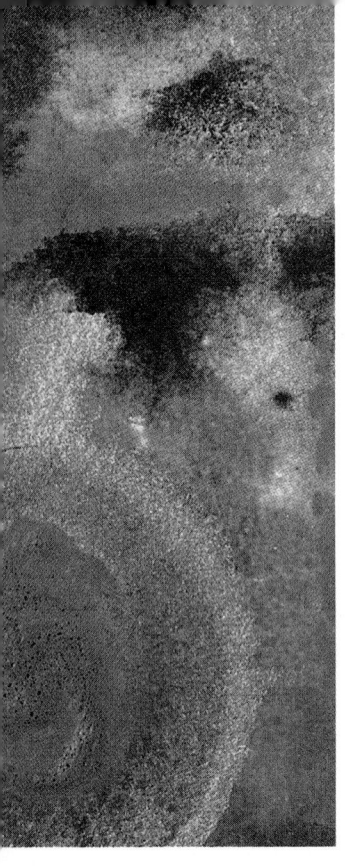

COMPONENT CHAPTER C

RISK MANAGEMENT AND INSURANCE

PROTECTION AGAINST RISK

All businesses face the risk of loss. Fire, lawsuits, accidents, natural disasters, theft, illness, disability, and death are common occurrences that can devastate any business—large or small—that is unprepared. Of course, managers cannot guard against every conceivable threat of loss. Still, they know that in any given situation, the greater the number of outcomes that may occur, the greater their company is at *risk*.

Understanding Risk

Risk is a daily fact of life for both businesses and individuals. Most businesses accept the possibility of losing money in order to make money. In fact, risk prompts people to go into business in the first place. Although the formal definition of **risk** is the variation, based on chance, in possible outcomes of an event, it's not unusual to sometimes hear the term used to mean exposure to loss. This second definition is helpful, because it explains why people purchase **insurance,** a contractual arrangement whereby one party agrees to compensate another party for losses.

Speculative risk refers to those exposures that offer the prospect of making a profit or loss—such as investments in stock. Because in most cases speculative risks are not insurable, the idea is to identify the risks, take steps to minimize them, and provide for the funding of potential losses. **Pure risk,** on the other hand, is the threat of loss without the possibility of gain. Disasters such as an earthquake or a fire at a manufacturing plant are examples of pure risk. Nothing good can come from an exposure to pure risk.

An **insurable risk** is one that meets certain requirements in order for the insurer to provide protection, whereas an **un-**insurable risk is one that an insurance company will not cover (see Exhibit C.1). For example, most insurance companies are unwilling to cover potential losses that can occur from general economic conditions such as a recession. Such uncertainties are beyond the realm of insurance. In general, a risk is insurable if it meets these requirements:

- *The loss must be accidental and beyond the insured's control.* For example, a fire insurance policy excludes losses caused by the insured's own arson, but losses caused by an employee's arson would be covered.

- *The loss must be financially measurable.* Although the loss of an apartment building is financially measurable, the loss suffered by having an undesirable tenant is not.

- *A large number of similar cases must be subject to the same peril.* In order for the likelihood of a loss to be predictable, insurance companies must have data on the frequency and severity of losses caused by a given peril. If this information covers a long period of time and is based on a large number of cases or observations, the **law of large numbers** will usually allow insurance companies to predict accurately how many losses will occur in the future. For example, insurers keep track of the number of automobile accidents by age group in the United States so they can estimate the likelihood of a customer's becoming involved in a collision.

- *The risk should be spread over a wide geographical area.* Unless an insurance company spreads its coverage over a large geographical area or a broad population base, a single disaster might force it to pay out on all its policies at once. Consider Hurricane Andrew. This catastrophe caused over $16.3 billion in insured losses, the largest dollar amount of damage claims

INSURABLE	**UNINSURABLE**
Property risks: Uncertainty surrounding the occurrence of loss from perils that cause 1. Direct loss of property 2. Indirect loss of property	Market risks: Factors that may result in loss of property or income, such as 1. Price changes, seasonal or cyclical 2. Consumer indifference 3. Style changes 4. Competition offered by a better product
Personal risks: Uncertainty surrounding the occurrence of loss due to 1. Premature death 2. Physical disability 3. Old age	Political risks: Uncertainty surrounding the occurrence of 1. Overthrow of the government 2. Restrictions imposed on free trade 3. Unreasonable or punitive taxation 4. Restrictions on free exchange of currencies
Legal liability risks: Uncertainty surrounding the occurrence of loss arising out of 1. Use of automobiles 2. Occupancy of buildings 3. Employment 4. Manufacture of products 5. Professional misconduct	Production risks: Uncertainties surrounding the occurrence of 1. Failure of machinery to function economically 2. Failure to solve technical problems 3. Exhaustion of raw-material resources 4. Strikes, absenteeism, labor unrest
	Personal risks: Uncertainty surrounding the occurrence of 1. Unemployment 2. Poverty from factors such as divorce, lack of education or opportunity, loss of health from military service

EXHIBIT C.1

INSURABLE AND UNINSURABLE RISK

Insurance companies consider some pure risks insurable. They usually view speculative risks as uninsurable. (Some pure risks, such as flood and strike, are considered uninsurable.)

ever made on the insurance system from a single natural event. Even though all insured claims for the damage caused by Hurricane Andrew were honored, many insurers now restrict the amount of insurance they provide in Florida.[1]

■ *The possible loss must be financially serious to the insured.* An insurance company could not afford the paperwork involved in handling numerous small **claims** (demands by the insured that the insurance company pay for a loss) of a few dollars each; nor would a business be likely to insure such a small loss. For this reason, many policies have a clause specifying that the insurance company will pay only that part of a loss greater than an amount stated in the policy. This amount, the **deductible,** represents small losses (such as the first $250 of covered repairs) that the insured has agreed to absorb.

Managing risk is indeed an important part of running a business. The process of reducing the threat of loss from uncontrollable events and funding potential losses is called **risk management,** which includes assessing risk, controlling risk, and financing risk by shifting it to an insurance company or by self-insuring to cover possible losses.

Assessing Risk

One of the first steps in managing risk is to identify where it exists. Those areas of risk in which a potential for loss exists, called **loss exposures,** fall under four headings: (1) loss of property

James Slover, head of risk management for Sizzler USA, lived a nightmare when 65 people fell ill and a toddler died following a food-borne illness outbreak linked to a franchised Sizzler restaurant in Milwaukee, Wisconsin in 2000. Slover worked closely with health department officials to determine how the outbreak occurred and help the franchisee deal with complex insurance issues and an independent investigation. Each year food-borne illnesses are responsible for 76 million sicknesses, 325,000 hospitalizations, and 5,200 deaths. For most food service companies, the first step in effective risk management is identifying the potential food-safety risks.

Theft and destruction of company information are two loss exposures that more and more companies are taking seriously. "High-tech crime is the wave of the future," says Lewis Schiliro, head of the FBI's computer crime department. According to a recent FBI survey of 563 corporations, 49 percent acknowledged unauthorized use of their computer systems.

(due to destruction or theft of tangible or intangible assets), (2) loss of income (either through decreased revenues or through increased expenses resulting from an accidental event), (3) legal liability to others, including employees, and (4) loss of the services of key personnel (through accidental injury or death).

Consider just one of the many loss exposures that a manufacturer of stuffed toys must face: First, the manufacturer must identify the ways a consumer (most likely a child) can be injured by a stuffed toy. The child might choke on button eyes, get sick from eating the stuffing, or have an allergic reaction to any material in the toy. Second, the company must identify any possible flaws in the production or marketing of the toy that might lead to one of these injuries. For example, a child may have an allergic reaction to the toy if its materials are not carefully tested for allergenic substances, if impurities enter the toy during manufacture, or if the toy is not properly packaged (allowing foreign substances to reach it). Third, the manufacturer must analyze these possibilities in order to predict product liability losses accurately.

Once you have identified your potential for risk, you have three reasonable choices: you can accept risk, eliminate or control it, or shift the responsibility for it.

Controlling Risk

Whereas some companies choose to fully accept the financial consequences of a loss themselves—especially when the potential loss costs are small or can be financed by the company itself—others choose to control risk by using a number of *risk-control techniques* to minimize the organization's losses:

■ *Risk avoidance.* A risk manager might try to eliminate the chance of a particular type of loss. With rare exceptions, such risk avoidance is not practical. The stuffed-toy manufacturer could avoid being sued for a child's allergic reaction

by not making stuffed toys, but, of course, the company would also be out of business.

■ *Loss prevention.* A risk manager may try to reduce (but not totally eliminate) the *chance* of a given loss by removing hazards or taking preventive measures. Security guards at banks, warnings on medicines and dangerous chemicals, and safety locks are examples of loss prevention measures.

■ *Loss reduction.* A risk manager may try to reduce the *severity* of the losses that do occur. Examples include installing overhead sprinklers to reduce damage during a fire and paying the medical expenses of an injured consumer to reduce the likelihood of litigation and punitive damages.

■ *Risk-control transfer.* A risk manager may try to eliminate risk by transferring to some other person or group either (1) the actual property or activity responsible for the risk or (2) the responsibility for the risk. For example, a firm can sell a building to eliminate the risks of ownership.

Of course, not all risk is controllable. Thus, many companies will shift risk to an outside insurance company or self-insure against risk.

Shifting Risk to an Insurance Company

Insurance is an intangible good—a contingent promise to be delivered in the future. When companies purchase insurance, they transfer a group's (but not an individual's) predicted losses to an insurance pool. The pool combines the cost of the potential losses to be financed and then redistributes them back to

Avoiding accidents and injuries through such measures as protective clothing is an important step in managing corporate risk.

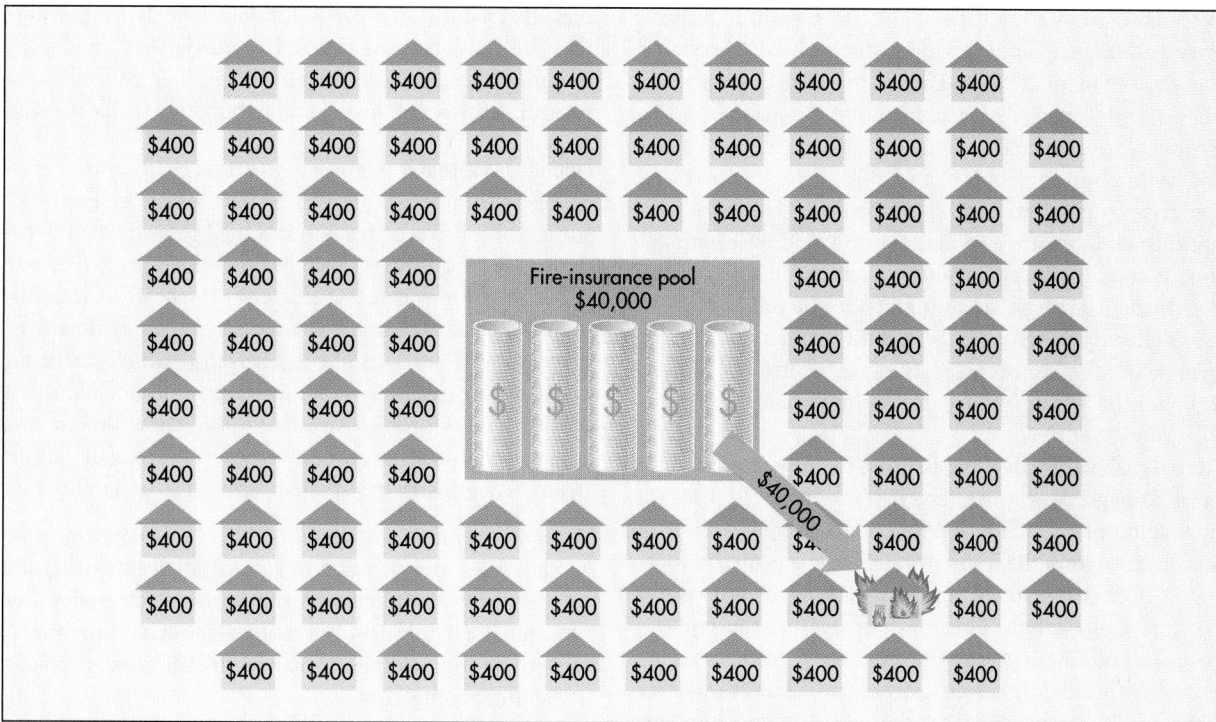

EXHIBIT C.2

HOW INSURANCE WORKS

An insurance company covers the cost of a policyholder's loss out of the premiums paid by a large pool of policyholders. Thus, if 100 policyholders pay $400 each to insure against fire damage, the insurance company can afford to compensate one policyholder who actually suffers fire damage with $40,000.

the individuals exposed (in advance) by charging them a fee known as an **insurance premium.**

Actuaries determine how much income insurance companies need to generate from premiums by compiling statistics of losses, predicting the amount needed to pay claims over a given period, and calculating the amount needed to cover these expenses plus any anticipated operating costs. Keep in mind that insurance companies don't count on making a profit on any particular policy, nor do they count on paying for a single policyholder's losses out of the premium paid by that particular policyholder. Rather, the insurance company pays for a loss by drawing the money out of the pool of funds it has received from all its policyholders in the form of premiums (see Exhibit C.2). In this way, the insurance company redistributes the cost of predicted losses from a single individual or company to a large number of policies.

If you were starting a business, what types of insurance would you need? To some extent, the answer to that question would depend on the nature of your business and your potential for loss. In general, however, you would probably want to protect yourself against the loss of property, loss of income, liability, and loss of services of key personnel (see Exhibit C.3).

Property Insurance Property loss can have a variety of causes, including accidental damage, natural disaster, and theft. Property can also be lost through employee dishonesty and nonperformance. When a cannery in California ships jars of pizza sauce by a truck to New York, for example, the goods face unavoidable

RISK	PROTECTION
Loss of property	
Due to destruction or theft	Fire insurance
	Disaster insurance
	Marine insurance
	Automobile insurance
Due to dishonesty or nonperformance	Fidelity bonding
	Surety bonding
	Credit life insurance
	Crime insurance
Loss of income	Business interruption insurance
	Extra-expense insurance
	Contingent business-interruption insurance
Liability	Comprehensive general liability insurance
	Automobile liability insurance
	Workers' compensation insurance
	Umbrella liability insurance
	Professional liability insurance
Loss of services of key personnel	Key-person insurance

EXHIBIT C.3

BUSINESS RISKS AND PROTECTION

Here are some of the more common types of business insurance purchased.

risks in transit. One wrong turn could cover a whole hillside with broken glass and gallons of sauce, which would represent a sizable loss to the manufacturer. The factory itself is vulnerable to fire, flood, and (especially in California) earthquake.

Property insurance covers the insured for physical damage to or destruction of property and also for its loss by theft. When purchasing property insurance, the buyer has three coverage options: replacement cost, actual cash value, or functional replacement cost. **Replacement-cost coverage** means that the insurer promises to pay an amount equal to the full cost of repairing or replacing the property even if the property was old or run-down before the loss occurred. Because the insured is often better off after the loss, the premium for this type of coverage is generally quite expensive.

Actual cash value coverage assumes that the property that was lost or damaged was worth less than new property because of normal aging or use. Thus, the insurance company will pay the amount that allows the insured to return the property to its same state before the incident. Sometimes, however, it does not pay to restore a property to its same state because the replacement cost of a building is greater than its market value (as is often the case with older, inner-city structures). **Functional-replacement-cost coverage** allows for the substitution of modern construction materials such as wall board instead of plaster to restore a property to a similar, functioning state.

Consequential Loss Insurance When a disaster strikes, such as a fire or a flood, property loss is only one part of the story. Disasters not only disrupt the business operation; they often result in temporary shutdown, costing the company far more than the equipment repairs or replacement of damaged stock. That's because expenses continue—salaries, interest payments, rent—even though the company is not earning revenues. Disruption also results in extra expenses: leasing of temporary space, paying overtime to meet work schedules with a reduced capacity, buying additional advertising to assure the public that the business is still a going concern. In fact, a prolonged interruption of business could even cause bankruptcy.

For this reason, many companies carry *consequential loss insurance.* Available coverage includes **business-interruption insurance,** which protects the insured against lost profits and pays continuing expenses when a fire or other disaster causes a company to shut down temporarily; **extra-expense insurance,** which pays the additional costs of maintaining the operation in temporary quarters; and **contingent business-interruption insurance,** which protects against a company's loss of profit due to the misfortune of another business, such as a fire or other disaster that interrupts the operation of an important supplier or the closing of an anchor store in the mall where the business is located.

Many companies discovered the value of business-interruption insurance when the Alfred P. Murrah Federal Building in Oklahoma City was bombed. Small firms in a 50-block area sustained about $500 million worth of damage from the explosion. However, Hogan Information Services, an Oklahoma City firm that collects nationwide credit-reporting information for compa-

nies and creditors, was closed for only three days following the explosion. That's because Hogan had purchased business-interruption insurance, and Kemper, Hogan's insurer, paid all the costs for relocating the company to another building, six blocks away.[2]

Liability Insurance Liability insurance provides protection against a number of perils. **Liability losses** are financial losses suffered by firms or individuals held responsible for property damage or for injuries suffered by others. In general, liability losses arise from three sources: (1) the costs of legal damages awarded by a court to the injured party if the company is found negligent; (2) the costs of a legal defense, which can be quite expensive; and (3) the costs of loss prevention or identifying potential liability problems so they may be handled in an appropriate way. To accommodate theses sources of liability, the insurance industry has created these types of liability policies:

■ *Commercial general liability.* This basic coverage automatically provides protection against all forms of liability not specifically excluded under the terms of the policy. Examples would be liability for operations on business premises, product liability, completed operations, and operations of independent contractors.

■ *Product liability.* Manufacturers of a product have a legal duty to design and produce a product that will not injure people in normal use. In addition, products must be packaged carefully and accompanied by adequate instructions and warnings so consumers may use them properly and avoid injury. If these duties are not fulfilled and result in an injured user, a potential for a product liability lawsuit exists. **Product liability coverage** protects insured companies from being threatened financially when someone claims that one of their products caused damage, injury, or death.

■ *Automobile liability.* Many companies also carry insurance that specifically covers liability connected with any vehicles owned or operated by the company. Some states have **no-fault insurance laws,** which means that all parties involved in an automobile accident receive compensation for their injuries from their own insurer, regardless of who causes the accident. According to current no-fault plans, after some threshold of damage has been reached, the injured party may revert to the liability system to seek compensation for loss. In some cases this threshold is so low that the term *no-fault* hardly seems descriptive.[3]

■ *Professional liability.* Also known as *malpractice insurance* or *errors and omissions insurance,* **professional liability insurance** covers people who are found liable for professional negligence. Because this type of coverage protects professionals from financial ruin if sued by dissatisfied clients, it is very expensive.

■ *Employment practices liability.* Recent increases in employee lawsuits and hefty judgments against employers have generated increased interest in employment practices liability insurance. Such insurance reimburses employers for defense costs, settlements, and judgments arising from employment claims related to discrimination, sexual harassment, wrongful termination, breach of employment contract, negligent eval-

The crash of an Air France supersonic Concorde jet, which killed all passengers and crew in addition to several people on the ground, is an airline's and insurers' worst nightmare. Estimates of property and liability insurance payments range from about $150 million to $350 million.

uation, failure to employ or promote, wrongful discipline, deprivation of career opportunity, wrongful infliction of emotional stress, and mismanagement of employee benefits.[4]

■ *Umbrella liability.* Because many liability policies have limits, or maximum amounts that may be paid out, businesses sometimes purchase **umbrella policies** to provide coverage after underlying liability policies have been exhausted. Sometimes an umbrella policy is called *excess liability insurance.*

Key-Person Insurance Sometimes one executive or employee has expertise or experience that is crucial to the company's operation. If a business loses this key person by illness, disability, death, or unplanned retirement, the effect may be felt in lost income. **Key-person insurance** can be purchased to protect a company against the financial impact of losing such a key employee under the circumstances described. Part of identifying the key-employee exposure is developing an estimate of where, at what cost, and how quickly a replacement may be hired and trained. For example, when fashion designer Gianni Versace was murdered, his key-man policy paid $21 million to his company.[5]

Self-Insuring Against Risk

Self-insurance is becoming an increasingly popular method of insuring against risk. Because self-insurance plans are not subject to state regulation, mandates, and premium taxes (typically 2 percent), companies that use **self-insurance** often save quite a bit of money. Deciding to self-insure with a liability reserve fund means putting aside a certain sum each year to cover predicted liability losses. Unless payments to the self-insurance fund are calculated scientifically and paid regularly, a true self-insurance system does not exist.

Keep in mind that self-insurance differs greatly from "going bare," or having no reserve funds. Self-insurance implies an attempt by business to combine a sufficient number of its own similar exposures to predict the losses accurately. It also implies

that adequate financial arrangements have been made in advance to provide funds to pay for losses should they occur. For instance, companies that self-insure often set aside a revenue or self-insurance contingency fund to cover any unexpected or large losses. That way, if disaster strikes, companies won't have to borrow funds to cover their losses, or be forced out of business. In addition, they generally protect themselves from unexpected losses or disasters by purchasing excess insurance from commercial insurers, called *stop-loss insurance.* This additional insurance is designed to cover losses that would exceed a company's own financial capabilities.

Experts advise companies to consider self-insurance plans only if they are prepared to handle the worst-case scenario (usually the point at which stop-loss insurance kicks in) and to use self-insurance only as a long-term strategy. That's because in some years the cost to self-insure will be lower than the cost of commercial insurance, whereas in other years it will be higher. In the long run, however, statistics show that the good and bad years should average out in the company's favor.[6]

Monitoring the Risk-Management Program

Risk management is an ongoing activity. Managers must periodically reevaluate the company's loss exposures by asking these questions: What does the company have? What can go wrong? What's the minimum we need to stay in business? What's the best way to protect the company's assets?[7] By answering these questions, managers can then revise a company's risk-management program to address changing needs and circumstances. Of course, smart managers recognize that risk management is really everybody's job. Practically every employee can take steps to reduce a company's exposure to risk by preventing it or controlling it.

Most self-insurers protect themselves from disasters by purchasing stop-loss insurance.

■ EMPLOYEE INSURANCE

Besides protecting company property and assets, many businesses look out for the well-being of employees by providing them with health, disability, workers' compensation, and life insurance coverage. Disease and disability may cost employees huge sums of money unless they are insured. In addition, death carries the threat of financial hardship for an employee's family.

Health Insurance

Today approximately 62 percent of employees are covered by a company health insurance plan.[8] Employers who provide group health insurance typically cover the employee and eligible dependents. Traditionally, group insurance includes health expense coverage as well as a coverage guaranteeing income in the event of a disabling illness or injury. Most group policies place limits on the amount they will pay for mental health and substance abuse claims. Exhibit C.4 lists the most common types of health expense coverage offered by employers.[9]

The Rising Cost of Medical Care   Employers typically pay a large portion of the premium costs of health insurance for their employees; however, as costs rise, many employers are shifting more of the cost burden to employees by requiring them to pay a larger portion of their own premiums and larger deductibles through a payroll deduction plan. Small companies often get hit the hardest. Because their insurance groups are smaller, premiums tend to be more costly, forcing some small companies to drop health insurance altogether.

Several factors have led to the escalating costs of health care. Some observers assert that the most significant factor is *cost shifting*, whereby hospitals and doctors boost their charges to private paying patients and their insurers to make up for the shortfall in government reimbursements for their Medicare and

Cutting health care costs by improving employees' health is the goal of the Hewlett Packard Fitness Center.

Medicaid patients.[10] Other factors causing the escalation of insurance premiums include the high costs and increased use of medical technology like MRI scanners, the high costs of professional liability insurance, increased hospital operating costs, and costly state mandates such as the one signed into law by the state of New York, which requires health insurance companies and HMOs to cover up to 15 chiropractic visits per year.[11] Remember, when hospitals and doctors increase their charges, and when states mandate certain benefit coverage, health insurance premiums go up.

Cost Containment Measures   To help keep the cost of employee health insurance in line, companies have adopted a variety of cost-containment practices. These include preadmission testing (to qualify health insurance applicants), second opinions, home health care, hospice care (long-term home care for the terminally ill), and generic drugs. Many companies have also established worksite disease-prevention programs, referred to as "wellness programs" or "wellcare," because studies show that keeping employees healthy reduces absenteeism and lowers health costs.

Another way companies choose to contain their health insurance costs is by joining **health maintenance organizations (HMOs),** which are comprehensive, prepaid, group-practice medical plans in which consumers pay a set fee (called a capitation payment) and in return receive most of their health care at little or no additional costs. Because the capitation payment does not change with usage, HMOs shift the risk from the employer to the health-care provider. Unlike hospitals and doctors in private practice, which charge on a fee-for-service basis, HMOs charge a fixed fee with which they must cover all their expenses. Certain HMOs (called "open HMOs") allow members the option of using hospitals and doctors outside the network. These variations are actually a form of **managed care** programs where employers (usually through an insurance carrier) set up their own network of doctors and hospitals that agree to discount the fees they charge in return for the flow of patients.

Basic medical	Designed to pay for most inpatient and some outpatient hospital costs
Major medical	Protects the insured against catastrophic financial losses by covering medical expenses that exceed the coverage limits of the basic policies
Disability income	Designed to protect against the loss of short-term or long-term income while the insured is disabled as a result of an illness or accident
Medicare supplemental	Designed specifically to supplement benefits provided under the Medicare program
Long-term care	Designed to cover stays in long-term care facilities

EXHIBIT C.4

COMMON TYPES OF HEALTH INSURANCE

Here are five of the most common types of health insurance policies sold by insurers.

As an alternative to HMOs, some employers opt for **preferred-provider organizations (PPOs),** health care providers that contract with employers, insurance companies, or other third-party payers to deliver health care services to an employee group at a reduced fee. In most companies, employees are not required to use preferred providers, but they are offered incentives to do so—such as reduced deductibles, lower co-payments, and wellcare. Preferred-provider organizations not only save employers money but also allow them to control the quality and appropriateness of services provided. However, employees are restricted in their choice of hospitals and doctors, and preventive services are generally not covered.

National Health Insurance The rising costs of health care has employers and employees alike clamoring for reform. The problem is getting more attention from Congress, which has been struggling with the issue for over a decade. Much of the debate on health care reform focuses on the idea of *national health care,* which is generally interpreted as some form of centralized government support or control. One of the strongest motivations for national health care is the goal of providing coverage for people who either aren't covered by employer programs or can't afford to cover themselves. England, Canada, and many other countries have national health care programs; however, many of these programs are struggling to stay afloat because of the need to increase taxes to pay for escalating health care costs.

National health care proposals have generally met with strong opposition in the United States for a variety of reasons. Some people want to let free-market forces drive the system; others believe the only way to get everyone covered is through government intervention. Some argue that a centralized, so-called single-payer system is the best way to make health care more efficient and more widely available, but opponents are skeptical that any government program—particularly one as massive as national health care—could ever be efficient. In fact, because of the huge amounts of money involved, any changes to the current system are likely to meet opposition from somebody, whether it's health-care professionals, insurance companies, taxpayers, employers, or employees.

Disability Income Insurance

Disability income insurance, which replaces income not earned because of illness or accident, is often included as part of the health insurance package provided by employers. Such policies are designated as either short-term or long-term, depending on the period for which coverage is provided. Short-term policies are more common and provide a specific number of weeks of coverage (often 30), after a brief waiting or elimination period—a period that must elapse before an employee is eligible to receive insurance payments. The purpose of the elimination period is to exclude payments for minor illness. Long-term disability income, on the other hand, provides a number of years of protection after a substantial elimination period has elapsed (generally six months of continuous disability).

The amount of disability payment depends on whether the disability is partial or total, temporary or permanent, short-term or long-term. In general, the amount received is decreased by the amount of disability payments received from Social Security. To encourage employees to return to work as soon as possible, some policies will continue partial payments if an employee is able to perform some type of work, even if the employee is unable to maintain the same pace of career advancement or hours of labor per week as before the disability.

Workers' Compensation Insurance

As Chapter 2 points out, each year thousands of workers die or are injured permanently because of job-related injuries. **Workers' compensation insurance** pays the medical bills of employees who are hurt or become ill as a result of their work. It covers loss of income by occupationally injured or diseased workers, full payment of medical expenses, and rehabilitation expenses for these workers. Plus, it provides death benefits to the survivors of any employee killed on the job. In most cases, it covers both full- and part-time employees.

Workers' compensation insurance is required by U.S. law, and the benefits are enumerated in the workers' compensation statute. Premiums for workers' compensation insurance are based on the employer's payroll and past experience. Thus, employers with relatively good safety results will pay lower workers' compensation insurance rates than employers with poor safety records. This approach rewards loss prevention and loss reduction efforts. Insurers also classify employers by industry, giving recognition to the fact that some industries involve more danger to workers than others. For instance, an employer in a mining industry would pay higher rates than an employer in the food services industry.

Life Insurance

One of the most unfortunate circumstances that could strike a family would be the loss of its main source of income. Life insurance policies provide some protection against the financial problems associated with premature death by paying predetermined amounts to **beneficiaries** when the covered individual dies.

There are many types of life insurance, and each is used for a variety of purposes. For example, *credit life insurance* is required by many lending institutions to guarantee that a mortgage or other large loan will be paid off in the case of the borrower's death.[12] Some life insurance policies provide a type of savings fund for retirement or other purposes by building a *cash value* from excess premiums. In some policies, owners can borrow against the cash value by paying interest to the insurer (sometimes at a lower rate than banks charge), and they can withdraw the accumulated cash value in one lump sum or in annual payments if they want to end the policy.

Term insurance, as the name implies, covers a person for a specific period of time—the term of the policy. If the insured outlives the period, no payment is made by the insurer, and the policy has no cash value. Group life insurance is term insurance that is commonly purchased by employers for their employees. It may generally be renewed without the proof of insurability (also known as guaranteed renewable), but not past the age of 65. **Whole life insurance** provides a combination of insurance and savings. The policy stays in force until the insured dies, provided that the premiums are paid. In addition to paying death benefits, whole life insurance accumulates cash value. Because this type of insurance tends to be more expensive than term insurance, it is not typically provided by employers.

Variable life insurance was developed in response to the soaring inflation of the late 1970s and early 1980s. The difference between variable life insurance and whole life insurance is that variable is most often associated with an investment portfolio because the underlying investments are securities, and the policy owner has some investment choice. If the insured's investment decisions are good, the policy's cash value and death benefit (the amount paid at death) will increase. On the other hand, if the investments do poorly, the cash value may drop to $0 and the death benefit may decrease—although not below the original amount purchased (the face value) as long as the policy remains in force and accumulates cash value.

Universal life insurance is also a flexible policy. It allows the insured to buy term insurance and invest an additional amount with the insurance company. Premiums on a universal life insurance policy are used to fund, in essence, term insurance and a savings account. The accumulated premium payments produce a cash value, which then earns two types of interest: a guaranteed interest rate specified in the contract, and an excess interest rate if policy conditions are met. The interest that accumulates on the savings portion of the policy is pegged to current money-market rates (but generally guaranteed to stay above a certain level). Premium payments may vary too, depending on the insured's preferences and as long as cash value is large enough to fund the term-insurance portion of the policy. Because of low market interest rates, this type of policy has lost popularity during the past few years.

■ SOCIAL INSURANCE PROGRAMS

When most people think of insurance, they think of the kind of insurance purchased from a private insurance company. Actually, the largest single source of insurance in the United States is the government, which accounts for nearly half of the total insurance premiums collected for all types of coverage combined. More than a quarter of the federal government's revenue comes from social insurance receipts.[13] Most social insurance programs are designed to protect people from loss of income, either because they have reached retirement age or because they have lost their jobs or become disabled. Unlike private insurance, which is voluntarily chosen by the insured, government-sponsored programs are compulsory.

Social Security

Social Security was created by the federal government following the Great Depression of the 1930s. Officially known as Old-Age, Survivors, Disability, and Health Insurance, this program covers just about every wage earner in the United States.

The basic purpose of the Social Security program is to provide a minimum level of income for retirees, their survivors, and their dependents, as well as for the permanently disabled. The program also provides hospital and supplemental medical insurance—known as Medicare—for people age 65 and over. Social Security benefits vary, depending on a worker's average indexed monthly earnings and number of dependents. The program is funded by a payroll tax paid half by workers and half by their employers. In most cases, these taxes are automatically deducted from each paycheck. Self-employed people pay the full amount of the tax as part of their federal income tax liability. It's important to note that Social Security is not a needs-based program; every eligible person is entitled to the benefits of the system, regardless of financial status.[14]

The future of Social Security is questionable. According to the most recent annual report of the Social Security trustees, payments to recipients will start to exceed receipts in 2015, and trust fund assets will be exhausted in 2037, although annual payroll taxes will be able to finance some benefits.[15] Increased longevity and a low birth rate are the chief causes for this financial dilemma. In the past, the system worked because a far greater number of workers supported every retiree, and many potential beneficiaries died before collecting their first check. This is no longer the case.[16]

Several alternative solutions have been proposed to restore the system's financial stability. These include increasing the tax rate paid by employees and employers, subjecting more earnings of higher-paid workers to the tax, subjecting all Social Security benefits to the federal income tax, and replacing some or all of the current system with privately funded individual retirement accounts.

Unemployment Insurance

Under the terms of the Social Security Act of 1935, employers in all 50 states finance special **unemployment insurance** to benefit employees who are unemployed. The cost is borne by employers. Currently, the unemployment insurance program is a joint federal–state program, with about 90 percent of the funding coming from the states.

The unemployment insurance program is designed to meet the peril of short-term unemployment caused by the business cycle and other factors over which workers have little control. Thus, an employee who becomes unemployed for reasons not related to performance is entitled to collect benefits—typically for 26 weeks, which may be extended in periods of very high unemployment. Because the United States is currently enjoying its lowest jobless rate in 30 years, state unemployment insurance trust funds are reporting fat surpluses. Another contributing factor to this surplus is the growing use of a temporary workforce. Contingent and part-time workers now make up roughly one-third of the U.S. workforce and most are ineligible for unemployment benefits.[17]

TEST YOUR KNOWLEDGE

QUESTIONS FOR REVIEW

1. What is the difference between pure risk and speculative risk?

2. What are the five characteristics of insurable risks?

3. What are the four types of loss exposure?

4. How can you control risk?

5. What is the difference between workers' compensation insurance and disability income insurance?

QUESTIONS FOR ANALYSIS

6. How do insurance companies calculate their premiums?

7. What is self-insurance and why is it becoming an increasingly popular risk-shifting technique?

8. Why is it a good idea to purchase consequential loss insurance?

9. If you were starting a new accounting practice with 15 employees, what types of insurance might you need?

10. Allstate Insurance recently announced that it will begin selling insurance through a toll-free number and the Web in addition to using traditional insurance agents. At the same time, Internet insurance marketplaces such as InsWeb and Quicken provide consumers with insurance quotes from a number of competing insurance companies. How do consumers benefit by using Internet insurance marketplaces for quotes instead of using traditional insurance agents? Why might a potential insurance customer still need to talk to an insurance agent?[18]

11. A recent survey by the Society of Chartered Property Casualty Underwriters rated ethical behavior as the number-one attribute insurance industry employers look for in job candidates when making hiring decisions.[19] Why is ethics of such critical concern in the insurance industry? (Hint: think about the nature and length of term of the product.)

CHAPTER GLOSSARY

actual cash value coverage
Property insurance in which the insurer pays for the replacement cost of property at the time of loss, less an allowance for depreciation

actuaries
People employed by an insurance company to compute expected losses and to calculate the cost of premiums

beneficiaries
People named in a life insurance policy who receive the proceeds of an insurance contract when the insured dies

business-interruption insurance
Insurance that covers losses resulting from temporary business closings

claims
Demands for payments from an insurance company because of some loss by the insured

contingent business-interruption insurance
Insurance that protects a business from losses resulting from losses sustained by other businesses such as suppliers or transportation companies

deductible
Amount of loss that must be paid by the insured before the insurer will pay for the rest

disability income insurance
Short-term or long-term insurance that protects an individual against loss of income while that individual is disabled as the result of an illness or accident

extra-expense insurance
Insurance that covers the added expense of operating the business in temporary facilities after an event such as a fire or a flood

functional-replacement-cost coverage
Property insurance that allows for the substitution of construction materials to restore a property to a similar, functioning state

health maintenance organizations (HMOs)
Prepaid medical plans in which consumers pay a set fee in order to receive a full range of medical care from a group of medical practitioners

insurable risk
Risk for which an acceptable probability of loss may be calculated and that an insurance company might, therefore, be willing to cover

insurance
Written contract that transfers to an insurer the financial responsibility for losses up to specified limits

insurance premium
Fee that the insured pays the insurer for coverage against loss

key-person insurance
Insurance that provides a business with funds to compensate for the loss of a key employee by unplanned retirement, resignation, death, or disability

law of large numbers
Principle that the larger the group on which probabilities are calculated, the more accurate the predictive value

liability losses
Financial losses suffered by a business firm or individual held responsible for property damage or injuries suffered by others

loss exposures
Areas of risk in which a potential for loss exists

managed care
Health care set up by employers (usually through an insurance carrier) in which networks of doctors and hospitals agree to discount the fees they charge in return for the flow of patients

no-fault insurance laws
Laws limiting lawsuits connected with auto accidents

preferred-provider organizations (PPOs)
Health care providers offering reduced-rate contracts to groups that agree to obtain medical care through the providers' organization

product-liability coverage
Insurance that protects companies from claims for injuries or damages that result from use of a product the company manufactures or distributes

professional liability insurance
Insurance that covers losses arising from damages or injuries caused by the insured in the course of performing professional services for clients

property insurance
Insurance that provides coverage for physical damage to or destruction of property and for its loss by theft

pure risk
Risk that involves the chance of loss only

risk
Uncertainty of an event or exposure to loss

replacement-cost coverage
Property insurance in which the insurer pays for the full cost of repairing or replacing the property rather than the actual cash value

risk management
Process used by business firms and individuals to deal with their exposures to loss

self-insurance
Accumulating funds each year to pay for predicted liability losses, rather than buying insurance from another company

speculative risk
Risk that involves the chance of both loss and profits

term insurance
Life insurance that provides death benefits for a specified period

umbrella policies
Insurance that provides businesses with coverage beyond what is provided by a basic liability policy

unemployment insurance
Government-sponsored program for assisting employees who are laid off for reasons not related to performance

uninsurable risk
Risk that few, if any, insurance companies will assume because of the difficulty of calculating the probability of loss

universal life insurance
Combination of term life insurance policy and a savings plan with flexible interest rates and flexible premiums

variable life insurance
Whole life insurance policy that allows the policyholder to decide how to invest the cash value

whole life insurance
Insurance that provides both death benefits and savings for the insured's lifetime, provided premiums are paid

workers' compensation insurance
Insurance that partially replaces lost income and that pays for employees' medical costs and rehabilitation expenses for work-related injuries

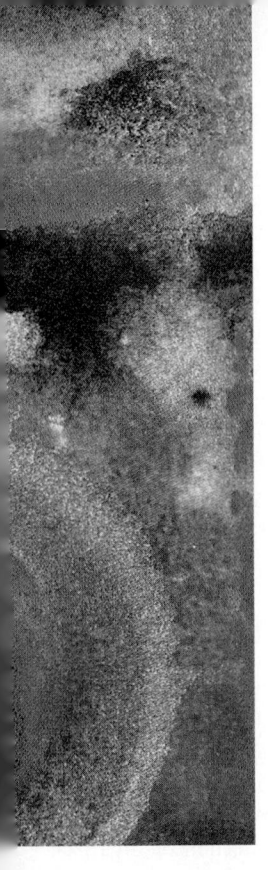

CAREERS IN BUSINESS AND THE EMPLOYMENT SEARCH

■ THINKING ABOUT YOUR CAREER

Getting the job that's right for you takes more than sending out a few letters and signing up with the college placement office. Planning and research are important if you want to find a company and a position that suit you. Before you limit your job search to a particular industry or functional specialty, analyze what you have to offer and what you hope to get from your work. Then you can identify employers who are likely to want you and vice versa.

What Do You Have to Offer?

What are your marketable skills? You can analyze them in three steps.

First, jot down 10 achievements you're proud of, such as learning to ski, taking a prize-winning photo, tutoring a child, or editing the school paper. Look carefully at each of these achievements. What specific skills did they demand? For example, leadership skills, speaking ability, and artistic talent may have helped you coordinate a winning presentation to the college administration. As you analyze your achievements, you'll begin to recognize a pattern of skills. Which of them might be valuable to potential employers?

Second, look at your educational preparation, work experience, and extracurricular activities. What kinds of jobs are you qualified to do on the basis of your knowledge and experience? What have you learned from volunteer work or class projects that could benefit you on the job? Have you held any offices, won any awards or scholarships, or mastered a second language?

Third, take stock of your personal characteristics so that you can determine the type of job you'll do best. Are you aggressive, a born leader, or would you rather follow? Are you outgoing, articu-

late, great with people, or do you prefer working alone? Make a list of what you believe are your four or five most important qualities.

For help with figuring out your interests and capabilities, consult your college placement office or career guidance center. Many schools administer tests designed to help you identify your interests, aptitudes, and personality traits. Although these tests won't reveal the "perfect" job for you, they'll help you focus on the types of work that best suit your personality. Another terrific career resource is the Prentice Hall Student Success SuperSite at www.prenhall.com/success. Log on and take the career assessment tests, visit the career doctor, learn about internships, networking, part-time jobs, and more.

What Do You Want to Do?

Knowing what you *can* do is one thing. Knowing what you *want* to do is another. Don't lose sight of your own values. Discover the things that will bring you satisfaction and happiness on the job.

■ *Decide what you'd like to do every day.* Talk to people in various occupations. You might consult relatives, local businesses, or former graduates (through your school's alumni relations office). Read about various occupations. Start with your college library or placement office. One of the liveliest books aimed at college students is Lisa Birnbach's *Going to Work.* Another useful source is the 13-volume *Career Information Center* encyclopedia of jobs and careers. Also consider how much independence you want on the job, how much variety you like, and whether you prefer to work with products, machines, people, ideas, figures, or some combination. Do you like physical work, mental work, or a mix? Constant change or predictable routine? Another terrific resource is the online *Career Development*

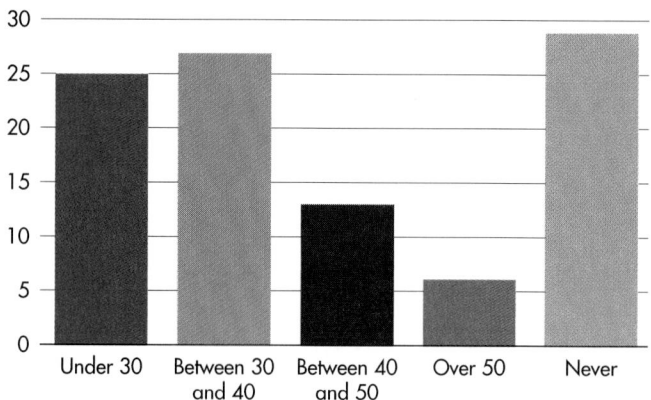

Asked of 2,000 college students and recent graduates, March 2000

EXHIBIT D.1

WHO WANTS TO BE A MILLIONAIRE?

A survey of 2,000 college students and recent graduates reports that more than half expect to make their first million before age 40.

Manual at the University of Waterloo. Go to www.prenhall.com/mescon, select Component Chapter D, then select "Student Resources," and click on the name of the site.

■ *Establish some specific compensation targets.* What do you hope to earn in your first year on the job? What kind of pay increase do you expect each year? What's your ultimate earnings goal? Would you be comfortable with a job that pays on commission, or would you prefer a steady paycheck? What occupations offer the kind of money you're looking for? Are these occupations realistic for someone with your qualifications? Are you willing to settle for less money in order to do something you really love? Are your salary expectations in line with the data in Exhibits D.1 and D.2? Consider where you'd like to start, where you'd like to go, and the ultimate position you'd like to attain. How soon after joining the company would you like to receive your first promotion? Your next one? What additional training or preparation will you need to achieve them?

■ *Consider the type of work environment you'd prefer.* Think in broad terms about the size and type of operation you find appealing, the location you prefer, the facilities you envision, and especially the corporate culture you're most comfortable with. Do you like the idea of working for a small, entrepreneurial operation or a large company? A profit-making company or a nonprofit organization? A service business or a manufacturing operation? Do you want a predictable work schedule or flexible, varied hours? Would you enjoy a seasonally varied job such as education (which may give you summers off) or retailing (with its selling cycles)? Would you like to work in a city, a suburb, a small town, or an industrial area? Do you favor a particular part of the country or a country abroad? Do you like working indoors or outdoors? Is it important to you to work in an attractive place, or will simple, functional quarters suffice? Do you need a quiet office to work effectively, or can you concentrate in a noisy, open setting? Is access to public transportation or freeways important? Would you be happy in a well-defined hierarchy, where roles and reporting relationships are clear, or would you prefer a less structured situation? What qualities do you want in a boss? Are you looking for a paternalistic organization or one that fosters individualism? Do you like a competitive environment or one that rewards teamwork?

SEEKING EMPLOYMENT OPPORTUNITIES AND INFORMATION

Whether your major is business, biology, or political science, once you know what you have to offer and what you want, you can start finding an employer to match. If you haven't already committed yourself to any particular career field, review the career tables at the end of this chapter (see Exhibits D.11A–G on pages 549–555.) and other sources of employment information to find out where the job opportunities are. Which industries are

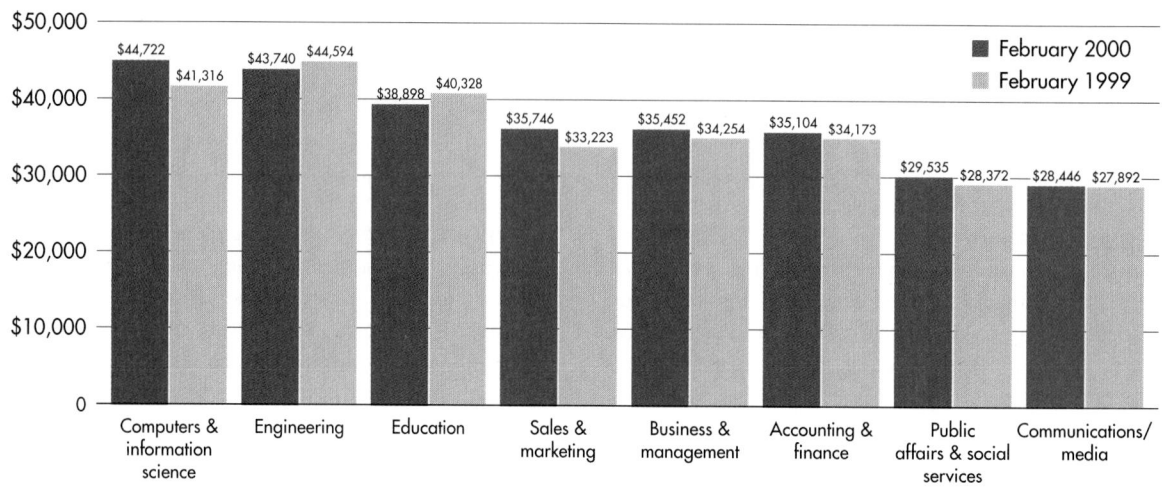

EXHIBIT D.2

SHOW ME THE MONEY

On average, starting salaries are highest for college grads pursuing careers in computers and information services and engineering.

strong? Which parts of the country are booming, and which specific job categories offer the best prospects for the future?

As you look at the career tables, consider employment trends and job possibilities for the occupations that interest you. Your opportunities for finding the perfect job will be affected by the demands of the marketplace. Are jobs plentiful or scarce in your chosen field of work? Is the number of jobs in your field of interest projected to grow or decline? The information in these tables has been compiled from the *Occupational Outlook Handbook,* a nationally recognized source of career information published by the U.S. Bureau of Labor Statistics. Revised every two years, the handbook (available in print and online at stats.bls.gov/ocohome.htm) describes what workers do on the job, working conditions, the training and education needed, earnings, and expected job prospects in a wide range of occupations.[1] Consider some of the following career areas:

■ *Careers in Management.* Today's business environment requires the skills of effective managers to reduce costs, streamline operations, develop marketing strategies, and supervise workers. As discussed in Chapter 6, managers perform four basic functions: planning, organizing, leading, and controlling. Facing increased competition, many businesses are becoming more dependent on the expertise of outside management consultants—one of the fastest-growing occupations of all jobs through the year 2006 (see Exhibit D.11A). Outside management consultants perform many important tasks, but chief among them is evaluating operating conditions and making recommendations to improve effectiveness. To find out more about what you can do with a degree in management and the typical courses management majors take, log on to the Prentice Hall Student Success SuperSite at www.prenhall.com/success/MajorExp/management.html.

■ *Careers in Human Resources.* As discussed in Chapters 10 and 11, human resources managers plan and direct human resource activities that include recruiting, training and development, compensation and benefits, employee and labor relations, health and safety. Additionally, human resources managers develop and implement human resources systems and practices to accommodate a firm's strategy and to motivate and manage diverse work forces. Large numbers of job openings are expected in the human resources field through 2006 (see Exhibit D.11B). Efforts to recruit quality employees and to provide more employee training programs should create new human resources positions. With a vast supply of qualified workers and new college graduates, however, the job market for human resources is likely to remain competitive.

■ *Careers in Computers and Information Systems.* Job opportunities abound for trained information technology workers. As competition and advanced technologies force companies to upgrade and improve their computer systems, the number of computer-related positions continues to escalate. Computer jobs hold the top spots in the fastest-growing occupations and rank among the top 20 in the number of newly created jobs through 2006 (see Exhibit D.11C). Within the computer field, only two categories of jobs are expected

to decrease: computer operators and data entry clerks. More user-friendly computer software has greatly reduced the need for operators and data entry processors, but displaced workers who keep up with changing technology should have few problems moving into other areas of computer support. To find out more about careers in computer science and information systems, log on to the Prentice Hall Student Success SuperSite at www.prenhall.com/success/MajorExp/index.html, and select Computer Science or Information Technology.

■ *Careers in Sales and Marketing.* Increasing competition in products and services should create greater needs for effective sales and marketing personnel in the future (see Exhibit D.11D). The number of securities and financial services sales representatives is projected to increase much faster than average to meet the needs of the growing numbers of investors putting their money into stocks, bonds, and other securities. Employment for insurance and real estate agents, however, is expected to grow more slowly than average. Computer technology will allow established agents to increase their sales volume and eliminate the need for additional marketing personnel in these fields. For additional information on the types of courses marketing majors take and what you can do with a degree in marketing see Chapters 12 through 15 and log on to the Prentice Hall Student Success SuperSite at www.prenhall.com/success/MajorExp/marketing.html.

■ *Careers in Finance and Accounting.* As Chapters 16 and 17 point out, accountants and financial managers are needed in almost every industry. Most positions in finance and accounting are expected to grow as fast as the average for all occupations through 2006 (see Exhibit D.11E). Three exceptions—bill and account collectors, financial planners, and loan officers/counselors—expect faster than average growth, stemming from projected increases in the number of loans and investments. Continued growth in the economy and population is expected to create more demand for trained financial personnel. To find out more about careers in finance and accounting, log on to the Prentice Hall Student Success SuperSite at www.prenhall.com/success/MajorExp/index.html, and select finance or accounting.

■ *Careers in Economics.* As Chapter 1 points out, economists study how society distributes scarce resources such as land, labor, raw materials, and machinery to produce goods and services. They conduct research, collect and analyze data, monitor economic trends, and develop forecasts. Economists are needed in many industries and spend time applying economic theory to analyze issues that are important to their firms. For example, they might analyze the effects of global economic activity on the demand for the company's product, conduct a cost-benefit analysis of the projects the company is considering, or determine the effects of government regulations or taxes on the company. Employment of economists is expected to grow about as fast as the average for all occupations, with the best opportunities in private industry—especially research, testing, and consulting firms—as more companies contract out for economic research services. To find out more about what you can do with a degree in economics and the typical courses economic majors take, log on to the Prentice Hall Student Success SuperSite at www.prenhall. com/success/MajorExp/economic.html.

■ *Careers in Communications.* As businesses recognize the need for effective communications with their customers and the public, employment of communications personnel is expected to grow as fast or faster than the average for all occupations through 2006 (see Exhibit D.11F). Recent college graduates may face keen competition for entry positions in communications as the number of applicants is expected to exceed the number of job openings. Newly created jobs in the ever-expanding computer world—such as graphic designers for Web sites or technical writers for instruction manuals—are expected to improve the career outlook for new communications graduates through 2006.

■ *Careers in Electronic Commerce.* Employees with knowledge and experience in electronic commerce are in high demand. Consult this text's E-Business in Action online supplement at www.prenhall.com/mescon, for special coverage of "Preparing for a Career in E-Business." There you will find dedicated e-commerce personal values tests, career information, and self-quizzes that will help you explore the opportunities that exist in this exciting field.

Keep in mind that job growth varies widely by education and training requirements. Jobs that require college degrees, for example, are expected to grow substantially in the near future. Categories that do not require a college degree are projected to grow slower than average through 2006 (see Exhibit D.3). Moreover, the hottest jobs in today's business world demand

technological and computer skills. Even if you're interested in finance, human resources, or marketing positions, you'll need basic computer skills to snare the best jobs in your desired field of work. As business becomes increasingly dependent on technology, computer-related careers have become the fastest-growing occupations among all jobs in the workforce (see Exhibit D.4).

Sources of Employment Information

In addition to the *Occupational Outlook Handbook,* you can find career information in a number of professional and trade journals in the career fields that interest you. Talk to people in these fields. You may be able to network with executives in your field by joining or participating in student business organizations, especially those with ties to real-world organizations such as the American Marketing Association or the American Management Association.

Keep abreast of business and financial news by subscribing to a major newspaper and scanning the business pages every day. Watch television programs that focus on business, such as *Wall Street Week.* You can find information about the future for specific jobs in *The Dictionary of Occupational Titles* (U.S. Employment Service), and the employment publications of Science Research Associates.

Once you've identified a promising career field, compile a list of specific organizations that appeal to you. Consult directories of employers such as *The College Placement Annual* and *Career: The Annual Guide to Business Opportunities.* Write to selected companies and ask for an annual report and any descriptive brochures or newsletters. Check to see if the organization you're interested in maintains a Web site. Such Web sites generally include a company profile, press releases, financial informa-

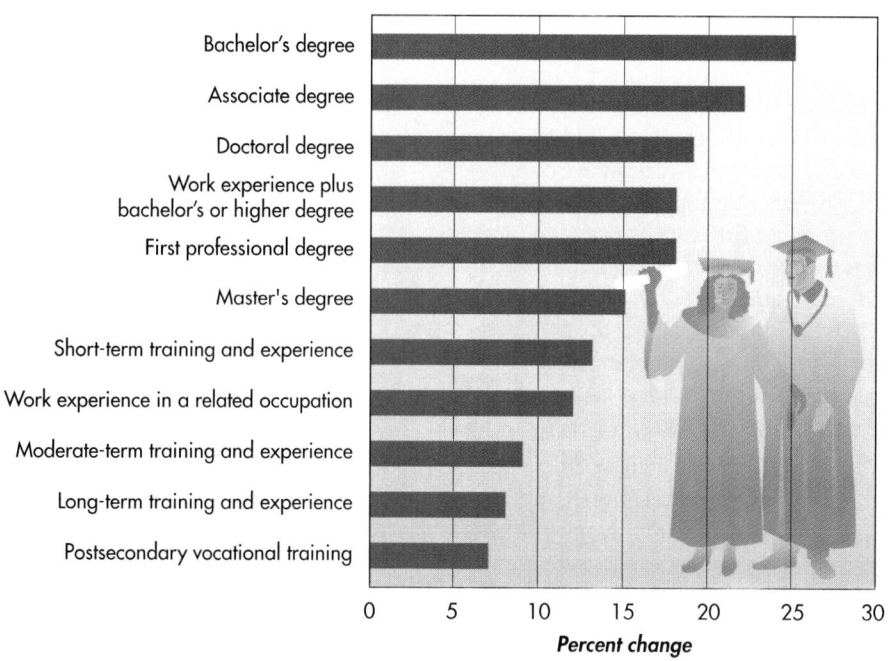

EXHIBIT D.3

JOB GROWTH BY EDUCATION AND TRAINING

Research by the Bureau of Labor Statistics shows that earning a bachelor's degree pays off.

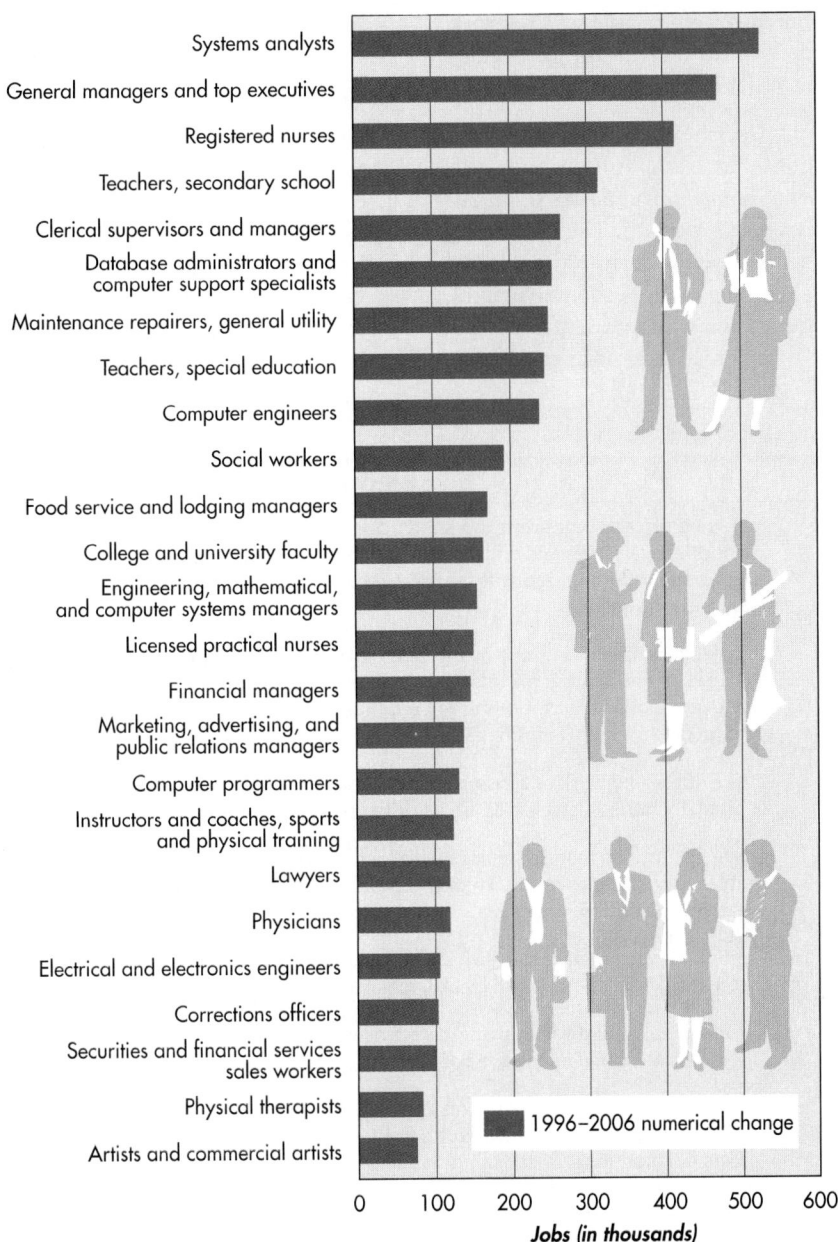

Systems analysts
General managers and top executives
Registered nurses
Teachers, secondary school
Clerical supervisors and managers
Database administrators and computer support specialists
Maintenance repairers, general utility
Teachers, special education
Computer engineers
Social workers
Food service and lodging managers
College and university faculty
Engineering, mathematical, and computer systems managers
Licensed practical nurses
Financial managers
Marketing, advertising, and public relations managers
Computer programmers
Instructors and coaches, sports and physical training
Lawyers
Physicians
Electrical and electronics engineers
Corrections officers
Securities and financial services sales workers
Physical therapists
Artists and commercial artists

■ 1996–2006 numerical change

0   100   200   300   400   500   600

Jobs (in thousands)

EXHIBIT D.4

THE 25 FASTEST-GROWING OCCUPATIONS

The 25 occupations with the largest and fastest employment growth, higher than average pay, and lower than average unemployment will account for 5 million new jobs, or 27 percent of all job growth between 1996 and 2006. Of the 25 occupations, 18 require at least a bachelor's degree.

tion, and employment opportunities. If possible, visit some of the organizations on your list, contact their human resources departments, or talk with key employees.

You can find ads for specific job openings by looking in local and major newspapers and by visiting your college placement office. Of course, a source of growing importance to your job search is the World Wide Web. An increasing number of large and small companies are posting job openings on the Internet.

Employment Information on the Web

The World Wide Web offers an amazing amount of employment information.[2] Is the Web the answer to all your employ-

ment dreams? Perhaps . . . or perhaps not. But as the Web grows, the employment information it provides is constantly expanding. For helpful hints and useful Web addresses, you can consult innumerable books such as *What Color Is Your Parachute?* by Richard Nelson Bolles.

When you're dealing with the Internet, the one thing you can count on is rapid change. Using the Web effectively in your job search will depend on how well you prepare your job-search strategy, how many employers (especially in your field) accept the Web as a source of potential employees, and how quickly current resources expand and adapt to the ever-changing Web environment. The Web offers information not only from employers seeking applicants but also from people seeking work. You can use the World Wide Web for a variety of job-seeking tasks in addition to searching for job openings (see Exhibit D.5):

■ *Finding career counseling.* Use the Web to analyze your skills and work expectations. For example, begin your self-assessment with the *Keirsey Temperament Sorter II,* an online personality test at www.keirsey.com/. The Web offers job-seeking pointers and counseling from online career centers, many of which are run by colleges and universities. Make sure the advice you get is useful and sensible, since some career centers are commercial sites. One good com-

mercial site is Monster.com: the Job-smart Coach at campus.monster. com/experts/bradley.

■ *Making contacts.* Use the Web to locate and communicate with potential employers. One way to locate people is through Usenet newsgroups dedicated to your field of interest. Newsgroup members can leave and send messages on an electronic bulletin board. You might also try listservs (or Internet mailing lists). These discussion groups mail each message to every member's e-mail address. Commercial systems such as Prodigy, America Online, and CompuServe have their own special interest discussion groups (called

WEB SITE	DESCRIPTION AND FEATURES
America's Career InfoNet www.acinet.org/	A good place to begin your job search, this site can help you make more informed career decisions. Learn about typical wages and employment trends across occupations and industries. Check education, knowledge, and skills requirements for most occupations. Site includes links to multiple career resources available on the Internet.
America's Job Bank www.ajb.dni.us/	This site is operated jointly by the U.S. Department of Labor and by 1,800 local employment service offices. The listing of jobs is large (almost 1 million). After searching by keywords, locations, or other options, you can get detailed descriptions of job requirements, salaries, and instructions on how to apply. Includes a list of links to over 600 employer Web sites—a great way to get information about companies.
Career-Builder www.careerbuilder.com/	Site offers a network of career services, job search information, and tips on how to succeed once you're hired. Includes a database of job openings by state with links to company profiles.
Career Magazine www.careermag.com/	Site features job hunting topics such as interviewing, networking, and preparing résumés. Includes searchable index of job openings, employer profiles, résumé bank, news items, and calendars for job fairs and campus recruiting.
Career Resource Center www.careers.org/	Site is a directory of career Web sites categorized by employers, learning resources, career reference resources, career services, and by U.S. regions.
Careers.wsj.com www.careerjournal.com/	Great place to find who's hiring, career news, and resources. Updated weekly, this site is sponsored by *The Wall Street Journal Interactive Edition* with content from the *National Business Employment Weekly.*
Careers in Business www.careers-in-business.com/	Site provides free information on a wide variety of business careers and is designed to help you select a satisfying career in the business world. Posts job openings by company name and by industry. Focuses on careers in accounting, finance, and marketing.
Headhunter.net www.headhunter.net	Site includes career resources center, calendar of upcoming career fairs, job hunting tips, ideas to improve your résumé, and latest job openings posted by employers. In addition, you can post your own résumé to their online database.
JOBTRAK www.jobtrak.com/	JOBTRAK has formed partnerships with over 800 college and university career centers to offer a comprehensive suite of services to both job seekers and employers. More than 3,000 new jobs are added to JOBTRAK's database daily. Many postings are aimed at entry-level candidates.
Monster.com www.monster.com/	Monster offers more than 175,000 job listings, plus company profiles that contain all the job listings for each company, in addition to the ability to apply online. The site includes tips on writing résumés and cover letters. Heavily marketed, it attracts many employers.
USA Careers www.usacareers.opm.gov/	This site was developed jointly by the U.S. Office of Personnel Management and a consortium of federal agencies. Offers self-assessment, career planning, and job search tools. Includes a listing of job opportunities in the public sector job market and other opportunities worldwide.
Yahoo! Classifieds classifieds.yahoo.com/	Site offers extensive listing of companies by U.S. city. You can post, clip, or store job ads. Customized "my ads" page allows you to check how many times your ad was viewed by prospective buyers. For career-related information click on link to Yahoo! Careers at careers.yahoo.com/.

EXHIBIT D.5

TWELVE PLACES TO START YOUR ONLINE JOB SEARCH

Begin your job search with these helpful online career resources.

Special Interest Groups, RoundTables, Clubs, Forums, or Bulletin Boards). E-mail allows you to communicate quickly and nonintrusively for requesting information or contacting a potential employer.

■ *Researching companies.* By visiting a company's Web site, you can find out its mission, products, annual reports, employee benefits, and job openings. You can locate company Web sites through URLs (Web addresses), links from other sites, or search engines such as Alta Vista, Lycos, Yahoo!, or Excite.

■ *Posting your résumé online.* You can post your résumé online either through an index service or on your own homepage. To post your résumé on an index service, you'll need to adapt it to an electronic format and transmit it by mail, fax, modem, or e-mail (see "Adapting Your Résumé to an Electronic Format" later in this chapter). Once your information is input into the service's database, your résumé will be sent to any employers whose requests match key words in your information. Posting your résumé on your own homepage allows you to retain a nicer-looking format. You can even include sound or video clips and links to papers you've written or recommendations you've received.

Using the World Wide Web to find employment allows you to respond directly to job postings (without going through recruiters), post résumés (tailored to match the skills and qualifications necessary to fill a particular position), send résumés through e-mail (which is faster and less expensive than printing and mailing them), send focused cover letters directly to the executives doing the hiring, and quickly gain detailed information about prospective employers. Most campus placement offices are retooling to help you take advantage of Web opportunities. Still, experts claim that at least 10 million U.S. employers don't think of the Internet when it's time to hire. In short, the Web cannot replace other techniques for finding employment; it's just one more tool in your overall strategy.

For any job, your ultimate goal is an interview with potential employers. The fastest way to obtain an interview is to get a referral from someone you know. In fact, many companies pay their employees handsome referral bonuses if they recommend a candidate who subsequently is hired and stays for a designated period of time.[3] Some organizations recruit students for job openings by sending representatives to college campuses for interviews, usually coordinated by the campus placement office. Employers also recruit candidates through campus publications and the employment bureaus operated by some trade associations. Unsolicited résumés can also be vital for obtaining interviews. Most companies will keep unsolicited résumés on file or scan them into a database.[4]

■ PREPARING YOUR RÉSUMÉ

A **résumé** is a structured, written summary of a person's education, employment background, and job qualifications. It's a form of advertising, designed to stimulate an employer's interest in meeting you and learning more about you. A good résumé inspires the prospective employer to pick up the phone and ask you to come in for an interview. Your objective in writing your résumé is to create interest rather than tell everything about yourself. If hints leave the reader wanting more, a potential employer will have more reasons to reach for the phone.

Build the reader's interest by calling attention to your best features and downplaying your weaknesses, without distorting or misrepresenting the facts.[5] A good résumé conveys seven specific qualities that employers seek. It shows that a candidate (1) thinks in terms of results, (2) knows how to get things done, (3) is well-rounded, (4) shows signs of progress, (5) has personal standards of excellence, (6) is flexible and willing to try new things, and (7) possesses strong communication skills. As you put your résumé together, think about how the format, style, and content convey these seven qualities.

Controlling the Format and Style

A typical recruiter devotes less than 45 seconds to each résumé before tossing it into either the "maybe" or the "reject" pile. In fact, most recruiters scan rather than read a résumé from top to bottom. If your résumé doesn't *look* sharp, and if you don't grab the reader's interest in the first few lines, chances are nobody will read it carefully enough to judge your qualifications.

To give your résumé a sharp look, use a clean typeface on high-grade, letter-size bond paper (in white or some light earth tone). Make sure that your stationery and envelope match. Leave ample margins all around, and be certain any corrections are unnoticeable. Avoid italic typefaces, which can be difficult to read, and use high-quality printing.

In general, try to write a one-page résumé. If you have a great deal of experience and are applying for a higher-level position, you may prepare a somewhat longer résumé. Give yourself enough space to present a persuasive, accurate portrait of your skills and accomplishments.

Lay out your résumé so that the information is easy to grasp.[6] Break up the text with headings that call attention to various aspects of your background, such as work experience and education. Underline or boldface key points, or set them off in the left margin. Use indented lists to itemize your most important qualifications. Leave plenty of white space, even if you're forced to use two pages. Pay attention to mechanics and details. Make sure that headings and itemized lists are grammatically parallel and that grammar, spelling, and punctuation are correct.

Write in a simple and direct style to save your reader time. Use short, crisp phrases instead of whole sentences, and focus on what your reader needs to know. Absolutely avoid using the word *I*. You might say, "Coached a Little League team to the regional playoffs" or "Managed a fast-food restaurant and four employees."

Think about your résumé from the employer's perspective. Ask yourself: What key qualifications will an employer be looking for? Which of these are my greatest strengths? What will set me apart from other candidates? What are my greatest accomplishments, and what was produced as a result? Then tailor your résumé to appeal to the employer's needs.

Tailoring the Contents

Most potential employers expect to see certain items in any résumé. The bare essentials are name and address, academic credentials, and employment history. Otherwise, it's up to you to emphasize your strongest, most impressive qualifications and combine your experiences into a straightforward message that communicates what you can do for your potential employer.[7] Don't exaggerate, don't alter the past or claim skills you don't have, and don't dwell on negatives. By focusing on your strengths, you can convey the desired impression without distorting the facts.

Choosing the Best Organizational Plan

Your résumé should emphasize information that has a bearing on your career objective and should minimize or exclude any that is irrelevant or counterproductive. Adopt an organizational plan—chronological, functional, or combination—that focuses on your strongest points. The "right" choice depends on your background and goals.

- *Chronological résumés.* The most common and most traditional type of résumé is the **chronological résumé.** The "Work Experience" section dominates the chronological résumé in the most prominent slot, immediately after the name and address and the career objective. Develop this section by listing your jobs sequentially in reverse order, beginning with the most recent position. Under each listing, describe your responsibilities and accomplishments, giving the most space to the most recent positions. If you're a recent college grad, focus attention on your academic credentials by putting your educational qualifications before your experience. The key advantages of the chronological pattern are (1) employers are familiar with it and can easily find things; (2) it highlights growth and career progression; and (3) it highlights employment continuity and stability.[8] The chronological approach is especially appropriate if you have a strong employment history and are aiming for a job that builds on your current career path (see Exhibit D.6).

- *Functional résumés.* In a **functional résumé,** you organize your résumé around a list of skills and accomplishments and then identify your employers and academic experience in subordinate sections. This pattern stresses individual areas of competence, and it's useful for people who are just entering the job market, people who want to redirect their careers, and people who have little continuous career-related experience. The key advantages of this organizational pattern are (1) it helps readers clearly see what you can do for them, rather than having to read through job descriptions to find out; (2) it allows job seekers to emphasize an earlier job experience; and (3) it deemphasizes lack of career progress or lengthy unemployment. Bear in mind that many seasoned employment professionals are suspect of this résumé style; they assume candidates who use it are trying to hide something.

- *Combination résumés.* A combination résumé includes the best features of the chronological and functional formats. This format emphasizes a candidate's skills and accomplishments while including a complete job history. Nevertheless, it is not commonly used and has two major disadvantages: (1) It tends to be longer, and (2) it can be repetitious because you may have to list your accomplishments and skills in both the functional section and the chronological job descriptions.

Adapting Your Résumé to an Electronic Format

Along with a traditional, paper résumé, you'll need an electronic version to submit to potential employers by e-mail or via the Internet. You may also need an HTML-coded document to post as a Web page should you choose to go that route.

Most Fortune 1000 companies today encourage applicants to submit electronic or scannable résumés. By scanning these résumés into their electronic database, companies can narrow down the pile of applicants quickly.

Electronic or scannable résumés should convey the same information as a traditional résumé, but the format and style must be computer-friendly. This means you must eliminate any graphics, boldface print, underlines, italics, small print, and formatting codes such as tab settings.[9] To change your traditional paper résumé into a scannable one, you convert it into plain text (ASCII) format, provide a list of key words, and balance common language with jargon (see Exhibit D.7).

- *Convert your résumé to ASCII format.* ASCII is a common plain-text language that allows your résumé to be read by any scanner and accessed by any computer regardless of the word-processing software you used to prepare the document. All word-processing programs allow you to save files as plain text. To convert your résumé to an ASCII plain-text file, remove all formatting such as bolding, centering, bullets, and graphic lines, and use a popular typeface such as Times, Helvetica, or Courier with a 10- to 14-point font size. To indicate a bullet, use an asterisk or a lowercase letter *o*. Add some blank spaces (rather than tabs) to align text and a few blank lines to create headings and separate paragraphs, as white space allows scanners and computers to recognize when one topic ends and another begins.

- *Provide a list of key words.* Emphasize certain key words to help potential employers select your résumé from the thousands they scan. When employers scan résumés, they generally search for nouns, because verbs tend to be generic rather than specific to a particular position or skill. To maximize the number of matches, or "hits," include a key word summary of 20 to 30 words and phrases that define your skills, experience, education, and professional affiliations. Place this list right after your name and address. A key word summary for an accountant, for example, might include these terms: Accountant, Corporate Controller, Fortune 1000, Receivables, Payables, Inventory, Cash Flow, Financial Analysis, Payroll Experience, Corporate Taxes, Activity Based Accounting, Problem Solving, Computer Skills, Excel, Access, Networks, HTML, Peachtree, Quick Books, BA Indiana University–Accounting, CPA, Dean's List, Articulate, Team Player, Flexible, Willing to Travel, Fluent Spanish.

- *Balance common language with current jargon.* To maximize hits between your résumé and an employer's search, use words that potential employers will understand. For example, don't call a keyboard an input device. Also, use only common abbreviations such as BA or MBA. Include the important buzz words in your field. You can find appropriate buzz words in the classified ads of major newspapers such as

---

ROBERTO CORTEZ
5687 Crosswoods Drive
Falls Church, Virginia 22046

Home: (703) 987-0086   Office: (703) 549-6624

OBJECTIVE

Accounting management position requiring a knowledge of international finance

EXPERIENCE

**March 1997
to present**

Staff Accountant/Financial Analyst, Inter-American Imports
(Alexandria, VA)

- Prepare accounting reports for wholesale giftware importer ($15 million annual sales)
- Audit financial transactions with suppliers in 12 Latin American countries
- Create computerized models to adjust accounts for fluctuations in currency exchange rates
- Negotiate joint-venture agreements with major suppliers in Mexico and Colombia
- Implement electronics funds tranfer for vendor disbursements, improving cash flow and eliminating payables clerk position.

**October 1993
to March 1997**

Staff Accountant, Monsanto Agricultural Chemicals
(Mexico City, Mexico)

- Handled budgeting, billing, and credit-processing functions for the Mexico City branch
- Audited travel/entertainment expenses for Monsanto's 30-member Latin American sales force
- Assisted in launching an online computer system to automate all accounting functions

EDUCATION

1991 to 1993

MBA with emphasis in international business
George Mason University (Fairfax, Virginia)

1987 to 1991

BBA, Accounting
University of Texas, Austin

INTERCULTURAL AND TECHNICAL SKILLS

- Fluent in Spanish and German
- Traveled extensively in Latin America
- Excel • Access • HTML • Visual Basic

EXHIBIT D.6

CHRONOLOGICAL RÉSUMÉ

Roberto Cortez calls attention to his most recent achievements by setting them off in list form with bullets. The section titled "Intercultural and Technical Skills" emphasizes his international background, fluency in Spanish, and extensive computer skills—all of which are important qualifications for his target position.

the *Wall Street Journal* and in résumés that are posted online. Be careful to check and recheck the spelling, capitalization, and punctuation of any jargon you include, and use only those words you see most often.

If an employer gives you an option of submitting a scannable résumé by mail, by fax, or by e-mail, choose e-mail. Sending your résumé by e-mail in a plain-text format puts your résumé directly into the employer's database, bypassing the scanning process. If you send your résumé in a paper format by regular mail or by fax, you still run the risk that a scanning program will create an error when reading your résumé.

If you submit your résumé by e-mail, don't attach it as a separate document. Most human resources departments won't accept attached files because of concern about computer viruses. Instead, paste your résumé into the body of your e-mail message, using the "insert text file" command to bring the ASCII-formatted résumé into the file. Always include reference numbers or job ad numbers in the subject line of your e-mail if they are available.

If you're posting your electronic résumé to an employer's online résumé builder, copy and paste the appropriate sections from your electronic file directly into the employer's form. Doing so will avoid rekeying and will eliminate errors.

Roberto Cortez
5687 Crosswoods Drive
Falls Church, Virginia 22046
Home: (703) 987-0086   Office: (703) 549-6624
RCortez@silvernet.com

KEY WORDS

Financial executive, accounting management, international finance, financial
analyst, accounting reports, financial audit, computerized accounting model,
exchange rates, joint-venture agreements, budgets, billing, credit processing,
online systems, MBA, fluent Spanish, fluent German, Excel, Access, Visual Basic,
team player, willing to travel

OBJECTIVE

Accounting management position requiring a knowledge of international finance

EXPERIENCE

Staff Accountant/Financial Analyst, Inter-American Imports (Alexandria, Virginia)
March 1997 to present
o Prepare accounting reports for wholesale giftware importer, annual sales of
$15 million
o Audit financial transactions with suppliers in 12 Latin American countries
o Create computerized models to adjust for fluctuations in currency exchange
rates
o Negotiate joint-venture agreements with suppliers in Mexico and Colombia
o Implement electronic funds transfer for vendor disbursements, improving cash
flow and eliminating payables clerk position

Staff Accountant, Monsanto Agricultural Chemicals (Mexico City, Mexico)
October 1993 to March 1997
o Handled budgeting, billing and credit-processing functions for the Mexico City
branch
o Audited travel/entertainment expenses for Monsanto's 30-member Latin
American sales force
o Assisted in launching an online computer system to automate all accounting
functions

EDUCATION

MBA with emphasis in international business, George Mason University (Fairfax,
Virginia), 1991 to 1993

BBA, Accounting, University of Texas, Austin, 1987 to 1991

INTERCULTURAL AND TECHNICAL SKILLS

Fluent in Spanish and German
Traveled extensively in Latin America
Excel, Access, HTML, Visual Basic

An attractive and fully formatted hard copy of this document is available upon
request.

EXHIBIT D.7

ELECTRONIC RÉSUMÉ

Because some of his target employers will be scanning his résumé into a database, and because he wants to submit his résumé via e-mail or post it on the Internet, Roberto Cortez created an electronic résumé by changing his formatting and adding a list of key words. However, the information remains essentially the same and appears in the same order.

If you fax your electronic résumé, set your machine to "fine" mode to result in a higher-quality printout on the receiving end. If you're mailing your résumé, you may want to send both a well-designed traditional résumé and a scannable one. Attach Post-it Notes, labeling one copy "visual résumé," and the other "scannable résumé."

Preparing Your Application Letter

The purpose of your cover letter is to get the reader interested enough to read your résumé. Always send the two together because each has a unique job to perform.

Before you write your application letter, learn something about the organization you're applying to. When composing the letter, show that you've done your homework. Imagine yourself in the recruiter's situation and show how your background and talents will solve a particular company problem or fill a need. The more you can learn about the organization, the better you'll be able to capture the reader's attention and convey your desire to join the company.[10] The letter in Exhibit D.8 makes an impression by focusing on the employer's needs.

During your research, find out the name, title, and department of the person you're writing to. Reaching and ad-

Glenda S. Johns

Home: 457 Mountain View Road, Clear Lake, IA 50428 (515) 633-5971
College: 1254 Main Street, Council Bluffs, IA 51505 (712) 438-5254

June 16, 2001

Ms. Patricia Downings, Store Manager
Wal-Mart
840 South Oak
Iowa Falls, Iowa 50126

Dear Ms. Downings:

You want retail clerks and managers who are accurate, enthusiastic, and experienced. You want someone who cares about customer service, who understands merchandising, and who can work with others to get the job done. When you're ready to hire a manager trainee or a clerk who is willing to work toward promotion, please consider me for the job.

Working as a clerk and then as an assistant department manager in a large department store has taught me how challenging a career in retailing can be. Moreover, my AA degree in retailing (including work in such courses as retailing, marketing, and business information systems) will provide your store with a well-rounded associate. Most important, I can offer Wal-Mart's Iowa Falls store more than my two years' of study and field experience. You'll find that I'm interested in every facet of retailing, eager to take on responsibility, and willing to continue learning throughout my career. Please look over my résumé to see how my skills can benefit your store.

I understand that Wal-Mart prefers to promote its managers from within the company, and I would be pleased to start out with an entry-level position until I gain the necessary experience. Do you have any associate positions opening up soon? Could we discuss my qualifications? I will phone you early next Wednesday to arrange a meeting at your convenience.

Sincerely,

Glenda Johns

Glenda Johns

Enclosure

EXHIBIT D.8

APPLICATION LETTER

In her unsolicited application letter, Glenda Johns manages to give a snapshot of her qualifications and skills without repeating what is said in her résumé.

---

dressing the right person is the most effective way to gain attention. Always avoid phrases such as "To Whom It May Concern" and "Dear Sir."

Following Up on Your Application

If your application letter and résumé fail to bring a response within a month or so, follow up with a second letter to keep your file active. This follow-up letter also gives you a chance to update your original application. Even if you receive a letter acknowledging that your application will be kept on file, don't hesitate to send a follow-up letter after three months. Such a letter demonstrates that you are sincerely interested in working for the organization and that you are persistent in pursuing your goals and upgrading your skills to make yourself a better employee—and it might just get you an interview.

INTERVIEWING WITH POTENTIAL EMPLOYERS

Approach job interviews with a sound appreciation of their dual purpose: The organization's main objective is to find the best person available for the job; the applicant's main objective is to find the job best suited to his or her goals and capabilities.

In general, the easiest way to connect with a big company is through your campus placement office; the most efficient way to approach a smaller business is by contacting the company directly. In either case, you move to the next stage and prepare to meet with a recruiter during an **employment interview,** a formal meeting during which an employer and an applicant ask questions and exchange information to see whether the applicant and the organization are a good match.

Most employers conduct two or three interviews before deciding whether to offer a person a job. The first interview, generally held on campus, is the **preliminary screening interview,** which helps employers eliminate unqualified applicants from the hiring process. Those candidates who best meet the organization's requirements are invited to visit company offices for further evaluation. Some organizations make a decision at that point, but many schedule a third interview to complete the evaluation process before extending a job offer.

Because the interview takes time, start seeking interviews well in advance of the date you want to start work. It takes an average of ten interviews to get one job offer. If you hope to have several offers to choose from, you can expect to go through 20 or 30 interviews during your job search.[11] Some students start their job search as early as nine months before graduation. Early planning is even more crucial during downturns in the economy because many employers become more selective when times are tough.

What Employers Look For

In general, employers are looking for two things: proof that a candidate can handle a specific job and evidence that the person will fit in with the organization. Employers are usually most concerned with the candidate's experience, intelligence, communication skills, enthusiasm, creativity, and motivation.

- *Qualifications for the job.* The interviewer may already have some idea of whether you have the right qualifications, based on a review of your résumé. During the interview, you'll be asked to describe your education and previous jobs in more depth so that the interviewer can determine how well your skills match the requirements. In many cases, the interviewer will be seeking someone with the flexibility to apply diverse skills in several areas.[12]

- *Personality traits.* A résumé can't show whether a person is lively and outgoing, subdued and low-key, able to take direction, or able to take charge. Each job requires a different mix of personality traits, so the task of the interviewer is to find out whether a candidate will be effective in a particular job.

- *Physical appearance.* Clothing and grooming reveal something about a candidate's personality and professionalism. Even in companies where interviewers may dress casually, show good judgment by dressing (and acting) in a professional manner. Interviewers also consider such physical factors as posture, eye contact, handshake, facial expression, and tone of voice.

- *Age.* Job discrimination against middle-aged people is prohibited by law, but if you feel your youth could count against

you, counteract its influence by emphasizing your experience, dependability, and mature attitudes.

- *Personal background.* You might be asked about your interests, hobbies, awareness of world events, and so forth. You can expand your potential along these lines by reading widely, meeting new people, and participating in discussion groups, seminars, and workshops.

- *Attitudes and personal style.* Openness, enthusiasm, and interest are likely to impress an interviewer. So are courtesy, sincerity, willingness to learn, and a positive, self-confident style—all of which help a new employee adapt to a new workplace and new responsibilities.

What Applicants Need to Find Out

What things should you find out about the prospective job and employer? By doing a little advance research and asking the right questions during the interview, you can probably find answers to these questions and more:

- Are these my kind of people?
- Can I do this work?
- Will I enjoy the work?
- Is this job what I want?
- Does the job pay what I'm worth?
- What kind of person would I be working for?
- What sort of future can I look forward to with this organization?

How to Prepare for a Job Interview

It's perfectly normal to feel a little anxious before an interview. Don't worry too much, however; preparation will help you perform well. Here are some pointers to guide that preparation:

- *Do some basic research.* Learning about the organization and the job is important because it enables you to review your résumé from the employer's point of view.

- *Think ahead about questions.* Most job interviews are essentially question-and-answer sessions: You answer the interviewer's questions about your background, and you ask questions of your own to determine whether the job and the organization are right for you. By planning for your interviews, you can handle these exchanges intelligently (see Exhibits D.9 and D.10). Of course, you don't want to memorize responses or sound overrehearsed.

- *Bolster your confidence.* By overcoming your tendencies to feel self-conscious or nervous during an interview, you can build your confidence and make a better impression. If some aspect of your background or appearance makes you uneasy, correct it or exercise positive traits to offset it, such as warmth, wit, intelligence, or charm. Instead of dwelling on your weaknesses, focus on your strengths so that you can emphasize them to an interviewer.

- *Polish your interview style.* Confidence helps you walk into an interview and give the interviewer an impression of poise, good

COLLEGE

- What courses in college did you like most? Least? Why?
- Do you think your extracurricular activities in college were worth the time you devoted to them? Why?
- When did you choose your college major? Did you ever change your major? If so, why?

- Do you feel you did the best scholastic work you are capable of?
- Which of your college years was the toughest? Why?

EMPLOYMENT HISTORY

- What jobs have you held? Why did you leave?
- What percentage of your college expenses did you earn? How?
- Why did you choose your particular field of work?
- What are the disadvantages of your chosen field?
- Have you served in the military? What rank did you achieve? What jobs did you perform?

- What do you think about how this industry operates today?
- Why do you wish to change employment?
- What do you like the least about your current position?
- What goals do you expect to achieve in your current job that you have not already accomplished?

THE NEW POSITION

- Why do you think you would like this particular type of job?
- What are your expectations of this position?
- What do you anticipate will be the most challenging aspects of this job?

- What can you contribute to this position?
- What would be your first goal in this position?
- How would you handle a 10 percent budget cut in your area of responsibility?

PERSONAL ATTITUDES AND PREFERENCES

- Do you prefer to work in any specific geographical location? If so, why?
- How much money do you hope to be earning in five years? In ten years?
- What do you think determines a person's progress in a good organization?

- What personal characteristics do you feel are necessary for success in your chosen field?
- Tell me a story.
- Do you like to travel?
- Do you think grades should be considered by employers? Why or why not?

WORK HABITS AND COMPANY "FIT"

- Are you a team player, or are you more satisfied working alone?
- What type of boss do you prefer?
- Have you ever had any difficulty getting along with colleagues or supervisors? With other students? With instructors?
- Would you prefer to work in a large or a small organization? Why?
- How do you feel about overtime work?
- What have you done that shows initiative and willingness to work?

- Do you praise the contributions of others?
- What characteristics do you believe an outstanding employee should possess? A peer? A supervisor?
- How would you handle a "problem" employee?
- How would you deal with a colleague who has competed with you for a position, feels better qualified than you, and now works for you?

CAREER GOALS

- What are your long-term goals?
- How have you moved from each stage in your career to the next?

- What factors are most important to you in terms of job satisfaction?
- When do you anticipate a promotion?

EXHIBIT D.9

COMMON INTERVIEW QUESTIONS

Prepare for a job interview in advance by thinking about your answers to these questions.

manners, and good judgment. In the United States, you're more likely to be invited back for a second interview or offered a job if you maintain eye contact, smile frequently, sit in an attentive position, and use frequent hand gestures. These nonverbal signals convince the interviewer that you're alert, assertive, dependable, confident, responsible, and energetic.[13] Work on eliminating speech mannerisms such as "you know," "like," and "um." Speak in your natural tone, and try to vary the pitch, rate, and volume of your voice to express enthusiasm and energy.

- *Plan to look good.* The best policy is to dress conservatively. Wear the best-quality businesslike clothing you can, preferably in a dark, solid color. Avoid flamboyant styles, colors, and prints. Clean, unwrinkled clothes, well-shined shoes, neatly styled and combed hair, clean fingernails, and fresh breath help make a good first impression. Don't spoil the effect by smoking cigarettes before or during the interview. Finally, remember that one of the best ways to look good is to smile at appropriate moments.

- What are this job's major responsibilities?

- What qualities do you want in the person who fills this position?

- Do you want to know more about my related training?

- What is the first problem that needs the attention of the person you hire?

- What are the organization's major strengths? Weaknesses?

- Who are your organization's major competitors, and what are their strengths and weaknesses?

- What makes your organization different from others in the industry?

- What are your organization's major markets?

- Does the organization have any plans for new products? Acquisitions?

- What can you tell me about the person I would report to?

- How would you define your organization's managerial philosophy?

- What additional training does your organization provide?

- Do employees have an opportunity to continue their education with help from the organization?

- Would relocation be required, now or in the future?

- Why is this job now vacant?

EXHIBIT D.10

APPLICANT QUESTIONS FOR INTERVIEWERS

Learn as much as you can about potential employers by asking these questions.

■ *Be ready when you arrive.* Be sure you know when and where the interview will be held. Take a small notebook, a pen, a list of your questions, a folder with two copies of your résumé, an outline of your research findings about the organization, and any correspondence about the position. You may also want to take a small calendar, a transcript of your college grades, a list of references, and, if appropriate, samples of your work. After you arrive, relax. You may have to wait, so bring something to read or to occupy your time (the less frivolous or controversial, the better).

How to Follow Up After the Interview

Touching base with the prospective employer after the interview, either by phone or in writing, shows that you really want the job and are determined to get it. It also brings your name to the interviewer's attention again and reminds him or her that you're waiting to know the decision.

The two most common forms of follow-up, the thank-you message and the inquiry, are generally handled by letter. But a phone call can be just as effective, particularly if the employer favors a casual, personal style. Express your thanks within two days after the interview, even if you feel you have little chance for the job. In a brief message, acknowledge the interviewer's time and courtesy, convey your continued interest, and

ask politely for a decision. If you're not advised of the interviewer's decision by the promised date or within two weeks, you might make an inquiry, particularly if you don't want to accept a job offer from a second firm before you have an answer from the first. Assume that a simple oversight is the reason for the delay, not outright rejection.

Building Your Career

Having the right skills is one way to build toward a career. Employers seek people who are able and willing to adapt to diverse situations, who thrive in an ever-changing workplace, and who continue to learn throughout their careers. In addition, companies want team players with strong work records and leaders who are versatile. Many companies encourage managers to get varied job experience.[14] In some cases, your chances of being hired are better if you've studied abroad or learned another language. Many employers expect college graduates to have a sound understanding of international affairs, and they're looking for employees with intercultural sensitivity and an ability to adapt in other cultures.[15]

Compile an employment portfolio. Get a three-ring notebook and a package of plastic sleeves that open at the top. Collect anything that shows your ability to perform, such as classroom or work evaluations, certificates, awards, and papers you've written. An employment portfolio serves as an excellent resource when writing your résumé and provides employers with tangible evidence of your professionalism.

As you search for a permanent job that fulfills your career goals, take interim job assignments, participate in an internship program, and consider temporary work or freelance jobs. Not only will these temporary assignments help you gain valuable experience and relevant contacts, but they will also provide you with important references and with items for your portfolio.[16] Employers will be more willing to find (or even to create) a position for someone they've learned to respect, and your temporary or freelance work gives them a chance to see what you can do.

If you're unable to find actual job experience, work on polishing and updating your skills. Network with professional colleagues and friends who can help you stay abreast of your occupation and industry. While you're waiting for responses to your résumé or your last interview, take a computer course or gain some other educational or life experience that would be difficult while working full time. Become familiar with the services offered by your campus career center (or placement office). These centers offer individual placement counseling, credential services, job fairs, on-campus interviews, job listings, advice on computerized résumé-writing software, workshops in job-search techniques, résumé preparation, interview techniques, and more.[17]

Once an employer hires you and you're on the job, don't think you've reached the end of the process. The best thing you can do for your long-term career is to continue learning. Listen to and learn from those around you who have experience. Be ready and willing to take on new responsibilities, and actively pursue new or better skills. Employers appreciate applicants and employees with willingness and enthusiasm to learn, to listen, and to gain experience.

EXHIBITS D.11A–G

Career charts on the following pages indicate the duties, qualifications, salary levels, and career outlook through 2006 for selected jobs in management, human resources, computers and information systems, sales and marketing, finance and accounting, communications, and other business careers.

JOB TITLE	DUTIES	QUALIFICATIONS	SALARY	THROUGH 2006
Building services/ facilities manager	Oversees physical aspects of facilities	Bachelor's degree; background in management, architecture, or real estate	Average: $53,800	Average growth
Chief executive officer, public company	Formulates policies; directs operations	Bachelor's degree or higher	Median: $714,000	Average growth
Chief executive officer, nonprofit organization	Sets strategies to meet objectives; directs operations	Bachelor's degree or higher	Average: less than $135,000	Average growth
Clerical supervisor	Supervises duties of clerical and administrative staff	Office and supervisory skills	Median: $28,900	Average growth
Food and beverage director	Directs food service operations	College degree or training in hotel/restaurant management	Average: $43,000	Average growth
Hotel manager	Responsible for overall operations of hotel	College degree or postsecondary training in hotel/restaurant management	Average: $54,000+ bonuses	Average growth
Industrial production manager	Oversees production staff and equipment	Varies; most manufacturers prefer college degree in business or engineering	Average: $60,000	Slight decline
Management analyst/ consultant	Collects and analyzes data; recommends and implements ideas	Master's degree in business plus 5 years of experience	Entry: $35,200; median: $39,500	Faster than average
Merchandise buyer/manager	Obtains highest-quality items at lowest possible cost	Bachelor's degree in business	Average: $33,200 for buyers (higher for managers)	Slower than average
Office/administrative service manager	Coordinates and directs office support services	Associate or bachelor's degree in business or management	Average: $41,400	Average growth
Property manager	Organizes, staffs, and manages real estate operations	College degree in real estate, finance, or business	Median: $28,500	Average growth

EXHIBIT D.11A

CAREERS IN MANAGEMENT

JOB TITLE	DUTIES	QUALIFICATIONS	SALARY	OUTLOOK THROUGH 2006
Affirmative action/ EEO specialist	Investigates and resolves EEO grievances; files EEO reports	College degree preferred; familiarity with laws and regulations necessary	Median: $38,200	Likely to remain competitive
Compensation and benefits director	Oversees pay and evaluation systems; develops and coordinates employee benefits program	Master's degree in human resources, labor relations, or business recommended	Median: $90,500	Likely to remain competitive
Employee assistance specialist	Assists with employee programs ranging from safety to child care	College degree preferred	Median: $39,00	Likely to remain competitive
Employee benefits specialist	Handles employee benefit programs; assists employees with filing claims	College degree preferred; certification in employee benefits desirable	Median: $38,300	Likely to remain competitive
Employment interviewer	Searches for promising job applicants; screens, interviews, and tests applicants	High school diploma sufficient	Entry: $25,300; commissions possible	Average growth
Human resources information systems specialist	Develops and applies computer programs to process personnel information	Bachelor's degree in computer science, math, or information systems	Median: $38,800	Faster than average growth
Human resources manager	Oversees all personnel activities: employment, compensation, benefits, training, and employee relations	College degree preferred; master's degree in human resources desirable	Median: $64,400	Likely to remain competitive
Industrial/labor relations director	Forms labor policy; oversees labor relations; negotiates bargaining agreements	College degree preferred; graduate study in labor relations may be necessary	Median: $106,100	Likely to remain competitive
Interviewing clerk	Assists with forms, applications, and questionnaires	High-school diploma	Median: $18,512	Faster than average growth
Job analyst	Collects and examines detailed data about job duties to prepare job descriptions	College degree in business or human resources	Median: $39,600	Likely to remain competitive
Occupational health and safety manager	Detects and corrects unsafe machinery or working conditions	Training in applicable laws or safety procedures; college degree may be required	Median: $36,140	Slower than average growth
Payroll and timekeeping clerk	Computes wages for payroll records, usually by computer	High school diploma necessary; higher degree favored	Median: $23,100	Little or no change
Personnel clerk	Maintains employee records	High school diploma necessary; higher degree favored	Median: $23,100	Little or no change
Recruiting manager	Recruits and interviews employees; advises on hiring decisions	College degree preferred	Median: $63,800	Likely to remain competitive
Training specialist	Plans, organizes, and directs training activities; evaluates training effectiveness	College degree in business, human resources, or personnel administration	Median: $37,200	Likely to remain competitive

EXHIBIT D.11B

CAREERS IN HUMAN RESOURCES

JOB TITLE	DUTIES	QUALIFICATIONS	SALARY	OUTLOOK THROUGH 2006
Computer-aided design (CAD) specialist	Develops and designs products with computer-aided design (CAD) software	Portfolio with formal CAD training or certification; associate or bachelor's degree in specialty field	Median: $30,680	Faster than average growth
Computer engineer	Designs hardware, software, networks, and processes; develops and tests systems	Bachelor's degree in computer science, computer engineering, or electrical engineering	Entry: $39,722	Much faster than average growth
Computer operator	Oversees the operation of computer hardware systems	Minimum of high school diploma; some postsecondary education or training may be required	Median: $22,400	Sharp decline expected
Computer programmer	Writes, tests, and maintains software programs; updates and expands existing programs	Bachelor's or two-year degree in computer-related field	Median: $40,100	Faster than average growth
Computer support specialist	Provides assistance and advice to computer users; interprets problems and provides technical support	Bachelor's degree in computer-related field	Entry: $25,000–$36,500 for help-desk support technicians	Much faster than average growth
Computer systems analyst	Designs computer solutions to meet needs; plans and develops new systems or revises existing resources to new operations	Bachelor's degree in computer-related field	Entry: $36,261; median: $46,300	Fastest-growing occupation of all jobs
Computer systems manager	Plans, coordinates, and directs computer programming, hardware, system design, and software	Bachelor's degree in computer-related field; master's degree often preferred	Median entry: $60,900; average range: $33,000–$100,000+	Much faster than average growth
Data entry clerk/word processor	Enters information into computers or word processors	High school graduate with skills in keyboarding and/or computer software packages	Entry: $18,100	Decline expected
Database administrator	Implements computer databases; coordinates changes and tests; plans and coordinates security	Bachelor's degree in computer-related field	Entry: $54,000–$67,500	Much faster than average growth
Information systems manager	Installs, configures, and supports systems or portions of systems	Bachelor's degree in computer-related field	Entry: $36,261	Much faster than average growth
Software developer	Designs and develops software; creates custom software applications	Bachelor's degree in computer-related field	Range: $49,000–$67,500	Much faster than average growth
Webmaster	Responsible for all aspects of maintaining Web site	Knowledge of HTML, Java, and/or specific databases; experience desirable	Range: $40,000–$90,000	Much faster than average growth

EXHIBIT D.11C

CAREERS IN COMPUTERS AND INFORMATION SYSTEMS

JOB TITLE	DUTIES	QUALIFICATIONS	SALARY	OUTLOOK THROUGH 2006
Account executive	Maintains and services accounts	Bachelor's degree in business with marketing emphasis	Entry for marketing majors: $29,000	Faster than average growth
Advertising sales representative	Markets advertising services	College degree in business, advertising, or marketing	Median: $26,000	Much faster than average growth
Insurance agent/broker	Sells and services insurance policies; helps policyowners settle claims	College graduate with proven sales ability	Median commissions: $31,500	Slower than average growth
Manufacturers' and wholesale sales representative	Markets products or services to manufacturers or to wholesale and retail establishments	High school diploma with desire to sell	Median: $36,100; commissions possible	Average growth
Marketing manager	Develops detailed marketing strategies; directs the sale of products and services	College degree in almost any major; certification desirable	Median: $46,000; bonuses possible	Faster than average growth
Marketing research analyst	Researches and analyzes data of past sales to predict future sales	Graduate degree in business, economics, marketing, or statistics	Median entry: $35,000 with master's degree	Average growth
Real estate agent/broker	Solicits property listings; sells properties; negotiates and conducts real estate transactions	License required; most states require 30–90 classroom hours; continuing education needed for license renewal	Median commissions: $31,500	Slower than average growth
Retail sales manager	Serves customers, supervises workers, and coordinates retail operations	Associate or bachelor's degree preferred	Median: $24,400	Slower than average growth
Sales representative, business services	Sells business products and services	High school diploma with proven sales record	Median: $30,264; commissions possible	Much faster than average growth
Stockbroker/securities sales representative	Advises investors on stocks, bonds, and market conditions; conducts buy/sell orders	College degree and sales ability; state license	Median: $38,800 (commissions after licensure)	Much faster than average growth
Travel agent	Organizes and schedules travel activities	Minimum of high school diploma; formal or specialized training desirable	Entry: $16,400; commissions possible	Faster than average growth

EXHIBIT D.11D

CAREERS IN SALES AND MARKETING

JOB TITLE	DUTIES	QUALIFICATIONS	SALARY	OUTLOOK THROUGH 2006
Accountant/ auditor	Prepares, analyzes, and verifies financial reports and taxes	Bachelor's degree in accounting or related field	Entry: $29,400	Average growth
Actuary	Determines probabilities of income or loss based on various risk factors	Bachelor's degree in math, actuarial science, business, accounting, or statistics	Entry: $37,600	Slower than average growth
Bank examiner	Investigates financial institutions to enforce laws and regulations; approves mergers and acquisitions	Bachelor's degree	Median: $36,140	Slower than average growth
Bank teller	Services banking customers by processing money, checks, and other financial items	High school diploma	Median: $16,300	Little or no change
Bill and account collector	Ensures that customers pay overdue accounts; locates and notifies customers of delinquent accounts	High school diploma	Median: $21,320	Much faster than average growth
Bookkeeper/ accounting clerk	Maintains financial data in computer and paper files	High school diploma	Median: $20,700	Little or no change
Budget analyst	Reviews, analyzes, and interprets financial data; makes recommendations for future	Bachelor's degree in accounting, finance, business, public administration, or economics	Entry: $24,000–$38,700	Average growth
Controller	Directs preparation of all financial reports; oversees accounting, audit, or budget departments	Bachelor's degree in accounting, finance, business, public administration, or economics	Range: $47,000–$138,000	Average growth
Cost estimator	Compiles and analyzes data on factors that influence costs	Bachelor's degree in construction management, engineering, math, accounting, or related field	Entry: $20,000–$31,949	Average growth
Credit analyst	Establishes credit rating criteria; determines credit ceilings and monitors credit extensions	Bachelor's degree in finance, accounting, economics, or business	Average: $40,500	Average growth
Financial manager	Oversees cash flow; monitors credit extensions; assesses risk of transactions; and analyzes investments	Minimum of bachelor's degree in finance or related field; master's degree preferred	Median: $40,700	Average growth
Financial planner	Determines financial objectives and analyzes data; develops and implements financial plans	College graduate with sales experience	Median: $38,800	Much faster than average growth
Insurance underwriter	Identifies and analyzes risk of loss; establishes premium rates and writes policies	College degree in business administration, finance, or accounting	Median: $31,400	Slower than average growth
Loan officer/ counselor	Prepares, analyzes, and verifies loan applications; extends credit; helps borrowers with loan transactions	Bachelor's degree in finance, economics, or related field	Mortgage loan: $30,600–$73,000; consumer loan: $28,900–$48,000	Faster than average growth
Loan and credit authorizer	Reviews credit histories and obtains data to determine creditworthiness of loan applicants	No specific training needed; on-the-job training usually provided	Average: $24,000–$24,700	Slight decline
Operations research analyst	Applies mathematical principles to organizational problems; evaluates options and chooses best alternative	Master's degree in operations research or management science and bachelor's in computer science or math	Median: $42,400	Slower than average growth
Treasurer	Prepares financial reports and ensures compliance with tax and regulatory requirements	Bachelor's degree in accounting, finance, business, public administration, or economics	Total compensation with bonuses: $122,500	Average growth

EXHIBIT D.11E

CAREERS IN FINANCE AND ACCOUNTING

JOB TITLE	DUTIES	QUALIFICATIONS	SALARY	OUTLOOK THROUGH 2006
Advertising/public relations manager	Directs advertising activities and communication of information	Bachelor's degree in advertising, journalism, or public relations	Entry for advertising majors: $27,000; median for managers: $46,000	Faster than average growth
Graphic designer	Creates artistic works to communicate ideas; designs images with computer software	Portfolio with training through bachelor's or master's degree in fine arts or graphic design	Median: $27,100	Faster than average growth
Public relations specialist	Creates favorable attitudes through effective communications	College degree in journalism, public relations, advertising, or communications	Median: $34,000	Faster than average growth
Radio news announcer	Researches, prepares, and presents news; interviews news guests; reports on community activities	Successful audition and broadcast journalism training from college or technical school	Average: $31,251	Slight decline; keen competition
Reporter/correspondent	Gathers and reports information; investigates issues and composes reports	Bachelor's degree in journalism	Median entry: $23,296	Decline expected; keen competition
Technical writer	Prepares understandable scientific and technical information for nontechnical audiences	College degree in communications, English, journalism, or specialized field	Median: $44,000	Faster than average growth
Television news anchor	Presents news stories; introduces videotapes news or live transmission from reporters	Successful audition and broadcast journalism training from college or technical school	Average: $65,520	Keen competition
Writer/editor	Communicates ideas and information; develops material for publication or broadcasts	College degree in communications, English, or journalism	Average entry: $21,000	Faster than average growth

EXHIBIT D.11F

CAREERS IN COMMUNICATIONS

JOB TITLE	DUTIES	QUALIFICATIONS	SALARY	OUTLOOK THROUGH 2006
Environmental protection specialist	Conducts investigations to ensure that food, water, and air comply with government standards	Bachelor's degree in environmental health or physical or biological sciences; some states require license	Average: $52,940 (federal government employee)	Slower than average growth
Industrial designer	Develops and designs manufactured products using computer-aided industrial design (CAID) software	Bachelor's degree in related field	Average entry: $27,000	Faster than average growth
Insurance adjuster	Investigates claims; inspects damage; negotiates and settles claims	College degree preferred with major in any field; many states require license	Median: $22,880	Faster than average growth
Quality assurance inspector/manager	Examines and inspects products or services to ensure high standards of quality	Varies by employer and specific job function; usually a combination of experience and education	Average: $47,020 (federal government employee)	Slower than average growth
Records clerk	Maintains and updates records; enters data into computer and performs basic data analysis	High school diploma	Median: $17,100–$23,700	Little or no change

EXHIBIT D.11G

OTHER BUSINESS CAREERS

TEST YOUR KNOWLEDGE

QUESTIONS FOR REVIEW

1. What things should you consider when planning and thinking about your career?

2. What are some helpful sources of employment and company information?

3. What qualities does an effective résumé possess?

4. How do the three organizational approaches for résumés differ?

5. How should you prepare for a job interview?

QUESTIONS FOR ANALYSIS

6. Take one of the online job skills assessment tests offered at the Prentice Hall Student SuperSite at www.prenhall.com/success/CareerPath. What did you learn about yourself after taking this test? How do these kinds of tests help you plan for a career in business?

7. What should you try to find out about a prospective job and employer before accepting a job offer?

8. What key attributes do most employers look for in job candidates?

9. How can you use the Internet to facilitate your job search?

10.  Perform an Internet Job search for a career that interests you using the resources listed in Exhibit D.5. What types of helpful career-related information did you find at these Web sites?

11. You'd rather not explain why you quit last summer's job as a telephone sales representative. Should you omit this position from your résumé? Can you mention it without revealing why you quit? If a prospective employer asks you what you did last summer, how will you respond?

CHAPTER GLOSSARY

chronological résumé
Most traditional type of résumé, listing employment history sequentially in reverse order so that the most recent experience is listed first

employment interview
Formal meeting during which an employer and an applicant ask questions and exchange information to see whether the applicant and the organization are a good match

functional résumé
Résumé organized around a list of skills and accomplishments, subordinating employers and academic experience in order to stress individual areas of competence

preliminary screening interview
Meeting between an employer's representative and a candidate for the purpose of eliminating unqualified applicants from the hiring process

résumé
Form of advertising that lists a person's education, employment background, and job qualifications in order to obtain an interview

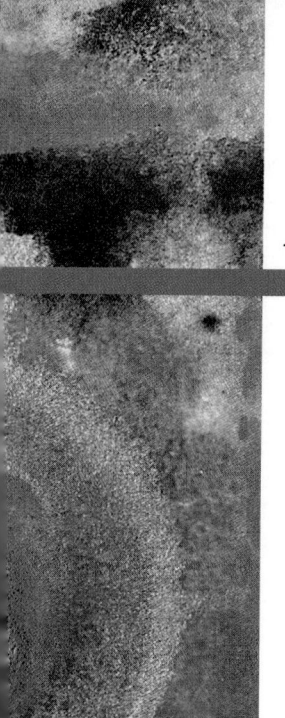

Appendix

YOUR BUSINESS PLAN

GETTING STARTED WITH BUSINESS PLANPRO SOFTWARE

Business PlanPro (BPP) software is a template for crafting a winning business plan. The software is designed to stimulate your thinking about the many tasks and decisions that go into planning and running a business. The software does not do your thinking for you; instead, it leads you through a thought process by asking you to respond to questions about your business and to provide data for the preformatted tables and charts. Accompanying instructions, examples, and sample business plans provide you with a full range of assistance you can use to draft your own comprehensive business plan. By working through the exercises at the end of each text part, you will gain a practical skill for your business career.

When installing the software disk be sure to install the *Getting Started* manual. This electronic guide is in a PDF format and can be read by using Adobe Acrobat Reader software. You can download the software for free by visiting the Adobe Acrobat Web site at www.adobe.com/products/acrobat/read step.html. To read the online *Getting Started* manual, open the Adobe Acrobat Reader software and then the Getting Started file. This file is located in the Bus PlanPro files, which are stored in the Pas file folder in your Program files.

NAVIGATING THE SOFTWARE

One of the best ways to become familiar with the BPP software is by navigating one of the BPP sample business plans. The BPP start-up screen offers you four choices. Click on Open a Sample Plan and select any sample plan. Read the *Getting Started* manual to learn about the different screen modes available in BPP. Navigate the sample plan as you read about the features avail-

able in each mode. As with most software, you have multiple options for accessing the same information. Once you navigate a few sample business plans, you'll see how easy it is to get around. You will use the same navigational process to enter information for your own business plan.

To access the text mode option, select Your Text icon from the Plan Manager Screen. Use the Previous and Next buttons at the bottom of the Text screen to move back and forward through the sample plan. To view related tables and charts, click on the Text Manager tab. Then click on the Go To Table or Go To Chart buttons.

If you prefer to view topics in your own sequence, access the plan outline by clicking on the Plan Outline icon at the bottom of your screen. To read a specific section of a sample plan, simply double click on its topic heading. You can return to the plan outline at any time by clicking on that icon.

The Task Manager (also accessed from the Plan Outline screen) is another way to navigate a business plan. The Task Manager uses descriptive headings to direct you to sections in the business plan that address related topics. For example, access the Task Manager in the sample plan and select Competitive Edge in the Your Marketing Plan section to read about how the company will gain a competitive edge in the marketplace. Click on the Plan Outline icon at the bottom of the screen, then click on the Plan Outline tab to find the related section in the plan outline.

You may find it helpful to print out a full copy of the sample plan you have selected and review it as you navigate its contents on your screen. This way you can see how the software uses the information to construct a formal business plan. To print out the sample plan, click on the Printer icon at the Plan Manager screen. Make sure both the Print Tables and Print Chart boxes are checked. You may print the plan to your screen by selecting the Preview option or you may print it on paper.

CREATING A WINNING BUSINESS PLAN

The exercises included at the end of each text part use the knowledge you've gained from reading that text part. Each exercise has two tasks: Think Like a Pro tasks require you to navigate the software, find and review information in the sample business plans, and evaluate and critique some of the thinking that went into these plans. By reviewing these sample plans with a critical eye you will begin to sharpen your own business planning skills. Create Your Own Business Plan tasks are an opportunity for you to apply your business planning skills to create your own winning business plan. So begin thinking now about the type of business you'd like to own or manage someday. Then develop and refine your business strategies as you work through the exercises.

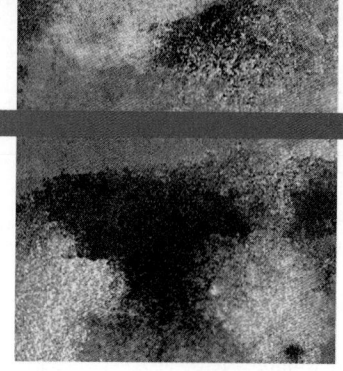

REFERENCES

■ Notes

CHAPTER 1

1. Kara Swisher, "Behind the Portal," *Wall Street Journal,* 17 April 2000, R74–R76; Brent Schlender, "How a Virtuoso Plays the Web," *Fortune,* 6 March 2000, F79–F83; Brent Schlender, "The Customer Is the Decision-Maker," *Fortune,* 6 March 2000, F84–F86; Joseph Nocera, "Do You Believe? How Yahoo! Became a Blue Chip," *Fortune,* 7 June 1999, 76–92; Linda Himelstein, Heather Green, Richard Siklos, and Catherine Yang, "Yahoo! The Company, the Strategy, the Stock," *Business Week,* 7 September 1998, 661; Jonathan Littman, "Driven to Succeed: The Yahoo Story," *Upside,* September 1998, 70–75; Carol Pickering, "A Tale of Two Startups," *Forbes,* 5 October 1998, 85; Steven Levy, "Surfers, Step Right Up!," *Newsweek,* 25 May 1998, 74–82; Steve Rosenbush, "How Can Tim Koogle Stay So Cool in the Face of AOL's Assault," *Business Week E.Biz,* 15 May 2000, EB27; Ben Elgin and Linda Himelstein, "The Word at Yahoo! Yikes!" *Business Week,* 30 October 2000, 63; Quentin Hardy, "The Killer Ad Machines," *Forbes,* 11 December 2000, 168–178.

2. IBM 1997 Annual Report online, *Annual Report Gallery,* [accessed 21 April 1999] www.reportgallery.com.

3. Everette James, "Services—U.S. Firms Are Leaders in the Global Economy," *Business America,* April 1998, 5–7.

4. U.S. Department of Commerce, Bureau of Economic Analysis Web site, beadata.bea.doc.gov/bea/dn2/gpoc.htm [accessed 24 September 1999]; "Fortune 1000 Ranked Within Industry," *Fortune,* 26 April 1999, F51–F73.

5. *Survey of Current Business* (Washington, D.C.: GPO, November 1997), Table B8, 132; Infoplease Almanac, Infoplease.com, [accessed 22 September 1999], www.infoplease.com/ipa/A0302230.html.

6. *Statistical Abstract of the United States, 1996* (Washington, D.C.: GPO, 1996), 56–59, 394, 396.

7. George Hager, "Fast-Growing Internet Industry Surges Startling 62%," *USA Today,* 6 June 2000, A1.

8. Thomas Stewart, "Brain Power," *Fortune,* 17 March 1997, 105–110; "Post-Capitalist Society," Soundview Executive Book Summaries 17, no. 3 (March 1995).

9. James Wilfong and Toni Seger, *Taking Your Business Global* (Franklin Lakes, N.J.: Career Press, 1997).

10. Robert L. Heilbroner and Lester C. Thurow, *Economics Explained* (New York: Simon & Schuster, 1994), 29–30.

11. Heilbroner and Thurow, *Economics Explained,* 250.

12. Heilbroner and Thurow, *Economics Explained,* 250.

13. Collin McMahon, "Russians at a Critical Crossroad," *Chicago Tribune,* 29 August 1998, 1; Patricia Kranz, "Russia; Is There a Solution?" *Business Week,* 7 September 1998, 27–29; Robert J. Samuelson, "Global Capitalism, R.I.P?" *Newsweek,* 14 September 1998, 40–42; Emily Thorton, "Russia—What Happens When Markets

Fail," *Business Week,* 26 April 1999, 50–52; Bruce Nussbaum, "Time to Act," *Business Week,* 14 September 1998, 34–37.

14. Larry Derfner, "The Fight over Privatization: Netanyahu Has Pledged to End Israel's," *The Jewish Week,* 9 August 1996, 14+; "Israel to Privatize 49% of El Al Airlines," *New York Times,* 2 June 1998, C5; Pierre Tran, "Air France Head Hopes for Privatization," *Reuters Business Report,* 8 June 1997, 6; Nathan Gardels, "Socialism Fate Awaits the Welfare State," *New Perspectives Quarterly,* 22 March 1996, 2; "Air France Shares Jump on First Day of Trading," *New York Times,* 23 February 1999, C3; Greg Steinmetz, "Her Majesty May Sell Part of London's Tube, Angering Some in U.K.," *Wall Street Journal,* 14 October 1999, A1, A12.

15. Erik Eckholm, "Chinese Restate Goals to Reorganize State Companies," *New York Times,* 23 September 1999, A10; Mark L. Clifford, Dexter Roberts, Joyce Barnathan, and Pete Engardio, "Can China Reform Its Economy?" *Business Week,* 29 September 1997, 116–123; Nicholas D. Kristof and Sheryl WuDunn, "The World's Ills May Be Obvious, But Their Cure Is Not," *New York Times,* 15 February 1999, [accessed 16 February 1999], www.nytimes.com/library/world/ global/021699global-econ.html; Dexter Roberts, "China's New Revolution," *Business Week,* 27 September 1999, 72–78.

16. Gary Hamel and Jeff Sampler, "The E-Corporation," *Fortune,* 7 December 1998, 81–92.

17. Brian O'Reilly, "The Rent-a-Car Jocks Who Made Enterprise #1," *Fortune,* 28 October 1996, 125–128.

18. Jeff Wise, "How Skiboarding Became the New Snowboarding," *New York Times Magazine,* 21 March 1999, 58–61.

19. Joel Brinkley, "U.S. Judge Says Microsoft Violated Antitrust Laws with Predatory Behavior," *New York Times,* 4 April 2000, A1, C12; Merrill Goozner, "Microsoft Is Ruled an Illegal Monopoly, *Chicago Tribune,* 4 April 2000, sec. 1, 1, 16; Ted Bridis and John R. Wilke, "Judge Orders Microsoft Broken in Two, Imposes Tough Restriction on Practices," *Wall Street Journal,* 8 June 2000, A3, A12; "Judge Suspends Restrictions on Microsoft," *Wall Street Journal,* 21 June 2000, A3; John R. Wilke and Rebecca Buckman, "Justices Decline Early Look at Microsoft," *Wall Street Journal,* 27 September 2000, A3, A17.

20. Jon Van, "WorldCom, Sprint Fold Under Heft of Scrutiny," *Chicago Tribune,* 14 July 2000, sec.3, 1.

21. Patrick M. Reilly, "Barnes & Noble Closes Book on Attempt to Buy Ingram Amid FTC Objections," *Wall Street Journal,* 3 June 1999, B16.

22. Martin Kasindorf and Ken Fireman, "The Clinton Budget/2002 Solution," *Newsday,* 7 February 1997, A4; Gilbert C. Alston, "Balancing the Federal Budget," *Los Angeles Times,* 14 February 1997, B8; Jennifer Oldham, "The Budget Battle; Deficit and Debt: A Primer," *Los Angeles Times,* 6 January 1996, D1; Brian Naylor, Jacki Lynden, and Robert Siegel, "House Budget Debate," 1997 National

Public Radio, 30 July 1997; U.S. Department of Treasury Web site, [accessed 19 April 1999], www.treas.gov.

23. Robert Kuttner, "What's Wrong With Paying Off the National Debt?" *Business Week*, 15 May 2000, 35; Budget of the United States Government Fiscal Year 2001, [accessed 21 April 2000], w3.access.gpo.gov/usbudget/index.html.

24. Kathleen Madigan, "Keep Your Nest Egg Safe—Watch Housing Data," *Business Week*, 17 April 2000, 208–210.

25. Elia Kacapyr, "The Well-Being Index," *American Demographics*, February 1996, 32–35; Beth Belton, "U.S. Brings Economy into Information Age," *USA Today*, 17 March 1999, B1.

26. Rona Gindin, "Dealing With a Multicultural Workforce," *Nation's Restaurant News*, September–October 1998, 31, 83; Howard Gleckman, "A Rich Stew in the Melting Pot," *Business Week*, 31 August 1998, 76+.

27. Nanette Byrnes and Paul C. Judge, "Internet Anxiety," *Business Week*, 28 June 1999, 79–88.

28. Robert D. Hof, Gary McWilliams, and Gabrielle Saveri, "The Click Here Economy," *Business Week*, 22 June 1998, 122–128.

29. Michael Moynihan, *The Coming American Renaissance* (New York: Simon & Schuster, 1987), 25.

30. William A. Sahlman, "The New Economy is Stronger Than You Think," *Harvard Business Review*, November–December 1999, 99–106.

31. Sahlman, "The New Economy Is Stronger Than You Think," 99–106.

32. Michael van Biema and Bruce Greenwald, "Managing Our Way to Higher Service-Sector Productivity," *Harvard Business Review*, July/August 1997, 87–95.

33. Moynihan, *The Coming American Renaissance*, 42–43; "Through Seven Decades, Tracking Business and the World," *Business Week*, 4 October 1999, 118A–118P.

34. Adapted from Tariq K. Muhammad, "Leaders in the Digital Economy," *Black Enterprise*, March 1999, 73–77; [accessed 13 April 2000]; *The New Economy Index*, www.neweconomyindex.org/section1_page05.html; Sahlman, "The New Economy Is Stronger Than You Think," 99–106; Mohanbir Sawhney, "Making New Markets," *Business 2.0*, March 2000, 202–208; Dale D. Buss, "Embracing Speed," *Nation's Business*, June 1999, 12–17; Eric Ransdell, "Network," *Fast Company*, September 1999, 208–224; James W. Michaels, "How New Is the New Economy?" *Forbes*, 11 October 1999, 48–49; Jeffrey E. Garten, "What Could Go Wrong in the New Economy," *Business Week*, 13 December 1999, 28+; Bob Tedeschi, "A New Concept for Web Sellers: Profitability," *New York Times*, 24 April 2000, C1, C15; Lee Gomes, "Copycats," *Wall Street Journal*, 17 April 2000, R43; *The New Economy Index*, [accessed 13 April 2000], www.neweconomyindex.org/section1_page06.html Bernard Wysocki Jr., "Need for Profits Pares the Dot-Coms' Options," *Wall Street Journal*, 1 May 2000, A1; Christina Brinkley, "Hyatt Plans Internet Firm With Marriott," *Wall Street Journal*, 2 May 2000, A3, A6; Robert L. Simison, Fara Warner, and Gregory L. White, "GM, Ford, DaimlerChrysler to Create a Single Firm to Supply Auto Parts," *Wall Street Journal Interactive Edition*, [accessed 28 February 2000], interactive.wsj.com/articles/SB951493383958527087.htm; Dale Buss, "What's the Matter With Kids Today," *Wall Street Journal*, 22 May 2000, R23; Alan Murray, "For Policy Makers, Microsoft Suggest Need to Recast Models," *Wall Street Journal*, 6 June 2000, A1, A8; Nanette Byrnes, "Eyeballs, Bah! Figuring Dot-Coms' Real Worth," *Business Week*, 30 October 2000, 62.

35. Adapted from Kendall Hamilton, "Getting Up, Getting Air," *Newsweek*, 13 May 1996, 68.

COMPONENT A

1. Jason Zien, "Measuring the Internet," *About.com*, 13 July 1999 [accessed 17 July 1999] internet.about.com/library/weekly/1999/aa071399a.htm; "FAST Aims for Largest Index," *Search Engine Watch*, 4 May 1999, [accessed 17 July 1999] searchenginewatch.internet.com/sereport/99/05-fast.htm.

2. Ernest L. Maier, Anthony J. Faria, Peter Kaatrude, and Elizabeth Wood, *The Business Library and How to Use It* (Detroit: Omnigraphics, 1996), 84–97; Matt Lake, "Desperately Seeking Susan OR Suzie NOT Sushi," *New York Times*, 3 September 1998, D1, D7.

3. Anne Zieger, "Enterprise Computing: IP Telephony Gets Real," *InfoWorld*, 5 January 1998, 20; Laura Kujubu, "Telcos Answer Wake-Up Call from Internet," *InfoWorld*, 15 December 1997, 19.

4. David Morse, ed., *CyberDictionary: Your Guide to the Wired World* (Santa Monica, Calif.: Knowledge Exchange, 1996), 113.

5. Morse, *CyberDictionary*, 233.

6. Charlene Marmer Solomon, "Sharing Information Across Borders and Time Zones," *Global Workforce*, March 1998, 13–18; Eryn Brown, "9 Ways to Win on the Web," *Fortune*, 24 May 1999, 112.

7. Material for this section was taken from Courtland L. Bovée and John V. Thill, *Business Communication Today*, 6th ed. (Upper Saddle River, N.J.: Prentice Hall, 1999), 348–352.

8. Samuel Greengard, "Extranets Linking Employees with Your Vendors," *Workforce*, November 1997, 28–34.

9. Andy Reinhardt, "The Paperless Manual," *Business Week e.Biz*, 18 September 2000, EB92.

10. Robert D. Hof, Gary McWilliams, and Gabrielle Saveri, "The Click Here Economy," *Business Week*, 22 June 1998, 122–128; Tim McCollum, "End Your Internet Anxieties Now," *Nation's Business*, April 1999, 19–26.

11. Robert D. Hof, David Welch, Michael Arndt, Amy Barrett, and Stephen Baker, "E-Mall for Business," *Business Week*, 13 March 2000, 32–34.

12. Steffano Korper and Juanita Ellis, *The E-Commerce Book: Building the E-Empire* (San Diego, Calif.: Academic Press, 2000), 80; Rodes Fishburne, Alex Frankel, Michelle Jeffers, Scott Lajoie, and Lee Patterson, "Voices of the Revolution," *Forbes ASAP*, 21 February 2000, 80–86.

13. Gary L. Neilson, Bruce A. Pasternack, and Albert J. Viscio, "Up the E Organization," *Strategy & Business*, First Quarter 2000, 52–61; Peter Fingar, Harsha Kumar, and Tarun Sharma, *Enterprise E-Commerce* (Tampa, Fla.: Meghan-Kiffer Press, 2000), 48–53; Ravi Kalakota and Marcia Robinson, *E-Business Roadmap for Success* (Reading, Mass.: Addison-Wesley, 1999), 2–3; Stewart Alsop, "E or Be Eaten," *Fortune*, 8 November 1999, 87.

14. Kalakota and Robinson, *E-Business Roadmap for Success*, 1–7; IBM E-Business Web site [accessed 10 March 2000], www.ibm.com/e-business/info; Korper and Ellis, *The E-Commerce Book: Building the E-Empire*, 4–5; Christina Ford Haylock and Len Muscarella, *Net Success* (Holbrook, Mass.: Adams Media Corporation, 1999), 10–11.

15. Korper and Ellis, *The E-Commerce Book: Building the E-Empire*, 4.

16. Korper and Ellis, *The E-Commerce Book: Building the E-Empire*, 232.

17. Kalakota and Robinson, *E-Business Roadmap for Success*, 2.

18. Kalakota and Robinson, *E-Business Roadmap for Success*, 15.

19. Kalakota and Robinson, *E-Business Roadmap for Success*, 22–23.

20. Bill Laberis, "Jumping the E-Gun," *Ent*, 8 September 1999, 46; Jim Thompson, "EBay Outage Could Strike You," *Boardwatch*, August 1999, 68.

21. Efraim Turban, Jae Lee, David King, and H. Michael Chung, *Electronic Commerce, A Managerial Perspective* (Upper Saddle River, N.J.: Prentice Hall, 2000), 15–16.

22. Walid Mougayar, *Opening Digital Markets* (New York: McGraw-Hill, 1998), 29–35.

23. Laurie Windham, *Dead Ahead* (New York: Allworth Press, 1999), 31–32.

24. Turban et al., *Electronic Commerce, A Managerial Perspective*, 15–16.

CHAPTER 2

1. Roger Rosenblatt, "The Root of All Good: Reaching the Top by Doing the Right Thing," *Time*, 18 October 1999, 88–91; Stan Friedman, "Apparel with Conscience: The Givers," *Apparel Industry Magazine*, June 1999, 78–79; Andrea Adelson, "Wedded to Its Moral Imperatives," *New York Times*, 16 May 1999, 9; Michael Lear-Olimpi, "Management Mountaineer," *Warehousing Management*, January–February 1999, 23–30; Jennifer Bellantonio, "Fighting the Good Fight," Sporting Goods Business, 1999, S18–S22; Larry Armstrong, "Patagonia Sticks to Its Knitting," *Business Week*, 7 December 1998, 68; Nancy Rivera Brooks, "Companies Give Green Power the Green Light," *Los Angeles Times*, 27 September 1998, D8; Charlene Marmer Solomon, "A Day in the Life of Terri Wolfe: Maintaining Corporate Culture," *Workforce*, June 1998, 94–95; Jacqueline Ottman, "Proven Environmental Commitment Helps Create Committed Customers," *Marketing News*, 2 February 1998, 5–6; Dawn Hobbs, "Patagonia Ranked 24th by Magazine," *Los Angeles Times*, 23 December 1997, B1; Jim Collins, "The Foundation for Doing Good," *Inc.*, December 1997, 41–42; Paul C. Judge, "It's Not Easy Being Green," *Business Week*, 24 November 1997, 180; Melissa Downing, "A Lean, Green Fulfillment Machine," *Catalog Age*, June 1997, 63; Staci Bonner, "Patagonia, A Green Endeavor," *Apparel Industry Magazine*, February 1997, 46–48; Polly LaBarre, "Patagonia Comes of Age," *Industry Week*, 3 April 1995, 42–48; John Steinbreder, "Yvon Chouinard, founder and owner of the Patagonia Outdoor . . ." *Sports Illustrated*, 2 November 1991, 200.

2. Thomas Easton and Stephan Herrera, "J&J's Dirty Little Secret," *Forbes*, 12 January 1998, 42–44.

3. Easton and Herrera, "J&J's Dirty Little Secret," 42–44.

4. "For Heavy Drinkers, a Written Warning," *New York Times Abstracts*, 27 October 1998, sec. F, 8 [accessed 24 May 1999]. djnr.com/cgi-binDJ.

5. Dan Carney, "Fraud on the Net," *Business Week E.Biz*, 3 April 2000, EB58–EB64.

6. John Galvin, "The New Business Ethics: Cheating, Lying, Stealing, 15 May 2000, 86–99.

7. Jeffrey L. Seglin, "Dot.Con," *Forbes ASAP*, 21 February 2000, 135; Jerry Useem, "New Ethics . . . or No Ethics," *Fortune*, 20 March 2000, 83–86.

8. "FCC, Slam Door on This Idea," *Los Angeles Tribune*, 27 September 1999, 6; "Customer Complaints On Phone Slamming, Cramming Seen Rising," *Wall Street Journal*, 30 August 1999, B10.

9. Amy Zipkin, "Getting Religion On Corporate Ethics," *New York Times*, 18 October 2000, C1, C10.

10. John S. McClenahen, "Your Employees Know Better," *Industry Week*, 1 March 1999, 12–14.

11. Betsy Stevens, "Communicating Ethical Values: A Study of Employee Perceptions," *Journal of Business Ethics*, June 1999, 113–120.

12. Milton Bordwin, "The Three R's of Ethics," *Management Review*, June 1998, 59–61.

13. Mark Seivar, personal communication, 2 April 1998; "1-800-Justice or 1-800-Rat-fink," *Reputation Management*, March–April 1995, 31–34; Margaret Kaeter, "The 5th Annual Business Ethics Awards for Excellence in Ethics," *Business Ethics*, December 1993, 26–29.

14. "Does It Pay to Be Ethical?" *Business Ethics*, March–April 1997, 14–16; Don L. Boroughs, "The Bottom Line on Ethics," *U.S. & World Report*, 20 March 1995, 61–66.

15. Douglas S. Barasch, "God and Toothpaste," *New York Times Magazine*, 22 December 1996, 28.

16. Edward O. Welles, "Ben's Big Flop," *Inc.*, September 1998, 40+; Constance L. Hays, "Getting Serious at Ben & Jerry's," *New York Times*, 22 May 1998, C1, C3.

17. Welles, "Ben's Big Flop," 40+; Hays, "Getting Serious at Ben & Jerry's," C1, C3.

18. Constance L. Hays, "Ben & Jerry's To Unilever, With Attitude," *New York Times*, 13 April 2000, C1, C20; Fred Bayles, "Reviews In On Ben & Jerry's Sweet Deal," *USA Today*, 20 April 2000, 3A.

19. See letters in *New York Times*, 25 August 1918, and *New York Herald*, 1 October 1918.

20. Michael A. Verespej, "Why They're the Best," *Industry Week*, 16 August 1999, 102–109.

21. Thomas A. Fogarty, "Corporations Use Causes for Effect," *USA Today*, 10 November 1997, 7B; Peaceworks Web site [accessed 22 June 1999], www.peaceworks.net; Florence Fabricant, "A Young Entrepreneur Makes Food, Not War," *New York Times*, 30 November 1996, sec. International Business, 21.

22. Wal-Mart Web site [accessed 22 June 1999], www.walmart foundation.org/cmn.html; Microsoft Web site [accessed 22 June 1999], www.microsoft.com/giving/pages/O-givann.htm; American Express Web site [accessed 22 June 1999], www6.americanexpress.com/corp/ philanthropy/community.asp.

23. Carrie Shook, "Dave's Way," *Forbes*, 9 March, 1998, 126–127.

24. Anna Muoio, ed., "Ways to Give Back," *Fast Company*, December–January 1998, 113+.

25. William H. Miller, "Cracks in the Green Wall," *Industry Week*, 19 January, 1998, 58–65.

26. "Why Ford Came Clean," *Newsweek*, 22 May 2000, 50.

27. Gil Adams, "Cleaning Up," *International Business*, February 1996, 32; Susan Moffat, "Asia Stinks," *Fortune*, 9 December 1996, 120–132; Pete Engardio, Jonathan Moore, and Christine Hill, "Time For a Reality Check in Asia," *Business Week*, 2 December 1996, 58–66.

28. Michael Castleman, "Tiny Particles, Big Problems: Our Air Is Cleaner, Yet the Body Count Climbs," *Sierra*, 21 November 1995, 26.

29. Chris Bury and Ted Koppel, "The Ad Campaign and the Kyoto Summit," *ABC Nightline*, 9 December 1997; Peter Passell, "Trading on the Pollution Exchange," *New York Times*, 24 October 1997, C1, C4; Julia Flynn, Heidi Dawley, and Naomi Freundlich, "Green Warrior in Gray Flannel," *Business Week*, 6 May 1996, 96.

30. Kirk Spitzer, "Companies Divert Enough Waste to Fill Five Astrodomes," *Gannett News Service*, 2 November 1995; Michael Satchell, Betsy Carpenter, Kenan Pollack, "A New Day for Earth Lovers," *U.S. News & World Report*, 24 April 1994, 58–62.

31. David Brinkerhoff, "Honda Unveils Electric Car to Rival GM Version," *Reuters Business Report*, 3 January 1997; "Manhattan Beach Offers Free Charging for Electric Cars," *Los Angeles Times*, 27 March 1997, B5; Howard Rothman, "Interview: Amory Lovins," *Business Ethics*, March–April 1996, 34–36.

32. Joseph Weber, "3M's Big Cleanup," *Business Week*, 5 June 2000, 96–98.

33. Dan Charles, "Industrial Symbiosis," *Morning Edition (NPR)*, 31 July 1997.

34. "Money to Burn?" *The Economist* 345, 6 December 1997; Donna Beckley, "Industrial Pollution Still Haunts Hudson, Group Says," *Gannet News Service*, 24 September 1996, S12; Jim Bradley, "Buying High, Selling Low," *E Magazine*, 17 July 1996, 14–15; Brian Doherty, "Selling Air Pollution," *Reason*, 1 May 1996, 32–37; Bill Nichols, "Four Years of Work, Debate Produce First Phase of EPA's Cluster Rules," *Pulp & Paper*, 1998, 71+.

35. Satchell, Carpenter, and Pollack, "A New Day for Earth Lovers," 58–62.

36. Spitzer, "Companies Divert Enough Waste to Fill Five Astrodomes," *Electric Library*, Online, [accessed 28 July 1997].

37. "The IW Survey: Encouraging Findings," *Industry Week*, 19 January 1998, 62.

38. Constance L. Hays, "Since 70's the World Has Become Safer for Consumerism," *New York Times*, 5 January 1998, C6.

39. Daniel Eisenberg and Adam Zagorin, "Firestone's Rough Road," *Time*, 18 September 2000, 38–40; Joann Muller and Nicole St. Pierre, "How Will Firestone and Ford Steer Through This Blowout?" *Business Week*, 28 August 2000, 54+.

40. Laura Shapiro, "The War of the Labels," *Newsweek*, 5 October 1992, 63, 66.

41. Karen Friefeld, "As Subtle As a Slap In the Face: New Ad Campaign Makes Certain Its Messages are Absolutely Clear," *Newsday*, 21 May 1995, A56.

42. Chris Burritt, "Fallout From the Tobacco Settlement," *Atlanta Journal and Constitution*, 22 June 1997, A14; Jolie Solomon, "Smoke Signals," *Newsweek*, 28 April 1997, 50–51; Marilyn Elias, "Mortality Rate Rose Through '80s," *USA Today*, 17 April 1997, B3; Mike France, Monica Larner, and Dave Lindorff, "The World War on Tobacco," *Business Week*, 11 November 1996; Richard Lacayo, "Put Out the Butt, Junior," *Time*, 2 September 1996, 51; Elizabeth Gleick, "Smoking Guns," *Time*, 1 April 1996, 50.

43. Anne Faircloth, "Denny's Changes Its Spots," *Fortune*, 13 May 1996, 133–142; Nicole Harris, "A New Denny's—Diner By Diner," *Business Week*, 25 March 1996, 166–168; Eric Smith, "Not Paid in Full," *Black Enterprise*, April 1996, 16; Mark Lowery, "Denny's New Deal Ends Blackout," *Black Enterprise*, 20 February 1995, 43; "Denny's Does Some of the Right Things," *Business Week*, 6 June 1994, 42; "Making Amends at Denny's," *Business Week*, 21 November 1994, 47.

44. "Does It Pay to Be Ethical?" *Business Ethics*, March–April 1997, 15.

45. John A. Byrne, Leslie Brown, and Joyce Barnathan, "Directors in the Hot Seat," *Business Week*, 8 December 1997, 100, 102, 104.

46. Suzanne Wooley, "The Hustlers Queue Up On the Net," *Business Week*, 20 November 1995, 146–148.

47. Robert Pear, "U.S. Proposes Rules to Bar Obstacles to the Disabled," *New York Times*, 22 January 1991, A1, 12.

48. "Vital Facts 1999," OSHA Web site, [accessed 29 September 1999], www.osha-slc.gov/OSHAFacts/OSHAFacts.html.

49. Yochi J. Dreazen, "New OSHA Proposal Enrages Businesses," *Wall Street Journal*, 8 November 2000, A2, A6; Robert Manor, "OSHA's Ergonomic Rules Rile Business," *Chicago Tribune*, 14 November 2000, sec. 1, 1.

50. Wendy Bounds and Hilary Stout, "Sweatshop Pact: Good Fit or Threadbare?" *Wall Street Journal*, 10 April 1997, A2; Ellen Neuborne, "Nike to Take a Hit In Labor Report," *USA Today*, 27 March 1997, B1; William J. Holstein et al., "Santa's Sweatshop," *U.S. News & World Report*, 16 December 1996, 50–60; Stephanie Strom, "From Sweetheart to Scapegoat," *New York Times*, 27 June 1996, C1, 16; Nancy Gibbs, "Cause Celeb: Two High-Profile Endorsers Are Props in a Worldwide Debate Over Sweatshps and the Use of Child Labor," *Time*, 17 June 1996; Ellen Neuborne, "Labor's Shopping List: No Sweatshops," *USA Today*, 5 December 1995, B1; Bob Herbert, "A Sweatshop Victory," *New York Times*, 22 December 1995, A15.

51. Skip Kaltenheuser, "Bribery Is Being Outlawed Virtually Worldwide," *Business Ethics*, May–June 1998, 11; Thomas Omestad, "Bye-bye to Bribes," *U.S.News & World Report*, 22 December 1997, 39, 42–44.

52. Kate Murphy, "Fighting Pollution—And Cleaning Up, Too," *Business Week*, 19 January, 1998, 90.

53. Martin Walker, "How Green Is Europe?" *Europe*, February 1998, 26, 28–29.

54. Del Jones, "FBI: Spies Cost U.S. Firms $2B a Month," *USA Today*, 10 February 1999, 2B.

55. Andrew Tanzer, "Tech-Savvy Pirates," *Forbes*, 7 September 1998 [accessed 28 June 1999], www.forbes.com/forbes/98/0907/6205162a.htm; Richard Rapaport, "Singapore Sting," *Forbes*, 7 April 1997 [accessed 28 June 1999], www.forbes.com/asap/97/0407/084.htm.

56. Barrie McKenna, "OECD Creates Corporate Conduct Code: Governance Principles Range from Shareholders' Rights to Responsibilities of Directors," *The Globe and Mail*, 29 April 1999, B13 [accessed 28 June 1999] nrstg2p.djnr.com.

57. Adapted from James Lardiner, "I Know What You Did Last Summer," *U.S. News and World Report*, April 19, 1999, 55–56; "The End of Privacy," *The Economist*, 1 May 1999, 21–23; Daniel Eisenberg, "Who's Reading Your Bills?" *Time*, September 6, 1999, 54–55; Leslie Miller and Elizabeth Weise, "FTC Studies Profiling by Web Sites," *USA Today*, 8 November 1999, 1A–2A; Elizabeth Weise, "How the Cookies Can Crumble," *USA Today*, 15 February 2000, 3D; Heather Green, Mike France, Marcia Stepanek, and Amy Borrus, "Online Privacy; It's Time for Rules in Wonderland," *Business Week*, 20 March 2000, 83–96; Julia Angwin, "A Plan to Track Web Use Stirs Privacy Concern," *Wall Street Journal*, 1 May 2000, B1, B18; Justin Matlick, "Don't Restrain Trade in Information," *Wall Street Journal*, 2 December 1999, A22; Amy Borrus, "Internet Privacy: Congress Starts Feeling the Heat," *Business Week*, 15 May 2000, 59; Amy Borrus, "Online Privacy: Congress Has No Time to Waste," *Business Week*, 18 September 2000, 54.

58. Geanne Rosenberg, "Truth and Consequences," *Working Woman*, June/August 1998, 79–80.

CHAPTER 3

1. Trek's Web site, www.trekbikes.com [accessed 26 May 2000]; Michele Wucker, "Keep on Trekking," *Working Woman*, December/January 1998, 32–36; Christopher Elliott, "Zero Defects through Design," *Chief Executive*, 1998, 36–38; Randy Weston, "Trek Design System Cranks Out Changes," *Computerworld*, 15 December 1997, 37.

2. John Alden, "What in the World Drives UPS?" *International Business*, March/April 1998, 6–7; UPS Web site, ups.com [accessed 16 May 2000].

3. "Getting It Right in Japan," *International Business*, May–June 1997, 19.

4. Gary M. Wederspahn, "Exporting Corporate Ethics," *Global Workforce*, January 1997, 29–30; Dana Milbank and Marcus W. Brauchli, "Greasing Wheels," *Wall Street Journal*, 29 September 1995, A1, A7.

5. James Wilfong and Toni Seger, *Taking Your Business Global* (Franklin Lakes, N.J.: Career Press, 1997), 289.

6. Jules Abend, "Jockey Colors Its World," *Bobbin*, February 1999, 50–54.

7. Ricky W. Griffin and Michael W. Pustay, *International Business* (Reading, Mass.: Addison-Wesley, 1999), 415.

8. "Padgett Surveys Franchise/Small Business Sectors," *Franchising World*, March–April 1995, 46; John Stansworth, "Penetrating the Myths Surrounding Franchise Failure Rates—Some Old Lessons for New Business," *International Small Business Journal*, January–March 1995, 59–63; Laura Koss-Feder, "Building Better Franchise Relations," *Hotel & Motel Management*, 6 March 1995, 18; Carol Steinberg, "Franchise Fever," *World Trade*, July 1992, 86, 88, 90–91; John O'Dell, "Franchising America," *Los Angeles Times*, 25 June 1989, sec. IV, 1.

9. One World Web site, www.oneworldalliance.com/ [accessed 16 May 2000].

10. Lewis M. Simons, "High-Tech Jobs for Sale," *Time*, 22 July 1996, 59.

11. Alden, "What in the World Drives UPS?" 6–7.

12. Ernest Beck and Emily Nelson, "As Wal-Mart Invades Europe, Rivals Rush to Match Its Formula," *Wall Street Journal*, 6 October 1999, A1, A6.

13. "Foreign Investment in U.S. Reaches 54.4 Billion Dollars in 1995," *Xinhua News Agency*, 1996.

14. Thomas G. Condon and Kurt Badenhausen, "Spending Spree," *Forbes*, 26 July 1999, 208–18.

15. *Big Emerging Markets: 1996 Outlook* (Washington D.C.: GPO, 1996); Nicholas D. Kristof and Sheryl WuDunn, "The World's Ills May Be Obvious, But Their Cure Is Not," *New York Times*, 18 February 1999, www.nytimes.com/library/world/global/021699global-econ.html [accessed 19 February 1999].

16. Holley H. Ulbrich and Mellie L. Warner, *Managerial Economics* (New York: Barron's Educational Series, 1990), 190.

17. Patrick Lane, "World Trade Survey: Why Trade Is Good for You," *The Economist*, 3 October 1998, S4–S6.

18. Bureau of Economic Analysis Web site, www.bea.doc.gov/bea/di/tradgs-d.htm [accessed 15 May 2000].

19. Maria Mallory, "Wheels of Fortune," *U.S. News & World Report*, 4 March 1996, 49–50.

20. "Overview of the Economy," Bureau of Economic Analysis Web site, www.bea.doc.gov/bea/glance.htm [accessed 15 May 2000]; Table 1—U.S. International Transactions, Bureau of Economic Analysis Web site, www.bea.doc.gov/bea/di/bopq/bop1./htm [accessed 27 October 1999].

21. Robert J. Samuelson, "Trading with the Enemy," *Newsweek*, 1 April 1996, 41; Amy Borrus, Pete Engardio, and Dexter Roberts, "The New Trade Superpower," *Business Week*, 16 October 1995, 56–57; David A. Andelman, "Marco Polo Revisited," *American Management Association*, August 1995, 10–12; John Greenwald, "Get Asia Now, Pay Later," *Time*, 10 October 1994, 61; Simons, "High-Tech Jobs for Sale," 59.

22. James Cox, "Tariffs Shield Some U.S. Products," *USA Today*, 6 May 1999, 1B.

23. Eric Schmitt, "U.S. Backs off Sanctions, Seeing Poor Effect Abroad," *New York Times*, 31 July 1998, A1, A6; Robert T. Gray, "Book Review," *Nation's Business*, January 1999, 47.

24. "Saudi Arabia Hopes to Join WTO by 2002," *Reuters Business Report*, 3 August 1997.

25. "Airbus to Resume Talks on Status," *New York Times*, 5 May 1999, C4; Daniel Michaels, "Airbus Industrie's Partners Are Close to Establishing a Single Corporation," *Wall Street Journal*, 8 June 2000, A20; Daniel Michaels, "Country by Country—Flying High," *Wall Street Journal*, 25 September 2000, R18.

26. "Japanese Steelmakers Face U.S. Penalties In Antidumping Case," *Wall Street Journal*, 3 August 2000, C19.

27. James Cox, "Tariffs Shield Some U.S. Products," *USA Today*, 6 May 1999, 1B, 2B.

28. "APEC Ministers Commit to Sustainable Development," *Xinhau News Agency*, 11 June 1997; Fred C. Bergsten, "An Asian Push for World-Wide Free Trade: The Case For APEC," *The Economist*, 6 January 1996, 62; "U.S. Must Press to Reduce Trade Barriers in Asia, Pacific, Congress Told," *Gannett News Service*, 1995.

29. Michael M. Phillips, "One by One," *Wall Street Journal*, 26 April 1999, R4, R7.

30. Christopher Koch, "It's a Wired, Wired World," *Webmaster*, March 1997, 50–55.

31. Masaaki Kotabe and Maria Cecilia Coutinho de Arruda, "South America's Free Trade Gambit," *Marketing Management*, Spring 1998, 39–46.

32. "Grand Illusions," *The Economist*, 4 March 1995, 87; Bob Davis, "Global Paradox: Growth of Trade Binds Nations, But It Also Can Spur Separatism," *Wall Street Journal*, 20 June 1994, A1, A6; Barbara Rudolph, "Megamarket," *Time*, 10 August 1992, 43–44; Peter Truell, "Free Trade May Suffer from Regional Blocs," *Wall Street Journal*, 1 July 1991, A1.

33. Patrice M. Jones, "Leaving Trade Pact's Woes Behind," *Chicago Tribune*, 10 May 2000, sec. 3, 42.

34. Rafael A. Lecuona, "Economic Integration: NAFTA and MERCOSUR, A Comparative Analysis," *International Journal on World Peace*, December 1999, 27–49.

35. Emeric Lepourte, "Europe's Challenge to the U.S. in South America's Biggest Market," *Christian Science Monitor*, 8 April 1997, 19; Mario Osava, "Mercosur: Free Trade with Europe More Advantageous Than FTAA," *Inter Press English News Wire*, 6 May 1997; Robert Maynard, "At a Crossroads in Latin America," *Nation's Business*, April 1996, 38–39; Gregory L. Miles and Loubna Freih, "Join the Caribbean Revolution," *International Business*, September 1994, 42–54; Matt Moffett, "Spreading the Gospel," *Wall Street Journal*, 28 October 1994, R12.

36. Lecuona, "Economic Integration: NAFTA and MERCOSUR, A Comparative Analysis.

37. Joel Russell, "NAFTA in the Real World," *Hispanic Business*, June 1996, 22–28; Scot J. Paltrow, "NAFTA's Job Impact Slight, Study Says," *Los Angeles Times*, 19 December 1996, D3.

38. "Sweden Says EU Enlargement Outweighs NATO Expansion," *Xinhau News Agency*, 16 July 1996; Helene Cooper, "The Euro: What You Need to Know," *Wall Street Journal*, 4 January 1999, A5, A6.

39. Thomas Kamm, "EU Certifies Participants for Euro," *Wall Street Journal*, 26 March 1998, A14.

40. Thane Peterson, "The Euro," *Business Week*, 27 April 1998, 90–94; Joan Warner, "The Great Money Bazaar," *Business Week*, 27 April 1998, 96–98; Gail Edmondson, "Industrial Evolution," *Business Week*, 27 April 1998, 100–101.

41. Bill Spindle, "A Flip of the Coins: Yen Dances, Euro Won't," *Wall Street Journal*, 10 May 2000, A21, A23.

42. Joshua Kurlantzick, "The Big Mango Bounces Back: Economic Recovery in Thailand and Southeast Asia," *World Policy Journal*, Spring 2000, 79–85.

43. Tom Petruno and Art Pine, "Indonesian Currency Fall Deepens Asia Crisis," *Los Angeles Times*, 9 January 1998, A1.

44. Pete Engardio, Christina Hoag, and Peter Coy, "Deja Vu?" *Business Week*, 21 December 1998, 34–35.

45. Mark Whitehouse, "Capital Flight Remains Draining Problem for Russia," *Wall Street Journal*, 19 April 1999, A19.

46. Jeffrey D. Sachs, "Rule of the Ruble," *New York Times*, 4 June 1998, A27; Richard Lacayo, "IMF to the Rescue," *Time*, 8 December 1997, 37–39; Paul Krugman, "Saving Asia: It's Time to Get Radical," *Fortune*, 7 September 1998, 75–80.

47. "IMF to East Asia: OOPS!" *Business Week*, 29 May 2000, 60; Sachs, "Rule of the Ruble"; Lacayo, "IMF to the Rescue."

48. Sachs, "Rule of the Ruble"; Lacayo, "IMF to the Rescue."

49. Nicholas D. Kristof and David E. Sanger, "How U.S. Wooed Asia to Let Cash Flow In," *New York Times* Web site www.nytimes.com/library/world/global/021699global-econ.html [accessed 15 February 1999]; Paul Krugman, "Saving Asia: It's Time to Get Radical," *Fortune*, 7 September 1998, 75–80; Phillips, "One by One."

50. Kristof and Sanger, "How U.S. Wooed Asia to Let Cash Flow In."

51. Kurlantzick, "The Big Mango Bounces Back: Economic Recovery in Thailand and Southeast Asia"; Diane Brady and Jonathan Moore, "Happy Days Are Here Again? Not Quite," *Business Week*, 27 September 1999, 44–45; Peter Montagnon, "Catching the Next Wave," *Financial Times*, 28 December 1999, 10+.

52. Kristof and WuDunn, "The World's Ills May Be Obvious, But Their Cure Is Not."

53. Jean-Michael Paul, "Asian Economies May Suffer a Relapse," *Wall Street Journal*, 5 May 1999, A22; Michael Schuman, "Korea's Fast Recovery Suggests That Reform Isn't the Only Answer," *Wall Street Journal*, 14 May 1999, A1, A6.

54. Neela Banerjee, "Good News and Bad News on the Economy of Russia," *New York Times on the Web*, www.nytimes.com/library/financial/122099outlook-russ.html [accessed 28 February 2000]; Patricia Kranz and Margaret Coker, "The Tidal Wave of Cash Gushing Out of Russia," *Business Week*, 13 September 1999, 158.

55. Laurence Zuckerman, "Boeing's Leaders Losing Altitude," *New York Times,* 13 December 1998, BU1, 11.

56. Rob Norton, "Not So Fast: The Little Crisis That Couldn't," *Fortune,* 17 April 2000, 100; Justin Fox, "Forecast for the U.S. Economy: Still Mostly Sunny," *Fortune,* 15 February 1999, 92–98; David E. Sanger, "U.S. Trade Deficit Soared in '98, Reaching Record $168.8 Billion," *New York Times,* 20 February 1999, A1, B2; Michael M. Phillips, "How Long Can the U.S. Stay Immune to What Ails the Economy?" *Wall Street Journal,* 5 February 1999, A1, A10.

57. Phillips, "How Long Can the U.S. Stay Immune to What Ails the Economy?"

58. Adapted from Neal E. Boudette, "In Europe, Surfing a Web of Red Tape," *Wall Street Journal,* 29 October 1999, B1; Mark Landler, "Asia-Pacific: In China, Malaysia, and Singapore, Freedom and Control Dance a Digital Minute," *Strategy & Business,* First Quarter 2000, 72–75; Terry McCarthy, "China's Internet Gold Rush," *Time,* 28 February 2000, 50–51; James Cox, "E-Opportunity Abounds in China," *USA Today,* 27 April 2000, 3B; Martin Vander Weyer, "Globalism vs. Nationalism vs. E-business The World Debates," *Strategy & Business,* First Quarter 2000, 63–72; Walid Mougayar, *Opening Digital Markets* (New York: McGraw-Hill, 1998), 39–41; Stephanie Gruner, "Late to the Party," *Wall Street Journal,* 12 July 1999, R25; Andersen Consulting, "Europe Poised for Take-Off," Anderson Consulting Web site, www.ac.com/ecommerce/ecom_efuture.html [accessed 2 May 2000]; David H. Freedman, "The Maybe Restoration," *Forbes ASAP,* 21 February 2000, 55–62; Peter Landers, "Electronics E-Commerce in Japan is Held Back by Retail Traditions," *Wall Street Journal,* 30 March 2000, A22; Mohanbir Sawhney and Sumant Mandal, "Go Global," *Business 2.0,* May 2000, 178–215; Julie Schmitt, "Tech Tripping on Tradition," *USA Today,* 25 March 1999, 3B; Jim Rohwer, "Japan's Quiet Corporate Revolution," *Fortune,* 30 March 1998, 82–92; Irene M. Kunii and Brian Bremner, "Will Technology Leave Japan Behind?" *Business Week,* 31 August 1998, 124–26; Julie Schmit, "Asia's Culture Hampers Internet Commerce," *USA Today,* 16 February 1999, 6B; "On the Continent, On the Cusp," *New York Times,* 14 May 2000, sec. 3, 1,18–19; Julie Schmit, "Japan Undergoes E-Makeover," *USA Today,* 19 April 2000, 1B, 2B; Justin Fox, "Surprise! Europe Has Web Fever," *Fortune,* 12 June 2000, 219–24; Ken Belson, "Asia's Internet Deficit," *Business Week E.Biz,* 23 October 2000, 106–110.

59. Courtland L. Bovée and John V. Thill, "Should Companies Stress English Only On the Job?" *Business Communication Today,* 6th ed. (Upper Saddle River, N.J.: Prentice Hall, 2000), 74.

60. Adam Zagorin, "The Great Banana War," *Time,* 8 February 1999, www.pathfinder.com [accessed 11 May 1999].

61. "USAJobs: International Trade Specialist," USA Jobs Web site, www.usajobs.opm.gov/wfjic/jobs/BL2896.htm [accessed 17 June 1999].

CHAPTER 4

1. Christopher Palmeri, "Is Idealab! Running Dry?" *Business Week,* 5 June 2000, EB50; Rhonda L. Rundle, "Idealab! Registers for Stocking Offering; Welch Joins Board," *Wall Street Journal,* 21 April 2000, B6; James Lardner, "Ideas on the Assembly Line," *U.S. News & World Report,* 20 March 2000, 48–50; Rhonda L. Rundle, "Idealab! Receives Funds from Firms Totaling $1 Billion," *Wall Street Journal,* 14 March 2000, B8; Karen Kaplan, "At Idealab, Rewards Outweigh the Risks," *Los Angeles Times,* 13 March 2000, C1; Arlene Weintraub and Jennifer Reingold, "That's One Hot Incubator," *Business Week,* 13 March 2000, 42–43; Warren S. Hersch, "The 1999 Top 25 Executives: Deeppockets," *Computer Reseller News,* 15 November 1999, 167; Emily Barker, "Bright Lights, Big Opportunity," *Inc.,* 14 September 1999, 22; Larry Armstrong, "They Thought We Were Crazy," *Business Week,* 8 March 1999, 38; Ann Marsh, "Warring Wallets," *Forbes,* 28 December 1998, 103; Larry Armstrong and Ronald Grover, "Bill Gross, Online Idea Factory," *Business Week,* 29 June 1998, 100; Ann Marsh, "Promiscuous Breeding," *Forbes,* 7 April 1997, 74–77; "Ideas by the Gross," *Inc.,*

February 1997, 50; Jerry Useem, "The Start-up Factory," *Inc.,* February 1997, 40–52; "Hatching Ideas," *Upside,* December 1996, 30; Joseph Nocera, "Bill Gross Blew Throught $800 Million in 8 Months And He's Got Nothing to Show For It," *Fortune,* 5 March 2001, 71–82.

2. David Birch, "Thinking About Tomorrow," *Wall Street Journal,* 24 May 1999, R30–R31.

3. Claudia H. Deutsch, "When a Big Company Hatches a Lot of Little Ideas," *New York Times,* 23 September 1998, D4.

4. "Matters of Fact," *Inc.,* April 1985, 32.

5. David Leonhardt, "Big Airlines Should Follow Midwest's Recipe," *Business Week,* 28 June 1999, 40; Stephenie N. Mehta, "Small Talk," *Wall Street Journal,* 23 May 1996, R28–R30.

6. Michael Moeller, Steve Hamm, and Timothy J. Mullaney, "Remaking Microsoft," *Business Week,* 17 May 1999, 106–16.

7. Timothy D. Schelhardt, "David in Goliath," *Wall Street Journal,* 23 May 1996, R14; Deutsch, "When a Big Company Hatches a Lot of Little Ideas."

8. Donna Fenn, "The Buyers," *Inc.,* June 1996, 46–52.

9. Brian O'Reilly, "The New Face of Small Business," *Fortune,* 2 May 1994, 82–88.

10. "The Facts About Small Business 1999," U.S. Small Business Administration, Office of Advocacy, SBA Website [accessed 5 June 2000] www.sba.gov/ADVO/stats/facts99.pdf.

11. Janice Castro, "Big vs. Small," *Time,* 5 September 1988, 49; Steve Solomon, *Small Business USA* (New York: Crown, 1986), 124.

12. Lloyd Gite and Dawn M. Baskerville, "Black Women Entrepreneurs on the Rise," *Black Enterprise,* August 1996, 73–74.

13. Rachel Beck, *Wall Street Journal Interactive Edition—Small Business Suite,* 28 March 1998, [accessed 21 April 1998] interactive. wsj.com/public/currentarticles/SB891025783545694000.htm.

14. Bill Meyers, "It's a Small-Business World," *USA Today,* 30 July 1999, B1, B2.

15. James Lardner and Paul Sloan, "The Anatomy of Sickly IPOs," *U.S. News and World Report,* 29 May 2000, 42; Hoover's Online [accessed 2 June 2000] www.hoovers.com/hoov/ipo/features/mainstats.html.

16. "Small Businesses Skeptical of Internet Impact," *NUA Internet Surveys,* 1 June 2000, [accessed 1 June 2000] www.nua.ie/surveys/ index.org; "U.S. Small Businesses Spending More Online," *NUA Internet Surveys,* 17 May 2000 [accessed 1 June 2000] www.nua.ie/ surveys/index.org.

17. Joshua Macht, "The Two Hundred Million Dash," *Inc. Technology 1997,* 16 September 1997, 48–55.

18. Tim McCollum, "A High-Tech Edge for Home Offices," *Nation's Business,* December 1998, 52–54.

19. *Inc. Special Edition—The State of Small Business 1997,* 20 May 1997, 112; James Wilfong and Toni Seger, *Taking Your Business Global* (Franklin Lakes, N.J.: Career Press, 1997), 84.

20. "The Facts About Small Business 1999," U.S. Small Business Administration, Office of Advocacy, SBA Website [accessed 5 June 2000] www.sba.gov/ADVO/stats/facts99.pdf.

21. Stephanie Armour, "Many Turn to Start-Ups for Freedom," *USA Today,* 8 June 1998, 1B, 2B; "The Top 500 Women-Owned Businesses," *Working Woman,* May 1998, 50.

22. Jane Fritsch, "Big in Small Business, Straining to Grow," *New York Times,* 23 September 1998, D2; "Report on Statistical Information About Women-Owned Businesses," *U.S. Small Business Administration,* October 1998 [accessed 31 May 2000] www.sba.gov/ library/reportsroom.html; "SBA FY1999 Annual Performance Report," *U.S. Small Business Administration* [accessed 31 May 2000] www.sba.gov/aboutsba/indexreports.html; "Report on Statistical Information About Minority-Owned Businesses," [accessed 31 May

2000] www.sba.gov/library/reportsroom.html; "The Facts About Small Business 1999," U.S. Small Business Administration, Office of Advocacy, SBA Website [accessed 5 June 2000] www.sba.gov/ADVO/stats/facts99.pdf.

23. Gordon Fairclough, "P&G to Slash 13,000 Jobs, Shut 10 Plants," *Wall Street Journal,* 10 June 1999, A3, A10.

24. Carolyn Brown, "How to Make Your Ex-Boss Your Client," *Black Enterprise,* 30 April 1994, 951.

25. Wilfong and Seger, *Taking Your Business Global,* 78–80; Kelly J. Andrews, "Born or Bred?" *Entrepreneurial Edge* 3 (1998): 24–28.

26. Jane Applegate, *Succeeding in Small Business* (New York: Plume/Penguin, 1992), 1.

27. Lisa J. Moore and Sharon F. Golden, "You Can Plan to Expand or Just Let It Happen," *U.S. News & World Report,* 23 October 1989, 78; John Case, "The Origins of Entrepreneurship," *Inc.,* June 1989, 56.

28. Norm Brodsky, "Caveat Emptor," *Inc.,* August 1998, 31–32; "Why Buy a Business?" CCH Toolkit Web site, [accessed 20 May 1999] aol.toolkit.cch.com/text/PO1_0820.asp.

29. Dale Buss, "New Dynamics for a New Era," *Nation's Business,* January 1999, 45–48.

30. Roberta Maynard, "Choosing a Franchise," *Nation's Business,* October 1996, 56–63.

31. Latonya West, "Success Is Convenient," *Minorities in Business,* [undated], 22–26.

32. Jeffrey A. Tannenbaum, "Taking a Bath," *Wall Street Journal,* 22 June 1998, 27.

33. Heath Row, "Great Harvest's Recipe for Growth," *Fast Company,* December 1998, 46–48.

34. Roberta Maynard, "The Changing Landscape," *Nation's Business,* January 1997, 54–55.

35. "Small Business Answer Card 1998," Small Business Administration, Office of Advocacy, SBA Website [accessed 5 June 2000] www.sba.gov/ ADVO/stats/answer.pdf.

36. Joseph W. Duncan, "The True Failure Rate of Start-Ups," *D&B Reports,* January–February 1994; Maggie Jones, "Smart Cookies," *Working Woman,* April 1995, 50–52; Janice Maloney, "Failure May Not Be So Bad After All," *New York Times,* 23 September 1998, 12.

37. Jerry Useem, "The Secret of My Success," *Inc.,* May 1998, 67–80.

38. Maloney, "Failure May Not Be So Bad After All."

39. Gerda D. Gallop and Roz Ayres-Williams, "Five Things You Should Know Before Starting a Business," *Black Enterprise,* September 1998, 66–72.

40. SCORE Web site [accessed September 18, 1997] www.score.org; J. Tol Broome Jr., "SCORE's Impact on Small Firms," *Nation's Business,* January 1999, 41–43.

41. Broome, "SCORE's Impact on Small Firms"; Robert McGarvey, "Peak Performance," *American Way,* July 1996, 56–60.

42. Loren Fox, "Hatching New Companies," *Upside,* February 2000, 144–52.

43. Dale Buss, "Bringing New Firms out of Their Shell," *Nations Business,* March 1997, 48–50; Fox, "Hatching New Companies."

44. Buss, "Bringing New Firms out of Their Shell."

45. Jonathan Katz, "Hatching Ideas," *Industry Week,* 18 September 2000, 63–65.

46. James Lardner, "Ideas on the Assembly Line Thanks to Internet Incubators, Starting a New Business May Never Be the Same," *U.S. News & World Report,* 20 March 2000, 48–50.

47. McGarvey, "Peak Performance."

48. Juan Hovey, "Risky Business," *Industry Week,* 15 May 2000, 75–76.

49. Sharon Nelton, "Coming to Grips with Growth," *Nation's Business,* February 1998, 26–32.

50. Nelton, "Coming to Grips with Growth."

51. Nelton, "Coming to Grips with Growth."

52. Nelton, "Coming to Grips with Growth."

53. Michael Selz, "Here's the Problem," *Wall Street Journal—Breakaway Special Report Winter 1999,* 22 February 1999, 12.

54. Bob Zider, "How Venture Capital Works," *Harvard Business Review,* November/December 1998, 131–39.

55. Barbara Darrow, "Touched By An Angel," *Computer Reseller News,* 17 April 2000, 152, 156.

56. Jill Andresky Fraser, "Where Has All the Money Gone?" *Inc.,* April 2000, 101–10.

57. Darrow, "Touched By An Angel," 152, 156.

58. Jane Easter Bahls, "Cyber Cash; "Startup Financing: Finding an Angel to Get Going," CCH Business Owners Toolkit Web site, [accessed 20 May 1999] aol.toolkit.cch.com/columns/Starting/225-99AngelR.asp.

59. Darrow, "Touched By An Angel," 152,156.

60. Rodney Ho, "Banking on Plastic," *Wall Street Journal,* 9 March 1998, A1, A8.

61. Joel Russell, "Credit Card Capitalism," *Hispanic Business,* March 1998, 40.

62. Henry Wichmann Jr., Charles Harter, and H. Charles Sparks, "Big Cash for Small Business," *Journal of Accountancy,* July 1999, 64–72.

63. Wilfong and Seger, *Taking Your Business Global,* 20.

64. Ronaleen R. Roha, "Big Loans for Small Businesses," *Changing Times,* April 1989, 105–09; "Small Loans, Big Problems," *Economist,* 28 January 1995, 73; Elizabeth Kadetsky, "Small Loans, Big Dreams," *Working Woman,* February 1995, 46–49; Reid Rutherford, "Securitizing Small Business Loans: A Banker's Action Plan," *Commercial Lending Review,* Winter 1994–1995, 62–74.

65. Roha, "Big Loans for Small Businesses," 105.

66. Susan Hodges, "Microloans Fuel Big Ideas," *Nation's Business,* February 1997, 34–35.

67. Karen Gutloff, "Five Alternative Ways to Finance Your Business," *Black Enterprise,* March 1998, 81–85.

68. Roberta Maynard, "Are You Ready to Go Public," *Nation's Business,* January 1995, 30–32.

69. Robert A. Mamis, "Face to Face—Andy Klein," *Inc.,* July 1996, 39–40; Sharon Nelton, "Using the Internet to Find Funds," *Nation's Business,* August 1998, 35–36.

70. "E-Business Case Studies," IBM Web site [accessed 10 March 2000] www.ibm.com/e-business/case_studies/dsm.phtml.

71. C. J. Prince, "This Little Company Went to Market," *Chief Executive,* April 1999, 22.

72. Nelton, "Using the Internet to Find Funds."

73. Stephanie Gruner, "When Mom & Pop Go Public," *Inc.,* December 1996, 66–73.

74. Adapted from J. William Gurley, "Startups, Beware: Obey the Law of Supply and Demand," *Fortune,* 29 May 2000, 278; William M. Bulkeley and Jim Carlton, "E-Tail Gets Derailed: How Web Upstarts Misjudged the Game," *Wall Street Journal,* 5 April 2000, A1, A6; Leslie Kaufman, "After Taking a Beating, Dot-Coms Now Seek Financial Saviors," *New York Times,* 18 April 2000, C1, C18; Kevin Maney, "Net Start-Ups Pull Out of the Garage," *USA Today,* 1 October 1999, 1B, 2B; Matt Krantz, "E-Retailers Run Low on Fuel," *USA Today,* 26 April 2000, 1B, 2B; "Survival of the Fastest," *Inc. Tech,* 16 November 1999, 44–58; Darnell Little, "Peapod Is in a Pickle," *Business Week,* 3 April 2000, 41; Heather Green, Nanette Byrnes, Norm Alster, and Arlene Weintraub, "The Dot.Coms Are Falling to Earth," *Business Week,* 17

April 2000, 48–49; John A. Byrne, "The Fall of a Dot-Com," *Business Week*, 1 May 2000, 150–60; Stephanie N. Mehta, "As Investors Play VC, It's Dot-Com Doomsday," *Fortune*, 1 May 2000, 40–41; David P. Hamilton and Mylene Mangalindan, "Angels of Death," *Wall Street Journal*, 25 May 2000, A1, A8; Luisa Kroll, "When the Music Stops," *Forbes*, 15 May 2000, 182; Chris Farrell, "Death of the Dot-Coms?" *Business Week*, 22 May 2000, 104E6; John Steele Gordon, "The Golden Spike," *Forbes ASAP*, 21 February 2000, 118–22; Eric W. Pfeiffer, "Where are We in the Revolution?" *Forbes ASAP*, 21 February 2000, 68–70; James Lardner and Paul Sloan, "The Anatomy of Sickly IPOs," *U.S. News and World Report*, 29 May 2000, 42; Hillary Stout, "Crunch Time," *Wall Street Journal*, 7 June 2000, B1; Jerry Useem, "Dot-Coms—What Have We Learned?" *Fortune*, 30 October 2000, 82–104; Heather Green and Norm Alster, "Guess What—Venture Capitalists Aren't Geniuses," *Business Week*, 10 July 2000, 98; Thomas E. Weber, "What Were We Thinking?" *Wall Street Journal*, 18 July 2000, B1, B4; Greg Ip, Susan Pulliam, Scott Thurm, and Ruth Simon, "The Color Green," *Wall Street Journal*, 14 July 2000, A1, A8; "Business Brief—Value America: Bankruptcy—Code Filing is Made by the Company," *Wall Street Journal*, 14 August 2000, B2.

75. Patti Bond, "Hispanics Display Growing Muscle in Entrepreneurship," *Atlanta Journal-Constitution*, 11 July 1996, B1.

CHAPTER 5

1. Adapted from Kinko's Web site, [accessed 13 December 1998] www.kinkos.com/info; Shawn Tully, "A Better Taskmaster Than the Market," *Fortune*, 26 October 1998, 277–86; Laurie J. Flynn, "For the Officeless, A Place to Call Home," *New York Times*, 6 July 1998, 1, 4; Michele Marchetti, "Getting the Kinks Out," *Sales and Marketing Management*, March 1997, 56–64; "Man of Few Words," *Sales and Marketing Management*, March 1997, 63; "Kinko's Improves Image of Businesses with Top-Notch Proposals and Presentations Capabilities; Presentations a Growing Percentage of Customer Work at Kinko's," *Business Wire*, 28 September 1997; "Kinko's Strengthens Office Product Assortment," *Discount Store News*, 17 November 1997, 6, 70; Ann Marsh, "Kinko's Grows Up—Almost," *Forbes*, 1 December 1997, 270–72; "Kinko's Strikes Deal for Mideast Growth," *Graphic Arts Monthly*, January 1998, 22; Lori Ioannou and Paul Orfalea, "Interview: The Brains Behind Kinko's," *Your Company*, 1 May 1999, 621.

2. Norman M. Scarborough and Thomas W. Zimmerer, *Effective Small Business Management* (Upper Saddle River, N.J.: Prentice Hall, 2000), 84.

3. James W. Cortada, "Do You Take This Partner," *Total Quality Review*, November–December 1995, 11.

4. Laurence Zuckerman, "UPS Hears Market's Song, and Plans to Sell Some Stock," *New York Times*, 22 July 1999, A1, C23.

5. Vivien Kellerman, "A Growing Business Takes the Corporate Plunge," *New York Times*, 23 July 1994, sec. Your Money, 31.

6. Noshua Watson, "The Lists," *Fortune*, 17 April 2000, 289–95.

7. Scarborough and Zimmerer, *Effective Small Business Management*, 90.

8. Robert G. Goldstein, Russell Shapiro, and Edward A. Hauder, "So Many Choices of Business Entities—Which One Is Best for Your Needs?" *Insight (CPA Society)*, February/March 1999, 10–16.

9. Rana Dogar, "Crony Baloney," *Working Woman*, January 1997; Richard H. Koppes, "Institutional Investors, Now in Control of More Than Half the Shares of U.S. Corporations, Demand More Accountability," *National Law Journal*, 14 April 1997, B5; John A. Byrne, "The Best & Worst Boards," *Business Week*, 25 November 1996, 82–84; Anthony Bianco, John Byrne, Richard Melcher, and Mark Maremont, "The Rush to Quality on Corporate Boards," *Business Week*, 3 March 1997, 34–35.

10. Cliff Edwards, "President of United Airlines Resigns Under Union Pressure—Edwardson Steps Down to Sidestep Turmoil," *Denver Rocky Mountain News*, 19 September 1998, 2B.

11. Gary Strauss, "From Public Service to Private Payday," *USA Today*, 17 April 2000, 1B, 2B.

12. Geoffrey Colvin, "America's Worst Boards," *Fortune*, 17 April 2000, 241–48.

13. David A. Nadler, "10 Steps to a Happy Merger," *New York Times*, 15 March 1998, BU14.

14. Peter Passell, "Do Mergers Really Yield Big Benefits?" *New York Times*, 14 May 1998, C1, C2.

15. "Merger Mania, Sobering Statistics," *The Economist*, 20 June 1998, 89.

16. Alex Taylor III, "More Mergers. Dumb Idea," *Fortune*, 15 February 1999, 26–27.

17. Nadler, "10 Steps to a Happy Merger"; Glenn Rifkin, "How IBM and Lotus Work Together," *Strategy and Business*, Third Quarter 1998, 42–61.

18. J. Robert Carleton, "Cultural Due Diligence," *Training*, November 1997, 67–75; "How to Merge," *The Economist*.

19. Almar Latour, "Detroit Meets a Worker Paradise," *Wall Street Journal*, 3 March 1999, B1, B4.

20. Michael Oneal, Brian Bremner, Jonathan B. Levine, Todd Vogel, Zachary Schiller, and David Woodruff, "The Best and Worst Deals of the '80s," *Business Week*, 15 January 1990, 52.

21. Irving W. Bailey II and Alvin H. Schechter, "The Corporation as Brand: An Identity Dilemma," *Chief Executive*, October 1994, 421.

22. Stephen Labaton, "800-Pound Gorillas," *New York Times*, 11 June 2000, sec. 4, 1.

23. Labaton, "800-Pound Gorillas."

24. William Glasgall, John Rossant, and Thane Peterson, "The Citicorp-Travelers Deal May Point the Way to the Future of Financial Services," *Business Week*, 20 April 1998, 35–37.

25. Martin Peers, Nick Wingfield, and Laura Landro, "AOL, Time Warner Set Plan to Link in Mammoth Merger," *Wall Street Journal*, 11 January 2000, A1, A6; Thomas E. Weber, Martin Peers, and Nick Wingfield, "Two Titans in a Strategic Bind Bet on a Futuristic Megadeal," *Wall Street Journal*, 11 January 2000, B1, B12; "AOL and Time Warner Will Merge to Create World's First Internet-Age Media and Communications Company," America Online Web site, [accessed 11 January 2000] media.web.aol.com/media/press.cfm.

26. Jeffrey Taylor, "Alarm Bells," *Wall Street Journal*, 12 May 1998, A1, A8; Tim Jones and Frank James, "FCC Head: No Ring of Certainty for Deal," *Chicago Tribune*, 13 May 1998, sec. 1, 1, 22; Jeffrey A. Tannenbaum, "The Consolidators: Acquisitive Companies Set Out to 'Roll Up' Fragmented Industries," *Wall Street Journal*, 3 March 1997, A1; Jon Van, "Ameritech Deal Targets Stocks over Consumers," *Chicago Tribune*, 12 May 1998, sec. 1, 1, 10.

27. Scott McCartney and Bill Adair, "Merger Talk Fills Skies and Airline Regulators Have a Juggling Act," *Wall Street Journal*, 8 June 2000, A1, A16.

28. Eleena De Lisser, "Banking on Mergers," *Wall Street Journal*, 24 May 1999, R25.

29. Stephen Labaton, "U.S. Set to Clear a Merger between Exxon and Mobil," *New York Times*, 27 November 1999, A1, B2.

30. Merrill Goozner and John Schmeltzer, "Mass Exodus Hits Corporate Names," *Chicago Tribune*, 12 May 1998, sec. 3, 1, 3; Bill Vlasic, "The First Global Car Colossus," *Business Week*, 18 May 1998, 40–43; Abid Aslam, "Exxon-Mobil Merger Could Poison the Well," *Inter Press Service English News Wire*, 2 December 1998, Electric Library [accessed 2 June 1999]; Agis Salpukas, "Do Oil and Bigger Oil Mix?" *New York Times*, 2 December 1998, C1, C4.

31. Steve Lipen, "Concentration: Corporations' Dreams Converge in One Idea: It's Time to Do a Deal," *Wall Street Journal*, 26 February 1997, A1, A8.

32. "Business: Pfizer's Prize," *Economist*, 12 February 2000, 69; Nikheil Deogun and Robert Langreth, "P&G Walks Away From Merger Talks Stock Decline Prompts End to Warner-AHP Link; Bidder Pfizer Bolstered," *Wall Street Journal*, 25 January 2000, A3.

33. Joann S. Lublin, " 'Poison Pills' Are Giving Shareholders a Big Headache, Union Proposals Assert," *Wall Street Journal*, 23 May 1997, C1.

34. Thomas Mulligan, "ITT Takes Starwood Offer," *Los Angeles Times*, 13 November 1997, D2; Kathleen Morris, "Behind the New Deal Mania," *Business Week*, 3 November 1997, 36.

35. Martha Groves and Stuart Silverstein, "Levi Strauss Offers Year's Pay as Incentive Bonus," *Los Angeles Times*, 13 June 1996, A1.

36. Michael Hickins, "Searching for Allies," *Management Review*, January 2000, 54–58.

37. Hickins, "Searching for Allies," 54–58.

38. Gary Dessler, *Management*, 2d ed.(Upper Saddle River, N.J.: Prentice Hall, 2001), 45.

39. Adapted from Jennifer Reingold, "Dot.Com Boards Are Flouting the Rules," *Business Week*, 20 December 1999, 130–34; Edward O Welles, "Not Your Father's Industry," *Inc.*, January 1999, 25–28; Peter Elkind, "The New Role of Directors," *Fortune*, 20 March 2000, 116–18; Karen Jacobs, "Running Boards," *Wall Street Journal*, 6 April 2000, R4.

40. "Entrepreneurs across America," *Entrepreneur Magazine Online* [accessed 12 June 1997] www.entrepreneurmag.com/entmag/50states5.hts.

CHAPTER 6

1. Jared Sandberg, "Case Study," *Newsweek*, 24 January 2000, 31–36; Fred Vogelstein, "The Talented Mr. Case," *U.S. News & World Report*, 24 January 2000, 41–42; David Lieberman, "Merger Fulfills Needs of Each," *USA Today*, 11 January 2000, 1B–2B; Kara Swisher, "How Steve Case Morphed into a Media Mogul," *Wall Street Journal*, 11 January 2000, B1, B12; Thomas E. Weber, Martin Peers, and Nick Wingfield, "Two Titans in a Strategic Bind Bet on a Futuristic Megadeal," *Wall Street Journal*, 11 January 2000, B1, B12; Joshua Cooper Ramo, "How AOL Lost the Battles But Won the War," *Time*, 22 September 1997, 46.

2. Richard L. Daft, *Management*, 4th ed. (Fort Worth, Tex.: Dryden Press, 1997), 8.

3. Courtland L. Bovée, John V. Thill, Marian Burk Wood, and George P. Dovel, *Management* (New York: McGraw-Hill, 1993), 220; David H. Holt, *Management: Principles and Practices*, 2d ed. (Upper Saddle River, N.J.: Prentice Hall, 1990), 10–12; James A. F. Stoner, *Management*, 4th ed. (Upper Saddle River, N.J.: Prentice Hall, 1989), 15–18.

4. Gillian Flynn, "A Flight Plan for Success," *Workforce*, July 1997, 72–28.

5. Norman M. Scarborough and Thomas W. Zimmerer, *Effective Small Business Management* (Upper Saddle River, N.J.: Prentice Hall, 2000), 41–56.

6. Stephen P. Robbins, *Managing Today* (Upper Saddle River, N.J.: Prentice Hall, 1997), 452.

7. David Bank and Don Clark, "Microsoft Broadens Vision Statement Beyond PCs," *Wall Street Journal*, 23 July 1999, A3, A4.

8. Leonard Goodstein, Timothy Nolan, and J. William Pfeiffer, *Applied Strategic Planning* (New York: McGraw-Hill, 1993), 169–92.

9. Aimee L. Stern, "Management: You Can Keep Your Staff on the Competitive Track If You . . . Inspire Your Team with a Mission Statement," *Your Company*, 1 August 1997, 36.

10. Toni Mack and Mary Summers, "Danger: Stealth Attack," *Forbes*, 25 January 1999, 88–92.

11. Joshua Cooper Ramo, "How AOL Lost the Battles But Won the War," *Time*, 22 September 1997, 46.

12. Scarborough and Zimmerer, *Effective Small Business Management*, 50.

13. Daft, *Management*, 221–23, 260–62.

14. Judy A. Smith, "Crisis Communications: The War on Two Fronts," *Industry Week*, 20 May 1996, 136; John F. Reukus, "Hazard Communication," *Occupational Hazards*, February 1998, 39; Kim M. Gibson and Steven H. Smith, "Do We Understand Each Other?" *Journal of Accountancy*, January 1998, 53.

15. Timothy Aeppel, Clare Ansberry, Milo Geyelin, and Robert L. Simison, "Road Signs: How Ford, Firestone Let the Warnings Slide By as Debacle Developed," *Wall Street Journal*, 6 September 2000, A1; Joann Muller, David Welch, Jeff Green, Lorraine Woellert, and Nicole St. Pierre, "A Crisis of Confidence," *Business Week*, 18 September 2000, 40–42.

16. William Echikson, Stephen Baker, and Dean Frost, "Things Aren't Going Better with Coke," *Business Week*, 28 June 1999, 49; Janine Reid, "Keeping a Crisis From Going Bad to Worse," *Air Conditioning, Heating & Refrigeration News*, 24 January 2000, 41+.

17. Edward A. Robinson, "America's Most Admired Companies," *Fortune*, 3 March 1997, 68; Susan Chandler, "Crisis Management: How TWA Faced the Nightmare," *Business Week*, 5 August 1996, 30; Kerri Selland, "Experts Say Corporations Ill-Prepared for Crises," *Reuters*, 23 July 1996; Thomas S. Mulligan, "TWA Garners Weak Marks for Crisis Management," *Los Angeles Times*, 20 July 1996, D1; Tom Incantalupo, "TWA's Image Polishing," *Newsday*, 23 July 1996, A49.

18. Michael Moeller, Steve Hamm, and Timothy J. Mullaney, "Remaking Microsoft," *Business Week*, 17 May 1999, 106–16.

19. Stephanie Armour, "Once Plagued by Pink Slips, Now They're in Driver's Seat," *USA Today*, 14 May 1998, 1B–2B.

20. Daft, *Management*, 219–21.

21. Gary A. Yukl, *Leadership in Organizations*, 2d ed. (Upper Saddle River, N.J.: Prentice Hall, 1989), 9, 175–76.

22. Daniel Goleman, "What Makes a Leader?" *Harvard Business Review*, November–December 1998, 92–102; Shari Caudron, "The Hard Case for Soft Skills," *Workforce*, July 1999, 60–66.

23. Daft, *Management*, 498–99.

24. Michael A. Verespej, "Lead, Don't Manage," *Industry Week*, 4 March 1996, 58.

25. Stratford Sherman, "Secrets of HP's 'Muddled' Team," *Fortune*, 18 March 1996, 116–20.

26. Daniel Goleman, "Leadership That Gets Results," *Harvard Business Review*, March–April 2000, 78–90.

27. Stephen P. Robbins and David A. De Cenzo, *Fundamentals of Management*, 2d ed. (Upper Saddle River, N.J.: Prentice Hall, 1998), 55–56; James Waldroop and Timothy Butler, "The Executive as Coach," *Harvard Business Review*, November–December 1996, 113.

28. Kathryn Tyler, "Scoring Big in the Workplace," *HR Magazine*, June 2000, 96–106.

29. "The Advantage of Female Mentoring," *Working Woman*, October 1991, 104.

30. Ram Charan and Geoffrey Colvin, "Why CEOs Fail," *Fortune*, 21 June 1999, 69–78.

31. James A. Belasco and Ralph C. Stayer, *Flight of the Buffalo* (New York: Warner Books, 1993), 138.

32. Michael Been and Nitin Nohria, "Cracking the Code of Change," *Harvard Business Review*, May–June 2000, 133–41.

33. Michael Barrier, "Managing Workers in Times of Change," *Nation's Business*, May 1998, 31–32.

34. J. Robert Carleton, "Cultural Due Diligence," *Training*, November 1997, 67–75.

35. Joanne Cole, "Flying High at Southwest," *HR Focus*, May 1998, 8+.

36. Kostas N. Dervitsiotis, "The Challenge of Managing Organizational Change," *Total Quality Management*, February 1998, 109–22.

37. George Taninecz, "Borg-Warner Automotive," *Industry Week,* 19 October 1998, 44–46.

38. Bovée et al., *Management,* 680.

39. Michael A. Verespej, "Stability Before Growth," *Industry Week,* 15 April 1996, 12–16.

40. James R. Lackritz, "TQM Within Fortune 500 Corporations," *Quality Progress,* February 1997, 69–72.

41. David Sirota, Brian Usilaner, and Michelle S. Weber, "Sustaining Quality Improvement," *Total Quality Review,* March–April 1994, 23; Joe Batten, "A Total Quality Culture," *Management Review,* May 1994, 61; Rahul Jacon, "More Than a Dying Fad?" *Fortune,* 18 October 1993, 66–72.

42. Lackritz, "TQM Within Fortune 500 Corporations."

43. Robert L. Katz, "Skills of an Effective Administrator," *Harvard Business Review,* September–October 1974. Reprinted in *Paths Toward Personal Progress: Leaders Are Made, Not Born* (Boston: Harvard Business Review, 1983), 23–35; Mike Dawson, "Leaders Versus Managers," *Systems Management,* March 1995, 32; R. S. Dreyer, "Do Good Bosses Make Lousy Leaders?" *Supervision,* March 1995, 19–20; Michael Maccoby, "Teams Need Open Leaders," *Research-Technology Management,* January–February 1995, 57–59.

44. Courtland L. Bovée and John V. Thill, *Business Communication Today,* 6th ed. (Upper Saddle River, N.J.: Prentice Hall, 2000), 4.

45. Daft, *Management,* 128; Kathryn M. Bartol and David C. Martin, *Management* (New York: McGraw-Hill, 1991), 268–72.

46. Bartol and Martin, *Management,* 268–72; Ricky W. Griffin, *Management,* 3d ed. (Boston: Houghton Mifflin, 1990), 131–37.

47. Robbins, *Managing Today,* 72.

48. Adapted from George Anders, "The Auctioneer," *Wall Street Journal,* 22 November 1999, R68–R70; George Anders, "The View From the Top," *Wall Street Journal,* 12 July 1999, R52; James M. Citrin and Thomas J. Neff, "Digital Leadership," *Strategy & Business,* First Quarter 2000, 42–50; Gary L. Neilson, Bruce A. Pasternack, and Albert J. Viscio, "Up the E-Organization," *Strategy and Business,* First Quarter 2000, 52–61; Beverly Goldberg and John G. Sifonis, "Focusing Your E-Commerce Vision," *American Management Association International,* September 1998, 48–51; Christian Ford Haylock and Len Muscarella, *Net Success* (Holbrook, Mass: Adams Media Corporation, 1999), 12; James Herman, "What Is an E-Strategy?" *Business Communication Review,* April 2000, 24–26; Rosabeth Moss Kanter, "Are You Ready to Lead the E-Cultural Revolution?" *Inc.,* February 2000, 43–44; Steve Hamm, "How to Jump-Start Your E-Strategy," *Business Week,* 5 June 2000, EB96–EB100; Laurie Windham, *Dead Ahead,* (New York: Allworth Press, 1999), 108; Debbie Howell, "Webvan: The Grocer with a Business Plan That Delivers," *Dsn Retailing Today,* 8 May 2000, 117–18; Chris Nadherny and Spence Stuart, "The New E-Leaders," *Chief Executive,* February 2000, 59; Diane Brady, "Wanted: Eclectic Visionary with a Sense of Humor," *Business Week,* 28 August 2000, 143–44.

49. "Starters: Spearing the Best," *Bon Appetit,* March 1997, 20; Mary Alice Kellogg, "The Reel Dish," *Bon Appetit,* March 1997, 38.

CHAPTER 7

1. American Express Company's Web site www.americanexpress. com; [accessed 29 July 2000] Sally Richards, "Make the Most of Your First Job," *Informationweek,* 21 June 1999, 183–86; Tim Greene, "American Express: Don't Leave Home to Go to Work," *Network World,* 8 March 1999, 25; Mahlon Apgar IV, "The Alternative Workplace: Changing Where and How People Work," *Harvard Business Review,* May/June 1998, 121–30; "How Senior Executives at American Express View the Alternative Workplace," *Harvard Business Review,* May/June 1998, 132–33; Michelle Marchetti, "Master Motivators," *Sales and Marketing Management,* April 1998, 38–44; Carrie Shook, "Leader, Not Boss," *Forbes,* 1 December 1997, 52–54.

2. Richard L. Daft, *Management,* 4th ed. (Fort Worth, Tex.: Dryden Press, 1997), 358.

3. Rob Goffee and Gareth Jones, "What Holds the Modern Company Together?" *Harvard Business Review,* November–December 1996, 134–45.

4. Peter F. Drucker, "Management's New Paradigms," *Forbes,* 5 October 1998, 152–76.

5. Stephen P. Robbins, *Managing Today!* (Upper Saddle River, N.J.: Prentice Hall, 1997), 193; Daft, *Management,* 320.

6. Stephen P. Robbins and David A. De Cenzo, *Fundamentals of Management,* 2d ed. (Upper Saddle River, N.J.: Prentice Hall, 1998), 201; Daft, *Management,* 321.

7. "Sharing Knowledge Through BP's Virtual Team Network," *Harvard Business Review,* September–October 1997, 152–53.

8. Alan Webber, "The Best Organization Is No Organization," *USA Today,* 13A; Eve Tahmincioglu, "How GM's Team Approach Works," *Gannett News Service,* 24 April 1996, S11.

9. Fred R. David, *Strategic Management,* 6th ed. (Upper Saddle River, N.J.: Prentice Hall, 1997), 225; Kathryn M. Bartol and David C. Martin, *Management* (New York: McGraw-Hill, 1991), 352.

10. Jeanne Dugan, Alison Rea, and Joseph Weber, "The BW 50: Business Week's Performance Rankings of the S&P 500 Best Performers," *Business Week,* 24 March 1997, 80.

11. Daft, *Management,* 325.

12. Bartol and Martin, *Management,* 345.

13. Courtland L. Bovée, John V. Thill, Marian Wood, George Dovel, *Management* (New York: McGraw-Hill, 1993), 285.

14. Bartol and Martin, *Management,* 370–71.

15. Gary Izumo, "Teamwork Holds Key to Organization Success," *Los Angeles Times,* 20 August 1996, D9; Daft, *Management,* 328–29; David, *Strategic Management,* 223.

16. John A. Byrne, "The Horizontal Corporation," *Business Week,* 20 December 1993, 76–81; "Is a Horizontal Organization for You?" *Fortune,* 3 April 1995, 96; Rahul Jacob, "The Struggle to Create an Organization for the 21st Century," *Fortune,* 3 April 1995, 90–96.

17. Steven Burke, "Acer Restructures into Six Divisions," *Computer Reseller News,* 13 July 1998, 10; Acer America Web site [accessed 20 July 2000] www.acer.com/aac/about/profile.htm.

18. Daft, *Management,* 332, 328–29; David, *Strategic Management,* 223; Bartol and Martin, *Management,* 376.

19. Dan Dimancescu and Kemp Dwenger, "Smoothing the Product Development Path," *Management Review,* 1 January 1996, 36.

20. Dimancescu and Dwenger, "Smoothing the Product Development Path."

21. Robbins, *Managing Today!* 209; Daft, *Management,* 333–36.

22. Daft, *Management,* 340–43; Robbins, *Managing Today!* 213–14.

23. Donna Fenn, "Managing Virtual Employees," *Inc.,* July 1996, 91.

24. Daft, *Management,* 340–43; Robbins, *Managing Today!,* 213–14.

25. "The Horizontal Organization," *Soundview Executive Book Summaries* 21, no. 3, (March 1999): 1–8.

26. "The Horizontal Organization."

27. "The Horizontal Organization."

28. Daft, *Management,* 352–53; Richards, *Strategic Management,* 217; Bartol and Martin, *Management,* 357–58.

29. Daft, *Management,* 338.

30. Stephen P. Robbins, *Essentials of Organizational Behavior,* 6th ed. (Upper Saddle River, N. J.: Prentice Hall, 2000), 105.

31. Daft, *Management,* 591; Robbins, *Managing Today!,* 295.

32. "Microsoft Teamwork," *Executive Excellence,* 6 July 1996, 6–7.

33. Jeffrey Pfeffer, "When It Comes to 'Best Practices'—Why Do Smart Organizations Occasionally Do Dumb Things?" *Organizational Dynamics,* 1 June 1996, 33; LaMar A. Trego, "Reengineering Starts with a 'Clean Sheet of Paper,' " *Manage,* 1 July 1996, 17.

34. Daft, *Management,* 594–95; Robbins and De Cenzo, *Fundamentals of Management,* 336; Robbins, *Managing Today!* 309.

35. Pfeffer, "When It Comes to 'Best Practices.' "

36. Scott Kirsner, "Every Day, It's a New Place," *Fast Company,* April–May 1998, 132–34.

37. Daft, *Management,* 594; Robbins and De Cenzo, *Fundamentals of Management,* 336.

38. Jenny C. McCune, "On the Train Gang: In the New Flat Organizations, Employees Who Want to Be Competitive Must Be Versatile Enough to Perform a Variety of Tasks," *Management Review,* 1 October 1994, 57.

39. Daft, *Management,* 594; Robbins and De Cenzo, *Fundamentals of Management,* 338; Robbins, *Managing Today!* 310–11.

40. Seth Lubove, "Destroying the Old Hierarchies," *Forbes,* 3 June 1996, 62–64.

41. W. V. Bussmann, "Making a Difference at Chrysler," *Business Economics,* July 1998, 10–12.

42. Ellen Neuborne, "Companies Save, But Workers Pay," *USA Today,* 25 February 1997, B1; Daft, *Management,* 594; Robbins and De Cenzo, *Fundamentals of Management,* 338; Robbins, *Managing Today!* 310.

43. Richard Moderow, "Teamwork Is the Key to Cutting Costs," *Modern Healthcare,* 29 April 1996, 138.

44. Daft, *Management,* 594.

45. Robbins, *Essentials of Organizational Behavior,* 109.

46. Deborah L. Duarte and Nancy Tennant Snyder, *Mastering Virtual Teams* (San Francisco: Jossey-Bass Publishers, 1999), 23.

47. "Sharing Knowledge Through BP's Virtual Team Network," *Harvard Business Review,* September–October 1997, 152–53.

48. Daft, *Management,* 612–15.

49. Robbins, *Essentials of Organizational Behavior,* 98.

50. Ross Sherwood, "The Boss's Open Door Means More Time for Employees," *Reuters Business Report,* 30 September 1996.

51. Neuborne, "Companies Save, But Workers Pay," B2; Charles L. Parnell, "Teamwork: Not a New Idea, But It's Transforming the Workplace," *Vital Speeches of the Day,* 1 November 1996, 46.

52. Robbins and De Cenzo, *Fundamentals of Management,* 151.

53. Larry Cole and Michael Cole, "Why is the Teamwork Buzz Word Not Working?" *Communication World,* February/March 1999, 29; Patricia Buhler, "Managing in the 90s: Creating Flexibility in Today's Workplace," *Supervision,* January 1997, 24+; Allison W. Amason, Allen C. Hochwarter, Wayne A. Thompson, and Kenneth R. Harrison, "Conflict: An Important Dimension in Successful Management Teams," *Organizational Dynamics,* Autumn 1995, 20+.

54. "Team Players," *Executive Excellence,* May 1999, 18.

55. Robbins and De Cenzo, *Fundamentals of Management,* 334–35; Daft, *Management,* 602–03.

56. Robbins, *Managing Today!* 297–98; Daft, *Management,* 604–07.

57. Thomas K. Capozzoli, "Conflict Resolution—A Key Ingredient in Successful Teams," *Supervision,* November 1999, 14–16.

58. Daft, *Management,* 609–12.

59. Steven Crom and Herbert France, "Teamwork Brings Breakthrough Improvements in Quality and Climate," *Quality Progress,* March 1996, 39–41.

60. David, *Strategic Management,* 221.

61. Phyllis Gail Doloff, "Beyond the Org Chart," *Across the Board,* February 1999, 43–47.

62. Stephanie Armour, "Failure to Communicate Costly for Companies," *USA Today,* 30 September 1998, 1A.

63. Reid Goldsborough, "Text Demands Respect on the Web," *Advertising Age,* 31 July 2000, 44; Reid Goldsborough, "Words of the Wise," *Link-Up,* September/October 1999, 25–26; Lisa Barbadora, "The Do's and Don'ts of Writing Content for the Web," *B to B,* 11 September 2000, 23; "Writing for the Web," Sun Microsystems Web site, [accessed 23 October 2000] www.sun.com/980713/webwriting; "Writing for the Web," Useit Web site, [accessed 23 October 2000] www.useit.com/papers/webwriting; Jack Powers, "Writing for the Web, Part 1," *Electric Pages,* [accessed 28 June 2000] www.electric-pages. com/articles/wftw1.htm.

64. Donna Fenn, "Teams: Formula for Success," *Inc.,* May 1996, 111.

CHAPTER 8

1. Adapted from Michael O'Neill, "There's Something About Cisco," *Fortune,* 15 May 2000, 114–38; Karl Taro Greenfeld, "Do You Know Cisco?" *Time,* 17 January 2000, 72–74; Julie Pitta, "The Cisco Kid," *Forbes,* 10 January 2000, 108–10; Andy Reinhardt, "Meet Mr. Internet," *Business Week,* 13 September 1999, 129–40; Marguerite Reardon, "Sizzling Cisco," *Informationweek,* 28 February 2000, 46–61; Henry Goldblatt, "Cisco's Secrets," *Fortune,* 8 November 1999, 177–84; Andy Reinhardt, "John T. Chambers," *Business Week,* 27 September 1999, EB52; Glenn Drexhage, "How Cisco Bought It's Way to the Top," *Corporate Finance,* May 1999, 26–30; Jodi Mardesich, "Cisco's Plan to Pop Up in Your Home," *Fortune,* 1 February 1999, 119–20; Richard L. Brandt, "President and CEO of Cisco Systems: John Chambers—On the Future of Communications and the Failure of Deregulation," *Upside,* October 1998, 122–33; Andrew Kupfer, "The Real King of the Internet," *Fortune,* 7 September 1998, 84–93; Eric Neer, "Cisco," *Fortune,* 5 February 2001, 91–96; Edward Iwata, "Juniper Attacks Cisco With 'Smart Bomb' Accuracy." *USA Today,* 30 January 2001, 66-72.

2. Kim Komando, "Taking Control of Info Overload," *USA Today,* 16 June 1999, 6D.

3. Bill Gates, *Business @ the Speed of Thought* (New York: Warner Books, 1999), 3.

4. Larry Long and Nancy Long, *Computers,* 6th ed. (Upper Saddle River, N.J.: Prentice Hall, 1999), MIS 5.

5. Kathryn M. Bartol and David C. Martin, *Management* (New York: McGraw-Hill, 1991), 703–05.

6. Richard L. Daft, *Management,* 4th ed. (Fort Worth, Tex.: Dryden, 1997), 688.

7. Kayte VanScoy, "Get Inside Your Customers' Heads," *SmartBusinessMag.Com,* June 2000, 100–114.

8. John W. Verity, "Coaxing Meaning out of Raw Data," *Business Week,* 3 February 1997, 134.

9. Daft, *Management,* 686.

10. Daft, *Management,* 687.

11. Bartol and Martin, *Management,* 709–10.

12. David Morse, ed., *CyberDictionary* (Santa Monica, Calif.: Knowledge Exchange, 1996), 19.

13. Long and Long, *Computers,* 21–22.

14. Paul C. Judge, "Artificial Imagination," *Business Week,* 18 March 1996, 60.

15. John Woram, "Feature: PC: Talk to Me!—Voice Recognition is Starting to Make Some Noise," *Windows,* 1 November 1997, 208; Walter S. Mossberg, "Dragon Systems Take a Giant Step in Speech Recognition," *Wall Street Journal,* 12 June 1997, B1; Long and Long, *Computers,* 137.

16. Long and Long, *Computers,* CORE 18.

17. Mark Halper, "Bigiron.com: Why Merrill Lynch, J.C. Penney, Wells Fargo, and Others Turned Their Old Mainframe Computers into Hot Web Servers," *Forbes ASAP,* 2 June 1997, 38–39.

18. Long and Long, *Computers,* CORE 19.

19. "IBM's Powerful Supercomputer," *Wall Street Journal,* 29 June 2000, B8.

20. Gene Bylinksy, "The Digital Factory," *Fortune,* 14 November 1994, 92–110.

21. Timothy Trainor and Diane Krasnewich, *Computers!* (New York: McGraw-Hill, 1989), 90.

22. Laurie Flynn, "CD-ROMs: They're Not Just for Entertainment," *New York Times,* 24 April 1994, sec. f, 10; Nancy K. Herther, "CD-ROM at Ten Years: The Technology and the Industry Mature," *Online,* March/April 1995, 86–93.

23. Long and Long, *Computers,* CORE 117, 122.

24. Long and Long, *Computers,* CORE 161.

25. Scott Leibs, "Think Before You Link," *Industry Week,* 17 April 2000, 22–27.

26. Brent Schlender, "Damn the Torpedoes! Full Speed Ahead," *Fortune* (European Edition), 10 July 2000, 39–52.

27. G. Christian Hill, "First Voice, Now Data," *Wall Street Journal,* 20 September 1999, R4; Nicole Harris, "All Together Now," *Wall Street Journal,* 20 September 1999, R10; G. Christian Hill, "Siber-Talk," *Wall Street Journal,* 20 September 1999, R27.

28. Michael Krantz, "Wired for Speed," *Time,* 23 September 1996, 54–55; Michael Krantz, "The Biggest Thing Since Color?" *Time,* 12 August 1996, 42–43.

29. Richard Des Ruisseaux, "Tech," *Gannett News Service,* 30 March 2000, ARC.

30. Salina Khan, "Gadgets Help You Get Out of Line," *USA Today,* 20 December 1999, 3B.

31. Janet Guyon, "The World Is Your Office," *Fortune,* 12 June 2000, 227–34.

32. Samuel Greengard, "How Secure Is Your Data?" *Workforce,* 52–60; Nikhil Hutheesing and Philip E. Ross, "Hackerphobia," *Forbes,* 23 March 1998, 150–54.

33. Rob Kaiser, "FBI Hunts Hackers Who Hit Microsoft," *Chicago Tribune,* 28 October 2000, sec. 1, 1, 3.

34. Elisa Williams, "Workplace Web Cops on the Watch," *Chicago Tribune,* 1 June 1998, B1, B8.

35. Julie Deardorff, "With Voice Mail, You Never Know Who's Listening," *Chicago Tribune,* 6 July 1998, 1, 8.

36. John Galvin, "Cheating, Lying, Stealing," *SmartBusinessMag.Com,* June 2000, 86–99.

37. Ira Sager, Steve Hamm, Neil Gross, John Carey, and Robert D. Hof, "Cyber Crime," *Business Week,* 21 February 2000, 37–42.

38. Kevin Maney, "Tainted Love," *USA Today,* 5 May 2000, 1B–2B.

39. Sager et al., "Cyber Crime."

40. Adapted from Marco R. Della Cava, "Wireless Nation," *USA Today,* 25 August 1999, 1A–2A; Stephen Baker, "Reach Out and Sell Someone," *Business Week e.biz,* 7 February 2000, EB50–EB52; Stephen H. Wildstrom, "Novel, but Still Far from Neat-O," *Business Week,* 10 April 2000, 24; Janet Guyon, "The World Is Your Office," *Fortune,* 12 June 2000, 227–34; John Ellis, "Digital Matters," *Fast Company,* July 2000, 302–06; Stephen Baker, Neil Gross, Irene M. Kunii, and Roger O. Crockett, "The Wireless Internet," *Business Week,* 29 May 2000, 136–44; Roger O. Crockett, "Wowing the Wireless Set," *Business Week e.biz,* 5 June 2000, EB16; Scott Woolley, "Telecommunications," *Forbes,* 10 January 2000, 160–61; David Wessel, "Gadget Envy," *Wall Street Journal,* 3 August 2000, B1; Gautam Naik and Almar Latour, "M-Commerce: Mobile and Multiplying," *Wall Street Journal,* 18 August 2000, B1, B4.

CHAPTER 9

1. Lidia Kelly, "For Krispy Kreme, Doughnuts a Delicacy," *The Arizona Republic,* 20 June 2000, D1; Avital Louria Hahn, "Krispy Kreme IPO Brings Jelly-Filled to a Dot-Com World," *The Investment Dealers' Digest: IDD,* 17 January 2000, 9, 14; Karyn Strauss, "Looking to Raise Dough . . . The Public Way: Krispy Kreme Goes for IPO," *Nation's Restaurant News,* 3 January 2000, 26; Charles Fishman, "The King of Kreme," *Fast Company,* October 1999, 268–78; Scott McCormack, "Sweet Success," *Forbes,* 7 September 1998; Chuck Martin, "For the Love of a Good Doughnut: Krispy Kremes Gain Status Across the Nation," *Gannett News Service,* 10 September 1997; Fred Faust, "Doughnuts Holing on in Munch Crunch," *St. Louis Post-Dispatch,* 21 July 1997, 12; Paul Brown and Robert Siegel, "Krispy Kreme History," *All Things Considered,* National Public Radio, 17 July 1997.

2. Roberta A. Russell and Bernard W. Taylor III, *Operations Management: Focusing on Quality and Competitiveness,* 2d ed. (Upper Saddle River, N.J.: Prentice Hall, 1998), 21.

3. Justin Martin, "Are You As Good As You Think You Are?" *Fortune,* 30 September 1996, 143–44; "Creating Greater Customer Value May Require a Lot of Changes," *Organizational Dynamics,* Summer 1998, 26.

4. Diane Brady, Katie Kerwin, David Welch, Louise Lee, and Rob Hof, "Customizing for the Masses," *Business Week,* 20 March 2000, 130B–130F.

5. John Greenwald, "Cruise Lines Go Overboard," *Time,* 11 May 1998, 42–45.

6. Joseph G. Monks, *Operations Management, Theory and Problems* (New York: McGraw-Hill, 1987), 77–78.

7. Mark M. Davis, Nicholas J. Aquilano, and Richard B. Chase, *Fundamentals of Operations Management* (Boston: Irwin McGraw-Hill, 1999), 241–42.

8. Jae K. Shim and Joel G. Siegel, *Operations Management* (Hauppauge, N.Y.: Barron's Educational Series, 1999), 206.

9. Monks, *Operations Management, Theory and Problems,* 2–3.

10. Shim and Siegel, *Operations Management,* 206.

11. Monks, *Operations Management, Theory and Problems,* 125.

12. Davis, Aquilano, and Chase, *Fundamentals of Operations Management,* 254; Richard L. Daft, *Management,* 4th ed. (Fort Worth, Tex.: Dryden Press, 1997), 718.

13. Kathryn M. Bartol and David C. Martin, *Management* (New York: McGraw-Hill, 1991), 307–08.

14. Roger Crockett, "Chow (On) Line," *Business Week E.Biz,* 5 June 2000, EB 84–90.

15. Larry E. Long and Nancy Long, *Introduction to Computers and Information Systems,* 5th ed. (Upper Saddle River, N.J.: Prentice Hall, 1997), AT 84.

16. Stuart F. Brown, "Giving More Jobs to Electronic Eyes," *Fortune,* 16 February 1998, 104B–104D.

17. "IBM and Dassault Awarded Boeing CATIA Contract," *CAD/CAM Update,* 1 January 1997, 1–8.

18. Russell and Taylor III, *Operations Management,* 211

19. "CAD/CAM Industry Embracing Intranet-Based Technologies," *Computer Dealer News* 12 (28 November 1996): 21.

20. Drew Winter, "C3P: New Acronym Signals Big Change at Ford," *Ward's Auto World* 32 (1 August 1996): 34; Thomas Hoffman, "Ford to Cut Its Prototype Costs," *Computerworld,* 30 September 1996, 65; Drew Winter, "Massive Changes Coming in Computer Engineering," *Ward's Auto World* 32 (1 April 1996): 34.

21. Davis, Aquilano, and Chase, *Fundamentals of Operations Management,* 64; Russell and Taylor, *Operations Management,* 257–58.

22. Russell and Taylor, *Operations Management,* 255–56.

23. John H. Sheridan, "Agile Manufacturing: Stepping Beyond Lean Production," *Industry Week,* 19 April 1993, 30–46.

24. Brian McWilliams, "Re-engineering the Small Factory," *Inc. Technology,* 1 (1996): 44–5.

25. Neal M. Goldsmith and Ed Rosenfeld, "Shooting the Rapids—Business Process Reengineering Can Be a Wild Ride, But There Are a Number of Tools and Services Available to Help Companies Manage Change and Maximize Growth," *Information Week,* 25 November 1996, 65; John H. Sheridan, "Lessons from the Best," *Industry Week,* 19 February 1996, 16–17; Bartol and Martin, *Management,* 688.

26. Jon E. Hilsenrath, "Parts Shortages Hamper Electronics Makers Surging Demand Shows Flaw in Just-in-Time Chains," *Wall Street Journal,* 7 July 2000, B5.

27. Shim and Siegel, *Operations Management,* 326.

28. Russell and Taylor, *Operations Management,* 712–33.

29. Patricia W. Hamilton, "Getting a Grip on Inventory," *D&B Reports,* March–April 1994, 32.

30. Robert O. Knorr and John L. Neuman, "Quick Response Technology: The Key to Outstanding Growth," *Journal of Business Strategy,* September–October 1992, 63.

31. Russell and Taylor, *Operations Management,* 652–53.

32. Karl Ritzler, "A Mercedes Made from Scratch," *Atlanta Journal and Constitution,* 30 May 1997, S1.

33. Del Jones, "Training and Service at Top of Winners' List," *USA Today,* 17 October 1996, 5B.

34. John A. Byrne, "Never Mind the Buzzwords. Roll up Your Sleeves," *Business Week,* 22 January 1996, 84.

35. Davis, Aquilano, and Chase, *Fundamentals of Operations Management,* 177–79; Russell and Taylor, *Operations Management,* 131.

36. William M. Carley, "Charging Ahead: To Keep GE's Profits Rising, Welch Pushes Quality-Control Plan," *Wall Street Journal,* 13 January 1997, A1, A6.

37. Russell and Taylor, *Operations Management,* 131.

38. Hugh D. Menzies, "Global Guide: Quality Counts When Wooing Overseas Clients," *Your Company,* 1 June 1997, 64; Michael E. Raynor, "Worldwide Winners," *Total Quality Management,* July–August 1993, 43–48; Greg Bounds, Lyle Yorks, Mel Adams, and Gipsie Ranney, *Beyond Total Quality Management: Toward the Emerging Paradigm* (New York: McGraw-Hill, 1994), 212; Russell and Taylor, *Operations Management,* 115–16.

39. Ronald Henkoff, "Boeing's Big Problem," *Fortune,* 12 January 1998, 96–103; James Wallace, "How Boeing Blew It," *Sales and Marketing Management,* February 1998, 52–57; John Greenwald, "Is Boeing out of Its Spin?" *Time,* 13 July 1998, 67–69; John T. Landry, "Supply Chain Management: The Case for Alliances," *Harvard Business Review,* November–December 1998, 24–25.

40. Davis, Aquilano, and Chase, *Fundamentals of Operations Management,* 382.

41. Russell and Taylor, *Operations Management,* 440.

42. Landry, "Supply Chain Management."

43. Timothy M. Laseter, "Balanced Sourcing the Honda Way," *Strategy and Business,* Fourth Quarter 1998, 24–31.

44. George Taninecz, "Forging the Chain," *Industry Week,* 15 May 2000, 40–46.

45. David Woodruff, Ian Katz, and Keith Naughton, "VW's Factory of the Future," *Business Week,* 7 October 1996, 52, 56.

46. Saul Hansell, "Is This the Factory of the Future?" *New York Times,* 26 July 1998, sec. 3, 1, 12–13; Pete Engardio, "Souping Up the Supply Chain," *Business Week,* 31 August 1998, 110–12; John A. Byrne, "Management By Web," *Business Week,* 28 August 2000, 84–96.

47. Gene Bylinsky, "For Sale: Japanese Plants in the U.S." *Fortune,* 21 February 2000, 240B–240D.

48. Hansell, "Is This the Factory of the Future?"; Engardio, "Souping Up the Supply Chain."

49. Hansell, "Is This the Factory of the Future?"; Engardio, "Souping Up the Supply Chain."

50. Laurence Zuckerman, "The Jet Wars of the Future," *New York Times,* 9 July 1999, C1, C5.

51. Adapted from J. William Gurley, "Big Company.com: Should You Start a B2B Exchange?" *Fortune,* 3 April 2000, 260+; Peter D. Henig, "Revenge of the Bricks," *Red Herring,* August 2000, 121–34; Daniel Lyons, "B2Bluster," *Forbes,* 1 May 2000, 122–26; Steven Kaplan and Mohanbir Sawhney, "E-hubs: The New B2B Marketplaces," *Harvard Business Review,* May–June 2000, 97–100; Robert D. Hof, "Who Will Profit From the Internet Agora?" *Business Week E.Biz,* 5 June 2000, EB56–EB62; Joseph B. White, "Getting Into Gear," *Wall Street Journal,* 17 April 2000, R65; Douglas A. Blackmon, "Where the Money Is," *Wall Street Journal,* 17 April 2000, R30–R32; Edward Iwata, "Despite the Hype, B2B Marketplaces Struggle," *USA Today,* 10 May 2000, 1B–2B; Jack Trout, "Stupid Net Tricks," *Business 2.0,* May 2000, 76–77; John W. Verity, "Invoice? What's an Invoice?" *Business Week,* 10 June 1996, 110–12; Christina Binkley, "Hyatt Plans Internet Firm with Marriott," *Wall Street Journal,* 2 May 2000, A3, A6; Clint Willis, "B2B . . . to Be?" *Forbes ASAP,* 21 August 2000, 125–30; Jason Anders, "Yesterday's Darling," *Wall Street Journal,* 23 October 2000, R8.

52. "How Microsoft Reviews Suppliers," *Fast Company,* 17 [accessed 3 September 1998] fastcompany.com/online/17/msoftreviews.html.

53. Gary Hoover, Alta Campbell, and Patrick J. Spain, eds., *Hoover's Handbook of American Business 1994* (Austin, Tex.: Reference Press, 1994), 268–69, 712–13, 1092–93; State and County Demographic and Economic Profiles, U.S. Census Bureau [accessed 14 August 2000] www.census.gov/datamap/www/ index.html.

CHAPTER 10

1. Charles Fishman, "Moving Toward a Balanced Work Life," *Workforce,* March 2000, 38–42; Joanne Cole, "Case Study: SAS Institute Inc. Uses Sanity as Strategy," *HR Focus,* May 1999, 6; Charles Fishman, "Sanity Inc.," *Fast Company,* January 1999, 85–96.

2. Fishman, "Moving Toward a Balanced Work Life."

3. Stephanie Armour, "Workplace Hazard Gets Attention," *USA Today,* 5 May 1998, B1.

4. "Finding and Keeping Talent in the Internet Age," *Chief Executive,* February 2000, 32–34.

5. Michael A. Verespej, "Balancing Act," *Industry Week,* 15 May 2000, 81–85.

6. Dennis C. Kinlaw, "What Employees See Is What Organizations Get," *Management Solutions,* March 1988, 38–41.

7. John McMorrow, "Future Trends in Human Resources," *HR Focus,* September 1999, 8–9.

8. Robert B. Reich, "The Company of the Future," *Fast Company,* November 1998, 124–50.

9. Donald J. McNerney, "Creating a Motivated Workforce," *HR Focus* 73, 1 August 1996, 1+.

10. Frederick Herzberg, *Work and the Nature of Man* (New York: World, 1971).

11. Douglas McGregor, *The Human Side of Enterprise* (New York: McGraw-Hill, 1960).

12. Reich, "The Company of the Future."

13. Kelly Barron and Ann Marsch, "The Skills Gap," *Forbes,* 23 February 1998, 44–45; "Nine HR Challenges for 1999," *HR Focus,* December 1998, 1, 14–16.

14. U.S. Bureau of Labor Statistics, *Employment Statistics* [accessed 23 August 1999] www.bls.gov.

15. Aaron Bernstein, "We Want You to Stay. Really," *Business Week,* 22 June 1998, 67–72; Carol Kleiman, "The New Loyalty: A Work in Progress," *Chicago Tribune,* 15 August 1999, sec. 6, 1.

16. Barron and Marsch, "The Skills Gap."

17. Greg Jaffe and Douglas A. Blackmon, "Just in Time. When UPS Demanded Workers, Louisville Did the Delivering," *Wall Street Journal,* 24 April 1998, A1, A10; James Ott, "UPS Hub 2000 at Louisville Marks New Airport Era," 20 July 1998, 47+.

18. Jennifer Laabs, "Has Downsizing Missed Its Mark?" *Workforce,* April 1999, 31–38.

19. Aaron Bernstein, "We Want You to Stay. Really."

20. Jennifer Laabs, "The New Loyalty: Grasp It. Earn It. Keep It." *Workforce,* November 1998, 35–39.

21. Emily Thornton, "No Room at the Top," *Business Week,* 9 August 1999, 50; Michael A. Lev, "Lifetime Jobs May Be at Death's Door as Japan Tradition," *Chicago Tribune,* 11 October 1998, sec. 5, 1, 18.

22. John Greenwald, "Spinning Away," *Time,* 26 August 1996, 30–31.

23. Stephanie Armour, "Blame It on Downsizing, E-Mail, Laptops, and Dual-Career Families," *USA Today,* 13 March 1998, B1; Jennifer Laabs, "Workforce Overload," *Workforce,* January 1999, 30–37.

24. Michelle Conlin, Peter Coy, Ann Therese, and Gabrielle Saveri, "The Wild New Workforce," *Business Week,* 6 December 1999, 39–44.

25. Sue Shellenbarger, "More Executives Cite Need for Family Time as Reason for Quitting," *Wall Street Journal,* 11 March 1998, B1.

26. Richard L. Daft, *Management,* 4th ed. (Fort Worth, Tex.: Dryden Press, 1997), 771.

27. Stephanie Armour, "Workplace Demands Taking Up More Weekends," *USA Today,* 24 April 1998, B1; Laabs, "Workforce Overload."

28. Armour, "Workplace Demands Taking Up More Weekends."

29. Laabs, "Workforce Overload."

30. Michael A. Verespej, "Stressed Out," *Industry Week,* 21 February 2000, 30–34.

31. Verespej, "Balancing Act."

32. John W. Newstrom and Keith Davis, *Organizational Behavior: Human Behavior at Work,* 9th ed. (New York: McGraw-Hill, 1993), 345.

33. Jennifer Bresnehan, "The Elusive Muse," *CIO Enterprise,* 15 October 1997, 52; Kerry A. Dolan, "When Money Isn't Enough," *Forbes,* 18 November 1996, 164–70.

34. Toby B. Gooley, "A World of Difference," *Logistics Management and Distribution Report,* June 2000, 51–55; William H. Miller, "Beneath the Surface," *Industry Week,* 20 September 1999, 13–16.

35. Steven Greenhouse, "Foreign Workers at Highest Level in Seven Decades," *New York Times,* 4 September 2000, A1, A12.

36. "Work Force Facts," *Chicago Tribune,* 10 September 2000, sec. 6,1.

37. Nina Munk, "Finished at Forty," *Fortune,* 1 February 1999, 50–66.

38. Munk, "Finished at Forty."

39. Munk, "Finished at Forty."

40. Gooley, "A World of Difference."

41. Joan Crockett, "Winning Competitive Advantage Through a Diverse Workforce," *HR Focus,* May 1999, 9–10.

42. Joan Crockett, "Winning Competitive Advantage Through a Diverse Workforce."

43. "Is There Really Still A Gender Pay Gap?" *HR Focus,* June 2000, 3–4.

44. Linda Himelstein and Stephanie Forest, "Breaking Through," *Business Week,* 17 February 1997, 64; "Study Says U.S. Women Make Workplace Gains," *Reuters Business Report,* 2 January 1997; Martha Groves, "Women Still Bumping Up Against Glass Ceiling," *Los Angeles Times,* 26 May 1996, D1; Christopher Farrell, "Women in the Workplace: Is Parity Finally in Sight?" *Business Week,* 9 August 1999, 35.

45. Daft, *Management,* 462–63.

46. Joseph White and Carol Hymowitz, "Broken Glass: Watershed Generation of Women Executives Is Rising to the Top," *Wall Street Journal,* 10 February 1997, A1, 6; Andrea Adelson, "Casual, Worker-Friendly, and a Moneymaker, Too: At Patagonia, Glass Ceiling Is Sky-High," *New York Times,* 30 June 1996, sec. Earning It, 8; Joan S. Lublin, "Women at Top Still Are Distant from CEO Jobs," *Wall Street Journal,* 28 February 1996, B1, 12; "Firm's Diversity Efforts Even the Playing Field," *Personnel Journal,* January 1996, 56; Himelstein and Forest, "Breaking Through," 64–70; Groves, "Women Still Bumping Up Against Glass Ceiling," D1, 5; Farrell, "Women in the Workplace"; Reed Abelson, "A Push from the Top Shatters a Glass Ceiling," *New York Times,* 22 August 1999, Y21, Y23.

47. Michael Barrier, "Sexual Harassment," *Nation's Business,* December 1998, 15–19.

48. Marianne Lavelle, "The New Rules of Sexual Harassment," *U.S. News & World Report,* 6 July 1998, 30–31.

49. Mahlon Apgar IV, "The Alternative Workplace: Changing Where and How People Work," *Harvard Business Review,* May–June 1998, 121–36.

50. Genevieve Capowski, "The Joy of Flex," *Management Review,* March 1996, 13.

51. Charles Fishman, "Moving Toward a Balanced Work Life."

52. Charlene Marmer Solomon, "Flexibility Comes out of Flux," *Personnel Journal,* June 1996, 38–40.

53. Solomon, "Flexibility Comes Out of Flux."

54. Shari Caudron, "Workers' Ideas for Improving Alternative Work Situations," *Workforce,* December 1998, 42–46; Carol Leonetti Dannhauser, "Who's in the Home Office?," *American Demographics,* June 1999, 50–56.

55. Dannhauser, "Who's in the Home Office?"

56. Apgar, "The Alternative Workplace."

57. Apgar, "The Alternative Workplace."

58. Melanie Warner, "Working at Home—The Right Way to Be a Star in Your Bunny Slippers," *Fortune,* 3 March 1997, 166; Lin Grensing-Pophal, "Employing the Best People—From Afar," *Workforce,* March 1997, 30–32.

59. Kemba J. Dunham, "Telecommuters' Lament," *Wall Street Journal,* 31 October 2000, B1, B8.

60. Lisa Chadderdon, "Merrill Lynch Works—At Home," *Fast Company,* April–May 1998, 70–72.

61. Caudron, "Workers' Ideas for Improving Alternative Work Situations."

62. Caudron, "Workers' Ideas for Improving Alternative Work Situations."

63. Thomas A. Kochan and Harry C. Katz, *Collective Bargaining and Industrial Relations* (Homewood, Ill.: Irwin, 1988), 165.

64. Linda Grant, "How UPS Blew It," *Fortune,* 29 September 1997, 29–30; Shari Caudron, "Part-Timers Make Headline News—Here's the Real HR Story," *Workforce,* November 1997, 40–50.

65. Catherine Yang et al., "Low-Wage Lessons," *Business Week,* 11 November 1996, 108–10.

66. Martha Irvine, "Organizing Twentysomethings," *Los Angeles Times,* 7 September 1997, D5.

67. Kochan and Katz, *Collective Bargaining and Industrial Relations,* 173.

68. Michael A. Verespej, "What's Behind the Strife?" *Industry Week,* 1 February 1999, 58–62; Keith Bradsher, "General Motors and the U.A.W. Agree on End to Strike," *New York Times,* 29 July 1998, A1, C6.

69. *World Almanac and Book of Facts* (New York: Scripps Howard, 1989), 161.

70. Susan Carey, "United Grapples With Summer of Widespread Discontent," *Wall Street Journal,* 8 August 2000, A2; Laurence Zuckerman and Matthew L. Wald, "Crisis for Air Traffic System: More Passengers, More Delays," *New York Times,* 5 September 2000, A1, C12.

71. Stephanie Overman, "Unions: New Activism or Old Adversarial Approach?" *HR Focus*, May 1999, 7–8; Laurence Zuckerman, "Pilots Lose a Battle, Not the War," *New York Times*, 17 April 1999, B1, B14.

72. Eugene H. Methvin, "The Union Label: With the Level of Union Violence on the Rise, Congress Must, Again, Deal with the Courts," *National Review*, 29 September 1997, 47; Anya Sacharow, "Walking the Line in Detroit," *Newspapers*, 22 July 1996, 8–13.

73. Paul D. Staudohar, "Labor Relations in Basketball: The Lockout of 1998–99," *Monthly Labor Review*, April 1999, 3–9; Herman, *Collective Bargaining and Labor Relations*, 61; "NLRB Permits Replacements During Legal Lockout," *Personnel Journal*, January 1987, 14–15.

74. David Field, "Airline Chief Has Become Key Figure in Labor Dispute," *USA Today*, 6 March 1997, B1, B2; Donna Rosato, "American Airlines Pilots Ask to Extend Deadline for Talks," *USA Today*, 18 March 1997, 2B; David Field, "Clinton Unlikely to Act Unless Both Sides Ask," *USA Today*, 10 February 1997, 2A.

75. Glenn Burkins, "Labor-Union Membership Increases for Second Year in Row to 16.48 Million," *Wall Street Journal*, 20 January 2000, A2; Michael Barone, "The Unions Go Public," *U.S. News & World Report*, 4 October 1999, 30.

76. International Labour Organization, *World Labour Report*, 4 November 1997 [accessed 7 November 1997] www.ilo.org.

77. Lloyd G. Reynolds, Stanley H. Masters, and Colletta H. Moser, *Labor Economics and Labor Relations*, 11th ed. (Upper Saddle River, N.J.: Prentice Hall, 1998), 497; Indiana University News Bureau, "Trends in U.S. Labor Movement," *Futurist*, January–February 1996, 44; Barbara Presley Noble, "Reinventing Labor: An Interview with Union President Lynn Williams," *Harvard Business Review*, July–August 1993, 115–25.

78. Aaron Bernstein, "Sweeney's Blitz," *Business Week*, 17 February 1997, 56–62; Marc Levinson, "It's Hip to Be Union," *Newsweek*, 8 July 1996, 44–45; James Worsham, "Labor Comes Alive," *Nation's Business*, February 1996, 16–24; E. Edward Herman, *Collective Bargaining and Labor Relations*, 4th ed. (Upper Saddle River, N.J.: Prentice Hall, 1998); Michael Hickins, "Unions: New Activism or Old Adversarial Approach?" *HR Focus*, May 1999, 7–8.

79. Stephanie Armour, "Start-Ups Face More Grind Than Glamour," *USA Today*, 12 July 1999, B1; Karl Taro Greenfeld, "Living the Late Shift," *Time*, 28 June 1999, 46–47; Rosabeth Moss Kanter, "Are You Ready to Lead the E-Cultural Revolution?" *Inc.*, February 2000, 43–44; Michelle Conlin, "Give Me That Old-Time Economy," *Business Week*, 24 April 2000, 99–104; Meryl Davids, "The IPO CEO's Reality," *Chief Executive*, January 2000, 22–26; Stephanie Armour, "Companies Recruiting Former Employees," *USA Today*, 2 February 2000, B1.

80. Ed Emde, "Employee Values Are Changing Course," *Workforce*, March 1998, 83–84.

81. "US West Labor Strike Ends," *CNNfn, CNN Interactive* [accessed 31 August 1998] cnnfn.com:80/hotstories/companies/9808/31/uswest.

CHAPTER 11

1. Brenda Paik Sunoo, "Blending a Successful Workforce," *Workforce*, March 2000, 44–48; Karyn Strauss, "Perron: Jamba's Juiced for Growth, Plans IPO," *Nation's Restaurant News*, 24 January 2000, 1, 76; Karyn Strauss, "Report: Smoothie Indies Face Rocky Road as Chains Slurp Up Market Share," *Nation's Restaurant News*, 14 June 1999, 8, 138; "Best Healthy Choice Menu Selection: Jamba Juice: Jambola Bread is on the Rise," *Nation's Restaurant News*, 24 March 1999, 168; Michael Adams, "Kirk Perron: Jamba Juice," *Restaurant Business*, 15 March 1999, 38; Victor Wishna, "Leaving for Good," *Restaurant Business*, 1 May 2000, 64–74.

2. Joanne Cole, "Permatemps Pose New Challenges for HR," *HR Focus*, December 1999, 7–8; Sharon R. Cohany, "Workers in Alternative Employment Arrangements: A Second Look," *Monthly Labor Review*, November 1998, 3–21.

3. Felicia Jefferson and Don Bohl, "CBR Minisurvey: Part-Time and Temporary Employees Demand Better Pay and More Benefits," *Compensation and Benefits Review*, November–December 1998, 20–24.

4. "Microsoft Moves to Curb Use of Temporary Workers," *Wall Street Journal*, 3 July 2000, B2.

5. Steven Greenhouse, "Equal Work, Less-Equal Perks," *New York Times*, 30 March 1998, C1, C6; Aaron Bernstein, "When Is a Temp Not a Temp?" *Business Week*, 7 December 1998, 90–92.

6. William J. Stevenson, *Production Operations Management*, 6th ed. (Boston: Irwin McGraw-Hill, 1999), 698; Laurie Edwards, "When Outsourcing is Appropriate," *Wall Street and Technology*, July 1998, 96–98.

7. George Donnelly, "Recruiting, Retention, and Returns," *CFO Magazine*, March 2000 [accessed 10 April 2000] www.cfonet.com/html/Articles/CFO/2000/00MArecr.html.

8. Audrey Arthur, "How Much Should Employees Know?" *Black Enterprise*, October 1997, 56; Anthony Ramirez, "Name, Résumé, References. And How's Your Credit? *New York Times*, 31 August 1997, F8.

9. Jonathan Segal, "When Norman Bates and Baby Jane Act Out at Work," *HR Magazine* 41, 1 February 1996, 31; Jenny C. McCune, "Companies Grapple with Workplace Violence," *Management Review*, March 1994, 52–57.

10. Ellis Henican, "Nightmare at Saks Fifth Ave.," *Newsday*, 5 June 1996, A2.

11. "Substance Abuse in the Workplace," *HR Focus*, February 1997, 1, 41; Tyler D. Hartwell, Paul D. Steele, and Nathaniel F. Rodman, "Workplace Alcohol-Testing Programs: Prevalence and Trends," *Monthly Labor Review*, June 1998, 27–34.

12. Randall S. Schuler, *Managing Human Resources* (Cincinnati, Ohio: South-Western College Publishing, 1998), 386.

13. Katharine Mieszkowski, "Report from the Future," *Fast Company*, February–March 1998, 28–30.

14. Tonia L. Shakespeare, "High-Tech Training, Wal-Mart Style," *Black Enterprise*, July 1996, 54.

15. Michael Barrier, "Develop Workers—and Your Business," *Nation's Business*, December 1998, 25–27.

16. Kevin Dobbs, "Tires Plus Takes the Training High Road," *Training*, April 2000, 56–63.

17. Adolph Haasen and Gordon F. Shea, *A Better Place to Work* (New York: American Management Association, 1997), 19–20.

18. Bill Roberts, "://Training Via the Desktop://" *HR Magazine*, August 1998, 98–104.

19. Gina Imperato, "How to Give Good Feedback," *Fast Company*, September 1998, 144–56.

20. Kate Ludeman, "How to Conduct Self-Directed 360," *Training and Development*, July 2000, 44–47; Cassandra Hayes, "To Tell the Truth," *Black Enterprise*, December 1998, 55.

21. Imperato, "How to Give Good Feedback."

22. Bradely R. Schiller, *State Minimum Wage Laws: Youth Coverage and Impact* (Washington, D.C.: George Mason University, 1994).

23. Jeff Kersten, "Gain Sharing in College Station," *PM: Public Management*, May 1998, 19.

24. Ellen Neuborne, "Meeting Goals Just Got More Rewarding," *USA Today*, 15 October 1996, B1–B2.

25. Bobette M. Gustafson, "Skill-Based Pay Improves PFS Staff Recruitment, Retention, and Performance," *Healthcare Financial Management*, January 2000, 62–63; Rosalie Webster, "Both Sides of the Coin," *New Zealand Management*, November 1998, 122; Genevieve Capowski, "HR View Online," *HR Focus*, June 1998, 2.

26. Karen Jacobs, "The Broad View," *Wall Street Journal*, 10 April 1997, R10; Schuler, *Managing Human Resources*, 386.

27. Keith H. Hammonds, Wendy Zellner, and Richard Melcher, "Writing a New Social Contract," *Business Week,* 11 March 1996, 60; Don L. Boroughs, "The Bottom Line on Ethics," *U.S. News & World Report,* 20 March 1995, 63–65; Dawn Gunsch, "Benefits Leverage Hiring and Retention Efforts," *Personnel Journal,* November 1992, 91–92, 94–97.

28. Fiona Jebb, "Flex Appeal," *Management Today* (London), July 1998, 66–69; Milton Zall, "Implementing a Flexible Benefits Plan," *Fleet Equipment,* May 1999, B4–B8.

29. "Employees Prefer Finding Their Own Health Care Coverage," *Employee Benefit Plan Review,* March 2000, 49.

30. "Employers Pass Along More Health-Care Costs," *HR Focus,* May 2000, 12.

31. Jan Ziegler, "Why Work Where You Can't Get Coverage?" *Business and Health,* June 2000, 61–62.

32. Richard D. Pearce, "The Small Employer Retirement Plan Void," *Compensation and Benefits Management,* Winter 1999, 51–55.

33. Arleen Jacobius, "Retirement Programs Cover 70 Percent of Employees," *Pensions and Investments,* 31 May 1999, 25.

34. James H. Dulebohn, Brian Murray, and Minghe Sun, "Selection Among Employer-Sponsored Pension Plans: The Role of Individual Differences," *Personnel Psychology,* Summer 2000, 405–32.

35. George Van Dyke, "Examining Your 401k," *Business Credit,* January 2000, 59.

36. Dulebohn et al., "Selection Among Employer-Sponsored Pension Plans."

37. Michael Arndt, "Will United's Woes Spread?" *Business Week,* 13 November 2000, 180–92.

38. Floyd Norris, "Pilot Woes: Why Employee Ownership Didn't Help UAL," *New York Times,* 11 August 2000, C1; Michael Arndt, "The Industry Will Pay for United's Deal With Pilots," *Business Week,* 18 September 2000, 52.

39. Sara Nathan, "Stock Options Not Only for Top Dogs," *USA Today,* 23 July 1999, 3B.

40. Del Jones, "More Workers Get Options, Too," *USA Today,* 7 April 1999, 3B.

41. Gillian Flynn, "Employees Need an FMLA Brush-up," *Workforce* 76, no. 4 (April 1997): 101–104; Barbara Presley Noble, "At Work: We're Doing Just Fine, Thank You," *New York Times,* 20 March 1994, 25.

42. "Workplace Briefs," Gannett News Service, 24 April 1997; Julia Lawlor, "The Bottom Line," *Working Woman,* July–August 1996, 54–58, 74–76.

43. Stephanie Armour, "Employers Stepping Up in Elder Care," *USA Today,* 3 August 2000, 3B.

44. Sue Shellenbarger, "Employees Who Value Time as Much as Money Now Get Their Reward," *Wall Street Journal,* 22 September 1999, B1.

45. Del Jones, "Firms Take New Look at Sick Days," *USA Today,* 8 October 1996, 8B.

46. William Atkinson, "Wellness, Employee Assistance Programs: Investments, Not Costs," *Bobbin,* May 2000, 42–48.

47. Atkinson, "Wellness, Employee Assistance Programs."

48. Atkinson, "Wellness, Employee Assistance Programs"; Kevin Dobbs, Jack Gordon, and David Stamps, "EAPs Cheap But Popular Perk," *Training,* February 2000, 26.

49. "50 Benefits and Perks That Make Employees Want to Stay Forever," *HR Focus,* July 2000, S2–S3.

50. Edward Iwata, "Staff-Hungry Tech Firms Cast Exotic Lures," *USA Today,* 1 February 2000, B1.

51. Valerie L. Williams and Jennifer E. Sunderland, "New Pay Programs Boost Retention," *Workforce,* May 1999, 36–40.

52. "Well No, They Won't Go," *CA Magazine,* April 1999, 11.

53. "Well No, They Won't Go."

54. Rodney Ho, "AT&T's Offer of $10,000 May Test Entrepreneurship of Laid-Off Workers," *Wall Street Journal,* 12 March 1997; David Fischer and Kevin Whitelaw, "A New Way to Shine Up Corporate Profits," *U.S. News & World Report,* 15 April 1996, 55.

55. Gillian Flynn, "Why Rhino Won't Wait Until Tomorrow," *Personnel Journal,* July 1996, 36–39.

56. Efraim Turban, Jae Lee, David King, and H. Michael Chung, *Electronic Commerce, A Managerial Perspective* (Upper Saddle River, N.J.: Prentice Hall, 2000), 164–68; Marlene Piturro, "The Power of E-Cruiting," *Management Review,* January 2000, 33–38; "Online Recruiting: What Works, What Doesn't," *HR Focus,* March 2000, 11–15; "More Pros and Cons to Internet Recruiting," *HR Focus,* May 2000, 8; Christopher Caggiano, "The Truth About Internet Recruiting," *Inc.,* December 1999, 156; Peter Buxbaum, "Where's Dilbert?" *Chief Executive* [accessed 2 March 2000] www.chiefexecutive.net/mag/150tech/part1c.htm; James R. Borck, "Recruiting Systems Control Résumé Chaos," *InfoWorld,* 24 July 2000, 47–48; Bill Leonard, "Online and Overwhelmed," *HR Magazine,* August 2000, 36–42; Milton Zall, "Internet Recruiting," *Strategic Finance,* June 2000, 66–72; "Why Your Web Site Is More Important Than Ever to New Hires," *HR Focus,* June 2000, 9; Rachel Emma Silverman, "Recruiters' Hunt for Résumés Is Nocturnal Game," *Wall Street Journal,* 20 September 2000, B1–B4.

57. Sal D. Rinalla and Robert J. Kopecky, "Recruitment: Burger King Hooks Employees with Educational Incentives," *Personnel Journal,* October 1989, 90–99.

CHAPTER 12

1. Jane Eisinger, "Capitalizing on Corporate Success," *Association Management,* February 2000, 47–49; Mike McNamee, "Isn't There More to Life Than Plastic?" *Business Week,* 22 November 1999, 173–76; Charles Fishman, "This is a Marketing Revolution," *Fast Company,* May 1999, 204–18; Leslie Goff, "Surviving the Data Minefield," *Computerworld,* 24 August 1998, 49–50.

2. "AMA Board Approves New Marketing Definition," *Marketing News,* 1 March 1985, 1.

3. Al Ries and Jack Trout, *The 22 Immutable Laws of Marketing* (New York: HarperCollins, 1994), 19–25.

4. Kevin Maney, "Consumers Latch onto Speedy Way to Get Gas," *USA Today,* 26 February 1998, 8B.

5. Fred Hapgood, "Death of the Salesman," *Inc. Tech,* no. 3 (1998): 95–98.

6. Hal Lancaster, "Managing Your Career: Giving Good Service, Never an Easy Task, Is Getting a Lot Harder," *Wall Street Journal,* 9 June 1998, B1.

7. Terry G. Vavra, "The Database Marketing Imperative," *Marketing Management* 2, no. 1 (1993): 47–57.

8. Suzanne Oliver, "Spoiled Rotten," *Forbes,* 15 July 1996, 70–73; "Skymall's Web Sales Take Flight as Shares Soar Nearly Threefold," *Wall Street Journal,* 29 December 1998, B9.

9. Peter Fingar, Harsha Kumar, and Tarun Sharma, Enterprise E-Commerce (Tampa, Fla.: Meghan-Kiffer Press, 2000), 24, 109.

10. Pierre M. Loewe and Mark S. Bonchek, "The Retail Revolution," *Management Review,* April 1999, 38–44.

11. Laurie Windham, *Dead Ahead* (New York: Allworth Press, 1999), 80–85.

12. Barbara Whitaker, "House Hunting with Cursor and Click," *New York Times,* 24 September 1998, D1, D5.

13. Janet Willen, "The Customer Is Wrong," *Business97,* October–November 1997, 40–42; William H. Davidow and Bro Uttal,

Total Customer Service: The Ultimate Weapon (New York: Harper & Row, 1989), 8; Valarie A. Zeithaml, A. Parasuraman, and Leonard L. Berry, *Delivering Quality Service* (New York: Free Press, 1990), 9; George J. Castellese, "Customer Service . . . Building a Winning Team," *Supervision,* January 1995, 9–13; Erica G. Sorohan and Catherine M. Petrini, "Dumpsters, Ducks, and Customer Service," *Training and Development,* January 1995, 9.

14. Peter Burrows, "HP: No Longer Lost in Cyberspace?" *Business Week,* 31 May 1999, 124, 126.

15. Avery Comarow, "Broken? No Problem," *U.S. News & World Report,* 11 January 1999, 68–69.

16. Ronald B. Lieber, "Storytelling: A New Way to Get Close to Your Customer," *Fortune,* 3 February 1997, 102–10.

17. Steve Schriver, "Customer Loyalty: Going Going . . ." *American Demographics,* September 1997, 20–23.

18. Scott Woolley, "Get Lost, Buster," *Forbes,* 23 February 1998, 90; Jon Van, "$5 Question: When Does Not Calling Not Add Up?" *Chicago Tribune,* 8 April 1999, sec. 1, 1, 14.

19. Mary J. Cronin, *Doing More Business on the Internet* (New York: Van Nostrand Reinhold, 1995), 13.

20. Eryn Brown, Mary J. Cronin, Ann Harrington, and Jane Hodges, "9 Ways to Win on the Web," Fortune, 24 May 1999, 112–25.

21. Joshua Macht, "The New Market Research," *Inc.,* July 1998, 87–94.

22. Louisa Wah, "The Almighty Customer," *Management Review,* February 1999, 16–22.

23. Thomas A. Stewart, "A Satisfied Customer Isn't Enough," *Fortune,* 21 July 1997, 112–13.

24. David C. Edelman, "Satisfaction Is Nice, But Share Pays," *Marketing Management* 2, no. 1 (1993): 8–13.

25. Oren Harari, "Six Myths of Market Research," *Management Review,* April 1994, 48–51.

26. Robert Passikoff, "Loyal Opposition—The Limits of Customer Satisfaction," *Brandweek,* 3 March 1997, 17.

27. Pamela G. Hollies, "What's New in Market Research," *New York Times,* 15 June 1986, sec. 3, 19; Phyllis M. Thornton, "Linking Market Research to Strategic Planning," *Nursing Homes,* January–February 1995, 34–37; Harari, "Six Myths of Market Research."

28. Raymond R. Burke, "Virtual Shopping: Breakthrough in Marketing Research," *Harvard Business Review,* March–April 1996, 120–31.

29. Harry S. Dent Jr., "Individualized Marketing," *Small Business Reports,* April 1991, 36–45.

30. Janet Novack, "The Data Miners," *Forbes,* 12 February 1996, 96–97; Don Peppers and Martha Rogers, *Enterprise One to One* (New York: Doubleday, 1997), 120–21.

31. Wah, "The Almighty Customer"; James Lardner, "Your Every Command," *U.S. News & World Report,* 5 July 1999, 44–46.

32. Charles Fishman, "This is a Marketing Revolution," *Fast Company,* May 1999, 206–18.

33. William S. Hopkins and Britton Manasco, "The Coming Customer Free-For-All," *New York Times Supplement—Customer Relationships in a Wired World,* 14 February 2000, CU1–CU2.

34. Diane Brady, "Why Service Stinks," *Business Week,* 23 October 2000, 118–28.

35. Don Peppers, Martha Rogers, and Bob Dorf, "Is Your Company Ready for One-To-One Marketing?" *Harvard Business Review,* January–February 1999.

36. Owen Thomas, "Dell's Premier Pages," *Ecompany,* August 2000, 77; Brown et al., "9 Ways to Win on the Web."

37. Tom Content, "Nike Lets You Be a Shoemaker," *USA Today,* 22 November 1999, 14B.

38. James Lardner, "Your Every Command," *U.S. News & World Report,* 5 July 1999, 44–46.

39. Lardner, "Your Every Command."

40. Peppers and Rogers, *Enterprise One to One,* 145–46.

41. Malcolm H. B. McDonald, "Ten Barriers to Marketing Planning," *Journal of Product and Brand Management,* Fall 1992, 51–64.

42. Vanessa O'Connell, "Changing Tastes Dent Campbell's Canned-Soup Sales," *Wall Street Journal,* 28 April 1998, B1, B25.

43. Norihiko Shirouzu, "Japan's High-School Girls Excel in Art of Setting Trends," *Wall Street Journal,* 24 April 1998, B1, B7.

44. Leslie Kaufman, "Playing Catch-Up at the On-Line Mall," *New York Times,* 21 February 1999, sec. 3, 1, 6; Gary Samuels, "CD-ROMs First Big Victim," Forbes, 28 February 1994, 42–44; Richard A. Melcher, "Dusting Off the Britannica," *Business Week,* 20 October 1997, 143–146.

45. "Setting a Fast Pace for the Wireless Web," *Business Week,* 18 September 2000, 48.

46. Malcolm McDonald and John W. Leppard, *Marketing by Matrix* (Lincolnwood, Ill.: NTC, 1993), 10; H. Igor Ansoff, "Strategies for Diversification," *Harvard Business Review,* November–December 1957, 113–24; H. Igor Ansoff, *Corporate Strategy* (New York: McGraw-Hill, 1965).

47. Alex Taylor III, "How to Murder the Competition," *Fortune,* 22 February 1993, 87, 90.

48. Scott Hays, "Exceptional Customer Service Takes the 'Ritz' Touch," *Workforce,* January 1999, 99–102.

49. Ann Oldenburg, "Market Responds Slowly to a Growing Population," *USA Today,* 18 March 1998, 9D.

50. David Shani and Sujana Chalasani, "Exploring Niches Using Relationship Marketing," *Journal of Business and Industrial Marketing,* no. 4 (1993): 58–66.

51. Michael J. Weiss, *The Clustering of America* (New York: Harper & Row, 1988), 41.

52. Don Peppers and Martha Rogers, "One-to-One Business Travel," *Inside 1to1,* 17 September 1998 [via e-mail 16 September 1998].

53. Shani and Chalasani, "Exploring Niches Using Relationship Marketing."

54. Courtland L. Bovée, Michael J. Houston, and John V. Thill, *Marketing,* 2d ed. (New York: McGraw-Hill, 1994), 224.

55. Daniel Roth, "First: From Poster Boy to Whipping Boy," *Fortune,* 6 July 1998, 28–29.

56. Gary Armstrong and Philip Kotler, *Marketing an Introduction,* 5th ed. (Upper Saddle River, N.J.: Prentice Hall, 2000), 201–4.

57. Faye Brookman, "Brushing Up," *Supermarket Business,* February 1998, 57–62; Laurie Freeman, "Maintaining the Momentum," *Supermarket Business,* February 1999, 57–58.

58. Kotler, *Marketing Management,* 294–97.

59. Adapted from William S. Hopkins and Britton Manasco, "Lands' End Enlivens Interactions on the Web," *New York Times Supplement—Customer Relationships in a Wired World,* 14 February 2000, CU10–CU11; Katrina Brooker, "First: The Nightmare Before Christmas," *Fortune,* 24 January 2000, 24–25; Carlton van Putten, "Keeping Customers Online," *HP Professional,* September 1999, 20–21; Laurie Windham, *Dead Ahead* (New York: Allworth Press, 1999), 33–34; Ellen Neuborne, "It's the Service, Stupid," *Business Week E.Biz,* 3 April 2000, EB18; Doug Bartholomew, "Service to Order," *Industryweek,* 3 April 2000, 19–22; Maryanne Murray Buechner, "How'd They Do?" *Time,* 24 January 2000, B1–B4; Mary Beth Grover, "Lost In Cyberspace," *Forbes,* 8 March 1999, 124–28; Bruce Horovitz, "Web Site Helps Untangle Mess of E-Customer Service," *USA Today,* 16 August 1999, 7B; John Dodge, "A Customer-Service Mantra Can Rebound on E-Tailers, Wall Street Journal Interactive Edition, 18

January 2000 [accessed 28 February 2000], http://interactive.wsj.com; Rebecca Quick, "Returns to Sender," *Wall Street Journal,* 17 July 2000, R8; Laura Bly, "Personal Touch Hits Turbulence on the Web," *USA Today,* 20 June 2000, 5D; Zehanya Gene Senyak, "Talk Shops," *Business 2.0,* 13 June 2000, 187–89; Robert Berner, "Customer Service—Lands' End," *Business Week E.Biz,* 18 September 2000, EB84–EB85; Lorrie Grant, "Customer Service Shortfall Cuts Into Net Sales," *USA Today,* 1 June 1999; George Anders, "At Your Service," *Wall Street Journal,* 17 April 2000, R12, R16; Jennifer Rewick, "Clinching the Holiday E-Sale," *Wall Street Journal,* 9 October 2000, B1, B22.

60. Adapted from John Case and Jerry Useem, "Six Characters in Search of a Strategy," *Inc.,* March 1996, 46–49.

61. Fred Vogelstein, "Corporate America Loves the Weather," *U.S. News & World Report,* 13 May 1998, 48.

CHAPTER 13

1. Michael Schrage, "Martha Stewart: Living Well on the World Wide Web," *Adweek,* 14 February 2000, IQ18–IQ30; Diana Brady, "Martha Inc.: Inside the Growing Empire of America's Lifestyle Queen," *Business Week,* 17 January 2000, 63–72; Robert Barker, "How Tasty is Martha's IPO?" *Business Week,* 6 September 1999, 108; Andrew Wahl, "Home Economics," *Canadian Business,* 27 August 1999, 18; Don Hogsett, "Martha Cooks Up an IPO," *Home Textiles Today,* 9 August 1999, 1, 21; Ann Smith, "A Living Brand," *Progressive Grocer,* November 1998, 21–22; Deborah Spence, "Marketing Martha By E-Mail," *Folio: The Magazine for Magazine Management,* 1 March 1998, 33.

2. Philip Kotler and Gary Armstrong, *Principles of Marketing,* 9th ed. (Upper Saddle River, N.J.: Prentice Hall, 2001), 296.

3. Gary Hamel, *Lessons in Leadership Lecture,* Northern Illinois University, 23 October 1997.

4. "Preparing for a Point to Point World," *Marketing Management* 3, no. 4 (Spring 1995): 30–40.

5. Al Ries and Jack Trout, "Focused in a Fuzzy World," *Rethinking the Future* (London: Nicholas Brealey Publishing, 1997), 183.

6. Bill Saporito, "Can Nike Get Unstuck?" *Time,* 30 March 1998, 48–53.

7. Michele Rosen, "Apple Escapes PC Market Crunch," *Forbes Digital Tool,* 15 April 1999 [accessed 16 June 1999] www.forbes.com/tool/html/99/apr/0415/mu2.htm.

8. John C. Dvorak, "Razor's with No Blades," *Forbes,* 18 October 1999, 168.

9. Marcia Mogelonsky, "Product Overload?" *American Demographics,* August 1998, 65–69.

10. Lisa Bannon, "Goodbye, Dolly: Mattel Tries to Adjust as 'Holiday Barbie' Leaves Under a Cloud," *Wall Street Journal,* 7 June 1999, A1, A8; Dana Canedy, "Beyond Barbie's Midlife Crisis," *New York Times,* 6 April 1999, C1, C8.

11. Jacob M. Schlesinger, "Firms Strive to Improve Basic Products," *Wall Street Journal,* 8 October 1985, B1.

12. "New Product Winners—And Losers," *In Business,* April 1985, 64.

13. Yumiko Ono, "Kraft Searches Its Cupboard for Old Brands to Remake," *Wall Street Journal,* 12 March 1996, B1, B4.

14. Tom Peters, "We Hold These Truths to Be Self-Evident," *Organizational Dynamics,* 1 June 1996, 27–32.

15. Tom Peters, *Lessons In Leadership Lecture.*

16. Bruce Horovitz and Melanie Wells, "Well-Known Products Try for Comeback," *USA Today,* 2 May 1995, B1.

17. Tim Stevens, "Lights, Camera, Innovation," *Industry Week,* 19 July 1999, 32–38.

18. Tim Stevens, "Idea Dollars," *Industry Week,* 16 February 1998, 47–49.

19. Tona Mack, "Let the Computer Do It," *Forbes,* 10 August 1987, 94.

20. *The New Economy Index* [accessed 13 April 2000] www.neweconomyindex.org/section1_page06.html.

21. Gary Armstrong and Philip Kotler, *Marketing an Introduction,* 5th ed. (Upper Saddle River, N.J.: Prentice Hall, 2000), 234.

22. Roberta Bernstein, "Food for Thought," *American Demographics,* May 2000, 39–42.

23. Armstrong and Kotler, *Marketing an Introduction,* 235.

24. Armstrong and Kotler, *Marketing an Introduction,* 206.

25. Bruce Horovitz, "Would You Like Fires with That Cappuccino?" *USA Today,* 22 September 2000, 1A.

26. Tim O'Brien, "Disneyland Paris Caters to European Tastes, Lowers Costs and Refines Service," *Amusement Business,* 5 May 1997, p. 18; "Disneyland Paris: How Beauty Became a Beast," *Reputation Management,* March–April 1995, 35–37.

27. Zachary Schiller, "Make It Simple," *Business Week,* 9 September 1996, 96–104; Katrina Brooker, "Can Procter & Gamble Change Its Culture, Protect Its Market Share, and Find the Next Tide?" *Fortune,* 26 April 1999, 146–52.

28. Tara Parket-Pope, "Custom-Made," *Wall Street Journal,* 26 September 1996, R22–R23.

29. Ernest Beck and Rekha Balu, "Europe Is Deaf to Snap! Crackle! Pop!" *Wall Street Journal,* 2 June 1998, B1, B12.

30. Thomas K. Grose, "Brand New Goods," *Time.com,* 1 November 1999 [accessed 17 February 2001] www.time.com/time/magazine/article/0,9171,33124-1,00.html.

31. Constance L. Hays, "No More Brand X," *New York Times,* 12 June 1998, C1, C4.

32. Kelly Barron, "The Cappuccino Conundrum," *Forbes,* 22 February 1999, 54–55.

33. Nina Munk, "Gap Gets It," *Fortune,* 3 August 1998, 68–82.

34. Diane Brady, "Why Tommy Hilfiger Is So Like, Um, 1998," *Business Week,* 24 April 2000, 55.

35. Melanie Wells, "Red Baron," *Forbes,* 3 July 2000, 151–60.

36. Jagdish N. Sheth and Rajendra S. Sisodia, "Feeling the Heat," *Marketing Management* 4, no. 2 (Fall 1995): 9–23.

37. Claudia H. Deutsch, "Will That Be Paper or Pixel?" *New York Times,* 4 August 2000, C1, C4.

38. David Leonhardt, "Cereal-Box Killers Are on the Loose," *Business Week,* 12 October 1998, 721.

39. Dean Takahashi, "Intel Steps Up Use of Price Cuts to Protect Its Turf and to Expand," *Wall Street Journal,* 9 June 1998, B6.

40. Terril Yue Jones, "Fearing the Old Shoddy Image," *Forbes,* 12 January 1998 [accessed 16 June 1999] www.forbes.com/forbes/98/0112/6101064a.htm.

41. Thomas T. Nagle, "Managing Price Competition," *Marketing Management,* 2, no. 1 (1993): 38–45; Sheth and Sisodia, "Feeling the Heat," 21.

42. Gurumurthy Kalyanaram and Ragu Gurumurthy, "Market Entry Strategies: Pioneers Versus Late Arrivals," *Strategy & Business,* Third quarter 1998 [accessed 16 June 1999] www.strategy-business.com.

43. Tim Klass, "Web Bookstores Discount Bestsellers," *Associated Press Online,* 17 May 1999 [accessed 21 May 1999] www.cbsmarketwatch.com.

44. Edwin McDowell, "Winging It, with Internet Fares," *New York Times,* 7 March 1999, sec. 3, 1, 10.

45. Douglas A. Blackmon, "Price Buster," *Wall Street Journal,* 17 July 2000, R12, R26; Indrajit Sinha, "Cost Transparency: The Net's Real Threat to Prices and Brands," *Harvard Business Review,* March–April 2000, 43–50; Laurie Windham, *Dead Ahead* (New York: Allworth Press, 1999), 188–90; Bill Gates, "The Price of the Future," *Executive Excellence,* March 1999, 8; "Faster! Better! Cheaper?" *Business 2.0,* 1 April 2000 [accessed online 23 April 2000] www.business2.com/

articles/2000/04/content/numbers.html; "Survey: E-Commerce: In the Great Web Bazaar," *The Economist*, 26 February 2000, S40–S44; Fred Hapgood, "The Corporate Flea Market," *Inc. Tech*, no. 3 (1999): 90–99; Elizabeth Weise, "Sizing Up Web Shoppers for the Perfect Fit," *USA Today*, 21 April 1999, 4D; Philip Kotler and Gary Armstrong, *Principles of Marketing*, 9th ed. (Upper Saddle River, N.J.: Prentice Hall, 2001), 372–73; Salina Khan, "Travel Sites Aim Discounts at First Timers," *USA Today*, 9 October 2000, 1B; Tami Luhby, "Ticket to Success Proves Fleeting for Priceline.com," *Chicago Tribune*, 8 October 2000, sec. 5, 1–2; Peter Coy and Pamela L. Moore, "A Revolution in Pricing? Not Quite," *Business Week*, 20 November 2000, 48–49; Jessica Davis, "American Consumers Will Force E-Tailers to Just Say No to Dynamic Pricing," *InfoWorld*, 9 October 2000, 116; David P. Hamilton, "The Price Isn't Right," *Wall Street Journal*, 12 February 2001, R8, R10.

46. Joanne Lipman, "Do Toll Phone Services Play Fair by Advertising Directly to Kids?" *Wall Street Journal*, 7 July 1989, B1.

47. Amy Olmstead, "Economics of On-Line Trading: Clicking for Dollars," *New York Times Magazine*, 11 April 1999, 30; Sean T. Kelly, "The Top Ten Discount Brokers," *Time Digital*, 17 May 1999, 38–39.

CHAPTER 14

1. Barbara F. Thompson, "The Home Depot," *Library Journal*, 1 February 2000, 30; Bruce Upbin, "Profit in a Big Orange Box," *Forbes*, 24 January 2000, 122–27; Sara Rose, "Building a Powerhouse," *Money*, December 1999, 62–64; Julia King, "E-retailers Take Time to Nail Down Virtual Shelves, Service," *Computerworld*, 6 September 1999, 1, 99; Dan Hanover, "It's Not a Threat, Just a Promise," *Chain Store Age*, September 1999, 176; "Home Depot Tells Vendors to Stay Off the 'Net," *Industrial Distribution*, September 1999, 21, 28; Katrina Booker, "First: Awfully Nervous," *Fortune*, 16 August 1999, 28–29; Matthew Budman, "Built from Scratch: How a Couple of Regular Guys Grew the Home Depot from Nothing to $30 Billion," *Across the Board*, June 1999, 61; Roy S. Johnson, "Home Depot Renovates," *Fortune*, 23 November 1998, 200–204.

2. Neil Gross, "The Supply Chain: Leapfrogging a Few Links," *Business Week*, 22 June 1998, 140–42.

3. Lisa H. Harrington, "The New Warehousing," *Industry Week*, 20 July 1998, 52, 54, 57–58.

4. Saul Hensell, "Is This the Factory of the Future?" *New York Times*, 26 July 1998, sec. 3, 1, 12.

5. Lisa Chadderdon, "How Dell Sells on the Web," *Fast Company*, September 1998, 58, 60.

6. Gregory L. White, "GM Is Forming Unit to Buy Dealerships," *Wall Street Journal*, 24 September 1999, A3; Joann Muller, "Meet Your Local GM Dealer: GM," *Business Week*, 11 October 1999, 48.

7. Leslie Kaufman, "As Big Business, Wal-Mart Propels Changes Elsewhere," *New York Times*, 22 October 2000, 1, 24.

8. Philip Kotler and Gary Armstrong, *Principles of Marketing*, 9th ed. (Upper Saddle River, N.J.: Prentice Hall, 2001), 435.

9. "Hallmark, a New Name in Mass Retailing," *Supermarket Business*, March 1997, 84; Daniel Roth, "Card Sharks," *Forbes*, 7 October 1996, 14; Julie Rygh, "Hallmark Cards Find Success with New Expressions Brand," *Knight-Ridder/Tribune Business News*, 31 August 1997, 831B0958.

10. Warren Cohen, "Same Price.com," *U.S. News & World Report*, 25 May 1998, 59; Joseph Conlin, "The Art of the Dealer Meeting," *Sales and Marketing Management*, February 1997, 761.

11. Michael S. Katz and Jeffrey Rothfeder, "Crossing the Digital Divide," *Strategy & Business*, First Quarter 2000, 26–41; Anne Stuart, "Clicks & Bricks," *CIO*, 15 March 2000, 76–84.

12. "1997 Economic Census: Advance Summary Statistics for the United States 1997 NAICS Basis," U.S. Census Bureau, 16 March 1999 www.census.gov/epcd/wwww/advanc1ahtm [accessed 7 June 1999].

13. Marcia Stepanek, "Middlemen: Rebirth of the Salesman," *Business Week*, 22 June 1998, 146–47.

14. "1997 Economic Census," U.S. Census Bureau.

15. Linnea Anderson, "Industry Zone: Industry Snapshot: Retail & Wholesale," Hoover's Online[accessed 7 June 1999] www.hoovers.com/features/industry/retail.html

16. Anderson, "Industry Zone."

17. Bruce Horovitz, "Trend Shrinks Store Sizes to Save Money, Satisfy Customers," *USA Today*, 9 August 1999, B1.

18. William M. Bulkeley, "Category Killers Go From Lethal to Lame in the Space of a Decade," *Wall Street Journal*, 9 March 2000, A1, A8.

19. Paul Klebnikov, "Trouble in Toyland," *Forbes*, 1 June 1998, 56, 58, 60; I. Jeanne Dugan, "The Corporation: Strategies: Can Toys "R" Us Get on Top of Its Game?" *Business Week*, 7 April 1997, 124.

20. Mike Troy, "Wal-Mart Supercenters: The Combo with the Midas Touch," *DSN Retailing Today*, 8 May 2000, 113–14; Wendy Zellner, "Look Out, Supermarkets—Wal-Mart Is Hungry," *Business Week*, 14 September 1998, 98, 100

21. William J. Holstein and Kerry Hannon, "They Drop Till You Shop," *U.S. News & World Report*, 21 July 1997, 51–52; Marci McDonald, "The Pall in the Mall," *U.S. News and World Report*, 18 October 1999, 64–67.

22. Holstein and Hannon, "They Drop Till You Shop."

23. Michelle Pacelle, "The Aging Shopping Mall Must Either Adapt or Die," *Wall Street Journal*, 16 April 1996, B1, B14.

24. Jennifer Steinhauer, "It's a Mall . . . It's an Airport," *New York Times*, 10 June 1998, B1, B4; Chris Woodyard, "Hamlets Feature Fewer Rivals, Higher Profits," *USA Today*, 3 February 1998, B1, B2.

25. Ginia Bellafante, "That's Retail-tainment!" *Time*, 7 December 1998, 64–65.

26. Julia King, "Retailers, Manufacturers Find Ways to Co-exist on Electronic Frontier," *Computerworld*, 17 May 1999 [accessed 21 May 1999] www.computerworld.com/home/print.nsf/all/990517a69e.

27. Philip Kotler, *Marketing Management*, 9th ed. (Upper Saddle River, N.J.: Prentice Hall, 1997), 567.

28. King, "Retailers, Manufacturers Find Ways to Co-exist."

29. Richard A. Feinberg, "Sobering Thoughts on Cybermalls," *Computerworld*, 14 April 1997, 35.

30. Susan Chandler, "Opening the Retail Gates for PCs," *Chicago Tribune*, 27 October 1999, B1, B2.

31. "Value of U.S. DM Driven Sales Compared to Total U.S. Sales," Direct Marketing Association [accessed 8 June 1999] www.thedma.org/services1/charts/dmsales_ussales.html.

32. Lorrie Grant, "Stores with Doors Not Passe," *USA Today*, 4 August 1999, 3B.

33. Grant, "Stores with Doors Not Passe."

34. Catherine Romano, "Telemarketing Grows Up," *Management Review*, June 1998, 31–34.

35. Nanette Byrnes, "Avon, The New Calling," *Business Week*, 18 September 2000, 136–40; Emily Nelson and Ann Zimmerman, "Avon Goes Store to Store," *Wall Street Journal*, 18 September 2000, B1, B4.

36. Joseph B. White, "What Works?" *Wall Street Journal*, 23 October 2000, R4.

37. Chris Woodyard and Lorrie Grant, "E-tailers Dash to Wild, Wild Web," *USA Today*, 13 January 1999, B1, B2.

38. Paul McDougall, "Dell Mounts Internet Push to Diversify Revenue," *Informationweek*, 10 April 2000, 32; Phil Waga, "Dell's Prowess on the Net," *Gannett News Service*, 23 November 1999, 11; Lisa Chadderdon, "How Dell Sells on the Web," *Fast Company*, September 1998, 58, 60; William J. Holstein, Susan Gregory Thomas, and Fred Vogelstein, "Click 'Til You Drop," *U.S. News & World Report*, 7 December 1998, 42–45.

39. Heather Page, "Open for Business," *Entrepreneur,* December 1997, 51–53.

40. Kelly J. Andrews, "Value-Added E-Commerce," *Entrepreneurial Edge,* 3 (1998), 62–64.

41. Jason Anders, "Yesterday's Darling," *Wall Street Journal,* 23 October 2000, R8.

42. Daniel S. Janal, "Net Profit Now," *Success,* July–August 1997, 57–63.

43. Tariq K. Muhammad, "Marketing Online," *Black Enterprise,* September 1996, 85–88.

44. Holstein, Thomas, and Vogelstein, "Click 'Til You Drop."

45. Patricia Gallup, "You, Me, and All Those Others Just Like Us," *Inc.,* 15 May 1998, 51–52; PC Connection Catalog, vol. 4, no. 6B, 1994, 2–3.

46. Lisa H. Harrington, "Coping with Adolescence," *Industry Week,* 19 October 1998, 110, 112, 114, 117; "Neiman Marcus Selects Circle as Global Logistics Supplier," Circle International, 21 April 1999 [accessed 8 June 1999] www.circleintl.com/news/releases/Neiman.html.

47. Ronald Henkoff, "Delivering the Goods," *Fortune,* 28 November 1994, 64–78.

48. Edward O. Welles, "Riding the High-Tech Highway," *Inc.,* March 1993, 72–85.

49. Colleen Gourley, "Retail Logistics in Cyberspace," *Distribution,* December 1996, 29; Dave Hirschman, "FedEx Starts Up Package Sorting System at Memphis Tenn. Airport," *Knight-Ridder/Tribune Business News,* 28 September 1997, 928B0953; "FedEx and Technology—Maintaining a Competitive Edge," *PresWIRE,* 2 December 1996.

50. Saul Hansell, "For Amazon, a Holiday Risk: Can It Sell Acres of Everything?" *New York Times,* 28 November 1999, sec. 3, 1, 15; Katrina Brooker, "Amazon vs. Everybody," *Fortune,* 8 November 1999, 120–28.

51. Steffano Korper and Juanita Ellis, *The E-Commerce Book: Building the E-Empire* (San Diego, Calif.: Academic Press, 2000), 71–72.

52. IBM e-Business Web site, [accessed 10 March 2000], www.ibm.com/e-business/info.

53. Marcia Stepanek, "Closed, Gone to the Net," *Business Week,* 7 June 1999, 113–14.

54. Barbara Boydston, "Ticket, Please," *Wall Street Journal,* 17 July 2000, R38, R42.

55. Rebecca Quick, "Returns to Sender," *Wall Street Journal,* 17 July 2000, R8; Greg Farrell, "Clicks-and-Mortar World Values Brands," *USA Today,* 5 October 1999, B1,B2; Ranjay Gulati and Jason Garino, "Get the Right Mix of Bricks and Clicks," *Harvard Business Review,* May-June 2000, 107–14; Anne Stuart, "Clicks & Bricks," *CIO,* 15 March 2000, 76–84; Jason Anders, "Sibling Rivalry," *Wall Street Journal,* 17 July 2000, R16; William M. Bulkeley, "Clicks and Mortar," *Wall Street Journal,* 17 July 2000, R4; Allanna Sullivan, "From a Call to a Click," *Wall Street Journal,* 17 July 2000, R30; Suein L. Hwang, "Clicks and Bricks," *Wall Street Journal,* 17 April 2000, R8, R10; Jeffrey Rothfeder, "Toys 'R' Us Battles Back," *Strategy & Business,* Second Quarter 2000; Dennis K. Berman and Heather Green, "Cliff Hanger Christmas," *Business Week E.Biz,* 23 October 2000, EB30–EB38; Jerry Useem, "Dot-Coms What Have We Learned?" *Fortune,* 30 October 2000, 82–104.

56. Bill Gates, *Business @ the Speed of Thought* (New York: Warner Books, 1999), 76; Elizabeth Weise, "Sizing Up Web Shoppers for the Perfect Fit," USA Today, 21 April 1999, 4D.

57. Paul Dean, "Auto Makers Shift into New Gear," *Los Angeles Times,* 15 January 1997, E1, E6.

58. Bill Dedman, "Holiday Vigil for FedEx Customers," *New York Times,* 8 November 1998, sec. 3, 4.

CHAPTER 15

1. Floorgraphics Web site [accessed 9 August 2000] www.floorgraphics.com; John Grossman, "Upstarts: Nontraditional

Ads," *Inc.,* March 2000, 23–26; David Wellman, "Floor 'Toons," *Supermarket Business,* 15 November 1999, 47; Skip Wollenberg, "Advertising Finds New Canvases," *Boulder News,* 1 June 1999 [accessed 8 April 2000] community.bouldernews.com/business/01bads.html; "Floor Show," *Dallas Morning News,* 4 September 1998, 11D.

2. Timothy E. Moore, "Subliminal Advertising: What You See Is What You Get," *Journal of Marketing,* Spring 1982, 38–47; Jack Haberstroh, "Can't Ignore Subliminal Ad Charges," *Advertising Age,* 17 September 1984, 3, 42, 44.

3. Chris Adams, "FDA Tells Glaxo to Halt Airing Flu Commercial," *Wall Street Journal,* 14 January 2000, B3.

4. Michele Marchetti, "What a Sales Call Costs," *Sales and Marketing Management,* September 2000, 80–82.

5. Direct Marketing Association Web site [accessed 23 November 1997] www.the-dma.org/services1/libres-home1b.shtml.

6. Gary Armstrong and Philip Kotler, *Marketing: An Introduction* (Upper Saddle River, N.J.: Prentice Hall, 2000), 409.

7. Beth Belton, "Technology is Changing Face of U.S. Sales Force," *USA Today,* 9 February 1999, 1A, 2A.

8. David Prater, "The Third Time's the Charm," *Sales and Marketing Management,* September 2000, 100–104; Armstrong and Kotler, *Marketing an Introduction,* 454.

9. "Rethinking the Sales Force," *Soundview Executive Book Summaries,* Pt. 3, vol. 21, no. 7 (July 1999): 1–8.

10. Dennis K. Berman, "From Cell Phones to Sell Phones," *Business Week,* 11 September 2000, 88–90.

11. Paul Duke Jr., and Ronald Alsop, "Advertisers Beginning to Play Off Worker Concern over Job Security," *Wall Street Journal,* 1 April 1988, A11; Ronald Alsop, "More Food Advertising Plays on Cancer and Cardiac Fears," *Wall Street Journal,* 8 October 1987, 33; George E. Belch and Michael A. Belch, *Introduction to Advertising and Promotion Management* (Homewood, Ill.: Irwin, 1990), 186.

12. Thomas R. King, "Pitches on Value Stick in Consumers' Minds," *Wall Street Journal,* 4 June 1990, B1.

13. Mark Hyman, "The Yin and Yang of the Tiger Effect," *Business Week,* 16 October 2000, 110.

14. Richard Sandomir, "Tiger Woods Signs Pact with American Express," *New York Times,* 20 May 1997, C1.

15. Weld Royal, "A Brand New Pitch," *Industry Week,* 6 March 2000, 41–42.

16. Janet Neiman, "The Trouble with Comparative Ads," *Adweek's Marketing Week,* 12 January 1987, 4–5; Joseph B. White, "Ford Decides to Fight Back in Truck Ads," *Wall Street Journal,* 28 February 1989, B1, B6.

17. Berman, "From Cell Phones to Sell Phones," 88–90.

18. "Direct Hit," *The Economist,* 9 January 1999, 55–57.

19. Sarah Lorge, "Banner Ads vs. E-Mail Marketing," *Sales and Marketing Management,* August 1999, 15.

20. Christine Blank, "Beating the Banner Ad," *American Demographics,* June 2000, 42–44.

21. Roger Reece, "The New Generation of Integrated Inbound/ Outbound Telemarketing Systems," *Telemarketing,* March 1995, 58–65; Malynda H. Madzel, "Outsourcing Telemarketing: Why It May Work for You," *Telemarketing,* March 1995, 48–49; "Despite Hangups, Telemarketing a Success," *Marketing News,* 27 March 1995, 19.

22. Bruce Horovitz, "Telemarketers on Hold," *USA Today,* 24 August 1999, 1A; Jerry Cerasale, "Pertinent New and Pending Legislation for Telephone Marketers," *Call Center Solutions,* November 1999, 104–7.

23. Bruce Haring, "Step Right Up for the Next Push in Remote Control," *USA Today,* 15 September 1999, 7D.

24. Nadya Labi, "Tae-Bo or Not Tae-Bo?" *Time,* 15 March 1999, 77.

25. Timothy R. Hawthorne, "Opening Doors to Retail Stores," *Direct Marketing,* January 1998, 48–51.

26. "Direct Marketing Industry Electronic Media Survey Results March 1999," Direct Marketing Association Web site [accessed 26 October 2000] www.the-dma.org/library/publications/electronicmedia99.shtml.

27. Jennifer Gilbert, "Really Booming Net Grabs $3.6 Billion," *Advertising Age,* 5 June 2000, 44, 52.

28. Efraim Turban, Jae Lee, David King, and H. Michael Chung, *Electric Commerce a Managerial Perspective* (Upper Saddle River, N.J.: Prentice Hall, 2000), 120.

29. Rebecca Quick, "E-Tailers Say, 'Bah, Humbug!' to Lavish Ads," *Wall Street Journal,* 22 September 2000, B1, B4.

30. Jennifer Rewick, "Beyond Banners," *Wall Street Journal,* 23 October 2000, R38.

31. "Promotional Trends Survey Caps Two Decades," *Cox Direct,* 14 September 1998 [accessed 24 May 1999] www.justdelivered.com/itm/pressreleases/pr-091498.htm.

32. "Coupons, Samples Drive Consumer Shopping Decisions," Cox Direct, 8 September 1998 [accessed 24 May 1999] www.justdelivered.com/itm/pressreleases/pr-090898-2.htm.

33. Paulette Thomas, "'e-Clicking' Coupons On-Line Has a Cost: Privacy," *Wall Street Journal,* 18 June 1998, B1, B8.

34. Micheline Maynard, "Ford Follows GM's Lead into Coupon Competition," *USA Today,* 24 April 1998, B1.

35. John Philip Jones, "The Double Jeopardy of Sales Promotions," *Harvard Business Review,* September–October 1990, 145–52; Laurie Petersen, "The Pavlovian Syndrome," *Adweek's Marketing Week,* 9 April 1990, P6–P7; "Coupons—Still the Shopper's Best Friend," *Progressive Grocer,* February 1995, SS11.

36. William M. Bulkeley, "Rebates' Secret Appeal to Manufacturers: Few Customers Actually Redeem Them," *Wall Street Journal,* 10 February 1998, B1, B8.

37. Lisa Z. Eccles, "Point of Purchase Advertising," *Advertising Age Supplement,* 26 September 1994, 1–6.

38. "Effective Sampling Strategies," *Sales Marketing Network* [accessed 7 November 2000] www.info-now.com/html/1022dir1.asp.

39. Mark Kleinman, "Olympics Beats Sponsor Goal By 50%," *Marketing,* 7 September 2000, 1.

40. Bob Tedeschi, "Running a Joint Promotion with Yahoo, Pepsi is in the Internet Generation," *New York Times,* 3 April 2000, C11.

41. Betsy Morris, "The Brand's the Thing," *Fortune,* 4 March 1996, 72–86.

42. Kate Bertrand, "Trade Shows Can Be Global Gateways," *Advertising Age's Business Marketing,* March 1995, 19–20; "Trade Shows: An Alternative Method of Selling," *Small Business Reports,* January 1985, 67.

43. Paul Holmes, "Public Relations," *Adweek's Marketing Week,* 11 September 1989, 234–35.

44. Kathryn Kranhold and Stephen Power, "Bridgestone Turns to Ketchum to Redo Image After Tire Recall," *Wall Street Journal,* 12 September 2000, A4.

45. Verne Gay, "Milk, the Magazine," *American Demographics,* February 2000, 32–33.

46. Armstrong and Kotler, *Marketing: An Introduction,* 405.

47. Wendy Zellner, "Southwest's New Direction," *Business Week,* 8 February 1999, 58–59; Jennifer Lawrence, "Integrated Mix Makes Expansion Fly," *Advertising Age—Special Integrated Marketing Report,* 4 November 1993, S10–S12.

48. Janet Smith, "Integrated Marketing," *American Demographics,* November 1995, 62.

49. Mark Maremont, "How Gillette Brought Its Mach3 to Market," *Wall Street Journal,* 15 April 1998, B1, B4; Jeremy Kahn, "Gillette Loses Face," *Fortune,* 8 November 1999, 147–48.

50. David J. Morrow, "From Lab to Patient, by Way of Your Den," *New York Times,* 7 June 1998, sec. 3, 1, 10.

51. Adapted from "Boston Consulting Group: E-commerce Sites Still Failing Shoppers," *NUA Internet Surveys* [accessed 22 April 2000] www.nua.ie/surveys; Laurie Windham, *Dead Ahead* (New York: Allworth Press, 1999), 27–47; Brian Hurley and Peter Birkwood, *A Small Business Guide to Doing Big Business on the Internet* (Bellingham, Wash.: International Self-Counsel Press, 1996), 124–34; "Design a Better Web Site," *Journal of Accountancy,* August 1998, 18; Anita Dennis, "A Home on the Web," *Journal of Accountancy,* August 1998, 29–31; Laura Morelli, "Writing for a Global Audience on the Web," *Marketing News,* 17 August 1998, 16; Yuri and Anna Radzievsky, "Successful Global Web Sites Look Through Eyes of the Audience," *Advertising Age's Business Marketing,* January 1998, 17; Sari Kalin, "The Importance of Being Multiculturally Correct," *Computerworld,* 6 October 1997, G16–G17.

52. Adapted from Heather Chaplin, "Smell My Candie's," *American Demographics,* August 1999, 64–65.

CHAPTER 16

1. Arthur Schatzman, co-owner, Dental Limited, personal communication, December 2000.

2. Elizabeth MacDonald, "U.S. Accounting Board Faults Global Rules," *Wall Street Journal,* 18 October 1999, A1.

3. Jeffrey E. Garten, "Global Accounting Rules? Not So Fast," *Business Week,* 5 April 1999, 26; MacDonald, "U.S. Accounting Board Faults Global Rules."

4. John Von Brachel, "AICPA Chairman Lays the Foundation for the Future," *Journal of Accountancy,* November 1995, 64–67.

5. Tom Kennedy Smith, "The Changing Face of Accounting Services," Corporate Report—Minnesota, 1 August 1996, 61.

6. Melody Petersen, "Shortage of Accounting Students Raises Concern on Audit Quality," *New York Times,* 19 February 1999, C1, C3.

7. Richard Melcher, "Where Are the Accountants?" *Business Week,* 5 October 1998, 144–46.

8. Jennifer Reingold and Richard A. Melcher, "Then There Were Four," *Business Week,* 3 November 1997, 37; Sallie L. Gaines, "KPMG and Ernst Call Off Merger," *Chicago Tribune,* 14 February 1998, B1,B3.

9. Ralph Saul, "Keeping the Watchdog Healthy," *Financial Executive,* November–December 1995, 10–13; Melcher, "Where Are the Accountants?"

10. Daniel McGinn, "Sherlocks of Finance," *Newsweek,* 24 August 1998, 38–39.

11. Robert Stuart, "Accountants in Management—A Globally Changing Role," *CMA Magazine,* 1 February 1997, 5.

12. Jack L. Smith, Robert M. Keith, and William L. Stephens, *Accounting Principles,* 4th ed. (New York: McGraw-Hill, 1993), 16–17.

13. Stanley Zarowin, "The Future of Finance," *Journal of Accountancy,* August 1995, 47–49.

14. Frank Evans, "A Road Map to Your Financial Report," *Management Review,* October 1993, 39–47.

15. Jeremy Kahn, "Presto Chango! Sales Are Huge!" *Fortune,* 20 March 2000, 90–96; Robert D. Hershey Jr., "Brave New Math Tests Limits of Accounting," *New York Times,* 20 March 2000, E-37; Norm Alster, "Cooking the Books," *Upside Today,* 12 January 2000 [accessed 27 October 2000] www.upside.com Elizabeth MacDonald, "SEC to Boost Accounting-Fraud Attack, Work More With Criminal Prosecutors," *Wall Street Journal,* 8 December 1999, A6; Catherine Yang, "Earth to Dot-Com Accountants," *Business Week,* 3 April 2000,

40–41; Elizabeth MacDonald, "Are Those Revenues for Real?" *Forbes,* 29 March 2000, 108–10.

16. Adapted from "Technology: Sound Chamber," *Newsweek,* 13 May 1996, 10.

CHAPTER 17

1. "Intuit, Metiom Plan Internet Marketplace for Small Businesses," *Wall Street Journal,* 11 September 2000, B8; Khanh T. L. Tran, "Intuit Beats Estimate for Quarter," *Wall Street Journal,* 24 May 2000, B6; Orla O'Sullivan, "Intuit's Opening Portals," *USBanker,* January 2000, 26; Glenn Coleman, "The Battle for Your Money," *Money,* December 1999, 134–40; Kathleen Murphy, "He Wants You to Pay Your Bills on the Web: An Interview with Intuit CEO Bill Harris," *Internet World,* 15 August 1999, 22–26; Tim McCollum, "End Your Internet Anxieties Now," *Nation's Business,* April 1999, 18–22; Steve Klinkerman, "The Perils of Progress," *Banking Strategies,* March–April 1999, 20–26; David Diamond, "Can Intuit Remake Itself on the Net?" *Upside,* September 1998, 96–100; Steve Hamm, "This Intuit Hunch May Pay Off," *Business Week,* 15 June 1998, 123; Edward W. Desmond, "Intuit Online," *Fortune,* 13 April 1998, 149–52; Eryn Brown, "Is Intuit Headed for a Meltdown?" *Fortune,* 18 August 1997, 200–202.

2. David H. Bangs Jr., "Financial Troubleshooting," *Soundview Executive Book Summaries* 15, no. 5 (May 1993).

3. Dean Foust, "The Check is in the E-Mail," *Business Week,* 30 October 2000, 120–22.

4. Bruce Horovitz and Chris Woodyard, "Quaker Oats' $1.4 Billion Washout," *USA Today,* 28 March 1997.

5. Mandy Andress, "Smart Is Not Enough: Cards Must Also Be Easy and Useful," *InfoWorld,* 16 October 2000, 94; Mary Shacklett, "American Express' Blue is Setting the Pace in U.S. Smart Card Market," *Credit Union Magazine,* September 2000, 16A–17A.

6. Beth Kwon, "Need Stamps, Stocks, Plane Tickets? Step Up to an ATM," *Newsweek,* 25 January 1999, 15; Kara K. Choquette, "Super ATMs Sell Lift Tickets, Exchange Currencies," *USA Today,* 19 January 1998, B1; Connie Guglielmo, "Here Come the Super-ATMs," *Fortune,* 14 October 1996, 232–34.

7. Thomas McCarroll, "No Checks. No Cash. No Fuss?" *Time,* 9 May 1994, 60–61.

8. Scott Woolley, "Virtual Banker," *Forbes,* 15 June 1998 [accessed 28 July 1999] www.forbes.com/forbes/98/0615/6112127a.htm; Dean Foust, "Will Online Banking Replace the ATM?" Yahoo! Internet Life, November 1998, 114–18.

9. "FDIC Statistics on Banking: Number of FDIC-Insured Commercial Banks, 1934 Through 1999," FDIC Databank [accessed 12 December 2000] www2.fdic.gov/hsob/SelectRpt.asp?EntryTyp510.

10. Stephan Labaton, "Accord Reached on Lifting Depression-Era Barriers Among Financial Industries," *New York Times,* 23 October 1999, A1, B4.

11. Patrick McGeehan, "Merrill Lynch Is Set to Move into Banking," *New York Times,* 26 January 2000, C1, C6.

12. Leah Nathans Spiro, "The Coca-Cola of Personal Finance," *Business Week,* 20 April 1998, 37–38; Joseph Nocera, "E-Banking Is Necessary—Banks Are Not," *Fortune,* 11 May 1998, 84–85; Glenn Coleman, "The Battle for Your Money," *Money,* December 1999, 134–40; Lorrie Grant, "Retail King Gets Thrifty Idea," *USA Today,* 30 June 1999, B1.

13. Sharon Nelton, "You Can Bank on the Personal Touch," *Nation's Business,* June 1999, 49–51.

14. "Important Banking Legislation," FDIC [accessed 28 July 1999] www.fdic.gov/publish/banklaws.html; "Interstate Branching," The Federal Reserve Board [accessed 23 July 1999] www.bog.frb.fed.us/generalinfo/isb.

15. Robert A. Rosenblatt, "Border Crossing," *Los Angeles Times,* 5 June 1994, D1, D4.

16. Jeffrey E. Garten, "The Fed Should Look Farther Than Its Own Backyard," *Business Week,* 31 August 1998, 18.

17. Laura Cohn, "Are T-Bills Y2K Insurance?" *Business Week,* 26 July 1999, 34.

18. Jathon Sapsford, "Consumers Take Notice of Online Banks," *Wall Street Journal,* 28 November 2000, C1, C19; Lauren Bielski, "Online Banking Yet to Deliver," *American Bankers Association, ABA Banking Journal,* September 2000, 6, 12+; Adam Romber, "World's Best Internet Banks," *Global Finance,* August 2000, 15–31; Heather Timmons, "Online Banks Can't Go It Alone," *Business Week,* 31 July 2000, 86–87; Mark Skousen, "Online Banking's Goodies," *Forbes,* 12 June 2000, P366+; Paul S. Nadler, "Fact and Fiction in Internet Banking," *The Secured Lender,* May–June 2000, 44–48; Tony Stanco, "Internet Banking—Some Big Players, But Little Returns So Far," *Boardwatch,* March 2000, 86–90; Carrick Mollenkamp, "Old-Line Banks Advance in Bricks-vs.-Clicks Battle," *Wall Street Journal,* 21 January 2000, C1; Christine Dugas, "Internet Bank Piques Interest with Rate Offer," *USA Today,* 27 April 1999, 1B; Christine Dugas, "Virtual Banks Get Real, Offer Deals to Woo Customers," *USA Today,* 13 April 2000, 12B; John Hechinger, "Check It Out," *Wall Street Journal,* 12 February 2001, R28.

19. Joseph B. Cahill, "Regulators Discover There Is No There at a 'Virtual' Bank," *Wall Street Journal,* 1 September 1998, A1, A6.

CHAPTER 18

1. Mike Hoffman, "Let's Get Physical," *Inc.,* 17 October 2000, 168–169; Louise Lee, "Tricks of E*Trade," *Business Week E.Biz,* 7 February 2000, EB18–EB31; Louise Lee, "Not Just Clicks Anymore," *Business Week,* 28 August 2000, 226–227; "The Story of E*Trade," E*Trade [accessed 28 April 1999] www.etrade.com; "More Secure Securities," E*Trade [accessed 28 April 1999] www.etrade.com; Kathleen Ohlson, "E*Trade Revenue Soars, Losses Continue," *Computerworld,* 20 April 1999 [accessed 28 April 1999] www.computerworld.com/home/news.nsf/all/9904202etrade; Saul Hansell, "Trading on E*Trade's Success," *New York Times,* 16 March 1999, C1, C11; Leah Nathans Spiro, "Will E*Trade Move Beyond E*Tragedy?" *Business Week,* 22 February 1999, 118; Sharon Machlis, "Glitch Snuffs Out Online Broker for Hours," *Computerworld,* 4 February 1999 [accessed 28 April 1999] www.computerworld.com/home/news.nsf/all/9902044etrade; Kimberly Weisul, "E*Trade Snafu Results in $4 Million Earnings Hit," *Investment Dealer's Digest,* 14 July 1997, 6–7; "E*Trade Solidifies Industry Leadership by Adding over 1,000,000 Net New Active Accounts in 12 months," E*Trade, 13 October 1999 [accessed 10 December 1999] www.etrade.com; Paul Beckett, "E*Trade Cases Net in Search of Alliances," *Wall Street Journal,* 20 March 2000, C1, C2.

2. "An Investor's Guide to Corporate Bonds: How Big Is the Market and Who Buys?" Bond Market Association [accessed 27 July 1999] www.investinginbonds.com/info/igcorp/big.htm.

3. David Rynecki, "CBOT Gazes into the Pit," *Fortune,* 15 May 2000, 279–94.

4. Harvey Shapiro, "You Gotta Have a Style," *Hemispheres,* July 1997, 53–55.

5. Martin L. Leibowitz and Stanley Kogelman, "Asset Allocation Under Shortfall Constraints," *Journal of Portfolio Management,* Winter 1991, 18–23.

6. Neil Weinberg, "The Big Board Comes Back from the Brink," *Forbes,* 13 November 2000, 274–81; New York Stock Exchange Web site [accessed 21 December 2000] www.nyse.com.

7. NASDAQ Web Site [accessed 20 December 2000] www.marketdata.nasdaq.com/asp/Sec1Summary.asp.

8. James K. Glassman, "Manager's Journal: Who Needs Stock Exchanges? Not Investors," *Wall Street Journal,* 8 May 2000, A42.

9. NASDAQ Web site [accessed 21 December 2000] www.nasdaq.com/about/nnm1.stm; American Stock Exchange Web

site [accessed 21 December 2000] www.amex.com/about/amex_listus. stm; New York Stock Exchange Web site [accessed 21 December 2000] www.nyse.com/listed/listedr.html.

10. Greg Ip, "Big Board Overhauls Its Standards," *Wall Street Journal,* 5 June 1998, C1, C16.

11. Julie Bort, "Trading Places," *Computerworld,* 27 May 1996, 1051.

12. Fred Vogelstein, "A Virtual Stock Market," *U.S. News & World Report,* 26 April, 1999, 47–48.

13. Weinberg, "The Big Board Comes Back from the Brink."

14. Diana B. Henriques, "Stock Markets, Facing Threats, Pursue Changes," *New York Times on the Web,* 6 March 1999 [accessed 7 March 1999] www.nytimes.com/library/financial/030799market-changes.htm.

15. Mike McNamee and Paula Dwyer, "A Revolt at NASD?" *Business Week,* 2 August 1999, 70–71.

16. Weinberg, "The Big Board Comes Back from the Brink."

17. Michael Schroeder and Randall Smith, "Sweeping Change in Market Structure Sought," *Wall Street Journal,* 29 February 2000, C1.

18. Rynecki, "CBOT Gazes into the Pit."

19. David Barboza, "In Chicago's Trading Pits, This May Be the Final Generation," *New York Times,* 6 August 2000, sec. 3, 1, 12.

20. Lee Copeland, "After-Hours Trading," *Computerworld,* 27 March 2000, 57.

21. Copeland, "After-Hours Trading."

22. Rebecca Buckman, "Making the Trade: What Now?" *Wall Street Journal Online Investing,* 14 June 1999, R6.

23. Leah Nathans Spiro, "Bullish on the Internet," *Business Week,* 14 June 1999, 45–46.

24. Nanette Byrnes, "How Schwab Grabbed the Lion's Share," *Business Week,* 28 June 1998, 88.

25. John R. Dorfman, "Crash Courses," *Wall Street Journal,* 28 May 1996, R12–R13.

26. Katrina Brooker, "Could the Dow Become Extinct?" *Fortune,* 15 February 1999, 194–95; Anita Raghavan and Nancy Ann Jeffrey, "What, How, Why—So What Is the Dow Jones Industrial Average, Anyway?" *Wall Street Journal,* 28 May 1996, R30; E. S. Browning, "New Economy Stocks Join Industrials," *Wall Street Journal,* 27 October 1999, C1, C15.

27. Jeffrey M. Laderman, "Why It's So Tough to Beat the S&P," *Business Week,* 24 March 1997, 82–83.

28. E. S. Browning, "Journal Goes 'Decimal' With Nasdaq Tables," *Wall Street Journal,* 2 August 2000, C1; "SEC Orders Decimal Stock Prices," *Chicago Tribune,* 29 January 2000, sec. 2, 2.

29. David Diamond, "The Web's Most Wanted," *Business 2.0,* August 1999, 120–28.

30. Thor Valdmanis and Tom Lowry, "Wall Street's New Breed Revives Inside Trading," *USA Today,* 4 November 1999, 1B.

31. Joseph Nocera, "No Whispering Allowed," *Money,* December 2000, 71–74; Heather Timmons, "The Full Disclosure Rule Could Mean More Secrets," *Business Week,* 9 October 2000, 198; Lee Clifford, "The SEC Wants to Open the Info Vault," *Fortune,* 13 November 2000, 434.

32. Amy Feldman, "The Seedy World of Online Stock Scams," *Money,* February 2000, 143–48.

33. Feldman, "The Seedy World of Online Stock Scams"; Aaron Lucchetti, "Some Web Sites Getting Tough on Stock Chat," *Wall Street Journal,* 28 May 1999, C1, C20; Rebecca Buckman, "NASD Maps War on Claims on Internet," *Wall Street Journal,* 24 March 1997, B98W.

34. Adapted from Pallavi Gogoi, "Rage Against Online Brokers," *Business Week E.Biz,* 20 November 2000, EB98–EB102; Christopher Farrell, "Online or Off, the Rules Are the Same," *Business Week,* 22 May 2000, 148–49; Andrew Fraser, "The Great Equalizer," *Wall Street Journal,* 12 June 2000, R6; Stephen Labaton, "On-Line Trades Rise and So Do the Complaints," *New York Times,* 28 January 1999, A1, C21; Paula Dwyer, "What to Do When Your Online Broker Screws Up," *Business Week,* 19 June 2000, 257–58.

35. Valdmanis and Lowry, "Wall Street's New Breed Revives Inside Trading."

36. Labaton, "On-line Trades Rise and So Do the Complaints."

COMPONENT CHAPTER B

1. William H. Miller, "Growth of Government," *Industry Week,* 21 September 1998, 83–94.

2. Joel Brinkley, "U.S. Judge Says Microsoft Violated Antitrust Laws with Predatory Behavior," *New York Times,* 4 April 2000, A1, C12; Merrill Goozner, "Microsoft Is Ruled an Illegal Monopoly," *Chicago Tribune,* 4 April 2000, sec.1, 1, 16; Ted Bridis and John R. Wilke, "Judge Orders Microsoft Broken in Two, Imposes Tough Restriction on Practices," *Wall Street Journal,* 8 June 2000, A3, A12; "Judge Suspends Restrictions on Microsoft," *Wall Street Journal,* 21 June 2000, A3; John R. Wilke and Rebecca Buckman, "Justices Decline Early Look at Microsoft," *Wall Street Journal,* 27 September 2000, A3, A17.

3. Henry R. Cheeseman, *Business Law,* 4th ed. (Upper Saddle River, N.J.: Prentice Hall, 2001), 899.

4. "Hundt Calls Internet Key to Competition," *Newsbytes News Network,* 28 August 1997; Susan Benkelman, "Free Cyberspeech Ruling Strikes Indecency Law," *Newsday,* 26 June 1997, A5; "FCC Paper Seeks to Limit Internet Regulation," *Newsbytes News Network,* 31 March 1997.

5. "The United States: The Electric Acid Test," *The Economist,* 25 September 1999, 29–30.

6. Wendy M. Beech, "Deregulation: Bonanza or Bust?" *Black Enterprise,* May 1998, 93–99; Tim Jones, "Consumers Yet to See Benefits of Telecom Act," *Chicago Tribune,* 28 January 2001, sec. 1, 1, 14.

7. Agis Salpukas, "California's Effort to Promote Plan for Electricity Is Off to a Slow Start," *New York Times,* 26 February 1998, C1, C6; James Worsham, "States Plug In to Deregulation," *Nation's Business,* April 1998, 66.

8. Robert J. Samuelson, "The Joy of Deregulation," *Newsweek,* 3 February 1997, 39.

9. Internal Revenue Service, Form 1120 Instructions for 2000 [accessed 15 January 2000] www.irs.ustreas.gov/prod/ forms_pubs/ instruct/index.html.

10. *Survey of Current Business* (Washington, D.C.: GPO, December 1997), D8.

11. Carl Weiser, "Lobbying: Players Say It's More Than Fat Cats, Money, Back-Room Deals," *Gannett News Service,* 4 June 1997.

12. Melinda Henneberger, "An Arm Twister's Dream Job," *New York Times,* 24 June 1997, C1.

13. Richard L. Berke, "Donors to Parties Sidestepped Rules," *New York Times,* 18 May 1991, sec. b, 7.

14. Cheeseman, *Business Law,* 67.

15. Cheeseman, *Business Law,* 182.

16. Caroline E. Mayer, "FTC Challenges Antibacterial Claims," *Washington Post,* 17 September 1999, A91.

17. "Stone Settles FTC Price Fix Charger," *Pulp & Paper,* April 1998, 19.

18. Elizabeth MacDonald, "SEC Alleges KPMG Violated Rules by Auditing Client of Former Affiliate," Wall Street Journal Interactive Edition [accessed 5 December 1997] www.wsj.com.

19. George A. Steiner and John F. Steiner, *Business, Government, and Society* (New York: McGraw-Hill, 1991), 149.

20. Mike France, "Order in the Business Court," *Business Week,* 9 December 1996, 138–140.

21. Cheeseman, *Business Law,* 91.

22. Jacqueline Bueno, "Home Depot to Fight Sex-Bias Charges," *Wall Street Journal,* 19 September 1997, B5; Edward Felsenthal, "Punitive Awards Are Called Modest, Rare," *Wall Street Journal,* 17 June 1996, B2.

23. Cheeseman, *Business Law,* 93.

24. "For the Record, What's the Beef, Oprah," *London Free Press,* 14 February 1998, F5; Deborah Frazier, "Cattlemen Have Beef with Oprah—Stock Raisers Angry That TV Host Maligned Food They're Proud Of," *Denver Rocky Mountain News,* 21 January 1998, 30A; "United States: No Beef with Oprah," *The Economist,* 7 March 1998, 29; Scott Baldauf, "In Oprah Trial, Food Libel Charges Prove Hard to Swallow," *Christian Science Monitor,* 27 February 1998, 3.

25. Bartley A. Brennan and Nancy K. Kubasek, *The Legal Environment of Business* (New York: McGraw-Hill, 1990), 184.

26. "Reasonable Product-Liability Reform," *Nation's Business,* 1 September 1997, 88.

27. David J. Morrow, "Maker of Diet Pill Agrees to Pay $3.75 Billion to Settle Liability Case," *New York Times* Web site [accessed 8 October 1999] www.nytimes.com.

28. Thomas W. Dunfee, Frank F. Gibson, John D. Blackburn, Douglas Whitman, F. William McCarty, and Bartley A. Brennan, *Modern Business Law* (New York: Random House, 1989), 569.

29. "Reasonable Product-Liability Reform"; Stephen Blakely, "Getting a Handle on Liability Coverage," *Nation's Business,* 1 September 1997, 87; John M. Broder, "Clinton Vetoes Bill to Limit Product-Liability Lawsuits," *Los Angeles Times,* 3 May 1996, A1.

30. Cheeseman, *Business Law,* 184.

31. Ethan A. Blumen, "Legal Land Mines," *Business 96,* June–July 1996, 53.

32. Dunfee et al., *Modern Business Law,* 284–97; Brennan and Kubasek, *The Legal Environment of Business,* 125–27; Douglas Whitman and John William Gergacz, *The Legal Environment of Business,* 2d ed. (New York: Random House, 1988), 196–97; *The Lawyer's Almanac* (Englewood Cliffs, N.J.: Prentice Hall Law & Business, 1991), 888.

33. Brennan and Kubasek, *The Legal Environment of Business,* 128.

34. James Bates, "Disney Settles Up with Its Former Studio Boss," *Los Angeles Times,* 8 July 1999, 1; Bruce Orwall, "Katzenberg Wins Round in Lawsuit with Walt Disney," *Wall Street Journal,* 20 May 1999, B161.

35. Roy Furchgott, "Opposition Builds to Mandatory Arbitration at Work," *New York Times,* 20 July 1997, F11; Barry Meier, "In Fine Print, Customers Lose Ability to Sue," *New York Times,* 10 March 1997, A1, C7.

36. Cheeseman, *Business Law,* 364–366, 446.

37. Cheeseman, *Business Law,* 588.

38. Brennan and Kubasek, *The Legal Environment of Business,* 160.

39. Del Jones, "Businesses Battle Over Intellectual Property," *USA Today,* 2 August 2000, 1B, 2B.

40. "Apple Computers: Apple Secures Worldwide Injunctions Against Daewoo and eMachines," *M2 Presswire,* 8 March 2000, 1.

41. Mike Snider, "Law Targets Copyright Theft Online," *USA Today,* 18 December 1998, A1.

42. Tariq K. Muhammad, "Real Law in a Virtual World," *Black Enterprise,* December 1996, 44.

43. Cheeseman, *Business Law,* 456–57.

44. Ronald A. Anderson, Ivan Fox, and David P. Twomey, *Business Law* (Cincinnati: South-Western Publishing, 1987), 635.

45. Cheeseman, *Business Law,* 575.

46. Dale Kasler, "Carson's Department Store Chain Manager Stronger After Bankruptcy," *Gannett News Service,* 21 November 1994.

47. "Business and Finance," *Wall Street Journal,* 29 December 2000, A1; Kevin Helliker, "Montgomery Ward to End 128-Year Run in Retailing," *Wall Street Journal,* 29 December 2000, A3.

COMPONENT CHAPTER C

1. "Hurricanes and the Insurance Crisis," *American Business Review,* 21 September 1997, 21; Matt Walsh, "Deeper Pockets," *Forbes,* 26 September 1994, 42–44.

2. John S. DeMott, "Think Like A Risk Manager," *Nation's Business,* June 1995, 30–32.

3. Mark S. Dorfman, *Introduction to Risk Management and Insurance,* 6th ed. (Upper Saddle River, N.J.: Prentice Hall, 1999), 322–23.

4. Branda Paik Sunno, "After Everything Else—Buy Insurance," *Workforce,* October 1998, 45–50.

5. Judy Feldman, "What Daredevil CEO's Can Cost," *Money,* April 1999, 321.

6. Laura M. Litvan, "Switching to Self-Insurance," *Nation's Business,* March 1996, 16–21; Joseph B. Treaster, "Protecting Against the Little Risks," *New York Times,* 31 December 1996, C1, C15.

7. John S. DeMott, "Think Like a Risk Manager," *Nation's Business,* June 1995, 30–32.

8. "Employees Prefer Finding Their Own Health Care Coverage," *Employee Benefit Plan Review,* March 2000, 49.

9. Dorfman, *Introduction to Risk Management and Insurance,* 505.

10. Sidney Marchasin, "Cost Shifting: How One Hospital Does It," *Wall Street Journal,* 9 December 1991, A10.

11. "Health Reform Continues on the State Level," *Employee Benefit Plan Review,* December 1997, 48–49.

12. *1991 Life Insurance Fact Book, Update* (Washington, D.C.: American Council of Life Insurance, 1991), 4.

13. Martin Kasindorf and Ken Fireman, "The Clinton Budget/2002Solution," *Newsday,* 7 February 1997, A04; Mark R. Greene and James S. Trieschmann, *Risk and Insurance* (Cincinnati: South-Western Publishing, 1988), 81.

14. Dorfman, *Introduction to Risk Management and Insurance,* 524.

15. Jon Forman, "Rescue in the Balance," *Barron's,* 18 December 2000, 54; Jane Bryant Quinn, "A Challenge, Not a Crisis," *Newsweek,* 3 July 2000, 26.

16. Doug Bandow, "Let Big Business Fix Social Security," *Fortune,* 8 December 1997, 56–60.

17. Lorraine Woellert, "A New Safety Net for the New Economy," *Business Week,* 28 February 2000, 157.

18. Bob Tedeschi, "E-Commerce Report," *New York Times,* 20 March 2000, C12; Bethany McLean, "Death of a Salesman," *Fortune,* 17 April 2000, 212–22.

19. Amada Levin, "Ethics Rates Highest When Hiring Insurance Staff," *National Underwriter,* 12 April 1999, 4, 65.

COMPONENT CHAPTER D

1. Bureau of Labor Statistics, *1998–99 Occupational Outlook Handbook* [accessed 10 August 1999], www.bls.gov/ocohome.htm, Webmaster career information from Excite Careers, Internet Industry Focus [accessed 10 August 1999] careers.excite.com/cgi-cls/display.exe?xc-xca+Career+WetFeet1Industry+HiTech_InternetWebmaster.

2. Richard Nelson Bolles, *The 1997 What Color Is Your Parachute?* (Berkeley, Calif.: Ten Speed Press, 1996), 129–66; Karen W. Arenson, "Placement Offices Leave Old Niches to Become Computerized Job Bazaars," *New York Times,* 17 July 1996, B12; Lawrence J. Magid, "Job Hunters Cast Wide Net Online," *Los Angeles Times,* 26 February 1996, 20; Richard Van Doren, "On-Line Career Advice Speeds Search for Jobs," *Network World,* 4 March 1996, 54; Alex Markels, "Job Hunting Takes Off in Cyberspace," *Wall Street Journal,* 20 September 1996, B1, B2;

Michael Chorost, "Jobs on the Web," *Hispanic*, October 1995, 50–53; Zane K. Quible, "Electronic Résumés: Their Time Is Coming," *Business Communication Quarterly* 58, no. 3 (1995): 5–9; Margaret Mannix, "The Home-Page Help Wanteds," *U.S. News & World Report*, 30 October 1995, 88, 90; Pam Dixon and Silvia Tiersten, *Be Your Own Headhunter Online* (New York: Random House, 1995), 53–69; Michele Himmelberg, "Internet an Important Tool in Employment Search," *San Diego Union-Tribune*, 7 September 1998, D2; Richard N. Bolles, "Career Strategizing, or What Color Is Your Web Parachute?" *Yahoo! Internet Life*, May 1998, 116–22; Valerie Frazee, "Online Job Services Explode," *Personnel Journal*, August 1996, 21.

3. Christoper Caggiano, "Recruiting Secrets," *Inc.*, October 1998, 29–42; Donna Fenn, "The Right Fit," *Inc. 500*, 1997, 1041.

4. Caggiano, "Recruiting Secrets."

5. Pam Stanley-Weigand, "Organizing the Writing of Your Résumé," *Bulletin of the Association for Business Communication* 54, no. 3 (September 1991): 11–12.

6. Janice Tovey, "Using Visual Theory in the Creation of Résumés: A Bibliography," *The Bulletin of the Association for Business Communication* 54, no. 3 (September 1991): 97–99.

7. Sal Divita, "If You're Thinking Résumé, Think Creatively," *Marketing News*, 14 September 1992, 29.

8. Richard H. Beatty and Nicholas C. Burkholder, *The Executive Career Guide for MBAs* (New York: Wiley, 1996), 133.

9. William H. Baker, Kristen DeTienne, and Karl L. Smart, "How Fortune 500 Companies Are Using Electronic Résumé Management Systems," *Business Communication Quarterly*, 61, no. 3 (September 1998): 8–19.

10. William J. Banis, "The Art of Writing Job-Search Letters," *CPC Annual, 36th Edition* 2 (1992): 42–50.

11. Banis, "The Art of Writing Job-Search Letters," 42–50.

12. Joel Russell, "Finding Solid Ground," *Hispanic Business*, February 1992, 42–44, 46.

13. Robert Gifford, Cheuk Fan Ng, and Margaret Wilkinson, "Nonverbal Cues in the Employment Interview: Links Between Applicant Qualities and Interviewer Judgments," *Journal of Applied Psychology* 70, no. 4 (1985): 729.

14. Amanda Bennett, "GE Redesigns Rungs of Career Ladder," *Wall Street Journal*, 15 March 1993, B1, B3.

15. Robin White Goode, "International and Foreign Language Skills Have an Edge," *Black Enterprise*, May 1995, 53.

16. Nancy M. Somerick, "Managing a Communication Internship Program," *Bulletin of the Association for Business Communication* 56, no. 3 (1993): 10–20.

17. Cheryl L. Noll, "Collaborating with the Career Planning and Placement Center in the Job-Search Project," *Business Communication Quarterly* 58, no. 3 (1995): 53–55.

■ Illustration and Text Credits

CHAPTER 1

6 Exhibit 1.1, U.S. Department of Commerce, Bureau of Economic Analysis [accessed 24 September 1999], beadata.bea.doc.gov/bea/dn2/gpoc.htm.

7 Exhibit 1.2, Noshua Watson, "Scarce Labor: Then and Now," *Fortune*, 15 May 2000, 496.

9 Exhibit 1.3, Adapted from Christopher Caggiano, "Will the Real Bootstrappers Please Stand Up?" *Inc.*, August 1995, 34; Mike Hofman, "Capitalism—A Bootstrappers' Hall of Fame," *Inc.*, August 1997, 54–57; 1999 Amazon.com Annual Report, Amazon Web site-Investor Relations [accessed 10 June 2000], www.amazon.com.

11 Exhibit 1.4, Adapted from Chris Woodyard, "Firms Stretch Travel Dollars," USA Today, 16 March 1999, sec. B, 1–2. Ted Bridis and John R. Wilke, "Judge Orders Microsoft Broken in Two, Imposes Tough Restrictions on Practices," *Wall Street Journal*, 8 June 2000, A3, A12.

16 Exhibit 1.6, Adapted from Budget of the United States Government Fiscal Year 2001, w3.access.gpo.gov/usbudget/index.html [accessed 21 April 2000].

17 Exhibit 1.7, Adapted from Roger LeRoy Miller, *Economics Today and Tomorrow* (New York: McGraw-Hill, 1999), 354.

19 Exhibit 1.8, Adapted from "100 Years of Innovation," *Business Week*, Summer 1999, 8+; Richard B. Brewer, "Is Biotech the Next High Tech?" *Forbes ASAP*, 31 May 1999, 60–62; *Inc. 20th Anniversary Issue*, 1999, 42–66; *Wall Street Journal Small Business*, 24 May 1999, R1–R30; Mark Borden, "Thinking About Tomorrow," *Fortune*, 22 November 1999, 170+.

22 Exhibit 1.9, "From GM to Cisco In Just Four Decades," *Business Week*, 7 February 2000, 40.

23 Focusing on E-Business Today: Adapted from "Competing in the Digital Age: How the Internet Will Transform Business," Booz-Allen & Hamilton Web site, www.bah.com/greatideas/pptdata/index.htm [accessed 21 April 1999].

COMPONENT CHAPTER A

32 Exhibit A.1, Adapted from *Search Engines Fact and Fun*, [accessed 11 March 1998], searchenginewatch.internet.com/facts/major.html; "Getting Started—What You Need to Know to Begin Using the Internet," *Fortune Technology Buyer's Guide*, Winter 1998, 232–240; Matt Lake, "Desperately Seeking Susan OR Suzie NOT Sushi," *New York Times*, 3 September 1998, D1, D7; "Notable Websites," *Fortune Technology Buyer's Guide*, Winter 1999; Stephen H. Wildstrom, "Search Engines with Smarts," *Business Week*, 8 February 1999, 22.

36 Exhibit A.3, Charles V. Callahan and Bruce A. Pasternack, "Corporate Strategy in the Digital Age," *Strategy and Business*, Second Quarter [accessed 21 April 2000], www.strategy-business.com/research/99202/page2.html.

37 Exhibit A.4, Adapted from Craig Fellenstein and Ron Wood, *Exploring E-Commerce, Global E-Business, and E-Societies* (Upper Saddle River, N.J.: Prentice Hall, 2000), 28.

38 Exhibit A.5, Adapted from Peter Fingar, Harsha Kumar, and Tarun Sharma, *Enterprise E-Commerce* (Tampa, Fla.: Meghan-Kiffer Press, 2000), 228–229; Laurie Windham, *Dead Ahead* (New York: Allworth Press, 1999), 57; Craig Fellenstein and Ron Wood, *Exploring E-Commerce, Global E-Business, and E-Societies* (Upper Saddle River, N.J.: Prentice Hall, 1999), 34.

CHAPTER 2

45 Recruiting the Thief to Protect the Jewels: Adapted from Karl Taro Greenfeld, "Meet the Napster," *Time*, 2 October 2000, 60–68; Jeremy Kahn, "Napster Legal Is a Tough Job for Boies," *Fortune*, 2 October 2000, 50–54; Adam Cohen and Bill Joy, "A Crisis of Content," *Time*, 2 October 2000, 68–73; Andrew Richard Albanese, "Napster: It's Not Just for Music," *Publishers Weekly*, 21 August 2000, 35–36; Spencer E. Ante, Steven V. Brull, Dennis K. Berman, and Mike France, "Inside Napster," *Business Week*, 14 August 2000, 112–120; Shawn Tully, "Big

Man Against Big Music," *Fortune*, 14 August 2000, 186–192; Adam Cohen, "Taps for Napster?" *Time*, 31 July 2000, 34–35; Don Clark, Anna Wilde Mathews, and Martin Peers, "Key Change: Napster Ruling Shifts Balance of Power Back to Music Industry," *Wall Street Journal*, 28 July 2000, A1; Fred Vogelstein, "Is It Sharing or Stealing?" *U.S. News & World Report*, 12 June 2000, 38–40; Kevin Maney, "File-Sharing Software May Transform the Net," *USA Today*, 7 June 2000, 1B–2B; Stephen Levy, "The Noisy War over Napster," *Newsweek*, 5 June 2000, 46–53; Jack Ewing, "A New Net Powerhouse," *Business Week*, 13 November 2000, 46–52; Thomas E. Weber, "Using 'Peer-to-Peer' To Make Net Smarter and More Productive," *Wall Street Journal*, 13 November 2000, B1. Lee Gomes, "Napster is Told to End Violations Quickly," *Wall Street Journal*, 7 March 2001, A3, A14.

46 Exhibit 2.1, Adapted from Manuel G. Velasquez, *Business Ethics: Concepts and Cases* (Upper Saddle River, N.J.: Prentice Hall, 1998), 87; Joseph L. Badaracco, Jr., "Business Ethics: Four Spheres of Executive Responsibility," *California Management Review*, Spring 1992, 64–79; Kenneth Blanchard and Norman Vincent Peale, *The Power of Ethical Management* (Reprint, 1989; New York: Fawcett Crest, 1991), 7–17; John R. Boatright, *Ethics and the Conduct of Business* (Upper Saddle River, N.J.: Prentice Hall, 1996), 35–39, 59–64, 79–86.

47 Exhibit 2.2, Adapted from *The Institute of Electrical and Electronics Engineers*, [accessed 21 July 1999], ieeeusa.org/documents/career/career_library/ethics.html.

48 Exhibit 2.3, "American Workers Do the Right Thing," *HR Focus*, March 1999, 4.

50 Exhibit 2.4, Weld Royal, "Real Expectations," *Industry Week*, 4 September 2000, 32.

56 Firestone and Ford: Failure to Yield . . . or Asleep at the Wheel?: Adapted from Joann Muller, David Welch, and Jeff Green, "Would You Buy One?" *Business Week*, 25 September 2000, 46–47; Timothy Aeppel, Stephen Power, and Milo Geyelin, "Firestone Breaks with Ford over Tire Pressure," *Wall Street Journal*, 22 September 2000, A3; Keith Naughton and Mark Hosenball, "Ford Vs. Firestone," *Newsweek*, 18 September 2000, 26–33; Keith Naughton, "Spinning Out of Control," *Newsweek*, 11 September 2000, 58; Stephen Power and Bob Simison, "Firestone Knew of Tire Safety Problems," *Wall Street Journal*, 7 September 2000, A3; Timothy Aeppel, Clare Ansberry, Milo Geyelin, and Robert L. Simison, "Road Signs: How Ford, Firestone Let the Warnings Slide By as Debacle Developed," *Wall Street Journal*, 6 September 2000, A1; Robert L. Simison, Norihiko Shirouzu, and Timothy Aeppel, "Ford Says It Knew of Venezuelan Tire Failures in 1998," *Wall Street Journal*, 30 August 2000, A3; Robert L. Simison, Norihiko Shirouzu, Timothy Aeppel, and Todd Zaun, "Pressure Points: Tension Between Ford and Firestone Mounts Amid Recall Efforts," *Wall Street Journal*, 28 August 2000, A1.

59 Exhibit 2.6, Workplace Killers, USA Snapshot, *USA Today*, 28 September 1999, B1.

61 Focusing on E-Business Today: Adapted from Heather Green, Mike France, Marcia Stepanek, and Amy Borrus, "Online Privacy: It's Time for Rules in Wonderland," *Business Week*, 20 March 2000, 83–96.

65 The Shady Side of the Olympics: Adapted from Mark Hosenball, "A New Olympics Mess," *Newsweek*, 20 September 1999, 28–29; Joan M. Steinauer, "Tarnished Gold?" *Incentive*, July 1999, 18–21; Terry Carter, "Wide World of Payola," *ABA Journal*, March 1999, 18; Mark Starr and Andrew Murr, "Blame Rolls Downhill: New Salt Lake Sins," *Newsweek*, 15 February 1999, 54–55; Christopher Dickey, Andrew Murr, and Russell Watson, "No More Fun and Games," *Newsweek*, 1 February 1999, 34–36; "International: City of Latter-Day Scandal," *Economist*, 30 January 1999, 42; "International: Gold Without Honour," *Economist*, 30 January 1999, 41–42; Matt Bai and Andrew Murr, "Go for the Greed," *Newsweek*, 25 January 1999, 30–33; Robert Sullivan, "How the Olympics Were Bought," *Time*, 25 January 1999, 38–42; Nadya Labi, "The Olympics Turns Into a Five-Ring Circus," *Time*, 11 January 1999, 33.

CHAPTER 3

70 Exhibit 3.1, "Going Global Has Its Barriers," *USA Today*, 3 May 2000, B1.

74 How to Avoid Business Blunders Abroad: Adapted from David Ricks, "How to Avoid Business Blunders Abroad," *Business*, April–June 1984, 3–11.

75 Exhibit 3.2, Brian Zajac, "Spanning the World," *Forbes*, 26 July 1999, 202–206.

76 Exhibit 3.3, *Big Emerging Markets: 1996 Outlook* (Washington, DC.: GPO, 1996), [accessed 17 July 1997], http://www.statusa.gov/itabems.htm.

78 Exhibit 3.4, adapted from U.S. Bureau of Economic Analysis Web site: Table 2—U.S. Trade in Goods, [accessed 15 May 2000], http://www.bea.doc.gov/bea/di/bopq/bop2-4.htm; Table 3—Private Service Transactions, [accessed 15 May 2000].

79 Exhibit 3.5, James Cox, "Tariffs Shield Some U.S. Products," *USA Today*, 6 May 1999, 1B [graph source is Grant Jerding, *USA Today*].

87 Focusing on E-Business Today exhibit source: "On the Continent, on the Cusp," *New York Times*, 14 May 2000, sec 3, 1,8. {Exhibit appears on page 1 of article.}

91 Doing Everybody's Wash—Whirlpool's Global Lesson: Adapted from Regina Fazio Maruca, "The Right Way to Go Global," *Harvard Business Review*, March–April 1994, 135-145; Deborah Duarte and Nancy Snyder, "From Experience: Facilitating Global Organizational Learning in Product Development at Whirlpool Corporation," *Journal of Product Innovation Management* 14, no. 1 (January 1997): 48-55; Joe Jancsurak, "Whirlpool: U.S. Leader Pursues Global Blueprint," *Appliance Manufacturer* 45, no. 2 (February 1997): G21; Carl Quintanilla, "Despite Setbacks, Whirlpool Pursues Overseas Markets," *Wall Street Journal*, 9 December 1997, B4; Ian Katz. "Whirlpool: In the Wringer." *Business Week*, 14 December 1998, 831; Gale Cutler, "Asia Challenges Whirlpool Technology," *Research Technology Management*," September-October 1998, 4-6; "Whirlpool Europe and Tupperware Europe Announce Strategic Alliance," Whirlpool Investor Relations, 28 April 1999, Whirlpool Web site, [accessed 5 May 1999], http://www.whirlpoolcorp.com; Sallie L. Gaines, "Washer War Spins on Investor Cycle," *Chicago Tribune*, 31 October 1999, sec. 5, 1, 7.

94 Mastering Global and Geographical Skills, Part 1: Adapted from Ian Katz, "Adios, Argentina—Hello, Brazil," *Business Week*, 17 January 2000, 56+.

96 Face-Off, Part 1: Douglas A. Blackmon and Diane Brady, "Just How Hard Should A U.S. Company Woo A Big Foreign Market?" *Wall Street Journal*, 6 April 1998, A1, A6; Douglas A. Blackmon, "FDX is Revamping Sales Operations in Wake of Weak Profit, UPS Gains," *Wall Street Journal Interactive Edition*, 17 December 1999, interactive.wsj.com; Brian O'Reilly, "UPS Vs. FedEx," *Fortune*, 7 February 2000, 101–12; [author], "FedEx: Going Nowhere Fast in Cyberspace," *BusinessWeek Online*, 31 January 2000, www.businessweek.com/2000/00_05/b3666124.htm; Douglas A. Blackmon, "Speed Limits," *Wall Street Journal*, 4 November 1999, A1, A16; Kelly Barron, "Logistics in Brown," *Forbes*, 10 January 1000, 78–83; Rick Brooks, "UPS Is Planning Pack-and-Ship Stores In Test Aimed at Luring New Customers," *Wall Street Journal*, 17 February 2000, B2; James F. Peltz, "A Stronger UPS Reinvents Itself," *Los Angeles Times*, 26 March 2000, C1, C4; Rick Brooks, "UPS Seeks to Chip Away at FedEx's Big Lead in China," *Wall Street Journal*, 16 May 2000, B4; Rick Brooks, "Postal Service, FedEx in Talks to Share Tasks," *Wall Street Journal*, 7 September 2000, B1, B4; Rick Brooks, "UPS to Fight Plans for FedEx, Post Office Deal," *Wall Street Journal*, 8 September 2000, A8; Nikhil Deogun and Rick Brooks, "FedEx, Looking to Grow on the Ground, Is in Talks to Buy American Freightways," *Wall Street Journal*, 13 November 2000, A17; Kristen S. Krause, "UPS Buys Mail Boxes Etc.," *Traffic World*, 12 March 2001, 32.

CHAPTER 4

100 Exhibit 4.1, Small Business Answer Card 1998, Small Business Administration, Office of Advocacy, SBA Web site, [accessed 5 June 2000], www.sba.gov/ADVO/stats/answer.pdf.

102 Exhibit 4.2, Adapted from Carrie Dolan, "Entrepreneurs Often Fail as Managers," *Wall Street Journal*, 15 May 1989, B1. Reprinted by permission of The Wall Street Journal, © 1989 Dow Jones & Company, Inc. All rights reserved worldwide.

104 Exhibit 4.3, Anne R. Carey and Grant Jerding, USA Snapshot, *USA Today*, 26 March 1998, B1.

105 Exhibit 4.4, Adapted from Carol Lawson, "Life's Miraculous Transmissions," *New York Times*, 6 June 1996, B3; Nancy Rotenier, "La Tempesta," *Forbes*, 18 December 1995, 134–35; Anne Murphy, "Entrepreneur of the Year," *Inc.*, December 1995, 38–51; Christina F. Watts and Loyde Gite, "Emerging Entrepreneurs," *Black Enterprise*, November 1995, 100–110; Marc Ballon, "Pretzel Queen," *Forbes*, 13 March 1995, 112–13; Robert La Franco, "Beach Bum Makes Good," *Forbes*, 19 June 1995, 80–82; Carla Goodman, "Medical Garb With a Smile," *Nation's Business*, May 1999, 65–67.

106 Create a Winning Business Plan: Adapted from Stanley R. Rich and David E. Gumpert, *Business Plans That Win $$$* (New York: Harper Row, 1985); J. Tol Broome Jr., "How to Write a Business Plan," *Nation's Business*, February 1993, 29–30; Albert Richards, "The Ernst & Young Business Plan Guide," *R & D Management*, April 1995, 253; David Lanchner, "How Chitchat Became a Valuable Business Plan," *Global Finance*, February 1995, 54–56; Marguerita Ashby-Berger, "My Business Plan–And What Really Happened," *Small Business Forum*, Winter 1994–1995, 24–35.

107 Are You Crazy?: Adapted from "Secrets of a Start-Up," *Success*, September 1998, 61; Martha Vissner, "Phoneomenon," *Success*, September 1998, 62; Marc Ballon, "Concierge Makes Hay in Corporate Fields," *Inc.*, September 1998, 23–25; Michelle Conlin, "It's in the Bag," *Forbes*, 28 December 1998, 86, 90.

108 Exhibit 4.5, Adapted from Norman M. Scarborough and Thomas W. Zimmerer, *Effective Small Business Management*, (Upper Saddle River, N.J: Prentice Hall, 2000), 8–13.

111 Exhibit 4.8, Adapted from Norman M. Scarborough and Thomas W. Zimmerer, *Effective Small Business Management* (Upper Saddle River, N.J: Prentice Hall, 2000), 27–29.

117 Focusing on E-Business Today: Edward C. Baig, "Web Sites Help Newbies Take Big Step," *USA Today*, 16 November 1999, 3B (graph by Julie Stacey).

122 Why Is Papa John's Rolling in Dough?: Adapted from Ron Ruggles, "John Schnatter: Mom Never Thought There'd Be Days Like This, But Papa John's CEO Is Rolling in Dough," *Nation's Restaurant News*, January 2000, 158–160; Amy Zuber, "Papa John's European Expansion to Mushroom via Perfect Pizza Buy," *Nation's Restaurant News*, 13 December 1999, 8; Alynda Wheat, "Striking It Rich the Low-Tech Way," *Fortune*, 27 September 1999, 86; Amy Zuber, "Papa John's Acquires Minnesota Pizza Co.," *Nation's Restaurant News*, 12 April 1999, 4, 91; Anne Field, "Piping-Hot Performance," *Success*, March 1999, 76–80; John Greenwald, "Slice, Dice, and Devour," *Time*, 26 October 1998, 64–66; Papa John's Web site, [accessed 2 June 2000], www.papajohns.com.

CHAPTER 5

126 Exhibit 5.1, Adapted with the permission of Simon & Schuster, Inc. from the Macmillan college text, *The Legal Environment of Business*, 2nd ed., by Charles R. McGuire. Copyright © 1986, 1989 by Merrill Pubishing, an imprint of Macmillan College Publishing Company, Inc., 216.

128 Exhibit 5.2, Adapted from "Business Enterprise," *Statistical Abstract of the United States, 1999*, 545.

134 How Cisco Bought Its Way to the Top: Adapted from Andy Server, "There's Something About Cisco," *Fortune*, 15 May 2000, 114–38; Henry Goldblatt, "Cisco's Secrets," *Fortune*, 8 November 1999, 177–81; Kimberly Caisse, "Cisco's Buying Binge Goes On," *Computer Reseller News*, 4 January 1999, 123, 128; Stacy Collett, "A Guide to Cisco's Acquisition and Investment Strategy," *Computerworld*, 4 October 1999, 20+; Glenn Drexhage, "How Cisco Bought Its Way to the Top," *Corporate Finance*, May 1999, 26–30.

136 Merger of Equals or Global Fender Bender?: Erick Schonfeld, "Have the Urge to Merge? You'd Better Think Twice," *Fortune*, 31 March 1997, 114–16; Phillip L. Zweig et al., "The Case Against Mergers," *Business Week*, 30 October 1995, 122–30; Kevin Kelly et al., "Mergers Today, Trouble Tomorrow?" *Business Week*, 12 September 1994; "How to Merge," *The Economist*, 9 January 1999, 21–23; "Study Says Mergers Often Don't Aid Investors," *New York Times*, 1 December 1999, C9.

139 Focusing on E-Business Today, "The List: Boardroom Basics," *Business Week*, 29 May 2000, 14.

144 DaimlerChrysler: Do Mergers Threaten Management's Responsibility to Shareholders?: Adapted from Bill Vlasic and Bradley A. Stertz, "How the DaimlerChrysler Marriage of Equals Got Taken for a Ride," *Business Week*, 5 June 2000, 86–92; Jeffrey Ball and Scott Miller, "Full Speed Ahead: Stuttgart's Control Grows With Shakeup at DaimlerChrysler," *Wall Street Journal*, 24 September 1999, A1, A8; Robert L. Simison and Scott Miller, "Making Digital Decisions," *Wall Street Journal*, 24 September 1999, B1, B4; Keith Bradsher, "A Struggle Over Culture and Turf at Auto Giant," *New York Times*, 25 September 1999, B1, B14; Message from DaimlerChrysler Chairmen to Company Employees, *Wall Street Journal*, 24 September 1999, A15; Joann Muller, Kathleen Kerwin, and Jack Ewing, "Man With a Plan," *Business Week*, 4 October 1999, 34–35; Frank Gibney Jr., "Worldwide Fender Bender," *Time*, 24 May 1999, 58–62; Daniel McGinn and Stefan Theil, "Hands On the Wheel," *Newsweek*, 12 April 1999, 49–52; Alex Taylor III, "The Germans Take Charge," *Fortune*, 11 January 1999, 92–96; Barrett Seaman and Ron Stodghill II, "The Daimler-Chrysler Deal: Here Comes the Road Test," *Time*, 18 May 1999, 66–69; Bill Vlasic, Kathleen Kerwin, David Woodruff, Thane Peterson, and Leah Nathans Spiro, "The First Global Car Colossus," *Business Week*, 18 May 1998, 40–43; Joann Muller, "Lessons From a Casualty of the Culture Wars," *Business Week*, 29 November 1999, 198; Rovert McNatt, "Chrysler: Not Quite So Equal," *Business Week*, 13 November 2000, 14.

148 Face-Off, Part 2: Nick Wingfield, "Amazon to Cut Product Offerings, Plans to Drop Unprofitable Items," *Wall Street Journal*, 2 February 2001, B6; Courtland Bovée and John Thill, *Business in Action* (Upper Saddle River, N.J.: Prentice Hall, 2001), 304, 324; David D. Kirkpatrick, "Online Superstore Pushes Into Digital," *New York Times*, 7 August 2000, C1, C6; Rebecca Quick, "Barnes & Noble and Its Online Sibling Enter Alliance Linking 'Bricks and Clicks,'" *Wall Street Journal*, 27 October 2000, B10; Avital Louria Hahn, "Barnes & Noble.com Gearing Up to Pose a Threat to Amazon," *The Investment Dealers' Digest*, 25 September 2000, 13–14; Diane Brady, "How Barnes & Noble Misread the Web," *Business Week*, 7 February 2000, 63; Connie Guglielmo, "Don't Write Off Barnes & Noble Just Yet," *Upside Today*, 21 April 2000 [accessed 23 April 2000], www.upside.com/Ebiz/38fceae10. html; Don Steinberg, "Smart Business 50," *smartbusinessmag.com*, November 2000, 121+; Katrina Brooker, "Amazon vs. Everybody," *Fortune*, 8 November 1999, 120–28; Doreen Carvajal, "Trying to Read a Hazy Future," *New York Times*, 18 April 1999, sec. 3, 1, 12; Michael S. Katz and Jeffrey Rothfeder, "Crossing the Digital Divide," *Strategy and Business*, First Quarter 2000, 26–41; Robert D. Hof, Debra Sparks, Ellen Neuborne, and Wendy Zellner, "Can Amazon Make It?" *Business Week*, 10 July 2000, 92–97; Ephraim Schwartz, "Amazon, Toys "R" Us In E-Commerce Tie-Up," *Infoworld*, 14 August 2000, 31; David Stodder, "Dancing With the Elephant," *Intelligent Enterprise*, 18 August 2000, 14–16; "Industry Leaders Advance in Lockstep," *DSN Retailing Today*, 7 August 2000, 44, 54; Karen J. Bannan, "Book Battle," *Adweek*, 28 February 2000, 90–94; Jacqueline Doherty, "Amazon.bomb," *Barron's*

31 May 1999, 25+; Peter S. Cohan, *e-Profit* (New York: American Management Association, 2000), 80, 82; "Barnes & Noble.com Buys Fatbrain," *Wall Street Journal,* 14 September 2000, B18; Raymond Hennessey, "E-Commerce (A Special Report): On the Battlefield—An Unfinished Story: Borders Group Was a Case Study of 'Too Late to the Net'; Maybe It Wasn't Too Slow After All," *Wall Street Journal,* 17 July 2000, R44.

CHAPTER 6

154 Exhibit 6.3, Adapted from Dell Computer homepage [accessed 15 June 1999] www.dell.com/corporate/vision/mission.htm.

160 Exhibit 6.5, Adapted from and reprinted by permission of *Harvard Business Review,* an exhibit from "How to Choose a Leadership Pattern" by Robert Tannenbaum and Warren H. Schmidt, May–June 1973. Copyright © 1973 by the President and Fellows of Harvard College, all rights reserved.

161 How Michael Dell Works His Magic: Adapted from Michael A. Verespej, "Michael Dell's Magic," *IW,* 16 November 1998, 57–64; Richard Murphy, "Michael Dell," *Success,* January 1999, 50–53.

163 How Much Do You Know About the Company's Culture?: Adapted from Andrew Bird, "Do You Know What Your Corporate Culture Is?" *CPA Insight,* February/March 1999, 25–26; Gail H. Vergara, "Finding a Compatible Corporate Culture," *Healthcare Executive,* January/February 1999, 46–47; Hal Lancaster, "To Avoid a Job Failure, Learn the Culture of a Company First," *Wall Street Journal,* 14 July 1998, B1.

165 Exhibit 6.7, Adapted from Courtland Bovée et al. *Management* (New York: McGraw-Hill, 1993) 678.

168 Exhibit 6.8, Stuart Crainer, "The 75 Greatest Management Decisions Ever Made," *Management Review,* November 1998, 17–23.

173 The Ax Falls on Chainsaw Al: James R. Fisher Jr., "Profits and People," *Executive Excellence,* January 2000, 18; Jenny Anderson, "Al Gets the Chainsaw," *Institutional Investor,* October 1999, 224; John A. Byrne, "Chainsaw: He Anointed Himself America's Best CEO," *Business Week,* 18 October 1999, 128; "Al Dunlap: Booted for Being a Shareholder Hero," *Fortune,* 26 April 1999, 413; Martha Brannigan, "Best and Worst Performing Companies: Worst 1-Year Performer: Sunbeam Corp," *Wall Street Journal,* 25 February 1999, R7; Geoffrey Colvin, "America's Most Hated," *Director,* September 1998, 35; Matthew Schifrin, "The Sunbeam Soap Opera: Act VI," *Forbes,* 6 July 1998, 44–45; John A. Byrne, "How Al Dunlap Self-Destructed," *Business Week,* 6 July 1998, 58; Daniel Kadlec, "Chainsaw Al Gets the Chop," *Time,* 29 June 1998, 46–47; David Morrison and Kevin Mundt, "Chainsaw Al Gets the Ax. What's Next for Sunbeam?" *Wall Street Journal,* 22 June 1998, A22; Jonathan R. Laing, "And Take the Chainsaw with You!" *Barron's,* 22 June 1998, 13–14; "Business: Exit Bad Guy," *The Economist,* 20 June 1998, 70–75; Patricia Sellers, "Exit for Chainsaw?" *Fortune,* 8 June 1998, 30–31; James R. Hagerty and Martha Brannigan, "Inside Sunbeam: Raindrops Mar Dunlap's Parade," *Wall Street Journal,* 22 May 1998, B1.

CHAPTER 7

182 Exhibit 7.4, Adapted from Steven Burke, "Acer Restructures into Six Divisions," *Computer Reseller News,* 13 July 1998, 10.

186 Mervyn's Calls SWAT Team to the Rescue: Adapted from Peter Carvonara, "Mervyn's Calls in the SWAT Team," *Fast Company,* April–May 1998, 54–56; Richard Halverson, "Ulrich Delivers Ultimatum to Mervyn's: Improve Sales Performance, or Else," *Discount Store News,* 26 October 1998, 3, 126.

190 Exhibit 7.6, Exhibit from *Management, Fourth Edition,* by Richard L. Daft, copyright © 1977 by Harcourt Inc., reproduced by permission of the publisher.

192 Office Ethics: Teams Make It Hard to Tattle: Adapted from Stephanie Armour, "Office Ethics: Teams Make It Hard to Tattle," *USA Today,* 17 February 1998.

195 Focusing on E-Business Today, Adapted from "Writing for the Web," Sun Microsystems Web site [accessed 23 October 2000] www.sun.com/980713/webwriting.

199 Harley-Davidson—From Dysfunctional to Cross-Functional: Adapted from Kevin R. Fitzgerald, "Purchasing at Harley Links Supply with Design," *Purchasing,* 13 February 1997, 56–57; Machan Dyan, "Is the Hog Going Soft?" *Forbes,* 10 March 1997, 114–15; Ronald B. Lieber, "Selling the Sizzle," *Fortune,* 23 June 1997, 80; Clyde Fessler, "Rotating Leadership at Harley-Davidson: From Hierarchy to Interdependence," *Strategy & Leadership,* July–August 1997, 42–43; Tim Minahan, "Harley-Davidson Revs Up Development Process," *Purchasing,* 7 May 1998, 44S18–44S23; Michael A. Verespej, "Invest in People," *Industry Week,* 1 February 1999, 6–7; Leslie P. Norton, "Potholes Ahead?" *Barron's,* 1 February 1999, 16–17; Mark A. Brunelli, "How Harley-Davidson Uses Cross-Functional Teams," *Purchasing,* 4 November 1999, 148; Rich Teerlink, "Harley's Leadership U-Turn," *Harvard Business Review,* July–August 2000, 43+; Joe Singer and Steve Duvall, "High Performace Partnering By Self-Managed Teams in Manufacturing," *Engineering Management Journal,* December 2000, 9–15.

CHAPTER 8

210 Exhibit 8.6, Adapted from James A. O'Brian, *Introduction to Information Systems,* 7th ed. (Burr Ridge, Ill.: Irwin, 1994), 25.

211 Using Information to Make a ScrubaDub Difference: Adapted from "Success, One Customer at a Time," The Inc./Cisco Growing With Technology Awards [accessed 31 July 2000] www.inc.com/custom_publishing/cisco/wash.html; Scrubadub Car Wash Web site [accessed 31 July 2000] www.scrubadub.com.

218 Exhibit 8.9, Adapted from Larry Long and Nancy Long, *Introduction to Computers and Information* Systems, 5th ed. (Upper Saddle River, N.J.: Prentice Hall, 1997), CORE 165–168.

220 Wait, Don't Punch That Computer Monitor: Adapted from Stephanie Armour, "Technology's Burps Give Workers Heartburn," *USA Today,* 16 August 1999, 1B, 2B; "COMPAQ: Employees Get 'IT' Out of Their Systems," *M2 Presswire,* 27 May 1999; Jack Gordon, Kim Kiser, Michele Picard, and David Stamps, "Take That, You @!%#!* Machine!" *Training,* May 1999, 20.

221 Exhibit 8.10, John Galvin, "Cheating, Lying, Stealing," *SmartBusinessMag.Com,* June 2000, 86–99.

222 Focusing on E-Business Today exhibit, Robert O. Crockett, "Wowing the Wireless Set," *Business Week E.Biz,* 5 June 2000, EB16.

227 How Nokia Rings Up Profits: Stephen Baker with Inka Resch and Roger O. Crockett, "Nokia's Costly Stumble," *Business Week,* 14 August 2000, 42; "Business: Star Turn," *The Economist,* 5 August 2000, 60; Maryanne Murry Buechner, "Making the Call," *Time,* 29 May 2000, 64–65; Justin Fox, "Nokia's Secret Code," *Fortune,* 1 May 2000, 160–74; Adrian Wooldridge, "Survey: Telecommunications: To the Finland Base Station," *The Economist,* 9 October 1999, S23–S27; Stephen Baker and Robert McNatt, "Now Nokia is Net Crazy," *Business Week,* 5 April 1999, 6; "Jorma Ollila: Finn Fatale," *Business Week,* 11 January 1999, 78; Stephen Baker with Roger O. Crockett and Neil Gross, "Nokia," *Business Week,* 10 August 1998, 54; Stephen Baker, John Shinal, and Irene M. Kunii, "Is Nokia's Star Dimming?: *Business Week,* 22 January 2001, 66–72.

CHAPTER 9

233 Exhibit 9.2, Adapted from Mark M. Davis, Nicholas J. Aquilano, and Richard B. Chase, *Fundamentals of Operations Management* (Boston: Irwin McGraw-Hill, 1999), 7.

239 Exhibit 9.4, Adapted from Courtland L. Bovee, et al., *Management* (New York: McGraw-Hill, 1993), 648; Roberta S. Russell and Bernard W. Taylor III, *Operations Management: Focusing on Quality and Competitiveness,* 2d ed. (Upper Saddle River, N.J.: Prentice Hall, 1998), 294.

238 A Bike That Really Travels: Adapted from Lisa Marshall, "A Bike That Really Travels," *Boulder Daily Camera,* June 1999, Bike Friday Web site [accessed 11 August 2000] www.bikefriday.com/reviews.cfm?ID=1; Tim Stevens, "Pedal Pushers," *Industry Week,* 17 July 2000, 46–52.

239 Exhibit 9.5, Adapted from Gerald H. Graham, *The World of Business* (Reading, Mass.: Addison-Wesley, 1985), 1999.

245 Chek Lap Kok's Turbulent Takeoff: Adapted from Bruce Dorminey, "Overconfidence, Poor Planning Led to Hong Kong Airport Woes," *Aviation Week & Space Technology,* 15 February 1999, 53+; Sherrie E. Zhan, "No Kudos for Chek Lap Kok Airport," *World Trade,* October 1998, 32+; Martyn Warwick, "Not Tried, Not Tested," *Communications International,* August 1998, 24+; "Hong Kong Opens New Airport," *Material Handling Engineering,* August 1998, 12+; "Trouble-Shooting at Chek Lap Kok," *Transportation & Distribution,* August 1998, 12; Bruce Dorminey and Carole A. Shifrin, "Hong Kong Investigates What Went Wrong," *Aviation Week & Space Technology,* 20 July 1998, 45+; Megan Scott, "Vendors Take Blame for System Woes," *Computerworld,* 20 July 1998, 29–32; Kristin S. Krause, "Order out of Chaos," *Traffic World,* 20 July 1998, 23–24; Murray Hiebert, "Opening-Day Blues," *Far-Eastern Economic Review,* 16 July 1998, 62–63; Mark Landler, "Problems Continue to Mount at New Hong Kong Airport," *New York Times,* 9 July 1998, C6; Michael Mecham, "In Hong Kong, There's Still Room to Expand," *Aviation Week & Space Technology,* 27 March 2000, 44–46.

247 Exhibit 9.7, Adapted from National Institute of Standards and Technology, *National Quality Program, Award Criteria,* http://nist.gov/public_affairs/guide/qpage.htm [accessed 11 February 1998].

249 Focusing on E-Business Today, Jack Trout, "Stupid Net Tricks," *Business 2.0,* May 2000, 76–77.

254 Porsche—Back in the Fast Lane: "The Stars of Europe: Turnaround Artists: Wendelin Wiedeking," *Business Week,* 19 June 2000, 186; Tom Mudd, "Back in High Gear," *Industry Week,* 21 February 2000, 38–46; Matthew Karnitschnig, "That Van You're Driving May Be Part Porsche," *Business Week,* 27 December 1999, 72; Peter Morgan, "Back to Winning Ways," *Professional Engineering,* 28 April 1999, 30–31; Karen Abramic Dilger, "Gear Up and Go," *Manufacturing Systems,* A24–A28; "Porsche Gears Up for Faster Parts Distribution," *Material Handling Engineering,* July 1998, 34–40; Richard Feast, "The Road Ahead for Porsche," *Independent,* 6 September 1996, 17.

258 Face-Off, Part 3: Adapted from Laurence Zuckerman, "A Wing-and-Wing Race," *New York Times,* 1 December 1999, C1, C2; Gail Edmondson, Janet Rae-Dupree, and Kerry Capell, "How Airbus Could Rule the Skies," *Business Week,* 2 August 1999, 54; Paulo Prada and David Gauthier-Villars, "Airbus Sales Hit a Record $17.2 Billion," *Wall Street Journal,* 30 January 2001, A14; Laurence Zuckerman, "The Jet Wars of the Future," *New York Times,* 9 July 1999, C1, C5; Adapted from John Tagliabue, "Airbus Industrie Is Considering a Very Big Bet," *New York Times,* 14 July 2000, C1, C6; Daniel Michaels, "Giant Jet Gets Orders It Required," *Wall Street Journal,* 30 November 2000, A17, A19; Alex Taylor III, "Blue Skies for Airbus," *Fortune,* 2 August 1999, 102–8. Laurence Zuckerman, "A Wing-and-Wing Race," *New York Times,* 1 December 1999, C1, C2; Paulo Prada and David Gauthier-Villars, "Airbus Sales Hit a Record $17.2 Billion," *Wall Street Journal,* 30 January 2001, A14; Daniel Michaels and Jeff Cole, "Taking Tons Off the World's Biggest Passenger Jet," *Wall Street Journal,* 19 January 2001, B1, B4; Jeff Cole, "Wing Commander," *Wall Street Journal,* 10 January 2001, A1, A12; Daniel Michaels, "Giant Jet Gets Orders It Required," *Wall Street Journal,* 30 November 2000, A17, A19; Andy Reinhardt, John Rossant, and Frederik Balfour, "Boeing Gets Blown Sideways," *Business Week,* 16 October 2000, 62; Jerry Useem, "Boeing vs. Boeing," *Fortune,* 2 October 2000, 148–160; Daniel Michaels, "Some Airbus Clients Worry About Jumbo Jet's Impact," *Wall Street Journal,* 24 July 2000, A21; John Tagliabue, "Airbus Industrie Is Considering a Very Big

Bet," *New York Times,* 14 July 2000, C1, C6; Daniel Michaels, "Flying High," *Wall Street Journal,* 25 September 2000, R18, R19; Daniel Michaels, "Europe's Airbus Ready to Spread Wings as a Company," *Wall Street Journal,* 23 June 2000, A15; Jeff Cole, "Flight of Fancy," *Wall Street Journal,* 3 November 1999, A1, A10; Gail Edmondson, Janet Rae-Dupree, and Kerry Capell, "How Airbus Could Rule the Skies," *Business Week,* 2 August 1999, 54; Alex Taylor III, "Blue Skies for Airbus," *Fortune,* 2 August 1999, 102–8; Laurence Zuckerman, "The Jet Wars of the Future," *New York Times,* 9 July 1999, C1, C5; Adapted from John Tagliabue, "Airbus Industrie Is Considering a Very Big Bet," *New York Times,* 14 July 2000, C1, C6; Daniel Michaels, "Giant Jet Gets Orders It Required," *Wall Street Journal,* 30 November 2000, A17, A19; Alex Taylor III, "Blue Skies for Airbus," *Fortune,* 2 August 1999, 102–108; J. Lynn Lunsford, "Boeing Plans Longer-Range Model of 747," *Wall Street Journal,* 13 April 2001, A3, A6.

CHAPTER 10

265 Exhibit 10.3, Adapted from *Management,* 4th ed. by Richard L. Daft, copyright © 1997 by Harcourt Inc., reproduced by permission of the publisher.

265 Exhibit 10.4, Douglas McGregor, *The Human Side of Enterprise* (New York: McGraw-Hill, 1960).

267 Exhibit 10.5, Jennifer Laabs, "The New Loyalty: Grasp It. Earn It. Keep It," *Workforce,* November 1998, 35–39.

269 Chuckle While You Work: Adapted from Erika Rasmusson, "A Funny Thing Happened on the Way to Work," *Sales and Marketing Management,* March 1999, 97–98; Peter Baker, "Work: Have Fun. And That's An Order," *The Observer,* 3 January 1999, 11+; Melanie Payne, "Chuckle While You Work," *San Diego Union-Tribune,* 19 October 1998, E1–E2; Maggie Jackson, "Corporate America Lightens Up: Laughing Workers Are Happy Workers," *The Salt Lake Tribune,* 4 May 1997, E1; Diane E. Lewis, "Employers Find Humor Can Improve Morale, Profits," *Boston Globe,* 1 April 1997, C5; R. J. King, "Here's A Laugh: Speaker Shows How Office Humor Helps," *Detroit News,* 15 February 1996, B3; Katy Robinson, "Use Laughter to Brighten Your Office," *Idaho Statesman,* 18 October 1995, 1.

273 Exhibit 10.6, From *USA Today* Snapshot, "9-to-5 Not for Everyone," *USA Today,* 13 October 1999, B1.

274 Is Telecommuting Right For You?: Adapted from Bronwyn Fryer, "WorkShop," *Working Woman,* April 1997, 59–60; Lisa Chadderdon, "Merrill Lynch Works—at Home," *Fast Company,* April–May 1998, 70–72; Peg Verone, "House Rules," *Success,* July 1998, 22–23.

280 Focusing on E-Business Today, "Finding and Keeping Talent in the Internet Age," *Chief Executive,* February 2000, 32–34.

285 Delivering Better Employment-Management Relations at UPS: John D. Schulz, "In Love with Hoffa," *Traffic World,* 1 May 2000, 34: "UPS Agrees to Create Another 2,000 Jobs Under Teamsters Pact," *Wall Street Journal,* 31 March 2000, A8; David Rocks, "UPS: Will This IPO Deliver?" *Business Week,* 15 November 1999, 41; "UPS's 4th Quarter Results Cap Year of Leadership in Key Growth Areas," UPS news release, 18 February 1999 [accessed 6 April 1999] www.ups.com/bin/ shownews.cgi?19990218earnings; Robert J. Grossman, "Trying to Heal the Wounds," *HR Magazine,* September 1998, 85–92; John Schmeltzer, "A Year After UPS Strike, Its Rivals Are Real Victors," *Chicago Tribune,* August 2, 1998, sec. 5, 1, 2; "UPS, Pilots Quickly Reach Agreement," *Logistics Management and Distribution Report,* February 1998, 26–27; Shari Caudron, "Part-Timers Make Headline News—Here's the Real HR Story," *Workforce,* November 1997, 40–50; and Linda Grant, "How UPS Blew It," *Fortune,* 29 September 1997, 29–30.

CHAPTER 11

292 Are Temp Workers Becoming a Full-Time Headache?: Adapted from "Microsoft Moves to Curb Use of Temporary Workers," *Wall*

Street Journal, 3 July 2000, B2; Pat Curry, "Help in a Hurry," *Industry Week,* 15 May 2000, 69–72; Aaron Bernstein, "When Is a Temp Not a Temp?" *Business Week,* 7 December, 1998, 90–92; Daniel Eisenberg, "Rise of the Permatemp," *Time,* 12 July 1999, 48+; Aaron Bernstein, "Now, Temp Workers Are a Full-Time Headache," *Business Week,* 31 May 1999, 46+; Barb Cole-Gomolski, "Reliance on Temps Creates New Problems," *Computerworld,* 31 August 1998, 1, 85; "Temp Work Force Rising Up for Benefits," *Salt Lake Tribune,* 30 June 1999, B5; John Cook, "Temp Ruling Far Reaching," *Seattle Post,* 14 May 1999, B1; Dan Richman, "Despite Changes, Microsoft's Temp Force Precariously Discontent," *Seattle Post,* 12 June 1999, A1; Jennifer Laabs, "Microsoft Battles Permatemp Issue," *Workforce,* March 1999, 16; Aaron Bernstein, "TempWars: Why Microsoft May Cry Uncle," *Business Week,* 15 November 1999, 48.

294 Exhibit 11.4, USA Today Snapshot "Checking Out New Hires," *USA Today,* 18 May 2000, B1.

303 It's Okay to Fall Asleep on the Job: Adapted from Anna Mulrine, "Take a Nap; It's on the House," *U.S.News & World Report,* 20 July 1998, 61; Janet Gemignani, "The Latest Productivity Booster," *Business and Health,* September 1997, 12+; "Take an Afternoon Nap on Your Way to the Top," *Management Today,* March 1998, 12–13; Shane McLaughlin, "A Real Dream Job," *Inc.,* January 1999, 80+; Mark Sabourin, "Sleeping on the Job," *OH & S Canada,* June–July 1998, 32–37.

304 Exhibit 11.6, USA Today Snapshot "Life Is Not Shabby at the Top," *USA Today,* 12 July 1999, B1.

306 Focusing on E-Business Today, Christopher Caggiano, "The Truth about Internet Recruiting," *Inc.,* December 1999, 156.

311 Brewing Up People Policies at Starbucks: Adapted from Jennifer Ordonez, "Starbucks' Schultz to Leave Top Post, Lead Global Effort," *Wall Street Journal,* 7 April 2000, B3; Karyn Strauss, "Howard Schultz: Starbucks' CEO Serves a Blend of Community, Employee Commitment," *Nation's Restaurant News,* January 2000, 162–63; Carla Joinson, "The Cost of Doing Business?" *HR Magazine,* December 1999, 86–92; "Interview with Howard Schultz: Sharing Success," *Executive Excellence,* November 1999, 16–17; Kelly Barron, "The Cappuccino Conundrum," *Forbes,* 22 February 1999, 54–55; Naomi Weiss, "How Starbucks Impassions Workers to Drive Growth," *Workforce,* August 1998, 60–64; Scott S. Smith, "Grounds for Success," *Entrepreneur,* May 1998, 120–26; "Face Value: Perky People," *The Economist,* 30 May 1998, 66; Howard Schultz and Dori Jones Yang, "Starbucks: Making Values Pay," *Fortune,* 29 September 1997, 261–72.

314 Face-Off, Part 4: Adapted from Ann Zimmerman, "Carved Out: Pro-Union Butchers at Wal-Mart Win a Battle, Lose War," *Wall Street Journal,* 11 April 2000, A1; Charlie Cray, "Wal-Mart Cuts the Union," *Multinational Monitor,* April 2000, 4; Wendy Zellner and Aaron Bernstein, "Up Against the Wal-Mart," *Business Week,* 13 March 2000, 76–78; "Wal-Mart Decides to End Meat Cutting at 180 of Its Stores," *Wall Street Journal,* 6 March 2000, B16; J.C. Conklin, "Wal-Mart Workers at Texas Outlet Vote to Join Union," *Wall Street Journal,* 24 February 2000, B12; Amy Feldman, "How Big Can It Get?" *Money,* December 1999, 158–164; "United States: Wal-Mart Wins Again," *The Economist,* 2 October 1999, 33; Bob Ingram, "Labor Laboratory," *Supermarket Business,* 15 August 2000, 1, 10; Mike Troy, "Wal-Mart to Open 48 at Yearend," *DSN Retailing Today,* 1 January 2001, 5; Mark Tosh, "In Good Faith?" *Progressive Grocer,* February 1999, 24–32. Data for table is from Mike Troy, "Wal-Mart to Open 48 at Yearend," *DSN Retailing Today,* 1 January 2001, 5; "United States: Wal-Mart Wins Again," *The Economist,* 2 October 1999, 33; Mark Tosh, "In Good Faith?" *Progressive Grocer,* February 1999, 24–32. Adapted from Table 718: Labor Union Membership, by Sector: 1983–1999, U.S. Census Bureau, Statistical Abstract of the United States: 1999, [accessed 13 February 2000], http://www.census.gov/statab; Yochi J. Dreazen, "Percentage of U.S. Workers in a Union Sank to Record Low of 13.5% Last Year," *Wall Street Journal,* 19 January 2001, A2; Mark Tosh, "In Good Faith?" *Progressive Grocer,* February 1999, 24–32.

CHAPTER 12

318 Exhibit 12.1, Gary Armstrong and Philip Kotler, *Marketing an Introduction,* 5th ed. (Upper Sadle River, N.J.: Prentice Hall, 2000), 5 (Figure 1.1—Core marketing concepts).

320 Exhibit 12.3, Gary Armstrong and Philip Kotler, *Marketing an Introduction,* 5th ed. (Upper Saddle River, N.J.: Prentice Hall, 2000), 19.

321 Exhibit 12.4, Adapted from Mary J. Cronin, *Doing More Business on the Internet* (New York: Van Nostrand Reinhold, 1995), 61.

323 Exhibit 12.5, Joan O. Fredericks and James M. Salter, "Beyond Customer Satisfaction," *Management Review,* May 1995, 29.

327 Move Over Boomers and Gen Xers: Here Comes Generation Y: Adapted from Ellen Neuborne, "Generation Y," *Business Week,* 15 February 1999, 80–88; Mary Purpura and Paolo Pontoniere, "A Look at the New N-Gen of the Economy," *Los Angeles Times,* 20 April 1988, D4; Molly O'Neill, "Feeding the Next Generation," *New York Times,* 14 March 1998, B1, B14.

331 Questionable Marketing Tactics on Campus: Adapted from Christine Dugas, "Colleges Target Card Solicitors," *USA Today,* 12 March 1999, B1; Lisa Toloken, "Turning the Tables on Campus," *Credit Card Management,* May 1999, 76–79; "Credit Cards Given to College Students a Marketing Issue," *Marketing News,* 27 September 1999, 38.

334 Exhibit 12.9, Gary Armstrong and Philip Kotler, *Marketing an Introduction,* 5th ed. (Upper Saddle River, N.J.: Prentice Hall, 2000), 201.

336 Focusing on E-Business Today, Rebecca Quick, "Returns to Sender," *Wall Street Journal,* 17 July 2000, R8.

341 Is Levi Strauss Coming Apart at the Seams?: Louise Lee, "Can Levi's Be Cool Again?" *Business Week,* 13 March 2000, 144, 148; Shawn Meadows, "Levi Shifts On-line Strategy," *Bobbin,* January 2000, 8; Luisa Kroll, "Denim Disaster," *Forbes,* 29 November 1999, 181; Stacey Collett, "Channel Conflicts Push Levi to Halt Web Sales," *Computerworld,* 8 November 1999, 8; Nina Munk, "How Levi's Trashed a Great American Brand," *Fortune,* 12 April 1999, 83–90; Betsy Spethmann, "Can We Talk?" *American Demographics,* March 1999, 42–44; Wayne D'Orio, "Clothes Make the Teen," *American Demographics,* March 1999, 34–37; Murray Forseter, "Levi's Weaves a Tangled Web," *Chain Store Age,* January 1999, 10; Suzette Hill, "Levi Strauss & Co.: Icon in Revolution," *Apparel Industry Magazine,* January 1999, 66–69; Luisa Kroll, "Digit Denim," *Forbes,* December 28, 1998, 102–03; "Keep Reinventing the Brand or Risk Facing Extinction," *Marketing,* 25 February 1999, 5; Suzette Hill, "Levi Strauss Puts a New Spin on Brand Management," *Apparel Industry Magazine,* November 1998, 46–47; Linda Himelstein, "Levi's is Hiking Up Its Pants," *Business Week,* 1 December 1997, 70–75.

CHAPTER 13

346 Exhibit 13.1, Courtland Bovee, Michael Houston, and John V. Thill, *Marketing,* Second Edition (New York: McGraw-Hill, 1994), p. 240.

348 Exhibit 13.2, Adapted from Charles D. Schewe, *Marketing Principles and Strategies* (New York: McGraw-Hill, 1987).

351 After You: Sometimes It Pays to Be Second: Adapted from Minda Zetlin, "When It's Smarter to Be Second to Market," *Management Review,* March 1999, 30–34; Jim Collins, "Best Beats First," *Inc.,* August 2000, 48–51.

352 Exhibit 13.4, Adapted from Charles D. Schewe, *Marketing Principles and Strategies* (New York: McGraw-Hill, 1987).

355 Winning at the Name Game: Adapted from Brad Stone, "Losing the Name Game," *Business Week,* 8 June 1998, 44; David Gross, "The Name Game," *Hemispheres,* July 1997, 42–49; Cacilie Rohwedder, "Global Products Require Name-Finders," *Wall Street Journal,* 11 April 1996, B6; Roberta Maynard, "What's In a Name," *Nation's Business,* September 1994, 54; Small Business Administration, "Packaging Your Business: How to Harness Image as a Marketing Tool," *Small Business Success Series—Volume IX—Improving Your Business* [accessed 7

September 2000] www.sba.gov/library/pubs.htm success9; Judy Strauss and Raymond Frost, *E-Marketing,* 2d ed. (Upper Saddle River, N.J.: Prentice Hall, 2001), 135.

362 Focusing on E-Business Today, "Prices, eMarketplace, and the Future of B-to-B," Business 2.0 online [accessed 12 September 2000] http://www.business2.com/content/research/numbers/2000/09/12/18581.

366 Saturn's Bumpy Ride: Gregory L. White, "Late to the Fair, Saturn Is Set to Unveil Small SUV," *Wall Street Journal,* 6 October 2000, B1, B4; David Welch, "Say it Ain't So, Saturn," *Business Week,* 24 July 2000, 10; Alex Taylor III, "Wrong Turn at Saturn," *Fortune,* 24 July 2000, 371–72; "Saturn Plans Layoffs at Delaware Plant on Lackluster Sales," *Wall Street Journal,* 26 May 2000, B10; David Welch, "Hard at Work under Saturn's Hood," *Business Week,* 21 February 2000, 118; David Welch, "Running Rings Around Saturn," *Business Week,* 21 February 2000, 114–18; Gregory L. White, "GM's Saturn Unit Temporarily Closes Plants on Slow Sales, Launch Problems," *Wall Street Journal,* 7 January 2000, A4; Mike Arnholt, "Saturn Grows Up," *Ward's Auto World,* July 1999, 43–45; Kathleen Kerwin with Keith Naughton, "A Different Kind of Saturn," *Business Week,* 5 July 1999, 28; Jeff Green, "Saturn's 'L' Pitch: 'Next Big Thing,'" *Brandweek,* 14 June 1999, 8; Greg Gardner, "Is This the End of Saturn?" *Ward's Auto World,* September 1998, 41; William J. Holstein, "Well, Not So Different," *U.S. News & World Report,* 3 August 1998, 46–47; Jennifer Laabs, "Saturn Workers Vote to Retain Innovative Risk-and-Reward Pay Package," *Workforce,* May 1998, 14; Kathleen Kerwin, "Why Didn't GM Do More for Saturn?" *Business Week,* 16 March 1998, 62; Sarah Lorge, "Saturn," *Sales and Marketing Management,* October 1997, 63.

CHAPTER 14

370 Exhibit 14.1, Adapted from Philip Kotler, *Marketing Management,* 10th ed. (Upper Saddle River, N.J.: Prentice Hall, 2000), 491.

374 Exhibit 14.3, Gary Armstrong and Philip Kotler, *Marketing an Introduction,* 5th ed. (Upper Saddle River, N.J.: Prentice Hall, 2000), 335.

376 Exhibit 14.4, Adapted from Charles D. Schewe, *Marketing Principles and Strategies* (New York: McGraw-Hill, 1987), 294. Reprinted by permission of the publisher.

376 Smart Car Dealers Say, "Follow That Mouse": Adapted from Karen Lundegaard, "Putting On the Brakes," *Wall Street Journal,* 23 October 2000, R6, R9; Evan R. Hirsh, Louis F. Rodewig, Peter Soliman, and Steven B. Wheeler, "Changing Channels in the Automotive Industry," *Strategy &Business,* First Quarter 1999 [accessed 9 February 2000] www.strategy-business.com/strategy/99105/page1.html; David Welch, "Car Dealers Say: Follow That Mouse," *Business Week,* 10 April 2000, 106,110; John Dodge, "Shifting Gears," *Wall Street Journal,* 12 July 1999, R40; Alex Taylor III, "Detroit Goes Digital," *Fortune,* 17 April 2000, 170–74; Bethany McLean, "Revenge of the Car Salesman: The Internet Is a Lemon," *Fortune,* 27 November 2000, 146–56.

380 REI's Perfect Blend of Retail and E-Tail Channels: Mike Troy, "REI.com Scales On-Line Heights," *DSN Retailing Today,* 8 May 2000, 6; Kellee Harris, "Online Travel Revs Up Revenues," *Sporting Goods Business,* 1 February 2000, 16; Lawrence M. Fisher, "REI Climbs Online: A Clicks-and-Mortar Chronicle," *Strategy&Business,* First Quarter 2000 [accessed 13 October 2000] www.strategy-business.com/casestudy/00111; "REI Scales New Heights with Second-Generation Web Sites and IBM," IBM E-Business Case Studies [accessed 10 March 2000] www.ibm.com/e-business/case_studies/rei.phtml; Kristin Carpenter, "REI.com," *Sporting Goods Business,* 6 July 1999, 57; David Orenstein, "Retailers Find Uses for Web Inside Stores," *Computerworld,* 11 January 1999, 41; Sharon Machlis, "Outdoor Goods Seller Creates Outline Outlet," *Computerworld,* 14 December 1998, 51–53; Kerry A. Dolan, "Backpackers Meet Bottom Line," *Forbes,* 16 November 1998, 161; Kristin Carpenter, "REI Venturing Out with Off-Price Web Site," *Sporting Goods Business,* 10 August 1998, 22.

381 Gateway's Big Gamble: Adapted from Robery Scally, "Gateway: The Crown Prince of Clicks-and-Mortar," *Retailing Today,* 8 May

2000, 75–76; Steven V. Brull, "Gateway's Big Gamble," *Business Week E.Biz,* 5 June 2000, EB26–EB30; Ephraim Schwarz, "Gateway Chief Is Looking Beyond Hardware," *InfoWorld,* 5 June 2000, 18; "Gateway to the Future," *Discount Merchandiser,* April 2000, 23; Anne Newman, "Gateway: Going for Bricks and Mortar," *Business Week,* 6 March 2000, 54; G. Pierre Goad, "Bricks n' Clicks," *Far Eastern Economic Review,* 6 July 2000, 39.

382 Exhibit 14.6, USA Today Snapshot "What Lures Online Shoppers?" *USA Today,* 23 November 1999, B1.

CHAPTER 15

402 Exhibit 15.2, Adapted from Courtland L. Bovée and John V. Thill, *Marketing* (New York: McGraw-Hill, 1992), 590.

406 Exhibit 15.3, "Leading National Advertisers," *Advertising Age,* 25 September 2000, S4.

415 Exhibit 15.7, Adapted from O.C. Ferrell and Geoffrey Hirt, *Business in a Changing World,* 3d ed. (Boston, Mass., Irwin McGraw-Hill), 2000), 346.

416 Focusing on E-Business Today, "Internet at a Glance," *Business 2.0,* 26 September 2000, 228.

424 Face-Off, Part 4: Adapted from Sharon Cleary, "Hungry for Profits," *Wall Street Journal,* 23 October 2000, R54; David Henry, "Online Grocers Must Change Buyer Habits, Keep Costs Down," *USA Today,* 30 March 2000, 3B; Keith Ferrell, "Food Fight Anyone?" *Chief Executive,* January 2000, 48–49; Victoria Griffith, "Focus: Online Grocers-From Homeruns to Webvan to Peapod," *Strategy and Business,* First Quarter 2000, 90–91; George Anders and Robert Berner, Webvan's Splashy Stock Debut May Shake Up Staid Grocery Industry—Some Traditional Food Chains are Testing Online Retailing, But So Far, Very Cautiously," *Wall Street Journal,* 8 November 1999, B1; Randall E. Stross, "Only a Bold Gamble Can save Webvan Now," *Wall Street Journal,* 2 February 2001, A9; Stacy Perman, "I George Shaheen, Promise to Do My Best, to Do My Duty to God and My Country, to Help Other People, and to Beat the Living Crap Out of the Competition," www.ecompany.com, September 2000, 147–154; Chet Dembeck, "Why Webvan Will Win the Online Grocery War," *E-Commerce Times,* 19 April 2000 [accessed online 14 February 2001] http://www.ecommercetimes.com; Rusty Weston, "Return of the Milkman," *Upside,* April 2000, 100–108; Connie Guglielmo, "Can Webvan Deliver? E-Commerce News,* 31 January 2000 [accessed online 7 June 2000] http://www.zdnet.com/ecommerce/stories/main; George Anders, "Co-Founder of Borders to Launch Online Megagrocer," *Wall Street Journal,* 22 April 1999, B1, B4; Ameet Sachdev, "Peapod Buys Rival's Operations, Exits 4 Cities," *Chicago Tribune,* 8 September 2000, sec 3, 3; Dick Satran, "Peapod's Woes Casting Shadow on Rivals," *Chicago Tribune,* 3 April 2000, sec. 4, 9; Debbie Howell, "Food: National E-Tailers Lead the Way," *Discount Store News,* 13 December 1999, 25, 61; "Webvan Bags HomeGrocer.com," *Frozen Food Age,* August 2000, 1, 45; Sid L., Huff and David Beckow, "Homegrocer.com (A Case Study)," *Ivey Business Journal,* May/June 2000, 90–95; Paul Bubny, "Not Yet Clicking," *Supermarket Business,* 15 July 2000, 65–66; "Business Brief—Webvan Group Inc.: Layoffs at Site are Planned," *Wall Street Journal,* 21 February 2001, B8.

424 Face-Off, Part 4, exhibit: Adapted from *Hoovers Online,* [accessed 22-February 2001], http://hoovers.com/co/capsule; Nick Wingfield, "Can These Dot-Coms Be Saved?—Cash Supply Shrinks While Webvan Losses Continue," *Wall Street Journal,* 25 January 2001; Nick Wingfield, "Webvan Expects Revenue to Miss Goals," *Wall Street Journal,* 10 January 2001.

424 Face-Off, Part 4, exhibit: Adapted from Paul Bubny, "Net Yet Clicking," *Supermarket Business,* 15 July 2000, 65-66; Stacy Perman, "I George Shaheen, Promise to Do My Best, to Do My Duty to God and My Country, to Help Other People, and to Beat the Living Crap out of the Competition," www.ecompany.com, September 2000, 147–154;

Connie Guglielmo, "Can Webvan Deliver? E-Commerce News, 31 January 2000, [accessed online 7 June 2000], http://www.zdnet.com/ecommerce/stories/main.

CHAPTER 16

429 Exhibit 16.1, Adapted from Joyce Thomas, "The Future—It Is Us," *Journal of Accountancy*, December 1998, 23.

430 Exhibit 16.2, Adapted from Gary Siegel and Bud Kulesza, "The Practice of Management Accounting," *Management Accounting*, April 1996, 20; "Up the Ladder of Success," *Journal of Accountancy*, November 2000, 24.

CHAPTER 17

462 Surprise! You've Been Swiped: Adapted from Tom Lowry, "Thieves Swipe Credit with Card Readers," *USA Today*, 28 June 1999, 1B; Elaine Shannon, "A New Credit-Card Scam," *Time*, 5 June 2000, 54–55; Linda Punch, "Card Fraud: Down But Not Out," *Credit Card Management*, June 1999, 30–42; Bill Orr, "Will E-Commerce Reverse Card Fraud Trend?" *American Bankers Association*, April 2000, 59–62.

463 Exhibit 17.5, Scott Woolley, "Virtual Banker," *Forbes*, 15 June 1998 [accessed 28 July 1999] http://www.forbes.com/forbes/98/0615/6112127a.htm; "Why Banks Don't Want to See You," *USA Today*, 17 February 1998, B1.

465 How Will You Be Paying for That?: Adapted from Julia Angwin, "E-Commerce: The Lessons We've Learned—E Money: And How Will You Be Paying for That?" *Wall Street Journal*, 23 October 2000, R37; Stacy Collett, "New Online Payment Options Emerging," *Computerworld*, 31 January 2000, 6; Kenneth Kiesnoski and Bob Curley, "Digital Wallets: Card issuers Seek to Ease Web Shopping," *Bank Systems and Technology*, October 1999, 26–34; Thomas E. Weber, "On the Web, the Race for a Better Wallet," *New York Times*, 16 December 1998, B1, B4.

468 Exhibit 17.6, "Money Stock and Debt Measures," Federal Reserve Release, 29 July 1999 [accessed 3 August 1999] http://www.bog.frb.fed.us/releases/H6/.

469 Exhibit 17.8 Adapted from *Statistical Abstract of the United States* (Washington, D.C.: GPO, 1999), 521.

470 Focusing on E-Business Today, Christine Dugas, "Virtual Banks Get Real, Offer Deals to Woo Customers," *USA Today*, 13 April 2000, 12B (graph is by Marcy E. Mullins, *USA Today*; graph source is Cyber Dialogue).

475 Baking Up Millions at Top of the Tree: Adapted from Tom Duffy, "Baking Up Millions," *Self-Employed Professional*, May–June 1997, 22–27; Carole Matthews, "Grassroots Marketing," *Self-Employed Professional*, May–June 1997, 22; "Gordon: The 6-Foot 9-Inch Pieguy . . ." Top of the Tree Baking Company, [accessed 24 March 1999] www.gordonpies.com/gordons3.htm; Michael Friedman, "Will Mrs. Smith's Acquisition Yield Array of Healthy Choice Desserts?" *Frozen Food Age*, April 1996, 5–6; John Duggleby, "Half-Baked Celebrity Raises Cash, Sells Pies to Erase $1 MM Debt," *The Edward Lowe Report*, March 2000, 1–2.

CHAPTER 18

481 Are Tracking Stocks on Track?: Adapted from Alan Levinsohn, "Tracking Stock," *Strategic Finance*, September 2000, 62–67; Susan Scherreik, "Tread Carefully When You Buy Tracking Stocks," *Business Week*, 6 March 2000, 182–84; Gretchen Morgenson, "Tracking Stocks' Luster Masks Risk and Conflict of Interests," *New York Times*, 12 December 2000, C1, C12; Peter Coy, "Tracking Stocks Are Accidents Waiting to Happen," *Business Week*, 2 August 1999, 33.

489 Exhibit 18.3, Fred Vogelstein, "A Virtual Stock Market," *U.S. News and World Report*, 26 April 1999, 47–48; Exhibit is on page 48—Robert Kemp USN&WR.

490 Exhibit 18.4, "The Big Picture," *Business Week*, 31 January 2000, 8; Data: Lemelson-MIT Awards Program.

496 Exhibit 18.8, "How to Read the Monthly Performance Tables," *Wall Street Journal*, 5 June 2000, R2.

497 Exhibit 18.9, Richard Korman, "Mining for Nuggets of Financial Data," *New York Times*, 21 June 1998, BU5.

498 Exhibit 18.10, Amy Feldman, "The Seedy World of Online Stock Scams," *Money*, February 2000, 143–48.

499 Focusing on E-Business Today, SEC Web site, [accessed 21 December 2000], http://www.sec.gov/consumer/jdatacom.htm.

502 Floored by Technology at the New York Stock Exchange: Peter Grant, "Big Board Signs Letter with State, City to Build $780 Million New York Home," *Wall Street Journal*, 21 December 2000, A8; Greg Ip and Peter Grant, "Deals & Deal Makers: NYSE's Deal for Staying in New York Draws Fire," *Wall Street Journal*, 6 December 2000, C22; Neil Weinburg, "The Big Board Comes Back from the Brink," *Forbes*, 13 November 2000, 274–280; Pimm Fox, "Floored by Technology," *Computerworld*, 23 October 2000, 41; "Stock Exchanges: The Battle for Efficient Markets," *The Economist*, 17 June 2000, 69–71; Marcia Trombly, "Under Pressure, the NYSE Moves Online," *Computerworld*, 27 March 2000, 48; Marcia Vickers, "Getting Off the NYSE Floor," *Business Week*, 7 February 2000, 80–81; Randall Smith, "Will NYSE Get Bowled Over by Rivals?" *Wall Street Journal*, 19 January 2000, C1; Hal Lux, "Grasso Seeks a Floor Plan," *Institutional Investor*, January 2000, 42–43; Greg Ip and Randall Smith, "Tense Exchange: Big Board's Members Face Off on the Issue of Automated Trading," *Wall Street Journal*, 15 November 1999, A, 1, 6; William P. Barrett, "End of an Era," *Forbes*, 11 October 1999, 121–126.

508 Face-Off, Part 5: Adapted from Randall Smith and Charles Gasparino, "Late to the Party: What Took Merrill Lynch So Long to Respond to the Web?" *Wall Street Journal*, 17 July 2000, R34; Leah Nathans Spiro, "Merrill's E-Battle," *Business Week*, 15 November 1999, 256–266; Andrew Rafalaf, "Can Merrill Overcome Its Legacy?" *Wall Street & Technology*, September 1999, 20-28; Shawn Tully, "Will The Web Eat Wall Street?" *Fortune*, 2 August 1999, 112–118; Patrick McGeehan, "Merrill Lynch Is Set to Move Into Banking," *New York Times*, 1 February 2000, C1, C6; Greg Ip and Rebecca Buckman, "The Web Snares Investors, Shifting Wall Street's Focus," *Wall Street Journal Interactive* [accessed 2 January 2000] http://www.interactive.wsj.com; Fred Vogelstein, "Can't Beat'Em," *U.S. News & World Report*, 14 June 1999, 42–44; James Kim and David Rynecki, "Merrill Lynch Hears Net's Call Firm Breaks Tradition, Integrates Cyber-Trading With Broker Service," *USA Today*, 2 June 1999, 01B; Robert Preston, "Merrill, HP The Latest to Confront Online-Selling Demons," *Internetweek*, 7 June 1999, 7; Thomas Hoffman, "Merrill Lynch Bows to Low-Cost Net Trading," *Computerworld*, 7 June 1999, 20; Louise Lee, "When You're No. 1, You Try Harder," *Business Week E.Biz*, 18 September 2000, EB88; Pui-Wing Tam and Randall Smith, "Schwab to Acquire U.S. Trust, Bringing in High-End Clients," *Wall Street Journal Interactive* [accessed 14 January 2000] http://www.interactive.wsj. com; Rebecca Buckman, "Schwab, Once A Predator, Is Now Prey," *Wall Street Journal*, 8 December 1999, C1; Paul J. Lim, "Broker Wars: The Battle Heats Up; Schwab, Merrill Plans Blur Industry's Lines," *Los Angeles Times*, 28 November 1999, 1; Erick Schonfeld, "Schwab Puts It All Online," *Fortune*, 7 December 1998, 94–100; Matthew Schifrin, "Cyber-Schwab," *Forbes*, 5 May 1997, 42–43; David S. Pottruck, "Same People. Same Values. Same Stationery. Different Company," *Wall Street Journal*, 28 December 1999, B10; Nanette Byrnes, "How Schwab Grabbed the Lion's Share," *Business Week*, 28 June 1999, 88; John Galvin, "Charles Schwab: Hey, Let's Transform the Company," *Smartbusinessmag.com*, November 2000, 124–125; Charles Schwab, "What's Best for Your Customers?" *Executive Excellence*, February 2000, 20.

508 Face-Off Exhibit, adapted from Merrill Lynch Web site, Financial Report Fact Book, [accessed 1 March 2001], http://www.ir.ml.com/; Charles Schwab Web site, 1999 Annual Report, [accessed 1 March 2001], http://www.aboutschwab.com/annualreport99/

financialhighlights/content.htm; Charles Schwab, "What's Best for Your Customers?" *Executive Excellence,* February 2000, 20; John Galvin, "Charles Schwab: Hey, Let's Transform the Company," *Smartbusinessmag.com,* November 2000, 124–125.

508 Face-Off Exhibit, adapted from Charles Schwab Corporation 1999 annual report, [accessed 1 March 2001], http://www. aboutschwab.com/; Charles Schwab, "What's Best for Your Customers?" *Executive Excellence,* February 2000, 20; John Galvin, "Charles Schwab: Hey, Let's Transform the Company," *Smartbusinessmag.com,* November 2000, 124–125.

COMPONENT CHAPTER B

516 Exhibit B.5, Adapted from Bartley A. Brennan and Nancy Kubasek, *The Legal Environment of Business* (New York: Macmillan, 1988), 24; Douglas Whitman and John Gergacz, *The Legal Environment of Business,* 2d ed. (New York: Random House, 1988), 22, 25.

522 Exhibit B.7, Adapted from Richard A. Brealey and Steward C. Myers, *Principles of Corporate Finance,* 4th ed. (New York: McGraw-Hill, 1991), 761–765.

COMPONENT CHAPTER D

536 Exhibit D.1, Nancy Shepherdson, "Life's A Beach 101," *American Demographics,* May 2000, 56–64.

536 Exhibit D.2, Nancy Shepherdson, "Life's A Beach 101," *American Demographics,* May 2000, 56–64.

538 Exhibit D.3, Bureau of Labor Statistics, [accessed 4 August 1999], www.bls.gov/images/ocotj10.gif.

539 Exhibit D.4, Bureau of Labor Statistics, [accessed 4 August 1999], www.bls.gov/images/ocotj08.gif.

■ Photo Credits

CHAPTER 1

page 2: Ronald W. Weir/ZEFA/Corbis/Stock Market; page 3: Michael Scumann/Corbis/SABA Press Photos, Inc.; page 6: Dakota Studios/Liaison Agency, Inc.; page 10: Joe Traver/Liaison Agency, Inc.; page 14: Michael Scumann/Corbis/SABA Press Photos, Inc.; page 15: Dennis Brack/Black Star; page 35: Joe Traver/Liaison Agency, Inc.

CHAPTER 2

page 42: David Woodfall/Stone; page 43: Pictor; page 49: Toby Talbot/AP/Wide World Photos; page 50: Marilynn K. Yee/NYT Permissions; page 53: Liaison Agency, Inc.; page 55: Mark Graham; page 57: Liaison Agency, Inc.

CHAPTER 3

page 68: Hugh Sitton/Stone; page 69: Reuters/Jacky Naegelen/Archive Photos; page 75: Greg Girard/Contact Press Images Inc.; page 80: Robert Sorbo/Corbis/Sygma; page 82: ©Daemmrich/The Image Works; page 84: Archive Photos; page 86: Misha Japaridze/AP/Wide World Photos.

CHAPTER 4

page 98: Peter Beck/Corbis/Stock Market; page 99: Amy C. Etra; page 101: Michael L. Abramson; page 103: T. Michael Keza Photography; page 104: Philip Saltonstall; page 110: Matrix International, Inc.; page 112: T. Michael Keza Photography; page 115: Steve Rawls Photography; page 116: Richard Howard Photography.

CHAPTER 5

page 124: Walter Hodges/Stone; page 125: Dan Lamont Photography; page 129: Michael Carroll Photography; page 130: Captured by Jodi Jacobson; page 131: Giboux/Liaison Agency, Inc.; page 137: Stuart Ramson/AP/Wide World Photos; page 138: Richard Drew/AP/Wide World Photos.

CHAPTER 6

page 150: Jim Cummins/Corbis/Stock Market; page 151: Reuters/Fred Prouser/Archive Photosl; page 155: Susan Ragan/AP/Wide World Photos; page 157: Thierry Charlier/AP/Wide World Photos; page 159: Etienn De Malglaive/Liaison Agency, Inc.; page 162: AP/Wide World Photos.

CHAPTER 7

page 176: Masterfile Corporation; page 177: Valrie Massey/Photo 20-20, Inc.; page 184: Rob Crandall/Stock Boston; page 185: Jay Daniel/Photo 20-20, Inc.; page 188: John Coletti/Stock Boston; page 191: Stephen Simpson/FPG International LLC; page 194: Charles Gupton/Stone.

CHAPTER 8

page 202: Henrik Montgomery/Pressens Bild/Retna, Ltd.; page 203: Laura Rauch/AP/Wide World Photos; page 213: Ann States/Corbis/SABA Press Photos, Inc.; page 215: John Maier, Jr./The Image Works; page 219: Todd Buchanan; page 221: Tom McCarthy/Rainbow.

CHAPTER 9

page 230: Mark Bolster/International Stock Photography Ltd.; page 231: Jim West/Impact Visuals Photo & Graphics, Inc.; page 234: Jonathan Atkin; page 240: AP/Wide World Photos; page 246: Reuters/Larry Chan/Archive Photos; page 248: Mark Richards/PhotoEdit; page 248: Sven Kaestner Stringer/AP/Wide World Photos.

CHAPTER 10

page 260: Masterfile Corporation; page 261: SAS Institute, Inc.; page 269: Nancy Pierce for The New York Times; page 270: Brian Coats Photography; page 271: Bill Sikes/AP/Wide World Photos; page 272: Bob Marshak/Photofest; page 277: Donna McWilliam/AP/Wide World Photos.

CHAPTER 11

page 288: Telegraph Colour Library/FPG International LLC; page 289: Amy C. Etra/PhotoEdit; page 294: Bob Daemmrich/The Image Works; page 295: Grant/Monkmeyer Press; page 296: page 300: PhotoEdit; Joe Raymond; page 304: Jason Grow/Corbis/SABA Press Photos, Inc.

CHAPTER 12

page 316: Churchill & Klehr Photography; page 317: LWA-Dann Tardif/Corbis/Stock Market; page 323: Michael Newman/PhotoEdit; page 326: Rhoda Sidney/PhotoEdit; page 333: David Young-Wolff/Stone.

CHAPTER 13

page 344: Patrick Ramsey/International Stock Photography Ltd.; page 345: Lynsey Addario/AP/Wide World Photos; page 347: Jeff Zelevansky/AP/Wide World Photos; page 348: Ted Rice; page 350: Kyoko Hamada; page 354: David Kampfner/Liaison Agency, Inc.

CHAPTER 14

page 368: Art Montes De Oca/FPG International LLC; page 369: Robert Holmgren Photography ; page 379: Jim Argo; page 380: Michael Newman/PhotoEdit; page 381: Jean-MichelBertrand/A Perfect Exposure; page 384: Kristine Larsen; page 385: David Burnett/Contact Press Images Inc.

CHAPTER 15

page 396: Jack K. Clark/The Image Works; page 397: Bill Cramer Photography; page 398: ad used with permission from Leo Burnett U.S.A., a Division of Leo Burnett Company, Inc.; page 400: Robin Nelson/Black Star; page 401: Michael Newman/PhotoEdit; page 405: Karen Leitza/Karin Leitza; page 412: Marilyn Yee / NYT Pictures.

CHAPTER 16

page 426: Jose Pelaez Photography/Corbis/Stock Market; page 427: Janice B. Terry Photography; page 431: SuperStock, Inc.; page 434: Bob Firth Photography/International Stock Photography Ltd.; page 440: Terry Vine/Stone; page 442: Olathe Daily News, Todd Feeback/AP/Wide World Photos.

CHAPTER 17

page 456: Shotgun/Corbis/Stock Market; page 457: Robbie McClaran/Corbis/SABA Press Photos, Inc.; page 463: Peter Cade/Stone; page 466: Michael Krasowitz/FPG International LLC; page 452: Jim Cummins/FPG International LLC.

CHAPTER 18

page 478: Poulides/Thatcher/Stone; page 479: Ann Dowie/New York Times Pictures; page 480: Ron Sherman/Ron Sherman, Photographer; page 483: BellSouth Corporation; page 485: Mark Joseph/Stone; page 490: Jeffrey MacMillan, U. S. News & World Report; page 491: Pat Sullivan/AP/Wide World Photos; page 492: James Leynse/Corbis/SABA Press Photos, Inc.; page 498: Ruby Washington/New York Times Pictures.

COMPONENT CHAPTER B

page 511: James Leynse/Corbis/SABA Press Photos, Inc.; page 517: ©Forrest MacCormack 2000; page 521 (top left): Liaison Agency, Inc.; page 521 (bottom right): Peter Cosgrove/AP/Wide World Photos.

COMPONENT CHAPTER C

page 525: Nick Ut/AP/Wide World Photos; page 526 (top left): Stan Godlewski; page 526 (bottom right): Stone; page 529: Francois Mori/AP/Wide World Photos; page 529: Susan Holtz; page 530: Jason Grow/Corbis/SABA Press Photos, Inc.

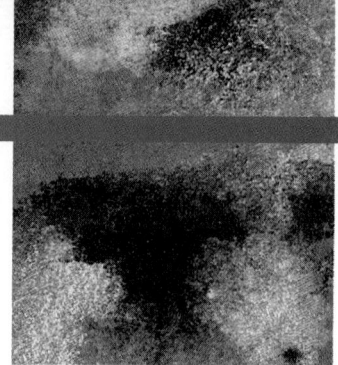

GLOSSARY

A

absolute advantage A nation's ability to produce a particular product with fewer resources per unit of output than any other nation

accountability Obligation to report results to supervisors or team members and to justify outcomes that fall below expectations

accounting Measuring, interpreting, and communicating financial information to support internal and external decision making

accounting equation Basic accounting equation stating that assets equal liabilities plus owners' equity

accounts receivable turnover ratio Measure of the time a company takes to turn its accounts receivable into cash, calculated by dividing sales by the average value of accounts receivable for a period

accrual basis Accounting method in which revenue is recorded when a sale is made and expense is recorded when it is incurred

acquisition Form of business combination in which one company buys another company's voting stock

activity ratios Ratios that measure the effectiveness of the firm's use of its resources

actual cash value coverage Property insurance in which the insurer pays for the replacement cost of property at the time of loss, less an allowance for depreciation

actuaries People employed by an insurance company to compute expected losses and to calculate the cost of premiums

administrative law Rules, regulations, and interpretations of statutory law set forth by administrative agencies and commissions

administrative skills Technical skills in information gathering, data analysis, planning, organizing, and other aspects of managerial work

advertising Paid, nonpersonal communication to a target market from an identified sponsor using mass communications channels

advocacy advertising Ads that present a company's opinions on public issues such as education and health

affirmative action Activities undertaken by businesses to recruit and promote women and minorities, based on an analysis of the workforce and the available labor pool

agency Business relationship that exists when one party (the principal) authorizes another party (the agent) to enter into contracts on the principal's behalf

agents and brokers Independent wholesalers that do not take title to the goods they distribute but may or may not take possession of those goods

analytic system Production process that breaks incoming materials into various component products and divisional patterns simultaneously

application software Programs that perform specific functions for users, such as word processing or spreadsheet analysis

arbitration Process for resolving a labor-contract dispute in which an impartial third party studies the issues and makes a binding decision

artificial intelligence Ability of computers to reason, to learn, and to simulate human sensory perceptions

asset allocation Method of shifting investments within a portfolio to adapt them to the current investment environment

assets Any things of value owned or leased by a business

auction exchange Centralized marketplace where securities are traded by specialists on behalf of investors

audit Formal evaluation of the fairness and reliability of a client's financial statements

authority Power granted by the organization to make decisions, take actions, and allocate resources to accomplish goals

authorization cards Sign-up cards designating a union as the signer's preferred bargaining agent

authorized stock Shares that a corporation's board of directors has decided to sell eventually

autocratic leaders Leaders who do not involve others in decision making

automated teller machines (ATMs) Electronic terminals that permit people with plastic cards to perform simple banking transactions 24 hours a day without the aid of a human teller

B

balance of payments Sum of all payments one nation receives from other nations minus the sum of all payments it makes to other nations, over some specified period of time

balance of trade Total value of the products a nation exports minus the total value of the products it imports, over some period of time

balance sheet Statement of a firm's financial position on a particular date; also known as a statement of financial position

bandwidth Maximum capacity of a data transmission medium

bankruptcy Legal procedure by which a person or a business that is unable to meet financial obligations is relieved of debt

banner ads A rectangular graphic display on a Web page that is used for advertising and linked to an advertiser's Web page

barriers to entry Factors that make it difficult to launch a business in a particular industry

bear market Falling stock market

behavior modification Systematic use of rewards and punishments to change human behavior

behavioral segmentation Categorization of customers according to their relationship with products or response to product characteristics

beneficiaries People named in a life insurance policy who receive the proceeds of an insurance contract when the insured dies

blue-chip stock Equity issued by large, well-established companies with consistent records of stock price increases and dividend payments

board of directors Group of people, elected by the shareholders, who have the ultimate authority in guiding the affairs of a corporation

bond Method of funding in which the issuer borrows from an investor and provides a written promise to make regular interest payments and repay the borrowed amount in the future

bonus Cash payment, in addition to the regular wage or salary, that serves as a reward for achievement

bookkeeping Record keeping, clerical aspect of accounting

bookmark A browser feature that places selected URLs in a file for quick access, allowing you to automatically return to the Web site by clicking on the site's name

Boolean operators The term *boolean* refers to a system of logical thought developed by the English mathematician George Boole; it uses the operators AND, OR, and NOT

boycott Union activity in which members and sympathizers refuse to buy or handle the product of a target company

brand A name, term, sign, symbol, design, or combination of those used to identify the products of a firm and to differentiate them from competing products

brand awareness Level of brand loyalty at which people are familiar with a product; they recognize it

brand insistence Level of brand loyalty at which people will accept no substitute for a particular product

brand loyalty Commitment to a particular brand

brand manager The person who develops and implements a complete strategy and marketing program for a specific product or brand

brand mark Portion of a brand that cannot be expressed verbally

brand names Portion of a brand that can be expressed orally, including letters, words, or numbers

brand preference Level of brand loyalty at which people habitually buy a product if it is available

breach of contract Failure to live up to the terms of a contract, with no legal excuse

break-even analysis Method of calculating the minimum volume of sales needed at a given price to cover all costs

break-even point Sales volume at a given price that will cover all of a company's costs

broadbanding Payment system that uses wide pay grades, enabling the company to give pay raises without promotions

broker Individual registered to sell securities

browser Software, such as Netscape Navigator or Microsoft's Internet Explorer, that enables a computer to search for, display, and download the multimedia information that appears on the World Wide Web

budget Planning and control tool that reflects expected revenues, operating expenses, and cash receipts and outlays

bull market Rising stock market

bundling Combining several products and offering the bundle at a reduced price

business Activity and enterprise that provides goods and services that a society needs

business agent Full-time union staffer who negotiates with management and enforces the union's agreements with companies

business cycle Fluctuations in the rate of growth that an economy experiences over a period of several years

business law Those elements of law that directly influence or control business activities

business plan A written document that provides an orderly statement of a company's goals and how it intends to achieve those goals

business-interruption insurance Insurance that covers losses resulting from temporary business closings

business-to-business e-commerce Electronic commerce that involves transactions between companies and their suppliers, manufacturers, or other companies

business-to-consumer e-commerce Electronic commerce that involves transactions between businesses and the end user or consumer

buyers' market Marketplace characterized by an abundance of products

C

calendar year Twelve-month accounting period that begins on January 1 and ends on December 31

canned approach Selling method based on a fixed, memorized presentation

capacity planning A long-term strategic decision that determines the level of resources available to an organization to meet customer demand

capital The physical, human-made elements used to produce goods and services, such as factories and computers; can also refer to the funds that finance the operations of a business

capital budgeting Process for evaluating proposed investments in select projects that provide the best long-term financial return

capital gains Difference between the price at which a financial asset is sold and its original cost (assuming the price has gone up)

capital investments Money paid to acquire something of permanent value in a business

capital structure Financing mix of a firm

capital-intensive businesses Businesses that require large investments in capital assets

capitalism Economic system based on economic freedom and competition

cash basis Accounting method in which revenue is recorded when payment is received and expense is recorded when cash is paid

category killers Discount chains that sell only one category of products

cause-related marketing Identification and marketing of a social issue, cause, or idea to selected target markets

CD-ROMs Storage devices that use the same technology as music CDs; popular because of their low cost and large storage capacity

cellular layout Method of arranging a facility so that parts with similar shapes or processing requirements are processed together in work centers

central processing unit (CPU) Core of the computer, performing the three basic functions of arithmetic (addition, etc.), logic (comparing numbers), and control/communication (managing the computer)

centralization Concentration of decision-making authority at the top of the organization

certification Process by which a union is officially recognized by the National Labor Relations Board as the bargaining agent for a group of employees

certified management accountants (CMAs) Accountants who have fulfilled the requirements for certification as specialists in management accounting

certified public accountants (CPAs) Professionally licensed accountants who meet certain requirements for education and experience and who pass a comprehensive examination

chain of command Pathway for the flow of authority from one management level to the next

channel captain Channel member that is able to influence the activities of the other members of the distribution channel

chat A form of interactive communication that enables computer users in separate locations to have real-time conversations. Usually takes place at Web sites called chat rooms

checks Written orders that tell the customer's bank to pay a specific amount to a particular individual or business

chief executive officer (CEO) Person appointed by a corporation's board of directors to carry out the board's policies and supervise the activities of the corporation

chief information officer (CIO) Top corporate executive with responsibility for managing information and information systems

chronological résumé Most traditional type of résumé, listing employment history sequentially in reverse order so that the most recent experience is listed first

claims Demands for payments from an insurance company because of some loss by the insured

client/server system Computer system design in which one computer (the server) contains software and data used by a number of attached computers (the clients); the clients also have their own processing capabilities, and they share certain tasks with the server, enabling the system to run at optimum efficiency

close the books The act of transferring net revenue and expense account balances to retained earnings for the period

closing Point at which a sale is completed

coaching Helping employees reach their highest potential by meeting with them, discussing problems that hinder their ability to work effectively, and offering suggestions and encouragement to overcome these problems

co-branding Partnership between two or more companies to closely link their brand names together for a single product

code of ethics Written statement setting forth the principles that guide an organization's decisions

cognitive dissonance Anxiety following a purchase that prompts buyers to seek reassurance about the purchase; commonly known as buyer's remorse

cohesiveness A measure of how committed the team members are to their team's goals

collateral Tangible asset a lender can claim if a borrower defaults on a loan

collective bargaining Process used by unions and management to negotiate work contracts

commercial paper An IOU, backed by the corporation's reputation, issued to raise short-term capital

commercialization Large-scale production and distribution of a product

commissions Payments to employees equal to a certain percentage of sales made

committee Team that may become a permanent part of the organization and is designed to deal with regularly recurring tasks

commodities Raw materials used in producing other goods

common carriers Transportation companies that offer their services to the general public

common law Law based on the precedents established by judges' decisions

common stock Shares whose owners have voting rights and have the last claim on distributed profits and assets

communism Economic system in which all productive resources are owned and operated by the government, to the elimination of private property

comparative advantage theory Theory that states that a country should produce and sell to other countries those items it produces more efficiently

comparative advertising Advertising technique in which two or more products are explicitly compared

compensating balance Portion of an unsecured loan that is kept on deposit at the lending institution to protect the lender and increase the lender's return

compensation Money, benefits, and services paid to employees for their work

competition Rivalry among businesses for the same customer

competitive advantage Ability to perform in one or more ways that competitors cannot match

competitive advertising Ads that specifically highlight how a product is better than its competitors

computer-aided design (CAD) Use of computer graphics and mathematical modeling in the development of products

computer-aided engineering (CAE) Use of computers to test products without building an actual model

computer-aided manufacturing (CAM) Use of computers to control production equipment

computer-integrated manufacturing (CIM) Computer-based systems, including CAD and CAM, that coordinate and control all the elements of design and production

conceptual skills Ability to understand the relationship of parts to the whole

conglomerate mergers Combinations of companies that are in unrelated businesses, designed to augment a company's growth and to diversify risk

consent order Settlement in which an individual or organization promises to discontinue some illegal activity without admitting guilt

consideration Negotiated exchange necessary to make a contract legally binding

consolidation Combination of two or more companies in which the old companies cease to exist and a new enterprise is created

consumer buying behavior Behavior exhibited by consumers as they consider and purchase various products

consumer market Individuals or households that buy goods or services for personal use

consumer price index (CPI) Monthly statistic that measures changes in the prices of about 400 goods and services that consumers buy

consumer promotion Sales promotion aimed at final consumers

consumer-to-consumer e-commerce Electronic commerce that involves transactions between consumers

consumerism Movement that pressures businesses to consider consumer needs and interests

contingency leadership Adapting the leadership style to what is most appropriate, given current business conditions

contingent business-interruption insurance Insurance that protects a business from losses resulting from losses sustained by other businesses such as suppliers or transportation companies

continuity Pattern according to which an ad appears in the media; it can be spread evenly over time or concentrated during selected periods

contract Legally enforceable exchange of promises between two or more parties

contract carriers Specialized freight haulers that serve selected companies under written contract

controller Highest-ranking accountant in a company, responsible for overseeing all accounting functions

controlling Process of measuring progress against goals and objectives and correcting deviations if results are not as expected

convertible bonds Corporate bonds that can be exchanged at the owner's discretion into common stock of the issuing company

cooperative advertising Joint efforts between local and national advertisers, in which producers of nationally sold products share the costs of local advertising with local merchants and wholesalers

core competence Distinct skills and capabilities that a firm has or does especially well so that it sets the firm apart from its competitors

corporation Legally chartered enterprise having most of the legal rights of a person, including the right to conduct business, to own and sell property, to borrow money, and to sue or be sued; owners of the corporation enjoy limited liability

cost accounting Area of accounting focusing on the calculation of manufacturing and storage costs of products for use or sale in a business

cost of capital Average rate of interest a firm pays on its combination of debt and equity

cost of goods sold Cost of producing or acquiring a company's products for sale during a given period

cost per thousand (CPM) Cost of reaching 1,000 people with an ad

coupons Certificates that offer discounts on particular items and are redeemed at the time of purchase

creative selling Selling process used by order getters, which involves determining customer needs, devising strategies to explain product benefits, and persuading customers to buy

credit cards Plastic cards that allow the customer to buy now and pay back the loaned amount at a future date

crisis management System for minimizing the harm that might result from some unusually threatening situations

critical path In a PERT network diagram, the sequence of operations that requires the longest time to complete

cross-functional teams Teams that draw together employees from different functional areas

cross-promotion Jointly advertising two or more noncompeting brands

currency Bills and coins that make up the cash money of a society

current assets Cash and items that can be turned into cash within one year

current liabilities Obligations that must be met within a year

current ratio Measure of a firm's short-term liquidity, calculated by dividing current assets by current liabilities

customer divisions Divisional structure that focuses on customers or clients

customer service Efforts a company makes to satisfy its customers to help them realize the greatest possible value from the products they are purchasing

customs duties Fees imposed on goods brought into the country; also called import taxes

D

damages Financial compensation to an injured party for loss and suffering

data Recorded facts and statistics; data need to be converted to information before they can help people solve business problems

data communications Process of connecting computers and allowing them to send data back and forth

data mining Sifting through huge amounts of data to identify what is valuable to a specific question or problem

data warehousing Building an organized central database out of files and databases gathered from various functional areas, such as marketing, operations, and accounting

database A collection of related data that can be cross-referenced in order to extract information

database marketing Process of building, maintaining, and using customer databases for the purpose of contacting customers and transacting business

day order Any order to buy or sell a security that automatically expires if not executed on the day the order is placed

dealer exchange Decentralized marketplace where securities are bought and sold by dealers out of their own inventories

debentures Corporate bonds backed only by the reputation of the issuer

debit cards Plastic cards that allow the bank to take money from the user's demand-deposit account and transfer it to a retailer's account

debt ratios Ratios that measure a firm's reliance on debt financing of its operations (sometimes called leverage ratios)

debt-to-equity ratio Measure of the extent to which a business is financed by debt as opposed to invested capital, calculated by dividing the company's total liabilities by owners' equity

debt-to-total-assets ratio Measure of a firm's ability to carry long-term debt, calculated by dividing total liabilities by total assets

decentralization Delegation of decision-making authority to employees in lower-level positions

decertification Process employees use to take away a union's official right to represent them

decision making Process of identifying a decision situation, analyzing the problem, weighing the alternatives, choosing an alternative and implementing it, and evaluating the results

decision support system (DSS) Information system that uses decision models, specialized databases, and artificial intelligence to assist managers in solving highly unstructured and nonroutine problems

deductible Amount of loss that must be paid by the insured before the insurer will pay for the rest

deed Legal document by which an owner transfers the title, or ownership rights, to real property to a new owner

deflation Economic condition in which prices fall steadily throughout the economy

delegation Assignment of work and the authority and responsibility required to complete it

demand Buyers' willingness and ability to purchase products

demand curve Graph of relationship between various prices and the quantity demanded at each price

demand deposit Money in a checking account that can be used by the customer at any time

democratic leaders Leaders who delegate authority and involve employees in decision making

demographics Study of statistical characteristics of a population

departmentalization Grouping people within an organization according to function, division, matrix, or network

departmentalization by division Grouping departments according to similarities in product, process, customer, or geography

departmentalization by function Grouping workers according to their similar skills, resource use, and expertise

departmentalization by matrix Assigning employees to both a functional group and a project team (thus using functional and divisional patterns simultaneously)

departmentalization by network Electronically connecting separate companies that perform selected tasks for a small headquarters organization

depreciation Accounting procedure for systematically spreading the cost of a tangible asset over its estimated useful life

deregulation Removal or relaxation of rules and restrictions affecting businesses

direct mail Advertising sent directly to potential customers, usually through the U.S. Postal Service

direct marketing Direct communication other than personal sales contacts designed to effect a measurable response

direct public offering (DPO) Sale of shares of a company's stock directly to investors instead of going through underwriters

disability income insurance Short-term or long-term insurance that protects an individual against loss of income while that individual is disabled as the result of an illness or accident

discount pricing Offering a reduction in price

discount rate Interest rate charged by the Federal Reserve on loans to commercial banks and other financial institutions

discount stores Retailers that sell a variety of goods below the market price by keeping their overhead low

discretionary order Market order that allows the broker to decide when to trade a security

discrimination In a social and economic sense, denial of opportunities to individuals on the basis of some characteristic that has no bearing on their ability to perform in a job

discussion mailing lists E-mail lists that allow people to discuss a common interest by posting messages that are received by everyone in the group

disk drive Most common mechanism for secondary storage; includes both hard disk drives and floppy disk (diskette) drives

dispatching Issuing work orders and schedules to department heads and supervisors

distortion Misunderstanding that results when a message passes through too many links in the organization

distribution centers Warehouse facilities that specialize in collecting and shipping merchandise

distribution channels Systems for moving goods and services from producers to customers; also known as marketing channels

distribution mix Combination of intermediaries and channels a producer uses to get a product to end users

distribution strategy Firm's overall plan for moving products to intermediaries and final customers

diversification Assembling investment portfolios in such a way that a loss in one investment won't cripple the value of the entire portfolio

diversity initiatives Company policies designed to enhance opportunities for minorities and to promote understanding of diverse cultures, customs, and talents

dividends Distributions of corporate assets to shareholders in the form of cash or other assets

domain name The portion of an Internet address that identifies the host and indicates the type of organization it is

double-entry bookkeeping Way of recording financial transactions that requires two entries for every transaction so that the accounting equation is always kept in balance

download Transmitting a file from one computer system to another; on the Internet, bringing data from the Internet into your computer

drop shippers Limited-service merchant wholesalers that assume ownership of goods but don't take physical possession; commonly used to market agricultural and mineral products

dumping Charging less than the actual cost or less than the home-country price for goods sold in other countries

dynamic pricing Charging different prices depending on individual customers and situations

E

earnings per share Measure of a firm's profitability for each share of outstanding stock, calculated by dividing net income after taxes by the average number of shares of common stock outstanding

ecology Study of the relationships between living things in the water, air, and soil, their environments, and the nutrients that support them

economic indicators Statistics that measure variables in the economy

economic system Means by which a society distributes its resources to satisfy its people's needs

economics The study of how society uses scarce resources to produce and distribute goods and services

economies of scale Savings from manufacturing, marketing, or buying in large quantities

electronic business (e-business) A company that has transformed its key business processes to incorporate Internet technology into every phase of the operation

electronic commerce (e-commerce) The general term for the buying and selling of goods and services on the Internet

electronic communication networks (ECNs) Internet-based networks that match up buy and sell orders without using a middleman

electronic data interchange (EDI) Information systems that transmit documents such as invoices and purchase orders between computers, thereby lowering ordering costs and paperwork

electronic funds transfer systems (EFTS) Computerized systems for performing financial transactions

e-mail Communication system that enables computers to transmit and receive written messages over electronic networks

embargo Total ban on trade with a particular nation (a sanction) or of a particular product

employee assistance programs (EAPs) Company-sponsored counseling or referral plans for employees with personal problems

employee benefits Compensation other than wages, salaries, and incentive programs

employee stock-ownership plan (ESOP) Program enabling employees to become partial owners of a company

employment at will Employer's right to keep or terminate employees as it wishes

employment interview Formal meeting during which an employer and an applicant ask questions and exchange information to see whether the applicant and the organization are a good match

enterprise resource planning (ERP) A comprehensive database system that includes information about the firm's suppliers and customers as well as data generated internally

entrepreneurs People who accept the risk of failure in the private enterprise system

equilibrium price Point at which quantity supplied equals quantity demanded

ethical dilemma Situation in which both sides of an issue can be supported with valid arguments

ethical lapse Situation in which an individual makes a decision that is morally wrong, illegal, or unethical

ethics The rules or standards governing the conduct of a person or group

euro A planned unified currency used by European nations that meet certain strict requirements

exchange process Act of obtaining a desired object from another party by offering something of value in return

exchange rate Rate at which the money of one country is traded for the money of another

excise taxes Taxes intended to help control potentially harmful practices or to help pay for government services used only by certain people or businesses

exclusive distribution Market coverage strategy that gives intermediaries exclusive rights to sell a product in a specific geographical area

executive information system (EIS) Similar to decision support system but customized to strategic needs of executives

expenses Costs created in the process of generating revenues

expert system Computer system that simulates the thought processes of a human expert who is adept at solving particular problems

exporting Selling and shipping goods or services to another country

express contract Contract derived from words, either oral or written

external data Data acquired from sources outside the company

extra-expense insurance Insurance that covers the added expense of operating the business in temporary facilities after an event such as a fire or a flood

extranet Similar to an intranet, but extending the network to select people outside the organization

factors of production Basic inputs that a society uses to produce goods and services, including natural resources, labor, capital, entrepreneurship, and knowledge

family branding Using a brand name on a variety of related products

fiber optic cable Cable that transmits data as laser-generated pulses of light; capable of transmitting data at very fast speeds

file transfer protocol (FTP) A software protocol that lets you copy or move files from a remote computer—called an FTP site—to your computer over the Internet; it is the Internet facility for downloading and uploading files

financial accounting Area of accounting concerned with preparing financial information for users outside the organization

financial analysis Process of evaluating a company's performance and analyzing the costs and benefits of a strategic action

financial control The process of analyzing and adjusting the basic financial plan to correct for forecasted events that do not materialize

financial futures Legally binding agreements to buy or sell financial instruments at a future date

financial management Effective acquisition and use of money

financial plan A forecast of financial requirements and the financing sources to be used

firewall Computer hardware and software that protects part or all of a private computer network attached to the Internet by preventing public Internet users from accessing it

first-line managers Those at the lowest level of the management hierarchy; they supervise the operating employees and implement the plans set at the higher management levels; also called supervisory managers

fiscal policy Use of government revenue collection and spending to influence the business cycle

fiscal year Any 12 consecutive months used as an accounting period

fixed assets Assets retained for long-term use, such as land, buildings, machinery, and equipment; also referred to as property, plant, and equipment

fixed costs Business costs that remain constant regardless of the number of units produced

fixed-position layout Method of arranging a facility so that the product is stationary and equipment and personnel come to it

flat organizations Organizations with a wide span of management and few hierarchical levels

flexible manufacturing system (FMS) Production system using computer-controlled machines that can adapt to various versions of the same operation

flextime Scheduling system in which employees are allowed certain options regarding time of arrival and departure

floating exchange rate system World economic system in which the values of all currencies are determined by supply and demand

foreign direct investment (FDI) Investment of money by foreign companies in domestic business enterprises

foreign exchange Trading one currency for the equivalent value of another currency

form utility Consumer value created by converting raw materials and other inputs into finished goods and services

formal communication network Communication network that follows the official structure of the organization

forward buying Retailers' taking advantage of trade allowances by buying more products at discounted prices than they hope to sell

franchise Business arrangement in which a small business obtains rights to sell the goods or services of the supplier (franchisor)

franchisee Small-business owner who contracts for the right to sell goods or services of the supplier (franchisor) in exchange for some payment

franchisor Supplier that grants a franchise to an individual or group (franchisee) in exchange for payments

free riders Team members who do not contribute sufficiently to the group's activities because members are not being held individually accountable for their work

free trade International trade unencumbered by restrictive measures

free-market system Economic system in which decisions about what to produce and in what quantities are decided by the market's buyers and sellers

frequency Average number of times that each audience member is exposed to the message (equal to the total number of exposures divided by the total audience population)

full-service merchant wholesalers Merchant wholesalers that provide a wide variety of services to their customers, such as storage, delivery, and marketing support

functional résumé Résumé organized around a list of skills and accomplishments, subordinating employers and academic experience in order to stress individual areas of competence

functional teams Teams whose members come from a single functional department and that are based on the organization's vertical structure

functional-replacement-cost coverage Property insurance that allows for the substitution of construction materials to restore a property to a similar, functioning state

G

gain sharing Plan for rewarding employees not on the basis of overall profits but in relation to achievement of goals such as cost savings from higher productivity

Gantt chart Bar chart used to control schedules by showing how long each part of a production process should take and when it should take place

general expenses Operating expenses, such as office and administrative expenses, not directly associated with creating or marketing a good or a service

general obligation bond Municipal bonds backed by the issuing agency's general taxing authority

general partnership Partnership in which all partners have the right to participate as co-owners and are individually liable for the business's debts

generally accepted accounting principles (GAAP) Professionally approved U.S. standards and practices used by accountants in the preparation of financial statements

generic products Products characterized by a plain label, with no advertising and no brand name

geodemographics Method of combining geographical data with demographic data to develop profiles of neighborhood segments

geographic divisions Divisional structure based on location of operations

geographic segmentation Categorization of customers according to their geographical location

glass ceiling Invisible barrier attributable to subtle discrimination that keeps women out of the top positions in business

globalization Tendency of the world's economies to act as a single interdependent system

goal Broad, long-range target or aim

goods-producing businesses Businesses that produce tangible products

graphical user interface (GUI) A user-friendly program that enables computer operators to enter commands by clicking on icons and menus with a mouse

gross domestic product (GDP) Dollar value of all the final goods and services produced by businesses located within a nation's borders; excludes receipts from overseas operations of domestic companies

gross national product (GNP) Dollar value of all the final goods and services produced by domestic businesses; includes receipts from overseas operations and excludes receipts from foreign-owned businesses within a nation's borders

gross profit Amount remaining when the cost of goods sold is deducted from net sales; also known as gross margin

growth stocks Equities issued by small companies with unproven products or services

H

hardware Physical components of a computer system, including integrated circuits, keyboards, and disk drives

health maintenance organizations (HMOs) Prepaid medical plans in which consumers pay a set fee in order to receive a full range of medical care from a group of medical practitioners

hedge To make an investment that protects the investor from suffering loss on another investment

holding company Company that owns most, or all, of another company's stock but that does not actively participate in the management of that other company

homepage The primary Web site for an organization or individual; the first hypertext document displayed on a Web site

horizontal coordination Coordinating communication and activities across departments

horizontal mergers Combinations of companies that are direct competitors in the same industry

hostile takeover Situation in which an outside party buys enough stock in a corporation to take control against the wishes of the board of directors and corporate officers

human relations Interaction among people within an organization for the purpose of achieving organizational and personal goals

human resources All the people who work for an organization

human resources management (HRM) Specialized function of planning how to obtain employees, oversee their training, evaluate them, and compensate them

hygiene factors Aspects of the work environment that are associated with dissatisfaction

hyperlink A highlighted word or image on a Web page or document that automatically allows people to move to another Web page or document when clicked on with a mouse

hypertext markup language (HTML) The software language used to create, present, and link pages on the World Wide Web

hypertext transfer protocol (HTTP) A communications protocol that allows people to navigate among documents or pages linked by hypertext and to download pages from the World Wide Web

I

implied contract Contract derived from actions or conduct

importing Purchasing goods or services from another country and bringing them into one's own country

incentives Cash payments to employees who produce at a desired level or whose unit (often the company as a whole) produces at a desired level

income statement Financial record of a company's revenues, expenses, and profits over a given period of time

incubators Facilities that house small businesses during their early growth phase

index number Percentage used to compare such figures as prices or costs in one period with those in a base or standard period

industrial distributors Wholesalers that sell to industrial customers rather than to retailers

inflation Economic condition in which prices rise steadily throughout the economy

informal communication network Communication network that follows the organization's unofficial lines of activity and power

informal organization Network of informal employee interactions that are not defined by the formal structure

initial public offering (IPO) Corporation's first offering of stock to the public

injunction Court order prohibiting certain actions by striking workers

insider trading The attempt to benefit from stock market fluctuations by using unpublicized information gained on the job

institutional advertising Advertising that seeks to create goodwill and to build a desired image for a company rather than to sell specific products

institutional investors Companies that invest money entrusted to them by others

insurable risk Risk for which an acceptable probability of loss may be calculated and that an insurance company might, therefore, be willing to cover

insurance Written contract that transfers to an insurer the financial responsibility for losses up to specified limits

insurance premium Fee that the insured pays the insurer for coverage against loss

integrated marketing communications (IMC) Strategy of coordinating and integrating communications and promotions efforts with customers to ensure greater efficiency and effectiveness

intellectual property Intangible personal property, such as ideas, songs, trade secrets, and computer programs, that are protected by patents, trademarks, and copyrights

intensive distribution Market coverage strategy that tries to place a product in as many outlets as possible

intentional tort Willful act that results in injury

interactive advertising Customer–seller communication in which the customer controls the amount and type of information received

interlocking directorates Situations in which members of the board of one firm sit on the board of a competing firm

internal auditors Employees who analyze and evaluate a company's operations and data to determine their accuracy

internal data Data acquired from company sources such as internal records and documents

international law Principles, customs, and rules that govern the international relationships between states, organizations, and persons

Internet A worldwide collection of interconnected networks that enables users to share information electronically and provides digital access to a wide variety of services

Internet service provider (ISP) A company that provides access to the Internet, usually for a monthly fee, via telephone lines or cable; ISPs can be local companies or specialists such as America Online

interpersonal skills Skills required to understand other people and to interact effectively with them

intrafirm trade Trade between global units of a multinational corporation

intranet A private network, set up within a corporation or organization, that operates over the Internet and may be used to link geographically remote sites

inventory Goods kept in stock for the production process or for sales to final customers

inventory control System for determining the right quantity of various items to have on hand and keeping track of their location, use, and condition

inventory turnover ratio Measure of the time a company takes to turn its inventory into sales, calculated by dividing cost of goods sold by the average value of inventory for a period

investment portfolios Assortment of investment instruments

ISO 9000 Global standards set by the International Organization for Standardization establishing a minimum level of acceptable quality

issued stock Authorized shares that have been released to the market

J

job analysis Process by which jobs are studied to determine the tasks and dynamics involved in performing them

job description Statement of the tasks involved in a given job and the conditions under which the holder of the job will work

job enrichment Reducing work specialization and making work more meaningful by adding to the responsibilities of each job

job redesign Designing a better fit between employees' skills and their work to increase job satisfaction

job sharing Splitting a single full-time job between two employees for their convenience

job specification Statement describing the kind of person who would be best for a given job—including the skills, education, and previous experience that the job requires

joint venture Cooperative partnership in which organizations share investment costs, risks, management, and profits in the development, production, or selling of products

just-in-time (JIT) system Continuous system that pulls materials through the production process, making sure that all materials arrive just when they are needed with minimal inventory and waste

K

key-person insurance Insurance that provides a business with funds to compensate for the loss of a key employee by unplanned retirement, resignation, death, or disability

knowledge Expertise gained through experience or association

knowledge-based pay Pay tied to an employee's acquisition of skills; also called skill-based pay

L

labor federation Umbrella organization of national unions and unaffiliated local unions that undertakes large-scale activities on behalf of their members and that resolves conflicts between unions

labor unions Organizations of employees formed to protect and advance their members' interests

labor-intensive businesses Businesses in which labor costs are more significant than capital costs

laissez-faire leaders Leaders who leave the actual decision making up to employees

law of large numbers Principle that the larger the group on which probabilities are calculated, the more accurate the predictive value

layoffs Termination of employees for economic or business reasons

lead time Period that elapses between the ordering of materials and their arrival from the supplier

leading Process of guiding and motivating people to work toward organizational goals

lease Legal agreement that obligates the user of an asset to make payments to the owner of the asset in exchange for using it

leverage Technique of increasing the rate of return on an investment by financing it with borrowed funds

leveraged buyout (LBO) Situation in which individuals or a group of investors purchase a company primarily with debt secured by the company's assets

liabilities Claims against a firm's assets by creditors

liability losses Financial losses suffered by a business firm or individual held responsible for property damage or injuries suffered by others

licensing Agreement to produce and market another company's product in exchange for a royalty or fee

limit order Market order that stipulates the highest or lowest price at which the customer is willing to trade securities

limited liability companies (LLCs) Organizations that combine the benefits of S corporations and limited partnerships without the drawbacks of either

limited partnership Partnership composed of one or more general partners and one or more partners whose liability is usually limited to the amount of their capital investment

limited-service merchant wholesalers Merchant wholesalers that offer fewer services than full-service merchant wholesalers; they often specialize in particular markets, such as agriculture

line of credit Arrangement in which the financial institution makes money available for use at any time after the loan has been approved

line organization Chain-of-command system that establishes a clear line of authority flowing from the top down

line-and-staff organization Organization system that has a clear chain of command but that also includes functional groups of people who provide advice and specialized services

liquidity The level of ease with which an asset can be converted to cash

liquidity ratios Ratios that measure a firm's ability to meet its short-term obligations when they are due

lobbies Groups that try to persuade legislators to vote according to the groups' interests

local advertising Advertising sponsored by a local merchant

local area network (LAN) Computer network that encompasses a small area, such as an office or a university campus

locals Relatively small union groups, usually part of a national union or a labor federation, that represent members who work in a single facility or in a certain geographic area

lockout Management tactic in which union members are prevented from entering a business during a strike in order to force union acceptance of management's last contract proposal

logistics The planning, movement, and flow of goods and related information throughout the supply chain

long-term financing Financing used to cover long-term expenses such as assets (generally repaid over a period of more than one year)

long-term liabilities Obligations that fall due more than a year from the date of the balance sheet

loss exposures Areas of risk in which a potential for loss exists

M

M1 That portion of the money supply consisting of currency and demand deposits

M2 That portion of the money supply consisting of currency, demand deposits, and small time deposits

M3 That portion of the money supply consisting of M1 and M2 plus large time deposits and other restrictive deposits

mail-order firms Companies that sell products through catalogs and ship them directly to customers

mainframe computer A large and powerful computer, capable of storing and processing vast amounts of data

managed care Health care set up by employers (usually through an insurance carrier) in which networks of doctors and hospitals agree to discount the fees they charge in return for the flow of patients

management Process of coordinating resources to meet organizational goals

management accounting Area of accounting concerned with preparing data for use by managers within the organization

management by objectives (MBO) A motivational tool whereby managers and employees work together to structure personal goals and objectives for every individual, department, and project to mesh with the organization's goals

management information system (MIS) Computer system that supplies information to assist in managerial decision making

management pyramid Organizational structure comprising top, middle, and lower management

mandatory retirement Required dismissal of an employee who reaches a certain age

manufacturing resource planning (MRP II) Computer-based system that integrates data from all departments to manage inventory and production planning and control

margin trading Borrowing money from brokers to buy stock, paying interest on the borrowed money, and leaving the stock with the broker as collateral

market People or businesses who need or want a product and have the money to buy it

market indexes Measures of security markets calculated from the prices of a selection of securities

market makers Dealers in dealer exchanges who sell securities out of their own inventories so that a market is always available for buyers and sellers

market order Authorization for a broker to buy or sell securities at the best price that can be negotiated at the moment

market segmentation Division of total market into smaller, relatively homogeneous groups

market share A firm's portion of the total sales in a market

marketable securities Stocks, bonds, and other investments that can be turned into cash quickly

marketing Process of planning and executing the conception, pricing, promotion, and distribution of ideas, goods, and services to create exchanges that satisfy individual and organizational objectives

marketing concept Approach to business management that stresses customer needs and wants, seeks long-term profitability, and integrates marketing with other functional units within the organization

marketing intermediaries Businesspeople and organizations that channel goods and services from producers to consumers

marketing mix The four key elements of marketing strategy: product, price, distribution (place), and promotion

marketing research The collection and analysis of information for making marketing decisions

marketing strategy Overall plan for marketing a product

mass customization Producing customized goods and services through mass production techniques

mass production Manufacture of uniform products in great quantities

matching principle Fundamental principle requiring that expenses incurred in producing revenue be deducted from the revenues they generate during an accounting period

material requirements planning (MRP) Method of getting the correct materials where they are needed, on time, and without carrying unnecessary inventory

materials handling Movement of goods within a firm's warehouse terminal, factory, or store

mean Sum of all items in a group, divided by the number of items in the group

media Communications channels, such as newspapers, radio, and television

media mix Combination of various media options that a company uses in an advertising campaign

media plan Written plan that outlines how a company will spend its media budget, including how the money will be divided among the various media and when the advertisements will appear

median Midpoint, or the point in a group of numbers at which half are higher and half are lower

mediation Process for resolving a labor-contract dispute in which a neutral third party meets with both sides and attempts to steer them toward a solution

mentor Experienced manager or employee with a wide network of industry colleagues who can explain office politics, serve as a role model for appropriate business behavior, and help other employees negotiate the corporate structure

merchant wholesalers Independent wholesalers that take legal title to goods they distribute

merger Combination of two companies in which one purchases the other, assuming control of all property and liabilities

microcomputer Smallest and least-expensive class of computers; often referred to as a personal computer

microprocessor Advanced integrated circuit that combines most of the basic functions of a computer onto a single chip

middle managers Those in the middle of the management hierarchy; they develop plans to implement the goals of top managers and coordinate the work of first-line managers

mission statement A statement of the organization's purpose, basic goals, and philosophies

missionary salespeople Salespeople who support existing customers, usually wholesalers and retailers

mobile commerce (m-commerce) Transaction of electronic commerce using wireless devices and wireless Internet access instead of PC-based technology

mode Number that occurs the most often in any series of data

modem Hardware device that allows a computer to communicate over a regular telephone line

monetary policy Government policy and actions taken by the Federal Reserve Board to regulate the nation's money supply

money Anything generally accepted as a means of paying for goods and services

money-market funds Mutual funds that invest in short-term securities

monopolistic competition Situation in which many sellers differentiate their products from those of competitors in at least some small way

monopoly Market in which there are no direct competitors so that one company dominates

morale Attitude individuals have toward their job and employer

motivation Force that moves someone to take action

motivators Factors of human relations in business that may increase motivation

multimedia Typically used to mean the combination of more than one presentation medium—such as text, sound, graphics, and video

multinational corporations (MNCs) Companies with operations in more than one country

municipal bonds Debt issued by a state or a local agency; interest earned on municipal bonds is exempt from federal income tax and from taxes in the issuing jurisdiction

mutual funds Pools of money raised by investment companies and invested in stocks, bonds, or other marketable securities

N

NASDAQ (National Association of Securities Dealers Automated Quotations) National over-the-counter securities trading network

national advertising Advertising sponsored by companies that sell products on a nationwide basis; refers to the geographic reach of the advertiser, not the geographic coverage of the ad

national brands Brands owned by the manufacturers and distributed nationally

national union Nationwide organization made up of local unions that represent employees in locations around the country

natural resources Land, forests, minerals, water, and other tangible assets usable in their natural state

need Difference between a person's actual and ideal states; provides the basic motivation to make a purchase

need-satisfaction approach Selling method that starts with identifying the customer's needs and then creating a presentation that addresses those needs; this is the approach used by most professional salespeople

negligence Tort in which a reasonable amount of care to protect others from risk of injury is not used

negotiable instrument Transferable document that represents a promise to pay a specified amount

net income Profit earned or loss incurred by a firm, determined by subtracting expenses from revenues; also called the bottom line

network Collection of computers, communications software, and transmission media (such as telephone lines) that allows computers to communicate

news conference Gathering of media representatives at which companies announce new information; also called a press briefing

news release Brief statement or video program released to the press announcing new products, management changes, sales performance, and other potential news items; also called a news release

no-fault insurance laws Laws limiting lawsuits connected with auto accidents

norms Informal standards of conduct that guide team behavior

not-for-profit organizations Firms whose primary objective is something other than returning a profit to their owners

O

objective Specific, short-range target or aim

office automation systems (OAS) Computer systems that assist with the tasks that people in a typical business office face regularly, such as drawing graphs or processing documents

oligopoly Market dominated by a few producers

open order Limit order that does not expire at the end of a trading day

open-market operations Activity of the Federal Reserve in buying and selling government bonds on the open market

operating expenses All costs of operation that are not included under cost of goods sold

operating systems Class of software that controls the computer's hardware components

operational plans Plans that lay out the actions and the resource allocation needed to achieve operational objectives and to support tactical plans; usually defined for less than one year and developed by first-line managers.

order getters Salespeople who are responsible for generating new sales and for increasing sales to existing customers

order processing Functions involved in preparing and receiving an order

order takers Salespeople who generally process incoming orders without engaging in creative selling

organization chart Diagram showing how employees and tasks are grouped and where the lines of communication and authority flow

organization structure Framework enabling managers to divide responsibilities, ensure employee accountability, and distribute decision-making authority

organizational culture A set of shared values and norms that support the management system and that guide management and employee behavior

organizational market Customers who buy goods or services for resale or for use in conducting their own operations

organizing Process of arranging resources to carry out the organization's plans

orientation Session or procedure for acclimating a new employee to the organization

outsourcing Subcontracting work to outside companies

over-the-counter (OTC) market Network of dealers who trade securities that are not listed on an exchange

owners' equity Portion of a company's assets that belongs to the owners after obligations to all creditors have been met

P

par value Arbitrary value assigned to a stock that is shown on the stock certificate

parallel processing Use of multiple processors in a single computer unit, with the intention of increasing the speed at which complex calculations can be completed

parent company Company that owns most, or all, of another company's stock and that takes an active part in managing that other company

participative management Sharing information with employees and involving them in decision making

partnership Unincorporated business owned and operated by two or more persons under a voluntary legal association

pay for performance Accepting a lower base pay in exchange for bonuses based on meeting production or other goals

penetration pricing Introducing a new product at a low price in hopes of building sales volume quickly

pension plan Company-sponsored program for providing retirees with income

performance appraisal Evaluation of an employee's work according to specific criteria

perpetual inventory System that uses computers to monitor inventory levels and automatically generate purchase orders when supplies are needed

personal property All property that is not real property

personal selling In-person communication between a seller and one or more potential buyers

persuasive advertising Advertising designed to encourage product sampling and brand switching

philanthropic Descriptive term for altruistic actions such as donating money, time, goods, or services to charitable, humanitarian, or educational institutions

physical distribution All the activities required to move finished products from the producer to the consumer

picketing Strike activity in which union members march at company entrances to persuade nonstriking employees to walk off the job and to persuade customers and others to cease doing business with the company

place marketing Marketing efforts to attract people and organizations to a particular geographical area

place utility Consumer value added by making a product available in a convenient location

planned system Economic system in which the government controls most of the factors of production and regulates their allocation

planning Establishing objectives and goals for an organization and determining the best ways to accomplish them

point-of-purchase display Advertising or other display materials set up at retail locations to promote products to potential customers as they are making their purchase decisions

political action committees (PACs) Groups formed under federal election laws to raise money for candidates through employee contributions

pollution Damage to or destruction of the natural environment caused by the discharge of harmful substances

positioning Using promotion, product, distribution, and price to differentiate a good or service from those of competitors in the mind of the prospective buyer

possession utility Consumer value created when someone takes ownership of a product

power of attorney Written authorization for one party to legally act for another

preferred stock Shares that give their owners first claim on a company's dividends and assets after all debts have been paid and whose owners do not have voting rights

preferred-provider organizations (PPOs) Health care providers offering reduced-rate contracts to groups that agree to obtain medical care through the providers' organization

preliminary screening interview Meeting between an employer's representative and a candidate for the purpose of eliminating unqualified applicants from the hiring process

premiums Free or bargain-priced items offered to encourage consumers to buy a product

press relations Process of communicating with reporters and editors from newspapers, magazines, and radio and television networks and stations

price elasticity A measure of the sensitivity of demand to changes in price

price-earnings ratio (p/e ratio) Stock's current market price divided by issuer's annual earnings per share; also known as the price-earnings multiple

primary data Data gathered for the study of a specific problem

primary market Market where firms sell new securities issued publicly for the first time

primary storage device Storage for data and programs while they are being processed by the computer

prime interest rate (prime) Lowest rate of interest charged by banks for short-term loans to their most creditworthy customers

principal Amount of a debt, excluding any interest

private accountants In-house accountants employed by organizations and businesses other than a public accounting firm; also called corporate accountants

private brands Brands that carry the label of a retailer or a wholesaler rather than a manufacturer

private carriers Transportation operations owned by a company to move only its own products

private corporation Company owned by private individuals or companies

privatizing The conversion of public ownership to private ownership

problem-solving team Informal team of 5 to 12 employees from the same department who meet voluntarily to find ways of improving quality, efficiency, and the work environment

process control systems Computer systems that use special sensing devices to monitor conditions in a physical process and make necessary adjustments to the process

process divisions Divisional structure based on the major steps of a production process

process layout Method of arranging a facility so that production tasks are carried out in separate departments containing specialized equipment and personnel

product Good or service used as the basis of commerce

product advertising Advertising that tries to sell specific goods or services, generally by describing features, benefits, and, occasionally, price

product divisions Divisional structure based on products

product layout Method of arranging a facility so that production proceeds along a line of workstations

product liability The capacity of a product to cause harm or damage for which the producer or seller is held accountable

product life cycle Four basic stages through which a product progresses: introduction, growth, maturity, and decline

product line A series of related products offered by a firm

product mix Complete list of all products that a company offers for sale

product-liability coverage Insurance that protects companies from claims for injuries or damages that result from use of a product the company manufactures or distributes

production Transformation of resources into goods or services that people need or want

production and operations management (POM) Coordination of an organization's resources for the manufacture of goods or the delivery of services

production control systems Computer systems that manage production by controlling production lines, robots, and other machinery and equipment

production forecasts Estimates of how much of a company's goods and services must be produced in order to meet future demand

professional liability insurance Insurance that covers losses arising from damages or injuries caused by the insured in the course of performing professional services for clients

profit Money left over after expenses and taxes have been deducted from revenue generated by selling goods and services

profit sharing System for distributing a portion of the company's profits to employees

profitability ratios Ratios that measure the overall financial performance of a firm

program evaluation and review technique (PERT) A planning tool that managers of complex projects use to determine the optimal order of activities, the expected time for project completion, and the best use of resources

promotion Wide variety of persuasive techniques used by companies to communicate with their target markets and the general public

promotional mix Particular blend of personal selling, advertising, direct marketing, sales promotion, and public relations that a company uses to reach potential customers

promotional strategy Statement or document that defines the direction and scope of the promotional activities that a company will use to meet its marketing objectives

property Rights held regarding any tangible or intangible object

property insurance Insurance that provides coverage for physical damage to or destruction of property and for its loss by theft

prospecting Process of finding and qualifying potential customers

prospectus Formal written offer to sell securities that sets forth the facts that an investor needs to make an informed decision

protectionism Government policies aimed at shielding a country's industries from foreign competition

proxy Document authorizing another person to vote on behalf of a shareholder in a corporation

psychographics Classification of customers on the basis of their psychological makeup

public accountants Professionals who provide accounting services to other businesses and individuals for a fee

public corporation Corporation that actively sells stock on the open market

public relations Nonsales communication that businesses have with their various audiences (includes both communication with the general public and press relations)

pull strategy Promotional strategy that stimulates consumer demand, which then exerts pressure on wholesalers and retailers to carry a product

purchasing Acquiring the raw materials, parts, components, supplies, and finished products needed to produce goods and services

pure competition Situation in which so many buyers and sellers exist that no single buyer or seller can individually influence market prices

pure risk Risk that involves the chance of loss only

push strategy Promotional approach designed to motivate wholesalers and retailers to push a producer's products to end users

Q

qualified prospects Potential buyers who have both the money needed to make the purchase and the authority to make the purchase decision

quality A measure of how closely a product conforms to predetermined standards and customer expectations

quality assurance System of policies, practices, and procedures implemented throughout the company to create and produce quality goods and services

quality control Routine checking and testing of a finished product for quality against an established standard

quality of work life (QWL) Overall environment that results from job and work conditions

quick ratio Measure of a firm's short-term liquidity, calculated by adding cash, marketable securities, and receivables, then dividing that sum by current liabilities; also known as the acid-test ratio

quotas Fixed limits on the quantity of imports a nation will allow for a specific product

R

rack jobbers Merchant wholesalers that are responsible for setting up and maintaining displays in a particular section of a retail store

random-access memory (RAM) Primary storage devices allowing a computer to access any piece of data in such memory at random

rate of return Percentage increase in the value of an investment

ratio analysis Use of quantitative measures to evaluate a firm's financial performance

reach Total number of audience members who will be exposed to a message at least once in a given period

read-only memory (ROM) Special circuits that store data and programs permanently but don't allow users to record their own data or programs; a common use of ROM is for the programs that activate start-up routines when the computer is turned on

real property Land and everything permanently attached to it

recession Period during which national income, employment, and production all fall

recruiting Process of attracting appropriate applicants for an organization's jobs

relationship marketing A focus on developing and maintaining long-term relationships with customers, suppliers, and distributors for mutual benefit

reminder advertising Advertising intended to remind existing customers of a product's availability and benefits

replacement-cost coverage Property insurance in which the insurer pays for the full cost of repairing or replacing the property rather than the actual cash value

reserve requirement Percentage of a bank's deposit that must be set aside

responsibility Obligation to perform the duties and achieve the goals and objectives associated with a particular position

retailers Firms that sell goods and services to individuals for their own use rather than for resale

retained earnings The portion of shareholders' equity earned by the company but not distributed to its owners in the form of dividends

return on investment (ROI) Ratio between net income after taxes and total owners' equity; also known as return on equity

return on sales Ratio between net income after taxes and net sales; also known as profit margin

revenue bond Municipal bonds backed by revenue generated from the projects financed with the bonds

revenues Amount earned from sales of goods or services and inflow from miscellaneous sources such as interest, rent, and royalties

risk Uncertainty of an event or exposure to loss

risk management Process used by business firms and individuals to deal with their exposures to loss

robots Programmable machines that can complete a variety of tasks by working with tools and materials

roles Behavioral patterns associated with or expected of certain positions

routing Specifying the sequence of operations and the path the work will take through the production facility

résumé Form of advertising that lists a person's education, employment background, and job qualifications in order to obtain an interview

S

S corporation Corporations with no more than 75 shareholders that may be taxed as a partnership; also known as a subchapter S corporation

salaries Fixed weekly, monthly, or yearly cash compensation for work

sales promotion Wide range of events and activities (including coupons, rebates, contests, in-store demonstrations, free samples, trade shows, and point-of-purchase displays) designed to stimulate interest in a product

sales support personnel Salespeople who facilitate the selling effort by providing such services as prospecting, customer education, and customer service

scheduling Process of determining how long each production operation takes and then setting a starting and ending time for each

scientific management Management approach designed to improve employees' efficiency by scientifically studying their work

scrambled merchandising Policy of carrying merchandise that is ordinarily sold in a different type of outlet

search engines Internet tools for finding Web sites on the topics of your choice

secondary data Data previously produced or collected for a different purpose

secondary market Market where subsequent owners trade previously issued shares of stocks and bonds

secondary storage Computer storage for data and programs that aren't needed at the moment

secured bonds Bonds backed by specific assets

secured loans Loans backed up with something of value that the lender can claim in case of default, such as a piece of property

securities Instruments such as stocks, bonds, options, futures, and commodities

selective credit controls Federal Reserve's power to set credit terms on various types of loans

selective distribution Market coverage strategy that uses a limited number of outlets to distribute products

self-insurance Accumulating funds each year to pay for predicted liability losses, rather than buying insurance from another company

self-managed teams Teams in which members are responsible for an entire process or operation

sellers' market Marketplace characterized by a shortage of products

selling expenses All the operating expenses associated with marketing goods or services

service businesses Businesses that provide intangible products or perform useful labor on behalf of another

setup costs Expenses incurred each time a producer organizes resources to begin producing goods or services

sexism Discrimination on the basis of gender

sexual harassment Unwelcome sexual advances, request for sexual favors, or other verbal or physical conduct of a sexual nature within the workplace

shareholders Owners of a corporation

shop steward Union member and employee who is elected to represent other union members and who attempts to resolve employee grievances with management

short selling Selling stock borrowed from a broker with the intention of buying it back later at a lower price, repaying the broker, and pocketing the profit

short-term financing Financing used to cover current expenses (generally repaid within a year)

sinking fund Account into which a company makes annual payments for use in redeeming its bonds in the future

skimming Charging a high price for a new product during the introductory stage and lowering the price later

small business Company that is independently owned and operated, is not dominant in its field, and meets certain criteria for the number of employees and annual sales revenue

smart cards Plastic cards that include an embedded chip to store money drawn from the user's demand-deposit account and information that can be used for purchases

social audit Assessment of a company's performance in the area of social responsibility

social responsibility The idea that business has certain obligations to society beyond the pursuit of profits

socialism Economic system characterized by public ownership and operation of key industries combined with private ownership and operation of less-vital industries

software Programmed instructions that drive the activity of computer hardware

sole proprietorship Business owned by a single individual

span of management Number of people under one manager's control; also known as span of control

special-purpose teams Temporary teams that exist outside the formal organization hierarchy and are created to achieve a specific goal

specialty advertising Advertising that appears on various items such as coffee mugs, pens, and calendars, designed to help keep a company's name in front of customers

specialty store Store that carries only a particular type of goods

speculative risk Risk that involves the chance of both loss and profits

speculators Investors who purchase securities in anticipation of making large profits quickly

speech-recognition system Computer system that recognizes human speech, enabling users to enter data and give commands vocally

stakeholders Individuals or groups to whom business has a responsibility

standards Criteria against which performance is measured

stare decisis Concept of using previous judicial decisions as the basis for deciding similar court cases

start-up companies New ventures

statement of cash flows Statement of a firm's cash receipts and cash payments that presents information on its sources and uses of cash

statistical process control (SPC) Use of random sampling and control charts to monitor the production process

statistical quality control (SQC) Monitoring all aspects of the production process to see whether the process is operating as it should

statistics Factual data that can be presented in numerical form

statutory law Statute, or law, created by a legislature

stock Shares of ownership in a corporation

stock certificate Document that proves stock ownership

stock exchanges Location where traders buy and sell stocks and bonds

stock options Contract allowing the holder to purchase or sell a certain number of shares of a particular stock at a given price by a certain date

stock specialist Intermediary who trades in a particular security on the floor of an auction exchange; "buyer of last resort"

stock split Increase in the number of shares of ownership that each stock certificate represents

stop order An order to sell a stock when its price falls to a particular point to limit an investor's losses

strategic alliance Long-term relationship in which two or more companies share ideas, resources, and technologies in order to establish competitive advantages

strategic plans Plans that establish the actions and the resource allocation required to accomplish strategic goals; usually defined for periods of two to five years and developed by top managers

strict product liability Liability for injury caused by a defective product when all reasonable care is used in its manufacture, distribution, or sale; no fault is assigned

strike Temporary work stoppage by employees who want management to accept their union's demands

strikebreakers Nonunion workers hired to replace striking workers

subsidiary corporations Corporations whose stock is owned entirely or almost entirely by another corporation

supercomputers Computers with the highest level of performance, often boasting speeds greater than 12 trillion calculations per second

supply Specific quantity of a product that the seller is able and willing to provide

supply curve Graph of relationship between various prices and the quantity supplied at each price

supply-chain management Integrating all of the facilities, functions, and processes associated with the production of goods and services, from suppliers to customers

synthetic system Production process that combines two or more materials or components to create finished products; the reverse of an analytic system

T

table Grid for displaying relationships between words and numbers, particularly many precise numbers

tactical plans Plans that define the actions and the resource allocation necessary to achieve tactical objectives and to support strategic plans; usually defined for a period of one to three years and developed by middle managers

tall organizations Organizations with a narrow span of management and many hierarchical levels

target markets Specific customer groups or segments to whom a company wants to sell a particular product

tariffs Taxes levied on imports

task force Team of people from several departments who are temporarily brought together to address a specific issue

tax accounting Area of accounting focusing on tax preparation and tax planning

tax credit Direct reduction in the amount of income tax owed by a person or business; granted by a government body for engaging or not engaging in selected activities

tax deduction Direct reduction in the amount of income on which a person or business pays taxes

team A unit of two or more people who share a mission and collective responsibility as they work together to achieve a goal

technical salespeople Specialists who contribute technical expertise and other sales assistance

technical skills Ability and knowledge to perform the mechanics of a particular job

telecommuting Working from home and communicating with the company's main office via computer and communication devices

telemarketing Selling or supporting the sales process over the telephone

Telnet A way to access someone else's computer (the host computer) and to use it as if it were right on your desk

term insurance Life insurance that provides death benefits for a specified period

termination Act of getting rid of an employee through layoffs or firing

test marketing Product-development stage in which a product is sold on a limited basis—a trial introduction

Theory X Managerial assumption that employees are irresponsible, unambitious, and distasteful of work and that managers must use force, control, or threats to motivate them

Theory Y Managerial assumption that employees like work, are naturally committed to certain goals, are capable of creativity, and seek out responsibility under the right conditions

time deposits Bank accounts that pay interest and require advance notice before money can be withdrawn

time utility Consumer value added by making a product available at a convenient time

top managers Those at the highest level of the organization's management hierarchy; they are responsible for setting strategic goals, and they have the most power and responsibility in the organization

tort Noncriminal act (other than breach of contract) that results in injury to a person or to property

total quality management (TQM) Comprehensive, strategic management approach that builds quality into every organizational process as a way of improving customer satisfaction

trade allowance Discount offered by producers to wholesalers and retailers

trade credit Credit obtained by the purchaser directly from the supplier

trade deficit Unfavorable trade balance created when a country imports more than it exports

trade promotions Sales-promotion efforts aimed at inducing distributors or retailers to push a producer's products

trade salespeople Salespeople who sell to and support marketing intermediaries by giving in-store demonstrations, offering samples, and so on

trade shows Gatherings where producers display their wares to potential buyers

trade surplus Favorable trade balance created when a country exports more than it imports

trademark Brand that has been given legal protection so that its owner has exclusive rights to its use

trading blocs Organizations of nations that remove barriers to trade among their members and that establish uniform barriers to trade with nonmember nations

transaction Exchange between parties

transaction processing system (TPS) Computerized information system that processes the daily flow of customer, supplier, and employee transactions, including inventory, sales, and payroll records

Treasury bills Short-term debt issued by the federal government; also referred to as T-bills

Treasury bonds Debt securities issued by the federal government that mature in 10 to 30 years

Treasury notes Debt securities issued by the federal government that mature within 1 to 10 years

trend analysis Examination of data over a sufficiently long period so that regularities and relationships may be detected, analyzed, and used as the basis for forecasts

tying contracts Contracts forcing buyers to purchase unwanted goods along with goods actually desired

U

umbrella policies Insurance that provides businesses with coverage beyond what is provided by a basic liability policy

unemployment insurance Government-sponsored program for assisting employees who are laid off for reasons not related to performance

Uniform Commercial Code (UCC) Set of standardized laws, adopted by most states, that govern business transactions

uniform resource locator (URL) Web address that gives the exact location of an Internet resource

uninsurable risk Risk that few, if any, insurance companies will assume because of the difficulty of calculating the probability of loss

unissued stock Authorized shares that are to be released in the future

universal life insurance Combination of term life insurance policy and a savings plan with flexible interest rates and flexible premiums

Universal Product Codes (UPCs) A bar code on a product's package that provides information read by optical scanners

unlimited liability Legal condition under which any damages or debts attributable to the business can also be attached to the owner because the two have no separate legal existence

unsecured loan Loan requiring no collateral but a good credit rating

upload To send a file from your computer to a server or host system

U.S. savings bonds Debt instruments sold by the federal government in small denominations

Usenet newsgroups One or more discussion groups on the Internet where people with similar interests can post articles and reply to messages

utility Power of a good or service to satisfy a human need

V

variable costs Business costs that increase with the number of units produced

variable life insurance Whole life insurance policy that allows the policyholder to decide how to invest the cash value

venture capitalists Investment specialists who provide money to finance new businesses or turnarounds in exchange for a portion of the ownership, with the objective of making a considerable profit on the investment; also called VCs

vertical marketing system (VMS) Planned distribution channels in which members coordinate their efforts to optimize distribution activities

vertical mergers Combinations of companies that participate in different phases of the same industry (e.g., materials, production, distribution)

vertical organization Structure linking activities at the top of the organization with those at the middle and lower levels

virtual teams Teams that use communication technology to bring geographically distant employees together to achieve goals

vision A viable view of the future that is rooted in but improves on the present

W

wages Cash payment based on the number of hours the employee has worked or the number of units the employee has produced

wants Things that are desirable in light of a person's experiences, culture, and personality

warehouse Facility for storing inventory

warranty Statement specifying what the producer of a product will do to compensate the buyer if the product is defective or if it malfunctions

Web site A related collection of files on the World Wide Web

wheel of retailing Evolutionary process by which stores that feature low prices gradually upgrade until they no longer appeal to price-sensitive shoppers and are replaced by new low-price competitors

whole life insurance Insurance that provides both death benefits and savings for the insured's lifetime, provided premiums are paid

wholesalers Firms that sell products to other firms for resale or for organizational use

wide area network (WAN) Computer network that encompasses a large geographic area

wireless transceivers Small hardware attachments that enable a computer to transmit and receive data

work specialization Specialization in or responsibility for some portion of an organization's overall work tasks; also called division of labor

worker buyout Distribution of financial incentives to employees who voluntarily depart, usually undertaken in order to reduce the payroll

workers' compensation insurance Insurance that partially replaces lost income and that pays for employees' medical costs and rehabilitation expenses for work-related injuries

working capital Current assets minus current liabilities

workstation Class of computers with the basic size and shape of microcomputers but with the speed of traditional midsize computers; often used for design, engineering, and scientific applications

World Wide Web (Web) A hypertext-based system for finding and accessing Internet resources such as text, graphics, sound, and other multimedia resources

wrongful discharge Firing an employee with inadequate advance notice or explanation

Y

yield Income received from securities, calculated by dividing dividend or interest income by market price

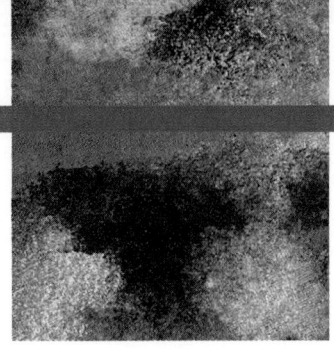

NAME / ORGANIZATION / BRAND / COMPANY INDEX

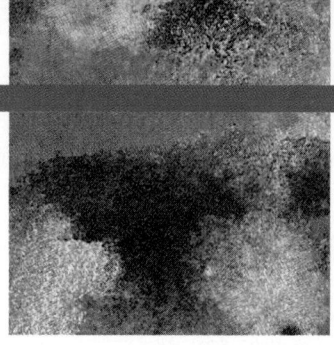

SUBJECT INDEX

TAKE AN INSIDE LOOK AT
BUSINESS TODAY!

**EXPLORE THE CHALLENGES COMPANIES ARE FACING
AS THEY CONDUCT E-BUSINESS TODAY!**

- What's New About the New Economy?
- Who Will Win the Great E-Commerce Privacy Debate?
- Roadblocks on the European and Asian Superhighways
- Why Are the Dot-Coms Falling to Earth?
- The New Breed of Dot-Com Directors
- Seven Habits of Highly Effective E-Managers
- Strategies for Smart Web Writing
- Going Mobile: Are You Ready for the Exciting Future of M-Commerce?
- What's All the Buzz about B2B?
- The Reality of Working for an E-Business Start-Up
- The Truth about Job Recruiting on the Internet
- It Takes More Than a Web Site
- A Revolution in Electronic Pricing? Not Yet
- Clicks and Mortar: Bridging the Physical and Virtual Worlds
- How to Create a Winning Web Site
- Are Those E-Business Revenues for Real?
- Cyberbanks Hit a Brick Wall
- As Online Trading Rises, So Do the Number of Complaints

**CHOOSE SIDES IN THE FACE-OFF BATTLES OF INDUSTRY RIVALS WHO
ADOPT DIFFERENT STRATEGIES TO GAIN A COMPETITIVE ADVANTAGE**

- **FedEx vs. UPS**
  - Fighting a Battle in the Sky and on the Ground
  - Duking It Out in China
  - FedEx Goes Postal
  - Betting on the Future of E-Commerce

- **Barnesandnoble.com vs. Amazon**
  - Barnesandnoble.com Tiptoes into the Internet Arena
  - Amazon Takes on the World
  - Barnesandnoble.com Sticks with Books
  - The Literary Titans Duke It Out in Cyberspace